The Borzoi Reader in American Politics

Consulting Editor:

Douglas W. Rae *Yale University*

Consultants:

Herbert Jacob *Northwestern University*

Charles O. Jones *University of Pittsburgh*

Clara Penniman *University of Wisconsin*

David Price *Yale University*

Douglas W. Rae *Yale University*

Ruth C. Silva *Pennsylvania State University*

Alfred A. Knopf New York

The Borzoi Reader in American Politics

Edited with Introductions by

Edward Keynes *Pennsylvania State University*

David Adamany *Wesleyan University*

TO OUR PARENTS

THIS IS A BORZOI BOOK

Published by Alfred A. Knopf, Inc.

 Published in the United States by Alfred A. Knopf, Inc., New York, and simultaneously in Canada by Random House of Canada Limited, Toronto. Distributed by Random House, Inc., New York.

ISBN: 0-394-31133-7

Library of Congress Catalog Card Number: 79-159553

Manufactured in the United States of America.

First Edition

987654321

Preface

Having both first taught American politics as graduate students at the University of Wisconsin, our perspective on the American political system and our interest in undergraduate teaching stem from those years. At a time when the life of that great university is imperiled, we wish to acknowledge how deeply we are in its debt and to express our hope that violence and turmoil will not overshadow its continuing contribution to teaching and scholarship in America.

We are only too well aware that collections on American politics already fill more than a large bookshelf. The decision to edit still another was prompted by a belief that our format distinguishes itself in three ways that might make this volume useful to undergraduates.

First, we have emphasized in Part I the political values that have historically inhered in American culture. Political institutions channel and distribute power. But ultimately the political values of a society are greater determinants of its course than are its political institutions. We endeavor to supply the reader a broad sample of those values.

Second, we sought to broaden the basis for our choice of readings by seeking the counsel of colleagues. Before undertaking this volume we received an advisory bibliographical essay from a political scientist of note in each major field included here. We are grateful for their thoughtful contributions. David Price of Yale University advised us on political thought and culture; Douglas W. Rae of Yale University on parties, interest groups, and elections; Charles O. Jones of the University of Pittsburgh on the Congress; Ruth C. Silva of Pennsylvania State University on the presidency; and Herbert Jacob of Northwestern University on the judiciary. In addition, we received from Clara Penniman of the University of Wisconsin an advisory essay for a chapter on state politics which we subsequently eliminated because of space limitations. Her contribution to this volume occurred time and again as we incorporated her recommendations in various chapters to show the impact of federalism on the institutions of national government.

Third, we decided to preface each part with an extensive essay setting a framework for the readings and raising evaluative questions in a context of democratic theory. We hope these essays will provide an integrating framework and provoke normative questions for students. We are confident they will provide a foil for many of our teaching colleagues who are in sharp disagreement with our biases.

In this entire undertaking we are grateful for the critical comments of Douglas Rae who served as editor and advisor. The encouragement and editorial assistance of Arthur Strimling, Barry Rossinoff, and Susan Gilbert of Random House-Alfred A. Knopf were indispensable. More important, we are impressed at their insistence that this volume serve educational goals before commercial ones. Kevin V. Mulcahy contributed significantly as research assistant and bibliographer.

Our greatest debt, however, is to our students who over the years have enlivened our thinking about American politics by their thoughtful insights, penetrating questions, and healthy skepticism.

To all who have contributed, we express gratitude. From those who use this volume we invite comment and criticism. Our aspiration is that this reader will in some way contribute to the teaching of American politics, and we readily accept responsibility for the gap between that aspiration and this final product.

E. K.
D. W. A.

February 1971
State College, Pennsylvania
Middletown, Connecticut

Contents

American Politics in the Twenty-First Century

Future, Present, and Past

Many books on American politics begin with an inquiry into the American past. They examine the constitutional basis of American politics, then analyze the development of the dominant political values and institutions of the culture. Next they attempt to assess the impact of traditional values on contemporary politics and government. Surely these are important aspects to consider. However, by beginning with them, a subtle, but pervasive, bias is introduced, one that assumes that traditional values, namely the norms of liberal democracy (such as majority rule and individual and minority rights) either will or should continue to inform the national political debate in the decades ahead. Whether this is wishful thinking or reasoned expectation is often unclear.

Although we, too, discuss these elements in later sections of this anthology, we begin by posing a different set of questions. During the remainder of the twentieth century, the nation, like other industrial societies, will confront several basic problems of survival. Three fundamental problems, in our opinion, stand out in relief against all others. The first, as Aldous Huxley observed in 1931, is the problem of overpopulation and overcrowding. The second is the management of rapid technological innovation and social change. The third is the maintenance of peace in an age of indescribable destructive capacity. We begin by asking how these problems and their solutions will affect, alter, or replace traditional American values and institutions.

We are aware of many other problems facing the national community—racism, urban decay, domestic violence, and governmental reform. But the problems of population, technology, and peace remain paramount, for if they are not resolved, survival, much less the good life, in the twenty-first century seems remote. To some extent these problems are transpolitical (that is, beyond, or greater than, the scope of politics). Their solutions, however, involve political choices: the assignment of national priorities in the use and distribution of society's resources. Thus, although our inquiry may seem speculative, a flight of fancy to some, it is not outside the realm of national politics.

Overpopulation and Overcrowding

In reexamining his earlier reflections on the *Brave New World,* Aldous Huxley wrote a decade ago:

> On the first Christmas Day the population of our planet was about two hundred and fifty millions—less than half the population of modern China. Sixteen centuries later, when the Pilgrim Fathers landed at Plymouth Rock, human numbers had climbed to a little more than five hundred millions. By the time of the signing of the Declaration of Independence, world population had passed the seven hundred million mark. In 1931, when I was writing *Brave New World,* it stood at just under two billions. Today, only twenty-seven years later, there are two billion eight hundred million of us. And tomorrow—what?[1]

Recent developments—improved sanitation, modern drugs, new surgical techniques—have stimulated world population growth. While human numbers continue to climb, pressures on the environment also mount. With world populations on the rise, there will soon be competition (individually and collectively) for living space, clean air and water, and a share of the earth's mineral and industrial wealth. Of course, the rate of population growth and attendant pressures on the environment are not evenly dispersed over the planet. But in the United States these pressures are beginning to be felt in the largest cities: in the megalopolis of the Northeast from Cape Hatteras, North Carolina, to Boston; in the Midwestern triangle from Cleveland through Indianapolis to Chicago; and in the great southern California urban sprawl from Los Angeles to San Diego. Soon other parts of the country will start to feel the pressures of population on the environment.

In addition to the domestic consequences of overpopulation, there will be serious international population problems. With rapidly growing populations and relatively limited natural and industrial resources, many underdeveloped nations will continue to grow poorer. In Egypt, for example, the increased productive capacity created by the Aswan High Dam has already been outstripped by the country's population growth. Rapidly growing populations and relatively limited productive capacities mean that more people will go to bed hungry every night. Moreover, the gap between industrialized and underdeveloped nations will grow larger, rather than smaller, with each passing year. These trends will promote greater world tensions as whole races and nations struggle to survive. The next twenty-five years, for these and other reasons, will probably be less secure than the past quarter century.

World population growth, in our opinion, will soon pose difficult, if not impossible, choices for relatively wealthy nations, such as the United States

1 Aldous Huxley, *Brave New World Revisited* (New York: Harper & Row, 1958), p. 8.

and the Soviet Union. If population growth continues at the present rate or accelerates, despite the pill and other contraceptive devices, the decision will have to be made whether whole races and nations will survive or perish. Our society has never had to face such decisions. Is it capable of making such choices? Do the traditional liberal values offer any guidelines for making these decisions?

Closely related to the problems of population quantity, as Huxley observed, is the equally vexing problem of population quality. Is the mental and physical quality of the population improving or declining? What is the ratio, in Huxley's terms, of the Alpha Pluses to the Alphas and the Betas? Is the average I.Q. greater or lower than it was when Huxley wrote *Brave New World*? If increased populations mean greater competition for scarce resources, then some part of the population will not receive the daily nutritional requirements essential for mental and physical well-being. Surely, under such conditions the quality of the race will decline. Each succeeding generation will become less well fed, housed, and clothed. These conditions threaten both the quality and survival of the race.

Population growth has social, economic, political, and biological consequences. Inasmuch as overcrowding is not uniform (more pronounced in the Northeast corridor, the Midwestern triangle, and the southern California sprawl), its effects will be felt differentially in various regions of the country. As life in the vast urban centers becomes increasingly unbearable, mass migrations to the less populated hinterlands of America will occur—to the Great Plains of the midlands and the high plateaus and mountains of the Northwest. These mass migrations will at first relieve the most severe pressures of urban populations on their environment. With further population growth and the attendant pollution of these once open spaces, the problems of overcrowding—foul air, dirty water, and littered land—must again be faced. Eventually, the Great Plains and the mountains will no longer be able to sustain life.

These mass migrations will also require the development of more marginal areas at great social, economic, and political costs. Mass population movements will necessitate the organization of individual human skills and resources as well as the mobilization of industrial and technological capabilities. New towns and cities will have to be created, old industries moved, and new ones for domestic refugees developed. Obviously, if these new communities are to avoid some of the problems confronted by the older, dying cities in the megalopolis, they must be organized according to wholly new principles of urban and environmental planning. New forms of transportation, sewage disposal, and electric power or other energy sources must be developed. New techniques for recycling wastes and industrial by-products must be invented. In other words, creative energies must be mobilized in a way demanded by no previous crisis, war, or depression.

To accomplish these Promethean tasks, the thousands and the millions, in the words of Father Teilhard de Chardin, will have to be organized. New forms of social organization will be required to replace shattered family, neighborhood, play, and work groups and associations. In twenty-first-century America social relations will increasingly become the business of the state. Freedom of movement will probably be restricted. The right to procreate may be limited. Under the conditions of twenty-first-century life, what will happen to the individual's traditional rights—the rights to privacy and freedom of action, movement, and association? Certainly the individual's living space will be narrower than it is today. In sum, we are suggesting that survival in the twenty-first century and beyond will require a new social, economic, and political order that is an anathema to the traditional values of America.

Technological Change

The problems associated with continued population growth are matched by equally vexing problems created by rapid technological innovation. Technological innovation, the application of scientific knowledge to industry, has had both beneficial and harmful consequences for twentieth-century America. The atomic research that led to the production of the first atom bomb during World War II also resulted in the generation of cheap electric power in the postwar era. Similarly, chemical and biological research during wartime led to the development of chemical-biological weapons as well as to drugs with curative properties. Scientific knowledge, as the past twenty-five years demonstrate, can be employed constructively and destructively by democratic as well as authoritarian societies.

The past quarter century was also marked by the haphazard application of science to industry. Many technological developments, often the results of war-related research, occurred without foresight or planning. Thus, jet aircraft developed at the end of World War II were introduced into commercial aviation in the 1960s. New jetliners, which carried more passengers with greater efficiency through longer distances, soon contributed to increased noise levels and air pollution in the large cities. Other discoveries also have had dramatic, but unintended, consequences. Thalidomide, a drug designed to relieve hypertension (especially during pregnancy) resulted in birth defects to the users' children. Only recently have the more harmful pesticides been revealed. Although these discoveries were initially thought to be beneficial, their harmful consequences were not realized until they were employed on a mass scale.

Rapid technological change may lead to disastrous consequences for a society precisely because of the pressure to introduce new products as soon as they are discovered. The desire to relieve pain, cure illness, make food plentiful and inexpensive, and ease the burdens of this generation, have frequently jeopardized the future of unborn generations. And the cries to introduce new wonder drugs are likely to grow louder as these discoveries accelerate with expanding scientific knowledge. Only a greater amount of public control can prevent technological suicide.

The problem of controlling or channeling technological innovation has an even more complex dimension. During the past century there has been an accelerated rate of change as well as rapid technological development. This phenomenon is best understood by comparing the rate of development of firearms with that of aircraft. Sometime between 1324 and 1354—no one is sure of the exact date—the first reliable weapon fired with gunpowder was developed. This event occurred several centuries after the discovery of gunpowder itself. Approximately three hundred years after the discovery of gunpowder (*c.* 1469), the first "hand gun," the arquebus, was introduced. In 1517 the original matchlock firing mechanism of the arquebus was replaced by the more reliable and controllable wheel lock. Over a hundred years later, in 1610, the flintlock was introduced, which allowed a soldier to fire his gun without blowing himself up in the process. Not until the early nineteenth century, however, did a Scottish clergyman invent percussion gunpowder. Shortly thereafter, when the British army developed a percussion cap, gunnery entered the modern era.

During the nineteenth century three other developments, which occurred in close succession, changed the science of gunnery. In the early 1800s rifling replaced the smooth-bore technique of gun manufacture. Rifling, or grooving, made the flight of the bullet truer, or more precise. In 1836 breechloading was introduced, which increased the rate of fire because guns no longer had to be loaded from the business end, a time-consuming activity. By the 1890s magazines, or repeating mechanisms, were invented. The repeating rifle, which could fire up to ten rounds without reloading, greatly increased the individual soldier's firing power. This power was further enhanced by smokeless powder, metal cartridge cases, and the compound bullet. On the eve of World War II most armies possessed a reliable rifle that weighed no more than ten pounds, had bolt action, and fired a bullet more than a mile and one-half.

Although three hundred years elapsed between the invention of gunpowder and its application to weaponry and another three hundred years passed before a reliable firing mechanism was developed, in the fifty years between 1862 and 1913 fire power was increased by more than twenty times. By 1917 the German army, which supplied its infantry divisions with 270 light and heavy machine guns, revolutionized warfare through the multiplication of fire power. The machine gun's rapid introduction, however, preceded necessary adjustments in military tactics. As a result, casualties rose dramatically in frontal infantry assaults against heavily fortified and well-armed trenches. The rate of technological innovation had surpassed the pace of human adaptation.

The history of combat aircraft during the past sixty-eight years reveals the acceleration in the rate of technological change even more dramatically. On December 17, 1903, the Wright brothers successfully flew a biplane driven by a 12-horsepower engine for 12 seconds through an air distance of 500 feet. A little more than ten years later, at the beginning of World War I, Michelin developed a combat aircraft for France that could fly 78 mph at an altitude of 6,500 feet for a distance of 370 miles. By the end of the war France possessed an airplane that could fly 112 mph to an altitude of 16,400 feet with a 435-mile combat range.

In the next two decades aircraft technology continued to develop rapidly in Europe and the United States. At the beginning of World War II the German Focke-Wulf fighter streaked through the skies at 389 mph at 18,000 feet. Just before Germany's defeat in 1945, the Heinkel jet fighter flew to an altitude of 19,700 feet at 522 mph with a 410-mile combat range. Within five years the U.S. B-47 Stratojet was in service over Korea flying at 630 mph with a 45,000-foot maximum ceiling and a 3,870-mile combat range. By the mid 1960s the U.S. F 111-A darted through the skies at more than twice the speed of sound. Each decade between 1900 and 1970 was marked by rapid increases in the speed, range, and maximum altitude of combat and civilian aircraft.

In contrast to the rather slow development of the gun, improvements in aircraft technology were swift. The introduction of new manufacturing processes, metal alloys, fuels, and power plants permitted and encouraged technological innovation. Today new weapons systems, including conventional aircraft, jets, and missiles, can be created in a relatively short time. Some weapons-system experts calculate that a new system can be deployed within four to five years of its initial development. In other words, time dimensions have been diminished from centuries, to decades, to years by the application of scientific knowledge to practical problems. Today, weapons systems and other innovations can be introduced more rapidly than the capacity to absorb and adjust to these advances. Acceleration in the rate of technological change has made it difficult, if not impossible, to plan for orderly, systematic change, for with every passing year there is less time to foresee unintended consequences, harmful side effects, and the next round of technological developments.

Ironically, whereas technological change occurs rapidly in some industries and nations, it seems to crawl at a snail's pace in other areas. New technological developments in food production, for example, are introduced and accepted more slowly than are changes in weapons systems. Because food production is highly fragmented, among other reasons, greater amounts of lead time are required to introduce new products and techniques. As a result, even assuming that dramatic new foods and production techniques are developed in the next several years, it may not be possible to avoid worldwide famine sometime after 1975. Changes in farming made in the next several years would not produce bumper crops in time to save the races and nations that face starvation in the coming decades. Just as rapid technological change in some areas may be dangerous, technological inflexibility in others may be equally disastrous. Thus, greater control over the rate of technological innovation is required for survival in the twenty-first century.

The Maintenance of Peace

A third major problem, closely related to population growth and technological change, is the need to maintain peace or to channel aggression in an age of indescribable destructive capacity. During the twentieth century weapons have been created that have changed the character of war. In previous centuries it was possible to discriminate between combatants and noncombatants in a theater of war. Although whole cities have been destroyed in the past (witness Carthage), the tools of war were far more limited in their destructive capacity. As late as World War I it was still possible to distinguish between civilians and soldiers.

With World War II, however, the character of warfare changed in several dramatic ways. First, warfare is now conducted behind the front lines as well as in the trenches and foxholes. Each soldier is maintained by numerous support troops in rear areas far from the battlefield. These armed forces, in turn, rely on civilian populations to produce essential war goods: clothing, ammunition, foodstuffs, personal equipment, and military hardware. A large army draws upon a society's industrial capacity to wage total war. The same factories that produce ball bearings for bicycles may also manufacture ball bearings for jeeps, tanks, and self-propelled artillery. Second, modern weapons frequently do not permit military strategists and tacticians to discriminate between civilians and soldiers. The effects of atomic and thermonuclear bombs cannot be limited to the immediate battle zone. In March 1954 a 20-kiloton thermonuclear blast (a relatively small one, equivalent to 20,000 tons of TNT) produced enough fallout to contaminate a 7,000 square-mile area (20 miles upwind, 200 miles downwind, and 40 miles across). The effects of a thermonuclear explosion are numerous: structural blast damage, intense thermal burns, initial gamma radiation, and long-term residual radiation.

World War II, as Raymond Aron has observed, ushered in an era of *total war*. It was followed by a quantitative and qualitative arms race that produced bigger and better bombs that offered more bang for the buck and new delivery systems that were difficult to interdict—supersonic bomber aircraft; soft, intermediate-range ballistic missiles; hardened intercontinental ballistic missiles; missiles with multiple warheads; and antimissile missile systems. Today the United States and the Soviet Union possess, or can produce, enough destructive force to bring about total annihilation. Although many of these weapons have been poised for almost ten years, their very destructiveness has thus far provided a major deterrent. Both superpowers have come to realize that the employment of strategic weapons to resolve political conflicts is the final nonpolitical act.

However concerned the superpowers may be about the use of thermonuclear weapons, they have not been able to prevent their proliferation. Some efforts have been made to limit the spread of strategic weapons: test-ban treaties, nonproliferation treaties, strategic-arms-limitation talks. But these conferences and agreements do not involve and bind all nations. France and China continue to develop and test new weapons and delivery systems. The United States and the Soviet Union detonate underground thermonuclear devices, which are not covered by the test-ban treaty. Some developing nations, such as Israel, continue to conduct laboratory tests and develop the industrial techniques necessary for the production of strategic weapons. Agreements signed by numerous nations thus far have not appreciably slowed the pace of the arms race. The hands on the doomsday clock continue to race toward the hour of midnight.

The question, so often raised, is whether the hands on the clock can be turned back. Clearly, weapons of mass destruction cannot be eliminated. Their existence is rooted in the knowledge and productive capacities of the industrial-technological society. Can the knowledge of atomic energy and the thermonuclear warheads be wrenched from a society that requires atomic energy to run its factories, heat its homes, and light its schools? To pose such questions is to ask whether a return to the preatomic age is possible. These are unrealistic thoughts.

The facts suggest that the capacity to make war—total war—is rooted in the very nature of the technological society. There are many views on the causes of war. Some analysts—Sigmund Freud, for example—view war as an essential element of man's inherently aggressive nature. If they are correct and war is a part of man's inherent nature, then man's natural condition is a state of war. Other analysts argue that conflict is a product of social organization. Therefore, new forms of social organization are required to reduce the probability of violent conflict. Whether war is a function of man's nature, technology, or social organization, it is clearly a recurring problem of world civilization. Since the beginning of the twentieth century, wars have almost continuously plagued the world. In addition to two major wars, countless little wars have erupted in all parts of the world. Even the most ardent apostles of peace would have to admit that we are not close to the kingdom of heaven.

The fact is that the decades ahead appear to be more perilous than the immediately preceding period. In the coming decades the proliferation, if not the universalization, of the means of mass or total warfare will be witnessed. Although small powers will not possess means adequate to destroy great nations, they may employ their limited arsenals to trigger the thermonuclear stockpiles of the superpowers. By precipitating great-power action, even the smallest nuclear nation could destroy life on earth. Proliferation of nuclear and thermonuclear weapons will also increase the probability of thermonuclear accident and miscalculation. The universalization of thermonuclear weapons will move the hands of the doomsday clock even closer to midnight.

Several Political Questions

The problems of population quantity and quality, technological innovation, and the maintenance of peace are not unique to the United States. They are broad, human problems, shared by all nations in varying degrees. Both the traditional values of liberal democracy and the social, economic, and political institutions that rest upon those values are called into question by the human problems that must be faced in the twenty-first century. Such values as privacy and individual freedom, privately owned means of production in a competitive market economy, localism and federalism in government, limited government operating on a principle of compromise and broad consensus, and majority-rule decision making may be in sharp conflict with the need for long-range planning, policy decisions rooted in highly technical considerations, an economy of scarcity, and a high degree of centralized social control by government over both the whole territory of the nation and many areas of human conduct formerly regarded as private rather than public.

A central value of liberal democracy is individual freedom, but the problem of population quantity and quality requires constraints on the most intimate relationships among individuals. In recent years the courts have expanded the safeguards of personal liberty. In striking down state regulation of birth control, the Supreme Court declared the marital relationship to be beyond governmental interference. The same principle has inspired lower courts to void laws against abortion. Because of decisions such as these, an area of privacy has been created that cannot be breached for the contrary purpose: to impose public limits on procreation. It is also doubtful whether indirect limits on population—such as negative tax incentives for more than two children per family—would be effective in a land of economic plenty. Furthermore, liberal values imbedded in community thought and in many religious faiths would be deeply offended by governmental limits upon childbearing.

Similar problems arise with regard to population distribution. The right to travel is now regarded as a right of national citizenship by the courts and is deeply cherished by the largest number of Americans. Will restrictions upon the selection of a home and upon travel from one section of the nation to another be tolerable to the American public? An age-old struggle has been for sufficient affluence to permit free travel and free choice of occupation and residence. The compromising of these freedoms to save future generations will be difficult to sell to those with contemporary expectations, and in a democracy only the majority's agreement permits the imposition of such limits.

Economic values, too, will be severely dislocated by the solutions to the problems of population and technology. Although state tax incentives have long been weighed in the calculations of business location, mandatory limits on business mobility in order to assure more even population distribution is a dramatic departure from the economic controls of the past. Also, new product lines will be restricted or banned outright because their consequences are unknown or because the resources they use do not accord with a set of national priorities—despite the existence of a sufficient consumer market to make the production of such goods or services profitable. The permissibility of economic and certain social activities will soon be measured by the effect on the natural environment. This, again, will be a sharp departure from the assumption of the past that resources are available almost without limit for human consumption. The imposition of rigid controls upon private economic activity of all kinds will directly confront the deeply held liberal democratic belief in private property rights and private choice in economic matters, both by producers and consumers.

Not only do the problems of the twenty-first century require solutions that run counter to traditional liberal democratic values, they challenge the basic assumptions about governmental organization that derive from those values. Localism and federalism become obstacles to survival rather than institutional arrangements permitting broad participation by the public in governments close to them, allowing variations in public policy to accommodate regional differences in demography and values, and encouraging policy experimentation by subunits of the nation. Centralized planning, national social and economic priorities, and social control consistent with such comprehensive overviews of national interest all require strong and aggressive central government.

The traditional tendency of liberal democracy to be essentially conservative in its view of government—to regard government as a broker between dynamic economic and social forces and institutions in the society—becomes quickly outdated within a context of scarcity that does not allow the waste that is a concomitant of self-centered striving by private social and economic institutions. The brokerage role of government must give way to an aggressive stance in which the government directs, rather than referees, the activities and institutions of society.

Checks and balances within the national government also become an obstacle to planning, to the demarcation of priorities, and to centralized social control. The important function of the separation of powers has been to impose a brake on progress so that new policies would be adopted only after long deliberation and after acceptance by a nearly consensual majority. In this process the legitimacy of the governmental system is the paramount value served by widely approved policies. But the speed-up in technology makes obsolete a checks-and-balance decision-making process designed more to win consensus than to direct dynamic change.

The internal structures of the three branches of the national government suffer similar defects. The Congress, as we indicate in Part III, is predominantly an institution of dispersed power. Congressional constituencies and the process of recruiting congressmen create strong tendencies toward localism. The bicameral system, with each house based on a vastly different principle of representation, tends to slow legislation and to require such numerous compromises that swift and comprehensive direction of affairs is difficult. Moreover, the vesting of broad authority in committee chairmen selected on the seniority principle subjects the fate of legislation to the biases of a single official, who often does not represent majority opinion in the country or the Congress.

The presidency and the Supreme Court are also institutions of dispersed power, although they are not as apparently decentralized as is the Congress. The executive branch, which seems centrally controlled, is interlaced with conflicts among the bureaus and departments, each supported by a complex of client groups that it serves. The links of the agencies to their clientele groups and to committees in Congress often render them more responsive to private and legislative wills than to the leadership of the President. Even in the executive office, presidential leadership is curbed by the limits on the President's time, energy, intellectual resources, knowledge, and interests. The President's staff and the agencies of the executive office may be in conflict over policy; only when the President takes a strong and insistent position will all his subordinates move together toward his announced policy objectives.

The Supreme Court, in spite of contemporary charges to the contrary, remains a passive institution, which must wait for adversaries to approach the bench. Yet even when decisions are made, they are subject to modification or nonenforcement when they are reinterpreted by the lower courts and a host of governmental agencies at the local, state, and national levels.

Political parties also do not offer a vehicle for bridging the separation and fragmentation of power in order to establish and then execute a set of national priorities. The party system, as explained in Part II, is centered around city halls, county courthouses, and state capitols. Localism is the dominant feature of American parties. Moreover, coalition building, rather than program formulating, is the primary art of the American politician.

Even if the dreams of party reformers became reality and the two parties were vehicles of clearly defined political programs that the voters could choose between on election day, the efficacy of party as a leadership instrument in the twenty-first century seems doubtful indeed, for the value of elections as instruments of government becomes doubtful. The ideal—most pronounced in the Jacksonian tradition—that all citizens are competent to decide policy at the polls and to hold office gives way in the face of highly complex and technical problems. The average citizen finds it increasingly difficult to understand the choices he is offered. And even if the parties present coherent policy alternatives, the formulation of these choices involves a host of prior policy decisions by technicians and scientists. The decisions remaining for the citizen become nominal. Thus, the whole concept of popular rule, majority decision, and the accountability of government is threatened as the policy-making role of technicians increases. Not only does power slip away from the people at the polls, but their elected representatives find it increasingly difficult to keep their hands on the throttles of government as the problems requiring solutions become more scientific and technical and, therefore, become the domain of experts rather than of generalists.

The future of traditional representative politics seems bleak indeed. The traditional checks on government become obstructions to governing. Localism and federalism are eroded; and the previously dispersed power centers within the three branches become increasingly centralized. The limits on government historically imposed by private social, economic, religious, and political institutions fall away as pervasive social control prevails. The political parties, with their widely decentralized power bases, become even less useful in policy making. The capacity of individuals to make choices about policy and the traditional majority-rule principle are both impaired by the technical nature of public problems.

Power becomes more centralized, less fettered, and increasingly the preserve of technocrats. All the problems we have examined require solutions that involve a high degree of social control. To limit the quantity of populations, quotas on family size will probably be needed. To assure population quality, selective breeding may have to be accepted. To guarantee rational technological change, the development and introduction of new agricultural and industrial techniques must be closely regulated. To channel aggressive tendencies and limit destructive capacities, extreme limitations on national sovereignty may have to be accepted and even the cherished myth about the permanence of the nation-state may have to be given up. Will this be intolerable? In terms of traditional values of personal liberty and freedom of action, these are intolerable outcomes. Measured against another standard—human survival—they may be acceptable, even desirable, limitations on individual selfishness.

These problems and their solutions suggest that traditional liberal democracy, the idea of the limited state that imposes only minimal restraints on individual and group competition, is neither possible nor desirable in the decades ahead. But how will the new order appear? Will it provide only the ennui, or boredom, that comes with homogeneity? Will the next age, as Father Chardin asks, offer only the sameness and sterility of an anthill? In fact, is a new world order possible? Surely a new order would require voluntary acceptance by the world powers, small and large, since the price of forced agreement is thermonuclear holocaust. What is the appropriate balance between individual freedom and collective action in the twenty-first century? Who will decide all of these questions: a Platonic elite? And, finally, *quis custodiet ipsos custodes,* who will guard the guardians?

one

American Political Thought and Culture

Commenting in 1835 on the American character, the French aristocrat Alexis de Tocqueville wrote, "The passions that stir the Americans most deeply are commercial and not political ones, or rather they carry a trader's habits over into the business of politics." Tocqueville, who was primarily concerned with the consequences of mass society on the future of political liberty, nevertheless exposed a central feature of the American political culture. As political scientist Gabriel Almond has remarked, American political culture is secular or multivalued. Having as its foundation a pluralistic social base, it has been a bargaining and experimental culture. In other words, American politics has had the earmarks of a game, a game in which the players enter the political marketplace to bargain or exchange resources rather than to convert or proselytize each other. Other observers, including Joseph Schumpeter and Louis Hartz, have described the political culture as "liberal," or one that assures continuity in the competitive political marketplace.

An understanding of America's political culture is essential to an analysis of its political institutions, because the former shaped the latter and established the limits or boundaries within which political struggles and contests have been conducted. The political culture, the society's central myth and values, has also acted as both a stimulus for reform and a gatekeeper against rapid social change. As a stimulus for reform, its values have been manipulated by various groups to criticize political institutions. Presidential nominating conventions, the electoral college, and congressional rules of procedure, for example, have been tested for conformity with the culture's ideals. The use of violence by groups—unions and industry as well as blacks and rednecks—has been similarly tested. Violence has been rejected as a legitimate form of protest because it threatens the resolution of conflict through competition in the political marketplace, a central value of the culture.

Before the American political culture can be described and its impact on political institutions explored, students of American government must first understand what is meant by culture in general and political culture in particular. The following definitions of these key terms, however, should be viewed as illustrative rather than exhaustive. There are two fundamental ways of describing a society's culture. The first method defines it as a central belief or value system—the central organizing myth. It is the collection of beliefs held by the members of a society that gives its institutions legitimacy. Thus in the United States, equality, that is, equality of opportunity, is a norm or expectation against which social institutions are evaluated. Institutions whose practices conform with the norm have a high degree of legitimacy conferred upon them by Americans. The second method defines culture as the actual pattern of behavior in the society: It is the distribution of behaviors relative to the established norms or central values. This approach attempts to account for observed departures from society's norms or expectations. The existence of two approaches emphasizes the inherent tension between idealized belief systems and actual behavior patterns in societies.

In every society there are a number of organizing myths and patterns of behavior. Some are concerned with a religious system; others with the pattern of economic exchange. Although these beliefs and behaviors are important and often impinge on the political system, they can be distinguished from the particular values and acts that are related to a society's public life or order.

The major concern in this section is the set of beliefs and behaviors that legitimate politics, or the making of public policy in the United States. These patterns of belief and behavior are taken to be the American political culture. By so limiting the field of inquiry, these values can be described and their development can be analyzed. In this way, students of American politics can begin to evaluate the congruence, disparity, or both, between the central myths and the political practice.

The Rules of Liberal Politics

Beginning with Tocqueville, observers of American politics have emphasized its secular, multivalued, or pluralistic basis. The constitutional foundation of American politics promotes a bargaining and pluralistic, rather than a preaching or proselytizing, political culture. It is argued that numerous constitutional limitations—the electoral college, the original, indirect method of electing senators, the prohibitions of the Bill of Rights—protect the rights of minorities and individuals and thereby assure the legitimacy of opposition, a central article of faith. The American party system promotes political marketplace competition through the operation of two national parties, both vying for the electorate's support. Political interest groups, which abound in American public life, also compete for a share of the public's resources. Competition in politics is generally regarded as essential to the liberal, secular, or pluralistic polity's maintenance. In fact, it is the cardinal principle of political liberalism.

Although liberals such as Joseph Schumpeter emphasize the importance of competitive political processes and institutions, they are aware of the need for some level of agreement or consensus. This consensus is based on the rules of the political game, which govern the limits and forms of political competition. It is a procedural rather than a substantive consensus, and an important element in it is the government's role in society. The purpose of the government, liberals urge, is to establish a framework within which political competition may occur. A major function of the government is to guarantee that the rules of political competition, agreed to by previous generations—especially the generation of saints who established the constitutional system—are adhered to by the competitors. Thus, a second major tenet of liberalism is defined: limited government, a public order that will do little more than provide the minimum security necessary for interest group competition to continue unimpeded.

The entire system rests on this general agreement, which includes such values as rule by majorities, protection of individual and minority rights, and fundamental fairness, a particularly British idea. Rule by majorities, however, does not require that a majority of the citizens decide each political issue; it simply dictates that majority rule shall be an operational principle or useful means of government. Protection of individual and minority rights, while stated as a constitutional absolute, also operates within certain limitations; namely, they may be suspended when the survival of the polity is at stake. Fundamental fairness, that elusive British notion, means only that settled procedures, agreed upon in advance, may be used in political contests; the rules may not be changed in midstream.

In the United States, the fundamental consensus is almost exclusively procedural rather than substantive. Although there is a generally recognized need to reconcile the competing values of individual liberty and collective welfare, there is little agreement on specific, substantive goals or the priority of national needs. Furthermore, there are no standards against which questions of distributive justice may be evaluated. Students of American politics rarely ask who *should* win or lose. Rather they tend to ask who *actually* wins or loses in political contests. How much has the oil industry won or lost in the latest revision of the tax laws? What has labor gained from the expansion of Social Security coverage? When political debate is cast in these terms, questions of distributive justice are much easier to answer. The national interest is no more nor less than the outcome of the political struggle. The terms of the temporary truce agreed upon by the participants in the struggle appear in the form of congressional acts, presidential orders, and court decisions. The Supreme Court's early interpretation (Slaughter House cases, 1873) of the Fourteenth Amendment's due process clause illustrates this emphasis. The Court narrowed the substantive and, by inference, expanded the procedural meaning of due process. The procedural emphasis of American political discourse makes discussions of national goals or priorities seem vacuous. The fact is that the American political vocabulary almost precludes discussions of substantive justice.

The American Political Culture: Genesis

Until recently most Americans accepted the dominance of procedural consensus without question. The American value system, as Daniel Boorstin argues, has a quality of "givenness," a compelling historical necessity. With the exception of the Civil War, the basic value system has remained intact and unquestioned for almost two hundred years. It has survived wars, depressions, the industrial revolution, and rapid technological innovation. There are numerous explanations of this basic stability. Two, however, stand out in relative importance. The first is the nation's almost uninterrupted historic continuity, a historic continuity that not even a revolution, a civil war, and a major depression destroyed. The second is the nation's relative prosperity. This prosperity has permitted great social mobility and has channeled citizens' attention away from public objects toward private concerns, which could be pursued in relative security. Since they were neither threatened by external forces nor pressed by economic scarcity, Americans had little reason to question liberal values. In this environment the development of American liberal democracy was incremental, almost unconscious, without a doctrinaire rationale. It is to this mode of development that students of American politics must turn if they are to understand the origin and operation of contemporary political institutions and the crisis in contemporary liberal democracy.

The American Revolution, as Louis Hartz and Daniel Boorstin note, was not a subspecies of the European political and social revolution. American revolutionaries did not overthrow an oppressive aristocracy. The revolution did not result in mass social upheaval, characteristic of both the French and the Russian revolutions. It was a colonial rebellion undertaken with great reluctance and hesitation. Curiously, it emphasized the continuity of British values, traditions, and institutions. American revolutionaries, such as they were, attempted to restore or reaffirm such traditional English liberties as trial by jury and representative government. The general thrust of the revolution was conservative—that is, conservative of liberal values. Revolution in the United States was an act of historic continuity rather than a rupture with tradition.

If the American Revolution was an act of historic continuity, it follows that the postrevolutionary period, though politically unsettled, cannot be compared to the Bonapartist putsch that followed the French Revolution. George Washington certainly was not a Napoleon Bonaparte. Although governmental instability existed and some uprisings occurred, mass unrest and turbulence did not grip the nation in a wave of fear or panic. Furthermore, governmental instability under the Articles of Confederation was soon recognized and dealt with in a lawyer-like manner by the delegates who convened in Philadelphia in 1787 to temper the excesses of mass democracy. Alexander Hamilton and other Federalists have been criticized as antidemocrats. But their constitutional system actually promoted the conservative side of liberalism: stability and continuity, the economic basis of the developing class structure, and the general freedom of commercial and entrepreneurial action within a free and protected national trade area. Some observers have argued that the Federalists emphasized these values to the detriment of mass democracy. But no matter how much the Federalists tilted the competitive system in their favor, they did not reject the basic premises of liberalism.

The constitutional system created in 1787 both restrained mass democracy and promoted governmental inaction or self-restraint. By deliberately fragmenting or dispersing power throughout the federal system, many of the constitutional delegates hoped to frustrate popular sovereignty. The indirect election of senators, the limited presidential veto, the confirmation of presidential appointments by the Senate, and the electoral college—the so-called checks-and-balance system—were all devices to insulate government from direct mass intervention. These techniques also served to prevent, or at least to retard, governmental action. They served as brakes on rapid social, economic, and political change. In other words, the legal craftsmen who wrote the Constitution created a governmental system that could do little more than secure "interest group" liberalism. In addition, their constitutional framework stated the basic conditions under which that interest group struggle would take place. The two great political movements of eighteenth-century America, the revolution and the Constitutional Convention, conserved and further articulated the major tenet of American liberalism: political marketplace competition. But, it was the basic conditions of American life that promoted the system's survival. Relative isolation from the great power conflicts that shattered Europe allowed Americans to turn their energies toward exploitation of the economic resources that the continent offered. The expansion of commerce in a free trade area, the continuing settlement of new lands in the West, and a nascent industrial revolution promoted economic security. Absorbed with the tasks of economic development, there was little need or time for most Americans to question the legitimacy of the system. Unlike the European industrial revolution, with its charnel houses, incipient American capitalism did not press class upon class in the competition for resources and living space.

While the Federalists emphasized the conservative side of liberalism, the Jeffersonian Republicans and the Jacksonians who followed represented its popular orientation. Both Jefferson and Jackson, who claimed at various times in their political careers to favor popular participation in government, expanded the powers of the presidency and the national government. Thus, they helped to vitiate the very conditions that maximized popular control of government. In his effort to avoid a direct confrontation with England, Jefferson ordered an embargo in 1808, which hastened the development of the industrial system by forcing American commerce and industry to substitute domestic products for imports no longer available to American consumers. The embargo undermined the agrarian arcadia in which the independent farmers could directly participate in government. Thomas Jefferson's Louisiana Purchase pushed the nation down the road toward the European industrial system that further expanded both the national government and the president's power and he abhorred. By employing Alexander Hamilton's means, the national government's expansive powers, Jefferson unwittingly moved the nation a long way toward the Federalists' objectives: a centralized and industrialized national political system.

Jefferson and Jackson's major objective, according to Arthur Schlesinger, was to promote "the struggle among competing groups for the control of the state." Only through open competition, free access to the political marketplace, could political liberty be preserved. Jackson's war with Nicholas Biddle and the Second Bank of the United States was an attempt to maintain a balance among groups in American public life. It is doubtful that Jackson opposed the national bank in principle. Rather, he opposed the excessive influence that Biddle and the bank possessed—their easy access to the nation's resources, which impaired the government's role as an arbiter among competing interests in society. Although numerous reforms during the Jackson epoch—the national party conventions, expansion of the franchise, and the spoils system—emphasized the popular side of American liberalism, the expansion of presidential and national governmental power foreshadowed the demise of limited government. As later events revealed, vast governmental powers would be necessary to maintain the historic balance or equilibrium of interests in American public life.

The theory of limited government, that is, of government as an arbiter of interests, also found expression in John C. Calhoun's *A Disquisition On Government,* first published in 1851. In contrast to the positive thrust of Jackson's policies, Calhoun's theory of the concurrent majority was a negative statement of American political pluralism, and, as Peter Drucker has noted, it has been a major organizing principle of American politics. Simply stated, Calhoun's theory is that every major interest in the United States—economic and sectional—should have a veto over the policies that affect it directly. Calhoun was neither the first nor the last analyst of American politics to discover interest group pluralism in the United States. Not unlike the Federalists, who preceded him, and contemporary American pluralists, such as Robert A. Dahl and David B. Truman, Calhoun elevated interest group pluralism to a "basic principle of free government," emphasizing the importance of multiple group interests and power centers as a restraint on absolute government. In fact, Calhoun concluded that the only way to assure the national community's survival and to prevent tyranny is through the concurring voice of the whole polity.

Within a decade after the *Disquisition* first appeared, however, the procedural consensus upon which the theory of the concurrent majority rested collapsed. The Civil War marked its first major test. Under the strain of sectional and economic conflicts, the procedural consensus proved inadequate in reconciling fundamental substantive debates in American politics. The Civil War also represented an important rupture in the "normal," or "natural," course of American history, marking the failure of the political system to reconcile competing substantive values within the framework of the traditional rules. Moreover, the rupture was not a temporary one.

The Civil War gave expression to two powerful forces in American culture that had remained suppressed for more than fifty years: racism and violence. In the first epoch, from the Constitutional Convention to the Civil War, the Negro was regarded in law and in fact as an article of real property. Two clauses of the Constitution tacitly recognized the slave's status. The first, in Article I, apportioned representation among the states in the House of Representatives by "adding to the whole number of persons . . . three fifths of all other persons." The second, in Article IV, provided for the return of indentured servants and fugitive slaves "on claim of the party to whom such service or labor may be due." In 1857, in the Dred Scott case, the Supreme Court confronted the issue of the Negro's status. Chief Justice Taney, speaking for the majority, raised the question squarely when he asked: "can a negro, whose ancestors were imported into this country and sold as slaves, become a member of the political community . . . and as such become entitled to all the rights, and privileges, and immunities, guarantied . . . to the citizen." In answering his own question, Taney excluded the Negro from the American political community, noting that at the time of the Constitutional Convention the Negro was "considered as a subordinate and inferior class of beings who had been subjugated by the dominant race . . . and had no rights or privileges but such as those who held the power and the government might choose to grant them." Thus, the Supreme Court seemed to close the door permanently on the Negro, assigning him to an inferior position outside the national political community.

Although the war changed the Negro's legal-constitutional status, it did not make him a member of the political community. The post-Civil War constitutional amendments (the thirteenth, fourteenth, and fifteenth) terminated slavery, expanded citizenship, and prohibited the deprivation of citizens' rights "on account of race," guaranteeing legal and political, rather than social and economic, equality. The Declaration's promises of life, liberty, and the pursuit of happiness for all men still lay beyond the black man's reach. In the Reconstruction period a few attempts were made to improve the Negro's status. With the end of Reconstruction and the restoration of civil government in the South, however, the Negro was assigned a new inferior social and political status and, once again, was marked as a pariah, a caste, apart from the national political community.

By the end of the nineteenth century, the Negro was excluded from political participation in a number of states. Poll taxes, white primaries, literacy tests, and grandfather clauses were employed effectively to exclude both Negroes and poor whites from political participation in southern states. Political exclusion was accompanied by racial segregation in transportation; in places of public accommodation such as hotels, theaters, and restaurants; and in public institutions such as schools and hospitals. The races were socially separated in a way uncontemplated prior to the war. Jim Crow statutes and practices created two Americas separated by an invisible but formidable barrier.

In 1896 the Supreme Court legitimated and institutionalized the two Americas in a landmark decision (*Plessy v. Ferguson*) that upheld the constitutionality of "separate but equal" facilities in intrastate railway transportation. The Court answered the charge that racial separation in places of public accommodation violated the equal protection clause of the Fourteenth Amendment by arguing that although the amendment's purpose was "to enforce the absolute equality of the two races before the law . . . in the nature of things it could not have been intended to abolish distinctions based upon color, or to enforce social, as distinguished from political, equality, or a comingling of the two races upon terms unsatisfactory to either." The Plessy decision, providing a legal-constitutional basis for racial segregation in education and places of public accommodation for more than fifty years, separated the two races physically and socially, undermined political consensus, promoted the existence of two political cultures of unequal status, and fostered a subject political culture among black Americans.

Although Negro organizations, such as the National Association for the Advancement of Colored People, arose in the twentieth century to challenge the legal-constitutional status of the separate but equal doctrine as well as other patterns of legal-political discrimination, their efforts were largely unsuccessful prior to World War II. In a series of decisions between 1944 and 1954, however, the Supreme Court undermined the constitutional basis for the two Americas. A major breakthrough occurred in 1944 (see *Smith v. Allwright*) when the Court overturned the constitutionality of the white primary in Texas as a deprivation of the "right of citizens to vote on account of color." Shortly after (in 1948) the Supreme Court, overturning a long line of precedents to the contrary, invalidated states' enforcement of discriminatory covenants in the sale of private housing as a violation of the equal protection clause of the Fourteenth Amendment (see *Shelley v. Kraemer*). This decision struck at the legal basis of residential discrimination in many cities in the North and East. In 1950 the Court began to attack racial discrimination in higher education by denying the possibility of separate but equal physical facilities in graduate and professional training (see *McLaurin v. Oklahoma* and *Sweatt v. Painter*). The most important blow to the doctrine occurred in 1954 (see *Brown v. Board of Education of Topeka, Kansas*), when, in a landmark decision that will long be remembered for its potential social consequences, the Court unanimously ruled that separate but physically equal facilities in primary and secondary education were inherently unequal. In an opinion that stirred the national community's conscience, Chief Justice Earl Warren concluded that the separation of black children "from others of similar age and qualifications solely because of their race generates a feeling of inferiority as to their status in the community that may affect their hearts and minds in a way unlikely ever to be undone." With this and other decisions made in the decade between 1944 and 1954, long-rooted patterns of segregation in American public life began to reverse.

As the history of the black struggle since 1954 reveals, however, the task of liberation remains incomplete. The black people's movement, though marked by internal conflict, has passed through several phases since the Brown decision. At first many black leaders (Whitney Young and Roy Wilkins, for example) focused their efforts and hopes on the courts and started a round of litigation to implement the Brown decision. Other black leaders, most notably Martin Luther King, Jr., frustrated by a lethargic President and Congress, began in the early 1960s a series of nationwide, nonviolent demonstrations. Attempting to awaken the nation's conscience to correct more than a hundred years of discrimination, black leaders challenged the consensus of the political system through direct action. Without the resources of money and prestige, they substituted bodies for direct access to the corridors of power.

Between 1957 and 1965 Congress finally responded with a series of civil rights acts. While these measures held forth the promise of *eventual* membership in the national political community, Congress placed the primary burden on the courts, where further delays frequently occurred. By 1965 many blacks were convinced that their grievances were once again being ignored by white America. Against this backdrop of inaction and frustration, they rejected political action as a means of making their claims and, instead, began to advocate the case of black separatism. Some blacks turned to violence and other forms of direct confrontation as a means of attaining otherwise unrealizable objectives.

The many years of frustration finally burst with the Watts riots of 1965, which were followed in 1966 and 1967 by similar riots in Newark, Detroit, Houston, Jackson, Tampa, Cincinnati, and Atlanta. In all, more than twenty-three major American cities experienced mass violence in the spring and summer of 1967. In the wake of these riots, the American political community finally became conscious of the existence of mass unrest among black Americans. After one hundred years of subjugation, black Americans were making their presence felt in the form of violent action. Only when blacks directly questioned the system's procedural consensus—only when the rules of the game were threatened—did the political community awaken.

Since 1965 the cry of black power has challenged many traditional rules. Black militants have demonstrated that the rules of liberal politics are applied to, and accepted by, white rather than black Americans. Rapp Brown, Eldridge Cleaver, and other black militants have not only destroyed many of the cherished myths of liberalism, but they have also shown how fragile the consensus of American public life is. Moreover, they have made white America painfully aware of its greatest failure since the Civil War—its inability to create a liberal society whose Constitution is truly color blind. These problems, first exposed during the Civil War and exacerbated in the period of rapid industrialization that followed, have posed a major challenge to the future of liberalism in the twentieth century.

The Civil War was also a prelude to the forces of industrialization and technological innovation that would continue to test the adequacy of the liberal political consensus in the twentieth century. In the decades between the end of the Civil War and World War I, forces that reshaped public life—the country's industrial machine and the great public corporations—were born. It was in this period that the American farmer was forced into the national credit system, and that both farmers and laboring men organized on a broad scale

—the Grange and the American Federation of Labor—to restore the historic balance that had existed in a much simpler era, an era in which individual laborers could still bargain independently with small entrepreneurs.

The postbellum period marked an increasing concentration of wealth and a growing disparity between the top and bottom of the economic system. The emergence of the great corporation not only encouraged concentration of wealth, but also promoted concentration of political power, since the dispersal of stock, along with such devices as garnered proxies, allowed relatively small groups of men to control the corporations. Exercising a disproportionate share of political influence, some industries—railroads, steel, oil, and coal—controlled state legislatures and, through the legislatures, dictated the choice of United States senators. For a time it appeared that the government of the United States was indentured to the nation's corporations. The historic balance of forces among competing interests was threatened in a way unimagined by the Jeffersonians and Jacksonians. Historically given rules, such as free and open competition (access to the political marketplace), were jeopardized by the new forms of power and modes of economic organization. It was against this backdrop that a series of reform movements entered the American political arena.

Richard Hofstadter, in his introduction to *The Age of Reform*, wrote, "Just as the cycle of American history running from the Civil War to the 1890's can be thought of chiefly as a period of industrial and continental expansion and political conservatism, so the age that has just passed, running from about 1890 to the second World War, can be considered an age of reform." In this latter period three great reform movements captured the public's attention in an attempt to restore a balance of interests within the liberal, democratic procedural consensus. The first movement, Populism, was an agrarian revolt that reached its zenith in the mid-1890s. Progressivism, an even more diffuse, middle-class movement, spanned the decade prior to World War I. The New Deal, the last of the great reform movements, was cut short by the nation's preparations for World War II. Although each of these reform movements differed in important ways and was not internally homogeneous, they all accepted and operated within the rules of the game to redistribute power and influence in the political system. Their objective was the restoration of a competitive society: the use of governmental power against the new industrial corporations.

In the 1890s agrarian protest movements emerged in American politics. Concentrated in the Midwest and the South, agrarian reformers responded to the farmer's new status in the economy. The farmer still perceived his role in terms of the independent yeoman myth that the Jeffersonians had promoted in the early nineteenth century, according to which the yeoman-farmer was democracy's lynch pin, its independent, rational man. Self-sufficient, the yeoman-farmer produced what he consumed and sold his small surplus in an immediate market. Under these conditions the yeoman-farmer had not participated extensively in the nation's market economy and credit system. With the Civil War, however, the American farmer's independent status declined. A new surplus agriculture, required by the manpower shortage resulting from the Civil War and the nation's industrialization and made possible by advances in farm machinery, changed the farmer's status from independent yeoman to dependent businessman. The need for expensive farm machinery and large tracts of land for its effective use placed the farmer in direct contact with the nation's credit system. The production of surplus cash crops such as wheat also made him part of regional, national, and, later, international markets. Farmers were forced to deal directly with railroads and grain elevators, essential elements in the new agriculture, and with the large corporations that bought and processed their agricultural products.

Under such conditions the discrepancy between the yeoman myth and the farmer's dependent status became apparent. To deal with the new conditions, farmers pursued several strategies. Some called for public regulation of railroads and grain elevators; others for cooperative ownership of these facilities; still others for public ownership of them. Thus, agrarian reformers attempted to restore the individual farmer's position vis-à-vis the large corporations. Their solutions, for the most part, were well within the accepted framework of the political system, but relatively few Populists saw their plight as a reflection on the basic structure or operation of the system. Even fewer perceived, or admitted, that farmers and laboring men were confronted by the same condition: a political system that allowed the capitalist interest to appropriate power with few limitations.

Some Populists like William Jennings Bryan attained national prominence, but failed to capture control of American political institutions because they were unable to consolidate their gains in several states and regions. More radical Populists also were largely unsuccessful in galvanizing rural discontent into a proletarian movement allied with labor and other urban interests. The basic structure of the political system finally anesthetized discontent. Populist discontent reached its apogee in William Jennings Bryan's 1896 presidential campaign and then faded from the American political scene. Like other reform movements, many of the Populists' demands subtly found their way into the political programs of the two major parties. The Populists were not entirely unsuccessful in curbing some of the excesses of capitalism; their reform program left a residue that continued to shape subsequent political contests and upon which later reformers capitalized.

In contrast to the agrarian, Populist movement, the Progressives, as Richard Hofstadter has noted, were urban and middle class. Or, as William Allen White wrote in his autobiography, "If the Progressives were a party of protest, they were not in the least proletarian . . . the movement which Theodore Roosevelt led in 1912 was in the main in its heart of hearts *petit bourgeois:* little businessmen, professional men, well-to-do farmers, skilled artisans from the upper brackets of organized labor." Just as Billy Sunday and Dwight L. Moody brought the religious revival to the city, reform political leadership passed from William Jennings Bryan of the Platte River country to Theodore Roosevelt of Oyster Bay, New York. The Progressive movement, which culminated in the 1912 presidential election, was largely a middle-class movement whose energies were focused on style and status issues: the politics of governmental reform and the restoration of the position of the small entrepreneurial class. Not unlike the Populists, the Progressives were a diverse political group. They counted among their numbers noisy muckrakers such as Ida Tarbell, pragmatic reformers such as Teddy Roosevelt, and strident political evangelists such as Robert LaFollette, Sr.

The Progressives entered the American political arena at a time when post-Civil War changes in labor, business, industry, and agriculture were consolidated. As the decades following the Civil War marked the genesis of American corporate capitalism, the turn of the century witnessed its apotheosis. Americans living between 1890 and 1910 saw the birth of Standard Oil, U.S. Steel, and the Tobacco Trust, whose power and organization further undermined both economic and political competition. The individual entered the economic and political marketplace without the vast resources available to the nation's corporations. Clearly, without some form of governmental intervention, the historic equilibrium of interests could not be restored. Even with governmental regulation of the economy, some Progressives feared that the task was hopeless.

In addition to undermining or destroying the balance of interests in American society, the new economic order irreversibly altered the class structure. The petite bourgeoisie (shopkeepers and small manufacturers) and the independent professionals (lawyers, doctors, and university professors) were displaced by the crass new men of wealth as society's ruling class. The petite bourgeoisie could only read in horror about James Hazen Hyde's 1902 dinner party for Ambassador Cambon of France, which, according to Walter Lord, cost the Equitable Assurance Society's investors and policyholders $12,600. Attempting to top this extravaganza, Hyde, in 1905, imported Madame Gabrielle Réjane and her theater company from Paris, hired the forty-piece orchestra of the Metropolitan Opera House for the evening, and converted Louis Sherry's restaurant into a "reasonable replica" of the Versailles Palace. As the corporation's structure had separated management, ownership, and control, so the rapid development of the industrial system destroyed the relation between wealth and social status. In a society in which fortunes were made and lost quickly, wealthy men, often without inherited social status, used their newly acquired wealth in bizarre social forms and frequently employed raw force in politics. The social status of the older middle class was no match for the capitalists' wealth and power.

The position of the older middle class was also threatened by the emergence of a new immigrant-laboring class in the United States. Beginning in 1890 a new pattern of immigration flooded the country with southern and eastern Europeans searching for streets paved with gold in the United States; Jews, Poles, Russians, and Italians came in great waves for almost thirty years. Immigrating from folk or peasant societies whose political cultures differed markedly from Anglo-American and western European liberal democratic societies, these new immigrants were easily manipulated by American capitalists—in whose industries they sweated—and by urban political machines. The Irish, Poles, Italians, and other immigrant groups trouped to the machine's colors, and, in turn, the urban machine looked after their needs, providing jobs, food, coal, homes, and protection from the police. Tammany's men were on hand to attend all of the rights of passage—baptisms, confirmations, weddings, and funerals. The machine was a great social insurance agency in the days before Franklin Roosevelt's New Deal nationalized and bureaucratized the Social Security system.

Caught between the new upper class's quest for power and the machine-manipulated lower classes, the older middle class turned to a new round of reform to reclaim its status and power within the framework of liberal democracy. The Progressives were their spokesmen in the struggle to restore the historic balance of interests in American society. Although the Progressives were concerned with the problems of labor and the consumer, they focused their energies on the disproportionate power of the trusts and on governmental reform. They siphoned vital energies out of class conflicts by dwelling on style issues. The Progressives, as Richard Hofstadter has argued, represented a class, or status, politics attempting to operate within the framework of interest group liberalism.

In an effort to reduce the influence of the trusts on government, Theodore Roosevelt employed for the first time the powers granted under the Sherman Antitrust Act. Although he did not dismantle the trusts, as his critics eagerly pointed out, his noisy pronouncements had an important symbolic value: they represented his commitment to interest group liberalism. In fact, he did not intend to dismantle the trusts, but simply to limit their influence on government through public exposure, just as the muckrakers were doing in the nation's press. Roosevelt, in contrast to the more radical muckrakers, stood as "a counterpoise to the fat materialism of the wealthy and the lurking menace of the masses." Theodore Roosevelt employed the presidency as a balance wheel, or an arbiter of interests, in the American political system.

Other Progressives (Robert LaFollette, Sr., in Wisconsin, Hiram Johnson of California, and the Farmer Labor leaders in Minnesota) were equally concerned with the loss of popular control of government. Everywhere the "interests" seemed to own state governments and manipulate the urban masses. Thus, the Progressives called for broad procedural reforms in local, state, and national politics, urging more democracy in order to cure democracy's ills. They argued for direct primaries to take nominations out of the hands of party bosses who controlled district, state, and national nominating conventions, and for the popular election of United States senators, who, they concluded, were the tools of predatory interests that controlled their selection through the state legislatures. The initiative, referendum, and recall were also championed as instruments of popular control and responsible government.

In retrospect, some of the Progressives' reforms actually further eroded, rather than promoted, popular control of government. The direct primary, for example, probably reduced popular participation in the nominating process, especially in minority parties that operate in one-party states. Furthermore, the very same bosses who had controlled the conventions now focused their attention on the primaries. Well-organized urban machines profited from the direct primary; with platoons of merchandisable votes, urban bosses like Boise Penrose were in a better position to dictate the selection of senators, governors, and presidents. A few reforms, such as the expansion of state civil service systems, also undermined responsible party government. Some governors, as in Wisconsin, were virtually stripped of their patronage power, which left them defenseless in their battles with recalcitrant party members in the legislature. In later periods, when popularly elected governors confronted malapportioned legislatures, the patronage system would have been a powerful resource in important public policy struggles.

Some of the Progressives' reforms were not widely accepted, and others often became enmeshed in a variety of local and state issues. The initiative, referendum, and recall never became popular in the East. In highly partisan Pennsylvania, for example, nonpartisan election of local and judicial officers was employed for a limited time in third-class cities, but this ended shortly after World War I. In Minnesota, nonpartisan election of county officers became tangled in the prohibition issue; a few state senators attempted to kill the bill in the 1913 session by including legislative positions on the nonpartisan ballot, but the liquor interests secured passage of the measure in the House. Minnesota's nonpartisan legislature was more the result of a historic accident than of the reform impulse. However much their reforms were resisted or confused by local and state issues, the Progressives' objectives remained constant: the adjustment of the new industrial order to the free marketplace. Their efforts centered on reform of governmental institutions in an attempt to restore political marketplace competition.

The Progressives reached their zenith in Teddy Roosevelt's "Bull Moose" presidential campaign of 1912 and soon faded from the scene as an organized national political movement. They were somewhat more successful than the Populists in capturing control of state governments, but, like them, they were unable to seize control of Congress or the presidency. Since some of their reforms found their way into state statutes and constitutions, they, too, were able to curb some of the excesses of capitalism. Whether these governmental reforms actually restored political marketplace competition and popular control of government is doubtful. Nevertheless, the impact of Progressivism continued to be felt long after it faded from the political scene.

Progressivism as an organized movement may have come to an end after the 1912 presidential election, but it began a political debate that informed the New Deal's program a generation later. The 1912 election debate between Theodore Roosevelt and Woodrow Wilson underscored many of the differences in position among Progressives. Roosevelt always had accepted the necessity for large-scale economic organization. His action against the trusts, especially in the Great Northern Securities case, was welcomed by many businessmen who found Great Northern's power obnoxious. He had always enjoyed the support of a large segment of the business community, which recognized the symbolic nature of his antitrust program. His objective was not control, but business regulation through the exercise of the power of the president and the national government in actively arbitrating among interests; his objective was not the destruction of the corporate-industrial economy, but its preservation within the liberal democratic framework.

These views were articulated by Herbert Croly (founder of the *New Republic),* Walter Lippman, and other "New Nationalist" Progressive intellectuals. Croly emphasized that when government had intervened in the past, urged on by old nationalists such as Alexander Hamilton, it had entered the contest on behalf of "the special interests"; but he argued that public power could also be employed to bring the great corporations under governmental control according to Jeffersonian objectives and that continued laissez-faire policies would only further serve the special interests. Governmental power, he concluded, must be expanded to make property interests serve human needs. Thus, New Nationalist Progressives like Croly argued for the use of the Constitution's commerce clause as a national police power to regulate wages, hours, conditions of employment, and child labor in order to make corporate industry serve the nation's interests.

In contrast to the New Nationalist Progressives, Woodrow Wilson, as Arthur S. Link has written, called for a "New Freedom." Wilson, a Progressive Jeffersonian believing in a return to laissez-faire individualism, argued that the government's power should be "used only to sweep away privileges and artificial barriers to the development of individual energies, and to preserve and restore competition in business." He did not believe that the government had a responsibility to assure individual and group welfare. In his inaugural address Wilson characterized his administration as a "work or restoration." "Our duty," he said, "is to cleanse, to reconsider, to restore, to correct the evil, without impairing the good." In a series of messages to Congress, he defined the major tasks of restoration. His New Freedom program would restore the yeoman-farmer's position by making the credit system just. It would revive competitive, entrepreneurial capitalism by breaking up the trusts and monopolies, which sapped individual initiative. In a special address to Congress on January 20, 1914, Wilson concluded, "We are all agreed that 'private monopoly is indefensible and intolerable,' and our programme is founded upon that conviction." Woodrow Wilson was in search of Jefferson's republic of independent yeomen-farmers and small businessmen. It was the government's responsibility to do no more than cleanse the evil of bigness and restore the older, more perfect order.

Wilson's hopes for the return to Jeffersonian ideals were expressed by Louis D. Brandeis, who shared the President's misgivings about bigness in industry and government, and who believed in the restoration of economic and political individualism once the government had purged monopoly. He accepted intervention by the government only insofar as it was designed to overthrow private monopoly and restore the free competition of small business. Although Brandeis and other Jeffersonians were not insensitive to the plight of labor, they did not accept vigorous governmental intervention to secure individual welfare; instead they believed that if economic monopoly were destroyed, many social ills and problems that plagued the workingman would be resolved. Not unlike Croly, Brandeis was Wilson's resident intellectual, providing rationale for the New Freedom.

The debate between Theodore Roosevelt and Woodrow Wilson represents a major dividing line for twentieth-century liberals. On the one side are liberal politicians and intellectuals who accept the new industrial order and the government's responsibility to regulate and humanize American capitalism. Later New Deal economic theoreticians such as Adolphe Berle would argue that the government must intervene to spread or redistribute the costs of capitalism. On the other side are Jeffersonian-Wilsonian individualists who urge the government to cleanse the nation and restore a more pristine and sanguine climate. This debate, which surfaced in the 1912 presidential election, has continued to preoccupy American liberals and conservatives. At times the debate has been blurred by the rush of events, but it always has reemerged as a focal point of controversy.

The debate among Progressives over the government's role as an arbiter of interests was soon cut short by United States involvement in World War I.

Not only did the war absorb national energies and bring both reform and restoration to a halt, but it also required the organization of the nation's productive capacities by the government. Woodrow Wilson, the apostle of American individualism, was forced to accept extensive government regulation and control of the economy to successfully prosecute the war. Among other wartime measures, Wilson accepted the need for censorship of the press, government propaganda, and alien and sedition laws. World War I was America's first real exercise in total mobilization. And, as Woodrow Wilson knew, total mobilization would not be conducive to liberty.

The political debate interrupted by the war was not resumed in the 1920s. Although some Americans, most notably farmers, experienced a postwar slump, the decade opened with the promise of unlimited prosperity. Disillusioned by the war, which had destroyed the political optimism of the Gilded Age, many Americans turned away from politics and public discourse to lose themselves in an orgy of self-indulgence. It was an era in which America convinced itself, in the words of the Frenchman Emil Coué, "Day by day in every way I am getting better and better." The new technology provided exciting diversions. On November 20, 1920, the nation's first commercial broadcast station, KDKA in Pittsburgh, Pennsylvania, ushered in the age of the radio. In the 1920s millions of Americans also thrilled to the silent screen performances of Rudolph Valentino and Clara Bow. The new Model T Ford also provided an evening's entertainment out on the town. All these not only provided diversions, but they also changed America's daily habits.

A new America was in the making. Americans witnessed the application of technological innovation to industry, which, like industrialization and corporate organization, would require governmental intervention and control. Regulation of interstate transportation would soon be followed by public licensing of the air waves and the establishment of routes for the fledgling commercial aviation industry. The issue that remained unresolved in the political and intellectual hiatus of the 1920s was whether the new adjustments could take place within the liberal democratic framework or whether fundamental changes in American life would require new forms of governmental organization and different political rules. Was liberalism equal to the task that lay ahead? Or, would a new collective order be needed to manage the nation's problems? Unfortunately, the economic bubble burst in 1929 before these important questions could be examined in public discourse.

On March 4, 1933, when Franklin Roosevelt became the thirty-second President of the United States, the nation was in the throes of the Great Depression. The new President, realizing the proportions of the crisis, called for "action, and action now" in his inaugural address. However forceful Roosevelt's appeal for action appeared to millions of Americans, many observers, according to Arthur Schlesinger, Jr., disagreed about his objectives. While Roosevelt's contemporaries and recent historians concur that his immediate objective was to ameliorate the Depression's effects on the nation, there is little consensus on the rationale of his administration or his long-range purpose. Did Roosevelt intend to cure the nation's economic ills by simply restoring the health of the corporate-industrial economy? Did he hope to construct a new social order based either on Brandeis' individualism or on a new collectivism? Or was Franklin Roosevelt, like his cousin Theodore, just an arbiter among competing interests in American society? Roosevelt's significance cannot be measured simply by analyzing his contribution to restoring economic prosperity or his wartime leadership. He must also be understood in terms of the consequences of his administration for the future of American liberalism. In the fourteen years that Franklin Roosevelt was President, contemporary American society was born.

The New Deal, like Populism and Progressivism, included many diverse elements. There were the vigorous social and economic planners like Rexford Guy Tugwell, the economist, and Arthur Morgan, the Tennessee Valley Authority (TVA) director, who accepted and welcomed the government's responsibility to comprehensively plan and organize the society's future. In the new utopia there would be a whole nation of model towns like Norris, Tennessee (the community built by the TVA). There also were the Brandeisian individualists, such as Felix Frankfurter and his "red hot dogs" Benjamin Cohen and Thomas Corcoran, who "urged a return to a more competitive society, not to the anarchy of unreconstructed profiteering, but to 'regulated competition.'" As with the Progressives and the Populists, these two views were fought out within the administration, amid attempts to restore economic order, rarely resulting in a decisive victory for one side or the other. Instead, dominance shifted gradually from the Tugwell liberals to the Brandeisians. The general change in the direction of the New Deal has prompted Arthur Schlesinger, Jr., William E. Leuchtenberg, and other recent American historians to argue that there were actually two New Deals. The first began with the first hundred days and lasted until 1935. The second New Deal opened with the second hundred days and continued until preparations for the war intervened. These two New Deals are characterized by differences in orientation to the government's role in society.

The purpose of the first New Deal was to restore the economic health of the nation through vigorous governmental intervention and regulation of the economy. Its major landmarks were the Agricultural Adjustment Administration, the Securities and Exchange Commission, the National Industrial Recovery Administration (NIRA), the Federal Deposit Insurance Corporation, and the Home Owners Loan Corporation. Although each of these agencies had multiple purposes, their central objective was the restoration of the corporate-capitalist order through governmental action. The Agricultural Adjustment Act established a system of farm price supports, which ultimately pumped money into the industrial economy. Shortly thereafter the government created the Farm Credit Administration to refinance defaulted farm mortgages. Inasmuch as the Agricultural Adjustment Act was directed toward the support of staple crops like grains, the government's program dealt a death blow to the small and marginal farmers and hastened the development of the corporate farm. The Home Owners Loan Act saved thousands of small home owners from forced sales, but it also aided larger real estate interests by redeeming defaulted mortgages with government bonds. The Glass-Steagall banking bill, which established the Federal Deposit Insurance Corporation, aided bankers by insuring bank deposits. The Securities and Exchange Act of 1934 established the Securities and Exchange Commission to prevent future manipulation of the stock market by insiders and to regulate trading practices in the nation's stock exchanges. Each of these measures attempted to rescue a particular sector of the economy through regulation and support. Their purpose—to restore corporate-industrial capitalism—was essentially conservative.

The clearest and most comprehensive example of the conservatism of the New Deal was the National Industrial Recovery Act. Simply stated in its declaration of policy, its purpose was to

> . . . provide for the general welfare by promoting the organization of industry for the purpose of cooperative action among trade groups, to induce and maintain united action of labor and management under adequate governmental sanctions and supervision, to eliminate unfair competitive practices, to promote the fullest possible utilization of the present productive capacity of industries, to avoid undue restriction of production (except as may be temporarily required), to increase the consumption of industrial and agricultural products by increasing purchasing power, to reduce and relieve unemployment, to improve standards of labor, and otherwise to rehabilitate industry and to conserve natural resources.

In order to attain a state of cooperative capitalism, Congress authorized the President to establish competitive codes for each major industry. The codes actually were drawn by representative trade groups and associations in each industry to assure protection for consumers, competitors, and employees. Theoretically the codes were subject to the President's approval. Although they were designed to promote industrial cooperation by creating competitive conditions, many critics charged that they actually promoted monopoly, since the codes were drawn by trade associations dominated by the leading businesses and corporations of each industry. In addition to establishing the conditions of cooperative competition, Section 7 (a) of the act specifically guaranteed to employees collective-bargaining rights. The NIRA attempted to organize the whole economy to avoid the waste of cut-throat competition.

The significance of the NIRA, however, goes far beyond the terms of the statute. It was more than a venture in government intervention or regulation; it was a bold experiment in corporate statism. Under the NIRA's aegis, public policy was determined by the major economic interests of society: labor, business, and industry. It established representation along economic, or functional, lines and institutionalized the access of powerful interest groups to the governmental process, each group practically being given a veto power over the government's business-industrial policy. The NIRA also further blurred the line between the public and private sectors in American society by delegating public policy-making power to private groups, which were not even theoretically responsible or accountable to the electorate. Had the NIRA succeeded, it would have drastically altered the government's role as an arbiter among interests. It would have further promoted "a series of private governments."

The beginning of a change in the purpose and direction of the New Deal was seen in 1935. In 1935–1936 the United States Supreme Court delivered the NIRA's death sentence, invalidated the first Agricultural Adjustment Act, criticized the Securities and Exchange Commission for conducting Star Chamber proceedings, struck down the Guffey Coal Act (which attempted to regulate the interstate coal industry), and overturned the municipal bankruptcy act (which allowed municipalities to appeal to federal bankruptcy courts to readjust their debts). "By Black Monday [the day on which the Court killed the NIRA]," writes William Leuchtenberg, "the President had already begun to move decisively in a new direction." In June 1935, as Leuchtenberg observes, Roosevelt sent five important bills to Congress: the Social Security bill, the Wagner labor measure, a banking bill, a public utilities bill, and a "soak the rich" tax scheme. If the nation's corporate rich and their allies on the Court would not cooperate with the administration in curing the ills of the new economic order, then Roosevelt would control, restrict, and, in some cases, dismantle the giants. Thus, during the second hundred days Franklin Roosevelt appeared to turn away from a regulatory solution toward the Wilsonian-Brandeisian approach of restoring economic individualism. The second New Deal was more of an attempt to turn back the clock than a revolution.

The first important bill passed during the second hundred days was Senator Robert Wagner, Sr.'s National Labor Relations Act. Congress empowered the newly created National Labor Relations Board (NLRB) to determine collective-bargaining units and agents. The NLRB also prohibited business and industry from interfering with employees' rights to organize collective-bargaining units or unions and, as Leuchtenberg notes, brought the government's weight to bear on the side of the unions in their battle with corporate capitalism. On August 14, 1935, Congress passed the Social Security Act. This act, perhaps the least radical measure of the second hundred days, was based on the private insurance principle. It established a national government insurance company, the Social Security Administration, and helped to redistribute the costs of social insurance. A third measure, the Banking Act of 1935, centralized the nation's banking system by giving the Federal Reserve Board of Governors greater control over the system's regional banks. By increasing the board's power over rediscount rates and reserve requirements, the government's control of monetary and banking policy was expanded. On August 26, Congress passed still another bill that was a presidential "must," the Wheeler-Rayburn or Public Utilities Holding Company Act, which attempted to restrict monopoly in public utilities ownership by prohibiting holding companies twice removed from operating companies. It also permitted the Securities and Exchange Commission to break up holding companies of the first degree when they were not in the public interest. The Holding Company Act was the clearest attempt to apply Brandeisian principles to public regulation. Roosevelt also attempted to redistribute "wealth and power" with the passage of the wealth tax act, which increased gift, estate, and capital stock taxes, instituted an excess-profits tax, and markedly increased the surtax. Roosevelt was unsuccessful, however, in pushing through the most progressive parts of his tax reform proposal.

The second New Deal is sometimes viewed as a radical change, or departure, in American politics. However radical its techniques were, its objectives were even more conservative than the first New Deal. Rather than accept the new corporate-industrial order, Roosevelt attempted to curb, or temper, industrial growth and concentration. He accepted Brandeis' objective—the restoration of the individual's position in society; but he did not employ Brandeis' means. Roosevelt was willing to use the government's broad powers to promote the individual's welfare and security. The methods of the second New Deal were those of Andrew Jackson and Theodore Roosevelt, not of Thomas Jefferson and Woodrow Wilson. The second New Deal profoundly changed the relation between man and his government by making the latter directly responsible for the former's welfare.

Taken together, the first and second New Deals represent a confused period in the development of American liberal democracy. The two schools of liberalism represented by Brandeis and Tugwell were continually at odds, as in the 1935 dispute between the President and the Supreme Court, but they rarely confronted each other in the kind of public debate found in the 1912 presidential campaign. Neither side was entirely successful in persuading Congress or the President to accept its position without reservation. Many major pieces of legislation, such as the 1935 tax act, represented broadly acceptable compromises rather than clear-cut victories for either side. The greatest failure of the New Deal was that it did not clearly chart the future course of American liberalism. Instead, many programs were simply accepted as expedients in dealing with the nation's economic crisis. Rarely were their consequences for the future of liberal democracy examined.

The pressures that generated the demand for "action, and action now" absorbed the nation's energies and suppressed public debate over the future. Public discourse soon was curtailed by involvement in a global war that required even greater governmental control of human and economic resources than either the Depression or World War I. Before the theoreticians of liberal democracy could assess the impact of the New Deal on the future of liberalism, they were assailed by external threats and attacks. The war years constitute a hiatus during which the future of liberalism remained in doubt. A question that remains is whether, after the interregnum of the Depression and World War II, the dedication to political marketplace competition is adequate or relevant as the nation approaches its second centennial.

Summary and Conclusion

Today, after almost two hundred years of acceptance, Americans are beginning to question the adequacy of liberalism as an organizing myth or rationale. If liberalism has been successful for so long, why should Americans question its adequacy today? For two centuries it prescribed a useful method—that of the marketplace—for resolving political conflicts. Liberals translated economic marketplace competition into political language. Eighteenth-century liberals institutionalized it in American politics. The Constitution elevated it to a central myth, or rationale. Liberal formulas—majority rule, minority and individual rights, checks and balances—provided Americans with techniques for resolving political contests. But liberalism did not provide them with an agenda; it did not tell them which controversies should be resolved. It left the nation without a set of priorities or the means to establish them.

During the past two centuries liberalism has had to adjust to significant changes in the economic and social environment that have challenged its fundamental premises. In the republic's first phase, which lasted approximately from the revolution to the Civil War, inequalities in society were relatively dispersed. Few large-scale economic aggregates existed in the incipient stage of American capitalism, and the government's role as arbiter was between individual and small entrepreneurial interests. It was also a period of economic plenty and relatively great social mobility. Few men questioned the continued existence of society or called for the government to promote or restore the economic order. Under these conditions, the government could remain relatively passive as an arbiter and liberalism unquestioned.

Liberalism entered a new phase with the Civil War. The war, which was a reflection of the inadequacy of the procedural consensus in resolving major economic and social conflicts, ushered in a new stage in America's economic and social development. During the forty years that followed the war, the nation's business-industrial system was created. In response to these changes, both the American farmer and laborer organized in an effort to restore the historic balance of interests. New forms of social organization in labor, business, industry, and agriculture posed a major problem for American liberalism. In a laissez-faire system, the government could no longer remain passive if the cherished open political marketplace was to be preserved. The government would have to intervene to restore equilibrium in the competitive struggle. Both the Populist and Progressive reform movements were attempts to restore this historic balance. Instead, however, they eased the birth pangs of the new corporate-industrial order. The Populists and Progressives ameliorated some of the worst excesses of capitalism, but they did not restore Jefferson's individualistic ideals.

The New Deal further recognized and assured the permanence of corporate capitalism. Franklin Roosevelt used the presidency to balance major interests in society against each other and to humanize the new corporate-industrial society. Though his means were often inconsistent and his own house was divided, Roosevelt's purpose was to conserve the corporate order, which was accomplished by making the government a partner rather than an arbiter among relatively powerful and equal interests. Conservation was achieved by institutionalizing the access of these interests to the governmental process, by making them part of the ruling coalition. The regulatory agencies of the New Deal were the cooptive mechanisms of the new corporate state. Many New Deal liberals were satisfied that through these mechanisms they had provided the techniques necessary to assure the survival of liberalism. If they could not restore *individual* marketplace competition, they could at least assure competition among "countervailing" elites and groups in American public life. New Deal liberals were satisfied that they had solved society's major problems by adjusting individualism and collective welfare and reconciling corporate-industrialism and liberalism through a series of incremental programs and techniques.

Once again liberals substituted process, or technique, for substance. They did not address themselves to major problems confronting American society because they believed that these problems had been, or easily could be, resolved through established processes, formulas, and institutions. Instead of considering the possibility that liberal rhetoric, vocabulary, and political rules were no longer adequate, they relied upon the largesse of an expanding economy to resolve existing inequities. If some groups—blacks, migrant workers, and unskilled workers (Marx's lumpen proletariat)—had been left out of the governing coalition, they, at least, could be given a share of the pie in an expanding economy. But liberals did not consider the possibility that the pie either would not expand significantly or fast enough to match the rising expectations of these groups. Thus, many were unprepared for Watts and the post-Watts revolution in American politics.

Similarly, many were unprepared for the violence that gripped American life in the last decade. Their emphasis on consensual politics, on the peaceful and orderly resolution of conflict, deluded liberals into ignoring America's violent past development which is studded with acts of violence: civil and international war, race riots and lynchings, labor union warfare, Indian wars, range wars, organized crime, political assassination, ghetto riots, and, most recently, violence and civil disorder on the nation's college and university campuses. In addition to these acts of public violence, the police blotters of every major city are filled with accounts of private violence: rape, murder, assault, battery, arson, and child abuse, among other acts. Although public and private violence are everyday occurrences in the United States, liberal thinkers and politicians have ignored this major theme in American life. Violence simply did not fit into the liberal framework; it violated the norms of peaceful conflict resolution.

Furthermore, in the post-World War II era two major issues absorbed the attention of liberals: external security and internal subversion. These issues allowed major substantive controversies to go unnoticed and unresolved until they overwhelmed the nation in the 1960s. Many liberals were preoccupied with securing democracy abroad and curbing Soviet expansionism in Europe, arguing that the future of liberalism depended directly on the nation's external security, that the more threatened America was abroad, the more difficult it would be to maintain an open, competitive society at home. The nation's preoccupation with internal subversion in the early 1950s seemed to bear out the liberals' arguments. While liberal intellectuals were confronted with the problems of securing world order through peaceful or controlled competition, they also were busy at home fending off attacks on the procedural rules from the far Left and Right, overlooking growing substantive problems in American society.

As the nation approaches its second centennial celebration, several unresolved substantive problems confront Americans: the vast inequalities that some critics of capitalism argue have become greater in the past quarter of a century. At the bottom of the system are great numbers of Americans who do not share in the nation's prosperity—the black man, the Mexican-American, the migrant worker, and the unskilled laborer—who neither participate in governing the new order nor receive its rewards. What part should these groups play in making public policy? What is their fair share of the system's rewards? While liberalism has been incapable of answering these questions, because it is a procedural rather than a substantive political theory, disorganized and inchoate groups at the bottom are capable of questioning the procedural consensus, which, indeed, has been rocked by the nation's failure to resolve these substantive inequities.

A new condition of environmental scarcity raises further questions about the adequacy of the procedural consensus. As man presses against his environment, can liberal democracy provide techniques to adjust the fundamental conflicts posed by such problems as population quantity and quality? Thus far, liberal democracy has operated in an environment of economic plenty, but steadily growing populations imply further crowding of living space, increased pressure on environmental resources, and relatively greater economic scarcity. How many people can the nation support in the twenty-first or twenty-second century? Under what material and social conditions should future generations of Americans live? What kind of population shall America have? Population quantity and quality are two fundamental problems that must be resolved shortly if society is to survive in the next century. Is liberal democratic government equal to the task? Does liberalism, as a process theory of government, provide the standards against which fundamental issues can be satisfactorily evaluated and resolved?

The future, it would seem, does not augur well for liberalism in America. Confronted with major substantive problems (social injustice, vast inequalities of opportunity, monumental environmental issues), large numbers of Americans have begun to question the adequacy or the relevance of liberalism in the decades ahead. Recognizing the discrepancies between promises and the conditions of public life, some Americans have openly challenged the procedural consensus through direct and, sometimes, violent protest. In contrast to major reform movements in the past, contemporary protests challenge the very rules of the political game, and liberalism's underlying premises. While aging liberals fear this generation's attacks on cherished ideas and values, they must turn their intellectual energies to the problems of a just society.

In the selections that follow, historians and political scientists explore the development of America as a liberal society, raising numerous questions about the future of liberalism in a highly complex industrial order. The selections in this part also provide useful yardsticks against which American political institutions—Congress, the presidency, the courts, parties, and pressure groups—can be evaluated. Do these institutions promote a liberal society? Are they useful in solving such fundamental problems as race relations and management of environmental resources? Or, are new political institutions required to solve major social problems? The basic questions raised provide many keys to understanding American politics today.

1

The American Revolution: Revolution Without Dogma

DANIEL J. BOORSTIN

In the following selection, Daniel J. Boorstein views the American Revolution as a conservative political movement, an affirmation of British political institutions. American revolutionaries neither rejected English political traditions nor accepted the general revolutionary theories then popular in France. The American Revolution, he argues, resulted from a constitutional debate over the nature of imperial government. The revolutionaries only reluctantly seceded from the British Empire, and their rebellion neither destroyed an oppressive feudal aristocracy nor created a new social order. Boorstin concludes that the American Revolution was not a "species of the genus 'Revolution'" but a conservative colonial rebellion.

The conservative nature of the revolution, the absence of an oppressive aristocracy, and the political continuity in the period following secession explain the basic stability and liberal value structure of the American political system. The revolutionaries' objectives were to conserve traditional English liberties, such as trial by jury, free speech, assembly, petition, and representative government, that are central to the interest group pluralism of today. The absence of a hereditary aristocracy, and other factors, such as economic plenty, promoted social mobility. Mass man's acceptance of these liberal values, it is hypothesized, rests upon his sharing in the economic plenty of the system. America's political tradition is conservative of liberal values and rests on mass consensus.

Daniel Boorstin, author of The Lost World of Thomas Jefferson *(1948),* The Americans: The Colonial Experience *(1958),* America and the Image of Europe *(1960), and* The Image *(1962), is Distinguished Service Professor of*

History at the University of Chicago. In 1961–1962 he held the first chair in American history at the Sorbonne, and in 1964–1965 he was a Fellow of Trinity College, Cambridge.

I. Some Peculiarities of Our Revolution

The most obvious peculiarity of our American Revolution is that, in the modern European sense of the word, it was hardly a revolution at all. The Daughters of the American Revolution, who have been understandably sensitive on this subject, have always insisted in their literature that the American Revolution was no revolution but merely a colonial rebellion. The more I have looked into the subject, the more convinced I have become of the wisdom of their naïveté. "The social condition and the Constitution of the Americans are democratic," De Tocqueville observed about a hundred years ago. "But they have not had a democratic revolution." This fact is surely one of the most important of our history.

A number of historians (J. Franklin Jameson and Merrill Jensen, for example) have pointed out the ways in which a social revolution, including a redistribution of property, accompanied the American Revolution. These are facts which no student of the period should neglect. Yet it seems to me that these historians have by no means succeeded in showing that such changes were so basic and so far-reaching as actually in themselves to have established our national republican institutions. When we speak of the Revolution therefore, we are still fully justified in referring to something other than what Jameson's disciples mean by "the American Revolution as a social movement." If we consider the American Revolution in that sense, it would not be a great deal more notable than a number of other social movements in our history, such as Jacksonianism, populism, progressivism, and the New Deal. Moreover, in so far as the American Revolution was a social movement, it was not much to be distinguished from European revolutions; and the increasing emphasis on this aspect of our history is but another example of the attempt to assimilate our history to that of Europe.

The Revolution, as the birthday of our nation, must mean something very different from all this. It is the series of events by which we separated ourselves from the British Empire and acquired a national identity. Looking at our Revolution from this point of view, what are some features which distinguish it from the French Revolution of 1789 or the other revolutions to which western European nations trace their national identity? And, especially, what are those peculiarities which have affected the place of theory in our political life?

1. First, and most important, the United States was born in a *colonial* rebellion. Our national birth certificate is a Declaration of Independence and not a Declaration of the Rights of Man. The vast significance of this simple fact is too often forgotten. Compared even with other colonial

Reprinted in abridged form from *The Genius of American Politics* by Daniel J. Boorstin (Chicago: The University of Chicago Press, 1953, p.p. 68–98, by permission of the author and The University of Chicago Press.

rebellions, the American Revolution is notably lacking in cultural self-consciousness and in any passion for national unity. The more familiar type of colonial rebellion—like that which recently occurred in India—is one in which a subject people vindicates its local culture against foreign rulers. But the American Revolution had very little of this character. On the contrary, ours was one of the few conservative colonial rebellions of modern times.

* * *

. . . the American Revolution [was] in the minds of most of its leaders an affirmation of the tradition of British institutions. The argument of the best theorists of the Revolution—perhaps we should call them lawyers rather than theorists—was not, on the whole, that America had institutions or a culture superior to that of the British. Rather their position, often misrepresented and sometimes simply forgotten, was that the British by their treatment of the American colonies were being untrue to the ancient spirit of their own institutions. The slogan "Taxation without Representation Is Tyranny" was clearly founded on a British assumption. As James Otis put it in his pamphlet, *The Rights of the British Colonies* (1764), he believed "that this [British] constitution is the most free one, and by far the best, now existing on earth: that by this constitution, every man in the dominions is a free man: that no parts of His Majesty's dominions can be taxed without their consent: that every part has a right to be represented in the supreme or some subordinate legislature: that the refusal of this would seem to be a contradiction in practice to the theory of the constitution."

According to their own account, then, the Americans were to have forced on them the need to defend the ancient British tradition; to be truer to the spirit of that tradition than George III and Lord North and Townshend knew how to be. They were fighting not so much to establish new rights as to preserve old ones: "for the preservation of our liberties . . . in defence of the freedom that is our birthright, and which we ever enjoyed till the late violation of it" (Declaration of Causes of Taking up Arms, July 6, 1775). From the colonists' point of view, until 1776 it was Parliament that had been revolutionary, by exercising a power for which there was no warrant in English constitutional precedent. The ablest defender of the Revolution—in fact, the greatest political theorist of the American Revolution—was also the great theorist of British conservatism, Edmund Burke.

2. Second, the American Revolution was *not* the product of a nationalistic spirit. We had no Bismarck or Cavour or any nationalist philosophy. We were singularly free from most of the philosophical baggage of modern nationalism.

Perhaps never was a new nation created with less enthusiasm. To read the history of our Revolution is to discover that the United States was a kind of *pis aller*. This fact explains many of the difficulties encountered in conducting the Revolution and in framing a federal constitution. The original creation of a United States was the work of doubly reluctant men: men reluctant, both because of their local loyalties—to Virginia, Massachusetts, Rhode Island, and New York—and because of their imperial loyalty. The story of the "critical period" of American history, of the Articles of Confederation and the Constitution, tells of the gradual overcoming of this reluctance. It was overcome not by any widespread conversion to a nationalist theory—even *The Federalist* papers are conspicuously lacking in such a theory—but by gradual realization of the need for effective union.

In the period of the American Revolution we do discover a number of enthusiasms: for the safety and prosperity of Virginia or New York, for the cause of justice, for the rights of Englishmen. What is missing is anything that might be called widespread enthusiasm for the birth of a new nation: the United States of America. Until well into the nineteenth century, Jefferson—and he was not alone in this—was using the phrase "my country" to refer to his native state of Virginia.

3. Our Revolution was successful at the first try. This is equally true whether we consider it as a revolt against British rule or as a movement for republican federalism. There was no long-drawn-out agitation, no intellectual war of attrition, of the sort which breeds dogmas and intransigence. Thomas Paine's *Common Sense*, which is generally considered "the first important republican tract to be issued in America . . . the first to present cogent arguments for independence," did not appear until January 10, 1776. Down to within six months of the break, few would have considered independence; and even then the colonists had only quite specific complaints. There had been no considerable tradition in America either of revolt against British institutions or of republican theorizing.

The political objective of the Revolution, independence from British rule, was achieved by one relatively short continuous effort. More commonly in modern history (take, for example, the European revolutions of the nineteenth century) any particular revolt has been only one in a long series. Each episode, then, ends on a note of suspense which comes from the feeling that the story is "to be continued." Under those circumstances, challenges to constituted authority follow one another, accumulating their ideological baggage.

In France, for example, 1789 was followed by 1830 and 1848 and 1870; a similar list could be made for Italy, Germany, and perhaps Russia. Such repetition creates a distinctive revolutionary tradition, with continued agitation keeping alive certain doctrines. Repeated efforts provide the dogmatic raw material for a profusion of later political parties, each of which rallies under the banner of one or another of the defeated revolutions or of a revolution yet to be made. But, properly speaking, 1776 had no sequel, and needed none. The issue was separation, and separation was accomplished.

II. How We Have Been Led to Ignore These Peculiarities

The student who comes for the first time to the literature of our Revolution is liable to be disappointed by the dull and legalistic flavor of what he has to read. Although the American Revolution occurred in an age which throughout Europe was laden with philosophic reflection and important treatises, our Revolution was neither particularly rich nor particularly original in its intellectual apparatus. The documents of that era, as Moses Coit Tyler described them, are "a vast morass of technical discussion, into which, perhaps, no living reader will ever follow the writer, from which, in fact, the writer himself never emerges alive."

Orators, textbook-writers, and other

tradition-makers have been hard put to it to find those ringing phrases, the battle-cries and philosophical catch-words, which slip smoothly off the tongue, remain fixed in the memory, and uplift the soul. This helps explain why a few phrases and documents have been overworked and why even these have always been read only in part or out of context. The first two paragraphs of the Declaration of Independence have been worn thin; few bother to read the remaining thirty. People have grasped at "life, liberty, and the pursuit of happiness," forgetting that it was two-thirds borrowed and, altogether, only part of a preamble. We have repeated that "all men are created equal," without daring to discover what it meant and without realizing that probably to none of the men who spoke it did it mean what we would like it to mean. Or we have exploited passages in the "speeches" of Patrick Henry, which were actually composed less by Henry than by his biographers.

The proper slogan of the Revolution—if, indeed, there was a slogan—was "No Taxation without Representation." Such words are far too polysyllabic, far too legalistic, to warm the popular heart. But if we compare them with the "Liberty, Equality, Fraternity" of the French Revolution and the "Peace, Bread, and Land," of the Russian, we have a clue to the peculiar spirit of the American Revolution. It is my view that the major issue of the American Revolution was the true constitution of the British Empire, which is a pretty technical legal problem. This notion is supported by Professor Charles H. McIlwain, who, in his admirable little book on the American Revolution, comes closer than any other recent historian to the spirit of our Revolutionary age.

In that age men were inclined to take their opponents at their word; the Revolutionary debate seems to have been carried on in the belief that men meant what they said. But in this age of Marx and Freud we have begun to take it for granted that, if people talk about one thing, they must be thinking about something else. Ideas are treated as the apparatus of an intellectual sleight-of-hand, by which the speaker diverts the audience's attention to an irrelevant subject while he does the real business unobserved. To study the Revolutionary debate is then to try to see (in the phrase of one historian) how "the colonists modified their theory to suit their needs." From such a point of view, there is perhaps never much political or legal thought worth talking about; to be realistic we should focus our discussion on hormones and statistics.

But such an approach would bleach away the peculiar tone of our history and empty our Revolution of its unique significance. Therefore, even at the risk of seeming naïve, I should like to consider the outlandish possibility that men like Jefferson and Adams all along meant what they were saying, that is, that the Revolution had something to do with the British constitution.

* * *

III. The Conservatism of the Revolution

* * *

The feature to which I want to direct your attention might be called the "conservatism" of the Revolution. If we understand this characteristic, we will begin to see the Revolution as an illustration of the remarkable continuity of American history. And we will also see how the attitude of our Revolutionary thinkers has engraved more deeply on our national consciousness a belief in the inevitability of our particular institutions, or, in a word, our sense of "givenness."

The character of our Revolution has nourished our assumption that whatever institutions we happened to have here (in this case the British constitution) had the self-evident validity of anything that is "normal." We have thus casually established the tradition that it is superfluous to the American condition to produce elaborate treatises on political philosophy or to be explicit about political values and the theory of community.

I shall confine myself to two topics. First, the manifesto of the Revolution, namely, the Declaration of Independence; and, second, the man who has been generally considered the most outspoken and systematic political philosopher of the Revolution, Thomas Jefferson. Of course, I will not try to give a full account of either of them. I will attempt only to call your attention to a few facts which may not have been sufficiently emphasized and which are especially significant for our present purpose. Obviously, no one could contend that there is either in the man or in the document nothing of the cosmopolitan spirit, nothing of the world climate of opinion. My suggestion is simply that we do find another spirit of at least equal, and perhaps overshadowing, importance and that this spirit may actually be more characteristic of our Revolution.

First, then, for the Declaration of Independence. Its technical, legalistic, and conservative character, which I wish to emphasize, will appear at once by contrast with the comparable document of the French Revolution. Ours was concerned with a specific event, namely, the separation of these colonies from the mother-country. But the French produced a "Declaration of the Rights of *Man* and the Citizen." When De Tocqueville, in his *Ancien Régime* (Book I, chap. iii), sums up the spirit of the French Revolution, he is describing exactly what the American Revolution was not:

> The French Revolution acted, with regard to things of this world, precisely as religious revolutions have acted with regard to things of the other. It dealt with the citizen in the abstract, independent of particular social organizations, just as religions deal with mankind in general, independent of time and place. It inquired, not what were the particular rights of the French citizens, but what were the general rights and duties of mankind in reference to political concerns.
>
> It was by thus divesting itself of all that was peculiar to one race or time, and by reverting to natural principles of social order and government, that it became intelligible to all, and susceptible of simultaneous imitation in a hundred different places.
>
> By seeming to tend rather to the regeneration of the human race than to the reform of France alone, it roused passions such as the most violent political revolutions had been incapable of awakening. It inspired proselytism, and gave birth to propagandism; and hence assumed that quasi religious character which so terrified those who saw it, or, rather, became a sort of new religion, imperfect, it is true, without God, worship, or future life, but still able, like Islamism, to cover the earth with its soldiers, its apostles, and its martyrs [trans. John Bonner (New York, 1856), pp. 26 f.].

In contrast to all this, our Declaration of Independence is essentially a list of specific historical instances. It is directed not to the regeneration but only to the "opinions" of mankind. It is closely tied to time and place; the special affection for "British brethren" is freely admitted; it is concerned with the duties of a particular king and certain of his subjects.

Even if we took only the first two paragraphs or preamble, which are the most general part of the document, and actually read them as a whole, we could make a good case for their being merely a succinct restatement of the Whig theory of the British revolution of 1688. . . . To be understood, its words must be annotated by British history. This is among the facts which have led some historians (Guizot, for example) to go so far as to say that the English revolution succeeded twice, once in England and once in America.

The remaining three-quarters—the unread three-quarters—of the document is technical and legalistic. That is, of course, the main reason why it remains unread. For it is a bill of indictment against the king, written in the language of British constitutionalism. "The patient sufferance of these Colonies" is the point of departure. It deals with rights and franchises under British charters. It carefully recounts that the customary and traditional forms of protest, such as "repeated Petitions," have already been tried.

The more the Declaration is reread in context, the more plainly it appears a document of imperial legal relations rather than a piece of high-flown political philosophy. The desire to remain true to the principles of British constitutionalism up to the bitter end explains why, as has been often remarked, the document is directed against the king, despite the fact that the practical grievances were against Parliament; perhaps also why at this stage there is no longer an explicit appeal to the rights of Englishmen. Most of the document is a bald enumeration of George III's failures, excesses, and crimes in violation of the constitution and laws of Great Britain. One indictment after another makes sense only if one presupposes the framework of British constitutionalism. How else, for example, could one indict a king "for depriving us in many cases, of the benefits of Trial by Jury"?

We can learn a great deal about the context of our Revolutionary thought by examining Jefferson's own thinking down to the period of the Revolution. We need not stretch a point or give Jefferson a charismatic role, to say that the flavor of his thought is especially important for our purposes. He has been widely considered the leading political philosopher of the Revolution. Among other things, he was, of course, the principal author of the Declaration of Independence itself; and the Declaration has been taken to be the climax of the abstract philosophizing of the revolutionaries. Because he is supposed to be the avant-garde of Revolutionary thought, evidence of conservatism and legalism in Jefferson's thought as a whole is especially significant.

. . . Neither in the letters which Jefferson wrote nor in those he received do we discover that he and his close associates—at least down to the date of the Revolution—showed any conspicuous interest in political theory. We look in vain for general reflections on the nature of government or constitutions. The manners of the day did require that a cultivated gentleman be acquainted with certain classics of political thought; yet we lack evidence that such works were read with more than a perfunctory interest. To be sure, when Jefferson prepares a list of worthy books for a young friend in 1771, he includes references to Montesquieu, Sidney, and Bolingbroke; but such references are rare. Even when he exchanges letters with Edmund Pendleton on the more general problems of institutions, he remains on the level of legality and policy, hardly touching political theory. Jefferson's papers for the Revolutionary period (read without the hindsight which has put the American and the French revolutions in the same era of world history) show little evidence that the American Revolution was a goad to higher levels of abstract thinking about society. We miss any such tendency in what Jefferson and his associates were reading or in what they were writing.

On the other hand, we find ample evidence that the locale of early Jeffersonian thought was distinctly *colonial;* we might even say *provincial.* And we begin to see some of the significance of that fact in marking the limits of political theorizing in America. By 1776, when the irreversible step of revolution was taken, the colonial period in the life of Jefferson and the other Revolutionary thinkers was technically at an end; but by then their minds had been congealed, their formal education completed, their social habits and the cast of their political thinking determined. The Virginia society of the pre-Revolutionary years had been decidedly derivative, not only in its culture, its furniture, its clothes, and its books, but in many of its ideas and—what is more to our purpose—in perhaps most of its institutions.

It is an important and little-noted fact that for many American thinkers of the period (including Jefferson himself) the cosmopolitan period in their thought did not begin until several years *after* their Revolution. Then, as representatives of the new nation, some of them were to enter the labyrinth of European diplomacy. Much of what we read of their experiences abroad even in this later period would confirm our impression of their naïveté, their strangeness to the sophisticated Paris of Talleyrand, the world of the *philosophes.* In Jefferson's particular case, the cosmopolitan period of his thought probably did not begin much before his first trip abroad as emissary to France in 1784.

When John Adams had gone, also to France, a few years earlier on his first foreign mission, he thought himself fresh from an "American Wilderness." Still more dramatic is the unhappy career of John Marshall, who was an innocent abroad if there ever was one. The career of Franklin, who was at least two generations older than these Revolutionary leaders, is something of an exception; but even in his case much of his charm for the salons of Paris consisted in his successful affectation of the character of a frontiersman.

The importance of this colonial framework in America, as I have already suggested, was to be enormous, not only from the point of view of Revolutionary thought, but in its long-run effect on the role of political theory in American life. The legal institutions which Americans considered their own and which they felt bound to master were largely borrowed. Jefferson and John Adams, both lawyers by profession, like their English contemporaries, had extracted much of their legal knowledge out of the crabbed pages of Coke's *Institutes.*

Now there were the elegant lectures of Sir William Blackstone, published as the four-volume *Commentaries on the Laws of England,* appearing between 1765 and 1769. It was this work of the ultra-conservative interpreter of English law that for many years remained the bible of American lawyers and, for several generations of them, virtually their whole bookish education. Blackstone's *Commentaries,* as Burke remarked in his Speech on Conciliation, had even by 1775 sold nearly as many copies in America as in England. American editions were numerous and popular; despite copious emendations and contradicting footnotes, Blackstone's original framework was faithfully preserved. Lincoln (as Carl Sandburg describes him), sitting barefoot on a woodpile in Illinois, fifty years later, reading the volumes of the conservative English lawyer—which he called the foundation of his own legal education—is a symbol of that continuity which has characterized our thinking about institutions. For our present purposes, the significant fact is that such a work as the *Commentaries* and the institutions which it expounded could continue to dominate the legal thinking of a people who were rebelling against the country of its origin.

During the very years when the Revolution was brewing, Jefferson was every day talking the language of the common law. We cannot but be impressed not only, as I have remarked, at the scarcity in the Jefferson papers for these years of anything that could be called fresh inquiry into the theory of government but also by the legalistic context of Jefferson's thought. We begin to see that the United States was being born in an atmosphere of legal rather than philosophical debate. Even apart from those technical legal materials with which Jefferson earned his living, his political pieces themselves possess a legal rather than a philosophical flavor.

A Summary View of the Rights of British America (July, 1774), which first brought Jefferson wide notice and which was largely responsible for his momentous choice on the committee to draft a declaration of independence, is less a piece of political theory than a closely reasoned legal document. He justifies the American position by appeal to the Saxon precedent: "No circumstance has occurred to distinguish materially the British from the Saxon emigration." It was from this parallel of the Americans with the Saxons, who also had once conquered a wilderness, that Jefferson draws several important legal consequences.

Jefferson's draft of the "new" Virginia Constitution of 1776 reveals a similar legalistic spirit: his Preamble comprised no premises of government in general, but only the same specific indictments of George III which were to be the substance of the Declaration of Independence. Jefferson actually describes the powers of the chief administrator as, with certain exceptions, "the powers formerly held by the king."

Jefferson's solid achievements in the period up to the Revolution were thus mainly works of legal draftsmanship. The reputation which he first obtained by his *Summary View,* he was to substantiate by other basic documents like the Virginia Constitution and by a host of complex public bills like those for dividing the county of Fincastle, for disestablishing the Church of England, for the naturalization of foreigners, and for the auditing of public accounts. Jefferson was equally at home in the intricacies of real-property law and in the problems of criminal jurisdiction. One of the many consequences of the neglect of American legal history has been our failure to recognize the importance of this legal element in our Revolutionary tradition. Jefferson's chef d'œuvre, a most impressive technical performance, was his series of Bills for Establishing Courts of Justice in Virginia. These bills, apparently drafted within about ten days in late 1776, show a professional virtuosity which any lawyer would envy.

The striking feature of these lawyerly accomplishments to those of us fed on clichés about the Age of Reason is how they live and move and have their being in the world of the common law, in the world of estates tail, bills in chancery, writs of supersedeas, etc., and not in the plastic universe of an eighteenth-century *philosophe*. Our evidence is doubly convincing, for the very reason that Jefferson was something of a reformer in legal matters. Yet even in his extensive projects of reform, he was eager to build on the foundation of the common law; for example, in his plan for the reform of the law of crimes and punishments. His tenacious conservatism appears in bold relief when we remind ourselves that Jefferson was a contemporary of Bentham, whose first important work, the *Fragment on Government,* also appeared in 1776.

But Jefferson did not found his reforms on any metaphysical calculus—rather on legal history and a continuity with the past. Even when he opposed feudal land tenures, he sought support from British sources. In the *Summary View* he had noted that feudal tenures were unknown to "our Saxon ancestors." "Has not every restitution of the antient Saxon laws had happy effects?" To have preserved the feudal tenures would actually have been, in Jefferson's words, "against the practice of our wise British an cestors. . . . Have not instances in which we have departed from this in Virginia been constantly condemned by the universal voice of our country?" (August 13, 1776; *Papers,* ed. Julian P. Boyd [Princeton, 1950], I, 492). Jefferson asked: "Is it not better now that we return at once into that happy system of our ancestors, the wisest and most perfect ever yet devised by the wit of man, as it stood before the 8th century?"

It is worth noting that Jefferson, who was to be the principal political philosopher of the Revolution, was given leadership in the important technical project of legal codification and reform in his native state of Virginia. Had he died at the end of 1776, he would probably have been remembered as a promising young lawyer of reformist bent, especially talented as a legal draftsman. In both houses of the Virginia legislature he had received the highest number of ballots in the election of members of the committee of legal revisers. The gist of the report of that committee (which included Edmund Pendleton, George Wythe, and George Mason, three of the ablest legal scholars on the continent, all active in the Revolution) is significant for our purposes. Jefferson himself recalled some years later that the commission had determined "not to meddle with the common law, i.e., the law preceding the existence of the statutes, further than to accommodate it to our new principles and circumstances."

Jefferson's philosophic concern with politics by the outbreak of the Revolution (actually only the end of his thirty-third year) was the enthusiasm of a reflective and progressive colonial lawyer for the traditional rights of Englishmen. To be sure, Jefferson did go further than some of his fellow-lawyers in his desire for legal reform—of feudal tenures, of entails, of the law of inheritance, of criminal law, and of established religion—yet even these projects were not, at least at that time, part of a coherent theory of society. They remained discrete reforms, "improvements" on the common law.

Jefferson's willingness to devote himself to purification of the common law must have rested on his faith in those ancient institutions and a desire to return to their essentials. This faith shines through those general maxims and mottoes about government which men took seriously in the eighteenth century and which often imply much more than they say. Jefferson's personal motto, "Rebellion to Tyrants Is Obedience to God," expresses pretty much the sum of his political theory—if, indeed, we should call it a "theory"—in this epoch. It was this motto (which Jefferson probably borrowed from Franklin, who offered it in 1776 for the Seal of the United States) that Jefferson himself proposed for Virginia and which he used on the seal for his own letters. But when we try to discover the meaning of the slogan to Jefferson, we find that it must be defined by reference less to any precise theology than to certain clear convictions about the British constitution. For who, after all, was a "tyrant"? None other than one who violated the sacred tenets of the ancient common law. Jefferson made his own view clear in the device which he suggested for the obverse of the United States seal: figures of "Hengist and Horsa, the Saxon chiefs from whom we claim the honor of being descended, and whose political principles and form of government we have assumed" (quoted by John Adams to Mrs. Adams, August 14, 1776; *Familiar Letters* [New York, 1875], p. 211).

In the Revolutionary period, when the temptations to be dogmatic were greatest, Jefferson did not succumb. The awareness of the peculiarity of America had not yet by any means led Jefferson to a rash desire to remake all society and institutions. What we actually discern is a growing tension between his feeling of the novelty of the American experience, on the one hand, and his feeling of belonging to ancient British institutions, on the other.

* * *

It would be possible to multiply examples of the importance of the continuing legal framework in the thought of other leaders of the Revolution. Few would be more interesting than John Adams, another of the authors of the Declaration of Independence. During the Revolutionary era, he elaborated a theory of the British Empire and developed in detail the notion of an unconstitutional act. His thought in this era has been characterized by Randolph G. Adams as that of a "Britannic Statesman."

IV. Revolution Without Dogma: A Legacy of Institutions

We begin to see how far we would be misled, were we to cast American events of this era in the mold of European history. The American Revolution was in a very special way conceived as both a vindication of the British past and an affirmation of an American future. The British past was contained in ancient and living institutions rather than in doctrines; and the American future was never to be contained in a theory. The Revolution was thus a prudential decision taken by men of principle rather than the affirmation of a theory. What British institutions meant did not need to be articulated; what America might mean was still to be discovered. This continuity of American history was to make a sense of "givenness" easier to develop; for it was this continuity which had made a new ideology of revolution seem unnecessary.

Perhaps the intellectual energy which American Revolutionaries economized because they were not obliged to construct a whole theory of institutions was to strengthen them for their encounter with nature and for their solution of practical problems. The effort which Jefferson, for example, did not care to spend on the theory of sovereignty he was to give freely to the revision of the criminal law, the observation of the weather, the mapping of the continent, the collection of fossils, the study of Indian languages, and the doubling of the national area.

The experience of our Revolution may suggest that the sparseness of American political theory, which has sometimes been described as a refusal of American statesmen to confront their basic philosophical problems, has been due less to a conscious refusal than to a simple lack of necessity. As the British colonists in America had forced on them the need to create a nation, so they had forced on them the need to be traditional and empirical in their institutions. The Revolution, because it was conceived as essentially affirming the British constitution, did not create the kind of theoretical vacuum made by some other revolutions.

The colonial situation, it would seem, had provided a *ne plus ultra* beyond which political theorizing did not need to range. Even Jefferson, the greatest and most influential theorist of the Revolution, remained loath to trespass that boundary, except under pressure: the pressure of a need to create a new federal structure. Mainly in the realm of federalism were new expedients called for. And no part of our history is more familiar than the story of how the framers of the federal Constitution achieved a solution: by compromise on details rather than by agreement on a theory.

There is hardly better evidence of this fact than the character of *The Federalist* papers themselves. Nearly everything about them illustrates or even symbolizes the way of political thinking which I have tried to describe. *The Federalist or, The New Constitution* consists of essays written by Alexander Hamilton, James Madison, and John Jay and published one at a time in certain New York journals between late 1787 and early 1788. They had a simple practical purpose: to persuade the people of the state of New York to ratify the recently drawn federal Constitution. The eighty-five numbers were written, like any series of newspaper articles, to be read separately, each essay being a unit. Their object is summarized by Hamilton in No. 1:

> I propose, in a series of papers, to discuss the following interesting particulars:—The utility of the UNION to your political prosperity—The insufficiency of the present Confederation to preserve that Union—The necessity of a government at least equally energetic with the one proposed, to the attainment of this object—The conformity of the proposed Constitution to the true principles of republican government—Its analogy to your own State constitution—and lastly, The additional security which its adoption will afford to the preservation of that species of government, to liberty, and to property.

If, indeed, *The Federalist* may be considered a treatise on political theory, it differs from other important works of the kind, by being an argument in favor of a particular written constitution. In this it is sharply distinguished from the writings of Plato, Aristotle, Hobbes, Locke, Rousseau, and J. S. Mill, which give us either systematic theories of the state or wide-ranging speculation. The organization of *The Federalist* papers is practical rather than systematic: they proceed from the actual dangers which confronted Americans to the weaknesses of the existing confederation and the specific advantages of the various provisions of the new constitution.

While the individual essays are full of wisdom, we must not forget, as Sir William Ashley reminds us, that "*The Federalist* has come to stand out more distinctly in the public view because of the oblivion that has befallen the torrent of other controversial writings of the same period." *The Federalist* essays are too often treated as if they comprised a single logical structure. They were a collaborative work mainly in the sense that their authors agreed on the importance of adopting the new constitution, not in the sense that the authors start from common and explicit philosophic premises. Hamilton, Madison, and Jay differed widely in personality and in philosophic position: individually they had even favored some other institutions than those embodied in the Constitution. But they had accepted the compromises and were convinced that what was being offered was far superior to what they already had. To read *The Federalist* is to discover the wisdom of Calhoun's observation that "this admirable federal constitution of ours . . . is superior to the wisdom of any or all of the men by whose agency it was made. The force of circumstances, and not foresight or wisdom, induced them to adopt many of its wisest provisions" (*Works,* ed. R. K. Cralle [New York, 1888], IV, 417).

The Revolution itself, as we have seen, had been a kind of affirmation of faith in ancient British institutions. In the greater part of the institutional life of the community the Revolution thus required no basic change. If any of this helps to illustrate or explain our characteristic lack of interest in political philosophy, it also helps to account for the value which we still attach to our inheritance from the British constitution: trial by jury, due process of law, representation before taxation, habeas corpus, freedom from attainder, independence of the judiciary, and the rights of free speech, free petition, and free assembly, as well as our narrow definition of treason and our antipathy to standing armies in peacetime. It also explains our continuing—sometimes bizarre, but usually fortunate—readiness to think of these traditional rights of Englishmen as if they were indigenous to our continent. In the proceedings of the San Francisco Vigilance Committee of 1851, we hear crude adventurers on the western frontier describing the technicalities of habeas corpus as if they were fruits of the American environment, as natural as human equality.

2

The Founding Fathers: An Age of Realism

RICHARD HOFSTADTER

In the following essay, Richard Hofstadter argues that although the Founding Fathers were "unwilling to turn their backs upon republicanism," they wanted to avoid the excesses of mass democracy. Their objective was to create a balanced or mixed form of government that would prevent the tyranny of both the aristocracy and the masses. Inasmuch as they were convinced that men were inherently evil or wicked (today we would say aggressive), they searched for a constitutional formula that would preserve traditional liberty by "checking vice with vice." Because they could scarcely change man's inherent aggressive character, they were forced to construct a political system that would at least restrain his excesses.

The governmental system they created was not democratic; it did not assure mass control. Indeed, in many ways—the indirect election of senators and the President, the limited executive veto, and the implied review powers of the courts—it limited the democratic or mass man. Furthermore, the system possessed the virtue of protecting property, a cardinal eighteenth-century liberty.

The Founding Fathers' concern for the protection of property can easily lead one to a Marxist, class analysis of the Federalist period in American history. Before making this leap, as Hofstadter warns, it should be noted that property, especially real estate, was widely dispersed in the United States at the end of the eighteenth century. Therefore, the protection of property was a society-wide rather than a narrow class interest. Only insofar as inequalities became cumulative rather than dispersed would such an interpretation of American society be valid.

Hofstadter is the author of Academic Freedom in the Age of the College *(1955),* Social Darwinism in American Thought *(1955),* Anti-Intellectualism in American Life *(1963),* The Paranoid Style in American Politics *(1968), and* The Progressive Histories *(1968). He was Professor of American History at Columbia University, had been a Fulbright and Guggenheim Fellow, and had received a Pulitzer Prize in history.*

Wherever the real power in a government lies, there is the danger of oppression. In our Government the real power lies in the majority of the community. . . .

James Madison

Power naturally grows . . . because human passions are insatiable. But that power alone can grow which already is too great; that which is unchecked; that which has no equal power to control it.

John Adams

Long ago Horace White observed that the Constitution of the United States "is based upon the philosophy of Hobbes and the religion of Calvin. It assumes that the natural state of mankind is a state of war, and that the carnal mind is at enmity with God." Of course the Constitution was founded more upon experience than any such abstract theory; but it was also an event in the intellectual history of Western civilization. The men who drew up the Constitution in Philadelphia during the summer of 1787 had a vivid Calvinistic sense of human evil and damnation and believed with Hobbes that men are selfish and contentious. They were men of affairs, merchants, lawyers, planter-businessmen, speculators, investors. Having seen human nature on display in the market place, the courtroom, the legislative chamber, and in every secret path and alleyway where wealth and power are courted, they felt they knew it in all its frailty. To them a human being was an atom of self-interest. They did not believe in man, but they did believe in the power of a good political constitution to control him.

This may be an abstract notion to ascribe to practical men, but it follows the language that the Fathers themselves used. General Knox, for example, wrote in disgust to Washington after the Shays Rebellion that Americans were, after all, "men—actual men possessing all the turbulent passions belonging to that animal." Throughout the secret discussions at the Constitutional Convention it was clear that this distrust of man was first and foremost a distrust of the common man and democratic rule. As the Revolution took away the restraining hand of the British government, old colonial grievances of farmers, debtors, and squatters against merchants, investors, and large landhold-

From *The American Political Tradition,* by Richard Hofstadter, pp. 3–17. Copyright 1948 by Alfred A. Knopf, Inc. Reprinted by permission of the publisher and Jonathan Cape Ltd.

ers had flared up anew; the lower orders took advantage of new democratic constitutions in several states, and the possessing classes were frightened. The members of the Constitutional Convention were concerned to create a government that could not only regulate commerce and pay its debts but also prevent currency inflation and stay laws, and check such uprisings as the Shays Rebellion.

Cribbing and confining the popular spirit that had been at large since 1776 were essential to the purposes of the new Constitution. Edmund Randolph, saying to the Convention that the evils from which the country suffered originated in "the turbulence and follies of democracy," and that the great danger lay in "the democratic parts of our constitutions"; Elbridge Gerry, speaking of democracy as "the worst of all political evils"; Roger Sherman, hoping that "the people . . . have as little to do as may be about the government"; William Livingston, saying that "the people have ever been and ever will be unfit to retain the exercise of power in their own hands"; George Washington, the presiding officer, urging the delegates not to produce a document of which they themselves could not approve simply in order to "please the people"; Hamilton, charging that the "turbulent and changing" masses "seldom judge or determine right" and advising a permanent governmental body to "check the imprudence of democracy"; the wealthy young planter Charles Pinckney, proposing that no one be president who was not worth at least one hundred thousand dollars—all these were quite representative of the spirit in which the problems of government were treated.

Democratic ideas are most likely to take root among discontented and oppressed classes, rising middle classes, or perhaps some sections of an old, alienated, and partially disinherited aristocracy, but they do not appeal to a privileged class that is still amplifying its privileges. With a half-dozen exceptions at the most, the men of the Philadelphia Convention were sons of men who had considerable position and wealth, and as a group they had advanced well beyond their fathers. Only one of them, William Few of Georgia, could be said in any sense to represent the yeoman farmer class which constituted the overwhelming majority of the free population. In the late eighteenth century "the better kind of people" found themselves set off from the mass by a hundred visible, tangible, and audible distinctions of dress, speech, manners, and education. There was a continuous lineage of upper-class contempt, from pre-Revolutionary Tories like Peggy Hutchinson, the Governor's daughter, who wrote one day: "The dirty mob was all about me as I drove into town," to a Federalist like Hamilton, who candidly disdained the people. Mass unrest was often received in the spirit of young Gouverneur Morris: "The mob begin to think and reason. Poor reptiles! . . . They bask in the sun, and ere noon they will bite, depend upon it. The gentry begin to fear this." Nowhere in America or Europe—not even among the great liberated thinkers of the Enlightenment—did democratic ideas appear respectable to the cultivated classes. Whether the Fathers looked to the cynically illuminated intellectuals of contemporary Europe or to their own Christian heritage of the idea of original sin, they found quick confirmation of the notion that man is an unregenerate rebel who has to be controlled.

And yet there was another side to the picture. The Fathers were intellectual heirs of seventeenth-century English republicanism with its opposition to arbitrary rule and faith in popular sovereignty. If they feared the advance of democracy, they also had misgivings about turning to the extreme right. Having recently experienced a bitter revolutionary struggle with an external power beyond their control, they were in no mood to follow Hobbes to his conclusion that any kind of government must be accepted in order to avert the anarchy and terror of a state of nature. They were uneasily aware that both military dictatorship and a return to monarchy were being seriously discussed in some quarters—the former chiefly among unpaid and discontented army officers, the latter in rich and fashionable Northern circles. John Jay, familiar with sentiment among New York's mercantile aristocracy, wrote to Washington, June 27, 1786, that he feared that "the better kind of people (by which I mean the people who are orderly and industrious, who are content with their situations, and not uneasy in their circumstances) will be led, by the insecurity of property, the loss of confidence in their rulers, and the want of public faith and rectitude, to consider the charms of liberty as imaginary and delusive." Such men, he thought, might be prepared for "almost any change that may promise them quiet and security." Washington, who had already repudiated a suggestion that he become a military dictator, agreed, remarking that "we are apt to run from one extreme to the other."

Unwilling to turn their backs upon republicanism, the Fathers also wished to avoid violating the prejudices of the people. "Notwithstanding the oppression and injustice experienced among us from democracy," said George Mason, "the genius of the people is in favor of it, and the genius of the people must be consulted." Mason admitted "that we had been too democratic," but feared that "we should incautiously run into the opposite extreme." James Madison, who has quite rightfully been called the philosopher of the Constitution, told the delegates: "It seems indispensable that the mass of citizens should not be without a voice in making the laws which they are to obey, and in choosing the magistrates who are to administer them." James Wilson, the outstanding jurist of the age, later appointed to the Supreme Court by Washington, said again and again that the ultimate power of government must of necessity reside in the people. This the Fathers commonly accepted, for if government did not proceed from the people, from what other source could it legitimately come? To adopt any other premise not only would be inconsistent with everything they had said against British rule in the past but would open the gates to an extreme concentration of power in the future. Hamilton saw the sharp distinction in the Convention when he said that "the members most tenacious of republicanism were as loud as any in declaiming the vices of democracy." There was no better expression of the dilemma of a man who has no faith in the people but insists that government be based upon them than that of Jeremy Belknap, a New England clergyman, who wrote to a friend: "Let it stand as a principle that government originates from the people; but let the people be taught . . . that they are not able to govern themselves."

II

If the masses were turbulent and unregenerate, and yet if government must be founded upon their suffrage and consent, what could a Constitution-maker do? One thing that the Fathers did not propose to do, because they thought it impossible, was to change the nature of man to conform with a more ideal system. They were inordinately confident that they knew what man always had been and what he always would be. The eighteenth-century mind had great faith in universals. Its method, as Carl Becker has said, was "to go up and down the field of history looking for man in general, the universal man, stripped of the accidents of time and place." Madison declared that the causes of political differences and of the formation of factions were "sown in the nature of man" and could never be eradicated. "It is universally acknowledged," David Hume had written, "that there is a great uniformity among the actions of men, in all nations and ages, and that human nature remains still the same, in its principles and operations. The same motives always produce the same actions. The same events always follow from the same causes."

Since man was an unchangeable creature of self-interest, it would not do to leave anything to his capacity for restraint. It was too much to expect that vice could be checked by virtue; the Fathers relied instead upon checking vice with vice. Madison once objected during the Convention that Gouverneur Morris was "forever inculcating the utter political depravity of men and the necessity of opposing one vice and interest to another vice and interest." And yet Madison himself in the *Federalist* number 51 later set forth an excellent statement of the same thesis:[1]

Ambition must be made to counteract ambition. . . . It may be a reflection on human nature that such devices should be necessary to control the abuses of government. But what is government itself, but the greatest of all reflections on human nature? If men were angels, no government would be necessary. . . . In framing a government which is to be administered by men over men, the great difficulty lies in this: you must first enable the government to control the governed; and in the next place oblige it to control itself.

Political economists of the laissez-faire school were saying that private vices could be public benefits, that an economically beneficent result would be providentially or "naturally" achieved if self-interest were left free from state interference and allowed to pursue its ends. But the Fathers were not so optimistic about politics. If, in a state that lacked constitutional balance, one class or one interest gained control, they believed, it would surely plunder all other interests. The Fathers, of course, were especially fearful that the poor would plunder the rich, but most of them would probably have admitted that the rich, unrestrained, would also plunder the poor. Even Gouverneur Morris, who stood as close to the extreme aristocratic position as candor and intelligence would allow, told the Convention: "Wealth tends to corrupt the mind and to nourish its love of power, and to stimulate it to oppression. History proves this to be the spirit of the opulent."

What the Fathers wanted was known as "balanced government," an idea at least as old as Aristotle and Polybius. This ancient conception had won new sanction in the eighteenth century, which was dominated intellectually by the scientific work of Newton, and in which mechanical metaphors sprang as naturally to men's minds as did biological metaphors in the Darwinian atmosphere of the late nineteenth century. Men had found a rational order in the universe and they hoped that it could be transferred to politics, or, as John Adams put it, that governments could be "erected on the simple principles of nature." Madison spoke in the most precise Newtonian language when he said that such a "natural" government must be so constructed "that its several constituent parts may, by their mutual relations, be the means of keeping each other in their proper places." A properly designed state, the Fathers believed, would check interest with interest, class with class, faction with faction, and one branch of government with another in a harmonious system of mutual frustration.

In practical form, therefore, the quest of the Fathers reduced primarily to a search for constitutional devices that would force various interests to check and control one another. Among those who favored the federal Constitution three such devices were distinguished.

The first of these was the advantage of a federated government in maintaining order against popular uprisings or majority rule. In a single state a faction might arise and take complete control by force; but if the states were bound in a federation, the central government could step in and prevent it. Hamilton quoted Montesquieu: "Should a popular insurrection happen in one of the confederate states, the others are able to quell it." Further, as Madison argued in the *Federalist* number 10, a majority would be the most dangerous of all factions that might arise, for the majority would be the most capable of gaining complete ascendancy. If the political society were very extensive, however, and embraced a large number and variety of local interests, the citizens who shared a common majority interest "must be rendered by their number and local situation, unable to concert and carry into effect their schemes of oppression." The chief propertied interests would then be safer from "a rage for paper money, for an abolition of debts, for an equal division of property, or for any other improper or wicked project."

The second advantage of good constitutional government resided in the mechanism of representation itself. In a small direct democracy the unstable passions of the people would dominate lawmaking; but a representative government, as Madison said, would "refine and enlarge the public views by passing them through the medium of a chosen body of citizens." Representatives chosen by the people were wiser and more deliberate than the people themselves in mass assemblage. Hamilton frankly anticipated a kind of syndical paternalism in which the wealthy and dominant members of every trade or industry would represent the others in politics. Merchants, for example, were "the natural representatives" of their employees and of the mechanics and artisans they dealt with. Hamilton expected that Congress, "with too few exceptions to have any influence on the spirit of the government, will be composed of landholders, merchants, and men of the learned professions."

The third advantage of the government the Fathers were designing was pointed out most elaborately by John Adams in the first volume of his *Defence of the Constitutions of Government of the United States of America,* which reached Philadelphia while the Convention was in session and was cited with approval by several delegates.[2] Adams believed that the aristocracy and the democracy must be made to neutralize each other. Each element should be given its own house of the legislature, and over both houses there should be set a capable, strong, and impartial executive armed with the veto power. This split assembly would contain within itself an organic check and would be capable of self-control under the governance of the executive. The whole system was to be capped by an independent judiciary. The inevitable tendency of the rich and the poor to plunder each other would be kept in hand.

III

It is ironical that the Constitution, which Americans venerate so deeply, is based upon a political theory that at one crucial point stands in direct antithesis to the main stream of American democratic faith. Modern American folklore assumes that democracy and liberty are all but identical, and when democratic writers take the trouble to make the distinction, they usually assume that democracy is necessary to liberty. But the Founding Fathers thought that the liberty with which they were most concerned was menaced by democracy. In their minds liberty was linked not to democracy but to property.

What did the Fathers mean by liberty? What did Jay mean when he spoke of "the charms of liberty"? Or Madison when he declared that to destroy liberty in order to destroy factions would be a remedy worse than the disease? Certainly the men who met at Philadelphia were not interested in extending liberty to those classes in America, the Negro slaves and the indentured servants, who were most in need of it, for slavery was recognized in the organic structure of the Constitution and indentured servitude was no concern of the Convention. Nor was the regard of the delegates for civil liberties any too tender. It was the opponents of the Constitution who were most active in demanding such vital liberties as freedom of religion, freedom of speech and press, jury trial, due process, and protection from "unreasonable searches and seizures." These guarantees had to be incorporated in the first ten amendments because the Convention neglected to put them in the original document. Turning to economic issues, it was not freedom of trade in the modern sense that the Fathers were striving for. Although they did not believe in impeding trade unnecessarily, they felt that failure to regulate it was one of the central weaknesses of the Articles of Confederation, and they stood closer to the mercantilists than to Adam Smith. Again, liberty to them did not mean free access to the nation's unappropriated wealth. At least fourteen of them were land speculators. They did not believe in the right of the squatter to occupy unused land, but rather in the right of the absentee owner or speculator to pre-empt it.

The liberties that the constitutionalists hoped to gain were chiefly negative. They wanted freedom from fiscal uncertainty and irregularities in the currency, from trade wars among the states, from economic discrimination by more powerful foreign governments, from attacks on the creditor class or on property, from popular insurrection. They aimed to create a government that would act as an honest broker among a variety of propertied interests, giving them all protection from their common enemies and preventing any one of them from becoming too powerful. The Convention was a fraternity of types of absentee ownership. All property should be permitted to have its proportionate voice in government. Individual property interests might have to be sacrificed at times, but only for the community of propertied interests. Freedom for property would result in liberty for men—perhaps not for all men, but at least for all worthy men.[3] Because men have different faculties and abilities, the Fathers believed, they acquire different amounts of property. To protect property is only to protect men in the exercise of their natural faculties. Among the many liberties, therefore, freedom to hold and dispose property is paramount. Democracy, unchecked rule by the masses, is sure to bring arbitrary redistribution of property, destroying the very essence of liberty.

The Fathers' conception of democracy, shaped by their practical experience with the aggressive dirt farmers in the American states and the urban mobs of the Revolutionary period, was supplemented by their reading in history and political science. Fear of what Madison called "the superior force of an interested and overbearing majority" was the dominant emotion aroused by their study of historical examples. The chief examples of republics were among the city-states of antiquity, medieval Europe, and early modern times. Now, the history of these republics—a history, as Hamilton said, "of perpetual vibration between the extremes of tyranny and anarchy"—was alarming. Further, most of the men who had overthrown the liberties of republics had "begun their career by paying an obsequious court to the people; commencing demagogues and ending tyrants."

All the constitutional devices that the Fathers praised in their writings were attempts to guarantee the future of the United States against the "turbulent" political cycles of previous republics. By "democracy," they meant a system of government which directly expressed the will of the majority of the people, usually through such an assemblage of the people as was possible in the small area of the city-state.

A cardinal tenet in the faith of the men who made the Constitution was the belief that democracy can never be more than a transitional stage in government, that it always evolves into either a tyranny (the rule of the rich demagogue who has patronized the mob) or an aristocracy (the original leaders of the democratic elements). "Remember," wrote the dogmatic John Adams in one of his letters to John Taylor of Caroline, "democracy never lasts long. It soon wastes, exhausts, and murders itself. There never was a democracy yet that did not commit suicide."[4] Again:

> If you give more than a share in the sovereignty to the democrats, that is, if you give them the command or preponderance in the . . . legislature, they will vote all property out of the hands of you aristocrats, and if they let you escape with your lives, it will be more humanity, consideration, and generosity than any triumphant democracy ever displayed since the creation. And what will follow? The aristocracy among the democrats will take your places, and treat their fellows as severely and sternly as you have treated them.

Government, thought the Fathers, is based on property. Men who have no property lack the necessary stake in an orderly society to make stable or reliable citizens. Dread of the propertyless masses of the towns was all but universal. George Washington, Gouverneur Morris, John Dickinson, and James Madison spoke of their anxieties about the urban working class that might arise some time in the future—"men without property and principle," as Dickinson described them—and even the democratic Jefferson shared this prejudice. Madison, stating the problem, came close to anticipating the modern threats to conservative republicanism from both communism and fascism:

> In future times, a great majority of the people will not only be without landed but any other sort of property. These will either combine, under the influence of their common situation—in which case the rights of property and the public liberty will not be secure in their hands—or, what is more probable, they will become the tools of opulence and ambition, in which case there will be equal danger on another side.

What encouraged the Fathers about their own era, however, was the broad dispersion of landed property. The small land-owning farmers had been troublesome in recent years, but there was a general conviction that under a properly made Constitution a *modus vivendi* could be worked out with them. The possession of moderate plots of property presumably gave them a sufficient stake in society to be safe and responsible citizens under the restraints of balanced government. Influence in government would be proportionate to property: merchants and great landholders would be dominant, but small property-owners would have an independent and far from negligible voice. It was "politic as well as just," said Madison, "that the interests and rights of every class should be duly represented and understood in the public councils," and John Adams declared that there could be "no free government without a democratical branch in the constitution."

The farming element already satisfied the property requirements for suffrage in most of the states, and the Fathers generally had no quarrel with their enfranchisement. But when they spoke of the necessity of founding government upon the consent of "the people," it was only these small property-holders that they had in mind. For example, the famous Virginia Bill of Rights, written by George Mason, explicitly defined those eligible for suffrage as all men "having sufficient evidence of permanent common interest with and attachment to the community"—which meant, in brief, sufficient property.

However, the original intention of the Fathers to admit the yeoman into an important but sharply limited partnership in affairs of state could not be perfectly realized. At the time the Constitution was made, Southern planters and Northern merchants were setting their differences aside in order to meet common dangers—from radicals within and more powerful nations without. After the Constitution was adopted, conflict between the ruling classes broke out anew, especially after powerful planters were offended by the favoritism of Hamilton's policies to Northern commercial interests. The planters turned to the farmers to form an agrarian alliance, and for more than half a century this powerful coalition embraced the bulk of the articulate interests of the country. As time went on, therefore, the main stream of American political conviction deviated more and more from the antidemocratic position of the Constitution-makers. Yet, curiously, their general satisfaction with the Constitution together with their growing nationalism made Americans deeply reverent of the founding generation, with the result that as it grew stronger, this deviation was increasingly overlooked.

There is common agreement among modern critics that the debates over the Constitution were carried on at an intellectual level that is rare in politics, and that the Constitution itself is one of the world's masterpieces of practical statecraft. On other grounds there has been controversy. At the very beginning contemporary opponents of the Constitution foresaw an apocalyptic destruction of local government and popular institutions, while conservative Europeans of the old regime thought the young American Republic was a dangerous leftist experiment. Modern critical scholarship, which reached a high point in Charles A. Beard's *An Economic Interpretation of the Constitution of the United States,* started a new turn in the debate. The antagonism, long latent, between the philosophy of the Constitution and the philosophy of American democracy again came into the open. Professor Beard's work appeared in 1913 at the peak of the Progressive era, when the muckraking fever was still high; some readers tended to conclude from his findings that the Fathers were selfish reactionaries who do not deserve their high place in American esteem. Still more recently, other writers, inverting this logic, have used Beard's facts to praise the Fathers for their opposition to "democracy" and as an argument for returning again to the idea of a "republic."

In fact, the Fathers' image of themselves as moderate republicans standing between political extremes was quite accurate. They were impelled by class motives more than pietistic writers like to admit, but they were also controlled, as Professor Beard himself has recently emphasized, by a statesmanlike sense of moderation and a scrupulously republican philosophy. Any attempt, however, to tear their ideas out of the eighteenth-century context is sure to make them seem starkly reactionary. Consider, for example, the favorite maxim of John Jay: "The people who own the country ought to govern it." To the Fathers this was simply a swift axiomatic statement of the stake-in-society theory of political rights, a moderate conservative position under eighteenth-century conditions of property distribution in America. Under modern property relations this maxim demands a drastic restriction of the base of political power. A large portion of the modern middle class—and it is the strength of this class upon which balanced government depends—is propertyless; and the urban proletariat, which the Fathers so greatly feared, is almost one half the population. Further, the separation of ownership from control that has come with the corporation deprives Jay's maxim of twentieth-century meaning even for many propertied people. The six hundred thousand stockholders of the American Telephone & Telegraph Company not only do not acquire political power by virtue of their stockownership, but they do not even acquire economic power: they cannot control their own company.

From a humanistic standpoint there is a serious dilemma in the philosophy of the Fathers, which derives from their conception of man. They thought man was a creature of rapacious self-interest, and yet they wanted him to be free—free, in essence, to contend, to engage in an umpired strife, to use property to get property. They accepted the mercantile image of life as an eternal battleground, and assumed the Hobbesian war of each against all; they did not propose to put an end to this war, but merely to stabilize it and make it less murderous. They had no hope and they offered none for any ultimate organic change in the way men conduct themselves. The result was that while they thought self-interest the most dangerous and unbrookable quality of man, they necessarily underwrote it in trying to control it. They succeeded in both respects: under the competitive capitalism of the nineteenth century America continued to be an arena for various grasping and contending interests, and the federal government continued to provide a stable and acceptable medium within which they could contend; further, it usually showed the wholesome bias on behalf of property which the Fathers expected. But no man who is as well abreast of modern science as the Fathers were of eighteenth-century science believes any longer in unchanging human nature. Modern humanistic thinkers who seek for a means by which society may transcend eternal conflict and rigid adherence to property rights as its integrating principles can expect no answer in the philosophy of balanced government as it was set down by the Constitution-makers of 1787.

NOTES

1. Cf. the words of Hamilton to the New York ratifying convention: "Men will pursue their interests. It is as easy to change human nature as to oppose the strong current of selfish passions. A wise legislator will gently divert the channel, and direct it, if possible, to the public good."
2. "Mr. Adams' book," wrote Benjamin Rush, often in the company of the delegates, "has diffused such excellent principles among us that there is little doubt of our adopting a vigorous and compounded Federal Legislature. Our illustrious Minister in this gift to his country has done us more service than if he had obtained alliances for us with all the nations of Europe."
3. The Fathers probably would have accepted the argument of the Declaration of Independence that "all men are created equal," but only as a legal, not as a political or psychological proposition. Jefferson himself believed in the existence of "natural aristocrats," but he thought they were likely to appear in any class of society. However, for those who interpreted the natural-rights philosophy more conservatively than he, the idea that all men are equal did not mean that uneducated dirt farmers or grimy-handed ship calkers were in any sense the equals of the Schuylers, Washingtons, or Pinckneys. It meant only that British colonials had as much natural right to self-government as Britons at home, that the average American was the legal peer of the average Briton. Among the signers of the Constitution, it is worth noting, there were only six men who had also signed the Declaration of Independence.
4. Taylor labored to confute Adams, but in 1814, after many discouraging years in American politics, he conceded a great part of Adams's case: "All parties, however loyal to principles at first, degenerate into aristocracies of interest at last; and unless a nation is capable of discerning the point where integrity ends and fraud begins, popular parties are among the surest modes of introducing an aristocracy."

3

Traditions of Democracy

ARTHUR M. SCHLESINGER, JR.

In the following excerpt, Arthur Schlesinger, Jr., argues that liberal capitalism is rooted in the traditions of the Jefferson and Jackson eras. The Jacksonians, according to Schlesinger, attempted to democratize American capitalism, to make it more humane so that it might better serve the national interest. The Jacksonians and, later, Franklin D. Roosevelt represent the democratic side of American liberalism, which tempered the self-seeking aspects of capitalism. This democratic spirit may have ebbed in certain periods—as it did during the American Civil War and Reconstruction, for example—but it has never been permanently impaired. The Populist revolts of the 1890s, the Progressive movement before World War I, and the New Deal represent the indestructibility of the Jacksonian ideal.

Although American liberal democracy presumes a limitation on the scope of governmental activity, it also requires the maintenance of political competition. Jacksonians, Populists, Progressives, and New Deal Democrats understood these fundamental requirements. Nevertheless, they also knew that the emergence of large industrial corporations, trusts, and conglomerates required governmental action, that is, the expansion of the government's scope of action, to restore the historic balance of competition in American public life. These reform movements may not have succeeded, but they were justifiable within the context of the American political tradition. Indeed, Schlesinger's The Age of Jackson, *from which the following excerpt comes, may be viewed as a historic justification of the New Deal.*

Schlesinger is the author of the three-volume The Age of Roosevelt *(1957–1960),* A Thousand Days *(1965),*

The Bitter Heritage *(1966), and* The Crisis of Confidence *(1969). He is Albert Schweitzer Professor of Humanities at the City College of New York and has received a Pulitzer Prize (1945) and a National Book Award (1965). From 1961 to 1964 he was a special assistant to the President of the United States.*

The tradition of Jefferson and Jackson might recede, but it could never disappear. It was bound to endure in America so long as liberal capitalistic society endured, for it was the creation of the internal necessities of such a society. American democracy has come to accept the struggle among competing groups for the control of the state as a positive virtue—indeed, as the only foundation for liberty. The business community has been ordinarily the most powerful of these groups, and liberalism in America has been ordinarily the movement on the part of the other sections of society to restrain the power of the business community. This was the tradition of Jefferson and Jackson, and it has been the basic meaning of American liberalism.

1

Yet the tradition clearly went into eclipse for some years after the Civil War. There had risen up before the war a party of industrial control, with smooth-running organization, energetic leadership, an active program and a solid economic base. Then the new and more terrible program of slavery had burst forth, mobilizing the loyalties and capacities of men of good will. The antislavery crusade thus drained off the energies, diverted the enthusiasm and destroyed the party of Jacksonian democracy.

* * *

This quiescence of the Jacksonian tradition, the breakup of the Jacksonian organization, the death of the Jacksonian leaders, disarmed liberalism for the postwar struggles. In the meantime the impulse of the business community toward protective coloration, begun by Seward, Weed and Greeley in the thirties, came to triumphant culmination. By capturing the Republican party the business community captured the prestige of representing freedom and democracy. The technique of "waving of bloody shirt"—that is, of freeing the slaves again every fourth year—enabled the Republicans long to submerge the fact that they were becoming the party of monopoly and wealth. Thus, for some time after the war, the pressing economic issues were kept out of national politics. When the country returned once more to the problems which had preoccupied the thirties, the radical democrats were forgotten, their experiments unknown, their philosophy sunk in oblivion. The continuities of reform had been broken.

2

At the same time new complexities, which the Jacksonians did not have to face, were weakening the faith of even some democrats in the efficacy

Reprinted from *The Age of Jackson* by Arthur M. Schlesinger, Jr., chap. 37, pp. 505–523, by permission of Little, Brown and Co.

of the radical democratic solution—in the efficacy, that is, of unlimited reliance on popular government. Of these, the most serious was the rise of a rootless, bewildered, unstable population, the creation, on the one hand, of the spread of industrialism, and, on the other, of the rapid increase of immigration. Starting on a large scale in the eighteen-forties, thousands of Europeans, ill-educated, tractable, used to low economic standards, unused to political liberty, began flocking to American shores. There they mingled with native Americans in the large cities and mill towns, all living a scanty and desperate life at day labor, all driven into a herd, imprinted with the same mold, and subjected to a barrage of insecurities which restricted their freedom of choice and undermined their responsibility. The "people" were being degraded into the "mass," bound together, not by common loyalties and aspirations, but by common anxieties and fears.

The political consequences of the rise of this new population were plain and terrifying. The "masses," huddled together in the slums, seemed no longer, in any real sense, to be free. As voters they were either at the beck and call of their employers, or else the dupes of unscrupulous demagogues. "Bread and circuses" appeared to be once more the formula for political success. Mike Walsh was a symbolic figure, exhibiting the good and the evil in the new mass politician: on the one hand, an honest fervor for popular rights; on the other, the methods of an accomplished political gangster—the Spartan Band and brawls in the streets and corruption at the polls ("vote early and vote often").

Yet Mike Walsh at least did, in his erratic way, have the people on his mind; but what of the men who took over Walsh's methods without his saving honesty? The rise of bosses like Fernando Wood in New York was profoundly alarming to believers in democracy.

Even more alarming in the long run were the men who took over Walsh's fervor, trumpeting their love of democracy and liberty, mainly in order to gain the power to destroy it. In New York, George Wilkes, fancy man, gossip monger, salesman of obscene literature, became an ardent Communist and wrote pamphlets extolling the Internationale and the Paris Commune. Yet the lineage from William Leggett to Mike Walsh to Walsh's pal Wilkes was straight, and much of Wilkes's appeal was couched in almost Jacksonian language.[1] Similarly in Massachusetts the unscrupulous Ben Butler became a noisy "radical," in 1884 the presidential nominee of the Anti-Monopoly party, and he too was in direct line of descent from Jacksonianism.

Many Jacksonians, reading these portents, began to succumb to the old Jeffersonian fears of the city and the industrial proletariat. In 1864 Gideon Welles and Preston King, expressing to each other their disgust that New York City could send Fernando Wood to Congress, got into a discussion of the limits of radical democracy.

"The whole city of New York," exclaimed Welles, "is alike leprous and rotten.... How can such a place be regenerated and purified? What is the remedy?" He confessed a reluctant belief that "in such a vicious community free suffrage was abased, and it was becoming a problem whether there should not be an outside movement, or some restriction on voting to correct palpable evil in municipal government."

King, as Welles put it, maintained

the old faith. "The evil will correct itself," the veteran radical stoutly declared. "After they have disgraced themselves sufficiently and loaded themselves with taxes and debt, they will finally rouse to a sense of duty, and retrieve the city from misrule."

For a moment Welles felt the "old enthusiasm of former years" return with King's unquestioning conviction. He recalled those happy days "when in the security of youth I believed the popular voice was right, and that the majority would come to right results in every community; but alas! experience has shaken the confidence I once had. In an agricultural district, or a sparse population the old rule holds," he conceded; but in the large cities? The "floating mass" seemed to him no safe depository of power. "Some permanent element is wanting in our system."[2]

Even the superb confidence of Walt Whitman was faltering. As he looked out on the post-Civil War world, as he saw "the shallowness and miserable selfism of these crowds of men, with all their minds so blank of high humanity and aspiration—then comes the terrible query, and will not be denied, Is not Democracy of human rights humbug after all?" Did these people "with hearts of rags and souls of chalk" have the grandeur of vision for self-government? He did not know; he would not "gloss over the appaling dangers of universal suffrage," but at bottom he was still convinced that the people would save themselves; he too still maintained the old faith.[3]

Yet democracy was certainly facing a problem which no rhetoric of majority rule could assuage. The rise of the masses gave the democratic appeal a sinister ambivalence. It could be employed with as much passion, and with many fewer scruples, by the Fernando Woods, the Ben Butlers and the George Wilkeses, the corrupt bosses, the proto-fascists and the proto-communists, as by the honest democrat. If democratic leadership could not solve the crucial economic problems, would not the masses, seeking in despair everywhere for relief, turn in the end to the man who would provide apocalyptic promises of everything?

The returns are not yet in. But the tired liberalism of Gideon Welles clearly exaggerated the imminence of disaster. The faith of Preston King and Walt Whitman in the recuperative capacity of American democracy, in its tendency toward self-correction, was still justified (in great part, of course, because of the natural endowments of economic wealth and geographical isolation). The people have not yet altogether become the "floating mass," and the "floating mass" itself is not beyond redemption. The future thus became a race between the radical democracy, trying to build a society which would eliminate anxiety and despair, and the black infectious taint of fear, which would demoralize the people and create the drive toward security at any price—as Whitman saw it, "the battle advancing, retreating, between democracy's convictions, aspirations, and the people's crudeness, vice, caprices."[4] Three quarters of a century after Gideon Welles's forebodings, the radical democracy in America still preserved, by some herculean exertions, a small but important advantage.

3

We have seen how the growth of impersonality in economic relations enhanced the need for the intervention of government. As the private conscience grew increasingly powerless to impose effective restraints on the methods of business, the public conscience, in the form of the democratic government, had to step in to prevent the business community from tearing society apart in its pursuit of profit. The rise of the "mass," by increasing the proportion of society only fitfully capable of making responsible decisions, added to the compulsion for state action. Yet by origin and creed the tradition of Jefferson was vigorously antistatist; and the conflict raised new problems for democratic thought.

This mistrust of government had roots deep in the American past. Many of the colonists, as Van Buren pointed out, had arrived with vivid recollections of the persecutions suffered by Puritan, Huguenot, Hussite and Dutch ancestors, which, "gradually stimulated into maturity and shape by the persevering injustice of the mother country, became political opinions of the most tenacious and enduring character." The first motive of American democracy was hostility against what was felt to be insupportable tyranny, and the war with Britain confirmed democracy in its suspicion of the state. Moreover, for people in the shadow of the Middle Ages, the history of liberty had been the history of the capture of guarantees and immunities from the state; and in the American republic itself, most interference by the central government—United States Bank, internal improvements, tariff—had been for the benefit of the business community. The instinct of democrats was thus to insist on the constitutional bounds of the state. Their experience of government and their reading of history, as Van Buren put it, destroyed all hope that "political power could be vested in remote hands, without the certainty of its being abused."[5]

"That government is best, which governs least," "The world is too much governed"—the mottoes repectively of the *Democratic Review* and the *Washington Globe*—expressed forcibly the prevailing antigovernmental complex. The corollary was that what government was necessary should be in the hands of the states. "The man who chiefly desires to preserve the rights of the States, and he whose interests are concentrated in perpetuating the rule of the many," as the *Democratic Review* said in 1844, "must, under our political system, use the same means to attain their ends."[6] George Bancroft observed that it was Jackson's deep conviction that "strict construction is required by the lasting welfare of the great labouring classes of the United States."[7]

These emotions about State rights and the evil of government were absorbed into and fortified by what may be called the "Jeffersonian myth." Every great social movement, as Sorel has reminded us, generates its "social myth"—the "body of images capable of evoking instinctively all the sentiments which correspond to the different manifestations" of the movement. Such a myth, though it purports to deal with the future, is by no means to be taken as a blueprint. It "must be judged as a means of acting on the present; any attempt to discuss how far it can be taken literally as future history is devoid of sense." The myths are "not descriptions of things, but expressions of a determination to act."[8] It is thus idle to refute a myth, since it exists as an emotional entirety whose essential function is to mobilize men for action.

Jackson in his vindication of his presidency to the Senate displayed some of the resources of the Jeffersonian myth. It had been his purpose, he said, "to heal the wounds of the

Constitution and preserve it from further violation; to persuade my countrymen, so far as I may, that it is not in a splendid government supported by powerful monopolies and aristocratical establishments that they will find happiness or their liberties protection, but in a plain system, void of pomp, protecting all and granting favors to none, dispensing its blessings, like the dews of Heaven, unseen and unfelt save in the freshness and beauty they contribute to produce."[9] The imagery discloses the underlying pattern: the Constitution undefiled vs. the Constitution violated; plain government vs. splendid government; equal rights vs. powerful monopolies; the dews of heaven, in freshness and beauty, vs. "aristocratical establishments," with their suggestions of monarchy, wealth and decadence.

The Jeffersonian myth thus implanted and sustained in the minds of its followers a whole set of social choices: simplicity vs. ostentation; frugality vs. extravagance; rectitude vs. laxity; moderation vs. luxury; country vs. city; virtuous farmer or mechanic vs. depraved capitalist or demoralized day laborer; plain homely government vs. sumptuous complicated government; economy vs. debt; strict construction vs. loose construction; State rights vs. huge federal power; decentralization vs. concentration; democracy vs. aristocracy; purity vs. corruption.

This body of values and images animated and deepened the appeals of Jefferson, John Taylor, Jackson, Van Buren and the other Jeffersonians. They were operating in terms of a great common vision, strong, simple and satisfying, evoking the emotions which hope, memory or experience had endeared to millions of Americans, and thrusting in sharp and ugly relief the invading armies of industrialism and aristocracy. The existence of this myth in the background of the mind gave its component parts—not least the belief in the evil of government—a strong and almost sacred status.

4

Yet change brought a growing divergence between the myth and the actuality. We have seen how the pat contrasts between country and city, honest farmer and demoralized laborer, were tripped up by the realities of Jacksonian politics. In the realm of government the divergence became acute with respect to the antigovernmental complex. The neat formulas of antistatism simply failed to work. Invented as protective doctrines against aristocratic despotism, they became an embarrassment when the radical party got into power itself. Jefferson ignored them when he felt strong executive action to be necessary, and in the quiet of his retirement he even developed a general rationale for overstepping the Jeffersonian limitations.[10]

The administration of Jackson accentuated the complexities which underlay the deceptively simple maxims of the *Globe* and the *Democratic Review*. Granted that competition free from government intervention constituted the ideal economy, what was the Jeffersonian obligation when that freedom resulted in the growth of monopolies which destroyed competition? The Jacksonian answer was government intervention—to restore the conditions of competition; that is, to "heal the wounds of the Constitution" and re-establish the principles of government in their original purity. As John L. O'Sullivan put it, "A good deal of positive government may be yet wanted to undo the manifold mischiefs of past mis-government."[11] Thus, the Jacksonians, under the banner of antistatism, could carry on a vigorous program of government intervention, and Jackson, ruling in the name of weak government, ended up by leaving the presidency stronger than it had ever been before.

Some of the details of the Jacksonian policy, however, caused orthodox Jeffersonians distinct discomfort, even those who managed to swallow such deviations as the Nullification Proclamation or the removal of the deposits.

The struggle to reconcile the Jeffersonian myth and the Jacksonian fact was fought out most candidly in the pages of the *Democratic Review.* The first issue contained a glowing and trustful statement of the Jeffersonian position, with the theory of weak government imbedded as the keystone. But what was the status of this theory in face of an army of corporations hostile to democracy? O'Sullivan wrestled with this difficulty in a casuistical article in the second number, eventually confining the theory to the federal government alone and vehemently attacking the Supreme Court for limiting the power of state governments over business.

But was this much help? After the banks suspended in May, 1837, a trade-union meeting in Philadelphia had declared in a typical outburst, "On the question of the currency, we have no confidence in the State administrations generally. . . . we hereby call upon the national administration to take all such measures as it shall judge the most expedient."[12] Where did this leave O'Sullivan's revised theory? He perceived the difficulty, and the third number carried a somewhat embarrassed article justifying the robustness of Jackson's presidency, but hoping devoutly that "those great powers resident in the Executive arm, may never again be called forth into activity."[13]

And so it went. Jeffersonian fundamentalists got off the bandwagon early. Even a Jacksonian like Orestes A. Brownson could in certain moods exclaim with alarm at Jackson's "tendency to Centralization and his evident leaning to *Bureaucraticy*. . . . We are making more rapid strides towards . . . Centralization and to the Bureaucratic system than even the most sensitive nullifier has yet suspected."[14]

It is no wonder that the attempt to defend Jacksonianism in terms of that government being best which governed least excited only the derision of the Whigs. To them Jacksonian policy consisted simply, as Caleb Cushing described it, of "the meddlesome interference of General Jackson in the business of the country, his prurient tampering with the currency under the pretext of reforming it," and so on.[15] The talk about restoring constitutional purity seemed a cynical pretext for reckless government intervention.

The vital point underlying this bandying of accusations is that "intervention" is not an absolute. It is always a question of whose ox is gored. Government *must* act; it cannot rest in Olympian impartiality. Even "governing least" is likely to be government for the benefit of the strongest group in the community. The crucial question is not, Is there "too much" government? but, Does the government promote "too much" the interests of a single group? In liberal capitalist society this question has ordinarily become in practice, Is the government serving the interests of the business community to the detriment of the nation as a whole? This has been the irrepressible conflict of capitalism: the struggle on the part of the business community to dominate the state, and on the part of the rest of society, under the leadership of "liberals," to check the political ambitions of business.

The real issue between the Whigs and Jackson was, thus, not freedom of enterprise. Both parties would concede that enterprise should be free, would claim always to be acting to protect this freedom, and each, when in possession of the state, would unhesitatingly intervene in business, on its own behalf and in the name of "freedom," by destroying United States Banks or establishing protective tariffs. The champions of Jeffersonianism were eager for government to suppress small notes and institute a ten-hour day, while the Hamiltonians would flourish free-trade principles when questions of trade-unionism or corporation control were brought up. If the men of the thirties and forties really accepted the antistatist maxims they constantly invoked, they would not have been in political parties at all, but in lonely huts around country ponds like the one man of the day who believed radically that that government was best which governed least.

The question was not principles but power: was a "liberal" government, in fact, strong enough to act contrary to the wishes of the business community? And in the struggle over this basic question conservatism or liberalism would adopt any myth, and has adopted most which promised to promote its cause. This is not to impugn the honesty of belief in the visions excited by the myth, for no great social movement can exist without such stimulus and support. The myth, it should never be forgotten, expresses only the "determination to act." The ends of action lie necessarily in an inscrutable future.

5

There were, in fact, certain "strong government" strains implicit in Jeffersonianism from the start. Jefferson himself could refer to "the protecting hand of the legislature." Speaking of the distresses caused by paper money, he would declare that they could not fail to "engage the interposition of the legislature."[16] The decisions of Marshall's Court, safeguarding corporations from the operations of state laws, intensified the Jeffersonian tendency to aggrandize the state governments. "The restoration of public supremacy," observed Charles Jared Ingersoll, arguing for legislative control over charters of incorporation, "is the great desideratum."[17] A Democratic Justice from Virginia, Philip P. Barbour, firmly and emphatically expanded the police power of the states against the disciples of Marshall.[18]

Once government was conceded some virtue in the states, it was difficult not to extend a little of the exoneration to the federal government. Some functions were simply too important to be confided to the states. As Thomas Hart Benton remarked of the currency, it should not be trusted to any authority "but the highest and most responsible which was known to our form of government"—the people's government at Washington.[19] The experience of the eighteen-thirties, when, from a Jacksonian point of view, state governments were exceedingly unreliable and the federal government was the stronghold of democracy, increased the tendency toward tolerance.

The pivotal conception in this redirection of the liberal tradition was expressed very ably by Taney in his Charles River Bridge decision. "The object and end of all government," he declared, "is to promote the happiness and prosperity of the community by which it is established; and it can never be assumed, that the government intended to diminish its power of accomplishing the end for which it was created."[20]

Now this remark appalled no Jacksonians and delighted no Hamiltonians; yet it foreshadowed a basic shift in the Jeffersonian theory, in the direction of Hamiltonianism. For Taney's maxim could hardly be distinguished from observations made by Hamilton and Marshall:—

> Now it appears to the Secretary of the Treasury that this *general principle* is *inherent* in the very *definition* of government, and *essential* to every step of the progress to be made by that of the United States, namely: That every power vested in a government is in its nature *sovereign*, and includes, by *force* of the *term*, a right to employ all the *means* requisite and fairly applicable to the attainment of the *ends* of such power, and which are not precluded by restrictions and exceptions specified on the Constitution, or not immoral, or not contrary to the *essential ends* of political society.[21]

> Let the end be legitimate, let it be within the scope of the Constitution, and all means which are appropriate, which are plainly adapted to that end, which are not prohibited, but consist with the letter and spirit of the Constitution, are constitutional.[22]

Jeffersonianism, if it were to follow the lead of the Taney formula, must abandon a good deal of its abhorrence of the state. And what other lead could it follow? Was not Jackson's administration—was not Taney's very decision—a confession that Jeffersonianism required Hamiltonian means to achieve its ends?

Jacksonian democracy lacked, however, a great creative political philosopher, who would perceive the essential drift of the Taney doctrine, formulate its implications and restate basically the principles of the liberal faith. The Jeffersonian myth was so persuasive, and Jacksonian action could be so plausibly explained as hewing the way back to original principles, that few were prepared to face the vital gap in the Jeffersonian argument. Yet this gap had to be faced. For if, in the ideal state, government was to be confined to the narrowest possible sphere, what was there to prevent the proliferation of the very monopolies that would, at some later date, require the active intervention of the government? Without a strong government, in other words, how could the people ever hope to deal with the business community? A Jeffersonian would answer that at least the "aristocracy" could do less harm in control of a weak government than a strong one. But under a weak government would not economic power gain the aristocracy all the control they needed? And was not the whole moral of the Jacksonian experience that only a strong people's government could break up the power of concentrated wealth?

But the Jeffersonians refused to admit this final step. Each energetic employment of the government for Jeffersonian ends was for them an exception, a transition stage, irrelevant to theory. In fact, they dared not acknowledge the true answer. They had to suppress it. The birth of democracy in revolt against tyranny had a traumatic effect on Jeffersonian democracy, coloring it with morbid fears of despotism, conditioning it to hate the state, inducing a whole complex of fantasies about government, which made it impossible for Jeffersonians to accept its necessity and drove them to hide what they were doing under a cabalistic repetition of the slogans of antistatism.

This persistence of the Jeffersonian

myth during the Jacksonian period had, moreover, great immediate advantages. Indeed, the very fact of its persistence was presumptive proof of its necessity. It corresponded more accurately and profoundly to the needs of the people than any alteration could have. In particular, it united, for more or less harmonious action over a long period, two essentially unfriendly groups: on the one hand, those opposing the business community from the point of view of the *rentier* class, the landed aristocracy, North as well as South; and on the other, those opposing it from the point of view of the small farmer and workingman. Their differences in interest, social status and ultimate hopes were concealed by their common absorption in the slogans and images of Jeffersonianism.

Small points occasionally betrayed the basic divergence. The first group, for example, exulted in the word "conservative," like Calhoun, Cooper, Taney, Hawthorne, the middle Brownson, and regarded themselves primarily as guardians of the sacred flame, cherishing the purest essence of the Jeffersonian past. The other group exulted in the word "radical," like Van Buren, Bancroft, Blair, Benton, the early Brownson, and regarded themselves as crusaders, out to realize the full values of the Jeffersonian tradition. The first group was defensive in outlook, fundamentally oriented in favor of a vanishing order, and on its behalf assisting in assaults on the aggressive sections of the existing order, while the second was itself aggressive, interested above all in transforming the existing order according to the Jeffersonian faith. The alliance broke down when the emergence of slavery, presenting the basic challenge, called the bluff of the "conservative" Jeffersonians.

6

But, in the long run, the failure to codify the Jacksonian deviations was unfortunate for American liberalism. With Jackson's mighty personality removed and the lessons of his presidency unlearned, his party tended to relapse into the antistatist formulas. The Jeffersonian myth was allowed to linger on, gaining a certain venerability and sanctity; and as a strong government became more clearly the necessary instrument of greater democracy, the business community rushed to fortify itself behind the antigovernmental parts of the Jeffersonian tradition. Ever since, conservatives have been turning to the Jeffersonian myth for weapons to defeat Jefferson's essential purposes. When the antistatist formulas are invoked today, it is ordinarily in defense of the very interests which Jefferson was using them to attack.

After the Civil War, conservatism, draping itself in the mantle of Jefferson and assuming the credit for destroying slavery, stared down the pretensions of any other group to stand for "democracy." Liberalism, deprived of the social myth which had united and sustained it before the war, was left uncertain and incoherent. Men of liberal inclination had nothing with which to mobilize their forces against the rule of the business community.

It was this sense of democratic impotence, intensified by the cynicism of postwar politics, which caused Walt Whitman to define "our fundamental want to-day"—a new faith, "permeating the whole mass of American mentality, taste, belief, breathing into it a new breath of life, giving it decision . . . radiating, begetting appropriate teachers, schools, manners, and, as its grandest result, accomplishing . . . a religious and moral character beneath the political and productive and intellectual bases of the States."

Whitman was demanding, among other things, a new social myth, which would serve the liberal tradition as the Jeffersonian myth had served it before the war. He recognized keenly how "the great literature," as he called it, "penetrates all, gives hue to all, shapes aggregates and individuals, and, after subtle ways, with irresistible power, constructs, sustains, demolishes at will." Unless radical democracy could thus inaugurate "its own perennial sources, welling from the centre for ever, its strength will be defective, its growth doubtful, and its main charm wanting." He announced the time had come for "a native expression-spirit . . . sternly taking command, dissolving the old, sloughing off surfaces, and from its own interior and vital principles, reconstructing, democratizing society." Whitman himself made the greatest sustained attempt to create the "single image-making work," but the need he had perceived could be filled only secondarily by literature. As he saw at other times, "the exercise of Democracy" contained the greatest promise for salvation. The very struggle for liberty and equality was immensely valuable; "strength it makes & lessons it teaches," and from it would emerge the great men who would renew and incarnate democratic ideals.[23]

In the end, exercise rather than literature saved democracy. A century of bitter experience in the democratic fight finally led liberalism to uncover what the Jeffersonians had buried: the need for a strong government. The impotence of the Jeffersonian state to realize Jeffersonian ends first became clear in the economic field, as it grew increasingly apparent that workingmen required protection from the mercies of their employers. Jackson and Van Buren sponsored the ten-hour day and worried over the power of businessmen to drive wages below subsistence. As George Bancroft declared in 1854, *laissez faire* might solve problems of international trade, "but its abandonment of labor to the unmitigated effects of personal competition can never be accepted as the rule for the dealings of man to man. . . . The good time is coming, when humanity will recognise all members of its family as alike entitled to its care; when the heartless jargon of overproduction in the midst of want will end in a better science of distribution."[24]

Such aspirations, in last analysis, called for government to take a much more active role in economic life. One of the first to acknowledge the inadequacy of the Jeffersonian view was the rascally but thoroughly intelligent Ben Butler of Massachusetts. While he had been "dazzled with the brilliancy of Jackson's administration," he wrote in his autobiography, "I early had sense enough to see that it conflicted, in a very considerable degree, with the teachings of Jefferson." The conclusion seemed obvious. "As to the powers and duties of the government of the United States, I am a Hamiltonian Federalist. As to the rights and privileges of the citizen, I am a Jeffersonian Democrat."[25]

Slowly the liberal tradition was overhauled, and the twentieth century saw the final disappearance of the Jeffersonian inhibitions. The Hamiltonian progressivism of Theodore Roosevelt ushered in a period of energetic government. Woodrow Wilson understood even more plainly the need for executive vigor and government action. Franklin D. Roosevelt carried out these tendencies more decisively than Wilson, and the New Deal achieved the emancipation of liberalism from this aspect of the Jeffersonian myth. By 1941 Roosevelt could observe that the criteria of the liberal party were its beliefs in "the wisdom and efficacy of the will of the great majority" and in the "duty" of government intervention.[26]

7

The final rejection of the Jeffersonian case for weak government does not mean that liberalism must herewith commit itself inextricably to the philosophy of government intervention. That would be to create a myth as misleading as Jeffersonian antistatism. Roosevelt himself has pointed to one obvious danger. "We have built up new instruments of public power. In the hands of a people's Government this power is wholesome and proper. But in the hands of political puppets of an economic autocracy such power would provide shackles for the liberties of the people."[27]

Some who talk about the infallibility of "planning" should ponder these words. So long as democracy continues, the government will periodically change hands; and every accretion to the power of the state must be accounted as a weapon of a future conservatism as well as of a present liberalism. It is not too much to anticipate that the fortunes of interventionism may duplicate the fortunes of free enterprise, and what began as a faith for liberals end up as a philosophy for conservatives.[28]

The problem of liberalism is rather to preserve as much variety within the state as is consistent with energetic action by the government. The chief enemy of variety, and thus of liberty, is likely to be that group which is most powerful and consequently needs liberty least. In American history that group has ordinarily been (though it may not always be so in the future) the business community. The judgment of American liberalism has been that it was best for the whole society, including the capitalists, that their power be constantly checked and limited by the humble members of society. The Jacksonian attempt to carry out this judgment challenged two other theories of society, which had able advocates both a century ago and today.

One was the theory of Federalism: that, since this is a capitalistic society, the class most interested in its security and prosperity is the capitalist class, which thus should have the most power. The theory has survived every test but experience. It simply has not worked. Since the Federalist party the American business community appears to have lost its political capacity: it has not been, in the strict sense, a ruling class. In placid days political power naturally gravitates to it as the strongest economic group in the state; but through American history it has been unable to use that power very long for national purposes. Moved typically by personal and class, rarely by public, considerations, the business community has invariably brought national affairs to a state of crisis and exasperated the rest of society into dissatisfaction bordering on revolt.

It is this moment of crisis which can unite the weaker groups and frighten the business community sufficiently to bring "liberalism" into power. Every great crisis thus far in American history has produced a leader adequate to the occasion from the ranks of those who believe vigorously and seriously in liberty, democracy and the common man. The sense of public responsibility, the ability to inspire national confidence, the capacity to face imperative issues, seem in this country to have been largely the property of the great democratic leaders, while in England, for example, the people have been able in crises to turn to the aristocracy for truly national government.

In the past, when liberalism has resolved the crisis and restored tranquillity, conservatism has recovered power by the laws of political gravity; then it makes a new botch of things, and liberalism again must take over in the name of the nation. But the object of liberalism has never been to destroy capitalism, as conservatism invariably claims—only to keep the capitalists from destroying it.

This essential conservatism of American liberalism brings it into conflict with the second antagonistic theory: the theory of socialism, which in the Fourierite form excited so many intellectuals in the eighteen-forties. This theory would say that capitalism is hopelessly wrong in principle, and salvation can lie only in its total abolition and the formation of new collectivisms. In the century since Jackson, socialism has far outstripped Federalism as the hope of mankind. Yet the history of the past decade has perhaps made it harder to respond to its promise with enthusiasm. The search for a New Order is somewhat less inspiring now that we have seen in practice what such New Orders are likely to be. As yet, none have shown much capacity to reconcile liberty with their various forms of regimentation; indeed, all have dispensed quite cheerfully with the liberal virtues. Perhaps those may not be the virtues of the future, but that has not yet been demonstrated.

In a time like the middle of the twentieth century, when the pressures of insecurity have driven people to the extremes of hope and anxiety, the Jacksonian experience assumes special interest. Its details are, of course, obsolete, but its spirit may be instructive. In an age dominated by the compulsive race for easy solutions, it is well to remember that, if social catastrophe is to be avoided, it can only be by an earnest, tough-minded, pragmatic attempt to wrestle with new problems as they come, without being enslaved by a theory of the past, or by a theory of the future.

For Jefferson and Jackson the demands of the future—whatever readjustments they may compel for our government and our economy—will best be met by a society in which no single group is able to sacrifice democracy and liberty to its own interests. "It will never be possible for any length of time for any group of the American people, either by reason of wealth or learning or inheritance or economic power," declared Roosevelt in 1936, perhaps a trifle optimistically, "to retain any mandate, any permanent authority to arrogate to itself the political control of American public life. This heritage . . . we owe to Jacksonian democracy—the American doctrine that entrusts the general welfare to no one group or class, but dedicates itself to the end that the American people shall not be thwarted in their high purpose to remain the custodians of their own destiny."[29]

The Jacksonian attitude presumes a perpetual tension in society, a doubtful equilibrium, constantly breeding strife and struggle: it is, in essence, a rejection of easy solutions, and for this reason it is not always popular. One of the strongest pressures toward the extremes, whether of socialism or of conservatism, is the security from conflict they are supposed to insure.

But one may wonder whether a society which eliminated struggle would possess much liberty (or even much real stability). Freedom does not last long when bestowed from above. It lasts only when it is arrived at competitively, out of the determination of groups which demand it as a general rule in order to increase the opportunities for themselves. To some the picture may not be consoling. But world without conflict is the world of fantasy; and practical attempts to realize society without conflict by confiding power to a single authority have generally resulted (when they have taken place on a larger stage than Brisbane's phalansteries) in producing a society where the means of suppressing conflict are rapid and efficient.

"Sometimes it is said that man can not be trusted with the government of himself," said Jefferson. "Can he, then, be trusted with the government of others? Or have we found angels in the forms of kings to govern him?" "The unfortunate thing," adds Pascal, "is that he who would act the angel acts the brute."[30] The great tradition of American liberalism regards man as neither brute nor angel.

NOTES

1. Wilkes, *Defence of the Paris Commune, with Some Account of the Internationale,* 44–45.
2. Welles, *Diary,* I, 524.
3. Whitman, "Notes for Lectures on Democracy and 'Adhesiveness,'" Furness, *Whitman's Workshop,* 57; "Democratic Vistas," *Prose,* 198.
4. Whitman, "Democratic Vistas," 198.
5. Van Buren, *Political Parties,* 51, 54.
6. "True Theory and Philosophy of Our System of Government," *Democratic Review,* XV, 232 (September, 1844).
7. Bancroft's eulogy in B. M. Dusenberry, comp., *Monument to the Memory of General Andrew Jackson,* 44.
8. Georges Sorel, *Reflections on Violence* (London, n.d.), 137, 135–136, 32.
9. Jackson, "Protest to the Senate," April 15, 1834, Richardson, ed., *Messages and Papers,* II, 92–93.
10. See Jefferson's important letter to J. B. Colvin, September 20, 1810, *Works,* XII, 418–422. "To lose our country by a scrupulous adherence to written law, would be to lose the law itself, with life, liberty, property and all those who are enjoying them with us; thus absurdly sacrificing the end to the means. . . . The line of discrimination between cases may be difficult; but the good officer is bound to draw it at his own peril, and throw himself on the justice of his country and the rectitude of his motives." Probably this statement describes accurately the necessities of leadership in a democracy. A kind of power is required in crises which would be dangerous normally and which rests ultimately on popular approval. In any case, Jefferson's statement certainly applies accurately to the behavior of himself, Jackson, Lincoln, Wilson and the Roosevelts in major crises. Jefferson evidently regarded the Constitution as an instrument to prevent bad action but not, in cases of emergency, to prevent good.
11. O'Sullivan, "Note," *Democratic Review,* XII, 583 (May, 1843).
12. *Washington Globe,* May 18, 1837.
13. "Executive Usurpation," *Democratic Review,* I, 290 (February, 1838).
14. *Boston Reformer,* August 4, 1837.
15. Cushing in the House, September 25, 1837, *Register of Debates,* 25 Congress 1 Session, 889. In 1834 William Leggett complained, "The attempts of the democracy to reassume their rights are clamorously denounced as usurpations of the rights of others; and all their efforts to restore the government to its original purity, stig-

matized as encroachments on its long established principles." *New York Evening Post*, October 23, 1834. The skepticism of the conservatives is understandable.
16. Jefferson to W. C. Rives, November 28, 1819, Jefferson, *Writings* (Ford), X, 151 n., 150.
17. "Speech of Charles J. Ingersoll. In the Convention of Pennsylvania," *Democratic Review*, V, 99 (January, 1839).
18. See, especially, Barbour's opinion in *City of New York v. Miln*, 11 Peters 139.
19. Benton, *Thirty Years' View*, I, 450.
20. *Charles River Bridge v. Warren Bridge*, 11 Peters 547.
21. Hamilton to Washington, February 23, 1791, Hamilton, *Works*, III, 446.
22. *McCulloch v. Maryland*, 4 Wheaton 421.
23. Whitman, "Democratic Vistas," *Prose*, 199–200, 202, 236, 218; "Notes for Lectures on Democracy and Adhesiveness,' " Furness, *Whitman's Workshop*, 57, 58.
24. Bancroft, *The Necessity, the Reality, and the Promise of the Progress of the Human Race*, 34.
25. Butler, *Butler's Book*, 85.
26. Roosevelt went on to cite Lincoln's version of the remark we have noted in Taney, Hamilton and Marshall: "the legitimate object of government is to do for a community of people whatever they need to have done, but cannot do at all, or cannot do so well, for themselves, in their separate and individual capacities." Roosevelt, *Public Papers*, VII, xxix–xxx.
27. Roosevelt, *Public Papers*, V, 16.
28. Now that a past liberalism has become a present conservatism, it will be of increasing interest to observe how much less outraged businessmen become over a bureaucracy under their own control.
29. Roosevelt, *Public Papers*, V, 198.
30. Jefferson's First Inaugural, Richardson, *Messages and Papers*, I, 322; Pascal, *Pensées* (Everyman), 99.

4

A Key to American Politics: Calhoun's Pluralism

PETER F. DRUCKER

In this article, Peter F. Drucker examines John C. Calhoun's theory of the "concurrent majority," which, Drucker claims, is the organizing principle of American politics. Stated simply, the idea of the concurrent majority is that every major interest in the United States—sectional and economic—should have a veto over public policies that affect it directly. Calhoun's importance with respect to his analysis of interest group pluralism in United States politics, Drucker concludes, is that he elevated interest group pluralism to a "basic principle of free government" and emphasized the importance of multiple group interests and power centers as a restraint on absolute government.

Drucker discusses interest group pluralism as it may restrain absolute government but asks if it is adequate to the task of establishing national priorities or promoting the ever elusive "national interest." He questions whether a nation beset by foreign and domestic crises can survive the push and pull of diverse and often discordant voices, if the major consequence of interest group pluralism is governmental inaction. Drucker is aware that a society totally subservient to the concurrent majority is subject to severe strains and disintegrations, and he points out that many contemporary critics of American politics are convinced that Calhoun's veto groups are the source of major problems in the political system.

Drucker, a German-born economist, is the author of The End of Economic Man *(1939),* The New Society *(1950),* The Future of Industrial Man *(1942),* America's Next Twenty Years *(1957),* The Age of Discontinuity *(1969), and a number of other monographs and articles. He has taught at New York University and has served as a management consultant to numerous United States corporations.*

The American party system has been under attack almost continuously since it took definite form in the time of Andrew Jackson. The criticism has always been directed at the same point: America's political pluralism, the distinctively American organization of government by compromise of interests, pressure groups and sections. And the aim of the critics from Thaddeus Stevens to Henry Wallace has always been to substitute for this "unprincipled" pluralism a government based as in Europe on "ideologies" and "principles." But never before—at least not since the Civil War years—has the crisis been as acute as in this last decade; for the political problems which dominate our national life today, foreign policy and industrial policy, are precisely the problems which interest and pressure-group compromise is least equipped to handle. And while the crisis symptoms: a left-wing Third Party and the threatened split-off of the Southern Wing, are more alarming in the Democratic Party, the Republicans are hardly much better off. The 1940 boom for the "idealist" Wilkie and the continued inability to attract a substantial portion of the labor vote, are definite signs that the Republican Party too is under severe *ideological* pressure.

Yet, there is almost no understanding of the problem—precisely because there is so little understanding of the basic principles of American pluralism. Of course, every politician in this country must be able instinctively to work in terms of sectional and interest compromise; and the voter takes it for granted. But there is practically no awareness of the fact that organization on the basis of sectional and interest compromise is both the distinctly American form of political organization and the cornerstone of practically all major political institutions of the modern U.S.A. As acute an observer as Winston Churchill apparently does not understand that Congress works on a basis entirely different from that of Britain's Parliament; neither do nine out of ten Americans and 999 out of a 1000 teachers of those courses in "Civics." There is even less understanding that sectional and interest-group pluralism is not just the venal expediency of that stock-villain of American folklore, the "politician" but that it in itself is a basic ideology, a basic principle—and the one which is the very foundation of our free society and government.[1]

I

To find an adequate analysis of the principle of government by sectional and interest compromise we have to go back almost a hundred years to John C. Calhoun and to his two political treatises[2] published after his death in 1852. Absurd, you will say, for it is practically an axiom of American history that Calhoun's political theories, subtle, even profound though they may have been, were reduced to absurdity and irrelevance by the Civil War. Yet, this "axiom" is nothing but a partisan vote of the Reconstruction Period. Of course, the specific occasion for which Calhoun formulated his theories, the Slavery issue, has been decided; and for the constitutional veto power of the states over national legislation, by means of which Calhoun proposed to formalize the principle of sectional and interest compromise,

From *Review of Politics* (1948). From *Men, Politics and Society*, forthcoming, by Peter F. Drucker.

was substituted in actual practice the much more powerful and much more elastic but extra-constitutional and extra-legal veto power of sections, interests and pressure groups in Congress and within the parties.[3] But *his basic principle itself: that every major interest in the country, whether regional, economic or religious, is to possess a veto power on political decisions directly affecting it,* the principle which Calhoun called—rather obscurely—"*the rule of concurrent majority,*" has become the organizing principle of American politics. And it is precisely this principle that is under fire today.

What makes Calhoun so important as the major key to the understanding of American politics, is not just that he saw the importance in American political life of sectional and interest pluralism; other major analysts of our government, Tocqueville, for instance, or Bryce or Wilson, saw that too. But Calhoun, perhaps alone, saw in it more than a rule of expediency, imposed by the country's size and justifiable by results, if at all. He saw in it a basic principle of free government.

> Without this (*the rule of concurrent majority based on interests rather than on principles*) there can be . . . no constitution. The assertion is true in reference to all constitutional governments, be their forms what they may: It is, indeed, the negative power which makes the constitution,—and the positive which makes the government. The one is the power of acting;—and the other the power of preventing or arresting action. The two, combined, make constitutional government.
>
> . . . it follows, necessarily, that where the numerical majority has the sole control of the government, there can be no constitution . . . and hence, the numerical, unmixed with the concurrent majority, necessarily forms, in all cases, absolute government.
>
> . . . The principle by which they (governments) are upheld and preserved . . . in constitutional governments is *compromise;*—and in absolute governments is *force. . . .*[4]

And however much the American people may complain in words about the "unprincipled" nature of their political system, by their actions they have always shown that they too believe that without sectional and interest compromises there can be no constitutional government. If this is not grasped, American government and politics must appear not only as cheap to the point of venality, they must appear as utterly irrational and unpredictable.

II

Sectional and interest pluralism has molded all American political institutions. It is the method—entirely unofficial and extra-constitutional—through which the organs of government are made to function, through which leaders are selected, policies developed, men and groups organized for the conquest and management of political power. In particular it is the explanation for the most distinctive features of the American political system: the way in which the Congress operates, the way in which major government departments are set up and run, the qualifications for "eligibility" as a candidate for elective office, and the American party structure.

To all foreign observers of Congress two things have always remained mysterious: the distinction between the official party label and the "blocs" which cut across party lines; and the power and function of the Congressional Committees. And most Americans though less amazed by the phenomena are equally baffled.

The "blocs"—the "Farm Bloc," the "Friends of Labor in the Senate," the "Business Groups," etc.—are simply the expression of the basic tenet of sectional and interest pluralism that major interests have a veto power on legislation directly affecting them. For this reason they must cut across party lines—that is, lines expressing the numerical rather than the "concurrent" majority. And because these blocs have (a) only a negative veto, and (b) only on measures directly affecting them, they cannot in themselves be permanent groupings replacing the parties. They must be loosely organized; and one and the same member of Congress must at different times vote with different blocs. The strength of the "blocs" does not rest on their numbers but on the basic mores of American politics which grant every major interest group a limited self-determination—as expressed graphically in the near-sanctity of a senatorial "filibuster." The power of the "Farm Bloc" for instance, does not rest on the numerical strength of the rural vote—a minority vote even in the Senate with its disproportionate representation of the thinly populated agricultural states—but on its "strategic" strength, that is on its being the spokesman for a recognized major interest.

Subordination of a major interest is possible; but only in a "temporary emergency." Most of the New Deal measures were, palpably, neither temporary nor emergency measures; yet their sponsors had to present them, and convincingly, as "temporary emergency measures" because they could be enacted only by over-riding the extra-constitutional veto of the business interests.

Once the excuse of the "temporary emergency" had fully lost its plausibility, that major interest could no longer be voted down; and the policy collapsed. By 1946, for instance, labor troubles could be resolved only on a basis acceptable to both labor and employer: higher wages *and* higher prices. (Even if a numerical majority had been available to legislate against either party—and the business group could probably still have been voted down two and a half years ago—the solution had to be acceptable to both parties.)

The principle of sectional and interest compromise leads directly to the congressional committee system—a system to which there is no parallel anywhere in the world. Congress, especially the House, has largely abdicated to its committees because only in the quiet and secrecy of a committee room can sectional compromise be worked out. The discussion on the floor as well as the recorded vote is far too public and therefore largely for the folks back home. But a committee's business is to arrive at an agreement between all major sectional interests affected; which explains the importance of getting a bill before the "right" committee. In any but an American legislature the position of each member, once a bill is introduced, is fixed by the stand of his party which, in turn, is decided on grounds that have little to do with the measure itself but are rather dictated by the balance of power within the government and by party programs. Hence it makes usually little difference which committee discusses a bill or whether it goes before a committee at all. In the United States, however, a bill's assignment to a specific committee decides which interest groups are to be recognized as affected by the measure and therefore entitled to a part in writing it ("who is to have standing before the committee"), for each committee represents a specific constellation of interests. In many cases this first decision therefore decides the fate of a proposed measure, especially as the compromise worked out by the committee is generally accepted once it reaches the floor, especially in the House.

It is not only Congress but every individual member of Congress himself who is expected to operate according to the "rule of concurrent majority." He is considered both a representative of the American people and responsible to the national interest and a delegate of his constituents and responsible to their particular interests. Wherever the immediate interests of his constituents are not in question, he is to be a statesman; wherever their conscience or their pocketbooks are affected, he is to be a business agent. This is in sharp contrast to the theory on which any parliamentary government is based—a theory developed almost two hundred years ago in Edmund Burke's famous speech to the voters at Bristol—according to which a member of Parliament represents the commonweal rather than his constituents. Hence in all parliamentary countries, the representative can be a stranger to his constituency—in the extreme, as it was practiced in Weimar Germany, there is one long national list of candidates who run in all constituencies—whereas the Congressman in this country must be a resident of his constituency. And while an American Senator considers it a compliment and an asset to be called "Cotton Ed Smith," the Speaker of the House of Commons not so long ago severely reprimanded a member for calling another member—an official of the miners' union—a "representative of the coal miners."

The principle of sectional and interest pluralism also explains why this is the only nation where Cabinet members are charged by law with the representation of special interests—labor, agriculture, commerce. In every other country an agency of the government—any agency of the government—is solemnly sworn to guard the public interests against "the interests." In this country the concept of a government department as the representative of a special interest group is carried down to smaller agencies and even to divisions and branches of a department. This was particularly noticeable during the war in such fights as that between OPA—representing the consumer—and the War Production Board representing the producer, or, within WPB between the Procurement branches speaking for the war industries and the Civilian Requirements Branch speaking for the industries producing for the "home front."

The mystery of "eligibility"—the criteria which decides who will make a promising candidate for public office—which has baffled so many foreign and American observers, Bryce for instance—also traces back to the "rule of the concurrent majority." Eligibility simply means that a candidate must not be unacceptable to any major interest, religious or regional group within the electorate; it is primarily a negative qualification. Eligibility operates on all levels and applies to all elective offices. It has been brilliantly analyzed in "Boss" Flynn's *You're the Boss.* His classical example is the selection of Harry Truman as Democratic vice-presidential candidate in 1944. Truman was "eligible" rather than Wallace, Byrnes or Douglas precisely because he was unknown; because he was neither Easterner nor Westerner nor Southerner, because he was neither New Deal nor Conservative, etc., in short because he had no one trait strong enough to offend anybody anywhere.

But the central institution based on sectional pluralism is the American party. Completely extra-constitutional, the wonder and the despair of every foreign observer who cannot fit it into any of his concepts of political life, the American party (rather than the states) has become the instrument to realize Calhoun's "rule of the concurrent majority."

In stark contrast to the parties of Europe, the American party has no program and no purpose except to organize divergent groups for the common pursuit and conquest of power. Its unity is one of action, not of beliefs. Its only rule is to attract—or at least not to repel—the largest possible number of groups. It must, by definition, be acceptable equally to the right and the left, the rich and the poor, the farmer and the worker, the Protestant and the Catholic, the native and the foreign-born. It must be able to rally Mr. Rankin of Mississippi and Mr. Marcantonio of New York—or Senator Flanders and Colonel McCormick—behind the same presidential candidate and the same "platform."

As soon as it cannot appeal at least to a minority in every major group (as soon, in other words, as it provokes the veto of one section, interest or class) a party is in danger of disintegration. Whenever a party loses its ability to fuse sectional pressures and class interests into one national policy—both parties just before the Civil War, the Republican Party before its reorganization by Mark Hanna, both parties again today—the party system (and with it the American political system altogether) is in crisis.

It is, consequently, not that Calhoun was repudiated by the Civil War which is the key to the understanding of American politics but that he has become triumphant since.

The apparent victors, the "Radical Republicans," Thaddeus Stevens, Seward, Chief Justice Chase, were out to destroy not only slavery and states rights but the "rule of the concurrent majority" itself. And the early Republican Party—before the Civil War and in the Reconstruction Period—was indeed determined to substitute principle for interest as the lodestar of American political life. But in the end it was the political thought of convinced pluralists such as Abraham Lincoln and Andrew Johnson rather than the ideologies of the Free Soilers and Abolitionists which molded the Republican Party. And ever since, the major development of American politics has been based on Calhoun's principle. To this the United States owes the strength as well as the weaknesses of its political system.

III

The weaknesses of sectional and interest compromise are far more obvious than its virtues; they have been hammered home for a hundred years. Francis Lieber, who brought the dominant German political theories of the early nineteenth century to this country, attacked pluralism in Calhoun's own state of South Carolina a century ago. Twenty years later Walter Bagehot contrasted, impressively, General Grant's impotent administration with those of Gladstone and Disraeli to show the superiority of ideological party organization. The most thorough and most uncompromising criticism came from Woodrow Wilson; and every single one of the Professor's points was amply borne out by his later experience as President. Time has not made these weaknesses any less dangerous.

There is, first of all, the inability of a political system based on the "rule of the concurrent majority" to resolve conflicts of principles. All a pluralist system can do is to deny that "ideological" conflicts (as they are called nowadays) do exist. Those conflicts, a pluralist must assert are fundamentally either struggles for naked power or friction between interest groups which could be solved if only the quarreling parties sat down around a conference table. Perhaps, the most perfect, because most naive, expression of this belief remains the late General Patton's remark that the Nazis were, after all, not so very different from Republicans or Democrats. (Calhoun, while less naive, was just unable to understand the reality of "ideological" conflict in and around the slavery problem.)

In nine cases out of ten the refusal to acknowledge the existence of ideological conflict is beneficial. It prevents fights for power, or clashes of interests, from flaring into religious wars where irreconcilable principles collide (a catastrophe against which Europe's ideological politics have almost no defense). It promotes compromise where compromise is possible. But in a genuine clash of principles—and, whatever the pluralists say, there *are* such clashes—the "rule of concurrent majority" breaks down; it did, in Calhoun's generation, before the profound reality of the slavery issue. A legitimate ideological conflict is actually aggravated by the pluralists' refusal to accept its reality: the compromisers who thought the slavery issue could be settled by the meeting of good intentions, or by the payment of money, may have done more than the Abolitionists to make the Civil War inevitable.

A weakness of sectional and interest pluralism just as serious is that it amounts to a principle of inaction. The popular assertion "it's better to make the wrong decision than to do nothing at all," is, of course, fallacious; but no nation, however unlimited its resources, can have a very effective policy if its government is based on a principle that orders it to do nothing important except unanimously. Moreover, pluralism increases exorbitantly the weight of well organized small interest groups, especially when they lobby *against* a decision. Congress can far too easily be high-pressured into emasculating a bill by the expedient of omitting its pertinent provisions; only with much greater difficulty can Congress be moved to positive action. This explains, to a large extent, the eclipse of Congress during the last hundred years, both in popular respect and in its actual momentum as policy-making organ of government. Congress, which the Founding Fathers had intended to be the central organ of government—a role which it fulfilled up to Andrew Jackson—became the compound representative of sections and interests and, consequently, progressively incapable of national leadership.

Pluralism gives full weight—more than full weight—to sections and interests; but who is to represent the national welfare? Ever since the days of Calhoun, the advocates of pluralism have tried to dodge this question by contending that the national interest is equal to the sum of all particular interests, and that it therefore does not need a special organ of representation. But this most specious argument is contradicted by the most elementary observation. In practice, pluralism tends to resolve sectional and class conflicts at the expense of the national interest which is represented by nobody in particular, by no section and no organization.

These weaknesses had already become painfully obvious while Calhoun was alive and active—during the decade after Andrew Jackson, the first President of pluralism. Within a few years after Calhoun's death, the inability of the new system to comprehend and to resolve an ideological conflict—ultimately its inability to represent and to guard the national interest—had brought catastrophe. For a hundred years and more, American political thought has therefore resolved around attempts to counteract if not to overcome these weaknesses. Three major developments of American constitutional life were the result: the growth of the functions and powers of the President and his emergence as a "leader" rather than as the executive agent of the Congress; the rise of the Supreme Court, with its "rule of law," to the position of arbiter of policy; the development of a unifying ideology—the "American Creed."

Of these the most important—and the least noticed—is the "American Creed." In fact I know of no writer of major importance since Tocqueville who has given much attention to it. Yet even the term "un-American" cannot be translated successfully into any other language, least of all into "English" English. In no other country could the identity of the nation with a certain set of ideas be assumed—at least not under a free government. This unique cohesion on principles shows, for instance, in the refusal of the American voter to accept Socialists and Communists as "normal" parties, simply because both groups refuse to accept the assumption of a common American ideology. It shows, for another example, in the indigenous structure of the American labor movement with its emphasis on interest pressure rather than on a political philosophy. And this is also the only country in which "Civics" could be taught in schools—the only democratic country which believes that a correct social philosophy could or should be part of public education.

In Europe, a universal creed would be considered incompatible with a free society. Before the advent of totalitarianism, no European country had ever known anything comparable to the flag salute of the American school child.[5] For in Europe all political activity is based on ideological factions; consequently, to introduce a uniform ideology in a European country is to stamp out *all* opposition. In the United States ideological homogeneity is the very basis of political diversity. It makes possible the almost unlimited freedom of interest groups, religious groups, pressure groups, etc.; and in this way it is the very fundament of free government. (It also explains why the preservation of civil liberties has been so much more important a problem in this country—as compared to England or France, for instance.) The assumption of ideological unity gives the United States the minimum of cohesion without which its political system simply could not have worked.

IV

But is even the "American dream" enough to make a system based on the "rule of the concurrent majority" work today? Can pluralism handle the two major problems of American politics—the formulation of a foreign policy, and the political organization of an industrial society—any more successfully than it could handle the slavery issue? Or is the American political system as much in crisis as it was in the last years of Calhoun's life—and for pretty much the same reasons?

A foreign policy can never be evolved by adding particular interests—regional, economic or racial—or by compromising among them; it must supersede them. If Calhoun's contention that the national interest will automatically be served by serving the interests of the parts is wrong anywhere, it is probably wrong in the field of foreign affairs.

A foreign policy and a party system seem to be compatible only if the parties are organized on programmatic grounds, that is on principles. For if not based on general principles, a foreign policy will become a series of improvisations without rhyme or reason. In a free society, in which parties compete for votes and power, the formulation of a foreign policy may thus force the parties into ideological attitudes which will sooner or later be reflected in their domestic policies too.

This was clearly realized in the early years of the Republic when foreign policy was vital to a new nation, clinging precariously to a long seaboard without hinterland, engaged in a radical experiment with new political institutions, surrounded by the Great Powers of that time, England, France and Spain, all of them actually or potentially hostile. This awareness of foreign policy largely explains why the party system of the Founding Fathers—especially of Hamilton—was an ideological one; it also explains why the one positive foreign-policy concept this country developed during the entire nineteenth century—the Monroe Doctrine—was formulated by the last two politically active survivors of the founding generation, Monroe and John Quincy Adams. No matter how little Calhoun himself realized it, his doctrine would have been impossible without the French Revolution and the Napoleonic Wars which, during the most critical period of American integration, kept its potential European enemies busy. By 1820, the country had become too strong, had taken in too much territory, to be easily attacked; and it was still not strong enough, and far too much absorbed in the development of its own interior, to play a part in international affairs. Hence Calhoun, and all America with him, could push foreign policy out of their minds—so much so that this is the only country in which it is possible to write a comprehensive work on an important historical period without as much as a mention of foreign affairs, as Arthur M. Schlesinger, Jr. managed to do in his *The Age of Jackson.*

But today foreign policy is again as vital for the survival of the nation as it ever was during the administrations of Washington and Jefferson. And it has to be a foreign *policy,* that is, a making of decisions; hence neither "isolationism" nor "internationalism" will do. (For "internationalism"—the search for formulae which will provide automatic decisions, even in advance—is also a refusal to have a foreign policy; it may well have done this country, and the world, as much harm as "isolationism"—perhaps more.) To survive as the strongest of the Great Powers, the United States might even have to accept permanently the supremacy of foreign policies over domestic affairs, however much this may go against basic American convictions, and indeed against the American grain. But no foreign policy can be evolved by the compromise of sectional interests or economic pressures; yet neither party, as today constituted, could develop a foreign policy based on definite principles.

The other great national need is to resolve the political problems of an industrial society. An industrial society is by nature ultrapluralistic, because it develops class and interest groups that are far stronger, and far more tightly organized, than any interest group in a pre-industrial age. A few big corporations, a few big unions, may be the actually decisive forces in an industrial society. And these groups can put decisive pressure on society: they can throttle social and economic life.

The problem does not lie in "asocial behavior" of this or that group but in the nature of industrial society which bears much closer resemblance to feudalism than to the trading nineteenth century. Its political problems are very similar to those which feudalism had to solve—and failed to solve. It is in perpetual danger of disintegration into virtually autonomous fiefs, principalities, "free cities," "robber baronies" and "exempt bishoprics"—the authority and the interest of the nation trampled underfoot, autonomous groups uniting to control the central power in their own interest or disregarding government in fighting each other in the civil conflict of class warfare. And the alternative to such a collapse into anarchy or civil war—the suppression of classes and interest groups by an all-powerful government—is hardly more attractive.

An industrial society cannot function without an organ able to superimpose the national interest on economic or class interests. More than a mere arbiter is needed. The establishment of the "rules of civilized industrial warfare," as was done by both the Wagner Act and the Taft-Hartley Act, tries to avoid the need for policies by equalizing the strength of the conflicting sections; but that can lead only to deadlock, to collusion against the national interest or, worse still, to the attempt to make the national authority serve the interest of one side against the other. In other words, an industrial society cannot fully accept Calhoun's assumption that the national good will evolve from the satisfaction of particular interests. An industrial society without national policy will become both anarchic and despotic.

Small wonder that there has been increasing demand for a radical change which would substitute ideological parties and programmatic policies for the pluralist parties and the "rule of the concurrent majority" of the American tradition. Henry Wallace's Third-Party Movement, while the most publicized, may well be the least significant development; for third parties are, after all, nothing new in our political history. But for the first time in a hundred years there is a flood of books—and by serious students of American government—advocating radical constitutional reform. However much Senator Fulbright, Henry Hazlitt and Thomas Fineletter disagree on details, they are one in demanding the elimination—or at least the limitation—of the "rule of the concurrent majority," and its replacement by an ideological system functioning along parliamentary lines. More significant even may be Walter Reuther's new unionism with its blend of traditional pressure tactics and working-class, that is ideological, programs and aims.

V

Yet all these critics and reformers not only fail to ask themselves whether an ideological system of politics would really be any better equipped to cope with the great problems of today—and neither the foreign nor the industrial policy of England, that most successful of all ideologically organized countries, look any too successful right now; the critics also never stop to consider the unique strength of our traditional system.

Our traditional system makes sure that there is always a legitimate government in the country; and to provide such a government is the first job of any political system—a duty which a great many of the political systems known to man have never discharged.

It minimizes conflicts by utilizing, rather than suppressing conflicting forces. It makes it almost impossible for the major parties to become entirely irresponsible: neither party can afford to draw strength from the kind of demagogic opposition, without governmental responsibility, which perpetually nurtures fascist and communist parties abroad. Hence, while the two national parties are willing to embrace any movement or any group within the country that commands sufficient following, they in turn force every group to bring its demands and programs into agreement with the beliefs, traditions and prejudices of the people.

Above all, our system of sectional and interest compromise is one of the only two ways known to man in which a free government and a free society can survive—and the only one at all adapted to the conditions of American life and acceptable to the American people.

The central problem in a free government is that of factions, as we have known since Plato and Aristotle. Logically, a free government and factions are incompatible. But whatever the cause—vanity and pride, lust for power, virtue or wickedness, greed or the desire to help others—factionalism is inherent in human nature and in human society. For 2000 years the best minds in politics have tried to devise a factionless society—through education (Plato), through elimination of property (Thomas More), through concentration on the life of the spirit outside of worldly ambition (the political tradition of Lutheranism). The last great attempt to save freedom by abolishing factions was Rousseau's. But to create the factionless free society is as hopeless as to set up perpetual motion. From Plato to Rousseau, political thought has ended up by demanding that factions be suppressed, that is, that freedom, to be preserved, be abolished.

The Anglo-American political tradition alone has succeeded in breaking out of this vicious circle. Going back to Hooker and Locke, building on the rich tradition of free government in the cities of the late middle ages, Anglo-American political realism discovered: that if factions cannot be suppressed, they must be utilized to make a free government both freer and stronger. This one basic concept distinguishes Anglo-American political theory and practice from continental European politics, and accounts for the singular success of free and popular governments in both countries. Elsewhere in the western world the choice has always been between extreme factionalism which makes government impotent if not impossible and inevitably leads to civil war, and autocracy which justifies the suppression of liberty with the need for effective and orderly government. Nineteenth-century France with its six revolutions, or near revolutions, stands for one, the totalitarian governments of our time for the other alternative of continental politics.

But—and this is the real discovery on which the Anglo-American achievement rests—factions can be used constructively only if they are encompassed within a frame of unity. A free government on the basis of sectional interest groups is possible only when there is no ideological split within the country. This is the American solution. Another conceivable solution is to channel the driving forces, the vectors of society, into ideological factions which obtain their cohesion from a program for the whole of society, and from a creed. But that presupposes an unquestioned ruling class with a common outlook on life, with uniform mores and a traditional, if not inherent, economic security. Given that sort of ruling class, the antagonist in an ideological system can be expected to be a "loyal opposition," that is, to accept the rules of the game and to see himself as a partner rather than as a potential challenger to civil war. But a ruling class accepted by the people as a whole, and feeling itself responsible to the people as a whole, cannot be created by fiat or overnight. In antiquity only Rome, in modern times only England, achieved it. On the Continent, all attempts to create a genuine ruling class have failed dismally.

In this country, the ruling-class solution was envisaged by Alexander Hamilton and seemed close to realization under the presidents of the "Virginia Dynasty." Hamilton arrived at his concept with inescapable consistency; for he was absorbed by the search for a foreign policy and for the proper organization of an industrial society—precisely the two problems which, as we have seen, pluralism is least equipped to resolve. But even if Hamilton had not made the fatal mistake of identifying wealth with rulership, the American people could not have accepted his thesis. A ruling class was incompatible with mass immigration and with the explosive territorial expansion of nineteenth-century America. It was even more incompatible with the American concept of equality. And there is no reason to believe that contemporary America is any more willing to accept Hamilton's concept, Mr. James Burnham's idea of the managerial elite notwithstanding. This country as a free country has no alternative, it seems, to the "rule of the concurrent majority," no alternative to sectional pluralism as the device through which factions can be made politically effective.

It will be very difficult, indeed, to resolve the problems of foreign and of industrial policy on the pluralist basis and within the interest-group system, though not provably more difficult than these problems would be on another, ideological, basis. It will be all the harder as the two problems are closely inter-related; for the effectiveness of any American foreign policy depends, in the last analysis, on our ability to show the world a successful and working model of an industrial society. But if we succeed at all, it will be with the traditional system, horse-trading, log-rolling and politicking all included. An old saying has it that this country lives simultaneously in a world of Jeffersonian beliefs and in one of Hamiltonian realities. Out of these two, Calhoun's concept of "the rule of the concurrent majority" alone can make one viable whole. The need for a formulated foreign policy and for a national policy of industrial order is real—but not more so than the need for a real understanding of this fundamental American fact: the pluralism of sectional and interest compromise is the warp of America's political fabric—it cannot be plucked out without unravelling the whole.

NOTES

1. A perfect illustration was the outraged amazement with which most book reviewers greeted Edward J. Flynn's *You're the Boss*—a simple and straight recital of facts every American should really have known and understood all along.
2. *A Disquisition on Government;* and *A Discourse on the Constitution and Government of the United States.*
3. Calhoun's extreme legalism, his belief that everything had to be spelled out in the written Constitution—a belief he shared with his generation—is one of the major reasons why the importance of his thesis has not been generally recognized. Indeed it is of the very essence of the concept of "concurrent majority" that it cannot be made official and legal in an effective government—the express veto such as the UN Charter gives to the Great Powers makes government impossible.
4. Quotations from *A Disquisition on Government* (Columbia, S.C., 1852), pp. 35 to 37.
5. The perhaps most profound discussion of the American ideological cohesion can be found in the two decisions of the Supreme Court on the compulsory flag salute, and in the two dissents therefrom, which deserve high rating among American state papers.

5

The Reform Impulse in American Politics

RICHARD HOFSTADTER

In this excerpt, Richard Hofstadter argues that the period from 1890 to the end of the 1930s encompassed three major reform movements in American politics: the Populists, the Progressives, and the New Deal Democrats. Although these movements had much in common, they were distinguishable episodes in the development of American political culture. The Populist movement expressed the discontent of farmers and businessmen with the changes in the American economy at the end of the nineteenth century. The Progressive movement was an optimistic, middle-class effort to restore "economic individualism" and "political democracy" by destroying the "great corporation" and the "corrupt political machine." The New Deal, born in the Great Depression, was rooted in these two prior reform movements but lacked the Populists' radicalism and the Progressives' optimism. The objectives of all three reform movements were, nevertheless, to restore an earlier, simpler dream: a society based on open, individual competition.

Each of these reform movements was, of course, a diverse phenomenon. Each included intellectuals, propagandists, and common men. The Progressives may have been concerned about restoring popular control over government, but they also emphasized nativistic American values and were fiercely isolationist. The Populists were an agrarian movement that attempted to restore the American farmer's economic independence. The New Deal had its Harold Ickes, but it also had its Raymond Moley. Thus, though all three movements spanned the range of values from liberalism to conservatism and radicalism to reaction, their major thrust was in the direction of political reform.

Just as the cycle of American history running from the Civil War to the 1890's can be thought of chiefly as a period of industrial and continental expansion and political conservatism, so the age that has just passed, running from about 1890 to the second World War, can be considered an age of reform. The surge of reform, though largely turned back in the 1890's and temporarily reversed in the 1920's, has set the tone of American politics for the greater part of the twentieth century. The reform movements of the past sixty-five years fall readily into three main episodes, the first two of which are almost continuous with each other: the agrarian uprising that found its most intense expression in the Populism of the 1890's and the Bryan campaign of 1896; the Progressive movement, which extended from about 1900 to 1914; and the New Deal, whose dynamic phase was concentrated in a few years of the 1930's.

* * *

Our conception of Populism and Progressivism has in fact been intimately bound up with the New Deal experience. The Populist-Progressive age came to an end only with the first World War, and by the time we began to get serious histories of that age, we had been plunged into a new phase of reform brought about by the Great Depression. The views, therefore, of Populism and Progressivism that one finds in histories written during and shortly after the New Deal era bear inevitably the stamp of this second wave of reform. This is not merely to say that they were usually sympathetic, but that they were pervaded by the assumption that in some way the New Deal was both an analogue and a lineal descendant of the Populist-Progressive tradition, an assumption which is by no means totally false but which tends none the less to direct our attention away from essential differences and hence seriously to distort the character of our history. I have been at some pains to emphasize these differences.

I should perhaps explain the unusually broad sense in which I use the terms "Populism" and "Progressivism." By "Populism" I do not mean only the People's (or Populist) Party of the 1890's; for I consider the Populist Party to be merely a heightened expression, at a particular moment of time, of a kind of popular impulse that is endemic in American political culture. Long before the rebellion of the 1890's one can observe a larger trend of thought, stemming from the time of Andrew Jackson, and crystallizing after the Civil War in the Greenback, Granger, and anti-monopoly movements, that expressed the discontents of a great many farmers and businessmen with the economic changes of the late nineteenth century. The Populist spirit captured the Democratic Party in 1896, and continued to play an important part in the politics of the Progressive era. While its special association with agrarian reforms has now become attenuated, I believe that Populist thinking has survived in our own time, partly as an undercurrent of provincial resentments, popular and "democratic" rebelliousness and suspiciousness, and nativism.

Similarly, by "Progressivism" I mean something more than the Progressive (or Bull Moose) Party formed by the Republican insurgents who supported Theodore Roosevelt for the presidency in 1912. I mean

Excerpts from the Introduction to *The Age of Reform*, by Richard Hofstadter, pp. 3–22.

rather that broader impulse toward criticism and change that was everywhere so conspicuous after 1900, when the already forceful stream of agrarian discontent was enlarged and redirected by the growing enthusiasm of middle-class people for social and economic reform. As all observant contemporaries realized, Progressivism in this larger sense was not confined to the Progressive Party but affected in a striking way all the major and minor parties and the whole tone of American political life. It was, to be sure, a rather vague and not altogether cohesive or consistent movement, but this was probably the secret of its considerable successes, as well as of its failures. While Progressivism would have been impossible without the impetus given by certain social grievances, it was not nearly so much the movement of any social class, or coalition of classes, against a particular class or group as it was a rather widespread and remarkably good-natured effort of the greater part of society to achieve some not very clearly specified self-reformation. Its general theme was the effort to restore a type of economic individualism and political democracy that was widely believed to have existed earlier in America and to have been destroyed by the great corporation and the corrupt political machine; and with that restoration to bring back a kind of morality and civic purity that was also believed to have been lost.

* * *

The Populist and Progressive movements took place during a rapid and sometimes turbulent transition from the conditions of an agrarian society to those of modern urban life. Standing much closer to the completion of this change, we have in some respects a clearer judgment of its meaning, but we are likely to lose sight of the poignancy with which it was experienced by earlier generations. The American tradition of democracy was formed on the farm and in small villages, and its central ideas were founded in rural sentiments and on rural metaphors (we still speak of "grass-roots democracy"). . . . the American was taught throughout the nineteenth and even in the twentieth century that rural life and farming as a vocation were something sacred. Since in the beginning the majority of the people were farmers, democracy, as a rather broad abstraction, became in the same way sacrosanct. A certain complacency and self-righteousness thus entered into rural thinking, and this complacency was rudely shocked by the conquests of industrialism. A good deal of the strain and the sense of anxiety in Populism results from this rapid decline of rural America.

And yet it is too little realized that the farmers, who were quite impotent as a special interest when they were numerous, competing, and unorganized, grew stronger as they grew relatively fewer, became more concerted, more tenaciously organized and self-centered. One of the clichés of Populism was the notion that, whatever the functions of the other vocations, the function of the farmer was pre-eminent in importance because he fed, and thus supported, all the others. Although it has been heard somewhat less frequently of late, and a counter-ideology of urban resentment has even begun to appear, our national folklore still bears the heavy imprint of that idea. In reality something like the opposite has become true—that the rest of us support the farmer; for industrial and urban America, sentimentally and morally committed to the ideal of the family farm, has undertaken out of its remarkable surpluses to support more farm-owners on the farm than it really needs under modern agricultural technology. It is in part because of the persistence of our agrarian traditions that this concession to the farmers arouses less universal antagonism than do the efforts of other groups menaced by technological changes—say, the musicians and the building-trades workers—to set up artificial safeguards for themselves. . . .

Another circumstance attending the rise of Populism and Progressivism in America was unique in the modern world. Here the industrialization and urbanization of the country were coupled with a breakdown in the relative homogeneity of the population. American democracy, down to about 1880, had been not only rural but Yankee and Protestant in its basic notions, and such enclaves of immigrants as had thus far developed were too small and scattered to have a major nationwide impact upon the scheme of its civic life. The rise of industry, however, brought with it what contemporaries thought of as an "immigrant invasion," a massive forty-year migration of Europeans, chiefly peasants, whose religions, traditions, languages, and sheer numbers made easy assimilation impossible. Populism and Progressivism were in considerable part colored by the reaction to this immigrant stream among the native elements of the population. Out of the clash between the needs of the immigrants and the sentiments of the natives there emerged two thoroughly different systems of political ethics . . . One, founded upon the indigenous Yankee-Protestant political traditions, and upon middle-class life, assumed and demanded the constant, disinterested activity of the citizen in public affairs, argued that political life ought to be run, to a greater degree than it was, in accordance with general principles and abstract laws apart from and superior to personal needs, and expressed a common feeling that government should be in good part an effort to moralize the lives of individuals while economic life should be intimately related to the stimulation and development of individual character. The other system, founded upon the European backgrounds of the immigrants, upon their unfamiliarity with independent political action, their familiarity with hierarchy and authority, and upon the urgent needs that so often grew out of their migration, took for granted that the political life of the individual would arise out of family needs, interpreted political and civic relations chiefly in terms of personal obligations, and placed strong personal loyalties above allegiance to abstract codes of law or morals. It was chiefly upon this system of values that the political life of the immigrant, the boss, and the urban machine was based. In many ways the struggles of the Progressive era were influenced by the conflict between the two codes elaborated on one side by the highly moral leaders of Protestant social reform and on the other by the bosses, political professionals, and immigrant masses. Since they stemmed from different views not only of politics but of morals and even of religion, it is hardly surprising that the conflicts of the period, often so modest in actual substance, aroused antagonisms so intense and misunderstandings so complete.

The political values and the ideas of government that had been formed in the rural Yankee world were profoundly influenced by entrepreneurship and the ideal of individual success. The side of the left in American political history—that is, the side of popular causes and of reform—had always been relatively free of the need or obligation to combat feudal traditions and entrenched aristocracies. It had neither revolutionary traditions, in the bourgeois sense (the American Revolution itself was a legalistic and socially conservative affair), nor proletarianism and social democracy of the kind familiar in all the great countries of the West in the late nineteenth century. American traditions of political revolt had been based upon movements against monopolies and special privileges in both the economic and the political spheres, against social distinctions and the restriction of credit, against limits upon the avenues of personal advancement. Because it was always possible to assume a remarkable measure of social equality and a fair minimum of subsistence, the goal of revolt tended to be neither social democracy nor social equality, but greater opportunities. At the turn of the century the world with which the majority even of the reformers was most affectionately familiar was the passing world of individual enterprise, predominantly small or modest-sized business, and a decentralized, not too highly organized life. In the Progressive era the life of business, and to some degree even of government, was beginning to pass from an individualistic form toward one demanding industrial discipline and engendering a managerial and bureaucratic outlook. The protests of reformers against this state of affairs often took the form of demands for the maintenance of the kind of opportunity that was passing rather than for the furtherance of existing tendencies toward organization. Most Americans who came from the Yankee-Protestant environment, whether they were reformers or conservatives, wanted economic success to continue to be related to personal character, wanted the economic system not merely to be a system for the production of sufficient goods and services but to be an effectual system of incentives and rewards. The great corporation, the crass plutocrat, the calculating political boss, all seemed to defy these desires. Success in the great corporation seemed to have a very dubious relation to character and enterprise; and when one observed the behavior of the plutocracy, it seemed to be inversely related to civic responsibility and personal restraint. The competitive process seemed to be drying up. All of society was felt to be threatened—not by economic breakdown but by moral and social degeneration and the eclipse of democratic institutions. This is not to say, however, that the men of the age gave way to despair; for they believed that, just as the sinner can be cleansed and saved, so the nation could be redeemed if the citizens awoke to their responsibilities. This mood of hope, in which the Progressive agitations were conducted, lasted until the first World War.

The next episode in the history of reform, the New Deal, was itself a product of that overorganized world which had so much troubled the Progressives. The trend toward management, toward bureaucracy, toward bigness everywhere had gone so far that even the efforts of reform itself had to be consistent with it. Moreover, as the New Deal era went on, leadership in reform had to be shared increasingly with an organized working class large enough to make important demands and to wield great political power. The political and moral codes of the immigrant masses of the cities, of the political bosses, of labor leaders, of intellectuals and administrators, now clashed with the old notions of economic morality. Some of the social strata and many of the social types that had seen great merit in the more limited reforms of the Progressive era found themselves in a bewildering new situation and, especially after the passing of the most critical depression years, grew increasingly offended by the novelties with which they were surrounded. The New Deal, with its pragmatic spirit and its relentless emphasis upon results, seemed to have carried them farther than ever from the kind of society in which economic life was linked to character and to distinctively entrepreneurial freedoms and opportunities.

In the attempts of the Populists and Progressives to hold on to some of the values of agrarian life, to save personal entrepreneurship and individual opportunity and the character type they engendered, and to maintain a homogeneous Yankee civilization, I have found much that was retrograde and delusive, a little that was vicious, and a good deal that was comic. To say this is not to say that these values were in themselves nonsensical or bad. The ideal of a life lived close to nature and the soil, the esteem for the primary contacts of country and village life, the cherished image of the independent and self-reliant man, even the desire (for all the snobberies and hatreds it inspired) to maintain an ethnically more homogeneous nation—these were not negligible or contemptible ideals, and to those who felt most deeply about them their decline was a tragic experience that must be attended to with respect even by those who can share it only through some effort of the imagination. My comments, then, on the old agrarian and entrepreneurial aspirations are not intended to disparage them as ultimate values but to raise some safeguards against the political misuse of them that was and sometimes still is attempted, and perhaps to shed some indirect light on the methods by which that part of them that is still meaningful can be salvaged.

In find that I have been critical of the Populist-Progressive tradition—more so than I would have been had I been writing . . . fifteen years ago. I say critical, but not hostile, for I am criticizing largely from within. The tradition of Progressive reform is the one upon which I was reared and upon which my political sentiments were formed, as it is, indeed, the tradition of most intellectuals in America. Perhaps because in its politics the United States has been so reliably conservative a country during the greater part of its history, its main intellectual traditions have been, as a reaction, "liberal," as we say—that is, popular, democratic, progressive. For all our conservatism as a people, we have failed to develop a sound and supple tradition of candidly conservative thinking. As Lionel Trilling remarks in *The Liberal Imagination*, our conservatives, with only a few exceptions, have not sought to express themselves in ideas, as opposed to action; they have only manifested "irritable mental gestures which seek to resemble ideas." The American businessman is expected to be a conservative in his politics. The conservative American politician can expect widespread recognition, frequently a long tenure in office, and usually a rewarding sense of public usefulness, even though we usually reserve our highest acclaim for the politician who has in him a touch of the liberal reformer. A conservative politician who has sufficient gifts—

Theodore Roosevelt is the best example—can in fact enjoy both respectability and the financial support of the great interests and all the satisfactions of the conservative role in public affairs and yet exert his maximal influence by using the rhetoric of progressivism and winning the plaudits of the reformers. In times past, however, the conservative intellectual, and with him the conservative politician who attempted to give to his actions the support of reasoned belief, has been rather out of touch with the main lines of thought and with the primary public that he wanted to reach. The flow of criticism between conservatives and liberals in the United States has been somewhat blocked, with the consequence that men on both sides have grown excessively complacent about their intellectual positions. In the absence of a formidable and reasoned body of conservative criticism, liberals have been driven, for that exercise of the mind which intellectuals seek, to self-criticism, which has been of less value to them than powerful and searching opposition.

In our own day, perhaps for the first time since the 1890's, this situation is changing, for there are some signs that liberals are beginning to find it both natural and expedient to explore the merits and employ the rhetoric of conservatism. They find themselves far more conscious of those things they would like to preserve than they are of those things they would like to change. The immense enthusiasm that was aroused among American intellectuals by such a circumspect and sober gentleman as Adlai Stevenson in 1952 is the most outstanding evidence of this conservatism. Stevenson himself remarked during the course of his campaign that the liberals have become the true conservatives of our time. This is true not because they have some sweeping ideological commitment to conservatism (indeed, their sentiments and loyalties still lie mainly in another direction) but because they feel that we can better serve ourselves in the calculable future by holding to what we have gained and learned, while trying to find some way out of the dreadful impasse of our polarized world, than by dismantling the social achievements of the past twenty years, abandoning all that is best in American traditions, and indulging in the costly pretense of repudiating what we should not and in fact cannot repudiate.

My criticisms of the Populist-Progressive tradition, in so far as they are at all tinctured by conservatism, are no doubt in part a response to this mood. I do not like to think of these criticisms as being associated with the "New Conservatism" of our time, which seems so modish that I find myself uncomfortable with it. The use of such a term as "*New* Conservatism" only suggests to me how uneasy Americans still are in the presence of candidly conservative ideas. I should have thought that anything that was good in conservatism was very old indeed, and so that finest of American conservatives, John Adams, would tell us if he could. To propagate something called "*New* Conservatism" sounds to me too much like the crasser forms of salesmanship. It is in itself a capitulation to the American demand for constant change, and hence a betrayal of conservatism at the outset. We Americans love to have everything labeled "new" and "big," and yet what is of most value in conservatism is its feeling for the past and for nuances of thought, of administration, of method, of meaning, that might be called "little." What appeals to me in the New Conservatism, in so far as anything does at all, is simply the old liberalism, chastened by adversity, tempered by time, and modulated by a growing sense of reality. Hence, to the degree that I have been critical in these pages of the Populist-Progressive tradition, it is criticism that aims to reveal some of the limitations of that tradition and to help free it of its sentimentalities and complacencies —in short, to carry on with a task so largely shirked by its opponents that it must be performed by its supporters.

It would be unfair not to add—indeed, to emphasize as much as it is possible to do here—that most of the failings in the liberal tradition that have attracted my interest are also failings of American political culture in general, and that they are usually shared by American conservatives. The most prominent and pervasive failing is a certain proneness to fits of moral crusading that would be fatal if they were not sooner or later tempered with a measure of apathy and of common sense. Eric Goldman, in his history of American reform, *Rendezvous with Destiny,* criticizes Progressive intellectuals for propagating a moral relativism that, by making all moral judgments the products of particular locales and particular historical situations, eventually undermined confidence in the significance of moral judgments as such. "The real trouble with us reformers," he quotes J. Allen Smith as having said, "is that we made reform a crusade against standards. Well, we smashed them all and now neither we nor anybody else have anything left." This accusation has, in my view, a certain pertinence to some liberals in our time, and particularly to those who were known a few years ago as "totalitarian liberals"—that is, to the type of professed liberals who failed to demand of their own side the civic principles they expected of others, who exempted movements deemed to be "historically progressive" from the moral judgments to which all other movements were subjected, and who in particular denied or granted special indulgences to the barbarities and tyrannies of Soviet politics that they freely recognized and condemned in the fascist countries. But this kind of thing, lamentable as it was, has not been the characteristic failing of most modern American reform movements, and certainly was not widely characteristic of the Populist-Progressive thinking of the period from 1890 to 1917. My criticism of the Progressivism of that period is the opposite of Smith's—not that the Progressives most typically undermined or smashed standards, but that they set impossible standards, that they were victimized, in brief, by a form of moral absolutism. It is possible that the distinction between moral relativism and moral absolutism has sometimes been blurred because an excessively consistent practice of either leads to the same practical result—ruthlessness in political life.

A great part of both the strength and the weakness of our national existence lies in the fact that Americans do not abide very quietly the evils of life. We are forever restlessly pitting ourselves against them, demanding changes, improvements, remedies, but not often with sufficient sense of the limits that the human condition will in the end insistently impose upon us. This restlessness is most valuable and has its most successful consequences wherever dealing with *things* is involved, in technology and invention, in productivity, in the ability to meet needs and provide comforts. In this sphere we have surpassed all other peoples. But in dealing with human beings and institutions, in matters of morals and politics, the limits of this undying, absolutist restlessness quickly become evident. At the so-called grass roots of American politics there is a wide and pervasive tendency to believe—I hasten to add that the majority of Americans do not habitually succumb to this tendency—that there is some great but essentially very simple struggle going on, at the heart of which there lies some single conspiratorial force, whether it be the force represented by the "gold bugs," the Catholic Church, big business, corrupt politicians, the liquor interests and the saloons, or the Communist Party, and that this evil is something that must be not merely limited, checked, and controlled but rather extirpated root and branch at the earliest possible moment. It is widely assumed that some technique can be found that will really do this, though there is always likely to be a good deal of argument as to what that technique is. All too often the assumption prevails among our political and intellectual leaders that the judgment of the people about such things must of necessity be right, and that it is therefore their own business not to educate the public or to curb its demands for the impossible but to pretend that these demands are altogether sensible and to try to find ways to placate them.

So we go off on periodical psychic sprees that purport to be moral crusades: liberate the people once and for all from the gold bugs, restore absolute popular democracy or completely honest competition in business, wipe out the saloon and liquor forever from the nation's life, destroy the political machines and put an end to corruption, or achieve absolute, total, and final security against war, espionage, and the affairs of the external world. The people who attach themselves to these several absolutisms are not always the same people, but they do create for each other a common climate of absolutist enthusiasm. Very often the evils they are troubled about do exist in some form, usually something can be done about them, and in a great many historical instances something has been done. It is the merit of our reform tradition that it has usually been the first to point to the real and serious deficiencies in our economic system and that it has taken the initiative in making improvements. It is its limitation that it often wanders over the border between reality and impossibility. This was, I believe, preeminently true of the Progressive generation. It is hardly an accident that the generation that wanted to bring about direct popular rule, break up the political machines, and circumvent representative government was the same generation that imposed Prohibition on the country and proposed to make the world safe for democracy.

I believe it will be clear that what I am trying to establish is not that the Populist and Progressive movements were foolish and destructive but only that they had, like so many things in life, an ambiguous character. Of their substantial net value in the main stream of American political experience I have no doubt. There has always been in the United States a struggle against those forces which were too exclusively preoccupied with the organization of economic life and the milking of our resources to give much thought to the human costs or to expend much sympathy on the victims of their work. It has been the function of the liberal tradition in American politics, from the time of Jeffersonian and Jacksonian democracy down through Populism, Progressivism, and the New Deal, at first to broaden the numbers of those who could benefit from the great American bonanza and then to humanize its workings and help heal its casualties. Without this sustained tradition of opposition and protest and reform, the American system would have been, as in times and places it was, nothing but a jungle, and would probably have failed to develop into the remarkable system for production and distribution that it is. If we were to follow the history of but one issue alone—that of taxation in all its aspects—we would be quickly reminded of the enormous debt we owe to the liberal tradition for shifting the costs of society to those who are best able to bear them. Fifty or sixty years ago our social system had hardly begun to be touched by the gentle hands of remorse or reform. Today, as a result of an unintended, intermittent, and usually hostile collaboration of the opposing forces of matter-of-fact profit-seeking, engineering, and salesmanship on one hand and dissent and reform on the other, it has been altered and softened in countless ways. The place of the Progressive tradition in this achievement is so secure that it should now be possible to indulge in some critical comments without seeming to impugn its entire value.

While it is always both feasible and desirable to formulate ideal programs of reform, it is asking too much to expect that history will move, so to speak, in a straight line to realize them. Liberal intellectuals, who have rather well-rationalized systems of political beliefs, tend to expect that the masses of people, whose actions at certain moments in history coincide with some of these beliefs, will share their other convictions as a matter of logic and principle. Intellectuals, moreover, suffer from a sense of isolation which they usually seek to surmount by finding ways of getting into rapport with the people, and they readily succumb to a tendency to sentimentalize the folk. Hence they periodically exaggerate the measure of agreement that exists between movements of popular reform and the considered principles of political liberalism. They remake the image of popular rebellion closer to their heart's desire. They choose to ignore not only the elements of illiberalism that frequently seem to be an indissoluble part of popular movements but also the very complexity of the historical process itself. In theory we may feel that we can in most cases distinguish without excessive difficulty between reforms that are useful remedies for the evils and abuses of our society and changes that are in fact only additions to or aggravations of such abuses. Popular movements do not always operate with the same discrimination, and it is often hard to tell when such a movement has passed beyond the demand for important and necessary reforms to the expression of a resentment so inclusive that it embraces not only the evils and abuses of a society but the whole society itself, including some of its more liberal and humane values. One can hardly read such works as Reinhard Luthin's recent study of twentieth-century American demagogy or Albert D. Kirwan's treatise on Mississippi politics, *Revolt of the Rednecks,* without finding abundant evidence of this coexistence of illiberalism and reform, and of its continuity in our history.

These points are, I believe, applicable to the history of twentieth-century

American reform movements. We tend, for instance, to think of both Populism and Progressivism in connection with the many ways in which they can be considered precursors of the more useful reforms of the New Deal era. Actually, . . . the spirit of the Progressive era was quite different from that of the New Deal. While there are genuine points of similarity and continuity, which I do not wish to deny or minimize, my own interest has been drawn to that side of Populism and Progressivism—particularly of Populism—which seems very strongly to foreshadow some aspects of the cranky pseudo-conservatism of our time. Somewhere along the way a large part of the Populist-Progressive tradition has turned sour, become illiberal and ill-tempered. Since most of my concern . . . has been with the period before 1917, and since the greater part of this souring process took place after 1917, and even after 1930, I have not attempted to deal in any detail with this transformation. And yet I think it might well be a leading preoccupation of any history of American political movements since the first World War. What I have tried to do, in my treatment of the earlier history of reform, is to show that this process of deconversion from reform to reaction did not require the introduction of anything wholly new into the political sensibilities of the American public but only a development of certain tendencies that had existed all along, particularly in the Middle West and the South.

Such tendencies in American life as isolationism and the extreme nationalism that usually goes with it, hatred of Europe and Europeans, racial, religious, and nativist phobias, resentment of big business, trade-unionism, intellectuals, the Eastern seaboard and its culture—all these have been found not only in opposition to reform but also at times oddly combined with it. One of the most interesting and least studied aspects of American life has been the frequent recurrence of the demand for reforms, many of them aimed at the remedy of genuine ills, combined with strong moral convictions and with the choice of hatred as a kind of creed. The history of this characteristic of our political experience has never been studied on the folk level, but it has been reflected in the caliber of our leadership. One finds it, for instance, in the families of the two Charles A. Lindberghs, and the two Martin Dieses, where in both cases the fathers were Populistic or Progressive isolationists and the sons became heroes of the extreme right. One finds it in the careers of such Western and Midwestern Senators as Burton K. Wheeler, Gerald P. Nye, Lynn Frazier, and William Lemke, and in such Southerners as Tom Watson, Pitchfork Ben Tillman, Cole Blease, James K. Vardaman, and Huey Long. Nor is it confined to practical politics. It has its representatives in literature, like Jack London, and in journalism, like William Randolph Hearst.

We have all been taught to regard it as more or less "natural" for young dissenters to become conservatives as they grow older; but the phenomenon I am concerned with is not quite the same, for it involves not so much the progression from one political position to another as the continued coexistence of reformism and reaction; and when it takes the form of a progression in time, it is a progression very often unattended by any real change in personal temper. No doubt the precise line between useful and valid criticism of any society and a destructive alienation from its essential values is not always easy to draw. Some men, and indeed some political movements, seem to live close to that line and to swing back and forth across it more than once in their lives. The impulses behind yesterday's reform may be put in the service of reform today, but they may also be enlisted in the service of reaction.

I am fully aware of the dangers of overemphasizing here the resemblances and the continuities between the currents of political feeling that trouble liberals today and their counterparts in earlier reform movements —the danger of becoming too present-minded to have a sound sense of historical veracity, of pushing an insight beyond the bounds of its valid application. Populism, for all its zany fringes, was not an unambiguous forerunner of modern authoritarian movements; nor was Progressivism, despite the fallible concept of mass democracy it sometimes sought to advance, an unambiguous harbinger of our most troublesome contemporary delusions. Among those things which must be kept in mind when we think of the period between 1890 and 1917 is that it had about it an innocence and relaxation that cannot again be known, now that totalitarianism has emerged. Mr. Dooley, one of the shrewdest commentators of that age, saw its character quite clearly when he said, even at the height of the Progressive ferment: "Th' noise ye hear is not th' first gun iv a rivolution. It's on'y th' people iv the United States batin' a carpet."

* * *

6

The Roosevelt Reconstruction: Retrospect

WILLIAM E. LEUCHTENBERG

In the following selection, William E. Leuchtenberg analyzes Franklin D. Roosevelt's "revolutionary" impact on American politics in expanding the president's powers and in changing the relationship between the national government and the individual citizen. Under Roosevelt, according to Leuchtenberg and other historians of the period, the government assumed a responsibility for the individual citizen's welfare; unemployment insurance, old-age and survivors insurance, and public housing marked the new relationship between man and his government in the 1930s. In spite of these revolutionary changes, Roosevelt's New Deal was essentially a conservative movement. Its objective was the restoration of liberal capitalism. The major purpose of the National Industrial Recovery Administration, for example, was the revitalization of a competitive industrial system. Thus, the New Deal did not attempt to replace capitalism; it simply sought to make it more humane by spreading the costs of industrialization throughout the society.

The effect of the New Deal, however, went beyond the relationship of man and his government. Groups were included in the governmental process that had never been part of the ruling coalition: the hyphenate Americans, labor unions, and other urban groups. Although New Dealers may be criticized for leaving out significant minorities—Negroes and Mexican-American migrant workers, for example—they greatly expanded participation in the governmental process. The New Deal is a watershed in American political development because it marked an end to the White-Anglo-Saxon-Protestant monopoly of power, prestige, and status in American public life and the emergence of the new men of politics, whom Robert Dahl has called the "ex-plebes."

Leuchtenberg is the author of Flood Control Politics *(1953),* The Perils of Prosperity *(1958),* The Great Age of Change *(1964), and* New Deal and Global War *(1964). He is Professor of History at Columbia University and has served with the United States Social Security Administration and as a consultant to the Ford Foundation.*

In eight years, Roosevelt and the New Dealers had almost revolutionized the agenda of American politics. "Mr. Roosevelt may have given the wrong answers to many of his problems," concluded the editors of *The Economist.* "But he is at least the first President of modern America who has asked the right questions." In 1932, men of acumen were absorbed to an astonishing degree with such questions as prohibition, war debts, and law enforcement. By 1936, they were debating social security, the Wagner Act, valley authorities, and public housing. The thirties witnessed a rebirth of issues politics, and parties split more sharply on ideological lines than they had in many years past. "I incline to think that for years up to the present juncture thinking Democrats and thinking Republicans had been divided by an imaginary line," reflected a Massachusetts congressman in 1934. "Now for the first time since the period before the Civil War we find vital principles at stake." Much of this change resulted simply from the depression trauma, but much too came from the force of Roosevelt's personality and his use of his office as both pulpit and lectern. "Of course you have fallen into some errors—that is human," former Supreme Court Justice John Clarke wrote the President, "but you have put a new face upon the social and political life of our country."[1]

Franklin Roosevelt re-created the modern Presidency. He took an office which had lost much of its prestige and power in the previous twelve years and gave it an importance which went well beyond what even Theodore Roosevelt and Woodrow Wilson had done. Clinton Rossiter has observed: "Only Washington, who made the office, and Jackson, who remade it, did more than [Roosevelt] to raise it to its present condition of strength, dignity, and independence."[2] Under Roosevelt, the White House became the focus of all government—the fountainhead of ideas, the initiator of action, the representative of the national interest.

Roosevelt greatly expanded the President's legislative functions. In the nineteenth century, Congress had been jealous of its prerogatives as the lawmaking body, and resented any encroachment on its domain by the Chief Executive. Woodrow Wilson and Theodore Roosevelt had broken new ground in sending actual drafts of bills to Congress and in using devices like the caucus to win enactment of measures they favored. Franklin Roosevelt made such constant use of these tools that he came to assume a legislative role not unlike that of a prime minister. He sent special mes-

Abridgment of Chapter 14, "The Roosevelt Reconstruction: Retrospect," from *Franklin D. Roosevelt and the New Deal* by William E. Leuchtenberg. Copyright © 1963 by William E. Leuchtenberg. By permission of Harper & Row, Publishers, Inc.

sages to Congress, accompanied them with drafts of legislation prepared by his assistants, wrote letters to committee chairmen or members of Congress to urge passage of the proposals, and authorized men like Corcoran to lobby as presidential spokesmen on the Hill. By the end of Roosevelt's tenure in the White House, Congress looked automatically to the Executive for guidance; it expected the administration to have a "program" to present for consideration.[3]

Roosevelt's most important formal contribution was his creation of the Executive Office of the President on September 8, 1939. Executive Order 8248, a "nearly unnoticed but none the less epoch-making event in the history of American institutions," set up an Executive Office staffed with six administrative assistants with a "passion for anonymity."[4] In 1939, the President not only placed obvious agencies like the White House Office in the Executive Office but made the crucial decision to shift the Bureau of the Budget from the Treasury and put it under his wing. In later years, such pivotal agencies as the Council of Economic Advisers, the National Security Council, and the Central Intelligence Agency would be moved into the Executive Office of the President. Roosevelt's decision, Rossiter has concluded, "converts the Presidency into an instrument of twentieth-century government; it gives the incumbent a sporting chance to stand the strain and fulfill his constitutional mandate as a one-man branch of our three-part government; it deflates even the most forceful arguments, which are still raised occasionally, for a plural executive; it assures us that the Presidency will survive the advent of the positive state. Executive Order 8248 may yet be judged to have saved the Presidency from paralysis and the Constitution from radical amendment."[5]

Roosevelt's friends have been too quick to concede that he was a poor administrator. To be sure, he found it difficult to discharge incompetent aides, he procrastinated about decisions, and he ignored all the canons of sound administration by giving men overlapping assignments and creating a myriad of agencies which had no clear relation to the regular departments of government.[6] But if the test of good administration is not an impeccable organizational chart but creativity, then Roosevelt must be set down not merely as a good administrator but as a resourceful innovator. The new agencies he set up gave a spirit of excitement to Washington that the routinized old-line departments could never have achieved. The President's refusal to proceed through channels, however vexing at times to his subordinates, resulted in a competition not only among men but among ideas, and encouraged men to feel that their own beliefs might win the day. "You would be surprised, Colonel, the remarkable ideas that have been turned loose just because men have felt that they can get a hearing," one senator confided.[7] The President's "procrastination" was his own way both of arriving at a sense of national consensus and of reaching a decision by observing a trial by combat among rival theories. Periods of indecision—as in the spring of 1935 or the beginning of 1938—were inevitably followed by a fresh outburst of new proposals.[8]

Most of all, Roosevelt was a successful administrator because he attracted to Washington thousands of devoted and highly skilled men. Men who had been fighting for years for lost causes were given a chance: John Collier, whom the President courageously named Indian Commissioner;

Arthur Powell Davis, who had been ousted as chief engineer of the Department of the Interior at the demand of power interests; old conservationists like Harry Slattery, who had fought the naval oil interests in the Harding era. When Harold Ickes took office as Secretary of the Interior, he looked up Louis Glavis—he did not even know whether the "martyr" of the Ballinger-Pinchot affair was still alive—and appointed him to his staff.[9]

The New Dealers displayed striking ingenuity in meeting problems of governing. They coaxed salmon to climb ladders at Bonneville; they sponsored a Young Choreographers Laboratory in the WPA's Dance Theatre; they gave the pioneer documentary film maker Pare Lorentz the opportunity to create his classic films *The Plow That Broke the Plains* and *The River*. At the Composers Forum-Laboratory of the Federal Music Project, William Schuman received his first serious hearing. In Arizona, Father Berard Haile of St. Michael's Mission taught written Navajo to the Indians.[10] Roosevelt, in the face of derision from professional foresters and prairie states' governors, persisted in a bold scheme to plant a mammoth "shelterbelt" of parallel rows of trees from the Dakotas to the Panhandle. In all, more than two hundred million trees were planted—cottonwood and willow, hackberry and cedar, Russian olive and Osage orange; within six years, the President's visionary windbreak had won over his former critics.[11] The spirit behind such innovations generated a new excitement about the potentialities of government. "Once again," Roosevelt told a group of young Democrats in April, 1936, "the very air of America is exhilarating."[12]

Roosevelt dominated the front pages of the newspapers as no other President before or since has done. "Frank Roosevelt and the NRA have taken the place of love nests," commented Joe Patterson, publisher of the tabloid New York *Daily News*. At his very first press conference, Roosevelt abolished the written question and told reporters they could interrogate him without warning. Skeptics predicted the free and easy exchange would soon be abandoned, but twice a week, year in and year out, he threw open the White House doors to as many as two hundred reporters, most of them representing hostile publishers, who would crowd right up to the President's desk to fire their questions. The President joshed them, traded wisecracks with them, called them by their first names; he charmed them by his good-humored ease and impressed them with his knowledge of detail.[13] To a degree, Roosevelt's press conference introduced, as some observers claimed, a new institution like Britain's parliamentary questioning; more to the point, it was a device the President manipulated, disarmingly and adroitly, to win support for his program.[14] It served too as a classroom to instruct the country in the new economics and the new politics.

Roosevelt was the first president to master the technique of reaching people directly over the radio. In his fireside chats, he talked like a father discussing public affairs with his family in the living room. As he spoke, he seemed unconscious of the fact that he was addressing millions. "His head would nod and his hands would move in simple, natural, comfortable gestures," Frances Perkins recalled. "His face would smile and light up as though he were actually sitting on the front porch or in the parlor with them." Eleanor Roosevelt later observed that after the President's death people would stop her on the street to say "they missed the way the President used to talk to them. They'd say 'He used to talk to me about my government.' There was a real dialogue between Franklin and the people," she reflected. "That dialogue seems to have disappeared from the government since he did."[15]

For the first time for many Americans, the federal government became an institution that was directly experienced. More than state and local governments, it came to be *the* government, an agency directly concerned with their welfare. It was the source of their relief payments; it taxed them directly for old age pensions; it even gave their children hot lunches in school. As the role of the state changed from that of neutral arbiter to a "powerful promoter of society's welfare," people felt an interest in affairs in Washington they had never had before.[16]

Franklin Roosevelt personified the state as protector. It became commonplace to say that people felt toward the President the kind of trust they would normally express for a warm and understanding father who comforted them in their grief or safeguarded them from harm. An insurance man reported: "My mother looks upon the President as someone so immediately concerned with her problems and difficulties that she would not be greatly surprised were he to come to her house some evening and stay to dinner." From his first hours in office, Roosevelt gave people the feeling that they could confide in him directly. As late as the Presidency of Herbert Hoover, one man, Ira Smith, had sufficed to take care of all the mail the White House received. Under Roosevelt, Smith had to acquire a staff of fifty people to handle the thousands of letters written to the President each week. Roosevelt gave people a sense of membership in the national community. Justice Douglas has written: "He was in a very special sense the people's President, because he made them feel that with him in the White House they shared the Presidency. The sense of sharing the Presidency gave even the most humble citizen a lively sense of belonging."[17]

When Roosevelt took office, the country, to a very large degree, responded to the will of a single element: the white, Anglo-Saxon, Protestant property-holding class. Under the New Deal, new groups took their place in the sun. It was not merely that they received benefits they had not had before but that they were "recognized" as having a place in the commonwealth. At the beginning of the Roosevelt era, charity organizations ignored labor when seeking "community" representation; at the end of the period, no fund-raising committee was complete without a union representative. While Theodore Roosevelt had founded a lily-white Progressive party in the South and Woodrow Wilson had introduced segregation into the federal government, Franklin Roosevelt had quietly brought the Negro into the New Deal coalition. When the distinguished Negro contralto Marian Anderson was denied a concert hall in Washington, Secretary Ickes arranged for her to perform from the steps of Lincoln Memorial. Equal representation for religious groups became so well accepted that, as one priest wryly complained, one never saw a picture of a priest in a newspaper unless he was flanked on either side by a minister and a rabbi.

The devotion Roosevelt aroused owed much to the fact that the New Deal assumed the responsibility for guaranteeing every American a minimum standard of subsistence. Its relief programs represented an advance over the barbaric predepression practices that constituted a difference not in degree but in kind. One analyst wrote: "During the ten years between 1929 and 1939 more progress was made in public welfare and relief than in the three hundred years after this country was first settled." The Roosevelt administration gave such assistance not as a matter of charity but of right. This system of social rights was written into the Social Security Act. Other New Deal legislation abolished child labor in interstate commerce and, by putting a floor under wages and a ceiling on hours, all but wiped out the sweatshop.[18]

Roosevelt and his aides fashioned a government which consciously sought to make the industrial system more humane and to protect workers and their families from exploitation. In his acceptance speech in June, 1936, the President stated: "Governments can err, Presidents do make mistakes, but the immortal Dante tells us that divine justice weighs the sins of the cold-blooded and the sins of the warm-hearted in different scales.

"Better the occasional faults of a Government that lives in a spirit of charity than the constant omission of a Government frozen in the ice of its own indifference." Nearly everyone in the Roosevelt government was caught up to some degree by a sense of participation in something larger than themselves. A few days after he took office, one of the more conservative New Deal administrators wrote in his diary: "This should be a Gov't of humanity."[19]

The federal government expanded enormously in the Roosevelt years. The crisis of the depression dissipated the distrust of the state inherited from the eighteenth century and reinforced in diverse ways by the Jeffersonians and the Spencerians. Roosevelt himself believed that liberty in America was imperiled more by the agglomerations of private business than by the state. The New Dealers were convinced that the depression was the result not simply of an economic breakdown but of a political collapse; hence, they sought new political instrumentalities. The reformers of the 1930's accepted almost unquestioningly the use of coercion by the state to achieve reforms.[20] Even Republicans who protested that Roosevelt's policies were snuffing out liberty voted overwhelmingly in favor of coercive measures.[21]

This elephantine growth of the federal government owed much to the fact that local and state governments had been tried in the crisis and found wanting. When one magazine wired state governors to ask their views, only one of the thirty-seven who replied announced that he was willing to have the states resume responsibility for relief.[22] Every time there was a rumored cutback of federal spending for relief, Washington was besieged by delegations of mayors protesting that city governments did not have the resources to meet the needs of the unemployed.

* * *

Under the New Deal, the federal government greatly extended its power over the economy. By the end of the Roosevelt years, few questioned the right of the government to pay the farmer millions in subsidies not to grow crops, to enter plants to conduct union elections, to regulate business enterprises from utility companies to air lines, or even to compete directly with business by generating and distributing hydroelectric power. All of these powers had been ratified by the Supreme Court, which had even held that a man growing grain solely for his own use was affecting interstate commerce and hence subject to federal penalties.[23] The President, too, was well on his way to becoming "the chief economic engineer," although this was not finally established until the Full Employment Act of 1946. In 1931, Hoover had hooted that some people thought "that by some legerdemain we can legislate ourselves out of a world-wide depression." In the Roosevelt era, the conviction that government both should and could act to forestall future breakdowns gained general acceptance. The New Deal left a large legacy of antidepression controls—securities regulation, banking reforms, unemployment compensation—even if it could not guarantee that a subsequent administration would use them.[24]

In the 1930's, the financial center of the nation shifted from Wall Street to Washington. In May, 1934, a writer reported: "Financial news no longer originates in Wall Street." That same month, *Fortune* commented on a revolution in the credit system which was "one of the major historical events of the generation." "Mr. Roosevelt," it noted, "seized the Federal Reserve without firing a shot." The federal government had not only broken down the old separation of bank and state in the Reserve system but had gone into the credit business itself in a wholesale fashion under the aegis of the RFC, the Farm Credit Administration, and the housing agencies. Legislation in 1933 and 1934 had established federal regulation of Wall Street for the first time. No longer could the New York Stock Exchange operate as a private club free of national supervision. In 1935, Congress leveled the mammoth holding-company pyramids and centralized yet more authority over the banking system in the federal government. After a tour of the United States in 1935, Sir Josiah Stamp wrote: "Just as in 1929 the whole country was 'Wall Street-conscious' now it is 'Washington-conscious.' "[25]

Despite this encroachment of government on traditional business prerogatives, the New Deal could advance impressive claims to being regarded as a "savior of capitalism." Roosevelt's sense of the land, of family, and of the community marked him as a man with deeply ingrained conservative traits. In the New Deal years, the government sought deliberately, in Roosevelt's words, "to energize private enterprise." The RFC financed business, housing agencies underwrote home financing, and public works spending aimed to revive the construction industry. Moreover, some of the New Deal reforms were Janus-faced. The NYA, in aiding jobless youth, also served as a safety valve to keep young people out of the labor market. A New Deal congressman, in pushing for public power projects, argued that the country should take advantage of the sea of "cheap labor" on the relief rolls. Even the Wagner Act and the movement for industrial unionism were motivated in part by the desire to contain "unbalanced and radical" labor groups. Yet such considerations should not obscure the more important point: that the New Deal, however conservative it was in some respects and however much it owed to the past, marked a radically new departure. As Carl Degler writes: "The conclusion seems inescapable that, traditional as the words may have been in which the New Deal expressed itself, in actuality it was a revolutionary response to a revolutionary situation."[26]

* * *

Commentators on the New Deal have frequently characterized it by that much-abused term "pragmatic." If one means by this that the New Dealers carefully tested the consequences of ideas, the term is clearly a misnomer. If one means that Roosevelt was exceptionally anti-ideological in his approach to politics, one may question whether he was, in fact, any more "pragmatic" in this sense than Van Buren or Polk or even "reform" Presidents like Jackson and Theodore Roosevelt. The "pragmatism" of the New Deal seemed remarkable only in a decade tortured by ideology, only in contrast to the rigidity of Hoover and of the Left.

The New Deal was pragmatic mainly in its skepticism about utopias and final solutions, its openness to experimentation, and its suspicion of the dogmas of the Establishment. Since the advice of economists had so often been wrong, the New Dealers distrusted the claims of orthodox theory —"All this is perfectly terrible because it is all pure theory, when you come down to it," the President said on one occasion—and they felt free to try new approaches.[27] Roosevelt refused to be awed by the warnings of economists and financial experts that government interference with the "laws" of the economy was blasphemous. "We must lay hold of the fact that economic laws are not made by nature," the President stated. "They are made by human beings."[28] The New Dealers denied that depressions were inevitable events that had to be borne stoically, most of the stoicism to be displayed by the most impoverished, and they were willing to explore novel ways to make the social order more stable and more humane. "I am for experimenting . . . in various parts of the country, trying out schemes which are supported by reasonable people and see if they work," Hopkins told a conference of social workers. "If they do not work, the world will not come to an end."[29]

Hardheaded, "anti-utopian," the New Dealers nonetheless had their Heavenly City: the greenbelt town, clean, green, and white, with children playing in light, airy, spacious schools; the government project at Longview, Washington, with small houses, each of different design, colored roofs, and gardens of flowers and vegetables; the Mormon villages of Utah that M. L. Wilson kept in his mind's eye—immaculate farmsteads on broad, rectangular streets; most of all, the Tennessee Valley, with its model town of Norris, the tall transmission towers, the white dams, the glistening wire strands, the valley where "a vision of villages and clean small factories has been growing into the minds of thoughtful men."[30] Scandinavia was their model abroad, not only because it summoned up images of the countryside of Denmark, the beauties of Stockholm, not only for its experience with labor relations and social insurance and currency reform, but because it represented the "middle way" of happy accommodation of public and private institutions the New Deal sought to achieve. "Why," inquired Brandeis, "should anyone want to go to Russia when one can go to Denmark?"[31]

Yet the New Deal added up to more than all of this—more than an experimental approach, more than the sum of its legislative achievements, more than an antiseptic utopia. It is true that there was a certain erosion of values in the thirties, as well as a narrowing of horizons, but the New Dealers inwardly recognized that what they were doing had a deeply moral significance however much they eschewed ethical pretensions. Heirs of the Enlightenment, they felt themselves part of a broadly humanistic movement to make man's life on earth more tolerable, a movement that might someday even achieve a cooperative commonwealth. Social insurance, Frances Perkins declared, was "a fundamental part of another great forward step in that liberation of humanity which began with the Renaissance."[32]

Franklin Roosevelt did not always have this sense as keenly as some of the men around him, but his greatness as a President lies in the remarkable degree to which he shared the vision. "The new deal business to me is very much bigger than anyone yet has expressed it," observed Senator Elbert Thomas. Roosevelt "seems to really have caught the spirit of what one of the Hebrew prophets called the desire of the nations. If he were in India today they would probably decide that he had become Mahatma—that is, one in tune with the infinite."[33] Both foes and friends made much of Roosevelt's skill as a political manipulator, and there is no doubt that up to a point he delighted in schemes and stratagems. As Donald Richberg later observed: "There would be times when he seemed to be a Chevalier Bayard, *sans peur et sans reproche,* and times in which he would seem to be the apotheosis of a prince who had absorbed and practiced all the teachings of Machiavelli." Yet essentially he was a moralist who wanted to achieve certain humane reforms and instruct the nation in the principles of government. On one occasion, he remarked: "I want to be a *preaching President*—like my cousin."[34] His courtiers gleefully recounted his adroitness in trading and dealing for votes, his effectiveness on the stump, his wicked skill in cutting corners to win a point. But Roosevelt's importance lay not in his talents as a campaigner or a manipulator. It lay rather in his ability to arouse the country and, more specifically, the men who served under him, by his breezy encouragement of experimentation, by his hopefulness, and—a word that would have embarrassed some of his lieutenants—by his idealism.

The New Deal left many problems unsolved and even created some perplexing new ones. It never demonstrated that it could achieve prosperity in peacetime. As late as 1941, the unemployed still numbered six million, and not until the war year of 1943 did the army of the jobless finally disappear. It enhanced the power of interest groups who claimed to speak for millions, but sometimes represented only a small minority.[35] It did not evolve a way to protect people who had no such spokesmen, nor an acceptable method for disciplining the interest groups. In 1946, President Truman would resort to a threat to draft railway workers into the Army to avert a strike. The New Deal achieved a more just society by recognizing groups which had been largely unrepresented—staple farmers, industrial workers, particular ethnic groups, and the new intellectual-administrative class. Yet this was still a halfway revolution; it swelled the ranks of the bourgeoisie but left many Americans—sharecroppers, slum dwellers, most Negroes—outside of the new equilibrium.

Some of these omissions were to be promptly remedied. Subsequent Congresses extended social security, authorized slum clearance projects, and raised minimum-wage standards to keep step with the rising price level. Other shortcomings are understandable. The havoc that had been done before Roosevelt took office was so great that even the unprecedented measures of the New Deal did not suffice to repair the damage. Moreover, much was still to be learned, and it was in the Roosevelt years that the country was schooled in how to avert another major depression. Although it was war which freed the government from the taboos of a balanced budget and revealed the potentialities of spending, it is conceivable that New Deal measures would have led the country into a new cycle of prosperity even if there had been no war. Marked gains had been made before the war spending had any appreciable effect. When recovery did come, it was much more soundly based because of the adoption of the New Deal program.

Roosevelt and the New Dealers understood, perhaps better than their critics, that they had come only part of the way. Henry Wallace remarked: "We are children of the transition—we have left Egypt but we have not yet arrived at the Promised Land." Only five years separated Roosevelt's inauguration in 1933 and the adoption of the last of the New Deal measures, the Fair Labor Standards Act, in 1938. The New Dealers perceived that they had done more in those years than had been done in any comparable period in American history, but they also saw that there was much still to be done, much, too, that continued to baffle them. "I believe in the things that have been done," Mrs. Roosevelt told the American Youth Congress in February, 1939. "They helped but they did not solve the fundamental problems. . . . I never believed the Federal government could solve the whole problem. It bought us time to think." She closed not with a solution but with a challenge: "Is it going to be worth while?"[36]

"This generation of Americans is living in a tremendous moment of history," President Roosevelt stated in his final national address of the 1940 campaign.

"The surge of events abroad has made some few doubters among us ask: Is this the end of a story that has been told? Is the book of democracy now to be closed and placed away upon the dusty shelves of time?

"My answer is this: All we have known of the glories of democracy—its freedom, its efficiency as a mode of living, its ability to meet the aspirations of the common man—all these are merely an introduction to the greater story of a more glorious future.

"We Americans of today—all of us—we are characters in the living book of democracy.

"But we are also its author. It falls upon us now to say whether the chapters that are to come will tell a story of retreat or a story of continued advance."[37]

NOTES

1. The Editors of the Economist, *The New Deal* (New York, 1937), p. 149; Representative Robert Luce to Herbert Claiborne Pell, November 14, 1934, Pell MSS., Box 7; Elliott Roosevelt (ed.), *F.D.R.: His Personal Letters, 1928–1945* (2 vols., New York, 1950), I, 723.
2. Clinton Rossiter, *The American Presidency* (Signet edition, New York, 1956), p. 114.
3. *Ibid.*, pp. 81–84; Edward S. Corwin, *The President: Office and Powers 1787–1957* (New York, 1957), pp. 274–275. Yet despite the growth of the Presidency, this was a period in which Congress had great influence. Much of the specific New Deal legislation was the consequence of the work of a Robert Wagner or a Robert La Follette, Jr. The expansion of the Presidency resulted in a reinvigoration of the whole political system.

4. Luther Gulick, cited in Rossiter, *American Presidency,* p. 96.
5. Rossiter, *American Presidency,* p. 100. Cf. Emile Giraud, *La Crise de la democratie et le renforcement du pouvoir exécutif* (Paris, 1938).
6. "At times Roosevelt acted as if a new agency were almost a new solution. His addiction to new organizations became a kind of nervous tic which disturbed even avid New Dealers." Arthur Schlesinger, Jr., *The Coming of the New Deal* (Boston, 1959), p. 535. Schlesinger has an excellent discussion of Roosevelt's administrative talent.
7. Elbert Thomas to Colonel E. LeRoy Bourne, January 6, 1934, Elbert Thomas MSS., Box 23.
8. Richard Neustadt, *Presidential Power* (New York, 1960), pp. 156–158.
9. In Roosevelt's first year in office, he signed an order restoring Glavis to the civil service status he had lost when President Taft fired him. Ironically, Ickes found Glavis as intolerable a subordinate as Taft had, and concluded that he had "been very unjust to Ballinger all of these years." *The Secret Diary of Harold Ickes* (3 vols., New York, 1954), III, 111.
10. John Collier to Louis Brandeis, April 5, 1937, Brandeis MSS., SC 19.
11. H. H. Chapman, "Digest of Opinions Received on the Shelterbelt Project," *Journal of Forestry,* XXXII (1934), 952–957; Bristow Adams, "Some Fence!" *Cornell Countryman,* XXXII (1934), 4; *Science News Letter,* CXXXIV (1938), 409; "Prairie Tree Banks," *American Forester,* CXLVII (1941), 177.
12. Samuel Rosenman (ed.), *The Public Papers and Addresses of Franklin D. Roosevelt* (13 vols., New York, 1938–50), V, 165.
13. Elmer Cornwell, Jr., "Presidential News: The Expanding Public Image," *Journalism Quarterly,* XXXVI (1959), 275–283; "The Chicago Tribune," *Fortune,* IX (May, 1934), 108; *Editor and Publisher,* March 4, 1933; Thomas Stokes, *Chip Off My Shoulder* (Princeton, 1940), p. 367.
14. Erwin Canham, "Democracy's Fifth Wheel," *Literary Digest,* CXIX (January 5, 1935), 6; Douglass Cater, *The Fourth Branch of Government* (Boston, 1959), pp. 13–14, 142–155; James Pollard, *The Presidents and the Press* (New York, 1947), pp. 773–845.
15. Frances Perkins, *The Roosevelt I Knew* (New York, 1946), p. 72; Bernard Asbell, *When F.D.R. Died* (New York, 1961), p. 161.
16. Felix Frankfurter, "The Young Men Go to Washington," *Fortune,* XIII (1936), 61; E. W. Bakke, *Citizens Without Work* (New Haven, 1940), pp. 52–53.
17. Richard Neuberger, "They Love Roosevelt," *Forum and Century,* CI (1939), 15; Corwin, *The President,* p. 471; William O. Douglas, *Being an American* (New York, 1948), p. 88.
18. Josephine Chapin Brown, *Public Relief 1929–1939* (New York, 1940), p. ix; Thomas Paul Jenkin, *Reactions of Major Groups to Positive Government in the United States, 1930–1940* (University of California Publications in Political Science [Berkeley and Los Angeles, 1945]), p. 284.
19. *Public Papers,* V, 235; J. F. T. O'Connor MS. Diary, June 25, 1933.
20. Paul Carter has noted the change in the social gospel. The editors of *The Baptist,* he has written, "recognized that the transfer of social privilege involves the use of social coercion, a fact which the Right and Center of the old Social Gospel had not always faced up to." Carter, "The Decline and Revival of the Social Gospel" (unpublished Ph.D. dissertation, Columbia University, 1954).
21. On the compulsory Potato Act, only six Republicans (and just nine Democrats) voted in opposition.
22. *Today,* III (January 12, 1935), 4.
23. Wickard *v.* Filburn, 317 U.S. 111 (1942).
24. Sidney Hyman, *The American President* (New York, 1954), pp. 263–264; Carl Degler, *Out of Our Past* (New York, 1959), pp. 391–393. In a few pages, Degler has written the best analysis of the permanent significance of the New Deal.
25. Ferdinand Lundberg, "Wall Street Dances to Washington's Tune," *Literary Digest,* CXVII (May 12, 1934), 46; "Federal Reserve," *Fortune,* IX (May, 1934), 65–66, 125; Sir Josiah Stamp, "Six Weeks in America," *The Times* (London), July 4, 1935.
26. *Public Papers,* IX, 11; Walter Pierce to Bureau of Publicity, Democratic National Committee, January 4, 1940, Pierce MSS., File 7.1; Robert Wagner to Harold McCollom, April 24, 1935, Wagner MSS.; Sidney Lens, *Left, Right & Center* (Hinsdale, Ill., 1949), pp. 286 ff.; Degler, *Out of Our Past,* p. 416. Not only did the New Deal

borrow many ideas and institutions from the Progressive era, but the New Dealers and the Progressives shared more postulates and values than is commonly supposed. Nonetheless, the spirit of the 1930's seems to me to be quite different from that of the Progressive era.

27. *Public Papers,* II, 269. "In the months and years following the stock market crash," Professor Galbraith has concluded, "the burden of reputable economic advice was invariably on the side of measures that would make things worse." John Kenneth Galbraith, *The Great Crash* (Boston, 1955), pp. 187–188. For a typical example, see N. S. B. Gras to Edward Costigan, July 22, 1932, Costigan MSS., V.F. 1.
28. *Public Papers,* I, 657. The Boston *Transcript* commented: "Two more glaring misstatements of the truth could hardly have been packed into so little space." J. Joseph Huthmacher, *Massachusetts People and Politics, 1919–1933* (Cambridge, 1959), p. 244. Cf. Eccles, *Beckoning Frontiers,* p. 73.
29. *Public Papers,* II, 302; V, 497; Josephine Chapin Brown, *Public Relief,* p. 152. Cf. Clarke Chambers, "FDR, Pragmatist-Idealist," *Pacific Northwest Quarterly, LII* (1961), 50–55; F. S. C. Northrop, *The Meeting of East and West* (New York, 1947), p. 152; Jacob Cohen, "Schlesinger and the New Deal," *Dissent,* VIII (1961), 466–468.
30. Tugwell, *Battle for Democracy,* p. 22. This is a vision caught, in different ways, in the paintings of Paul Sample, Charles Sheeler, Grant Wood, and Joe Jones.
31. Marquis Childs, *Sweden: The Middle Way* (New Haven, 1936); David Lilienthal to George Fort Milton, July 9, 1936; Milton to F.D.R., July 8, 1936, Milton MSS., Box 20; Irving Fisher to F.D.R., September 28, 1934, Fisher MSS.; John Commons to Edward Costigan, July 25, 1932, Costigan MSS., V.F. 1; Arthur Schlesinger, Jr., *The Politics of Upheaval* (Boston, 1960), p. 221.
32. Frances Perkins, "Basic Idea Behind Social Security Program," *The New York Times,* January 27, 1935.
33. Thomas to Colonel E. LeRoy Bourne, January 6, 1934, Elbert Thomas MSS.
34. Donald Richberg, *My Hero* (New York, 1954), p. 279; Schlesinger, *Coming of New Deal* (Boston, 1959), p. 558.
35. Henry Kariel, *The Decline of American Pluralism* (Stanford, 1961).
36. Henry Wallace, *The Christian Bases of World Order* (New York, 1943), p. 17; Dorothy Dunbar Bromley, "The Future of Eleanor Roosevelt," *Harper's,* CLXXX (1939), 136.
37. *Public Papers,* IX, 545.

7

Liberal Democracy and Social Control

ANDREW HACKER

In the following essay, Andrew Hacker argues that liberal democracy was the instrument of power of America's middle- and upper-middle-class governors. For over a century and a half the values of individual liberty and limited government protected the ruling classes and were accepted by the masses. This acceptance was based upon a carefully nurtured deference system, which has since been destroyed by mass immigration from Europe and the expansion of the economy. Mass immigration brought to the United States vast numbers of people who did not share the Anglo-American liberal values and deference system; economic plenty elevated the new men to positions of power in the era of the New Deal.

If America's older ruling class relied upon a deference system, what legitimates the present power of the governors? Hacker asserts that deference has been replaced by the engineering of consent, the manipulation of the masses through the media of communication. "The American public . . . is kept content with congenial work, a feeling of participation, a high pattern of consumption, and the general belief that they live in the best of all possible societies." What is the consequence of this redistribution of power in American public life? Hacker concludes that the new men of power, who are themselves the products of a liberal society, have unwittingly destroyed the "ideals" of liberal democracy.

Hacker, Professor of Political Science at Cornell University, has been a Social Science Research Council Fellow (1954–1955) and a Ford Foundation Fellow (1962–1963). He is the author of Political Theory *(1961),* Congressional Districting *(1963), and* The Study of Politics *(1963), and the co-author of* Politics and Government in the U.S. *(1965).*

Liberal democrats, like all those who elect to paddle in the placid waters of liberalism, show a charming imperviousness to the existence of power. It is the ingenuousness which permitted the ideology of individualism to flourish for well over a century in the Western world. But all chickens—political as well as others—eventually come home to roost; and the failure to imbibe the home truths set down by such ungentlemanly characters as Thrasymachus, Machiavelli, and Pareto now accounts for the dilemmas, reconsiderations, and tortured defenses of liberal democracy which we see abounding on all sides.

Liberal democracy—that uneasy compromise which was never a compromise at all—is, from the moral standpoint, the worthiest of political creeds.[1] It can arouse the enthusiasm of the humane, the heretical, and the responsible: in short, of all men of good will. But the tenets of liberal democracy can only be a guide for governors and governed in a community if there exists a halcyon situation in which the traditional status system is placidly taken for granted by all in the community. Only in this way can attention be focussed on the preservation of liberties and the encouragement of individual development. For social arrangements set the stage for the allocation of power, interests, and status. As long as these arrangements are not questioned in their fundamentals, then the conditions for promoting the liberal democratic ethic are possible of attainment. It goes without saying that any community must maintain a consensus if it is to survive. The question to be explored continually, then, is what propositions must be agreed upon. The startling fact of our time is that there are fundamental propositions about the allocation of power which were sublimely taken for granted heretofore and which are now being called to the bar to defend themselves. That they have no ultimate defense is the tragedy of liberal democracy in the modern world.

Liberal democracy in America never had a politics. It was essentially an upper-middle-class and upper-class creed. Unable, through ignorance—or unwilling, because of sensibility—to make explicit its class basis, its proponents persuaded themselves that the ideology was accepted on its merits. In point of fact, it was the class and not the ideology which was accepted. Liberal democracy, the creed of that class, was the received ideology simply because the men who promulgated it were the men who had deference automatically and unquestioningly accorded to them. The liberal democratic tradition in America has had an infinitely smaller constituency than we prefer to believe. The man in the street accepted political, economic, and social arrangements the basis for which he did not in the least perceive or comprehend. If he occasionally rebelled at them, it was not for the purpose of furthering individual liberty in the liberal democratic sense; it was rather status or

Reprinted from *American Political Science Review,* 51 (December 1957), 1009–1026, by permission of the author and the American Political Science Association.

interest revolt in the name of popular or direct democracy. For if liberal democracy never had a politics it never had to have one either. The classes, which supplied the personnel for the positions of power and prestige, had the built-in means of control which exist in any stratified society. In short, the basis of power of liberal democracy has traditionally been deference to a ruling class.

I. The Class Basis of Liberal Democracy

Whether we like to admit it or not, a society which encourages the full flowering of individual liberty is, and can only be, a stratified society. Such encouragement requires a strong measure of tolerance on the part of those with power. The man in the street, as John Stuart Mill never ceased repeating, is fearful of the unusual and the idiosyncratic. It is only a secure class which can afford to set down the conditions which allow for non-conformist behavior. This means that social controls must exist which, on one side of the coin, will allow a ruling class to exercise the significant power without having to worry about the emotional insecurities of the mass of men; and, on the other, will divert the mass of men from questioning the fact that a small class has arrogated to itself the privilege of deciding what forms of behavior are to be tolerated.

For almost a century and a half, America had just such an unquestioned class. It ruled the country without having to worry about public opinion or popular emotion. And the social control which permitted this class to hold informal sway was the very traditional one of deference. Deference here is not to be thought of as an Old World retainer tugging at his forelock as the lord of the manor drives by. It means more simply that the bulk of the community defers to a small section and does not think to question that this class will hold the important positions and make the vital decisions. America has had such a class, and to it has been delegated national power in its economic, political, and social aspects. These "old" Americans possess, for the most part, some common characteristics. First of all, they are "WASPs"—in the cocktail party jargon of the sociologists. That is, they are white, they are Anglo-Saxon in origin, and they are Protestant (and disproportionately Episcopalian). To their Waspishness should be added the tendency to be located on the Eastern seaboard or around San Francisco, to be prep school and Ivy League educated, and to be possessed of inherited wealth. Talcott Parsons has generalized about such a group:

> There is a continuing tendency for earlier economic developments to leave a 'precipitate' of upper groups, the positions of whose members are founded in the achievements of their ancestors, in this case relatively recent ones. By historical necessity these groups are strongest in the older parts of the country. Hence the cities of the Eastern seaboard have tended to develop groups that are the closest approach we have—though still very different from their European equivalent—to an aristocracy. They have generally originated in business interests, but have taken on a form somewhat similar to the mercantile aristocracies of some earlier European societies, such as the Hanseatic cities.[2]

There is no point in belaboring the definitional question of whether or not this group or groups constitutes a "class." What is being said is simply that it was these people who, without serious question on anyone's part, entered, *au naturel,* the positions of power in the political and economic worlds. They provided the presidential candidates, the diplomatic personnel, the cabinet officers, the judges and influential lawyers, and the heads of the important banks, investment houses, commercial interests, and the boards of directors of many of the great corporations. They also, of course, dominated the churches and the institutions of higher learning. In short, it was this group which exercised national power. Of course, immigrants gained access to seats of municipal power quite soon; and on the frontiers of the economy trails were blazed by men who, if of old American stock, did not spring from the ruling class. But the power of the city politician was localized, and the Robber Baron was too busy on the industrial front to worry much about national politics and social arrangements. At all events, we must not overestimate the national power of the city boss or the entrepreneur, despite their flamboyant behavior and the publicity which attended it.[3] In reality, it was members of the traditional ruling group who made the decisions which set the tone and atmosphere in which American politics was to be conducted. It is, of course, true that this pool of the privileged was not a caste. Failure to possess any one of the requisites mentioned above did not debar a potential entrant. Certainly, inherited wealth did not have to go back further than one generation. Analogy with the European aristocracies is, as Parsons points out, misleading. A better comparison would be with what has been referred to in contemporary Britain as "The Establishment."[4] The basis of this group is partly family, education, and social standing; but it is also to be defined in terms of a set of position-holders, or role-players. As long as people from a narrow and specified background have virtually automatic access to the seats of power, then we are speaking of a "ruling class." When recruitment for these positions is based primarily on talent, the power inherent in the roles does not necessarily diminish, but it would be more proper to refer to an "elite." However, one of the "talents" demanded for ascendency may often be possession of the manners and attitudes acquired only through the breeding and education gained by virtue of membership in the dominant class.

At all events, nothing is lost if we refer to an old ruling class in American life. This group did not possess the corporate self-awareness of the British aristocracy. Furthermore, it would be idle to accuse its members of any conspiratorial designs. If there were common objectives and common outlooks among this ruling class, it was simply because those who belonged to it were pretty much the same kind of people. Through constant contacts in clubs, churches, boards of directors, governmental bodies, and in each others' homes, they informed one another of what was going on. But again it must be stressed that such transmission, consultation, and concert can hardly be construed as "a plot against the people." Rather it was a spontaneous—and oftentimes childlike—effort to perform the tasks and duties they sincerely believed to be theirs by right.

The spontaneous character of this activity ought to be apparent if we consider it in its ideological aspect. The promotion of liberal democracy was one of the chief endeavors of the old ruling class. This was not for the sake of that ideology's own intrinsic beauty, nor was it for the purpose of giving the mass of the community an opportunity to develop their potentialities. Rather, the idea of a limited government was for their own class benefit. The reasons for this, on the economic side, are quite clear. But in the process, this class came to defend the Bill of Rights, the common law, and the whole idea of decency, civility, and fair play—in short, the framework of liberal democracy. The judges and lawyers who came from this class were willing to interpret the Constitution in such a way that dissenters would be allowed free rein to express their thoughts. This tolerance, however, came not from any abstract love for civil liberties.[5] It is simply that the ruling class itself counted *among its own members* individuals who possessed radical views and who tended to display idiosyncratic behavior. In order to protect its own kind, it was prepared to give strength to the law by ensuring that the Bill of Rights was a living doctrine. Tolerance, therefore, was an internalized class tolerance. The Harvard atheist of good family, the transcendental rebel with manners and breeding, the Utopian socialist who paid heed to the rules of gentlemanly intercourse—these were, after all, "our kind of people" and had to be safeguarded from the coercive power both of the state and of society in general.

The whole rationale of the liberal democratic scheme—incorporating the ideas of individual liberty and limited government—was that it could work as long as it had only to protect a particular section of the community. It takes power to guarantee freedom. And the power of the ruling class was exercised only to carve out an area of freedom for its own members. On the one hand, it shaped the law so that property rights and freedom of expression would be sanctioned; on the other, it kept the emotions of the majority at bay. It is vital to take note of this because there are many who believe that the protection of the Bill of Rights ought to be extended to cover *all* men and not simply a privileged few. In abstract terms this, of course, is a worthy belief. But what must be confronted is the question of *who,* if there is no established ruling class, is to defend the liberties of the larger constituency of citizens which has developed. It must not be thought that their fellow-citizens, or the state, or even the courts are in a position to protect *any* dissident whatsoever. Certainly, in the past, the nonconformist, if he was simply an average citizen, was not so protected. This privilege was reserved for a few.

For the Constitutional gentlemen who acted as the guardians of the common law and the Bill of Rights were traditionally in a position where they could well form a bulwark around those in need of such a hedge. If the Overseers of Harvard College or the Justices of the Supreme Court wished to condone an unpopular act, the deference they commanded stood between them and the breath of popular criticism. And even if at times, the deference showed a tendency to wear thin, the established position of these lawyers, judges, educators, and businessmen in the social and economic structure gave them the ability to ignore the clamorings of the ordinary man. The ruling class, then, combined civility and power. Educated in a humane tradition, conscious of the value of free expression, and willing to protect their own sort, they shaped the instruments of law and social institutions so that at least the civil liberties of a few were protected.[6] The man on the street might well wonder at the wisdom of tolerating such behavior. But he did not consider it his province to question his exclusion from participating in making these mysterious judgments.

Furthermore, it must be stressed that the ruling class was quite conscious of the limitations on its power. It made no effort to educate the population to the *merits* of liberal democracy. Nor did it seek to protect those outside its own membership. The civil liberties of the trade union organizer in Colorado, of the Negro in Alabama, of the disabled factory worker in Pennsylvania or of the nonconformist professor of economics in a small Midwestern college—these persons were not considered proper materials for defense. Had the ruling class sought, say, to put its power behind the radicals of the I.W.W. it would have so endangered its foundation of deference that the existence of the class itself would come into question. Courts, universities, boards of directors all drew a firm line as to who would merit their help. This could not be otherwise. The dynamics of American growth let the ruling class know in no uncertain terms that its power had perceptible limitations.

It is proper, therefore, when speaking of the defense of liberal democracy to ask just *who* the defenders are. In the first century of our Republic's existence, one could readily point to these guardians: the old ruling class. Through the deference accorded to them and by virtue of their established economic power, they were able to carry the shield for those they chose to protect. The existence of these people cannot be taken for granted. Liberal democracy would have had no meaning without their intervention and interpretation. And if this class was needed to give meaning to the idea of freedom, then one has to ask how long liberal democracy can last without the presence of its protectors.

II. The New Men

It is common knowledge that the power of the old American ruling class has diminished over the past fifty years. There are at least two major reasons for the toppling of the traditional hegemony and the rise of new men of power. These are the Americanization of the immigrant and the expansion of the economy.

The deference which was accorded to the old ruling class was founded on the premise that our doors would always be open to new arrivals from Europe.[5] For this flood of immigration ensured the continued existence of a large mass of people who were, in reality, second-class citizens. To be sure, in municipal politics they might sell their votes to the machine. But above this level they would not—nor would their party bosses—think to question national leadership. This proletariat for a generation provided an acquiescent base for the old family rulers. The process is made clear in the party of the immigrant: the Democrats. Ed Flynn might boss the Bronx, but he would defer to Franklin D. Roosevelt (of Harvard); Carmine De Sapio rides behind Averill Harriman (of Yale); and Jake Arvey cleared the way for Adlai Stevenson (of Princeton). The seeming inconsonance of the fact that the party of the immigrant accepted old-stock patricians as its leaders is good evidence of the deference that was paid to the *ancien regime*. And as long as this unquestioning attitude was bolstered by the arrival of boatloads of new immigrants the old families stood secure.

More important, in many ways, was the fantastic expansion of the economy. For with tremendous expansion could go tremendous waste. There is little doubt that the old ruling class produced many brilliant leaders. But it also produced its fair share of uninspired mediocrities. A man who went effortlessly to Groton, Harvard College, and Harvard Law School then went on, without strain, to a Wall Street law firm and perhaps to a Cabinet post in time. If he had ability, it was strictly a matter of genetic probability. Yet success was not hard to achieve, for his only competition was from members of his own class. And the rules which governed this competition were those of gentlemen. The talented Harvard "poor boy," even if Protestant and Anglo-Saxon, was not urged to enter this race which was not a race. And the application of the brilliant Fordham Law School graduate was not even considered. Such an imperviousness to talent could be afforded. The rate of expansion and innovation in our economy was such that the casual, the amateur, and even the stupid in high places were cushioned by automatic profits and prestige. It was possible, and thought preferable, to have the "right" man rather than the best men. The law, for example, was conducted among gentlemen in a leisurely way. There was no imperative that the Cravath firm had to have the best tax man. Taxes, like everything else, were far simpler in those days; and at all events, it was better to preserve traditions of civility by associating with people of one's own kind. The price of tolerating mediocrity was not high; and organizational life was sufficiently cushioned so that efficiency did not have to be the chief value.

These conditions allowed the ruling class to rule, and to rule according to its own standards of what constituted meritorious leadership. As a result, these rulers were ill-instructed in the grammar of power. It is altogether explainable that we never produced a Machiavelli or a Burke to set down the rudimentary facts of political life. From Henry Adams to Woodrow Wilson to Dean Acheson, the old-stock leaders have assumed that they stood or fell on their intelligence, honesty, or administrative skill. Never did they ask the forbidden question: "*Why* should men follow me? *Me* of all people?" It took an Edmund Burke, who was always on the fringes of Britain's Establishment to see that deference to a ruling class can be maintained only by consciously fostering the sentiments of habit, custom, and prejudice. The opium of religion, and the myth of the natural superiority of prescriptive rulers, Burke said quite frankly, must be maintained in the minds and hearts of the common people if it is to be assured that they will continue to defer to their betters. Yet the American ruling class had to do without the superstitious—and feudal—basis of its European counterparts.[8] This meant that its power could last only as long as the patterns of deference held up of their own strength. And just as unrestricted immigration and an exuberantly expanding economy were its mainstays, so changes in these areas led to the decline of the old ruling class.

For once the barriers to new Americans were closed, our second-class citizenry began to disappear. With the closing off of immigration it was soon evident that a race of "pure" Americans, without benefit of hyphens, would develop. The last generations to come in during the decades before the gate clanged shut would, for a time, remain humble and deferential. But they would be the last. From then on, their children and grandchildren would become full-blooded and first-class citizens. This new citizenry would be able to take at face value the rhetoric of equality. The son of the Irish truck-driver and the grandson of the Italian shoemaker can find no compelling reason to think of themselves as other than Americans. Already the Scandinavians and the Germans have lost their ethnic identity. The Slavs and Jews are well on the way to assimilation. In a brief span, only the Negroes, Mexican-Americans, and Puerto Ricans will stand outside the pale.[9]

By all traditional lights, these new Americans are arrogant.[10] It was arrogant of the Boston Irish to want one of their own—a Curley—as their mayor rather than a Beacon Hill Brahmin. This new arrogance is coming into its own; and it is now beyond the bounds of control. No longer can deference be counted on as a means of political and social control. The old families have had to join combat with the new. No one can be sure whether it was the Secretary of the Army or the Wisconsin Senator who won the televised battle several years ago, but it is certain that for all his New England heritage, Stevens was not the hands-down victor. The point is not that the *ancien regime* had had its day. Centuries of prestige are not dashed in an hour. Rather the regime must now face the competition of classes which once knew their proper station. It can no longer count on automatic respect—or automatic anything at all.

Furthermore, our economy has reached a stage of complexity and consolidation where talent is needed and talent is rewarded. The American dream of open opportunity has extended to areas—important areas—never available before to large sections of the population. In an earlier day, as was pointed out, the Wall Street law firm did not suffer if it had something less than the best tax man. Today, however, talent is at a premium in the upper ranks of business and the professions, while sixteen years of full employment have forced employers to abandon many discriminatory bars in order to secure sufficient qualified help in respectable lower rank occupations—which may in turn afford entry to the upper ranks. And so citadels once closed to the child of the immigrant are now opening. It is vital to remind ourselves that it is only since 1940 that banks, investment houses, the diplomatic service, and established industries and universities have opened their positions of power and responsibility to others than those of old American stock. Twenty years ago Americans of Irish, Italian, Slav, and Jewish antecedents were simply not recruited, admitted, or welcomed.

All this is changing. New men, of both immigrant and old stock, are being admitted with greater frequency. Our society and our economy are more complex, more competitive, and more sophisticated. To stand the pace brought on by the complexity of the tasks we must perform, fewer and fewer organizations can afford to keep on those of mediocre competence. In fields ranging from medicine to advertising, from accounting to personnel, from educational administration to the ministry, from the foreign service to journalism—in all of these, skills are required. Even old family firms and partnerships must let in new men (hopefully a son-in-law, but usually not). For without these hands, the ship will surely founder in highly competitive waters. The new men are energetic. They have to be, and they have had to be. But the expenditure of this energy is at a price. The psychic cost is high. For the man who has had to run, to push, and to fight develops an outlook towards himself and towards society quite at variance from that of the man who has easily had power and responsibility thrust upon him.

The *ancien regime* was a leisure class. To be sure, many of its members toiled mightily in the vineyard. But their upbringing and even their adult years were devoid of the pressures imposed on the new men of today. That leisure enabled them to study—not necessarily in a formal, but often in a disciplined, way—the responsibilities and obligations which were to be theirs. The lawyer had, of course, to serve his client. But he was able to serve the common law and the Constitution at the same time. The educational administrator took seriously the claims of "useless" scholarship as well as those of useful preparation for life. In short, men of leisure were able to regard their power as an instrument for transmitting traditional values as well as an instrument for performing particular tasks at hand.[11] These values were sustained by a class which could ignore the demands of career-building and organizational competition. For it is plain enough that there is all too frequently a conflict between, let us say, defending the Bill of Rights and earning a dollar or winning a vote. Simple exhortation is not enough to lead a man to strike a blow for the one at the risk of losing the other. He must first be sure that he is in a position to make a short-run sacrifice for the long-term good.

The new men are not cushioned either by status or by private incomes. If we ask the newly arrived man—who, let it be said, is never completely sure that he has arrived—to take a stand on fundamental liberties, we are asking too much of him. One may, with good reason, demand that a Senator from an old Cincinnati family or a Boston lawyer of wealth and standing stake a claim in defense of the First Amendment. But to ask this of a bright young politician from California or an engineer who has risen through the ranks of an automobile company is asking the impossible. The distinction is not one of character or personality. What distinguishes a Taft from a Nixon is what separates the old from the new men. As Shils point out, the new

> American elites in business, politics, publicity and learning tend to come great geographical distances from the places of their birth to the places where they work and achieve. The great size of the country makes the loss of local ties in the leadership of the country a common phenomenon. Moreover, the cultures, the professional and social milieu into which the newly ascended leaders come, do not ordinarily possess powerful traditions which impose themselves firmly on most new-comers. There is no aristocratic or gentry pattern of life to which newcomers can clearly aspire and which they can definitely assimilate.[12]

The new men have neither family nor wealth nor geographical ties to support them. They have only their talent. And the talent must be a "marketable" one: it must accommodate itself to the demands of customers, voters, and colleagues. The *ancien regime* did not have to worry about the market. Either the customer-voter would docilely take what was offered; or, if he had the presumption to refuse the offering, he could be ignored with impunity.

The objective needs of the man in the street have not changed over the years. It is doubtful if he is more tolerant of the unusual or unknown than was his grandfather. What has changed is the fact that more and more of our men of power *must* be directed in their actions by these popular demands, whims, and caprices. We are entering a more perfect democracy in that the customer-voter is now, more than ever before, "always right." The new lawyer, for instance, is not so secure that he can ignore the wishes of his clients. Neither is the new broker or corporation president or university professor. And the stark fact is that a larger and larger proportion of market demands, be they economic or social or political, are in conflict with the traditional values of liberal democracy. The law has ceased to be a profession and has become an arm of our corporate economy. The chief reason for this transformation is to be found in the new lawyers, who know full well that they have no personal choice other than to serve their clients. The modern university cannot be expected to hold up the flag of liberal education against the cries of students—and their future employers—for vocational or pre-professional training. The few institutions which hold out for the traditional values can do so because they are so prestigious and so financially cushioned that they can ignore market demands. But to think that the small New England college will set the future standard for the new campuses of state universities being created in the middle and far west is wishful thinking. While many professors at such campuses might like to follow such a lead, their institution cannot afford to. More and more they will be forced to imitate, and with success, the pattern set by a Michigan State University. What the defenders of liberal education fail to concern themselves with are the structural conditions under which such education—and institutions imparting such education—can flourish. The first condition is internal strength: and power to do the right is hardly bestowed by exhortation. For strength is the strength to ignore the market. Is there not a high positive correlation between size of endowment and whether or not a private institution kept on a professor who pleaded the Fifth Amendment? Today neither the institutions, nor the professors, nor the students, are in a position to tell the consuming public to go to the devil.

America, then, is more democratic than ever before. Careers are open to the talents, and not by virtue of an Horatio Alger-like break. But the new men of power have, in their climb, had no time to develop a sense of responsibility toward what have been our traditional standards—our liberal democratic values. Furthermore, these new men are always personally insecure. They cannot rely on traditional patterns of deference to maintain their power. For they have no family ties or inherited wealth to bolster their careers. But what is more crucial is that deference to the old ruling class has all but ceased to exist in the popular mind. Indeed, just as the new men show small respect for the family connections of those they have joined, so this attitude is spreading throughout society.[13] Despite the fact that we live in a period of prosperity, there is a slackening indulgence of the old rich. Those who are admired are those on their way up. Talent—especially talent in "human relations"—is what is held up as the noteworthy achievement.

But if the new men are admired, they are admired only for the duration of the popular appeal which they evoke for their personal performances. As individuals, the new men cannot be said to command deference in the traditional sense of that word. This means, as will be seen, that they must seek other forms of control. The members of the *ancien regime,* who were habitually deferred to simply because of their class connection, never had to concern themselves with control. They ruled; they were obeyed. Their interest was in administration and the pursuit of the right as they saw it. The new men, on the other hand, have been given the instrument of power without a built-in form of control. It is not guaranteed to them that habitual deference will be accorded by those over whom they must exercise power. This potentially anarchic situation necessitates the calling forth of a set of political arrangements far different from those found in traditional societies. The theories of John Locke and John Stuart Mill are not of much use here. What must be called forth is the Machiavellian prescription, as old as Thrasymachus and as new as the latest public relations handbook. For the new men are only able to rule because of what they *do*—not because of what they *are.* The new men are not anything as individuals. All they possess is their wits. For this reason they must think constantly of ways in which to achieve not the deference of the man in the street, for that is impossible to acquire in our age, but simply his obedience.

III. From Deference to Manipulation

It is the constant effort at gaining consent which explains the importance of public relations and the use of communications media in modern politics. No longer can a would-be leader or his organization assume continual deference on the part of the public. Control cannot be taken for granted, it must be engineered at every juncture. What we have, then, is the replacement of social control by means of deference with social control by manipulation. Whereas in the past, the man in the street habitually followed those situated above him in the social structure, today, because the barriers of the old structure have crumbled, our men of power must consciously and premeditatedly condition those who fall beneath them.[14]

The rise of professional public relations and the development of sophisticated communication techniques, while fascinating as subjects of study in and for themselves, must be viewed in perspective. The "engineering of consent" is necessary on the part of the new men simply because the obedience of the man in the street cannot be taken for granted, nor even less left to chance. The managers of a great corporation, for example, cannot assume that the public will feel that what is good for the corporation will be good for the country. Instead, the managers will have to work overtime conditioning underlying attitudes so that the community will not bring itself to the point where it might question the mode of operation, or even the very existence, of the company. The same is true of trade, professional, and other powerful organizations. The chief aim of public relations is to throw sand in the public's eyes. Talk about scientific progress rather than profits. Talk about ownership by millions of stockholders rather than the power of a few managers. Talk about the success stories of the fortunate few rather than the thwarted ambitions of those left behind. And, most important, talk of the institution as if the decision of its managers contained no element of power, but rather were the natural and rational outcome of an overriding desire to serve consumers. The principal technique of public relations, then, is never to discuss a case on its own merits. In fact, the highest desideratum is to persuade the public that the organization has no power whatsoever. The body in question is to be viewed purely as a service entity: rather like a national Lion's Club. It should be known by its immediate products—the dashing style of the automobile, the polite voice of the telephone operator—and not by its power as a social institution.

That the public is susceptible to manipulation such as this ought not to be surprising. There is no good reason to suppose that the average American citizen of our time is any more able to withstand such organized powers of persuasion than any other average person in history has been able to exempt himself from the exercise of concerted manipulative power. Nor does the practice of manipulation render this country any less a democracy. Democracy describes a system based on the free consent of the governed. If this consent is engineered, it certainly does not make it any the less consent. And it is doubtful if it is any the less free for its being the product of manipulation. To be sure, there is a difference between liberal democracy and what is coming to be called "mass" democracy. But inasmuch as the former variety is dependent on the unquestioned authority of the old ruling class we have discussed, it ought to be clear that as an ideology it is increasingly anachronistic. What must concern us, therefore, is the consequences to liberal democracy inherent in the coming mass democracy.[15]

First of all, it must be noted that there has not been any widening or deepening of the basis of power in America. Rather, power has been transferred from one group to another. That is, with the descent from exclusive power of the old ruling class, and the concomitant necessity of sharing their power with the new elite, it cannot be argued that the public at large has gained anything in the process. All that can be said is that where once, because of ingrained habit and custom, he consented to arrangements by reason of deference, now, because of conscious and premeditated conditioning, he consents to arrangements by reason of manipulation. The factors operating on him are different. But his powerlessness remains constant. The average American of our day gives his consent not to prescription and the works of men long dead, but to a system of power which is controlled by men who are alive and among us. Both deference and manipulation are similar in that they are control. Both permit a few men to rule many men.

The American public, then, is kept content with congenial work, a feeling of participation, a high pattern of consumption, and the general belief that they live in the best of all possible societies. Such a public can be led to a state of satisfaction with its other-directed—non-economic, non-political—existence.[16] This public is composed of those who have neither the talent nor the will to compete for positions of control. They remain where they are, not because they are discriminated against, but because they prefer the easy life. These are, in short, the organization men. And they are not much different from the little men who have populated the streets of a thousand lands since the dawn of history.[17]

Of more concern to us are the exceptions—the new men of power—who rise above the happy and placid life of the engineered existence. The new men who should command our attention are not the run of the mill organization men.[18] Rather, they are the engineers. The new engineer is not simply a modern Henry Ford, a wizard with an assembly line and a part-time tinkerer with watches. Rather, he applies the principles of his calling—and he probably does not regard them as principles—to the order of human as well as material resources. Ever pragmatic, he is willing to learn and develop new techniques the better to accomplish the job at hand. Human engineering, therefore, becomes his major consideration. Not simply the workers at the bench, but higher managers must be treated like fragile mechanisms: their egos must be pampered lest the workings of the whole machine go awry. The feeling of participation, the feeling of being consulted, the feeling of self-esteem—all of these must be nurtured if the optimum output is to be achieved.[19] The science of committee procedure, the catalyst of modern management, is the skill most demanded of the human engineer. All must be allowed to believe that they are part of the team, be it the informal-turned-formal group on the factory floor, or the board of directors itself. These principles, too, are applied to the areas of community relations and public relations. People must be managed. They are not intractable; but their pliability must not be approached too facilely. Human resources can be controlled. However it is a full-time task and few if any of its aspects can be taken for granted.

IV. Conclusion

The new engineers are the focus of power in the emerging American society. They are the ones who have replaced the old ruling class. They are not a class in the old sense, although they are developing into an "Establishment" along a number of significant lines. The new men stand, furthermore, in stark contrast to the tens of thousands of well-rounded, well-adjusted people in middle-management. We know a little about how they differ from their immediate subordinates in terms of personality characteristics. We know a little about how they, rather than others, are recruited for the top echelons. But by and large we must rest content with saying that, as in all ages, they take the leading positions because they are best able to deal with the particular problems at hand. Foxes rather than lions, to use Pareto's distinction, they can meet the imperatives of a time which calls for the sophisticated manipulation of men's attitudes and sensibilities.[20] This minority is the key to American politics and society. Its members are not so much typical as prototypical of the new men who are found not only in industry, but in politics and the military. They are aware of the need for, and familiar with the ways to achieve, control. Controllers rather than controlled, they find their own satisfactions in their careers and in providing the happiness of others. Unlike David Riesman's egoistic "saving remnant," this group does not flee from responsibility.[21] It dimly understands that its role is the important one. The new men must forfeit their own happiness and serve the happiness of a public which cannot and will not plan its own existence. The new men work overtime at their job; they develop ulcers and nervous tensions; they neglect their families, outside interests, and the pursuit of culture. But they do their task with imagination and vigor. It is no understatement to say that they are carrying the rest of us on their backs.

The new men are our new rulers. They are intelligent, but not cultured. They are tolerant in informal social relations, but they have no compassion for those who are subject to political injustice. The American tradition, for them, probably began in 1945. Values are judged not by their place in the prescriptive scheme of things, but by their current utility. For the new men it would be suicide to regard individuals as ends in themselves: they must always be viewed as resources to be managed. Liberty deals not with freedom of expression or with protection from tyranny by the state: rather it is the complex of conditions under which organizational ends can be pursued and organizational order maintained. And truth becomes an image of the world which ordinary men are capable of comprehending without too much strain on their imaginations.

These definitions obviously appear anomalous. But this is simply because the words are the vocabulary of liberal democracy and their content is not. With the rise of the new men the conditions necessary for liberal democracy have seen their day. This means that we must turn to a new set of prescriptions. The focus must be on control and the controllers.[22] The "Legend of the Grand Inquisitor" —*with* its stress on responsibility— has more meaning in prescriptive terms than the legend of the town meeting. The controllers are not men without souls. They are not philistines by nature. And there is good reason to believe that, in time, they can be civilized. But at this point they are simply busy. And if, in their furious activity, they are unknowingly breaking the idols of liberal democracy, we ought to think twice before we complain. For the new men are the products of equality of opportunity. If we *really* believe that careers ought to be open to the talents, regardless of background or adherence to traditional values, then we must accept the new ascendency with a good grace.

NOTES

1. "Liberal democracy," for present purposes, must be defined briefly and arbitrarily. It describes both an ideology and an institutional system; and its appeal is to those who claim to be fearful alike of the consequences of elite rule and of direct democracy. Both ideology and institutions, therefore, postulate a dynamic equilibrium between two values: (1) majority rule and human equality, *i.e.,* that each shall count for one in political arrangements and that self-government, with the majority decision prevailing, is the best government; and (2) individual rights and constitutional guarantees, *i.e.,* that there shall be an optimum area in which neither government nor society shall interfere with the individual in his pursuit of activities he thinks good. Both these values, Liberal Democrats postulate, are crucial: neither must be allowed to overwhelm the other. The means by which a majority is to be brought to respect minorities, and the areas in which individuals are to be left unhindered, as well as the methods for ensuring that in "proper" cases a majority shall have its way—these questions are open to constant discussion, compromise, and accommodation. This creed seems to be the received doctrine among academic political scientists; and the juxtaposition of majority rule and individual liberty is the alpha and omega of most introductory courses and textbooks. For the definitive exposition, see J. Roland Pennock, *Liberal Democracy: Its Merits and Prospects* (New York, 1950).

2. "Social Strains in America," in Daniel Bell, ed., *The New American Right* (New York, 1955), p. 125.
3. The American mythology, of course, is that most nineteenth-century businessmen were shrewd, ill-tutored freewheelers like Jay Gould and Daniel Drew. In fact, studies in entrepreneurial history show that, for the most part, the men who headed the great enterprises were from a privileged background. See Mabel Newcomer, *The Big Business Executive* (New York, 1955), and W. Lloyd Warner and James C. Abegglen, *Big Business Leaders in America* (New York, 1955). For an evaluation and comparison of these studies, see Morroe Berger, "The Business Elite: Then and Now," "*Commentary,* Vol. 22 (October, 1956), pp. 367–74.
4. See Henry Fairlie, "Political Commentary," *Spectator,* Vol. 195 (September 23, 1955), pp. 379–81; and (October 21, 1955), pp. 516–17.
5. This point has been well made by John Roche in his "Communication" in the *American Political Science Review,* Vol. 51 (June, 1957), pp. 484–88. Roche also discusses the lack of a libertarian strand in the American tradition in his excellent articles, "We've Never Had More Freedom," *New Republic,* Vol. 134 (January 23, 1956), pp. 12–15; (January 30, 1956), pp. 13–16; and (February 6, 1956), pp. 13–15. If it seems outrageous to suggest that a ruling class was only concerned with keeping its own children out of trouble, a recent example may bring this unwelcome truth home. Contrast, for a moment, the reaction of the upper-middle-class liberal to the indictment, trial, and conviction of Alger Hiss, on the one hand, and of the Rosenbergs, on the other. In terms of the overall record, there may be equal reason to wonder at the justice of both convictions. Yet the good people who were (and still are) much aroused about the treatment of Hiss seem to find it difficult to worry about the Rosenbergs, or Morton Sobell. Would it be too much to suggest that this is because Hiss was one of the "right people"—in terms of stock, education, manner, etc.,—whereas the Rosenbergs were not? There are, of course, all sorts of complicating factors which bedevil a comparison of the two cases. Yet in light of the contemporary liberal reaction—or lack of it—to the plight of the Rosenbergs, perhaps the limited civil liberties vistas of the old ruling class become more plausible.
6. For a good statement of the tone and propriety which developed under the aegis of gentlemanly politics, see Edward Shils' chapter entitled, significantly, "The Deformation of Civility," in his *The Torment of Secrecy* (Glencoe, Illinois, 1956), pp. 153–175: "As long as the political ruling classes were recruited from the aristocracy or from the classes whose conduct was guided by an aristocratic ideal of life, there was an inevitable diffuseness in their range of interest and in their attitude towards their major tasks. The aristocrat was expected to act like a gentleman, to be interested in the administration of his estate, to be interested in sports and proficient in military skills, and he was naturally expected to take his place in the government of the country, locally and nationally" (p. 156).
7. There has been surprisingly little written by political scientists on the political implications of the Americanization process. The task appears to have been left to journalists and members of other academic disciplines. Samuel Lubell's *The Future of American Politics* (New York, 1952) and *The Revolt of the Moderates* (New York, 1956) are good essays in casual empiricism. William S. White's " 'Consensus American': A Portrait" in *The New York Times Magazine* (November 25, 1956) is an interesting attempt at a theory. Perhaps the best analyses (brilliant when read individually and chaotic when read at one sitting) are the papers by Peter Viereck, David Riesman, Richard Hofstadter, Seymour Lipset, Nathan Glazer, Talcott Parsons, and Daniel Bell in *The New American Right, op. cit.* While this book is a discussion of the McCarthyite-nativist fringe, much of the analysis can be applied to a far larger segment of the American population.
8. Louis Hartz, *The Liberal Tradition in America* (New York, 1955).
9. Even the assimilation pattern of Jews—long thought a special case—is going according to form. See Oscar Handlin, "What Will U.S. Jewry Be Like in 2000?", *The National Jewish Monthly,* Vol. 71, No. 9 (May, 1957), pp. 5, 32–33. And for a glimpse of the way middle-class Negroes are preparing themselves for the immersion, see E. Franklin Frazier, *Black Bourgeoisie* (Glencoe, Illinois, 1957).
10. "Arrogance" is certainly the word which comes immediately to mind when one

reads, say, Peter Viereck's *The Unadjusted Man* (Boston, 1956), or Walter Lippman's *The Public Philosophy* (Boston, 1955). It is the view of both "conservative" and "liberal" liberal democrats that humility ought to be the most noticeable characteristic of the man in the street. However, Viereck's flaming indictment of direct democracy ends up being not so much clarion as pathetic. Down deep, Viereck must know that the ruling class he so respects will never again command the deference of the American public.

11. To be sure, there were free-wheeling entrepreneurs, who lived on the frontiers of our economy in the nineteenth century, and who had no sense of responsibility to society or to posterity in the prescriptive sense. And no one expected them to. But we must not overestimate their numbers (see the references above, note 3); and we must also recall that many of them, like Rockefeller and Harriman, founded family dynasties. Thus a John D. Rockefeller, Jr. was put in a position where he could serve his fellow men in conservationist and philanthropic endeavors. And the five grandsons have carried on the "tradition" from Latin America to Winrock, Arkansas. The family character of nineteenth century and early twentieth century enterprise made it possible for these families to develop responsible second and third generations. Today's men of power have little opportunity to do this for their sons. This means that each successive industrial ruler is, in a real sense, a self-made man. Each one has made the climb himself and in doing this has not had the leisure or security to develop a sense of *noblesse oblige* which, some might wish, would inform his exercise of power. See Daniel Bell, "The Break-Up of Family Capitalism," *Partisan Review*, Vol. 24 (Spring, 1957), pp. 317–20.

12. *Op. cit.*, p. 79. A number of recent novels juxtapose the new and the old men quite neatly. Louis Auchincloss's *The Great World and Timothy Colt* (Boston, 1956) shows how a Wall Street law firm undergoes this transition in its leading personnel. The senior partner, a venerable figure on the style of Oliver Wendell Holmes, is forced to admit to partnership a Fordham Law School graduate. The latter has not one iota of feeling for the legal profession's prescriptive responsibilities (we can just imagine what *his* response would be if he were asked to defend a Communist under a Smith Act indictment); but he is highly skilled in bringing in the kind of business a large firm needs to survive. When the patrician dies, it is inevitable that the new man will take over complete charge. The firm will be successful; but success will be judged by an entirely different standard. The legal ethic of the old regime will be looked on as a curiosity; perhaps a worthy relic, but hardly attuned to modern needs. On the other side of the street, Cameron Hawley's *Cash McCall* (Boston, 1955) shows just how the new manipulator is capable of meeting problems which are totally incomprehensible to the old-style businessman. It is significant that when the editors of *Business Week* gave this book to several top executives to read and asked them to discuss the "moral problem" raised by the existence of Cash, most of them saw nothing unusual in his activities—but if there was, it could be remedied by changing the current tax laws! No. 1372 (December 17, 1955), pp. 104–114.

13. That traditional American class relationships have little meaning not only to the man-in-the-street, but also to his wife in the split-level house, is brought out by Elizabeth Janeway in her review of Diana Barrymore's *Too Much, Too Soon* in *The New York Times Book Review*, April 7, 1957. Miss Janeway was commenting on what is wanted in novel-reading today: "Today's mass audience finds fiction hard going. Very few people, I think, really read for escape; most readers are anxious to learn about the world and their place in it. But the old mythology of class and social relationship on which the novel has relied for the last two hundred years is neither interesting nor pertinent to the mass audience, for the mass audience stands outside that crumbling structure. . . . The ordinary members of 'the lonely crowd' need stories which will help them understand and control their lives, they need signposts to behavior and meaning as much as men always have. And a new mythology is consequently being created for them. Like all mythologies in the beginning, it is based on particular events. When the reader asks, 'Did this really happen?' it is able to reply, 'Oh yes, it did. I really knew this Unforgettable Character. This is a direct quote from Marilyn Monroe.' "

14. See, for example, Stanley Kelley, *Professional Public Relations and Political Power* (Baltimore, 1956) and Vance Packard, *The Hidden Persuaders* (New York, 1957).

Both of these studies show that when expert technicians work from a basis of power, persuasion can be effectively engineered on a mass scale. The elements of manufactured obedience are well outlined in Edward Bernays, ed., *The Engineering of Consent* (Norman, Oklahoma, 1955). However, it is a big mistake to overestimate the extent to which people can be influenced from a long distance. Penetration can be deeper, and hence more lasting and effective, if it is conducted on the individual or small-group level. For there the processes of persuasion can be especially tailored to the needs of the individual person who is the object of attack. Certainly, the small-group approach is the basis of the "human relations" techniques in industry and the effectiveness of psychotherapy rests on its person-to-person relationship. For a discussion of the latter, see my "A Political Scientist Looks at Psychotherapy," *The International Journal of Social Psychiatry,* Vol. 2 (Summer, 1956), pp. 23–33.

15. The changing character of democracy in our century has been the chief concern of such writers as E. H. Carr and C. Wright Mills. Carr is concerned with the shift in ideological underpinning which has accompanied the transition from "individualism" to "mass democracy," *The New Society* (London, 1951), ch. 4; and Mills, in what is certainly the most important chapter of his much misunderstood *The Power Elite* (New York, 1956), discusses the differences between a "public" and a "mass" as the human raw materials for a democratic society. For liberal democracy required, as a citizenry, a "public." But as mass characteristics infuse this public, so a liberal democracy is transformed into a mass democracy. The citizen of the latter society must be managed by his rulers rather than be led by his leaders. Hence there arises the need for a "power elite" which comes into being not because of the lust for power on the part of its individual members, but because such a group is ready to perform certain functions which society requires (ch. 13). Neither Mills nor Carr goes into the dynamics which transform a public into a mass. A good analysis of this process, in economic and psychological terms, is to be found in Erich Fromm's *The Sane Society* (New York, 1955). See, in particular, his discussion of alienation, at pp. 120–52.
16. The starkest fact—for students of politics—in the spate of sociological essays now appearing, is the acquiescent *powerlessness* of the people who inhabit the emerging middle-class. For the members of the lonely crowd, politics is a spectator sport; for the organization men, patterns of life and work are determined by an amoral institution; for the exurbanite, participation is social or civic, rather than partisan; and for all, the fruits of a surfeit of honey are sufficient exchange for removal from the decision-making process. See David Riesman, *The Lonely Crowd* (New Haven, 1950); William H. Whyte, Jr., *The Organization Man* (New York, 1956); A. C. Spectorsky, *The Exurbanites* (Philadelphia, 1955); Russell Lynes, *A Surfeit of Honey* (New York, 1957). To be sure, these people have power in the very special sense that they compel decision-makers to frame policies in such a way that they will be acceptable to the "market" (be it economic, political, or social). But the consequence is that decision-makers strive to *anticipate* reactions rather than waiting for the political-economic "customer" to make his wishes known.
17. If we claim that the average man of our time is content with the amenities of his placid, middle-class existence, we must also go on to insist that he is, in point of fact, soft. He has little in the way of internal strength and he possesses few resources—either material or psychic—of his own. The fact that these people are willing to allow themselves to be carried is made clear in an episode in Sloan Wilson's *The Man in the Grey Flannel Suit* (New York, 1955). Hopkins, the ulcerous network president, finally states an unpleasant fact of life to Tom Rath, the nice young man who wants to take it easy: " 'Somebody has to do the big jobs! This world was built by men like me! To really do a job, you have to live it body and soul! You people who just give half your mind to your work are riding on our backs!' "
18. Standing out like a sore thumb in *The Organization Man* is the chapter called "The Executive: Non-Well-Rounded Man." (ch. 11) Here we are allowed a glimpse of the top three men in the nation's 300 largest corporations. Their lives and personalities present a sharp contrast to those of the middle-management men depicted in the remainder of the book. One wonders if, in fact, the well-adjusted organization men will be recruited into the highest echelon at all.

19. The classic statement is Russell Davenport, "The Greatest Opportunity on Earth," *Fortune,* Vol. 40 (October, 1949), pp. 65ff. See also Alpheus T. Mason's analysis of this trend, "Business Organized as Power," the *American Political Science Review,* Vol. 44 (June, 1950), pp. 323–42.
20. For an elaboration, see my "Utopia, Inc.," *The Commonweal,* Vol. 65 (February 8, 1957), pp. 479–81.
21. This is the title of an essay in *Individualism Reconsidered* (Glencoe, Illinois, 1954), pp. 99–120. Riesman tells the would-be autonomous or self-directed man to find his satisfactions in highly personalized activities. Indeed, it is rather difficult to discover the difference between "autonomy," which Riesman thinks good, and "marginal differentiation," which Riesman implies is rather hollow. The solution-via-abdication is illustrated in Ernst Pawel's novel, *The Dark Tower* (New York, 1957), where the hero concludes that he cannot meet the standard of success in his corporation or the standard of good citizenship in his suburb, and hence packs up his family and finds a country-editor job for himself in the Rockies. The point about the new men is that, unlike Pawel's hero, they find their brand of autonomy by attaining the heights where they can exercise power within the framework of the organization. The climb may, in one sense, appear to be morally and intellectually debilitating. But in another it can be viewed as the only road to freedom in today's society.
22. A fascinating attempt to evolve a new set of prescriptions for a new society and a new citizenry is to be found in the work of B. F. Skinner. The whole of his philosophy is in his Utopian novel, *Walden Two* (New York, 1948). A briefer statement is his "Freedom and Control of Man" in *The American Scholar,* Vol. 25 (Winter, 1955–56), pp. 47–65. Also of value is a two-man symposium between Skinner and Carl R. Rogers, in which Skinner defends his ideas against a variety of criticisms: "Some Issues Concerning the Control of Human Behavior," *Science,* Vol. 124 (November 30, 1956), pp. 1057–66.

8

Welfare Liberalism and Social Change

TOM HAYDEN

In the excerpt that follows, Tom Hayden argues that American welfare liberalism is incapable of fundamental reform. Social legislation during the past thirty years may have improved the quality of American life, but most reforms have proven to be, in his words, either "illusory or token." In reality, he says, the trend is toward more racial segregation and greater disparity between the rich and the poor.

The failures of welfare liberalism are also reflected in a foreign policy that internationalizes inequality and exploitation. American intervention in Vietnam, as in other countries around the world, has thwarted the possibility for genuine reform and social change. He concludes that welfare liberalism at home and abroad are techniques for co-opting the discontented and preventing revolutionary change.

Hayden, formerly a student at the University of Michigan, is one of the original organizers of the radical Students for a Democratic Society. He has also been active in the civil rights movement as a worker in the rural South and the urban northern ghetto.

I

Americans find it unthinkable that their country can be corrupt at the center, guilty as a society of inhuman

From *The Great Society Reader*, edited by Marvin E. Gettleman and David Mermelstein, pp. 477-501.

behavior. This is true even among American reformers, most of whom hold that discrimination, poverty, and foreign intervention are simply flaws in a generally humanitarian record. While the massacre of the Vietnamese grinds on, while Negro uprisings spread to every city, while the public looks back on August 6 as Luci's wedding and Hiroshima is forgotten, the progressive American—he may be a liberal businessman, university president, technical assistance expert, or trade unionist—is perhaps uneasy but remains basically complacent, secure in the justness of our objectives at home and abroad.

Since early in the century, the task of American leaders has been to make "peace," "self-determination" and the promise of a better life the language that explains American purposes. Probably none of them has ever willfully deprived a man of food or killed another in cold blood; they order political and economic suppression and murder—by gas, napalm, or nuclear weapons—only as a means of realizing peace and preserving democracy.

Until the day their language changes to that of naked power, it is easy to assume they are not fiends but honorable men. This is the assumption that makes reformers hope for their country. But it is sheer indulgence not to confront the consequences of our leaders' actions. We need to stop giving weight to protestations of good intentions, and to examine instead the worth of American words in the light of American deeds.

The general contradiction most worth examining is between the philosophy and the practice of the liberal-welfare state that has been constructed at home and is now being forcibly exported to other parts of the world. It is the belief in our commitment to welfare that, more than anything else, allows our honorable men to sleep at night while other men are murdered, jailed or hungry.

II

The legitimacy gained by the industrial unions, the welfare legislation passed in the thirties and forties, and now the civil rights and antipoverty reforms of the sixties—these are seen as part of a long sweep toward a society of economic and social justice. But there is, in fact, little evidence to justify the view that the social reforms of the past thirty years actually improved the quality of American life in a lasting way, and there is much evidence which suggests that many of the reforms gained were illusory or token, serving chiefly to sharpen the capacity of the system for manipulation and oppression.

Look closely at the social legislation upon which the notion of domestic improvement is based. The Wagner Act was supposed to effect unionization of workers; but today the unionized labor force is shrinking with the automation of the mass-production industries, and millions of other workers, never organized, are without protection. The Social Security laws were supposed to support people in distress, but today many are still not covered, and those who are solely dependent on Social Security payments cannot make ends meet. Unemployment compensation policies were supposed to aid men in need of jobs, but today many are still without coverage, while benefits represent a smaller and smaller share of the cost of living. The Employment Act of 1946 was supposed to guarantee federal action to provide a job for every American who needed one, but in 1966 the official (understated) unemployment rate is close to 5 per cent, and may be over 30 per cent for young men in the ghettos. The 1949 Public Housing Act, sponsored by conservative Robert Taft, was to create 800,000 low-cost units by 1953, but today less than half that number have been constructed, and many of them are beyond reach of the poor. The difficult struggle to enact even a token policy of public medical care, the hollow support for public education, the stagnation and starvation of broader programs for health, recreation and simple city services—all this suggests that the welfare state is more machinery than substance.

The trend is *toward,* not away from, increased racial segregation and division, greater unemployment for Negroes than whites, worse educational facilities in the slums, less job security for whites, fewer doctors for nearly everyone: in essence, the richest society in all history places increasing pressures on its "have nots" despite all talk of the "welfare state" and "Great Society." The real subsidies go to the housebuilders, farmers, businessmen, scholars, while comparatively, there are only scraps for the poor. The welfare recipient who cannot purchase decent furniture will not take much comfort in knowing she is one of the "richest" poor people in the world. America's expanding affluence is still built on a system of deep inequalities.

The quality of the welfare state is well illustrated by the sluggish way it responds to pressure for modest civil rights reform. It required the slaughter of little girls, a bloodbath in Montgomery and Birmingham, Southern racist violence against Northern whites—students and ministers—an outbreak of Negro rebellion across the North, and the organization of an independent political party in Mississippi before the Administration and Congress began to move on the civil rights front. But even that gave little hope of real progress. The 1965 Civil Rights Bill actually shrinks the legitimate power of the federal government.[1] Under the law, the call for concrete action remains an option of the Attorney General; the burden of proof and time-consuming procedures is placed on local Negroes; no effective protection is provided civil rights workers against violence and intimidation. The rejection by Congress of the 1966 bill must be interpreted as a reflection of the national mood toward further change.

Seen in this context, the 1965 antipoverty program should evoke little optimism. The amount of money allotted is a pittance, and most of it is going to local politicians, school boards, welfare agencies, housing authorities, professional personnel and even the police; its main thrust is to shore up sagging organizational machinery, not to offer the poor a more equitable share of income and influence. Meaningful involvement of the poor is frustrated by the poverty planners' allegiance to existing local power centers. In reality, the poor only flavor the program. A few are co-opted into it, but only as atomized individuals. They do not have independent organizational strength, as do the machines and social agencies.[2]

Some of the more sophisticated poverty planners believe that the involvement of the poor is essential to effective programs; thus the heavy emphasis on, and debate about, the need for "maximum feasible participation" of the poor. This policy concept rests upon the conviction that the modern poor cannot be socialized upward and into the mainstream of American life in the tradition of the earlier immigrants.

The slavery period has left the Negro poor, according to this view, without the tight-knit culture, the economic skills, and the expanding market opportunities that were so common in the life of the immigrants. The result is the breakdown of the family, at least in its function of preparing the young to take their places in the slots offered by the established industrial machine.

Though it is not officially put this way, the poverty program thus seeks to be a substitute parent more than a meal ticket, an agency of socialization more than of welfare. Not only is this the conception that underlies the Job Corps camps and the new batteries of "psychological service" counsellors; it underlies the Community Action Program as well.

Self-organization, the development of skills, helping oneself through social action, are supposedly the means by which the ghetto residents ("the target population") will be rehabilitated. The amount and kind of conscious stress on this process vary from city to city. One view is evident in testimony given to a congressional subcommittee by Denton Brooks, director of the Chicago antipoverty program. Asked whether the tactics of conflict, such as rent strikes, might be necessary for progress, his answer was negative for this reason:

> Once you get the interaction of all groups, once you have a policy that something should be done for the poor, once this becomes a national policy, then you work on a problem and find a positive solution. *Then the need for protest is eliminated.*[2]

The practical impact of such policies was explained by Father Theodore R. Gibson, assigned as federal trouble-shooter for Newark in the summer of 1965. Gibson was convinced that the antipoverty program was the key to racial peace in Newark this summer. . . . "All the things I saw that would make for trouble got their answer in the antipoverty program," asserted the Community Relations Service representative. "What saved the community more than anything else was the involvement of so many people in so many things. *Even members of the most militant groups," he said, "were so busy working on antipoverty projects that they had little time to stir up dissension.*"[3]

Many of the poverty planners concede that progress will involve some element of conflict and that the poor cannot be painlessly assimilated into the greater society. The feeling is that change can be accomplished through a "dialogue" between the poor and the powerful, in which the poor assert their needs as clearly as necessary. But while dialogue is promoted, final decisions remain in traditional hands. Sargent Shriver encourages "representative neighborhood advisory organizations" to give "advice on programs," which can then be "channeled" to the community action agency. This is all Shriver sees as necessary to give neighborhood people "an effective voice in the conduct and administration of neighborhood-based programs."[4]

The poverty program, in short, assumes the poor are groups of damaged individuals who need charity, relief, technical aid, or retraining. What the program cannot accept is the possibility that the poor are "natives" pitted against "colonial" structures at home that exclude and exploit them. One such "native" in Newark is Mrs. Joanne Robinson who made the following definitive comment after her first antipoverty meeting:

> It seemed to me the meeting was run by politicians, whereas I thought it should

> be run by the poor people themselves. I didn't feel free to stand up and say anything really. It was as if they wanted who they knew in, and no strangers. If you join something, you want to feel part of it, and the people at the poverty meeting just didn't give you a chance to feel part of it. It was like you're an outsider looking in.

Welfare liberalism has brought new insecurities to the American exploited. The poor are without the effective ability to control any economic resources in the welfare state. Antipoverty funds are controlled "from above" by city or federal officials. There is no unionization of tenants or welfare clients to provide financing and protection. Unable to gather independent capital from the public sector, the poor are considered unqualified for credit by banks and lending institutions. This lack of meaningful economic power divides the contemporary poor from earlier immigrant generations, who entered an expanding economy and formed unions and co-ops to advance their interests. Lacking any security or power, the "left out" whites and the poor Negroes are more likely to vote for their "masters"—those who control the public housing, welfare, and unemployment checks—or not vote at all, rather than risk an independent political initiative.

The "colonial power" maintains control of the ghetto from the outside, through the police, social agencies, and a cultivated group of colonized natives ("Uncle Toms"). The idea is conveyed, by every means, that only the governors are qualified to govern, that the only chance for self-gain, even survival, lies in trying to be like the governors, that protest is a sign of maladjustment and furthermore can never succeed. This colonialism is as real as the more traditional colonialism of Britain and France, despite our official national ideology of equality. SNCC field secretary Charlie Cobb puts it this way:

> If I were trying to run things my way, I would do everything that I could to teach everybody that they were not able to run things like me. I would teach that to build something else meant that whoever wanted to do it would have to become like me. I would finally teach that I was the only person who knew enough to make other people like me. If I could manage all that, I wouldn't have to let people know they were slaves. It would be very important that the slavery I imposed be couched in my definition of freedom, and remain unseen in order that rebellion remained stifled, and my control intact.[5]

III

American foreign policy, in Vietnam in particular, stems from the same framework of thought that determines domestic welfarism. "America is building a curious empire," writes John McDermott, "a kind which has never before been seen. It is committed not to the exploitation of native peoples but to their welfare."[6] The policy of the Open Door still governs. The US denies any colonial desire, that is, direct political control of other nations. Nor does the American government claim an interest in draining other economies for our prosperity; all that is desired is that other nations remain "open" to American trade and investment. Yet in Vietnam the US finances roughly 85 per cent of the Saigon budget and is the real force holding the Ky government in power. How can these words and deeds be consistent?

Strikingly, New Dealers were among the group that initiated American activity in Vietnam when it became certain that the French would withdraw. In addition to liberal reformers like Wolf Ladejinsky, intellectuals from Michigan State University under the auspices of the CIA were intimately involved in building up the position of Ngo Dinh Diem. A passion for social reform evidently inspired these men; even General Lansdale of the Central Intelligence Agency spoke of the need for a "revolutionary alternative" to Communism for the Vietnamese people. For several years, the American public read about the "miracle of social reform" in Vietnam.[7]

As with the New Deal, the need for a Vietnamese welfare state was defined in reaction to a threat to the social order, in this case from the Communist-led Vietminh who controlled most of Vietnam in 1954. This primary concern made two priorities precede all others: an effective police force and a stable anti-Communist government. "Sink or swim with Ngo Dinh Diem" became the watchword and (with MSU help) guns, anti-riot equipment and 10,000 American advisers were brought into Saigon. The underlying rationale was that no matter how bad Diem might be, at least improvements were possible under his government, whereas Communism would bring the end of any possibilities at all.

So the US developed a government and an army. In Saigon, a prosperous urban economy was envisioned, in which American aid would allow the Vietnamese to purchase American imports, mostly automobiles, perfumes, and other luxury items—thus creating a consumer market for American business. The strategic reason for this, as some officials observed, was to develop a new urban class in Vietnam that would identify with the government receiving the American support.

There were two problems with this economic program: (1) a new privileged class developed that was too corrupt to become a successful "nationalist" alternative to Communism; (2) the tremendous spending of American dollars has as much as doubled the Saigon cost of living in a single year.

But the real contest, most officials knew, would be in the countryside, where the bulk of the people live. The first obstacle in reaching the peasants, however, was a deep prejudice. The "prosperous" urban South Vietnamese looked with disgust upon the rural people; the French had called them *les jaunes;* and common American views were summed up as early as 1948 by Congressman Lyndon Johnson who warned that "any yellow dwarf with a pocket knife" might threaten American interests in Asia.

There is little difference today, though the United States dares not suggest racial reasons for the war. Pvt. Dennis Mora, a Puerto Rican facing three years of hard labor for refusing to fight in Vietnam, told a military court that his instructor in basic training said to "kill as many Asians as we could" and the reason for going to Vietnam was because "those small brown people were too small to carry a B.A.R. [Browning Automatic Rifle]."[8] American-trained Mobile Unit Teams take the same attitude across the border in Thailand; Alex Campbell reported that civic action has "flopped badly" there because its administrators are viewed by the peasants as tax-collectors and "have a bad habit of calling the peasants to their faces filthy, uncivilized pigs, making them squat on the ground in their presence, and making them call any policeman 'master.'"[9]

Despite this fundamental bias, some of the American planners had great dreams for the countryside. First, however, the rural areas had to be "pacified," an unusually frank term describing a plan borrowed from the unsuccessful French. The plan involved moving vast numbers of peasants from their villages into barricaded fortresses, usually despite their will and after "weeding out" subversives. But the total US plan involved more than uprooting the rural population and eliminating its traditional village government structure. Here welfarism entered to help the natives. Schools and health clinics were to be established in every hamlet, and land reform was to give the natives their own plot of land and economic security. Both the Kennedy and Johnson Administrations have had to keep coming up with new programs for the welfare of the peasants while abandoning equally hopeful older programs that had died without ever being put into effect.

The carrying out of these plans involved horrors which may never be fully recorded. Despite tuberculosis, malaria, trachoma, and more recently, bubonic plague, all spread by the war, the US has barely succeeded in bringing medical equipment to the few areas under its control. Despite mass illiteracy, despite the fact that South Vietnamese young people cannot join the civil service without a high school diploma, in US-controlled areas only a fraction of the young will finish high school. The land reform program was intended to create rent control and sell plots of ground to individual peasants; but of the million acres that Ky plans to dispose of in this way, after ten years of promises, almost all of it has been parceled out already to peasants by the National Liberation Front. After an equally long period of "tax reform," the Saigon government collects less than 20 per cent of its budget from the South Vietnamese people (and even those revenues stem from American-generated income).

Ky and his government are *part of the American system,* not foreigners to it. More aid is given to Saigon than any state in the US; American businessmen, doctors and teachers are settled there; the South Vietnamese army is paid with the same funds that pay for the National Guard here; no one can deny that the whole structure of the Saigon government would collapse if American support were withdrawn; the strategic hamlets are no different from, if less stable than, the reservations where American Indians are kept.

Yet good men—liberal men—carry forward this Asian Great Society, as Hubert Humphrey calls it, year after year (or its counterpart in Latin America and Africa). Their clinching argument in support of the war in Vietnam still is that reform is underway. This is maintained despite the fact that the United States has never supported a real social revolution, but, as in Cuba, China, and recently the Dominican Republic, has been violently opposed.

What seems to happen is this: because "aid" is aimed at stopping Communism, it finds its way into the pockets of politicians whose invariable corruption matters less to American supporters than staunch anti-Communist views. As paternal as the domestic poverty program—"we are trying to create Joneses for the people to keep up with" is how the US aid officer in Laos puts it—the reforms inevitably fail to attract popular support. When insurgency, Communist-inspired or not, begins to threaten the pro-US ruling group, however decadent the rulers, the Americans call for military suppression. In the "counter-insurgency" which follows, counter-revolutionary violence takes priority—in deed, not in rhetoric—over any social construction. Americans begin to torture for freedom. What we are offering to the third world under the label of welfarism is a sophisticated barbarism. Yet Peace Corps officials can seriously consider organizing "social revolution" in Latin America, and Robert Kennedy can encourage a "new left." These men are sincere. What can they mean?

IV

One way of understanding the welfare state is through its processes of institutionalized reform. Perhaps because of its Madisonian political traditions or its prosperity, America allows substantial dissent, as shown, for example, in the history of the labor or civil rights movements. Yet there are profound continuities that the tradition of dissent has not interrupted significantly: private corporation privilege, imperialist intervention abroad, racial and class prejudice. Reform seems to follow a typical pattern, challenging the society for a time but always adjusting to these status quo facts.

In the postwar period, reformers have tended to be of two types. The first are the professionals, men located in government agencies, teaching, journalism, law, social work. The second are the activists, located in reform, civil rights, and labor politics. Their types often blend, for instance, as former civil rights activists take desk jobs in the War on Poverty, or as professors begin to join demonstrations. Both the professional and the activist assume that the leadership of American society can be "enlightened" and improved through a combination of political pressure and skilled maneuver.

The term "professionalized reform" was coined by Daniel Moynihan to describe one part of this postwar pattern of change. In his view, the poverty program was created by a handful of concerned professionals rather than by an existing or threatening social movement. These poverty planners typify a "new class" precisely because they plan, they study the general needs of the system rather than defending a narrow interest. Less and less do they require "the masses" to bring issues to their attention; research makes possible a kind of "early warning system" for the country's elite.[10]

Certainly this view reflects a real development. The poverty legislation was conceived by a small circle of men, just as New Deal reforms were conceived by a "brain trust." Michael Harrington's book helped to inspire it, just as earlier muckrackers focused attention on social needs. The personal compassion of JFK and LBJ made the programs possible, just as the plight of "one-third of a nation" troubled FDR. Such opportunities for "professionalized reform" are becoming more numerous than in earlier periods because of the expanding class of professional and service personnel taking part in the administration of society.

But it is not clear that these groups add more than sophistication and a white collar image to the status quo. They in fact develop their own "vested interests," as do even the social workers. Not being "of" the ghetto or the working class, they depend on information about the poor filtered through organizations of people similar to themselves. Their proposals for reform are developed not by the people who must live with the reforms (the poor themselves), but by planners with one eye on the census data and another on the political barometer. The consequence of the "new professionalism" tends to be, at best, patchwork (a young woman receives a skill through the Neighborhood Youth Corps, but her new earning power leads to a separation from her husband who is earning less) and, at worst, new public funds to shore up existing bureaucracies of the "welfare industry."

Yet these men might style themselves "participatory democrats," and so we must look at what they mean. The democracy they envision stems from modern thinking about organized society. Large-scale groups, from universities to business corporations, have been concerned increasingly with the "psychological" welfare of their employees and clients, trying to find the causes of low morale, alienation and revolt. It has become a dictum that the individual is a better citizen, worker, or student if he identifies with the large institution. In this view, grievances are primarily described as a result of misunderstanding and faulty organizational adjustment, rather than as problems of injustice. Where injustice is granted, it is seen as resulting from "backward" elements in an advanced system, such as Southern "rednecks," labor "thugs," or "savage" South Vietnamese army officers. The presupposition is that all problems can be negotiated. Society has reached the period of postrevolution. Racial violence, civil war, terror, and disruptive demonstrations are not needed if men are willing to give negotiation a try. Seen this way, violence reflects what are essentially merely personality struggles and power "grabs." Says a *New York Times* editorial, for instance:

> Any leader there [in Vietnam] must always be on the defensive against his own generals and against potentially disruptive forces, such as the political leaders of the Buddhists and Catholics, the intellectuals and the outs who would like to get in and grab the power and the rewards that go with politico-military favor in South Vietnam.[11]

This is part of the reason why a liberal can sanction the use of napalm or send police with tear gas into the ghetto when the situation becomes "difficult." This is the thinking, too, that leads Sargent Shriver to celebrate the rebirth of democracy when thousands of the poor are hired as "subprofessionals," or Job Corpsmen successfully learn to be gas station attendants. Something much broader than specific property rights or a narrow organizational interest is being defended. Rather, a system of administering property and organization, a way of doing things, is projected, by men who have been trained to see the world in the same way in the universities, business firms and the Defense Department. The confidence in "managerialism" may be the closest thing to an ideology in our society.

This "professionalized reform" is a companion to the work of the activist reformers. The professionals see themselves as anticipating or translating the people's needs for the government; the activists "represent" those needs and petition the professionals and the government to do something. These activist-reformers begin with the view that the American masses are "apathetic" and can only be roused because of simple material needs or during short periods of great enthusiasm. The masses most likely to move, it is said, are those who have gained something already: the unionized workers, registered voters, property owners. Those less likely to move are the people on the absolute bottom with nothing to lose, for they are too damaged to be the real motor of change.

From this rough description of the masses, liberals go on to argue the need for certain sorts of organizations. The masses need skilled and responsible leaders, they insist. It is best if these leaders have rank-and-file experience and operate within a formally democratic system. But this grass-roots flavor must not obscure the necessity for leaders to lead, that is, to put forward a program, a set of answers that guides the movement. And because they monopolize leadership experience, it soon appears to these leaders that they alone are qualified to maintain the organization.

The perilous position of the movement, due to attacks from centralized business and political forces, adds a further incentive for a top-down system of command. The need for alliances with other groups, created in large part through the trust which sets of leaders develop for each other, also intensifies the trend toward vertical organization. Finally, the leaders see a need to screen out anyone with "Communist-oriented" views, since such individuals are presumably too skilled to be allowed to operate freely within the movement. Slowly an elite is formed, calling itself the liberal-labor community. It treats the rank-and-file as a mass to be molded; sometimes thrust forward into action, sometimes held back. A self-fulfilling pattern emerges: because the nature of the organization is elitist, many people react to it with disinterest or suspicion, giving the leadership the evidence it needs to call the masses apathetic.

The pressures which influence these leaders come, not primarily from below, but from the top, from the most powerful men in the country. Sometimes bluntly and sometimes subtly, the real elite grooms responsible trade union and civil rights leaders. The leaders' existence comes to depend upon the possibility of receiving attention from the President or some top aide, and they judge organizational issues with an eye on this possibility. There is usually no question about the leaders' primary loyalty to the "national interest" as defined by the Administration, even though they always believe their judgments are independently made. Thus most of the civil rights leadership in 1964, fearing the Goldwater movement and hoping for civil rights legislation from a victorious Johnson Administration, called for a "moratorium" on mass demonstrations. The labor leadership performed the same function for the same reasons during World War II; the irony is that their critics in that period included A. Philip Randolph and Bayard Rustin, two Negroes who pushed for the 1964 moratorium.

Some on the left tend to see each piece of social legislation as a victory which strengthens the "progressive" forces. They see a step-by-step transformation of society as the result of pushing for one "politically acceptable" reform after another. But it appears that the American elite has discovered a long-term way to stabilize or cushion the contradictions of our society. It does this through numerous forms of state intervention, the use of our abundant capacity for material gratification, and the ability to condition nearly all the information which people receive. And if this is the case, then more changes of the New Deal variety will not be "progressive" at all. Except for boosting the relative income of a few, this entire reformist trend has weakened the poor under the pretense of helping them and strengthened elite rule under the slogan of curbing private enterprise. In fostering a "responsible" Negro and labor leadership and bringing it into the pseudo pluralist system of bargaining and rewards, a way has been found to contain and paralyze the disadvantaged and voiceless people.

Defenders of the welfare state—professional or activist—say that its critics overlook (1) the political and material gains that have been made for the poor under its auspices, and (2) the relative freedom to continue organizing protest that it guarantees. The point, however, is not to deny the gains. No economic improvement or civil liberty, however small, should be underestimated. But it is something else to point to those gains in defense of an entire system. In the first place, the gains are minute in relation to what the American productive system could make available to its people. Second, the very security of those gains is not guaranteed without continuous militant pressure. Third, the struggle for those gains left most white workers with more security but at the price of remaining racist in outlook, while still working under alienating conditions. Fourth, the process of reform seemed to undermine the spirit of insurgency itself by institutionalizing and limiting it.

Consider the caseworker who tells the client she should have died in slavery, and the civic action worker who calls the peasant an uncivilized pig; the policeman beating the Negro even after he collapses unconscious; the administrator ordering shock treatment for the mental patient screaming about his rights; the executive looking for a black prostitute during lunch; the professor interviewing an Asian official while a beaten prisoner lies on the floor; the worker reading about the machine that will replace him; the judge at juvenile court deciding to put away the young delinquent until she is 21; the landlord come with the constable to evict the tenants on rent strike. These are the everyday realities of a society that preaches liberal intentions.

We see, then, that welfare liberalism is more than a system of co-optation, more than an air-conditioned nightmare. It is also a system that punishes, with whatever violence is necessary, those who balk at its embrace. In this sense its liberalism is a façade over a more coercive conservative core.

The need is not to expand the welfare state, not to incorporate the "backward" parts into it, but to replace it altogether with a political economy that serves, rather than denies, the needs of the poor and millions of other people in this country and abroad. But replacing the political economy is not a negotiable issue arrived at through institutional reform. It is a revolutionary issue, resolved by building new institutions to replace the old. What then can be done.

V

The welfare state, with all its elaborate mechanisms for containing protest, still is ridden with instabilities. Conservative forces attempt to keep social services at a minimum and their administration under archaic patronage systems. The poor, including those who are semi-employed, live in conditions that generate protest and violence. The more America becomes involved in the Vietnam-type war, the deeper these conflicts at home tend to become.

But not only the poor are affected adversely by these developments. The hypocrisy of America's role in the world is a source of discontent among intellectuals and professionals. These seeds of conflict can only become more deeply planted because of

America's firm counterrevoluntionary policy. There may be a short-range flexibility possible in foreign affairs, but American policy is spiraling toward a nuclear finale. In order to carry out this global policy—which requires elite control of foreign policy, massive military spending, artificial attempts at consenus, etc.—it will be necessary to repress or neglect many groups seeking change through legitimate means at home. Thus a loose opposition to "welfare imperialism" can be expected to emerge from those groups that have little to say but much to lose in an American empire. Already insurgency is a growing pattern among the poor, the students, and the new professionals.

The Negro Revolt and Movements of the Poor

The youth of Watts and the Mississippi sharecroppers are the most visible and inspiring representatives of an awakening that is taking place among the Negro poor. Their perspective centers on Negro liberation, but they are interested as well in a movement of all the powerless and exploited.

The Southern movement stems from the conditions of the Black Belt. The people's strength comes from a stable system of family life and work, built up over generations within the framework of exploitation. Politics is new and fresh for them; they have not experienced the hollow promises of an opportunistic liberal-Negro machine. Their opposition's naked brutality keeps them constantly in a crisis framework. The broadening of their movement into Arkansas, Alabama, Louisiana, Georgia, the Carolinas, and Virginia, already underway, can be expected to challenge fundamentally the national coalition directing the Democratic Party. Already the Democrats are trying to groom moderate and liberal politicians to provide an "alternative" to the segregationists and the independent Freedom Democratic Party. Probably this effort will succeed, in the sense that political moderates will begin to compete for electoral power and leadership of the civil rights forces, mostly basing their strength in the cities, among privileged Negroes. The FDP, as a structure, may be absorbed into the national party, if only because it has no other, more effective place to go. But since the new Southern power structure will not solve the problems of poverty and race, which have plagued the North for generations, there is very little chance that this movement of poor people will be entirely coopted or crushed.

In the black ghettos of the North, organizers face different obstacles. There work is often deadening, family life distorted: "proper" political channels are sewers; people are used to, and tired of, party organizers exploiting them. The civil rights movement does not touch these hundreds of ghettos in a deep way because of the religious and the middle-class nature of its program and leadership, though the televised Southern brutality does create much bitterness in the North. However, the Harlem rent strikes, the activities of Malcolm X and the spread of "riots" are clear evidence that there are in the ghettos people prepared to take action. Some of them are of Southern background; some are housewives with wasted talents; some are youth with no future for their energy; some are junkies and numbers men with little loyalty to their particular game. Different as the forms of their discontent may be, the discontent itself is general to the ghetto and can be the spring for action. Under present conditions, political movements among these people are likely to be based on a race consciousness that is genuine and militant—and that is based on the failure of whites to act in favor of equal rights. It will be partly violent for, as the Negro has learned too well, force is required when dialogue does not work. The ghetto consciousness, however, is intertwined with the consciousness of being both poor and powerless. Almost of necessity, the demands that the ghetto poor put forward are also potentially in the interest of the white poor, as well as of middle class professionals who depend on the expansion of the public sectors of the economy.

But will white working class and poor people take up these issues that the "Negro problem" by its nature tends to raise? SNCC sees poor whites as potentially their major ally within the United States (other revoluntionary movements in the world perhaps being their main allies). The evidence for this hope is negative, but inconclusive. Poor whites, such as those in Appalachia, who are truly irrelevant to the modern economy, tend to see their plight (sometimes with accuracy) as personal rather than social: a function of sickness, bad luck, or psychological disorder. Poverty is not seen as the fate of a class, but only as the fate of individuals, each shamed into self-blame by their Protestant ideology. Working class whites, on the other hand, are more likely to be conscious of their problems as a group, but they tend to defend their scarce privileges—jobs, wages, education for their children—against what they see as the onslaught of Negro competition. While "backlash" did not split the alliance of white working people with the Democratic Party in 1964, it does serve as a barrier to an alliance with the Negro poor. But it is foolish to be rigid about these notions. Whites *are* being organized, on a mass basis, in areas of Appalachia where there exists a common culture and an industrial union tradition, and where the blame for misery can be laid to the coal operators, the conservative United Mine Workers, and the government. They also have been organized in Cleveland and Chicago.

But these organizing efforts were led by local people or independent organizers outside the structure of the labor movement. Today there are millions of workers trapped by the organizational framework of the AFL-CIO. Their unrest at times moves the international unions slightly, but the internationals are more dependent on government and business than on their own members, and, in addition, they seem to possess effective techniques for curbing shop revolts. It is not simply the "better objective conditions" that split the white from the Negro poor, but the existence of trade unions, which actively distort the better aspirations of their members. Economic and social conditions, of course, are not improving and workers' discontent is evidenced by the recent wave of rank-and-file revolts. But whether this discontent spurs a coalition of poor whites with Negroes depends, most of all, on whether a way can be found to organize workers independent of AFL-CIO routines. Concretely, that means democratic control by the workers of their union locals, and the entry of those locals into political activities and coalitions on the community level. It also means community action and organization among the millions of low-paid workers presently outside the labor movement.

The crucial importance of community work can only be grasped if one understands the sorts of ideas the American poor have about themselves. They operate with a kind of split consciousness. On the one hand, poor people know they are victimized from every direction. The facts of life always break through to expose the distance between American ideals and personal realities. This kind of knowledge, however, is kept undeveloped and unused because of another knowledge imposed on the poor, a keen sense of dependence on the oppressor. This is the source of that universal fear that leads poor people to act and even to think subserviently. Seeing themselves to blame for their situation, they rule out the possibility that they might be qualified to govern themselves and their own organizations. Besides fear, it is their sense of inadequacy and embarrassment that destroys the possibility of revolt. At the same time, this set of contradictory feelings results in indirect forms of protest all the time: styles of dress and language, withdrawal from political life, defiance of the boss's or the welfare worker's rules and regulations.

There can be no poor people's movement in any form unless the poor can overcome their fear and embarrassment. What is required is a certain kind of organizing that tries to make people understand their own worth and dignity. This work depends on the existence of "material issues" as a fundamental organizing point—high rents, voting rights, unpaved roads, and so on—but it moves from there into the ways such issues are related to personal life. The organizer spends hours and hours in the community, listening to people, drawing out their own ideas, rejecting their tendency to depend on him for solutions. Meetings are organized at which people with no "connections" can be given a chance to talk and work out problems together—usually for the first time. All this means fostering in everyone that sense of decision-making power which American society works to destroy. Only in this way can a movement be built which the Establishment can neither buy off nor manage, a movement too vital ever to become a small clique of spokesmen.

An organizational form that suggests the style of such a movement is the "community union," involving working-class and poor people in local insurgency. Open and democratic, the community union offers a real alternative to the kind of participation permitted in civil rights groups, trade unions and Democratic party machines. It might take a variety of forms: block clubs, housing committees, youth groups, etc. The union's insistence on the relevance of "little people," as well as its position outside and against the normal channels, would create a rooted sense of independence among the members.

The chance for short-term political success for these groups is small. The people are gerrymandered, they are not stable residents of their districts, they often are afraid of or misunderstand complex election procedures, they are cynical about elections; those who do vote are usually uncritical supporters of the Democratic Party, which is carefully organized in ghetto areas.

A community union would seek positions of political power only where really possible and where insurgency, not merely the status of an individual, might be advanced. Among the possibilities are neighborhood or municipal elections "close" to the people's experience. Where the group could not realistically seek power in that sense, it would build up at least the power of resistance at the point where colonial power is used against them, by the police, the landlords, the caseworkers who have to enter the community to do business. Besides being the only counterforce to intruding colonial authority, the community union can be a center where people can combine strength, provide services and help each other, and develop the skills of organization. By proving in practice a genuine interest in the people's welfare, by stressing the outside character of the exploiters, and by building up services and democratic activities of its own, the community union might eventually be in a position to win political power with a movement capable of using it. If not, it can be a permanent center of resistance.

A Student Movement

If poor people are in the movement because they have nothing to gain in the status system, students are in it because, in a sense, they have gained too much. Most of the active student radicals today come from middle to upper middle class professional homes. They were born with status and affluence as facts of life, not goals to be striven for. In their upbringing, their parents stressed the right of children to question and make judgments. And then these students so often encountered social institutions that denied them their independence and betrayed the democratic ideals they were taught. They saw that men of learning were careerists; that school administrators and ministers almost never discussed the realities the students lived with; that even their parents were not true to the ideals they taught the young.

It was against this background that young people became concerned about war, racism and inequality in the early sixties. By now, the empty nature of existing vocational alternatives has pushed several hundreds of these students into community organizing. Working in poor communities is a concrete task in which the split between job and values can be healed. It is also a position from which to expose the whole structure of pretense, status, and glitter that masks the country's real human problems. And, finally, it is a way to find people who want to change the country, and possibly can do so.

After the civil rights activities culminating in the 1964 Mississippi Summer Project and Northern summer projects, students began to find ways to create movements around other problems as well. The Berkeley Free Speech Movement and the April 1965 March on Washington to End the War in Vietnam were major departures from the inconsequential student government politics of five years before. On many campuses now students are beginning to form unions of their own, as well as independent study programs pointed in the direction of "free universities," projects located in the student community similar in direction to neighborhood organizing projects. In addition, by mobilizing antiwar activity, students are encountering their friends working among the poor. These efforts are threading the several protest movements in the country into a grassroots coalition with students in one of the leading roles.

The fact is that student protest is becoming a normal, even legitimate, part of society. The danger involved is that the Establishment is looking for a solution that can be for students what the Wagner Act was to workers:

a concession giving approval to the new student status while attempting to channel it in a "safe" direction. Private and public agencies are developing programs to "harness the energy of young people": VISTA and the Peace Corps, the Teaching Corps, "national service" ideas, etc. On the other hand, an opportunity is opened up, because the student desire for a meaningful vocation is being considered worth subsidizing. No doubt many students will boycott opportunities to be the social workers for imperialism's victims. Others will be swallowed up. Others will try these opportunities out to test their limits.

In other words, students are being treated in a way similar to previous emerging political forces. Whether the process of "institutionalized reform" can work on the affluent will be an interesting question. There is ample reason to believe that students as a rule will choose comfort over radical vocations. But on the other hand, students are rebelling against both materialism and manipulations; that is, against the root of the process by which insurgency is usually met. The society may have to choose between its counterrevolutionary policy and satisfying the desires of its younger generation.

There is a second danger facing the student movement: that of disintegration due to failure. The expanding Vietnam war may exhaust, embitter, or end in crushing the new activists. In the years 1960–1963 the student movement drew its health from the assumption that society could allow change. The war, by closing the hope for change, has exposed this assumption as naïve. If the war continues to spread, and if the majority remains comfortable, campus activism may further adopt the "opting-out" posture of the hippies. But if the expanding war causes much greater discomfort for the majority, there will be a massive right-wing demand to repress students and minorities. At any rate, even if the war is somehow ended, it has erased so much middle class innocence that a renewed student movement would perhaps be far more radical.

Middle-Class Insurgents

A centralized and commercial society wastes the talents and energies of millions of individuals. Some of these are women who are excluded from male-dominated vocations. Some are people with human values who cannot assert them effectively within organizations attached to the Cold War consensus. Some were politically active in the thirties, but faded away when popular movements declined. Some are part of the postwar generation which missed the experience of a radical movement altogether, and who are lodged uneasily in publishing houses, universities, and labor bureaucracies. In general, these are the professionals whose priorities are met inadequately by an inhuman society. They have a degree of conscience and shame; they want more than Moynihan's "professionalized reform."

The new movements are opening up great possibilities for these professionals to give their service directly (though some will take lucrative jobs with the Peace Corps and the poverty program). Community groups need lawyers, researchers, planners, doctors, newspapermen—in numerous ways. But these same professionals have a struggle of their own as well, against the wholesale co-option of their institutions by the national government. Professors joining students against the administration, welfare workers and teachers forming unions, muckrakers dissenting from the mass media imagery: these actions contribute to the general pressure on an Administration that talks of a Great Society while budgeting for nuclear weapons. This professional insurgency is bound to increase as the newest generation of student activists graduates and moves out of the university into careers.

VI

A Summary Word

It would be foolish to make of these speculations predictions-to-live-by. Revolutionaries are often among the last to know whether they are succeeding. In the 1930s radicals were surprised by the staying power of a capitalism that they had thought doomed. In the 1960s radicals may yet be surprised by the collapse of a welfare-capitalism that now seems flexible but invulnerable.

At any rate, humane opposition to the American welfare empire must be constructed not in speculative theory, but in action. Ideas, after all, are welcome commodities, easily absorbed in the new system. Only through combined action will ordinary men create the beginning of a different society. The experience and practice of solidarity is a deeper form of opposition to the welfare empire than any radical critique. Only a community contributing its own movements and institutions can fill the vacuum of local political life that the authoritarian society creates. Only men who know themselves to be capable decision-makers can consider fighting for a thoroughly democratic society. Only men able to improvise and invent vocations of their own will be prepared to demand, and live in, a decentralized, automated society of the future. Only men with experience in a universe of mixed races and cultures will be able to shed national chauvinism and ethnocentrism. Furthermore, masses of men will only be persuaded of change when some of them create a compelling, if very imperfect, example of what the future might be.

The real alternative to bureaucratic welfarism is to be found budding in the experience of men who form communities—whether a freedom school, a community union, a teach-in, or a wildcat strike—to struggle as equals for their own self-determination. Such communities come and go, existing at their best during intense periods of solidarity. But even where they fail to achieve institutional reality, these communities become a permanent part of this generation's consciousness of the possible. The new society still takes shape in the womb of the old.

NOTES

1. This power was established long ago in such codes as Section 242, Title 18, providing for criminal prosecution of people acting under cover of law to violate the constitutional rights of others.
2. *Hearings before the Subcommittee on the War on Poverty Program,* Committee on Education and Labor, House of Representatives, 89th Congress, 1st session, 1965, p. 327. Emphasis added.
3. *Newark News* (September 14, 1965). Emphasis added.
4. *Hearings before the Subcommittee on the War on Poverty Program,* Committee on

Education and Labor, House of Representatives, 89th Congress, 1st session, 1965, p. 78.
5. Charlie Cobb, "Whose Society Is This?," *New Republic* (December 18, 1965), pp. 13–15.
6. *The Nation* (July 25, 1966).
7. This aspect of CIA activity is documented in a number of sources, such as David Wise and Thomas B. Ross, *The Invisible Government* (New York, 1964), and the essay by Robert Scheer in Marvin E. Gettleman (ed.), *Vietnam: History, Documents and Opinions* . . . (New York, 1965), pp. 235–53. But the activity of the CIA is more extensive than most Americans have suspected, including its support of the National Student Association, and a wide range of other nominally independent organizations. (See the revelations in *Ramparts,* February, 1967.) The effects of this have been well analyzed by Robert Kopkind, "CIA: The Great Corruptor," *New York Review of Books* (March 23, 1967). President Johnson himself was forced to make some public declaration of policy on this matter, and on March 29, 1967, he ordered the CIA to halt its aid to certain private groups, except when justified on grounds of "overriding national security." Johnson did not, however, state that the CIA would refrain from promoting the overthrow by force and violence of governments it does not like.—M. and M., Eds.
8. *New York Times* (September 8, 1966).
9. "Thailand: Is This Something to Fall Back On?," *New Republic* (March 26, 1966).
10. Cf. Andrew Kopkind, "The Future Planners," *New Republic* (February 25, 1967).
11. *New York Times* (March 14, 1966).

9

The Myths of Coalition

STOKELY CARMICHAEL AND CHARLES V. HAMILTON

In the following excerpt from Black Power, *Stokely Carmichael and Charles V. Hamilton argue that the politics of coalition, alliances of black groups under the direction of white leaders, have failed to achieve the Negro's objective. Although individual whites have been useful to blacks, coalition politics actually have resulted in the perpetuation of patterns of white dominance and co-optation of black men in the white man's culture. The authors urge blacks to organize their own interest group coalitions. White men may still be useful, but they should not be allowed to define the black man's experience and determine his value.*

Advocates of "black power" such as Carmichael and Hamilton have often been accused of advocating revolutionary political objectives and tactics. The authors' plea, however, is quite conventional. They argue that social and economic pluralism be extended to the domain of politics. Only when "blacks and whites . . . accept each other as co-equal partners and . . . identify their goals as politically and economically similar . . ." will the promise of political pluralism be fulfilled in America.

Carmichael, former head of the Student Nonviolent Coordinating Committee, was born in Trinidad in 1941 and moved to New York City at the age of eleven. While a freshman at Howard University in Washington, D.C., he became involved in the civil rights movement as a "freedom rider." Due to his role in demonstrating against segregation in places of public accommodation he was arrested twenty-seven times. He is author of a forthcoming book entitled Stokely Speaks: Black Power Back to Pan-Africanism. *Charles V. Hamilton was Professor of Government at Columbia University and has served as head of Lincoln University's political science department.*

There is a strongly held view in this society that the best—indeed, perhaps the only—way for black people to win their political and economic rights is by forming coalitions with liberal, labor, church and other kinds of sympathetic organizations or forces, including the "liberal left" wing of the Democratic Party. With such allies, they could influence national legislation and national social patterns; racism could thus be ended. This school sees the "Black Power Movement" as basically separatist and unwilling to enter alliances. Bayard Rustin, a major spokesman for the coalition doctrine, has written:

> Southern Negroes, despite exhortations from SNCC to organize themselves into a Black Panther Party, are going to stay in the Democratic party—to them it is the party of progress, the New Deal, the New Frontier, and the Great Society—and they are right to stay.[1]

Aside from the fact that the name of the Lowndes County Freedom Party is *not* the "Black Panther Party," SNCC has often stated that it does not oppose the formation of political coalitions *per se;* obviously they are necessary in a pluralistic society. But coalitions with whom? On what terms? And for what objectives? All too frequently, coalitions involving black people have been only at the leadership level; dictated by terms set by others; and for objectives not calculated to bring major improvement in the lives of the black masses.

. . . we propose to reexamine some of the assumptions of the coalition school, and to comment on some instances of supposed alliance between black people and other groups. In the process of this treatment, it should become clear that the advocates of Black Power do *not* eschew coalitions; rather, we want to establish the grounds on which we feel political coalitions can be viable.

The coalitionists proceed on what we can identify as three myths or major fallacies. *First,* that in the context of present-day America, the interests of black people are identical with the interests of certain liberal, labor and other reform groups. Those groups accept the legitimacy of the basic values and institutions of the society, and fundamentally are not interested in a major reorientation of the society. Many adherents to the current coalition doctrine recognize this but nevertheless would have black people coalesce with such groups. The assumption—which is a myth—is this: what is good for America is automatically good for black people. *The second myth* is the fallacious assumption that a viable coalition can be effected between the politically and economically secure and the politically and economically insecure. *The third myth* assumes that political coalitions are or can be sustained on a moral, friendly, sentimental basis; by appeals to conscience. We will examine each of these three notions separately.

The major mistake made by exponents of the coalition theory is that they advocate alliances with groups which have never had as their central goal the necessarily total revamping of the society. At bottom, those groups accept the American system and want only—if at all—to make peripheral, marginal reforms in it. Such reforms are inadequate to rid the society of racism.

Here we come . . . to an important point . . . : the overriding sense of supe-

From Black Power, by Stokely Carmichael and Charles V. Hamilton, pp. 59-84. Copyright © 1967 by Stokely Carmichael and Charles Hamilton. Reprinted by permission of Random House, Inc. and Jonathan Cape Ltd.

riority that pervades white America. "Liberals," no less than others, are subjected and subject to it; the white liberal must view the racial scene through a drastically different lens from the black man's. Killian and Grigg were correct when they said in *Racial Crisis in America:*

> . . . most white Americans, even those white leaders who attempt to communicate and cooperate with their Negro counterparts, do not see racial inequality in the same way that the Negro does. The white person, no matter how liberal he may be, exists in the cocoon of a white-dominated society. Living in a white residential area, sending his children to white schools, moving in exclusively white social circles, he must exert a special effort to expose himself to the actual conditions under which large numbers of Negroes live. Even when such exposure occurs, his perception is likely to be superficial and distorted. The substandard house may be overshadowed in his eyes by the television aerial or the automobile outside the house. Even more important, he does not perceive the subjective inequalities inherent in the system of segregation because he does not experience them daily as a Negro does. Simply stated, the white American lives almost all of his life in a white world. The Negro American lives a large part of his life in a white world also, but in a world in which he is stigmatized [p. 73].

Our point is that no matter how "liberal" a white person might be, he cannot ultimately escape the overpowering influence—on himself and on black people—of his whiteness in a racist society.

Liberal whites often say that they are tired of being told "you can't understand what it is to be black." They claim to recognize and acknowledge this. Yet the same liberals will often turn around and tell black people that they should ally themselves with those who can't understand, who share a sense of superiority based on whiteness. The fact is that most of these "allies" neither look upon the blacks as co-equal partners nor do they perceive the goals as any but the adoption of certain Western norms and values. Professor Milton M. Gordon, in his book, *Assimilation in American Life,* has called those values "Anglo-conformity" (p. 88). Such a view assumes the "desirability of maintaining English institutions (as modified by the American Revolution), the English language, and English-oriented cultural patterns as dominant and standard in American life." Perhaps one holding these views is not a racist in the strict sense of our . . . definition, but the end result of his attitude is to sustain racism. As Gordon says:

> The non-racist Anglo-conformists presumably are either convinced of the *cultural* superiority of Anglo-Saxon institutions as developed in the United States, or believe simply that regardless of superiority or inferiority, since English culture has constituted the dominant framework for the development of American institutions, newcomers should expect to adjust accordingly [pp. 103–104].

We do not believe it possible to form meaningful coalitions unless both or all parties are not only willing but believe it absolutely necessary to challenge Anglo-conformity and other prevailing norms and institutions. Most liberal groups with which we are familiar are not so willing at this time. If that is the case, then the coalition is doomed to frustration and failure.

The Anglo-conformity position assumes that what is good for America—whites—is good for black people. We reject this. The Democratic Party makes the same claim. But the political and social rights of black people have been and always will be negotiable and expendable the moment they conflict with the interests of their "allies." A clear example of this can be found in the city of Chicago, where Mayor Daley's Democratic "coalition" machine depends on black support and unfortunately black people vote consistently for that machine. Note the results, as described by Banfield and Wilson in *City Politics:*

> The civic projects that Mayor Daley inaugurated in Chicago—street cleaning, street lighting, road building, a new airport, and a convention hall, for example —were shrewdly chosen. They were highly visible; they benefited the county as well as the city; for the most part they were noncontroversial; they did not require much increase in taxes; and they created many moderately paying jobs that politicians could dispense as patronage. The *mayor's program conspicuously neglected the goals of militant Negroes,* demands for the enforcement of the building code, and (until there was a dramatic exposé) complaints about police inefficiency and corruption. *These things were all controversial, and, perhaps most important, would have no immediate, visible result; either they would benefit those central-city voters whose loyalty could be counted upon anyway* or else (as in the case of police reform) they threatened to hurt the machine in a vital spot [p. 124; author's italics].

As long as the black people of Chicago—and the same can be said of cities throughout the country—remain politically dependent on the Democratic machine, their interests will be secondary to that machine.

Organized labor is another example of a potential ally who has never deemed it essential to question the society's basic values and institutions. The earliest advocates of unionism believed in the doctrine of *laissez faire.* The labor organizers of the American Federation of Labor (AFL) did not want the government to become involved in labor's problems, and probably for good reason. The government then—in the 1870's and 1880's—was anti-labor, pro-management. It soon became clear that political power would be necessary to accomplish some of the goals of organized labor, especially the goals of the railroad unions. The AFL pursued that power and eventually won it, but generally remained tied to the values and principles of the society as it was. They simply wanted in; the route lay through collective bargaining and the right to strike. The unions set their sights on immediate bread-and-butter issues, to the exclusion of broader goals.

With the founding and development of mass industrial unionism under the Congress of Industrial Organizations (CIO), we began to see a slight change in overall union orientation. The CIO was interested in a wider variety of issues—foreign trade, interest rates, even civil rights issues to an extent—but it too never seriously questioned the racist basis of the society. In *Politics, Parties and Pressure Groups,* Professor V. O. Key, Jr. has concluded: ". . . on the fundamental question of the character of the economic system, the dominant labor ideology did not challenge the established order." Professor Selig Perlman wrote: ". . . it is a labor movement upholding capitalism, not only in practice, but in principle as well."[2] Organized labor, so often pushed as a potential ally by the coalition theorists, illustrates the pitfalls of the first myth; as we shall see later in this [essay], its history also debunks the second myth.

Yet another source of potential alliance frequently cited by the exponents of coalitions is the liberal-reform movement, especially at the local political level. But the various reform-politics groups—particularly in New

York, Chicago and California—frequently are not tuned in to the primary goals of black people. They establish their own goals and then demand that black people identify with them. When black leaders begin to articulate goals in the interest of black people *first,* the reformers tend, more often than not, to term this "racist" and to drop off. Reformers push such "good government" programs as would result in posts being filled by professional, middle-class people. Wilson stated in *The Amateur Democrat,* "Blue-ribbon candidates would be selected, not only for the important, highly visible posts at the top of the ticket, but also for the less visible posts at the bottom" (p. 128). Black people who have participated in local reform politics—especially in Chicago—have come from the upper-middle class. Reformers generally reject the political practice of ticket balancing, which means that they tend to be "color blind" and wish to select candidates only on the basis of qualifications, of merit. In itself this would not be bad, but their conception of a "qualified" person is usually one who fits the white middle-class mold. Seldom, if ever, does one hear of the reformers advocating representation by grass-roots leaders from the ghettos; these are hardly "blue-ribbon types. Again, when reformers push for elections at large as opposed to election by district, they do not increase black political power. "Blue-ribbon" candidates, government by technical experts, elections at large—all these common innovations of reformers do little for black people.

Francis Carney concludes from his study of California's liberal-reform Democratic clubs[3] that although those groups were usually strong on civil rights, they were nonetheless essentially middle-class oriented. This could only perpetuate a paternalistic, colonial relationship—doing *for* the blacks. Thus, even when the reformers are bent on making significant changes in the system, the question must be asked if that change is consistent with the views and interests of black people—as perceived by those people.

Frequently, we have seen that a staunch, militant stand taken by black leaders has frightened away the reformers. The latter could not understand the former's militancy. "Amateur Democrats (reformers) are passionately committed to a militant stand on civil rights, but they shy away from militant Negro organizations because they find them 'too race-conscious'" (p. 285), says Wilson in *The Amateur Democrat,* citing as one example the Independent Voters of Illinois, who felt they could not go along with the desire of some black members to take a very strong, pro-civil rights and anti-Daley position. The liberal-reform politicians have not been able fully to accept the necessity of black people speaking forcefully and for themselves. This is one of the greatest points of tension between these two sets of groups today; this difference must be resolved before viable coalitions can be formed between the two.

To sum up our rejection of the first myth . . . the political and economic institutions of this society must be completely revised if the political and economic status of black people is to be improved. We do not see how those same institutions can be utilized—through the mechanism of coalescing with some of them—to bring about that revision. We do not see how black people can form effective coalitions with groups which are not willing to question and condemn the racist institutions which exploit black people; which do not perceive the need for, and will not work for, basic change. Black people cannot afford to assume that what is good for white America is automatically good for black people.

The second myth we want to deal with is the assumption that a politically and economically secure group can collaborate with a politically and economically insecure group. Our contention is that such an alliance is based on very shaky grounds. By definition, the goals of the respective parties are different.

Black people are often told that they should seek to form coalitions after the fashion of those formed with so-called Radical Agrarians—later Populists—in the latter part of the nineteenth century. In 1886, the Colored Farmers' Alliance and Cooperative Union was formed, interestingly enough, by a white Baptist minister in Texas. The platform of this group was similar to that of the already existing Northern and Southern Farmers' Alliances, which were white. But upon closer examination, one could see substantial differences in interests and goals. The black group favored a Congressional bill (The Lodge Federal Elections Bill) which aimed to guarantee the voting rights of Southern black people; the white group opposed it. In 1889, a group of black farmers in North Carolina accused the Southern Alliance of setting low wages and influencing the state legislature to pass discriminatory laws. Two years later, the Colored Alliance called for a strike of black cotton pickers. Professors August Meier and Elliot Rudwick ask a number of questions about these two groups, in *From Plantation to Ghetto:*

> Under what circumstances did Negroes join and to what extent, if any, was participation encouraged (or even demanded) by white employers who were members of the Southern Alliance? . . . Is it possible that the Colored Alliance was something like a company union, disintegrating only when it became evident that the Negro tenant farmers refused to follow the dictates of their white employers? . . . And how was it that the Alliance men and Populists were later so easily led into extreme anti-Negro actions? In spite of various gestures to obtain Negro support, attitudes such as those exhibited in North Carolina and on the Lodge Bill would argue that whatever interracial solidarity existed was not firmly rooted [pp. 158–59].

The fact is that the white group was relatively more secure than the black group. As C. Vann Woodward writes in *Tom Watson, Agrarian Rebel,* "It is undoubtedly true that the Populist ideology was dominantly that of the landowning farmer, who was, in many cases, the exploiter of landless tenant labor" (p. 18). It is difficult to perceive the basis on which the two could coalesce and create a meaningful alliance for the landless, insecure group. It is no surprise, then, to learn of the anti-black actions mentioned above and to realize that the relation of blacks to Populists was not the harmonious arrangement some people today would have us believe.

It is true that black people in St. Louis and Kansas backed the Populists in the election of 1892, and North Carolina blacks supported them in 1896. But it is also true that the Populists in South Carolina, under the leadership of "Pitchfork" Ben Tillman, race-baited the black man. In some places—like Georgia—the Populists "fused" with the lily-white wing of the Republican Party, not with the so-called black-and-tan wing.

Or take the case of Tom Watson. This Populist from Georgia was at one time a staunch advocate of a united front between Negro and white farmers. In 1892, he wrote: "You are kept apart that you may be separately fleeced of your earnings. You are made to hate each other because upon that hatred is rested the keystone of the arch of financial despotism which enslaves you both. You are deceived and blinded that you may not see how this race antagonism perpetuates a monetary system which beggars both."[4]

But this is the same Tom Watson who, only a few years later and because the *political* tide was flowing against such an alliance, did a complete turnabout. At that time, Democrats were disfranchising black people in state after state. But, as John Hope Franklin recorded in *From Slavery to Freedom,* "Where the Populists were unable to control the Negro vote, as in Georgia in 1894, they believed that the Democrats had never completely disfranchised the Negroes because their votes were needed if the Democrats were to stay in power. This belief led the defeated and disappointed Tom Watson to support a constitutional amendment excluding the Negro from the franchise—a complete reversal of his position in denouncing South Carolina for adopting such an amendment in 1895" (p. 218).

Watson was willing to ally with white candidates who were anti-Democratic-machine Democrats. With the black vote eliminated, the Populist stood to hold the balance of power between warring factions of the Democratic Party. Again C. Vann Woodward spells it out in his book, *Tom Watson, Agrarian Rebel:*

> He [Watson] . . . pledged his support, and the support of the Populists, to any anti-machine, Democratic candidate running upon a suitable platform that included a pledge to "a change in our Constitution which will perpetuate white supremacy in Georgia."
>
> How Watson managed to reconcile his radical democratic doctrine with a proposal to disfranchise a million citizens of his native state is not quite clear.
>
> "The white people dare not revolt so long as they can be intimidated by the fear of the Negro vote," he explained. Once the "bugaboo of Negro domination" was removed, however, "every white man would act according to his own conscience and judgment in deciding how he shall vote." With these words, Watson abandoned his old dream of uniting both races against the enemy, and took his first step toward the opposite extreme in racial views [pp. 371–72].

At all times, the Populists and Watson emerge as politically motivated. The history of the period tells us that the whites—whether Populists, Republicans or Democrats—always had their own interests in mind. The black man was little more than a political football, to be tossed and kicked around at the convenience of others whose position was more secure.

We can learn the same lesson from the politics of the city of Atlanta, Georgia today. It is generally recognized that the black vote there is crucial to the election of a mayor. This was true in the case of William B. Hartsfield, and it is no less true for the present mayor, Ivan Allen, Jr. The coalition which dominates Atlanta politics has been described thus by Professor Edward Banfield in *Big City Politics:*

> The alliance between the business-led white middle class and the Negro is the main fact of local politics and government; only within the limits that it allows can anything be done, and much of what is done is for the purpose of holding it together [p. 35].

Mayor Hartsfield put together a "three-legged stool" as a base of power. The business power structure, together with the "good government"-minded middle class that takes its lead from that power structure is one leg. The Atlanta press is another. The third leg is the black community. But something is wrong with this stool. In the first place, of course, the third leg is a hollow one. The black community of Atlanta is dominated by a black power structure of . . . "leaders" . . . concerned primarily with protecting their own vested interests and their supposed influence with the white power structure, unresponsive to and unrepresentative of the black masses. But even this privileged group is economically and politically insecure by comparison with the other two forces with whom they have coalesced. Note this description by Banfield:

> Three associations of businessmen, *the leadership of which overlaps greatly,* play important parts in civic affairs. The Chamber of Commerce launches ideas which are often taken up as official city policy, and it is always much involved in efforts to get bond issues approved. The Central Atlanta Association is particularly concerned with the downtown business district and has taken the lead in efforts to improve expressways, mass transit, and urban renewal. Its weekly newsletter is widely read and respected. *The Uptown Association is a vehicle used by banks and other property owners to maintain a boundary line against expansion of the Negro district. To achieve this purpose it supports nonresidential urban renewal projects* [pp. 31–32, author's italics].

Atlanta's substantial black bourgeoisie cannot compete with that line-up.

The political and economic interests causing the white leaders to enter the coalition are clear. So is the fact that those interests are often diametrically opposed to the interests of black people. We need only look at what the black man has received for his faithful support of politically and economically secure "alliance partners." Banfield puts it succinctly: "Hartsfield gave the Negro practically nothing in return for his vote" (p. 30). That vote, in 1957, was nine-tenths of the 20,000 votes cast by black people.

In 1963, a group of civic leaders from the black community of Southeast Atlanta documented the injustices suffered by that community's 60,000 black people. The lengthy list of grievances included faults in the sewerage system, sidewalks needed, streets which should be paved, deficient bus service and traffic control, substandard housing areas, inadequate parks and recreation facilities, continuing school segregation and inadequate black schools. Their report stated:

> Atlanta city officials have striven to create an image of Atlanta as a rapidly growing, modern, progressive city where all citizens can live in decent, healthful surroundings. This image is a blatant lie so long as the city provides no health clinics for its citizens but relies entirely upon inadequate county facilities. It is a lie so long as these health clinics are segregated and the city takes no action to end this segregation. Because of segregation, only one of the four health clinics in the South side area is available to over 60,000 Negroes. This clinic . . . is small, its equipment inadequate and outdated, and its service dangerously slow due to general overcrowding.

In 1962, the city employed 5,663 workers, 1,647 of them black, but only 200 of those did other than menial work. The document lists twenty-two departments in which, of 175 equipment operators in the Construction Department, not one was black. The city did not even make a pretense of belief in "getting ahead by burning the midnight oil": there was only one public library in the community, a single room with 12,000 volumes (mostly children's books) for 60,000 people.[5]

This is what "coalition politics" won for the black citizens of one sizeable community. Nor had the situation in Atlanta's ghettos improved much by 1966. When a so-called riot broke out in the Summerhill community, local civic groups pointed out that they had deplored conditions and called the area "ripe for riot" many months earlier.

Black people must ultimately come to realize that such coalitions, such alliances have *not* been in their interest. They are "allying" with forces clearly not consistent with the long-term progress of blacks; in fact, the whites enter the alliance in many cases precisely to impede that progress.

Labor unions also illustrate very clearly the treacherous nature of coalitions between the economically secure and insecure. From the passage of the Wagner Act in 1935 (which gave unions the right to organize and bargain collectively), unions have been consolidating their position, winning economic victories for their members, and generally developing along with the growing prosperity of the country. What about black workers during this time? Their status has been one of steady deterioration rather than progress. It is common knowledge that the craft unions of AFL (printers, plumbers, bricklayers, electrical workers) have deliberately excluded black workers over the years. These unions have taken care of their own—their white own. Meanwhile, the unemployment rate of black workers has increased, doubling, in some cases, that of white workers. The unions themselves were not always innocent bystanders to this development:

> . . . The war has been over twenty years now, and instead of more Negroes joining labor unions, fewer are doing so; for the Negro, increased unionization has in too many instances meant decreased job opportunity. . . .
>
> When the International Brotherhood of Electrical Workers became the collective bargaining agent of the Bauer Electric Company in Hartford, Connecticut in the late forties, the union demanded and got the removal of all Negro electricians from their jobs. The excuse was advanced that, since their union contract specified "whites only," they could not and would not change this to provide continued employment for the Negroes who were at the plant before the union was recognized. Similar cases can be found in the Boilermakers' Union and the International Association of Machinists at the Boeing Aircraft Company in Seattle.[6]

Precisely *because* of union recognition, black workers *lost* their jobs.

The situation became so bad that in 1959 black workers in the AFL-CIO, under the leadership of A. Philip Randolph, organized the Negro American Labor Council (NALC). Some black workers, at least, finally accepted the reality that they had to have their own black representatives if their demands were to be made—not to mention being met. The larger body did not particularly welcome the formation of this group. Randolph told the NAACP convention in June, 1960 in St. Paul, Minnesota that "a gulf of misunderstanding" seemed to be widening between the black community and the labor community. He further stated: "It is unfortunate that some of our liberal friends, along with some of the leaders of labor, even yet do not comprehend the nature, scope, depth, and challenge of this civil rights revolution which is surging forward in the House of Labor. They elect to view with alarm practically any and all criticisms of the AFL-CIO because of racial discrimination."[7]

It has become clear to many black leaders that organized labor operates from a different set of premises and with a different list of priorities, and that the status of black workers does not occupy a high position on that list. In fact, they are highly expendable, as in the political arena. Note the following observation:

> . . . the split has even deeper causes. It arises out of the Negro's declaration of independence from white leadership and white direction in the civil rights fight—the Negro view today is that the whites, in labor or in other fields, are unreliable race campaigners when the chips are down, and that only the Negro can carry through to race victories.
>
> "Negro trade unionists and workers must bear their own cross for their own liberation. They must make their own crisis decisions bearing upon their life, labor, and liberty," Randolph told the NAACP.[8]

The Negro American Labor Council itself, however, suggests that such realizations may not be sufficient. It is our position that a viable group cannot be organized *within* a larger association. The sub-group will have to acquiesce to the goals and demands of the parent; it can only serve as a conscience-pricker—because it has no independent base of power from which to operate. Coalition between the strong and the weak ultimately leads only to perpetuation of the hierarchical status: superordinance and subordinance.

It is also important to note that the craft unions of the AFL were born and consolidating their positions at the same time that this country was beginning to expand imperialistically in Latin America and in the Philippines. Such expansion increased the economic security of white union workers here. Thus organized labor has participated in the exploitation of colored peoples abroad and of black workers at home. Black people today are beginning to assert themselves at a time when the old colonial markets are vanishing; former African and Asian colonies are fighting for the right to control their own natural resources, free from exploitation by Western and American capitalism. With whom will economically secure, organized labor cast its lot—with the big businesses of exploitation or with the insecure poor colored peoples? This question gives additional significance—a double layer of meaning—to the struggle of black workers here. The answer, unfortunately, seems clear enough.

We cannot see, then, how black people, who are massively insecure both politically and economically, can coalesce with those whose position is secure—particularly when the latter's security is based on the perpetuation of the existing political and economic structure.

The third myth proceeds from the premise that political coalitions can be sustained on a moral, friendly or sentimental basis, or on appeals to conscience. We view this as a myth because we believe that political relations are based on self-interest: benefits to be gained and losses to be avoided. For the most part, man's politics is determined by his evaluation of material good and evil. Politics results from a conflict of interests, not of consciences.

We frequently hear of the great moral value of the pressure by various church groups to bring about passage of the Civil Rights Laws of 1964 and 1965. There is no question that significant numbers of clergy and lay groups participated in the successful lobbying of those bills, but we should be careful not to overemphasize the value of this. To begin with, many of those religious groups were available only until the bills were passed; their sustained moral force is not on hand for the all-important process of ensuring federal implementation of these laws, particularly with respect to the appointment of more federal voting registrars and the setting of guidelines for school desegregation.

It should also be pointed out that many of those same people did not feel so morally obliged when the issues struck closer to home—in the North, with housing, as an example. They could be morally self-righteous about passing a law to desegregate southern lunch counters or even a law guaranteeing southern black people the right to vote. But laws against employment and housing discrimination—which would affect the North as much as the South—are something else again. After all, ministers—North and South—are often forced out of their pulpits if they speak or act too forcefully in favor of civil rights. Their parishioners do not lose sleep at night worrying about the oppressed status of black Americans; they are not morally torn inside themselves. As Silberman said, they simply do not want their peace disrupted and their businesses hurt.

We do not want to belabor the church in particular; what we have said applies to all the other "allies" of black people. Furthermore, we do not seek to condemn these groups for being what they are so much as we seek to emphasize a fact of life: they are unreliable allies when a conflict of interest arises. Morality and sentiment cannot weather such conflicts, and black people must realize this. No group should go into an alliance or a coalition relying on the "good will" of the ally. If the ally chooses to withdraw that "good will," he can do so usually without the other being able to impose sanctions upon him of any kind.

Thus we reject the last myth. . . . Some believe that there is a conflict between the so-called American Creed and American practices. The Creed is supposed to contain considerations of equality and liberty, at least certainly equal opportunity, and justice. The fact is, of course, that these are simply words which *were not even originally intended* to have applicability to black people: Article I of the Constitution affirms that the black man is three-fifths of a person.[9] The fact is that people live their daily lives making practical day-to-day decisions about their jobs, homes, children. And in a profit-oriented, materialistic society, there is little time to reflect on creeds, especially if it could mean more job competition, "lower property values," and the "daughter marrying a Negro." There is no "American dilemma," no moral hang-up, and black people should not base decisions on the assumption that a dilemma exists. It may be useful to articulate such assumptions in order to embarrass, to create international pressure, to educate. But they cannot form the basis for viable coalitions.

What, then, are the grounds for viable coalitions?

Before one begins to talk coalition, one should establish clearly the premises on which that coalition will be based. All parties to the coalition must perceive a *mutually* beneficial goal based on the conception of *each* party of his *own* self-interest. One party must not blindly assume that what is good for one is automatically —without question—good for the other. Black people must first ask themselves what is good *for them,* and then they can determine if the "liberal" is willing to coalesce. They must recognize that institutions and political organizations have no consciences outside their own special interests.

Secondly, there is a clear need for genuine power bases before black people can enter into coalitions. Civil rights leaders who, in the past or at present, rely essentially on "national sentiment" to obtain passage of civil rights legislation reveal the fact that they are operating from a powerless base. They must appeal to the conscience, the good graces of the society; they are, as noted earlier, cast in a beggar's role, hoping to strike a responsive chord. It is very significant that the two oldest civil rights organizations, the National Association for the Advancement of Colored People and the Urban League, have constitutions which specifically prohibit partisan political activity. (The Congress of Racial Equality once did, but it changed that clause when it changed its orientation in favor of Black Power.) This is perfectly understandable in terms of the strategy and goals of the older organizations, the concept of the civil rights movement as a kind of liaison between the powerful white community and the dependent black community. The dependent status of the black community apparently was unimportant since, if the movement proved successful, that community was going to blend into the white society anyway. No pretense was made of organizing and developing institutions of community power within the black community. No attempt was made to create any base of organized political strength; such activity was even prohibited, in the cases mentioned above. All problems would be solved by forming coalitions with labor, churches, reform clubs, and especially liberal Democrats.

. . . It should . . . already be clear that the building of an independent force is necessary; that Black Power is necessary. If we do not learn from history, we are doomed to repeat it, and that is precisely the lesson of the Reconstruction era. Black people were allowed to register, to vote and to participate in politics, because it was to the advantage of powerful white "allies" to permit this. But at all times such advances flowed from white decisions. That era of black participation in politics was ended by another set of white decisions. There was no powerful independent political base in the southern black community to challenge the curtailment of political rights. At this point in the struggle, black people have no assurance—save a kind of idiot optimism and faith in a society whose history is one of racism—that if it became necessary, even the painfully limited gains thrown to the civil rights movement by the Congress would not be revoked as soon as a shift in political sentiments occurs. (A vivid example of this emerged in 1967 with Congressional moves to undercut and eviscerate the school desegregation provisions of the 1964 Civil Rights Act.) We must build that assurance and build it on solid ground.

We also recognize the potential for limited, short-term coalitions on relatively minor issues. But we must note that such approaches seldom come to terms with the roots of institutional racism. In fact, one might well argue that such coalitions on subordinate issues are, in the long run, harmful. They could lead whites and blacks into thinking either that their long-term interests do *not* conflict when in fact they do, or that such lesser issues are the *only* issues which can be solved. With these limitations in mind, and a spirit of caution, black people can approach possibilities of coalition for specific goals.

Viable coalitions therefore stem from four preconditions: (a) the recognition by the parties involved of their respective self-interests; (b) the mutual belief that each party stands to benefit in terms of that self-interest from allying with the other or others; (c) the acceptance of the fact that each party has its own independent base of power and does not depend for ultimate decision-making on a force outside itself; and (d) the realization that the coalition deals with specific and identifiable—as opposed to general and vague—goals.

The heart of the matter lies in this admonition from Machiavelli, writing in *The Prince:*

> And here it should be noted that a prince ought never to make common cause with one more powerful than himself to injure another, unless necessity forces him to it. . . . for if he wins you rest in his power, and princes must avoid as much as possible being under the will and pleasure of others.[10]

Machiavelli recognized that "necessity" might at times force the weaker to ally with the stronger. Our view is that those who advocate Black Power should work to minimize that necessity. It is crystal clear that such alliances can seldom, if ever, be meaningful to the weaker partner. They cannot offer the optimum conditions of a political *modus operandi.* Therefore, if and when such alliances are unavoidable, we must not be sanguine about the possibility of their leading to ultimate, substantial benefit for the weaker force.

Let black people organize themselves *first,* define their interests and goals, and then see what kinds of allies are available. Let any ghetto group contemplating coalition be so tightly organized, so strong, that—in the words of Saul Alinsky—it is an "indigestible body" which cannot be absorbed or swallowed up.[11] The advocates of Black Power are not opposed to coalitions per se. But we are *not* interested in coalitions based on myths. To the extent to which black people can form *viable* coalitions will the end results of those alliances be lasting and meaningful. There will be clearer understanding of what is sought; there will be greater impetus on all sides to deliver, because there will be *mutual* respect of the power of the other to reward or punish; there will be much less likelihood of leaders selling out their followers. Black Power therefore has no connotation of "go it alone." Black Power simply says: enter coalitions only *after* you are able to "stand on your own." Black Power seeks to correct the approach to dependency, to remove that dependency, and to establish a viable psychological, political and social base upon which the black community can function to meet its needs.

At the beginning of our discussion of Black Power, we said that black people must redefine themselves, state new values and goals. The same holds true for white people of good will; they too need to redefine themselves and their role.

Some people see the advocates of Black Power as concerned with ridding the civil rights struggle of white people. This has been untrue from the beginning. There is a definite, much-needed role whites can play. This role can best be examined on three different, yet interrelated, levels: educative, organizational, supportive. Given the pervasive nature of racism in the society and the extent to which attitudes of white superiority and black inferiority have become embedded, it is very necessary that white people begin to disabuse themselves of such notions. Black people, as we stated earlier, will lead the challenge to old values and norms, but whites who recognize the need must also work in this sphere. Whites have access to groups in the society never reached by black people. They must get within those groups and help perform this essential educative function.

One of the most disturbing things about almost all white supporters has been that they are reluctant to go into their own communities—which is where the racism exists—and work to get rid of it. We are not now speaking of whites who have worked to get black people "accepted," on an individual basis, by the white society. Of these there have been many; their efforts are undoubtedly well-intended and individually helpful. But too often those efforts are geared to the same false premises as integration; too often the society in which they seek acceptance of a few black people can afford to make the gesture. We are speaking, rather, of those whites who see the need for basic change and have hooked up with the black liberation movement because it seemed the most promising agent of such change. Yet they often admonish black people to be non-violent. They should preach non-violence in the white community. Where possible, they might also educate other white people to the need for Black Power. The range is great, with much depending on the white person's own class background and environment.

On a broader scale, there is the very important function of working to reorient this society's attitudes and policies toward African and Asian countries. Across the country, smug white communities show a poverty of awareness, a poverty of humanity, indeed, a poverty of ability to act in a civilized manner toward non-Anglo human beings. The white middle-class suburbs need "freedom schools" as badly as the black communities. Anglo-conformity is a dead weight on their necks too. All this is an educative role crying to be performed by those whites so inclined.

The organizational role is next. It is hoped that eventually there will be a coalition of poor blacks and poor whites. This is the only coalition which seems acceptable to us, and we see such a coalition as the major internal instrument of change in the American society. It is purely academic today to talk about bringing poor blacks and poor whites together, but the task of creating a poor-white power block dedicated to the goals of a free, open society—not one based on racism and subordination—must be attempted. The main responsibility for this task falls upon whites. Black and white *can* work together in the white community where possible; it is not possible, however, to go into a poor Southern town and talk about "integration," or even desegregation. Poor white people are becoming more hostile—not less—toward black people, partly because they see the nation's attention focused on black poverty and few, if any, people coming to them.

Only whites can mobilize and organize those communities along the lines necessary and possible for effective alliances with the black communities. This job cannot be left to the existing institutions and agencies, because those structures, for the most part, are reflections of institutional racism. If the job is to be done, there must be new forms created. Thus, the political modernization process must involve the white community as well as the black.

It is our position that black organizations should be black-led and essentially black-staffed, with policy being made by black people. White people can and do play very important supportive roles in those organizations. Where they come with specific skills and techniques, they will be evaluated in those terms. All too frequently, however, many young, middle-class, white Americans, like some sort of Pepsi generation, have wanted to "come alive" through the black community and black groups. They have wanted to be where the action is—and the action has been in those places. They have sought refuge among blacks from a sterile, meaningless, irrelevant life in middle-class America. They have been unable to deal with the stifling, racist, parochial, split-level mentality of their parents, teachers, preachers and friends. Many have come seeing "no difference in color," they have come "color blind." But at this time and in this land, color *is* a factor and we should not overlook or deny this. The black organizations do not need this kind of idealism, which borders on paternalism. White people working in SNCC have understood this. There are white lawyers who defend black civil rights workers in court, and white activists who support indigenous black movements across the country. Their function is not to lead or to set policy or to attempt to define black people to black people. Their role is supportive.

Ultimately, the gains of our struggle will be meaningful only when consolidated by viable coalitions between blacks and whites who accept each other as co-equal partners and who identify their goals as politically and economically similar. At this stage, given the nature of the society, distinct roles must be played. The charge that this approach is "anti-white" remains as inaccurate as almost all the other public commentary on Black Power. There is nothing new about this; whenever black people have moved toward genuinely independent action, the society has distorted their intentions or damned their performance. . . .

NOTES

1. Bayard Rustin, "Black Power and Coalition Politics," *Commentary* (September, 1966).
2. Selig Perlman, "The Basic Philosophy of the American Labor Movement," *Annals of the American Academy of Political & Social Science*, Vol. 274 (1951), pp. 57–63.
3. Francis Carney, *The Rise of the Democratic Clubs in California*, Eagleton Institute Cases in Practical Politics, New York: McGraw-Hill, 1959.
4. Tom Watson, "The Negro Question in the South," *Arena*, Vol. 6 (1892), p. 548.
5. "The City Must Provide. South Atlanta: The Forgotten Community," Atlanta Civic Council, 1963.
6. Myrna Bain, "Organized Labor and the Negro Worker," *National Review* (June 4, 1963), p. 455.
7. "Labor Negro Division Widens," *Business Week* (July 9, 1960), p. 79.
8. Bain, *op. cit.*
9. "Representatives and direct Taxes shall be apportioned among the several States which may be included within this Union, according to their respective Numbers, which shall be determined by adding to the whole Number of free Persons, including those bound to Service for a Term of Years, and excluding Indians not taxed, three-fifths of all other Persons."
10. Niccolo Machiavelli, *The Prince and the Discourses*, New York: Random House (Modern Library), 1950, p. 84.
11. Saul Alinsky speaking at the 1967 Legal Defense Fund Convocation in New York City, May 18, 1967.

SELECTED BIBLIOGRAPHY

Bachrach, Peter. *The Theory of Democratic Elitism.* Boston: Little, Brown, 1967. Provides a comprehensive review and critique of various elite theories. Argues that "democratic elitism" is inconsistent with the tenets of classical democratic theory. Concedes that major governmental decisions are made by a small, qualified elite, but calls for wider participation in decision making. Redefines political decision making to include private institutions that allocate resources for society.

Bell, Daniel, ed. *The Radical Right.* New York: Doubleday, 1963. Maintains that the conventional categories of American political analysis are of little help in understanding such phenomena as McCarthyism. Argues that American politics are essentially pragmatic or experimental. Further argues that the conversion of discrete political issues into ideologies can only undermine democratic society. Concludes that despite their danger, developments such as McCarthyism are the price a free society must pay for its openness.

Dahl, Robert A. *Who Governs.* New Haven, Conn.: Yale University Press, 1961. Argues that power in New Haven and other American communities is pluralistic. Emphasizes the importance of competing elites, the noncumulative distribution of resources, and a general commitment to democratic game rules for the survival of liberal democracy. Concludes that, although citizens are not equally influential, all citizens ultimately have a voice in the government.

Ekrich, Arthur. *The Decline of American Liberalism.* London: Longmans, Green, 1955. Defines liberalism as a habit of mind or a set of attitudes that includes representative government and the widest possible freedom, both economic and intellectual. Maintains that conservatism in the 1950s was only the most recent example of the decline of liberalism. Concludes that liberal values have lost their importance in American life and thought.

Hartz, Louis. "American Political Thought and the American Revolution," *American Political Science Review,* 46 (June 1952), 321–342. Discusses early American political thought in terms of its consensual and liberal character. Asserts that the absence of economic and class cleavages, typical of Europe, made revolutionary radicalism unnecessary. Views the American Revolution as strangely "conservative." Liberal in content, American thought has since become conservative in form. Concludes that the ideological consensus allows Americans to reduce questions of politics to matters of technique.

Hofstadter, Richard. "The Pseudo-Conservative Revolt," *American Scholar,* 24 (Winter 1954–1955), 9–27. Applies the term "pseudo-conservative" to right-wingers who, unlike other conservatives, reject American traditions and institutions. Argues that right-wingers are driven by status anxieties and a search for identity. Concludes that the right-wing revolt is given to expressions of vague discontent rather than specific programmatic demands.

Hunter, Floyd. *Community Power Structure.* New York: Doubleday, 1963. Argues that community elites are small, closed crowds or groups in and out of the formal governmental structure. Finds that a pyramidal power structure exists in American communities. Concludes that the power structure is cohesive, shares a common set of values, and agrees on important community decisions.

Huntington, Samuel P. "Conservatism as an Ideology: Its Place in America Today," *American Political Science Review,* 51 (June 1957), 454–473. Maintains that conservatism is not, as the aristocratic theory suggests, the monopoly of a particular class in history. Views conservatism as situational, that is, arising from a distinct historical challenge. Argues that Soviet Communism presents such a challenge to American institutions. Concludes that liberals must become conservative to protect the institutions they have created.

Kariel, Henry S. *The Decline of Pluralism.* Stanford: Stanford University Press, 1961. Maintains that corporate giants have emerged as private political regimes under a system of public government designed for a preindustrial society. Critically analyzes contemporary organizational practices. Argues that pluralism is outmoded because contemporary organizations are oligarchically governed hierarchies; believes that they place unjustifiable limits on constitutional democracy.

Kornhauser, William. *The Politics of Mass Society.* New York: Free Press, 1959. Maintains that democratic society is threatened by the direct accessibility of elites and masses to each other. Argues that intervening groups, such as trade unions, political parties, and churches, constitute an important buffer between elites and masses. Concludes that such intervening structures would prevent mobilization of the masses by elites and mass dominance of elites.

Levy, Leonard W. "Liberty and the First Amendment: 1790–1800," *American Historical Review,* 68 (October 1962), 22–37. Discusses the "breakthrough" in American thought with respect to freedom of speech and the press as promoted by Republican opposition to the Sedition Act. Maintains that the Sedition Act provoked Republicans to question seditious libel as a crime and to develop the idea that free government requires freedom of political discourse.

Lowi, Theodore. *The End of Liberalism.* New York: Norton, 1969. Indicts both the old liberal-conservative debate as irrelevant and interest group liberalism as the "ersatz political formula" that has arisen to take the place of classical liberalism. Argues that costs of interest group liberalism include the atrophy of institutions of popular control, an erosion of governmental responsibility and legitimacy, the reenforcement of tendencies toward oligarchy in private organizations, and a bias in favor of groups that are already a part of the pluralistic equilibrium. Suggests that a corrective focus would include a new definition of the public interest.

Lynd, Staughton. *Intellectual Origins of American Radicalism.* New York: Pantheon, 1968. Traces the roots of present-day radicalism from the political expressions of the American Revolution and the abolitionist movement. Maintains that a continuous radical tradition existed in America prior to the formation of an industrial proletariat or Marxist theory. Holds that the interpretation of the Declaration of Independence by pre-Civil War radicals has much in common with contemporary radicalism.

McClosky, Herbert. "Conservatism and Personality," *American Political Science Review,* 52 (March 1958), 27–45. Attempts to demonstrate empirically the relation between personality and conservatism. Argues that the modal conservative is psychologically timid, is distrustful of differences, fears change, dreads disorder, is intolerant of nonconformity, and derogates reason and intellectuality.

Meyers, Marvin. "The Jacksonian Persuasion," *American Quarterly,* 5 (Spring 1953), 3–15. Stresses the symbolic content of the Jacksonian movement. Argues that the Jacksonians were, above all, restorationists motivated by an illusory vision of republican virtue and rustic simplicity. Concludes that their appeals to the people and attacks on the money power should be viewed as a reaction against emerging economic and political forms and the decline of the "sturdy, independent, citizen-toiler."

Mills, C. Wright. *The Power Elite.* New York: Oxford University Press, 1965. Develops the concept of the ruling elite into a theory of community and national power. Argues that American military, business-industrial, and political elites are unified and coordinated. Accepts the need for centralized direction in a complex society, but argues that the power elite must be made responsible. Concludes that the intelligentsia is capable of making the power elite responsible.

Polsby, Nelson W. *Community Power and Political Theory.* New Haven, Conn.: Yale University Press, 1963. Argues that the reputational methods of locating power employed by Mills and Hunter are invalid. Asserts that their findings with respect to the power elite are an artifact of the reputational method. Concludes that a pluralist interpretation of American public life accurately describes contemporary American politics.

Prothro, J. W., and C. M. Grigg. "Fundamental Principles of Democracy: Bases of Agreement and Disagreement," *Journal of Politics,* 24 (May 1960), 276–294. Analyzes the importance of fundamental consensus of "principles" for the survival of democracy. Maintains that general assertions of principle evaporate when applied to specific issues and problems.

Reimer, Neil. "Two Conceptions of the Genius of American Politics," *Journal of Politics,* 20 (November 1958), 695–717. Argues that America is more indebted to past theory and is less a product of the present American landscape than Daniel Boorstin suggests. Maintains that there has been a greater continuity in American political thought than Boorstin admits and that past theory has shaped American political institutions. Concludes that the genius of American politics is not simply the result, as Boorstin maintains, of the "unprecedented opportunities of this continent," but also of conscious, explicit theory.

Rose, Arnold. *The Power Structure.* New York: Oxford University Press, 1967. Attacks the "economic-elite" dominance hypothesis of C. Wright Mills and Floyd Hunter as a caricature of American society. Denies the thesis that there is a unified power structure in the United States dominated by an economic elite. Argues that economic elites are subordinated to political authorities. Concludes that the power structure is highly complex and that elites are less than monolithic entities.

Schlesinger, Arthur M., Jr. *The Crisis of Confidence.* Boston: Houghton Mifflin, 1969. Sees the American people as shaken from a placid faith in its virtue and invulnerability by events that have challenged its leadership and resources. Defines the problems facing the society with special reference to individual violence, the cold war, and Vietnam. Discusses the role of students, intellectuals, and political leaders (especially the President) in solving these problems.

Schumpeter, Joseph. *Capitalism, Socialism, and Democracy.* 3rd ed. New York: Harper & Row, 1962. Examines the classical liberal theories of democracy. Analyzes the shortcomings of classical liberalism. Advances a theory of democracy based on the existence of competitive elites.

Spitz, David. "Power and Personality: The Appeal to the Right Man in Democratic States," *American Political Science Review,* 52 (March 1958), 840–897. Discusses the appeal for "the right man" to govern, the man who would achieve justice and secure liberty. Raises the problem of identifying "the right man." Maintains that although democracy does not guarantee that so-called right men will govern, it is preferable for that purpose to other methods of selection. Concludes that the logic of democracy requires that all men are admitted to the contest for power on equal terms.

Walker, Jack L. "Critique of the Elitist Theory of Democracy," *American Political Science Review,* 60 (June 1966), 285–305. Asserts that pluralist models of American politics convert classical democratic theory from a radical ideal to a conservative apology for the status quo. Argues that political apathy is not a prerequisite for political stability. Concludes that the pluralistic models of Dahl and Truman are inadequate to the task of evaluating contemporary American problems.

Wilson, G. W. "Democracy and the Modern Corporation," *Western Political Quarterly,* 13 (March 1960), 45–56. Examines the relation between public democracy and the existence of large corporations. Argues that the modern corporation has created conditions that are incompatible with free and open marketplace competition. Maintains that the corporation is inherently undemocratic. Concludes that powerful restraints are needed to check corporate power.

two

Parties, Interest Groups, and Elections

No aspect of American politics is so badly understood as the linkage of the people to their government. Essential components of this linkage are political parties, elections, and interest groups. Maligned and distrusted as these are, they constitute the most important—though far from the only—conduits through which Americans impose their will upon the formal institutions of government and through which, conversely, the politicians seek to lead public opinion toward support for the policies they espouse.

No observer of American politics asserts that parties, interest groups, and elections serve perfectly to reflect the "popular will," that illusive and perhaps only imaginary guidepost in a democracy. Indeed, the defects and inadequacies and occasional corruptions of these processes are so widely known as to create the contrary image: instead of serving democracy well the political process undermines representative government. For every political commentator who, along with Clinton Rossiter, asserts that in America there is "no democracy without politics, no politics without parties,"[1] there is a legion of detractors who believe that politicians are bosses, that parties are machines, that interest groups are selfish and corrupt, that the electorate is ignorant or vicious, that elections are manipulated by the professional pitchmen of Madison Avenue or bought by the perpetual reincarnations of Boss Tweed, and that politics is the tragedy of American democracy. It is against this background that students of American politics study the linkage institutions of the nation. The writers in this part, although wedded to the system they describe, are not without critical comment. Even so, they are generally more favorable or at least more charitable toward politics and politicians than is the citizenry at large.

The Parties

Stephen K. Bailey describes American parties as "a mystic maze," noting that "the closer one gets to our two great national parties, the more difficult it is to find them." One problem is, of course, the carelessness with which Americans use the word "party." They seldom recognize that each American party exists in three different forms: the voters who identify themselves with the party constitute the party and the electorate; the leaders and workers who form the party organization are the party of the activists; and the elected officials, candidates, and appointed governmental officers are the party in government. Each segment of the party has its own goals and concerns, and within each there is also a wide diversity in objectives and style. Thus, each major party is a difuse, decentralized, and loosely articulated coalition of voters, activists, and officeholders.

The most damaging sterotype of parties occurs when Americans speak of the party of the activists. They often view party workers as the venial and petty creatures of political bosses who steal from the public treasury and share their ill-gotten gains with their followers. Yet Frank Sorauf points out that the desire to promote favored public policies, the social and psychological satisfactions gained from party work, and the attachment to party as an institution are incentives for party activism fully as important as job patronage, preferments in the form of contracts or business arrangements, and advancement in

[1] Clinton Rossiter, *Parties and Politics in America* (Ithaca: Cornell University Press, 1960), p. 1.

political careers. These incentives to activism differ from place to place and time to time; nevertheless, the party organization is built upon a blend of them rather than upon any single motivation.

The old-style political machine was probably characterized by a large element of "material incentives" such as patronage and preferments. Machine politics was a stepping stone to status for those who lacked the wealth and professional credentials that marked the American elites. But the desire to promote policies that would benefit neighbors, ethnic brethren, and coreligionists also moved the traditional politicos. To this extent, at least, policy incentives were important. The social satisfactions derived from the fraternity spirit of the political clubhouse were as great a factor as any in attracting and holding people to the traditional political machine; the pleasures of association for immigrants and workingmen who had no other ties to the community cemented allegiance to the machine as no other incentive could.

The decline of the old-style political machine has been carefully analyzed by Fred Greenstein, and his thesis seems validated by the defeat in recent years of some of the most persistent of the old-style machines, such as those in New York, Philadelphia, and Pittsburgh. Only the legatees of Boss Hague's Jersey City machine, the powerful organization of Chicago's Mayor Daley, and the incredible Albany regime of "Uncle Dan" O'Connell remain unbowed. And even in these cities the erosion of the old politics is well advanced.

Whereas material incentives dominate the old-style machine, concern with policy and ideology takes precedence in the reform political clubs that have emerged since World War II. An exaltation of the antiorganization ethic and a policy-directed politics can be found in the reform Democratic clubs in New York; in the California Democratic Clubs and the California Republican Assembly; in the state party organizations in Michigan, Minnesota, and Wisconsin; in scores of less visible reform efforts around the country; and in the jerry-built National Democratic Coalition which arose from the ruins of the presidential campaigns of Eugene McCarthy and Robert F. Kennedy.

These political movements draw heavily on the upper middle classes. In this respect, the new reformers are in the tradition of the Progressives of the early years of the century. Their concerns are not with patronage or preferments, but rather with political issues, usually on the national level. The commitment of time, energy, and talent of the reform politicians can be enormous, and when on occasion there is an issue or a candidate of broad appeal, such as the Vietnam war issue and the McCarthy candidacy of 1968, the narrow base of reform activists becomes an important locus for broadly based protest activism.

The strengths of reform politics, however, are also its weaknesses. Because issue incentives are the mainstay of activism, changes in issues or discouragement at the slowness of political change take their toll on the clubs' ranks. Precisely because the "amateur" politicians are not dependent on politics for their standing in the community or for their income, they often drift away to other causes or activities. The reformers are, in the phrase of ward politician George Washington Plunkitt, only "mornin' glories." Furthermore, their intense focus on issues often renders them ineffective; they allow debate of the issues and passage of resolutions to take precedence over the unromantic tasks of registration, canvassing, and getting out the vote upon which the control of government—and, ironically, public policy—turn. The style of the issue-oriented political organizations has tended to narrow their base, especially among the Democrats. The minority groups about whom liberal ideologues are so often concerned may find more relevance in the old-style politics that provides social services, jobs, and mediation between the citizen and the bureaucracy than in the new politics of foreign policy, civil liberties, and the preservation of the environment. Even the leaders of the minority groups feel alienated by the upper-middle-class style of the reform politicians, illustrated by the bitter complaint of a black political leader in Los Angeles that the reformers' idea of a political meeting was a wine-tasting party.

Somewhere between the urban machines with their orientation toward material incentives and the reform clubs with their emphasis on policy incentives lie the vast majority of American party organizations. Leon Epstein has characterized the largest number of these as "skeletal." They consist of only a handful of activists, often too few to fill all the precinct and county committee posts established by statute and party rules. In few local party organizations are the essential tasks of registration, canvassing, membership solicitation, fund raising, record keeping, and recruitment performed with any vigor; in many, these tasks are not even attempted. The absence of party organization, rather than its effectiveness, is the most notable characteristic of great stretches of the country.

In skeletal parties the mix of incentives almost certainly runs heavily to social and psychological satisfactions. Many activists are socialized into party work at an early age by their parents. For them, affiliation with party is as natural as affiliation with civic clubs and religious sodalities. The standing in the community of a party position, especially when such standing costs little energy, is another attractive feature of party activism. But even in the skeletal party there may also be a surprising extent of policy orientation; this finding in the study by Lewis Bowman and his collaborators of precinct and ward leaders in Massachusetts and North Carolina—states not particularly noted for issue-oriented politics—challenges the easy assumption that American politics is rooted in essentially materialistic motivations.

Another widespread misconception about American politics is that party organization is hierarchical in structure and leadership. Civics texts too often portray American parties as neat pyramids with the national party chairmen at the apex, followed in descending order by the national party committees, the state party committees and chairmen, the congressional district committees and chairmen, the county and city committees and chairmen, and the ward and precinct clubs. In this political mirage, the barking of orders in backrooms at the top brings obedient responses throughout the ranks. No image could be further from reality.

The American parties are more like a mosaic than a pyramid. Each party unit is a separate piece with its own individual place in the whole. In a mosaic some pieces are larger, more brightly colored, more crucial to the design, and more polished than others. So it is with party units. Some are more effective in marshaling votes and may therefore lie nearer the center of party politics, particularly if the votes they deliver are numerous and for the "right" candidates. But each unit stands essentially by itself, for the incentives of politics are primarily local. Where material incentives remain important, it is the patronage of the city hall and the county courthouse that sustains the machine, not the few jobs that are bestowed by a president. For Mayor Daley's Chicago organization, thousands of city jobs and thousands more on the Cook County payroll provide the incentives for party work. For parties whose important incentives are social and psychological, the association with fellow partisans at the local level is important. Even for issue-oriented activists, the local party unit is the main arena, since it is there that issues are discussed, aspirants heard, and resolutions passed.

Parties are decentralized in yet another way. The main resources of politics are accumulated at the local level. The workers gather in local units. The money is often raised by local committees. Convention delegates who select candidates and construct platforms are chosen in local caucuses. Local primaries, because they are poorly attended by the electorate, are often influenced by the activists, who are more important opinion leaders in the primary than in the general election, where turnout is greater and party label provides voters with a tool for easily making ballot choices. Registration, canvassing, and getting out the vote are all local activities, conducted by local party units without significant assistance from those whose titles suggest higher standing in the party organization.

Where party leaders in the higher ranks have significant incentives at their command, they may effectively organize an army of local party committees. In Pennsylvania, where there are as many as 50,000 state patronage jobs, and in Indiana, where the number reaches 8,000, material incentives are available for building statewide machines. Ordinarily, though, party leadership at the higher levels must rely on less tangible incentives to bring together and activate the many independent elements in the political army. The charisma of the candidates, the policy stands by party leaders, the personal loyalties built on mutual deference and respect, and the deeply ingrained sense of party loyalty are the glue that holds in place—albeit uncertainly—party mosaic.

When the glue dissolves, there is little that party leaders can do. The southern Democratic leaders who sulked over the national party's civil rights commitments in every election from 1948 through 1968 could not be punished by the national party chairman because the resources and strength of American party politics are local and the rebels rather than the "leaders" are in the strategic positions. Similarly, the intractable conservative supporters of Senator Robert A. Taft who bolted the Eisenhower candidacy in 1952 were beyond reach and almost beyond reproach by national party leaders. When incentives are unavailable, when issues divide the party, when candidates are lackluster, when the harmony of personal relationships is disrupted, or when attachment to the party declines, the coalition that usually assembles under the same partisan banner comes apart easily. Party leadership in America, then, demands the artful orchestration of thousands of fiercely independent players by improvising a score that allows each player a worthy role and emphasizes common concerns rather than rivalries.

A third widely held misconception about American politics is that there is no difference between the parties. This complaint is not new; at the turn of the century, Englishman James Bryce asserted that the parties were like two empty wine bottles, differing only by label. The contemporary public continues this prejudice. How can Republicans claim to be different from Democrats when they embrace liberals such as Senators Jacob Javits and Clifford Case on the one hand and conservatives such as Senators Barry Goldwater and Roman Hruska on the other? The Democrats span the political spectrum too—from Edward Kennedy to James Eastland.

Both parties are clearly coalitions; each encompasses in its electoral base, its organization, and its range of officeholders, every shade and hue of political philosophy and program. Yet the "centers of gravity"—to borrow Stephen K. Bailey's apt phrase—are different. The work of McClosky and his collaborators shows that Democrats tend to be more "liberal" on regulation of the economy, social welfare endeavors, and civil rights. This same pattern appears in voting in the Congress. Despite the mavericks in both parties, when the roll calls are intoned the Democrats, with the exception of their southern wing, tend to favor a larger role for government in attacking social and economic problems while the Republicans, following an antigovernment bias, tend to prefer less governmental interference. Indeed, if the pattern discovered by McClosky and his coauthors in 1957–1958 remains intact today, Democratic leaders cluster around issue stances to the left of most of their followers while Republican activists prefer policies quite distinctly to the right of their election-day supporters. The party organizations, then, may actually be more sharply separated than are the voters; and the parties, instead of being too similar, may in fact be as clearly differentiated as the electorate will allow.

Within each party the differences on policy may be related to party rank or role. Edmond Costantini found that among California Democrats, ideological stance is closely related to party position.[2] Officeholders and candidates on the one hand and state-level party officials on the other tend to be "centrist" in their views, apparently to strike postures that appeal to the moderate electorate. Those prominent in congressional district party organizations (measured by their selection to the 1960 California national convention delegation) were more liberal than the higher echelon leaders; and those nominated for convention delegation seats by congressional district caucuses but not selected were more liberal still. Thus, while the centers of gravity of the two parties differ distinctively, it may also be true (at least in the issue-oriented, reform-style Democratic party of California) that within the party top strategists and candidates are under pressure from party activists to take more ideological stances while also being pulled by the electorate toward the center. The complete triumph of the activist perspective may doom the party at the polls, as the nomination of Barry Goldwater in 1964 testifies. But the spurning of ideology may have equally damaging consequences if it alienates the core of activists who are so important in waging campaigns; this was certainly one of Hubert Humphrey's burdens in 1968.

Candidates and officeholders play a mediating role in the party system. They must balance their responsibilities to party, constituency, and conscience as they campaign and govern. The role of the party in government is examined later in the discussions of the Congress and the presidency. But it is useful in this section to warn of the vast chasm between rhetoric about the duty of public service and the painful performance of that duty. The lofty appeal

[2] Edmond Costantini, "Intraparty Attitude Conflict: Democratic Party Leadership in California," *Western Political Quarterly*, 16 (December 1963), 956–972.

John F. Kennedy made to the graduates of Syracuse University, urging them to become active in politics, translates into the discouraging, exhausting, lonely campaign for office in an opposition-dominated district such as the First District in Massachusetts, where James McGregor Burns aspired unsuccessfully to graduate from the classrooms of Williams to the cloakrooms of Congress. The stark absence of the party from Burns' campaign reaffirms the skeletal nature of so much of American party organization, and suggests strongly that the lack of cohesive, policy-oriented parties in government, so strongly complained about by reformers, is a consequence of the ineffectiveness in nominations and elections of the shrivelled grass roots of American party organization.

Burns describes American politics as four-party politics and declares that democracy is deadlocked by this system. The "presidential wings" of both parties derive from the more liberal elements within them. They are rooted in the great metropolitan states of the nation, whose vast electoral vote blocs swing easily from one party to the other in response to policy stances that appeal to the diverse vote groups of the big-state electorates. The "congressional parties," on the other hand, are rooted in safer, more homogeneous one-party districts, far removed from the dynamics of change in fast-growing, problem-ridden metropolitan America. The seniority system installs old men in power, and it takes them from the stable rather than from the changing districts, from areas of social agreement rather than from areas of political conflict. These power holders are essentially conservative, unchallenged in their baliwicks by the opposition, unresponsive to grass-roots party organizations with strong orientations toward national policy, and independent of the elected leaders of their own party.

Thus, while there are distinct differences between the centers of gravity of the two parties in government, the structure of the government enthrones the most conservative members of each party in critical positions in the Congress. Neither the President, nor the majority of the party caucus, nor whatever party organizations may exist back home can compel these men to "represent" the party's national position in their discharge of responsibilities. So the party in government is fragmented and often deadlocked, far from the ideal of a cohesive unit enacting a program mandated in the party's name by the electorate.

How nearly politics conforms to the ideal, however, depends distinctly on one's choice of ideals. Many will argue that public officials should not follow the party line but should instead be guided by the wishes of their constituents or by their own consciences. Democratic congressmen from South Carolina have different constituencies than Democratic congressmen from California, and it would be a corruption of representative government, the argument goes, to compel them to vote as their party leaders do. The vast diversity in American politics reflects the social, economic, and political conditions of the American people. To maintain major party status, each party must encompass widely differing views. National politics is the bargaining and compromising of these divergences, perhaps—but not always—within the structure of the party, so that the results of the government serve all the people in some measure, though none of them fully. Party cohesion is gained by mutual understanding, not by the power of party organizations at the grass roots or of party leaders in the government. And while reformers insist on a need for more direct, decisive action by cohesive, issue-oriented parties, the present process can be defended as having secured continued peace in America by striking balances between competing forces; it compromises the most deeply felt differences rather than tearing the fabric of a consensual society by giving total policy victories to one segment of the nation and total defeats to another.

Just as the party of the activists is, upon close examination, many parties—ranging from the old-style urban machine to the amateur reform clubs—so the party in government is neither the cohesive, disciplined policy-making organ of the reformers nor an atomized collection of officials bearing only by chance the same party label. The desire to win draws officeholders together in common efforts to make policies that will capture public approval. The tools of leadership inherent in party posts in Congress and in the presidency add further elements of cohesion. Skillful use of these tools heightens the effectiveness of the party; so does communication from party activists back home, particularly when party organizations are vigorous and issue-oriented. Finally, the effectiveness of the party in government depends on the common commitments to issues and the constituency preferences of the party members. The policies adopted by elected party officials, the pledges made by party aspirants for office, the attitudes of the activists, and the preferences of the voters combine to fill James Bryce's differently labeled bottles with wines that are distinguishable from one another if not totally different.

Voters, Parties, and Elections

The impact of party organizations upon elections may be declining as the strength of political machines wanes. Party workers continue to make an impact, however, through their canvassing, telephone calling, literature distributions, and get-out-the-vote campaigns. In 1968, for example, about 25 percent of American voters reported being contacted by a worker in behalf of one of the candidates or parties. The number was obviously higher in locales with strong party structures. Despite studies showing that active party canvassing may affect the voting decisions of as many as 10 percent of the electors in presidential elections and of even larger numbers in lesser races, the full effect of party activity on voters is difficult to measure precisely.

Furthermore, American parties play a large role in determining election outcomes through the illusive concept of party identification. As Greenstein points out, party identification—the self-image of party membership by the individual voter—is the most important element in the dynamic of electoral choice. Nearly three out of four Americans identify themselves as Democrats or Republicans. This is their "standing decision" about electoral matters; in most circumstances their ballot on election day will be cast for candidates running under the banner of the party with which they identify. Of course, party identification is not the sole element in a voter's decision. His orientation to candidates and issues also influences him. Moreover, since most elections in America are settled by a small percentage of the votes, the impact of candidate, and issues is often great enough to provide the margin between victory and defeat for parties and their candidates.

Despite this flexibility in the electoral system, the commitment to party by so many Americans has a substantial stabilizing effect on national politics. Party identification tends to be a lifelong commitment. Indeed, it becomes stronger with advancing age. Furthermore, the party identification of parents is one of the most important influences on the eventual choice of their children. Party identification tends therefore to be quite stable. Once a party has gained the adherence of a majority of the American population, it remains the dominant party for an extended period. The Republican party, for example, maintained dominance for almost seven decades—from 1860 to 1930. Even when the Republicans were cast from office in 1912 and 1916, when Democrat Woodrow Wilson gained the presidency, they retained the loyalty of the vast majority of Americans. Since 1930, the Democrats have commanded the majority support, despite the Republican breakthroughs for Eisenhower in 1952 and 1956 and for Nixon in 1968. The point may be that the American political system is one of political eras, demarked by great events, such as the Civil War and the Great Depression, that dramatically alter party identifications among voters and create a new party majority in the nation. During any political era, party politics is reasonably stable and predictable. The public policy of the nation is mainly responsible to whatever groups, interests, and political values compose the majority party.

Seen in the context of political eras more or less dominated by a majority party, the observation that the major parties are dissimilar, at least in their centers of gravity, becomes central to an understanding of American politics. Greenstein's tabular presentation of the "sociology of the electorate" offers insight into the dominant stream of contemporary politics. The Democrats are the majority party in the present political era. Their electoral coalition can be seen from Greenstein's figures to draw most heavily from the grade- and high-school educated, the blue-collar workers, the big-city dwellers, the Catholics, and the minority racial groups. In short, it is a coalition of the socially and economically "disadvantaged," who seek to improve their opportunities for enjoying America's promise and abundance through favorable governmental programs. The Democratic party's domestic liberalism, its "progovernment bias," is an apparent response to the aspirations of the dominant elements in its electoral base. This responsiveness provides one of the key links between the people and their government. It is not so much a popular mandating of particular programs as a general commitment, reflected in the party's actions in government, to the social and economic interests of those groups who provide the votes.

The same analysis applies, of course, to the Republicans. Drawing most heavily from the established segments of society—the college educated, the professionals and businessmen, the residents of small towns and cities, and the ethnic and religious groups that arrived in the early waves of immigration —the Republican party tends to be more conservative, more reluctant to redistribute wealth and social standing, more committed to existing private institutions and the established order in society. Although it has been the minority party in recent decades, the Republican party coalition was the majority party during the decades when American capitalism came of age, when the cleavages of the Civil War dominated the society, when Americans were still pioneering to the West and settling in the small towns and cities, and when aspiring immigrant groups either had not yet developed their political muscle or were content, for reasons mainly removed from national policies and programs, to support old-style machines of either party. The Republican party's time, as Kevin Phillips and other Republican intellectuals argue, may have come again in an era when the drive for social and economic reform is slackening and when many of those who constituted the old Democratic coalition, having reached the status of "haves" rather than "have nots," prefer a party less committed to altering the distribution of money and standing in America.

In pointing out differences between the parties, it is imperative to recall that while their centers of gravity are different, both parties are coalitions encompassing all views and groups in America. Like the range of political philosophy among party activists and officeholders in each party, the sociology of the electorate confirms this. Although most union members vote Democratic, some vote Republican; although most professionals and businessmen are Republicans, the Democrats gain the votes of a minority. Thus each party, despite the distinct nature of its electorate and its consequent approach to public policy, must pay heed to those who are not its primary constituents in order to retain support among those groups. In seeking election victories, the parties work to expand their base, to win votes among groups ordinarily associated with the opposition as well as among the groups from which they draw most of their adherents; in the process they strive to accommodate many policy preferences, to moderate policy orientations, and thus to become truly "national" political parties. This unslackening drive to develop broader appeals on policy causes the parties simultaneously to have different centers of gravity but not totally different constituencies, programs, or identifications. As links between the electorate and government, each party represents, although in different measures, almost all segments and opinions in the nation.

Interest Groups

Major parties in America play the electoral game first and foremost. They compete for control of the government under their own banners by fielding candidates, marshaling voters, making appeals on issues, personalities, or whatever else will attract support, and they test their own success by whether their candidates win a plurality at the polls. Interest groups do not shun the electoral arena, but they do not directly participate either. Their goals are limited mainly to policies or decisions that affect their members, or at least those members in control. Occasionally an interest group defines a broad national program that has many of the trappings of a party platform—such is the case with American labor. But even an interest group with comprehensive goals directs its greatest efforts to the particular issues that closely affect the group's members. Thus, for labor unions, matters of collective bargaining, wages, hours, and working conditions take precedence over foreign policy and farm subsidies.

Interest groups may not be active in politics at all. If they can achieve their objectives by private means, such as negotiation or reciprocal denial of goods and services or competition in the marketplace, they prefer to keep government out of their affairs. But often the losers in these private conflicts seek governmental intervention to redress the balance. This is a process which E. E. Schattschneider calls the "socialization of conflict."[3] The losers seek to force the issue into the public arena, where they hope the addition of new participants will bring a different result. It is only when interest groups—associations formed around common goals or institutions—become engaged in this socialization of conflict that they become "political" interest groups, operating in the public arena.

The American political landscape is crowded with political interest groups. There are literally tens of thousands seeking to impose their values and objectives on the community through the instrument of government. Business is the most highly organized segment of society with its numerous trade associations, chambers of commerce, and political action committees; but the list of organized interests ranges from such obvious groups as labor unions, farm organizations, and ethnic and racial associations to such virtually invisible entities as the Shore and Beach Preservation Association.

The proliferation of political interest groups is undoubtedly encouraged by the decentralized structure of the American government. There are many governmental forums in which a group, defeated elsewhere, can seek to right the balance. The federal system provides innumerable opportunities. Thus it is that the temperance forces in the United States have succeeded in banning alcoholic beverages in many of the nation's towns, counties, and cities (and until recently several states), even after being rebuffed nationally by the repeal of the Eighteenth Amendment. Similarly, the profusion of governmental institutions at each level of government provides many separate skirmishing opportunities. For many years those who favored racial segregation found that they could win battles in the Congress by means of the seniority system, which yielded key committee chairmanships to conservatives, and the filibuster, even though the President was committed to desegregation. In turn, those who favored desegregation, seeking a new forum in which they could win, ultimately took their struggle into the Supreme Court and succeeded, as one of the selections in Part V illustrates.

The nature of the party system also contributes to the profusion of interest groups. The broad coalition nature of parties and their lack of internal cohesion requires that advocates of causes seek alternative methods for advancing their goals within the government. Both the endless flight to government of the losers in interest conflicts and the steady expansion of governmental concerns require the mobilization of political interest groups to protect the common interests of groups of citizens. The strong constitutional sanction of the right to petition the government adds to the tendency toward interest groups in American politics, since the activities of such groups precisely fit the purpose, if not the intent, of the First Amendment.

The strength of interest groups depends heavily on their membership and leadership. It is commonly observed that groups with large memberships are advantaged, since they can make themselves felt in elections. Labor unions, for example, derive much of their influence from their large numbers. A membership that is well off, well educated, and of high status adds force to

[3] E. E. Schattschneider, *The Semisovereign People* (New York: Holt, Rinehart and Winston, 1960), p. 7.

a group. One reason the American Medical Association has been successful is that its members are prestigious within their communities and are financially able to support extensive pressure campaigns for their own interests. A group with an educated and articulate membership that understands the structure of American politics can petition the government more effectively than can other groups. The distribution of membership can also be important. Members spread over a large number of electorally marginal districts or states may benefit a group, since many elected officials will want to obtain the group's support. A skilled leadership capable of holding its membership together and familiar with the structure of the government also adds to the effectiveness of a political interest group. Perhaps most important to such a group is internal agreement on and commitment to its objectives.

Just as these attributes strengthen a political interest group, their absence weakens its effectiveness. A group may also be weakened by opposition from other groups that seek to maintain the status quo or limit the extent of the changes. The law, too, imposes limitations on each interest group by requiring it to register, report its sources of income and its expenditures, and declare the legislation it supports. However, the most significant constraint on interest groups is deeply rooted public antipathy. Surveys show that Americans distrust most such groups, and that even those who acknowledge their membership in groups that advance political objectives display a high level of suspicion of lobbying activities. A political interest group whose methods are too aggressive or indiscreet may bring upon itself a tide of public hostility that will strengthen its opponents and cause public officials to repudiate its goals. This was the case in 1956, when President Eisenhower vetoed a natural gas bill whose substantive provisions he approved; lobbyists for the industry had used methods of dubious morality to obtain the bill's passage.

Political interest groups employ a wide range of tactics in pursuit of their objectives. The most commonly known technique is of course "lobbying," from which the whole activity of interest groups has gained its name. Derived from the practice of interest group representatives standing about in the lobbies of the legislature to discuss their objectives with the members, lobbying is the attempt to persuade legislators to a certain view. Lobbyists appear before legislative committees, interview legislators, conduct letter-writing campaigns, circulate petitions, present resolutions by groups "back home," and bring delegations to the capitol. The forming of coalitions with like-minded groups and logrolling, in which groups trade support for each other's objectives, are among the tactics they employ to build strength in the legislature.

Executives, too, are subject to lobbying, since they play a major role in the legislative process, appoint executive officials to administer laws crucial to interest groups, and formulate and administer the budgets upon which hangs the effectiveness of most governmental activity. Interest groups are active in the courts as well. Judicial interpretation of statutory language may turn a legislative defeat into a victory, and challenges to the constitutionality of legislative or administrative action may undo adverse decisions in other forums. The test case and the amicus curiae brief are common activities of interest groups, as are attempts to influence judicial appointments (or elections, in the case of many state judges), to place favored views of the law in strategic locations such as legal journals, and to select for litigation those courts likely to take a view of the law that is congenial to the group's interests.

Overarching all these activities are attempts to persuade the public. Many associations engage in public relations campaigns to win public support for their objectives. The now famous "Reddy Kilowat" was a device to persuade people that the electric power provided by privately owned utilities was the cheapest item in the family budget, and that, concomitantly, there was no need for the expansion of such public power projects as the Tennessee Valley Authority.

Interest groups participate in political campaigns as well as in more general appeals. They endorse candidates whose records they favor and announce the endorsements both to their members and to the public. Some groups contribute financially to the campaigns of favored candidates; most notable among the "big givers" are labor's Committee on Political Education, the Business and Industry Political Action Committee, and the political action arm of the American Medical Association. Registration drives, canvassing, and other chores commonly attributed to political parties may also be undertaken by interest groups seeking to "reward their friends and punish their enemies," in the phrase of Samuel Gompers of the American Federation of Labor. In addition, the house organ of an interest group can promote the candidacies of the group's allies in the government and criticize its enemies. Furthermore, the group's meetings can be opened as platforms for its endorsed candidates; indeed, the key to the union hall, the Chamber of Commerce convention, or the Farmer's Union Cooperative station may be available to endorsed candidates only.

All these activities are designed to bring the policies of the government into line with the aspirations of citizens—at least those citizens organized into political interest groups. To the extent that political interest groups effectuate the constitutional freedom to petition the government, they scarcely seem objectionable. Furthermore, in a society whose ethos stresses the accountability of officials to the people and the role of citizens in the political life of their country, political interest groups appear to provide a convenient vehicle for the citizen who wants to engage in politics, represent his views to the government, and hold his representatives responsible for their actions. But political interest groups do not operate evenly in the population. Some are far more advantaged by the system than others. Through interest groups, the weight of individual citizens in the governmental process may become more uneven rather than more fully represented. The "scope and bias of the pressure system," in Schattschneider's persuasive phrase, is what is objectionable to the thoroughgoing democrat. It is this scope and bias in all of the linkage processes that has drawn the ire of American political reformers.

Parties, Pressure Groups, and Elections in Perspective

Many of the "functions" that Clinton Rossiter attributes to America's two great parties can be credited to political interest groups as well. Parties and interest groups both recruit political leaders and involve themselves in staffing the government. While parties take a more direct role in nominating candidates and waging their campaigns, interest groups also participate. Both parties and interest groups advance programs, although the emphasis on policy in interest groups may be greater than in parties, where platforms are often designed to capture votes rather than prescribe the direction of the government. Both serve as buffers and adjusters in meeting the problems that citizens often have with their government, such as obtaining a passport and applying for veterans' benefits. Political interest groups, like parties, serve as centers for political education. And, like parties, they may have a symbolic function, insofar as many Americans identify themselves politically with their church or farm organization as well as with their political party.

But the greatest role of American parties cited by Rossiter is precisely the role that political interest groups do not share, or at least do not share significantly—that is, the consensus-building function. For as Rossiter points out, "the parties have been the peacemakers of the American community, the unwitting but forceful suppressors of the 'civil-war potential' we carry always in the bowels of our diverse nation."[4] The coalition nature of parties, their insistence on appealing to all views and groups, and their commitment to electoral success rather than ideological rectitude have been widely praised by political scientists. By striving for compromises that give something to everyone, but not everything to anyone, the parties encourage "working within the system" and avoid the complete alienation of segments of the community from the political process. Fraternal feuds do not become fratricide as long as Edward Kennedy and James Eastland find themselves under the common umbrella of the Democratic party and Jacob Javits and Barry Goldwater find themselves under the Republican parasol. Political interest groups are more single minded; they are not usually moderated in their aspirations by the need to accommodate the contrary view within their own ranks. In short, the catalysts of policy conflict in America are pressure groups rather than parties, and this "nearly formless political process in which parties with too little power and interest groups with too much purpose struggle riotiously" is perhaps "the price of union."

This formulation of the linkage process draws sharp criticism from Schattschneider and Bailey. "[T]he most powerful special interests want private settlements," Schattschneider argues, "because they are able to dictate the outcome as long as the conflict remains private. . . . It is the function of public authority to modify private power relations by enlarging the scope of the conflict."[5] Parties should be the instrument of this enlargement, for their battles are fought before the entire public and decided in contests in which every elector is a proper participant.

The parties need more clearly differentiated policy stands and the tools to convert campaign rhetoric to governmental action. For without governmental effectiveness by parties, special interest groups are able, by taking up defensive positions in the highly decentralized political system, to prevent public interference with the private outcomes they have dictated. The labyrinthine quality of the American government serves well the defensive strategies of special interest groups, since the friendly interpretation of hostile legislation by an administrative agency or a court, the veto power of a sympathetic executive, the insistence on delay through the filibuster, and a

[4] Rossiter, *op. cit.*, p. 59.

[5] Schattschneider, *op. cit.*, p. 40 (emphases deleted).

host of other sticking points prevent affirmative action to modify private power relations.

Furthermore, in the words of a Bob Dylan song, "the times they are a changin'." The four-party, deadlocked "government of fits and starts" will no longer suffice. As a world power, America must face the issue of war or peace. In the midst of a revolution by minority groups and young people against domestic policies and "the establishment," there is greater need than before for "a flow of imaginative, informed, consistent, and power-related responses to pressing national and world issues," and these responses must be accountable to a national majority. Parties that ameliorate differences instead of offering choices are no longer appropriate, and party reformers have insisted on a long agenda of changes to make parties "relevant" to the changing times.

But the agenda of change offered by Bailey and other "responsible party" advocates may still miss the mark; the "upper-class bias of the pressure system" noted by Schattschneider may indeed be a bias of the whole system.[6] Schattschneider points out the "overwhelming evidence that participation in voluntary organizations is related to upper social and economic status." It is the well off and the well educated, those most likely to resist change, who write their congressmen, join pressure groups, contribute funds to politics, and otherwise participate in the pressure system. This same problem may affect party government as well. With the decline of the old-style machine, which co-opted the powerless into its ranks, party politics also becomes increasingly an activity of those in the upper statuses. The most "responsible" and "issue-oriented" parties are those mass membership organizations whose activists are predominantly upper-middle class and whose biases on policy and political style may be far removed from those of the great majority of Americans.

The upper-middle-class bias in political activism is the result not only of the greater understanding of politics that derives from more formal education and of the heightened sense of political efficacy that accompanies standing in the community, but also of the advantage in political resources. If prestige, wealth, and education increase political effectiveness, then the upper-middle class is advantaged in political resources as well as in political knowledge and will. The only major resource the lower classes have is numbers, which without ample skill, knowledge, and money cannot be organized for maximum electoral impact.

The narrowness of the political system extends to American elections. There is a correlation between social and economic status and voting that is similar to, if not so pronounced as, the relationship between social class and participation in voluntary associations. Those who are somewhat better established in the system are apparently motivated to participate in it. Furthermore, among much of the middle and upper classes voting is considered a civic duty, while among many of the poor, the black, and the young, alienation and apathy discourage voting. Education increases the understanding of registration requirements, the governmental system, and the importance of voting. Furthermore, income, social standing, and education, highly correlated among themselves, seem together to engender a feeling of political efficacy—the ability to affect the government by one's own actions, which is a crucial factor

[6] *Ibid.*, p. 32.

in whether people cast ballots. Registration and residency requirements often work against the disadvantaged, since they are frequently transient. The young move around while in college and in their first years of employment, and members of minority groups tend to move regularly in search of better jobs or more favorable living conditions. The minimum voting age of twenty-one, long prevailing in all but four states, has disqualified a large number of young people who are deeply concerned about contemporary affairs. At this writing, a revised Voting Rights Act enfranchising citizens at eighteen years of age has been enacted into law and is being tested in the Supreme Court. Moreover, literacy tests, poll taxes, and a variety of discriminatory devices have ousted most Negroes in the South and some in the North from electoral participation. The end of these barriers as a result of the 1965 Voting Rights Act has not been fully accomplished, since economic and social pressures against black voting in the South remain strong (although Negro registration has increased about 1.8 million since the act became law).

The sociology of voting tells the story in dramatic fashion. In 1964, 88 percent of the college educated voted, compared to only 68 percent of the high school educated. Ballots were submitted by 75 percent of the professionals and businessmen, but by only 50 percent of the unskilled workers. Among white Americans participation was 79 percent; among black Americans, only 64 percent. Among those under thirty-five, 68 percent voted, compared to 80 percent of those fifty-five and over.

The bias of the linkage system becomes quite apparent. Participation by the groups most anxious for change is lowest in interest groups, somewhat, but probably not significantly, higher in the party of the activists, and highest in the electoral process. But even in the electoral process, participation is far greater among the well off than among the distressed. It is not surprising that the easy tactics of confrontation have captured the imagination of many groups in America—of welfare mothers, black militants, and the radical young. There appears to be a contagion of confrontation, for the police in Chicago have shown themselves as capable of rioting as the blacks in Watts. And the "hard hats" have apparently learned—if somewhat more slowly than the radicals who physically assault prowar speakers on college campuses—that intimidation can be achieved by a good beating. What seems obvious is that participation in confrontations may be easier, more satisfying to the ego, and, because of mass media, more visible than participation in the traditional linkage processes. Furthermore, the antisystem rhetoric of left-wing protesters and the difficulties of registering, canvassing, and getting out the vote, when compared to the organizing of a street rally, tend to siphon off political energy from such incremental political modes as pressure groups, parties, and electoral activities. It is also clear that effective substitutes have not been found for the old techniques for engendering participation in parties and elections, especially the old-style party machine.

Advocates of party reform, along with Schattschneider and Bailey, believe that sharper distinctions between the parties, more cohesive party action in policy making, and revitalization of local party organizations around ideological incentives will not only improve national policy making through the party system, but will also engender broader participation by providing more meaningful choices and more concrete policy results through partisan conflict.

In some respects Bailey's prescriptions for party reform have gained acceptance, but in most aspects, the passing of time has weakened rather than strengthened the party system.

The preliminary signs of party reshuffling that Bailey reports in his essay have become more distinct in the subsequent years. The enfranchisement of large numbers of blacks in the South, the identification of some southern Democrats with the national liberal Democratic party, and the "southern strategy" of Barry Goldwater have all powered a Republican resurgence in the former Confederacy and in the Border States. The new breed of southern Republicans is flanking the Democrats from the right; and, while many old-time southern Democratic officeholders continue in the traditional conservative mold, the Democrats are increasingly taking moderate or moderately liberal positions in the South. In a region whose politics is somewhat more conservative than that of the nation, the southern Democrats are nonetheless becoming the more liberal of the two parties. At the same time that there is a revival of two-partyism in the South, the competitive status of the Democratic party in the Midwest and in the great expanse from the Mississippi River to the Rocky Mountains has been confirmed. Indeed, in the off-year of 1970, these formerly staunch Republican bastions were the site of the greatest Democratic successes.

But if the party reformers were shrewd foretellers of intensified and more consistently issue-oriented electoral competition, their aspirations for stronger party organization have gone unfulfilled. The mass membership party constructed around purposive incentives has not grown as a force on the American political scene. The membership strength of the New York and California political clubs and the citizen parties in Minnesota, Michigan, and Wisconsin has not expanded, and indeed in several places party strength has plummeted.

Commentators on political parties, such as Leon D. Epstein[7] and Frank J. Sorauf,[8] have argued that changes in society have made obsolete the traditional role of party organizations. The incentives and indeed the effectiveness of the old-style party machine are gone, as Greenstein points out. The new middle-class parties—where they exist at all—are unlikely to be as thorough and effective in the tasks of voter registration, canvassing, and getting out the vote. The issue-oriented activists within the party "may wish to act only selectively on behalf of candidates whose issue positions are congruent with theirs."[9] Most important, mass media have increasingly displaced precinct workers as links between office seekers and voters.

> [T]he new techniques [of politics] involve increasing use, and increasingly skilled use, of the mass media for political and other kinds of communication. Their use is advanced by material developments, especially in television, and by behavioral research in popular responses. Moreover, increased formal education and a pervasive home-centered middle-class life style make for a large audience that is responsive to direct appeals about politics as about everything else. An organizational apparatus intervening between candidates and voters may be less necessary, or at any rate less efficient, as a vote-getting device.[10]

[7] Leon D. Epstein, *Political Parties in Western Democracies* (New York: Praeger, 1967), esp. chap. 9.
[8] Frank J. Sorauf, *Party Politics in America* (Boston: Little, Brown, 1968), esp. chap. 18.
[9] *Ibid.*, p. 427.
[10] Epstein, *op. cit.*, p. 233.

The essential resources of the new political style are money and technical skills. The mass membership, ideological party envisioned by party reformers provides neither. Mass parties, even as highly developed as those in Europe, have in recent years been unable to fund campaigns from membership subscriptions, and the studies of American mass parties show that they receive little of their money (as low as 7 percent, in the case of Wisconsin) from membership dues.

The party of the activists seems, therefore, on the wane. The population is not as responsive to old-style political techniques, and the parties are unable to wage such traditional campaigns. The public is better educated and more issue oriented with the consequence that allegiances to party are weakened in favor of more selective commitments to issues and candidates. The development of the media as the most important information sources about public affairs has placed media technicians above party activists in the process of political persuasion. And the failure of political parties—especially the Democratic party—to provide financial resources effectively has further weakened their role in the election campaigns of their candidates.

Just as the party of the activists is undergoing dramatic changes in the media age, the contemporary era is filled with signs of new directions in electoral politics. Among the most provocative commentaries is Kevin P. Phillips' *The Emerging Republican Majority.*[11] The core of his argument is that America is once again in a critical election period, with 1964 and 1968 marking the first phase of a realignment that will return the Republicans to the majority party, status they enjoyed from 1860 until the Roosevelt New Deal coalition was forged in the economic disaster of the Great Depression.

The elements of this new Republican majority lie mainly in the South and in the Great Plains. George Wallace's American Independent party is viewed by Phillips as one of those halfway houses that occur in American history when a large element of the electorate needs a vehicle for eschewing its former party to join a new one. According to Phillips, the vast majority of the Wallace voters are incipient Republicans. Goldwater's victory in the Deep South in 1964 and the combined Wallace-Nixon vote in both the Confederacy and the Border States presage Republican hegemony throughout the area. In the Great Plains, the Republicans are already the majority, and their dominance will be strengthened as voters repudiate stagnant liberal economic and social programs and reject the confrontation tactics of the college activists and black militants who are catered to by the liberal establishment.

The shift to the suburbs of formerly Democratic ethnic and economic groups also signifies a shift to Republicanism. These groups once favored redistribution of the wealth through New Deal social and economic legislation, but in recent years they have "been elevated by prosperity to middle-class status and conservatism."[12]

> The emerging Republican majority spoke clearly in 1968 for a shift away from the sociological jurisprudence, moral permissiveness, experimental residential, welfare and educational programing and massive federal spending by which the Liberal (mostly Democratic) Establishment sought to propagate liberal institutions and ideology. . . . The dominion of this impetus is inherent in the list of Republican-

[11] Kevin P. Phillips, *The Emerging Republican Majority* (New Rochelle, N.Y.: Arlington House, 1969).
[12] *Ibid.*, p. 470.

trending groups and potentially Republican Wallace electorates of 1968: Southerners, Borderers, Germans, Scotch-Irish, Pennsylvania Dutch, Irish, Italians, Eastern Europeans and other urban Catholics, middle-class suburbanites, Sun Belt residents, Rocky Mountain and Pacific Interior populists. Democrats among these groups were principally alienated from their party by its social programs and increasing identification with the Northeastern Establishment and ghetto alike.[13]

The bastions of liberal Republicanism in New York, New England, and Michigan have been written off by Phillips: these areas will be forfeited to the Democrats as the Republicans construct a new conservative majority in the South (including Texas), the Border States, and Great Plains. The Pacific Coast states (California, Washington, and Oregon), the Non-Yankee Northeast (Pennsylvania, New Jersey, Delaware, and Maryland), the Upper Mississippi Valley (Iowa, Minnesota, and Wisconsin), and the Ohio-Mississippi Valley (Ohio, Indiana, Illinois, Missouri, Kentucky, and West Virginia) are the battlegrounds where presidential elections will be decided (see Map 1). Here

Map 1 The Emerging Republican Majority

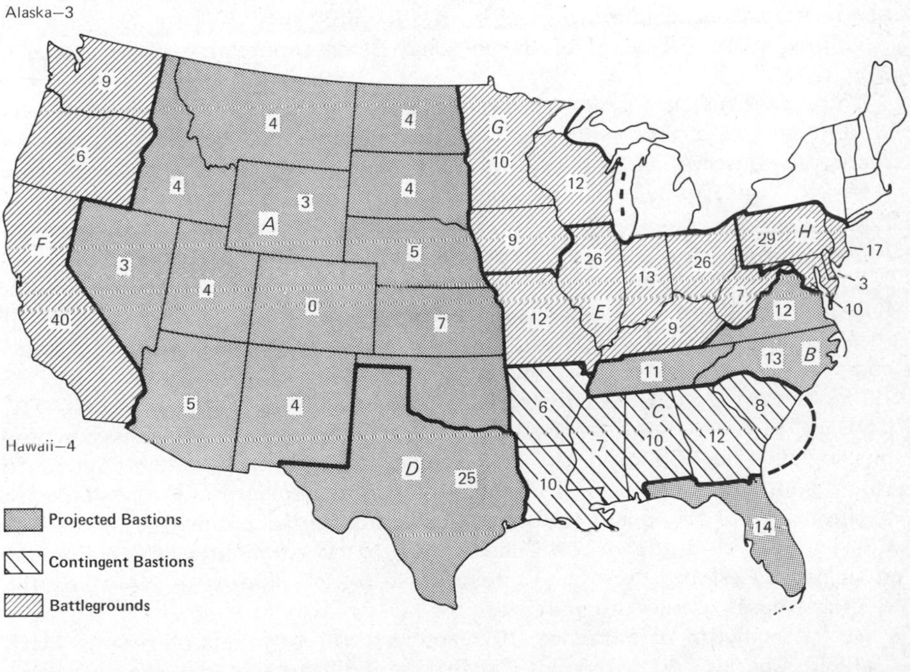

Source: Kevin Phillips, *The Emerging Republican Majority* (New Rochelle, N.Y.: Arlington House, 1969), p. 472. Copyright © 1969 by Arlington House, New Rochelle, New York and used with permission.

Areas *A, B,* and *D* are projected Republican bastions after the realigning election of 1968. Area *C* is shifting to the Republicans through the halfway house of George Wallace's American Independent party. Areas *E, F, G,* and *H* are marginal areas in which defections among lower-middle-class Democrats have given the Republicans an edge. Only in the Pacific Northwest and Upper Mississippi River Valley areas is Democratic strength about equal to the Republican voting power. The unshaded areas (New York, New England, and Michigan) are conceded by Phillips to the Democrats.

[13] *Ibid.*, p. 471.

the revolt of newly arrived suburbanites, drawn from the ethnic and economic lower-middle classes, formerly Democratic, will give the Republicans a critical advantage.

In Phillips' view the Democratic party will become the minority liberal party in the South, the vehicle of wealthy liberals in the upper-class suburbs and fashionable neighborhoods of the big cities, and the choice of defecting Republican Yankees and Scandinavians in rural areas and small cities in New York, New England, and the Pacific Northwest who were formerly the electoral base for the liberal Republicanism of Wendell Willkie and Nelson Rockefeller.

The Democrats will also remain the party of 90 percent of the nation's black voters. This, Phillips asserts, is an important element in the building of the emerging Republican majority, for in the South, Negro Democrats drive the majority whites into the GOP; and in the North, their domination of the big cities alienates the lower-middle-class Democrats who have found new homes in suburbia. "Abandonment of civil rights enforcement would be self-defeating," says Phillips. "Maintenance of Negro voting rights in Dixie, far from being contrary to GOP interests, is essential if southern conservatives are to be pressured into switching to the Republican Party—for Negroes are beginning to seize control of the national Democratic Party in some Black Belt areas."[14]

To prevent the Democrats from reuniting the Roosevelt coalition around its traditional core of economic issues, the Republicans must pursue a "successful moderate conservatism" that will dispel blue collar fears that the Republican party will undermine programs such as Social Security, Medicare, collective bargaining, and aid to education that have an obvious and well-perceived importance to the upwardly mobile lower-middle classes.

Phillips' book is more than a description of a new era in American politics, it is a prescription for Republican strategy as well. Phillips was an assistant to John N. Mitchell, now attorney general, who in turn was Richard Nixon's campaign manager and most influential advisor. The Nixon strategy for the 1970 off-year elections heavily reflected the imprint of Phillips' thesis. The decision to name Southerners to the Supreme Court and to disavow the bussing of school children, the deliberate efforts of Vice-President Agnew to woo a southern constituency and to put northern Democrats on the defensive on the issues of crime and student disruption, and the repudiation of Senator Charles Goodell in favor of Conservative party candidate James Buckley strongly suggest the President's intention to follow Phillips in reshaping the electoral bases of the two parties.

Recent criticism of administration policy from such Republicans as Mark Hatfield, Charles Percy, and Edward Brooke indicates that the liberals within the Republican party fear for themselves the consequences of a strategy that moves the center of gravity in the Republican party to the right and deliberately forsakes the party's liberal wing. The liberal criticism of Phillips and his southern strategy gains weight from the results of the 1970 election. Ironically, Republican victories were most prominent in the East, while the Democrats made gains—especially in gubernatorial elections—in the South,

[14] *Ibid.*, p. 464.

Midwest, and Great Plains, precisely the targets of the Phillips' strategy.

Within a year after the publication of Phillips' book, Richard M. Scammon and Ben J. Wattenberg published *The Real Majority*[15] disputing Phillips' thesis. Recognizing the dramatic realignment of 1932, Scammon and Wattenberg argue nonetheless that beginning in 1948 American politics has been essentially tideless: since World War II each party has won three presidential elections and the Democrats have won a clear majority of the presidential votes only once. The Democrats have, of course, shown much greater strength in Congress in which they have been given a majority by the voters in nine of the twelve sessions. The basic economic issue upon which the Democratic majority was built during the Great Depression continues to be important. Any faltering of the economy, particularly when unemployment rises sharply, triggers a Democratic resurgence.

Scammon and Wattenberg detect, however, the rise of another major issue that cross-cuts the economic issue. It is the social issue, and it has at least five salients. First is the deepening concern about the nation's rising crime rate. Second is racial division in the nation, especially to the extent that violence and black militancy have displaced the former nonviolent civil rights movement as the most visible manifestation of the struggle of minority groups for equality. Third is "kidlash," the adverse reaction of most Americans to campus disruption, youth life styles (long hair, short skirts, foul language, and the disregard of traditional manners in social relations), and drugs. The growing diversity in values, particularly the more common availability of explicitly sexual literature and films and the increase in nonmarital sexual intimacy, is a fourth element; and related to it is the resentment of many Americans who work hard to support families and pay taxes against the rise of an ethic in which work and most traditional personal responsibilities are scorned. Finally, the Vietnam protest movement has contributed to the emergence of the social issue. Polls clearly show that Americans overwhelmingly (in magnitudes of more than 90 percent on most issues) reject such aspects of the social issue as drug use, college disruptions, pornography sent through the mails, and new judicial decisions expanding the rights of criminal defendants.

Scammon and Wattenberg take a close reading of the demography of the American electorate. The young, the poor, and the black (and other racial minorities) are by no means a majority of the population. Moreover, differentials in vote turnout work against them to reduce even further their influence at the polls. Summing up these demographic explorations, Scammon and Wattenberg say of the electorate,

> In all: unyoung, unpoor, unblack. Furthermore, the young and the poor are unmonolithic in their Presidential voting behavior. Six in seven voters are over thirty. Nine out of ten are unpoor. Nine out of ten are white. Because there is some duplication—a young poor black man, for example—a fair guess is that seven of ten American voters are neither young, nor poor, nor black.[16]

And in caricaturing the average American voter they write,

15 Richard M. Scammon and Ben J. Wattenberg, *The Real Majority* (New York: Coward-McCann, 1970).

16 *Ibid.*, p. 57.

Middle Voter is a forty-seven-year-old housewife from the outskirts of Dayton, Ohio, whose husband is a machinist. . . .

To know that the lady in Dayton is afraid to walk the streets alone at night, to know that she has a mixed view about blacks and civil rights because before moving to the suburbs she lived in a neighborhood that became all black, to know that her brother-in-law is a policeman, to know that she does not have the money to move if her new neighborhood deteriorates, to know that she is deeply distressed that her son is going to a community junior college where LSD was found on the campus—to know all this is the beginning of contemporary political wisdom.[17]

Thus, it is on the social issue that Middle Voter's longstanding Democratic allegiance might falter. From 1964 to 1969, Americans reversed themselves in political labeling. In the former year they identified themselves 49 percent as liberals and 46 percent as conservatives; five years later as 33 percent liberal or moderately liberal and 51 percent conservative or moderately conservative. In the main, this new conservatism is based on the social issue, for on such matters as discrimination against blacks and Indians, aid to education, the living conditions of those in slums, and the plight of the elderly, Americans generally show a high recognition of the problem and support government action to address it.

What surfaces from the Scammon and Wattenberg analysis is not an emerging Republican majority, but a "real majority" consisting of middle Americans who are conservative on the social issue, likely to vote Democratic when the economy weakens, and basically liberal in dealing with many of the nation's pressing domestic problems. The typical voter who comprises this majority, they argue, is found most distinctly in "Quadcali"—the shaded states in Map 2 which account for a comfortable majority in the Electoral College. Quadcali is slightly more Catholic than the nation, and in many states it includes a larger proportion of the liberal young, the poor, and minority groups than does the electorate at large. These factors do not, however, significantly diminish the dominance of the Middle Voter in the crucial presidential states.

The real majority, then, is centrist. It favors New Deal economic programs and governmental action to solve national domestic problems. It is unsympathetic to crime, racial militancy, student disruptions, the new sexual mores, drugs, hippie life styles, and other elements encompassed within the rubric "social issue." But it is also not irrational in its approach to such matters. It apparently favors legislative steps to advance racial equality and it is willing to take some responsibility on an individual basis to achieve improved race relations. It also recognizes that drugs and crime are problems that need reasoned approaches more than vituperative political slogans. In a real sense, it is the traditional American political approach: progressive but not radical on economic matters, cautious but pragmatic on cultural and social concerns.

Many believe that 1970 was a testing year for the thesis of *The Real Majority*, which was widely read by politicians of both parties and taken to heart by liberal Democrats who regarded it as friendly advice from men basically sympathetic to their cause. (Mr. Scammon served as Director of the United States Bureau of the Census under President Kennedy and the authors describe themselves in their book as Independent Democrats.) Democrats

[17] *Ibid.*, p. 71.

Map 2 Quadcali

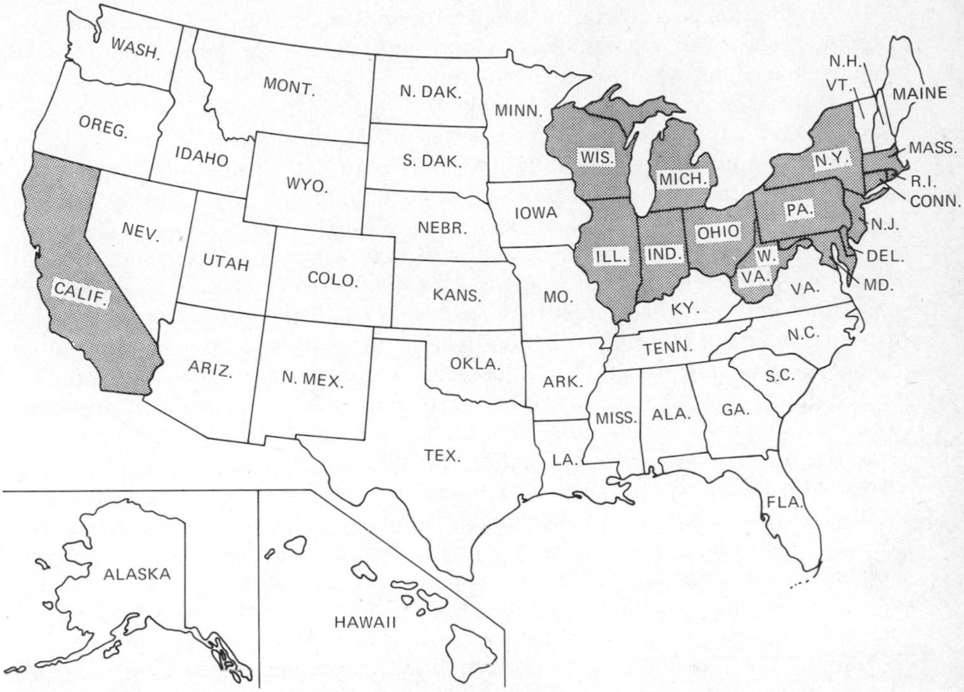

Source: Reprintod by permission of Cowaru-McCann, Inc. from *The Real Majority* by Richard M. Scammon and Ben J. Wattenberg. Copyright © 1970 by Richard M. Scammon and Ben J. Wattenberg.

emphasized the deteriorating condition of the national economy. And they confronted the social issue head-on by disavowing violence on campuses or in the streets while insisting on long-term attention to societal ills as well as short-term steps to uphold law and order. Democratic successess in 1970 suggest that the Scammon and Wattenberg thesis, which does not preclude either party from effectively taking up the centrist majority position, is a more accurate portrayal of contemporary electoral politics than Phillips' position which concedes to the Republicans national majority party status.

Walter Dean Burnham, who is an associate professor of political science at Washington University, concurs in the view that the party in the electorate is undergoing dramatic changes, but he sees a trend toward party "disaggregation" rather than toward realignment, on the one hand, or toward issue-oriented centrist politics, on the other.[18] He points to evidence that the traditional affiliation of voters with parties is in sharp decline. Through the quarter century from 1940 to 1965, polls showed that independents constituted between 20 percent and 22 percent of the electorate. In 1968 they had suddenly become

18 Walter Dean Burnham, "The End of American Party Politics," *Trans-Action,* 7 (December 1969), 12–22.

30 percent. This penchant for independence is sharpest among the young: 42 percent of those between twenty-one and twenty-nine years of age declare that they are independent rather than party identifiers, and this represents a 10 percent increase over the first half of the decade of the 1960s. Furthermore, in the population as a whole, independent identification has risen most sharply among those in the upper socioeconomic ranks where the largest numbers of staunch partisans were formerly found.

This trend poses a bleak outlook for democratic politics in America. Burnham argues that parties have served an important tension-management function in America by providing alternatives to the status quo when it has become intolerable to the electorate. In realigning elections such discontent is expressed by thrusting the minority party into power as a repudiation of existing conditions. The cycle of stability and realignment, Burnham argues, does not provide effectively for adaptive change by meeting new problems and absorbing emerging groups as they surface (and in this, his view is contrary to the consensus-building function widely attributed to parties by other political scientists). But it does at least provide some method for the populace to instigate a clear change in national direction when the status quo protected by majority party domination is no longer acceptable.

In the new period of disaggregation, Burnham warns that even this imperfect tension-management process is obsolete. He foresees, instead, a highly politicized society in which technological advances have reshaped the social structure into classes encompassing the technologically competent, the technologically obsolescent, and the technologically superfluous. In these circumstances, the middle groups (akin to the economically and socially besieged middle American of other commentators), pressed from both the top and bottom of the social system, become politically mobilized in a kind of urban populism, "a stance of organized hostility to blacks, student radicals, and cosmopolitan liberal elites."[19] This is, of course, similar to the dynamic force behind Kevin Phillips' emerging Republican majority and the ingredients of Scammon and Wattenberg's social issue. But rather than a stable Republican majority or a thrust toward centrist politics, this urban populism would more likely be a radical response to the issues of race, class, and life style. Stable party majorities assume a low level of politicization after realignment occurs and a high degree of passivity in the electorate, which maintains political allegiances as a matter of habit until the occurrence of another realigning period. Burnham's urban populism assumes a high level of political consciousness by the middle which manifests itself in "spasms of self-defense" in the electoral process.

Perhaps nothing shows the role of party in American life so clearly as these wide-ranging expressions of concern about the future of the American party system. Party has served as the main linkage institution in American politics. The party of the activists, more than any other political institution, has been responsible for mobilizing the American people for participation in elections. And elections themselves have been a force for the "socialization of conflict" so that the public monitors the policy decisions that would otherwise lie solely within the realm of private power relationships. Furthermore, the cycle

[19] *Ibid.*, p. 21.

of maintaining and realigning elections has combined in a crude way the stability and responsiveness that are essential to a democratic polity.

There is, of course, nothing sacred about parties, interest groups, and elections as linkage processes. But there is a need for some procedures and institutions by which clear and visible alternatives are posed for the public without simultaneously generating a level of conflict that destroys the consent of minorities in the decisions of the government and by which newly emerging groups can attain a place at the bargaining table. Traditional linkage institutions today are challenged by confrontation tactics and pervasive mass media. The continued efficacy of parties, interest groups, and elections is by no means certain. When established linkage institutions are in jeopardy, a democratic people must face anew the central question of democratic government: how shall the governors be made responsive to the governed?

10

The Political Party of the Activists

FRANK SORAUF

In the following excerpt from his text Party Politics in America, *Frank Sorauf describes the many incentives that draw people into party organizations. The pervasive notion that the crudest material incentives are uniformly the motive for party activism is dispelled by Sorauf. Both individuals and party organizations are likely to respond to a complex of incentives, the composition of which is of course an important determinant of the style of party organization and of the activities of the party. To a surprising extent, the material incentives described by Sorauf (patronage, preferments, political careers) are subordinate to social and psychological considerations and policy incentives in these organizations.*

Sorauf, a student of both constitutional law and political parties, is Professor of Political Science at the University of Minnesota. He has written Political Parties in the American System *(1964),* Party and Representation *(1963), and numerous articles in political science journals.*

Behind the imposing façades of the hierarchical structures the states create are the living, organizational realities of the political parties. . . . The statutes do indeed set limits and suggest outlines for party organization, but the questions of who staff the party, why and how they do, and how they act in the party's name are closer to the real world of political parties than all the statutory paragraphs put together. Where there is

From *Party Politics in America* by Frank Sorauf, pp. 82-90.

a gap between the reality of party organization and the mandates of a state law on party organization, it is because party organization is far more likely to reflect the goal-seeking behavior of men than even the most determined legislative plans.

While it may not always appear so to the politically cynical, the American major parties are purposive, goal-seeking organizations. As the most completely electoral parties in the democracies of the world, they are preeminently committed to the winning of elections and the capture of public office. . . . Additionally, the parties may choose to seek any number of short- and long-run goals—the spread of an ideology, the enactment of a set of public policies, or the easing of state regulation of political finance. But whatever the goal or goals, the political party must select means and strategies for their achievement, always choosing in the knowledge that the other major party and other political organizations are very likely trying similarly to achieve competing goals of their own.

The major political party as an organization, therefore, is a mechanism for uniting adherents in the pursuit of general goals or hierarchies (priorities) of goals. It recruits and mobilizes the resources and skills for political action. In the employment of those resources it works out a division of labor and a hierarchy of authority. Like any other complex organization it, too, has its leaders and followers, its own specialization of role and function, its own internal system of communication. And it is a decision-making apparatus in which choices must repeatedly be made about the mobilization of resources, the setting of strategies, and the deployment of assets. . . .

Goal-seeking, however, goes on within the party organization on a personal, individual level as well. Individual party leaders, workers, and members are in the party organization for some identifiable, if covert or implicit, set of reasons or motives. There must, in other words, be rewards or incentives . . . for devoting one's leisure time to party activity rather than the service of Kiwanis or Rotary or the improvement of one's golf game. And the recruitment of the right individuals with the right political skills remains the chief organizational problem of the parties.[1]

The System of Incentives

The American political parties have never operated primarily in a cash economy. They have rarely bought or hired the millions of man-hours of labor they need; even today paid staffs are small or non-existent in most party organizations, and it is a rare party chairman who draws even a pittance of a salary from the organization he serves. The great number of Americans active in the parties receive no cash in return for their often considerable time and skill. Even the earthy old custom of paying precinct workers on election day is vanishing. What is it, then, that induces party workers to lavish their hours and efforts on the affairs of the parties? If the parties' rewards and "payments" are not made in cash, in what coin are they made?

Patronage

Patronage, the use of appointive governmental positions to reward past party work and induce future labors, is hardly unique to the American political parties. Even today the municipal services of the Italian cities swarm with the partisans of the party or parties in political power. But very probably no other party system has over its history relied as systematically on it as the American. The easy confidence of the Jacksonians that no public task was so complex that it demanded experience, and their matching conviction that "to the victors go the spoils," set its tone and ethic early in the 19th century. From then to the present a vast array of public job-holders—from elevator operators and charwomen in city hall to American ambassadors in foreign capitals—have owed their appointment to political worthiness and the right political sponsorship.

Even with the explosive growth of government bureaucracy in this century the amount of patronage available to the parties has declined precipitously. The expansion of civil service and merit systems has been the chief reason. What was once a flourishing federal patronage—historians write of the hordes of ill-mannered job-seekers overrunning presidential inaugurations—has by now dwindled to something less than 1 per cent of the federal establishment.[2] There still remain the U.S. marshals, the collectors of customs, and the rural mail carriers, to mention a few of the classic federal patronage posts, but theirs is a shrinking roster. Similar declines have come, albeit more slowly, to the states and localities. While any number of states, counties, and cities have virtually abolished patronage (at least one governor of Wisconsin has estimated his available patronage positions at about a baker's dozen), it flourishes in others. Pennsylvania, for example, still has about 50,000 jobs available for reward, and a number of localities in that state have until very recently included jobs as teachers, police, and firemen within the local patronage. In fact, the country and city remain the chief centers of patronage. For example:

> A recent survey of Democratic party members in St. Louis indicates that more than 40 per cent hold or have held patronage jobs.[3]

> Almost three-fourths of the Democratic committeemen in Pittsburgh in the late 1950's held public jobs.[4]

And yet for every such example there are many others in which only a small fraction of party leadership is on the public payrolls.

The reasons for the decline of patronage as an incentive for party work go beyond the encroachments of civil service reform. The increasing complexities and importance of many appointive positions forces chief executives to seek skills as well as political merit. It is difficult enough to find ambassadors and heavy equipment operators with the desirable occupational skills without adding a set of political credentials. Also, at a time of relatively full employment the usually poorly paid patronage appointments seem greatly less attractive; the politics of patronage have always worked best among the depressed and disadvantaged. Most patronage positions do not tempt the educated, "successful," "respected" middle-class leadership the parties would like to attract. Furthermore, elected executives may use patronage to build their own political followings rather than the party apparatus; a sizeable percentage of the patronage of the Kennedy administration, for example, went to Democrats "for Kennedy before West Virginia."[5] Finally, the parties may not be able to use the patronage available to them. Especially when they win power after years of failure, they do not have the necessary administrative machinery, the list of job-seekers, or even the will to fire ruthlessly the opposing partisans and replace them with loyal followers.[6]

Perhaps in response both to the shrinking availability of patronage and to the party's shrinking need for it, recent years have seen the development of a new patronage variant: the "political non-job." One writer has recently summarized the development with equal parts of wit and insight:[7]

> The members of the new elite corps of American politics—the fund raisers, the intellectual counselors, "media coordinators," and leaders of the growing citizens' movements—are profitably employed already, with better pay and working conditions than government can offer. To them, the most appealing aspect of a public job is the prestige which sometimes accompanies it.
>
> Happily, political leaders have devised ways to bestow the status symbols of high office without the job itself. At Democratic national headquarters in Washington, where many such spilt-level appointments are routinely requisitioned and cleared, the new institution is known as "the honorary." Elsewhere it has been dubbed the patronage non-job, and it can range from nomination to a White House advisory committee to an invitation to be an honored member of an Air Force civic-inspection tour of California, arranged at the behest of your local Congressman.

So, while by 1961 count there were only 133 full-time appointive jobs available for patronage use in the Interior Department (many of them carrying, moreover, skill and experience qualifications), the Department had 49 advisory committees and commissions with a total membership of about 800, 52 of them presidential appointments (with which the recipient receives a parchment certificate signed by the President). The development, one should be clear, is not a novel one. The King or Queen's Honors List has in part served the same function for some time in Britain; and Kentucky has been appointing Colonels for almost as long.

Political Career

Elective political office has for many Americans all of the income, the responsibility, the prestige, and the excitement—not to mention the power—that most patronage positions do not. And since the political party offers an efficient, and in some cases the only, avenue to elective office, it was inevitable that the search for an elective political career would recruit new party activists or sustain that activity after other incentives had "worn off." In the middle 1950's, for instance, about half of a group of Wisconsin party officials from both parties said they either had been elected or defeated in a past try for elective office; 21 per cent declared that they "intended" to run, and 35 per cent "desired" to make a race for office.[8]

There exist those party organizations with such disciplined control over their primaries that they can and do "give" public office, especially at the state and local level, to loyal party workers. If the party dominates the politics of the area, control of the primaries makes public offices into an "elective patronage." The candidate is offered the chance to run and then does little more as the party organization runs up the necessary majorities. More commonly, party endorsements elsewhere carry enough weight and money to make running against the party's choice hazardous or difficult at the least. But regardless of party control over the primary, the party's ability to select its candidates from among its loyal workers depends on the degree of two-party competitiveness in the constituency. The greater the competitiveness the less the possibility of electing any "warm body" and the greater, therefore, the necessity of considering candidate appeal in addition to political worthiness.

But the would-be candidate needs more than the "nod," approval or selection by the party. He needs advice, know-how, manpower, and money —and in most parts of the country the party still remains a likely source of them. Service in the party, then, yields the skill, the experience, the connections, the approval, and the resources that any candidate needs. It is, of course, possible for the candidate without party ties to seek election, but for every one who does, there are hundreds or thousands of successful office-seekers who have party ties. And for the partisan who already holds office there is no easier way to assure reelection or to move to a more attractive office than by work in the party. So sedulous are the party's office-holders in currying the support of the party organizations that speculation over their aspirations and "moves" remains one of the most enduring intra-party recreations.

Preferments

The tangible, material rewards of politics may take, especially in the state and localities, a series of forms other than appointive or elective office. The active partisan or the financial "fat cat" may, for example, seek preference in the awarding of public contracts. In this respect, it is not accidental that the leaders of the construction industry should be so active politically in the states and localities which spend millions every year on roads and public buildings. Preference may take other forms: a tolerant or haphazard application of regulatory or inspection policies, the provision of unusually prompt or efficient public services (premiere snow and garbage removal, for example), a forgiving instrument of the law (e.g., the "fixed" traffic ticket), or the granting of a scarce public service (admission to crowded mental hospitals, for instance). It may also involve the granting of scarce "opportunities," such as liquor licenses or franchises. By "preferment," in other words, one means the gaining of special treatment or advantage, and it is dependent usually on the party's holding the administrative decision-making positions of government. It is partly in this sense that parties talk of "controlling" city hall, the county courthouse, or the state capitol.

One particularly unappealing form of political "preferment" is that given activities which operate on the shady side of the law. It may involve a calculated ignoring of prostitution, bookmaking, the numbers game, or traffic in drugs in return for some form of political support; in other forms it has involved the parties' taking a share of protection money or the proceeds from crime, vice, or the rackets. The link between crime and politics in New York, write Glazer and Moynihan, was "complex."[9]

> The politicians of course needed money; and political protection was on the whole more important to illegitimate than to legitimate businessmen. Other elements were mixed in. There was ethnic pride, which motivated a Frank Costello as much as it did a businessman who had not become rich as a bootlegger. There was a desire to help out relatives and friends. There was the fact that bootleggers, politicians, lawyers, judges, and policemen had all grown up on the block together, and had never lost touch. How was one to sort out the influences, and decide the significance of the fact that judges and ex-bootleggers and gamblers all sat around the same table to raise money for an orphan's home?

The prevalence of such an incentive to party effort is understandably difficult to estimate. Perhaps it suffices to say that it is probably less vital than the political cynics think and more important than the Pollyannas admit.

Socio-Economic Mobility

Political activity offers easy publicity (or notoriety) and contacts for those who seek them—young lawyers trying to build a practice, owners of food and watering spots, insurance and real estate brokers, storekeepers, and the socially ambitious. Party activity often opens up the contacts within the party and public life, and the easy publicity outside, that lead to prosperity in business or profession, to a new job or business opportunity, even to raised social status. It is a generally accepted form of self-advertisement. Writes one observer of the Philadelphia organization men:[10]

> One explanation of their motivation would locate the "boys' " essential urge in the factor known as "prestige." The truth is, many intellectuals and many members of the upper class who have come in contact with politicians argue that, for the Irish, Jewish, Italian bright boys who pursue it, politics is a "status-conferring" occupation. The Bill Greens and the Victor Blanes and the Aus Meehans, they point out, could no doubt have earned wealth and even the respect of their fellow-men by selling insurance, practicing law, and the like. But the one thing that they could not earn in these ways is "place" in the community. Politics gives them that.

In the tired American phrase, some people join the active ranks in the parties to "get ahead," whether they define getting ahead in terms of social or economic upward mobility.

Social and Psychological Satisfactions

The personal, non-material rewards of party activity are not easy to identify, and certainly they are not easy to measure. But one can sense the social rewards of politics in the camaraderie of the "gang" at party headquarters or the court house, and he can see it at a party dinner as the workers press around the great and near great of the party, hoping for a word of greeting or a nod of recognition. In the new style political clubs the attractiveness of the social life and friendship circle is explicit. "Many volunteers are rootless, transient newcomers searching the city for a means of associating with like-minded people."[11] The party organization offers an open and hospitable occasion for meeting people. But while the parties' clubs rely on the social incentives, those incentives are probably either secondary or they attract large numbers of low-activity partisans:

> Although many clubs in various cities offer their members reduced air fares to Europe on charter flights, a full schedule of social events, forums featuring prestigious speakers, and the opportunity to play the political game, and although some members join simply to find a mate quickly or get to Paris inexpensively, if the clubs should cease to define themselves as organizations devoted to liberalism or reformism or similar worthy causes, they could not for long sustain the interest of any but the handful who simply enjoy the company of others or like being district leader.[12]

At a more general level, almost all of the reported research on the motivations of party activists find that large numbers of them reply that they "like people" or that they "like politics."

Social satisfactions merge almost imperceptibly with the psychological. Political activity may bolster the sagging ego or sustain the demanding one.

> Like the theater, politics is a great nourisher of egos. It attracts men who are hungry for attention, for assurance that somebody loves them, for the soul-stirring

music of their own voices. . . . A main ingredient in the make-up of every successful politician is a thick slice of ham.[13]

Party work may offer the individual a cause or an enterprise with which to identify, a charismatic leader to follow, a round of activities which can lift him above the personally unrewarding tasks of the workaday world. The party may be a small island of excitement in a sea of routine. It may even offer an occasion for the manipulation or domination of others—a chance to decide or command, even an avenue for the projection of aggressions and hostilities.

Ideology and Policy Issues

Even the most casual soundings of party rhetoric these days indicate an increasing identification of partisans within the major parties as "liberals" and "conservatives." Behind these phrases lies a potent motivation to party activity: a commitment to clusters and patterns of related attitudes about government and politics—especially about the proper and desirable role of government in contemporary society. Other patterns of attitudes may be wrapped up in commitments to "good government" or "reform." On a more modest and limited scale the spur to activity may be concern for a single issue or interest (tax cuts, the war in Vietnam, the maintenance of local schools, the well-being of a neighborhood or a racial or ethnic group) or a single area of policy concern (foreign policy, civil rights, local planning and development). The "cause" may, indeed, be the reform or rehabilitation of the political party itself.

Just as the importance of the immediate, material, personal rewards of politics have recently declined, those of issue and ideology have increased. Even in Manhattan, long the fief of Tammany Hall, the trend is evident:

. . . there is a "new look" among today's political activists. They are "respectable," solid middle-class citizens. The party "hack" of fiction, films, and the traditional literature is hard to find among the young, well-educated, affluent, and socially acceptable committeemen—and women—of the nineteen-sixties. Concomitantly, both the nature of political motivation and the character of political activity have changed. The contemporary politician considers his party organization an instrument for effectuating policy rather than a haven of personal security. He tends to be more interested in social reform than in catering to individual constituents.[14]

In national politics the country in 1964 witnessed the capture of the Republican national party by partisans whose chief criterion for candidate and platform was frankly ideological.

The activist may also be drawn to the party by a more general civic ideology. A sense of political responsibility and obligation, a concept of the duty of a citizen, may impel him. Scholars who have questioned party officials and workers about their reasons or motives for working in the parties know the familiar answers. They were "asked" to serve, and they acceded out of a personal view of good citizenship. Often that response, in whatever words it may be couched, merely masks what the respondent feels are less acceptable motives. Often, however, it is an honest testament to the power of deeply ingrained civic values. Those values rarely operate alone, but they do reinforce and provide important rationalization for other goals and motives.

The Party Itself

Two final varieties of incentive, both essentially related to the party *per se*, must be mentioned. First of all, as a party activist works within the party, the health and well-being of the party itself become an incentive for work; the party becomes an end in itself. It retains its capacity for achieving the goals and rewards of politics, but at the same time its workers attach many of their loyalties and aspirations to it. The party's wins and losses become issues in and of themselves, and attacks on it are far more than attacks on its policies and activities. Secondly, it may be, as Robert Salisbury suggests in his study of St. Louis politicians, that large numbers of party activists participate "because they were brought up in a highly politicized atmosphere."15 The party

participant per family socialization was probably not exposed to involvement in other kinds of organizations, any more than a devout young communicant of the church would necessarily be taught to carry his devotion into other organizational settings.

Our findings suggest that much political behavior is to be explained as habitual. It is not directly derived from the intellectual, economic, social, or characterological features of the actors. It is an aspect of a life style that has been accepted uncritically since childhood by a relatively small number of people in the society. Party workers may gravitate to the party because they are accustomed to it and because through years of socialization they have invested loyalties in it.

No party organization depends on a single incentive, and very few individual partisans labor in the party for only one. The party organization relies on a varied series or "system" of incentives. That incentive system differs from organization to organization, and it differs within a single organization as well. One set of incentives may recruit the precinct workers while another lures the party leadership. Eldersveld reports that in Wayne County, Michigan, precinct chairmen depend heavily on the rewards of social contacts and associations, but party leadership in the county and congressional districts seeks immediate economic gain and ideological-philosophical rewards.16 The individual worker for his part is recruited by a congeries of incentives. He may, furthermore, shift his motivations in the course of party work. Part of the socialization process within the party organization may be to make the worker aware of the range of incentives open to him.

* * *

NOTES

 A similar "economizing" model of the American parties is developed in Anthony Downs, An Economic Theory of Democracy (New York: Harper, 1957).

2. On the federal patronage see Harvey C. Mansfield, "Political Parties, Patronage, and the Federal Government Service" in *The Federal Government Service* (New York: The American Assembly, 1954).

3. Robert H. Salisbury, "The Urban Party Organization Member," Public Opinion Quarterly, XXIX (Winter, 1965-66), p. 558.

4. William J. Keefe and William C. Seyler, "Precinct Politicians in Pittsburgh," Social Science, XXXV (1960), p. 28.

5. The phrase refers to those early Kennedy supporters who made a commitment to him before he won the important West Virginia presidential primary in May of 1960. It was an attempt to bypass those johnny-come-latelies who rushed to the Kennedy bandwagon after West Virginia.

6. On patronage see Daniel P. Moynihan and James Q. Wilson, "Patronage in New York

State, 1955–1959," *American Political Science Review,* LVIII (1964), pp. 286–301; James Q. Wilson, "The Economy of Patronage," *Journal of Political Economy,* LXIX (1961), pp. 369–380; and Frank J. Sorauf, "State Patronage in a Rural County," *American Political Science Review,* L (1956), pp. 1046–1056.

7. Don Oberdorfer, "The New Political Non-Job," *Harpers* (October, 1965), p. 108ff.
8. Leon D. Epstein, *Politics in Wisconsin* (Madison: Univ. of Wisconsin Press, 1958), pp. 91, 187.
9. Nathan Glazer and Daniel P. Moynihan, *Beyond the Melting Pot* (Cambridge: MIT Press, 1963), pp. 210–212.
10. James Reichley, *The Art of Government: Reform and Organization Politics in Philadelphia* (New York: Fund for the Republic, 1959), p. 104.
11. James Q. Wilson, *The Amateur Democrat* (Chicago: Univ. of Chicago Press, 1962), p. 165.
12. *Ibid.*
13. John Fischer, "Please Don't Bite the Politicians," *Harper's* (November, 1960), p. 16.
14. Robert S. Hirschfield, Bert E. Swanson, and Blanche D. Blank, "A Profile of Political Activists in Manhattan," *Western Political Quarterly,* XV (1962), p. 505.
15. Robert H. Salisbury, *op. cit.,* pp. 562, 564.
16. Samuel J. Eldersveld, *Political Parties: A Behavioral Analysis* (Chicago: Rand McNally, 1964), p. 278.

11

The Changing Pattern of Urban Party Politics

FRED I. GREENSTEIN

In the essay that follows, Fred I. Greenstein reports the social, economic, and political conditions in which the old-style political machine flourished and describes the decline of such machines with changes in urban life. Greenstein's comparison of the incentives that fueled the traditional machine and the orientations of the reform-club activists illustrates clearly Sorauf's point: that as the incentive structures of political organizations differ, their composition and activities differ. The limited effectiveness of the emergent reform clubs in canvassing voters is often cited by those who predict the imminent demise of the party of the activists.

Greenstein is Professor of Government at Wesleyan University. He has published Children in Politics *(1965), on the political socialization of youngsters in New Haven, Connecticut,* Personality and Politics *(1969), and* The American Party System and the American People *(1970), from which an excerpt on voting behavior appears later in this part.*

* * *

Highly organized urban political parties are generally conceded to be one of America's distinctive contributions to mankind's repertory of political forms. Just as the two major national parties in the United States are almost universally described in terms of their *dis*organization—their lack of an authoritative command structure—the municipal parties have, until recently, been characterized by most

Reprinted in abridged form from *The Annals* of the American Academy of Political and Social Science, 353 (May 1964), 1-13, by permission of the author and the publisher.

observers in terms of their hierarchical strength. E. E. Schattschneider once summarized this state of affairs in the memorable image of a truncated pyramid: a party system which is weak and ghostlike at the top and solid at the bottom.[1]

This essay deals with the disciplined, largely autonomous local political parties which sprang up in many American cities in the nineteenth century. Much of the literature on these political configurations is heavily pejorative, . . . Even the basic nomenclature, "boss" and "machine," is laden with negative connotations, although recently there has been a turn toward nostalgic romanticization of the "vanishing breed" of city bosses.[2]

Here . . . I shall . . . attempt . . . to delineate rather than to pass moral judgment: What was the nature of old-style urban party organization? Why did this political pattern develop and how did it operate? What contributed to its short-run persistence in the face of reform campaigns? Under what circumstances have such organizations disappeared and under what circumstances have they continued into the present day—or even undergone renaissances? What are the present-day descendents of old-style urban party organizations?

* * *

Old-Style Party Organization: Definitional Characteristics

Ranney and Kendall have persuasively argued that the imprecision and negative connotations of terms like "boss" destroy their usefulness. What, beyond semantic confusion, they ask, can come from classifying politicians into "bosses" versus "leaders"? Such a distinction leads to fruitless preoccupation with the purity of politicians' motives rather than the actuality of their behavior; it overestimates the degree to which figures of the past such as Richard Croker, William Tweed, and Frank Hague were free of public constraints; and it obscures the fact that *all* effective political leaders, whether or not they are popularly labeled as bosses, use quite similar techniques and resources.[3]

Granting these points, it still seems that a recognizable and noteworthy historical phenomenon is hinted at by the venerable terms "boss" and "machine." If the overtones of these terms make us reluctant to use them, we might simply speak of an "old style" of party organization with the following characteristics:

(1) There is a disciplined party hierarchy led by a single executive or a unified board of directors.
(2) The party exercises effective control over nomination to public office, and, through this, it controls the public officials of the municipality.
(3) The party leadership—which quite often is of lower-class social origins—usually does not hold public office and sometimes does not even hold formal party office. At any rate, official position is not the primary source of the leadership's strength.
(4) Rather, a cadre of loyal party officials and workers, as well as a core of voters, is maintained by a mixture of material rewards and *nonideological* psychic rewards—such as personal and ethnic recognition, camaraderie, and the like.[4]

The Rise of Old-Style Party Organization

This pattern of politics, Schattschneider comments, "is as American as the jazz band . . . China, Mexico,

South America, and southern Italy at various times have produced figures who played roles remotely like that of the American boss, but England, France, Germany, and the lesser democracies of Europe have exhibited no tendency to develop this form of political organization in modern times."[5] What then accounted for the development of old-style party organization in the United States?

The Crokers, Tweeds, and Hagues and their organizations probably could not have arisen if certain broad preconditions had not existed in American society and culture. These include the tradition of freewheeling individualism and pragmatic opportunism, which developed in a prosperous, sprawling new society unrestrained by feudalism, aristocracy, monarchy, an established church, and other traditional authorities. This is the state of affairs which has been commented on by countless observers, even before de Tocqueville, and which has been used to explain such disparate phenomena as the failure of socialism to take hold in the United States, the recurrence of popularly based assaults on civil liberties, and even the peculiarly corrosive form which was taken by American slavery.[6]

It also is possible to identify five more direct determinants of the form that urban party organization took in the nineteenth century, three of them consequences of the Industrial Revolution and two of them results of political institutions and traditions which preceded industrialization.

Massive Urban Expansion

Over a relatively brief span of years, beginning in the mid-nineteenth century, industrial and commercial growth led to a spectacular rise in the number and proportion of Americans concentrated in cities. A thumbnail sketch of urban expansion may be had by simply noting the population of urban and rural areas for each of the twenty-year periods from 1840 to 1920:

	Urban Population	*Rural Population*
	(in millions)	
1840	1.8	15.2
1860	6.2	25.2
1880	14.1	36.0
1900	30.1	45.8
1920	54.2	51.6

These statistics follow the old Census Bureau classification of areas exceeding 2,500 in population as urban. Growth of larger metropolitan units was even more striking. In 1840 slightly over 300,000 Americans lived in cities—or, rather, a single city, New York—with more than a quarter of a million residents; by 1920 there were twenty-four cities of this size, containing approximately 21 million Americans.

The sheer mechanics of supporting urban populations of this magnitude are, of course, radically different from the requirements of rural life. There must be extensive transportation arrangements; urban dwellers are as dependent upon a constant inflow of food and other commodities as an infant is on the ministrations of adults. A host of new administrative functions must be performed as the population becomes urbanized: street construction and maintenance, bridges, lighting, interurban transportation, sanitary arrangements, firefighting, police protection, and so forth. Overwhelming demands suddenly are placed on governments which, hitherto, were able to operate with a minimum of effort and activity.

Disorganized Forms of Urban Government

The forms of government which had evolved in nineteenth-century America were scarcely suitable for meeting the demands of mushrooming cities. Governmental structures reflected a mixture of Jacksonian direct democracy and Madisonian checks and balances. Cities had a multitude of elected officials (sometimes they were elected annually), weak executives, large and unwieldy councils and boards. The formal organization of the cities placed officials in a position permitting and, in fact, encouraging them to checkmate each other's efforts to make and execute policies. Since each official was elected by appealing to his own peculiar constituency and had little incentive to co-operate with his associates, the difficulties caused by the formal limitations of government were exacerbated. In a period when the requirements for governmental action were increasing geometrically, this was a prescription for chaos.

Needs of Businessmen

A third aspect of mid-nineteenth-century American society which contributed to the formation of old-style party organizations was the needs of businessmen. There was an increasing number of merchants, industrialists, and other businessmen, licit and illicit, who needed—and were willing to pay for—the appropriate responses from city governments. Some businessmen wanted to operate unrestrained by municipal authority. Others desired street-railway franchises, paving contracts, construction work, and other transactions connected with the very growth of the cities themselves.

Needs of Dependent Populations

The needs of the bulk of the nineteenth-century urban population were not for profits but for the simple wherewithal to survive and maintain a modicum of dignity. It is difficult in the relatively affluent society of our day to appreciate the vicissitudes of urban life several generations ago: the low wages, long hours, tedious and hazardous working conditions, and lack of security which were the lot of most citizens. Even for native-born Americans, life often was nasty and brutish. But many urbanites were first- and second-generation immigrants who, in addition to their other difficulties, had to face an alien culture and language. Between the Civil War and the First World War, the United States managed somehow to absorb 25 million foreigners.

Unrestricted Suffrage

Urban dwellers were not totally without resources for their own advancement. The American tradition of unrestricted male franchise was, in the long run, to work to their advantage. Although it doubtless is true that few city dwellers of the day were aware of the importance of their right to vote, politicians *were* aware of this. Because even the lowliest of citizens was, or could become, a voter, a class of politicians developed building upon the four conditions referred to above: the requirements of organizing urban life, the inability of existing governments to meet these requirements, and the presence of businessmen willing to pay for governmental services and of dependent voting populations in need of security from the uncertainties of their existence.

The old-style urban party leader was as much a product of his time and social setting as was the rising capitalist of the Gilded Age. Building on the conditions and needs of the day, the politician had mainly to supply his own ingenuity and co-ordinating ability in order to tie together the machinery of urban government. If a cohesive party organization could control nominations and elect its own agents to office, the formal fragmentation of government no longer would stand in the way of municipal activity. The votes of large blocs of dependent citizens were sufficient to control nominations and win elections. And the financial support of those who sought to transact business with the city, as well as the revenues and resources of the city government, made it possible to win votes. The enterprising politician who could succeed in governing a city on this basis was a broker *par excellence;* generous brokers' commissions were the rule of the day.

The importance of out-and-out vote-buying on election day as a source of voter support can easily be overestimated. Party organizations curried the favor of voters on a year-long basis. In a day when "better" citizens espoused philosophical variants of Social Darwinism, urban politicians thought in terms of an old-fashioned conception of the welfare state. In the familiar words of Tammany sachem George Washington Plunkitt:

What holds your grip on your district is to go right down among the poor families and help them in the different ways they need help. I've got a regular system for this. If there's a fire in Ninth, Tenth or Eleventh Avenue, for example, any hour of the day or night, I'm usually there with some of my election district captains as soon as the fire engines. If a family is burned out I don't ask whether they are Republicans or Democrats, and I don't refer them to the Charity Organization Society, which would investigate their case in a month or two and decide they were worthy of help about the time they are dead from starvation. I just get quarters for them, buy clothes for them if their clothes were burned up, and fix them up til they get things runnin' again. It's philanthropy, but it's politics, too—mighty good politics. Who can tell how many votes one of these fires bring me? The poor are the most grateful people in the world, and, let me tell you, they have more friends in their neighborhood than the rich have in theirs.[7]

With numerous patronage appointees (holders not only of city jobs but also of jobs with concerns doing business with the city), party organizations could readily administer this sort of an informal relief program. And, unlike many latter-day charitable and governmental relief programs, the party's activities did not stop with the provision of mere physical assistance.

I know every man, woman and child in the Fifteenth District, except them that's been born this summer—and I know some of them, too. I know what they like and what they don't like, what they are strong at and what they are weak in, and I reach them by approachin' at the right side.

For instance, here's how I gather in the young men. I hear of a young feller that's proud of his voice, thinks that he can sing fine. I ask him to come around to Washington Hall and join our Glee Club. He comes and sings, and he's a follower of Plunkitt for life. Another young feller gains a reputation as a baseball player in a vacant lot. I bring him into our baseball club. That fixes him. You'll find him workin' for my ticket at the polls next election day. Then there's the feller that likes rowin' on the river, the young feller that makes a name as a waltzer on his block, the young feller that's handy with his dukes—I rope them all in by givin' them opportunities to show themselves off. I don't trouble them with political arguments. I just study human nature and act accordin'.[8]

This passage reflects some of the ways in which party activities might be geared to the *individual* interests of voters. *Group* interests were at least as important. As each new nationality arrived in the city, politicians rather rapidly accommodated to it and brought it into the mainstream of political participation. Parties were concerned with the votes of immigrants virtually from the time of their arrival. Dockside naturalization and voter enrollment was not unknown.

But if the purpose of the politicians was to use the immigrants, it soon became clear that the tables could be turned. In Providence, Rhode Island, for example, a careful study of the assimilation of immigrant groups into local politics shows that, within thirty years after the arrival of the first representative of a group in the city, it began to be represented in the councils of one or both parties. Eventually, both of the local parties came to be dominated by representatives of the newer stocks. Thus, in 1864 no Irish names appear on the lists of Democratic committeemen in Providence; by 1876 about a third of the names were Irish; by the turn of the century, three-quarters were Irish. In time, the Republican party became the domain of politicians of Italian ancestry.[9] Perhaps the most dramatic example to date of urban party politics as an avenue of upward social mobility was in the antecedents of President Kennedy, whose great-grandfather was an impoverished refugee of the Irish potato famine, his grandfather a saloon keeper and a classical old-time urban political leader, his father a multimillionnaire businessman, presidential advisor, and ambassador to the Court of St. James's.

When the range of consequences of old-time party organizations is seen, it becomes apparent why moral judgments of "the boss and the machine" are likely to be inadequate. These organizations often were responsible for incredible corruption, but they also —sometimes through the very same activities—helped incorporate new groups into American society and aided them up the social ladder. The parties frequently mismanaged urban growth on a grand scale, but they *did* manage urban growth at a time when other instrumentalities for governing the cities were inadequate. They plied voters, who might otherwise have organized more aggressively to advance their interests, with Thanksgiving Day turkeys and buckets of coal. But, by siphoning off discontent and softening the law, they probably contributed to the generally pacific tenor of American politics. It seems fruitless to attempt to capture this complexity in a single moral judgment. One can scarcely weigh the incorporation of immigrant groups against the proliferation of corruption and strike an over-all balance.

Why Reformers Were "Mornin' Glories"

Stimulated by high taxes and reports of corruption and mismanagement on a grand scale, antiboss reform movements, led by the more prosperous elements of the cities, became increasingly common late in the nineteenth century. Compared with the regular party politicians of their day, reformers were mere fly-by-night dilettantes —"mornin' glories."[10] They lacked the discipline and the staying power to mount a year-long program of activities. Perhaps more important, the values of the reformers were remote from—in fact, inconsistent with—the values of the citizens whose support would be needed to keep reform administrations in office. Reformers ordinarily saw low taxes and business-like management of the cities as the exclusive aim of government. To the sweatshop worker, grinding out a marginal existence, these aims were at best meaningless, at worst direct attacks on the one agency of society which seemed to have his interests at heart.

The Decline of Old-Style Party Organization

Although in the short run old-style party organizations were marvelously immune to the attacks of reformers, in recent decades the demise of this political form has been widely acclaimed. Because of the absence of reliable trend data, we cannot document "the decline of the machine" with precision. The decline does seem to have taken place, although only partly as a direct consequence of attempts to reform urban politics. Events have conspired to sap the traditional resources used to build voter support and to make voters less interested in these resources which the parties still command.

Decline in the Resources of Old-Style Urban Politicians

Most obviously, job patronage is no longer available in as great a quantity as it once was. At the federal level and in a good many of the states (as well as numerous cities), the bulk of jobs are filled by civil service procedures. Under these circumstances, the most a party politician may be able to do is seek some minor form of preferment for an otherwise qualified job applicant. Furthermore, the technical requirements of many appointive positions are sufficiently complex to make it inexpedient to fill them with unqualified personnel.[11] And private concerns doing business with the cities are not as likely to be sources of partronage in a day when the franchises have been given out and the concessions granted.

Beyond this, many modern governmental techniques—accounting and auditing requirements, procedures for letting bids, purchasing procedures, even the existence of a federal income tax—restrict the opportunities for dishonest and "honest" graft. Some of these procedures were not instituted with the explicit purpose of hampering the parties. Legislation designed deliberately to weaken parties *has,* however, been enacted—for example, nomination by direct primary and nonpartisan local elections, in which party labels are not indicated on the ballot. Where other conditions are consistent with tight party organization, techniques of this sort seem not to have been especially effective; old-style parties are perfectly capable of controlling nominations in primaries, or of persisting in formally nonpartisan jurisdictions. But, together with the other party weakening factors, explicit antiparty legislation seems to have taken its toll.

Decline of Voter Interest in Rewards Available to the Parties

Even today it is estimated that the mayor of Chicago has at his disposal 6,000 to 10,000 city patronage jobs. And there are many ways of circumventing good government, antiparty legislation. An additional element in the decline of old-style organization is the increasing disinterest of many citizens in the rewards at the disposal of party politicians. Once upon a time, for example, the decennial federal census was a boon to those local politicians whose party happened to be in control of the White House at census time. The temporary job of door-to-door federal census enumerator was quite a satisfactory reward for the party faithful. In 1960 in many localities, party politicians found census patronage more bother than boon; the wages for this task compared poorly with private wages, and few voters were willing to put in the time and leg work. Other traditional patronage jobs—custodial work in city buildings, employment with departments of sanitation, street repair jobs—were becoming equally undesirable, due to rising levels of income, education, and job security.

An important watershed seems to have been the New Deal, which provided the impetus, at state and local levels as well as the federal level, for increased governmental preoccupation with citizen welfare. The welfare programs of party organizations were undercut by direct and indirect effects of social security, minimum wage legislation, relief programs, and collective bargaining. And, as often has been noted, the parties themselves, by contributing to the social rise of underprivileged groups, helped to develop the values and aspirations which were to make these citizens skeptical of the more blatant manifestations of machine politics.

Varieties of Contemporary Urban Politics

Nationally in 1956, the Survey Research Center found that only 10 per cent of a cross section of citizens reported being contacted personally by political party workers during that year's presidential campaign. Even if we consider only nonsouthern cities of over 100,000 population, the percentage is still a good bit less than 20.[12] This is a far cry from the situation which would obtain if party organizations were well developed and assiduous. But national statistics conceal a good bit of local variation. A survey of Detroit voters found that only 6 per cent of the public remembered having been approached by political party workers; in fact, less than a fifth of those interviewed even knew that there *were* party precinct officials in their district.[13] Reports from a number of other cities—for example, Seattle and Minneapolis—show a similar vacuum in party activity.[14]

In New Haven, Connecticut, in contrast, 60 per cent of the voters interviewed in a 1959 survey reported having been contacted by party workers.[15] The continuing importance of parties in the politics of this municipality has been documented at length by Robert A. Dahl and his associates.[16] New Haven's Mayor Richard C. Lee was able to obtain support for a massive urban redevelopment program, in spite of the many obstacles in the way of favorable action on such programs elsewhere, in large part because of the capacity of an old-style party organization to weld together the government of a city with an extremely "weak" formal charter. Lee commanded a substantial majority on the board of aldermen and, during the crucial period for ratification of the program, was as confident of the votes of Democratic aldermen as a British Prime Minister is of his parliamentary majority. Lee was far from being a mere creative creature of the party organization which was so helpful to him, but he also was effectively vetoed by the party when he attempted to bring about governmental reforms which would have made the mayor less dependent upon the organization to obtain positive action.[17]

Further evidence of the persistence of old-style party activities came from a number of other studies conducted in the late 1950's. For example, in 1957 party leaders from eight New Jersey counties reported performing a wide range of traditional party services, in response to an ingeniously worded questionnaire administered by Professor Richard T. Frost.[18]

Services Performed by New Jersey Politicians

The Service	*Percentage Performing It "Often"*
Helping deserving people get public jobs	72
Showing people how to get their social security benefits, welfare, unemployment compensation, etc.	54
Helping citizens who are in difficulty with the law. Do you help get them straightened out?	62

There was even some evidence in the 1950's of a rebirth of old-style urban party activities—for example, in the once Republican-dominated city of Philadelphia, where an effective Democratic old-style organization was put together. Often old-style organizations seem to exist in portions of contemporary cities, especially the low-income sections. These, like the reform groups to be described below, serve as factions in city-wide politics.[19]

Why old-style politics persists in some settings but not others is not fully clear. An impressionistic survey of the scattered evidence suggests, as might be expected, that the older pattern continues in those localities which most resemble the situations which originally spawned strong local parties in the nineteenth century. Eastern industrial cities, such as New Haven, Philadelphia, and many of the New Jersey cities, have sizable low-income groups in need of traditional party services. In many of these areas, the legal impediments to party activity also are minimal: Connecticut, for example, was the last state in the union to adopt direct primary legislation, and nonpartisan local election systems are, in general, less common in industrial cities than in cities without much manufacturing activity.[20] Cities in which weak, disorganized parties are reported—like Seattle, Minneapolis, and even Detroit (which, of course, *is* a manufacturing center of some importance)—are quite often cities in which nonpartisan institutions have been adopted.

Some New-Style Urban Political Patterns

In conclusion, we may note two of the styles of politics which have been reported in contemporary localities where old-style organizations have become weak or nonexistent: the politics of nonpartisanship and the new "reform" factions within some urban Democratic parties. Both patterns are of considerable intrinsic interest to students of local government. And, as contrasting political forms, they provide us with further perspective on the strengths and weaknesses of old-style urban politics.

The Politics of Nonpartisanship

The nonpartisan ballot now is in force in 66 per cent of American cities over 25,000 in population. Numerous styles of politics seem to take place beneath the façade of nonpartisanship. In some communities, when party labels are eliminated from the ballot, the old parties continue to operate much as they have in the past; in other communities, new local parties spring up to contest the nonpartisan elections. Finally, nonpartisanship often takes the form intended by its founders: no organized groups contest elections; voters choose from a more or less self-selected array of candidates.

In the last of these cases, although nonpartisanship has its intended effect, it also seems to have had—a recent body of literature suggests[21]—a number of unintended side effects. One of these is voter confusion. Without the familiar device of party labels to aid in selecting candidates, voters may find it difficult to select from among the sometimes substantial list of names on the ballot. Under these circumstances, a bonus in votes often goes to candidates with a familiar sounding name—incumbents are likely to be re-elected, for example—or even candidates with a favorable position on the ballot. In addition, campaigning and other personal contacts with voters become less common, because candidates no longer have the financial resources and personnel of a party organization at their disposal and therefore are dependent upon personal financing or backing from interest groups in the community.

Nonpartisan electoral practices, where effective, also seem to increase the influence of the mass media on voters; in the absence of campaigning, party canvassing, and party labels, voters become highly dependent for information as well as advice on the press, radio, and television. Normally, mass communications have rather limited effects on people's behavior compared with face-to-face communication such as canvassing by party workers.[22] Under nonpartisan circumstances, however, he who controls the press is likely to have much more direct and substantial effect on the public.

Ironically, the "theory" of nonpartisanship argues that by eliminating parties a barrier between citizens and their officials will be removed. In fact, nonpartisanship often attenuates the citizen's connections with the political system.

The Reform Democrats

The doctrine of nonpartisanship is mostly a product of the Progressive era. While nonpartisan local political systems continue to be adopted and, in fact, have become more common in recent decades, most of the impetus for this development results from the desire of communities to adopt city-manager systems. Nonpartisanship simply is part of the package which normally goes along with the popular city-manager system.

A newer phenomenon on the urban political scene is the development, especially since the 1952 presidential campaign, of ideologically motivated grass-roots party organizations within the Democratic party.[23] The ideology in question is liberalism: most of the reform organizations are led and staffed by college-educated intellectuals, many of whom were activated politically by the candidacy of Adlai Stevenson. In a few localities, there also have been grass-roots Republican organizations motivated by ideological considerations: in the Republican case, Goldwater conservatism.

New-style reformers differ in two

major ways from old-style reformers: their ideological concerns extend beyond a preoccupation with governmental efficiency alone (they favor racial integration and improved housing and sometimes devote much of their energy to advocating "liberal" causes at the national level); secondly, their strategy is to work within and take control of the parties, rather than to reject the legitimacy of parties. They do resemble old-style reformers in their preoccupation with the evils of "bossism" and machine politics.

There also is an important resemblance between the new reform politician and the old-style organization man the reformer seeks to replace. In both cases, very much unlike the situation which seems to be stimulated by nonpartisanship, the politician emphasizes extensive face-to-face contact with voters. Where reformers have been successful, it often has been by beating the boss at his own game of canvassing the election district, registering and keeping track of voters, and getting them to the polls.[24]

But much of the day-to-day style of the traditional urban politician is clearly distasteful to the new reformers: they have generally eschewed the use of patronage and, with the exceptions of campaigns for housing code enforcement, they have avoided the extensive service operations to voters and interest groups which were central to old-style party organizations. For example, when election district captains and other officials of the Greenwich Village Independent Democrats, the reform group which deposed New York Democrat County Leader Carmine DeSapio in his own election district, were asked the same set of questions about their activities used in the New Jersey study, strikingly different responses were made.

Services Performed by New York Reform Democrats[25]

The Service	*Percentage Performing It "Often"*
Helping deserving people get public jobs	0
Showing people how to get their social security benefits, welfare, unemployment compensation, etc.	5
Helping citizens who are in difficulty with the law. Do you help get them straightened out?	6

The successes of this class of new-style urban party politician have vindicated a portion of the classical strategy of urban party politics, the extensive reliance upon canvassing and other personal relations, and also have shown that under some circumstances it is possible to organize such activities with virtually no reliance on patronage and other material rewards. The reformers have tapped a pool of political activists used by parties elsewhere in the world—for example, in Great Britain—but not a normal part of the American scene. One might say that the reformers have "discovered" the British Labor constituency parties.

It is where material resources available to the parties are limited, for example, California, and where voter interest in these resources is low, that the new reformers are successful. In practice, however, the latter condition has confined the effectiveness of the reform Democrats largely to the more prosperous sections of cities; neither their style nor their programs seem to be successful in lower-class districts.[26] The areas of reform Democratic strength are generally *not* the areas which contribute greatly to Democratic pluralities in the cities. And, in many cities, the reformers' clientele is progressively diminishing as higher-income citizens move outward to the suburbs. Therefore, though fascinating and illuminating, the new reform movement must at least for the moment be considered as little more than a single manifestation in a panorama of urban political practices.[27]

Conclusion

The degree to which *old-style* urban party organizations will continue to be a part of this panorama is uncertain. Changes in the social composition of the cities promise to be a major factor in the future of urban politics. If, as seems possible, many cities become lower-class, nonwhite enclaves, we can be confident that there will be a continuing market for the services of the service-oriented old-style politician. Whether or not this is the case, many lessons can be culled from the history of party politics during the years of growth of the American cities—lessons which are relevant, for example, to studying the politics of urbanization elsewhere in the world.[28] In the nineteenth century, after all, the United States was an "emerging," "modernizing" nation, facing the problems of stability and democracy which are now being faced by countless newer nations.

NOTES

1. E. E. Schattschneider, *Party Government* (New York, 1942), pp. 162–169.
2. Among the better known accounts are Frank R. Kent, *The Great Game of Politics* (Garden City, N.Y., 1923, rev. ed., 1930); Sonya Forthall, *Cogwheels of Democracy* (New York, 1946); Harold F. Gosnell, *Machine Politics* (Chicago, 1937); and the many case studies of individual bosses. For a recent romanticization, see Edwin O'Connor's novel, *The Last Hurrah* (Boston, 1956).
3. Austin Ranney and Willmoore Kendall, *Democracy and the American Party System* (New York, 1956), pp. 249–252.
4. This last definitional criterion explicitly departs from the characterization of a "machine" in James Q. Wilson's interesting discussion of "The Economy of Patronage," *The Journal of Political Economy*, Vol. 59 (August 1961), p. 370n., "as that kind of political party which sustains its members through the distribution of material incentives (patronage) rather than nonmaterial incentives (appeals to principle, the fun of the game, sociability, etc.)." There is ample evidence that for many old-style party workers incentives such as "the fun of the game," "sociability," and even "service" are of central importance. See, for example, Edward J. Flynn, *You're the Boss* (New York, 1947), p. 22; James A. Farley, *Behind the Ballots* (New York, 1938), p. 237. . . . The distinction between "material" and "nonmaterial" incentives would probably have to be discarded in a more refined discussion of the motivations underlying political participation. So-called material rewards, at base, are nonmaterial in the sense that they are valued for the status they confer and for other culturally defined reasons.
5. *Op. cit.*, p. 106.
6. See, for example, Edward A. Shils, *The Torment of Secrecy* (Glencoe, Ill., 1956) and Stanley M. Elkins, *Slavery* (Chicago, 1959, reprinted with an introduction by Nathan Glazer, New York, 1963).
7. William L. Riordon, *Plunkitt of Tammany Hall* (originally published in 1905; republished New York, 1948 and New York, 1963; quotations are from the 1963 edition), pp. 27–28.
8. *Ibid.*, pp. 25–26.

9. Elmer E. Cornwell, Jr., "Party Absorption of Ethnic Groups: The Case of Providence, Rhode Island," *Social Forces,* Vol. 38 (March 1960), pp. 205–210.
10. Riordon, *op. cit.*, pp. 17–20.
11. Frank J. Sorauf, "State Patronage in a Rural County," *American Political Science Review,* Vol. 50 (December 1956), pp. 1046–1056.
12. Angus Campbell, Philip E. Converse, Warren E. Miller, and Donald E. Stokes, *The American Voter* (New York, 1960), pp. 426–427. The statistic for nonsouthern cities was supplied to me by the authors.
13. Daniel Katz and Samuel J. Eldersveld, "The Impact of Local Party Activity on the Electorate," *Public Opinion Quarterly,* Vol. 25 (Spring 1961), pp. 16–17.
14. Hugh A. Bone, *Grass Roots Party Leadership* (Seattle, 1952); Robert L. Morlan, "City Politics: Free Style," *National Municipal Review,* Vol. 38 (November 1949), pp. 485–491.
15. Robert A. Dahl, *Who Governs?* (New Haven, 1961), p. 278.
16. *Ibid.;* Nelson W. Polsby, *Community Power and Political Theory* (New Haven, 1963); Raymond E. Wolfinger, *The Politics of Progress.*
17. Raymond E. Wolfinger, "The Influence of Precinct Work on Voting Behavior," *Public Opinion Quarterly,* Vol. 27 (Fall 1963), pp. 387–398.
18. Frost deliberately worded his questionnaire descriptions of these services favorably in order to avoid implying that respondents were to be censured for indulging in "machine tactics." Richard T. Frost, "Stability and Change in Local Politics," *Public Opinion Quarterly,* Vol. 25 (Summer 1961), pp. 231–232.
19. James Q. Wilson, "Politics and Reform in American Cities," *American Government Annual, 1962–63* (New York, 1962), pp. 37–52.
Studies in Society and History, Vol. 5 (January 1963), pp. 219–221.
20. Phillips Cutright, "Nonpartisan Electoral Systems in American Cities," *Comparative Studies in Society and History,* Vol. 5 (January 1963), pp. 219–221.
21. For a brief review of the relevant literature, see Fred I. Greenstein, *The American Party System and the American People* (Englewood Cliffs, N.J., 1963), pp. 57–60.
22. Joseph T. Klapper, *The Effects of Mass Communication* (New York, 1960).
23. James Q. Wilson, *The Amateur Democrat* (Chicago, 1962).
24. There is another interesting point of resemblance between old- and new-style urban party politics. In both, an important aspect of the motivation for participation seems to be the rewards of sociability. Tammany picnics and New York Committee for Democratic Voters (CDV) coffee hours probably differ more in decor than in the functions they serve. An amusing indication of this is provided by the committee structure of the Greenwich Village club of the CDV; in addition to the committees dealing with the club newsletter, with housing, and with community action, there is a social committee and a Flight Committee, the latter being concerned with arranging charter flights to Europe for club members. See Vernon M. Goetcheus, *The Village Independent Democrats: A Study in the Politics of the New Reformers* (unpublished senior distinction thesis, Honors College, Wesleyan University, 1963), pp. 65–66. On similar activities by the California Democratic Clubs, see Robert E. Lane, James D. Barber, and Fred I. Greenstein, *Introduction to Political Analysis* (Englewood Cliffs, N.J., 1962), pp. 55–57.
25. Goetcheus, *op. cit.*, p. 138.
26. DeSapio, for example, was generally able to hold on to his lower-class Italian voting support in Greenwich Village; his opponents succeeded largely by activating the many middle- and upper-class voters who had moved into new high-rent housing in the district.
27. Probably because of their emphasis on ideology, the new reform groups also seem to be quite prone to internal conflicts which impede their effectiveness. One is reminded of Robert Michels' remarks about the intransigence of intellectuals in European socialist parties. *Political Parties* (New York, 1962, originally published in 1915), Part 4, Chap. 6.
28. On the significance of the American experience with old-style urban politics for the emerging nations, see Wallace S. Sayre and Nelson W. Polsby, "American Political Science and the Study of Urbanization," Committee on Urbanization, Social Science Research Council, mimeo. 1963, pp. 45–48.

12

Incentives for the Maintenance of Grassroots Political Activism

LEWIS BOWMAN, DENNIS IPPOLITO, AND WILLIAM DONALDSON

Lewis Bowman, Dennis Ippolito, and William Donaldson report in the following article that policy incentives and social and psychological satisfactions have greatly overshadowed material incentives as reasons for party activism by local party officials in Massachusetts and North Carolina. Party organizations are faced not only with the problem of recruiting activists but also with maintaining their allegiance. The authors discovered little difference in the incentives to activism cited by local party officials who intended to continue in party work and those who expected to leave their posts. The critical difference in maintaining party activism seems not to be incentives but rather the opinion that party officials have about the importance of their party offices.

In a society where party activity and party organizations are widely distrusted and disapproved by the public, there are likely to be insistent social pressures against party work and norms that demean the importance of party activism. In this atmosphere it is not surprising that local party officials are quickly discouraged and that turnover among them is high. Parties are faced with more than the difficult problem of recruiting workers; they must find ways to emphasize the dignity and importance of party work if they are to maintain their ranks.

Bowman and Ippolito are professors of political science at Emery University, and Donaldson is a member of the faculty at the University of Virginia. Bowman has published several articles on the recruitment and activities of party activists.

Table 1
What Local Party Officials Like Most About Their Positions (in percentages)

	Responses by Area and Party, First Response and Total Responses									
	Mass. 1st	*Dem. total*	*Mass. 1st*	*Rep. total*	*N. C. 1st*	*Dem. total*	*N. C. 1st*	*Rep. total*	*Total 1st*	*Total total*
Personal satisfaction and rewards	91	70	77	62	67	54	70	69	75	62
Being influential in the community	0	16	6	16	19	26	18	20	12	20
Being influential in the party	0	1	10	11	11	16	9	10	8	11
General party activities	9	13	7	11	3	4	3	1	5	7
	100	100	100	100	100	100	100	100	100	100
N=	(22)	(39)	(31)	(56)	(36)	(69)	(34)	(61)	(123)	(225)

Introduction

Relatively few persons become involved in party organizational work on a continuing basis.[1] An examination of the incentives systems involved in party work can help to explain this phenomenon. What do party officials like and dislike about party work? What are the incentives which tend to keep party officials active? And, of course, does discontinuity in party activism reflect the inability of the party to deliver the incentives which it offers (or which it socializes its activists to expect) or is it a reflection of particular and highly personal conflicts within the local organization? While the initial recruitment process has begun to receive increasing attention, little scholarly work has dealt with these questions at the grassroots level of party organization where an incentives system capable of maintaining the party organization over a period of time is likely to be quite different from that of national or even state party leadership.[2] If the local party is to function as an organization, it must provide incentives which are adequate to encourage party workers to continue their formal affiliation with the party over a substantial period of time.

In an effort to provide answers to some of these questions about incentives systems for party work, we conducted a survey of Democratic and Republican precinct party officials in selected areas—three Massachusetts and two North Carolina communities.[3]

Incentives to Party Organizational Work

A large majority of the local party officials said that they liked their post, because it provided them with certain personal satisfactions and rewards. Among such satisfactions and rewards are "self-improvement as a citizen," "the personal contacts which one can make," "it helps business," and the

Reprinted in abridged form from *Midwest Journal of Political Science*, 13 (February 1969), 126–139, by permission of the authors and the Wayne State University Press.

inevitable affinity of the inside dopesters—"I like being on the inside." Perhaps indicating the differing nature of party politics in the two states, the party officials in the Massachusetts communities were somewhat more inclined to articulate reasons of personal satisfaction than were their North Carolina counterparts. The Massachusetts Democrats in particular—while not varying significantly from the other sub-groups in terms of total responses to the question, "What do you like most about being a party official?"—gave an initial answer reflecting personal satisfactions or rewards in over ninety per cent of their responses. It is to be expected that local party officials in Massachusetts, where few duties (and apparently little power) are generally associated with their positions, would like their job because of general party activities (such as working at the polls, campaigning, etc.) and personal rewards rather than because of any inordinate party or community influence inherent in the positions. If the first response can be assumed to be the main reason for liking the position, the different perceptions by North Carolina and Massachusetts party officials of community or party influences as a concomitant of their positions are striking. None of the initial responses of Massachusetts Democrats and only sixteen per cent of the responses of Massachusetts Republicans were in terms of community or party influence. In North Carolina, however, thirty per cent of the Democrats and twenty-seven per cent of the Republicans thought that their positions put them in line to exert influence in matters of policy formation, candidate selection, criticism of party affairs, or community affairs. And, of course, the importance of community and party influence relative to personal satisfactions and rewards is particularly strong for North Carolina Democrats. Obviously, their perceived incentives

Table 2
What Local Party Officials Like Least About Their Positions (in percentages)

	Responses by Area and Party, First Response and Total Responses									
	Mass. 1st	*Dem. total*	*Mass. 1st*	*Rep. total*	*N. C. 1st*	*Dem. total*	*N. C. 1st*	*Rep. total*	*Total 1st*	*Total total*
Conflict within the party organization	27	35	11	14	27	29	42	39	26	29
Party tasks	33	25	36	38	19	21	12	9	24	23
Undue demand on time	0	0	25	26	31	21	19	23	21	19
Apathy of the people in the community	27	25	14	11	11	18	19	20	17	18
Non-organizational conflict	13	15	14	11	12	11	8	9	12	11
	100	100	100	100	100	100	100	100	100	100
N=	(15)	(20)	(28)	(35)	(26)	(38)	(26)	(31)	(95)	(124)

differ from those articulated by Massachusetts party officials, or even by their Republican counterparts in North Carolina.

Interesting variations also occurred when the local party officials were asked, "What do you like least about your position?" North Carolina Republicans, who had been involved in recent intra-party skirmishes between the Young Republicans and the older federal Republicans for control of the local party machinery, expressed concern about conflict within the party organization. Nearly one-half of their initial responses are of this nature. Among the Massachusetts Democrats, where internecine party conflict is not unusual, this type of reaction also was significant (thirty-five per cent of the total responses). Since the four party groups varied little in their dislike of non-organizational conflict, it is probable that the party officials were expressing a general dislike for conflict generated by particular local situations. The dislike of party tasks among the Massachusetts party officials, particularly Republicans, was apparently related to the fact that, in recent campaigns, a concerted effort was made to use the precinct chairmen in the solicitation of funds from the public. The differential responses of North Carolina and Massachusetts officials in terms of dislike of party tasks may have mirrored their differing perceptions of the influence of their position. It could be that a degree of perceived influence renders the performing of certain party tasks somewhat less objectionable. In a similar study of county party organizations in Nassau County, the same problem arose over fund-raising campaigns. It appeared, however, that the committeemen reacted more strongly against door-to-door solicitation then did zone leaders or assembly district leaders, although most of these officials did solicit funds. Thus, it may be that the more objectionable tasks which the activist performs need to be rationalized in personally meaningful terms such as power or influence in the party or community.[4]

The perceived and expressed reasons for liking and disliking their positions indicate that variations in extent, if not in type, characterize the attractions and dissatisfactions of party activism for party officials in these communities. In the aggregate, however, the personal rewards and satisfactions of party work appear to be the most important incentives among all officials. And, while it is clearly less important, the perception of situational or party influence apparently constitutes an important incentive. Particular situational and party differences, however, are somewhat more evident in terms of dissatisfactions with party work. Thus, for example, intra-party conflict and party tasks were of greater relevance for some local organizations than for others. And, for all officials, there was no particular dislike which predominated to the extent evidenced in the ranking of positive incentives.

The Rating of Particular Incentives

The responses of party officials to open-minded questions indicated a similar reaction toward positive or "satisfying" incentives and a varying ranking—depending on community or party—of negative or unsatisfactory aspects of party work. The local party leaders' responses to a series of closed-ended items reinforced the similarity relating to positive incentives. This battery of questions was initially used by Marvick and Nixon to differentiate between the motivations of Repub-

Table 3
The Importance of Incentives to the Local Party Officials* (in percentages)

	Massachusetts			*North Carolina*			*Total*		
Item	*Dem.*	*Rep.*	*Total*	*Dem.*	*Rep.*	*Total*	*Dem.*	*Rep.*	*Total*
1. Concern with public issues	87	88	88	95	91	93	92	89	91
2. Sense of community obligation	70	85	78	83	85	84	78	85	82
3. Strong party loyalty	74	58	66	46	56	51	56	49	53
4. Politics part of way of life	56	42	48	51	44	48	53	46	49
5. Making social contacts and friends	39	30	35	39	56	48	39	42	41
6. Fun and excitement of campaign	26	25	26	29	35	32	28	30	29
7. Personal friend of candidate	26	15	21	29	24	27	28	19	24
8. Being close to influential people	17	15	16	27	20	24	23	18	21
9. Furthering political ambition	13	5	9	10	3	7	11	4	8
10. Making business contacts	9	5	7	12	3	8	11	4	8
N=	(23)	(40)	(63)	(41)	(34)	(75)	(64)	(74)	(138)

* In percentages of those to whom the incentive was "very important."

lican and Democratic volunteer campaign workers in Los Angeles.[5] . . .

* * *

In order to relate these incentives to organizational theory, we assigned the incentives to the categories suggested by Clark and Wilson, who pointed out that three broad categories of incentives influence members of organizations: material, solidary, and purposive.[6] According to their definitions, the "material" incentives are tangible rewards such as money, or rewards easily transferable to money. The "solidary" incentives are intangible rewards which mainly result from the act of associating, and include socializing, group identification, member status, and fun-seeking. The "purposive" incentives are intangible—like the "solidary" incentives—but result generally from the stated ends of association rather than from mere association. Following these definitions we categorized as *material* incentives these items: "being close to influential people," "furthering political ambition," and "making business contacts"; *solidary* items included "strong party loyalty," "politics as part of a way of life," "making social contacts and friends," "the fun and excitement of campaigns," and "personal friend of a candidate"; the remaining items—"concern with public issues" and "sense of community obligation"—were classified as *purposive.*

As Table 4 indicates the differences by party and area in the importance of incentive categories were quite small. In each case, the relative ranking of the incentive categories was the same. Further, the small variations which occurred in the ranking of each incentive category by area and party appeared to be idiosyncratic. Of course, the fact that all four subgroups ranked the incentive categories in the same order—"purposive" incentives most important, "solidary" incentives next most important, "material" incentives least important—may be instructive. It could be that, at this party level, activists are more highly motivated by concerns about public issues, community obligation, and party loyalty and social contacts than by material gains. This might indicate as much about the availability of material incentives at the local level as it does about the idealism, loyalty, and conviviality of grassroots activists, but the rather consistent ordering of the responses among the sub-groups strongly suggests such an interpretation.

In dealing with incentives, then, the differences between the areas and the parties were relatively minor. Only in the case of "dislikes" relating to party work do the influences of party and specific locale appear to be of some importance. Thus, the perceptions of party officials relating to incentives indicate a degree of commonality relating to activism generally at the local level.

The Decision to Continue in the Party Post

Of those officials who had reached a decision, approximately two-thirds planned to continue in their party posts. The essential question, then, is whether the decision to continue or to quit is related to the categories of incentives or to likes and dislikes about the position.

In examining the "positive" incentives relating to party activism, it appeared that little variation occurred either among areas or among parties. A similar finding emerges when we contrast the perceived incentives of those who said they were going to continue in party office with those who plan to quit. As aggregates they differ slightly, if at all.

In terms of "dislikes," moreover,

Table 4
The Importance of Solidary, Purposive, and Material Incentives by Area and Party

	*Categories of Incentives (Grand Mean Score)**		
	Purposive	*Solidary*	*Material*
North Carolina Republicans	1.17	2.14	3.15
North Carolina Democrats	1.10	1.96	2.85
Massachusetts Republicans	1.21	2.15	3.39
Massachusetts Democrats	1.43	1.87	3.08
Total	1.18	2.01	3.12

* The possible ratings are: (1) "very important"; (2) "somewhat important"; (3) "not very important"; and (4) "not important at all." Thus, the higher the grand mean, the lower the incentive category in importance.

there are few substantial differences. Among those who plan to quit, "undue demand on time" apparently constitutes a greater burden than among those who plan to continue. Yet intra-party conflict, which is at least intuitively suggestive, is not a discriminating factor, at least as far as the aggregates are concerned.

A number of other factors, including such obvious ones as age and tenure in office, as well as type of recruitment and nature of first contest for office, were also examined, yet the differences here again were slight, and there was no evidence of a consistent pattern of differentiation between the groups.

Indeed, one of the few differences between those who plan to continue and those who plan to quit relates to the assessment of their party position. When asked to assess the personal importance of their party post, a substantially greater number of activists who plan to quit (fifty-four per cent) than activists who plan to continue (twenty-six per cent) characterized their position as "unimportant." Moreover, the differences between the two groups are consistent within each of the party and area sub-groups.

This evaluation of party position is reinforced by the differing evaluations of party loyalty as important incentives by the two groups. There are only two cases in the direct battery of incentive items in which some degree of variation is shown. One is the importance of personal friendship for a candidate, which is somewhat more important as an incentive for those who plan to quit than for those who plan to continue. And the second is the assessment of strong party loyalty. Fifty-eight per cent of the continuing activists rated this incentive as very important as opposed to only forty-five per cent of those activists who plan to quit. It is probable that these two factors are somewhat related. Personal friendship for a candidate may provide an impetus to party activism, but it is not likely to promote continuing activism in some cases without a reinforcement by and reorientation to party. And since not only the importance of party loyalty but also the importance of the party position is less for those who plan to quit, this type of reinforcement and reorientation might not have occurred.

What may be indicated, then, is a relative lack of party orientation on the part of some activists. Further, the problem could become more acute at this level of the party organization. As we noted earlier, the party officials with whom we are dealing do not hold positions which are particularly pow-

Table 5
Relation of Their Views of the Personal Importance of Party Post to the Party Officials' Plans to Continue in Office, by Area and Party (in percentages)

	Mass.				*N. Carolina*				*Totals*		
	Dem.		*Rep.*		*Dem.*		*Rep.*				
R says post is:	*Cont.*	*Quit**	*Cont.*	*Quit*	*Cont.*	*Quit*	*Cont.*	*Quit*	*Cont.*	*Quit*	*All*
Important	82	50	79	46	62	30	75	57	74	46	63
Unimportant	18	50	21	54	38	70	25	43	26	54	37
N=	(17)	(2)	(19)	(13)	(24)	(13)	(20)	(14)	(80)	(42)	(122)

* Relevant only for completeness because of the small number.

Table 6
The Importance of Various Incentives to the Local Party Officials Who Are Going to Continue in the Position, as Compared to Those Who Are Going to Quit* (in percentages)

Incentive	*Plan to Continue in Office*	*Plan to Quit the Office*
Purposive		
Concern with public issues	91	90
Sense of community obligation	80	83
Solidary		
Strong party loyalty	58	45
Politics part of way of life	48	50
Making social contacts and friends	42	40
Fun and excitement of the campaign	31	33
Personal friend of candidates	21	31
Material		
Being close to influential people	21	24
Making business contacts	9	7
Furthering political ambitions	8	7
N=	(80)	(42)

* In percentages of those answering "very important" when questioned about the incentive.

erful or influential; the officials' evaluations reflect this assessment. It is also clear that those who do plan to relinquish their party posts do not perceive and/or articulate political ambitions or other material incentives as particularly important. Indeed, both groups rank the incentive categories virtually the same.

The problem of maintaining activism at the local level, then, appears to have several components. First, in the areas studied here as elsewhere, purposive incentives are becoming increasingly important as an impetus to party activism. In maintaining such activism, however, the ability of the party either to "pay-off" on such incentives or to reinforce or reorient them becomes critical. Thus, for those who continue in party office, party loyalty and a high evaluation of the personal importance of party office may reflect, to some extent, a socialization of the activist. More tangible and direct personal benefits may simply not be relevant at the local party level in these areas. And, indeed, the chances for patronage or political advancement of any consequence in these areas are quite restricted. For some activists, however, initial attachment to the party or socialization which fosters such attachment both to the party in general and to the party position in particular may not be sufficiently strong.

Summary

It is clear that personal rewards and satisfactions are important incentives at the local level. The degree to which officials of both parties in North Carolina and Massachusetts articulate their positive responses to party work in these terms indicates this clearly. In addition, material incentives are relatively unimportant for all subgroups. This probably reflects the relative availability of such incentives,

Table 7
Relation of Types of Incentives to the Local Party Official's Plans to Continue or to Quit the Position

Incentive Category	*Plans to Continue*	*Plans to Quit*
	*Mean Score for Category of Incentive**	
Material	3.0	3.1
Solidary	1.9	2.0
Purposive	1.2	1.2
N=	(80)	(42)

* The possible ratings are: (1) "very important"; (2) "somewhat important"; (3) "not very important"; (4) "not important at all." Thus, the higher the mean, the lower the incentive category in importance.

the basic level of party structure with which we are dealing, and the changing character of the contemporary activist.

Discontinuity in party activism, however, is apparently unrelated to differing perceptions of incentives. To the extent that those who plan to continue differ from those who plan to quit, the essential difference appears to be related to the importance which they attach to their party position and their perceptions of party loyalty. For those to whom party loyalty is very important and for whom the party position is personally important, continued activism is more likely than among those whose party orientation and position orientation are less strong.

The local party, then, can attract activists through purposive incentives. But the maintenance of activism requires, to some extent, the eventual positive orientation of the activist toward the party as a group and toward his position in the party.[7] Where material incentives are either unavailable or largely irrelevant and where the party's ability to pay off in terms of purposive incentives is restricted, the importance of solidary incentives in general and of party attachment in particular becomes clear. The maintenance of activism appears to require that the party official find some personal value in his position, whether or not that position is actually powerful or influential.

NOTES

1. At the local level, there is no reliable estimate of continuous activism. Indeed, continuity would need some strict definition if we are to begin estimating turnover at the local level. In Eldersveld's study, it is reported that "At least half the top precinct mobiles in the Democratic party, and two-fifths in the Republican party, had brief political careers . . . [while] one-third of the top mobiles in both parties had been in the party continuously for at least 16 years." Samuel J. Eldersveld, *Political Parties: A Behavioral Analysis* (Chicago: Rand-McNally, 1964), p. 167. In Nassau County, New York, a sample of 85 executive committeemen revealed none who had decided to quit their party post. At the committeeman level, however, turnover in the Democratic party is nearly twenty per cent every two years and in the Republican party it is only slightly less. What this suggests is that measurement of continuous activism depends on the type of activists (careerists or noncareerists; mobiles or nonmobiles), the local party level (e.g., district chairmen or precinct chairmen), the party (majority or minority), and the area or political context within which the party is

working. On these last two points, see William J. Crotty, "The Party Organization and Its Activities," in *Approaches to the Study of Party Organization,* ed. William J. Crotty (Boston: Allyn and Bacon, 1968), pp. 251–60, 293.

2. For some recent analyses of the incentives systems at the local level, see Eldersveld, *op. cit.,* pp. 272–303; Robert S. Hirschfield, Bert E. Swanson, and Blanche D. Blank, "A Profile of Political Activists in Manhattan," *Western Political Quarterly,* 15 (September, 1962), pp. 489–506; Dwaine Marvick and Charles Nixon, "Recruitment Contrasts in Rival Campaign Groups," in *Political Decision-Makers,* ed. Dwaine Marvick (New York: Free Press, 1961), pp. 193–217; Robert H. Salisbury, "The Urban Party Organization Member," *Public Opinion Quarterly,* 29 (Winter, 1965–1966), pp. 350–64; also the general analysis in Frank J. Sorauf, *Party Politics in America* (Boston: Little, Brown and Company, 1968), pp. 82–90. There are clear signs of change in the incentives system at the local level—in particular, the importance of patronage and other material incentives is apparently decreasing—but, as Eldersveld notes, one should expect some "diversity in motivational patterns hierarchically, areally, and organizationally (p. 302)."
3. For purposes of this study, "local party official" has been defined as the Republican and Democratic precinct chairmen in the North Carolina communities and as the two highest ranking Republican and Democratic ward officials in the Massachusetts communities. The latter choice was occasioned by the organizational arrangement in Massachusetts, and while it presents some limited problems in comparability, all those designated are the "grassroots" party officials in both systems and are comparable in that important respect.
4. This and other references to Nassau County are drawn from a study of party leadership conducted during the summer and fall of 1966. See Dennis S. Ippolito, *Political Perspectives and Party Leadership: A Case Study of Nassau County, New York* (unpublished Ph.D. dissertation, University of Virgina: 1967).
5. Marvick and Nixon, *op. cit.,* p. 208. The question used is "People get involved in politics for different reasons. The following reasons have been given by some party officials with whom we have talked. How important are these reasons to you?" The individual items appeared in a different order in the questionnare than in Tables 3 and [6].
6. Peter Clark and James Q. Wilson, "Incentive Systems: A Theory of Organization," *Administrative Science Quarterly,* 6 (1961), pp. 129–166.
7. Eldersveld's findings suggest this also. As he notes, "The one striking consistency of perspectives emerging from this analysis is that those activists who were unable to articulate the goal of the party, and those who had no clear perception of their own role, were definitely inclined to be disillusioned motivationally (p. 293)." It is to be expected that indecision about party goals and lack of clear perception of one's role are not likely to sustain strong personal commitments to either. If this is the case, the need for reinforcement and reorientation becomes acute.

13

Issue Conflict and Consensus Among Party Leaders and Followers

HERBERT McCLOSKY, PAUL J. HOFFMANN, AND ROSEMARY O'HARA

The article by Herbert J. McClosky and others that follows has been widely cited, quoted, and reprinted. In it strong evidence is marshaled to undermine the common view that there are no important issue differences between the major American parties. Although this 1957–1958 survey of national convention delegates confirms that each party contains within its ranks leaders of every view on issues, it clearly shows that most Democratic leaders differ sharply from most Republican leaders, particularly on those economic issues that identify Democrats with the lower-income classes and the Republicans with the well-off.

The comparable study of the attitudes of voters reveals that they are not so sharply divided along party lines on these issues. Indeed, voters seem to have more moderate views on the issues than the leaders of either party; and if the electorate of both parties finds itself close to one or another of the party leadership cadres, it is to the Democrats. This strongly suggests that there is a congruence on policy between the majority of the electorate and the party they have entrusted with control of the government during most of the past four decades. Whether the conclusions drawn from this study remain valid in today's highly volatile politics, however, is problematic.

McClosky is Professor of Political Science and Research Psychologist at the University of California at Berkeley. He is coauthor of The Soviet Dictatorship *(1960) and has written articles in political science and psychology journals. The research for this study was conducted by McClosky and his collaborators with grants from the Social Science Research Council and the Rockefeller Foundation.*

American political parties are often regarded as "brokerage" organizations, weak in principle, devoid of ideology, and inclined to differ chiefly over unimportant questions. In contrast to the "ideological" parties of Europe—which supposedly appeal to their followers through sharply defined, coherent, and logically related doctrines—the American parties are thought to fit their convictions to the changing demands of the political contest.[1] According to this view, each set of American party leaders is satisfied to play Tweedledee to the other's Tweedledum.

I. Pressures Toward Uniformity and Cleavage

Although these "conclusions" are mainly derived from *a priori* analysis or from casual observations of anecdotal" data (little systematic effort having been made so far to verify or refute them), they are often taken as confirmed—largely, one imagines, because they are compatible with certain conspicuous features of American politics. Among these features is the entrenchment of a two-party system which, by affording both parties a genuine opportunity to win elections, tempts them to appeal to as many diverse elements in the electorate as are needed to put together a majority.[2] Since both parties want to attract support from the centrist and moderate segments of the electorate, their views on basic issues will, it is thought, tend to converge. Like giant business enterprises competing for the same market, they will be led to offer commodities that are in many respects identical.[3] It is one thing for a small party in a multi-party system to preserve its ideological purity, quite another for a mass party in a two-party system to do so. The one has little hope of becoming a majority, and can most easily survive by remaining identified with the narrow audience from which it draws its chief supporters; the other can succeed only by accommodating the conflicting claims of many diverse groups—only, in short, by blunting ideological distinctions.[4]

Constraints against enlarging intellectual differences also spring from the loosely confederated nature of the American party system, and from each national party's need to adjust its policies to the competing interests of the locality, the state, and the nation.[5] Many party units are more concerned with local than with national elections, and prefer not to be handicapped by clear-cut national programs. Every ambitious politician, moreover, hopes to achieve a *modus vivendi* tailored to the particular and often idiosyncratic complex of forces prevailing in his constituency, an objective rarely compatible with doctrinal purity.[6] Often, too, local politics are largely nonpartisan or are partisan in ways that scarcely affect the great national issues around which ideologies might be expected to form.[7] The development and enforcement of a sharply delineated ideology is also hindered by the absence in either party of a firmly established, authoritative, and continuing organizational center empowered to decide questions of doctrine and discipline.[8] Party affiliation is loosely defined, responsibility is weak or non-existent, and organs for indoctrinating or communicating with party members are at best rudimentary.

Cultural and historical differences may also contribute to the weaker

Reprinted in abridged form from *American Political Science Review*, 54 (June 1960), 406–427, by permission of the authors and the American Political Science Association.

ideological emphasis among American, as compared with European, parties. Many of the great historical cleavages that have divided European nations for centuries—monarchism *vs.* republicanism; clericalism *vs.* anticlericalism; democracy *vs.* autocracy, etc.—have never taken root in this country. Apart from the slavery (and subsequently the race) issue, the United States has not experienced the intense class or caste conflict often found abroad, and contests of the capitalism *vs.* socialism variety have never achieved an important role in American politics. In addition, never having known a titled nobility, we have largely been freed from the conflicts found elsewhere between the classes of inherited and acquired privilege.

Consider, too, the progress made in the United States toward neutralizing the forces which ordinarily lead to sharp social, and hence intellectual and political, differentiation. The class and status structure of American society has attained a rate of mobility equalling or exceeding that of any other long established society. Popular education, and other facilities for the creation of common attitudes, have been developed on a scale unequalled elsewhere. Improvements in transportation and communication, and rapid shifts in population and industry have weakened even sectionalism as a source of political cleavage. Rural-urban differences continue to exist, of course, but they too have been diminishing in force and have become less salient for American politics than the differences prevailing, for example, between a French peasant proprietor and a Parisian *boulevardier*.[9] In short, a great many Americans have been subjected in their public lives to identical stimuli—a condition unlikely to generate strong, competing ideologies.

The research reported here was designed not to refute these observations but to test the accuracy of the claim that they are sufficient to prevent differences in outlook from taking root in the American party system. We believed that the homogenizing tendencies referred to are strongly offset by contrary influences, and that voters are preponderantly led to support the party whose opinions they share. We further thought that the competition for office, though giving rise to similarities between the parties, also impels them to diverge from each other in order to sharpen their respective appeals. For this and other reasons, we expected to find that the leaders of the two parties, instead of ignoring differences alleged to exist within the electorate, would differ on issues more sharply than their followers would. We believed further that even in a brokerage system the parties would serve as independent reference groups, developing norms, values, and self-images to which their supporters could readily respond.[10] Their influence, we felt, would frequently exceed that of ethnic, occupational, residential and other reference groups. In sum, we proceeded on the belief that the parties are not simply spokesmen for other interest groups, but are in their own right agencies for formulating, transmitting, and anchoring political opinions, that they attract adherents who in general share those opinions, and that through a feedback process of mutual reinforcement between the organization and its typical supporters, the parties develop integrated and stable political tendencies. Other hypotheses will be specified as we present and analyze our findings.

II. Procedures

The questions considered in this paper were part of a large field study made in 1957–1958 on the nature, sources, and correlates of political affiliation, activity, and belief in the American party system (hereafter referred to as the PAB study)....

For our samples of party "leaders" we turned to the Democratic and Republican national conventions, largely because they are the leading and most representative of the party organs, their delegates coming from every part of the United States and from every level of party and government activity.... In the absence of comprehensive information about the characteristics of the party elites in America, no one can say how closely the convention delegates mirror the total party leadership. We felt it fair to assume, nevertheless, that the delegates represented as faithful a cross section of American party leadership as could be had without an extraordinary expenditure of money and labor. Using convention delegates as our universe of leaders also held some obvious advantages for research, since the composition of this universe (by name, address, party, state, sex, place of residence, and party or public office) can usually be ascertained from the convention calls. Of the 6,848 delegates and alternates available to be sampled, 3,193 actually participated; 3,020 (1,788 Democrats and 1,232 Republicans) completed and returned questionnaires that were usable in all respects.[11] The proportion of returns was roughly equivalent for both sets of party leaders.

The rank-and-file sample, which we wanted both for its intrinsic value and for its utility as a control group, was obtained by special arrangement with the American Institute of Public Opinion. In January 1958, Gallup interviewers personally distributed our questionnaire to 2,917 adult voters in two successive national cross-section surveys. Some 1,610 questionnaires were filled out and returned, of which 1,484 were completely usable. This sample closely matched the national population on such characteristics as sex, age, region, size of city, and party affiliation, and, though it somewhat oversampled the upper educational levels, we considered it sufficiently large and representative for most of our purposes. Of the 1,484 respondents, 821 were Democratic supporters (629 "pure" Democrats, plus 192 whom we classified as "independent" Democrats) and 623 were Republican supporters (479 "pure" Republicans, plus 144 "independent" Republicans). Forty respondents could not be identified as adherents of either party.

* * *

The questions most relevant for the present article were those which asked each respondent to express his attitudes toward twenty-four important national issues, and to state whether he believed support for each issue should be "increased," "decreased," or "remain as is." The list of issues and the responses of each sample will be found in Tables 2A through 2E, where for convenience of analysis, the issues have been grouped under five broad headings: Public Ownership, Government Regulation of the Economy, Equalitarianism and Human Welfare, Tax Policy and Foreign Policy.

... The index was built by assigning a weight of 1.0 to each "increase" response in the sample, of 0 to each "decrease" response, and of .50 to each "remain as is" (or "same") response. Thus the ratio-of-support score shown for any given sample is in effect a

Table 1
Average Differences in the Ratio-of-Support Scores Among Party Leaders and Followers for Five Categories of Issues

Category of Issues	*Democratic Leaders vs. Republican Leaders*	*Democratic Followers vs. Republican Followers*	*Democratic Leaders vs. Democratic Followers*	*Republican Leaders vs. Republican Followers*	*Democratic Leaders vs. Republican Followers*	*Republican Leaders vs. Democratic Followers*
a. Public ownership of resources	.28	.04	.06	.18	.10	.22
b. Government regulation of the economy	.22	.06	.08	.10	.12	.16
c. Equalitarianism, human welfare	.22	.05	.08	.21	.06	.25
d. Tax policy	.20	.06	.06	.20	.04	.26
e. Foreign policy	.16	.02	.05	.08	.07	.10
Avrage differences in ratio scores for all categories	.21	.04	.07	.15	.08	.20

Sample Sizes: Democratic Leaders, 1,788; Republican Leaders, 1,232; Democratic Followers, 821; Republican Followers, 623.

mean score with a possible range of 0 to 1.0, in which support for an issue increases as the scores approach 1.0 and decreases as they approach 0. In general, the scores can be taken to approximate the following overall positions: .0 to .25—strongly wish to reduce support; .26 to .45—wish to reduce support; .46 to .55—satisfied with the *status quo;* .56 to .75—wish to increase support; and .76 to 1.00—strongly wish to increase support. Note that the differences in degree suggested by these categories refer not to the *strength of feeling* exhibited by individuals toward an issue but rather to the *numbers of people* in a sample who hold points of view favoring or opposing that issue.

Because they include the "same" and "no code" as well as "increase" and "decrease" responses, our ratios of support sometimes flatten the differences between groups. Had we employed only the percentage scores for the "increase" or "decrease" responses, the differences between samples would in many instances have seemed larger. Nevertheless, the ratio of support offers so many advantages that we have employed it as our principal measure. For one thing, as the equivalent of a mean score, it takes into account all scores, omitting no respondent from the tabulation. For the same reason it enables us to assess the amount of dispersion or homogeneity exhibited by any sample and makes it easy to calculate significances of difference.[12] Reliance upon a single, uniform statistic also allows us to make ready comparisons not only *between* but *within* samples, and to determine quickly how large the differences actually are. By observing whether a ratio of support is above or below .50 we can see at once whether a particular group predominantly favors or opposes the issue in question, and how strongly it does so. The use of ratio scores also makes it possible to compare issues as well as groups, *e.g.*, to see whether one issue is more preferred than another.

* * *

A word of caution before we turn to the findings. The respondents were offered only the twenty-four issues that impressed us in February, 1957, as most significant and enduring. However, they may not all be as salient today as they seemed at that time....

The *form* of our issue questions may also be open for criticism, for space limitations prevented our subjects from indicating how strongly they felt and how much they knew about each of the issues. This deficiency, however, may be less important than it appears, since for the groups we most wanted to compare (*e.g.*, Democratic *vs.* Republican leaders), the degree of political knowledge and intensity is likely to be rather similar. The difficulty is greater when comparing leaders with followers, but is somewhat offset by controlling for education and socio-economic status....

Finally, one may wonder about the value of opinions stated on a questionnaire compared with the worth of views formally expressed by an organization or implicit in the actions of its leaders.... The controversy over the value of the two approaches is to some extent spurious, however, for they offer different perspectives on the same thing. In addition, considerable correspondence exists between the party positions evident in congressional roll calls and the privately expressed opinions of the party leaders in our study.[13]

III. Findings: Comparisons Between Leaders

No more conclusive findings emerge from our study of party issues than those growing out of the comparisons between the two sets of party leaders. Despite the brokerage tendency of the American parties, their active members are obviously separated by large and important differences. The differences, moreover, conform with the popular image in which the Democratic party is seen as the more "progressive" or "radical," the Republican as the more "moderate" or "conservative" of the two.[14] In addition, the disagreements are remarkably consistent, a function not of chance but of systematic points of view, whereby the responses to any one of the issues could reasonably have been predicted from knowledge of the responses to the other issues.

Examination of Tables 2A–2E and 3 shows that the leaders differ significantly on 23 of the 24 issues listed and that they are separated on 15 of these issues by .18 or more ratio points—in short, by differences that are in absolute magnitude very large. The two samples are furthest apart in their attitudes toward public ownership and are especially divided on the question of government ownership of natural resources, the Democrats strongly favoring it, the Republicans just as strongly wanting it cut back. The difference of .39 in the ratio scores is the largest for any of the issues tested. In percentages, the differences are 58 per cent (D) vs. 13 per cent (R) in favor of increasing support, and 19 per cent (D) vs. 52 per cent (R) in favor of decreasing support. Both parties preponderantly support public control and development of atomic energy, but the Democrats do so more uniformly.

Table 2A
Comparison of Party Leaders and Followers on "Public Ownership" Issues, by Percentages and Ratios of Support

	Leaders		Followers	
Issues	*Dem.* *N=1,788*	*Repub.* *N=1,232*	*Dem.* *N=821*	*Repub.* *N=623*
		(%s down)		
Public ownership of natural resources				
% favoring: Increase	57.5	12.9	35.3	31.1
Decrease	18.6	51.9	15.0	19.9
Same, n.c.*	23.8	35.2	49.7	49.0
Support ratio	.69	.30	.60	.56
Public control of atomic energy				
% favoring: Increase	73.2	45.0	64.2	59.4
Decrease	7.2	15.3	7.1	10.0
Same, n.c.	19.6	39.7	28.7	30.6
Support ratio	.83	.65	.79	.75
Mean support ratios for the public ownership category	.76	.48	.70	.66

* n.c.=no code.

V. O. Key, among others, has observed that the Republican party is especially responsive to the "financial and manufacturing community,"[15] reflecting the view that government should intervene as little as possible to burden or restrain prevailing business interests. The validity of this observation is evident throughout all our data, and is most clearly seen in the responses to the issues listed under Government Regulation of the Economy, Equalitarianism and Human Welfare, Tax Policy. Democratic leaders are far more eager than Republican leaders to strengthen enforcement of anti-monopoly laws and to increase regulation of public utilities and business. Indeed, the solidarity of Republican opposition to the regulation of business is rather overwhelming: 84 per cent want to decrease such regulation and fewer than .01 per cent say they want to increase it. Although the Democrats, on balance, also feel that government controls on business should not be expanded further, the differences between the two samples on this issue are nevertheless substantial.

The two sets of leaders are also far apart on the farm issue, the Democrats preferring slightly to increase farm supports, the Republicans wanting strongly to reduce them. The Republican ratio score of .20 on this issue is among the lowest in the entire set of scores. The magnitude of these scores somewhat surprised us, for while opposition to agricultural subsidies is consistent with Republican dislike for state intervention, we had expected the leaders to conform more closely to the familiar image of the Republican as the more "rural" of the two parties.[16] It appears, however, that the party's connection with business is far more compelling than its association with agriculture. The Republican desire to reduce government expenditures and to promote independence from "government hand-

Table 2B
Comparison of Party Leaders and Followers on "Government Regulation of the Economy" Issues, by Percentages and Ratios of Support

	Leaders		*Followers*	
	Dem. *N=1,788*	*Repub.* *N=1,232*	*Dem.* *N=821*	*Repub.* *N=623*
Issues	*(%s down)*			
Level of farm price supports				
% favoring: Increase	43.4	6.7	39.0	23.0
Decrease	28.1	67.4	27.6	40.3
Same, n.c.	28.5	25.8	33.4	36.7
Support ratio	.58	.20	.56	.41
Government regulation of business				
% favoring: Increase	20.2	0.6	18.6	7.4
Decrease	38.5	84.1	33.4	46.2
Same, n.c.	41.3	15.3	48.0	46.4
Support ratio	.41	.08	.43	.31
Regulation of public utilities				
% favoring: Increase	59.0	17.9	39.3	26.0
Decrease	6.4	17.6	11.1	12.0
Same, n.c.	34.6	64.5	49.6	62.0
Support ratio	.76	.50	.64	.57
Enforcement of anti-monopoly laws				
% favoring: Increase	78.0	44.9	53.2	51.0
Decrease	2.9	9.0	7.9	6.6
Same, n.c.	19.1	46.1	38.9	42.4
Support ratio	.88	.68	.73	.72
Regulation of trade unions				
% favoring: Increase	59.3	86.4	46.6	57.8
Decrease	12.4	4.5	8.9	10.6
Same, n.c.	28.3	9.2	44.5	31.6
Support ratio	.73	.91	.69	.74
Level of tariffs				
% favoring: Increase	13.0	19.2	16.6	15.2
Decrease	43.0	26.3	25.3	21.3
Same, n.c.	43.9	54.5	58.1	63.4
Support ratio	.35	.46	.46	.47
Restrictions on credit				
% favoring: Increase	24.8	20.6	26.1	25.7
Decrease	39.3	20.6	22.2	23.8
Same, n.c.	35.9	58.8	51.8	50.5
Support ratio	.43	.50	.52	.51
Mean support ratios for "government regulation of the economy" category	.59	.48	.58	.53

outs" prevails on the farm question as it does on other issues, while the Democratic preference for a more regulated economy in which government intervenes to reduce economic risk and to stabilize prosperity is equally evident on the other side. Party attitudes on this issue appear to be determined as much by ideological tendencies as by deliberate calculation of the political advantages to be gained by favoring or opposing subsidies to farmers. Comparison of our findings with Turner's earlier data on farm votes in Congress[17] suggests, in addition, that the sharp party difference on the farm issue is neither a recent development nor a mere product of the personal philosophy of the present Secretary of Agriculture.

Having implied that agricultural policies partly result from principle, we must note that on three other issues in this category (trade unions, credit, and tariffs), principle seems to be overweighed by old-fashioned economic considerations. In spite of their distaste for government interference in economic affairs, the Republicans almost unanimously favor greater regulation of trade unions and they are more strongly disposed than the Democrats toward government intervention to restrict credit and to raise tariffs. Of course, party cleavages over the credit and tariff issues have a long history,[18] which may by now have endowed them with ideological force beyond immediate economic considerations.[19] The preponderant Democratic preference for greater regulation of trade unions is doubtless a response to recent "exposures" of corrupt labor practices, though it may also signify that the party's perspective toward the trade unions is shifted somewhat.

The closer Republican identification with business, free enterprise, and economic conservatism in general, and the friendlier Democratic attitude toward labor and toward government regulation of the economy, are easily observed in the data from other parts of our questionnaire. Republican leaders score very much higher than Democratic leaders on, for example, such scales as economic conservatism, independence of government, and business attitudes. On a question asking respondents to indicate the groups from which they would be most and least likely to take advice, 41 per cent of the Democratic leaders but only 3.8 per cent of the Republican leaders list trade unions as groups from which they would seek advice. Trade unions are scored in the "least likely" category by 25 per cent of the Democrats and 63 per cent of the Republicans. Similarly, more than 94 per cent of the Republican leaders, but 56 per cent of the Democratic leaders, name trade unions as groups that have "too much power." These differences, it should be noted, cannot be accounted for by reference to the greater number of trade union members among the Democratic party leadership, for in the 1956 conventions only 14 per cent of the Democrats belonged to trade unions, and while an even smaller percentage (4 per cent) of the Republicans were trade unionists, this disparity is hardly great enough to explain the large differences in outlook. The key to the explanation has to be sought in the symbolic and reference group identifications of the two parties, and in their underlying values.

Nowhere do we see this more clearly than in the responses to the Equalitarian and Human Welfare issues. The mean difference in the ratio scores for the category as a whole is .22, a very large difference and one that results from differences in the expected direction on all six issues that make up the category. On four of these issues—federal aid to education, slum clearance and public housing, social security, and minimum wages—the leaders of the two parties are widely separated, the differences in their ratio scores ranging from .36 to .21. The percentages showing the proportions who favor increased sup-

Table 2C
Comparison of Party Leaders and Followers on "Equalitarian and Human Welfare" Issues, by Percentages and Ratios of Support

	Leaders		*Followers*	
	Dem. *N=1,788*	*Repub.* *N=1,232*	*Dem.* *N=821*	*Repub.* *N=623*
Issues		*(%s down)*		
Federal aid to education				
% favoring: Increase	66.2	22.3	74.9	64.8
Decrease	13.4	43.2	5.6	8.3
Same, n.c.	20.4	34.5	19.5	26.8
Support ratio	.76	.40	.85	.78
Slum clearance and public housing				
% favoring: Increase	78.4	40.1	79.5	72.5
Decrease	5.6	21.6	5.8	7.9
Same, n.c.	16.0	38.3	14.6	19.6
Support ratio	.86	.59	.87	.82
Social security benefits				
% favoring: Increase	60.0	22.5	69.4	57.0
Decrease	3.9	13.1	3.0	3.8
Same, n.c.	36.1	64.4	27.5	39.2
Support ratio	.78	.55	.83	.77
Minimum wages				
% favoring: Increase	50.0	15.5	59.0	43.5
Decrease	4.7	12.5	2.9	5.0
Same, n.c.	45.2	72.0	38.1	51.5
Support ratio	.73	.52	.78	.69
Enforcement of integration				
% favoring: Increase	43.8	25.5	41.9	40.8
Decrease	26.6	31.7	27.4	23.6
Same, n.c.	29.5	42.8	30.7	35.6
Support ratio	.59	.47	.57	.59
Immigration into United States				
% favoring: Increase	36.1	18.4	10.4	8.0
Decrease	27.0	29.9	52.0	44.6
Same, n.c.	36.9	51.7	37.6	47.4
Support ratio	.54	.44	.29	.32
Mean support ratios for "equalitarian and human welfare" category	.71	.50	.70	.66

port for these issues are even more striking. In every instance the Democratic percentages are considerably higher: 66 *vs.* 22 per cent (education); 78 *vs.* 40 per cent (slum clearance and housing); 60 *vs.* 23 per cent (social security); and 50 *vs.* 16 per cent (minimum wages). The Democratic leaders also are better disposed than the Republican leaders toward immigration: twice as many of them (36 per cent *vs.* 18 per cent) favor a change in policy to permit more immigrants to enter. The overall inclination of both party elites, however, is to accept the present levels of immigration, the Democratic ratio score falling slightly above, and the Republican slightly below, the midpoint.

More surprising are the differences

on the segregation issue, for, despite strong southern influence, the Democratic leaders express significantly more support for enforcing integration than the Republicans do. Moreover, the difference between the two parties rises from .12 for the national samples as a whole to a difference of .18 when the southern leaders are excluded. In his study of Congress, Turner found that the Republicans gave more support to Negro rights than the Democrats did.[20] The reversal of this finding in our data does not necessarily mean that a change has occurred since Turner made his study, but only that the votes of the congressional parties do not always reflect the private feelings of the national party leadership. Then, too, southern influence is disproportionately stronger in the Democratic congressional party than in the national Democratic organization as a whole, and disproportionately weaker in the Republican congressional party than in the Republican organization as a whole.

Examination of the actual magnitude of the ratio scores in this category reveals that the Republicans want not so much to abrogate existing social welfare or equalitarian measures as to keep them from being broadened. The Democrats, by comparison, are shown to be the party of social equality and reform, more willing than their opponents to employ legislation for the benefit of the underprivileged. Support for these inferences and for the greater liberalism of the Democrats can be found elsewhere in our data as well....

The self-images and reference group identifications of the two parties... should be noted in this connection. For example, many more Democratic than Republican leaders call themselves liberal and state that they would be most likely to take advice from liberal reform organizations, the Farmers' Union, and (as we have seen) from the trade unions; only a small number consider themselves conservative or would seek advice from conservative reform organizations, the National Association of Manufacturers, or the Farm Bureau Federation. The Republicans have in almost all instances the reverse identifications: only a handful regard themselves as liberal or would seek counsel from liberal organizations, while more than 42 per cent call themselves conservative and would look to the NAM or to conservative reform organizations for advice. Almost two-thirds of the Republicans (compared with 29 per cent of the Democrats) regard the Chamber of Commerce as an important source of advice. Businessmen are listed as having "too much power" by 42 per cent of the Democrats but by only 9 per cent of the Republicans. The Democrats are also significantly more inclined than the Republicans to consider Catholics, Jews, and the foreign born as having "too little power." While self-descriptions and reference group identifications often correspond poorly with actual beliefs—among the general population they scarcely correspond at all, in fact—we are dealing, in the case of the leaders, with a politically informed and highly articulate set of people who have little difficulty connecting the beliefs they hold and the groups that promote or obstruct those beliefs.

Our fourth category, Tax Policy, divides the parties almost as severely as do the other categories. The mean difference for the category as a whole is .20, and it would doubtless have been larger but for the universal unpopularity of proposals to increase taxes on small and middle income groups.

Table 2D
Comparison of Party Leaders and Followers on "Tax Policy" Issues, by Percentages and Ratios of Support

	Leaders		*Followers*	
Issues	*Dem.* *N=1,788*	*Repub.* *N=1,232*	*Dem.* *N=821* (*%s down*)	*Repub.* *N=623*
Corporate income tax				
% favoring: Increase	32.3	4.0	32.0	23.3
Decrease	23.3	61.5	20.5	25.7
Same, n.c.	44.4	34.5	47.5	51.0
Support ratio	.54	.21	.56	.49
Tax on large incomes				
% favoring: Increase	27.0	5.4	46.6	34.7
Decrease	23.1	56.9	13.8	21.7
Same, n.c.	49.9	37.7	39.6	43.6
Support ratio	.52	.24	.66	.56
Tax on business				
% favoring: Increase	12.6	1.0	24.6	15.9
Decrease	38.3	71.1	24.1	32.6
Same, n.c.	49.1	27.8	51.3	51.5
Support ratio	.37	.15	.50	.42
Tax on middle incomes				
% favoring: Increase	2.7	0.8	4.5	3.0
Decrease	50.2	63.9	49.3	44.3
Same, n.c.	47.1	35.3	46.2	52.6
Support ratio	.26	.18	.28	.29
Tax on small incomes				
% favoring: Increase	1.4	2.9	1.6	2.1
Decrease	79.2	65.0	77.5	69.6
Same, n.c.	19.4	32.1	20.9	28.3
Support ratios	.11	.19	.12	.16
Mean support ratios for "tax policy" category	.36	.19	.42	.38

Table 2D shows that the differences between the parties on the tax issues follow the patterns previously observed and that tax policy is for the Democrats a device for redistributing income and promoting social equality. Neither party, however, is keen about raising taxes for *any* group: even the Democrats have little enthusiasm for new taxes on upper income groups or on business and corporate enterprises. The Republican leaders are overwhelmingly opposed to increased taxes for *any* group, rich *or* poor. This can be seen in their low ratio scores on the tax issues, which range from only .15 to .24. But while they are far more eager than the Democratic leaders to cut taxes on corporate and private wealth, they are less willing to reduce taxes on the lower income groups. These differences, it should be remarked, are not primarily a function of differences in the income of the two samples. Although there are more people with high incomes among the Republican leaders, the disproportion between the two samples is not nearly

Table 2E
Comparison of Party Leaders and Followers on "Foreign Policy" Issues, by Percentages and Ratios of Support

Issues	Leaders Dem. N=1,788	Leaders Repub. N=1,232	Followers Dem. N=821	Followers Repub. N=623
	(%s down)			
Reliance on the United Nations				
% favoring: Increase	48.9	24.4	34.7	33.4
Decrease	17.6	34.8	17.3	19.3
Same, n.c.	33.5	40.7	48.0	47.3
Support ratio	.66	.45	.59	.57
American participation in military alliances				
% favoring: Increase	41.5	22.7	39.1	32.3
Decrease	17.6	25.7	14.0	15.4
Same, n.c.	40.9	51.6	46.9	52.3
Support ratio	.62	.48	.62	.58
Foreign aid				
% favoring: Increase	17.8	7.6	10.1	10.1
Decrease	51.0	61.7	58.6	57.3
Same, n.c.	31.1	30.7	31.3	32.6
Support ratio	.33	.23	.26	.26
Defense spending*				
% favoring: Increase	20.7	13.6	50.5	45.7
Decrease	34.4	33.6	16.4	15.4
Same, n.c.	44.8	52.8	33.0	38.8
Support ratio	.43	.40	.67	.65
Mean support ratios for "foreign policy" category (excl. defense spending)	.54	.39	.49	.47

* See footnote 22.

great enough to account for the dissimilarities in their tax views.

Of the five categories considered, Foreign Policy shows the smallest average difference, but even on these issues the divergence between Democratic and Republican leader attitudes is significant. Except for defense spending the Democrats turn out to be more internationalist than the Republicans, as evidenced in their greater commitment to the United Nations and to American participation in international military alliances like NATO. Twice as many Democrats as Republicans want the United States to rely more heavily upon such organizations, while many more Republicans want to reduce our international involvements. Both parties are predominantly in favor of cutting back foreign aid—a somewhat surprising finding in light of Democratic public pronouncements on this subject—but more Republicans feel strongly on the subject. Our data thus furnish little support for the claim that the parties hold the same views on foreign policy or that their seeming differences are merely a response to the demands of political competition.[21]

Nevertheless, it would be incorrect to conclude that one party believes in internationalism and the other in isolationism. The differences are far too small to warrant any such inference.

Traces of isolationism, to be sure, remain stronger in the Republican party than in the Democratic party.... The pattern of Republican responses . . . signifies, however, that the leaders of that party generally accept the degree of "internationalism" now in effect, but shrink from extending it further. Consider too, the similarities in the leaders' scores on defense spending, for despite their greater leaning toward isolationism, the Republicans are no more inclined than the Democrats to leave the country defenseless.[22]

In treating issues in the Elmira election study of 1948, Berelson, Lazarsfeld, and McPhee[23] found it helpful to distinguish between "style" and "position" issues. "Style" issues principally yield symbolic, psychological, or subjective gratifications, and have relatively intangible consequences; "position" issues reflect direct, personal and material interests, and have more objective consequences. According to the Elmira report, "position" issues (or what politicians might call "bread and butter" issues) divide voters more sharply than style issues. Most of the issues tested in the present study would have to be classified as "position" issues, but five of them—United Nations, international alliances, foreign aid, immigration, and segregation—could be classified as style issues. Four others—natural resources, atomic energy, education, and slum clearance—contain both symbolic and material elements and can best be described as "mixed."

Although the classification is crude, the findings it yields are generally consistent with the claims of the Elmira study. On the fourteen position issues—taxes, trade unions, tariffs, minimum wages, farm prices, social security, credit restrictions, and the regulation of business, public utilities and monopolies—Democratic and Republican leaders show an average ratio score difference of .21. On the style issues the two parties differ by .13—a significantly smaller difference. Largest of all, however, are the differences for the "mixed" issues, which average more than .30. This result should occasion little surprise, for when ideology and interest are *both* at work, partisanship is likely to be intensified. Several considerations could account for the superiority of position over style issues as causes of political cleavage: they are "bread and butter" issues, and are thus more often subject to pressure by organized interest groups; they have immediate and tangible consequences, which may lead politicians to pay greater attention to them than they do to issues whose payoff is more uncertain; and, finally, they are not so likely to be part of the common core of values upon which the community structure rests.

Comparison of the magnitude of the differences between groups can be seen in Table 3, where we have ranked the issues, high to low, according to the size of the difference between the groups being compared. By presenting a rank-order of differences for the two leader groups, for the two follower groups, and for the leaders and followers of each party, this table makes it possible to observe not only which issues most and least divide the several party groups, but whether they divide the leaders and followers in the same way.

Notice that the issues commonly thought to be most divisive do not always evoke the greatest cleavage between the parties. Immigration, tariffs, civil rights, monopoly control, and credit regulation fall toward the lower end of the rank order, while farm supports, federal aid to education, slum clearance, social security,

Table 3
Rank Order of Differences in the Support-Ratio Scores of Party Leaders and Followers*

Democratic vs. Republican Leaders — Issues	Diff. between ratio scores†	Democratic vs. Republican Followers — Issues	Diff. between ratio scores	Democratic Leaders vs. Followers — Issues	Diff. between ratio scores	Republican Leaders vs. Followers — Issues	Diff. between ratio scores
1. Natural resources	+.39	Farm supports	+.14	Immigration	+.25	Fed. aid to edu.	−.39
2. Farm supports	+.38	Gov't. reg. of business	+.12	Anti-monopoly	+.15	Taxes—large income	−.32
3. Fed. aid to edu.	+.37	Taxes—large income	+.10	Taxes—large income	−.15	Taxes—corp.	−.28
4. Taxes—corp.	+.33	Minimum wages	+.09	Taxes—business	−.13	Taxes—business	−.27
5. Reg.—business	+.33	Taxes—business	+.09	Reg. pub. util.	+.12	Natural resources	−.23
6. Taxes—large inc.	+.28	Reg. pub. util.	+.07	Tariffs	−.11	Pub. housing	−.23
7. Pub. housing	+.27	Taxes—corp.	+.07	Restrict. credit	−.09	Reg. business	−.22
8. Reg. pub. util.	+.26	Social security	+.07	Natural resources	+.09	Social security	−.22
9. Social security	+.23	Fed. aid to edu.	+.06	Fed. aid to edu.	−.08	Farm supports	−.22
10. Taxes—business	+.22	Reg. trade unions	−.05	Foreign aid	+.08	Minimum wages	−.18
11. Minimum wages	+.21	Natural resources	+.05	Reliance on U.N.	+.07	Reg. trade unions	+.17
12. Reliance on U.N.	+.21	Public housing	+.05	Minimum wages	−.05	Immigration	+.13
13. Anti-monopoly	+.20	Taxes—small income	−.04	Social security	−.05	Reliance on U.N.	−.12
14. Atomic energy control	+.18	American participation, NATO	+.04	Reg. trade unions	+.05	Enforce integration	−.12
15. Reg. trade unions	−.18	Atomic energy control	+.04	Atomic energy control	+.04	Taxes—middle income	−.11
16. American participation, NATO	+.13	Immigration	−.03	Farm supports	+.02	Atomic energy control	−.10
17. Enforce integration	+.12	Defense spending	+.02	Reg. business	−.02	American participation, NATO	−.10
18. Tariffs	−.11	Taxes—middle income	−.02	Enforce integration	+.01	Reg. public utilities	−.07
19. Foreign aid	+.10	Reliance on U.N.	+.02	Taxes—middle income	−.01	Anti-monopoly	−.04
20. Increase immigration	+.10	Tariffs	−.01	Taxes—corporation	−.01	Foreign aid	−.03
21. Taxes—small income	−.08	Enforce integration	−.01	Taxes—small income	−.01	Taxes—small income	+.03
22. Taxes—middle income	+.08	Restriction credit	+.01	American participation, NATO	−.01	Restriction credit	−.01
23. Restriction credit	−.07	Foreign aid	−.01	Public housing	.00	Tariffs	−.01
24. Defense spending	+.03	Anti-monopoly	.00	Defense spending	‡	Defense spending	‡

N's. Democratic Leaders: 1,788; Republican Leaders: 1,232; Democratic Followers: 821; Republican Followers: 623.

* The plus sign means that the first group listed in the heading is more favorable to the issue named than the second group; the minus sign means that the second group is the more favorable.

† Leaders and Followers cannot be compared on defense spending, for reasons given in footnote to Table 2E.

‡ Size of difference required for differences to be significant at .01 level: Democratic Leaders *vs.* Republican—.048; Democratic Followers *vs.* Republican Followers—.068; Democratic Leaders *vs.* Democratic Followers—.054; Republican Leaders *vs.* Republican Followers—.063.

minimum wages, public housing, and issues dealing with the regulation and taxation of business fall toward the upper end. Though by no means uniformly, the older, more traditional issues appear to have been superseded as sources of controversy by issues that have come into prominence chiefly during the New Deal and Fair Deal.

IV. Comparisons Between Followers

So far we have addressed ourselves to the differences between Democratic and Republican *leaders.* In each of the tables presented, however, data are included from which the two sets of party *followers* may also be compared.

The observation most clearly warranted from these data is that the rank-and-file members of the two parties are far less divided than their leaders. Not only do they diverge significantly on fewer issues—seven as compared with 23 for the leader samples—but the magnitudes of the differences in their ratio scores are substantially smaller for every one of the 24 issues. No difference is larger than .14, and on the majority of the issues the disparity is smaller than .05. Insofar as they differ at all, however, the followers tend to divide in a pattern similar to that shown by the leaders, the correlation between their rank orders being .72. All the issues on which the followers significantly disagree are of the "bread and butter" variety, the more symbolic issues being so remotely experienced and so vaguely grasped that rank-and-file voters are often unable to identify them with either party. Policies affecting farm prices, business regulation, taxes, or minimum wages, by contrast, are quickly felt by the groups to whom they are addressed and are therefore more capable of arousing partisan identifications. It should also be noted that while the average differences are small for all five categories, they are smallest of all for foreign policy—the most removed and least well understood group of issues in the entire array.[24]

Democratic and Republican followers were also compared on a number of scales and reference group questions. The results, while generally consistent with the differences between the leaders, show the followers to be far more united than their leaders on these measures as well. Even on business attitudes, independence of government, and economic conservatism, the differences are small and barely significant.... The average Democrat is slightly more willing than the average Republican to label himself a liberal or to seek advice from liberal organizations; the contrary is true when it comes to adopting conservative identifications. Only in the differential trust they express toward business and labor are the two sets of followers widely separated.

These findings give little support to the claim that the "natural divisions" of the electorate are being smothered by party leaders.[25] Not only do the leaders disagree more sharply than their respective followers, but the level of consensus among the electorate (with or without regard to party) is fairly high. Inspection of the "increase" and "decrease" percentage scores (Tables 2A–2E) shows that substantial differences of opinion exist among the electorate on only five of the 24 issues (credit restrictions, farm supports, segregation, and corporate and business taxes). Of course, voters may divide more sharply on issues at election time, since campaigns intensify party feeling and may also intensify opinions on issues. Available data from election studies allow no unequivocal conclusion on this point,[26] but even the party-linked differences found among voters during elections may largely be echoes of the opinions announced by the candidates—transient sentiments developed for the occasion and quickly forgotten.

V. Leader Conflict and Follower Consensus: Explanations

Considering the nature of the differences between the leader and follower samples, the interesting question is not why the parties fail to represent the "natural division" in the electorate (for that question rests on an unwarranted assumption) but why the party elites disagree at all, and why they divide so much more sharply than their followers.

Despite the great pressures toward uniformity we have noted in American society, many forces also divide the population culturally, economically, and politically. The United States is, after all, a miscellany of ethnic and religious strains set down in a geographically large and diverse country. Many of these groups brought old conflicts and ideologies with them, and some have tried to act out in the new world the hopes and frustrations nurtured in the old. Then, too, despite rapid social mobility, social classes have by no means been eliminated. No special political insight is needed to perceive that the two parties characteristically draw from different strata of the society, the Republicans from the managerial, proprietary, and to some extent professional classes, the Democrats from labor, minorities, low income groups, and a large proportion of the intellectuals.[27] Partly because the leaders of the two parties tend to overrespond to the modal values of the groups with which they are principally identified, they gradually grow further apart on the key questions which separate their respective supporters.[28] The Republican emphasis on business ideology is both a cause and a consequence of its managerial and proprietary support; the greater Democratic emphasis on social justice, and on economic and social levelling, is both the occasion and the product of the support the party enjoys among intellectuals and the lower strata. These interrelationships are strengthened, moreover, by the tendency for a party's dominant supporters to gain a disproportionate number of positions in its leadership ranks.[29]

The differences which typically separate Democratic from Republican leaders seem also to reflect a deep-seated ideological cleavage often found among Western parties. One side of this cleavage is marked by a strong belief in the power of collective action to promote social justice, equality, humanitarianism, and economic planning, while preserving freedom; the other is distinguished by faith in the wisdom of the natural competitive process and in the supreme virtue of individualism, "character," self-reliance, frugality, and independence from government. To this cleavage is added another frequent source of political division, namely, a difference in attitude toward change between "radicals" and "moderates," between those who prefer to move quickly or slowly, to reform or to conserve. These differences in social philosophy and posture do not always coincide with the divisions in the social structure, and their elements do not, in all contexts, combine in the same way. But, however crudely, the American parties do tend to embody these competing points of view and to serve as reference groups for those who hold them.

Party cleavage in America was no doubt intensified by the advent of the New Deal, and by its immense electoral and intellectual success. Not only did it weld into a firm alliance the diverse forces that were to be crucial to all subsequent Democratic majorities, but it also made explicit the doctrines of the "welfare state" with which the party was henceforth to be inseparably identified. Because of the novelty of its program and its apparently radical threat to the familiar patterns of American political and economic life, it probably deepened the fervor of its Republican adversaries and drove into the opposition the staunchest defenders of business ideology. The conflict was further sharpened by the decline of left-wing politics after the war, and by the transfer of loyalties of former and potential radicals to the Democratic party. Once launched, the cleavage has been sustained by the tendency for each party to attract into its active ranks a disproportionate number of voters who recognize and share its point of view.

Why, however, are the leaders so much more sharply divided than their followers? The reasons are not hard to understand and are consistent with several of the hypotheses that underlay the present study.

(1) Consider, to begin with, that the leaders come from the more articulate segments of society and, on the average, are politically more aware than their followers and far better informed about issues.[30] For them, political issues and opinions are the everyday currency of party competition, not esoteric matters that surpass understanding. With their greater awareness and responsibility, and their greater need to defend their party's stands, they have more interest in developing a consistent set of attitudes—perhaps even an ideology. The followers of each party, often ignorant of the issues and their consequences, find it difficult to distinguish their beliefs from those of the opposition and have little reason to be concerned with the consistency of their attitudes. Furthermore, the American parties make only a feeble effort to educate the rank-and-file politically, and since no central source exists for the authoritative pronouncement of party policy,[31] the followers often do not know what their leaders believe or on what issues the parties chiefly divide. In short, if we mean by ideology a coherent body of informed social doctrine, it is possessed mainly by the articulate leadership, rarely by the masses.

(2) Differences in the degree of partisan involvement parallel the differences in knowledge and have similar consequences. The leaders, of course, have more party spirit than the followers, and, as the election studies make plain, the stronger the partisanship, the larger the differences on issues. The leaders are more highly motivated not only to belong to a party appropriate to their beliefs, but to accept its doctrines and to learn how it differs from the opposition party. Since politics is more salient for leaders than for followers, they develop a greater stake in the outcome of the political contest and are more eager to discover the intellectual grounds by which they hope to make victory possible. Through a process of circular reinforcement, those for whom politics is most important are likely to become the most zealous participants, succeeding to the posts that deal in the formation of opinion. Ideology serves the instrumental purpose, in addition, of justifying the

heavy investment that party leaders make in political activity. While politics offers many rewards, it also makes great demands on the time, money, and energies of its practitioners—sacrifices which they can more easily justify if they believe they are serving worthwhile social goals. The followers, in contrast, are intellectually far less involved, have less personal stake in the outcome of the competition, have little need to be concerned with the "correctness" of their views on public questions, and have even less reason to learn in precisely what ways their opinions differ from their opponents'. Hence, the party elites recruit members from a population stratified in some measure by ideology, while the rank-and-file renews itself by more random recruitment and is thus more likely to mirror the opinions of a cross section of the population.

(3) Part of the explanation for the greater consensus among followers than leaders resides in the nature and size of the two types of groups. Whereas the leader groups are comparatively small and selective, each of the follower groups number in the millions and, by their very size and unwieldiness, are predisposed to duplicate the characteristics of the population as a whole. Even if the Republicans draw disproportionately from the business-managerial classes and the Democrats from the trade union movement, neither interest group has enough influence to shape distinctively the aggregate opinions of so large a mass of supporters. Size also affects the nature and frequency of interaction within the two types of groups. Because they comprise a smaller, more selectively chosen, organized, and articulate elite, the leaders are apt to associate with people of their own political persuasion more frequently and consistently than the followers do. They are not only less cross-pressured than the rank-and-file but they are also subjected to strong party group efforts to induce them to conform. Because their political values are continually renewed through frequent communication with people of like opinions, and because they acquire intense reference group identifications, they develop an extraordinary ability to resist the force of the opposition's arguments. While the followers, too, are thrown together and shielded to some extent, they are likely to mingle more freely with people of hostile political persuasions, to receive fewer partisan communications, and to hold views that are only intermittently and inconsistently reinforced. Since, by comparison with the leaders, they possess little interest in or information about politics, they can more easily embrace "deviant" attitudes without discomfort and without challenge from their associates. Nor are they likely to be strongly rewarded for troubling to have "correct" opinions. The followers, in short, are less often and less effectively indoctrinated than their leaders. The group processes described here would function even more powerfully in small, sectarian, tightly organized parties of the European type, but they are also present in the American party system, where they yield similar though less potent consequences.

(4) Political competition itself operates to divide the leaders more than the followers. If the parties are impelled to present a common face to the electorate, they are also strongly influenced to distinguish themselves from each other.[32] For one thing, they have a more heightened sense of the "national interest" than the followers do, even if they do not all conceive it in the same way. For

another, they hope to improve their chances at the polls by offering the electorate a recognizable and attractive commodity. In addition, they seek emotional gratification in the heightened sense of brotherhood brought on by the struggle against an "outgroup" whose claim to office seems always, somehow, to border upon usurpation. As with many ingroup-outgroup distinctions, the participants search for moral grounds to justify their antagonisms toward each other, and ideologies help to furnish such grounds. Among the followers, on the other hand, these needs exist, if at all, in much weaker form.

VI. Leaders Versus Followers

In comparing each party elite with its own followers we were mainly interested in seeing how closely each body of supporters shared the point of view of its leaders, in order to test the hypothesis that party affiliation, even for the rank-and-file, is a function of ideological agreement. In predicting that the parties would tend to attract supporters who share their beliefs, we expected, of course, to find exceptions. We knew that many voters pay little attention to the ideological aspects of politics and that, in Gabriel Almond's phrase, a party's more "esoteric doctrines" are not always known to its followers.[33] Nevertheless we were not prepared for the findings turned up by this phase of the inquiry, for the differences between leaders and followers—among the Republicans at least—are beyond anything we had expected. Indeed, the conclusion is inescapable that the views of the Republican rank-and-file are, on the whole, much closer to those of the Democratic leaders than to those of the Republican leaders. Although conflicts in outlook also exist between Democratic leaders and followers, they are less frequent or severe.

If we turn once again to the table of rank-order differences, we see that the Democratic followers differ significantly from their leaders on twelve of the 23 issues, and that the average difference in the ratio scores of the two samples is .07. Democratic leaders and Republican followers differ significantly on only eleven of the 23 issues, with an average difference between them of only .08. Notice, by contrast, that Republican leaders and followers diverge significantly on 18 of the 23 issues, and show an average difference of .16. To complete the comparison, the Republican leaders and Democratic followers were in disagreement on 19 of the 23 issues, their average difference being .20. As these comparisons make plain, there is substantial consensus on national issues between Democratic leaders and Democratic and Republican followers, while the Republican leaders are separated not only from the Democrats but from their own rank-and-file members as well.

Examination of the Democratic scores shows the leaders to be slightly more "progressive" than their followers on most of the issues on which differences appear. The leaders are, for example, more favorable to public ownership of natural resources, to regulation of monopolies and public utilities, to a reduction of tariffs, and to a liberalized credit policy. They are more internationalist on the foreign aid and United Nations issues and substantially more sympathetic to the maintenance and expansion of immigration. The results showing the relative radicalism of the two samples are not unequivocal, however, for on several issues—federal aid to education, minimum wages, and taxes on business enterprise and large incomes—the followers take the more radical view. Nor are the differences significant on such issues as atomic energy, slum clearance, segregation, farm price supports, government control of business and trade unions, and taxes on middle and small income groups. In general, the followers turn out more radical chiefly on a few of the "bread and butter issues"—a reflection, no doubt, of their lower socioeconomic status. When we control for occupation, the differences between Democratic leaders and followers on these issues largely disappear.

Consideration of the scores of Republican leaders and followers shows not only that they are widely separated in their outlooks but also that the leaders are uniformly more conservative than their followers. Only on the immigration issue is this trend reversed. The followers hold the more "radical" ideas on the two public ownership issues, on five of the six equalitarian and human welfare issues, on four of the seven regulation-of-the-economy issues, and on four of the five tax policy issues. They are also more willing to place greater reliance upon the U.N. and upon international military alliances. Observe that the largest differences occur on those issues which have most sharply separated New Deal–Fair Deal spokesmen from the hard core of the Republican opposition—federal aid to education, redistribution of wealth through taxes on business, corporations and the wealthy, public ownership of natural resources, public housing, regulation of business, social security, farm price supports, minimum wages, and trade union regulations.

In short, whereas Republican leaders hold to the tenets of business ideology and remain faithful to the spirit and intellectual mood of leaders like Robert A. Taft, the rank-and-file Republican supporters have embraced, along with their Democratic brethren, the regulatory and social reform measures of the Roosevelt and Truman administrations. This inference receives further support from the scores on our Party Ideology scale where, on a variety of attitudes and values which characteristically distinguish the leaders of the two parties, the Republican followers fall closer to the Democratic than to the Republican side of the continuum. Thus, in addition to being the preferred party of the more numerous classes, the Democrats also enjoy the advantages over their opponents of holding views that are more widely shared throughout the country.

Assuming the findings are valid, we were obviously wrong to expect that party differentiation among followers would depend heavily upon ideological considerations.[34] Evidently, party attachment is so much a function of other factors (*e.g.* class and primary group memberships, religious affiliation, place of residence, mass media, etc.) that many voters can maintain their party loyalties comfortably even while holding views that contradict the beliefs of their own leaders.

Still, we are not entitled to conclude that issue outlook has no effect on the party affiliation of ordinary members. It is conceivable, for example, that the Republican party has come to be the minority party partly because the opinions of its spokesmen are uncongenial to a majority of the voters. We have no way of knowing from our data—collected at only a single point in time—how many "normally" Republican voters, if any, have defected to the Democrats or fled into independency because they disapprove of

Republican beliefs. At the present stage of the analysis, we have no grounds for going beyond the proposition that political affiliation without conformity on issues is possible on a wide scale. In future analyses we shall attempt to learn more about the nature of the relationship between belief and party affiliation by stratifying voters according to the frequency with which they conform to the beliefs of their party leaders. We hope, in this way, to discover whether those who conform least are also less firm in their party loyalties.

VII. The Homogeneity of Support for Leaders and Followers

So far we have only considered conflict and agreement *between* groups. We should now turn to the question of consensus *within* groups. To what extent is each of our samples united on fundamental issues?

In order to assess homogeneity of opinion within party groups, standard deviation scores were computed on each issue for each of the four samples. The higher the standard deviation, of course, the greater the disagreement. The range of possible sigma scores is from 0 (signifying that every member of the sample has selected the same response) to .500 (signifying that all responses are equally divided between the "increase" and "decrease" alternatives). If we assume that the three alternative responses had been randomly (and therefore equally) selected, the standard deviations for the four samples would fall by chance alone around .410. Scores at or above this level may be taken to denote extreme dispersion among the members of a sample while scores in the neighborhood of .300 or below suggest that unanimity within the sample is fairly high. By these somewhat arbitrary criteria we can observe immediately (Table 4) that consensus within groups is greater on most issues than we would expect by chance alone, but that it is extremely high in only a few instances. Although the Republican leaders appear on the average to be the most united and the Democratic leaders the least united of the four groups, the difference between their homogeneity scores (.340 vs. .310) is too small to be taken as conclusive. The grounds are somewhat better for rejecting the belief that leaders are more homogeneous in their outlooks than their followers, since the hypothesis holds only for one party and not for the other.

While generalizations about the relative unity of the four samples seem risky, we can speak more confidently about the rank order of agreement *within* samples. In Table 4 we have ranked the issues according to the degree of consensus exhibited toward them by the members of each of the four party groups. There we see that the leaders of the Republican party are most united on the issues that stem from its connections with business—government regulation of business, taxes (especially on business), regulation of trade unions, and minimum wages. The Democratic leaders are most united on those issues which bear upon the support the party receives from the lower and middle income groups—taxes on small and middle incomes, anti-monopoly, slum clearance, social security, and minimum wages. The Republican leaders divide most severely on federal aid to education, slum clearance, U.N. support, segregation, and public control of atomic energy and natural resources; the Democratic leaders are most divided on farm prices, segregation, credit restrictions, immigration,

Table 4
Consensus Within Party Groups: Rank Order of Homogeneity of Support on Twenty-Four Issues

		Democratic Leaders		*Republican Leaders*		*Democratic Followers*		*Republican Followers*	
*Average Rank Order**	*Issue*	*Rank Order*	*Sigma*	*Rank Order*	*Sigma*	*Rank Order*	*Sigma*	*Rank Order*	*Sigma*
1	Tax on small incomes	1	.220	6	.270	1	.224	1	.250
2	Tax on middle incomes	3	.276	4	.248	6	.292	2	.278
3	Social security benefits	5	.282	8	.296	2	.266	3	.286
4	Minimum wages	6	.292	5	.268	4	.276	4	.294
5	Enforcement of anti-monopoly	2	.246	13	.321	8	.324	7	.314
6	Regulation of public utilities	8	.307	10	.300	10	.336	5.5	.310
7	Slum clearance	4	.276	23	.386	3	.274	5.5	.310
8	Regulation of trade unions	12	.356	3	.240	9	.331	15	.345
9	Government regulation of business	17	.376	1	.192	20	.363	8	.315
10	Tax on business	9	.338	2	.236	19	.362	16	.348
11	Level of tariffs	10	.350	16	.344	11	.338	9	.316
12	Public control of atomic energy	7	.302	20	.362	7	.312	13	.340
13	Federal aid to education	13	.360	24	.394	5	.283	11	.322
14	Foreign aid	19	.383	12	.317	12.5	.340	12	.340
15	Tax on large incomes	11	.356	9	.298	17	.358	22	.379
16	American participation in military alliances, NATO	14	.370	18	.351	14	.350	14	.344
17	Immigration into U.S.	21	.399	17	.345	12.5	.340	10	.318
18	Corporate income tax	16	.375	7	.284	21	.371	17	.361
19	Restrictions on credit	22	.400	14	.324	16	.358	18	.362
20	Defense spending	15	.371	15	.334	22	.380	21	.366
21	Public ownership of natural resources	20	.393	19	.354	15	.352	19	.362
22	Reliance on U.N.	18	.380	22	.384	18	.359	20	.365
23	Level of farm supports	24	.421	11	.306	23	.414	23	.397
24	Enforce integration	23	.416	21	.382	24	.418	24	.399

* The range of sigma scores is from .192 to .421, out of a possible range of .000 (most united) to .500 (least united). Hence, the lower the rank order the greater the unity on the issue named.

and the natural resources issue. Among the followers the patterns of unity and division are very similar, as attested by the high correlation of .83 between the rank orders of their homogeneity scores. Both Republican and Democratic followers exhibit great cohesion, for example, on taxes on small and middle incomes, social security, slum clearance, and minimum wages. Both divide rather sharply on segregation, farm price support, defense spending, U.N. support, and taxes on large incomes. The two sets of followers, in short, are alike not only in their opinions on issues but in the degree of unanimity they exhibit toward them.

* * *

In computing scores for homogeneity we were in part concerned to test the belief that political parties develop greatest internal solidarity on those questions which most separate them from their opponents. According to this hypothesis, external controversy has the effect of uniting the members further by confronting them with a common danger. Whether or not this hypothesis would be borne out in a study of small, sectarian parties we cannot say, but it receives no support from the present study of the American mass parties. Comparisons of the rank-order data in Tables 3 and 4 show that there is no consistent connection between interparty conflict and intraparty cohesion. The correlations between the rank orders of difference and the rank orders of homogeneity are in every case insignificant.[35]

Summary and Conclusions

. . . From the data yielded by this inquiry, the following inferences seem warranted.

1. Although it has received wide currency, especially among Europeans, the belief that the two American parties are identical in principle and doctrine has little foundation in fact. Examination of the opinions of Democratic and Republican leaders shows them to be distinct communities of co-believers who diverge sharply on many important issues. Their disagreements, furthermore, conform to an image familiar to many observers and are generally consistent with differences turned up by studies of Congressional roll calls. The unpopularity of many of the positions held by Republican leaders suggests also that the parties submit to the demands of their constituents less slavishly than is commonly supposed.

2. Republican and Democratic leaders stand furthest apart on the issues that grow out of their group identification and support—out of the managerial, proprietary, and high-status connections of the one, and the labor, minority, low-status, and intellectual connections of the other. The opinions of each party elite are linked less by chance than by membership in a common ideological domain. Democratic leaders typically display the stronger urge to elevate the lowborn, the uneducated, the deprived minorities, and the poor in general; they are also more disposed to employ the nation's collective power to advance humanitarian and social welfare goals (*e.g.*, social security, immigration, racial integration, a higher minimum wage, and public education). They are more critical of wealth and big business and more eager to bring them under regulation. Theirs is the greater faith in the wisdom of using legislation for redistributing the national product and for furnishing social services on a wide scale. Of the two groups of leaders, the Democrats are the more

"progressively" oriented toward social reform and experimentation. The Republican leaders, while not uniformly differentiated from their opponents, subscribe in greater measure to the symbols and practices of individualism, *laissez-faire,* and national independence. They prefer to overcome humanity's misfortunes by relying upon personal effort, private incentives, frugality, hard work, responsibility, self-denial (for both men and government), and the strengthening rather than the diminution of the economic and status distinctions that are the "natural" rewards of the differences in human character and fortunes. Were it not for the hackneyed nature of the designation and the danger of forcing traits into a mold they fit only imperfectly, we might be tempted to describe the Republicans as the chief upholders of what Max Weber has called the "Protestant Ethic."[36] Not that the Democrats are insensible to the "virtues" of the Protestant-capitalistic ethos, but they embrace them less firmly or uniformly. The differences between the two elites have probably been intensified by the rise of the New Deal and by the shift of former radicals into the Democratic party following the decline of socialist and other left-wing movements during and after the war.

3. Whereas the leaders of the two parties diverge strongly, their followers differ only moderately in their attitudes toward issues. The hypothesis that party beliefs unite adherents and bring them into the party ranks may hold for the more active members of a mass party but not for its rank-and-file supporters. Republican followers, in fact, disagree far more with their own leaders than with the leaders of the Democratic party. Little support was found for the belief that deep cleavages exist among the electorate but are ignored by the leaders. One might, indeed, more accurately assert the contrary, to wit: that the natural cleavages between the leaders are largely ignored by the voters. However, we cannot presently conclude that ideology exerts no influence over the habits of party support, for the followers do differ significantly and in the predicted directions on some issues. Furthermore, we do not know how many followers may previously have been led by doctrinal considerations to shift their party allegiances.

4. Except for their desire to ingratiate themselves with as many voters as possible, the leaders of the two parties have more reason than their followers to hold sharply opposing views on the important political questions of the day. Compared with the great mass of supporters, they are articulate, informed, highly partisan, and involved; they comprise a smaller and more tightly knit group which is closer to the wellsprings of party opinion, more accessible for indoctrination, more easily rewarded or punished for conformity or deviation, and far more affected, politically and psychologically, by engagement in the party struggle for office. If the leaders of the two parties are not always candid about their disagreements, the reason may well be that they sense the great measure of consensus to be found among the electorate.

5. Finding that party leaders hold contrary beliefs does not prove that they *act* upon these beliefs or that the two parties are, in practice, governed by different outlooks. . . . Until further inquiries are conducted . . . it seems reasonable to assume that the views held privately by party leaders can never be entirely suppressed but are bound to crop out in hundreds of large and small ways—in campaign

speeches, discussions at party meetings, private communications to friends and sympathizers, statements to the press by party officials and candidates, legislative debates, and public discussions on innumerable national, state, and local questions. If, in other words, the opinions of party leaders are as we have described them, there is every chance that they are expressed and acted upon to some extent. Whether this makes our parties "ideological" depends, of course, on how narrow we define that term. Some may prefer to reserve that designation for parties that are more obviously preoccupied with doctrine, more intent upon the achievement of a systematic political program, and more willing to enforce a common set of beliefs upon their members and spokesmen.

6. The parties are internally united on some issues, divided on others. In general, Republican leaders achieve greatest homogeneity on issues that grow out of their party's identification with business, Democratic leaders on issues that reflect their connection with liberal and lower-income groups. We find no support for the hypothesis that the parties achieve greatest internal consensus on the issues which principally divide them from their opponents.

In a sequel to this paper we shall offer data on the demographic correlates of issue support, which show that most of the differences presented here exist independently of factors like education, occupation, age, religion, and sectionalism. Controlling for these influences furnishes much additional information and many new insights but does not upset our present conclusions in any important respect. Thus, the parties must be considered not merely as spokesmen for other interest groups but as reference groups in their own right, helping to formulate, to sustain, and to speak for a recognizable point of view.

NOTES

1. Maurice Duverger, *Political Parties, Their Organization and Activity in the Modern State* (New York, 1955), p. 102.
2. The analysis of these and related tendencies associated with the American party system is ably set forth in Pendleton Herring, *The Politics of Democracy* (New York, 1940), p. 102 and *passim.* Also James M. Burns, *Congress on Trial: The Legislative Process and the Administrative State* (New York, 1949), p. 34.
3. See especially E. E. Schattschneider, *Party Government* (New York, 1942), p. 92 and *passim;* and V. O. Key, *Politics, Parties, and Pressure Groups,* 4th ed. (New York, 1958), ch. 8; Howard R. Penniman, *Sait's American Parties and Elections,* 5th ed. (New York, 1952), p. 162.
4. William Goodman, *The Two-Party System in the United States* (New Jersey, 1956), p. 43.
5. Duverger, *op. cit.,* pp. 187, 418.
6. Pendleton Herring, *op. cit.,* p. 133.
7. *American State Legislatures,* ed. Belle Zeller (New York, 1954); but see also Malcolm E. Jewell, "Party Voting in American State Legislatures," *American Political Science Review,* Vol. XLIX (Sept. 1955), pp. 773–91.
8. Report of the Committee on Political Parties, American Political Science Association, *Toward a More Responsible Two-Party System* (New York, 1950), *passim.*
9. Data bearing on these generalizations will be presented in companion articles which specifically deal with sectional and rural-urban influences on issue outlook.
10. *Cf.* James W. Prothro, Ernest Q. Campbell, and Charles M. Grigg, "Two Party Voting in the South: Class vs. Party Identification," *American Political Science Review,* Vol.

LII (March 1958), pp. 131–39. Also, Peter H. Odegard and E. Allen Helms, *American Politics: A Study in Political Dynamics* (New York, 1947 ed.), pp. 200–221.

11. This gratifyingly large number of returns of so lengthy and detailed a questionnaire was attained through a number of follow-up mailings and special letters. These and other procedures designed to check the adequacy of the sample will be fully described in the volume containing the report of the overall study. The difference in the number of returns from the two parties was largely a result of the greater number of Democratic delegates to begin with.
12. The measure of dispersion used for this purpose was the standard deviation, which was computed by using the scores of 0, .50 and 1.00 as intervals in the calculations. To avoid having to calculate separate significances of difference for each of the comparisons we wanted to observe, we simply made the assumption—erring on the side of caution—that the maximum variance of .50 had occurred in each instance. The magnitude of the significance of difference is, in other words, often greater than we have reported. The significance test used in this procedure was the critical ratio. Unless otherwise indicated, all the differences reported are statistically significant at or beyond the .01 level.
13. See, for example, the congressional roll-call results reported by Julius Turner, *Party and Constituency: Pressures on Congress*, The Johns Hopkins University Studies in Historical and Political Science Series, Vol. LXIX, No. 1 (1951). The complexities affecting the determination of party votes in Congress are thoroughly explored in David B. Truman, *The Congressional Party: A Case Study* (New York, 1959).
14. Conservatism is here used not in the classical but in the more popular sense, in which it refers to negative attitudes toward government ownership, intervention, and regulation of the economy; resistance to measures for promoting equalitarianism and social welfare through government action; identification with property, wealth, and business enterprise; etc.
15. Key, *op. cit.*, p. 239.
16. The friendlier attitude toward farmers among Democratic leaders than Republican leaders is borne out in the responses to several other questions used in the study. For example, the Republican leaders list farmers as having "too much power" far more frequently than do the Democratic leaders. Equally, the Democrats are significantly more inclined to regard farmers as having "too little power."
17. Turner, *op. cit.*, p. 64.
18. See John B. Johnson, Jr., *The Extent and Consistency of Party Voting in the United States Senate*, Ph.D. thesis, University of Chicago, 1943. By applying the Rice Index-of-Likeness to Senate votes, Johnson finds the tariff to have been the most partisan issue before the Congress in the years 1880–1940.
19. Corinne Silverman, "The Legislator's View of the Legislative Process," *Public Opinion Quarterly*, Vol. 18 (1954–55), p. 180.
20. Turner, *op. cit.*, p. 54.
21. *Cf.* Turner, *op. cit.*, p. 56, in which he found differences on foreign policy difficult to assess in Congress, partly because of its tie with the executive branch; see also, George Belknap and Angus Campbell, "Political Party Identification and Attitudes toward Foreign Policy," *Public Opinion Quarterly*, Vol. XV (Winter 1951–52), pp. 608–19.
22. The issue of defense spending has been kept separate from the other foreign policy issues because the magnitude of the scores for some of the leaders and all of the followers were obviously inflated by the launching of Sputnik I in November, 1957. The Sputnik incident occurred between the first and second wave of the leader survey and produced an increase in the number favoring defense spending of 40 per cent for the Democrats and 33 per cent for the Republicans. While this is a fascinating testimonial to the influence sometimes exercised by events on public opinion, its effect in this case was to distort scores in such a way as to make the leader and follower samples non-comparable. With proper caution, however, comparisons can be made between the Democratic and Republican leaders since both samples were affected in roughly the same way by Sputnik. For a similar reason we can also compare the Democratic followers with the Republican followers. Comparisons between leaders and followers on this issue cannot, however, be justified from our data.

23. Bernard R. Berelson, Paul F. Lazarsfeld, and William N. McPhee, *Voting* (Chicago, 1954), ch. 9.
24. For comparative data on party affiliation and issue outlooks among rank-and-file voters, see Angus Campbell, Phillip E. Converse, Warren E. Miller, and Donald E. Stokes, *The American Voter* (New York, 1960), especially chs. 8 and 9 dealing with issues and ideology. The text of this important report on the 1956 election study carried out by the Michigan Survey Research Center unfortunately reached us too late to be used to full advantage in the present analysis. The findings of the Michigan and the PAB studies, relative to the role of issues and ideology among the general population, corroborate and supplement each other to a very great degree.
25. *Cf.* Stephen K. Bailey, *The Condition of Our National Parties* (monograph), Fund for the Republic, 1959.
26. The data reported by the Elmira study of 1948 show the supporters of the two parties to be largely in agreement on issues. See *ibid.*, pp. 186, 190, 194, 211. The findings of the 1956 Michigan Survey suggest strongly that most voters, even at election time, do not know much about issues and are unable to link the parties with particular issues. Campbell and his associates conclude, for example, that "many people fail to appreciate that an issue exists; others are insufficiently involved to pay attention to recognized issues; and still others fail to make connections between issue positions and party policy." *The American Voter, op. cit.*, ch. 8.
27. For an analysis of the connection between intellectuals and liberal politics, see Seymour M. Lipset, *Political Man* (New York, 1960), ch. 10; also Paul F. Lazarsfeld and Wagner Thielens, Jr., *The Academic Mind* (Glencoe, 1958), chs. 1 and 2.
28. Samuel P. Huntington, "A Revised Theory of American Party Politics," *American Political Science Review*, Vol. XLIV (1950), p. 676.
29. PAB data supporting this generalization will be presented in a future publication.
30. For the effects of education on issue familiarity, see Campbell *et al., op. cit.*, ch. 8.
31. Schattschneider, *op. cit.; Toward a More Responsible Two-Party System, op. cit., passim.*
32. See E. E. Schattschneider, *Party Government, op. cit.*, p. 192.
33. Gabriel Almond, *The Appeals of Communism* (Princeton, 1954), pp. 5–6, and ch. 3.
34. See the discussion bearing on this conclusion in Campbell *et al., op. cit.*, chs. 8 and 9. Also, Avery Leiserson, *Parties and Politics, An Institutional and Behavioral Approach* (New York, 1958), pp. 162–66.
35. For an interesting set of comparative data on the relation of internal party cohesion to issue outlook, see Morris Davis and Sidney Verba, "Party Affiliation and International Opinions in Britain and France, 1947–1956," *Public Opinion Quarterly*, Winter 1960–61.
36. Max Weber, *Protestant Ethic and the Spirit of Capitalism* (London, 1948), ch. V.

14

The Profession of Politics

JOHN F. KENNEDY

In the following commencement address, delivered at Syracuse University on June 3, 1957, Senator John F. Kennedy remarks on the urgent public responsibilities of citizens. The idealism of Kennedy's remarks contrasts starkly with the reality of candidacy described by James MacGregor Burns in the next selection. The intellectual range and wit displayed in this speech are qualities that marked many of Kennedy's public utterances.

Anyone who is interested in the history of the United States Senate always feels a great sense of privilege and responsibility in coming to this state and to this part of the state. For New York has had a long parade of unusually distinguished men who served their nation in the Chamber of the Senate—and one of these of whom I am particularly reminded today was a very distinguished member of the opposite party—Elihu Root. His father was the second principal in the history of the Syracuse Academy—and Root himself was always fond of upstate New York. Perhaps one of the most dramatic moments of his life came in Utica in 1906 when as Secretary of State he agreed to speak for his party in this state. The opposition had imported a gang of hecklers to make his speech impossible. Having secured copies of his address in advance, they had instructions to start interruptions on particular lines—shouting, for example, on the first reference to the late President McKinley, "Let McKinley rest in peace," with the others roaring their approval. Unfortunately for the hecklers, the meeting was packed with

Root admirers and Hamilton College students; and the first one who started to interrupt was pushed in the face, and the rest were bodily threatened. Finally, when a great roar arose from the crowd to throw out one heckler, Root raised his right hand to quell the uproar, and in a powerful voice cried out: "No, let him stay—and learn!"

I trust that all of you will stay—I can only speculate as to how much you will learn—but I will welcome any heckling at the close of these ceremonies. I hope the example of Elihu Root will be an inspiration to all of those whom we honor on this solemn day of Commencement. For them, the pleasures, the values and the friendships of college days are coming to an end—the identical group sitting here this morning will probably never gather again—and the sands of time will gradually erase most of the memories which seem so important today.

But what concerns us most on these occasions is not what you graduates leave behind but what you take with you, what you will do with it, what contribution you can make. I am assuming, of course, that you are taking something with you, that you do not look upon this university as Dean Swift regarded Oxford. Oxford, he said, was truly a great seat of learning; for all freshmen who entered were required to bring some learning with them in order to meet the standards of admission—but no senior, when he left the university, ever took any learning away; and thus it steadily accumulated.

The high regard in which your education at Syracuse is held is evidenced by the intensive competition which rages between those hoping to benefit from it. Your campus is visited by prospective employers ranging from corporation vice-presidents to professional football coaches. Great newspaper advertisements offer inducements to chemists, engineers, and electronic specialists. High public officials plead for more college graduates to follow scientific pursuits. And many of you will be particularly persuaded by the urgent summons to duty and travel which comes from your local draft board.

But in the midst of all of these pleas, plans and pressures, few, I dare say, if any, will be urging upon you a career in the field of politics. Some will point out the advantages of civil service positions. Others will talk in high terms of public service, or statesmanship, or community leadership. But few, if any, will urge you to become politicians.

Mothers may still want their favorite sons to grow up to be President, but, according to a famous Gallup poll of some years ago, they do not want them to become politicians in the process. They may be statesmen, they may be leaders of their community, they may be distinguished lawmakers—but they must never be politicians. Successful politicians, according to Walter Lippmann, are "insecure and intimidated men," who "advance politically only as they placate, appease, bribe, seduce, bamboozle, or otherwise manage to manipulate" the views and votes of the people who elect them. It was considered a great joke years ago when the humorist Artemas Ward declared: "I am not a politician, and my other habits are good also." And, in more recent times, even the President of the United States, when asked at a news conference early in his first term how he liked "the game of politics," replied with a frown that his questioner was using a derogatory phrase. Being President, he said, is a "very fascinating experience . . . but the word 'politics' . . . I have no great liking for that."

Politics, in short, has become one of our most neglected, our most abused and our most ignored professions. It ranks low on the occupational list of a large share of the population; and its chief practitioners are rarely well or favorably known. No education, except finding your way around a smoke-filled room, is considered necessary for political success. "Don't teach my boy poetry," a mother recently wrote the headmaster of Eton; "Don't teach my boy poetry, he's going to stand for Parliament." The worlds of politics and scholarship have indeed drifted apart.

Unfortunately, this disdain for the political profession is not only shared but intensified in our academic institutions. To many universities and students we politicians represent nothing but censors, investigators and perpetrators of what has been called the "swinish cult of anti-intellectualism." To others, we are corrupt, selfish, unsavory individuals, manipulating votes and compromising principles for personal and partisan gain.

Teachers as well as students, moreover, find it difficult to accept the differences between the laboratory and the legislature. In the former, the goal is truth, pure and simple, without regard to changing currents of public opinion; in the latter, compromises and majorities and procedural customs and rights affect the ultimate decision as to what is right or just or good. And even when they realize the difference, most intellectuals consider their chief function to be that of the critic—and politicians are sensitive to critics (possibly because we have so many of them). "Many intellectuals," Sidney Hook has said, "would rather 'die' than agree with the majority, even on the rare occasions when the majority is right." Of course, the intellectual's attitude is partly defensive—for he has been regarded with so much suspicion and hostility by political figures and their constituents that a recent survey of American intellectuals by a national magazine elicited from one of our foremost literary figures the guarded response, "I ain't no intellectual."

But this mutual suspicion was not always the case—and I would ask those of you who look with disdain and disfavor upon the possibilities of a political career to remember that our nation's first great politicians were traditionally our ablest, most respected, most talented leaders, men who moved from one field to another with amazing versatility and vitality. A contemporary described Thomas Jefferson as "A gentleman of 32, who could calculate an eclipse, survey an estate, tie an artery, plan an edifice, try a cause, break a horse, dance a minuet, and play the violin."

Daniel Webster could throw thunderbolts at Hayne on the Senate Floor and then stroll a few steps down the corridor and dominate the Supreme Court as the foremost lawyer of his time. John Quincy Adams, after being summarily dismissed from the Senate for a notable display of independence, could become Boylston Professor of Rhetoric and Oratory at Harvard and then become a great Secretary of State. (Those were the happy days when Harvard professors had no difficulty getting Senate confirmation.)

This versatility also existed on the frontier. Missouri's first Senator, Thomas Hart Benton, the man whose tavern brawl with Jackson in Tennessee caused him to flee the state, was described with these words in his obituary: "With a readiness that was often surprising, he could quote from a Roman Law or a Greek philosopher, from Virgil's Georgics, The Arabian Nights, Herodotus or Sancho Panza, from the Sacred Carpets, the German reformers or Adam Smith; from Fenelon or Hudibras, from the financial reports of Necca or the doings of the Council of Trent, from the debates on the adoption of the Constitution or intrigues of the kitchen cabinet or from some forgotten speech of a deceased Member of Congress."

This link between American scholarship and the American politician remained for more than a century. A little more than one hundred years ago, in the Presidential campaign of 1856, the Republicans sent three brilliant orators around the campaign circuit: William Cullen Bryant, Henry Wadsworth Longfellow and Ralph Waldo Emerson. (Those were the carefree days when the "egg-heads" were all Republicans.)

I would urge therefore that each of you, regardless of your chosen occupation, consider entering the field of politics at some stage in your career. It is not necessary that you be famous, that you effect radical changes in the government or that you be acclaimed by the public for your efforts. It is not even necessary that you be successful. I ask only that you offer to the political arena, and to the critical problems of our society, which are decided therein, the benefit of the talents which society has helped to develop in you. I ask you to decide, as Goethe put it, whether you will be an anvil—or a hammer. The formal phases of the "anvil" stage are now completed for many of you, though hopefully you will continue to absorb still more in the years ahead. The question now is whether you are to be a hammer—whether you are to give to the world in which you were reared and educated the broadest possible benefits of that education.

It is not enough to lend your talents merely to discussing the issues and deploring their solutions. Most scholars, I know, would prefer to confine their attention to the mysteries of pure scholarship or the delights of abstract discourse. But "Would you have counted him a friend of Ancient Greece," as George William Curtis asked a century ago during the Kansas-Nebraska Controversy, "who quietly discussed the theory of patriotism on that Greek summer day through whose hopeless and immortal hours Leonidas and his three hundred stood at Thermopylae for liberty? Was John Milton to conjugate Greek verbs in his library, or talk of the liberty of the ancient Shumanites, when the liberty of Englishmen was imperilled?" No, the duty of the scholar—particularly in a republic such as ours—is to contribute his objective views and his sense of liberty to the affairs of his state and nation.

This is a great university, the University of Syracuse. Its establishment and continued functioning, like that of all great universities, has required considerable effort and expenditure. I cannot believe that all of this was undertaken merely to give the school's graduates an economic advantage in the life struggle. "A university," said Professor Woodrow Wilson, "should be an organ of memory for the state for the transmission of its best traditions. Every man sent out from a university should be a man of his nation, as well as a man of his time." And Prince Bismarck was even more specific—one-third of the students of German universities, he once stated, broke down from overwork; another third broke down from dissipation;

and the other third ruled Germany. (I leave it to each of you to decide which category you fall in.)

But if you are to be among the rulers of our land, from precinct captain to President, if you are willing to enter the abused and neglected profession of politics, then let me tell you—as one who is familiar with the political world—that we stand in serious need of the fruits of your education. We do not need political scholars whose education has been so specialized as to exclude them from participation in current events—men like Lord John Russell, of whom Queen Victoria once remarked that he would be a better man if he knew a third subject—but he was interested in nothing but the Constitution of 1688 and himself. No, what we need are men who can ride easily over broad fields of knowledge and recognize the mutual dependence of our two worlds.

I do not say that our political and public life should be turned over to college-trained experts who ignore public opinion. Nor would I adopt from the Belgian Constitution of 1893 the provision giving three votes instead of one to college graduates (at least not until more Democrats go to college). Nor would I give the University of Syracuse a seat in the Congress as William and Mary was once represented in the Virginia House of Burgesses.

But I do urge the application of your talents to the public solution of the great problems of our time—increasing farm foreclosures in the midst of national prosperity—record small business failures at a time of record profits—pockets of chronic unemployment and sweatshop wages amidst the wonders of automation—monopoly, mental illness, race relations, taxation, international trade, and, above all, the knotty complex problems of war and peace, of untangling the strife-ridden, hate-ridden Middle East, of preventing man's destruction by nuclear war or, even more awful to contemplate, by disabling through mutations generations yet unborn.

No, you do not lack problems or opportunities—you do not lack the ability or the energy; nor, I have tried to say, do you lack the responsibility to act, no matter what you have heard about the profession of politics. Bear in mind, as you leave this university and consider the road ahead, not the sneers of the cynics or the fears of the purists, for whom politics will never be an attraction—but bear in mind instead these words which are inscribed behind the Speaker's desk high on the Chamber Wall of the United States House of Representatives, inscribed for all to see and all to ponder, these words of the most famous statesman my state ever sent to the Halls of Congress, Daniel Webster: "Let us develop the resources of our land, call forth its power, build up its institutions, promote all its great interests and see whether we also in our day and generation may not perform something worthy to be remembered."

15

The Outsider Inside

JAMES MacGREGOR BURNS

To illustrate his thesis that American parties are too weak to govern, James MacGregor Burns tells in the following essay of his own campaign for Congress in the First District of Massachusetts. The party organization was totally inactive in the primary, could offer only minimal support in the general election, and was scarcely interested in the issues that he attempted to raise. Furthermore, the First District, like a vast majority of congressional districts across the United States, is so completely dominated by one party (in this case, the Republican) that the opposition poses little real threat. Burns argues that the lack of strong, issue-oriented party organizations and the imposing one-party bias in most congressional districts contributes to the "deadlock of democracy" because it separates the senior leadership of Congress from those political conditions that are the basis for the President's program. In addition, Burns forcefully portrays the hardships visited upon the aspirant for office in America.

Burns is A. Barton Hepburn Professor of Government at Williams College. He served as an adviser to President John F. Kennedy and has written numerous books, including Congress on Trial *(1949),* The Lion and the Fox *(1956),* John F. Kennedy: A Political Biography *(1959), and* Presidential Government: The Crucible of Leadership *(1966).*

. . . I must here declare an interest: I am a politician too. I am one of the ten thousand or so part-time politi-

From *The Deadlock of Democracy: Four-Party Politics in America* by James MacGregor Burns.

Published by Prentice-Hall, Inc., Englewood Cliffs, N.J.

cians in both parties who attend committee meetings, junket to national and state conventions as delegates, organize rallies, telephone voters, and attend endless coffee hours. And once, for almost a year, I was a full-time politician, when I ran for Congress as the Democratic nominee in the 1st Congressional District of Massachusetts. . . . Since no Democrat had carried this district for 60 years, and only one since the Civil War, hoping to be a Congressman was not my only reason for running. I wanted the sheer experience, and I wanted to advance my education.

I was especially curious about three things. How much help would I get from the party in which I had been active so long? To what extent would the various candidates campaign together or separately? Above all, was it possible for a congressional candidate to run on national isses?

The answer to the first question began to come very quickly. Although I had been chairman of my local Democratic committee, the Democratic party made no special effort to recruit or draft me—I recruited myself. If I had waited for the joyful sight of a party deputation urging me to make my contribution to statesmanship, I would still be waiting today. I could have arranged a fake draft, of course, but no one would have been fooled. This confirmed an old rule in politics; drafts do not just happen.

After I decided to run in the primary I soon found that I was very much on my own. Many of my Democratic party friends gave me a great deal of aid, but the party committees officially were neutral between me and my Democratic opponent. Lacking organized party help, I built in each city and town a personal organization of party committeemen, Young Democrats, independents, union leaders, civic group activists, and even a few Republicans. Meantime my Democratic opponent, and the scores of Democrats running for a dozen other nominations, busily constructed their own campaign organizations, all of which overlapped one another in a baffling mosaic of concentric and cross-cutting circles. A small army of Republicans was busily campaigning for their party's nominations too; at every clambake, steakbake, and cornbake, I and the rest of this host of rapacious vote seekers descended on the bewildered picnickers like locusts; sometimes we outnumbered them.

The nomination won, I plunged into the general election contest against the Republican nominee. The Democratic party committees now endorsed me, of course, but it was soon apparent that these committees as such could give me limited help. In the small Republican towns, where I most needed aid and sustenance, Democratic committees hardly existed. Where they did exist, they had small memberships, practically no funds, few workers outside their own committees, and a narrow range of action. And they had the impossible burden of trying to elect Democrats to more than a dozen posts, from Governor to probate judge and register of deeds. They lacked even enough money to put out adequate advertising for the party ticket as a whole. When I approached the party chairmen for funds, occasionally they asked me to contribute to them, or at least to buy tickets to a dinner they were putting on; evidently the candidates were supposed to support the party rather than vice versa. As a result of all this I continued to lean heavily on my own organization, now bolstered by more party regulars and also independents.

It was not the party organization but my personal following that distributed 30 or 40 thousand leaflets, mailed thousands of letters, rang countless doorbells, arranged coffee hours, put up posters, organized the climactic rallies, handed out cards at the polls.

There was an interesting mix of cooperation and conflict among the Democratic candidates for different offices. Each had his own organization, which he hesitated to share; each wanted help from the other; each had his exclusive sources of support that he could not or would not share. But there was a good deal of concerted activity too, especially between Democrats running in somewhat the same constituencies or holding a similar point of view. In my case I worked especially with Democrats running for state legislative offices in each district, because of our mutual interest in legislation, and with the candidate for United States Senator, who happened to be John F. Kennedy. We indulged, in short, in a continuous game of coattail grabbing (especially Mr. Kennedy's), but also in coattail avoidance.

Senator Kennedy could hardly have been more generous in extending his coattails to me. We made a film together, which I was allowed to put on television as much as I wished (and could afford), and we appeared together at party rallies and other ceremonials. Still, it was apparent that he was able to identify himself with issues in a way that I could not. It was not only that he was better known and had an ability to improvise in political situations—for example, taking the baton from a high school band leader and ending on the right beat. He had in eastern Massachusetts a big metropolitan area that gave him a solid and assured electoral foundation on which to base a politics of issues. And he could speak through a system of mass media that was organized on a state-wide basis.

My situation was quite different. The 1st District is a giant inverted saucer, with isolated cities dotting the rim and the center composed of mountains, trees, small towns, and Republicans. The two television stations covering the district were both outside the district—one was across the state line in New York—so that whenever I used television I was guaranteed an audience of which at least 75 per cent could not vote for me. The chief morning newspaper was published outside the district. Most of the evening papers were Republican, and while all but one or two were fair in their coverage, they were not effective vehicles for publicizing a coherent set of policies. The district—and I think this is true of many others—simply had no identity or coherence. Communicating with the voters was like trying to grab a handful of water. And my opponent would not debate with me.

I do not mean that we based all our efforts on an intellectual appeal. I preceded the main campaign with six months of door-to-door canvassing of carefully selected "local opinion leaders." We went in for the usual leaflets, matchbooks, bumper strips, blotters, sound trucks, and all the rest, and we even published our own newspaper in a city where the only newspaper, we felt, was not treating us fairly. But I hoped to supplement all this, and to give it some meaning, by relating campaign media to issues. Even our billboards urged that we "build jobs, schools, homes" rather than featuring just the name and picture.

My stand on issues did not interest the party regulars very much; it was enough for them that I was a Democrat. But I also needed strong independent support, and the independents or volunteers who became active in my campaign most decidedly were interested in issues. My talks to the regulars were reiterations of the party credo and were accepted as such. My talks to the mugwump type of independent provoked vigorous exchanges of ideas, and I was asked my opinions on unilateral disarmament, regulation of television, Israel-Arab relationships, population control, wire-tapping, and other subjects that might have seemed a bit esoteric to the regulars. The two groups never really met intellectually or physically. The mugwumps were wonderfully imaginative in thinking up publicity ideas and special campaign appeals and they arranged a magnificent climactic rally. But they did little of the pick-and-shovel work of the campaign, such as canvassing, registration work, driving voters to the polls, because they had never been geared into the operations of the local party organizations.

My chief memory of the campaign is a big room in some fraternal hall, with a bar in the rear—there always seemed to be a bar in the rear. After opening with the usual local references and pleasantries, I tried to deal emphatically with at least one national issue. I had to be emphatic to be heard over the buzz and laughter and tinkle of glasses at the bar. Although I was stressing bread-and-butter issues—this was a textile area caught in recession—I had to fight for my audience. And in the midst of my oratory someone was as likely as not to rise from a table in front of me, make his way noisily and unsteadily to the bar, and then, with all eyes following his uncertain progress, return triumphantly to his seat bearing four martinis.

This did not bother me. Who could doubt the relative importance of drink-in-hand compared to all the birds in the bush being discussed by a speaker whose name you hadn't quite caught. But it symbolized the overpowering emphasis in the campaign on immediate and local specifics. There was simply no way—I believe that we tried every method except sky-writing—to lift the campaign out of the grip of local forces, geography (where the candidate came from), or ethnic, personality, and religious factors. My education was completed election night with defeat. I won 45 per cent of the vote; significantly, I did best in the areas where my opponent and I had both been unknown before the election, but I did worst in the textile cities that needed my brand of policies, or so I thought, but that remembered my opponent's faithful errand-running as a state senator. Despite the intensive stumping of both of us, almost half the eligibles failed to vote. In the elections since, the 1st District has been faithful to [its Republican tradition.] Today it is more incorrigibly one-party than ever.

16

Interest Groups in the States

HARMON ZEIGLER

The essay by Harmon Zeigler that follows is drawn from a volume on American state politics, and it deals more with the role of interest groups in the states than in the national government. Zeigler's discussion is nonetheless significant for the study of national politics because it considers the relationship between social and economic variables (such as the extent of urbanism and per capita income), the strength of the political parties, and the influence attained by political interest groups. He finds that where parties are strong, interest groups are ordinarily weak. This seems to confirm the thesis of E. E. Schattschneider and others that the "socialization of conflict"—including the expansion of the role of parties in the government, both by making them more issue oriented and by increasing their internal discipline—takes power from the interest groups and spreads it more broadly in society.

Zeigler also confirms the allegation that interest groups rest on a narrow base in the population, which is heavily drawn from among the higher social and economic classes. Interest groups are not linkage institutions that directly represent the views of either a cross section or a large number of Americans, but, on the other hand, they may be useful for registering the views of those who feel most intensely about issues. The essential democratic consensus requires that majorities refrain from frequently enacting policies deeply repugnant to minorities; therefore, the existence of linkage institutions that reflect intensity rather than breadth of feeling is important. As Zeigler notes, many interest groups engage in political activity only sporadically; indeed, some groups come into existence to fight a particular cause and then disappear. This irregularity in pressure activity suggests that it is mainly when issues mean a great deal to the affected parties that interest groups seek to influence the government. Even in the representation of intense policy preferences, however, the upper-class bids of "the pressure group system" favors established minorities rather than disadvantaged segments of the population.

Finally, Zeigler views interest group activity as a form of communication and warns against considering lobbying to be contrary to public ethics. The most common and important activities of interest groups are reinforcing those already predisposed to their view, assisting the campaigns of those who share their policy preferences, providing information about legislation, and seeking broadly based public support. The occasional improprieties that so quickly gain the attention of the public misrepresent both the methods and the morals of political interest groups.

Zeigler, Professor of Political Science at the University of Oregon, is a specialist in the study of American interest groups. His writings include The Politics of Small Business *(1961),* Interest Groups in American Society *(1964),* Lobbying: Interaction and Influence in American State Legislatures *(1969), and a number of articles and monographs.*

* * *

Organizational Membership and Political Life

* * *

Attitudes Toward Organized Group Activity

Leaving aside for the moment the actual participation of Americans in formal organizations, we inquire first into their perceptions of the role of such organizations in the political process. Few people prefer to spend their free time in organizational activities. When asked to indicate what sorts of activities interested them most, the respondents in the Almond-Verba study rarely specified politics. In fact, participation in organizations such as unions, business associations, and professional associations received less mention than any other type of activity. . . . People who are normally unconcerned about politics may become active if threatened. Does this mean that the formal organization would be their choice of an instrument?

The evidence indicates that taking action through an organized group would be just about the last choice of those who would undertake any effort at achieving a satisfactory solution. When asked what they would do if a law were being considered by Congress which they believed to be unjust or harmful, the sample indicated the following choices: (1) contact elected leaders as an individual; (2) work through informal, unorganized groups; (3) do nothing; (4) vote; (5) work through a formal group; and (6) work through a political party. Clearly the individual and informal method is preferred, perhaps reflecting the distrust of organized activity. . . .

From *Politics in the American States,* edited by Herbert Jacob and Kenneth N. Vines, pp. 101–147.

A final aspect of the perception of group activity may be gleaned from perceptions of the most *effective* method of influencing a governmental decision. People apparently believe that group activity is very effective when considered in impersonal terms. By asking a question with no reference to personal reactions it was learned that the formation of a group was believed to be the best way to achieve success, followed by writing to government officials, working through personal and family connections, and forming a protest demonstration. It seems that group activity is perceived as a more effective device when undertaken by *others*. Does this reinforce suspicions about the questionable legitimacy of organized activity? The data do not provide an explicit answer to this question, but we can infer that the average person would not want to engage in "pressure politics" but believes that the "others" who do so are successful. Further clarification of this idea is given by the fact that 58 per cent of the sample indicated agreement with the statement that there are some people or groups having so much influence on the way government is run that the interests of the majority are ignored. What kinds of groups have this influence? According to the sample, big business or "the rich" rank first, followed by political parties and labor unions. When we examine these beliefs by income, we find that the high income groups think labor is more powerful than business and the low income groups think business is more powerful than labor.

Here again we see evidence of the belief that the other fellow is the one with power. If we examine the literature of organized groups we find that, with rare exceptions, the description of a particular group conflict is phrased in terms of power opponents with unlimited funds—an enemy whose defeat will require unusual loyalty and devotion among the members of the organization.

* * *

The Extent of Organized Membership

Having given a brief description of the attitudinal environment in which state interest groups operate, we turn our attention to the problem of finding out what kinds of people belong to organizations. The folk saying that "Americans are joiners" is supported by the findings of Almond and Verba. Of the five nations in which interviews were conducted, the American respondents indicated the highest de-

Table 1
Perceptions of Powerful Groups by Income of Respondents

	Per Cent Who Perceive Labor or Business as Powerful	
Income of Respondents	*Labor*	*Business*
$ 2,000–2,999 (99)*	16%	13%
3,000–4,999 (217)	10	15
5,000–7,499 (265)	13	21
7,500–9,999 (98)	13	21
10,000–14,999 (75)	18	15
15,000 or more (28)	22	16

* Number in parentheses indicates total number of respondents in each income group.

Table 2
Perceptions of Political Involvement

Type of Organization	*Per Cent of Membership Perceiving the Organization as Politically Involved*	*Total Number of Members in Sample*
Farm	71	29
Civic-Political	62	111
Professional	60	41
Business	55	40
Labor	50	136
Religious	35	180

gree of organizational membership (57 per cent).[1] However, only 24 per cent of the respondents believed the organizations to which they belonged were engaged in politics. As Almond and Verba themselves point out, this does not mean that the perception is in accordance with the reality. Organizations engaging in political activities may be perceived as non-political by their members. Further, organizations should not be categorized as political or non-political as though this were a static definition. Robert Lane, for example, is unwilling to categorize organizations as either political or non-political and prefers the term "quasi-political." In his study of the Connecticut Manufacturers Association, he found that the political involvement of the organization varied through time. By analyzing the content of its journal from 1937 to 1946 he found that attention to government-business relationships decreased while attention to problems of production increased. During the same period there was a steady rise in the political interest of unions.[2] . . .

Whether these perceptions reflect the actual extent of participation can be determined only by observation of the behavior of the particular organization at a given moment in history. It would be expected that during periods of organizational crisis (labor during the Taft-Hartley or Landrum-Griffith episodes and doctors during struggles over medical insurance) political involvement and corresponding perceptions of this involvement would increase.

Laying aside for the moment the categorizing of organizations according to perceptions of political activity, what do we know about *participation* in voluntary associations? Virtually no sample of national or local populations has failed to conclude that membership in voluntary organizations is greater among the upper socio-economic strata. Membership in organizations is positively correlated with high income and high educational attainment.[3] . . .

. . . Table 3 . . . indicates that people who live in cities of more than 100,000 population are more likely to belong to organizations than people who live in smaller towns. The main thrust of this evidence is that states with an urban, industrial economy are more likely to be characterized by an organization-oriented population than the more rural states whose population is more individualistic.

Returning to the perceived distinction between political and non-political organizations, we find the urban dominance remains. More of the members of perceived political organizations live in large towns than do the members of perceived non-political organizations.

Table 3
Urbanism and Organizational Membership; Variations According to Size of Town

	Per Cent Belonging to:		
Size of Town	*No Organizations*	*One or More Organizations*	*Number of Respondents*
Less than 5,000	45.7	54.3	297
5,000 to 100,000	41.7	58.3	247
100,000 or more	40.8	59.2	423

Characteristics of State Interest Groups

The survey data outlined above, while providing a general profile of the group affiliations of the American people, tells us nothing about the extent to which the organizations try to influence the state political process. This information must come from material provided by various states which require that lobbying organizations register with an agency of the state government. Before examining this material, some theoretical comments about the extent to which the formal institutions of American government influence the nature of state interest groups are in order. Clearly, the most significant institution of this type is the federal system.

The American federal system has contributed to the proliferation of interest groups at the state level. By creating numerous points of decision-making, federalism contributes to a diffusion of the political process. The federal system gives interest groups opportunities for their activities by increasing the number of points at which decisions are made. It does not follow, however, that all groups are equally concerned with state politics. The degree to which a group concerns itself with state politics may be understood to be a function of two factors: (1) the degree to which it has access to state decision-makers; and (2) the extent to which the decisions of state governments seem to affect the well-being of the group.

Successful access depends, in the first instance, on the ability of a group or its leaders to get a favorable response from those officials in a position to make a crucial decision. Access or lack of access cannot be linked directly to any set of circumstances or characteristics. However, it is likely that access is determined less by the skill or "pressure" of organized groups and more by the structure of the situation. . . .

As to the decisions of state governments and their impact on interest groups, one point ought to be made clear. As the federal government has expanded its role, the states have followed suit. Since the end of World War II, expenditures of state and local governments have increased more rapidly than the non-war expenditures of the federal government. Naturally, there are interest groups which are concerned about how this money is to be spent.

Those groups with resources at the state level and a clear stake in state politics are most likely to concentrate their efforts in state legislatures. Several examples will illustrate this point. In the South, segregationist groups have functioned almost as semi-official arms of the state government while Negro groups have been subjected to vigorous legal attacks and legislative investigation. In Louisiana, for example, Negroes believe that no legislators can be depended upon to initiate measures favorable to the Negro community when such a measure might come into conflict with the policy aims of whites.[4] Access to the national legislature is more easily achieved by Negroes. On the other hand, independent retailers anxious to prevent the growing dominance of chain stores were much more successful in persuading state legislatures to adopt restrictive taxes than they were in convincing Congress to adopt a national fair-trade law. . . .

Turning to the national government is not the only strategy available to those groups which are denied access to the state legislature. Within the state governments themselves there is the possibility of success. It has been suggested that the Supreme Court is the most effective arena for the presentation of claims by groups whose access to the Congress is restricted. Groups which are unable to influence the electoral, legislative, or administrative process may turn to the courts and, in the case of the Supreme Court, enjoy considerable success. This is especially true of the organizations representing minority groups such as the National Association for the Advancement of Colored People.[5] Is it true that groups disadvantaged through state legislation will perceive the state courts as accessible as they do national courts, or will the difference in values of state and national judges channel minority groups away from state courts? . . .

. . . Vines's study of Southern state courts and race relations sheds some light upon these questions.[6] He finds that Negroes prefer to avoid the state courts if possible since the Southern supreme court judges are elected officials with strong functional links to the state political system. The state supreme courts render decisions favorable to Negroes about one-third of the time, substantially less than the percentage of favorable dispositions by federal district courts in the South. Vines's research indicates that the state courts do not play the same role in the state political systems (at least in the South) as does the Supreme Court in the national political system. However, during the same period that the state supreme courts were deciding against Negroes two-thirds of the time, Southern state legislatures failed to pass a single bill favorable to Negroes. Further, state supreme court reversals of lower court decisions are, in over 90 per cent of the cases, favorable to Negroes. It may be suggested, therefore, that, relative to the other political institutions in the Southern states, the supreme courts have to some extent played the same role as does the Supreme Court in national politics.

A final point to be made has bearing on lobbying strategy. To what extent are the groups concerned with state policies coordinated by a national association? There appear to be relatively few examples of interstate coordination. Most groups probably operate without much national direction. Exceptions to the rule are, of course, available. The American Petroleum Industries Committee has branches in most state capitals and operates in a rather unitary fashion. The same can be said of the National Association of Real Estate Boards which worked through state legislatures to defeat rent control after the war, or the American Truckers Association which provides information to state truckers' associations in their opposition to taxes or length and

Table 4
Classification of Interest Groups in Selected States, 1964

State	*Business* %	*Single Bus. Corp.* %	*Labor* %	*Farm* %	*Prof.* %	*Reform* %	*Public Agency* %	*Religious and Ethnic* %	*Veteran* %	*Other* %
California (432)*	28.8	23.1	10.7	1.9	4.7	4.4	11.2	1.1	0	14.1
Florida (439)	18.7	28.2	20.1	2.3	5.7	1.1	10.3	1.0	0	12.6
Iowa (204)	36.3	10.8	8.8	2.9	5.3	6.9	7.4	7.8	1.5	12.3
Kentucky (59)	49.2	6.8	16.8	1.7	10.2	1.7	6.8	0	0	6.8
Maine (165)	40.0	16.4	8.5	3.0	5.4	2.4	14.6	.6	.6	8.5
Michigan (322)	19.9	35.4	8.1	2.1	12.1	5.0	11.2	1.6	1.2	3.4
Montana (180)	27.2	27.2	13.9	4.4	4.4	3.0	8.9	1.0	1.7	8.3
Nebraska (150)	35.3	13.3	4.7	5.3	9.1	4.7	11.3	1.3	1.0	14.0
South Dakota (92)	41.5	21.7	5.4	5.4	8.7	4.3	5.4	0	3.3	4.3
Kansas (41)	9.5	39.4	9.5	2.8	5.2	3.8	13.7	1.9	0	14.2
New York (174)	47.1	27.0	8.1	1.0	7.5	1.0	3.5	1.0	0	3.8
Ohio (173)	35.8	23.9	15.0	1.2	12.1	1.0	4.6	1.0	1.0	4.4
Pennsylvania (243)	32.8	30.8	10.3	1.0	12.4	1.2	7.8	1.6	0	2.1
Virginia (107)	18.7	62.6	8.4	3.7	1.9	0	1.0	0	0	3.7
Connecticut (175)	44.6	26.3	4.6	1.1	6.3	1.7	6.3	1.1	1.1	6.9
Indiana (136)	38.2	11.8	10.3	1.5	7.4	9.4	3.7	2.9	0	14.8
Rhode Island (60)	33.3	21.7	16.7	1.7	8.3	0	0	1.7	5.0	11.6

* Numbers in parentheses indicate total number of interest groups registered with the state.

weight limitations.[7] However, few groups have a large enough membership or treasury to allow very much planning. . . .

Is there any appreciable difference in the types of groups which appear before the legislatures of differing types of states? Information for all states is not available but the preceding table, which presents information on the types of organizations which register to lobby before selected state legislatures, is suggestive.[8]

Notice that, while the percentages vary considerably, in every state the registrations are dominated by business associations or single businesses or corporations. No matter what kind of economy [is] enjoyed by the state, the businesses dominate the *numerical* structure of lobbying. For example, 30.6 per cent of the population of South Dakota is employed in nonindustrial occupations while 1.8 per cent of the population of Connecticut is so employed. Yet 63 per cent of the South Dakota interests are either business associations or single businesses and 71 per cent of the Connecticut interests are in this category.

Does this mean that business generally has more access to state legislatures than to the national legislature? While many people believe this to be the case, it cannot be established solely from the magnitude of business lobbying. We could hardly justify a conclusion based upon the relation between magnitude of lobbying and power of lobbying units. Many of the registrations before the state legislatures are "one shot" affairs, and the lobbyist is not in attendance more than a few days during the session. However, evidence drawn from interviews with legislators also indicates that business groups are the most important contributors to the pressure system. This was true of states with such differing economic structures as Ohio, California, Tennessee, New Jersey, Michigan, and North Carolina.[9] Business associations are the most numerous group in Washington, as Schattschneider and Milbrath have established by different methods.[10] This means that the "business character of the pressure system," which Schattschneider discovered in examining groups engaged in lobbying before Congress, can also be extended to the states.

* * *

These data on the scope of state lobbying tell us nothing about the relative power of specific groups which might be numerically insignificant, but quite influential. The less than 3 per cent representation of farm groups in the Iowa legislature surely does not reflect the influence they might have. Indeed, the existence of relatively few groups interested in a particular policy area may actually indicate substantial cohesion and agreement among the group membership as opposed to the possible fragmentation of the membership of the more numerically significant groups. Also, it is impossible to know how many people are actually members of the various organizations. We would suspect that most of the organizations are rather small in membership, if the organizations listed in *National Associations of the United States* can be considered typical. Most of these organizations have a membership of less than one hundred.

* * *

The Politico-Economic Setting

. . . The argument is that within the states in which voluntary association membership should be the greatest the impact of interest groups on public policy is estimated to be the least. The greater participation in organizations in the urban states means that more group-anchored conflicts will come to the attention of the governmental decision-makers. The greater the number of demands which come to the attention of any single decision-making agency, the less likely will be the probability that any one set of demands will be able to maintain control over the content of policy.

The Link Between Economic and Political Variables

. . . If we maintain that the socio-economic structure of a state structures the behavior and importance of interest groups, is it not likely that other components of the political system, such as political parties, are influenced too? Also, it is probable that the strength of the party system itself may inhibit or encourage interest groups. To illustrate, it has long been suggested that strong party cohesion in legislative voting contributes to a weakness of interest groups. However, if we examine the causes of party voting we find that, with considerable variation, there is a relationship between legislative cohesion and party competition. Further, if we probe deeper, both legislative cohesion and party competition are related to the industrialization and urbanization of a state. Accordingly, it is best to treat economic and political variables as components in a single system, rather than as independent or dependent variables.

The following table describes the American states in terms of three *political* variables:[11] strength of inter-

Table 5
The Strength of Pressure Groups in Varying Political and Economic Situations

	Types of Pressure System[a]		
Social Conditions	*Strong*[b]	*Moderate*[c]	*Weak*[d]
Party Competition	*(24 states)*	*(14 states)*	*(7 states)*
One-Party	33.3%	0%	0%
Modified One-Party	37.5%	42.8%	0%
Two-Party	29.1%	57.1%	100.0%
Cohesion of Parties in Legislature			
Weak Cohesion	75.0%	14.2%	0%
Moderate Cohesion	12.5%	35.7%	14.2%
Strong Cohesion	12.5%	50.0%	85.7%
Socio-Economic Variables			
Urban	58.6%	65.1%	73.3%
Per Capita Income	$1900	$2335	$2450
Industrialization Index	88.8	92.8	94.0

a. Alaska, Hawaii, Idaho, New Hampshire, and North Dakota are not classified or included.
b. Alabama, Arizona, Arkansas, California, Florida, Georgia, Iowa, Kentucky, Louisiana, Maine, Michigan, Minnesota, Mississippi, Montana, Nebraska, New Mexico, North Carolina, Oklahoma, Oregon, South Carolina, Tennessee, Texas, Washington, Wisconsin.
c. Delaware, Illinois, Kansas, Maryland, Massachusetts, Nevada, New York, Ohio, Pennsylvania, South Dakota, Utah, Vermont, Virginia, West Virginia.
d. Colorado, Connecticut, Indiana, Missouri, New Jersey, Rhode Island, Wyoming.

est groups, strength of political parties, and legislative cohesion.*

The table also links these factors with three *economic* variables, urban population, per capita income, and percentage of the population employed in occupations other than agriculture, forestry, and fishing (industrialization). Taken together, these economic factors indicate the existence or absence of a heterogeneous society with its corresponding increase or decrease in group tensions. Thus, a state that has a high per capita income, a high percentage of its population employed in industrial occupations, and a high proportion of its population living in urban areas should exhibit a strong and active group life, but not necessarily a strong pressure group system. This idea becomes clear if we examine the table. With regard to political variables, pressure groups are strongest when political parties and legislative cohesion are weakest. Concerning the economic variables, we see that pressure groups are strongest in states with a relatively backward economy. Combining both types of variables, there are two patterns which emerge. The first pattern consists of strong pressure groups, weak parties (both electorally and legislatively), low urban population, low per capita income, larger proportion of the population engaged in non-industrial occupations. The second pattern consists of moderate or strong pressure groups, competitive parties, an urban, industrial economy. In short, there is a clear relation between pressure politics, party politics, and socio-economic structure.

There are, of course, notable exceptions. For example, California and Michigan are hardly non-industrial, non-urban states, yet they have strong pressure groups. Nevertheless, it can be argued that the pattern is sufficiently clear and that the deviant states do not destroy the pattern. In the strong pressure group category we find every state in the South, the very states where the economy is less developed and organizational memberships are the fewest. What is it about these states that produces a strong pressure group system? If we follow the theory developed so far, we would maintain that it is not the non-industrial nature of the economy per se which is a fundamental cause, but rather that such economies are normally *non-diverse.* That is to say, the economies of such states tend to be dominated by a single type of enterprise. Industrial economies tend to be less keyed to a particular set of businesses and are less likely to be monopolized.

* Because of certain methodological problems, the classification is subject to criticism. In deciding whether a state is characterized by strong, moderate, or weak pressure groups, questionnaires were sent to political scientists in each state. The limitations of this method are apparent. However, there is reason to assume that these evaluations are relatively accurate in view of the consistent patterns which appear in the economic and political factors associated with the three groups of states. The measure of legislative cohesion is taken from the same study but is not subject to the same criticism since objective evaluations of cohesion do exist. The extent of party competition, taken from Austin Ranney's classification, is appropriate since it relies only on state elections. One modification has been made in Ranney's classification. Modified one-party Democratic and modified one-party Republican are merged into a single category since the direction of the partisanship is of no concern.

* * *

Emerging Patterns of Group Conflict

The fact that interest groups thrive in non-industrial states does not mean that there is a *single* pattern of group activity. There are, in fact, four distinct patterns which emerge from the strong pressure group category of states. First, there is the "typical" strong pressure group pattern consisting of a non-diversified economy, relatively non-competitive party politics, and weak legislative cohesion. This pattern is descriptive of the Southern states and of non-Southern states with similar economic and political systems, such as Maine. In these states the strength of interest groups is achieved by means of an *alliance of dominant groups*. Next, there is a pattern with an equally non-diversified economy but with two-party politics and moderate legislative cohesion, such as in Montana. Here we find that a *single dominant interest* strengthens the pressure system. Thirdly, we find a pattern consisting of a non-diversified industrial economy, two-party politics, and strong legislative cohesion. The best example of this pattern is Michigan where there is a *conflict between two dominant groups*. Finally, California is an example of a diverse economy, two-party politics, and a weak legislative cohesion. A classic case of the free play of interest groups in a legislature unencumbered by demands originating from political parties, California is best described as the *triumph of many interests*. Note that these patterns have one of two characteristics in common. Either the economic structure of the state is non-diverse or the party system is weak. To understand how each of these systems operates, we shall explore them in some detail.

* * *

Contrasting Patterns: States Without a Dominant Pressure System

A strong party system contributes to a balancing of the power between parties and interest groups or, in some cases, to a clear dominance of the parties. If the strength of parties produces a more balanced distribution of power, we can expect to find that interest groups are vigorous and active, but clearly dependent upon parties for access to governmental decision-makers. Contributions are channeled to the candidate through the party organization, and it is to the party that the fealty of the candidate is owed. Further, there is a tendency for each party to develop its own constellation of interests from which support can be expected. These interests rarely attempt to persuade individual legislators to cast a favorable vote on a specific issue but rather devote their attention exclusively to party leaders. In these situations it is clear that the party is in control. In Connecticut, for example, parties are able to punish an interest group if its demands become intolerable.

In contrast to this pattern of cooperation, Missouri is an example of a genuinely low pressure system. Salisbury has described the pressure system of Missouri as one of *ad hoc* rather than permanent alliances. He finds that broad coalitions of groups in conflict with rival combinations do exist, but are a rare phenomenon.[12] The shifting, temporary issue-oriented alliances in Missouri cannot compete with the stable and competitive party system. Lacking a major economic cleavage, interest groups have not developed either the ability to work closely with a party as in Michigan or the power to circumvent and dominate the parties as in Maine or California. In fact, Missouri and California have similarly diverse economies. It is probable that, had California not undergone its unique historical development, its pressure system would have been as weak as Missouri's. Diffusion and fragmentation of power, a pluralistic situation endemic to most industrial, urban states, provides parties with the opportunity to function without severe competition from interest groups.

Lobbying as a Communications Process

In order to achieve success in state politics, the interest group must have access to key decision-makers. Up to this point, factors within the political and socio-economic system over which interest groups have no control have been described in terms of their impact upon the performance of groups. It is true that such factors structure and limit the activities of interest groups and that success or failure is probably more dependent upon the nature of the society than upon the skills or techniques of lobbyists. Nevertheless, it is within the power of interest groups to maximize whatever advantages accrue to them because of their place within a social system. A high status manufacturers' organization might sacrifice its initial advantage by lobbying techniques which offend the sensibilities of legislators or make it difficult for them to vote the way the organization would prefer. If, for example, such an organization publicly threatens to defeat all legislators who vote the "wrong" way, it may be necessary for these legislators to establish their independence by voting against the wishes of the organization. Access, then, does depend to some extent upon skills. In lobbying, as in any other profession, such skills are acquired by experience and practice. A pertinent question is: how experienced are state lobbyists?

The Characteristics of State Lobbyists

The available information does not present a picture of *most* state lobbyists as more professional at their job than the legislators are at theirs. In fact, the proportion of newcomers to the lobbying ranks seems to be about the same as the proportion of newcomers to the legislature. . . .

There are, without doubt, many experienced lobbyists just as there are experienced legislators. However, to lament the amateurism of the legislator is to forget that the lobbyist, mythology to the contrary, is not any more of a professional. Walter DeVries' study of lobbying in Michigan, for example, points out that the majority of lobbyists are not very frequent visitors to Lansing; only a core of regulars are really familiar with the vagaries of the legislative process. Of equal significance is that not very many lobbyists spend their full time in lobbying during the session. Patterson found that over 60 per cent of the Oklahoma lobbyists spend half their time or less engaged in lobbying. In North Carolina, 59 per cent of the lobbyists interviewed indicated that they spend no more than half their time in lobbying.[13]

Finally, there should be some mention of lobbying specialization. If it is to be argued that legislators do not have the time to become fully informed about specific areas of public policy and, therefore, look to representatives of the interested organizations to supply information (that is, in fact, a basic function of lobbying), then what can we say of the lobbyists who are on retainer from several organizations—in some cases dozens—to handle a particular problem? Approximately one-fourth of the lobbyists registering in the states represent more than one client. Judging from what little evidence can be gathered from the various changes in registration, most of the lobbyists with multiple clients change clients as the issues being debated before the legislature change. Thus, in one session lobbyists for brewers and bankers might return for the next session as lobbyists for bakers and butchers. . . .

What kinds of backgrounds do state lobbyists have? One striking difference between the backgrounds of state and national lobbyists is the relative absence of lawyers among the ranks of the state lobbyists. Milbrath found that most Washington lobbyists were lawyers, but in none of the states for which we have information is the proportion of lawyers this high. In Oklahoma, only four out of a sample of forty-three indicated law as their occupation. Twelve per cent of the Michigan lobbyists were lawyers; however, in Virginia and North Carolina the respective percentages were 46 and 41.[14] Whether the higher proportion of lawyers as lobbyists in Southern states is coincidence or reflective of the cultural or political structure of the South cannot be ascertained from so few cases. The largest single occupational category in both Oklahoma and North Carolina is that of full-time executive or employee of an association engaged in lobbying; in Virginia, association executives are second to lawyers. . . .

It would seem that interest groups would be anxious to employ people who had . . . knowledge, and that ex-legislators would be eagerly sought after. This may be the case, but relatively few ex-legislators ever become lobbyists. . . . This does not mean that ex-legislators are not useful as lobbyists. Indeed, DeVries' study suggests that there is a significant relationship between any amount of legislative experience and lobbying effectiveness. Thus, while a group employing an ex-legislator may have an advantage, very few groups are so fortunate. On the other hand, quite a few lobbyists have had some form of governmental or political experience. This experience may be at the executive level or perhaps at the local level. . . . Moreover, there is a significant relationship between *length* of government service and effectiveness: the longer the experience, the greater the effectiveness. The same sort of relationship exists with regard to experience in a political party. Milbrath noted that the Washington lobbyists find it useful to avoid partisan activity and that "the party with which a man identifies appears to be relatively unimportant in lobbying."[15] The competitive nature of Congress would make open partisanship hazardous, but in states in which one party can be relied upon to control the legislature the risks are less and the advantages considerable. . . . A strong party system does not necessarily mean the diminution of the influence of interest groups but may mean a channeling of pressure toward holders of party office rather than toward the party rank and file. This is the case in Michigan and Massachusetts, for example, where labor organizations serve frequently as auxiliaries to the parties.

Money: How Necessary for Access Is It?

In establishing a satisfactory relationship with a group of legislators, the use of money cannot be ignored but can be put in proper perspective. In the first place, it is relatively easy for journalists to nod knowingly at the magic power of money and assume that merely by uttering the word they have offered the insider's explanation of how legislation is enacted. What does money buy? How is money spent? These are questions frequently left unanswered. Consider for example the case of entertainment. Reports on various states such as Wisconsin, Florida, and Michigan suggest that lobbyists at the state level do more entertaining than do lobbyists in Washington.[16] However, it does not appear that lobbyists rate entertaining as high as other techniques and that its role is exaggerated by popular accounts. Also the style of entertaining is probably more circumspect than might be expected. While some lobbyists maintain an open bar for legislators, most entertaining seems to fall into the category of lunches for small groups or annual dinners for the entire legislature. It is likely that such affairs are more in the nature of creating access than in the discussion of explicit legislation. A lobbyist who relied upon entertaining exclusively would not be very successful; however, at least in Michigan, the more effective lobbyists spend more time entertaining than the less effective ones.

We can exclude overt bribery from our consideration of state lobbying because it is either extremely rare or impossible to substantiate. On the other hand, contributions to political campaigns can be an important part of group strategy. Realistically speaking, money does not win elections. If it did, Republicans would win more than they do. However, money can create a relationship of gratitude and trust. Politicians seeking public office have basic campaign costs to meet, and those organizations willing to meet some or all of these costs certainly can be assured of at least formal access to decision-makers. . . . we can compare the use of campaign contributions in states with competitive and non-competitive party systems. The basic difference seems to be that in the competitive systems the contributions are channeled to candidates through the party organization, while in one-party systems the contact between candidate and organization is not marred by an intermediary. Within the competitive systems, a distinction can be made between groups which contribute with a specific goal in mind and groups which make contributions because of general agreement with a political party. Turning to the first example, Andrew Hacker's study of the conflict between railroads and truckers in Pennsylvania is instructive. The truckers, undertaking a long and arduous campaign to repeal a state law limiting the weight of trucks to 45,000 pounds, contributed heavily to the campaigns of state legislators. The specific goal was the repeal of the law; the partisan sympathies of the trucking companies were of no concern. Therefore the $76,000 collected by the Pennsylvania Motor Truck Association was divided almost equally between the parties. It is clear that the organization expected to recoup this expenditure by revenue gained from a more favorable weight law, a point made by Hacker: "Many of the men who voted for S.615 (to increase the permissible weight of trucks) knew that they were doing so to repay a campaign debt or in anticipation of future contributions . . . they consciously made a bargain to limit their freedom in return for a payment."[17]

Such an unequivocal exchange is unlikely to take place in situations where groups with more continuing and long-range goals are giving the money. The best example is, of course, organized labor. Labor contributions usually flow through the offices of the Democratic party on a more or less permanent arrangement. Labor organizations are—because of their relatively large membership—also anxious to offer their services in the mobilization of voters for the Democratic party. Alexander Heard points out that the financial resources and potential voting strength of unions are concentrated in seventeen* states where the percentage of union members among persons of voting age equalled or exceeded the national percentage and in which the percentage of non-agricultural employees was thirty or more.[18] In such states as Massachusetts and Michigan, the collaboration between the unions and the Democratic party is complete to the point where the unions serve as auxiliary parties and assume many of the responsibilities of the formal party organization. . . . of Massachusetts, Lockard writes, "In some areas the Democratic party . . . will leave to labor almost the whole job of campaigning for state candidates, and in many campaigns the money labor gives is a very crucial factor in the Democratic effort."[19] In other states of the seventeen mentioned by Heard, the collaboration is less formal. In Washington, for example, the unions are friendly to the Democratic party but have not infiltrated to the extent of those in Michigan and Massachusetts. The point is that these contributions are probably not accompanied by explicit expectations. Also, it is likely that, at least in Michigan and Massachusetts, less money filters down to candidates to the state legislature and more ends up in the coffers of gubernatorial candidates.

In one-party states, the exchange between candidate and interest groups is more explicit in the absence of a party organization. Joseph Bernd's investigation of contributions in Georgia shows that about 50 per cent of the money received by major candidates for governor came from liquor dealers and highway contractors, both of which have clear and narrowly defined expectations.[20] Here, again, the money flows past the legislature to the place where it is thought it can do the most good.

While campaign contributions do form part of the strategy of those groups in state politics able to afford it, it would hardly be accurate to assume that it plays a more important role at the state than the national level. Certainly in terms of the total amount of money spent, the state political process would come off a poor second. However, it may be suggested that a little money goes a longer way at the state level, where candidates are personally less well-off and of lower general social status than are candidates to the national legislature.

Money may also be used in public relations campaigns but, with a few notable exceptions, state interest groups are not as concerned with the "new lobby" technique of mass persuasion. Examples of the use of public relations campaigns usually appear where the state interest groups have an affiliation with a national organization which provides much of the propaganda. For instance, the struggle over right-to-work laws has attracted national organizations which supply state units or sympathetic, but unaffiliated, organizations with literature, arrange for public meetings, and the like. The same set of circumstances seems to apply to the perennial conflict between trucking companies and railroads in which the representatives of the respective national associations have displayed an understandable interest. The relatively slight use of public relations at the state level is not difficult to understand. The indirect communication of the mass

* The states are: New York, Pennsylvania, California, Illinois, Ohio, Michigan, New Jersey, Indiana, Massachusetts, Missouri, Wisconsin, Washington, Minnesota, West Virginia, Oregon, Montana, and Nevada.

media, for example, is not presumed to be as persuasive as personal communication. Since the state legislators are generally more accessible than their national counterparts, the use of indirect methods to create a favorable climate of opinion is not really necessary. Daily attendance at the state capitol, the cultivation of key legislators, the establishment of feelings of respect and confidence on the part of those legislators who have authority in the area of interest to the lobbyist and his organization—these are the preferred techniques of experienced lobbyists.

The Advantage of the Defense

Groups whose basic goal is defensive and who are satisfied with the status quo and concern themselves primarily with maintaining it have a better chance of success than those who try to alter the existing distribution of values. In Michigan, high-status groups such as manufacturers or professional associations have been able to play the role of policeman with considerable success, while groups such as labor unions which are struggling for social change feel they are at a disadvantage. The coexistence of high-status groups and defensive posture is not coincidental, but does not necessarily mean that labor unions will usually be on the attack in the state legislatures. In Massachusetts, for example, the unions spend practically all their time in a consciously defensive set of maneuvers to prevent the opposition from *weakening* existing labor laws. Of course, labor's most consistent defensive position has been against right-to-work laws. In states listed by Heard as being those with the greatest concentration of union membership, the union lobbyists can play the role of policeman while it is the job of the business groups to induce the legislature to change the status quo. . . .

* * *

Lobbying Techniques: The Communication of Information

Turning now to the specific techniques of influence, a word of caution should be offered. We cannot assume that, merely because the more experienced lobbyists are more successful, their experience includes knowledge of the ways to manipulate legislators, to guide unpopular legislation through a series of hostile entrapments and, in general, to utilize "pressuring." In practice, the role of the skilled lobbyist is far less dramatic. Generally, his job can be little more than that of an agent serving to *communicate* the position of a group on a given issue to someone who he believes will have some control over the outcome.[21] Of course, it is also part of the lobbyist's job to communicate the notion of group power, but this is largely a matter determined without the intervention of lobbying skills. . . .

Recent studies of Washington lobbying all have a similar thrust: lobbying is very rarely directed at legislators who have taken a position in opposition to the desired goals of the group employing the lobbyist. Most contact between lobbyist and legislator is typically that of two partisans reinforcing agreement.[22] In this context, "pressure" is not a very useful concept. In the legislature, as with the general public, "pressure" is a tactic only opponents engage in. If the legislator and lobbyist have similar goals, communication is likely to be perceived as the legitimate expression of a sound point of view. Consequently, the feeling that the legislature is under considerable pressure (if the legislators feel this to be the case) probably indicates either that the lobbyists are talking to the wrong people or the legislator "has heard" of great pressure (on the part of his opponents. . . .

Choices of Strategies

In establishing a contact with a friendly legislator to transmit the position of his organization, the lobbyist has a choice of strategies. He can elect to operate primarily through the official channels of the legislature. Testimony at committee hearings is the most usually employed device of this type. The lobbyist can also try to develop a personal relationship with as many legislators as possible so that they will look upon him as reliable and dependable. If he is successful, the formal testimony of the hearing room can be supplemented with informal conversation. If he represents a wealthy organization the establishment of a personal relationship might be undertaken by means of entertainment—the "social lobby." Other methods of communication are more indirect. The lobbyist can urge members of his organization to write or contact a legislator personally, or his organization can engage in a long-range public relations campaign intended to impress both members and non-members in the hopes that some of these people will feel inclined to take action. Organizations may hope to establish communication through gratitude and invest funds in the campaigns of legislators. Needless to say, methods of establishing communication channels like the last mentioned are reserved to those few organizations affluent enough to undertake such activities on a continuing basis. Of course, an organization may try any combination of these methods but usually there is a distinct preference for one, depending both on the nature of the organization and the particular characteristics of the situation. It is also true that lobbying techniques depend to some extent upon the political system in which the lobbying takes place. For example, interest groups have been able to establish a more permanent web of interaction with administrative agencies than they have with the legislature because of the inherently monopolistic tendencies of administrative politics. At the state level, each agency will have responsibility for a narrowly defined set of operations and will come into almost daily contact with a clientele whose interests are affected by the agency's operations. Thrown into constant association with a specific clientele, administrators see very little of a more general public and gradually tend to identify their values with those of their clientele. The establishment of a set of mutually shared values between agency and clientele can be useful not only in turning legislative defeat into administrative victory but also in the pursuit of group goals through legislation. A combination of private interest group and public agency is a valuable one in the event that a group without access to the administrative agency tries to change the structure of power through the legislature.[23]

Because of the more unstructured nature of state legislatures, more time is devoted to the cultivation of valuable personal relationships. Consequently, the full-time, experienced lobbyists prefer to operate as what Patterson calls "contact men." In his article on Oklahoma, Patterson describes the contact man as one who:

. . . conceives of his job as primarily that of making contacts, personal acquaintanceships and friendships with various legislators, and of maintaining these contacts. The Contact Man provides a direct communications link between the interest group and the individual member of the legislature. When faced with a legislative problem for his group, the lobbyist with a Contact Man orientation is likely to propose as the solution the personal contacting of as many members of the legislative body as possible, directly presenting the interest group's case to them.[24]

... There is an interesting comparison that can be made with the national legislative process on the question of preferred lobbying techniques. Milbrath discovered that, while the Washington lobbyists feel direct personal communication to be their most effective method, they spend little of their time in direct conversations with legislators.[25] Thus it may well be that the state legislative process, because of its relative informality, facilitates the direct approach.

While it may be true that the state legislative process presents more opportunities for direct access to legislators, the contact men must be in a position to use this access to best advantage. Stated simply, there must be a sufficient amount of trust between legislator and lobbyist so that the legislator will feel that the statements of the lobbyist can be relied upon for their accuracy. Pressure groups are most readily accepted by legislators if they avoid a mere assertion of demands and provide information useful to legislators as they try to develop an accurate picture of the situation. Lobbyists who have established a reputation for reliability are more likely to be effective contact men than lobbyists whose reputation is for pressuring or threatening. An interesting example of how *not* to be a successful lobbyist comes from Colorado. In this case the Colorado Motor Carriers Association, in trying to defeat a gross ton-mile tax, relied upon the "old style lobby" techniques. Lavish entertainment, threats to defeat legislators at the polls, and even, it is said, threats to persuade bankers to call in overdue notes owed by legislators favoring the tax were prominent in this campaign. Legislators apparently were unimpressed by these efforts and they doubted the authenticity of the technical information supplied by the truckers' association. Threats to call a strike of truckers, to move trucking concerns out of the state, and to refuse to pay the new tax contributed further to a deterioration of the relationship between the interest group and the legislature. At any rate, the lobbyist responsible for the drive against the tax was dismissed.[26]

The Flow of Communication

The question of whom to contact is answered to some extent by the structure of the legislature and the role of the political party in determining legislative policy. Needless to say, lobbyists do not spend much time talking to legislators whom they regard as unimportant; they want to communicate with party leaders in states with strong party discipline and cohesion, and with the chairmen of standing committees in states with a tradition of committee dominance like that of Congress. In states where the parties and their satellite interest groups exist in a well defined system of interaction, the problem of access does not exist. Business groups can talk with Republicans and labor unions can talk with Democrats with confidence that their views will be taken seriously. It is in the legislatures without the control of a party organization that the job of locating and impressing the key decision-makers becomes acute. Jewell has noted that standing committees in state legislatures rarely exercise the independence typical of those of Congress. Most of the important bills are guided to a few committees dominated by a few legislators, usually party or faction leaders.[27] To establish and maintain access to these committees becomes a major goal of the state lobbyist and it is here that competition is keenest. In the frantic atmosphere of a legislature which meets only for a few months every other year, the rush of legislation makes the task of the lobbyist difficult. The simple question of time may become quite important. Consequently, the patient cultivation of good will can make the difference between talking to a legislator or waiting all day without so much as a glimpse: "The harassed member will give his ear to those advocates he knows and likes in preference to persons he knows only distantly."[28]

Limits on the Effectiveness of Techniques

This discussion of the techniques of the lobbyist should not obscure one fundamental point. The techniques of lobbying as practiced by a representative of an interest group are less important than the group itself in contributing to any given legislative outcome. In the words of the authors of *The Legislative System*, "... reasons connected with a group's claim to be represented or with its general political power appear ... to be more significant than reasons associated with its lobbying activities in the legislative arena itself."[29] General political power is, of course, difficult to define and is probably best understood as a subjective definition on the part of the individual legislator. Groups will rarely (if they are represented by experienced lobbyists) threaten a legislator with electoral defeat and they will rarely flaunt economic power openly. On the other hand, wealth or potential electoral strength are credited by legislators as being critical factors in the effectiveness of groups. One plausible explanation is that political power and representative quality in an organization are frequently perceived as being synonymous by legislators. For example, the Florida Dairy Products Association, an organization representing practically all the milk distributors in Florida, had a virtual monopoly on access to the house Public Health Committee which would never report out a bill opposed by the organization. Those who sought alterations in the laws governing the sale of milk in Florida did not go to the legislature or to one of its committees. They went first to the Florida Dairy Products Association. Why was this the case? Of course, the large milk distributors such as Sealtest, Borden's, and Foremost are economically powerful, but it is difficult to believe that the control of the legislative committee was due exclusively to wealth. The strength of the association was certainly not due to its voting strength. Rather, it is more likely that its influence was due to the willingness of the legislative committee to accord it, because of its representative quality, the role of legitimate spokesman for an economic interest.[30]

If we use the idea of the legislative acknowledgment of legitimacy as a source of influence, we can return once again to the idea of power as relative to the situation. An excellent illustration of this idea is provided by

Wilder Crane's study of bankers and the Wisconsin legislature. In this case, the issue was whether to allow banks to establish paying or receiving stations on parking lots within 1,000 feet of the bank. The Wisconsin Bankers Association opposed the bill and most of the larger Milwaukee banks hired their own lobbyists to voice their opposition. The bill was defeated and Crane's subsequent investigation led him to conclude that the activities of bankers formed the crucial factor in its defeat. Only 6 per cent of the legislators voted against what they believed to be the dominant pressure from bankers in their district. Further, many legislators took the initiative away from the lobbyists by contacting the bankers themselves to find out where they stood. This bill was perceived as being an issue on which bankers had a legitimate right to be heard. Other factors, such as rural-urban conflict or party loyalty, were not present in the situation and most of the conflict came from within the banking community. Since labor did not take a position, Democrats contacted bankers about as frequently as Republicans.[31] It can easily be seen that the power of the bankers was keyed to the particular situation and cannot be described as generalized power. When the legislature considers banking legislation it calls upon bankers. This simple explanation is most useful in understanding the play of groups upon the legislature. Given another set of circumstances—for example, the entrance of a competitive group of equal status into the competition, or another definition of the situation by the legislature—the position of the bankers may have been less prominent. Also, there are some issues on which no pressure group has very much to say. For example, questions of legislative reapportionment do not permit groups to play as significant a role as they might at other times.[32]

Conclusions

* * *

Considering the more immediate factors first, a basic conclusion is that lobbying skills are not as important as the legitimate claim of the group to represent a public that has a stake in the outcome of a given decision. Techniques can maximize the advantage gained from the according of legitimacy to a group, but cannot *create* this legitimacy. Hence, even in the short run, success or failure may be a function of forces beyond the control of the interest group.

In the long run, the strength of interest groups is governed by developments in other components of the system. We have described interest groups as part of a political and social system. A system consists of a set of interrelated parts. A change in one of the parts brings about a change in the others, or there is no system. Since we have concluded that the strength of interest groups varies with the strength of parties and the degree of industrialization and urbanization of a state, we can offer a prediction based upon changes in the other parts of the system. States are becoming more industrialized and urban. As the socio-political structure of the states changes, changes in the political structure will follow. Thus, political parties are becoming more competitive. The areas of one-party domination are becoming fewer. Consequently, we can say that it is probable that the independent influence of interest groups will *decline* in the future. As states without effective party organizations gradually develop party competition, part of the vacuum formerly filled by interest groups will be filled by political parties. In the South, where all states have strong interest groups, this process is underway. Pressure groups, like other systems of human endeavor, will continue to adjust to a change in environment.

NOTES

1. [Gabriel Almond and Sidney Verba, *The Civic Culture* (Princeton: Princeton University Press, 1963).] Voluntary association memberships in the other countries included in the study are: Great Britain, 47 per cent; Germany, 44 per cent; Italy, 29 per cent; Mexico, 25 per cent.
2. Robert E. Lane, *The Regulation of Businessmen* (New Haven: Yale University Press, 1954) pp. 53–54.
3. See Robert E. Lane, *Political Life* (New York: Free Press of Glencoe, 1959) pp. 76–79, for a summary of the evidence of this statement. See also Charles R. Wright and Herbert H. Hyman, "Voluntary Association Membership of American Adults: Evidence from National Sample Surveys," *American Sociological Review XXIII* (1958) 284–294. For a discussion of the implications of the data on organizational membership for group theory, see William C. Mitchell, "Interest Group Theory and 'Overlapping Memberships' " (Paper presented to the 1963 meeting of the American Political Science Association).
4. Diane Phillips, "Access to Governmental Machinery as It Is Perceived by Negro Leaders" (unpublished ms.) p. 6.
5. Walter Murphy, "The South Counterattacks: The Anti-NAACP Laws," *Western Political Quarterly XII* (1959) 372.
6. Kenneth N. Vines, "Southern State Supreme Courts and Race Relations," *Western Political Quarterly XVIII* (1965).
7. Robert Engler, *The Politics of Oil* (New York: Macmillan Co., 1961) pp. 381–384; House Select Committee on Lobbying Activities, *Hearings*, Housing Lobby, 81st Cong., 2d sess., 1950, pp. 681–682; Andrew Hacker, "Pressure Politics in Pennsylvania: The Truckers vs. the Railroads," in Alan F. Westin (ed.), *The Uses of Power* (New York: Harcourt, Brace & World, 1963) p. 355; Wayne Goodwin, "An Investigation of Pressure Group Activity of the Colorado Trucking Industry," M.A. thesis, University of Colorado, 1954, p. 46.
8. The following people were helpful in locating lobbying lists which were not immediately available: Ethan P. Allen, University of Kansas; James R. Bell, Sacramento State College; Alan L. Clem, University of South Dakota; Elmer E. Cornwell, Jr., Brown University; J. C. Davies, Bowdoin College; Wayne Francis, Syracuse University; Malcolm E. Jewell, University of Kentucky; Robert G. Scigliano, Michigan State University; R. D. Sloan, Jr., University of Nebraska.
9. For Ohio, California, Tennessee, and New Jersey, see John C. Wahlke, *et al.*, *The Legislative System* (New York: John Wiley and Sons, 1962) p. 315. The Michigan research is reported in Walter DeVries, *The Michigan Lobbyist: A Study in the Bases and Perceptions of Effectiveness*, Ph.D. dissertation, Michigan State University, 1960. The North Carolina findings are based on interviews with lobbyists rather than legislators. The interviews were conducted under the auspices of the Political Studies Program of the University of North Carolina. They were made available through the courtesy of Professor William J. Crotty, Department of Political Science, University of Georgia. The Political Studies Program is under the direction of Professor Donald R. Matthews.
10. E. E. Schattschneider, *The Semi-Sovereign People* (New York: Holt, Rinehart & Winston, 1960) p. 31. Lester Milbrath, *The Washington Lobbyists* (Chicago: Rand McNally & Co., 1963) pp. 30–31. Schattschneider examined the listings of *National Associations of the United States* while Milbrath interviewed a sample of lobbyists.
11. The classification of states according to strength of interest groups and legislative cohesion is taken from Belle Zeller (ed.), *American State Legislatures* (New York: Thomas Y. Crowell Co., 1954) pp. 190–191.

12. Nicholas A. Masters, Robert H. Salisbury, and Thomas H. Eliot, *State Politics and the Public Schools* (New York: Alfred A. Knopf, 1964) pp. 37–38.
13. DeVries, p. 36. See also John P. Hackett, "Lobbying in Rhode Island," *Providence Sunday Journal*, August 11, 1963.
14. DeVries, p. 63; North Carolina Political Studies Program; Thomas J. Moore, "An Analytical Study of Lobbying during the 1962 Session of the General Assembly of Virginia" (unpublished) p. 36. The last source was made available through the courtesy of Professor Spencer Albright of the University of Richmond.
15. Milbrath, p. 77.
16. Leon D. Epstein, *Politics in Wisconsin* (Madison: University of Wisconsin Press, 1958) p. 103. DeVries, p. 177. William C. Havard and Loren P. Beth, *The Politics of Misrepresentation* (Baton Rouge: Louisiana State University Press, 1962) pp. 235–236.
17. Hacker, p. 333.
18. Alexander Heard, *The Costs of Democracy* (Chapel Hill: University of North Carolina Press, 1960) p. 175.
19. Duane, Lockard, *New England State Politics* (Princeton: Princeton University Press, 1959) p. 163. See also Joseph LeVow Steinberg, "Labor in Massachusetts Politics: The Internal Organization of the C.I.O. and A.F.L. for Political Action, 1948–1955," Senior Honors thesis, Harvard University, 1956.
20. Joseph L. Bernd, *The Role of Campaign Funds in Georgia Primary Elections, 1936–1958* (Macon: The Georgia Journal, 1958) p. 3. Another good example of the explicit expectations which accompany contributions is the case of Ellis Arnall and an oil investor group. The investors agreed to provide strong backing for Arnall in his 1942 gubernatorial race against Eugene Talmadge because Talmadge failed to support statutory authorization for a pipeline project. See Bernd, pp. 4–5.
21. Bauer, de Sola Pool, and Dexter, pp. 422–433. See also Donald R. Matthews, *U.S. Senators and Their World* (Chapel Hill: University of North Carolina Press, 1960) pp. 177–178.
22. Frank Bonilla, "When is Petition 'Pressure'?" *Public Opinion Quarterly XX* (1956) 46–48.
23. J. Leiper Freeman, *The Political Process: Executive Bureau–Legislative Committee Relations* (Garden City, N.Y.: Doubleday and Co., 1955). On state administrative politics see the following: Harmon Zeigler, *The Florida Milk Commission Changes Minimum Prices* (New York: The Inter-University Case Program, 1963); Donald G. Balmer, *Interest Groups in Action: A Case Study of Oregon Milk Control, 1933–1954,* Ph.D. dissertation, University of Washington, 1956; William W. Boyer, "Policy-Making by Government Agencies," *Midwest Journal of Political Science IV* (1960) 267–288; James W. Fesler, "Independence of State Regulatory Agencies," *American Political Science Review XXXIV* (1940) 935–947.
24. Samuel C. Patterson, "The Role of The Lobbyist: The Case of Oklahoma," *Journal of Politics XXV* (1963) p. 83. See also Patterson, "The Role of the Labor Lobbyist" (Paper presented to the 1962 meeting of the American Political Science Association).
25. Milbrath, p. 215.
26. Goodwin, *loc. cit.*
27. Malcolm E. Jewell, *The State Legislature* (New York: Random House, 1962) p. 93.
28. Buchanan, p. 102.
29. Wahlke, *et al.*, p. 334.
30. Harmon Zeigler, *The Florida Miik Commission Changes Minimum Prices* reprinted in Edwin A. Bock (ed.), *State and Local Government: A Case Book* (University of Alabama Press, 1963) pp. 395–428.
31. Wilder Crane, Jr., "A Test of the Effectiveness of Interest Group Pressures on Legislators," *Southwestern Social Science Quarterly XLI* (1960) 335–340.
32. Malcolm E. Jewell (ed.), *The Politics of Reapportionment* (New York: Atherton Press, 1962) pp. 32–34. Gilbert Y. Steiner and Samuel P. Gove, *Legislative Politics in Illinois* (Urbana: University of Illinois Press, 1960) p. 116. See also Gordon Baker, *The Politics of Reapportionment in Washington State* (Eagleton Institute Cases in Practical Politics: New York: Holt, Rinehart & Winston, 1960).

17

Citizen Politics: The Behavior of the Electorate

FRED I. GREENSTEIN

In this selection from The American Party System and the American People, *Fred I. Greenstein analyzes the voting behavior of the American electorate. Different socioeconomic groups identify with different political parties, thus creating quite different constituencies to which the parties must be responsive. And there are sharp variations in voter turnout between groups. The choices made by individual voters are determined mainly by their attitudes toward issues, candidates, and parties. Stressing that party is the most important of these influences, Greenstein argues that there is a high correlation between voters' attitudes about the role of government and the party they support. Furthermore, voters overwhelmingly support the party that they believe will serve the policy interests of the sociological group (blue-collar workers, professionals and businessmen, farmers, and so forth) to which they belong. Greenstein's analysis shows that the choices of the much maligned American voter may be more intelligently grounded than is commonly credited, and that voting may consequently be a fairly effective linkage process.*

* * *

Who Supports Which Party in the United States?

By considering the electorate in terms of its group makeup, we add to our understanding of the citizen base of the American political system in . . . a way that begins to provide us with

From Fred I. Greenstein, *The American Party System and the American People,* Second Edition, © 1970, pp. 23–42. Reprinted by permission of Prentice-Hall, Inc., Englewood Cliffs, N.J.

preliminary insight into the functions served by the political parties. As is well known, each of the major parties tends to have a somewhat different clientele of supporters among the groups in society. When we look at group party-support patterns, it becomes clear that in spite of the paucity of political information and carefully considered opinions in the population, the citizen's vote *does* seem to relate his needs and interests to the actions of elected officials in a rational way.

For instance, let us analyze the congressional vote when, on July 20, 1967, the House of Representatives considered and rejected the "Rat Control and Extermination Act of 1967," which provided a $40 million program to help cities control rats. The House action was taken a week after serious ghetto rioting in Newark, New Jersey, and was widely criticized as an example of congressional insensitivity to the needs of the increasingly restive citizens of the urban slums. Although no single congressional roll-call can fully illustrate the differences between the American parties, this vote resembled many others in contemporary sessions of Congress. Of the 176 Congressmen who favored floor consideration of the bill, 154 were Democrats. Of the 207 Congressmen opposed to consideration of the bill, 148 were Republicans. Futhermore, 52 of the 59 opposing Democrats were from that party's southern wing.[1]

We can make a good bit of sense out of this House roll-call simply by examining patterns of group support for the parties in the electorate. Table 1 shows the voting behavior of American population groups in three elections which are instructive examples of the range of election outcomes that appear to be possible under contemporary political conditions: the very close 1948 "upset" election in which Democratic incumbent President Harry S. Truman defeated New York Governor Thomas E. Dewey (similarly close victories were achieved by Democrat John F. Kennedy in 1960 and by Republican Richard M. Nixon in 1968); the 1956 election in which Republican Dwight D. Eisenhower won by a substantial majority; and the 1964 election in which Democratic President Lyndon B. Johnson defeated his Republican adversary Barry Goldwater in a record landslide. Table 1, although it offers many illuminating insights into the distinctive characteristics of each of these elections, is perhaps most interesting for what it indicates about the *regularities* of party support. Using this table we can distinguish the group bases of each party—the hard-core groups that tend to support a party even in its lean years and the groups that the parties add to their coalitions in winning years.

For an indication of the Republican core, note the groups that gave a plurality of their support to the GOP not only in its winning year of 1956, but also in its losing year of 1948.[2] *Every* population group gave more support to the Democrats than to the Republicans in the Democratic avalanche of 1964, but even in that year the Republican core groups held more solidly for that party than did the rest of the population. These categories of consistent Republican voting are the professional and managerial occupations, the college-educated, and the residents of those areas that are so often thought to be the quintessence of Republicanism, America's towns and smaller cities. Also "carried" by the Republicans in both their winning year and the year when they were defeated by only a small margin are a pair of population groupings that

Table 1
The Voting of Major American Social Groups: Survey Research Center Findings in 1948, 1956, and 1964 Elections

	1948				1956				1964			
Group Characteristic	*Vote Rep.*	*Vote Dem.*	*Other*	*Not Voting*	*Vote Rep.*	*Vote Dem.*	*Other*	*Not Voting*	*Vote Rep.*	*Vote Dem.*	*Other*	*Not Voting*
Education												
Grade School	16%	35%	4%	45%	35%	24%	1%	40%	14%	54%	0%	32%
High School	29	34	4	33	41	34	1	26	22	54	—[a]	24
College	54	17	8	21	62	28	—	10	40	48	—	12
Occupation of head of family												
Professional and managerial	58	14	3	25	57	27	1	15	35	50	0	15
Other white-collar	38	38	5	19	48	30	1	21	30	54	0	16
Skilled and semiskilled	15	52	4	29	39	32	1	28	16	57	—	27
Unskilled	12	33	5	50	24	29	—	47	11	56	0	33
Farm operators	13	25	4	58	40	34	—	26	29	52	—	19
Trade union affiliation of head of family												
Member	13	55	5	27	36	39	2	23	12	68	0	20
Nonmember	32	26	4	38	46	25	1	28	28	47	0	25
Type of community												
Metropolitan areas	32	46	5	17	43	35	1	21	17	63	0	20
Towns and cities	30	28	5	37	46	25	1	28	28	50	—	22
Rural areas	12	25	4	59	38	29	1	32	23	52	—	25
Religion												
Protestant	28	25	5	42	44	25	1	30	29	47	—	24
Catholic	25	49	5	21	43	36	1	20	18	66	0	16
Race												
White	29	33	4	34	46	29	1	24	28	51	—	21
Negro	10	18	8	64	12	23	1	64	0	64	0	36

[a] Less than 0.5 per cent.
Source: National surveys conducted by the University of Michigan Survey Research Center. The 1948 and 1956 data are reported in Austin Ranney, *The Governing of Men* (New York: Holt, 1958), pp. 291–293. The 1964 data were furnished by the SRC.

are too large and amorphous to be treated as clienteles to which parties can appeal directly—Protestants and non-union members.

On the Democratic side we find three groups consistently providing a plurality of support for that party, even in the face of Eisenhower's 1956 triumph—unskilled workers, Negroes, and union members. Clearly, legislation designed to combat the consequences of urban decay and slums—like the Rat Control bill—is more likely to seem urgent to members of the Democratic core groups (especially the first two of them) than to those from the Republican-leaning strata of the population. Further evidence of this traditional Democratic coalition—which formed during the years of Franklin D. Roosevelt's New Deal—can be found by noting the additional groups picked up by the Democrats in 1948 and carried with special one-sidedness in 1964—Catholic (in many cases representatives of the ethnic groups which emigrated from Europe between the middle of the nineteenth century and World War I), residents of metropolitan areas, and the grade-school and high-school educated.

Although many Americans object to group analyses of political behavior—especially if they touch on social-class—group voting patterns have a long history in the United States. References to them can be found as far back as colonial times; in fact, the competition of social groups during the period of the Articles of Confederation was an important consideration in the minds of the Founding Fathers when the Constitution was framed.[3] Analysis of group voting is one of the standard tools of the working politician. . . . one of the most difficult tasks faced by an elected official is somehow to reach down to the grassroots and gain insight into his actual or potential sources of support. To do this effectively, it is necessary to find some means of categorizing the electorate, of pinpointing groups which may be responsive—or antagonistic—to different appeals. By necessity, therefore, working politicians become students of the sociology of the electorate. (As we shall see shortly, the politician's use of shorthand procedures for classifying and analyzing the public is paralleled by the voter's similar use of a number of elementary "simplifying" devices which make possible the act of political choice.)

Table 1, although it indicates the group bases of each party, also suggests that the popular objection to class interpretations of American politics has some merit. Neither party has exclusive "control" of any of the population groups. Each party is sufficiently heterogeneous to receive some support from all groups. And, from election to election, the winning party is capable of advancing within the groups which ordinarily provide the other party's supporters. Small-town voters were more Democratic in 1948—and, of course, in 1964—than in 1956; unskilled workers were more Republican in 1956 than in the two Democratic winning years.

There is a single important exception in Table 1 to the rule that no party monopolizes *all* of any group, applying to only one of the three elections there summarized. In 1964, the Survey Research Center interviewers did not encounter a single Negro Goldwater supporter. This is not to say that in the general population there were absolutely no black votes for the Republicans (although a few black precincts did in fact go 100 per cent for Johnson); it simply indicates that black voters were overwhelmingly pro-Democratic in that year.

The circumstances of the one-sided

Negro vote for Johnson in 1964 are instructive. Johnson had just actively presided over the passage of a major civil rights bill. Goldwater's vote against that bill had been widely publicized. In 1968 the Republican candidate also did very poorly among Negroes; the Survey Research Center found only 3 per cent black support for Nixon. One of Mr. Nixon's first political "signals" after assuming the Presidency (on the occasion of a ceremonial visit to the Washington black ghetto) was to let it be known that he hoped to establish his, and his party's, stock among Negroes. While it is easy to exaggerate the degree to which political leaders are moved by electoral calculations, it is worth noting that President Nixon's margin of victory had been so close that even a tiny splinter of the Negro vote was not to be scorned. Furthermore, the advantages of bidding for further support in this population group—strategically placed as it is in populous, closely competitive states—were obvious.[4]

Let us attempt to state the implications of voter sociology for democratic politics in a reasonably general fashion: *Under conditions of reasonably close balance between the parties, politicians who want to gain office have a substantial incentive to adopt what might be described as a "flexibly responsive" stance to the principal groups in the electorate.* They need to be sufficiently responsive to the central groups in their own clientele to hold the support of these groups and encourage them to turn out at the polls. At the same time, they have reason to be sufficiently flexible to win at least some votes from members of groups that supply the core constituents of the other party. Conditions of close party balance do not in fact obtain everywhere in the United States. . . . But in some political jurisdictions there *is* close party competition; in many others the minority party at least poses an occasional threat; and in the nation's most important jurisdiction, the presidential electorate arena, the party balance is sufficiently close to produce occasional outcomes like President Nixon's 1968 popular vote plurality of 0.68 of 1 per cent.

Such evenness of electoral balance encourages more than simple response to group demands; it encourages entrepreneurial efforts by politicians to anticipate (and shape) group desires even before they are fully crystallized. In such enterprising efforts by politicians to establish links with the diverse groups of the electorate we find a partial explanation of the seeming contradiction [that] . . . the American electorate appears to exercise considerable (though scarcely perfect) control over the political actions of its leaders—even though most members of the electorate appear to be strikingly low in political activity and attentiveness.

The Dynamics of Electoral Choice

The study of group voting takes us only part of the way to an understanding of electoral behavior. For a more thorough knowledge of the voter we must move to a level of analysis closer to his actual processes of choice—from voter sociology to voter psychology. What are the voter's motivations? What criteria guide his electoral choices?

George Price, a *New Yorker* cartoonist who specializes in acid commentary on man and his works, once memorably portrayed the decision-making of a totally criteria-less voter. Price sketched a voting booth, the curtains drawn. Spinning in the air over the booth was a flipped coin. . . . we might expect that for many citizens the act of voting is precisely as arbitrary as it was for Price's coin-flipping voter. But this clearly is not the case. If all voters were random in their choices none of the groups shown in Table 1 would vary far from a 50–50 split.

Once we establish the actual mental processes influencing voters' decisions, we can begin to explain the regularities in Table 1—the year-to-year consistencies in group voting patterns. It is unsatisfactory to attempt to explain such phenomena merely by observing the regularities in voting and advancing speculative inferences about what mental processes account for them. Apart from the logical circularity of inferring motivation from voting and then using the inferred motivations to explain the very same patterns of voting, it is also the case that voting statistics simply do not provide the information needed to accept or reject equally convincing speculative explanations of the same voting pattern. A group voting pattern may result, for example, from the conscious beliefs of group members that "party X has the interests of my group at heart," or the pattern may be a consequence of shared characteristics that lead the members of a group to vote together without conscious reference to their group membership. By directly observing voters' psychological orientations it becomes possible both to assess such competing explanations of voting regularities and to seek explanations for the fluctuations from election to election in group voting.

* * *

Although only a small fraction of the increasingly elaborate findings of voter psychologists can be touched on here, we may note some of the highlights. In general, the criteria which voters use to make their choices can be summarized under three headings, *issue orientation, candidate orientation,* and *party identification.*

Orientations Toward Issues and Electoral Choice

The voter who is highly issue-orientated gathers information and weighs the policy alternatives posed in a campaign, making his choice on the basis of his agreement or disagreement with the candidate's expressed views on the crucial problems of the day. This citizen doubtless fits best into the standard civics-book conception of how voters *should* make their choices. By and large, he will be an *"ideologue."* That is, he will have a reasonably self-conscious and overarching view of the good life, usually expressed in the form of a liberal or conservative philosophy.

Ideology provides a remarkably keen tool for assessing new political issues as they arise—the liberal or conservative ideologue will quite readily be able to decide where he stands on policies as diverse as parity price supports, offshore oil reserves, free trade—and possibly even free love. His need to be consistent will lead him to abandon a traditional party or a once-supported candidate if either should stray from the path of purity. But voting research suggests that ideologues are quite rare in the United States. Even people who simply *tend* to view the political world in liberal or conservative terms probably make up little more than a tenth of the electorate.

Nevertheless, issue orientation of a less thoroughgoing sort is sufficiently widespread to affect election outcomes significantly. In 1964, for example, 84 per cent of the voters who supported President Johnson in favoring Medicare also voted for Johnson, whereas he received the votes of only 37 per cent of Medicare's opponents, the remaining 63 per cent going for Senator Goldwater. Johnson received 86 per cent support from people agreeing with the statement "It's all right for the government to own some power plants"; but among those who believed that "electricity should be left to private business," there was about a 50–50 division in presidential vote. Also, Johnson received 80 to 90 per cent of the support of people who felt that the pace of civil rights advances was "about right" or "too slow," but his backing went down to 60 per cent among those who held that civil rights proponents were "pushing too fast."[5]

Findings of this sort serve to indicate that issue orientation does have an impact on voting. But at the same time, they underscore the imperfect nature of that impact: of the voters who were drawn to the kinds of views Senator Goldwater had been expressing on civil rights, more than half voted for President Johnson. There was a similar, if less substantial, vote for Johnson by people who took Goldwater's position on the other issues, as well as some Goldwater backing among those whose views matched the positions of President Johnson.

Orientations Toward Candidates and Electoral Choice

Few readers will be surprised to learn that the personal attractiveness (or unattractiveness) of a candidate may have a considerable effect on the behavior of voters—an effect which is independent of the policies espoused by the candidate. In recent decades the personal appeals of Presidents Roosevelt and Eisenhower were especially potent. The Eisenhower attraction has been carefully studied, both through examination of the many "trial-heat" presidential surveys conducted before Eisenhower stated a party affiliation or even avowed an interest in running for office, and by analysis of voter response during the two Eisenhower campaigns. "Liking Ike" seems to have resulted, to a remarkable degree, from perception of the General's personal attributes. The appeal of these qualities was especially great in a number of the population categories (e.g., high-school graduates) which ordinarily give strong support to the Democrats.[6]

In the Survey Research Center election studies, candidate orientation usually has been studied by tabulating the frequency of positive and negative references to the candidates in response to the questions "Is there anything about X that would make you want to vote *for* him?" and "Is there anything about X that would make you want to vote *against* him?" The SRC has consistently found that the higher a voter "scores" a candidate in answering these questions, the more likely the voter is to cast his ballot for that candidate.

It is easier to distinguish candidate orientation from issue orientation *analytically* than it is to disentangle these two classes of criteria in the "real world." To begin with, they influence each other; the voter who likes Ike will be predisposed to like what Ike likes; the voter who disagrees with Goldwater's military policy may generalize this into a criticism of Goldwater's alleged "personal impulsiveness." Second, some of the very statements that are made ostensibly about the merits and faults of candidates are in fact policy statements. For example, in 1960, one rather common reason given for liking Vice-

President Nixon was that "he will stop communism abroad," although those sympathetic to him were more likely to make vaguer and more personal observations about Nixon's political experience and his capacity to "handle world problems." An especially common reason given for *not* supporting Nixon's 1960 opponent, John F. Kennedy, was Kennedy's religion—a criterion which certainly illustrates the difficulty of distinguishing a candidate orientation from an issue orientation. In that year Kennedy received more accolades than Nixon in the category that is most often associated with candidate orientation—his "pleasing personality." In 1964, voters offered both of the criticisms of Senator Goldwater alluded to above, but a good number of them praised him for his "integrity." President Johnson, on the other hand, was approved of much more for his record of public service and for his experience than for such personal qualities as "integrity" (or "sincerity"); in many respects he seemed to profit mainly from the electorate's uneasiness both on personal and on issue grounds about his opponent.[7]

It is part of our political mythology that Americans generally "vote for the man." This notion is in need of a good bit of qualification. If electoral choices were made simply on the basis of candidates' personal characteristics, the voting of various groups would probably exhibit very little continuity from one election to the next—as manifested, for example, by the patterns of election returns from high- and low-income precincts, or from urban and rural sections of a state. But actually the continuities are impressive, except . . . when political parties are not a part of the electoral process. In 1896, for instance, the Democratic party virtually repudiated the conservative policies of its President, Grover Cleveland, and nominated William Jennings Bryan, a man who represented almost the antithesis of Cleveland. Nevertheless, a large proportion of Bryan's support came from precisely the same Democratic areas which had backed Cleveland four years earlier.[8] Evidently, virtually any candidate named by the Democrats would have been supported by these areas.

Identifications with Parties and Electoral Choice

The candidate- and issue-oriented voter to a considerable extent bases his vote on short-run factors tied to a specific election campaign. After all, not until summer of the presidential election year are candidates formally designated, even though occasionally one party's nominee (especially if he is an incumbent President) may be fairly well set in advance of the nominating conventions. Similarly, the debate over issues that has gone on during the 4 interelection years among the politically active members of the community notwithstanding, only when the nominees have been selected does it become clear *which* issues are to be emphasized by the candidates, and in what ways. Yet a remarkable proportion of voters regularly report that they make up their minds *before* the presidential nominating conventions, and many additional voters decide immediately after the conventions—that is, before the campaigns "officially" begin.[9]

On what basis are such election decisions made? For many citizens a vote is—in V. O. Key's words—a "standing decision" to support a particular political party. Party identification—the third criterion for electoral choice—is by far the strongest of the lot. If we were able to learn where a voter stood on just one of the three criteria—issues, candidates, and party—knowledge of the last would enable us to make the most accurate prediction of his vote. In any election some party identifiers—especially those whose loyalties are not strong—will vote for the opposing party, normally on the basis of issue or candidate preferences. But it is considerably more likely that a voter's choice on election day will be inconsistent with either of these preferences than it is that he will bolt his party.[10]

The term "party identification" refers to what might appear to be one of the simpler and more fragile phenomena—namely, the individual's subjective attachment to the Republicans or Democrats (or, in the case of an infinitesimal proportion of the electorate, to some other political party). This psychological orientation, which in fact proves to be durable and most influential, is measured in the University of Michigan voting studies simply by asking: "Generally speaking, do you usually consider yourself as a Republican, a Democrat, an independent, or what?"[11] The possession of a party identification should not be confused with a generalized belief that parties are a "good thing." While most Americans claim to prefer the present party system to various possible alternatives, by and large Americans do not think of the parties as performing the various positive functions many political scientists attribute to them.[12] There are many factors that might seem to discourage party identification in the United States in addition to the widespread negative attitudes toward partisanship and partisan conflict; for example, the American parties do not have formal membership procedures, and, as we have seen, many Americans are not deeply interested in politics. Nevertheless, *about 3 out of every 4 American adults identify with one or the other major political party.*

The somewhat complex set of findings in Table 2, which come from the SRC's study of the 1964 Johnson-Goldwater election, bear careful attention, in that they elegantly illustrate what is meant when we say party identification is the strongest determinant of voting. Table 2 shows the combined effect on voter's electoral choices of three variables: party identification, issue orientation, and the major regional factor that complicates American politics—the differences between the South and the rest of the nation.[13] The particular aspect of issue orientation dealt with is one that was far more sharply joined in 1964 than in most election years—that of welfare statism. The SRC respondents were asked whether they agreed that "the government in Washington should see to it that every person has a job and a good standard of living" (which was very much President Johnson's position), or whether "the government should just let each person get ahead on his own" (a central theme in Goldwater's political philosophy).

The reader should begin by looking at the . . . portion of the table which reports on the 378 northern Democrats in the SRC sample and shows the presidential votes of those who took a positive, negative, or neutral position on the question of whether the government should guarantee employment and a good standard of living. Starting from the entries furthest to the left in this portion of the table, we see that 36 per cent of the northern Democrats agreed with Johnson's "welfare state" position; of these, 35 per cent voted for Johnson and only 1 per cent for Goldwater. But moving

Table 2

The Great Impact of Party Identification: 1964 Presidential Vote by Party, Issue Position, and Region[a]

"In general, some people feel the government in Washington should see to it that every person has a good job and a good standard of living. Others think the government should just let each person get ahead on his own. Have you been interested enough in this to favor one side over the other?"

Vote	NORTH[a] Government should help	Depends, Don't know, No interest	Person get ahead on own		Totals	SOUTH[a] Government should help	Depends, Don't know, No interest	Person get ahead on own		Totals
	Northern Democrats (N=378)					Southern Democrats (N=204)				
Johnson	35%	26%	32%	=	93%	37%	22%	24%	=	83%
Goldwater	1	1	5	=	7	4	3	10	=	17
	36%	27%	37%	=	100%	41%	25%	34%	=	100%
	Northern Independents (N=181)					Southern Independents (N=41)				
Johnson	20%	23%	28%	=	71%	17%	7%	17%	=	41%
Goldwater	3	6	20	=	29	5	7	47	=	59
	23%	29%	48%	=	100%	22%	14%	64%	=	100%
	Northern Republicans (N=253)					Southern Republicans (N=53)				
Johnson	7%	8%	15%	=	30%	8%	0%	6%	=	14%
Goldwater	8	14	48	=	70	13	15	58	=	86
	15%	22%	63%	=	100%	21%	15%	64%	=	100%

[a] The South includes the eleven Confederate states, Oklahoma, Kentucky, West Virginia, and Maryland. The "North" includes all the remaining states except Alaska and Hawaii, which were not included in the sample.

Source: Angus Campbell, "Interpreting the Presidential Victory," *op. cit.*, p. 271.

to the right in the table, to the 37 per cent of northern Democrats who took the Goldwater position that the government should let a person "get ahead on his own," we find that this group of Democrats also went very strongly for Johnson: 32 to 5. Indeed, it is only when we move all the way across to the right-hand side of the upper-right portion of Table 2—the "anti-welfare state" southern Democrats—that we find any appreciable defection from a Democratic vote. Even this small group favored Johnson more than 2 to 1.[14]

Looking now at the bottom panels of the table, which report on Republican party identifiers, we find much the same story. In every instance—whether pro, con, or neutral concerning the "welfare state," whether in the North or the South—more Republican identifiers favored Goldwater than Johnson, even in the very heavily Democratic year of 1964. Sympathy with Johnson's views does lead to a high rate of defection. Among the handful of "pro-welfare state" northern Republicans (15 per cent of the northern GOP respondents) there is an almost even (8-to-7) split, and this is in striking contrast to the other Republican extreme—the "anti-welfare state" Southerners, who were overwhelmingly for Goldwater. But what the table delineates with special sharpness is the very strong tendency of voters to follow their party preferences. Given the number of party identifiers in the population, and the tendency of most of them to vote regularly for their party's nominee, it is not surprising that almost half of the voting public reports always having voted for the same party's candidates in presidential elections.[15]

In the United States an individual's identification is usually an evolutionary outcome of the largely inadvertent and unintended political learning that is absorbed from family, peer group, neighborhood, schools, and mass media, remarkably early in childhood. By the age of ten (fifth grade), more than one-half of all American children consider themselves little Republicans or Democrats, whereas at this age the capacities for abstraction that are necessary for issue orientation are largely unformed, and orientations toward candidates and political leaders in general are immature in the sense that children tend to be idealistically uncritical of those individuals in public life of whom they are aware.[16] Children do not invariably acquire the party preference held by their parents: a major national survey of high-school seniors and their parents reveals much more inter-generational political difference than would be suspected from the widespread reports by adults that they identify with the same party their parents supported. Nevertheless, among parents who are party identifiers there is a better than fifty-fifty chance that the child will hold the same party identification by the age of 17, at which time the incidence of party identification is still about 10 per cent lower than it is in the adult population. Of those children who do not share their parents' party loyalty, the greatest number have not formed party identifications. The relatively few children who actually "oppose" their parents in partisanship tend to balance each other out (4 per cent of the adolescent population appear to be Republican defectors from Democratic parents and 4 per cent to be Democrats from Republican backgrounds): by and large these are not principled departures or the consequences of adolescent rebellion, but rather the result of drift and what the report on this inquiry calls "lack of cue-

Table 3
Distribution of Party Identification: Findings from Seven National Surveys

Party Identification	*Oct. '52*	*Oct. '54*	*Oct. '56*	*Oct. '58*	*Oct. '60*	*Nov. '62*	*Oct. '64*	*Nov. '66*	*Oct. '68*
Strong Republican	13%	13%	15%	13%	14%	12%	11%	10%	9%
Weak Republican	14	14	14	16	13	16	13	15	14
Independent Republican	7	6	8	4	7	6	6	7	9
Independent	5	7	9	8	8	8	8	12	10
Independent Democrat	10	9	7	7	8	8	9	9	10
Weak Democrat	25	25	23	24	25	23	25	27	26
Strong Democrat	22	22	21	23	21	23	26	18	20
Apolitical, don't know	4	4	3	5	4	4	2	2	2
Total: (N)	100% (1614)	100% (1139)	100% (1772)	100% (1269)	100% (3021)	100% (1289)	100% (1571)	100% (1291)	100% (1558)

Source: John P. Robinson et al., *Measures of Political Attitudes* (Ann Arbor: Survey Research Center, Institute for Social Research, 1968), p. 496. Data for 1968 supplied by Survey Research Center.

giving and object saliency on the part of parents."[17]

Changes of party identification during adult life are rare; the few voters who change appear largely to be less-involved supporters of the parties; shifts out of and into each party evidently are of about the same magnitude, since the aggregate distribution of party identifications in the electorate as a whole is amazingly constant, setting the terms of partisan conflict for entire epochs. The present distribution appears to have formed in the early 1930's, when, under the stress of unemployment rates of as high as 25 per cent, the electorate shifted from a plurality of Republican identifiers to a Democratic plurality.[18] The precise contemporary pattern of party identification can be seen in Table 3, which summarizes statistics from nine national samplings conducted at two-year intervals, beginning with the Survey Research Center's first attempt to measure party identification. During that time a persistent three-quarters of the population was willing to express a party preference,[19] and the Democratic advantage—a 3-to-2 edge—was exceedingly consistent.

For the young child, party identification is so barren of supporting information that he may be able to say "I am a Republican" or "I am a Democrat" without even knowing the party of the incumbent President. One study found that it is not until seventh grade that even a few children differentiate between the parties in terms of what they stand for.[20] Some adults—but only a very few—manage to stay in this state of blissful ignorance. The meanings people learn to attribute to the parties are to a considerable degree consistent with the group voting regularities shown in Table 1. As Table 4 shows, the Democratic and Republican voting groups tend to see the appropriate party as "best" for their group.

When asked directly what they like about each party, most voters show an awareness—with varying degrees of sophistication—of the kinds of party differences we noted in the congressional voting on the Rat Control

Table 4
Voters' Views of Which Party Serves Their Group Best: January 1962

"As you feel today, which political party—the Democratic or Republican—do you think serves the interests of (business and professional people; white-collar workers; skilled workers; unskilled workers) best?" (Asked of members of each group.)

	Business and Professional	*White Collar*	*Skilled*	*Unskilled*
Democratic	22%	38%	59%	58%
Republican	51	23	13	12
No difference	13	25	16	13
No opinion	14	14	12	17
	100%	100%	100%	100%

Source: AIPO Releases, January 12, 14, and 17, 1962. Of the groups listed above, all but white-collar workers showed considerable stability over time in their perceptions of the parties, as revealed by Gallup polls during the decade from 1952 to 1962. The latter moved by slow stages to the division indicated above from the following 1952 division: Democratic, 28%; Republican, 44%; No difference, 12%; No opinion, 16%.

Bill of 1967. Only 12 per cent of the electorate present well-developed issue-based descriptions of the parties on a liberal–conservative basis, associating the Democrats with high levels of government spending and support of welfare policies, the Republicans with budget-cutting and lack of governmental regulation. But another 42 per cent differentiate the parties on a group basis linking the Democrats to "poor people" or "common folk" and the Republicans to business. Still another 24 per cent (making a total of 78 per cent of the electorate that has some way of distinguishing the parties from each other) are more fragmentary in their descriptions: most often, citizens in this last category advance what the SRC calls a "nature of the times" characterization of the parties. That is, they assert that the party tends to bring "good times" or "bad times" when it is in office. (The Democrats are seen as the party of prosperity by many voters—but also as the party of war. One of the greatest Republican assets, on the other hand, is the widespread belief that the GOP is the peace party.) Finally, even among the remaining 22 per cent of the electorate that does not advance explanations of how the parties differ from each other, party preferences sometimes are consistent with the typical preference of members of the voter's socio-economic group, simply because that group (via the family, peer-group, and neighborhood) provides the setting in which the preference is acquired.[21]

Party identifications seem to have such an impact on voting because they are, as it were, first on the scene. They typically form early in childhood and therefore can influence later learning about issues and candidates. Moreover, even among adults party identifications are temporally prior to issue and candidate orientations in that as new issues and candidates arise over the years they are perceived and judged by voters who already are possessed of party identifications. Thus party becomes not only a criterion for voting, but also a criterion for shaping the other criteria. Voters may describe their election choices in terms of their views of the issues and candidates and in doing so they may accurately portray their impressions of what has motivated them;

they are likely to fail to appreciate what often lies *behind* their issue and candidate preferences—party identifications and the group experiences which foster and reinforce partisanship.

The Political Significance of Party Identifications

Just as voting on the basis of issue orientation seems to many Americans to be closest to the ideal of citizen participation, so party voting seems to be furthest from that ideal. To many observers, party is a blind criterion for political choice—one which leads merely to "brand label" voting. Yet, if there is truth to the following observation of James Bryce, the pervasive influence of party on voting may not be unfortunate in terms of maintaining democracy and promoting political stability:

> To the great mass of mankind in all places public questions come in the third or fourth rank among the interests of life, and obtain less than a third or fourth of the leisure available for thinking. It is therefore rather sentiment than thought than the mass can contribute, a sentiment grounded on a few broad considerations and simple trains of reasoning; and the soundness and elevation of their sentiment will have more to do with their taking their stand on the side of justice, honour, and peace, than any reasoning they can apply to the sifting of the multifarious facts thrown before them, and to the drawing of the legitimate inferences therefrom.[22]

. . . Bryce's observation is to a considerable degree true—public evaluations of government and politics do tend to be confined to "broad considerations" and "simple trains of reasoning." That one of the most important of these considerations is party is probably of great consequence both for the political system and for the voter.

For the voter, party labels simplify the task of political choice to a remarkable degree. They enable him to respond to the infinitely complex events of the contemporary political world in terms of a few simple criteria. Without such criteria, detailed research on the issues of the day would be necessary to make any sort of meaningful electoral choice. Perhaps even more important than the usefulness of party labels as devices to simplify issue questions is their usefulness for sorting out candidates and public officials. Given the vast complexity of American government, with its divisions between executive and legislature and between the federal, state, and local levels, there is immense value to an instrument which enables the voter, in one burst of exertion, to evaluate all the public officials he must select. Without party labels choice becomes almost impossible, especially at the state and local levels, where dozens of public officials —down to the tax collector and the county sheriff—may be on the ballot.

Although party labels, and voting on the basis of party identifications, are great political simplifiers, they are not complete blinders. Where powerful issues and striking candidates have not emerged to become the focus of public attention, most of the electorate votes on a party basis. Under such circumstances, elections will be decided by the underlying distribution of party identifications in the population. By taking account of the 3-to-2 Democratic plurality among party identifiers—but also of the lower turnout rate of Democrats (due to the lower educational and occupational levels of their core supporters)—it has been estimated that there is a "natural" Democratic majority of about 53 per cent in any election which involves a ratification of party preferences.[23]

* * *

Party identifications do not wholly dominate voting, however. The actual vote fluctuates greatly around the "normal" expectation of 53 per cent Democratic, with Democrats receiving only 45 and 42 per cent of the vote in 1952 and 1956, respectively; a bare 50 per cent in 1960; and slightly under 43 per cent in the 1968 election, which also saw a vote of close to 14 per cent for a third-party candidate, former Alabama Governor George C. Wallace.

* * *

Thus, although the dead weight of voters' "standing decisions" has a major effect on election outcomes, the nation's electoral decision is also dependent on the voters' evaluations of current issues and candidates. Furthermore, the various elements in the equation of voting behavior—party identification, differential group turnout, response to current issues and candidates—are such as to make any single national election a matter of considerable uncertainty. This prevents the politicians from becoming complacent and stimulates the more politically interested and active members of the electorate to pay attention to the spectacle and drama of the campaign.

Although the outcomes of national elections are ordinarily in doubt, a result of the prevalence and stability of party identifications and of the link between party identifications and group voting differences is that many aspects of politics become predictable.[24] In the present era, Democrats—or at least northern Democrats—can be sure that their core support will come from citizens in the lower educational and blue-collar occupational levels. Republicans can generally be confident of their business, professional, college-educated, and small-town stalwarts.

Politicians in both parties are led to advance policies consistent with group interests by the need to maintain the backing of their core groups. This contributes to differentiation in the policies supported by leaders of both parties. At the same time, since each of the parties also needs—and seeks—support from the more or less uncommitted groups (such as white-collar workers and farmers) *and* from groups in the other party's coalition, party differences are not likely to be so sharp that changes in party control of government lead to radical reversals of governmental policy. The Republican return to office in 1953 after twenty years out of power, the Democratic return eight years later, and the Republican victory in 1968 did not lead to momentous shifts in the nation's domestic or international programs. The cross-cutting nature of party appeals also tends to keep political cleavage from reaching the point at which some elements of the public or leadership consider revolutions and *coups* preferable to elections because they do not care to risk the possibility that intolerable policies will be put into effect by their opponents.

NOTES

1. The bill was eventually passed as an amendment to the Partnership for Health Bill after public outcry against the original action. Other issues on which a conservative coalition of Republicans and southern Democrats voted against the Democratic President in 1967 were model cities, rent supplements, crime control, foreign aid,

budget cuts, and anti-poverty funding. See *Congressional Quarterly Weekly Report,* December 29, 1967, pp. 2649–2661. . .

2. A more detailed analysis would, of course, also deal with the overlap between categoric groups referred to earlier in this chapter—by determining, for example, whether college graduates at the lower occupational levels were as Republican in their voting as college graduates at the higher occupational levels. For an especially sophisticated analysis taking account of these factors see Angus Campbell et al., *The American Voter* (New York: Wiley, 1960), pp. 295–332.

3. The following episode from the period of the Articles of Confederation provides as good an example as any that politics based at least in part on social-class cleavages is not without precedent in America. The 1787 Massachusetts gubernatorial election, which followed Shays' Rebellion, has been described by historians as a struggle between a candidate representing the poor debtor classes, John Hancock, and a candidate of the state's more prosperous citizens, Governor James Bowdoin. (Bowdoin had ordered the suppression of the insurrection of the state's western farmers.)

Shortly after his defeat, Bowdoin's supporters reported the following breakdown of the vote in Boston:

	Bowdoin	*Hancock*
Physicians	19	2
Clergymen	2	0
Lawyers	17	3
Independent gentlemen	50	0
Merchants and traders	295	21
Printers	8	4
Tradesmen	328	279
Laborers, servants, etc.	5	466
	724	775

Not to be outdone, Hancock's forces reported their own analysis:

	Bowdoin	*Hancock*
Usurers	28	0
Speculators in public securities	576	0
Stockholders and bank directors	81	0
Persons under British influence	17	0
Merchants, tradesmen, and other "worthy" citizens	21	448
Friends of the Revolution	0	327
Wizards	1	0
	724	775

(*Massachusetts Centinel,* April 4 and 7, 1787, reprinted in Peter H. Odegard and E. Allen Helms, *American Politics* [New York: Harper, 1957], pp. 24, 25.)

4. That black voters had not suddenly become wholly wed to the Democrats was vividly illustrated in 1969 when Mayor John Lindsay of New York City, a Republican who had been defeated in his own party's primary election and who was running on the ticket of a New York third party (the Liberal Party), was re-elected with overwhelming support from black areas of the city. Lindsay was running against Democratic and Republican candidates who emphasized the kinds of "law and order" issues that came in the late 1960's to be seen by many voters as a surrogate for direction expression of racial antagonisms. The variability of voting among Negroes, a group low in the resources that normally make for effective political participation, provides a striking illustration of how group voting can serve to express citizens' needs and desires. For an essay arguing that, in general, voting studies tend to underestimate voter rationality, see V. O. Key, Jr., *The*

Responsible Electorate (Cambridge, Mass.: Harvard University Press, 1966). Also see the comments on Key's thesis, as well as the more general findings referred to in the text above, in the SRC report on the 1968 election: Philip E. Converse et al., "Continuity and Change in American Politics: Parties and Issues in the 1968 Election," *American Political Science Review,* Vol. 63 (December, 1969), pp. 1083–1105.

5. I am indebted to the University of Michigan Survey Research Center for providing these tabulations from its 1964 election study.
6. Herbert Hyman and Paul Sheatsley, "The Political Appeal of President Eisenhower," *Public Opinion Quarterly,* Vol. 17 (Winter, 1953–1954), pp. 443–460.
7. Angus Campbell, "Interpreting the Presidential Victory," in Milton C. Cummings, Jr., ed., *The National Election of 1964* (Washington, D.C.: The Brookings Institution, 1966), pp. 256–281.
8. Lee Benson, "Research Problems in American Historiography," in Mirra Komarovsky, ed., *Common Frontiers of the Social Sciences* (Glencoe, Ill.: The Free Press, 1957), pp. 162–163.
9. For example, in 1952, 35 per cent of a sample of voters report having decided before the conventions and another 39 per cent report having made up their minds at the time of the conventions. In 1960, 30 per cent report deciding before the conventions and another 30 per cent at the time of the conventions. In years when the renomination of the incumbent President is in the offing, even more voters may have made their choice before the conventions—57 per cent report having done so in 1956 and 40 per cent in 1964. These findings and much further useful presentation of Survey Research Center data are to be found in William H. Flanigan, *Political Behavior of the American Electorate* (Boston: Allyn and Bacon, 1968), p. 99 and passim.
10. Angus Campbell and Donald E. Stokes, "Partisan Attitudes and the Presidential Vote," in Eugene Burdick and Arthur J. Brodbeck, eds., *American Voting Behavior* (Glencoe, Ill.: The Free Press, 1959), pp. 356–357.
11. Following this the voter is asked if he considers himself either a strong Democrat or strong Republican. If he describes himself as an independent, he is asked if he "leans" toward one of the political parties.
12. The only systematic study in this area is Jack Dennis, "Support for the Party System by the Mass Public," *American Political Science Review,* Vol. 60 (September, 1966), pp. 600–615. The Dennis study is of a sample of Wisconsin citizens, and that state (because of its historical connections with Progressivism) may be somewhat more anti-party than the rest of the nation. Among Dennis' finding are that 54 per cent of Wisconsinites believe that "the parties do more to confuse the issues than to provide a clear choice on them," whereas only 20 per cent reject that assertion; 53 per cent agree with the statement "Our system of government would work a lot more efficiently if we could get rid of conflicts between parties altogether," and only 34 per cent disagree; 82 per cent choose voting for "the man regardless of his party label"; and so forth. That the Wisconsin findings are not wholly untypical of the rest of the nation is indicated by a 1968 Gallup national survey, which obtained virtually the identical distribution of attitudes on "voting for the man rather than his party." The national findings did, however, indicate that anti-partisanship does not extend itself to positive preferences for some other kind of party system: 67 per cent of the national population was "generally satisfied with the choice of parties we have now" and only 27 per cent favored a new party; and the 27 per cent was of such diverse backgrounds that it could not have readily been aggregated into a single third party. *Gallup Opinion Index,* October, 1968.
13. I follow the Survey Research Center's convenient, if geographically expansive usage, and refer to the non-South as "the North."
14. But this does clearly indicate what sociologists sometimes call a "structural effect." It has greater consequences for one's behavior to be a conservative Democrat in the South than elsewhere in the nation.
15. In a Survey Research Center 1966 poll, voters were asked, "Have you always voted for the same party or have you voted for different parties for President?" Of those respondents who had ever voted in a presidential election, 46 per cent reported that they had always voted for the same party; 5 per cent said they had "mostly" voted for the same party; and 49 per cent had voted for different parties. (Data supplied by the Survey Research Center.) Since Americans do not consider party voting a

positive virtue (see note 12), these statements probably underestimates the amount of straight party voting. A number of years earlier, preceding the exceptionally large number of Republican defections in the 1964 election, 50 per cent of a national sample reported always having voted for the same party's candidates. The contribution of party identifiers to this statistic was suggested by the fact that only 5 per cent of the self-styled independents reported such consistency. Angus Campbell et al., *The Voter Decides* (Evanston, Ill.: Row, Peterson, 1954), p. 18.

16. Robert D. Hess and Judith V. Torney, *The Development of Political Attitudes in Children* (Chicago: Aldine, 1967), esp. pp. 9 and 90. Fred I. Greenstein, *Children and Politics* (New Haven: Yale University Press, 1965), Chap. 4.
17. That is, the parties are not important to the parents and therefore the children are not exposed to enough partisan communication to learn what the parents' preferences are. M. Kent Jennings and Richard G. Niemi, "The Transmission of Political Values from Parent to Child," *American Political Science Review*, Vol. 62 (March, 1968), pp. 169–184.
18. The last previous realignments seem to have occurred in 1896, when a declining Republican plurality was substantially strengthened, and just after the Civil War, when the nation polarized into a Republican-dominated North and a Democratic South. On realignment see V. O. Key, Jr., "A Theory of Critical Elections," *Journal of Politics*, Vol. 17 (February, 1955), pp. 3–18, and Angus Campbell et al., *Elections and the Political Order* (New York: Wiley, 1966), Chap. 4.
19. With a slight slippage in the 1966 and 1968 findings (70 and 69 per cent respectively). This may be the beginning of a slow drift in the direction of the oft-proclaimed increasing "independence" of the electorate. It may also simply reflect temporary reactions to some of the political events of the 1960's, as well as the chance variability of plus or minus a few percentage points, which is the normal expectation from statistical sampling.
20. Greenstein, *Children and Politics*, p. 68.
21. Campbell et al., *The American Voter*, pp. 216–265; Campbell, "Interpreting the Presidential Victory," *op. cit.*, pp. 266–268; and the various issues of *Gallup Opinion Index*.
22. James Bryce, *The American Commonwealth*, 3rd ed. (New York: Macmillan, 1904), Vol. II, pp. 250–251.
23. Philip E. Converse et al., "Stability and Change in 1960: A Reinstating Election," *American Political Science Review*, Vol. 55 (June, 1961), pp. 269–280; Philip E. Converse, "The Concept of a Normal Vote," in Angus Campbell et al., *Elections and the Political Order*, pp. 9–39.
24. Recent research makes it clear that the rapid rise and fall in France of new political movements (many of them hostile to the democratic political order) is related to the weakness of voters' party ties. Less than 45 per cent of the French voters (in contrast to the 75 per cent of Americans) identify with parties. Philip Converse and Georges Dupeux, "Politicization of the Electorate in France and the United States," in Angus Campbell et al., *Elections and the Political Order*, pp. 269–291. Interestingly, research on the political orientations of French children complements the American research on this topic, showing that most French children have not formed a party preference by the age at which the typical American child has become a party identifier. See the discussion of "L'absence d'orientation partisane" in Charles Roig and Françoise Billon-Grand, *La Socialisation Politique des Enfants* (Paris: Armand Colin, 1968), pp. 92–102.

18

Classification of Presidential Elections

GERALD M. POMPER

In the following selection, Gerald M. Pomper reviews and revises the classification of presidential elections used by other political scientists, providing convenient categories to evaluate the impact of particular elections on the long-term political history of the nation. His study emphasizes the long periods of electoral stability in which one party dominates American politics. He classifies "maintaining elections" as those that preserve the partisan balance in the country; "deviating elections" as temporary defeats for the dominant party which do not end its long-term hold on a majority of the electorate; "realigning elections" as critical turning points at which the people reject the old majority party and in large numbers change their party allegiance to the former minority party; and "converting elections" as those in which a large number of voters change their party allegiance but leave the party's majority status unchanged.

By applying statistical techniques, Pomper describes both the periods of stability and change in the nation's political history and suggests the significance of the 1964 election in the flow of history. Concluding that 1964 was a converting election in which the Democratic majority was not dissipated, Pomper is at odds with Kevin Phillips' thesis that America is in a period of realignment from which a new Republican majority will emerge.

Pomper is Professor of Political Science at Rutgers University. He is the author of Nominating the President: The Politics of Convention Choice *(1963),* Elections in America *(1968), and numerous articles. An excellent discussion of the methodology of identifying realigning elections has been omitted from the following article only because it seemed inappropriate to the purpose of this book.*

* * *

Comparisons between elections can perhaps most usefully be focused on the enduring factors in American politics, the parties, and their sources of support. . . . Key pointed to "a category of elections . . . in which the decisive results of the voting reveal a sharp alteration of pre-existing cleavages within the electorate. Moreover, and perhaps this is the truly differentiating characteristic of this sort of election, the realignment made manifest in the voting in such elections seems to persist for several succeeding elections."[1]

Building on this concept, the authors of *The American Voter* suggested classifying elections into three categories: Maintaining, Deviating, and Realigning.[2] In the first two types of elections, there is no change in the basic patterns of party loyalty. In a Maintaining election, the "normal" majority party wins its expected victory; in Deviating cases, the minority party wins a short-lived tenure because of temporary factors, such as a popular candidate. In the Realigning election, much as in Key's critical election, the basis of voter cleavage is transformed.[3]

. . . As noted by Irish and Prothro,[4] the Michigan typology is based on two different dimensions which are not clearly distinguished. One of these dimensions is power, i.e. continuity or change in the party controlling the White House. The second dimension is electoral support, i.e. continuity or change in voter cleavages. Four combinations of these factors are possible, but the basic Michigan scheme includes but three.

The deficiency is due to ambiguous use of the Realigning category, applied to elections in which "the basic partisan commitments of a portion of the electorate change, and a new party balance is created."[5] This definition confuses two distinct effects: change in partisan commitments, and change in the party balance. Both results are evident when the former majority is displaced, as was the case in the period around the New Deal. It is also possible, however, that the reshuffling of voters can retain the same majority party, although it is now endorsed by a different electoral coalition. Partisan commitments change, while the party balance continues the same party as the majority.

The election of 1896, perhaps the classical critical contest, illustrates the problem. The Republican Party was the majority both before and after this watershed year, winning six of eight Presidential elections in each interval. The basis of its support changed significantly in 1896, even though the party balance was not affected. Given the ambiguities of their classification, the Michigan authors find it difficult to deal with this election. At one point, the contest is included in a series of Maintaining elections but, in the space of a few pages, it is discussed as Realigning.[6]

The classification represented in the diagram below separates the two aspects of elections. The horizontal axis is the power of the "normal" majority party. The vertical dimension is continuity or change in electoral cleavages.[7] The terms Maintaining and Deviating are used in a manner similar to that employed by the SRC. Realigning is reserved for elections in which a new majority party comes to power as the electorate substantially revises its loyalities. If the invention of a new label may be excused, Converting is offered as a term for elections in which the majority party retains its position, but there is considerable change in its voter base.

Reprinted from *Journal of Politics*, 29 (August 1967), 535–566, by permission of the publisher.

		Majority Party	
		Victory	*Defeat*
Electoral Cleavage	*Continuity*	"Maintaining"	"Deviating"
	Change	"Converting"	"Realigning"

Figure A
A Classification of Presidential Elections

The problem is one of assigning given elections to the proper category. The horizontal dimension presents no difficulties. There are only two possible outcomes, victory or defeat of the majority party, and these are historical facts. Complexities arise in regard to the vertical dimension, in knowing whether a particular result signifies electoral continuity or change. Since both are partially present in every contest, there can be no simple solution. Some reasonable means is needed to locate critical elections, by distinguishing a Maintaining from a Converting victory of the majority party, and discriminating between Deviating and Realigning triumphs of the minority. To deal with these questions, various statistical procedures are applied here to presidential state voting results. If these techniques are valid, they should be applicable to more extensive and detailed studies, using elections for other offices and using data more detailed than the state-wide results employed here.

* * *

A Survey of Presidential Elections

We . . . have five statistical measures available with which to classify elections. To summarize, an ideal Converting or Realigning election would be likely to show a low correlation to the immediately preceding election, to the average of four preceding elections and to the series of individual elections which both precede and follow it. The mean of state differences from the "normal" state votes and the standard deviation would tend to be high. In a Converting election, the majority party would retain its status; in a Realigning contest, the former minority would become dominant. In the model Maintaining or Deviating election, the opposite statistical results would be evident. The majority party would win the White House in the Maintaining case, but would be temporarily displaced in a Deviating contest. . . .

By all indications, the victory of Martin Van Buren in 1836 was a Converting election. There is a low correlation to the 1828 and 1832 votes, and sharp increases in the mean of state differences and the standard deviation. Historical evidence indicates a considerable change in the leadership of both parties, the center of gravity of the Democratic party moving away from the South toward the Middle Atlantic states. In the balloting, the basis of party support shifted strongly in the same direction. The Democrats gained 10 or more percentage points in the six New England states, and lost a similar proportion in 10 states, 7 of them slave areas. As McCormick writes of the South in particular, "Although the new alignments did not become firm in some states until after 1837, the basic outlines of what were to be the Democratic and Whig parties had been delineated."[8] By 1844, a period of electoral continuity is evident, relatively undisturbed by the plethora of third parties, the admission of new states, and the substitution of the Republicans as the principal opposition party in 1856.

The second break in electoral continuity resulted from the Civil War. The 1860 vote, in the face of the contemporary upheavals, bears a strong resemblance to the past. If we combine the Douglas and Breckinridge percentages, the total shows a correlation of .89 with the 1856 results. The party did not change its geographical support, in other words, but this support had divided into two opposing factions.

During the War and Reconstruction, changes in party loyalty became evident. The correlation coefficients tend to be low, whatever figure is used to represent the Democratic vote of 1860, and the same conclusion results if we compare later elections or use four-election averages. The net import of these statistics is a definite break in traditional bases of support. The Republican Party became dominant in the nation, making 1864 a Realigning election. The degree of Republican victory in this year is exaggerated by the absence of the Confederate states, but the signs of change are evident in the Northern states alone, as the Republicans assimilated former Whigs, Know-Nothings, Constitutional Unionists and even Democrats. The party bore the new name of Union in 1864, and "it is a much debated question," writes Dennis Brogan, whether it had much "in common with the agglomeration of 'Anti-Nebraska' men of 1854, or even with the Republican Party of 1856 or 1860."[9] Readjustments in the electorate continued for some time after 1864. Stability returned in 1876, when a considerable return to antebellum loyalties is evident.[10]

The post-Reconstruction system was not long-lived. Whatever measurement is used, a transformation of the political order is evident with the Populist movement of 1892 and the Bryan-McKinley presidential contest of 1896. The change is evident in both of these years, not only in 1896, which is often classified as the single crucial election of the period.[11] Transformations in party support were geographically widespread. Nineteen states changed more than 10 percentage points from their "normal" Democratic vote in 1896. Ten states showing Democratic losses were all located in the Northeast. Nine states with large Democratic gains were all in the South and West. Extensive changes also occurred within states and in the leadership of the parties, as evidenced in the splintering of each party and in the campaign appeals to social class.[12]

The Populist Party was a crucial element in the change. In 1892, Populist votes appear to have come largely from former Democrats; in 1896 many Populists then supported Bryan.[13] The decisive break of 1892–96, however, did not immediately result in the establishment of a new electoral coalition. Future years saw additional changes, and Republican dominance was sealed more firmly in 1900 than in the more-noticed first contest of McKinley and Bryan. Thus, 1896 was a great watershed, but it did not by itself fix the future contours of American politics.

Another change in the party system

took place, as is well-known, in the period 1924–36. The discontinuity is evident in the measures used here, but it is less dramatic than the revisions of earlier periods. Unlike previous changes, those associated with the time of the Depression and New Deal were not principally sectional in character. Realignment occurred in most states, along lines of social class, residence, and ethnicism.[14] Measurements of state-wide voting can capture some of these changes, but not in the fine detail of sample surveys.

To the extent that aggregate figures are useful, they point to 1924 as a transitional year, and the Progressive Party as a "halfway house" for those leaving their traditional party. Changes in this election are signified by the high mean of differences from "normal" state votes and high standard deviations. The Progressive vote probably came from former adherents of both major parties but there is some indication that it tended to be more from Republican loyalists.[15]

The transition to a Democratic majority extended over a number of elections, but the most critical appears to be 1928. The correlation coefficients for this election are the lowest for any 20th century contest before 1960. Al Smith lost 10 percentage points or more from the average Democratic vote in seven states, all of them Southern or Border. He gained strongly in seven other states, four of them urban and Catholic, the rest largely rural and Progressive. There was sufficient change in 1928 to constitute it a Realigning election, although the new Democratic majority did not become evident until 1932.[16] The new pattern was then continued for the next four contests.[17]

By the methods employed here, the four most recent presidential contests constitute another critical period, culminating in the 1964 Conversion of the dominant Democratic majority. Strains in the New Deal coalition were already evident in 1948, when the Dixiecrats temporarily split the party. There was no fundamental alteration in that year, but greater change is evident in 1952, when all of our measures indicate discontinuity from the past. Shifts toward the Republicans occurred in all social groups and in all parts of the nation. Geographical variations were evident within the general trend. Differences from the four-election averages were greatest in sixteen states, all in the South or Mountain regions.[18]

The 1964 election represents a radical break from past results, and the statistics strongly suggest that it was a Converting election, retaining the same Democratic party as the majority, but on a new basis of popular support. The correlation coefficients for this election are astoundingly low, given the generally moderate to high figures, even in the case of arbitrarily paired elections. The 1964 Democratic vote is positively related to that of only two years other than 1960, both involving third parties. Johnson's vote is related to Truman's vote alone in 1948 ($r=.65$), and to Douglas' vote alone in 1860 ($r=.40$). In all of these cases, the Democratic vote was highly sectional in character, and severely depressed in the South.

There was large variation from traditional Democratic levels in most states. Of course, the Democratic vote increased substantially, as Johnson gained the largest percentage of the total vote ever achieved by a Democrat. The important point is that the gains were not relatively equal in all states, as would tend to be the case if all areas were reacting only to the temporary oddities of Goldwaterism. The party vote decreased from its four-election average in the five Black Belt states of the South, while it increased over 18 percentage points in eleven states of the Northeast and five of the Midwest.

The final test of a critical election must remain persistence. In the final analysis, 1968 and 1972 will tell if the pattern of 1964 did constitute a true Converting election. It is possible that the great transfer of voters between the parties was only a temporary reaction to the admittedly unusual circumstances of the time. It would be quite remarkable if such were the case. The events of 1964 left their mark in the control of state legislatures by the Democrats, the passage of "great society" legislation, intensification of the civil rights movement, organizational changes and conflicts in both parties, and the memories of the voters. Republican strength in the South continued to grow in the 1966 elections. Democrats lost considerably last November, but these losses were not simply a return to pre-1964 voting patterns. Democrats were elected in areas of former party weakness, such as Maine and Iowa, but were defeated in traditional bastions such as Illinois and Minnesota. The future impact of "black power" and other developments is now uncertain, but clearly significant. Change, not simple continuity, seems evident.

* * *

. . . there is evidence that there has been change in party identifications as well. Belief in their immobility has been an unquestioned, but perhaps unjustified, article of faith. The evidence that party identification has been stable is largely based on aggregate figures from the surveys, not on analysis of individual behavior. We find, for example, that the proportion of Republicans from 1952 to 1964 always remained in the range of 24–32% of the total electorate.[19] It is therefore assumed that a given 24% of the voters were always Republicans, that 68% never identified with the G.O.P., and that only 8% ever changed their loyalties. This is a vital error, the same error which is often made in the analysis of aggregate voting data. In both cases, the net change between parties is assumed to be the total change.

* * *

. . . To measure stability in party identifications, it is necessary to examine the behavior of individuals, as the Michigan surveys have indeed done. Ideally, respondents to a previous survey should be reinterviewed, as in the 1960 study. Alternately, persons can be asked to recall past identifications, as was done in the 1956 and 1964 surveys.

The results are interesting. Of the 1956 sample, 18 percent indicated that they had changed their party loyalty at some time in the past. Compare this finding to that obtained upon reinterviewing in 1960. In the intervening four years, using the same categories as in 1956, 11 percent of the total group had changed their identifications. (Changes from Independent *to* either Democratic or Republican, or from strong to weak partisanship are not included, only changes *from* the two parties.) In other words, there was more than half as much change in party loyalty in the four-year period from 1956 to 1960 as in all of the years (perhaps twenty for the average respondent) in which the interviewees had been politically active before 1956.

In 1964 a different sample was interviewed, of which 22 percent indicated some change in party identification in the past. Changes at all elections, not only in the previous four years, are included here. It seems significant that, eight years further away from the realignments induced by the Depression and New Deal, stability in party loyalty had actually decreased in comparison to 1956.[20] Fuller analysis of these responses are necessary before any final conclusions are reached, but there does seem sufficient evidence, in the survey results themselves, to support a suspicion that party identification has not been unchanging, but rather that significant numbers of voters have been altering traditional loyalties.[21]

In recent elections, therefore, statistical analysis of state voting indicates considerable shifts in the geographical bases of party support. The extent of change found in sample surveys is less, but there are numerous clues in that material to justify a tentative belief that the 1964 Presidential contest was indeed a Converting election.

Conclusions

It is now possible to summarize our findings and to attempt a classification of presidential elections. It is obvious that categorization is not a simple matter, for elections are not always of one type or another. Some convenient simplifications are lacking. For example, change in voter loyalties does not fit any neat cyclical pattern, with change occurring after a fixed number of years.[22] There is a tendency, it is true, for critical elections to occur approximately once in every generation, but the length of time between these contests varies considerably. The party system which became stabilized in 1876 lasted only until 1888, while the different party system which began to appear in 1924 still greatly affects politics today. Electoral change is periodic, but the periods are irregular.

Difficulties also exist in isolating the turning points in these periods, the critical elections. It is apparent that electoral change is neither unheralded nor precipitate. In most cases, there is not a single critical election, sandwiched between two periods of great stability. Rather, there are times of unease preceding the most crucial year, and a period of assimilation after it. Typically, the critical election represents a break in electoral continuity, but does not result in the immediate establishment of a new and persistent voter coalition. Thus, the elections identified as critical here do not show high correlations with later ballots, but following contests do demonstrate this stability. Persistence comes after the critical election, and partially as a reaction to its upheavals.

* * *

Despite the many pitfalls, it may be suggestive to position elections within the categories offered in Figure A. The horizontal dimension clearly represents a nominal classification—the left and right sides are exclusive and exhaustive. The vertical dimension is more in the nature of a continuum—particular elections may not be clearly stable or critical, but may tend to an intermediate position. Therefore, the distinction between a Deviating and Realigning contest, or a Maintaining and Converting election, is somewhat subjective and arbitrary. The change which exists in every election is disguised, as is the existence of critical periods, rather than single crucial ballotings.

On the basis of the data developed here . . . the elections of 1836, 1896, and 1960–64 are classified as Converting, and those of 1864 and 1928–32 as Realigning. The victories of the first Harrison, Taylor, Lincoln in 1860, Cleveland, Wilson, and Eisenhower are considered Deviating, and the others are classified as Maintaining.[23] In order to isolate a small number of critical elections, fairly strict standards have been applied in making this classification. Modified standards would obviously change the designation of individual elections.

The most accurate characterization of our political history would be one of electoral eras. The life cycle of an electoral era typically begins with, or soon follows, a third-party election. The first such era began with the contest of 1836, in which the Democrats faced three opposition Whig candidates. The period came to an end in 1860 with the division of the Democratic party, and the nation. The next period ended with the emergence of the Populists in 1892, and the Republican dominance that began with the victories of McKinley began to disappear with the 1924 appearance of the LaFollette Progressives. The end of the New Deal era was heralded by the Democratic split of 1948.

Third parties arise when traditional loyalty seems inadequate to many voters. Often, the rise of third parties accompanies or precedes change in these loyalties sufficient to constitute a critical election. This election may continue the same party in power, on the basis of a realigned majority, or result in an overthrow of its power. The changes in the critical year itself, as we have seen, will not necessarily be permanent. Further readjustments are likely in succeeding contests.

After a time, stability is achieved. Stable periods tend to resemble earlier eras. Thus, after the adjustments which result from the critical election, correlations between paired elections of different periods are fairly high. For example, the correlation of the vote in 1876 and 1860 is .78; that in 1900 and 1888, .85; and that in 1932 and 1920, .80. Part of the process of readjustment is an apparent return by the voters in some states to past voting traditions. Even with the transformation of the electoral coalition, a strong degree of continuity is present.

The transition from one electoral era to another, resulting from considerable partisan movement by the voters, is an impressive manifestation of democratic control. Voters intervene decisively to change the political terms of reference. Party support and party programs become more congruent. Old policies and slogans are replaced by new, possibly more appropriate, appeals. The confusions of a waning order give way to the battle cries of an emergent party division. The Eisenhower elections did little to change the content of American politics from the dated themes of the New Deal. The Kennedy-Johnson administration, and the 1960–64 elections, did present new issues and conflicts. If 1964 did indeed constitute a Converting election, it may have provided the electoral foundation for the governmental resolution of long-standing issues.

NOTES

1. *Journal of Politics,* Vol. 17 (February, 1955), p. 4. The most notable works are those of the Survey Research Center, particularly Angus Campbell, *et al., The American Voter* (New York: Wiley, 1960) and *Elections and the Political Order* (New York: Wiley, 1966). A recent important work is V. O. Key, Jr., *The Responsible Electorate* (Cambridge: Harvard University Press, 1965).
2. *The American Voter,* pp. 531–538. The additional category, Reinstating, is best under-

stood as a sub-category of Maintaining. Cf. Philip Converse, *et al.*, "Stability and Change in 1960: A Reinstating Election," *American Political Science Review*, Vol. LV (June, 1961), pp. 269–280.

3. Further work by the same authors on this subject is included in chapters 4, 7 and 10 of *Elections and the Political Order*.
4. Marian Irish and James Prothro, *The Politics of American Democracy*, 3rd. ed. (Englewood Cliffs: Prentice-Hall, 1965), pp. 300–1.
5. *The American Voter*, p. 534; *Elections and the Political Order*, p. 74.
6. *The American Voter*, p. 531, places Republican victories from the Civil War to the 1920s in the Maintaining category, but on p. 536, the authors write of "the realignment accompanying the election of 1896." In *Elections and the Political Order*, p. 74, the existence of a Republican majority prior to 1896 seems to exclude this election as Realigning, but on p. 76, McKinley is grouped with Lincoln and Franklin Roosevelt as victors in Realigning contests.
7. The "normal" majority party must be assumed at some point in time from historical evidence. For example, we can make the rather safe assumption that the Democrats were the majority party after 1936. After the initial assumption, the election results will indicate when this majority status began and when other changes occurred. Emphasizing the success or failure of a given party, rather than change as such, avoids the need for a sub-category such as the SRC's Reinstating election. It also avoids the problems, inherent in Irish and Prothro's scheme, of dealing with two consecutive Deviating elections, as in 1912–16.
8. Cf. Richard P. McCormick, *The Second American Party System* (Chapel Hill: University of North Carolina Press, 1966), for an excellent account of the changes in the party system. The quotation is from p. 339.
9. *Politics in America* (New York: Harper and Row, 1954), p. 55. Cf. David Donald, *The Politics of Reconstruction* (Baton Rouge: Louisiana State University Press, 1965).
10. Correlation of the 1876 vote with that of Douglas in 1860 is −.19, but it is a high .78 with the combined Douglas and Breckinridge tallies.
11. Cf. MacRae and Meldrum, *op. cit.*, pp. 678–81. The change in 1892 did not come only in Western, silver states. Indeed, six of these "radical" states were excluded from the 1892 calculations here, since they were not in the Union in earlier elections.
12. Cf. Stanley L. Jones, *The Presidential Election of 1896* (Madison: University of Wisconsin Press, 1964).
13. A statistical indication of the source of Populist votes is the higher correlation of the 1892 vote with that of 1888 (.81) when Populist and Democratic votes are added together than when Democratic votes alone are considered (.71). The correlation of the combined 1892 vote with that of 1896 is .75, higher than the coefficient achieved if comparison is made to the Democratic vote alone, .54.
14. Cf. *The American Voter*, pp. 153–60; Samuel J. Eldersveld, "The Influence of Metropolitan Party Pluralities in Presidential Elections since 1920," *American Political Science Review*, Vol. XLIII (December, 1949), pp. 1189–1205; Samuel Lubell, *The Future of American Politics* (Garden City: Doubleday Anchor, 1956); Rutch C. Silva, *Rum, Religion and Votes* (University Park: Pennsylvania State University Press, 1962).
15. The coefficient for the Democratic vote alone in 1920 and 1924 is extremely high, .97. If the Progressive vote is added to the Democrats' for 1924, however, the correlation falls to .83.
16. Key, "A Theory of Critical Elections," and MacRae and Meldrum, also find 1928 to be critical. Smith gained votes in Massachusetts, Rhode Island, New York, Illinois, Wisconsin, Minnesota and North Dakota.
17. When change takes place over a number of years, classification of individual elections becomes awkward. It might be more precise to classify the 1928 election as a Converting or Deviating election to explain Hoover's victory, but it then becomes even more complicated to correctly appraise the 1932 results.
18. For indication of change within the South, cf. Donald S. Strong, "The Presidential Election in the South, 1952," *Journal of Politics*, Vol. 17 (August, 1955), pp. 343–89.
19. *Elections and the Political Order*, p. 13.
20. Percentages are calculated from the data in *The American Voter*, Table 7–2, p. 148; *Elections and the Political Order*, Table 12–2, p. 225; and Inter-University Consortium

for Political Research, *1964 Election Study Codebook*, Question 51, Deck 6, col. 11–12. SRC is now preparing further materials on this subject.

21. In a more recent publication, Angus Campbell writes, "The question which the 1964 vote raises is whether we are entering a period of party realignment. . . . There are indications in our survey data of a movement of this kind." However, this conclusion is also based on analysis of the distribution of party identifications, not on changes in these loyalties. Cf. "Interpreting the Presidential Victory," in Milton C. Cummings, Jr., *The National Election of 1964* (Washington: The Brookings Institution, 1966), esp. pp. 275–81.
22. Cyclical explanations are advanced in Louis Bean, *How to Predict Elections* (New York: Knopf, 1948).
23. Two tests define a critical election: correlation to the last election and to the four-election average of less than .70 (in the 19th century) or .80 (20th century); and a coefficient divided by the mean, with the result then multiplied by 100. Alternately, low correlation to the previous election alone, combined with a high mean (15 or greater) and high standard deviation (8 or greater), would definie a critical election.

19

Surge and Decline: A Study of Electoral Change

ANGUS CAMPBELL

In the excerpt that follows, Angus Campbell shows that in "high stimulus elections," those marked by heated controversy about candidates and issues, there is a high turnout of voters, including many with weak party identification. These voters and many partisans are influenced by the candidates and issues in casting their votes. However, in "low stimulus elections," such as off-year congressional elections, the outcome is decided mainly by the party identification of the electorate. One implication of his study, of course, is that the reliance by politicians and the press on the outcomes of low-stimulus congressional elections as indicators of presidential popularity may be badly misplaced. The continuing importance of the stable party identifications of most Americans is again underscored by Campbell's work.

*Campbell, Director of the Survey Research Center at the University of Michigan and Professor of Psychology and Sociology, is one of the world's leading experts on voting behavior. His numerous writings include coauthorship of important volumes on voting behavior and its impact on the political system—*The Voter Decides *(1954),* Group Differences in Attitudes and Votes *(1956),* The American Voter *(1960),* and Elections and the Political Order *(1966).*

The study of election statistics has revealed certain impressive regularities in the voting behavior of the American electorate. It has been pointed out by Key[1] that in presiden-

Reprinted from *Elections and the Political Order* by Angus Campbell (New York: Wiley, 1966), pp. 41–62, by permission of the publisher.

pointed out by Key[1] that in presidential elections since 1890 sharp upsurges in turnout have invariably been associated with a strong increase in the vote for one party, with little change in the vote for the other. Key also documents the well-known fact that since the development of the two-party system in 1860 the party which has won the Presidency has, with a single exception, always lost seats in the House of Representatives in the off-year election which followed.

The establishment of regularities of this kind through the use of aggregative data typically leaves unanswered the question as to why the regularity exists. We propose in this [essay] to demonstrate the manner in which survey data can be used to illuminate the nature of aggregative regularities and to present a theory of political motivation and electoral change which will comprehend both of these seemingly unrelated characteristics of the national vote.

The Nature of Electoral Change

Fluctuations in the turnout and partisanship of the vote in the national elections are primarily determined by short-term political forces which become important for the voter at election time. These forces move the turnout by adding stimulation to the underlying level of political interest of the electorate, and they move the partisanship of the vote from a baseline of "standing commitments" to one or the other of the two parties. In the following pages we will first review a series of propositions which elaborate this general statement and then turn to certain national surveys conducted by the Survey Research Center for relevant empirical evidence.

SHORT-TERM POLITICAL STIMULATION. Political stimulation in an election derives from several sources: the candidates, particularly those leading the ticket; the policy issues, foreign and domestic; and other circumstances of the moment. The intensity and character of this stimulation vary from one election to the next. There are occasions when none of these components of the world of politics seems important to the electorate, resulting in what we will refer to as a *low-stimulus* election. In other years dramatic issues or events may stir a great deal of interest; popular candidates may stimulate widespread enthusiasm. Such an election, in which the electorate feels the combined impact of these various pressures, we will speak of as a *high-stimulus* election.

The essential difference between a low-stimulus and a high-stimulus election lies in the importance the electorate attaches to the choice between the various party-candidate alternatives which it is offered. If the alternatives are generally seen as implying no important differences if one candidate or the other is elected, the stimulation to vote will be relatively weak. If the alternatives are seen as implying significantly different consequences, the stimulation to vote will be relatively high.[2] It may be assumed that in every election a certain air of excitement is created by the sheer noise level achieved by the mass media and the party apparatus. This type of direct stimulation undoubtedly has some impact that is independent of the particular alternatives which confront the voter and accounts for some of the variation in turnout from one election to another, but for the most part we may assume that the effectiveness of such stimulation varies in a dependent way with the significance the electorate attaches to the particular election decision at issue.

UNDERLYING POLITICAL INTEREST. The individual members of the electorate differ substantially in their level of concern with political matters, in their responsiveness to political stimulation, and in the salience of politics in their psychological environment. This level of interest is an enduring personal characteristic. We assume that it typically develops during the process of early socialization and, having reached its ultimate level, persists as a relatively stable attribute of the adult interest pattern. It is not simply a function of social or economic background; people of high and low interest are found at all levels of the electorate.

PARTY IDENTIFICATION. Political partisanship in the United States derives in large part from a basic psychological attachment to one of the two major political parties. . . . a large majority of the electorate identify with greater or less intensity as Republicans or Democrats, and this identification is impressively resistant to change. To the extent that they so identify, their political perceptions, attitudes, and acts are influenced in a partisan direction and tend to remain consistently partisan over time. Those members of the electorate without party attachment are free of this influence and are consequently less stable in their partisan positions from year to year.

TURNOUT. Differences in turnout from election to election are brought about by one or both of two causes, either by changes in the other-than-political circumstances which face the electorate on election day, or by variations in the level of political stimulation to which the electorate is subjected from one election to the next. The former factor can have only limited influence. We may assume that bad weather or an epidemic may affect the vote in restricted areas or even nationally on occasion, but such external considerations cannot reasonably be associated with the kind of fluctuation which we know to exist. It is, for example, quite untenable to suppose that the weather or the health of the electorate is always worse in off-year elections than in presidential years. The explanation of these and other fluctuations must lie in the changing motivation of the electorate.

A large proportion of the turnout in any national election consists of people whose level of political interest is sufficiently high to take them to the polls in all national elections, even those in which the level of political stimulation is relatively weak. These "core voters" are joined in a high-stimulus election by additional "peripheral voters," whose level of political interest is lower but whose motivation to vote has been sufficiently increased by the stimulation of the election situation to carry them to the polls. There remains a sizable fraction of the electorate which does not vote even in a high-stimulus election; some of these people are prevented from voting by poor health, failure to meet eligibility requirements, or conflicts of one sort or another. Others do not vote because their level of political interest is so low that no amount of political stimulation will motivate them to vote.

The turnout in any specific election is largely a question of how many of the less interested, less responsive people are sufficiently stimulated by the political circumstances of the moment to make the effort to vote.

An election in which a stirring issue or an attractive candidate makes the party-candidate choice seem unusually important may bring these peripheral voters to the polls in large numbers. In an election of lesser apparent importance and weaker total stimulation the participation of these peripheral voters declines, leaving the electoral decision largely to the high-interest core voters. A low-stimulus election is thus not simply a smaller version of a high-stimulus election; in the extent to which the peripheral voters differ from the core voters, the two elections may have quite different characteristics.

PARTISANSHIP. The partisan division of the vote in any particular election is the consequence of the summation of partisan forces on the voters. In every election there are superimposed on the underlying orientations the electorate has toward the two parties (party identifications) the contemporary elements of politics which tend to swing voters one way or the other. In a particular election these elements may be relatively weak and have little impact on the electorate. Despite the best efforts of the party publicists, the candidates may have little appeal, and the issues little apparent relevance to the basic interests of the electorate. In such a case the turnout would of course be low, and the division of the vote would approximate the underlying distribution of party identifications. In the absence of strong pressures associated with persons, issues, or circumstances prominent at the moment, party loyalty holds the adherents of the two parties to their respective tickets, and the independent voters divide their vote between the two. In other words, a low-stimulus election tends to follow party lines.

Contemporary events and personalities occasionally assume great importance for the public and exert a strong influence on the vote. The general increase in the motivation to vote in such an election will, as we have said, bring a surge of peripheral voters to the polls. It will also swing the partisan division of the vote toward the party which happens to be advantaged by the circumstances of the moment. It is very unlikely that a political situation which heightens the public's sense of the importance of choosing one party-candidate alternative or another will favor these alternatives equally. The circumstances which create a high-stimulus election may be expected to create simultaneously a strong differential in the attractiveness of the vote alternatives. Increases in turnout will consequently be accompanied by shifts in the partisanship of the vote.[3]

The partisan surge which characterizes a high-stimulus election consists of two components: (1) those peripheral voters for whom the stimulus of highly differentiated party-candidate alternatives provides the needed impetus to move them to the polls and who, depending on the strength of their party identification, are swung toward the ticket of the advantaged party, and (2) those core voters who are drawn from their normal position as Independents or identifiers with the disadvantaged party to the candidate of the party which is advantaged by the political circumstances of the moment. The number of voters who consistently turn out in presidential elections in support of their party's candidates is now sufficiently close to an equal balance between the two parties so that the movement of these two components of the partisan surge will almost certainly determine the outcome of any high-stimulus election.

If a high-stimulus election is followed by a low-stimulus election, the reduction in the general level of political stimulation will result in a decline in the total vote. There will also be a decline in the proportion of the vote received by the party advantaged by the political circumstances of the preceding high-stimulus year. This decline also consists of two components: (1) the dropout of those peripheral voters who had gone to the polls in the previous election, and who had given the advantaged party a majority of their votes, and (2) the return to their usual voting position of those core voters who had moved in the surge year from their normal position to support the advantaged party, the identifiers with the disadvantaged party moving back to the support of that party, and the Independents back to a position between the two parties. Those voters whose normal identification was with the advantaged party would, of course, support it in the high-stimulus election; of these, the less-involved peripheral voters would drop out in the subsequent low-stimulus election, and the core voters would continue to support their party.

THE CYCLE OF SURGE AND DECLINE. In the normal flow of events in American politics, fluctuations in turnout and partisanship follow the "natural" cycle which we have described. The long-run stability of the system depends on the underlying division of party loyalties. Short-term circumstances may swing large numbers of voters away from their usual partisanship or from a position of independence, but when the smoke has settled these people strongly tend to return to their former position, thus restoring the party balance to its former level. Only in the most extraordinary national crises has this cycle been broken, and a new balance of party strength created. Such elections, in which a basic realignment of party loyalties occurs, are rare in American electoral history. For the most part, fluctuations in the vote reflect the passing impact of contemporary events, and the subsequent decline toward the underlying division of partisanship after these events have lost their salience.

The Evidence

The study of individual change requires data from the same persons at different points in time. Such information can best be provided by a panel study covering the period in which the change took place. It can be obtained somewhat less satisfactorily by asking survey respondents to recall their attitudes or behavior at earlier points in time. Two surveys conducted by the Survey Research Center make available data regarding voting patterns which are relevant to our present concerns. The first of these was a study of the presidential election of 1952, in which a national sample of adults living in private households were asked to report their vote for President in 1952 and to recall their vote for President in 1948.[4] The second was a panel study of a similar national sample, interviewed first in 1956 and again in 1958, being asked on each occasion to report their vote in that year.

1948–1956: A Case of Electoral Surge

The presidential election of 1952 presents a unique opportunity for the study of electoral surge. The election of 1948 had seen one of the lowest turnouts of presidential voters in recent history with only 48.4 million voters. The proportion of eligible voters who turned out lagged far behind the record of peacetime presidential elections prior to the Second World War. In 1952, 61.6 million voters went to the polls, an increase of more than 25 percent above the total of the previous election. This great surge in turnout was associated, of course, with a tremendous increase in the vote received by the Republican presidential nominee, which far exceeded the increment in the Democratic vote.

THE INCREASE IN TURNOUT. The movement in the turnout of the vote from 1948 to 1952 was made up of four components. Of our sample interviewed in November 1952, 58 percent said they had voted in both 1948 and 1952; 6 percent said they had voted in 1948 but not in 1952; 15 percent said they had voted in 1952 but not in 1948; and 21 percent said they had not voted in either election.[5] When we examine the characteristics of these four segments of the electorate we find that the core voters who had voted in both elections and the peripheral voters who had voted in one election but not the other differed very little in respect to those variables which are usually found to be associated with turnout. In education, income, occupation, and sex the two kinds of voter were very similar, although they differed significantly from the persistent nonvoters in all these respects. The characteristic which does discriminate sharply between the core voters and the peripheral voters is their level of political interest.

Several indicators of political interest are available to us from our interviews; the one which is freest from the impact of the specific election we are studying is the respondent's report on his previous voting history. In the 1952 interview our respondents were asked, "In the elections for President since you have been old enough to vote, would you say that you have voted in all of them, most of them, some of them, or none of them?" We assume that people who vote in all elections, regardless of the highs and lows of political stimulation, must be relatively responsive to political matters, and those who have never voted must be relatively lacking in political interest.

We can also use the respondent's direct statement about his degree of interest in the current campaign. In October 1952 we asked the question, "Some people don't pay much attention to the political campaigns. How about you, would you say that you have been very much interested, somewhat interested, or not much interested in following the political campaigns so far this year?" This question does not give us as clean a measure of long-term interest in political activities as we would like, since it related to the 1952 campaign specifically. The effect of this specific reference almost certainly reduces the range of response we would expect from a more general question, because the impact of current political activities might be expected to raise the interest level of those at the bottom of the range more than those near the top. In other words, the differences we find between the different types of voter would probably be larger if this question were more general in its reference.

When we now compare the levels of interest shown by the four components of the 1956 electorate, we find a very consistent pattern. That part of the electorate which reported voting in both the 1948 and 1952 elections was far more responsive to the stimuli of politics than any of the other groups. This is especially impressive in the report of previous voting: 90 percent of those who voted in both elections said they had voted in all or most previous presidential elections, as compared to 66 percent of those who voted in 1948 but not in 1952, 23 percent of those who voted in 1952 but not 1948, and 6 percent of those who did not vote in either election. The interest of the 1948–1952 voters in the campaign then current, as expressed by their subjective report, was also higher than that of any of the other groups: 48 percent of those who voted in both elections said they were "very much interested in the campaign," as compared to 26 percent of those who voted in 1948 but not 1952, 31 percent of those who voted in 1952 but not 1948, and 14 percent of those who did not vote in either election.

On both these measures those people who were responsible for the major part of the difference in turnout between the two elections (the 1952 voters who had not voted in 1948) gave substantially less evidence of high political interest. Although they appear to come from the same strata of society, as the more persistent voters, they apparently are drawn from the less concerned and less attentive levels of the stratum to which they belong.

It is clear that the persistent nonvoters, those people whom even the high stimulation of the 1952 campaign could not move to the polls, are not prevented from voting by adventitious considerations of health or weather. For the most part, these people do not vote because their sensitivity to the world of politics is so low that political stimulation does not reach them. As one might expect, they come largely from the low-income and low-education groups. Two-thirds of them are women.

THE SWING IN PARTISANSHIP. The 1948 election may be taken as the prototype of a low-stimulus presidential election. In the absence of candidates, issues, or circumstances that might have aroused strong public interest in the choice of alternatives, the turnout was low, and the partisanship of the vote was determined largely by the established party loyalties of the voters. Of the total Democratic vote for President in 1948,[6] 74 percent came from Democratic Party identifiers, 20 percent from Independents, and 6 percent from Republican Party identifiers. Of the total Republican vote for President in 1948, 71 percent came from Republican Party identifiers, 23 percent from Independents, and 6 percent from Democratic Party identifiers.

The high-stimulus election in 1952 brought to the polls millions of voters who had not voted in 1948 and shifted the partisanship of the vote of a sizable proportion of those who had. We see in Table 1 that the two parties received almost equal support among those people who voted for the same party in both years. Although these consistent core voters made up well over half the voters in 1952, the decisive margin for Mr. Eisenhower was provided by two other groups, those who switched from a 1948 vote for Mr. Truman and those who had failed to vote in 1948. The former group appears to have been considerably larger than the latter, although it is likely that the overstatement of the 1948 vote to which we have referred makes our estimate of the number of new voters in 1952 somewhat lower than it actually was. The Democratic Party also appears to have lost a little

Table 1
Presidential Votes in 1948 and 1952 as Reported by Survey Research Center Sample in 1952 (N=1614)

Vote for President in 1948	*Vote for President in 1952*	*Percent*
Democratic	Democratic	23
Republican	Republican	24
Democratic	Republican	11
Republican	Democratic	1
Democratic	Did not vote	4
Republican	Did not vote	2
Did not vote	Democratic	6
Did not vote	Republican	8
Did not vote	Did not vote	21
		100

ground among the small proportion of 1948 voters who did not vote in 1952, but this figure is subject to the same overstatement, and we may assume that this component of the total shift of votes between 1948 and 1952 was not very significant.

We can illuminate the character of these movements considerably if we examine the degree and quality of the customary party identifications of the people in these groups of 1952 voters (Table 2). The greatest polarity of party attachment is found among those voters who supported the presidential candidates of the same party in both elections. The fact that the consistent Democratic vote is composed so heavily of Democratic Party identifiers conforms to our supposition regarding the high-stimulus surge. When the political tide is running against a party, it reduces that party to its loyal partisans; the party will lose most of the support it may have received at other times from Independent voters or from defectors from the other party. The advantaged party benefits from this partisan movement, particularly among the Independents and weak adherents of the opposite party who are not strongly held by feelings of party loyalty. This gain is apparent in the Democratic-Republican column of Table 2.

The party affiliations of the two groups of 1952 voters who had failed to vote in 1948 provide additional evidence of the interaction of party identification and the partisan pressures of a surge year. Those previous nonvoters who came to the support of Stevenson in 1952 were largely Democratic Party identifiers. The high stimulation of the 1952 campaign brought them out of their nonvoting status, but their party loyalty was sufficiently strong to resist the pro-Republican drift of the times. In contrast, the nonvoters who were inspired to vote for Eisenhower came from all party groups. Some of them were indifferent Republicans who had sat out the Dewey campaign; a large number were Independents; there was a sizable number of Democrats, although few of them called themselves "strong" Democrats. None of these people had voted in 1948, but they

Table 2
Party Identification of Components of the 1948 and 1952 Vote for President (in percent)

Party Identification	*1948:* / *1952:*	*Democratic* / *Democratic* (*N*=372)	*Republican* / *Republican* (*N*=385)	*Democratic* / *Republican* (*N*=172)	*Republican* / *Democratic* (*N*=17)	*Did Not Vote* / *Democratic* (*N*=105)	*Did Not Vote* / *Republican* (*N*=130)
Strong Democrat		48	*	19	(4)	36	5
Weak Democrat		33	4	36	(2)	43	23
Independent		17	23	31	(7)	20	29
Weak Republican		2	28	11	(3)	1	26
Strong Republican		*	45	3	(1)	†	15
Apolitical, other		*	*	†	†	†	2
		100	100	100	†	100	100

* Less than one-half of 1 percent.
† No cases.
Note. Figures in parentheses are number of persons rather than percent; number of cases is too small to support reliable estimates.

contributed significantly to the increase in turnout and the Republican surge in 1952.

The fact that only 1 percent of the electorate in 1952 moved against the Republican tide, from a Republican to a Democratic vote, provides an effective illustration of the nature of a partisan surge. Although the high level of stimulation in 1952 brought some peripheral Democrats to the defense of their party, there was no countervailing Democratic force beyond that of party loyalty to offset the powerful impact of candidates and issues which advantaged the Republican Party. This we believe to be the basic characteristic of a surge election; the conditions which give rise to a sharp increase in turnout invariably greatly favor one party over the other. The political circumstances which create the surge in turnout also produce the shift in partisanship.

1956–1958: A Case of Electoral Decline

One of the most dependable regularities of American politics is the vote decline in off-year congressional elections. The turnout in the off-year elections is invariably smaller than in the presidential elections which they follow, usually by a margin of over 25 percent of the presidential vote. Almost as dependable is the loss which the party which has won the White House in the presidential year suffers in the midyear election that follows. As we have observed, in every off-year election since the Civil War, with the exception of 1934, the presidential party has lost seats in the House of Representatives.

The vote for President in 1956 totaled 62 million; the vote for congressional candidates in 1958 was 45.7 million, a decline of slightly less than 25 percent from the vote cast two years earlier. President Eisenhower received nearly 58 percent of the popular vote in 1956. The Republican candidates for Congress in 1958 received 44 percent of the two-party vote, and the Republican Party lost 47 of the 200 seats it had held in the House of Representatives.

THE DECLINE IN TURNOUT. The off-year election of 1958 was a low-stimulus election. Within the framework of the American electoral system the off-year congressional contests must always present the electorate with a less intensely charged situation than the presidential elections which precede and follow. The election of a Congressman cannot have the importance to the average citizen that the election of a President has; the expected consequences of the election of one or the other congressional candidate cannot seem as great. Associated with this lesser significance is the fact that party activities are less intense, and the mass media somewhat quieter in off-year elections. The impact of the typical congressional election is considerably more muted than even the least exciting presidential election.

When we examine the components of the electorate in 1956 and 1958 we find the counterparts of the four segments of the electorate we identified in our 1952 survey. Of our panel interviewed in both 1956 and 1958, 56 percent said they had voted in both elections, 19 percent said they had voted in 1956 but not in 1958, 4 percent said they had voted in 1958 but not in 1956, and 21 percent said they had not voted in either election.[7]

Comparison of the core voters in 1956–1958 with those who voted only in 1956 reveals differences similar to those we observed in the core and peripheral components of the 1952 electorate. Those 1956 voters who dropped out in 1958 had somewhat more distinctive socioeconomic characteristics than the 1948 nonvoters who went to the polls in 1952. As compared to those who voted in both 1956 and 1958 they were of a somewhat lower status in occupation, income, and education. They were also younger. But these differences were small and very much less impressive than the differences in political interest which distinguished these groups: 92 percent of those who voted in both elections said they had voted in all or most previous presidential elections, as compared to 60 percent of those who voted in 1956 but not in 1958, 59 percent of those who voted in 1958 but not in 1956, and 17 percent of those who did not vote in either election.[8]

Involvement in the 1956 campaign, as expressed in the interviews in that year, was also much lower among those parts of the electorate which did note vote in either or both elections: 40 percent of those who voted in both elections said they were "very much interested" in the campaign, as compared to 21 percent of those who voted in 1956 but not in 1958, 33 percent of those who voted in 1958 but not in 1956, and 12 percent of those who did not vote in either election.

Thus it appears that the people who accounted for the decline in the vote in 1958 were politically similar to the people who increased the vote in 1952. They were in-and-out voters, with a very irregular history of previous voting performance and a low level of sensitivity to political affairs. They appear to form a rather inert reservoir of voters, available for service under conditions of high stimulation but not highly motivated by an intrinsic interest in politics. Activated to vote by the highly charged circumstances of the 1956 campaign, they were not sufficiently moved to go to the polls by the lesser impact of the congressional election. Without them, the core voters who had made up 75 percent of the vote in 1956 contributed virtually the entire vote (93 percent) in 1958.

THE SWING IN PARTISANSHIP. Like the presidential election of 1948, the congressional election of 1958 attracted a relatively low turnout. Without strong national candidates, pressing issues or circumstances to move the electorate, the voting decision was determined largely by the standing party loyalties of those voters sufficiently concerned with politics to go to the polls. The sources of the vote which the two parties commanded in 1958 resemble those from which they drew their vote in 1948, although there was apparently more crossing of party lines in the latter election than there had been in the former.[9] Of the total vote for Democratic Congressmen in 1958, 69 percent came from Democratic Party identifiers, 20 percent came from Independents, and 11 percent came from Republican Party identifiers. Of the total vote for Republican Congressmen in 1958, 65 percent came from Republican Party identifiers, 26 percent came from Independents, and 9 percent came from Democratic Party identifiers.

The substantial shift from the comfortable majority which Mr. Eisenhower received in 1956 to the Republican congressional defeat in 1958 was almost wholly accounted for by two segments of the electorate, that is, those Eisenhower supporters in 1956 who switched to a Democratic vote in 1958 and the considerable number of people who voted for President in 1956 but failed to vote in 1958. The

Table 3
Partisanship of the Vote in 1956 and 1958 (N = 1,354)

Vote for President in 1956	*Vote for Congressman in 1958*	*Percent*
Democratic	Democratic	22
Republican	Republican	22
Democratic	Republican	2
Republican	Democratic	11
Democratic	Did not vote	6
Republican	Did not vote	12
Did not vote	Democratic	3
Did not vote	Republican	1
Did not vote	Did not vote	21
		100

number of 1958 voters who had not voted in 1956 and of voters moving against the tide (Democratic to Republican) was much smaller than the two other groups (Table 3).

The similarities between Table 1 and Table 3 are striking, despite the fact that Table 1 compares succeeding presidential elections, and Table 3 compares a presidential election with a congressional election. We now find that when we distribute the party identifications of the people making up the major components of the 1956–1958 electorate, a table results which closely resembles Table 2 (see Table 4). We find again that those voters who support the same party through both low-turnout and high-turnout elections consist largely of people who identify themselves with that party. These are the core voters on whom each party relies. They were joined in 1956–58 by a sizable number of Independent voters, but by very few people who identified with the opposite party.

Those people who fail to vote in a low-stimulus election after having been brought to the polls in a preceding high-stimulus election provide a counterpart to those peripheral voters in Table 2 who did not vote in 1948 but did turn out in 1952. We see that they have comparable partisan characteristics. The smaller group, people who had voted for Stevenson in 1956 but did not vote in 1958, had strong Democratic Party attachments and closely resembled the 1948 nonvoters who went to the polls in 1952 to vote for Stevenson. Those 1956 Eisenhower voters who failed to vote in 1958, by contrast, were distinguished by having very few strong identifiers with either party. They include a high proportion of Independents and weak identifiers from each party, just as did the group of people who did not vote in 1948 but who turned out for Eisenhower in 1952. In all likelihood these two groups in 1958 consisted largely of people who had also failed to vote in the congressional election of 1954. They had been brought to the polls as peripheral voters by the stimulation of the 1956 election but dropped out again because of the weaker stimulus of the 1958 election. They contribute the major part of the surge and decline in turnout in these successive elections. Since these people tend to

Table 4

Party Identification of Components of the Vote for President in 1956 and Vote for Congressman in 1958 (in percent)

Party Identification	1956: 1958:	*Democratic* *Democratic* *(N=303)*	*Republican* *Republican* *(N=294)*	*Democratic* *Republican* *(N=21)*	*Republican* *Democratic* *(N=144)*	*Democratic* *Did Not Vote* *(N=89)*	*Republican* *Did Not Vote* *(N=159)*
Strong Democrat		50	1	(4)	13	41	6
Weak Democrat		31	4	(9)	27	37	17
Independent		15	26	(6)	30	17	36
Weak Republican		3	25	(2)	20	5	27
Strong Republican		*	44	†	8	†	14
Apolitical, other		1	†	†	2	†	†
		100	100	—	100	100	100

* Less than one-half of 1 percent.

† No cases.

Note. Figures in parentheses are number of persons rather than percent; number of cases is too small to support reliable estimates.

come to the polls more favorably disposed to one party than the other, they contribute to the partisan shift in a surge election, and their failure to vote in the succeeding election tends to reduce the proportion of the vote the previously advantaged party receives.

The other component of the shift in partisanship in both the 1952 and 1958 elections is the core voters who move from support of one party to the other. We saw in Table 2 that in 1952 the bulk of these people, moving then from a Democratic to a Republican vote, were Independents and weak partisans, and we see in Table 4 that the comparable group, moving in the opposite political direction, had the same characteristics. We assume that the large number of Democrats in the 1958 group were moving back to their "normal" party position after having supported Mr. Eisenhower in the 1956 election. The number of Republican identifiers in this group is larger than we would have anticipated and suggests that the partisan movement in 1958 cannot be entirely attributed to a normal decline toward standing party loyalties after the displacement of the vote in a surge year.[10]

Ticket Splitting and the Congressional Vote

A comparison of the vote for President and the vote for Congressman in the ensuing off-year election does not fully describe the movement of voters in this two-year election sequence. Because of the option which the American voter has of splitting his ticket, the relation of the presidential vote to the subsequent congressional vote may be very different from the relation of the vote for Congressman in a presidential year to the vote for Congressman in the subsequent off year. If we examine the consistency with which the 1956–1958 voting groups supported the ticket of the presidential candidate they preferred in 1956, we find convincing support for our earlier observations regarding the characteristics of these groups, and we discover a pattern of change in the congressional votes in the two elections quite different from what we found in the comparison of successive presidential and congressional votes.

Table 5 presents the 1956 voting patterns of the core and peripheral voters in the 1956 and 1958 elections. We see again that those voters who withstood the Republican surge in the 1956 election were strongly committed to the support of the Democratic Party, as indicated by their high level of straight-ticket voting. Fewer than 1 in 10 of the voters in the two major Democratic groups, those who voted for Stevenson in 1956 and a Democratic Congressman in 1958 and those who voted for Stevenson in 1956 but did not vote in 1958, split their 1956 vote at the national level. The consistent Republican voters also had a high record of straight-ticket voting, although not quite as high as the consistent Democrats because of the large number of Independents included among them. The other Republican group, the Eisenhower voters who did not go to the polls in 1958, had a notably smaller proportion of straight-ticket voters and a much larger proportion who split their tickets at the national level. We have seen that this group of peripheral voters who came to the polls in 1956 to vote for Mr. Eisenhower was made up of people of heterogeneous party background, including many Independents and a considerable number of weakly identified Democrats. Many of these latter

Table 5
1956 Voting Patterns of Major Voting Groups in the Vote for President in 1956 and Vote for Congressman in 1958 (in percent)

1956: / *1958:* / *1956 Voting Pattern*	*Democratic* *Democratic* *(N=289)*	*Republican* *Republican* *(N=286)*	*Democratic* *Republican* *(N=21)*	*Republican* *Democratic* *(N=140)*	*Democratic* *Did Not Vote* *(N=77)*	*Republican* *Did Not Vote* *(N=143)*
Voted straight ticket at national and local levels	68	60	(10)	26	66	46
Voted straight ticket at national level only	20	20	(5)	15	8	17
Split ticket at the national level	7	15	(6)	49	8	24
Did not vote complete ticket	3	1	*	3	13	8
Other	2	4	*	7	5	5
	100	100	*	100	100	100

* No cases.
Note. Figures in parentheses are number of persons rather than percent; number of cases is too small to support reliable estimates.

people obviously did not go all the way to the Republican position. Thirteen percent of this group (not shown specifically in Table 5) voted for Mr. Eisenhower but otherwise supported a straight Democratic ticket.

The 1956 Eisenhower voters who voted for a Democratic Congressman in 1958 present an especially interesting picture of ballot splitting. As we have seen, these core voters consist very largely of Democrats and Independents. Only a quarter of this group voted a straight Republican ticket in 1956, although they all voted for Mr. Eisenhower. A fifth of them voted a straight Democratic ticket except for President, and an additional quarter or more failed to vote a consistent Republican ticket at the national level. They responded to the personal appeal of Mr. Eisenhower as the Republican candidate in 1956, but they did not accept his party. When Mr. Eisenhower was not on the ballot in 1958, these people moved back to their usual party positions.

It is significant that both groups of peripheral voters, those who voted for either Eisenhower or Stevenson in 1956 but did not vote in 1958, contain a number of people who reported that they failed to vote a complete ticket on their presidential ballot. These are the only groups in which such voters appear in any significant frequency. This evidence of limited involvement in the vote is consistent with our earlier picture of the peripheral voter. Having less intrinsic interest in political matters and coming to the polls only when there is strong stimulation to do so, their concern about voting is inherently weak, in contrast to those voters who go to the polls whatever the circumstances.

The decline from the Republican Party's proportion of the presidential vote in 1956 to its proportion of the congressional vote in 1958 was associated with a considerably smaller decline from its congressional vote in 1956 to its congressional vote in 1958. As our data on ticket splitting make clear, the Republican congressional candidates in 1956 received far fewer votes than their standard-bearer, Mr. Eisenhower; they did not in fact achieve a majority of the popular vote. The decline of their congressional vote in 1958 from their congressional vote in 1956 was much smaller than the decline from the high mark of Mr. Eisenhower's vote, and the components of this decline differ somewhat from those of the decline from the presidential vote (Table 6).

It is clear that the dropout of the peripheral voters in 1958 had very little effect on the distribution of congressional votes in that year, since, at the same time they were giving Mr. Eisenhower a 2-to-1 margin of their votes in 1956, they were dividing their votes for Congressman about equally between the two parties. We would ordinarily expect this component of the vote to have greater importance than it had in 1958. In most elections that the electorate is strongly motivated to vote, we would expect the congressional vote for the advantaged party to swing along with the presidential vote. It was precisely the failure of this joint movement to occur, however, which made the 1956 election remarkable and resulted, for the first time in over a hundred years, in the election of a President of one party and both houses of Congress of the other. The Republican surge in 1956 was largely an Eisenhower surge.

In the absence of any influence from the dropout of 1956 voters, the major contribution to the rather small decline in the vote received by Republican congressional candidates in the

Table 6
Partisanship in the Congressional Vote in 1956 and 1958 (N = 1301)

Vote for Congressman in 1956	*Vote for Congressman in 1958*	*Percent*
Democratic	Democratic	25
Republican	Republican	19
Democratic	Republican	3
Republican	Democratic	6
Democratic	Did not vote	9
Republican	Did not vote	8
Did not vote	Democratic	4
Did not vote	Republican	2
Did not vote	Did not vote	24
		100

two elections was made by party switchers. There were movements in both directions from one election to the next, but there were twice as many changes from Republican to Democratic candidates as from Democratic to Republican. It is probable that part of the 3 percentage point Democratic advantage in this shift reflects the "coattail" effect which Mr. Eisenhower exerted on the 1956 election.[11] Some of these people were Democrats who had gone over to Mr. Eisenhower in 1956 and had voted his party ticket. But when Mr. Eisenhower was no longer on the ballot in 1958 they returned to their usual party choice.

The fact that the off-year elections typically reduce the congressional strength of the party which has won the Presidency two years earlier is readily understandable within the terms of our description of surge and decline. As long as there is no significant shift in the distribution of standing party attachments within the electorate, the decline in turnout in an off-year election will almost certainly be associated with a decline in the proportion of the vote received by the presidential party. If the partisan pressures of the presidential election have induced any movement toward the winning candidate among the Independents and members of the opposing party, this movement will recede in the following congressional election, partly because of the dropout of voters who had supported the ticket of the winning presidential candidate and partly because of the return to their usual voting positions of those Independents and opposing partisans who had switched during the presidential year.

The one clear reversal of this pattern which has occurred in the last hundred years is instructive. The House of Representatives that was elected with Mr. Roosevelt in 1932 had 310 Democratic members; in the 1934 elections this majority was extended to 319 members, although the turnout in 1934 was approximately 18 percent lower than it had been in 1932. According to our understanding of the nature of electoral decline, this could not have happened if the basic division of party loyalties was constant during this period. There is substantial reason to believe, however, that the distinguishing feature of American politics in the early 1930's was a realignment in the basic strength of the two parties. The economic collapse associated with the Hoover Administration brought millions of Independents and Republicans into the Democratic Party, not as temporary supporters but as long-term committed adherents. The Democratic gain in the 1934 election reflected a period of political conversion that gradually changed the Democratic Party from the minority party, which it had been since at least 1896, into the majority party of today. Such mass realignments of party identification, however, are very infrequent in American politics; more commonly the distribution of party loyalties remains stable despite the ups and downs of individual elections. Swings away from the basic division of party loyalties in high-turnout elections tend to swing back in the low-turnout elections which follow.

Conclusion

We have presented a theory of the nature of electoral change that is specifically intended to comprehend and explain two well-established regularities of American voting behavior, the highly partisan character of upsurges in turnout in presidential elections and the characteristic loss which the party winning the Presidency suffers in the ensuing off-year elections. We have proposed that fluctuations in turnout and partisanship result from a combination of short-term political forces, superimposed on the underlying level of political interest and on the long-standing psychological attachments of the electorate to the two parties. We have been able to present data from two election sequences, one illustrating electoral surge and the other decline. Additional evidence from other electoral situations would obviously be desirable, but the data in hand give convincing support to our understanding of the dynamics of voting change.

Our discussion has dealt entirely with electoral change within the American political system. We think it likely that the basic concepts which we have relied on in this analysis—political stimulation, political interest, party identification, core voters and peripheral voters, and high- and low-stimulus elections—are equally applicable to the understanding of political behavior in other democratic systems. But it is apparent that political behavior in other societies takes place within different institutional forms than those in the United States, and that they would have to be taken into account if we were to attempt an analysis in those societies comparable to the one presented here.

NOTES

1. V. O. Key, Jr., *Politics, Parties, and Pressure Groups*, Fourth Edition, New York: Thomas Y. Crowell, 1958, p. 638.
2. Anthony Downs uses the term "expected party differential" to express the degree of importance the voter attaches to the difference between the various party-candidate alternatives offered. See his *Economic Theory of Democracy*, New York: Harper, 1957, Chap. 3.
3. We omit from consideration in this [essay] shifts in the partisanship of the vote which occur in periods of stable turnout. Substantial shifts of this kind can be

found in the history of American elections, as for example in the presidential elections of 1928 and 1932, and they pose interesting questions as to how a shift in the absence of a surge in turnout differs from a shift which accompanies a voting surge. We will be concerned exclusively with the latter type of partisan change in the present discussion.

4. A detailed report of this study appears in A. Campbell, G. Gurin, and W. E. Miller, *The Voter Decides*, Evanston, Ill.: Row, Peterson, 1954.
5. There is a clear discrepancy between these reports and the election statistics for 1948 and 1952. Survey reports of turnout are always higher than the proportion of total vote to the total adult population, partly because surveys do not cover the institutional, military, and "floating" populations and partly because some respondents report a vote they did not cast. In the present case, the report of the 1952 vote does not appear to be greatly overstated, but the recall of the 1948 vote is more seriously inflated. The proportions saying they voted in both elections or in 1948 but not 1952 are probably both somewhat high. This introduces some distortion in the relative size of the different components of the vote and some restraints on the uses we can make of the data.
6. All references to voting in 1948 are based on the respondent's recall of this event when interviewed in 1952. Those few individuals who reported having voted for Thurmond or Wallace in 1948 are included in the Democratic vote.
7. We again have some problem of overreport of voting in the low-turnout election. This has the effect of understating the size and importance of the group of 1956 voters who dropped out in 1958. However, since the 19 percent of our sample who place themselves in this category are very unlikely to include individuals who actually voted in 1958, we can regard this as a relatively pure group for analytical purposes, remembering that it is somewhat smaller in size than it should be.
8. The differences in these data from those obtained in 1952 derive in large part from the fact that in this case we are grouping voters according to their performance in a presidential and a congressional election, and in the previous case we were grouping voters according to their performance in two successive presidential elections. The 1952 data are further influenced by the fact that about one-fourth of those 1952 voters who had not voted in 1948 were too young to vote in that year. Since the 1956–1958 sample is a panel, there is no comparable group in the 1958 data.
9. A number of factors might be expected to contribute to party crossing in the congressional elections. The personal impact of the Congressman in his district is not likely to equal that of a highly publicized presidential candidate, but it may be rather intense within a more limited range of individual voters. Over time a Congressman may establish sufficient personal contacts to have a visible effect on the vote. The repeated reelection of Congressmen in some districts tends to give them the character of nonpartisan fixtures: they attract cross-party votes which a less well-established candidate on the same ticket would not get. Of course, in those districts where a candidate runs without opposition, members of the minority party must cross party lines if they are to vote at all.
10. Losses going beyond the normal decline have occurred in other off-year elections and may be taken to reflect the development of circumstances unfavorable to the presidential party in the first two years of its term.
11. Additional coattail influence was undoubtedly felt among those people who voted for Eisenhower and a Republican Congressman in 1956 but did not vote in 1958. For a discussion of the nature of coattail voting, see W. E. Miller, "Presidential Coattails," *Public Opinion Quarterly*, 19, 353–368 (1955).

20

The Functions of American Parties

CLINTON ROSSITER

In the following essay, Clinton Rossiter describes the "functions" of American political parties. He dwells particularly on the role of the parties as "peacemakers." The parties bring together within their ranks the centrifugal forces—specifically sectionalism; class and calling; and race, religion, and ethnic origin—that might otherwise break apart the nation's precarious unity. It is the coalition nature of parties, demonstrated both in their vote bases and in their programs, that is for Rossiter their great contribution to America. Conceding that they are crippled as policy makers by their diversity, Rossiter nonetheless finds in this broadness a great virtue rather than a debilitating vice. He is at odds in this with Stephen K. Bailey, James MacGregor Burns, and the other party reformers.

Despite his low estimate of parties as engines of policy, Rossiter approves of many of their other activities—such as the recruitment of candidates and appointive officials, education of the electorate, and mediation between individuals and the government bureaucracy—and believes them to be essential to American democracy. Rossiter makes clear his belief that there are no alternatives presently available to take up the activities, no matter how haphazardly performed, of the parties, although he does not insist that this would be impossible. Yet if there is indeed a decline and imminent demise of parties, as predicted by Walter Dean Burnham, a salient question raised by Rossiter's praise of parties might be "who shall do the parties' work in the future?"

Rossiter, whose untimely death in 1970 deprived America of one of its most far-ranging and prolific political commentators, was John L. Senior Professor of American Institutions at

Cornell University. His books include Seedtime of the Republic *(1953),* Conservatism in America *(1955),* The American Presidency *(1956),* 1787: The Grand Convention *(1966),* Alexander Hamilton and the Constitution *(1964),* Marxism: The View from America *(1960).*

Parties, it could be argued, exist primarily to serve the interests of the men who lead or support them. They are justified by their fruits, by which I mean the fruits that are showered on the leaders in the form of power and on the supporters in the form of favors. This, however, is a crude and narrow view of the role of parties in our society; for whatever they may have been in their beginnings, parties are now public institutions rather than private preserves. They stand closer to Congress and the courts than they do, say, to the American Legion or General Motors or the A.F.L.-C.I.O. on the spectrum of social organization that runs from the very private to the totally official. They are justified by their functions, by which I mean functions that are performed as services to the entire nation. We tolerate and even celebrate their existence because they do things for us in the public realm that would otherwise be done poorly or not at all.

Let us turn now to look at our parties in this light. Let us describe the political and social functions of any party in any democracy, and see how well our particular parties have performed each of these functions in our peculiar democracy. Let us see, too, if there are any special, "characteristically American" functions that they have been called upon to perform or, more accurately, have performed without knowing it. Then perhaps we will be in a position to pass meaningful judgment on the quality of service rendered by the American party system to the American people.

The primary function of a political party in a democracy such as ours is to control and direct the struggle for power. From this function all others derive naturally. I trust that no apologies need be made for calling attention to the fact that the political process in a free country is essentially a conflict, limited and regularized but nonetheless relentless, among groups of men who have contradictory interests and more or less mutually exclusive hopes of securing them. . . .

It is one of the aspirations of democracy to bring this struggle as much as possible into the open. It is the great purpose of political parties, the handmaidens of democracy, to bring the struggle under control: to institutionalize it with organization, to channel it through nominations and elections, to publicize it by means of platforms and appeals, above all to stabilize it in the form of that traditional quadrille in which the Ins and the Outs change places from time to time on a signal from the voters. The parties did not create the struggle for power; it would go on merrily without them. It would go on, however, much less purposefully and effectively and openly, and we might well be more grateful to our own parties for their modest efforts to bring under benevolent control the eternal conflict of interests described by Madison in *The Federalist,* no. 10. Just how grateful we should be is a question I will try to answer at the end of this review of the functions of parties.

The first of what we might call the

subsidiary functions of a party in a democracy (subsidiary, that is, to the great, inclusive function we have just noted) is to act as an immense personnel agency. Constitutions make frugal provision for the election or appointment of persons to high office, but they extend no aid at all to those persons in and out of government who must act as recruiters. Statutes and ordinances bloom in profusion to create the rules and rewards of a civil service, but they offer to guaranty that the men on top of the permanent bureaucracy will be like-minded enough to give it a sense of cohesion or alert enough to the needs of the public to give it a sense of direction.

This is exactly where parties enter the picture decisively and why, all things considered, we could hardly do without them. Willingly and indeed eagerly they set up and operate the machinery that places men and women in public office, and they do it at four key points: *nominations*, for they are organized to do the preliminary sifting of aspirants to elective office or, if necessary, to go out and recruit them actively; *campaigns*, for they make known to the voting public the credentials and promises of the narrowed list of candidates; *elections*, for they can provide (in bulk and at small cost) the swarm of citizens needed to man the polls and count the votes; and *appointments*, for they are no less eager to assist in the selective process than they are in the elective process. Indeed, they can come up even more quickly with a reasonably qualified candidate for appointment as Secretary of State or district attorney or recorder of deeds than with an equally qualified candidate for election as President or assemblyman or county coroner.

There are, of course, other techniques for recruiting men and women into the service of the community. The machinery of election is vigorously nonpartisan in two states and many cities in the United States, and the machinery appears to work fairly well. In the case of nominations for local office a caucus of all interested citizens is often the most sensible method of narrowing the field. And it is hard to deny that we could push the line dividing partisan from career appointments in, let us say, the diplomatic service well up the ladder with no injury to efficiency or team-mindedness. Yet this is the way we have chosen to do this important job, and there is much to be said for the choice of agents we have made—the major parties. They bring order out of disorder, simplicity out of diversity, precision out of chaos. They comb the population for willing and (more often than legend would have it) able recruits; and, by placing their tags upon these aspirants for election or appointment, they help us all, even in a country where tags can sometimes be misleading, to make more rational choices.

How would we ever get through the process of electing a Congress if the parties did not take over the primaries and elections? How would the President ever find candidates for several thousand offices a year if his party's informal patronage machinery were not quick with suggestions? How would we go about filling the 750,000 (give or take 100,000) elective offices in the United States if we were a strictly nonpartisan people? If we do not get as many first-rate men as we should in Congress and the administration, in state legislatures and school boards, the blame must be laid at the doors of the people with their antipolitical mores and not of the politicians with their vulgar methods. The latter, after all, stay in business by pleasing the former, and up to now they seem to have pleased us well enough. This, in any case, is the wonderfully symbiotic relationship that we, like all other democracies, have created. The process of nomination and election needs parties to make it go; parties make nominations and fight elections or they are not parties at all. Small wonder that the parties have been given legal status throughout the United States and that the state legislatures have chosen increasingly to regulate their structure and operation in considerable detail.

Parties can also serve as important sources of public policy. They have no monopoly of this function, to be sure, nor should they in the kind of pluralistic society we identify with democracy. The great and small policies by which we live emerged first as special pleadings of an infinite variety of groups and persons, and we should be happy to live in a society in which organizations like N.A.M. or N.A.A.C.P. and men like Walter Lippmann or Bernard Baruch come up constantly with new proposals for our consideration. Yet the parties—and in this instance I include third parties—are perhaps best fitted of all agencies to convert formless hopes or frustrations into proposals that can be understood, debated, and, if found appealing, approved by the people. Because they are the only truly national, multi-interest, broadly based organizations active in our society (the only ones, indeed, that we can permit to be active), they are uniquely situated to originate policies themselves or to broaden the special pleadings of other men and groups. Their policies, moreover, are likely to be a little more realistic than those that emerge from the paid researches of interest groups, for any one policy must be fitted with dozens of others into a full program for governing the nation.

Thanks to the fuzzy nature of our political system, the major parties have not been especially effective in performing this function. In the words of the Committee on Political Parties of the American Political Science Association, "the American two-party system has shown little propensity for evolving original or creative ideas about public policy; it has even been rather sluggish in responding to such ideas in the public interest." The platforms of the parties, which are presumably the most eloquent statements they can make of their current intentions, have never been noted for originality or clarity. One cannot fail to be impressed by some of the reports of the Democratic Advisory Council or by the Report of the Republican Committee on Program and Progress, *Decisions for a Better America,* issued in September 1959, yet one is struck by the scarcity of concrete proposals in all these reports and bound to wonder if the members of these committees really speak with the voice of authority. Yet the remembrance of Wilson's New Freedom and Roosevelt's New Deal should be enough to convince us that parties can originate policies, and that their policies, unlike those of most interest groups, can cut a broad swath through American life. Wilson and especially Roosevelt took their policies wherever they found them, but some of the most important were first given form by lieutenants acting consciously as Democrats.

The point at which our parties may indeed have failed us in this matter of policies is not in originating or formulating or advertising them, but in converting them into the hard coin of purposeful law and skillful administration. Before we can go into that problem, however, we must take note of the function that makes it possible and even mandatory for parties in a democracy to put their policies into effect: the organization and operation of government. Within every true party there exists . . . a governmental party, a hard core of officeholders whose duty to the community goes beyond mere electioneering or even formulating policies. If this party has been victorious in the most recent election, it is expected to organize the legislative and executive branches and to run them with the aid of the appeals and disciplines of party loyalty. In the United States, of course, the ground rules of the Constitution make it necessary for a party to win several elections over a period of time in order to exercise the kind of over-all control that comes in one large bundle to the majority party (or coalition) under the rules of the parliamentary system, but in all democratic countries the principle is the same: every self-respecting party is, in effect, a miniature state that must be prepared to take over and operate the real state (or some portion of it) at the command of the electorate. A political organization unwilling to govern is not, by any definition, a party.

To cite the example closest to home, in 1956 we asked Mr. Eisenhower, in his capacity as victorious candidate for the Presidency under the aegis of the Republican party, to wield his own powers and to supervise the execution of the laws of the United States with the aid of a large team of men drawn almost exclusively from the ranks of his party. He and his colleagues promised us to operate the executive branch in a certain way and for certain purposes, and we, in effect, turned the levers of public power over to them. They also promised to account to us as a party in the next election for the way in which they had manipulated these levers—or so at least runs the theory of party responsibility in a democracy.

At the same time, and in a unique demonstration of political cussedness, we asked Mr. Rayburn and Senator Johnson, in their capacities as leaders of the victorious party in the congressional elections, to organize the two houses of our national legislature and run them with the help of all kinds of party machinery—floor leaders, whips, committee chairmen, policy committees, and the rest. This they were expected to do, as men have done for generations, with as much conviction and precision as one can ever get out of the American party system, and they, too, promised to be held accountable as a party. So it goes all down through the kaleidoscopic structure of government in the United States. Although we try to remove parts of it—a board here, a city there—from the arena of the party struggle, we rely overwhelmingly on our political parties to organize and operate the agencies of the public will. For example, in almost every state legislature where two-party politics exists at all, the majority party exercises tight control over formal organization and procedures. This is one of those things which, as some people like to say, is "done better in England," where constitutional government takes on the form, openly and proudly, of party government. Yet even in America we would be at a loss how to get on with the public business if the parties were not always around begging us to lease them the concession.

If we have few complaints about the technical competence with which our majority parties organize and operate the agencies of government, we have many, probably more than any other people in the democratic world, about the skill and dedication they bring to the process of making their own policies the policies of city or state or nation; and that, as I have already indicated, is one of the basic functions of a party in a democracy: to make concrete promises to the electorate and then, if invited by the electorate to govern, to make good on those promises. There are promises and promises, to be sure, and the imperatives of democracy demand that a major shift in public policy be carried through only by a clear majority in answer to a clear invitation. Yet if this function is not the essence of party government, what is? If parties will not take the lead in making policy for the community, what groups will? In the ideal democracy, it could be argued, responsible parties would exercise command, if never enjoy a monopoly, of the process of decision making. We would always know whom to punish for unkept promises and wrong guesses.

No country comes close to being an ideal democracy, and, in this instance at least, America does not come close at all. American parties are notoriously delinquent in keeping their promises to the electorate. We have become especially skeptical about the capacity of the majority party in Congress, no matter how smashing its most recent electoral triumph, to build new structures of law and administration out of the planks in its platform. To tell the truth, most of us do not find this skepticism hard to bear, and the complaints are voiced more in sorrow than in anger. The fact is that we have never been as willing as the British or Swedes or Belgians or even the Canadians to consign to partisan hands the great process of decision making for the nation. We seem to be happier with decisions that have been adopted on a bipartisan or, even better, nonpartisan basis, more willing to live with laws that have been approved finally by a majority of both parties in Congress—and for which neither party can properly take primary credit. Yet in adopting this easygoing attitude, we are hacking at the roots of responsible party government. If parties are not expected or encouraged to make good on their reasonable promises, then other groups less open in operation and accountable in fact—blocs and interest groups and loose coalitions of lobby-ridden legislators—will assume the authority to make public policy.

The last of what we might call the political functions of parties in a democracy is one that a party does not choose happily yet must accept willingly if the burden is thrust upon it. This is the delicate function, so necessary to democracy and so incomprehensible to autocracy, of "loyal opposition." It is, of course, the special province of the party that has lost the last election. The minority party is expected to organize itself in the legislature for the primary purpose of checking the majority party. Members of the party are not rigidly forbidden to be creative statesmen, and in any session many occasions will arise when they will join with the majority, as individuals or even as a party, in enacting measures that cut across partisan lines or do not appear as partisan at all. For the most part, however, their task is essentially negative in character and purpose. They must oppose the proposals of the majority, develop alternative proposals for the electorate to consider at the next election, and keep a close watch on those who are executing the laws under the direction of the majority party. Like any other task we assign to our parties, this function admits of abuse. Few politicians in the ranks of the minority pay careful attention to the rough line between responsible opposition and irresponsible pugnacity. Yet it is a function that we could ill do without, for so long as the majority party is expected to govern, so long must the minority party be encouraged to oppose.

American parties have had perhaps more success in opposing than in governing, which is a revealing commentary on the nature of our political system. In fact, it often seems that American politicians are happier out of power than in it. Like the great Constitution under which we live serenely, our political instinct seems to prefer restraint to power and delay to action. The minority, finding its role more congenial than does the majority, performs it with a relish that is usually missing in the activities of the governing party. The framers of the Constitution were concerned, on one hand, to construct a system of checks and balances and, on the other, to make it difficult for parties to arise and prosper. Would they be shocked or merely surprised to learn that one of the most effective checks in our enduring system of checks and balances is the party in opposition...?

To this list of the political functions of parties in a democracy we can add three others that might more accurately be described as social, since in performing them parties serve men in their roles as social rather than political animals. First, parties are important agencies in the educational process. The citizens of a free country must be instructed in the practices of democracy and kept informed on the issues of their times, not merely to become more forceful agents of public opinion and more skillful voters, but also to live more satisfying lives. Once they have finished the last stage of their formal education, they must rely on a battery of informal instruments ranging from Sunday afternoon television to word of mouth. Political parties are at best crude instruments of adult education, yet they can do much to compel study and discussion of important problems.

American parties have given over perhaps too much of their own responsibility for adult education to interest groups, yet our history is full of instances in which a party took the lead in educating the public to recognize and understand the facts of a new condition or trend in American life. The Republican party, speaking through men like Lincoln, did much to educate the nation in the true nature and implications of slavery. The Democratic party, speaking through Franklin Roosevelt and his friends, did even more to educate us in the proper relations of private enterprise and public authority. Third parties, too, although their student bodies have been limited, have scored real successes as educating agencies. The parties could certainly afford to do a great deal more in performing this function, especially in stimulating interest in politics. The "seminars" and "schools" now being run every year in several parts of the country could be multiplied many times over to the benefit of American minds and American democracy. Even these present modest efforts are welcome additions to the vast, jerry-built structure of adult education. The citizen who goes to school cautiously with our political parties can get an excellent education in subjects that really count.

Next, the parties serve a useful social purpose in acting as buffers and adjusters between individuals and society, especially as the latter intrudes into the lives of ordinary persons in the shape of impersonal political authority. The days are pretty well over when big and little bosses did much (for a consideration, to be sure) to soften the impact of the city on the sensibilities of helpless and ignorant people—when Nocky Johnson of Atlantic City kept a pile of coal to which any poor Negro could come for a free bagful; when George Washington Plunkitt handed out jobs along with free advice; when Frank Skeffington (or was it James Curley, or Spencer Tracy?) acted the part of the bountiful city squire; when Walter Lippmann doubted that the City of New York could ever be "as human, as kindly, as jolly as Tammany Hall"; and when Martin Lomasney of Boston spoke for all the old machines: "I think that there's got to be in every ward somebody that any bloke can come to—no matter what he's done—and get help. Help, none of your law and justice, but help."

Yet the parties are still important dispensers of those aids, favors, and immunities (for example, from prosecution of father for peddling without a license or son for breaking windows) that make it possible for men and women to live reasonably confident lives in a harsh environment. If poor Negroes in Atlantic City no longer need to be given coal, they do need help in obtaining unemployment compensation with which to buy coal. The more penetrating and complicated the power of government becomes, the more demand there is for skilled "adjusters," who might as well be politicians as priests or social workers. There is, of course, a seamy side to this function; politicians contribute more than their fair share to the corruptions and injustices of American life, in the country as well as in the city. Yet the fact that a function is performed corruptly is no decisive argument against its being performed in the first place. Men need buffers against both state and society, and they must take them as and where they find them. In the local organizations of political parties Americans have found buffers of uncommon efficiency. The lives of millions of Americans would have been much harder to bear if the parties had not done their work as agencies of social welfare.

Finally, parties serve a symbolic function—or should we start from the other direction and call it psychological?—by providing an object, large and friendly and often exciting, to which men can extend allegiance. Graham Wallas, in his memorable study of *Human Nature in Politics,* was perhaps the first observer to isolate and examine this function. Having taken note of the multitude of voters and of the psychical inability of any one voter to deal with more than a few men and ideas, he went on: "Something is required simpler and more permanent, something which can be loved and trusted, and which can be recognized at successive elections as being the same thing that was loved and trusted before; and a party is such a thing."

* * *

In the effectiveness with which they perform most of these political and social functions, parties in America fall well short of the ideal of democracy or even of the reality of parties in many other countries. They are especially ineffectual in the task of formulating policies and transforming them into government programs, and thus they get only low marks for their performance of the great, overriding function of channeling and disciplining the struggle for power. No matter how indulgently we judge them, we are bound to conclude that parties are not nearly as important factors in the decision-making process in America as they are in most other democracies. Blocs, interest groups, bipartisan coalitions, and nonpartisan elites all challenge the parties constantly for control of the key stages in the political process.

An American party is a relatively weak agent of decision and power primarily because it is . . . broad in appeal, moderate in outlook, loose-jointed in structure, tolerant in discipline, uncommitted in ideology, one of two parties in a political system that plays down principle and plays up accommodation. It is that kind of party for dozens of reasons. . . .

We would have to look first at the Constitution. . . . Almost every command, prohibition, or arrangement in this document has helped to dictate the direction in which our parties have developed. The division of power and even of sovereignty between nation and states is a major cause of decentralization in the parties. This fact of federalism, strengthened by the physical separation of the legislature and the executive, makes a mockery of all hopes for strong party discipline. The method of electing congressmen and, even more obviously, the President dooms the first two parties to lives of incessant compromise and all other parties to frustration. The Presidency itself, at once the most political and least political of offices, cuts across the neat lines of party responsibility. And the whole spirit of the Constitution, a document that remains even today a catalogue of limitations, insists so strongly that many decisions of a public character be taken by private persons and agencies that it is no wonder our parties are encouraged to be all things to all men in many areas of controversy.

Behind the Constitution stand the American people. . . . We are said to be a people with a prejudice against politics, and that may explain why our parties tolerate so many mavericks, men who claim to be "Americans first and party men second," even in the front ranks. We are said to be a people with a pragmatic cast of mind, and that may explain why we permit the parties to pursue their seemingly absurd ways, asking only that the results make sense. Above all we are said to be a people with scant respect for fine points of doctrine, and that goes far to explain the weakness of ideological commitment in our successful parties.

There are plenty of ideological Americans, and the number may be growing, but they are still far from numerous or ideological enough to force our parties to take stronger stands on doctrinal issues. A people's institutions must reflect the broad features of their character. If American parties have small use for sharply honed ideology, that is because so many Americans have even less. While the parties are by now both cause and effect of our refusal to engage in sharp distinctions of doctrine, the main influence has been visited by the people on the parties. If ideology does play a part in shaping the parties, it does it in a rough and offhanded way by forcing them to stand for many of the same principles. If we think only a few large thoughts about the nature of society and the purpose of government, we think them strongly—and we think them in common. The American consensus is unique in its virility and broad appeal. Our interests, which are many, are remarkably diverse;

our principles, which are few, are remarkably uniform. The natural product of this powerful national consensus is a pair of parties that overlap substantially in their attempts to prove their loyalty to it.

The last place in which we would look for an explanation of the peculiar nature of American parties, and thus of their undistinguished performance in the struggle for power, would be the history of the parties themselves. It is a fact of small repute but great moment—I would hail it as the paramount fact in this whole book—that our parties have had thrust upon them functions other and perhaps more important than those that are considered the natural functions of a party in a democracy....

To put the matter as simply as possible, they are the parties they are today because they have played a vital role in creating the unity of America. They are weak agents in the struggle for power because they have been strong agents in the course of our rise to nationhood. It has been their historic mission to hold the line against some of the most powerful centrifugal forces in American society, and their success in performing it can be measured with considerable accuracy in their peculiar habits. No one should pass judgment on American parties until he understands that fact and has reviewed the whole record of their achievements. Let us now move on with our own review by taking careful note of the contributions our major parties have made to national unity in checking the forces of disunity.

The first of these forces is sectionalism, which lies so deep in the American way of life and has exerted such an attraction on American minds and passions that the wonder is we are one country at all and not a parcel of squabbling Balkan states.... The Union got off to a shaky start; it was challenged boldly in the nineteenth century by every section of the country in turn; several sections seem to have been at perpetual odds with it. One section, indeed, as we will never be allowed to forget, made an agonizing attempt to break loose completely, and only the force of arms kept the eleven Southern states in the Union—or, as some prefer, brought them back into it.

What had kept them in the Union up to the break of 1861 and was to bring them back after 1865 was the force of politics, which has always been—next to a common language, common needs, and common memories—the most powerful centripetal force in American society. The parties, especially the Whigs before the Civil War and the Democrats both before and after, have acted as skillfull brokers of sectional interests. In their efforts to build up a majority in the country, they have reached out into all sections for support, have drawn on all sections for officeholders and voters, and have tried to make the special interests of each section the interests of the whole nation. Always adept at bargaining and compromise, the parties have gone far to build up an acceptable consensus among the elites in every part of the land. Needless to say, they have not always found this task easy. The Republicans, in particular, have had their troubles being a national party; even today there lingers upon them that scent of Northern and Western sectionalism that in 1856 alerted the sensitive nostrils of the South to the realization that the old rules no longer held and that the Union might be about to disintegrate.

The force of politics as a nationalizing influence demonstrated its historic importance most dramatically in its one hour of failure.... The failure of the Democrats to nominate Stephen A. Douglas at Charleston in the spring of 1860, the withdrawal of the slave-state delegations to Richmond and the Douglas men to Baltimore, and the consequent victory of the Republicans under Lincoln were a series of hammer blows that sent the Union sprawling. The fact for us to remember is that the last institution to break apart in the crisis of slavery and sectionalism was a political party—not a church or lodge or interest group—and the first to be reunited after the resolution of the crisis by force of arms was the same political party. By stretching out their hands for the votes of their old friends in the South in 1866 and 1868, the Democrats did more to restore the Union than did any other group or force in or out of power. To round out this revealing story of disunion and union, we might recall that the parties brought off the famous deal of 1877 that cemented the South politically in the Union. In return for an agreement by the Democrats not to challenge the shaky results of the election of 1876, the Republicans promised to withdraw federal troops from the South. This was a classic demonstration of the whole process I have been describing. The motives were impure and the purposes selfish; the methods of decision were not those we write about so glibly in our tracts and texts on democracy. Yet there can be no doubt that the chief object of benefaction was the American Union....

* * *

A second centrifugal force in American society against which the parties have held the line with success for us as well as for themselves—and with damage only to discipline and principle—is the divisive thrust of class and calling. Thanks to the happier social and economic climate of America, the free play of these closely related forces has never imperiled our unity half so dangerously as it has the unity of France, Italy, or even Britain. Yet the climate cannot be awarded all the credit for the limited impact on American unity of the eternal conflict of economic and social interests. The parties, too, have played their part in smothering the conflict. In the course of their unflagging search for the complicated formula of victory, they have appealed to all classes and interests as they have appealed to all sections, and almost every class and interest has wisely agreed that it is better to be a half-satisfied part of a rabble with some hope of victory than the dominant force in a disciplined army with no hope at all. Perhaps the class struggle in all its vigor and viciousness would never have come to tyrannize over America, yet there is no doubt that it has been kept even more safely at bay by the peculiar workings of our two-party system. So long as the Republicans bid powerfully for the votes of workingmen, so long as the Democrats can count on their share of businessmen and gentlemen, so long as both parties fall all over themselves wooing the increasingly perverse voters from the farms of America, this nation has less than other nations to fear from the always thinly veiled passions of social and economic division. Although our parties are perhaps more openly oriented to particular classes and economic interests than they were a generation ago, we are still far from a system in which the Haves and Have-Nots face each other suspiciously across a sharply drawn political line....

The third force of disunity which

the parties have done much to smother is the explosive power latent in the scrambled pattern of race, national origin, and religion. Almost every identifiable cultural group in American society has found a happier political home in one party than in the other. At least one major group in one part of the country, the Negroes in the South, has been fought off savagely by one of the parties, the Democrats. Still, the broad scheme of American politics has been one under which neither party could afford to write off any sizable group and under which most groups have divided evenly enough between the parties to create an illusion, and perhaps more than just an illusion, of unity amid diversity. Most of the particulars of this historic process are too well known to require extended comment: how millions of immigrants were given their first hearty welcome by a local boss; how the Democrats made good Americans out of Irishmen and the Republicans made equally good Americans out of Germans; how thousands of men shut off by a wall of prejudice from other paths to higher status made their way up the dizzy escalator of politics; how men of different tongues learned to speak the common language of politics; how Negroes in the North made progress in politics much faster than in any other area; how the parties tiptoed around the divisive issues of religion and thus gave them no chance to explode. Again one must confess that the picture is not all that pleasant. There is always something a little hard to swallow in the party ticket listing an upstate, old-stock Protestant for governor, a downstate Irish Catholic for lieutenant-governor, a suburban Jew for attorney-general, a large-city Italian for secretary of state, and a small-city Pole for comptroller, but if this kind of enterprise is one of the few to bring men of such diverse backgrounds together—and to invite each of their followings to cast a highly "tolerant" ballot—who can argue that the higher good of democratic unity has not been served, however casually and perversely?

In all these ways and in many more the parties have softened the rough edges of America's fabulous diversity. They have paid a stiff price in the coin of diminished reputation, for many articulate Americans continue to ask caustically, "Why don't they stand for anything different?"—indeed, "Why don't they stand for anything at all?" We have paid an even stiffer price in the coin of a nearly formless political process in which parties with too little power and interest groups with too much purpose struggle riotously over a darkling plain. Yet the feeling will not down that the price, although high, has not been exorbitant, and that what we have purchased with it—the unity of a free people—is more to be coveted than a politics that makes perfect sense. It would be helpful if more people realized that the peculiarities of our party system have been, in Herbert Agar's phrase, "the price of union," but perhaps it is better for us to live in a system we only dimly comprehend.

This, in any case, is the essence of our political history: the parties have been the peacemakers of the American community, the unwitting but forceful suppressors of the "civil-war potential" we carry always in the bowels of our diverse nation. Blessed are the peacemakers, I am tempted to conclude. They may never be called the children of God nor even inherit the earth, but they, after all, seek only to inherit the White House.

21

The Condition of Our National Political Parties

STEPHEN K. BAILEY

In the following essay, Stephen K. Bailey joins those advocates of "responsible political parties" who argue that the urgency and scope of national problems no longer permit the luxury of the highly diffuse and decentralized political process to which Americans have become accustomed. The parties, he asserts in a nine-point reform program, must become more issue oriented and more internally cohesive in order to enact and administer "imaginative, informed, consistent" public policy. Whether the diversity of America can be contained in two parties with well-defined policy objectives and a relatively high degree of internal cohesion, however, is immediately questionable.

Whether the coalition-building, consensus-creating function of parties should be abandoned for greater policy coherence and a higher degree of interparty conflict would certainly be challenged by many commentators on American political parties. But even if responsible parties are possible and desirable, the student of politics might entertain doubts as to whether Bailey's nine proposals for reform will advance those goals as far or as swiftly as he alleges.

Bailey is both a student and a practitioner of politics. He served as mayor of Middletown, Connecticut, while on the faculty of Wesleyan University. He has been an adviser to governors and presidents and most recently was appointed by Governor Rockefeller to the Board of Regents of the State of New York. Until his resignation in 1968, Bailey was Dean of the Maxwell Graduate School of Citizenship and Public Affairs at Syracuse University. Among his writings are Congress Makes a Law *(1950),* The New Congress *(1966), and a delightful article, in* Public Administration Review, *14 (Summer 1954), 202-204, entitled "A Structured Interaction for Harpsichord and Kazoo," which describes in a stream-of-consciousness style the incongruities in simultaneously teaching public administration and serving as mayor.*

The Parties and Responsible Power

The American government today suffers from three weaknesses:

1. its difficulty in generating sustained political power;
2. its difficulty in developing a flow of imaginative, informed, consistent, and power-related responses to pressing national and world issues;
3. its difficulty in making policy truly accountable to a national popular majority.

These are serious defects, not only because they interfere with wise and coherent governing in these dangerous days, but because they undermine the faith of the citizen in the reality or even the possibility of responsible representative government.

* * *

Is Leadership the Basic Issue?

To say that we need a new kind of political leadership may be true, but it begs the question. Where and how does political leadership arise in the United States? Who selects presidential and congressional candidates? How can the process of selection be improved? How can leadership be sustained? How can first-class political executives be found to run our great public departments? Why is their present tenure so ephemeral? By what means can presidential and congressional purposes be brought into a working relationship? And why cannot leadership be held more fully accountable to the desires of popular majorities?

All of these questions are related to the structural handicaps under which the American government now operates. At first glance, the problem seems to be constitutional—and in part it is. But the only two structural faults of the Constitution which really get in the way of responsible power in the national government are the 22nd Amendment, which limits the President to two terms, and the provisions for staggered elections. The only two constitutional reforms that this paper will suggest are the repeal of the 22nd Amendment and changes in the term of Members of the House from two to four years and of United States Senators from six to eight years (half the Senate coming up every four years at the same time as the presidential elections). The real problem is *political*. If our *political* institutions can be modernized by certain changes in statutory law and in political party rules, the old problems associated with separation of powers, checks and balances, and federalism would, it seems probable, largely disappear.

The root of the weakness is that while the two national parties for years have genuinely competed for

Reprinted from *The Condition of Our National Political Parties* by Stephen K. Bailey (Santa Barbara: The Fund for the Republic, 1959), by permission of the author and the Center for the Study of Democratic Institutions.

the Presidency they have not made a similar effort in the election of United States Senators and Members of the House of Representatives. Nor have they been of sufficient help to the President and the Congress in providing candidates of high quality for the grand patronage of departmental and agency direction. So long as we lack strong national parties operating as catalysts in the Congress, the executive branch, and the national government as a whole, and between the national government and state and local governments, power will continue to be dangerously diffused or, perhaps what is worse, will whip-saw between diffusion and presidential dictatorship.

The Natural Party Distinctions

Contrary to the view of many writers, the parties do not need to be strongly ideological or even strongly programmatic—that is, beholden to comprehensive and distinct sets of policies—in order to accomplish the kind of re-alignment of the party system that would stabilize the national power and help to make it responsible. There are vast areas of overlap in the rather vague programmatic shadows that our two great parties cast over the nation—and this is as it should be if consensus is to continue in the making of public policy and in the administration of foreign policy.

But the centers of gravity of the two parties are quite distinct. The Democratic party basically is a party of innovation, with a "pro-government" bias. The Republican party is an essentially "consolidating" party with a limited-government bias. The distinction has become blurred in the last two generations, largely because of the extreme economic and social conservatism of one-party areas in the South—a conservatism which has been reflected in the Congress through its seniority rules and some other carefully contrived rules and myths. But now, the peculiar condition which has smudged party images for so long is on its way out. The economic base of the solid South has shifted monumentally in the past fifteen years; one-party areas across the land are on the wane; the northern migration of the Negro is having vast political consequences.

Political reform does not include making the parties any more ideological than they are now. It does include making them competitive across the nation, allowing them to appeal to the natural ideological divisions within the population and within us as individuals. The stumbling block in this task is that neither party has a sufficiently unified structure to enable it to dramatize its program around its ideology; neither has the power, even if it had the right structure, to carry out the program; neither has sufficiently clear and unambiguous lines of political accountability running to the voters.

The Results of Party Diffusion

The structural limitations of the parties have grave consequences. First, they virtually insure a government by fits-and-starts. . . . In . . . recent times presidential requests for an adequate United States Information Agency budget have been listened to one year and ignored the next by the House Appropriations Committee. As a result, cultural officers abroad have had to spend much of their time hiring and firing—inflating and deflating programs like an accordion. This has made us look ridiculous as a nation, and has also made it extremely difficult for a coherent information program to develop as a vital element in our foreign policy. The same has been true of foreign economic aid.

Spasms in domestic policy have been equally obvious and equally unsettling. The executive department and the Congress have been unable to agree on any coordinated methods of applying the kind of devices needed to stabilize the economy and promote the goals of the Employment Act of 1946. Similar fits and starts have been noticeable in defense policy, atomic energy policy, welfare policy, and conservation policy. They have been quite as apparent when the Presidency and both Houses of Congress have been in one party as when the control of the government has been divided.

The second consequence of the structural limitations of the parties has been the lack of rationality and consistency in the substance of much public policy. In Paul Appleby's phrase, in this day and age someone or something has to "make a mesh of things." In a world in which, for example, the indiscriminate dumping of rice on the world market in order to ease a temporary glut in Louisiana could cost us the friendship of Burma, there are huge dangers in having unlinked centers of power making their own policy for the nation. And yet, parochial groups in the Congress (often in league with sections of the executive branch and with outside pressure groups) still carry an inordinate amount of power.

The third consequence of the absence of coherent party machinery truly responsive to popular majorities is that congressional compromise tends to fall with considerable regularity on the side of minority rather than majority interests. Committee chairmen from "safe," and often sparsely populated, one-party states and districts; the minority-weighted bipartisan rules committee; and the myths, rules, and influence structure which enable congressional leaders to ignore demands for greater majority representation in policy decisions—all these combine to inflate the power of minority interests at the expense of the national popular majority....

This is government by tollgate. It leads directly to consequence four: the increasing danger of public cynicism and apathy toward the Congress, partly because its power is too diffuse or too subtle to comprehend; partly because when the power *is* clearly identifiable it seems to work more consistently for minorities than for the majority.

The last and by no means the least important consequence stemming from the absence of a unified party structure is that desperately needed criticism of both domestic and foreign policy is dissipated and discouraged. There is no effective vehicle for responsible opposition criticism of programs; there is no machinery for anticipating the implications of social changes and their effects on policy....

In sum, the absence of effective party machinery in each House, and in the government generally, means that policy is frequently developed by an infinitely intricate system of barter and legerdemain.

Some defenders of America's traditional disorder have discounted the dangers to policy-making of these intermittencies and irresponsibilities. They argue that our survival suggests that presidential leadership and a congressional desire to cooperate during periods of crisis can save us in the future as they have in the past;

that the thermidor between crises allows the divergences in our society to have their day without being subject to the tyranny of a transient numerical majority; and that the accepted American tradition of government by extraordinary or concurrent majorities has not stopped innovation or social criticism, it has only slowed change, and in the process has insured a healthy unity behind public policy.

In relation to the past, these may be strong arguments. But are they addressed to a world of big bureaucracies, sustained cold wars, and chronic international and domestic crises? Are there any longer identifiable periods between crises? As long as the frontier was open and the spirit of laissez faire encouraged political parties to be barriers against government action, anarchy in program and uncontrolled shifts in power within the national government were of little consequence. For many years the parties were anti-governmental vehicles, so to speak, minimizing public policy and fencing off large sections of the population and of the domain for private exploitation and private dreams. But we are now in a very different world. As E. E. Schattschneider has pointed out:

"The revolution in communications, the dissolution of nationality blocs, the impact of the labor movement, urbanization, the revolution in public policy, the expansion of the practising electorate in recent years, and the new world position of the United States are only a few of the influences likely to give impetus to political reorganization in the present generation. It is obvious that the *purposes* of political organization are not what they once were. There was a time when it might have been said that the purpose of the party system, or large parts of it, was *obstruction*. In an era of perpetual crisis, political organization is reasonably certain to reflect the anxieties that now dominate all public life."

* * *

It is time for a stringent look at the national politics we have had, the kind of national politics we want, and the reasons for believing that our traditional party system, like a vast glacier, may now have reached the edge of the sea.

The Parties Today: A Mystic Maze

The closer one gets to our two great national parties, the more difficult it is to find them. If you contend that they exist in their quadrennial national conventions, you must be prepared to answer where they are between conventions. If you identify them with the national committee offices in Washington, or one of them with the White House, you will hear immediate disclaimers from the party leaders on Capitol Hill. If a temporary marriage should be negotiated between the party in Congress and the party's executive wing, the great cellular blocks of the party at the state and local levels might well ask embarrassing questions about the true locus of party power.

Perhaps the shortest route through the maze of national party structure begins with the presidential nominating conventions. These are the formal governing bodies of the parties, the selectors of national candidates and issues for the quadrennial elections. They are composed of delegates chosen in a variety of ways and responsible to a wide variety of power groups within the states and beyond the states; Governors, machine leaders, Senators, Members of Congress, pressure groups, individual presidential candidates and their followers, the incumbent President, and so on.

But national conventions generally last less than a week. In order to provide continuity and necessary machinery in the long years between conventions, both parties elect national committees to serve for four years from the adjournment of the conventions. Actually, each state delegation proposes the two national committeemen (one is a woman) who are "elected" by the convention.

The long history of the parties shows that it would be a mistake to suggest that the national committees have been at the power apex of their parties. "Although the party organization can be regarded as . . . capped by the national committee, it may be more accurately described as a system of layers of organization. Each successive layer—county or city, state, national—has an independent concern about elections in its geographical jurisdiction. Yet each higher level of organization, to accomplish its ends, must obtain the collaboration of the lower layer or layers of organization. That collaboration comes about, to the extent that it does come about, through a sense of common cause rather than the exercise of command."

But even this does not tell the whole story. In the case of election campaigns for the Senate and the House, for example, there is no one layer of the party organization clearly responsible for these campaigns. The groups that come closest are the respective party campaign committees in each House, but their power lies merely in the intermittent services and limited financial help they are able to offer; there is no hierarchical power or consistent influence here.

The formal organization [illegible] parties can be described, if [illegible] then, as a series of pyramids with a common base in the shifting sands of active party membership, and generally with no clear locus of power in or out of the government.

As Professor Key has pointed out, there are a number of reasons why the party system has had more *pluribus* than *unum:* "Both unity and disunity within the national organization have their roots in the diverse social, economic, and political interests in the party following. Yet another foundation of deconcentration of party leadership is the federal form of government. State and local party organizations are built up around the patronage of state and local government; and these organizations, particularly in cities and states dominated by one party, have a continuous life regardless of whether the party is in or out of power nationally. State and local patronage makes the local machine financially independent of the national headquarters and contributes to a spirit of independence. Federalism in our formal governmental machinery includes a national element independent of the states, but in our party organization the independent national element is missing. Party structure is more confederative than federal in nature. The state and local machines, built on state patronage, are allied with or paralleled by machines built around the patronage controlled by Senators and Representatives; and owing to the method of dispensation of this patronage, the resultant machines are almost as independent of central control as are the purely local organizations. Federalism in government tends to encourage confederation in the party's government.

This state of affairs might excite no special interest if it were not that [c]onfederation in the government of the parties has had a substantial effect on the conduct of the federal government. This effect can best be highlighted, perhaps, by trying to answer a deceptively simple question: On matters of national policy, what individual or group speaks with authority for each of the national parties?

Who Speaks for the Party?

Obviously, this question cannot be handled without first asking such prior questions as "where" and "when." When we speak of the national party, are we speaking of the in-party? The out-party?[1] The party in the Senate? The party in the House? The party as represented by its national committee? The party in quadrennial convention? All of these? Only some of these? And at what point in time?

Let us start with a presidential election year and a national convention. "Conventions," as Richard Rovere has written, ". . . are exercises in definition." The choice of the Presidency personifies the majority decision of the national convention, and in this respect the winning nominee speaks with special authority as a symbol of what the party stands for at that moment. The image may be particularly clear when an incumbent is renominated, since he usually has had a commanding influence over the drafting of the party platform. In any case, what the candidate decides to emphasize from (or outside of) the platform creates a more powerful image of party policy than the platform itself. From the moment of nomination until election, the presidential candidate is usually the undisputed voice of the party. This does not mean that the voice will necessarily be clear, but no other is likely to be clearer.

There is a circumstance, however, in which even this last generalization needs qualification. Special problems arise when an incumbent President and a new presidential nominee are of the same party. In 1952, for example, with Adlai Stevenson as the Democratic nominee but with Harry S. Truman still in the White House, a series of delicate issues developed over campaign strategy, organization, and policy. President Truman wanted Stevenson to retain Frank McKinney as chairman of the Democratic National Committee. Stevenson, however, exercised his influence to see to it that the Committee selected Stephen Mitchell. Once appointed, Mitchell set up office, as expected, in the Democratic National Committee headquarters in Washington. But Stevenson was still Governor of Illinois. His personal campaign had to be run from Springfield, Illinois. The question immediately arose, was Wilson Wyatt, as Stevenson's personal campaign manager, to give orders to Stephen Mitchell, the chairman of the National Committee? Chaos could have resulted if the answer to this had been no. Then, because of deteriorating relations between Springfield and the White House, Stephen Mitchell took pains to stress that President Truman was still the head of the party, that the Springfield headquarters was to be considered the Springfield office of the Democratic National Committee, and that one of the Committee's channels of authority would still run to the White House.

This resolution of a complex issue was verbal and political, but hardly organizational—and the National Committee found itself the center of a tug of war between the White House and Springfield. It was not until after the election that President Truman called Adlai Stevenson "the head of the nation's Democrats."

The President as Party Spokesman

Apart from the kind of conventions and campaigns that may create unusual ambiguities of the sort just mentioned, the recognized spokesman for a national party controlling the Presidency (the in-party) is the President himself. Not only does the magnificent singularity of the office give the incumbent an unparalleled vehicle for the construction of party programs and philosophy; he is also the accepted party leader.

"The President," as Clinton Rossiter has written, "dictates the selection of the national chairman and other top party officials, reminds his partisans in Congress that their legislative record must be bright if victory is to crown their joint efforts, delivers 'fight talks' to the endless procession of professionals who call upon him, and, through the careful distribution of the loaves and fishes of federal patronage, keeps the party a going concern. The loaves and fishes are not so plentiful as they were in the days of Jackson and Lincoln, but he is still a wholesale distributor of 'jobs for the boys.'"

The extent to which a President can create the image of a reasonably united party, depends, of course, on his capacity to make his own policy pronouncements dominant in the party. This is not always automatic, especially if the President is successfully blocked by powerful leaders of his own party in the Congress or is running out the last two years of his last term. But, even then, the power of his voice generally reduces the voices of self- or group-appointed party spokesmen to a subordinate level.

The Problem of the "Out-Party"

If the in-party has problems in creating a clear party image, the task is many times more difficult for the out-party. No real answer has yet been found to the question of who speaks for the party when it does not control the White House, or when no presidential campaign is in progress. Over the years, some of the major contenders for the job of out-party spokesman have been congressional leaders, national committee chairmen, national committee executive committees, ex-Presidents, defeated presidential candidates, *ad hoc* groups established by the national committees, congressional policy committees, congressional campaign committees, and, most recently, a permanent advisory council to a national committee.

The contention that the leaders of the out-party in Congress have the responsibility and the right to speak for their party has been staunchly defended by those leaders. But, in the years since World War II, intramural struggles between national committee chairmen and spokesmen on the one hand, and congressional leaders and staff on the other, have been staples in out-party politics, regardless of which party was "out." And even when the congressional leaders have reluctantly shared with national committees the job of constructing party policies for campaign purposes, there has been a tendency to insist, as Senate Republican leaders did in 1950, that the products should be limited to "a restatement of the aims and purposes of the Republican members of Congress." As *The New York Times* commented on this occasion, Republican Senate leaders "do not feel that the National Committee properly is a policy-making body, and, in off-year nonpresidential elections, the party members in Congress have to make their own issues without outside interference."

Obvious problems arise in having the congressional leaders speak for the out-party. Congress itself is bifurcated, and its power, as we have said, tends to gravitate into the hands of men who are not necessarily responsive to the party majorities. On occasion, the minority or majority leader in the Senate, or the Speaker or minority leader of the House, may claim to speak for his own party. But whether anybody inside or outside the Congress believes that the voice of the party has been heard in the land depends either upon coincidence with already accepted party formulations or upon the personal prestige and political virtuosity of these congressional spokesmen. Congress is not over being what Woodrow Wilson once called a "disintegrate ministry"; but even when the ministry is not disintegrate, it is rarely representative of either party's national popular majority. Even party leaders in the Congress chosen in caucuses of their own party are captives, willing or unwilling, of the feudal barons who immediately surround them. There are no party policy or steering committees in the House worthy of the name, and those in the Senate lack power and representativeness.

The result is that there are a large number of Democratic and Republican party members who may have no effective voice in the Congress (to say nothing of the White House) but who still feel that they should have a hand in determining their party's national policies. The national committee tends to represent the interests of members of the out-party who feel un- or under-represented in the Congress. In addition, it may be said that the out-party's national committee is the official representative of the party's *executive wing*.

The internal squabbles in both parties frequently look like constitutional fireworks—sparks set off by "separation of powers" and "checks and balances." But without further explanation, these principles are shallow and misleading. The real issue is that the government, in a generation of prolific services and equally prolific regulation, has become a vast arena in which group interests and personalities struggle for power without sufficient reference to questions of the long-range public interest. These groups and personalities use the pressure points and divergent party roles and constituencies of the President, the bureaucracy, the national committees, and the two Houses of Congress as instruments of access and finagle. This produces a politics of "boodle" and accommodation, but not a politics of responsible power and clear national purpose.

The Democratic Advisory Council

The absence of any fully accepted out-party national spokesman has led each party sporadically over the years to try to fill the vacuum. More than a generation ago, the Republicans established an Advisory Committee on Policies and Platform to help focus ideas and power prior to the 1920 convention. The Committee performed its function and died. Similar groups have been formed from time to time.

Perhaps the most noteworthy out-party voice in recent years has been the Democratic Advisory Council of the Democratic National Committee. Established by a resolution of the Executive Committee of the Democratic National Committee on November 27, 1956, the Council exists to provide "a collective voice for the Democratic Party, representing on a year-round basis the millions of Democrats who may or may not be represented in either House of the Congress." The official congressional leaders of the party have refused membership on the Council, but many of the party's national figures (e.g., Adlai Stevenson, Harry Truman, Herbert Lehman, Senator Hubert Humphrey, Governor G. Mennen Williams) belong, as do the members of the Executive Committee of the Democratic National Committee. The Council is helped in its deliberations by advisory committees of distinguished party intellectuals on such matters as foreign policy, domestic economic policy, labor policy, urban problems, science and technology, and party organization.

With their help, the Council has issued a series of statements on major issues facing the nation and the Congress. These pronouncements have not been accepted as party doctrine by the Democratic leaders in the Congress, but they have hardly been in a position to ignore them, if for no other reason than that each statement has had front-page treatment and editorial comment from leading newspapers.

* * *

Party Finance and Party Coherence

The problem of the out-party in developing a recognizable philosophy and coherent political program is further complicated by the disorganized state of its finances. Actually, the in-party is also haunted by the same spectre. Money-raising for national and congressional campaigns is such a jungle, and so choked with the vines of subterfuge to get around the Hatch Act and other unrealistic laws, that efforts to develop coherent national party organizations are seriously impeded.

It is an axiom of congressional campaigning, for example, that little direct financial help can be expected either from Washington (campaign committees on Capitol Hill or the national committees) or from state committees. There are, of course, exceptions but these are sufficiently rare to prove the rule. Since the party as party (no matter how defined) has not been a sure source of financial help to the man campaigning for a seat in the Senate or House, what obligation does he owe to it, or to programs endorsed by it?

And there is a further complication. Some support for congressional candidates may come in the form of what Senator Benton used to call "emotional money"—money given by friends and admirers, with no strings attached. But much of it comes from constituent interests, or powerful national interests, expecting, if not favors, at least sympathetic understanding and ready access. It makes little difference if the President or an advisory council to a national committee comes out with a strong plea for more liberal foreign economic policies in the interests of national security and world economic development so long as powerfully placed Representatives or Senators are beholden financially to narrow anti-foreign aid and trade interests in their constituencies.

Attempts by the national committees to raise money for "the party" have gone largely into the staggering costs of presidential campaigns, past or present. And even when, as in the case of the Republican National Finance Committee, a consolidated drive has been carried out for the benefit of the campaign committees of Congress, as well as for the national committee, no attempt has been made to develop any national party criteria for allocating the funds. Actually, none of the four congressional campaign committees purports to take any interest whatsoever in a congressional candidate's policy stand or his identification with a party majority. They are interested in electing "Republicans" period, or "Democrats" period.

It is true that both national committees have given increasingly large campaign contributions to congressional candidates in the form of services and advice. But these services have frequently caused frictions and jealousies between the national committees and the campaign committees of the Congress. As one careful student of the "Hill" campaign committees has noted, "In a large measure, the continued existence and importance of the senatorial and congressional campaign committees symbolize the desire of congressional leaders to protect their interests when they believe these interests to be counter to the ambitions of the national party organization." The linear mile that separates Capitol Hill from the White House also separates the campaign committees of Congress from the national committees of the two parties.

It is probable that the first national committee to develop a mass financial base sufficient to allow a spillover from presidential to legislative campaigns will have made the most important political break-through of the century. But this is still in the future, and will involve legal revision as well as monetary success.

These, then, are our national parties: unified for presidential contests, otherwise divided in power and lacking in definition; sporadically financed through various channels, subterfuges, and individual candidacies; peculiarly confused as out-parties; weak vehicles for executive-legislative cooperation as in-parties. They have performed valued services of reconciliation and compromise in our history—services which should not be underestimated. But the problem today is how to transcend these services in order to provide the government with sustained and responsible national power. How should our national party system be modified in order to make the parties effective instruments of our national purposes and needs?

Nine Political Reforms

One reason why it is safe to suggest that the national party system must be strengthened in order to bring sustained power in our government is that the safe-guards of the Constitution will continue to discourage any force that becomes so unified as to threaten our freedom. The American people hold firm to the sanctity of the Constitution. It is inconceivable that they would countenance a wholesale revision of the Constitution in the foreseeable future. No model of a new or improved party system that rests on substantial constitutional change is realistic.

* * *

What we are after is a national two-party system that will continue to have room for diversity and compromise but will nevertheless bring about more coherent and responsible programming by the executive and legislative branches and more coherent and responsible criticism of policy and administration. We are after a system that will make parties compete vigorously to find the right answers; that will organize political power at the national level so that it is adequate to carry out those answers; and that will make this power ultimately accountable to popular majorities.

This neither presumes nor suggests ideological or highly disciplined parties, although it does presume differences in the ideological propensities of each party and also presumes that party members who vote consistently against their own party's majority will not be favored with positions of party power inside or outside the Congress.

Various changes in state primary laws, in methods of choosing national convention delegates and national committee members, and in grass-roots political organization could have a profound influence on national party behavior. But, in my opinion, changes of this sort will come about rapidly only if prior attention is given to the following political reforms . . .

* * *

1. Broadly Based Financing

Nothing comes closer to the heart of party reform than financial reorganization. As already noted, candidates for Congress, incumbent or new, receive little or no financial aid either from their national committees or from their campaign committees on Capitol Hill. If the normal concerns of a Congressman with his constituency are reenforced by heavy campaign contributions from local interests, and if there are no direct countervailing pressures or inducements from the national party, it should not be surprising that the Congressman fails to give due weight to the national interest. On the other hand, if the national party were able to help finance even a small proportion of a Congressman's campaign, and thus reduce his dependency on local money, he might feel freer to weigh short-term local against long-term national interests or, more accurately, to weigh the special interests against the common interests within his own constituency.

* * *

. . . at least for sustaining operations the parties should depend heavily upon small gifts solicited by mail or by nationally sponsored party dinners.

To insure an increasingly responsible role for the national committees over national party finances, the Hatch Act provisions dealing with spending limitations for national campaigns should be repealed or realistically adjusted to meet the realities of political life. Furthermore, federal income-tax credits or exemptions should be allowed for individual contributions to the *national* organizations or candidates up to a certain amount.

The postage franking privilege and a block of network television time, radio time, and newspaper advertising space should be given to each national committee before each national election, to be financed by congressional appropriations and rigidly audited by the General Accounting Office.

2. Two-Party Competition

One of the most compelling reasons for the national committees to have more money is that greater riches may encourage more vigorous competition between the parties in all states and congressional districts in the country. Everything we know about one-party areas indicates that they tend to reflect minority interests and, through unopposed re-elections, produce Members of Congress who are pushed purely by seniority into positions of high and unrepresentative power.

"The variations in the degree to which the parties are competitive within their respective states condition in a major way the policy inclinations of Senators," V. O. Key writes. "Those from one-party states may be untouched by the great tides of national politics. On the other hand, Senators from close states may live under the strongest compulsion to collaborate among themselves in the promotion of the cause of their party nationally."

The more quickly the national party organizations succeed in stimulating opposition in districts and states where there is none, or in narrowing the margin of the dominant party's victory, the better chance there is of relating the Congress more closely to the interests of the national majority. The interests of a majority in one part of the nation are now more and more similar to the interests of majorities in all other parts of the nation, and the stimulation of political competition in all sections cannot help increasing the power of the national majority in the government as a whole. Furthermore, real party rivalries should tend to increase informed social criticism and encourage greater citizen interest and participation, including financial participation.

...There are extremely delicate problems involved in having representatives of the national committees insinuate themselves in this way into matters traditionally considered to be the prerogatives of the local organizations. But local party leaders are often unequipped to recruit and develop the type of people needed to understand and execute national programs. The help of national party representatives in this area could be of enormous long-range significance. And if the state committees can be encouraged to establish full-time party staffs in their state capitals, the job of the national committees and their regional representatives would be correspondingly easier.

As the national committees become stronger financially and organizationally, their prestige will also grow to the point where they could have a much more positive influence on the choice of congressional nominees. Until that time, their interests, and those of the country, would seem to be best served by a thoroughgoing drive to strengthen two-party competition in all parts of the country. . . .

3. Advisory Councils

At its best, an advisory council to an out-party's national committee can be a loyal opposition in the manner of the British shadow cabinet. The council obviously has less meaning for the in-party; although, even here, it is possible that a small group of discerning party members detached from direct governmental operations might bring fresh insights to the President. On the organizational level the in-party would profit by some such device to link the professional politician, as represented by the executive committee of the national committee, more closely to the policy functions of the President and the party in the Congress.

For both the out-party and the in-party an advisory council, unhampered by day-to-day governing, should be able to anticipate at least some of the kaleidoscope problems that arise almost daily in political affairs and provide more careful analyses of them than the over-burdened government official has time to do. Both parties could certainly use continuing intellectual labor directed towards the drafting of platforms for the conventions. Both parties could profit from systematically tapping the minds and talents of their most intelligent members outside the government bureaucracy.

Although the advisory councils should explicitly represent the executive wing of their parties, they should include in their membership, at least as non-voting observers, the congressional party leaders or their designates.

* * *

The two national conventions, as the ultimate governing bodies of the national parties, should formally sanction the establishment of advisory councils as permanent policy arms of the two national committees.

4. Party Clubs

The idea of having a "Democratic Club" and a "Republican Club" in Washington to house the national committees and congressional campaign staffs and to serve as a social headquarters for the parties has been considered off and on for many years by both parties. Actually, *ad hoc* party clubs presently exist in Washington—but only for social purposes. If these clubs were given greater dignity and larger facilities for housing disparate party staffs, they would unquestionably promote more coordinated and efficient party efforts, not by hierarchy but by propinquity. . . .

5. Congressional Terms

The constitutional provisions for staggered elections are a significant cause of the pullings and haulings in our national government. It is equally clear that a two-year term for the House is too short to turn a freshman member into an effective legislator or to avoid the harassing and expensive responsibilities of perpetual campaigning. The last election and the next election are often an indistinguishable blur. Furthermore, if a truly competitive two-party system should develop across the nation, there will be more frequent alternation of victorious candidates between the parties, thus shortening the tenure of any one Congressman.

A four-year term for the House, if it coincides with the presidential term, should have a number of important effects. Under normal conditions, it would insure the same political complexion for the House as the President's. It would reduce the continuous campaign and constituency pressures which a two-year term almost inevitably fosters. It would give Congressmen sufficient time to learn their trade and to make a substantial contribution to public life.

Also, if an eight-year term were provided for members of the Senate (half of them coming up for election every four years at the same time as the Presidency), the likelihood that the President would have a working majority in both Houses would be overwhelming. At the same time, the conservative utility of overlapping terms would be maintained with only a slight modification in the constitutional wish for continuity.

Enhancing the possibility of one-party control of the government would enhance the possibility of substantial governmental power and would unmistakably fix responsibility for governmental policy.

6. Party Policy Committees in the Congress

The Legislative Branch Appropriation Act of 1946 established party policy committees in the Senate after the

House of Representatives had rejected the idea in the Legislative Reorganization bill of that same year. The Democrats in the Senate have placed their majority leader in charge of their policy committee. Lyndon Johnson's power comes in large part from his own personal ability; but it seems certain that his leadership has been strengthened by his policy committee role. His power would more truly reflect the interests of the majority of his party in the Senate if the representative character of the policy committee were broadened and more caucuses were held. The Republican policy committee in the Senate is far more representative than its Democratic counterpart; what it needs is to be tied more closely to the operations of the Republican floor leader who is a member of the policy committee, but not its chairman.

With these changes, the example set by the Senate should be followed by the House of Representatives. Adequately staffed party policy committees should be elected in both Houses by caucus. In the House of Representatives, the Speaker should chair his party's committee; the minority leader should chair the minority party's committee. The majority policy committee should assume the functions of the House Rules Committee. Both policy committees should act as the committee on committees for their party, and should perform policy and steering functions presently scattered or moribund.

In order to bring greater cohesion to the handling of major presidential recommendations, the four policy committees should meet jointly for two weeks in late January and early February each year to conduct general hearings on the President's State of the Union message. The hearings should be widely covered by press, radio, and television; the leaders in the administration and in the out-party should be heard; and majority and minority reports should be issued for the general guidance of legislators and of the general public. These reports would demonstrate the differences in program between the parties and also the areas of national agreement.

These changes in the basic units of party power in the Congress are designed to make power more visible and more responsive to party majorities in each House than now obtains. But if they are to be effective they must be accompanied by the following reform.

7. Seniority

The principle of seniority has always been defended in the Congress on the ground that it is the only system for elevation to positions of power that has the virtue of being automatic. Congress, it is argued, is already so charged with tension and conflict that additional struggles for power would be dangerous to the underlying agreement upon which compromise and unity rest.

There is enough weight to this argument to suggest that if responsible majority rule can be achieved without destroying the impersonal attributes of the seniority system, the system should be kept. However, there seems to be no reason why a simple mathematical formula cannot be devised to give added seniority credit to legislators who come from competitive two-party districts and states. For example, a Member might receive two points for every *general* election in which his opponent received more than 20 per cent of the vote. Seniority would still rule, automatically, but power would tend to shift toward those Congressmen who come from districts in which vigorous two-party competition searches out the majority interest.

8. 22nd Amendment

The 22nd Amendment places a two-term limit on American Presidents. Its effect is to weaken the political power and influence of the President in his second term, particularly in his last two years. At a time when foreign policy and national defense hold apocalyptic potentialities, it is madness to retain in our Constitution an Amendment which *guarantees* fitful national power.

9. Executive Talent

The strength and responsiveness of the national government depend upon many factors, but one of the most basic requirements is a core of able political executives to direct the sprawling departments and agencies of the government. Present recruiting for these men is a hit-or-miss affair carried on at the departmental, presidential, congressional, and national party level.

No greater service could be performed by the national party committees, especially by their regional representatives, than to compile a continuing roster of good people in and out of the party organization for these strategic jobs. Selecting the right men, of course, would have to be done ultimately by the President in a full understanding of state and congressional party interests.

But the job is too important not to be undertaken systematically, and the national committees are the ones to do it.

The Traditional Conflicts

The contention that a political shift is inevitable in this country and that changes, such as those advocated above, in the traditional national party arrangements are now possible rests on a theory of politics supported by empirical evidence.

The theory, borrowed intact from Professor E. E. Schattschneider, is that politics is basically concerned with the expression and resolution of conflict. The relevant corollary of the theory is that if the nature of social conflict changes, either political institutions must adjust in order to reflect the new social impulses or society suffers the penalties which inertia and impairment of function exact. In a democratic society, the atmosphere is conducive to adjustment.

The parties historically have performed a variety of very valuable functions in American society. They have been functions of accommodation, compromise, and the peaceful transmission of power. Only rarely have the parties been concerned with insuring coherence of program or responsible power in the carrying out of program. Their lack of interest in national policies backed by national political power can be largely explained by the nature of the social conflicts with which they have had to deal. These traditional conflicts merit brief examination before we pass on to the contention of this paper that the character of the conflicts is changing and that the party system must change with it.

New and Old Settlers

One of the perennial conflicts in American history has been that between new and old settlers....

Historically, as one generation became settled and adjusted, it tended to look hostilely at new arrivals, particularly if the newcomers were from a different part of the old world, spoke a different language, or had a different religion. In the fourteen years before World War I, immigration rose to a peak of a million a year. In contrast to the nineteenth century immigration, the largest part of this million came from southern and eastern Europe: Italy, Poland, Russia, Hungary, Greece. Their attempts to find a life for themselves, especially in the urban areas of the East and Middle West; the resistances they met; the fears they created and suffered; the help local politicians gave them in exchange for their votes—all this has been and, although greatly modified by now, still is the stuff of American politics. Each group in turn has pursued the American dream; each in turn has found the upward ladder wobbly, and at times sticky. Part of the glory of our traditional party system has been that when other ladders were removed the political ladder was almost always open. But many crowded on the ladder at once; and as some of those below overtook those on the higher rungs, conflict was inevitable.

Sections and Classes

If the new and the old have warred, so have sections and classes....

* * *

The remnants of these ... regional struggles are still with us, especially in the Congress, but they have been complicated—sometimes modified, sometimes egregiously promoted—by far-ranging class conflicts between rich and poor, debtor and creditor, capital and labor, small farmers and big farmers. On a few occasions, these class collisions have got beyond the control of existing political machinery. But this has been rare. In the words of David Potter we have been a "people of plenty," and for much of our history the frontier has provided a real as well as a psychological safety-valve. What it could not provide, democratic politics by and large has provided: a redress of intolerable economic grievances.

The Negro Issue

In one form or another the Negro problem has always been with us. Like some vast geologic fault it has rendered the land unstable and created deep moral fissures. It was an issue in colonial days; it had to be compromised in the drafting of our Constitution. It was the emotional core of the Civil War. In the cruel and stupid days of reconstruction, the social and political inversions imposed by northern occupation terrified both whites and Negroes and left raw scars of fear, hatred, and anti-Republicanism.

The Negro issue has occupied a central place in the development of the national party organizations and in the formation of political alliances. Because the issue seemed until recently a "southern" problem, the Democratic party as the more national of the two parties had to live a precarious existence astride a two-headed donkey. It survived by promising the Presidency to the North and the Congress to the South. The Republican party, on the other hand, as a party operating effectively only in the North, was able to strike a bargain with southern Democrats which linked white supremacy and business supremacy in the policy labyrinths of the Congress. The bargain clouded the image of each party and put largely irresponsible power over policy in the hands of a southern Democratic–northern Republican coalition, buttressed by seniority and hallowed by carefully designed rules. None of this would have happened if the parties had not had to juggle the Negro issue. It has been the single most useful device of the economic conservatives to keep the political parties from becoming coherent instruments of majority rule.

Personal Ambitions

Like every country, America has known the conflicts of clashing personal ambitions. Politics is, among other things, a study of power and the powerful, of influence and the influential. Issues are often a cover for the struggle of personalities for deference and status. Politics is unintelligible without an understanding of the raw strivings of people for recognition. The struggles between ambitious politicians have left incradicable marks on the history of the national parties.

The Changes in the Conflicts

The national parties have become what they are because of these historical conflicts which they have had to settle, hide, or gloss over....

But what happens when the conditions of conflict change? For they are changing, and rapidly, in the United States.

The Social Changes

Take the struggle between the old and the new. We used to be able to tell the difference between old and new settlers by their accent, or dress, or occupational level. But we are fuller of hundred-per cent Americans every day and are rapidly reaching the time when nationality politics will be as anachronistic as the trolley car....

Or take sectional and class conflict. The heart has been cut out of sectionalism by vast changes in technology and communications which have dispersed industry and revolutionized agriculture. Where are the one-crop "Cotton Ed" Smiths of a few years back? The fact is that there are precious few one-crop areas left in America. And even where there are, as in some of the great agricultural regions of the Great Plains, technology is bringing a revolution of another kind. In the last five years almost four million people have left the farm. The forecast for reapportionment of congressional seats after the 1960 census suggests a dramatic decrease in rural representation in the United States Congress, and this trend will continue as the rise in population throws more and more people into metropolitan areas.

The movement in urban politics tends to be toward class rather than regional politics. But even class politics has changed. It is no longer a kind of rabble vs. gentry rivalry. Rather, among other things, it is national industry against highly bureaucratized and well-paid national labor. Senator Barry Goldwater of Arizona is not a regional figure. In the congressional elections of 1958, national giants contended in that sparsely populated desert state, and for national stakes.

What bothers the auto worker in Detroit bothers the auto worker in Los Angeles. What worries the businessman in Chicago worries his competitor in Boston. With transcontinental jet planes, the political or labor or industrial leader whose home is in

San Francisco is almost more accessible to his counterpart in New York than is a train traveler from Boston; and, in any case, distance has been obliterated by electricity, electronics, and the direct-dial telephone.

And what is happening to the Negro issue? It, too, is becoming nationalized. Today there are more Negroes in New York than in New Orleans; more in Detroit than in Birmingham, Alabama; more in Pittsburgh than in Little Rock; more in Los Angeles than in Richmond; more in Chicago than in Atlanta. The Negroes' locust-like migration to northern metropolitan centers may have brought new problems to city governments, but it has aroused a critical competition between the two major parties in the North and West to capture the Negro vote. In heavily populated, evenly divided states, a bloc shift of a few votes can mean thirty or forty electoral college votes for a presidential candidate.

Perhaps more than any one other factor, the northern migration of the Negro is working tremendous transformations in our political life. The South no longer can exercise a veto in either presidential convention. Some diehards may walk out in 1960, but the result will only be that they will risk losing what waning power they have in the Congress. For, in more than sixty congressional districts in the North and West, the Negro holds the political balance of power if he decides to bloc-vote; and in the South his political power is likely to increase steadily despite the present tensions.

As for the clash of personal political ambitions in the United States, they are being completely submerged by the international and domestic concerns of the American public. War and peace, inflation and depression, are both personal and universal issues; tariffs, taxes, foreign aid, military spending, federal reserve policies, and hosts of other national policies affect local economic activities across the land. Politicians who wish to become statesmen must be able to talk intelligently about issues that concern people in *all* constituencies. The extraordinary social and economic changes now going on are absorbing and transcending the old conflicts of personal ambitions.

The Party Changes

The shifts in the nature of the conflicts are reflected in the changes that are already taking place in our party system:

1. The number of one-party states and one-party congressional districts is dramatically declining.

* * *

2. The permanent staffs of the national party committees and the variety of committee functions have grown greatly during the past decade. Until World War II both national committees were served by skeletal staffs, except for the few months before national presidential elections. Today both of them maintain year-round staffs of between seventy-five and a hundred people. In election years this number doubles or triples. The annual budget of each committee amounts to almost a million dollars—a figure which skyrockets during election years.

3. Both national committees are doing everything within their power to spread their financial base. The evolution has been from fat-cats and expensive fund-raising banquets to mass appeals and direct-mail solicitation.

4. Almost unnoticed, a revolution has occurred in the "nationalization" of off-year senatorial and congressional campaigns. As recently as 1938,

the press and the public criticized President Roosevelt for campaigning in an off-year election. But in 1954, when both the President and the titular leader of the Democrats actively campaigned in their parties' congressional elections, both the newspapers and the voters seemed to accept the fact that it was perfectly all right for the executive wings of the parties to interest themselves actively in the outcome of the legislative contests. . . .

5. Since 1937, the Presidents have met regularly with party leaders in the Congress on matters of legislative priority and strategy. This has elevated the prestige and power of these men, particularly on matters of foreign policy and national defense. The passage of the Legislative Reorganization Act of 1946 further recognized the need for party leadership in the Congress, and succeeded to some degree in institutionalizing the leadership function in the Senate which established party policy committees with paid staffs.

6. The creation of the Democratic Advisory Council and the recent appearance of an embryonic Republican counterpart show a new concern in both parties for clarifying the party image. There is little doubt that, eventually, pronouncements of these "executive wings" of the parties will be more effective than similar attempts by congressional leaders or individual party spokesmen excepting the President.

The Conclusion

This far from exhaustive list of the responses of our political system to nationalizing forces represents only the beginnings of adaptation and adjustment. Our basic political institutions, and their relationships to each other and to the public, are in a state of flux. If we want a political system designed to give full play to America's political energies and to hold them within bounds set by a popular majority, we are obligated to modify the system still further.

The reforms outlined in these pages will not obviate America's continuing need for personal force and political virtuosity in the office of the Presidency and in top positions in the Congress. Nor will these or any other party reforms dispel the terrifying military, diplomatic, and social problems of our age. But they will help the parties toward stronger leadership in a more responsible framework than has been traditional. To paraphrase Emerson, they can help us to perceive the terror of life and to man ourselves to face it. In this apocalyptic age, can we ask for greater service from our political parties? We must not ask for less.

NOTE

1. "In-party" will be used to refer to the party which controls the Presidency regardless of whether it controls the Congress or either House thereof. "Out-party" is used throughout to refer to the party that does not control the White House, whether or not it controls either House or both Houses of Congress.

SELECTED BIBLIOGRAPHY

Berelson, Bernard, Paul Lazarsfeld, and William McPhee. *Voting*. Chicago: University of Chicago Press, 1954. A widely cited study of voter behavior in the 1948 election in Elmira, New York. Reports in depth the impact of the political campaign, especially as perceived through mass media. One of the most important works on voter behavior during the campaign.

Binkley, Wilfred E. *American Political Parties: Their Natural History.* 4th ed. New York: Knopf, 1962. The standard history of American parties. Treats the organizational development, policy stances, and election campaigns of the parties.

Campbell, Angus, Philip Converse, Warren Miller, and Donald Stokes. *The American Voter.* New York: Wiley, 1960. The classic work on voting behavior. Analyzes the impact of party identification, issue orientation, and candidate preference on the individual voter in the 1952 and 1956 elections. Examines the relationship between these factors on the one hand, and the social status of voters, the timing of voting decisions, and voter turnout, on the other. The authors' classification of presidential elections has been widely applied to American political history.

Clausen, Aage, Philip Converse, and Warren Miller. "Electoral Myth and Reality: The 1964 Election," *American Political Science Review,* 59 (June 1965), 321–336. Analyzes the Goldwater defeat in 1964. Concludes that the conservatives erred in believing that there is a large bloc of conservative voters who might be brought to the polls by "a choice, not an echo." Shows that Goldwater received more votes than those of people who agreed with him on ideological grounds because of party-identification voting.

Cotter, Cornelius P., and Bernard C. Hennessy. *Politics Without Power: The National Party Committees.* New York: Atherton Press, 1964. An examination of the two national committees and a discussion of their powerlessness in national politics. Confirms Schattschneider's description of American parties as a "truncated pyramid."

Dawson, Richard E., and James A. Robinson. "Inter-Party Competition, Economic Variables, and Welfare Policies in the American States," *Journal of Politics,* 25 (May 1963), 265–287. Argues that the level of welfare payments is related to economic variables rather than to the intensity of party competition.

Eldersveld, Samuel J. *Political Parties: A Behavioral Analysis.* Chicago: Rand McNally, 1964. A study of political parties based on interviews with Detroit party activists and citizens. Surveys the level of party activity by the party organization and assesses the impact on the voters. Describes differences in ideology between Democratic and Republican activists and between officials at different levels in the same party. Also describes the different social and economic backgrounds of both party activists and officials and their attitudes toward politics. Provides sharp insight into the internal diversities within each party. Also suggests important differences between them in policy, activity, and sources of workers.

Epstein, Leon D. *Political Parties in Western Democracies.* New York: Praeger, 1967. A far-ranging survey of the party systems of Western democracies. Rejects Duverger's theory that the future of political parties lies in the mass-membership parties found on the European left. Suggests that parties are the product of historical and contemporary social factors, and that the party of the activists may be withering away because media campaigning, the fund-raising that supports it, and the life-style and education of the electorate have reduced the effectiveness of grass-roots organizations and made them difficult to sustain.

Fenton, John H. *Midwest Politics.* New York: Holt, Rinehart and Winston, 1966. Classifies the six Midwestern states into issue-oriented party systems (Michigan, Minnesota, and Wisconsin) and job-oriented party systems (Illinois, Indiana, and Ohio). Considers the historical and social factors that contributed to the development of vastly different party politics in the two groups of states. Argues that these political styles have important consequences for public policy.

Fenton, John H., and Donald W. Chamberlayne. "The Literature Dealing with the Relationships Between Political Processes, Socioeconomic Conditions & Public Policies in the American States: A Bibliographical Essay," *Polity,* 1 (Spring 1969), 388–404. Argues that the extent of interparty competition is a significant independent variable in the levels of public services (welfare, Aid to Dependent Children, educational and general services) apart from socioeconomic conditions in the various states. Conflicts in view with the conclusions of Dawson and Robinson, *op. cit.,* that the intensity of electoral competition is not a major variable in state policy outputs.

Heard, Alexander. *The Costs of Democracy.* Chapel Hill: University of North Carolina Press, 1960. The standard work on political finance. Describes the amounts of money spent in the 1952 and 1956 elections, the sources of funds for the two parties, the techniques of raising funds, the uses of money, and the greater import of money in nomination than in general election campaigns. Surveys the policy options available for coping with the massive pressures on politicans to raise money, especially to finance media campaigning.

Holtzman, Abraham. *Interest Groups and Lobbying.* New York: Macmillan, 1966. A brief survey of the activities of American political interest groups, with comparisons to the role of pressure groups in Great Britain and Italy. Treats the relationship between interest group activity and the characteristics of American politics—especially the separation of powers, federalism, and undisciplined coalition parties.

Key, V. O., Jr. *American State Politics: An Introduction.* New York: Knopf, 1956. A classic study showing the impact of national balloting on state voting and making a persuasive argument against holding state elections in nonpresidential years. Suggests the negative impact of the long ballot on state government; shows that nominations in primary elections are not representative and at the same time sap the strength of the minority party so that it cannot offer effective general election opposition to the majority; and describes how effective policy making is often frustrated by divided party control of state government.

———. *Southern Politics.* New York: Knopf, 1950. A survey of the southern states analyzing the impact of race upon southern politics, the effect of southern one-partyism on national politics, and the consequences of transferring the struggle for control of the government from the general election to the primary. Provides an insight into the background of politics in the Old Confederacy and is rich with hypotheses about the consequences of one-party systems for democratic government, although it is no longer descriptive of southern politics. Fascinating vignettes of politics and politicians in the solid Democratic South.

Lockard, Duane. *New England State Politics.* Princeton, N.J.: Princeton University Press, 1959. A survey of politics in the six New England states with emphasis on the electoral bases of the parties, the cohesiveness and effectiveness of party organizations, the importance of parties in government, and the policy consequences of different kinds of party systems.

Milbrath, Lester. *The Washington Lobbyists.* Chicago: Rand McNally, 1963. An extensive survey of the recruitment and activities of Washington lobbyists, their effectiveness, and the groups they represent.

Rae, Douglas W. *The Political Consequences of Electoral Laws.* New Haven, Conn.: Yale University Press, 1967. A study of elections in twenty countries over a twenty-year period. Shows that there may be less difference between plurality and proportional election systems than their respective advocates insist. Finds that in both systems the largest parties gain disproportionate representation in the legislature, while the small parties do not win their just due. One of the few studies to probe effectively the relationship of institutional arrangements and political realities.

Schattschneider, E. E. *The Semi-Sovereign People.* New York: Holt, Rinehart and Winston, 1960. A plea for "the socialization of conflict" through effective, responsible political parties and the election system to overcome the narrow scope and upper-class bias of the powerful pressure system in America.

Sindler, Allan P. *Political Parties in the United States.* New York: St. Martin's Press, 1966. A concise survey of American parties with perceptive analysis of the consequences of various types of party systems (one-party bifactional competition, two-party competition, and so forth).

White, Theodore, H. *The Making of the President, 1960.* New York: Atheneum, 1961. The best of the "Making of the President" series. Captures the color of American presidential campaigning without forfeiting close observation of nomination and general election politics. Gives an especially provocative commentary on broad trends —though perhaps using less precise methods than those of political scientists.

Zeigler, Harmon, and Michael Baer. *Lobbying: Interaction and Influence in American State Legislatures.* Belmont, Cal.: Wadsworth Publishing Co., 1969. A survey of lobbyists and legislative lobbying in Massachusetts, Oregon, North Carolina, and Utah. Devotes attention to the recruitment and status of lobbyists and the relationship between lobbying and the party system. Also gives special attention to the perceptions of lobbying activity by lobbyists and the legislators they seek to influence.

three

The Congress

Congress: Liberal or Popular Institution

The decade of the 1960s witnessed a renewed interest in the Congress by scholars, journalists, and the public, an interest that was stimulated by the increased role of Congress in national policy making: the civil rights acts of 1960, 1964, and 1965; Medicare legislation; the Gulf of Tonkin Resolution; and the subsequent debates about the United States commitments in Vietnam. The visibility of congressional personalities—Lyndon B. Johnson, Hubert Humphrey, and Edmund Muskie, among others—also contributed to this renewed interest. In addition, the revelations of Bobby Baker's and Senator Thomas Dodd's activities added to mass awareness of Congress. While these events and personalities may have illuminated the existence of Congress, they did not necessarily help many citizens understand its role in the American political system.

At the same time that Senator Everett M. Dirksen (the former Republican floor leader) asserted that Congress was the citadel, the central institution, of American democracy, his colleague Senator Joseph S. Clark often said that Congress was both undemocratic and incapable of responding to national crises. There are, however, many meanings and interpretations of the word "democracy." Some students of American politics, including J. Austin Ranney and E. E. Schattschneider, believe that democracy means majority rule; that is, majorities should be capable of making decisions. Other observers—William S. White, for example—argue that democracy involves the reconciliation of majority rule and minority and individual rights through such representative institutions as Congress. At times Congress responds to broad national majorities, as in the first hundred days of Franklin D. Roosevelt's New Deal. At other times, a small band of men can prevent the passage of legislation, as the continuing post-World War II debate over civil rights legislation reveals. Whether Congress is seen as a democratic institution depends in the first instance upon one's definition of democracy.

Although some of the features of the congressional process promote majority rule, others protect the interests of minorities. On balance, the rules and structure of Congress can be employed by entrenched minorities to delay and frustrate congressional action. The seniority system, albeit an informal practice, places men from one-party, socially homogeneous, and usually conservative districts in command positions as committee chairmen; as such, they can kill or cripple legislation favored by a majority of their colleagues in the House and the Senate. In the Senate, the present cloture rule allows small minorities, whether liberal or conservative, to delay action on the floor through the filibuster, or unlimited debate. The House Rules Committee, for many years controlled by conservative Republicans and southern Democrats, bottled up controversial civil rights, federal aid to education, and social welfare legislation. Cumbersome procedures, such as the discharge petition and the calendar Wednesday procedure by which a bill may be taken from a committee's jurisdiction for floor action, make it difficult for even a determined majority to bring legislation to the floor over the objections of an equally determined minority. In the Senate, which conducts most of its business by unanimous consent, a single member's objections can bring the process to a standstill.

These rules of procedure, informal practices, and structures generally give the advantage in Congress to interests that favor the status quo. In 1957, for example, southern members of Congress employed the threat of a filibuster to wring important concessions from the backers of the first civil rights legislation in more than eighty years. Concerned by the effect of these and other dilatory tactics, the sponsors of the bill were forced to accept the deletion of Section III, granting important powers to the attorney general in civil rights suits. Although filibusters and the threat of filibusters have been employed to frustrate northern liberals, they have also been used by these same liberals to protect the Supreme Court. In the summer and fall of 1964 a coalition of northern liberals (Democrats and Republicans) rallied around the leadership of Senators Paul Douglas and William Proxmire to protect the Supreme Court's decision in *Reynolds v. Sims,* which eventually reversed legislative apportionments in more than half the states. These liberals filibustered Senator Dirksen's repeated attempts to overturn the Court's decision by limiting its jurisdiction over state legislative apportionment. After more than twenty years of criticizing conservatives for their use of dilatory tactics, liberals applied the same techniques to obtain their policy objectives.

There is a close relation between the frustration of policy preferences and demands for congressional reforms, as illustrated by debates over the rules, repeated attempts to change the rules, and use of the rules as shown above. Although some purists argue for congressional reform as a means of promoting majority rule in Congress, most reformers, however, are simply masking their real objectives behind the banner of reform. Frustrated by congressional inaction on civil rights and social welfare legislation, they argue for congressional changes that will make it easier to obtain action in these important fields. Their arguments for reform, however, are usually couched in terms of democratic theory, that is, the theory of majority rule.

In contrast to these arguments, political conservatives in and out of Congress claim that consistent majorities and minorities do not exist in the Senate and the House. Congress, they urge, is composed of shifting majorities and minorities. Coalitions arise, cohere, and are replaced by new blocs in Congress, each organized around specific issues and legislation. A member voting in the majority on one issue may find himself in the minority on another question. However persuasive this argument may be, it does not answer the majority-rule democrats, for there are several fundamental issues in American public life around which permanent majorities and minorities have formed. The most notable of these issues is race relations. The inability of Congress to resolve this basic problem belies the arguments of conservatives that a majority can work its will. A majority may eventually prevail, but in the interim major crises can undermine the national consensus and threaten the survival of the polity. The fact is that the protection of minority rights sometimes promotes minority rule. Thus, conservatives have used the minority and individual rights argument to protect their interests at the price of national stability.

Before the contribution of Congress to political democracy can be evaluated, students of American politics must also understand the role of Congress in the political system. What does Congress do? How does it perform its responsibilities? How does its structure—the parties and their elected leaders, the standing committees and their chairmen, and the rules of procedure—shape its role and performance? Obviously, Congress legislates, but legislation is only one of its functions. It also represents citizens' demands on their government, attempts to manage and resolve conflicts in the political system, and, hopefully, makes decisions that are regarded as legitimate or authoritative by the citizens. Thus, as Ralph K. Huitt has noted, Congress is more than a bill-and-resolution factory. Congress must do more than legislate; it must build a broad national consensus for the legislation it enacts.

Congress must perform all these activities without disintegrating in the process. In addition to resolving conflict and legislating for the political system, Congress must protect its internal structure and process. In order to understand how this fragile balance is maintained, students of American politics must examine how the members get to Capitol Hill, how they behave once they arrive, the "folkways" of the institution, the internal distribution of power and influence, the decision-making processes, and so on. Each of these factors partially explains the countervailing, centrifugal (dispersal of power), and centripetal (concentration of power) forces at work in both the Congress and the entire political system.

Congressional Recruitment and Congressional Behavior

The men who come to Congress are the products of a highly fragmented and localized recruitment system that centers around the constituency party. These party organizations operate in a variety of constituencies that range from highly competitive two-party districts to the one-party districts of the South described by V. O. Key, Jr. In some areas where local and state machines are strong, as in Connecticut, the party organization may actually recruit candidates. In other areas, such as South Carolina and Florida, where parties are fragmented, candidates may be recruited by rival factions or by groups of "friends and neighbors." Some House and Senate members come from relatively safe districts, while others have to nurture shifting electoral coalitions in closely contested campaigns.

If members wish to remain in Congress after the next election, they must be sensitive to the local constituencies from which they were recruited. Each member must calculate what percentage of time he must give to satisfy various interests in his constituency in order to remain in Congress. Each member performs this rough calculation in a variety of ways: by polling electors, by reading letters and telegrams from key constituents, by making frequent trips back home, and by talking to opinion makers and leaders in his state or district. Some members use all of these methods; others place their confidence in one or more particular method. However he informs himself, a member of Congress develops a cognitive map, a set of perceptions and an evaluation of his constituents' needs, wants, and desires; these help him to develop a set of roles or patterns of behavior in relation to constituents, pressure groups, executive agencies, the President, and other members of Congress. A member's behavior is, therefore, the result of various factors: his personality, his professional and political career, his public policy commitments, his perceptions of his constituency, and his relations with other participants in the legislative process. Many of these patterns are established well before he arrives on Capitol Hill.

Donald R. Matthews attempts to characterize senators' roles in terms of their career patterns prior to election and their behavior within the institution. He describes four basic role types: Patricians, Professionals, Amateurs, and Agitators. Both the Patricians and Amateurs come from relatively high-status positions in American society. The Patricians enter politics early and rise steadily, whereas the Amateurs tend to be self-made men whose public careers follow Horatio Alger-like success stories in business and industry. Both the Professionals and the Agitators lack the Patricians' and Amateurs' social status. In contrast to the Professionals, whose political careers are well established before they enter the Senate, the Agitators are newcomers to politics. Each type describes a different route to the Senate.

Each type also makes markedly different contributions to the Senate. The Patricians and the Professionals characteristically play the insider's role, adhering to the norms of the institution, eventually being accepted by the Inner Club or the Senate establishment, and ultimately assuming the institution's strategic posts. The Amateurs and, more frequently, the Agitators find it difficult to adjust to the norms of the institution. In fact, the Agitators, or outsiders—Joseph McCarthy, Robert LaFollette, Sr., Wayne Morse—deliberately violate the Senate's norms. Patricians and Professionals promote conflict resolution, whereas Amateurs and Agitators increase the level of conflict. Differences in career patterns and social background, as Matthews remarks, are important factors in explaining and analyzing congressional behavior.

The selection system is also an important determinant of congressional behavior, for it is both a screening device and a channel to office. The most important fact to remember about this system is that it is highly localized, which helps to explain the difficulty of building majority coalitions for particular pieces of legislation. This fact also explains why party leaders in Congress must plead, cajole, promise rewards, and sometimes threaten members with reprisals, which are often not credible, in order to pass a presidential program. Not only are congressional constituencies localized, but most members' electoral coalitions are different from that of the President. This is a result of the electoral college system, which places special emphasis on the President's ability to capture the large, populous, urban states of the North and East. These subtleties of the electoral process are among the most important centrifugal factors operating in Congress.

In addition to the electoral college, the American federal system itself separates congressional from presidential constituencies. The federal system has promoted a highly fragmented party structure; not only are the national committees of both parties powerless to discipline state party organizations, but the state parties are coalitions of local and, often, hostile groups. In the New York Democratic party, for example, upstate conservatives frequently engage in internecine wars with downstate liberals. In some districts in New York City, machine regulars compete with insurgent reformers for control of party clubs and organizations. These factors, among others, promote congressional parochialism. In contrast to the English parliamentarian's national orientation, the average member of Congress is the creature of local issues, interests, and party organizations. Members of Congress may be concerned with the national interest, but they perceive the nation's interests from the perspective of Brooklyn, New York; Jim Thorpe, Pennsylvania; and Pascagoula, Mississippi.

Numerous attempts have been made to characterize the relations between congressmen and their constituencies. But how do congressmen perceive their responsibilities to their constituencies? Edmund Burke, an eighteenth-century member of the English Parliament and a political philosopher, argued that a legislator is a free agent, a trustee who, although he should consider his constituents' views, must exercise his independent judgment in pursuing the nation's interests. In contrast to this view, the American post-revolutionary tradition emphasized the ultimate authority of the members' constituents. In fact, in the past some town meetings were assembled to instruct their legislators as to their demands. This tradition stresses the delegate role; a member of Congress is one who must merely carry out his constituents' expressed views. The delegate conception of a congressman's role poses several problems, however. First, it presumes that his constituents have views on every major subject. Second, it assumes that their views are relatively homogeneous. If a congressman's constituents either have no views or disagree, as is often the case, he cannot help but exercise his independent judgment.

In a complex and rapidly changing society, a legislator cannot always rely solely on his own judgment or slavishly follow his constituents' demands. A member of Congress is subject to numerous pressures from within and from outside his electoral constituency. Frequently he must reconcile these conflicting views in the legislative process. In addition to congressmen who regard themselves as trustees and delegates, there are members who view themselves as *politicos*. These congressmen recognize that it is sometimes possible and desirable to satisfy their constituents' demands and sometimes necessary to exercise their own judgment. The representative's task is to know what percentage of the time he can depart from his constituents' demands without committing electoral suicide.

However important the selection process may be in explaining congressional behavior, it does not account for everything that occurs in Congress. Both the folkways, or informal norms, and the rules of procedure are products of and affect the centrifugal and centripetal forces that shape congressional life. Some norms, most notably in the Senate, such as apprenticeship and institutional loyalty or patriotism promote internal cohesion. Other norms, such as courtesy and reciprocity, emphasize the individual member's political independence. These folkways promote the resolution of conflict in an institution whose selection system emphasizes each member's fundamental equality before the electorate, facilitate personal relations, and influence policy making.

Some norms, such as the Senate's apprenticeship rule, have a conservative impact on the institution. The apprenticeship norm discourages newer members, usually liberals and moderates, from speaking out on issues they feel strongly about. This norm appears to be less significant today than it was in the immediate postwar era, because the Kennedys (John F. and Robert), Joseph Clark, William Proxmire, and Wayne Morse undermined the rule of silence in the late 1950s. Other elements of the apprenticeship system are the acceptance of poor committee assignments by new members, which removes younger members from the vital centers of power, and the expectation that new members will show deference to their older brethren, which infuses the Senate with a conservative atmosphere. These norms narrow the range of conflict; preclude certain issues from public debate; and usually permit only safe, or manageable, issues to come to the floor.

Other norms, particularly the rule of specialization, provide a power base from which new members can operate. New members are encouraged to become policy, or subject-matter, experts and are reminded that the survival of the institution in a complex age depends on each member's performance of his specialized responsibilities. Thus, a new member can gain considerable influence as a result of the specialized knowledge he possesses. Birch Bayh, for example, attained early prominence because of his skillful work as Chairman of the Senate Judiciary Subcommittee on Constitutional Amendments. He had a decided impact on such issues as presidential succession, the jurisdiction of federal courts, and voting rights. The norm of specialization, as many members argue, also strengthens the position of Congress in dealing with the complex and highly specialized executive branch. If Congress is to play an effective policy-making role, its members must be encouraged to assume specialized legislative responsibilities. Thus, conformity to the institution's norms can have significant policy consequences.

As some students of Congress have observed, not all the members conform. In fact, one member, Senator William Proxmire, has consciously chosen to defy the Senate's norms. Senator Clark has also defied some of his colleagues' expectations, by, for example, refusing to grant unanimous consent to dispense with the reading of the previous day's journal, in order to demonstrate how undemocratic some rules can be. Occasionally Representative H. R. Gross has employed the dilatory rules of procedure to delay or prevent the passage of legislation.

What happens to the maverick or outsider? Can he be punished or disciplined? Ralph K. Huitt argues that the norms permit a number of alternative behaviors. Donald R. Matthews, on the other hand, insists that to be effective, to be an insider, one must go along or conform with the norms. The Matthews-Huitt debate is an important one, for it highlights the countervailing forces at work in Congress. Although nonconformity is not rewarded (with favors from the majority leader, such as a choice office suite), mavericks are rarely punished. This suggests that the norms are not rigidly enforced. But when are sanctions applied? The late Senator Joseph R. McCarthy often charged that the Department of State was rife with Communists, and once remarked that President Dwight D. Eisenhower was a dupe of the Communist conspiracy. He was not chastized by his brethren in the Senate for these remarks. However, when he finally demeaned the dignity of the Senate, his colleagues censured him. Thereafter they treated him as a pariah. The McCarthy censure case suggests that the members will, but are loathe to, discipline their colleagues, and that the norms permit a variety of legitimate behaviors.

Congressional rules of procedure also permit a variety of behaviors. In the Senate unlimited debate, or the filibuster, is a testimony to the omnipotence of a single member or a small group of senators. In 1963 Senator Wayne Morse talked for more than twenty-four hours in order to focus public attention on the communications satellite bill. Several marathon filibusters have been conducted by southern senators to prevent the passage of civil rights legislation.

A single member or a small group of members can bring the body to a standstill. However, this is rarely done. Although most members are aware that they can tie the body in knots by employing such devices as repeated quorum calls, they also recognize the importance of reciprocity in a collegial institution and wish to avoid later use of similar tactics against themselves.

The Structure of Power and Influence in Congress

Although many of these observations apply to both the House and the Senate, there are some important differences between the two bodies. The larger size of the House of Representatives has necessitated a greater reliance on the formal rules of procedure, allowing fewer opportunities for individual members to bring the floor proceedings to a grinding halt. Individual members have less opportunity to exhibit maverick tendencies, because of the more institutionalized structure of the House and its leadership. Moreover, the Speaker of the House seems to possess greater institutionalized power than the Senate's majority leader. Commenting on the majority leader's fluid system of influence, Lyndon Johnson once remarked that "power is where power goes" in the Senate. Despite these differences, both the norms and congressional rules of procedure exhibit the countervailing, centrifugal and centripetal, tendencies previously described.

Not unlike the electoral process, the folkways, and the rules, the structure of power, or influence, reveals similar countervailing tendencies in Congress. There are at least two sets of leaders in Congress: the chairmen of the standing committees (the seniority leaders) and the party leaders, which include the Speaker of the House, the majority and minority floor leaders and assistant leaders (or whips), and the heads of various party committees, such as the policy committee and the caucus. The leadership of Congress is collegial; no single individual monopolizes power in Congress. Because the leaders possess different power bases and public policy commitments and are subject to divergent pressures, they must bargain with each other and with the members in constructing majority coalitions. These coalitions are often transient and must be constructed around each new major piece of legislation. Much of a leader's time, energy, and other resources are spent in constructing and maintaining legislative coalitions.

Sometimes congressional leaders work at cross purposes. This may be explained by a more careful examination of the two sets of leaders. The elective leaders of both houses do not simply govern Congress as neutral arbiters, as does the Speaker of the English House of Commons. They are also their respective party's leaders and are subject to the pressures of partisan colleagues, the President (if their party happens to control the White House), and other party leaders outside of Congress. The elective leadership, as David B. Truman has observed, is in a mediate position; it is usually moderate in its political outlook and attempts to compromise the extremes within each party. The elective leadership is also at the center of a vast network of communications, from which it derives much of its influence. In large measure, with the exception of the Speaker of the House, the power of the elective leadership is personal rather than institutional.

The personal nature of the influence of elective leadership is easily revealed by comparing the styles of two recent Senate majority leaders, Lyndon B. Johnson and Mike Mansfield. Lyndon Johnson, as Rowland Evans and Robert Novak note, possessed a highly developed information network, at the center of which stood Bobby Baker (Secretary to the Majority). Johnson was a dynamic leader who exchanged favors for votes; pleaded with, threatened, and cajoled his colleagues; and collected political IOUs. He knew where the votes were and how to get them. Since 1960, when Johnson became Vice-President, Mike Mansfield has occupied the majority leader's office. By comparison, his style is quiet and unassuming; his leadership is low key. Instead of hammering out bargains in the Johnson fashion, Mansfield waits until the sense of the party emerges. Mansfield's intelligence system is not as highly developed as was the Johnson network. At times during Johnson's presidency Mansfield was so unsure of his votes that he had to call Johnson at the White House for a head count. In contrast to Johnson, as the majority leader, Mansfield is a political figure almost unknown outside of the Senate.

Lyndon Johnson was more than an effective majority leader; he left his stamp on the institution. When he became majority leader, the Senate was a quiet, unhurried place, a club that had remained almost unchanged for a century. Without rewriting a single rule, Lyndon Johnson changed the institution. In the period following his heart attack, he developed a style that reduced debate to a minimum. He wrenched unanimous consent agreements from liberals and conservatives to keep the Senate's business moving. Johnson frequently drove his colleagues relentlessly, working far into the night. Following his heart attack, he also introduced the "stop-and-go" technique. Ordered by his doctors to take frequent rests at his ranch, Johnson pushed his colleagues for several weeks and recessed the Senate for brief holidays. Even after he recovered, Johnson retained the stop-and-go technique in order to force action on major legislation.

However aggressive or persuasive an elected leader may be, he must come to terms with the seniority leaders—the committee chairmen—whose selection he cannot control. Committee chairmen are chosen by a process that tends to insulate them from the control of the elective leaders. At present, the informal practice dictates the selection of standing committee chairmen by their length of service within the party in each committee. Thus, when Senator Wayne Morse switched parties, he lost his seniority ranking within each of the standing committees on which he served. Although the proponents and opponents of the seniority system disagree about many of its consequences, they generally agree that the system favors the selection of chairmen from among representatives of one-party constituencies, because such members are usually returned to Congress one session after another, thereby accruing credit toward chairmanships and ranking memberships. Inasmuch as their tenure is more secure than that of congressmen from two-party constituencies, elected leaders can do little to discipline them. Because such members become committee chairmen, the control of elected leaders over Congress is seriously attenuated as a result of the seniority system.

Committee chairmen are further insulated from the control of elective leadership as a result of their life-and-death power over the flow of legislation in standing committees. A chairman's power derives from the rules and practices of the committee as well as from his personal influence among his colleagues. Some committee chairmen are empowered to fix meeting times. All committee chairmen have the power to fix agendas and to determine the order of hearings. Inasmuch as he presides at committee meetings, the chairman has the power to rule on motions, order votes, recognize members, and refuse to schedule additional meetings. Through his power to appoint committee staff and to direct their activities, the chairman determines the scope and direction of the legislative and oversight activities of the committee.

In addition to these powers over the full committee, a chairman also controls subcommittee activities. Though limited by the constraints of seniority, a chairman appoints subcommittee chairmen and assigns members to subcommittees. Because party ratios in subcommittees are more flexible than in full committees, the chairman's power of assignment is enhanced. Furthermore, the committee chairman refers legislation to subcommittees. He may even exercise his power more directly as an ex-officio member of all subcommittees under his committee's jurisdiction. Finally, he determines when a subcommittee's legislative recommendations will be considered by the full committee and who will manage a bill on the floor. In other words, the House and Senate rules give the committee chairman a large and only loosely grant of power, which strengthens the judicious chairman's control over his committee and insulate him from the influence of elective leadership.

The potential for conflict between elective and seniority leaders can be seen by examining the operations of the House Rules Committee. The Rules Committee has the authority to schedule controversial measures for floor action. For a number of years the committee was dominated by an eight-man (four Democrats and four Republicans) conservative coalition under the chairmanship of Democratic Representative Howard Smith. Under "Judge" Smith the committee acted as more than a scheduling committee or a "traffic cop." It was a major stumbling block, or graveyard, for many of President Kennedy's New Frontier programs in the early 1960s. After prolonged maneuvering, Speaker Sam Rayburn succeeded in first temporarily and then permanently expanding the size of the Rules Committee from twelve to fifteen. With the addition of two "moderate" to "liberal" members, the committee opened the gate for the President's programs. The struggle between the committee, on the one hand, and the Speaker and a majority of the House, on the other, nicely illustrates the tensions that are inherent in a collegial leadership whose power bases are divergent.

The diffusion of power in Congress, as illustrated by the tensions inherent in collegial leadership, creates a complex decision-making process. With sixteen Senate and twenty House standing committees, numerous foci of power exist. Because power is fragmented through committees and subcommittees, there are many points of access to congressional decision making. A single bill authorizing the expenditure of funds from the Treasury, for example, may be considered by several committees in each house. If each house passes it in a slightly different form, the differences must be resolved by a conference committee composed of members of both houses. This fragmented decision-making process affords political interest groups numerous opportunities at the committee stage to affect public policy. Inasmuch as committees differ in personnel and structure, equal access is not afforded to all groups in the political system.

Given their pivotal position in the legislative process in Congress, the committees hold life-and-death power over legislation. Therefore, a committee's subject-matter jurisdiction, which usually dictates the reference of bills, is not simply a technical question; it is a significant political issue. Attempts to alter the number of committees, to change their subject-matter jurisdictions, and in other ways to streamline the committee system are highly controversial political questions, for such reforms inevitably redistribute both internal power and access to congressional committees. As important as the subject-matter jurisdiction of a committee may be, it only partially explains the role of the committee in the legislative process. Jurisdiction defines the matters about which a committee may legislate; it does not indicate what a committee will recommend to its parent body.

Of equal importance in explaining the roles of committees are their personnel and structure. Several studies of congressional committees attest to the significance of the chairman's personality and political convictions. Since a chairman has the power to appoint subcommittee chairmen, to assign members to subcommittees, and to refer legislation, his personality and preferences are vitally important in congressional policy making. When A. Willis Robertson replaced J. William Fulbright as Chairman of the Senate Committee on Banking and Currency, the significance of the chairman's role was highlighted. Fulbright, according to John Bibby, was a permissive, or "service," chairman who aided subcommittee members in conducting critical investigations of executive agencies, such as the Federal Reserve Board. Senator Robertson, Bibby notes, was a "minority and restraining" chairman who used his power to prevent committee activity. Under Robertson, a fiscal and economic conservative, criticism of the Federal Reserve Board was muted. As this comparison shows, a chairman can determine his committee's activities by either encouraging or discouraging the interests of its members.

A committee's legislative activity is also a product of the interests, ideologies, personalities, and political needs of its members. The House Committee on Education and Labor in the postwar era (1945–1962), according to Richard F. Fenno, Jr., is a case in point. For a number of years the committee was unable to resolve intense controversies over aid to education. Federal aid was opposed by Republicans and southern Democrats for varying reasons. Republican committee members were concerned over the expansion of the power of the national government. Southern Democrats did not want governmental intervention to threaten racial segregation. Members of both parties were divided on the question of federal aid to private, especially church-related, schools. Thus, committee divisions were tightly drawn along political, ideological, and religious lines.

These controversies were intensified by the composition of the committee. The Republican leadership encouraged House members who were deeply committed to their positions and who came from safe districts to apply for a position on the committee. Democratic leaders chose equally contentious and committed committee members. In 1961 the Republicans were all white, Protestant, and came from predominantly white districts outside of the South and Border States. The Democrats included two women, seven Catholics, two Jews, and four southern and Border State members. The committee's chairman was a Negro, Adam Clayton Powell, and four Democratic committeemen had constituencies with substantial black populations. All of these conditions maximized existing controversies within the committee. It is easy to understand how and why federal aid to education died in the House Education and Labor Committee, with the leadership's tacit consent.

The structure of a committee may also shape its legislative activity. The House Committee on Agriculture, according to Charles O. Jones, is designed for conflict because the jurisdictions of its subcommittees are largely organized along commodity lines. This structure frequently pits members of different commodity subcommittees against each other on price-support legislation. The House Appropriations Committee, on the other hand, whose subcommittees parallel the jurisdictions of executive agencies, does not suffer from intense internal conflict. In addition, its subcommittees do not correspond to the constituency interests of its members as closely as do those of the Agriculture Committee. These two examples suggest that the structure of a committee is important in determining its capacity to resolve conflict over policy.

The leadership, personnel, and structure of committees reveal the conflicting, centrifugal and centripetal, tendencies found elsewhere in Congress. Although the committee chairman may act as a cohesive, centralizing force in a committee, he must share his power, influence, and authority with competing subcommittee chairmen and ranking members. An effective chairman may be able to overcome potential threats to a committee's cohesion by carefully structuring subcommittees that cut across existing lines of conflict. He may also reduce conflict by co-opting dissidents as subcommittee chairmen. At least one committee chairman, James Eastland of the Senate Committee on the Judiciary, seems to have maintained minimum cohesion by co-opting such potential dissidents as Birch Bayh, Edward Kennedy, and Joseph Tydings. Of course, a committee chairman may purchase cohesion at the price of losing control over his committee.

There are numerous factors that contribute to the unity or disunity of a committee. The similarity of members' backgrounds and political careers, the convergence of their policy commitments, and the esteem in which they hold the committee all contribute to the committee's internal cohesion and, ultimately, to its legislative success on the floor. A cohesive committee probably has a better chance of securing favorable floor action on its legislative proposals than one that is internally divided. Successful floor action requires the construction of broad majority coalitions within the framework of the legislative rules of procedure. The process of building such coalitions is more complex than shepherding a measure through the committee stage. Action on the floor is the distillation of all that has occurred in the legislative process. Liberals and conservatives, northerners and southerners, freshmen and veterans, the powerful and the powerless, the leaders and followers come to ratify the terms of numerous bargains that have been carefully negotiated over one or more sessions of Congress. With some controversial measures it may take several sessions to strike a bargain.

Two controversial measures, the Public Housing Act of 1949 and the Civil Rights Act of 1957, illustrate some of the problems in building consensus for major legislative breakthroughs in Congress. The Public Housing Act was first introduced in 1946, a decade after passage of the nation's first public housing measure (the United States Housing Act of 1937). It was immediately opposed by conservative real-estate and mortgage-banking interests, which were able to tie it up in committee for several sessions. Only after passage of the National Housing Act of 1948, a measure designed to assist the private housing industry, did opponents of federally assisted, local public housing relent. To gain acceptance for federally sponsored public housing, the sponsors of the measure were forced to offer numerous sweeteners to the private housing interests. After more than four years of bargaining and negotiation in Congress, interest group activities outside of Congress, and general public debate, the national government publicly stated its commitment to protect the individual's social welfare in the 1949 Public Housing Act. This measure represented a symbolic commitment, a major breakthrough of the government to secure the individual's welfare.

Between 1939 and 1957, numerous attempts were made by liberals in both houses to pass civil rights legislation. Their efforts were frustrated by a coalition of southern Democrats and conservative Republicans. Southern Democrats employed the threat of a filibuster, while conservative Republicans provided support on key procedural votes to kill the legislation. In 1956 the House finally passed a civil rights bill, which was bottled up in the Senate by a series of procedural devices that delayed action until the end of the session. Armed with a new House civil rights bill at the beginning of the next session, Senate liberals threatened to move for an end to unlimited debate, a major obstacle to the legislation's passage. Afraid of losing the filibuster weapon, southern Democrats finally agreed to a watered-down civil rights act.

Both measures, the Public Housing Act of 1949 and the Civil Rights Act of 1957, were controversial, landmark laws, reflecting a changing consensus in the American polity. They required the careful construction of a broad coalition among members of Congress, interested groups and associations, and an attentive public. Both acts were the results of numerous compromises and bargains made at every turn in the legislative process, and both required several sessions to make their way through that process. Their passage illustrates the need to build broad national coalitions to promote social, economic, and political change through the legislative process in Congress.

Conclusion

If a roll call of the House or Senate is the result of a fluid, complex process, can it be said that majorities or minorities govern? Certainly, majorities and minorities are not permanently fixed. Legislative coalitions wax and wane with issues or sets of issues. Today's minority may be tomorrow's majority. In such an environment, it is difficult to say who is responsible. Furthermore, if there are no permanent majorities and minorities, it is equally difficult to determine whether the process is democratic.

If the limited test of "majority rule" is applied, Congress is obviously undemocratic, for often majorities are prevented from deciding important questions. Democracy, as noted earlier, may involve the reconciliation of conflicting values, such as majority rule and minority and individual rights. But democracy involves more than a procedure for making decisions. It also requires citizens' satisfaction with decisions that are made by representative institutions. Finally, it could be argued that democracy, if it is to survive, requires a high degree of political stability. Therefore, Congress' performance should be evaluated against the attainment of several values: responsiveness to majorities, reconciliation of conflicts, procedural fairness, citizens' satisfaction, and political stability. The way in which Congress serves various, and sometimes conflicting, values is a recurring theme in the selections that follow.

22

The Politicians

DONALD R. MATTHEWS

In the following selection, Donald R. Matthews examines the sociological bases of political behavior. His keen interest in the social backgrounds and political careers of United States senators stems from the assumption that a verifiable relation exists between current political behavior and previous experience. Thus, senators' political careers are important determinants of their roles, styles, perceptions of political issues, and votes on legislation. Although few political scientists would deny that such relationships exist, they are often, as Matthews acknowledges, difficult to state precisely.

This excerpt examines the political careers of senators in the post-World War II era. Matthews argues that the recruitment patterns for office are diverse, reflecting the fragmented and pluralistic nature of American politics. He concludes that four basic senatorial types inhabit the Senate, each of which exhibits characteristic and different recruitment patterns and behaviors. They are Patrician, Professional, Amateur, and Agitator.

Matthews, a well-known analyst and observer of the United States Senate, is the author of The Social Background of Political Decision-Makers *(1954) and the coauthor of* Negroes and the New Southern Politics *(1966). He is currently on the staff of the Brookings Institution, Washington, D.C.*

In the Middletown of 1925 the Lynds found that politics and politicians were suspect. One businessman told

Reprinted from *U.S. Senators and Their World* by Donald R. Matthews (Chapel Hill: University of North Carolina Press, 1960), chap. 3, pp. 47–67, by permission of the publisher.

them, "Our politics smell to heaven, elections are dirty and unscrupulous, and our better citizens mostly don't mix in them." Another said, "No good man will go into politics here. Why should he? Politics is dirty. I would't mix in it here. Maybe if I was rich and independent I would, but I'd think twice about it even then."[1] Upon their return to Middletown ten years later the Lynds were greeted with the remark, "Whatever changes you may find elsewhere in Middletown, you will find that our politics and government are the same crooked shell game."[2]

Much the same attitudes are prevalent today. Recently a representative sample of the nation's electorate was asked, "If you had a son would you like to see him go into politics as a life's work when he gets out of school?" Sixty-eight per cent of the sample answered no, 21 per cent answered yes, and 11 per cent had no opinion. Even more significant are the reasons given by the respondents in support of their answers. Those who opposed a political career did so on the grounds that politics was crooked, unethical, and that the temptations of a political career were too great; that there were better opportunities in other lines of endeavor; and that a political career was too insecure. The principal reason given for favoring a political career by the 21 per cent of the sample who indicated such approval was the need for clean-minded men in politics to supplant the people that are in it now! All told, about half the American electorate, if this poll is to be trusted, believe that it is difficult to be an honest politician.[3]

Despite these public attitudes, the subjects of this study became politicians. Why? What incentives were strong enough to attract this group of generally able men and women into politics? Neither our understanding of human motivation (the psychologists working in contrived laboratory situations have not made much progress; how can we hope to do better?) nor our data permit a definitive answer to this question. We can, however, hazard a few more or less informed guesses.

Political Incentives

One incentive to political activity is the desire for prestige and power. This seems paradoxical when contrasted with the lurid public image of "politics" and "politicians" sketched in above, but the American public's picture of politicians has another side. The Gallup poll, for example, often asks a cross section of the voting population whom they most admire. Time and again, the most admired Americans include prominent politicians. High public office also possesses great prestige in the United States. One recent survey, which sought to discover the public's prestige-ranking of occupations, found that United States Supreme Court justices, state governors, cabinet members, diplomats, mayors of large cities, and United States representatives were rated among the top ten occupations in the country.[4] The normal incumbents of these offices are "politicians." While politicians as a class may not enjoy great prestige, many successful politicians do. The people often think that their politicians are different, that they are "good politicians," or not politicians at all.

Of course, politics is not the only way one can achieve power and prestige, but it is a particularly attractive one to some groups within the American population. Look, for example, at the position of a successful business or professional man in one of the nation's smaller cities and towns. Suppose that he is not content to be a big fish in a little pond; where can he turn? The upper reaches of the nation's corporate businesses are not open to him; the prominent law firms in the larger cities are not likely to bring him in as a partner. His opportunity to enter either of these worlds came at his graduation from college or law school. He did not take that option then. Where does he turn to assuage his lofty ambitions? Politics is always a possibility. Or take a member of an American ethnic group. The United States, he has been told, is the land of opportunity. One should strive to "get ahead." As a practical matter, his chances of getting ahead are not good. But in politics—especially, of course, if he lives in an area containing a concentration of voters with similar nationality or religious backgrounds—his foreign name, ancestry, and religion are a positive advantage. In this way politics furnishes an avenue of upward mobility for those groups whose opportunities in other lines of endeavor are poor.[5]

Another incentive to political activity is love of the game. Politics provides, even to the neophyte, a sense of power, excitement, camaraderie, a sense of being "in on things," a sense of importance. The strength of these psychic lures should not be underestimated. They may attract some people more than others—Harold Lasswell, for example, has suggested that politicians have a special need for such satisfactions because of an unusually low esteem of the self[6]—but they appeal to most people more than they are willing to admit.

Most politicians say that they are in politics to be of "public service." Much, perhaps most, of this can be dismissed as rationalization, but not all of it. Some men have such a clear-cut image of "the public interest" and such a strong emotional commitment to it that they decide to do something about it themselves.

Finally, there is the family influence. The evidence that our political attitudes are shaped early in life is impressive.[7] At least one-third of the senators came from politically oriented families. No less than 15 per cent of them were sons of politicians, and at least another 15 per cent had one or more members of their families active in politics during their formative years. A child born into such an environment is likely to be instilled with more favorable attitudes towards politics and politicians than the average American. Moreover, the right contacts and a familiar name can give him a considerable head-start in politics.

But *why* our subjects became politicians must remain an open question. More is known about *how* they became senators—although again not as much as we would like. Complete and reliable information is available only on the public offices the senators held. The data on the senators' activities in political parties and campaigns, the political situation in their states at the time of their nomination and election, and the senators' unsuccessful bids for elective office is too fragmentary to merit analysis. This means, unfortunately, that we are unable to deal with some of the most interesting and significant questions concerning the senators' political careers. It means that we are able to describe only the open political activity of the senators and only a part of that. Given these strict limitations on our data, what can be said about how these men became senators?

Getting Started in Politics

Most of the men who served as senators after World War II began their political careers early in life.

Table 1
Age at Achieving First Public Office

	Age Group				
	20-29	*30-39*	*40-49*	*50 plus*	*Totals*
All Senators	46%	30%	15%	9%	100% (177)
Northern and Western Democrats	47%	30%	22%	0%	100% (36)
Southern and Border Democrats	64%	22%	11%	4%	100% (55)
Republicans	35%	35%	14%	16%	100% (86)

Note: The age at achieving first public office of three senators is unknown. They have been omitted from this analysis.

Almost half of them held their first public offices before their thirtieth birthdays; a full three-quarters of them were public officials before they were forty years old (Table 1). Of course, these figures exaggerate the age at which the senators became politically active, for few persons achieve public office without prior years of work for a political party. We can assume, therefore, that the "average" senator probably became immersed in politics shortly after the completion of his education.

Nonetheless, a few politically precocious senators began their office-holding careers before they were old enough to vote; others did not start out until they were over sixty. Those who held their first public offices early in life tended to be sons of politicians; to have been born in families of relatively high occupational standing; to be minority group members rather than Yankee-Protestants; and to be farmers or lawyers rather than businessmen or professors. The Democrats, especially those from the one-party Southern and Border states, held their first public offices earlier in life than the Republicans.[8]

The senators' first public offices varied widely in their character and importance (Table 2). Almost exactly half of the senators began either as law-enforcement officers (prosecuting attorneys, judges, or marshals) or by serving in their state legislatures. While no other offices were nearly so popular at this stage in their careers,

Table 2
First Public Office Achieved

Type of Office	*Number*	*Percentage*
U.S. Senator	17	9%
State Governor	4	2
United States Representative	7	4
State Legislator	38	21
Statewide Elective Official	8	4
Local Elective Official	25	14
Law Enforcement	50	28
Administrative Official	26	14
Congressional Staff	5	3
	180	100%

a sizeable minority also started out by being elected to local office or appointed to some kind of administrative position.[9]

The ages of future senators had a great deal to do with the kinds of offices they first achieved. Those who entered politics as relatively young men usually began by serving as state legislators, in law-enforcement or in statewide or local elective offices, or as Congressional staff members. The older men tended to begin as senators, governors, United States representatives, or as some kind of administrator.[10]

The senators' occupations were also related to their first public offices. Half of the lawyers began as law-enforcement officers, a quarter of them as state legislators. No other offices came close to rivaling these two as the place for the Senate lawyers to begin. The other senators started out their political careers in a wider variety of public offices. Twenty-five per cent of the businessmen began as local elective officials, jobs which businessmen can combine with their regular occupations with relative ease. Nineteen per cent of the businessmen began as senators, another 19 per cent as state legislators, and 17 per cent as administrators. The farmers usually started out as state legislators (33 per cent), as local officials (25 per cent), as administrators or as senators (17 per cent each). The professors most often began in appointive administrative positions (43 per cent).

Levels of Political Activity

Once started, most senators stayed in politics. By the time they were elected to the Senate, they had held no fewer than 495 public offices, not counting re-elections to the same office. The mythical "average senator" had held about three public offices and had devoted ten years or approximately half his adult life to officeholding before arriving at the upper chamber. But again we find vast departures from these norms. Some of the senators had served in seven, eight, or nine offices for more than twenty-five years, virtually their entire adulthood. Others were completely without office-holding experience before their election or appointment to the Senate.

What kinds of men tended to be most politically active before their election to the Senate? What kinds of men were elected or appointed to the Senate with little previous experience?

There appear to be two major differences between the most and the least politically experienced senators. The first of these is occupational: the farmers and lawyers were the most politically active and experienced before their election to the Senate; the businessmen and professors were least politically experienced. The second difference is partisan: the Democrats, especially those from the Southern and Border states, were more active than the Republicans.

It would be hazardous to conclude, on the basis of this alone, that the senators' occupations and party affiliations caused these differences in levels of political activity. A larger number of Democrats than Republicans, for example, come from one-party states, where holding public office is less hazardous than in areas of vigorous partisan competition. Perhaps the difference between Democrats and Republicans is the result of this factor. But if one compares the Democrats with the Republicans from the same kinds of states as has been done in

Table 3
Percentage Spending More than 40 Per Cent of Pre-Senate Adult Years in Public Office, by Type of State Party System

Type of State Party System	*Northern and Western Democrats*	*Southern and Border Democrats*	*Republicans*	*All Senators*
Two-Party System	50% (32)	71% (7)	33% (58)	41% (97)
Modified One-Party System:				
Senator from Strong Party		57% (21)	50% (26)	53% (47)
One-Party System		63% (27)	50% (2)	62% (29)
All States	47% (36)	52% (55)	39% (88)	

Note: Senators from the weaker party in modified one-party states were omitted because of too few cases.

Table 3, one sees that the Southern Democrats tend to have been the most politically active; the non-Southern Democrats, the next most active; and the Republicans, the least active regardless of the party system in their states. A partisan and regional difference in level of political activity exists independent of the different numbers of Democrats and Republicans from one- and two-party areas. This raises a further point: does the difference in occupational makeup of the two parties explain the difference in political involvement of Democrats and Republicans? The answer is contained in Table 4. The farmers, lawyers, businessmen, and professors tend to have been politically active in that order within each party and section. Thus occupation does make a difference, even when the effects of party and section are controlled. But the Democrats also tend to be more active than the Republicans with the same occupations. Therefore, both a senator's party affiliation and his occupation affect the level of his political activity before becoming a senator.

Channels to the Senate

By the time they became senators, our 180 subjects had held almost every conceivable kind of public office. From this it might be inferred that almost any public office can serve as a likely steppingstone to the power and prestige of the Senate chamber. Such, however, is not the case.

. . . About 30 per cent of the senators were elected from the House; 20 per cent after serving as governors;

Table 4
Percentage Spending More than 40 Per Cent of Pre-Senate Adult Years in Public Office, by Occupation

Occupation	*Northern and Western Democrats*	*Southern and Border Democrats*	*Republicans*	*All Senators*
Lawyers	60% (20)	68% (37)	41% (39)	55% (96)
Businessmen	43% (7)	40% (10)	30% (36)	34% (53)
Farmers	0% (1)	80% (5)	71% (7)	69% (13)
Professors	0% (4)	0% (2)	0% (1)	0% (8)

17 per cent, administrators; 15 per cent, law-enforcement officers; and 10 per cent, as state legislators. Very few senators were elected from any other kind of office. When one stops to think that there were only 48 state governorships and 435 seats in the House, while there were many thousands of these other positions, it is clear that a far larger proportion of governors and congressmen were "promoted" to the Senate than is true of other officeholders. In this sense, the governorships and the House are the two major channels to the Senate.

The senators' occupations were definitely related to the channels they followed to the Senate (Table 5). The lawyers most often came up via the House of Representatives, with law-enforcement offices and governorships running a close second and third. Businessmen were usually elected to the Senate from administrative positions, with the governorships, the House, and "civilian" jobs tied for second place. Farmers were most often elected from governorships, with state legislatures running a poor second. All the professors with political experience came from administrative posts, local elective office, or the House.

The party system in the senator's state also seems to have had a great deal to do with the channel he followed to the Senate. Those from one-party states, of either the "pure" or "modified" variety, arrived via the two usual gateways far more often than did the men from two-party states. Sixty per cent of those from one-party, and 70 per cent of those from modified one-party states, were elected from either a governorship or a seat in the House; this was true of only 30 per cent of those from two-party states. The senators from two-party states were elected from a far wider range of less important offices or with no officeholding experience at all.[11]

Age at Election

The Senate of the United States is organized, in large part, on the basis of seniority. Given this principle of organization and the hard facts of the mortality tables, the age at which a man becomes a United States senator is of considerable importance. What factors influence the age at which these men are elected?

Table 5
Principal Occupation and Last Public Office

Last Public Office	*Lawyer*	*Businessman*	*Farmer*	*Professor*
None	2%	19%	15%	14%
Governor	21	19	38	0
U.S. Representative	30	19	15	29
State Legislator	7	9	23	0
Statewide Elected Office	2	0	0	0
Local Elected Office	1	11	0	29
Law Enforcement Office	22	2	0	0
Administrative Office	15	21	8	29
Congressional Staff	1	0	0	0
	100%	100%	100%	100%
	(97)	(53)	(13)	(7)

First of all, while there is a great deal of overlapping, the Democrats as a group became senators five or so years before the Republicans. It is conceivable that this difference is a reflection of a basic difference between the two major parties. On the other hand this association between political party and age of election to the Senate may be the result of some other factor. For instance, more Democrats than Republicans are elected to the Senate from one-party states; can the differences in ages of newly elected Democrats and Republicans be accounted for on the basis of the fact that members of the two parties tend to come from different kinds of state party systems? . . . The Democrats tend to be younger at their original election than the Republicans no matter what kind of state party system they came from.

Certain features of the senators' lives and careers also affected the stage in life at which they became senator. Those elected to the Senate especially early in life most often were born in families of relatively high social status. Professional men became senators at an earlier age than farmers or businessmen. And, as one might expect, the earlier in life the senators entered politics, the younger they were when elected to the Senate.

Types of Careers

So far we have found that the senators were, as a group, very politically active before their election or appointment to the Senate and that, as a group, these same men possessed unusually high social status. But not all senators possessed both of these characteristics. Logically, therefore, there are four possible combinations of social status and political activity to be found among the senators [see table].

	Social Status	*Political Activity*
1.	High	High
2.	High	Low
3.	Low	High
4.	Low	Low

When the senators are classified according to this scheme and examined with care, four distinct types of senatorial careers emerge.[12]

Patrician Politicians

About 7 per cent of the senators possessed both relatively high social status and relatively high political accomplishment before becoming senators. We shall call them Patrician Politicians.

The Patricians come from America's "old families," with the assured social positions, wealth, and security that this connection provides. They are also highly experienced politicians. "Public service," as political activity is known in these circles, tends to run in the family. More than half of the Patricians' fathers were in politics before them. All of them had numerous ancestors and relatives prominent in state or national politics before their time. Usually, they entered politics by running for a relatively minor elective office (about half of them for state legislatures and a quarter for law-enforcement offices) shortly after graduating from college or law school. Eighty-five per cent were officeholders while still in their twenties, and all of them were in public office before they were forty years old. Their rise to the Senate was steady and fairly rapid. A third were in their thirties when elected or appointed to the chamber; three-quarters of them were senators before they were fifty.

Senators Saltonstall and Lodge, both from Massachusetts, are good examples. They were born into the leading families of the Commonwealth. Both attended private schools and then Harvard University. Saltonstall practiced law for a few years in Boston before beginning (at the age of twenty-eight) an almost uninterrupted political career as alderman, assistant district attorney, state representative, speaker of the House, governor, and senator. Lodge, a government major at Harvard, began work as a reporter, correspondent, and editorial writer for the *New York Herald Tribune*. Then, moving back to Massachusetts, he began his political career by running for a seat in the state legislature when he was thirty-one years old. Only four years later he was a United States senator.

The Patricians tend to come from the Northeast and the South, portions of the country which most clearly contain "old family" strata. They are just as often Democrats as Republicans.

Amateur Politicians

Thirty-four per cent of the postwar senators were Amateur Politicians. They are distinguished from the Patricians by their far lower degree of political involvement and accomplishment before they became senators.

Most of the Amateurs came from middle-class families, although a few of them were from very well-to-do or working-class homes. They were quite successful businessmen (45 per cent), lawyers (33 per cent), and professors (10 per cent). More often than not, they were prosperous. As a group, they started political careers later in life than the other senators, about 60 per cent of them being over forty when they achieved their first public offices. Usually, they began their political careers by being appointed to an important executive position or being elected to a major public office. Indeed, a quarter of the Amateurs had held no previous public office when they became senators. Often they won their Senate seats via appointment to a vacancy rather than by election. They were the oldest group of senators at their entry into the chamber; almost a third of them were over sixty when they began their Senate careers.

An example is Homer E. Capehart. The son of an Algiers, Indiana, tenant farmer, Capehart went to work as a salesman immediately upon his graduation from high school. He was an almost immediate success. By the time he was in his early thirties, he was already president of the Capehart Corporation, manufacturers of radio, phonograph, and television equipment. Then, a rich man by the time he was forty, Capehart held a huge Republican rally at his large farm in Washington, Indiana. Seven years later, still with no officeholding experience, Capehart was elected to the Senate. Senator Kerr is another example. He made a fortune in oil and then entered active politics in his fifties by successfully running for governor of Oklahoma. Senator Murray was also a wealthy lawyer and businessman in his fifties before a job as chairman of the Montana Advisory Board for the WPA launched him on a political career. William Benton was a nationally known advertising executive before he was forty years old. Resigning from his firm of Benton and Bowles, he tried his hand at education (vice-president of the University of Chicago) and diplomacy (assistant secretary of state, United States delegate to numerous international conferences) before being appointed to the Senate to fill a vacancy.

All told, about 43 per cent of the Republicans were Amateurs; only a quarter of the Democrats followed this career line to the Senate. Paradoxically, the politically inexperienced Amateurs were most apt to become senators from two-party states, where politics is most competitive and the risks of a political career most severe. At the same time, the cost of a Senate campaign is also greater in these states, and the Amateurs are usually in a position to pay for a large share of their own campaigns. Moreover, in two-party states, the nomination process is more likely to be controlled by the party leadership than in one-party areas. Apparently, Amateurs fare better in such a situation than in a wide-open, every-man-for-himself primary contest in which a wide personal following is needed to secure a Senate nomination.

Professional Politicians

The most common type of senator is the Professional Politician—55 per cent of the postwar senators fall into this category. The Professionals were as politically involved and experienced as the Patricians but did not possess "old family" backgrounds. The majority of them trained as lawyers (64 per cent), the Professionals entered politics very early in life—usually as law-enforcement officers or state legislators. Their rise to the Senate was relatively slow but steady; most of them came up via the House of Representatives or state governorships. As a group, they were a little younger than the Amateurs and considerably older than the Patricians upon their first election to the Senate.

Alben Barkley's career is a fairly typical one. Born near Lowes, Kentucky, the son of a tenant farmer, the irrepressible "Veep" attended Marvin College in nearby Clinton and Virginia Law School. After only five years of private law practice, Barkley was elected prosecuting attorney of his county, then county judge, and then congressman. After more than two decades of officeholding experience, he was elected United States senator.

John Bricker of Ohio is another example. The son of a Mount Sterling, Ohio, farmer, Bricker attended college and law school at Ohio State University and then immediately plunged into politics as a city solicitor, assistant attorney general of Ohio, public utilities commissioner, attorney general of Ohio, and governor. By the time he was first elected to the Senate in 1947, Bricker had spent a total of twenty-five years in public office. Not all the other Professional Politicians in the Senate have had as extensive pre-Senate careers, but most of them at least approximate this pattern.

The Professional Politicians are the most numerous in both parties and in all types of states. However, 60 per cent of the Democrats were Professionals while only 45 per cent of the Republicans were so classified. They also tend to be elected from one-party areas more frequently than from two-party states.

Agitators

Occasionally, a senator is elected to the Senate without the inherited position of the Patricians, the solid record of business or professional accomplishment of the Amateurs, or the political accomplishments of the Professional Politicians. These men, the exceptions to the general rule that substantial prestige is requisite for Senate membership, may be called Agitators. They constituted 4 per cent of the senators during the postwar years.

The Agitators tend to have relatively low social origins. Usually lawyers, they started political careers early in life and were elected to the Senate while still relatively young; only the Patricians were younger than they at their election to the chamber. On the other hand, their nonpolitical careers were hardly distinguished, nor did they have much of a political record to show before they became senators. Usually, they rocketed into the chamber from relatively minor state or local public offices.

An excellent example is Glen Taylor of Idaho. After completing an eighth-grade education, Taylor went to work as a hired manager of motion-picture theaters, joined a dramatic stock company, and then struck out on his own as the guitar-playing leader of a second-rate hillbilly band. Inspired by the incongruous notion that he should be a congressman, the singing cowboy campaigned—hillbilly band and all—unsuccessfully for a seat in Congress in 1938 and in the Senate in 1940 and 1942. Badly beaten in politics, out of the good graces of the party leaders, unsuccessful as an entertainer, Taylor then got a job as a sheet-metal worker, which he held until the beginning of his successful 1945 campaign for the Senate.

A somewhat different case is presented by Sheridan Downey of California. Born in the Wyoming Territory—his father was the territory's Republican congressman for a while—Downey followed family tradition and became a lawyer. At first in Laramie and then in Sacramento, Downey was reasonably successful. But in 1928 his extensive real estate speculations caught up with him and he was financially ruined. Then the impoverished California lawyer suddenly experienced flashes of economic insight. Books and pamphlets *(Why I Believe in the Townsend Plan, Pensions or Penury)* followed, and Downey became active in the panacea fringe of California politics. Several unsuccessful campaigns as an EPIC and Townsendite candidate followed until his advocacy of wholesale pension plans as a Democrat overcame his lack of political experience and he was elected to the Senate in 1939.

The most famous young-man-in-a-hurry to be elected to the Senate in recent years was Joseph R. McCarthy of Wisconsin. Born into an Irish Catholic farming family, McCarthy left school at the age of fourteen to work as a hand on his father's farm. Subsequent stints as a self-employed chicken farmer and as a grocery clerk failed to satisfy his ambitions. Then at nineteen he returned to school. It must have been an ordeal for the man-sized Joe McCarthy to squeeze into the child-sized desks and to be forced into the company of fourteen-year-olds. The future senator not only bore this, but with considerable help from a sympathetic school superintendent, he completed the regular four-year high school course in one. Then, piecing together a living from night work in restaurants and gas stations with some financial aid from home, McCarthy went to Marquette University.

After graduating with an LL.B., McCarthy began legal practice in the small town of Waupaca, Wisconsin. His practice was so anemic that, according to his (unfriendly) biographers, he largely supported himself from his poker winnings. Politics, for which he had shown some flair at Marquette, seemed like a possible solution to his financial problems, but McCarthy was a Democrat in a normally Republican state. A losing campaign for district attorney on the Democratic ticket showed that the party was a blind alley, so when the struggling young lawyer was offered a job by a prosperous and respected Republican lawyer in nearby Shawano, he took it—and became a Republican. Several years later McCarthy was elected a circuit judge, the youngest man ever to be so honored in his state. Thus began one of the most rapid, and most ruthless, political careers in modern American politics. Seven years later—thirty months of which were spent in the United States Marines—McCarthy was a United States senator at the extraordinarily early age of thirty-seven. Few senators have gone so far so fast.

Normally, becoming a senator is a time-consuming and difficult task. The merits of those who aspire to the office are pretested in a rough and ready (and not entirely equitable) way by the necessity for a fairly distinguished career, either in or out of politics. The election of men to the Senate who have not distinguished themselves in either respect may well be a symptom of a breakdown in the regularized methods of senatorial recruitment in the United States. These men have "beaten the game." Sometimes this may have been because of fantastic good luck, but more often it would seem to have been the result of a willingness to resort to demagoguery and unscrupulous methods, to ignore "the rules of the game."

The Agitators are most frequently elected from the Western states. The reason for this is not at all clear, but perhaps this is because the social structure of the West is more "open," less stratified, than in the East and South. Moreover, in the Western states, the party leadership is relatively powerless to influence nominations. Agitators are not the kind of candidates likely to appeal to responsible party leaders. In the Southern one-party states, where party leaders have even less influence on the nomination process than in the West, the social structure is more highly stratified. The combination of a relatively fluid social structure with almost leaderless political parties seems to provide the conditions from which Agitators are most likely to emerge.

We have attempted to describe and analyze the senators' political careers up to the time of their election or appointment to the chamber. We have found that the "typical" senator started a political career shortly after graduating from college by being elected state legislator or becoming a prosecuting attorney or some other kind of law-enforcement officer. By the time he was elected to the Senate he had held three previous public offices and had spent about ten years or half of his adult life in public office. The chances are that he was elected to the Senate while, or shortly after, serving as a state governor or member of the House of Representatives.

But this "typical" picture is overly simple. For one thing, it may lead us to overlook the significant role of happenstance, drift, and just plain luck in senatorial careers, and it tells us very little about the politics of the senators' careers. In part, this is the result of inadequate information, but also it is an inherent weakness of studies such as this one which concentrates on career patterns. . . .

In the second place, the picture of the "typical" senator's political career, presented above, obscures the fact that the senators followed a wide variety of paths to the Senate. We have sought to overcome this limitation by describing and analyzing the *differences* in senatorial careers. The result has been not one "typical" senator but four—Patricians, Amateurs, Professionals, and Agitators.

* * *

NOTES

1. R. S. and H. M. Lynd, *Middletown* (New York: Harcourt, Brace and Company, 1929), p. 421.
2. R. S. and H. M. Lynd, *Middletown in Transition* (New York: Harcourt, Brace and Company, 1937), p. 319.
3. H. Cantril (ed.), *Public Opinion: 1935–46* (Princeton: Princeton University Press, 1951), p. 534.
4. "Jobs and Occupations: A Popular Evaluation," *Opinion News,* IX (September 1, 1947), 3–13. United States senator was not among the occupations the sample was asked to rate.
5. Cf., S. Lubell, *The Future of American Politics* (New York: Harper and Brothers, 1951), Ch. 4.
6. H. D. Lasswell, *Power and Personality* (New York: W. W. Norton, 1948).
7. H. Hyman, *Political Socialization* (Glencoe, Illinois: The Free Press, 1959). On the subject of this entire section see also H. Eulau, W. Buchanan, L. Ferguson, and J. C. Wahlke, "The Political Socialization of American State Legislators," *Midwest Journal of Political Science,* III (May, 1959), 188–206.
8. To say that so many factors are associated with an early start in politics is to beg the question: Which ones are the most important? It is possible, by a process of cross tabulation too lengthy and tedious to report fully here, to approximate an answer to this question.

   First of all, the earlier age at which Democrats launched officeholding careers was not the result of a larger proportion of them coming from one-party and modified one-party states. The Democrats from one-party states tended to be younger at their first public office than the one-party state Republicans, while the Democrats from two-party states were younger than Republicans from two-party states, and so on. Second, a senator's party affiliation is more closely and consistently related to his age at first public office than the type of party system in his state. Finally the Southern and Border Democrats were younger than the Northern and Western Democrats who in turn were younger than the Republicans, even when they all possessed similar personal backgrounds. Party and sectional affiliations, therefore, appear to be more important in influencing the age at which the senators launched officeholding careers than either the type of party system in their state or their personal backgrounds.
9. This classification of offices has been adapted from J. A. Schlesinger, *How They Became Governor* (East Lansing: Michigan State University Press, 1957). The criteria of inclusion in and exclusion from the categories may be found in *ibid.,* p. 10.
10. Ninety-four per cent of the senators whose first public office was state legislator achieved this office before they were forty years of age. Eighty-nine per cent of those who began as law-enforcement officers, 88 per cent beginning as state-wide elective officials, 80 per cent beginning as Congressional staff members, 71 per cent beginning as administrators, 50 per cent beginning as U.S. representatives, 33 per cent beginning as governors, and 6 per cent beginning as U.S. senators held their first public offices before their fortieth birthdays.
11. This is true in both political parties. The proportion of the senators whose last

public office was either governor or U.S. representative is as follows for each party and type of party system:

	Two-Party States	*Modified One-Party States*	*One-Party States*
Democrats	25%	67%	59%
Republicans	27%	73%	50%

12. This typology of careers, as is the case with so many others like it, is not particularly easy to "operationalize." Clear-cut examples of each type came quickly to mind, but when 180 senators must be assigned to one or the other category, some agonizing decisions have to be made. The following operational definitions were used:

Patrician Politicians are senators who came from "old families" and had served ten or more years in public office, or had been in office more than 30 per cent of their adult lives. (This alternative criterion was added so as not to introduce an age bias into the categories.)

Amateur Politicians are defined as those senators who had served less than ten years and less than 30 per cent of their adult years in public office.

Professional Politicians are senators who meet the public-service requirements of the Patricians but did not come from "old families."

Agitators have served less than ten years and less than 30 per cent of their adult lives in public office *and* have displayed little occupational attainment.

Distinguishing between Professionals and Patricians and between Amateurs and Agitators requires the exercise of subjective judgment concerning the senators' social origins and occupational attainments. In making these decisions, the author assigned a senator to the Patrician or Agitator category only if the evidence was overwhelmingly in favor of doing so. A more liberal interpretation of the definitions would have resulted in a larger number of Patricians and Agitators, a highly desirable consequence for purposes of statistical analysis. It would also have resulted, however, in a more heterogeneous group of senators in the Patrician and Agitator categories.

* * *

23

The Senate and the Club

WILLIAM S. WHITE

William S. White is one of the leading advocates of the establishment thesis of senatorial power. According to White and other proponents of this position, the Senate is governed by an inner circle, or establishment, which is composed of Democrats and Republicans, liberals and conservatives, and northerners and southerners, all Senate men, and all intensely loyal to the institution. Loyalty is, in fact, one of the principal requirements for admission to the club.

In the following excerpt, White describes the members of the Inner Club in the period following World War II. Some recent observers argue that the club no longer exercises a high degree of influence over the decision-making process in the Senate. Intense public controversies, particularly over the formulation of American foreign policy, and the emergence of a new senatorial type, exemplified by Robert F. Kennedy, have undermined its influence.

White, a former congressional correspondent for The New York Times, *is one of America's most astute journalistic observers of Congress. He is author of* The Taft Story *(1954),* Majesty and Mischief *(1961), and* The Professional *(1964).*

When one unexpectedly needs a room in a good, and crowded, hotel in New York like the Pierre, which is not so very long on tradition, his best course is to approach the clerk in masterful determination, allowing no other as-

From *Citadel: The Story of the U.S. Senate*, chap. 3.

sumption at all than that he will be accommodated. When such a need rises in a traditional hotel abroad, say Brown's in London, the wiser attitude is precisely the reverse. There it is better to approach the subject wearily and a bit hopelessly and to say to the clerk, of course I know it is hardly possible that you could find a place for me.

When one enters the House of Representatives, or becomes an official in the Executive Department, the sound attitude is not simply to put the best foot forward, but to stamp it for emphasis—in front of the photographers if any are present, and if official superiors are not. But when one enters the Senate he comes into a different place altogether. The long custom of the place impels him, if he is at all wise, to walk with a soft foot and to speak with a soft voice, and infrequently. Men who have reached national fame in less than two years in powerful non-Senatorial office—Saltonstall as Governor of Massachusetts, Duff as Governor of Pennsylvania for recent examples—have found four years and more not to be long enough to feel free to speak up loudly in the Institution. All the newcomer needs, if he is able and strong, is the passage of time—but this he needs indispensably, save in those rare cases where the authentic geniuses among Senate types are involved.

The old definition of the Senate as "the most exclusive club in the world" is no longer altogether applicable, as perhaps it never was. It *is*, however, both a club and a club within a club. By the newly arrived and by some of the others the privileges are only carefully and sparingly used. To the senior members—and sometimes they are senior only in terms of power and high acceptability—privilege is inexhaustible and can be pressed to almost any limit. I have seen one member, say a Lehman of New York, confined by niggling and almost brutal Senate action to the most literal inhibitions of the least important of all the rules. And again I have seen a vital Senate roll call held off by all sorts of openly dawdling time-killing for hours, in spite of the fact that supposedly it is not possible to interrupt a roll call once it is in motion, for the simple purpose of seeing that a delayed aircraft has opportunity to land at Washington Airport so that a motorcycle escort can bring, say a Humphrey of Minnesota in to be recorded.

Lehman was, of course, a member of the Outer Club, which is composed of all the Senate. But Humphrey is, in part by the mysterious operation of acceptability-by-association, in or very close to the Inner Club. The inequality indicated here has nothing to do with political belief or activity; both Lehman and Humphrey are liberal Democrats and both have records of distinction. Humphrey simply got along better.

The inner life of the Senate—and the vast importance to it of its internal affairs may be seen in the fact that it has on occasion taken longer to decide upon the proper salaries for a handful of Senate employees than to provide billions of dollars for the defense of the United States—is controlled by the Inner Club. This is an organism without name or charter, without officers, without a list of membership, without a wholly conscious being at all.

There is no list of qualifications for membership, either posted or orally mentioned. At the core of the Inner Club stand the Southerners, who with rare exceptions automatically assume membership almost with the taking of the oath of office. They get in, so to speak, by inheritance, but at their elbows within the core are others, Easterners, Midwesterners, Westerners, Republicans or Democrats.

The outer life of the Senate, in which all the members are theoretically more or less equal at the time of decision that comes when a roll-call vote is added up, is defined by its measurable actions on bills and on public policies. But this outer life, even in its most objective aspects, is not free of the subtle influence of the inner life of the Institution.

The inner life is in the command of a distinct minority within this place of the minority. This minority-within-a-minority is the Inner Club. This Inner Club, though in spirit largely dominated by the Southerners, is by no means geographic.

Those who belong to it express, consciously or unconsciously, the deepest instincts and prejudices of "the Senate type." The Senate type is, speaking broadly, a man for whom the Institution is a career in itself, a life in itself and an end in itself. This Senate type is not always free of Presidential ambition, a striking case in point having been the late Senator Taft. But the important fact is that when the Senate type thinks of the Presidency he thinks of it as only *another* and not as really a *higher* ambition, as did Taft and as did Senator Russell of Georgia when, in 1952, he sought the Democratic Presidential nomination.

The Senate type makes the Institution his home in an almost literal sense, and certainly in a deeply emotional sense. His head swims with its history, its lore and the accounts of past personnel and deeds and purposes. To him, precedent has an almost mystical meaning and where the common run of members will reflect twice at least before creating a precedent, the Senate type will reflect so long and so often that nine times out of ten he will have nothing to do with such a project at all.

His concern for the preservation of Senate tradition is so great that he distrusts anything out of the ordinary, however small, as for example a night session. Not necessarily an abstemious man (and sometimes a fairly bibulous one as a convivial character *within* the Institution) he will complain that such sessions, especially along toward the closing days of Congress, will be unduly tiring on the elders of the body. Often he really means here that prolonged meetings, tending as they do to send the most decorous of men out to the lounges for a nip, may wind up with one or more distinguished members taking aboard what never in the world would be called a few too many.

This Senate type knows, with the surest touch in the world, precisely how to treat his colleagues, Outer Club as well as Inner Club. He is nearly always a truly compassionate man, very slow to condemn his brothers. And not even the imminent approach of a great war can disturb him more than the approach of what he may regard as adequate evidence that the Senate may in one crisis or another be losing not the affection of the country (for which he has no great care) but the *respect* of the country.

He measures the degree of respect being shown by the country at any given time not wholly by what he reads and hears through the mass media, and not at all by the indicated attitude of any President, but by what is borne in upon his consciousness by his contact with what he considers to be the more *suitable* conveyors of *proper* public thought. He, the true Senate type, has this partiality toward the few as distinguished from the many all through his career even though he will hide it skillfully in his recurring tests at home when, up for re-election, he *must* depend upon the mass.

As the Southern members of the Inner Club make the ultimate decisions as to what is proper in point of manner—these decisions then infallibly pervading the Outer Club—so the whole generality of the Inner Club makes the decisions as to what *in general* is proper in the Institution and what *in general* its conclusions should be on high issues. These decisions are in no way overtly or formally reached; it is simply that one day the perceptive onlooker will discover a kind of aura from the Inner Club that informs him of what the Senate is later going to do about such and such.

For an illustration of the point, there was this small but significant incident in 1956: Some of the junior members had set out to put some Congressional check on the Central Intelligence Agency by creating an overseeing Joint Congressional Committee. A majority of the whole body became formally committed to the bill, and all seemed clear ahead. Suddenly, however, some of the patriarchs —among them the venerable Alben Barkley of Kentucky, who was soon to die in his seventy-ninth year while smiting the Republicans from a speaking platform at Washington and Lee University—found themselves disenchanted. They decided, for no very perceptible reason except that they felt they had been inadequately consulted, that a joint committee would not do at all. Under their bleak and languid frowns the whole project simply died; a wind had blown upon it from the Inner Club and its ertswhile sponsors simply left it.

The Senate type therefore—and his distillate as found in the Inner Club—is in many senses more an institutional man than a public man in the ordinary definition of such a personage. Some of the Senate's most powerful public men have not been truly Senate types. The late Senator Arthur Vandenberg of Michigan, for all his influence upon foreign relations after he had abandoned isolationism for internationalism, was never in his career a true Senate type, no matter how formidable he was as a public man. Incomparably the truest current Senate type, and incomparably the most influential man on the inner life of the Senate, Senator Russell of Georgia, has never had one-tenth Vandenberg's impact upon public and press in objective, or out-Senate, affairs.

Russell's less palpable and less measurable influence, however, was infinitely greater in the *Senate*, on all matters involving its inner being, than was Vandenberg's, as indeed was Taft's. For Russell could actually command the votes of others upon many matters, even some entirely objective matters. Vandenberg spoke to the country and occasionally to the world. Russell (and the other Senate types as well) speaks primarily to the Senate. Going back a good deal farther, Huey Long of Louisiana spoke also beyond the Senate, specifically to the discontented and the dispossessed outside, while one of his greatest critics of the time, Carter Glass of Virginia, spoke to the Senate, as Byrd of Virginia does to this day.

The non-Senate types, it thus may be seen, are in the end influential only to the degree that they may so instruct or so inflame a part of the public sufficiently large to insist upon this or that course of political conduct. The Senate type in the last analysis has the better of it. For not only does his forum generally resist change and all public pressure save the massive and enduring; it also will tend quickly to adopt *his* proposals unless they are quite clearly untenable.

The Senate Democratic leader in the Eighty-fourth Congress, Lyndon Johnson of Texas, once was able to pass more than a hundred bills, not all of them lacking in controversy, in a matter of a little more than an hour. There were a variety of reasons for this wholly untypical burst of speed in a body devoted to the leisurely approach. But the most important of these reasons was simply "Lyndon wants it." It is hardly necessary to add that "Lyndon" is preeminently a Senate type, so much so that, highly realistic politician though he is, he is quite unable to believe that the public is not in utter fascination of the parliamentary procedures of his Institution.

Again the Republican Senate leader, Knowland of California (and like Johnson he is senior only in terms of place and power and not in years) is a curious example of the power of the Senate type. Knowland, who inherited the leadership in a personal laying on of hands from the dying Senator Taft, was in both the Eighty-third and Eighty-fourth Congresses in what one might have thought to be a position scarcely likely to win him great popularity in his party or in the Senate.

A young Republican of the old school, he was faithful in his fashion to the newly arrived Republican in the White House, General Eisenhower, but he persisted, it will be recalled, in rebellious notions about Asian policy and about dealing with the world Communists. There were many times when, in the Senate and before the world, he was clearly contradicting an almost ecstatically popular Republican President of the United States and all the powerful forces in that President's train.

Outsiders could not quite see how Knowland could in these circumstances remain the President's party spokesman in the Senate. The Senate types, for their part, simply could not grasp what the outsiders were talking about. To the Inner Club it was sheer nonsense to talk of Knowland as the *President's* leader; plainly he was the *Senate's* leader, on one side of the aisle.

There arose some talk among the "Eisenhower Republicans" of trying to displace Knowland as leader. It died, embarrassedly, in the throats of its utterers before the stern reproof of the Senate type—in both parties, if it comes to that.

A man, therefore, may be a Senate type in good standing in the Inner Club if he is wholly out of step on fateful matters with his own Administration (as with Knowland on Asia in regard to Eisenhower). He may be the same if he is wholly out of step with his own party, as for illustration Byrd in regard to the regular Democrats who control the party nationally. He may be the same if, like McClellan of Arkansas he comes fortuitously and reluctantly to national attention only because he becomes involved in something widely televised, like the Army-McCarthy hearings.

Equally a man may be a powerful Senate type with never a great legislative triumph to his credit, by a mysterious chemical process that seems to be transforming now so relative a newcomer as Payne of Maine. Why such progress for Payne? It is a little awkward to explain; perhaps the explanation is that Payne, who was a rather hard-handed politician as Governor of Maine, simply generates a warmth about him because he so wholeheartedly performs, without fuss or trouble, such Senate chores as are handed over to him.

The converse is similarly so. William Fulbright of Arkansas, a Rhodes Scholar, an ex-university president, a young and literate man with many useful years ahead of him, was credited as a member of the House with promoting this country's turn to internationalism before the Second World War. He has been credited since in the Senate with many achievements, not the least of which is the cumulative achievement of an experience and a seniority that are very likely one day to make him chairman of the Foreign Relations Committee.

He is not, for all of this, quite a Senate type. Nor, for another example, is Paul Douglas of Illinois, with his academic background, his ability in the field of economics, and his not inconsiderable feat in winning reelection in 1954 over assistance given to his opponent by President Eisenhower. Is scholastic achievement or "intellectualism" then—considering the cases of Fulbright and of Douglas—some bar to the Inner Club? Not at all. For, standing well inside the doors of the Inner Club, at least, is Humphrey of Minnesota, who used to teach political science. And at the very heart of the Inner Club in the Eighty-fourth Congress sat the man with what many would consider the most truly intellectual character in the Senate, Eugene Millikin of Colorado.

Does being liberal put a barrier on the way to the Inner Club? No, for few in the Institution can be more liberal than the old indestructible, Senator Theodore Green of Rhode Island, a member of the very hierarchy of the Club.

Does being "unpopular" and remote keep out a man? No. The ordinary conversation of Carl Hayden of Arizona, whose manners are as leathery as his face, consists largely of sour grunts. And Hayden could very nearly be the president of the Club, if only it had officers.

Does wealth or social status count? Not really. One of those men in the Senate who are wholly without commercial instinct and must get along strictly on their salaries is Mike Mansfield of Montana. He spent his young years in the mines of Butte; he largely educated himself—and he, like Humphrey, is well across the threshold of the Inner Club. And, unlike Humphrey, Mansfield has no gift at all for gregariousness; at Senatorial parties one sees him standing aloof, his eyes and voice quiet, smoking his pipe and leaving as soon as departure is at all possible. Knowland, too, is less than a relaxed social being. Earnest, conscientious and loyal though he is, he is almost without a sense of humor—but not without a sense of tolerance.

Indeed, it may be that this is one of the keys to the qualities of the Senate type—tolerance toward his fellows, intolerance toward any who would in any real way change the Senate, its customs or its way of life. And, right or wrong, it is the moral force of these men that gives to them an ascendancy in the Institution which they never assert and which most of them do nothing consciously to promote.

It is, then, against all this background of the human facts in the case that answer must be made to the question whether and how the Senate is "the most exclusive club in the world" and whether, indeed, it is exclusive in the ordinary understanding at all.

Certainly there is in the common

definition nothing exclusive in a place in which a Taft, with his almost religious feeling about party orthodoxy, for years sat so amicably and by choice beside an Aiken of Vermont, whose Republicanism had, by Taft's standards, some sadly thin spots in its fabric. Where the son of an Alabama sharecropper, Sparkman of Alabama, has shared so many projects in social legislation with the rich, aloof Murray of Montana. Where the son of Huey Long, Senator Russell Long of Louisiana, so atypically carries on the dynasty by habitual quietude and responsibility in the seat that his father made so clangorous and so irresponsible. Where a Prescott Bush of Connecticut, late of St. George's School, Newport, R. I., and still later of Brown Brothers Harriman & Co. of Wall Street, has shared a forum with a Pastore of Rhode Island, late of the public schools of the city of Providence and of Northeastern University.

There *is*, however, for all of this, a quality of exclusiveness, too. Though some arrive more or less by accident in the Senate, most have worked a passage that has required more than luck, than money, than family or political position. In a sense at first there is the exclusiveness of success and then, as test succeeds test, the exclusiveness of both success and understanding. All these may be, and are, attained without reaching the final quality of exclusiveness that is involved in acceptance in the Inner Club.

To be in the Inner Club a man must be many things—some important and some mere accidents of life—but the greatest of these things is to have the character that will pass the severest scrutiny (if carried out blandly and seemingly casually) of which nearly five score highly understanding and humanly perceptive men are capable.

It is not character in the sense intended in the forms prepared by personnel offices. It has not got much to do with questions like "Does applicant drink?" or "Does he pay his bills?" It is character in the sense that only the true traditionalists will understand.

It is character in the sense that the special integrity of the person must be in harmony with, and not lesser in its way than, the special integrity of the Institution—the integrity of its oneness.

24

The Internal Distribution of Influence: The House

RICHARD F. FENNO, JR.

In this selection, Richard F. Fenno, Jr., examines the bases of influence in the House of Representatives. Insight into how the House resolves conflicts over public policy without destroying itself in the process is essential to an understanding of the internal distribution of influence in the House. The existence of power bases, or resources, does not mean that they will be employed by the members. If a member wants to be influential, he must convert potential power into actual power. Fenno's study points to the need for further research on the conditions under which members of Congress exercise power or influence.

Fenno, Professor of Political Science at the University of Rochester, is the author of The President's Cabinet *(1959),* The Power of the Purse *(1966), and the coauthor of* National Politics and Federal Aid to Education *(1962). He has also written numerous articles for leading professional journals, such as "President-Cabinet Relations" (1958) and "The House Committee on Appropriations" (1961), both in the* American Political Science Review.

Every action taken in the House of Representatives is shaped by that body's structure of influence. That structure, in turn, has emerged as a response to two very basic problems of organization. The first is the problem of decision-making. That is, who

From David B. Truman, ed., *The Congress and America's Future*, pp. 52–76, © 1965 by The American Assembly, Columbia University. Reprinted by permission of Prentice-Hall, Inc., Englewood Cliffs, N.J.

shall be given influence over what, and how should he (or they) exercise that influence? Influence can be defined simply as a share in the making of House decisions. The House's first problem, then, involves the distribution of these shares among its members and, hence, the creation of a decision-making structure.

The second organizational problem is that of holding the decision-making structure together so that the House can be maintained as an on-going institution. This is the problem of maintenance. How, in other words, should the members be made to work together so as to minimize disruptive internal conflicts? The House must be capable of making decisions, but it must not tear itself apart in the process. It is in response to these twin problems—decision-making and maintenance—that the House's internal structure of influence has developed. And it is by focusing on these two problems that the structure can best be understood.

Decision-Making

Shares in the making of House decisions are not distributed equally among the 435 members. Two sets of formal leadership positions have emerged: the decision-making positions, such as those on the committees, which have been established and maintained by the entire membership of the House, and those positions, such as majority leader and minority leader, which have been established and maintained by the members of the two congressional parties. These two structures of influence, the House structure and the party structure, do overlap—the position of the Speaker, for example, fits into both. But they are distinguishable. Those House members who occupy leadership positions in either structure or both possess the greatest potential for influence in the chamber. Some may not be able to capitalize on that potential; and it is wrong to assume that every man occupying a leadership position is, in fact, a leader. On the other hand, few members of the House become very influential without first occupying a formal leadership position in the House or party structures. Decision-making in the chamber must be described primarily in terms of these two interrelated structures.

House Structure

In 1963, 9,565 bills and 1,731 resolutions were introduced in the House, each calling for a decision. In that same year, one individual member alone reported having received 10,000 letters, kept 900 appointments in his office and attended 650 meetings, nearly all of which carried requests that he take action of some sort. Individually and collectively, House members are called upon to make decisions, sometimes within the space of a few hours, on matters ranging from national security to constituency service. In short, a body of 435 men must process a work load that is enormous, enormously complicated and enormously consequential. And they must do so under conditions in which their most precious resources, time and information, are in chronically short supply. The need for internal organization is obvious.

COMMITTEES, DIVISION OF LABOR AND SPECIALIZATION. To assist them in making their constituency-related decisions, members hire an office staff and distribute them between Washington and "the district." To meet the more general problems the House has developed a division of labor—a system of standing committees. To this they have added a few *ad hoc* select committees and, in conjunction with the Senate, a few joint committees. The 20 standing committees plus the Joint Committee on Atomic Energy provide the backbone of the House's decision-making structure. They screen out most of the bills and resolutions introduced in the House—10,412 out of 11,296 in 1963. On a small fraction, they hold hearings. In fewer cases still the committee will send a modified bill out to the floor of the House for final action. With a few important exceptions, the full House accepts the version of the bill produced by the committee. Decisions of the House for the most part are the decisions of its committees.

The authority of the committees in the chamber rests on the belief that the members of a committee devote more time and possess more information on the subjects within their jurisdiction than do the other congressmen. Specialization is believed to produce expertise. For the noncommittee member, reliance on the judgment of the experts on the committee is a useful short-cut in making his decisions. For the committee member, the deference of others is a source of influence. A man of whom it can be said that "he does his homework," "he knows what he's talking about," and "he knows more about that executive bureau than they do themselves" is a prestigeful figure in the House. Members pride themselves on producing, through specialization, a home-grown body of legislative experts to guide them in making their decisions and to serve as a counterweight to the experts of the executive branch. Carl Vinson, George Mahon, and Gerald Ford on military affairs, Wilbur Mills and John Byrnes on taxes, and John Fogarty on medical research are a few such men.

The conditions of committee influence vary. Members are likely to defer to a committee, for example, when the issues are technical and complicated, when large numbers do not feel personally involved, or when all committee members unite in support of the committee's proposal. Some or all of these conditions obtain for committees such as Armed Services and Appropriations, and doubtless help to account for the fact that their recommendations are seldom altered on the floor. Conversely, members are less likely to defer to the judgment of a committee when the issue is of a broad ideological sort, where national controversy has been stirred, or where the committee is not unanimous. These latter conditions frequently mark the work of the Committees on Education and Labor and on Agriculture. Under such circumstances committee influence may be displaced by the influence of party, of constituency, or of a member's social philosophy. Yet even here the committee can determine the framework for later decision-making, and members not on the committee may still be influenced by the factional alignments within the committee.

Committee claims to expertise stem not only from the individual talents of their leaders, but from the abilities of their professional staffs. One of the goals of the Legislative Reorganization Act of 1946 was to strengthen committee staffs. Within the limits of this law, and within budgetary limits voted each year by the House, staff selection is one of the important prerogatives of the committee chairman. Staff size, partisan composition, professional capacity, and duties will reflect his desires. Staff influence varies with the confidence which committee members, and especially the chairman, place in their abilities and their judgment. Where the desire to use a staff and confidence in it exists, staff members constitute a linchpin of internal committee decision-making. When these conditions are not present, it does not make much difference what kind of staff a committee has. Such staff influence as does exist in the House exists here—in the committees. One committee, the Joint Committee on Internal Revenue Taxation, functions primarily as the formal "holding company" for an expert staff which dominates decision-making in that field. In only a few cases does any member of a congressman's personal office staff enter the mainstream of legislative decision-making—in marked contrast to the situation in the Senate. Thus, to advocate larger staff in the House is to argue in favor of the division of labor, of subject-matter specialization, and of an increase in the influence of the twenty standing committees.

COMMITTEE LEADERSHIP AND ITS CONDITIONS. Acceptance of the division of labor as a necessity by House members makes it likely that committee leaders will have major shares in the making of House decisions. Who, then, are the committee leaders and how do their shares vary? In describing the committee-based leaders, it is easy to mistake form for substance. The most common pitfalls are to assume that invariably the most influential committee leaders are the chairmen and to infer that the vital statistics of these twenty individuals characterize committee leadership. Each committee chairman does have a formidable set of prerogatives—over procedure, agenda, hearings, subcommittee creation, subcommittee membership, subcommittee jurisdiction, staff membership, staff functions—which gives him a potential for influence. His actual influence in the House, however, will depend not only upon the prestige of his committee, but also upon his ability to capitalize on his potential and to control his committee. Consequently, many important committee leaders do not hold the position of chairman. They may be subcommittee chairmen, ranking minority members of committees or subcommittees, and occasionally members who hold no formal committee position.

Because House committees differ tremendously in power and prestige, committees like Ways and Means, Rules and Appropriations necessarily are more influential than committees like Post Office and Civil Service, House Administration, and District of Columbia. These differentials in influence are demonstrated by the House members themselves when, in seeking to change their committee assignments, they regularly trade the possibility of a chairmanship on a low-influence committee for a low-ranking position on a high-influence committee. Circumstance may, of course, alter the relative importance of committees, but at any point in time influential House leaders must be sought among the most influential House committees.

House leaders must be sought, too, among the subcommittee leaders of important House committees. The Committee on Appropriations, for example, divides its tasks among thirteen largely autonomous subcommittees, whose chairmen have as large a share in House decision-making as all but a few full committee chairmen. Thus the chairman of the Appropriations Subcommittee on Foreign Aid exercises more influence over that program than does the chairman of the Foreign Affairs Committee. And the equivalent statement can be made about a half-dozen other Appropriations subcommittee chairmen. When the Reorganization Act of 1946 reduced the number of standing committees from forty-eight to nineteen, it stimulated the growth and the importance of subcommittees. This outcome has obscured the realities of committee-based influence. Analyses of committee leadership which exclude the 123 (as of 1964) subcommittees can be but caricatures of the influence patterns in the House.

The influence of a committee leader in the House depends not only upon the relative power of his committee, but also upon how each committee or subcommittee makes its decisions. To be influential in the House a committee leader must first be influential in his committee. The patterns vary from autocracy to democracy. A chairman who is the acknowledged expert in his field, whose skill in political maneuver is at least as great as that of his colleagues, and who exploits his prerogatives to the fullest can dominate his committee or subcommittee. But his dominance may well proceed with the acquiescence of a majority of the committee. They may, and usually do, expect him to lead. Since a majority of any committee can make its rules, it is impossible for a chairman to dictate committee decisions against the wishes of a cohesive and determined majority of its members—at least in the long run. The acquiescence of his subcommittee chairmen will be especially crucial. On the other hand, since timing is of the essence in legislative maneuver, a short-run autocracy may be decisive in shaping House decisions. A successful chairman, however, must retain the support of his committee, and most chairmen are sensitive to pressures which may arise inside the committee for a wider distribution of internal influence. Long-term resistance to such pressures may bring about a revolt inside the committee which permanently weakens the influence of its chairman. Such revolts occurred, for instance, in the Committee on Government Operations in 1953 and in the Committee on Education and Labor from 1959 to 1961.

It is wrong to assume that most chairmen—even if they could—would monopolize decision-making in their committees. In most cases the creation of subcommittees means a sharing of influence inside the committee. Sharing can be kept to a minimum by designating subcommittees (sometimes simply by numbers) and giving them no permanent jurisdiction of any kind—as has been tried by chairmen of the committees on Armed Services and on the District of Columbia. Or the same result can be produced by withholding jurisdiction over certain bills for the full committee, as is sometimes done by the chairmen of the Armed Services and the Interstate and Foreign Commerce Committees. But where subcommittees are allowed a maximum of autonomy (Government Operations, Public Works, Appropriations, for example) the chairman may willingly provide leaders of his subcommittees with a base of influence in the House. In the Committee on Government Operations John Moss's Subcommittee on Foreign Operations and Government Information, and in the Committee on Public Works John Blatnik's Subcommittee on Rivers and Harbors come readily to mind. Although the former chairman of the Banking and Currency Committee used the system of numbered subcommittees without permanent jurisdiction as a method of controlling committee activity, he gave to Albert Rains a subcommittee with permanent jurisdiction over housing, thereby enabling Rains to become an influential subject-matter expert. In some cases committee or subcommittee chairmen who work harmoniously with their opposite numbers in the minority party invest the latter with a potential for House influence.

CHARACTERISTICS OF COMMITTEE LEADERS. The chairmen and ranking minority members of the standing committees attain their formal leadership positions through seniority. A variety of rules exist for determining seniority in the case of simultaneous appointments to a committee, but the rules of advancement from that time on are simple to understand and can be applied automatically. A chairman or ranking minority member who retains his party designation and gets re-elected is not removed from his leadership position.

Seniority, however, only partially governs the selection of subcommittee leaders. These positions are filled by the committee chairman (and by the ranking minority member for his side), and he retains sufficient authority over the subcommittee structure to modify the impact of seniority if he so desires. Once a committee member has been appointed to a subcommittee, he usually rises via seniority to become its chairman or ranking minority member. But the original assignment to subcommittees may not be made in accordance with seniority on the parent committee. It may be made on the basis of constituency interests (as is the case with the crop-oriented Agriculture subcommittees), on the basis of prior experience, or on the basis of the chairman's design for influencing subcommittee decisions.

Since the chairman may control subcommittee leadership by his power to determine their jurisdiction and to create or abolish subcommittees, his actions may infuse an important element of flexibility into the rigidities created by strict adherence to seniority. Thus chairmen of the Armed Services and the Post Office and Civil Service Committees have often operated with *ad hoc* subcommittes, hand-picked to consider a particular piece of legislation. The number of Appropriations subcommittees has varied from nine to fifteen since the Reorganization Act, and many of these changes resulted in giving or taking away a subcommittee chairmanship without regard for the claims of seniority.

Normal adherence to the rule of seniority means that by and large committee leaders have had long experience in dealing with their subject matter. Committee-based leadership is founded on subject-matter specialization, and committee-based influence in the House operates within subject-matter areas. Along with information and knowledge, the accumulated experience of committee leaders normally produces practical political wisdom on such matters as how to retain the support of a committee, when to compromise on the contents of a bill, when to take a bill to the floor, how to maneuver in debate, and how to bargain with the Senate in conference—all in a special subject-matter area.

Seniority practices also mean that formal committee leaders represent the traditional areas of party strength —especially the rural South and the rural Midwest and East. In 1964 the twenty Democratic chairmen represented primarily the party strongholds in the South (twelve) and to a smaller degree districts in the urban North (four). The ranking Republicans came in like proportions from rural districts in the Midwest and East (twelve) and from suburban constituencies (four). If one includes the formal subcommittee leaders from the half-dozen most prestigeful committees which have subcommittees (Appropriations, Armed Services, Foreign Affairs, Agriculture, Judiciary and Interstate and Foreign Commerce), the picture is similar.

What difference does it make to draw committee leaders from safe constituencies? Clearly such interests as can be identified with these areas of the country are advantaged by the makeup of committee leadership. The safest general description of those social interests is that they tend to be conservative, but even this is a gross oversimplification. The important question concerns how the committee chairmen in fact act on those matters which come before their particular committees. By itself the fact that leaders come from safe constituencies tells us only that they will respond to district sentiment that is clear and intense. In all other instances, however, such men remain freer than most other members to use their own judgment in legislative matters without fear of reprisal at the polls. All things being equal, a member who has flexibility of maneuver in the House will be more influential there than one whose constituency obligations leave him without elbow room.

Committee leaders, moreover, defy any easy typology. Representative Howard Smith, Chairman of the Rules Committee, is a prime example of the advantage given to conservative interests by a rural Southern chairman of a key committee. On the other hand, Carl Vinson of Georgia, Chairman of the Armed Services Committee and also a rural Southerner, wielded a critical influence on behalf of President Kennedy's New Frontier proposals. Wilbur Mills, Chairman of the Ways and Means Committee, who represents a rural Arkansas district, followed a pattern of action between these two—steering the Trade Act and the tax cut through his Committee and the House, but blocking Medicare legislation.

The committee structure is a decentralized decision-making system. A fully accurate description of who it is that benefits from the committee structure almost requires, therefore, a committee-by-committee, subcommittee-by-subcommittee, and leader-by-leader analysis.

RULES AND THE DISTRIBUTION OF INFLUENCE. What we have called the House structure of influence (as distinguished from the party structure) results not only from the division of labor by committees but also from the body of formal rules which superintend decision-making. One obvious requirement for the House is a body of rules sufficiently restrictive to prevent unlimited delay and to permit the members to take positive action. Such a set of rules must recognize both a majority's right to govern and a minority's right to criticize. Each is necessary if the rules are to be accepted by both. The accomplishment of this kind of balance is best evidenced by the extraordinary devotion to established rules and to procedural regularity which characterize every aspect of House action.

Increments of influence accrue to those leaders who understand House rules and can put them to use in their behalf. As they exist in the Constitution, in Jefferson's Manual, in the eleven volumes of Hinds's and Cannon's precedents, and in the forty-two Rules of the House, the procedures of the chamber represent as technical and complex a body of knowledge as any subject-matter area. Influence inside a committee may carry over to the House floor, but success on the floor requires additional skills. Primary among these are the ability to sense the temper of the House and the ability to use the Rules of the House to advantage. A Clarence Cannon, a Howard Smith, or an Albert Rains is a procedural specialist, quite apart from any subject-matter competence he may possess.

The official with the greatest potential for influence in the House, especially in matters of procedure, is the Speaker. Although his importance stems primarily from his position as leader of the majority party, he derives considerable influence from his position as the presiding officer of the House. In this capacity, he exercises a series of procedural controls over House activity. And some of these, in turn, provide opportunities to affect the substance of House decisions. He must recognize any member who wishes to speak on the floor; he rules on the appropriateness of parliamentary procedures; he determines the presence of a quorum; he selects the Chairman of the Committee of the Whole; he votes in case of a tie; he counts and announces votes; he decides in doubtful cases to which standing committee a bill will be assigned; he appoints special or select committees; he appoints the House members to each conference committee; and he maintains decorum in the chamber. The small element of discretion involved in any of these prerogatives occasionally affects legislation. The refusal, for example, of Speaker Sam Rayburn to entertain dilatory tactics before announcing the 203–202 vote extending the draft in 1941 may have prevented a different outcome.

Because the procedural controls of the Speaker extend fairly broadly across the stages through which legislative proposals must pass before they emerge as law, the scope of his procedural influence is probably more important than its weight at any one point. For most House leaders, however, the various decision-making stages represent boundaries which contain their influence. Committee leaders dominate the initial stage of review, reformulation and recommendation; the Committee on Rules and a few party leaders control the agenda stage; committee leaders, party leaders and a cluster of other interested members combine to dominate the floor debate and amending stage; a very few committee leaders speak for the House in the conference committee. At each stage a few members normally dominate decision-making. But from stage to stage and from bill to bill, dispersion, not concentration, of influence is the dominant pattern.

THE COMMITTEE ON RULES. No better illustration of these generalizations about influence—its concentration within stages and its dispersion across stages—exists than the Committee on Rules. This Committee owes its great influence in the chamber to the fact that it stands athwart the flow of legislation at one stage—the agenda stage. Since bills flow out of the standing committees and onto the various House calendars in considerable profusion, some mechanism is necessary for sending them to the floor in an orderly fashion. For most important bills these agenda decisions are made by the Rules Committee. By "granting a rule" to a bill the Committee takes it from a calendar, where action is uncertain, and sends it to the floor, where final action is assured. The rule for a bill specifies the length of the debate and the number and kinds of floor amendments to be allowed, and it may remove from challenge provisions which otherwise would violate standing House rules, such as the prohibition against legislation in an appropriation bill.

Commonly referred to as a toll gate or a traffic cop, the Committee obviously functions in the interest of an orderly and efficient flow of business. Just as obviously, however, the Rules Committee functions as a second substantive, policy-making committee for each bill which passes its way. Its fifteen members can exact concessions from the bill's sponsors as their price for granting a rule. Or, as they do on about a dozen bills each year, they can refuse to grant a rule altogether. The Committee thus can wield and threaten to wield a virtual veto over the decision-making process. The veto power is not absolute. Money bills from the Appropriations Committee do not require a rule. A number of bypasses, such as the discharge petition and Calendar Wednesday are available; but they are clumsy and hence are rarely attempted and hardly ever succeed. The members' devotion to procedural regularity contributes an essential underpinning to Rules Committee influence.

Since House decision is a composite of several formal (and countless informal) decisions, and since at each stage in decision-making a different cluster of House leaders may prevail, supporters of a given bill must build a series of majorities—in the substantive committee, in the Rules Committee, on the floor, and in conference—if they are to be successful. Opponents of a bill, however, need to build but a single majority—at any one stage in the process—to achieve their ends. The Committee on Rules in particular has lent itself to such defensive action. Thus in 1960, when for the first time in history both houses of Congress had passed a federal-aid-to-education bill and the Rules Committee refused to grant a rule so that the bill could go to conference, it was the only place in the entire Congress where opponents of federal aid could block a majority vote. But it was enough. The consequence, therefore, of the series of stages when accompanied by a corresponding dispersion of influence is to confer a substantial advantage on those interests in society that wish to preserve the *status quo*. House rules make it easier to stop a bill than to pass one.

Party Structure

The complex processes of majority-building involve a party structure of influence which is both different from and yet closely interwoven with the House structure of influence. Considered by itself, the House structure of influence is markedly decentralized—substantively in accordance with committee specialization and procedurally in accordance with a sequence of stages. The party groups organize decision-making across committees and across stages, thereby functioning as a centralizing force in the making of House decisions. Specifically, they organize to elect their own members to the formal leadership positions of the House, to superintend the flow of legislation within and across the various stages, and to determine the substance of policy. Generally, they organize to give some element of central direction to the process of majority building.

THE PARTIES AS CENTRALIZERS. On the record, such centralization as does occur in House decision-making comes about largely as a result of action taken by the party groups. On the other hand, the centralizing capacity of the parties is distinctly limited—so much so that in some ways the net of their activity is to add yet another decentralizing force to that of the House structure. It is a well-established fact that the voting patterns of House members can be explained better by knowing their party affiliation than by knowing anything else about them. On the other hand, it is an equally well-established fact that on many of the most controversial decisions House majorities must be made up of members of both parties. As organizing, centralizing forces inside the House, the parties have inherent strengths and inherent weaknesses.

Their strength rests in the fact that they are the most comprehensive groups in the House and in the fact that for most members the party is a meaningful source of identification, support, and loyalty. For most of its members, a party label stands for some things which they share in common—an emotional attachment, an interest in getting and keeping power, some perceptions of the political world and, perhaps, certain broad policy orientations. But the unitary party label also masks a pluralism of geographic, social, ideological, and organizational sources of identification, support, and loyalty. The roots of this pluralism lie outside the chamber, in the disparity of conditions under which the members are elected and in the decentralized organization of the parties nationally. As electoral organizations, the two parties are coalitions of diverse social interests and party organizations formed to elect governmental officials—especially the President. No national party hierarchy exists to control the nomination and election of House members or to control their decision-making activity once they are elected. Different House members owe their election to different elements in the party coalition, and they can be expected, in the interests of survival, to respond to their own special local sources of support. Each party label therefore papers over disparate factional blocs and conflicting policy viewpoints. Inside the House as well as outside, the parties remain loose coalitions of social interests and local party organizations.

MAJORITY PARTY LEADERSHIP. Since its members constitute an automatic majority in the House, the larger of the two parties has the greater potential for influence. If the members of the majority party could be brought into perfect agreement, they could produce majorities at every stage of decision-making and transform every party decision into a decision of the House. The fact is, of course, that they cannot. But they do come much closer to the goal than does the minority party. Their successes and failures at maintaining their internal unity and at organizing decision-making provide, therefore, the best insights into the strengths and weaknesses of the party groups in the House.

The majority party achieves its maximum degree of unity and, hence, its greatest success, in filling the leadership positions of the House with its own members. Technically, the whole House elects its Speaker, the chairmen of its standing committees, and the members of each committee. But so long as the majority party prefers to vote its own members into these positions in preference to members of the other party, the decisions are made within the majority party and are only ratified on the House floor. On few, if any, other votes can the majority party achieve unanimity.

The leaders selected inside the majority party—in the Democratic caucus or the Republican conference as the case may be—become leaders in the House. The Speaker, of course, is the prime example and represents the complete interweaving of House and party structure. His dual role gives him a centralizing potential far greater than that of any other member. His effectiveness, however, has varied with the formal authority vested in him by the House and the informal authority he could amass through political skill.

The most successful imposition of party influence upon the House has occurred under strong Speakers—men like Thomas Reed and Joseph Cannon. And the basis of their strength lay in the fact that their formal authority extended into critical areas of personnel and procedure. Speaker Cannon, for example, controlled the Rules Committee by sitting as its chairman. He controlled the substantive committees by selecting their chairmen and members—with or without regard to seniority as he saw fit. Given these and other controls, the majority party leader was able to dominate policy making in the House and become a party leader co-equal with the President. Since 1910, however, the Speaker's formal authority has been modest; and his centralizing influence has been more informal and interstitial than formal and comprehensive. Sam Rayburn's success as Speaker was a triumph of personal skill and only served to obscure the essential modesty of his formal powers.

The majority party elects another leader for the purpose of bringing party influence to bear on the making of House decisions, the majority floor leader. Both he and his counterpart in the minority party remain outside the official House structure. The fact that each of the last eight Speakers served previously as his party's floor leader suggests not only a close working relationship but also some similarity of personal qualifications. In the post-Cannon era, these qualifications have been those of the negotiator. Prime among them has been the recognized ability to command the trust, respect, and confidence of various party factions to the end that the tasks of informal negotiation among them will be facilitated. Successful Speakers and majority leaders are men who appeal personally to their fellow House members and not men whose main appeal is to party elements outside the House. They have been men whose devotion to the House was considered greater than any devotion to ideological causes. These characteristics improve the likelihood that formal party leaders can influence House decision-making. The Speaker and the majority floor leader constitute the nucleus of that somewhat amorphous group in the majority party known as "the leadership." Such centralization as the majority party is able to bring to House decision-making springs from them.

In barest organizational terms, the job of the majority floor leader is to manage the legislative schedule of the House by programming the day-to-day business on the floor. In so doing, he avails himself of the full range of the Speaker's procedural controls. He also avails himself of the party whip and his assistants who inform members of the schedule, take polls to assess party sentiment, round up members when a vote is to be taken, and generally channel communications between leaders and followers. In their execution, obviously, these scheduling and communications functions shade into the most crucial kinds of procedural concerns—setting legislative priorities, determining strategies of timing, planning parliamentary maneuver. And these functions, in turn, bring opportunities to affect the substance of decisions. The success of many a bill depends more upon when it is called up than on anything else. The effectiveness of the majority party in centralizing House decision-making depends upon its ability to control the procedural flow of legislation. Such success depends in turn upon the ability of the Speaker, the majority leader, and the whips to pool their resources to this end.

PARTY LEADERSHIP AND COMMITTEE PERSONNEL. Whether viewed as a control over personnel, procedure, or policy, one fundamental limitation on majority party influence in the House is the inability of its leaders to select committee chairmen. All committee chairmen do, of course, come from the majority party; but the only action which that party takes is to ratify the workings of seniority. More than anything else, this practice perpetuates the separation of House and party structures of influence. The subject-matter committees dominate policy making in their areas of specialization. The Rules Committee exercises a crucial influence over the flow of legislation. But to the degree that the majority party leaders cannot select the chairmen of these committees, their control over procedure and policy is restricted. When the leaders of the party and the committee leaders are in basic disagreement, centralized control is impossible. If in such circumstances unity between members of the same party is to be achieved at all, it must be brought about by the subtle processes of negotiation, bargaining, and compromise.

Lacking influence over the selection of committee chairmen, the most important control over committee personnel which remains within the purview of elective party leaders is that of filling committee vacancies. On the Democratic side, committee assignments are made by action of the Democratic members of the Ways and Means Committee. The selection of Democrats for that Committee, by the entire caucus, is among the most important decisions made in that party. Accordingly, Speaker Rayburn kept tight control over that process, screened the candidates carefully, and maintained his influence in all their subsequent deliberations. Committee assignments on the Republican side are made by a committee comprised of one member from each state which has a Republican congressman—with each member having as many votes as there are Republicans in his state's delegation. The party leader is the chairman of the group; he also chooses and then chairs the subcommittee which actually does the work. Thus Joseph Martin and Charles Halleck have exercised a direct influence on committee assignments.

These personnel decisions can have important consequences for House decision-making. If there are enough vacancies on a given committee, the impact of committee assignments on committee policy may be immediate—as happened in the filling of six vacancies on the Education and Labor Committee in 1959. In this case, a new majority was created which pushed a new set of rules through the committee, overrode the chairman, and got the first general aid-to-education bill in history through the House. If the policy balance is close, a single appointment may be decisive. Those Democrats who in 1962 defeated Representative Landrum's bid for a seat on the Ways and Means Committee, in caucus and against the wishes of Speaker McCormack, believed that the fate of President Kennedy's trade program, of his tax program, and of the Medicare bill might be at stake in that single assignment. But even if no short-run effect can be foreseen, changes in committee leadership and policy may be effected. So reasoned the Democrats with their five "liberal" appointments to the Appropriations Committee and the Republicans with their five "conservative" appointments to the Foreign Affairs Committee in 1963. It is important to understand that seniority is but one among a large number of criteria that custom prescribes for filling vacancies. Party leaders are not at all bound by it, and the process, therefore, has great potential as a means for impressing party influence on the House.

Typically, a formal party leader does not dictate to his "Committee on Committees." Rather he negotiates with them in making committee assignments. The reason for this is simply that the members of these important committees represent the various elements in the party coalition and, as such, may be important party leaders in their own right. Among the Democrats on the Ways and Means Committee are customarily found representatives of the big-city delegations (New York, Philadelphia, Chicago, Detroit), of key state delegations (California, Texas), and of regional groupings (New England, Southeastern, and Border states). The membership of the key Republican subcommittees will include representatives from all the large state delegations—New York, Pennsylvania, Ohio, California and Illinois. The most influential members of these committees—men like the late Thomas O'Brien, dean of the Illinois Democratic delegation, and Clarence Brown, veteran leader of the Ohio Republican delegation—are the leaders of party factions. These factions represent important sources of electoral strength and they are the building blocks of the party inside the House as well. In making party decisions, the Speaker and majority leader must always negotiate with the leaders of such coalition elements—thus, in effect, broadening "the leadership" itself into a kind of coalition.

PARTY LEADERSHIP AND POLICY MAKING. Further evidence of the fragmentation of party groups can be found in the attempts by each to organize for the making of policy. Formally the Democratic caucus can make such decisions and bind all House Democrats to vote as directed. But the exceptions are kept sufficiently broad so that no one is, in effect, under any constraint. Furthermore, so deep has been the cleavage between the northern and the southern factions of the party in recent years that the caucus never meets to discuss policy. To do so, say the leaders, would only heat up factional division and make their task of negotiation among the elements of the coalition more difficult. The Democrats also have a steering committee, a smaller group containing representatives of all factions—also designed to discuss and recommend policy positions. But for fear that it, too, might exacerbate disunities, it has not met in recent years.

The Republicans have a representative Policy Committee which has been active and whose chairman, at least, is recognized as a member of the Republican "leadership." Typically, however, its main function is one of facilitating communication among various Republican factions—East and Midwest, suburban and rural, young and old, liberal and conservative. Where a policy consensus already exists, the Policy Committee will state the party position. Where disagreement exists, the Policy Committee is powerless to make a statement of party policy—much less enforce one on its members. If dissident party members refuse to be bound by policy pronouncements worked out within the chamber, they are of course far less willing to listen to the counsels of party groups outside Congress, whether the national committees or such *ad hoc* groups as the Democratic Advisory Council and the All-Republican Conference.

Nothing makes clearer the decentralized nature of policy making by the congressional parties than an examination of certain other policy-oriented groups which exist within (and between) the parties. The most elaborate of these is the Democratic Study Group. These 125 northern and western liberals have concerted their efforts by settling policy positions, by organizing their own whip system to deliver the vote, and by looking even to the financing of House campaigns for like-minded individuals. Conservative southern Democrats also meet (now under the leadership of Omar Burleson of Texas) to discuss issues and strategy on matters of regional concern. Across the two parties, linked by the informal communications of their leaders, a coalition of Democrats and Republicans has operated off and on since 1938 as an informal policy alliance. Similarly the party delegations from each state meet to discuss and seek unity on policies of interest to them. In the Republican party especially, each "class" of first-term party members forms a group in whose meetings party policy is discussed. Smaller discussion groups—the Marching and Chowder Society, the Acorns—persist as forums in which sympathetic party members can talk shop. And, even more informally, members talk policy at regular coffee hours, during workouts in the gym, at poker games, in visits along the same corridor in the office buildings or between nearby Washington residences. The communication networks of congressmen are infinitely complex and, in the absence of two party hierarchies capable of making policy, all of these less formal sources of consultation become consequential for policy making.

Such policy leadership as comes to the party group comes most importantly from the President. To the members of his party in the House, his program provides a unifying, centralizing influence. It reduces the necessity for any active policy-making organ for his party. To the members of the other party, presidential initiatives furnish targets to shoot at. Activity is stirred among the minority party's policy making organs in an attempt to put together some coherent opposition. But, on the evidence, factionalism in the party which cannot claim the President remains more pronounced than in the party which can. The optimum conditions for policy leadership by the majority party in Congress occur when the President is of the same party. Under other conditions fragmentation is harder to check. Even under the best of circumstances, however, the limitations on the President, not in proposing but in disposing of his program, must be recognized. Since he does not control the electoral fortunes or the House careers of most of his own party members, he may not be able to give them what they most want or discipline them if they fail to follow him. He too, therefore, is normally cast in the role of a negotiator with the elements of his party coalition and, when necessary, with elements of the other party coalition.

MAJORITY BUILDING BY THE MAJORITY PARTY. The decisions with which the party groups are concerned thus are made by processes of negotiation and bargaining. Through these processes party leaders try to build and maintain the majorities they need to control House personnel, House procedure, and House policy. In the era since Speaker Cannon, the success of the majority party leaders has depended more on a mixed bag of resources than on any massive concentration of formal authority. Typically, in any effort at any stage, "the leadership" of either party can depend on a hard core of support within the party, based on a sympathy of views and overlaid with a sense of party loyalty. Members have, as well, an ingrained respect for the constituted authority of their party leader. All things being equal, party members feel more comfortable when they find it possible to be "with" the party leadership rather than against it. The negotiations of "the leadership" center on making this support possible for a majority of members.

A successful leader of the majority party will put his experience and his political intuition to work in assessing what is possible for key individuals on the committees and in factional blocs. At any point in time, he must make a judgment as to the "temper of the House," what its dominant sentiments are and what things it can or cannot accept. And the same is true for committees, for blocs, or for individuals. In making these assessments and then negotiating for support the effective Speaker avails himself of his own good personal relations with members, his reputation for fairness, for integrity, for trustworthiness, and for political judgment. He extends his own capacities by using the talents of those friends and protegés whom he locates in every House group. Through them he maintains a line into every committee, every bloc, and every informal group. With them, "the Speaker's boys," he shares his party leadership and, in return, secures a broader base of support than he might otherwise get. Through personal friendship—such as that which existed between Sam Rayburn and Joseph Martin—he maintains a line into the opposition party. Through these networks he identifies the views of others and calculates what concessions he can make before the costs exceed the benefits. He learns whether he can build a majority with his own party or must rely upon negotiations with the other party as well. He decides how partisan a tone he wishes to give to the contest. By adding up support in terms of large blocs, he can determine whether the policy he supports has a fighting chance. If it does not, he is likely to wait, for he will not willingly commit his prestige in a losing cause.

If the large bases of support have been secured and the task of majority building boils down to persuading a few waverers, the knowledge which the party leaders possess of individual idiosyncrasies plus the availability of rewards and punishments may then come into play. The leaders do, after all, influence committee assignments. Through the Congressional Campaign Committee they influence the distribution of campaign money often in small amounts but badly needed nonetheless. Through the Congressional Patronage Committee they influence the distribution of a few jobs. Through their procedural controls they may influence the disposition of bills on the Private Bill Calendar, the Consent Calendar, and bills passed by a suspension of the rules. Through their contact with the President they may be able to influence the disposition of a "pet project" of a given member—a dam, a post office, a research laboratory, a federal building. By manipulating rewards and punishments like these, the leaders can bargain for increments of support—in the committees or on the floor.

Majority party leaders negotiate in order to overcome the decentralizing tendencies of party factionalism and the committee system. It follows, then, that the sternest challenge to the centralizing capacities of "the leadership" arises when they confront a dissident party faction in control of an important committee. And, since "the leadership" is normally trying to construct a majority on behalf of some positive action, the greatest test of all occurs when an entrenched party faction uses the advantages of the rules to defend the *status quo*. In recent years the classic contests of this sort have occurred between the leadership of the majority Democratic party and the bipartisan coalition of Southern Democrats and Republicans operating from the bastion of the Committee on Rules.

* * *

Maintenance

Decentralized and yet distributing influence unequally among the 435 members, the decision-making structure of the House is essentially a semi-oligarchy. This semi-oligarchical structure has been in existence since shortly after the revolution of 1910. In order fully to understand that structure it is necessary finally to understand those internal processes by which it has maintained itself. Structural stability is the result, in brief, of internal processes which have served to keep the institution from tearing itself apart while engaged in the business of decision-making.

The disruption of the influence structure of the House is prevented through the existence of certain general norms of conduct which are widely held and widely observed by House members and which function to minimize internal conflicts. Foremost among these is the norm that members be devoted to the House as an institution, that they do not pursue internal conflicts to the point where the effectiveness of the House is impaired. Immediately after he is elected and sworn in, the Speaker customarily voices this norm and his total allegiance to it. Similarly, the minority party leader graciously accepts the results of the election, thereby symbolizing the minority commitment to the House as an institution. From this over-arching rule of conduct follows the norm that all formal rules and informal traditions of the House should be observed.

Two distinguishable clusters of such rules and traditions are of special importance to the preservation of the existing structure. One cluster functions to maintain harmony between those who hold leadership positions in the House and those who do not. It is the seniority-protegé-apprentice system of norms. A second cluster functions to maintain harmony among those members who hold leadership positions. This is the negotiation and bargaining system of norms. Together the two systems maintain the degree of centralization-decentralization which gives to the House its semioligarchical characteristics.

These clusters of norms represent what most members regard as proper behavior. By word and by example they are taught to the newcomers of the House in the earliest years of their tenure. Members who learn them well and whose behavior demonstrates an attachment to them are rewarded with increased influence. Conversely, members who seriously and persistently deviate from them are punished by diminution of their influence. Members may be denied or given the potential for leadership that goes with such formal positions as subcommittee leader or party leader. Or, if they are committee chairmen, rewards and punishments may affect their capacity to maximize the potential for influence. But for these socializing and sanctioning mechanisms, the structure of influence would be quite different from the one just described.

The Seniority-Protegé-Apprentice System

The seniority rules which govern the selection of committee chairmen draw a great deal of attention in commentaries on Congress. What does not draw attention is the fact that these rules are only the most visible ones out of a large and complex body of norms which superintend the House career of every member. Seniority governs ultimate leadership selection; but for all those who do not hold leadership positions, the rules which count represent the other side of the coin. Seniority rules rest on the basic assumption that a man must first spend time learning to be a representative, just as he learns any other occupation. Seniority signifies experience, and experience brings that combination of subject-matter knowledge and political wisdom which alone is held to qualify a man for leadership in the House. Before a member can be certified as an experienced senior member, he must first be an apprentice and a protegé.

* * *

The seniority-protegé-apprentice system emphasizes a gradual and well-modulated ascent to positions of formal leadership. In its early stages this process of leadership selection is affected by the behavior of the individual member and by the reaction of the leaders to him. The idea of a ladder is basic; but members are sorted out and placed on different career ladders. By their third term most members will be embarked on a House and party career that will follow a fairly predictable path. And in its climactic stage, the process is totally predictable, automatic, and quick. Custom has made this nearly as true for the succession from majority leader to Speaker as it has for the succession to committee chairmanships. The seniority-protegé-apprentice system is basically a system for minimizing conflict among members over who shall exercise influence and who shall not. Its apprentice norms damp down a potential conflict over leadership between newcomers and the more experienced members. Its rules for rewarding the newcomer with a predictable degree of influence keep most of those in mid-career reasonably satisfied with their prospects. Finally, at the point where conflict would be greatest, namely, where formal leadership positions are at stake, the system proscribes conflict entirely.

The seniority-protegé-apprenticeship system is a regulator of many relationships in the chamber—not merely a way of picking committee chairmen. The system must be considered in its entirety as it functions to stabilize the internal structure of influence. It must be considered, too, as a system which touches almost every activity of the House. Consequently, proposed changes in the seniority-protegé-apprentice system cannot be considered as minor. They would produce a new distribution of influence in the House.

The Negotiation and Bargaining System

An organization like the House, in which influence is distributed among forty or fifty different leaders, risks the danger of irreconcilable conflict among them. And it is to prevent such internecine struggle from destroying the institution that a system of norms has developed to govern the business of majority building.

The negotiation and bargaining system of norms defines for the members how majority building should proceed. The over-arching norm of this system is that compromise through negotiation be accepted as the proper way of making decisions in the chamber. No individual or group ought to expect to get exactly what it wants from the process. Each must "give a little and take a little" if majorities are to be built and the institution is to survive. A corollary of this norm is that all conflicts should be [as] de-personalized as possible and that policy disagreement should not produce personal animosities. Members should "disagree without being disagreeable." Only thus will it be possible to negotiate and bargain with one's colleagues on a continuing basis and construct new alliances with former opponents. From these basic norms of conduct flow other rules to govern those interactions between specific leaders or specific groups where conflict might be expected to arise.

* * *

Conflict is the very life blood of a decision-making body in a free society. Yet it is amazing how much of the time and energy of House members is devoted to the business of avoiding conflict. The reason for this is simple. Excessive conflict will disrupt and disable the entire internal structure. In the interests of stability, therefore, a cluster of norms calling for negotiation and bargaining is operative at every point where conflict might destroy the institution. In view of the criticisms frequently pointed at bargaining techniques—"back scratching," "log rolling," "pork barrelling," "vote trading"—it should be noted that these techniques are designed to make majority building possible. Negotiations in which exchanges of trust or exchanges of tangible benefits minimize conflict pervade every attempt to exercise influence in the chamber. If they were replaced with new rules of conduct, a wholly new structure for decision-making would have to be inaugurated in the House.

Conclusion

This essay has attempted to describe the existing structure of influence inside the House of Representatives. And it has used the problems of decision-making and maintenance as the vehicles for that description. The reader has been invited to view influence relationships in the House as they function to solve these two basic organizational problems. Present relations within and between committees and party units have been treated as one solution to the problem of decision-making. Seniority and bargaining norms have been considered in terms of their contribution to maintenance. Obviously, many other structural arrangements can be devised to deal with these same problems. The pre-1910 Speaker-centered structure comes most readily to mind. This essay, however, offers neither blueprints nor prescriptions. To those who may be concerned with alternative arrangements, the suggestion here is simply that they focus their attention on the twin problems of decision-making and maintenance.

* * *

25

Power in the House of Representatives

CLEM MILLER

In the letter that follows, Representative Clem Miller explores the dual nature of power in the House. He observes that power is both personal and institutional, or hierarchical. A representative's personal power is based on his ability to persuade his colleagues. His institutional power flows from the possession of key positions—the speakership, the majority leadership, and the standing committee chairmanships—and their attendant resources. Whether members actually employ personal or institutional resources or both to influence their colleagues is a matter of strategy and tactics, a pragmatic rather than a predictable decision.

Clem Miller was a member of Congress from the First District of California. Between 1959 and 1961, during his tenure as a member of the House of Representatives, he addressed a series of letters to friends and interested constituents on congressional activity. The purpose of these letters, according to John W. Baker, who collected and edited them, was "to transmit the flavor of Congress as savored by an articulate congressman."

Dear Friend:

This is basically a report on power in the House of Representatives. It must be tentative, as all such things are.

As I see it, power in the House is a personal thing. A congressman ac-

Reprinted by permission of Charles Scribner's Sons from *Member of the House: Letters of a Congressman*, pp. 110–112, by Clem Miller, edited by John W. Baker.

cedes to power by his own personal actions over a period of time. Having said that, let me quickly contradict myself by saying that power is also hierarchical in nature. Power adheres to committee chairmen, and filters slowly down to the lower ranks.

As I have reported previously, Congress is a collection of committees that come together in a Chamber periodically to approve one another's actions. The committee chairman or ranking minority member becomes the rallying point for his party in any debate on any given bill. Unlike other deliberative bodies, the Floor Leader for a piece of legislation is the committee chairman rather than the Majority Leader.

Members will frequently, and even customarily, follow a committee chairman against their own best interests and against the dictates of friendship or reason. A case comes vividly to mind. On the Landrum-Griffin Bill the chairman of the committee had agreed with the Republicans to sacrifice what seemed to him a good amendment in order to get their approval on the overall bill, thus forestalling a bitter battle. A minority of us on the committee made a vigorous Floor fight on this amendment which we also regarded as desirable. The facts, the presentation, and the merits were all on the side of a "yes" vote. Yet, on a standing vote, a good share of the Democrats stood up with the chairman to say "nay," although we felt no case had been made.

Such loyalty to committee chairmen may undergo revision in our next session. When the Landrum-Griffin Bill was up for vote, thirteen of the nineteen committee chairmen deserted the Speaker to favor the bill. This graphically illustrated the locus of power in the House. The Speaker, unable to deliver votes, was revealed in outline against the chairmen. This fact was not lost on Democratic Members. Last January the Speaker pledged that legislation would not be permitted to languish in committee or to be forestalled by the Rules Committee. The Landrum-Griffin Bill was mute evidence that this pledge could not be redeemed. Those who (with excellent hindsight) now criticize the agreement with the Speaker should be reminded that until the redemption of this pledge was made clear to all, no one could make a move.

The effect of this new appraisal may be detected in several unnoted votes after this time. For example, the Chairman of the Agriculture Committee opposed an amendment to an agricultural bill offered by a ranking Republican. He glanced around at the substantial Democratic membership arrayed behind him, but was dismayed to see seventy of them stand up with the Republican's forces to carry the amendment against the southern Democrats, 153–52.

Another interesting series of votes occurred on the second housing bill. The Republican proposed a series of limiting amendments. The southerners bounced up about forty strong to vote with the Republicans for the first amendment on a teller, pass-through count. The hostility on the part of other Democrats to this action was as visible as an unsheathed knife. Then, as each amendment came along fewer southerners arose with the Republicans, till at last there were only five left, conspicuously self-conscious.

If these are portents for the next session, and well they might be, chairmen will not be so successful in securing the automatic allegiance of their junior colleagues. This could mean some shift of power.

It is more likely, however, that any coalition of northern forces will have only limited success. Congressional government, by the design of our forefathers, does not encourage coordinate political action. A coalition of northerners, without interior lines of strength, is a tenuous thing. The very reason many are here is that they tend to be individualistic, hence not readily amenable to central authority. There is no unifying philosophy such as the issue of segregation is to the southerners. While northern Democrats have generally similar objectives, on any given vote there is enough disagreement among them to result in noticeable defection and frequent defeat.

Let us return to the analogy with warfare. The committees with their chairmen are like a string of forts. The northern coalition, as the attackers, are spread out, with poor communication and hence poor coordination. They have no base of power from which to menace the chairmen on the one hand, or to discipline their members on the other.

The greatest hazard to the besiegers, however, is the undependability of their coalition. They may have determined a strategy, only to discover that one of the barons has left the line with his levies to return home, or to sue for a separate peace with the defenders. Certain significant blocs of votes owe their primary and definitive allegiance to their city or state, and the outlines of broad policy always give way before local needs.

A graphic example comes to mind. On the vote to override Eisenhower's second public works veto, one leader who controlled four other votes on this issue held those votes out till the end. The vote was very close. We could all see him negotiating about something with the Majority Leader near the Speaker's rostrum. Finally, the bloc's votes were recorded in favor of the override. The results of the negotiations are not known to me. Perhaps it was a tour de force. But the lesson was there. If a leader were willing to jeopardize his party on such a major test of strength, it is not hard to see how much more this is true in lesser but still significant matters.

Very sincerely,

Clem Miller

26

Party Leadership: The Senate

RANDALL B. RIPLEY

Randall B. Ripley's analysis of party leadership in the Senate points to the important fact that Congress is not simply a decision-making organization or, as another student of the legislative process has observed, a bill-and-resolution factory. It is a partisan *decision-making body. Conflicts over public policy in Congress must be resolved within the context of its partisan organization. While party leaders are called upon to perform integrative tasks, such as building legislative majorities around specific legislation, they are often confronted by such centrifugal tendencies as the diffusion of power among elected leaders and committee chairmen. The tension between the integrative processes of building legislative majorities and the structural fragmentation of power among several leaders is one of the most important features of Congress.*

In the following excerpt, based largely on Brookings Institution round-table discussions held in 1965 with senators and their staffs, Ripley describes members' perceptions of recent party leaders. He provides some interesting contrasts between Lyndon B. Johnson's hard-driving style and Mike Mansfield's more subtle, persuasive techniques. Furthermore, he examines the operations of the various party committees in the Senate. Ripley, among others, concludes that the leadership performs a mediate role, attempting to broaden the areas of agreement among members through the techniques of compromise and bargaining. Finally, Ripley emphasizes the fluidity of party leadership in the Senate.

Ripley is Professor of Political Science at The Ohio State University. From 1964 to 1967 he was a Research Assistant at the Brookings Institution,

Washington, D.C., where he conducted several studies of Congress. He is the author of Party Leadership in the House of Representatives *(1967) and has also written articles for scholarly and professional journals, including "The Party Whip Organization in the House of Representatives" (1964) and "The Case of the House Democrats" (1966), both in the* American Political Science Review.

* * *

The structure of legislative life in the present Senate does not permit domination by party leaders, committee chairman, or senior senators. It also protects the Senate, at least psychologically, from domination by the executive branch or by the House of Representatives. Every senator, however new, may develop a specialization in which his opinion will be regarded as authoritative by the whole Senate. This [essay] analyzes the degree of influence over the Senate's legislative actions exercised by contemporary party leaders. Even in an individualistic situation the leaders retain some importance.

Identity of Party Leaders

The Democratic View

Democratic senators at present face a situation of diffuse, shifting, and unstable leadership. The formally elected Majority Leader is only *part* of the party's leadership.

The Democratic senators regard the main task of the formal leaders (Majority Leader, Whip, and Secretary of the Democratic Conference) as important, but quite limited. According to one senator, they "meet with the President once a week and sit down, therefore, with the Administration and Cabinet members who may be there. They bring back the viewpoint of the Executive and communicate what the Administration wants." But what the Administration wants constitutes only a small part of what the Senate does legislatively. According to a senior Democrat, "About 90 percent of the congressional activities are routine. They are things the President doesn't take a strong interest in. Ten percent would probably be of very special interest to the Administration, and that is where you have communication through the formal leadership."

In addition to the formal leaders, the senators most likely to be considered as part of the leadership are committee and subcommittee chairmen. Almost all Democratic senators are eligible to become part of the constantly shifting leadership group. This eligibility has expanded in the last few years because of the generational changes in the Senate (new men with different attitudes acquiring some seniority and the staunchest leaders of the "Old Guard" dead, retired, defeated, or ill and tired of combat) and because of the Majority Leader's permissive attitudes toward individual legislative activity.[1] A skillful Democratic senator is now in a position to make the most of the opportunities that come his way. Senator Edmund Muskie of Maine, for example, in 1963 became the chairman

Reprinted in abridged form from *Power in the Senate* by Randall B. Ripley (New York: St. Martin's Press, 1969), pp. 83–108, by permission of the publisher.

of two important subcommittees only four years after entering the Senate. Rapidly he used these positions to become *the* Senate authority on intergovernmental relations and air and water pollution. The central leaders, the chairmen of the parent committees, lobbyists, and bureaucrats all acknowledge his primacy.[2]

* * *

In addition to subject-matter experts, other types of Democrats are also leaders. First, there are men so generally revered in the Senate that they can speak with authority and lead other senators on substantive matters that come from a variety of committees. Second, there are men for whom junior senators feel special respect. The junior men are willing to take advice from some senators on a wide range of matters—including which committees to apply for—although they do not always follow it on substantive legislative matters. . . .

* * *

No Democratic senator is excluded permanently from this shifting leadership group, unless, as one southerner put it, "He has excluded himself. Some talk themselves out of it." Republicans can also become, especially in committee and through the sufferance of the majority party, a part of the leadership of the entire Senate. Party lines are sufficiently dim to permit strong Republican influence on a few specific matters. . . .

* * *

Democratic senators, then, look to various locations for leadership. They may look to the White House, the elected leadership, committee or subcommittee chairmen, or a network of generally respected senators, including a few Republicans. Virtually all senators, at least in the majority party, can aspire to lead on some matters. The formal leaders rapidly learn to live with a great deal of competition for the attention and loyalty of the members. Much of the "competitive" leadership activity, however, aims at results sought by the formal leaders.

The Republican View

The Republicans have a considerably different view of their leadership. They regard the formal leaders—and there are more of them in the Republican case—as much more important than Republican members of committees. This feeling is related to the high degree of activity and skill on the part of their Minority Leader, Everett Dirksen of Illinois. Dirksen generally overshadows Republicans with special expertise on committees. In 1964, for example, Dirksen named the seven Republican captains in charge of the different titles of the civil rights bill when it reached the floor, rather than letting them emerge naturally from the concerned committees.[3]

This feeling is also related to a general pattern of partisan inactivity and collusion with the Democratic chairmen on the part of most ranking Republican committee and subcommittee members. Senior Republicans on committees are less likely than senior Democrats to develop into "issue leaders." Hence the field is relatively clear for the formal leadership. At present, however, Republicans feel that there is less leadership activity than there should be for a minority party and that, although Dirksen is doing a fine job, he should not be called upon to operate almost alone.

The formal Republican leaders do not form a cohesive unit. Said one senior Republican, "The formal party leadership, like Topsy, just growed. We have a series of positions: the

Chairman of the Republican Conference, the Chairman of the Republican Policy Committee, the Floor Leader, and the Assistant Floor Leader or Whip. These men were not chosen at the same time, so there were particular reasons for the election of each."

The Republicans on committees develop into issue leaders only on relatively minor matters; the majority party monopolizes the important issues. Said one Republican,

> I was supposed to be the man to see about a specific kind of legislation, at least for the people who were for the bill. Interestingly enough, when the number of Republicans shrank so much, these same people who used to come to me are now searching over on the Democratic side for a person to do that. I have also tried to make myself acquainted with another specific problem, so I assume some people will be talking to me when it comes up. But these are minor things. These aren't the great issues.

Republicans do not become "issue leaders" on important issues in part because of lack of numbers. Said one member, "We are spread thinner in the Senate than in the House. We don't get as much chance to specialize." Another reason for the lack of Republican leadership on specific issues is the nonpartisan style of many of the minority party's ranking members on committees. . . .

* * *

In the Republican party, then, there is less chance for an individual senator to become important to the whole Senate as an issue leader. He may, however, be an important issue leader within his own party. And there are, of course, exceptional cases in which a Republican will be a Senate-wide leader on an important matter. In 1967, for example, freshman senator Charles Percy of Illinois emerged as such an exception in the housing field. The necessities of minority status generally help create a situation in which there are a number of central leaders who share as best they can the duties and responsibilities of providing guidance on substance to all Republicans. When they choose not to provide such guidance, Republican senators may have to look to Democratic colleagues for issue leadership.

Responsibility of Party Leaders

Democrats view their party leaders ideally as broadly responsible to the whole body of Democrats in the Senate, as well as to a Democratic President. There was, however, some disagreement over what responsibility meant in practice. Some felt that the leaders were in fact responsible to the Democratic Conference (all Democrats). Said one,

> They [the members of the conference] select the leaders and the leaders are going to have a reasonably satisfied majority of them, or they are not going to be there next time, so in that sense I would say they are responsible. Mike Mansfield has stated on a number of occasions that he is accountable to the Democratic majority.

Others questioned whether this formal responsibility meant anything. They observed that the conference has never replaced a sitting Democratic leader and that reelection to leadership posts is automatic. Said one,

> As a practical matter, the Democratic Conference meets very seldom. When it does, it is just for a rather broad presentation of some problem. I don't think you could say that the leadership is held responsible to the Conference. It is just not conceivable to me that the Conference

would meet and ask the Majority Leader to come before the Conference and answer for his conduct on something or other.

Republicans did not believe that their central leaders were held even formally responsible or accountable to the Republican Conference. They pointed out that Dirksen's predecessor as floor leader, William Knowland of California, was generally uncooperative and aloof, but that he was floor leader for five years and his tenure was terminated only by defeat at the polls, not by any action in the Republican Conference.

* * *

Styles of Leadership in the Contemporary Senate

Democrats

That there is no fixed style of operation that a floor leader must adopt is well illustrated by the contrast between Lyndon Johnson (floor leader, 1953-1961) and Mike Mansfield (floor leader, 1961-present).

Johnson operated "a highly personalized, intensive system of Senate rule adaptable to no successor."[4] He gradually developed control over a broad range of rewards and punishments, including committee assignments, office space, assignments to delegations scheduled to make foreign trips, campaign funds, the flow of information, and procedure. He relied heavily on unanimous consent agreements, aborted quorum calls, night sessions, and bursts of activity followed by periods of lethargy to move the Senate in directions he desired.

Crucial to Johnson's style was maintenance of a constant flow of information both to and from him. He wanted to know what all Democratic senators (and most of the Republicans) were thinking and doing. He reciprocated by telling them his plans for controlling the business of the Senate. Both in collecting and in distributing information Johnson relied heavily on Robert G. Baker, Secretary to the Majority.[5]

* * *

The Democratic participants said Johnson constantly checked their preferences and plans. He tried to sense dissent ahead of time and overcome it by negotiation. They viewed Johnson as an extremly aggressive—but conciliatory—Majority Leader. On the whole, his style of leadership met with favor because it got results. They liked the feeling of being led on some matters.

The Majority Leader since 1961, Mike Mansfield of Montana, is, in many ways, the opposite of Johnson. By nature he is unaggressive and unassuming. By choice, he often defers to the wishes of others in the party. At the round tables his fellow Democrats tended to view his leadership as lacking in many qualities they would have liked. The Democratic staff members who came to the round tables made a stronger case for the effectiveness of low-key leadership in the Senate.

Mansfield is uncomfortable with power. In discussing his Majority Leadership he said, "I have no power, no prestige, no influence."[6] He uses a "soft-sell."[7] Rather than meet a difficult issue head-on or even by deviousness he is likely to make straightforward compromises. For example, in 1964 he joined Dirksen in sponsoring a constitutional amendment that would have slowed the pace of legislative reapportionment. Mansfield did not like the proposal but commented that "It was a case of arriving at the best possible compromise in a question that is avalanching all over the country." It also allowed the Senate to consider adjourning, whereas a long fight would have made life in the Senate unpleasant by preventing a widely-desired adjournment.[8]

* * *

One specific limit on Mansfield's effectiveness is the highly restricted use he makes of his position in relation to collecting and distributing information vital to the smooth working of the Senate. A leader who dominates the flow of information can strengthen his hand. A leader who ignores the flow of information weakens his position.

Democratic members of the round tables insisted that even though Mansfield and the Whip, Russell Long of Louisiana, went to the White House once a week they brought almost no information back with them that they were willing to distribute. Furthermore, Mansfield and Long do not collect much information about the activities and preferences of their fellow Democrats. Mansfield stopped the practice of taking detailed polls or head counts on specific bills. The White House does its own polling in the Senate. What Mansfield learns is from the White House, but there is no evidence to suggest that he even seeks this information.

Another limit on what Mansfield can accomplish is his lack of rapport with the Whip, Long. Between 1961 and 1965, Whip Hubert Humphrey of Minnesota engaged in some of the activities that Mansfield avoided. But Long seems little interested in the customary activities of a formal party leader. Rather he is intent on developing his powers as chairman of the Finance Committee to their fullest potential. His methods for increasing this power strike many Democratic senators as excessively crude and bullying.[9] He does not conceive the Whip's job to be one that automatically makes him a lieutenant of the President or the Administration or even the Majority Leader. In early 1967, for example, Long denied on national television that he spoke for the President or necessarily agreed with him. In his March 4, 1967, newsletter to his constituents he asserted his independence by cataloging his disagreements with the President (most of which were also disagreements with Mansfield) and by stating that the principal reason that he was glad to be Whip was that it put him in a position to do more for Louisiana.

The differences between Long and Mansfield are, however, rooted more in personal difficulties than in policy disagreements.[10] Their lack of regard for each other is apparent in the daily workings of the Senate. For example, their open clash over Long's plan for financing presidential campaigns involved a conflict between personalities, not just a dispute over policy.[11] Inside the Democratic party, their dispute has had two results growing out of Mansfield's determination not to give Long any real control over party affairs or over floor business. First, Mansfield appointed four Assistant Whips who could represent him on the floor, thus avoiding Long.[12] Second, the third ranking Democrat in the leadership, Conference Secretary Robert Byrd of West Virginia, has become Mansfield's principal assistant, again bypassing Long.

Despite his evident shortcomings as a leader, Mansfield can also be effective in specific situations. He uses three techniques particularly well.

First, he uses the unanimous-consent agreement even more frequently than Johnson did. This gives him great flexibility to motion up matters with no notice and have them passed with few senators on the floor. This at least allows him to keep the Senate from falling behind in its disposition of business unless some major matter produces a filibuster.[13]

Second, because Mansfield is particularly solicitous of the minority party's members and rights he can count on some support from them, if not on substance at least on procedure. And some of the major accomplishments of the Senate during Mansfield's tenure, such as the Civil Rights Act of 1964, have been achieved only through close bipartisan cooperation, especially between Mansfield and Dirksen. Republicans are much more generous in their assessment of Mansfield than Democrats. John Williams of Delaware, for example, said that "When Lyndon was the leader, he liked to play tricks on you. The game was always trying to outfox Lyndon. But I would never try to pull anything like that on Mike. Why, he'd just turn around and say, 'The Senator is perfectly within his rights . . .' " George Aiken of Vermont, the senior Republican in the Senate, said, "There isn't a Republican who would raise a finger to hurt Mike."[14]

Third, largely because of his interest in orderly scheduling, Mansfield has kept at least some subtle pressure on the standing committees to be productive. Democratic staff members at the round tables were convinced that this technique was particularly useful in 1965, when the votes were present for Democratic programs and thus scheduling and orderliness took on extra importance. Two committee staff members argued the case for Mansfield:

He writes a letter to the chairman asking what big bills will be out and then he follows it up with telephone calls. Mansfield has put contact with committees on a regular basis. First of all, he and the Policy Committee staff checked the President's program and then they asked the committee chairmen early about what the bills are and then they keep steadily checking on the progress of them.

The Democratic Policy Committee calls me once a week: "When are you going to meet on this? When are you going to get this out? When are you going to do that?" So you can't say they are not exercising leadership. Nobody is more responsible for the President's program in the Senate than the Majority Leader. I think it is to Mr. Mansfield's credit that there isn't a lot of uproar on most of these bills.

The White House also made its own efforts to move legislation through the standing committees. Said one committee staff member, "Another thing that has been in evidence is White House calls. There was a time when the White House called and every secretary receiving such a call passed out. Now, once a day you get a call from the White House about some matter that they want to check on independently."

Republicans

The Republicans at the round tables regarded themselves as individualists who would not submit to the blandishments of a leader. As a senior man put it, "I think this is the nature of the people who get elected as Republicans. We are loners. We are proud of our ability to make up our own minds. I don't know when the pattern began to develop, but it was here when I came and it has never been changed."

The Republican leaders take account of these preferences and operate much of the time without attempting to achieve unity. When the present leader, Dirksen, does seek unity, he avoids affronting any of the members by violating the basic individualistic norms.

* * *

In both parties, then, the present leaders respect the desires of individual senators to be left alone much of the time, free from party demands. This enhances the bargaining weight of the individual senators on those occasions on which the leaders do make demands. Senators of both parties view their leaders as helpful servants more than as masters.

Party Committees

Democratic Committees

STEERING COMMITTEE. The Democratic Steering Committee is chaired by the floor leader and composed of seventeen members. The floor leader also nominates all of his fellow members, who are automatically approved by the Democratic Conference. Sitting members automatically continue on the committee. Most of the members of the Steering Committee are quite senior. In 1966 eight of them were committee chairmen.

The Steering Committee, guided but not bound by seniority, votes on assignments of Democratic senators to committees. There is no formal geographical representation on the committee, and the access of individual Democrats to the committee varies radically. The Democratic participants in the round tables were interested in altering the Steering Committee to give each member specific geographic responsibilities, so that each Democratic senator would be represented by someone on the committee. The participants felt that the present general balance between conservatives and liberals and between northerners and southerners on the committee was good.

Mansfield, in the eyes of his colleagues, has less influence on the Steering Committee than did Lyndon Johnson. Bobby Baker helped Johnson inspire applications for committees from the senators he favored for the openings.

POLICY COMMITTEE.[15] The Democratic Policy Committee is composed of nine senators and is chaired by the floor leader. He also appoints the members. Once a senator is made a member, he is automatically reappointed. The members of the committee are quite senior. Five of the nine members in 1966 were committee chairmen.

The job of the committee is to advise the Majority Leader on scheduling business for the floor, although it considers only some of the important bills. It has no power to veto bills that have been reported from standing committees; the final scheduling decision still lies with the Majority Leader. But it does give the Majority Leader some useful information on priorities, political considerations, and personal desires. . . .

* * *

Occasionally, the Policy Committee will examine the substance of a bill. A non-committee member described his experience in defending a bill coming from his subcommittee: "I had to go in and defend over again all of the substantive parts of the bill the substantive committee had already decided on and reported, and I thought the Policy Committee was simply to schedule it for the time when it would come to the floor."

* * *

CALENDAR COMMITTEE. For some years the Democrats had a three-man Calendar Committee that tried to keep the calendar moving in an orderly fashion and oversee it so that the interests of no individual senators were ignored or mistreated. In the last few years, however, the Calendar Committee has fallen into disuse. It is no longer composed of freshmen members with the time to spend on the floor. Furthermore, Mansfield's style of handling floor business—which involves picking and choosing, apparently at random, among bills ready for floor action—does not lend itself to review by a Calendar Committee. However, there was some feeling among the Democratic participants that this committee had earlier served the useful purpose of informing individual senators about the schedule and should be resuscitated.

CONFERENCE. The Democratic Conference is the formal name for all Democratic senators meeting together. It has a chairman (the Majority Leader) and a secretary. In the past, when it sometimes met as a caucus and made binding decisions, this group has had an important policy impact. During the first two years of Woodrow Wilson's presidency (1913–1915) the caucus reached its high point of activity. At that time it met, discussed issues and amendments on the major points of Wilson's legislative program, and took binding positions that guaranteed the success of those programs on the floor.[16] But since that time it has steadily declined in influence. At present, and for the past two or three decades, it has generally met only at the beginning of each Congress to ratify the present leadership's tenure in office or to elect new leaders if vacancies have occurred. The last successful attempt to oust an incumbent leader in this conference came in 1913.

Occasionally the conference will meet to discuss substantive matters, but not to take a party position. The Democrats at the round table testified that few senators came to these informal meetings, and when they did it was generally because there was disagreement over the best course of action on a specific matter.

* * *

Republican Committees

COMMITTEE ON COMMITTEES. The Republican leaders designate the chairman and members of the Committee on Committees. The full Conference of Republicans then automatically ratifies these choices. Except for the chairman, the members ordinarily serve only two years. The chairman, according to one senator, is usually "a rather senior senator. It has been someone who has been universally admired for fairness. Everybody respects him."

The committee's main function is to record preferences of senators and then allocate openings strictly on the basis of seniority. Its suggestions are formally approved by the full Republican Conference. It has some modest weight in preventing possible conflicts over assignments.

POLICY COMMITTEE.[17] The Republican Policy Committee in the Senate has developed along different lines from the Democratic Policy Committee. It has developed a staff, numbering eighteen in 1965, to help Republican senators with research on substantive matters.

The Policy Committee in 1965 was composed of eight party leaders and six Republican senators facing campaigns in 1966. The party leaders are automatically on the committee. The other members are nominated by the chairman of the Republican Conference and ratified by the conference.

The Policy Committee staff is, as one senator put it, "the party's staff in the Senate for general services, general research, reports on legislation, and development of material that could be used in campaigns."

The senators on the committee do not take party positions. They apparently do not meet as a committee. But the one project they undertake is to hold a lunch every Tuesday to which all Republican senators are invited.

A staff man described these meetings:

> It is completely informal. Senators Dirksen (Minority Leader), Hickenlooper (Chairman of the Policy Committee), and Saltonstall (Chairman of the Conference), in a sense, preside. Senator Dirksen gives a picture of what is coming up, some of the main issues as well. Senator Hickenlooper takes over for a certain area, Senator Saltonstall for another and then they ask for reports from other senators from their committees and pending legislation and what the problem may be and then it is a free-for all discussion on many things.

CONFERENCE. The Republican Conference includes all Republican senators, who elect their own chairman. In past years the conference has never been as important as was the Democratic Conference in 1913–1915. But it has usually held some meetings each year on policy matters and occasionally will attempt to state a party position, although such a position is not regarded as formally binding on individual Republican senators. In 1964, for example, the conference passed a resolution supporting the civil rights bill. In the final roll call on the floor, thirty Republicans voted for it and none against.

The Republican Conference, formally constituted, meets about six to eight times a year. At the formal meetings, organizational matters are often the topic of conversation. In 1965, for instance, the conference met two or three times on the proposed change in the seniority rule for committee assignments. It also meets on important legislative matters about three or four times a year. According to the round table participants, about 60 or 70 percent of the Republican senators attend these meetings. . . .

* * *

Impact of the Party Leaders

A summary of the impact of party leadership in the late 1940's and early and mid-1950's is still generally accurate for the Senate of the mid-1960's:

> On Capitol Hill everyone is a partisan. Yet the Democratic and Republican parties are quite different in the Senate. The Democrats incline toward a highly personalized rule by the floor leader; the Republicans, toward leadership by a handful of party officials. In neither party do the leaders conceive of their jobs as regularly requiring the development of an over-all legislative program or regular intervention into committee proceedings. Rather, their principal efforts are directed toward maximizing party unity during the floor consideration and voting on bills. . . .
>
> Party unity in the Senate is more the result of the correspondence of views of the senator and the actions of his party than the result of "pressure" from the leadership. However, the party leaders do have an effect on their parties' unity.[18]

Senators of both parties expect the party leaders to perform three main tasks. First, the leaders should state party positions on at least some legislative matters. The party leaders are viewed by many members as legitimate agents for taking party positions. Others insist that the party leaders should state a position only if a consensus in the party is present. Democrats saw their party leaders as spokesmen rather than molders of party positions. On the most important matters the leaders echoed the position taken by the President. On less important matters, party policy was decided in the standing committees by the Democratic members. The job of the leader was to enforce the work of the standing committees and present their legislative product as something that the party should endorse. Republicans, on the other hand, felt that Dirksen had a little more room for independent action but that he, too, was largely a spokesman, principally for the senior Republicans on standing committees.

Second, the members expect their leaders to make appeals for unity and loyalty on important bills. They do not, however, accept coercion as legitimate, nor do they think that the party leaders should interfere with the business of standing committees, aside from urging them to keep on schedule.

The typical appeal from Democratic leaders was, in the words of one member, "Can you help me out; we would like to get this passed." Johnson and Mansfield differed in personal style, but they both used noncoercive persuasion and appeal. Two members summarized the Johnson style:

A: He was in the cloak room or other places all the time.
B: He circulated.
A: He had his arm around you. He would say, "Beloved, can you help me?" You got the feeling that you would like to help him.

Another senator described the Mansfield style:

Mansfield is very gentle, but he will sometimes call a meeting of some eight or ten senators and have coffee and cookies in his office, and just talk over the legislation that is coming up and without making an outright plea, this can still probably be diagnosed as some sort of a pep meeting. This is the very soft sell for the Administration's position. He wants to get everybody together: "Let's don't have too many amendments, and we can't waste too much time on getting this bill passed."

Dirksen also uses a noncoercive appeal. He asks people to trust his judgment on a personal basis and to support his policy stands when possible. The potential weapons in the hands of the leadership—control over some limited campaign funds and control over committee assignments—are not, according to the Republicans, used to enforce party discipline on legislative matters.

Third, members of both parties expect their leaders both to distribute and to collect information on scheduling and on substance. Senators feel that the leaders operate somewhat haphazardly in this respect, but they do not demand a more carefully organized system. Democrats indicated, however, that they would like more advance notice on scheduling. Republicans, in contrast, felt that their Tuesday luncheons under Policy Committee sponsorship sufficed to distribute information to all senators. As one Republican put it, "At least there is a weekly contact with the leadership, face to face, and an opportunity to discuss the immediately pending legislation." Aside from the information dispensed at this weekly meeting, most information from the central leadership was likely to come from the Senate Minority Secretary. No members of either party felt that the leaders systematically collected information about what was going on in the Senate; however, they generally found the existing situation satisfactory.

The leaders of both parties in the present Senate play a limited role in restricting the options and choices of individual members. They clearly receive less deference and have a smaller impact on the members than the leaders in the House.[19] Individual senators are content with this situation. They are willing to make changes in the leadership structure and operations if the changes will enhance their own position, but the members have almost no concern for the strength of their parties as such. Greater power in the hands of the leaders might mean diminished power in the hands of individual senators.

NOTES

1. See Roger H. Davidson, David M. Kovenock, and Michael K. O'Leary, *Congress in Crisis: Politics and Congressional Reform* (Wadsworth, 1966), pp. 153–154.
2. See Martin Nolan, "Muskie of Maine," *Reporter,* July 13, 1967, pp. 44–46.
3. *Washington Post,* March 8, 1964.
4. Rowland Evans and Robert Novak, *Lyndon B. Johnson: The Exercise of Power* (New American Library, 1966), p. 95. See chapter 6 for an excellent general discussion of the "Johnson System." Comments here are based in part on that discussion. See also Ralph K. Huitt, "Democratic Party Leadership in the Senate," *American Political Science Review,* Vol. 55 (June 1961), pp. 333–344.
5. Baker continued some of his informational activities under Mansfield, but resigned the job in 1963 after various financial irregularities had been charged against him.
6. *Sunday Star* (Washington), January 8, 1967.
7. For a fine discussion of Mansfield's style see the story by Andrew J. Glass in the *Washington Post,* September 25, 1966.
8. See the *Washington Post,* August 13, 1964.
9. See the *Wall Street Journal,* May 2, 1967; and the *Sunday Star* (Washington), May 7, 1967.
10. For one version of a key incident leading to the break between Mansfield and Long see the *Washington Post,* September 25, 1966. "Mansfield was appalled when, during the final night of last year's Senate session . . . Long, having dined well but not wisely, had to be carried out of the chamber, flush-faced, by three of his brawny colleagues. . . . Well-informed senators contend the incident triggered a break with Long that cannot be repaired."
11. See the *Washington Post,* April 21, 1967; and the *Evening Star* (Washington), April 22, 1967.
12. See the Evans and Novak column in the *Washington Post,* January 19, 1966.
13. Mansfield has used this technique throughout his period as Majority Leader. See, for example, Floyd M. Riddick, "The Eighty-seventh Congress: First Session," *Western Political Quarterly,* Vol. 15 (June 1962), p. 261.
14. Quotations are from the *Washington Post,* September 25, 1966.
15. See Hugh A. Bone, *Party Committees and National Politics* (University of Washington Press, 1958), chapter 6; Bone, "An Introduction to the Senate Policy Committees," *American Political Science Review,* Vol. 50 (June 1956), pp. 229–359; and Malcolm E. Jewell, *Senatorial Politics and Foreign Policy* (University of Kentucky Press, 1962).
16. On this period see Randall B. Ripley, *Majority Party Leadership in Congress* (Little, Brown, 1969), chapter 3.
17. See Bone, *Party Committees;* Bone, "An Introduction to the Senate Policy Committees"; Jewell, *op. cit.;* and Jewell, "The Senate Republican Policy Committee and Foreign Policy," *Western Political Quarterly,* Vol. 12 (December 1959), pp. 966–980.
18. Donald R. Matthews, *U.S. Senators and Their World* (University of North Carolina Press, 1960), p. 145.
19. See Randall B. Ripley, *Party Leaders in the House of Representatives* (Brookings, 1967).

27

The Johnson Treatment

ROWLAND EVANS AND ROBERT NOVAK

In the brief excerpt that follows, Rowland Evans and Robert Novak describe Majority Leader Lyndon Johnson's highly personalized style. They observe that the Johnson treatment, a weapons arsenal that Johnson employed in his attempts to master the legislative process in the Senate, overwhelmed the Senator's colleagues in Congress. But the treatment, so successful in the Senate, was disastrous in the White House. Suited to the corridors of power in Congress, it seemed "crude" and "arrogant" as reported in the public press.

Rowland Evans is a syndicated columnist who has served with the Associated Press, the New York Herald Tribune, *and the* Washington Post. *He has also contributed articles to the* Saturday Evening Post, Harper's, Reporter, *and* New Republic. *Robert Novak, also a syndicated columnist, has been a congressional correspondent for the* Wall Street Journal *and a political columnist for the* New York Herald Tribune. *He is also the author of* The Agony of the G.O.P. *(1964).*

* * *

The Treatment could last ten minutes or four hours. It came, enveloping its target, at the LBJ Ranch swimming pool, in one of LBJ's offices, in the Senate cloakroom, on the floor of the Senate itself—wherever Johnson might find a fellow Senator within his reach. Its tone could be supplica-

Reprinted by permission of the World Publishing Company from *Lyndon B. Johnson: The Exercise of Power* by Rowland Evans and Robert Novak. An NAL book. Copyright © 1966 by Rowland Evans and Robert Novak.

tion, accusation, cajolery, exuberance, scorn, tears, complaint, the hint of threat. It was all of these together. It ran the gamut of human emotions. Its velocity was breathtaking, and it was all in one direction. Interjections from the target were rare. Johnson anticipated them before they could be spoken. He moved in close, his face a scant millimeter from his target, his eyes widening and narrowing, his eyebrows rising and falling. From his pockets poured clippings, memos, statistics. Mimicry, humor, and the genius of analogy made The Treatment an almost hypnotic experience and rendered the target stunned and helpless.

In 1957, when Johnson was courting the non-Senate Eastern liberal establishment, he summoned historian and liberal theoretician Arthur Schlesinger, Jr., down from his classroom at Harvard. Wary at the prospect of his first prolonged meeting with Johnson (whom he suspected of disdaining the liberal cause), Schlesinger had in his mind a long list of questions to ask Johnson. Never known for shyness, Schlesinger was nevertheless on his guard when he entered Johnson's Capitol office and sat in front of the great man's desk.

The Treatment began immediately: a brilliant, capsule characterization of every Democratic Senator: his strengths and failings, where he fit into the political spectrum; how far he could be pushed, how far pulled; his hates, his loves. And who (he asked Schlesinger) must oversee all these prima donnas, put them to work, knit them together, know when to tickle this one's vanity, inquire of that one's health, remember this one's five o'clock nip of Scotch, that one's nagging wife? Who must find the hidden legislative path between the South and the North, the public power men and the private power men, the farmers' men and the unions' men, the bomber-boys and the peace-lovers, the eggheads and the fatheads? Nobody but Lyndon Johnson.

Imagine a football team (Johnson hurried on) and I'm the coach, and I'm also the quarterback. I have to call the signals, and I have to center the ball, run the ball, pass the ball. I'm the blocker (he rose out of his chair and threw an imaginary block). I'm the tackler (he crouched and tackled). I'm the passer (he heaved a mighty pass). I have to catch the pass (he reached and caught the pass).

Schlesinger was sitting on the edge of his chair, both fascinated and amused. Here was a view of the Senate he had never seen before.

Johnson next ticked off all the bills he had passed that year, how he'd gotten Dick Russell on this one, Bob Kerr on that one, Hubert Humphrey on another. He reached into his desk drawer and out came the voting record of New Jersey's Clifford Case, a liberal Republican. You liberals, he told Schlesinger, are always talking about my record. You wouldn't question Cliff Case's record, would you? And he ran down the list and compared it to his voting record. Whatever Johnson had on those two lists, he came out with a record more liberal than Case's.

Johnson had anticipated and answered all of Schlesinger's questions. The leader rolled on, reiterating a theme common to The Treatment of that time. He'd had his heart attack, he said, and he knew he'd never be President. He wasn't made for the presidency. If only the Good Lord would just give him enough time to do a few more things in the Senate. Then he'd go back to Texas. That's where he belonged.

28

Leadership in the House of Representatives

GEORGE B. GALLOWAY

George B. Galloway's analysis of party leadership in the House of Representatives emphasizes the tensions inherent in collective leadership. The House breaks down into two types of leaders that exist in uneasy alliance: (1) the elected leaders such as the Speaker, each party's floor leaders, and the whips, and (2) the seniority leaders, or committee chairmen, and ranking minority members of each standing committee. As Galloway notes, patterns of tension and interaction have varied significantly in the 181-year history of the House. At times the Speaker of the House, as in the days of "Uncle" Joe Cannon, has provided highly centralized, even dictatorial, leadership. At other times, since the late 1930s, for example, the Speaker has vied for power with the chairman of the Rules Committee. For a time, after the revolt of 1909–1910, the majority leader assumed a prominent role in the House leadership cadre.

In the following excerpt, Galloway describes the development of the current leadership roles and examines such institutionalized party structures as the caucuses and the whip system. His description of the rather diffuse patterns of party control raises an important question about the House's role in a democratic society: If the leadership is so diffuse that it cannot act cohesively, can it promote responsible party government in the House of Representatives?

Galloway was a Senior Specialist in American Government and Public Administration in the Legislative Reference Service of the Library of Congress. He was a well-known advocate of congressional reform and, as such, participated in the passage of the Legislative Reorganization Act of 1946. In addition to his services at the Library of Congress, Galloway served on the staffs of other government agencies and private founda-

tions. He is the author of Congress at the Crossroad *(1946),* The Legislative Process in Congress *(1953),* Congressional Reorganization Revisited *(1956),* Congress and Parliament *(1958),* History of the House of Representatives *(1961), and numerous articles in the* American Political Science Review, *the* American Historical Review, *and the* Western Political Quarterly.

In order to perform its functions a legislative body must have some kind of a system of leadership. The House of Representatives has long had two types of formal leaders: (1) the "elective" leaders, including the Speaker and the majority and minority floor leaders; and (2) the "seniority" leaders, including the chairmen and ranking minority members of the standing committees.

During the first twenty years of congressional history the Speakers were mere figureheads. They presided over the House, to be sure, but actual legislative leadership and control were exercised by the Executive with the aid of trusted floor lieutenants, especially during the Jeffersonian regime. . . .

* * *

. . . in the beginning, "leadership was neither the prerogative of seniority nor a privilege conferred by the House; it was distinctly the gift of the president." During the Jeffersonian period the President kept a recognized leader in the House in order to see that members "voted right." Party caucus and House floor leader took their orders from the White House. "The infallibility of Jefferson in the political field was like unto that of the pope in the spiritual, and denial of his inspiration was heresy, punishable by political death. Good Republicans such as John Randolph, for instance, who insisted upon the right of independent judgment, were promptly read out of the party. It seemed a far cry to democracy when the President insisted upon doing the thinking for Congress and regulating the actions of its members."[1]

After Jefferson's retirement the balance of power shifted from the President to Congress. Several factors contributed to this transfer: the weakness and political incompetence of President Madison, a rebellion in the House against executive control, factional fights within the Cabinet, and the appearance on the legislative scene of the "war hawks" of 1812—that famous group of young and energetic men, including Calhoun and Clay, who became the new Speaker. It took some time for Henry Clay and his followers to restore party unity and recover control of the administration, but by the end of the second war with England they had succeeded in erecting a new system, based on the party caucus, in which legislative leadership was now the prerogative of a group of prominent men in the House of Representatives. No longer subject and submissive to the dictates of a strong President, Congress developed its own internal leadership structure. Under Henry Clay the speakership emerged as an office of greatly enhanced power and prestige. Merely chairman of the House and subordinate in actual influence to the floor leader during the Jeffersonian regime, the Speaker now became both presiding officer and leader of the majority party in the chamber. Meanwhile, the development of the standing committee system in 1816 and afterwards, with the appointment of

Reprinted from *Western Political Quarterly*, 12 (June 1959), 417–441, by permission of the University of Utah, Coypright holder, and Mrs. Galloway.

their chairmen by the Speaker, completed the transformation. "Thus, by 1825," as Harlow observes, "so far as its organization was concerned, the House of Representatives had assumed its present form."[2]

With the evolution of the committee system during the nineteenth century, and with the gradual delegation of functions by the House to these "little legislatures," their chieftains acquired enlarged powers and enhanced importance as leaders in the legislative process. The chairmanships of the great committees called for steering qualities of a high order. Those who demonstrated the most skillful generalship in the arts of floor management were promoted by the Speaker from one committee headship to another, gradually rising in the committee hierarchy to preside over Appropriations and Ways and Means, the most prized posts next to the speakership in the leadership structure of the House.

Thus, as the nineteenth century advanced, the leadership of the House came to be divided among the chairmen of its standing committees. The more numerous the committees and subcommittees, the more was leadership diffused. By 1885 Woodrow Wilson reported that "the House has as many leaders as there are subjects of legislation; for there are as many standing committees as there are classes of legislation. . . . The chairmen of the standing committees do not constitute a co-operative body like a ministry. They do not consult and concur in the adoption of homogeneous and mutually helpful measures; there is no thought of acting in concert. Each committee goes its own way at its own pace."[3]

Diffusion is still the characteristic feature of leadership in Congress. In practice, Congress functions not as a unified institution, but as a collection of autonomous committees that seldom act in unison. The system of autonomous committees and the selection of committee chairmen on the basis of seniority militate against the development of centralized legislative leadership and the adoption of a coherent legislative program. The function of leadership was dispersed in 1955 among the chairmen of more than 230 committees of all types in both houses: standing, special, joint, and subcommittees. Party caucuses or conferences are occasionally held to determine the party stand on legislative issues, but they are not binding. And party responsibility for policymaking is weakened by the operation of the seniority system.

Formally, the existence in the House of Representatives of 20 standing committee chairmen, plus the various political committees and elective leaders, gives an appearance of widespread diffusion of leadership functions in the first chamber. But, in practice, leadership in the House is more effectively centralized in the Speaker, the Rules Committee, and the floor leaders than in their senatorial counterparts. Several factors contribute to this result. These include the powers, prestige, and personal influence of the Speaker; the stricter rules of the House, the tighter organization of its business and debates; and the greater discipline of its members. The larger size of the House and the shorter term of office of representatives also combine to reduce the members' comparative independence.

The Office of the Speaker

In the American system of government the speakership of the national legislature is rated as the second most powerful office in the land. Only the presidency stands higher in the political hierarchy.

The Constitution says that: "The House of Representatives shall choose their Speaker and other officers," but remains silent upon his status and functions. Historians regard him as a direct descendant of the Speaker in the colonial Assemblies. Asher C. Hinds, former parliamentarian of the House, held that the Constitution did not create the Speaker, but merely adopted an existing officer. His office is thus a colonial heritage whose importance and influence have varied down through the passing years, depending upon the personal force of the incumbents.

Selection and Qualifications

We do not know what the intent of the founding fathers was with respect to the Speaker. They did not say whether he must be a member of the House, although he always has been. Nor did the framers say how he should be selected. At first he was elected by ballot, but since 1839 he has been chosen by voice vote, on a roll call. In 1809 it was held that the Speaker should be elected by a majority of all present, and in 1879 that he might be elected by a majority of those present, if a quorum.

In fact there is a discrepancy between the law and the practice in the choice of the Speaker. For in actual practice the Speaker is really chosen by the caucus of the majority party in the House whose choice is then ratified by the House itself. On the eve of the meeting of each new Congress the congressional parties hold caucuses or conferences at which they nominate their respective candidates for the elective offices in the House. On rare occasions there is a lively contest for the nomination for the speakership. On the eve of the Sixty-sixth Congress, for example, a spirited campaign was waged between Mr. Gillett of Massachusetts and Mr. Mann of Illinois. Gillett won. The contest is keenest in the caucus of the majority party because its nomination is equivalent to election in the House.

In nominating their candidates for the speakership the congressional parties usually lay stress on length of congressional service, among other factors. Long legislative experience is a criterion that seems to carry more weight in the twentieth century than it did in the nineteenth. Before 1896 the average length of congressional service before election to the Chair was seven years. Henry Clay of Kentucky and William Pennington of New Jersey were elected to the speakership on their first appearance in the House, something that would never happen in our time. Since 1896, however, the average length of service of Speakers has been about three times as long as before. "Uncle Joe" Cannon was elevated to the Chair in his thirty-first year in the House of Representatives. Champ Clark was chosen in his sixteenth year of service, Gillett in his twenty-seventh, Longworth in his twenty-first, and . . . Sam Rayburn, at the time of his first election was in his twenty-eighth year in the House.

Aside from long congressional service, the modern Speakers are men who have won the confidence and esteem not only of their own party, but also of the general membership of the House. They have usually served as chairmen of important committees of the House or as floor leaders. Thus, Speaker Rayburn was long chairman of the Committee on Interstate and Foreign Commerce and later was the Democratic floor leader.

It has been a long-standing custom of the House to re-elect a Speaker to that office as long as his party remains in control of the House and he retains his seat. Both Speaker Cannon and Speaker Clark were re-elected consecutively for four terms, until a change of party control took place. Mr. Rayburn was elected Speaker on September 16, 1940, and is now (1959) serving his eighth term, having held the office longer than any predecessor in the Chair.

Powers and Duties

The Speaker of the House derives his powers and duties from the Constitution, the rules of the House, previous decisions of the Chair, and general parliamentary law. He presides at the sessions of the House, announces the order of business, puts questions, and reports the vote. He also decides points of order and can prevent dilatory tactics, thanks to the earlier rulings of Speaker Reed. He appoints the chairman of the Committee of the Whole and the members of select and conference committees. He chooses Speakers pro tem and refers bills and reports to the appropriate committees and calendars. He also enjoys the privileges of an ordinary member of the House, and may vote and participate in debate on the floor

When Henry Clay took the Chair as Speaker on December 1, 1823, he described the duties of the office in terms that are still apropos today.

> They enjoin promptitude and impartiality in deciding the various questions of order as they arise; firmness and dignity in his deportment toward the House; patience, good temper, and courtesy towards the individual Members, and the best arrangement and distribution of the talent of the House, in its numerous sub-divisions, for the dispatch of the public business, and the fair exhibition of every subject presented for consideration. They especially require of him, in those moments of agitation from which no deliberative assembly is always entirely exempt, to remain cool and unshaken amidst all the storms of debate, carefully guarding the preservation of the permanent laws and rules of the House from being sacrificed to temporary passions, prejudices, or interests.

A Triple Personality

In contrast to his English counterpart, the Speaker of our House is a triple personality, being a member of the House, its presiding officer, and leader of the majority party in the chamber. As a member of the House he has the right to cast his vote on all questions, unlike the Vice President, who has no vote except in case of a tie. Usually, the Speaker does not exercise his right to vote except to break a tie or when he desires to make known how he stands on a measure. As a member, he also has the right to leave the Chair and participate in debate on the House floor as the elected representative of his district, unlike the Vice President, who may not do likewise in the Senate. The Speaker seldom exercises this right, but when he does, as on close party issues, the House fills up and everyone pays close attention.

As presiding officer of the House, the Speaker interprets the rules that the House has adopted for its guidance. Customarily he performs this duty as a judge, bound by the precedents created by prior decisions of the Chair. But in 1890 Speaker Reed broke with all past practice by refusing to entertain a motion on the ground that it was dilatory and by including members physically present but not voting in counting a quorum. With significant exceptions, appeals are in order from decisions of the Chair, but are seldom taken; when taken, the Chair is usually sustained.

The Speaker's power of recognition is now narrowly limited by House rules and conventions that fix the time for the consideration of various classes of bills; require recognition of the chairmen of the Appropriations and Ways and Means committees when they rise to move the consideration of appropriation and revenue bills; and allow committeemen in charge of other legislation to control all the time allotted for general debate. The Chair still has discretion, however, in determining who shall be recognized while a bill is being debated under the five-minute rule in Committee of the Whole; but then the Speaker is not in the Chair. He still has complete discretion also as to whom he will recognize to make motions to suspend the rules, on days when such motions are in order. The rules of the House may be suspended by a two-thirds vote on the first and third Mondays of the month and on the last six days of the session.

As party leader the Speaker prior to 1910 had certain additional powers: to appoint all standing committees and to name their chairmen; to select the members of the Rules Committee; and from 1858 to serve as its chairman. By the exercise of these powers he was in a position to influence greatly the action taken by the standing committees, the order of business in the House, and the character of the action taken by the House itself. His political powers evolved gradually during the nineteenth century, reaching a peak under the masterful leadership of Speakers Reed and Cannon. Taken together, the powers of the Speaker prior to 1910, as a member of the House, as its presiding officer, and as majority leader were so far-reaching that the speakership was regarded as second only in power and influence to the presidency, and as supreme in relation to the legislative process. After a long process of evolution the problem of leadership in the House of Representatives seemed to have been finally solved.

In the revolution of 1910, however, a coalition of Democrats and insurgent Republicans, led by George W. Norris, rebelled against the despotism of "Czar" Cannon, dethroned the Speaker from his post of power, and deprived him of most of the great powers he formerly possessed. They removed him from the Rules Committee of which he had formerly been chairman. They stripped him of the power to appoint the standing committees of the House and their chairmen, which he had exercised as a powerful weapon of party discipline. And they restricted his former right of recognition. This revolutionary reversal in the powers of the Speaker was swiftly accomplished and was described as "one of the most remarkable reversions of policy that has ever characterized a political system." The revolt was not so much against the principle of leadership as it was against the concentration of powers in the hands of a single individual who had exercised them in an arbitrary and autocratic manner.

Although the Speaker lost his power in the revolution of 1910 of appointing the standing committees of the House, he still appoints the select committees, the House members of conference committees, and the chairman of the Committee of the Whole. Prior to 1910, the Speaker controlled the House in collaboration with a coterie of trusted party lieutenants. Since 1910 the leadership of the House has been in commission. Despite the overthrow of Cannonism, the speakership thus continues to be the most powerful office in Congress.

* * *

Rayburn and Martin

Sam Rayburn and Joseph W. Martin, Jr., . . . previous Speakers of the House of Representatives, have enjoyed responsibilities beyond those of the typical Speaker of earlier days. Mr. Rayburn was a close friend and trusted adviser of both President Franklin D. Roosevelt and Harry S. Truman. Mr. Martin met with President Eisenhower in his weekly conferences at the White House with the Republican leaders of Congress.

William S. White, who covered Congress for the *New York Times,* has described the Speaker as "the second most influential elected official" in Washington today.

> Officially, his job is in many respects comparable to the job of heading any great corporation or enterprise. He is the ultimate chief of everything in the House, from the nature of its legislative program to the conduct of its dining room, and the direction of its personnel—hired and elected—is his endless concern.
>
> He performs this job with economy of motion, with scant and infrequent but heady praise for those about him, with a ready and easy delegation of authority and with a somewhat amused deference to perhaps the most temperamental of all men—a politician at work.
>
> The Speaker of the House has three main functions:
>
> (1) To perform as the responsible presiding officer (and in nearly every real sense the outright boss) of a parliamentary body.
>
> (2) To act as the head of [his] party in the House; its general manager, umpire and occasionally, in a rather hard-shelled way, as a paternal counselor, to whom many in the fold bring their troubles and ambitions. In this, he has also, and always, to keep a critical eye upon all the vast legislative mechanisms of the House, spurring on this laggard committee, reining in that over-zealous one—in short, taking personal responsibility for all the important business of the House.
>
> (3) To advise the highest personages in Washington on all manner of topics, at all times.[4]

The Majority Leader of the House of Representatives

In any numerous body leaders must arise or be chosen to manage its business and the American House of Representatives has long had its posts of leadership. Outstanding among them have been the Speaker, the floor leader, and the chairman of the Committee on Rules. The chairmen of Ways and Means and of Appropriations have also long been top leadership positions in the hierarchy of the House, followed by the chairmen of the other great standing committees of that body. This section will discuss the office of the majority leader of the House: its history, role, and relationships.

History of the Office

In the history of the evolution of the office of majority leader the year 1910 marks a major dividing point. For the reform of the House rules adopted in that year brought about a redistribution of the powers of the speakership and a significant change in the position of the floor leader.

During the nineteenth century the floor leader was customarily selected by the Speaker who often designated either his leading opponent within the party or the chairman of Ways and Means or of the Appropriations Committee or one of his faithful lieutenants. . . .

According to Riddick,

> in the House, the early titular floor leaders were at the same time the chairmen of the Ways and Means Committee. Before the division of the work of that committee, the duties of its chairmen were so numerous that they automatically became the

actual leaders, since as chairmen of that committee they had to direct the consideration of most of the legislation presented to the House. [Ways and Means handled both the revenue and the appropriations bills down to 1865.] From 1865 until 1896 the burden of handling most of the legislation was shifted to the chairman of the Appropriations Committee, who then was designated most frequently as the leader. From 1896 until 1910 once again the chairmen of the Ways and Means Committee were usually sought as the floor leaders.[5]

Since 1910 the floor leader has been elected by secret ballot of the party caucus. During the Wilson administrations the Democrats resumed their former practice of naming the chairman of Ways and Means as floor leader, but since the Seventy-second Congress (1931–33), when the Democrats recovered control of the House, their floor leaders have not retained their former committee assignments. John W. McCormack, who was elected Democratic floor leader on September 16, 1940, and who . . . held that office longer than any predecessor, resigned his seat on Ways and Means when he became majority leader. In 1919, when the Republicans captured control of the House, they elected as their floor leader the former chairman of Ways and Means and made him ex-officio chairman of their Committee on Committees and of their Steering Committee. He gave up his former legislative committee assignments in order to devote himself, with the Speaker, to the management of the business of the House.

Changes After 1910

As a result of the so-called "revolution of 1910," notable changes were made in the power structure of the House. Under "Uncle Joe" Cannon who had been Speaker since 1903, the Speaker was supreme and all-powerful. He dominated the Rules Committee which made the rules and was a law unto itself. The majority party caucus was seldom needed or used. The Speaker appointed the standing committees which were entirely free from control by a majority of the House, while the floor leader was a figurehead.

After the congressional elections of November, 1910, in which the Democrats won full control of the House, they held a party caucus on January 19, 1911, and chose Champ Clark as Speaker and Oscar Underwood as their floor leader and as chairman of the Ways and Means Committee. Under the new system that became effective in the 1911–12 session of the Sixty-second Congress, the Speaker was largely shorn of power and the majority party caucus became the dominant factor. The Rules Committee was controlled by the floor leader and the caucus; it made the rules and retained all its former powers. The Democratic members of Ways and Means organized the House by naming its standing committees.

Under Underwood the floor leader was supreme, the Speaker a figurehead. The main cogs in the machine were the caucus, the floor leadership, the Rules Committee, the standing committees, and special rules. Oscar Underwood became the real leader of the House. He dominated the party caucus, influenced the rules, and as chairman of Ways and Means chose the committees. Champ Clark was given the shadow, Underwood the substance of power. As floor leader, he could ask and obtain recognition at any time to make motions to restrict debate or preclude amendments or both. "Clothed with this perpetual privilege of recognition, and backed by his caucus," remarked a contemporary observer, "the floor leader had it in his power to make a Punch and Judy show of the House at any time."[6]

After World War I the party caucus gradually fell into disuse, the floor leader ceased to be chairman of Ways and Means, the standing committees continued to function as autonomous bodies, and the Rules Committee became a more influential factor in the power structure of the House. After 1937 this powerful committee ceased to function as an agent of the majority leadership and came under the control of a bipartisan coalition which was often able to exercise an effective veto power over measures favored by the majority party and its leadership.

The net effect of the various changes of the last thirty-five years in the power structure of the House of Representatives has been to diffuse the leadership, and to disperse its risks, among a numerous body of leaders. The superstructure which has come to control "overhead" strategy now includes the Speaker, the floor leader, the chairman of Rules, and the party whip. At a somewhat lower echelon behind this inner "board of strategy" are the chairman and the secretary of the party caucus or conference, the majority members of Rules who have grown from three to [ten], and the members of the Steering (Democratic) and Policy (Republican) committees and of the two Committees on Committees. Thus, the top leaders of the House are no longer "the chairmen of the principal standing committees," as Woodrow Wilson described them in 1885, although the chairmen still have large powers over bills within their jurisdiction.

So far as the position of floor leader is concerned, he no longer occupies the post of supremacy that Oscar Underwood held. There is no provision for his office in the standing rules of the House. Nevertheless, he stands today in a place of great influence and prestige, the acknowledged leader of the majority party in the chamber, its field general on the floor, number two man in the party hierarchy, and heir apparent to the Speaker himself. All the Speakers of the past quarter-century have been advanced to the speakership from the floor leadership position.

Qualifications and Previous Experience

After retiring from the House of Representatives where he represented Buffalo from 1897 to 1911, DeAlva Alexander wrote an informative history of that body which contains a series of character sketches of the floor leaders of the House from Griswold in 1800 to Underwood in 1911. Most of these mighty men of old are now forgotten, but to their contemporaries they were men of exceptional capacity. "In interesting personality and real ability the floor leader is not infrequently the strongest and at the time the best-known man in the House."

Alexander went on to give his own evaluation of the characteristics of a good leader as follows:

> It certainly does not follow that a floor leader is the most effective debater, or the profoundest thinker, or the accepted leader of his party, although he may be and sometimes is all of these. It should imply, however, that in the art of clear, forceful statement, of readily spotting weak points in an opponent's argument, and in dominating power to safeguard the interests of the party temporarily responsible for the legislative record of the House, he is the best equipped for his trade. It is neither necessary nor advisable for him to lead or even to take part in every debate. The wisdom of silence is a great asset. Besides, chairmen and members of other committees are usually quite

capable and sufficiently enthusiastic to protect their own measures. But the floor leader must aid the Speaker in straightening out parliamentary tangles, in progressing business, and in exhibiting an irresistible desire to club any captious interference with the plans and purposes of the majority.[7]

Thirteen men have held the office of floor leader of the House of Representatives since 1919. Six of them were Republicans: Mondell, Longworth, Tilson, Snell, Martin, and Halleck. Seven were Democrats: Garrett, Garner, Rainey, Byrns, Bankhead, Rayburn, and McCormack. Elevation to the floor leadership comes only after long service in the House. The Republican floor leaders had served, on the average, sixteen years in the chamber; the Democrats twenty-one years before their election. The combined average for the whole group was nineteen years previous service in the House. The long-run trend in point of previous House experience is downward, both McCormack and Halleck having been elected floor leader after serving only six terms in the House.

All the floor leaders since World War I have also enjoyed long service on some of the most eminent committees of the House. Of the six Republicans, three had served on the Rules Committee, two ranked high on Ways and Means, and one on the Appropriations Committee. Of the seven Democrats, three were high ranking on Ways and Means, two on Rules, one on Appropriations, and one (Rayburn) had been chairman of Interstate and Foreign Commerce.

Functions and Duties of Floor Leader

The standing rules of the House are silent on the duties of the floor leaders who, as we have seen, are selected by the caucus or conference of their respective parties. As his title indicates, the principal function of the majority leader is that of field marshal on the floor of the House. He is responsible for guiding the legislative program of the majority party through the House. In co-operation with the Speaker, he formulates and announces the legislative program, keeps in touch with the activities of the legislative committees through their chairmen, and stimulates the reporting of bills deemed important to the nation and the party. After conferring with the Speaker and majority leader, the majority whip customarily sends out a "whip notice" on Fridays to the party members in the House, indicating the order of business on the floor for the following week, and the majority leader makes an announcement to the same effect on the floor in response to an inquiry from the minority leader. The legislative program is planned ahead on a weekly basis according to the readiness of committees to report, the condition of the calendars, the exigencies of the season, and the judgment of the party leaders. Advance announcement of the weekly program protects the membership against surprise action.

The role of the majority leader was lucidly summarized in a statement inserted in the *Congressional Record* on May 11, 1928, when the Republicans were in power, by Representative Hardy of Colorado:

The floor leader, especially the leader of the majority side, has much to do with the legislative program. The majority leader, of course, represents the majority on the floor. Motions he makes are usually passed. He endeavors to represent the majority view and the majority follow his leadership. He leads in debate on administration matters and gives the House and the country the viewpoint of his party on the legislative program.

The leader keeps in touch with proposed legislation, the status of bills of importance, with the steering committee of which he is chairman, and with the attitude of the Rules Committee. He confers with committee chairmen and Members in general. The majority leader often confers with the President and advises with him regarding administrative measures. He takes to the President the sentiment of the party in the House and he brings to the party in the House the sentiment of the President. The majority leader acts also as chairman of the committee on committees and of the steering committee. . . .[8]

The Democratic party in the House set up its own Steering Committee in 1933, composed of the Speaker, floor leader, chairman of the party caucus, party whip, the chairmen of Ways and Means, Appropriations, and Rules, and one Representative from each of the fifteen zones into which the country is divided for party purposes, each such Representative being elected by the Democratic delegation in the House from the zone. The Steering Committee elects its own chairman, vice-chairman, and secretary and cooperates with the leadership in the planning and execution of party policy. In actual practice, nowadays, however, "the Democratic Steering Committee seldom meets and never steers," according to James F. Byrnes.

Various parliamentary procedures are employed by the floor leader in directing and expediting the legislative program. Much noncontroversial business on the Unanimous Consent Calendar is disposed of without debate and "without objection." The work of the House is sometimes described as "lawmaking by unanimous consent" because the floor leader uses this device to fix the program of business. Members know that it would be futile to object to his unanimous consent requests to consider legislation because the same end could be achieved via a special rule from the Committee on Rules. Similarly, if a member sought to bring up a matter out of its turn, without prior agreement with the leadership, the floor leader could defeat him by objecting.

The floor leader can also limit debate on a bill, if it tends to get out of control, by making the point of order that debate is not germane to the pending subject or by moving that all debate on the pending bill and all amendments thereto close in a certain time. By his temper and spirit he can also influence the tone of debate.

As the end of a session approaches, with many measures pressing for passage, the Speaker and the floor leader co-operate closely to avoid a last-minute jam. The procedural devices employed at this time are largely unanimous consent, special orders, and motions to suspend the rules which are in order on the last six days of a session and require a two-thirds vote. "There is a usual speeding up of the program during the last days. But there is also a tightening of control. In strong contrast to the Senate, the House remains a poised, businesslike body as it approaches adjournment. The men in the cab hold the legislative train steady to the very end of its run."[9] At the end of each session the floor leader customarily extends his remarks by inserting a record of its accomplishments, showing the major legislative actions taken and the number of public and private laws enacted, viewing with pride the role of the majority party in the legislative process.

* * *

Since the floor leader is responsible for the orderly conduct of the business of legislation on the floor, it is necessary for him to keep in close touch with the sentiment of the House and with the chairmen of committees that have under consideration bills of interest to the House, the country, and the party. To this end he holds frequent conferences with those concerned with prospective measures in order to compose any differences that may arise, as well as to plan the strategy and tactics of his campaign. Information as to party sentiment on a particular bill is also obtained, with the aid of the party whips, by polls of the state delegations.

Whip Organization

On the Democratic side the Whip Organization in the House consists of a chief whip who is appointed by the majority leader in consultation with the Speaker, and fifteen assistant whips who are selected by the Democratic representatives from as many zones into which the country is divided for party purposes. . . It is the whip's job to be present on the House floor most of the time the House is in session. He helps the majority leader keep tab on legislation, and he keeps the members advised of the legislative schedule. He attempts to make sure the members of his party are on the floor when a significant vote is imminent. On occasion the whip joins the Speaker and the majority leader in seeking to round up votes on an important issue.

On the Republican side the Whip Organization includes the chief whip who is elected by the Committee on Committees, three regional whips selected from three regions by the Republican whip, and ten assistant whips who are also appointed by the chief whip. . . .

Party Caucuses

Under the old system the congressional parties held frequent caucuses at which party policies were vigorously discussed and differences settled. Every major measure of a session was considered in party caucus and members were bound to abide by its decisions. The leadership then knew exactly where it stood, whether bills could be passed on the floor without amendment or whether compromises would have to be made. After Champ Clark became floor leader in 1909 the House Democrats held many binding caucuses and much of the success of the legislative program of the Wilson administration was attributed to the effective use of the caucus by the Democratic party in both houses of Congress. For many decades House Republicans also held frequent party conferences which, although they were not binding, made for a consensus among the party membership and helped a succession of strong G.O.P. Speakers and floor leaders to hold the party reins tightly.

Under the new system, however, party caucuses are seldom held except at the opening of a new Congress to nominate House officers and approve recommendations of the leadership for committee appointments. Perhaps party leaders nowadays consider these meetings too hazardous. The leadership cannot compel members to vote against their will or conscience nor can it discipline them by removal or demotion from committees. In latter years the floor leader has relied for the co-operation of his followers not upon the compulsion of party rules but upon his own powers of logic and persuasion and considerations of party welfare.

Under the new system the Floor Leader is dependent not upon his power under

> the rules, but upon his own personality and character, upon the esteem in which he is held in the House for his political sagacity and his wisdom as a statesman, and upon the natural instincts which prompt men belonging to a party, and held together by natural selfish instincts for mutual protection, for his success in harmonizing differences and thus being able to go into the House with a measure assured of sufficient support to secure its enactment . . . the Floor Leader has become the general manager of his party in the House, the counselor of his colleagues, the harmonizer of their conflicting opinions, their servant, but not their master.[10]

Summarizing, the function of a leader is to lead. In the case of a majority leader of a legislative assembly, leadership involves planning the legislative program, scheduling the order of business on the floor, supporting legislation calculated to implement the party's platform pledges, coordinating committee action to this end, and using his individual influence to keep the members of the party in the House in line with party policies. The majority leader's task is to steer his party in the House toward the formulation and adoption of policies and strategy designed to carry out the Administration's legislative program, where the House and the presidency are controlled by the same political party. As floor leader his function is to employ all the arts of parliamentary procedure to expedite the enactment of that program.

Under existing conditions in the Democratic party in the House of Representatives, this is a large order. For the party is deeply divided along sectional lines. It has both conservative and liberal members who wear the same party emblem, but lack a common political philosophy. Loyalty to local and sectional interests sometimes transcends a sense of responsibility to the national political party. Under these circumstances, the task of the party leader is difficult to accomplish. Who can lead where others will not follow? Who can discipline recalcitrant party members for failing to co-operate when effective sanctions are lacking? To be sure, Rule 2 of the House Democratic Caucus Rules provides that "any member of the Democratic Caucus of the House of Representatives failing to abide by the rules governing the same shall thereby automatically cease to be a member of the Caucus." And Rule 7 provides that "in deciding upon action in the House involving party policy or principle, a two-thirds vote of those present and voting at a Caucus meeting shall bind all members of the Caucus: provided, the said two-thirds vote is a majority of the full Democratic membership of the House. . . ." But for all practical purposes these rules are moribund.

Relations with Committees

During the nineteenth century, as already noted, the actual floor leader was often the chairman of Ways and Means prior to 1865 when this committee handled both the revenue and appropriation bills. In that year the supply bills were given to the Committee on Appropriations and thereafter the floor leader was often the chairman of Appropriations. When the Sixty-second Congress (1911–13) transferred the power to appoint committees from the Speaker to the Democratic members of Ways and Means, its chairman (Underwood) who was also floor leader thus acquired an indirect influence over legislation not enjoyed by his predecessors. Today Democratic vacancies on Ways and Means are filled by election by the party caucus which ratifies the choice of the party leadership which is thus able to exercise influence over tax and other legislation reported by that committee.

As already noted, the Republican floor leader serves as chairman of the Republican Committee on Committees of the House which has the task of filling its party vacancies on the legislative committees. This involves hearing the claims of interested candidates and deciding who should be chosen.

The floor leader on both sides of the House aisle is also a member of his party's Steering or Policy Committee. The Republican floor leader has been ex officio chairman of his Steering Committee. An interesting account of the role of the Republican Steering Committee several years ago was given by Representative Hardy of Colorado, as follows:

> An influential factor in government is the steering committee. It exerts a powerful influence but makes no effort to exhibit power. It works along diplomatic lines to feel out and consolidate sentiment for administration measures and procedure. It meets at the call of the chairman, and considers the welfare of the Government from the party point of view. It advises with the White House, the chairmen of important committees, the party leaders, and the Rules Committee. It helps to iron out differences, and to formulate the majority program in the House. The chairman of the Steering Committee is the floor leader. When the committee meets the Speaker sometimes and the chairman of the Rules Committee usually are invited in for consultation. . . .[11]

Relations between the leadership of the House and the Rules Committee have varied over the years. From 1890 to 1910 they were merged, for Rules was then a triumvirate composed of the Speaker and his two chief lieutenants, often the chairmen of Ways and Means and of Appropriations. After 1910 the speakership was "syndicated" and the leadership was separated from the members of the Committee on Rules who ceased to be the dominant figures in the House, although their chairman continued to be an important personality because of his position.[12] Writing in 1927 Hasbrouck said of the Rules Committee:

> It is the trump card of the Floor Leader, but he himself is not officially identified with it. True, he must appeal to the reason of 12 men, and win a majority of them to the support of his proposals. But the mainspring of action is not in the Rules Committee. The impulse comes from the Floor Leader after consultation with his "board of strategy" or, for purposes of more formal and routine action, with the Steering Committee.[13]

In 1937, the leadership lost control of the House Rules Committee, thanks to the seniority custom, when three of its Democratic members joined with the four Republican members to block floor consideration of controversial Administration bills. The coalition succeeded in preventing many New Deal–Fair Deal measures from reaching the House floor except by the laborious discharge route. After World War II a rising demand developed for reform of the Rules Committee whose powers were temporarily curbed during the Eighty-first Congress (1949–50) by adoption of the so-called "21-day rule." This rule strengthened the position of the chairmen of the legislative committees of the House vis-à-vis both the Rules Committee and the leadership. While it was in effect, the 21-day rule brought the anti-poll-tax bill to the House floor for a successful vote and forced action on the housing and minimum wage bills. It also enabled the House to vote for the National

Science Foundation, Alaska and Hawaii statehood legislation, and other important measures. Altogether, during the Eighty-first Congress eight measures were brought to the House floor and passed by resort to the 21-day rule, while its existence caused the Rules Committee to act in other cases. Repeal of this rule in January, 1951, restored the checkrein power of the Rules Committee which it has since exercised on various occasions. "Until the 21-day rule is restored," remarked Representative Holifield, "we can expect further situations in which a few men, strategically situated in the Rules Committee, can impose their will on the Congress and prevent the enactment of legislation deemed by the House majority to be essential to the security and welfare of this Nation."[14]

Today the Rules Committee is regarded as an important arm of the House leadership whose wishes it is expected to respect. Presumably it does so on most occasions. But "traditions of seniority and tenure have at times made certain of the majority members of the Rules Committee of the House somewhat out of tune with the larger portion of their party colleagues, with the result that there has been something of a cleavage between the actions of the Committee and the wishes of the core leadership of the party."[15]

The influence of the party leadership on the legislative committees of the House is suggestive, not coercive; informal, not official; tactful, not dictatorial. The floor leader seldom appears in person before committees, but he maintains close and friendly relations with their chairmen on matters of party policy, seeking to mediate between the wishes of the Administration and those of the committeemen. Prior to 1947, before the committee structure had been streamlined and jurisdictions clarified, leadership could influence the fate of a bill by referring it to a favorable or unfavorable committee; but freedom of choice in bill referrals was reduced by the Legislative Reorganization Act of 1946.

The practice of floor leaders regarding their own committee assignments has varied in recent times. Representative McCormack, now the [Speaker], voluntarily resigned from Ways and Means in 1940 when he was elected floor leader, on account of the strenuous duties of that office. But when the Republicans captured control of the House in the Eightieth Congress and Mr. McCormack became minority whip, he accepted membership on the Committee on Government Operations. . . . On the other hand, Mr. Martin, former Speaker and minority floor leader, has had no committee assignments (except to the Select Committee on Astronautics and Space Exploration in the Eighty-fifth Congress), while Mr. Halleck who was majority leader in the Eightieth, . . . Eighty-third, . . . [and] Eighty-sixth Congress[es], has served on the Rules, Administration, and Lobbying committees.

Relations with the President

For more than fifteen years now regular conferences have been held at the White House between the President and his party leaders in Congress—the so-called "Big Four": the Speaker and majority leader of the House and the Vice President and majority leader of the Senate, when they belong to the President's party. When, as during the Eighty-fifth and Eighty-sixth Congresses, opposing political parties control Congress and the presidency, the minority leaders attend these meetings at the White House which are usually weekly while Congress is in session, if the President is in town. These "Big Four" meetings have helped to bridge the gap between the legislative and executive branches of the national government created by our inherited system of separated powers.

Mutatis mutandis, they are the American counterpart of what Bagehot, referring to the British Cabinet, described as "the hyphen that joins, the buckle that fastens, the executive to the legislature." They are advantageous to both ends of Pennsylvania Avenue because they give congressional leaders an insight into the President's plans, while affording the President valuable counsel and guidance on the prospects of his legislative program. When of the same political party, the floor leaders are expected to serve as spokesmen for the Administration, although there have been a few noteworthy departures from this practice. On the House side, however during the Eighty-third Congress, Majority Leader Halleck successfully made the transition from opposition to administration leader and became the most effective champion in Congress of Eisenhower's program. In the White House those days "Charlie" Halleck was the best-liked man on Capitol Hill.

When President Roosevelt took office in 1933, he launched such a varied legislative program that it was necessary for him to keep in close touch with Congress through the leaders of both houses. He consulted with his party leaders and committee chairmen with respect to the New Deal measures before they were introduced as Administration bills, usually by the majority leaders. Sometimes he called the majority leader of the House or Senate individually to the White House to confer about some problem peculiar to one chamber or the other. After his return from trips abroad he sometimes asked the floor leaders of each house to brief him on legislative developments during his absence.

When opposing parties control the two branches, the President is more likely to discuss domestic legislative matters with the congressional leaders of his own party, although in the early days of the Eightieth Congress President Truman occasionally conferred with Messrs. Vandenberg, White, Martin, and Halleck, especially on legislation of a nonpartisan nature. In view of the vital role of Congress in the field of foreign relations, the President must sometimes take the leaders of both political parties in both houses into his confidence. In the days before World War II, when President Roosevelt was seeking to strengthen our defenses, he frequently conferred with both Democratic and Republican leaders in both houses of Congress. Such a conference was the famous night meeting at the White House late in July, 1939, when the President and Secretary of State Cordell Hull urged that Congress repeal the Embargo Act. Among those in attendance were the chairmen of the Foreign and Military Affairs committees, members of the Cabinet, and the majority and minority leaders of the House and Senate.

John McCormack's Service as Majority Leader

John W. McCormack has represented the Twelfth Massachusetts District in the House of Representatives since November 6, 1928. Twelve years later he was first elected majority leader of the House on September 16, 1940: an office which he . . . held [until his election as Speaker] except during the Republican Eightieth and Eighty-third Congresses when he served as minority whip. Thus, in 1958 he was serving his 29th year in the House and his 13th year as majority leader, longer than any predecessor in this post. For many years he was the faithful lieutenant of Presidents Roosevelt and Truman, and was responsible for steering through the House the vital legislation of the 1940's.

McCormack's incumbency of the floor leadership coincided with World War II and the postwar years. During the fateful forties Congress made many vital legislative decisions in important fields of public policy. The problem areas that called for legislative action included conversion and control over manpower, money, and supplies; labor policy, price control, monetary policy; military policy and the conduct of the war, foreign policy and postwar commitments, and reconversion to peace. Among the typical issues of congressional politics during this eventful decade were the efforts to achieve "equality of sacrifice," to "take the profits out of war," and to "freeze economic relationships," as well as wartime elections, the New Deal, and bureaucracy. Far from becoming an anachronism or merely a rubber stamp in providing funds and delegating powers to the President, the role of Congress in wartime increased rather than diminished. The national legislature considered simultaneously many facets of the war and postwar economy of the nation.

* * *

Representative McCormack was in the forefront of all these momentous wartime and postwar activities on Capitol Hill. Although deeply devoted to his political party, he always put national above party and personal interest. He believed that above all sections is the nation, and above all nations is humanity. He was very close, officially and personally, to Speaker Sam Rayburn for whom he felt deep respect and friendship. They assumed their respective offices on the same day back in 1940 and they functioned as a team thereafter. Mr. McCormack was frequently elected as acting Speaker pro tempore and presided over the House in Mr. Rayburn's absence.

Committee on Rules

Last but far from least in the political hierarchy is the House Committee on Rules, whose jurisdiction and powers make it an effective instrument of majority party or coalition control of legislative action. This political committee, which owes its existence to the constitutional right of the House to "determine the rules of its proceedings," was a select committee from 1789 to 1849, a standing committee during the Thirty-first and Thirty-second Congresses (1849–53), and again select from 1853 to 1880, when it converted itself into a standing committee for the second time and has so continued ever since. The Rules Committee has varied in size from five to fourteen members. At present it has twelve members, of whom eight are Democrats and four are Republicans. The Speaker was first made a member in 1858 and remained as such until his removal in 1910.

After the Speaker became a member of Rules in 1858 it gradually rose to a pre-eminent position in the congressional committee system. Thanks to a series of favorable rulings by the Speaker, the Committee on Rules acquired the power (a) to consider and report special orders; (b) to sit during sessions of the House; (c) to report matters not previously introduced, reported, or committed to it; and (d) to have its reports immediately considered. By the exercise of these powers the Rules Committee can sift the business coming from the other nineteen committees of the House and decide which bills shall have the right of way to consideration on the floor and the order in which they shall be taken up. Through its power to report new business it has original as well as secondary jurisdiction over the legislative agenda. By amending their measures as a condition of giving them a "green light" to the floor Rules can substitute its own judgment for that of the great legislative committees of the House on matters of substantive policy. It can also determine the duration of debate on a controversial measure and restrict the opportunity to amend it, thus expediting or delaying a final decision.

Moreover, since the Rules Committee is the only channel through which amendments of the rules can reach the House, it is able to prevent changes in the rules and so prevent parliamentary reform. In short, the Committee on Rules is to a large degree the governing committee of the House. To it the House has largely delegated the power to regulate procedure vested in itself by the Constitution.

Under Cannonism the House Rules Committee was a "sleeping giant," in Haines's apt phrase. But after Cannon was dethroned and the majority floor leader succeeded to the scepter, Rules became an active power. If a majority [8] of its members refuse to report a bill to the House, the other [427] are impotent to compel action. Only by the laborious discharge petition procedure, which requires 219 signatures, can the House force the Rules Committee to act upon any subject over which it has jurisdiction. It can dispose as it pleases, for example, of resolutions for special investigations and of proposed innovations in parliamentary practice.

Through special rules this powerful committee is able to advance directly, or to retard indirectly, any measure that it selects for passage or slaughter. Three kinds of special rules are handed down by the Rules Committee: (1) "gag rules" limiting amendment of pending measures; (2) rules permitting certain favored legislation to come before the House; and (3) rules that make certain bills the next order of business in order to obstruct others that otherwise would come up for consideration via the usual calendar route. By the exercise of its powers the Rules Committee can also function as a steering committee, steering the House in whatever direction the exigencies of the hour appear to demand.

Whether such concentration of political power in one committee is good or evil depends upon whose ox is gored. By some the practice is defended as a legitimate means for clearly fixing party responsibility and obtaining able and energetic guidance of legislative affairs. . . .

* * *

Those who in our own time believe in more definite fixation of party responsibility and in more effective legislative leadership, as means both of holding political parties accountable for the performance of campaign pledges and of correcting the existing dispersion of leadership in Congress, will presumably take a complacent view of the situation. Willoughby, for example, has suggested strengthening the Rules Committee by making its Republican and Democratic members the executive committee of the two caucuses in the House, with the power of selecting the chairmen of committees and making all committee assignments. If it were also given the function of formulating the parties' legislative programs, its collective responsibilty would be complete and the legislative command would be unified.

Those like Senator O'Mahoney, on the other hand, fear concentrated authority in any form and would, therefore, be vehemently opposed to any further steps in that direction. Others think that the Rules Committee should function only as a traffic director on the legislative highway, deciding the order of business but without authority to pass upon the merits of bills or to block the presentation of favorable committee reports to the House. Some members believe that unanimous committee reports should automatically have the right of way to the House floor.

Struggle over the 21-Day Rule

After World War II a rising demand developed for reform of the powers of the Committee on Rules. Rebellion against the "undemocratic and arbitrary dictatorship" of the Committee found expression in a letter that Representative Eberharter wrote his House colleagues in December, 1948.

> In theory the Rules Committee is a traffic director on the legislative highway, determining the order of business on the floor of the House. In practice this committee often allows bills to come before the House only on its own terms. It frequently usurps the functions of the regular legislative committees of the House by holding hearings and reviewing the merits of bills that have already been carefully studied by the proper legislative committees. A reform of this undemocratic system is long overdue. Congress is constantly engaged in a struggle for the respect of the people. The people never have and never will be able to understand how the will of a majority of the House of Representatives can be set aside by the judgment of a few men on a powerful committee.

The fight against the "obstructive tactics" of the Rules Committee finally came to a head on January 3, 1949, when the House adopted the so-called 21-day rule by a vote of 275 to 142. Under this rule the chairman of a legislative committee that had favorably reported a bill could call it up for House consideration if the Rules Committee reported adversely on it or failed to give it a "green light" to the House floor within 21 days. The 21-day rule remained in effect throughout the Eighty-first Congress (1949–50), despite a determined effort to repeal it early in the second session. A coalition led by Congressman Cox of Georgia was defeated on January 20, 1950, by a vote of 236 to 183. Eighty-five Southern Democrats voted for the Cox repeal resolution, while 64 Republicans sided with the Administration against their own leadership. The 21-day rule proved effective in preventing a permanent blockade of vital legislation by the Rules Committee until it was repealed in January, 1951.

Two opposing principles are involved in the struggle over the powers of the House Committee on Rules: whether legislative action should be controlled by a majority of the entire House, or whether the majority party should control through its nominal agent. Those who believe in the principle of majority rule by the Whole House favor reducing the Rules Committee to a traffic director on the legislative highway and adopting a more liberal discharge rule. Their fundamental objection to the existing setup is that it vests power in a small group of rules committeemen to prevent the House from considering and taking action upon measures not favored by the committee or the House leaders. Under the present system, they say, many cases arise where a bill or resolution that would receive favorable action by the House, if it had a chance to consider it, is killed in committee. Such a system, it is argued, denies the House its constitutional right to legislate and violates the principle of representative government.

On the other hand, those who believe that the party in power should control legislative action, as a means of fulfilling its responsibility to the electorate, favor strengthening party government in the House through a strong Rules Committee and a strict discharge rule. To curtail the authority of the committee, they assert, would (1) go far to destroy the effective working of party government and responsibility and (2) tend to facilitate the attempt of self-seeking special interests and minority groups to secure the passage of legislation detrimental to the general welfare.

While conceding the force of these objections, advocates of a change maintain that, under existing political conditions in the Rules Committee, it is possible for the will of the majority party, as expressed at the polls, to be frustrated by a hostile coalition within the committee. Under these circumstances, runs their argument, only a reform of the powers of the committee will, in crucial cases, enable the true majority will to prevail.

NOTES

1. Ralph V. Harlow, *The History of Legislative Methods in the Period Before 1825* (New Haven: Yale University Press, 1917), pp. 176–77.
2. *Ibid.*, p. 208.
3. Woodrow Wilson, *Congressional Government* (Boston: Houghton Mifflin, 1885), pp. 60–61.
4. William S. White, "Sam Rayburn—The Untalkative Speaker," *New York Times Magazine*, February 27, 1949, p. 48.
5. Floyd M. Riddick, *The United States Congress: Organization and Procedure* (Manassas, Va.: National Capitol Pubs., 1949), chap. v, "The Floor Leaders and Whips," p. 86n.
6. Lynn Haines, *Law Making in America* (Bethesda, Md.: L. Haines, 1912), pp. 15–16.
7. DeAlva S. Alexander, *History and Procedure of the House of Representatives* (Boston: Houghton Mifflin, 1916), chap. vii, "Floor Leaders," p. 109.
8. *Congressional Record*, 70th Cong., 1st Sess., p. 8439.
9. Paul H. Hasbrouck, *Party Government in the House of Representatives* (New York: Macmillan, 1927), p. 117.
10. George R. Brown, *The Leadership of Congress* (Indianapolis: Bobbs-Merrill, 1922), pp. 221–22, 224.
11. *Cannon's Precedents of the House of Representatives*, Vol. 8, Sec. 3626.
12. Atkinson and Beard, "The Syndication of the Speakership," *Political Science Quarterly*, September, 1911, p. 414.
13. Hasbrouck, *op. cit.*, pp. 95–96.
14. Hearings before the Senate Committee on Government Operations, on the Organization and Operation of Congress, June, 1951, p. 52.
15. Ernest S. Griffith, *Congress: Its Contemporary Role* (2d ed.; New York: New York University Press, 1956), p. 165.

29

The Seniority Rule in Congress

EMANUEL CELLER

The congressional seniority system has long been the target of journalists, political scientists, and some members of Congress, as it is in the following essay by Representative Emanuel Celler. It is often criticized as a cause of Congress' conservative legislative bias, the control of the committee system by either southern Democrats or midwestern Republicans, and the insulation of House and Senate committees from the control of the elective leadership of Congress. At the same time, the seniority system has been praised as a protection of minority rights and a deterrent to centralized dictatorship or "Cannonism." In truth, both its detractors and defenders have exaggerated their claims.

The seniority system, as Celler emphasizes, is a customary, or habitual, rather than a legally prescribed way of selecting committee chairmen. Although the system seems to be firmly entrenched, seniority in one's party in a standing committee has not always prevailed as the method for selecting committee chairmen. From 1789 to 1823, Celler notes, committee members were elected and the member having the greatest number (a plurality) of votes was designated as chairman. In this selection, Celler examines the system's operation, history, and political consequences and evaluates alternatives to the current method of selecting committee chairmen.

Celler has been a Democratic representative to the House since March 4, 1923. For a number of years he has been Chairman of the House Committee on the Judiciary. He is a graduate of Columbia College and the Columbia University School of Law.

It is a rare session of Congress that does not produce its share of proposals to abolish that perennial red herring—the so-called "seniority rule." This long-standing congressional tradition, under which the House and the Senate organize their working committees, has become as popular a target as sin itself. It is intermittently bombarded by Democrats and by Republicans, by liberals and by conservatives, depending largely upon whose ox is being gored.

I do not entirely understand why this should be so. True, it is sometimes expedient to explain the defeat of a locally popular measure in terms of the tyranny of a committee chairman. Also, able and energetic young men and women who come to Congress and find the best seats occupied will understandably chafe at the tardiness with which their talents are recognized and rewarded by assignments to coveted posts. Thus, a distinguished United States Senator, after two years of service, called the seniority rule a "straitjacket," described it as "rigid, inflexible, and unyielding," and urged its discontinuance as "the sole determinant of Congressional sovereignty and influence" in committee chairmanships and assignments. An example of the intermittent assaults upon congressional seniority is the joint resolution, H. J. Res. 253, of the 86th Congress, which would have rendered senators and representatives who have served twelve years ineligible for re-election for a two-year period.

But the tendency to attack the seniority principle has not been confined to members of Congress, nor, indeed, to politicians. Students of political science regularly excoriate the rule for theoretical imperfections which no method of selection designed by human beings could conceivably eliminate. Even members of the working press—practical men and women who know their way around Capitol Hill—fall in with this approach. The seniority bugaboo is always good for a couple of sticks on a dull Monday, or for a feature in the Sunday Supplement, predicting what the Hill "leadership" will or will not "permit," with the clear implication that the congressional power is too narrowly held and dictatorially exercised.

From the tone of some of its critics, one would suppose that the seniority principle is firmly entrenched and sanctified by law, and that little short of a constitutional amendment could dislodge it. Properly speaking, however, it is not a rule at all, but is rather a custom or convention. Although operative in both the Senate and the House for many years, it is embodied in no formal rule of either chamber. And, far from being sacrosanct, seniority has been overridden by both parties, when circumstances appear to require. Instances of this include the ouster of Stephen A. Douglas from the chairmanship of the Senate Committee on Territories in 1859, and the removal of Charles Sumner from the chairmanship of the Committee on Foreign Relations in 1871. It was a Democratic caucus that ousted Douglas, a Republican caucus that removed Sumner. Moreover, the rigor of the seniority rule has been modified in the current practice of Senate Democrats to allow no senator a second committee choice until each freshman shall have received at least one major committee assignment.

Reprinted from *Western Political Quarterly*, 14 (March 1961), 160–167, by permission of the University of Utah, Copyright holder.

Recurrent criticisms also create the impression that the seniority criterion has wrested control of legislation from the members of Congress and concentrated it in the hands of autocratic committee chairmen, for the gratification of their personal whims. Yet despite these repeated assertions, no steps are even taken to change the basic operation of the system. Like the weather, much is said, but nothing done about it.

Just what role does seniority actually play in the operation of Congress, and why, if it is as unsatisfactory as its critics assert, has it not long been abandoned?

My thirty-eight years of continuous service in the House of Representatives, spent first in acquiring the experience and understanding of legislative work which are implicit in "seniority," and more recently in the exercise of the responsibilities that go with a committee chairmanship, have given me a better than average opportunity to observe the working of the system. I believe that the seniority principle, though far from perfect, performs an indispensable function in the organization of the Congress, and that the alternatives that have been offered as a cure for its deficiencies would aggravate, rather than relieve them.

The significance and operation of the rule are best appraised against its history which, in turn, involves the history of the manner of selection of the members of standing committees. The first House of Representatives operated under a rule which placed the appointment of committees of three or less in the Speaker, larger committees being elected by the House. This proved unsatisfactory, and, at the opening of the second Congress it was specified that "The Speaker shall appoint committees until the House shall otherwise determine." By usage, the member first named to a committee served as its chairman.

Late in 1804, a vacancy in the House Committee on Claims was occasioned by the withdrawal from the committee of its chairman. Samuel W. Dana, of Connecticut, who was appointed "in his stead," maintained that this appointment placed him at the bottom of the committee's list with respect to the chairmanship, because he was last named to it. The Committee thought otherwise, claiming him as its chairman. In resolving the resulting impasse, the House framed a rule specifying that the first-named member of a committee should be its chairman and that order of appointment should govern succession, "unless the committee, by a majority of their number, elect a chairman." Although the Committee on Claims, availing itself of the last word which the closing clause of the rule gave it, elected Dana chairman, from that time the usage in the House, as among American lawmaking bodies generally, has been that the first-named member of a standing committee shall serve as its chairman.

Appointment of House committee members by the Speaker was under sporadic attack from 1806, when James Sloan of New Jersey unsuccessfully proposed that committees should be elected by the House, and their chairmen by the committees, until 1911, when the House "rebelled" against the rule of Speaker "Uncle Joe" Cannon, stripping him and his successors of the power of committee appointments. His autocratic power of appointment and the evils attendant thereupon should be sufficient reason for never reinstating such power in the Speaker of the House. The House rules have since provided that initial appointments and permanent vacancies both in the membership and the chairmanship of standing committees shall be made by the House itself.

This rule, however, inadequately reflects the actual practice, for though the House has reserved the prerogative of making appointments, the formal process of election amounts to little more than the assignment of newly elected members to committees and the occasional transfer of members from one committee to another. Even in this, the two parties tacitly accept each other's designations of majority and minority members. Actually, the Democrats' new assignments of members to fill vacancies on committees are made by majority vote of the Democratic members of the Ways and Means Committee. A Republican Committee on Committees, appointed by the Republican leadership more or less on a geographical basis, assigns the Republican members to fill vacancies on the House Committees. The House itself then confirms all new appointments to fill vacancies. Beyond this, a member who has served on a committee is regarded as entitled to continue to serve on it as long as he keeps his seat, and the seniority ladder determines the succession to the chairmanship.

In the Senate, standing committees have been appointed in various ways at different times: by ballot, by the President of the Senate, by the President pro tempore, or by the adoption of a full list of names submitted by the party leaders.

During the first thirty-four years (1789–1823) all Senate committees were appointed by ballot, and a plurality of votes determined the choice. According to John Quincy Adams, it was the prevailing practice of the Senate during this period that "the member having the greatest number of votes is first named, and as such is chairman."

From December 9, 1823, until April 15, 1826, the Presiding Officer appointed the committees. Appointment by ballot was the rule from April 15, 1826, to December 24, 1828. The President pro tempore appointed the committees of the Senate from December 24, 1828, to December 9, 1833, at which time the practice of appointment by ballot was resumed. From 1839 to 1845 the President pro tempore made the appointments. It was not until the 29th Congress (1845–46) that the Senate began to approve of lists of committees drawn up by party leaders. Since 1846 it has been the traditional practice (with occasional exceptions) for the Republican and Democratic committees on committees to draw up slates of committee assignments at the opening of each new Congress.

The procedure of the Senate in the appointment of committees is prescribed in a long-standing rule (Rule XXIV) which reads in part as follows:

> 1. In the appointment of the standing committees, the Senate, unless otherwise ordered, shall proceed by ballot to appoint severally the chairman of each committee, and then, by one ballot, the other members necessary to complete the same. A majority of the whole number of votes given shall be necessary to the choice of a chairman of a standing committee, but a plurality of votes shall elect the other members thereof. All other committees shall be appointed by ballot, unless otherwise ordered, and a plurality of votes shall appoint.

For upwards of a century, however, the significant phrase—"unless otherwise ordered"—has usually been invoked; and unanimous consent has been given to enable the majority party to determine the chairmanships of the standing committees. Seniority of committee service has long been the principal guide in making up the list of committee chairmanships. Writing in 1938, George H. Haynes, historian of the Senate, remarked: "In the shifting of chairmanships in the past half-century there probably has not been one instance in fifty where the caucus Warwicks have failed to place the crown upon this universally recognized 'heir apparent.' So assured is such an unchallenged succession that voters are often exhorted to consider it as a main reason for re-electing a Senator of great expectations."

The salient and long-established features of the committee system in the American Congress are thus seen to include length of uninterrupted tenure as the traditional determinant of choice in committee assignment, length of uninterrupted committee service as the rule of succession to a chairmanship, and minority party representation on committees roughly proportional to minority strength in the chamber. It may be noted that the bipartisan character of the committees was challenged by President Wilson as weakening party responsibility—a position reminiscent of Jefferson's asserted belief that only members in favor of a measure should be assigned to work on the committee charged with responsibility for its progress.

With respect to the designation of members to committees, moreover, John Quincy Adams believed that this should be by lot, a method which has not found favor in the United States or in Commonwealth countries but which is operative today in a number of Western European parliaments, notably those of France, Belgium, the Netherlands, and Italy.

As concerns the method of designating chairmen of standing committees, foreign countries today fall into two principal categories. The parliamentary organization and practice of the seventeen countries that compose the British Commonwealth are modeled on that of the Mother of Parliaments—the English House of Commons, where the practice appears to be for the Speaker to appoint the chairmen of standing committees.

Elsewhere among the fifty-seven parliaments that are members of the Interparliamentary Union, the general practice is for the chairmen of committees to be elected by the committees themselves. A curious departure is found in the Bundestag where chairmen of committees are allotted proportionally among the parties. The number of chairmen of committees allotted to a parliamentary party corresponds to the number of members of the different parliamentary parties. Chairmen of different committees are nominated by parliamentary parties on the basis of agreement between the parties. The chairman is then formally elected in committee. Up to the present, the chairmen proposed by the parliamentary parties have always been elected.

Appraisal of the American system against this background must take into account the realities of the legislative process. Neither house of Congress could conceivably give detailed attention to all the facets of its legislative program in regular session. Preliminary consideration of legislative proposals is therefore delegated to standing committees, which, with the aid of specialized subcommittees, study the bills, conduct investigations, hear and attempt to reconcile divergent needs and views, and finally report a measure to the full body. Thereafter the committee members perform their individual responsibilities in the ensuing debate. In addition, each committee has the task of keeping itself informed as to the effectiveness with which existing laws within its jurisdiction are being enforced.

What is more, legislation destined for ultimate enactment frequently fails of passage in the Congress in which it is initially introduced. Indeed, it is not unusual for legislative history of a measure to extend over more than two biennia. In such cases, although new bills must be introduced in each new Congress, the committee has a virtually continuing responsibility for managing, or processing, the legislative issue.

Against this background, the rationale of the seniority principle becomes evident. Over the years, manifestly, the effectiveness of a committee will bear a direct relationship to the stability of its personnel. If the legislative committees were to be reshuffled after each election—beyond what is necessitated by the retirement of members and the arrival of new ones—all issues pending unresolved in the House, and to a lesser degree those pending in the Senate would require consideration *de novo*. The time and effort necessarily expended by committee members in familiarizing themselves with the nature of the committee's work, the intricacies of its problems, and the identity and character of interested parties would indeed be lost. What has been said of the members applies with peculiar force to the committee's chairman. Upon the chairman rests the administrative responsibility for the committee's program and for the functioning of the subcommittees. He supervises the professional staff. Continued availability of the chairman's accumulated expertness, experience, and prestige is a central factor in a committee's effectiveness. Interruption of his tenure, other than is necessitated when the control of the Chamber passes from one political party to the other, would needlessly impair the efficiency of the committee's operations.

Fundamentally, the seniority system avoids the waste implicit in instability of committee composition and management. It invokes the presumption that, other things being equal, the man or woman with the greatest experience in a particular job is best fitted to participate and to lead in its performance. To quote Luce, in his work on legislative procedure, "Whatever the activity, we all know that experience counts for more than anything else, and promotion by seniority is nothing but the recognition of this." Since a senior congressman is more experienced than his junior, and since all congressmen aspire to posts of influence, choice of committee assignments may safely be left to seniority. Within a committee, similarly, since effectiveness is presumptively related to length of uninterrupted service, the seniority ladder properly defines the succession to the chairmanship.

The seniority criterion for selecting committee chairmen has the added virtue of being objective. It automatically eliminates the intrigues, deals, and compromises that characterize election campaigns. By the same token, committees are able to get down to work immediately, without having first to bind the wounds of disappointed aspirants to leadership.

To counter these salient advantages, opponents of the system offer two principal criticisms. The first is addressed to its alleged effect upon the functioning of the committees. Here it is contended that the capacity to achieve re-election has no necessary relation to the qualities ideally embodied in a chairman; that under a seniority rule the potential contribution of an exceptionally able young legislator is sacrificed to the entrenchment of an aging incumbent whose energies may be waning; and that the relative inviolability of the custom operates to immunize chairmen against retribution, no matter how arbitrary and dictatorial their conduct of office.

Each of these claims has surface plausibility—and each has been overstated. Although seniority, alone, does not guarantee superior ability, success in effectively serving the state or district remains an indispensable attribute of the perennially successful candidate for election. The most backward electorate will not indefinitely return a congressman who wholly fails to serve its needs. Such a man is retired, if not in an election, then in a primary contest. By and large, the so-called "safe" state or district is one that has been getting the kind of representation it wants. And inevitably, the affirmative qualities that keep a man in office do contribute to his effectiveness as a committee chairman.

Each of us must some day lay down his burdens, but nature has not uniformly decreed when this must be. Some men remain vigorous and effective in their eighties; others may fail at fifty. As stated by Gross in *The Legislative Struggle,*

> The seniority system has often been mistakenly attacked on the ground that it puts too much power in the hands of old men. This argument misses the real implications of the seniority system. Age alone does not cause diminution of mental vigor, alertness, and leadership ability. Nor does it mean that a man becomes more conservative. Some of the outstanding liberals in Congress have been old men who have fought valiantly despite the other handicaps of age.

I am reminded of Longfellow in "Morituri Salutamus":

> But why, you ask me, should this tale
>   be told
> To men grown old, or who are growing
>   old?
> It is too late! Ah, nothing is too late
> Till the tired heart shall cease to
>   palpitate.
> Cato learned Greek at eighty; Sophocles
> Wrote his grand Oedipus, and Simonides
> Bore off the prize of verse from his
>   compeers,
> When each had numbered more than
>   fourscore years,
> And Theophrastus, at fourscore and ten,
> Had but begun his "Characters of Men."
> Chaucer, at Woodstock with the
>   nightingales,
> At sixty wrote the Canterbury Tales;
> Goethe at Weimar, toiling to the last,
> Completed Faust when eighty years
>   were past.

Public servants with long tenure should be able to retire with a measure of security, and recent amendments of the retirement system make this increasingly possible for members of Congress. But most men know when they have had enough, and I fear that by imposing compulsory retirement of committee chairmen upon the attainment of any particular age we would as often lose as gain in terms of the vigor and capacity of the successor. With respect, also, to the criticism that able young legislators with special skills must today go too long without appropriate outlet for their talents, it is noteworthy that increasing use of subcommittees, as well as select committees, are enabling greater utilization of such members in chairmanships.

By far the most serious of this group of criticisms is that which implies arbitrary, one-man rule of committees. It is true that the prerogative of calling meetings and the control of agendas gives some chairmen wide powers, sometimes amounting to the practical equivalent of a veto. But it would be a mistake to attribute this to the seniority system. Seniority does no more than designate the chairman; it does not write the committee's rules of procedure, nor does it prescribe despotism in the conduct of the committee's affairs. Recent years have seen an increasing incidence of well-developed rules of procedure for the governance of committee business. It is always possible for the members of a committee to outvote its chairman. That this happens from time to time is wholesome. That it does not happen more often is as reasonably attributable to the respect and confidence with which the members regard their chairman as to any sinister implication of dictatorship. I believe that the charge of dictatorship is often an attempt to saddle the chairman with sole responsibility for the committee majority's unwillingness to act.

As Luce puts it: "Somebody must lead. If it is not the strong, it will be the weak. If it is not the experienced, it will be the inexperienced. Otherwise, chaos." Under any method of selection, the chairman will remain the committee's most powerful member. The cure for despotism, where it may still exist, is not to deprive the committee of the services of its most seasoned member, but to insist on democratic procedures. In this way, the committee itself can guarantee that the chairman will act as a guide and leader, responsive to the will of the majority, and not as a dictator.

The other major objection that has been leveled at the seniority system is that it concentrates the power implicit in chairmanships in congressmen from so-called one-party states and districts, at the expense of areas whose political complexion is mixed. It is further asserted that the prestige and influence of a high-seniority congressman becomes a political asset in warding off assaults upon his tenure, thus further entrenching him in office. Here, again, some truth and some exaggeration are encountered.

In a Democratic Congress, like the present one, the argument is usually illustrated by pointing to the preponderance of southerners, traditionally more conservative than northern and western Democrats, at the helms of the committees. It is true that of 36 standing committees in the House and the Senate, 21 are headed by men from the South. On the other hand, many important chairmanships are in the hands of northerners and westerners. Indeed, the dean at this writing among Senate Democrats, in his eighties, is the exceptionally able Senator Carl Hayden, chairman of the Committee on Appropriations, who speaks for Arizona. So, too, the states of Nevada, Washington, New Mexico, and Missouri, none of them classed as southern, are represented among Senate committee chairmanships.

In the House, likewise, the important Committees on Appropriations, Banking and Currency, Education and Labor, Foreign Affairs, Government Operations, Interior and Insular Affairs, Judiciary, Public Works, and Un-American Activities, are chaired by men from non-southern states, including New York, Illinois, Pennsylvania, Missouri, Kentucky, and Colorado. And four of the six House committee chairmen having the greatest length of uninterrupted service are from non-southern states. Numerous northerners are also chairmen of powerful subcommittees.

Withal, it cannot be denied that the seniority system produces some disproportion in the distribution of committee chairmanships. Whether this justifies abandonment of the rule raises the question whether the one-party districts can properly be penalized, simply for being able to make up their minds, by being deprived of the fruits that normally accrue from the acquisition of experience and expertness by their representatives. Such considerations tend to become academic, however, unless some satisfactory substitute for the existing rule can be found.

It is my conviction that the reason why the seniority principle has not long been abandoned lies not only in its demonstrable advantages but also in the difficulties that beset alternative proposals. I know of no substitute for the present system whose disadvantages would not outweigh its benefits. Proposals to require chairmen to step down at a specified age, or after a specified period of service, and to rotate chairmanships among committee members having a specified period of service would destroy continuity without necessarily producing more capable leadership. Proposals to elect chairmen in party caucuses would additionally give rise to campaigning with its attendant evils—again without any real assurance of the election of the best fitted candidate. Resort to secret ballot would slightly, but not wholly obviate this objection. The practice of foreign parliaments in which chairmen are predominantly elected by committee members may be appropriate in situations in which the members are themselves selected by lot. Such a system, however, makes knowledge or interest on the part of the committee members improbable. In systems like our own in which a premium has always been placed on continuity, election by committee members would be subject to all the infirmities of election by caucus. Appointment by the Speaker would generate inordinate pressures upon him from within and without Congress and would inordinately enlarge his power over legislation. I doubt whether the present Speaker would want such power. None of these alternatives would go to the real heart of the problem—the evolution of committee procedures that will guarantee democratic functioning.

I suspect that we shall continue to follow the custom of respecting seniority in the selection of congressional committee chairmen, not because it is perfect, but because it is better than any other method that has yet been proposed. And we could do much worse, for, to paraphrase Speaker Rayburn, the rules of both Houses of Congress are such that a determined majority can always work its will.

30

The House Appropriations Committee as a Political System: The Problem of Integration

RICHARD F. FENNO, JR.

In the following excerpt, Richard F. Fenno, Jr., examines the factors that account for the internal cohesion or integration of the House Committee on Appropriations. He also attempts to relate the committee's internal cohesion to the behavior of its members and their legislative activity on the floor of the House of Representatives. The internal cohesion, he concludes, is due to a number of factors including the members' consensus on the committee's role, the specialized and technical nature of the committee's subject-matter jurisdiction, the committee's attractiveness to the members of the House, and the stability of the committee's membership. These factors permit the committee's members to develop both shared expectations and shared behaviors.

If the committee is one of the most highly integrated in the House of Representatives, what are the consequences of its internal cohesion for appropriations policy in the House? Fenno asserts that the committee is highly successful in shepherding its appropriations recommendations through the House with relatively few changes on the floor, which, he concludes, is a result of the committee's integration. In contrast to the Appropriations Committee is the House Committee on Education and Labor, whose members often bitterly disagree about such controversial legislation as federal aid to sectarian schools and public school desegregation. This committee's lack of internal cohesion, it may be inferred, undermines its effectiveness on the floor of the House. If these conclusions are correct, then a committee's internal cohesion, as Fenno argues, may be essential in understanding the legislative process in Congress.

Studies of Congress by political scientists have produced a time-tested consensus on the very considerable power and autonomy of Congressional committees. Because of these two related characteristics, it makes empirical and analytical sense to treat the Congressional committee as a discrete unit for analysis. This paper conceives of the committee as a political system (or, more accurately as a political subsystem) faced with a number of basic problems which it must solve in order to achieve its goals and maintain itself. Generally speaking these functional problems pertain to the environmental and the internal relations of the committee. This study is concerned almost exclusively with the internal problems of the committee and particularly with the problem of self-integration.[1] It describes how one congressional committee—The Committee on Appropriations of the House of Representatives—has dealt with this problem in the period 1947–1961. Its purpose is to add to our understanding of appropriations politics in Congress and to suggest the usefulness of this type of analysis for studying the activities of any congressional committee.

The necessity for integration in any social system arises from the differentiation among its various elements. Most importantly there is a differentiation among subgroups and among individual positions, together with the roles that flow therefrom.[2] A committee faces the problem, how shall these diverse elements be made to mesh together or function in support of one another? No political system (or subsystem) is perfectly integrated; yet no political system can survive without some minimum degree of integration among its differentiated parts. Committee integration is defined as the degree to which there is a working together or a meshing together or mutual support among its roles and subgroups. Conversely, it is also defined as the degree to which a committee is able to minimize conflict among its roles and its subgroups, by heading off or resolving the conflicts that arise.[3] A concomitant of integration is the existence of a fairly consistent set of norms, widely agreed upon and widely followed by the members. Another concomitant of integration is the existence of control mechanisms (*i.e.*, socialization and sanctioning mechanisms) capable of maintaining reasonable conformity to norms. In other words, the more highly integrated a committee, the smaller will be the gap between expected and actual behavior.

This study is concerned with integration both as a structural characteristic of, and as a functional problem for, the Appropriations Committee. First, certain basic characteristics of the Committee need description, to help explain the integration of its parts. Second comes a partial description of the degree to which and the ways in which the Committee achieves integration. No attempt is made to state this in quantitative terms, but the object is to examine the meshing together or the minimization of conflict among certain subgroups and among certain key roles. Also, important control mechanisms are described. The study concludes with some comments on the consequences of Committee integration for appropriations politics and on the usefulness of further Congressional committee analysis in terms of functional problems such as this one.

Reprinted from *American Political Science Review*, 56 (June 1962), 310–324, by permission of the author and the American Political Science Association.

I

Five important characteristics of the Appropriations Committee which help explain Committee integration are (1) the existence of a well-articulated and deeply rooted consensus on Committee goals or tasks; (2) the nature of the Committee's subject matter; (3) the legislative orientation of its members; (4) the attractiveness of the Committee for its members; and (5) the stability of Committee membership.

Consensus

The Appropriations Committee sees its tasks as taking form within the broad guidelines set by its parent body, the House of Representatives. For it is the primary condition of the Committee's existence that it was created by the House for the purpose of assisting the House in the performance of House legislative tasks dealing with appropriations. Committee members agree that their fundamental duty is to serve the House in the manner and with the substantive results that the House prescribes. Given, however, the imprecision of House expectations and the permissiveness of House surveillance, the Committee must elaborate for itself a definition of tasks plus a supporting set of perceptions (of itself and of others) explicit enough to furnish day-to-day guidance.

The Committee's view begins with the preeminence of the House—often mistakenly attributed to the Constitution ("all bills for raising revenue," Art. I, sec. 7) but nevertheless firmly sanctioned by custom—in appropriations affairs.

It moves easily to the conviction that, as the efficient part of the House in this matter, the Constitution has endowed it with special obligations and special prerogatives. It ends in the view that the Committee on Appropriations, far from being merely one among many units in a complicated legislative-executive system, is *the* most important, most responsible unit in the whole appropriations process.[4] Hand in hand with the consensus on their primacy goes a consensus that all of their House-prescribed tasks can be fulfilled by superimposing upon them one, single, paramount task—*to guard the Federal Treasury.* Committee members state their goals in the essentially negative terms of guardianship—screening requests for money, checking against ill-advised expenditures, and protecting the taxpayer's dollar. In the language of the Committee's official history, the job of each member is "constantly and courageously to protect the Federal Treasury against thousands of appeals and imperative demands for unnecessary, unwise, and excessive expenditures."[5]

To buttress its self-image as guardian of public funds the Committee elaborates a set of perceptions about other participants in the appropriations process to which most members hold most of the time. Each executive official, for example, is seen to be interested in the expansion of his own particular program. Each one asks, therefore, for more money than he really needs, in view of the total picture, to run an adequate program. This and other Committee perceptions—of the Budget Bureau, of the Senate, and of their fellow Representatives—help to shape and support the Committee members in their belief that most budget estimates can, should and must be reduced and that, since no one else can be relied upon, the House Committee must do the job. To the consensus on the main task of protecting the Treasury is added, therefore, a consensus on the instrumental task of *cutting whatever budget estimates are submitted.*

As an immediate goal, Committee members agree that they must strike a highly critical, aggressive posture toward budget requests, and that they should, on principle, reduce them. In the words of the Committee's veterans: "There has never been a budget submitted to the Congress that couldn't be cut." "There isn't a budget that can't be cut 10 per cent immediately." "I've been on the Committee for 17 years. No subcommittee of which I have been a member has ever reported out a bill without a cut in the budget. I'm proud of that record." The aim of budget-cutting is strongly internalized for the Committee member. "It's a tradition in the Appropriations Committee to cut." "You're grounded in it. . . . It's ingrained in you from the time you get on the Committee." For the purposes of a larger study, the appropriations case histories of 37 executive bureaus have been examined for a 12-year period, 1947–1959.[6] Of 443 separate bureau estimates, the Committee reduced 77.2 per cent (342) of them.

* * *

To the major task of protecting the Treasury and the instrumental task of cutting budget estimates, each Committee member adds, usually by way of exception, a third task—*serving the constituency to which he owes his election.* This creates no problem for him when, as is sometimes the case, he can serve his district best by cutting the budget requests of a federal agency whose program is in conflict with the demands of his constituency.[7] Normally, however, members find that their most common role-conflict is between a Committee-oriented budget-reducing role and a constituency-oriented budget-increasing role. Committee ideology resolves the conflict by assigning top, long-run priority to the budget-cutting task and making of the constituency service a permissible, short-run exception. No member is expected to commit electoral suicide; but no member is expected to allow his district's desire for federal funds to dominate his Committee behavior.

Subject Matter

Appropriations Committee integration is facilitated by the subject matter with which the group deals. The Committee makes decisions on the same controversial issues as do the committees handling substantive legislation. But a money decision—however vitally it affects national policy—is, or at least seems to be, less directly a policy decision. Since they deal immediately with dollars and cents, it is easy for the members to hold to the idea that they are not dealing with programmatic questions, that theirs is a "business" rather than a "policy" committee. The subject matter, furthermore, keeps Committee members relatively free agents, which promotes intra-Committee maneuvering and, hence, conflict avoidance. Members do not commit themselves to their constituents in terms of precise money amounts, and no dollar sum is sacred—it can always be adjusted without conceding that a principle has been breached. By contrast, members of committees dealing directly with controversial issues are often pressured into taking concrete stands on these issues; consequently, they may come to their committee work with fixed and hardened attitudes. This leads to unavoidable, head-on intracommittee conflict and renders integrative mechanisms relatively ineffective.

The fact of an annual appropriations process means the Committee members repeat the same operations with respect to the same subject matters year after year—and frequently more than once in a given year. Substantive and procedural repetition promotes familiarity with key problems and provides ample opportunity to test and confirm the most satisfactory methods of dealing with them. And the absolute necessity that appropriations bills do ultimately pass gives urgency to the search for such methods. Furthermore, the House rule that no member of the Committee can serve on another standing committee is a deterrent against a fragmentation of Committee member activity which could be a source of difficulty in holding the group together. If a committee has developed (as this one has) a number of norms designed to foster integration, repeated and concentrated exposure to them increases the likelihood that they will be understood, accepted and followed.

Legislative Orientation

The recruitment of members for the Appropriations Committee produces a group of individuals with an orientation especially conducive to Committee integration. Those who make the selection pay special attention to the characteristics which Masters has described as those of the "responsible legislator"—approval of and conformity to the norms of the legislative process and of the House of Representatives.[8]

Key selectors speak of wanting, for the Appropriations Committee, "the kind of man you can deal with" or "a fellow who is well-balanced and won't go off half-cocked on things." A Northern liberal Democrat felt that he had been chosen over eight competitors because, "I had made a lot of friends and was known as a nice guy"—especially, he noted, among Southern Congressmen. Another Democrat explained, "I got the blessing of the Speaker and the leadership. It's personal friendships. I had done a lot of things for them in the past, and when I went to them and asked them, they gave it to me." A Republican chosen for the Committee in his first term recalled,

> The Chairman [Rep. Taber] I guess did some checking around in my area. After all, I was new and he didn't know me. People told me that they were called to see if I was—well, unstable or apt to go off on tangents . . . to see whether or not I had any preconceived notions about things and would not be flexible—whether I would oppose things even though it was obvious.

A key criterion in each of the cases mentioned was a demonstrable record of, or an assumed predisposition toward, legislative give-and-take.

The 106 Appropriations Committee members serving between 1947 and 1961 spent an average of 3.6 years on other House committees before coming to the Committee. Only 17 of the 106 were selected as first term Congressmen. A House apprenticeship (which Appropriations maintains more successfully than all committees save Ways and Means and Rules[9]) provides the time in which legislative reputations can be established by the member and an assessment of that reputation in terms of Appropriations Committee requirements can be made. Moreover, the mere fact that a member survives for a couple of terms is some indication of an electoral situation conducive to his "responsible" legislative behavior. The optimum bet for the Committee is a member from a sufficiently safe district to permit him freedom of maneuver inside the

House without fear of reprisal at the polls.[10] The degree of responsiveness to House norms which the Committee selectors value may be the product of a safe district as well as an individual temperament.

Attractiveness

A fourth factor is the extraordinarily high degree of attractiveness which the Committee holds for its members—as measured by the low rate of departure from it. Committee members do not leave it for service on other committees. To the contrary, they are attracted to it from nearly every other committee.[11] Of the 106 members of the 1947–1961 period, only two men left the Committee voluntarily; and neither of them initiated the move.[12] Committee attractiveness is a measure of its capacity to satisfy individual member needs—for power, prestige, recognition, respect, self-esteem, friendship, etc. Such satisfaction in turn increases the likelihood that members will behave in such a way as to hold the group together.

The most frequently mentioned source of Committee attractiveness is its power—based on its control of financial resources. "Where the money is, that's where the power is," sums up the feeling of the members. They prize their ability to reward or punish so many other participants in the political process—executive officials, fellow Congressmen, constituents and other clientele groups. In the eyes of its own members, the Committee is either the most powerful in the House or it is on a par with Ways and Means or, less frequently, on a par with Ways and Means and Rules. The second important ingredient in member satisfaction is the government-wide scope of Committee activity. The ordinary Congressman may feel that he has too little knowledge of and too little control over his environment. Membership on this Committee compensates for this feeling of helplessness by the wider contacts, the greater amount of information, and the sense of being "in the middle of things" which are consequent, if not to subcommittee activity, at least to the full Committee's overview of the federal government.

Thirdly, Committee attractiveness is heightened by the group's recognizable and distinctive political style—one that is, moreover, highly valued in American political culture. The style is that of *hard work;* and the Committee's self-image is that of "the hardest working Committee in Congress." His willingness to work is the Committee member's badge of identification, and it is proudly worn. It colors his perceptions of others and their perceptions of him.[13] It is a cherished axiom of all members that, "This Committee is no place for a man who doesn't work. They have to be hard working. It's a way of life. It isn't just a job; it's a way of life."

The mere existence of some identifiable and valued style or "way of life" is a cohesive force for a group. But the particular style of hard work is one which increases group morale and group identification twice over. Hard work means a long, dull, and tedious application to detail, via the technique of "dig, dig, dig, day after day behind closed doors"—in an estimated 460 subcommittee and full committee meetings a year. And virtually all of these meetings are in executive session. By adopting the style of hard work, the Committee discourages highly individualized forms of legislative behavior, which could be disruptive within the Committee. It rewards its members with power, but it is power based rather on work inside the Committee than on the political glamour of activities carried on in the limelight of the mass media. Prolonged daily work together encourages sentiments of mutual regard, sympathy and solidarity. This *esprit* is, in turn, functional for integration on the Committee. A Republican leader summed up,

> I think it's more closely knit than any other committee. Yet it's the biggest committee, and you'd think it would be the reverse. I know on my subcommittee, you sit together day after day. You get better acquainted. You have sympathy when other fellows go off to play golf. There's a lot of *esprit de corps* in the Committee.

The strong attraction which members have for the Committee increases the influence which the Committee and its norms exercise on all of them. It increases the susceptibility of the newcomer to Committee socialization and of the veteran to Committee sanctions applicable against deviant behavior.[14]

Membership Stability

Members of the Appropriations Committee are strongly attracted to it; they also have, which bears out their selection as "responsible legislators," a strong attraction for a career in the House of Representatives. The 50 members on the Committee in 1961 had served an average of 13.1 years in the House. These twin attractions produce a noteworthy stability of Committee membership. In the period from the 80th to the 87th Congress, 35.7 per cent of the Committee's membership remained constant. That is to say, 15 of the 42 members on the Committee in March, 1947, were still on the Committee in March, 1961.[15] The 50 members of the Committee in 1961 averaged 9.3 years of prior service on that Committee. In no single year during the last fourteen has the Committee had to absorb an influx of new members totalling more than one-quarter of its membership. At all times, in other words, at least three-fourths of the members have had previous Committee experience. This extraordinary stability of personnel extends into the staff as well. As of June, 1961, its 15 professionals had served an average of 10.7 years with the Committee.[16]

The opportunity exists, therefore, for the development of a stable leadership group, a set of traditional norms for the regulation of internal Committee behavior, and informal techniques of personal accommodation. Time is provided in which new members can learn and internalize Committee norms before they attain high seniority rankings. The Committee does not suffer from the potentially disruptive consequences of rapid changeovers in its leadership group, nor of sudden impositions of new sets of norms governing internal Committee behavior.

II

If one considers the main activity of a political system to be decision-making, the acid test of its internal integration is its capacity to make collective decisions without flying apart in the process. Analysis of Committee integration should focus directly, therefore, upon its subgroups and the roles of its members. Two kinds of subgroups are of central importance—subcommittees and majority or minority party groups. The roles which are most relevant derive from: (1) positions which each member holds by virtue of his subgroup attachments, *e.g.*, as subcommittee member, majority (or minority) party member; (2) positions which relate to full Committee membership, *e.g.*, Committee member, and the seniority rankings of veteran, man of moderate experience, and newcomer;[17] (3) positions which relate to both subgroup and full Committee membership, *e.g.*, Chairman of the Committee, ranking minority member of the Committee, subcommittee chairman, ranking subcommittee member. Clusters of norms state the expectations about subgroup and role behavior. The description which follows treats the ways in which these norms and their associated behaviors mesh and clash. It treats, also, the internal control mechanisms by which behavior is brought into reasonable conformity with expectations.

Subgroup Integration

The day-to-day work of the Committee is carried on in its subcommittees each of which is given jurisdiction over a number of related governmental units. The number of subcommittees is determined by the Committee Chairman, and has varied recently from a low of 9 in 1949 to a high of 15 in 1959. The present total of 14 reflects, as always, a set of strategic and personal judgments by the Chairman balanced against the limitations placed on him by Committee tradition and member wishes. The Chairman also determines subcommittee jurisdiction, appoints subcommittee chairmen and selects the majority party members of each group. The ranking minority member of the Committee exercises similar control over subcommittee assignments on his side of the aisle.

Each subcommittee holds hearings on the budget estimates of the agencies assigned to it, meets in executive session to decide what figures and what language to recommend to the full Committee (to "mark up" the bill), defends its recommendations before the full Committee, writes the Committee's report to the House, dominates the debate on the floor, and bargains for the House in conference committee. Within its jurisdiction, each subcommittee functions independently of the others and guards its autonomy jealously. The Chairman and ranking minority member of the full Committee have, as we shall see, certain opportunities to oversee and dip into the operations of all subcommittees. But their intervention is expected to be minimal. Moreover, they themselves operate importantly within the subcommittee framework by sitting as chairman or ranking minority member of the subcommittee in which they are most interested. Each subcommittee, under the guidance of its chairman, transacts its business in considerable isolation from every other one. . . .

* * *

All members of all subcommittees are expected to behave in similar fashion in the role of subcommittee member. Three main norms define this role; to the extent that they are observed, they promote harmony and reduce conflict among subcommittees.[18] Subcommittee autonomy gives to the House norm of *specialization* an intensified application on the Appropriations Committee. Each member is expected to play the role of specialist in the activities of one subcommittee. He will sit on from one to four subcommittees, but normally will specialize in the work, or a portion of the work, of only one. Except for the Chairman, ranking minority member and their confidants, a Committee member's time, energy, contacts and experience are devoted to his subcommittees. Specialization is, therefore, among the earliest and most compelling of the Committee norms to which a newcomer is exposed. Within the Committee, respect, deference and power are earned through subcommittee activity and, hence to a degree, through specialization. Specialization is valued further because it is well suited to the task of guarding the Treasury. Only by specializing, Committee members believe, can they unearth the volume of factual information necessary for the intelligent screening of budget requests. Since "the facts" are acquired only through industry an effective specialist will, perforce, adopt and promote the Committee's style of hard work.

Committee-wide acceptance of specialization is an integrative force in decision-making because it helps support a second norm—*reciprocity*. The stage at which a subcommittee makes its recommendations is a potential point of internal friction. Conflict among subcommittees (or between one subcommittee and the rest of the Committee) is minimized by the deference traditionally accorded to the recommendation of the subcommittee which has specialized in the area, has worked hard, and has "the facts." "It's a matter of 'You respect my work and I'll respect yours.' " "It's frowned upon if you offer an amendment in the full Committee if you aren't on the subcommittee. It's considered presumptuous to pose as an expert if you aren't on the subcommittee." Though records of full Committee decisions are not available members agree that subcommittee recommendations are "very rarely changed," "almost always approved," "changed one time in fifty," "very seldom changed," etc.

No subcommittee is likely to keep the deference of the full Committee for long unless its recommendations have widespread support among its own members. To this end, a third norm—*subcommittee unity*—is expected to be observed by subcommittee members. Unity means a willingness to support (or not to oppose) the recommendations of one's own subcommittee. Reciprocity and unity are closely dependent upon one another. Reciprocity is difficult to maintain when subcommittees themselves are badly divided; and unity has little appeal unless reciprocity will subsequently be observed. The norm of reciprocity functions to minimize inter-subcommittee conflict. The norm of unity functions to minimize intra-subcommittee conflict. Both are deemed essential to subcommittee influence.

One payoff for the original selection of "responsible legislators" is their special willingness to compromise in pursuit of subcommittee unity. The impulse to this end is registered most strongly at the time when the subcommittee meets in executive session to mark up the bill. Two ranking minority members explained this aspect of markup procedure in their subcommittees:

> If there's agreement, we go right along. If there's a lot of controversy we put the item aside and go on. Then, after a day or two, we may have a list of ten controversial items. We give and take and pound them down till we get agreement.

> We have a unanimous agreement on everything. If a fellow enters an objection and we can't talk him out of it—and sometimes we can get him to go along—that's it. We put it in there.

Once the bargain is struck, the subcommittee is expected to "stick together."

It is, of course, easier to achieve unity among the five, seven, or nine members of a subcommittee than among the fifty members of the full Committee. But members are expected wherever possible to observe the norm of unity in the full Committee as well. That is, they should not only defer to the recommendations of the subcommittee involved, but they should support (or not oppose) that recommendation when it reaches the floor in the form of a Committee decision. On the floor, Committee members believe, their power and prestige depend largely on the degree to which the norms of reciprocity and unity continue to be observed. Members warn each other that if they go to the floor in disarray they will be "rolled," "jumped," or "run over" by the membership. It is a cardinal maxim among Committee members that "You can't turn an appropriations bill loose on the floor." . . .

* * *

One of the most functional Committee practices supporting the norm of unity is the tradition against minority reports in the subcommittee and in the full Committee. It is symptomatic of Committee integration that custom should proscribe the use of the most formal and irrevocable symbol of congressional committee disunity—the minority report. A few have been written—but only 9 out of a possible 141 during the 11 years, 1947–1957. That is to say, 95 per cent of all original appropriations bills in this period were reported out without dissent. The technique of "reserving" is the Committee member's equivalent for the registering of dissent. In subcommittee or Committee, when a member reserves, he goes on record informally by informing his colleagues that he reserves the right to disagree on a specified item later on in the proceedings. He may seek a change or support a change in that particular item in full Committee or on the floor. But he does not publicize his dissent. The subcommittee or the full Committee can then make an unopposed recommendation. The individual retains some freedom of maneuver without firm commitment. Often a member reserves on an appropriations item but takes no further action. . . .

* * *

Disagreement cannot, of course, be eliminated from the Committee. But the Committee has accepted a method for ventilating it which produces a minimum of internal disruption. And members believe that the greater their internal unity, the greater the likelihood that their recommendations will pass the House.

The degree to which the role of the subcommittee member can be so played and subcommittee conflict thereby minimized depends upon the minimization of conflict between the majority and minority party subgroups. Nothing would be more disruptive to the Committee's work than bitter and extended partisan controversy. It is, therefore, important to Appropriations Committee integration that a fourth norm—*minimal partisanship*—should be observed by members of both party contingents. Nearly every respondent emphasized, with approval, that "very little" or "not much" partisanship prevailed on the Committee. One subcommittee chairman stated flatly, "My job is to keep down partisanship." A ranking minority member said, "You might think that we Republicans would defend the Administration and the budget, but we don't." Majority and minority party ratios are constant and do not change (*i.e.*, in 1958) to reflect changes in the strength of the controlling party. The Committee operates with a completely non-partisan professional staff, which does not change in tune with shifts in party control. Requests for studies by the Committee's investigating staff must be made by the Chairman and ranking minority member of the full Committee and by the Chairman and ranking minority member of the subcommittee involved. Subcommittees can produce recommendations without dissent and the full Committee can adopt reports without dissent precisely because party conflict is (during the period 1947–1961) the exception rather than the rule.

The Committee is in no sense immune from the temperature of party conflict, but it does have a relatively high specific heat. Intense party strife or a strongly taken presidential position will get reflected in subcommittee and in Committee recommendations. Sharp divisions in party policy were carried, with disruptive impact, into some areas of Committee activity during the 80th Congress and subsequently, by way of reaction, into the 81st Congress.[19] During the Eisenhower years, extraordinary presidential pleas, especially concerning foreign aid, were given special heed by the Republican members of the Committee.[20] Partisanship is normally generated from the environment and not from within the Committee's party groups. Partisanship is, therefore, likely to be least evident in subcommittee activity, stronger in the full Committee, and most potent at the floor stage. Studies which have focused on roll-call analysis have stressed the influence of party in legislative decision-making.[21] In the appropriations process, at any rate, the floor stage probably represents party influence at its maximum. Our examination, by interview, of decision-making at the subcommittee and full Committee level would stress the influence of Committee-oriented norms—the strength of which tends to vary inversely with that of party bonds. In the secrecy and intimacy of the subcommittee and full Committee hearing rooms, the member finds it easy to compromise on questions of more or less, to take money from one program and give it to another and, in general, to avoid yes-or-no type party stands. These decisions, taken in response to the integrative norms of the Committee are the most important ones in the entire appropriations process.

Role Integration

The roles of subcommittee member and party member are common to all.

Other more specific decision-making positions are allocated among the members. Different positions produce different roles, and in an integrated system, these too must fit together. Integration, in other words, must be achieved through the complementarity or reciprocity of roles as well as through a similarity of roles. This may mean a pattern in which expectations are so different that there is very little contact between individuals; or it may mean a pattern in which contacts require the working out of an involved system of exchange of obligations and rewards.[22] In either case, the desired result is the minimization of conflict among prominent Committee roles. Two crucial instances of role reciprocity on the Committee involve the seniority positions of old-timer and newcomer and the leadership positions of Chairman and ranking minority member, on both the full Committee and on each subcommittee.

The differentiation between senior and junior members is the broadest definition of who shall and who shall not actively participate in Committee decisions. Of a junior member, it will be said, "Oh, he doesn't count—what I mean is, he hasn't been on the Committee long enough." He is not expected to and ordinarily does not have much influence. His role is that of apprentice. He is expected to learn the business and the norms of the Committee by applying himself to its work. He is expected to acquiesce in an arrangement which gives most influence (except in affairs involving him locally) to the veterans of the group. Newcomers will be advised to "follow the chairman until you get your bearings. For the first two years, follow the chairman. He knows." "Work hard, keep quiet and attend the Committee sessions. We don't want to listen to some new person coming in here." And newcomers perceive their role in identical terms: "You have to sit in the back seat and edge up little by little." "You just go to subcommittee meetings and assimilate the routine. The new members are made to feel welcome, but you have a lot of rope-learning to do before you carry much weight."

* * *

Among the Committee's veterans, the key roles are those of Committee Chairman and ranking minority member, and their counterparts in every subcommittee. It is a measure of Committee integration and the low degree of partisanship that considerable reciprocity obtains between these roles. Their partisan status nevertheless sets limits to the degree of possible integration. The Chairman is given certain authority which he and only he can exercise. But save in times of extreme party controversy, the expectation is that consultation and cooperation between the chairman-ranking minority member shall lubricate the Committee's entire work. For example, by Committee tradition, its Chairman and ranking minority member are both *ex officio* voting members of each subcommittee and of every conference committee. The two of them thus have joint access at every stage of the internal process. A subcommittee chairman, too, is expected to discuss matters of scheduling and agenda with his opposite minority number. He is expected to work with him during the markup session and to give him (and, normally, only him) an opportunity to read and comment on the subcommittee report.[23] . . .

* * *

Where influence is shared, an important exchange of rewards occurs. The chairman gains support for his leadership and the ranking minority member gains intra-Committee power. The Committee as a whole insures against the possibility of drastic change in its internal structure by giving to its key minority members a stake in its operation. Chairmen and ranking minority members will, in the course of time, exchange positions; and it is expected that such a switch will produce no form of retribution nor any drastic change in the functioning of the Committee. Reciprocity of roles, in this case, promotes continued integration. . . .

* * *

Reciprocity between chairmen and ranking minority members on the Appropriations Committee is to some incalculable degree a function of the stability of membership which allows a pair of particular individuals to work out . . . personal accommodation[s]. . . . The close working relationship of Clarence Cannon and John Taber, whose service on the Committee totals 68 years and who have been changing places as Chairman and ranking minority member for 19 years, highlights and sustains a pattern of majority-minority reciprocity throughout the group.

Internal Control Mechanisms

The expectations which apply to subcommittee, to party, to veterans and to newcomers, to chairmen and to ranking minority members prescribe highly integrative behaviors. We have concentrated on these expectations, and have both illustrated and assumed the close correlation between expected and actual behavior. This does not mean that all the norms of the Committee have been canvassed. Nor does it mean that deviation from the integrative norms does not occur. It does. From what can be gathered, however, from piecing together a study of the public record on appropriations from 1947 to 1961 with interview materials, the Committee has been markedly successful in maintaining a stable internal structure over time. As might be expected, therefore, changes and threats of change have been generated more from the environment—when outsiders consider the Committee as unresponsive—than from inside the subsystem itself. One source of internal stability, and an added reason for assuming a correlation between expected and actual behavior, is the existence of what appear to be reasonably effective internal control mechanisms. Two of these are the socialization processes applied to newcomers and the sanctioning mechanisms applicable to all Committee members.

Socialization is in part a training in perception. Before members of a group can be expected to behave in accordance with its norms, they must learn to see and interpret the world around them with reasonable similarity. The socialization of the Committee newcomer during his term or two of apprenticeship serves to bring his perceptions and his attitudes sufficiently into line with those of the other members to serve as a basis for Committee integration. The Committee, as we have seen, is chosen from Congressmen whose political flexibility connotes an aptitude for learning new lessons of power. Furthermore, the high degree of satisfaction of its members with the group increases their susceptibility to its processes of learning and training.

For example, one half of the Committee's Democrats are Northerners and Westerners from urban constituencies, whose voting records are just as "liberal" on behalf of domestic social welfare programs as non-Committee Democrats from like constituencies. They come to the Committee favorably disposed toward the high level of federal spending necessary to support such programs, and with no sense of urgency about the Committee's tasks of guarding the Treasury or reducing budget estimates. Given the criteria governing their selection, however, they come without rigid preconceptions and with a built-in responsiveness to the socialization processes of any legislative group of which they are members. It is crucial to Committee integration that they learn to temper their potentially disruptive welfare-state ideology with a conservative's concern for saving money. They must change their perceptions and attitudes sufficiently to view the Committee's tasks in nearly the same terms as their more conservative Southern Democratic and Republican colleagues. What their elders perceive as reality (*i.e.*, the disposition of executives to ask for more money than is necessary) they, too, must see as reality....

* * *

The younger men, in this case the younger liberals, do learn from their

Committee experience. Within one or two terms, they are differentiating between themselves and the "wild-eyed spenders" or the "free spenders" in the House. "Some of these guys would spend you through the roof," exclaimed one liberal of moderate seniority. Repeated exposure to Committee work and to fellow members has altered their perceptions and their attitudes in money matters. Half a dozen Northern Democrats of low or moderate seniority agreed with one of their number who said: "Yes, it's true. I can see it myself. I suppose I came here a flaming liberal; but as the years go by I get more conservative. You just hate like hell to spend all this money.... You come to the point where you say, 'By God, this is enough jobs.' " These men will remain more inclined toward spending than their Committee colleagues, but their perceptions and hence their attitudes have been brought close enough to the others to support a consensus on tasks. They are responsive to appeals on budget-cutting grounds that would not have registered earlier and which remain meaningless to liberals outside the Committee. In cases, therefore, where Committee selection does not and cannot initially produce individuals with a predisposition toward protecting the Treasury, the same result is achieved by socialization.

Socialization is a training in behavior as well as in perception. For the newcomer, conformity to norms in specific situations is insured through the appropriate application, by the Committee veterans, of rewards and punishments. For the Committee member who serves his apprenticeship creditably, the passage of time holds the promise that he will inherit a position of influence. He may, as an incentive, be given some small reward early in his Committee career. One man, in his second year, had been assigned the task of specializing in one particular program. However narrow the scope of his specialization, it had placed him on the road to influence within the Committee....

* * *

At some later date, provided he continues to observe Committee norms, he will be granted additional influence, perhaps through a prominent floor role. A model Committee man of moderate seniority who had just attained to this stage of accomplishment, and who had suffered through several political campaigns back home fending off charges that he was a do-nothing Congressman, spoke about the rewards he was beginning to reap.

> When you perform well on the floor when you bring out a bill, and Members know that you know the bill, you develop prestige with other Members of Congress. They come over and ask you what you think, because they know you've studied it. You begin to get a reputation beyond your subcommittee. And you get inner satisfaction, too. You don't feel that you're down here doing nothing.

The first taste of influence which comes to men on this Committee is compensation for the frustrations of apprenticeship. Committee integration in general, and the meshing of roles between elders and newcomers in particular, rests on the fact that conformity to role expectations over time does guarantee to the young positive rewards—the very kind of rewards of power, prestige, and personal satisfaction which led most of them to seek Committee membership in the first place.

The important function of apprenticeship is that it provides the necessary time during which socialization can go forward. And teaching proceeds with the aid of punishments as well as rewards. Should a new member inadvertently or deliberately run afoul of Committee norms during his apprenticeship, he will find himself confronted with negative sanctions ranging in subtlety from "jaundiced eyes" to a changed subcommittee assignment. Several members, for example, recalled their earliest encounter with the norm of unity and the tradition against minority reports. One remembered his attempt to file a minority report. "The Chairman was pretty upset about it. It's just a tradition, I guess, not to have minority reports. I didn't know it was a tradition. When I said I was going to write a minority report, some eyebrows were raised. The Chairman said it just wasn't the thing to do. Nothing more was said about it. But it wasn't a very popular thing to do, I guess." He added that he had not filed one since.

Some younger members have congenital difficulty in observing the norms of the apprentice's role. In the 86th Congress, these types tended to come from the Republican minority. The minority newcomers (described by one of the men who selected them as "eight young, energetic, fighting conservatives") were a group of economy-minded individuals some of whom chafed against any barrier which kept them from immediate influence on Committee policy. Their reaction was quite different from that of the young Democrats, whose difficulty was in learning to become economy-minded, but who did not actively resent their lack of influence. One freshman, who felt that "The appropriations system is lousy, inadequate and old fashioned," recalled that he had spoken out in full Committee against the recommendations of a subcommittee of which he was not a member. Having failed, he continued to oppose the recommendation during floor debate. By speaking up, speaking in relation to the work of another subcommittee and by opposing a Committee recommendation, he had violated the particular norms of his apprentice role as well of the generally applicable norms of reciprocity and unity....

* * *

One internal threat to Committee integration comes from new members who from untutored perceptions, from ignorance of norms, or from dissatisfaction with the apprentice role may not act in accordance with Committee expectations. The seriousness of this threat is minimized, however, by the fact that the deviant newcomer does not possess sufficient resources to affect adversely the operation of the system. Even if he does not respond immediately to the application of sanctions, he can be held in check and subjected to an extended and (given the frequency of interaction among members) intensive period of socialization. The success of Committee socialization is indicated by the fact that whereas wholesale criticism of Committee operations was frequently voiced among junior members, it had disappeared among the men of moderate experience. And what these middle seniority members now accept as the facts of Committee life, the veterans vigorously assert and defend as the essentials of a smoothly functioning system. Satisfaction with the Committee's internal structure increases with length of Committee service.

An important reason for changing member attitudes is that those who have attained leadership positions have learned, as newcomers characteristically have not, that their conformity to Committee norms is the ultimate source of their influence inside the group. Freshman members do not as readily perceive the degree to which interpersonal influence is rooted in obedience to group norms. They seem to convert their own sense of powerlessness into the view that the Committee's leaders possess, by virtue of their positions, arbitrary, absolute, and awesome power. Typically, they say: "If you're a subcommittee chairman, it's your Committee." "The Chairman runs the show. He gets what he wants. He decides what he wants and gets it through." Older members of the Committee, however, view the power of the leaders as a highly contingent and revocable grant, tendered by the Committee for so long and only so long as their leaders abide by Committee expectations. In commenting on internal influence, their typical reaction is: "Of course, the Committee wouldn't follow him if it didn't want to. He has a great deal of respect. He's an able man, a hard-working man." "He knows the bill backwards and forwards. He works hard, awfully hard and the members know it." Committee leaders have an imposing set of formal prerogatives. But they can capitalize on them only if they command the respect, confidence and deference of their colleagues.

It is basic to Committee integration that members who have the greatest power to change the system evidence the least disposition to do so. Despite their institutional conservatism, however, Committee elders do occasionally violate the norms applicable to them and hence represent a potential threat to successful integration. Excessive deviation from Committee expectations by some leaders will bring counter-measures by other leaders. Thus, for example, the Chairman and his subcommittee chairmen exercise reciprocal controls over one another's behavior. The Chairman has the authority to appoint the chairman and members of each subcommittee and fix its jurisdiction. "He runs the Committee. He has a lot of power," agrees one subcommittee chairman. "But it's all done on the basis of personal friendship. If he tries to get too big, the members can whack him down by majority vote."

In the 84th Congress, Chairman Cannon attempted an unusually broad reorganization of subcommittee jurisdictions. The subcommittee chairman most adversely affected rallied his senior colleagues against the Chairman's action—on the ground that it was an excessive violation of role expectations and threatening to subcommittee autonomy. Faced with the prospect of a negative Committee vote, the Chairman was forced to act in closer conformity to the expectations of the other leaders. As one participant described the episode,

> Mr. Cannon, for reasons of his own, tried to bust up one of the subcommittees. We didn't like that. . . . He was breaking up the whole Committee. A couple of weeks later, a few of the senior members got together and worked out a compromise. By that time, he had seen a few things, so we went to him and talked to him and worked it out.

On the subcommittees, too, it is the veterans of both parties who will levy sanctions against an offending chairman. It is they who speak of "cutting down to size" and "trimming the whiskers" of leaders who become "too cocky," "too stubborn" or who "do things wrong too often." Committee integration is underwritten by the fact that no member high or low is permanently immune from the operation of its sanctioning mechanisms.

III

Data concerning internal committee activity can be organized and presented in various ways. One way is to use key functional problems like integration as the focal points for descriptive analysis. On the basis of our analysis (and without, for the time being, having devised any precise measure of integration), we are led to the summary observation that the House Appropriations Committee appears to be a well integrated, if not an extremely well integrated, committee. The question arises as to whether anything can be gained from this study other than a description of one property of one political subsystem. If it is reasonable to assume that the internal life of a congressional committee affects all legislative activity involving that committee, and if it is reasonable to assume that the analysis of a committee's internal relationships will produce useful knowledge about legislative behavior, some broader implications for this study are indicated.

In the first place, the success of the House Appropriations Committee in solving the problem of integration probably does have important consequences for the appropriations process. Some of the possible relationships can be stated as hypotheses and tested; others can be suggested as possible guides to understanding. All of them require further research. Of primary interest is the relationship between integration and the power of the Committee. There is little doubt about the fact of Committee power. Of the 443 separate case histories of bureau appropriations examined, the House accepted Committee recommendations in 387, or 87.4 per cent of them; and in 159, or 33.6 per cent of the cases, the House Committee's original recommendations on money amounts were the exact ones enacted into law. The hypothesis that the greater the degree of Committee unity the greater the probability that its recommendations will be accepted is being tested as part of a larger study.[24] House Committee integration may be a key factor in producing House victories in conference committee. This relationship, too, might be tested. Integration appears to help provide the House conferees with a feeling of confidence and superiority which is one of their important advantages in the mix of psychological factors affecting conference deliberations.

Another suggested consequence of high integration is that party groups have a relatively small influence upon appropriations decisions. It suggests, too, that Committee-oriented behavior should be duly emphasized in any analysis of Congressional oversight of administrative activity by this Committee. Successful integration promotes the achievement of the Committee's goals, and doubtless helps account for the fairly consistent production of budget-cutting decisions. Another consequence will be found in the strategies adopted by people seeking favorable Committee decisions. For example, the characteristic lines of contact from executive officials to the Committee will run to the chairman and the ranking minority member (and to the professional staff man) of the single subcommittee handling their agency's appropriations. The ways in which the Committee achieves integration may even affect the success or failure of a bureau in getting its appropriations. Committee members, for instance, will react more favorably toward an administrator who conforms to their self-image of the hard-working master-of-detail than to one who does not—and Committee response to individual administrators bulks large in their determinations.

Finally, the internal integration of this Committee helps to explain the extraordinary stability, since 1920, of appropriations procedures—in the face of repeated proposals to change them through omnibus appropriations, legislative budgets, new budgetary forms, item veto, Treasury borrowing, etc. Integration is a stabilizing force, and the stability of the House Appropriations Committee has been a force for stabilization throughout the entire process. It was, for example, the disagreement between Cannon and Taber which led to the indecisiveness reflected in the short-lived experiment with a single appropriations bill.[25] One need only examine the conditions most likely to decrease Committee integration to ascertain some of the critical factors for producing changes in the appropriations process. A description of integration is also an excellent base-line from which to analyze changes in internal structure.

All of these are speculative propositions which call for further research. But they suggest, as a second implication, that committee integration does have important consequences for legislative activity and, hence, that it is a key variable in the study of legislative politics. It would seem, therefore, to be a fruitful focal point for the study of other congressional committees.[26] Comparative committee analysis could usefully be devoted to (1) the factors which tend to increase or decrease integration; (2) the degree to which integration is achieved; and (3) the consequences of varying degrees of integration for committee behavior and influence. If analyses of committee integration are of any value, they should encourage the analysis and the classification of congressional committees along functional lines. And they should lead to the discussion of interrelated problems of committee survival. Functional classifications of committees (*i.e.*, well or poorly integrated) derived from a large number of descriptive analyses of several functional problems, may prove helpful in constructing more general propositions about the legislative process.

NOTES

1. On social systems, see: George Homans, *The Human Group* (New York, 1950); Robert K. Merton, *Social Theory and Social Structure* (Glencoe, 1957); Talcott Parsons and Edward Shils, *Toward A General Theory of Action* (Cambridge, 1951), pp. 190–234. Most helpful with reference to the political system has been David Easton, "An Approach to the Analysis of Political Systems," *World Politics* (April, 1957), pp. 383–400.
2. On the idea of subgroups as used here, see Harry M. Johnson, *Sociology* (New York, 1960), ch 3. On role, see specifically Theodore M. Newcomb, *Social Psychology* (New York, 1951), p. 280; see generally N. Gross, W. Mason and A. McEachern, *Explorations in Role Analysis: Studies of the School Superintendency Role* (New York, 1958). On differentiation and its relation to integration, see Scott Greer, *Social Organization* (New York, 1955).
3. The usage here follows most closely that of Robert Merton, *op. cit.*, pp. 26–29.
4. This and all other generalizations about member attitudes and perceptions depend heavily on extensive interviews with Committee members. Semi-structured interviews, averaging 45 minutes in length were held with 45 of the 50 Committee members during the 86th Congress. Certain key questions, all open-ended, were asked of all respondents. The schedule was kept very flexible, however, in order to permit particular topics to be explored with those individuals best equipped to discuss them. In a few cases, where respondents encouraged it, notes were taken during the interviews. In most cases notes were not taken, but were transcribed immediately after the interview. Where unattributed quotations occur in the text, therefore, they

are as nearly verbatim as the author's power of immediate recall could make them. These techniques were all used so as to improve *rapport* between interviewer and respondent.

5. "History of the Committee on Appropriations," House Doc. 299, 77th Cong., 1st sess., 1941–1942, p. 11.
6. The bureaus being studied are all concerned with domestic policy and are situated in the Agriculture, Interior, Labor, Commerce, Treasury, Justice and Health, Education and Welfare Departments. For a similar pattern of Committee decisions in foreign affairs, see Holbert Carroll, *The House of Representatives and Foreign Affairs* (Pittsburgh, 1958), ch. 9.
7. See, for example, Philip A. Foss, "The Grazing Fee Dilemma," Inter-University Case Program, No. 57 (University, Alabama, 1960).
8. Nicholas A. Masters, "House Committee Assignments," *American Political Science Review*, Vol. 55 (June, 1961), pp. 345–357.
9. In the period from 1947 through 1959 (80th to 86th Congress), 79 separate appointments were made to the Appropriations Committee, with 14 going to freshmen. The Committee filled, in other words, 17.7 per cent of its vacancies with freshmen. The Rules Committee had 26 vacancies and selected no freshmen at all. The Ways and Means Committee had 36 vacancies and selected 2 freshmen (5.6 per cent). All other committees had a higher percentage of freshmen appointments. Armed Services ranked fourth, with 45 vacancies and 12 freshmen appointed, for a percentage of 26.7. Foreign Affairs figures were 46 and 14, or 30.4 per cent; Un-American Activities figures were 22 and 7, or 31.8 per cent. *Cf.* Masters, *op. cit.*
10. In the 1960 elections, 41 out of the current 50 members received more than 55.1 per cent of the vote in their districts. By a common definition, that is, only 9 of the 50 came from marginal districts.
11. The 106 members came to Appropriations from every committee except Ways and Means.
12. One was personally requested by the Speaker to move to Ways and Means. The other was chosen by a caucus of regional Congressmen to be his party's representative on the Rules Committee. Of the 21 members who were forced off the Committee for lack of seniority during a change in party control, or who were defeated for reelection and later returned, 20 sought to regain Committee membership at the earliest opportunity.
13. A sidelight on this attitude is displayed in a current feud between the House and Senate Appropriations Committees over the meeting place for their conference committees. The House Committee is trying to break the century-old custom that conferences to resolve differences on money bills are always held on the Senate side of the Capitol. House Committee members "complain that they often have to trudge back to the House two or three times to answer roll calls during a conference. They say they go over in a body to work, while Senators flit in and out. . . . The House Appropriations Committee feels that it does all the hard work listening to witnesses for months on each bill, only to have the Senate Committee sit as a court of appeals and, with little more than a cursory glance, restore most of the funds cut." *Washington Post*, April 24, 1962, p. 1.
14. This proposition is spelled out at some length in J. Thibaut and H. Kelley, *The Social Psychology of Groups* (New York, 1959), p. 247, and in D. Cartwright and A. Zander, *Group Dynamics: Research and Theory* (Evanston, 1953), p. 420.
15. This figure is 9 per cent greater than the next most stable House committee during this particular period. The top four, in order, were Appropriations (35.7%), Agriculture (26.7%), Armed Services (25%), Foreign Affairs (20.8%).
16. The Committee's permanent and well integrated professional staff (as distinguished from its temporary investigating staff) might be considered as part of the subsystem though it will not be treated in this paper.
17. "Newcomers" are defined as men who have served no more than two terms on the Committee. "Men of moderate experience" are those with 3–5 terms of service. "Veterans" are those who have 6 or more terms of Committee service.
18. A statement of expected behavior was taken to be a Committee norm when it was expressed by a substantial number of respondents (a dozen or so) who represented both parties, and varying degrees of experience. In nearly every case, moreover,

no refutation of them was encountered, and ample confirmation of their existence can be found in the public record. Their articulation came most frequently from the veterans of the group.

19. See, for example, the internal conflict on the subcommittee dealing with the Labor Department. 93 *Cong. Record,* pp. 2465–2562 passim; 94 *Cong. Record,* pp. 7605–7607.
20. See, for example, the unusual minority report of Committee Republicans on the foreign aid appropriations bill in 1960. Their protest against Committee cuts in the budget estimates was the result of strenuous urging by the Eisenhower Administration. House Report No. 1798, *Mutual Security and Related Agency Appropriation Bill,* 1961, 86 Cong. 2nd sess. 1960.
21. David Truman, *The Congressional Party* (New York, 1959); Julius Turner, *Party and Constituency: Pressures on Congress* (Baltimore, 1951).
22. The ideas of "reciprocity" and "complementarity," which are used interchangeably here, are discussed in Alvin Gouldner, "The Norm of Reciprocity," *American Sociological Review* (April, 1960). Most helpful in explaining the idea of a role system has been the work of J. Wahlke, H. Eulau, W. Buchanan, L. Ferguson. See their study, *The Legislative System* (New York, 1962), esp. Intro.
23. See the exchange in 101 *Cong. Rec.,* pp. 3832, 3844, 3874.
24. *Cf.* Dwaine Marvick, "Congressional Appropriations Politics," unpublished manuscript (Columbia, 1952).
25. See Dalmas Nelson, "The Omnibus Appropriations Act of 1950," *Journal of Politics* (May, 1953).
26. This view has been confirmed by the results of interviews conducted by the author with members of the House Committee on Education and Labor, together with an examination of that Committee's activity in one policy area. They indicate very significant contrasts between the internal structure of that Committee and the Appropriations Committee—contrasts which center around their comparative success in meeting the problem of integration. The House Committee on Education and Labor appears to be a poorly integrated committee. Its internal structure is characterized by a great deal of subgroup conflict, relatively little role reciprocity, and minimally effective internal control mechanisms. External concerns, like those of party, constituency and clientele groups, are probably more effective in determining its decisions than is likely to be the case in a well-integrated committee. An analysis of the internal life of the Committee on Education and Labor, drawn partly from interviews with 19 members of that group, will appear in a forthcoming study, *Federal Aid to Education and National Politics,* by Professor Frank Munger and the author, to be published by Syracuse University Press. See also Nicholas R. Masters, *op. cit.,* note 8 above, pp. 354–555, and Seymour Scher, "Congressional Committee Members as Independent Agency Overseers: A Case Study," *American Political Science Review,* Vol. 54 (December 1960), pp. 911–920.

31

Bargaining in Congress

LEWIS A. FROMAN, JR.

In the following selection, Lewis A. Froman, Jr., examines the relation between the rules of the legislative game and the formation of majorities around specific legislation. He discusses how the two houses of Congress can be sufficiently integrated to make widely accepted policy decisions, given the highly dispersed and fragmented nature of congressional power. Some students argue that the leadership and party system act as sufficient integrative mechanisms. Although this may be true, the present party leaders operate within the framework of existing congressional rules of procedure, both formal and informal, which establish the limits within which the legislative struggle is conducted. Thus, the rules also constitute an integrative force in Congress, setting the boundaries of the struggle.

As Froman points out, legislative coalitions shift from one issue to the next at various stages in the consideration of a single measure. A good bargainer in Congress must be aware of these subtleties in the legislative process and must also be familiar with the relevant rules, for they are important instruments in building majority coalitions. At times, simple majorities may not be adequate, either because the rules dictate a greater number or a broad consensus is required for the acceptance of a policy, as in the case of United States policy in Vietnam. The bargaining process in Congress is designed to construct coalitions that will reflect a broad national consensus on public policy.

Froman, Professor of Political Science at the University of California at Irvine, is the author of Congressmen and Their Constituencies *(1963) and*

People and Politics *(1962). As an American Political Science Association Congressional Fellow (1963–1964), he has had the opportunity to observe Congress closely.*

Congress is an intricate and complex institution. Each body has its own sets of leaders, its own complex division of labor (essentially through the committee system), its own set of formal rules and procedures which define the various ways in which the "game" may be played, and its own set of informal rules which help to set the conditions under which certain actions will take place and will be considered legitimate and appropriate. As intricate and complex as congressional decision-making is, however, it is possible to make several generalizations about it.

First, . . . it is widely accepted that each house of Congress is a highly decentralized political institution in which power is widely dispersed. Although political party affiliation is undoubtedly the most important organizing and coordinating force within the institution, other pressures (such as constituency, state party delegation, committee loyalty, personal stands on issues, interest group activity, and leadership rewards and punishments) are crucial in understanding how decision-making takes place within Congress. Committees in Congress, for example, are almost entirely autonomous. In addition, for many committees (Appropriations, Public Works, and Governmental Operations in the House, for example) subcommittees are also relatively autonomous. This dispersion of autonomous political power means that actions taken by the committees are usually the actions which are taken by the parent body.

A second point concerning decision-making in Congress is that a general method of coordination of these autonomous units is a system of reciprocity. Committees, and committee members, tend not to interfere with the work of other committees. The number of amendments which are offered on the floor and the number of successful changes in bills on the floor vary considerably from bill to bill and committee to committee. If the committee is cohesive in its recommendation (especially if it is bipartisanly cohesive), and if the bill does not involve conflicting ideologies, then few amendments will be offered and few will be successful. There is a strong tendency for members to accept the work and expertise of the other committees. In return, of course, they expect little interference in their own work.

Third, legislative decision-making is serial, involving a number of different approvals. It proceeds in stages, from the introduction of a bill, to committee, to subcommittee, back to committee, to the Rules Committee (if in the House), to the floor, to the Committee of the Whole (in the House), to final passage. Many things can happen to a bill along the way. A single negative action may be sufficient to defeat the bill. Bringing a bill to the floor to final passage requires the most skillful negotiation. Agreements reached must be cumulative.

Fourth, this legislative process is also lengthy and time-consuming with many opportunities for delay. A major reason is that the relatively autonomous committees often consist of members with different kinds of constituents. This usually produces built-in conflict in each unit. Reaching agreement among members with varying preferences (sometimes quite intense preferences) is no easy task, even in a relatively small unit like a committee or subcommittee. Since there is very little over-all coordination or control by the leadership over matters still within committees, the speed with which legislation passes the House or Senate is in large measure determined by the nature of the conflict and the ability of those opposed to use the rules and structure of this complex organization. [The following table] shows the points at which delay and defeat may occur in the House of Representatives. A similar table, with some modifications, would illustrate the same points for the Senate.

Most criticisms of the House of Representatives center around these points of possible delay and defeat, especially those which can occur before the bill reaches the floor. Since the brunt of these arguments involves the idea that the majority should be able to work its will, criticisms center on the places where less than a majority may delay or defeat legislation. In the House, legislative committees and the Rules Committee come under strongest attack; in the Senate, legislative committees and the loose rules of floor debate, especially filibusters, raise the strongest objections.

Although there are methods by which committees may be by-passed, members are reluctant to invoke these procedures. Committee chairmen are powerful individuals. They can be very helpful to younger congressmen

Points at Which Delay or Defeat May Occur in the House

Delay	*Defeat*
Committee inaction in referring to a subcommittee	Committee inaction
Subcommittee inaction (prolonged hearings; refusal to report)	Negative vote in committee
Committee inaction (prolonged hearings; refusal to report)	Subcommittee inaction
Rules Committee inaction (refusal to schedule hearings; prolonged hearings; refusal to report)	Negative vote in subcommittee
	Rules Committee inaction
Slowness in scheduling the bill	
Floor action (demanding full requirements to the rules)	Negative vote in Rules Committee
reading of the journal	Defeat of rule on the floor
repeated quorum calls	
refusing unanimous consent to disperse with further proceedings under the call of the roll	Motion to strike enacting clause
	Motion to recommit
prolonging debate	
various points of order	Final passage

wishing special favors (committee assignments, private and public bills, help "downtown," etc.); they can also take positive steps to damage the effectiveness of other members in hundreds of small ways. They are not, in short, persons to be trifled with. To oppose a committee chairman one pays a price, and often one is never sure what the price might be.

In addition, all bills come from committees. If one committee is by-passed what is to prevent a member's own committee from being by-passed in the future when something which he feels strongly about is being delayed? Lacking a strong, centralized leadership with weapons to force decentralized units to act, reciprocity becomes an operating rule of no small importance in coordinating the activities of the House and Senate.

Reciprocity and comity as informal norms of Congress, however, only partially explain how agreements are reached in the House and Senate. How, then, are winning coalitions formed? For many bills a winning coalition is a majority coalition, but in other cases much larger coalitions are required (for example, Consent Calendar, Private Calendar, Suspension of the Rules, Cloture). But even when "only" a majority is necessary, the problem of coalition-building is complicated by the existence of multiple decision-points. The problem of putting together a majority coalition is not simply a problem of one coalition. Under normal circumstances there must be a majority in the subcommittee, a majority in the committee, a majority in the Rules Committee (if in the House), a majority to defeat amendments on the floor, often a majority against a recommittal motion, and a majority on final passage. These "majorities" involve different people in different situations at different points in time. The problems which arise in building a coalition may vary considerably at each of these decision-points.

There is also a problem of "intensity" involved in coalition-building. How intense the opposition is in part determines how intense the proponents must be to succeed. That is, given apathetic minority opposition, not much more than apathetic majority support is probably required for passage. However, given intense opposition, at least some among the proponents must also be intense at each of the steps in the decision-making process. For various reasons intense majorities rarely appear. On most bills majorities are the *result* of the legislative process, not the precondition for it. It is during the legislative process that the wide variety of interests and personalities bargain and compromise on a bill, and its provisions, which make it acceptable to at least a majority of the members. It is seldom that a majority would support a *specific* bill before it reaches Congress. There may be general agreement that some kind of legislation is necessary, although even this may not happen very often, but the particular provisions of the bill need to be worked out to gain wide support for the specific legislation which will have to be passed.

There are many reasons for the general absence of intense majorities. The first is simply the diversity of interests being represented in the House. Northerners differ from southerners, Republicans differ from Democrats, representatives from rural areas differ from those from urban areas.[1] This, coupled with an absence of ways to enforce party discipline, means that there are often as many views on public policy questions as there are congressmen.

The second reason for the absence of intense majorities is that, even if there were not various combinations of constituency differences, individual members differ from each other on what they consider to be important legislation. For example, if we take constituencies which have elected more than one member from the same party during a ten-year period, and compare them with constituencies which have elected the same member over the same period of time, we find the variation in voting in Congress by the elected representatives is greater for those constituencies which elected more than one member. This illustrates that even with party and constituency held constant, some variation in congressional voting still exists which may be attributed to the values and attitudes of particular members.[2]

Third, many issues are salient to only a few members. That is, given any issue, it not only affects different congressmen differently (as the first two reasons suggest), but it also will affect some congressmen hardly at all. Many congressmen will have little personal stake in the outcome of many bills and will not be intense about the issues. Most congressmen are specialists in only a few areas and are intensely concerned with only a few issues.

Fourth, few bills embody only a single issue. Most bills have multiple provisions. Congressmen, therefore, will be selective in their attention and support for the bill. They may be quite intense about some provisions, mildly interested in others, and not concerned at all about still others. Their support, then, during the negotiating process may be quite erratic depending upon what is left in the bill, what is taken out, and what is added.

Given this lack of intensity and dispersion of issue concern, few bills are centrally important to a majority of congressmen. Other values come into play in a congressman's behavior. Congressmen, like other people, have multiple values and play many games, and it is rare that any single game or set of values will lead to the sacrifice of every other value. Other games include: running for higher office, hoping for an executive appointment, getting a job outside of Congress, trying to be influential in the House, wanting a committee appointment, and wanting a particular bill which directly affects his constituency. Hence, coalitions are formed and reformed on a number of criteria as the issues come up. These coalitions have in them some people who are very intense all the way down to some members who are not intense at all. A member who is not intense about an issue will not sacrifice other values (like the chance for an important committee assignment). Issues, after all, are not considered in a vacuum. Many things are at stake, including a congressman's or committee's prestige, his relationships with the leadership (and all this entails in terms of institutional rewards), and, of course, his constituency interests. Political actions have costs, and different issue-contexts will affect many congressmen quite differently in how far they are willing to pursue their interest in the issue to the exclusion of other important values they may have.

For these reasons, then, minorities, through the committee system, are able to exercise power over legislation. Since the major power structure of the House is the committee system, and since most institutional rewards and punishments are channeled through the committees, members are naturally reluctant to take actions which are adverse to their potential interests.

To complicate this analysis even further, and to give some indication of the wide variety of variables which are involved, whether or not a bill passes Congress will depend upon:

1. what the bill is (that is, what the stakes of the game are);
2. how many members are intense in their support (the greater the number of intense members, the greater likelihood of passage);
3. the magnitude of intensity (the greater the intensity, the greater the likelihood of passage, assuming flexibility);
4. who the supporters are (leadership, committee chairmen, respected members, White House support);
5. where the supporters are located (on the committee to which the bill is assigned, on the subcommittee, on the Rules Committee);
6. and how many, how intense, who and where located is the opposition. These factors will also help to determine the kinds of procedures which will be employed to bring the bill to a vote (for example "normal" rules and procedures such as the regular Calendar vs. "abnormal" ones such as the discharge rule and Calendar Wednesday).

When certain combinations of these factors exist, one can predict whether or not a bill is in trouble, and even say approximately how much trouble. If it is known, for example, that those who favor the bill constitute a majority, that some are relatively intense, that the leadership favors passage, that neither the committee to which the bill is to be referred nor the Rules Committee is hostile to the bill, and that those who oppose the bill are few in number, not very intense, and not strategically located on the committee nor among committee chairmen or others in position of influence, then it can be expected that the bill will not have much difficulty on its way to final passage. If, however, just one or a few of these factors change, an entirely different situation confronts the proponents of the bill.

With almost any controversial bill, there will be one or more places along the decision-route which may be hostile. Given this state of affairs for most bills, there must exist some mechanism or set of mechanisms by which conflicts can be resolved or circumvented. The alternative to such a mechanism would undoubtedly be stalemate, inability to operate, and, in the future, either a change in the institution or a diminution of political power. The mechanism which helps to coordinate decentralized decision-making within Congress and which aids in coalition-building at the various decision-points is bargaining.

Bargaining as a Political Process

Bargaining as a mechanism of coordination and a device for building coalitions is an incredibly complex phenomenon and it will be useful at this point to make very clear just exactly how the term is being used.

First, bargaining is not just one thing, but a number of things. One very important distinction which separates two types of bargaining from the others is whether negotiation is involved. As Lindblom has pointed out, there are methods of coordination in decision-making which do not involve negotiation (defined as an actual interchange between two or more people).[3] Whether these forms of non-negotiated decision-making should even be called bargaining is a matter of definition. Our definition treats these as bargaining, but to distinguish them from bargaining in which negotiation is involved they will be called non-negotiated bargaining.

Second, bargains may vary as to whether they are implicit or explicit.[4] Bargains are implicit when the "counters" or "payoffs" being used are not known or are vague. Explicit bargaining involves known counters.

The following is a typology of bargaining with explanations of each type.[5]

Non-Negotiated Bargaining	*Negotiated Bargaining*
1. Unilateral action	3. Simple logrolling
2. Anticipated reaction	4. Time logrolling
	5. Compromise
	6. Side-payments

1. Unilateral Action

Unilateral action is a form of non-negotiated bargaining in which a decision-maker simply takes action without regard for its consequences or other decision-makers. There are many circumstances under which unilateral action may take place. Its most prevalent form probably occurs when a person issues an authoritative command or rule which he expects to be obeyed simply because he feels he is in a position of authority to issue the command. In some cases he may be quite correct. In other cases it may have been wise for him to negotiate with his subordinates and others who may be affected, or at least attempt to anticipate their reactions and take them into account.

Unilateral action may also occur out of naïveté or lack of knowledge. A decision-maker may simply not know that his decision will have certain effects on others, or he may not care.

Unilateral action is always an implicit bargain. There are no counters involved, or at least they are not considered by the decision-maker.

2. Anticipated Reaction

A second form of non-negotiated bargaining will be called anticipated reaction. As in unilateral action this form of bargaining does not involve an actual interchange between two or more people, but unlike unilateral bargaining the possible reactions of other decision-makers are taken into account in the decision. Anticipated reactions may be used when it does not appear necessary to negotiate or it is not possible to negotiate. A move is made with the reactions of others in mind but actual negotiation is not present. A lot of bargaining, especially at early stages, is probably of this type; it is also quite prevalent when bargaining is adversary in nature.

Anticipated reaction may be either explicit or implicit, but the line between the two may be quite thin. Schelling has done some interesting work with this problem and the circumstances under which anticipated reactions may be shaped and, therefore, predictable.[6] In some cases the anticipated reactions may be clear to the original decision-maker but not to the person whose reactions he is attempting to anticipate. In other cases they may be clear to both parties.

3. Simple Logrolling

The next four categories of bargaining are more widely considered to be bargaining, that is, forms which involve direct negotiation between two or more people.

A simple logroll is a negotiated bargain which takes the form "You give me what I want and I'll give you what you want." Simple logrolling occurs when there are a number of smaller projects, issues, or programs which can be put into one bill. The process simply requires mutual support, or at least mutual non-interference. The most important point to be made with simple logrolling, however, as compared with the next category, time logrolling, is that in simple logrolling the payoffs to the partners to the bargain occur at the same time.

By its very nature, then, simple logrolling is explicit. To engage in this type of bargain each of the parties has to know what he wants and what he is willing to support in return for support from others.

In the omnibus Rivers and Harbors Bill (pork barrel), bargaining is likely to involve simple logrolling and anticipated reaction. The process of building a coalition with a policy involving smaller, separate projects simply involves putting into the same bill a large number of these separate and independent projects. The norm here is reciprocity. If a congressman or senator is going to get his project (a wider river, a new or deeper harbor, etc.) he must not interfere in other people's projects.

4. Time Logrolling

Time logrolling is a negotiated bargain of the form "You support me now, and I'll support you some time in the future." Time logrolling involves the same kind of process as simple logrolling except the support or non-interference promised is, for one of the parties, in the future. For example, there may be at least two separate bills involved in the bargain, rather than a number of projects in one bill.

Logrolling over time may be either implicit or explicit. That is, the promised future support may be on some definite issue or bill, or the second part of the bargain may be left indefinite.

A classic example of logrolling occurred in 1964 when two logrolls occurred on the same bill. First, a simple logroll took place in the Senate when a wheat section was attached to an already House-passed Cotton Bill. Then, when the bill was returned to the House a time logroll took place. Those who wanted the Cotton-Wheat Bill logrolled with those who wanted the Food-Stamp Bill. The price for support by the urban Democrats for the Cotton-Wheat Bill was support by the rural Democrats for the Food-Stamp Plan. As part of the bargain the liberals even demanded that the Food-Stamp Bill be reported to the floor of the House first. If successful, they would support the Cotton-Wheat Bill.

5. Compromise

Compromise is a form of negotiated bargain of the general form "You want x, I want z, let's settle on y." A compromise normally occurs when a bill specifies a certain thing or a certain amount of something, others want less (or none at all), and to gain sufficient support a policy or figure between the two positions is accepted and agreed upon. This is the "half a loaf is better than no loaf at all" bargain.

Compromise is not usually a form of bargaining in the early stages of negotiation. Rather, unilateral action or anticipated reaction will probably be tried first. In fact, anticipated reaction is often used in conjunction with compromise in the sense that decision-makers may anticipate opposition and ask for more than they really want with a view to later compromise. This is probably a major strategy in the budgetary process,[7] as well as in the House-Senate bargaining. Alternatively, decision-makers may perceive strong opposition and ask for less than they really want as a way of avoiding later compromise and especially to circumvent the possibility that later compromise will not occur because they asked, originally, for too much.

The original proponents of the 1964 Civil Rights Bill were forced to modify the provisions of the bill as the bill went from subcommittee to full committee to the floor in the House, and then more compromise was necessary to meet the extraordinary majority (two-thirds) needed to break a filibuster in the Senate. As the bill was exposed to larger and larger groups with diverse interests it required modification to win the support of a coalition large enough to pass the bill. The major portions of the bill which were changed involved sections regulating how the courts, businesses, and places of accommodation were to deal with Negroes.

If and when bargaining reaches the stage of compromise, however, such bargaining is explicit. That is, various middle-ground positions are tried (the most obvious one being the exact middle) to see whether a mutually satisfactory point can be reached. Compromise obviously cannot occur between inflexible bargainers, for example, ideologues. Compromise requires that both sides be flexible. In the absence of such flexibility bargaining of quite a different sort may appear (i.e., side-payments).

6. Side-Payments

A probably less often used, but highly publicized type of bargaining takes the form of "You support me and I will reward you," or, alternatively, "You support me or else I will punish you." Side-payments are non-policy rewards and punishments such as personnel positions (federal judgeships, postmasterships, patronage appointments in general), institutional positions (committee assignments, subcommittee chairmanships and assignments, party positions), and resources (campaign contributions and aid, additional staff members, money-producing speaking engagements, travel).

Side-payments can be either negative or positive. For example, a person can threaten to withhold aid, or can threaten to take some positive but detrimental step, or he can promise aid. Side-payments may also be for the particular individual, or they may be put at the disposal of the particular individual to give to someone else.

Side-payments may be either implicit or explicit. That is, what is promised in return for support (or opposition) may be made quite clear, or it may be left in doubt.

Certain highly controversial issues might involve, to the extent that bargaining is possible at all, the politics of side-payments. This will be especially true if these issues take something away from one group and give an approximately equivalent amount to another group. There will be strong pressure to replace what was taken away with something else. Side-payments are ideally suited for such replacement. There will also be strong pressure toward compromise, weakening the bill in a number of ways.

Bargaining on highly controversial issues might also involve bargaining by unilateral action. Decision-makers, because of the heated nature of these issues, find it difficult to negotiate, and in the absence of negotiation it is possible to find attempts to do by unilateral action that which cannot be done by forms of bargaining involving negotiation.

These forms of bargaining, unilateral action, anticipated reaction, simple and time logrolling, compromise, and side-payments, represent six ways in which coordination may be achieved in decision-making.

Conditions Under Which Various Types of Bargaining Take Place

The conditions under which the various types of bargaining referred to above take place are many. We will be concerned with six major types: (1) historical circumstances, (2) structure of the group in which the decision-making takes place, (3) position of people in the group, (4) personality of people making the decisions, (5) the time sequence of decision-making, and (6) the issues in the decision-making.

1. Historical Circumstances

Certain committees and subcommittees in Congress have developed relatively standard and routine ways of handling the issues which come before them. Similarly, people in positions of leadership, unless they are new to their job, may have developed ways of handling problems which repeatedly come across their desks.[8] Hence it would be important to determine whether certain committees or other sub-groups in Congress have any patterns of bargaining.

For example, Richard Fenno has suggested that the Appropriations Committee in the House of Representatives has developed relatively standard norms of bargaining within the Committee. Generally, bargaining in the Appropriations Committee may be described as logrolling, anticipated reaction (mutual non-interference among the subcommittees, reciprocity) and compromise.[9] Other committees may exhibit quite different forms of bargaining. The Education and Labor Committee in the House when chaired by Representative Graham Barden was one in which unilateral action was prevalent, given the circumstances which produced an inability to be flexible in negotiation.[10]

Actually, "historical circumstances" is probably a catch-all which hides to some extent other underlying variables (such as personalities, norms, or modes of operations) which would be very helpful to know.

2. Structure of the Group

It would be interesting to know if different kinds of group structures facilitate or impede various forms of bargaining. For example, highly decentralized decision-making units, like Congress, probably facilitate bargaining by logrolling. Decision-structures which are bi-polar in nature (House vs. Senate) probably facilitate compromise. Highly structured hierarchical decision-units probably facilitate bargaining by unilateral action. Loosely structured, less permanent decision-structures probably impede logrolling over time and encourage charismatic leadership.

3. Position in the Group

Obviously, the more resources one has at his disposal the better able he is to bargain. Although most everyone has some resources, leaders probably have more resources than anyone else. This would be especially true in the use of unilateral action and side-payments, and only slightly less true of compromise. Anyone with a vote can logroll, however, and this along with anticipated reaction is likely to be the most prevalent form of bargaining among non-leaders.

4. Personality of Decision-Makers

The personalities of the decision-makers are probably also very important in determining the extent and kinds of bargaining which go on. We are all familiar with this at a casual level. For example, ideologues find it very difficult to compromise but not at all difficult to logroll; statesmen find it very difficult to logroll (each proposal must be examined on its merits) but may not find it difficult to compromise (we must do what is right for the most number of people); leaders in positions of authority may find it difficult to issue commands (unilateral action); unintelligent people may find it difficult to anticipate others' reactions; highly moral people find it difficult to engage in side-payments. A proliferation of such personality types would be enormously useful in analyzing the use of bargaining.

5. Time Sequence in Decision-Making

It may be that in many decision-making situations there is a sequence in which certain kinds of bargaining are tried before others. If the first types are unsuccessful, then others will be attempted. For example, in the preliminary stages of bargaining unilateral action and anticipated reactions may be employed. If these are unsuccessful, logrolling and compromise may be tried. If these in turn do not succeed then, and perhaps only then, will side-payments (probably the most costly of all bargains) be employed.

Another interesting time relationship is that of combinations of bargaining. For example, anticipated reaction may be employed purposely to set up a future bargaining situation of either compromise or logrolling. Leaders in the House may include a provision in a bill for trading purposes with the Senate. The leaders in the House will agree to delete its provision which is obnoxious to the Senate (and which the House leaders really did not want anyway) if the Senate leadership will, in turn, delete a provision which is unacceptable to the House. Or, the Senate may not include a provision in its bill because it is known that the House will not accept it. Other examples of combinations of bargaining will come readily to mind.

6. Type of Issue

There are a number of ways in which issues on types of policies may be distinguished.[11] The characteristic which will be of chief concern to us here is the extent of opposition which a bill generates in Congress. How divisive an issue is will structure, to a large extent, the way in which bargaining takes place.

How much opposition a bill will have is itself dependent upon several factors. We may say, for example, that the "newer" the program, the more "ideological" the program (especially in terms of a liberal-conservative dimension), the greater the probability that the program will touch on cleavages already existing in the society at large (such as race or religion), the less the acceptance of the bill by those who are to be directly affected by the program, and, the more the program deviates from past programs, the greater the opposition.

Rules, Issues, and Bargaining

The relationships among these many factors have a number of interesting consequences for the operation of decision-making in Congress. For example, we have already referred to the decentralized structure of Congress, the wide distribution of power within Congress, and the elaborate rules and procedures which require majorities at many points in the decision-making process. We have raised the question, given this decentralized system, how is coordination achieved? How are coalitions built? We have also suggested that the answer to this question is relatively complex. Generally speaking it is through bargaining that the many hurdles are overcome. But bargaining varies a good deal, and the difficulties in overcoming the hurdles also vary depending upon the kind of issue which is at stake, and the number, intensity, and location of the opposition.

On the basis of this discussion we can now draw some generalizations about the operation of Congress in a wider context. The kinds of issues which Congress is most admirably suited to handle are those which are relatively non-controversial. The fact that there are so many decision-points as a bill progresses through Congress, and the fact that most of these stages involve members with diverse interests, means that if a coalition is going to be put together it will probably be done, or it can best be done, by logrolling.

We also know that Congress is a relatively stable institution in which the membership remains relatively constant over a period of time. . . . This is especially true for the leadership of Congress. Simple logrolling, involving as it does bargains within a single bill at a single point in time, does not require a stable institution. Time logrolling, on the other hand does require that the participants remain over a period of time so that bargains can be fulfilled. Time logrolling, in a sense, requires that members expect other members to be around to fulfill their part of the bargain. Congress admirably guarantees that members, and again especially leaders who often tend to be recruited with safety of district in mind, will be in Congress from one session to the next.

On the other hand, Congress is less well equipped to handle issues which might raise strong opposition. We have suggested that such divisive issues are likely to have one or more of the following characteristics: new or ideological programs, or programs which bear on cleavages already existing in society, which are not acceptable to the groups directly affected, or which deviate markedly from past programs in the same area. Minorities are in positions, very often, to block such legislation. If they are in such a position, why should they bargain? If a group has a chance to win, there may be little incentive to take half a loaf when they can insure no loaf at all.

What has happened, then, on many controversial issues is that they have been delegated to some other agency of government. That is, because Congress itself finds it difficult to negotiate on these issues it will pass the buck to an administrative agency. Outside interests may themselves prefer the easier politics of administrative agencies rather than the labyrinthine and uncertain politics of Congress. Given a political system which allows relatively small minorities to prevail in situations in which they are intense (or at least to force a compromise) how much worse is this situation when relatively large numbers are intensely involved? The answer, very often, is stalemate.

Most issues which Congress handles are not likely to involve intense opposition. Pork barrel and subsidies are traditional rewards which congressmen and senators use to continue in office. Most congressmen and senators recognize this. Reciprocity through anticipated reactions is a prevalent form of bargaining on these kinds of issues. If intense opposition does arise, and if it is strategically located, it is usually possible to "overcome" the opposition through simple or time logrolling, compromise, or, if all else fails, side-payments. On very intense issues, given the nature of the decision-making apparatus in Congress, a majority coalition is difficult to put together—or, if not difficult to put together, difficult to exert against intense minorities strategically located. It forces congressmen and senators to employ rules and procedures which very often are not part of the "normal" decision-making process. This normal decision-making process is the very process which facilitates logrolling. What is required on very controversial issues is for congressmen and senators to be willing to bypass the "normal" decision-making process and violate the norms which make that process operative.

These considerations, then, bring up the question of rules and procedures and the strategies involved in their use. Bargaining is the informal process by which issues brought before Congress are handled. What kinds of bargains will be used will depend upon the nature of the issue, which in turn affects the number of people engaged in the conflict and the level of intensity of the conflict. However, the "game" played on any given issue takes place within the framework of rules and procedures. Which rules and procedures will be used, whether stalling will take place, whether unusual rules and procedures will be invoked, will depend upon the same factors that determine the kinds of bargaining which take place.

For example, we would expect the rules and procedures defined as part of the normal legislative process to be employed on most non-controversial issues. In the House of Representatives, for example, Consent and Suspension Calendars are used primarily for issues of this kind. If there is an intense opposition, the bill will probably not be able to "skip" the Committee on Rules. On highly controversial issues, extraordinary procedures (such as discharge or threat of discharge, and Calendar Wednesday) may have to be resorted to. If the issue cannot be resolved through the normal channels, if the bargains cannot be struck, and the rules cannot be made to work, the bill will languish in committee, or will be defeated somewhere along the line.

The same considerations apply to both houses even though their specific rules and procedures are considerably different. The "normal" legislative channels will be employed when logrolling, compromise, and side-payments are able to settle the conflict within the normal rules. When, however, issues are presented which create situations that break down the normal channels, when policies are presented to Congress which cannot be negotiated within the system of rules and procedures by bargaining, then other routes and procedures, the "abnormal" rules of the system, will be employed.

Decision-making in Congress, then, is an extremely complicated process. The rules, procedures, and strategies employed using alternative routes, are closely linked with the type of issue which Congress has before it, and the ability of the normal rules and procedures to contain the conflict within the normal bargaining procedures. Abnormal rules and procedures are resorted to only when the normal legislative system is not able to handle the conflict through bargaining.

NOTES

1. Lewis A. Froman, Jr., *Congressmen and Their Constituencies* (Chicago: Rand McNally, 1963), Chap. 7.
2. *Ibid.*, Chap. 8.
3. Charles E. Lindblom, *The Intelligence of Democracy* (New York: Free Press, 1965), esp. Chs. 1–5.
4. Lewis A. Froman, Jr., *People and Politics* (Englewood Cliffs: Prentice-Hall, 1962), Chap. 4.
5. For two other typologies of bargaining see Lindblom, *op. cit.*, Chaps. 1–5, and William H. Riker, *The Theory of Political Coalitions* (New Haven: Yale University Press, 1962), Chap. 5.
6. Thomas Schelling, *The Strategy of Conflict* (Cambridge, Mass.: Harvard University Press, 1960).
7. Aaron Wildavsky, *The Politics of the Budgetary Process* (Boston: Little, Brown, 1964).
8. For theories developed around this notion, see James G. March and Herbert A. Simon, *Organizations* (New York: Wiley, 1958), and David Braybrooke and Charles E. Lindblom, *A Strategy of Decision* (New York: Free Press of Glencoe, 1963). For an application see Wildavsky, *op. cit.*
9. Richard F. Fenno, Jr., "The House Appropriations Committee as a Political System: The Problem of Integration," *American Political Science Review*, vol. 56 (June, 1962), 310–24.
10. Richard F. Fenno, Jr., "The House of Representatives and Federal Aid to Education," in Robert L. Peabody and Nelson W. Polsby, eds., *New Perspectives on the House of Representatives* (Chicago: Rand McNally, 1963), pp. 195–237.
11. Lewis A. Froman, Jr., "The Categorization of Policy Contents," paper delivered at the Social Science Research Council's Conference on Public Policy, 1966.

32

Prologue to Reform

JOSEPH S. CLARK

Senator Joseph S. Clark, who has long advocated congressional reform, is among those who assert that Congress is both undemocratic and incapable of acting expeditiously in the face of domestic and international crises. According to its critics, Congress is undemocratic because its rules, procedures, and structure frustrate majority rule and often are used by a small, willful band of men—the members of the "establishment"—to block the passage of vital legislation. In order to make Congress responsive to broad national majorities, more efficient in the performance of its business, and more receptive to the President's programs, major reforms that involve a redistribution of internal influence are imperative.

In the following essay, Clark examines some of the conditions under which reorganization has occurred in the past. It is almost ironic that congressional reform, as Clark describes it, seems to have occurred when an intense majority in Congress desired a change in the institution's procedures and structures. If Congress is capable of reforming itself when an intense majority so desires, can it not also pass substantive legislation longed for by equally intense majorities? If the answer to this question is affirmative, then perhaps a reorganization of Congress is not what is needed. It may be argued that the dilatory rules of procedure are used by minorities and majorities to kill legislation they do not favor, and hence these rules act as a gatekeeper to prevent the consideration of unmanageable conflicts.

Clark has served as a United States senator from Pennsylvania (Democrat, 1956–1968) and as mayor of Philadelphia. During his years in Congress, he became one of the most articulate proponents of congressional reform.

Relations between Congress and the President are unsatisfactory. The internal structure of Congress is obsolete. The record of Congress through much of American history is dismal. Many members of Congress are too preoccupied with getting re-elected, and too harried by their lesser chores, to perform with any distinction the high public service for which they are chosen.

Surely it is possible to improve the situation—to make Congress responsible, democratic, workable, constructive. It is, indeed. But there are obstacles to be overcome. There are also precedents to guide us through the maze of reform.

The first obstacle is the political time lag which is such an imposing part of Congressional tradition. Public realization that a continuing, affirmative, national legislative policy is necessary is a relatively new thing in American politics. It had its origin in Wilson's New Freedom and reappeared during the early New Deal. Yet it took World War II and the Cold War of the 1950s to convince the American people that positive national governmental action must replace political laissez faire. But Congress, because of its method of selection and its ancient customs, has not yet caught up with prevailing creative public opinion. The political stalemate described by Samuel Lubell in *The Future of American Politics* and by James MacGregor Burns in *The Deadlock of Democracy* represents the facts of Congressional life today.

The customs, manners, rules and procedures of the Congress owe much to the American tradition of thinking in sectional and local social, economic and political terms. Americans, like most human beings, share a conviction that "The Lord helps those who help themselves." Until recently we were content to protect ourselves from alleged governmental restraint on our personal activities by Congressional devices designed to give minority interests (other than the Negro) a veto on the legislative process. The durability of these devices is also a tribute to the curious notion that to do nothing does not constitute a decision. The fear that the creation of a national legislature with the capacity to act might produce wrong decisions overlooks the fact that to do nothing in the modern world may itself represent a decision as disastrous as any affirmative action.

This strain of negativism runs deep. One may recall the interminable delays in enacting the constitutional amendments providing for the income tax, the direct election of Senators and women's suffrage; and how long we waited for child labor legislation, unemployment compensation and a host of economic and social welfare measures passed a generation earlier in most other Western democracies.

While Congressional political lag has always existed—indeed, through failure to solve the slavery question it played its part in bringing on the Civil War—it did not become glaringly apparent until the Great Depression of the 1930s. Prior to that time the system worked tolerably well. Each section got its interests taken care of by logrolling. Our wealth made the price supportable. World affairs did not require decisive action by the Congress. The really vital interests of the nation were not adversely affected. The system operated through a national legislature so organized that sectional and economic interests were able to protect themselves from objectionable government policy during a period in which no vigorous government policy of any kind was required in the national interest.

A governmental system that is not capable of producing a coherent legislative program is not likely to appear deficient to a people imbued with a firm distaste for strong government and not confronted with crisis. It produced a government that did not interfere with the expanding economy, which was then the main interest of most influential Americans. Understandably, it was not then perceived that an arrangement which gave minority interests a stranglehold on national policy through control over Congressional procedures might, when crisis arrived, prove to be inoperable.

It is in the nature of minorities, as Joseph Chamberlain once said, "to devise some ingenious machinery by which [they] may be saved from the natural consequences of being outnumbered." Such ingenious machinery is the very nerve center of the present control of the Congress. It will not do to defend this machinery as a protection against "the tyranny of the majority," for it is nothing of the sort. It is a built-in defense for maintaining a status quo no longer tenable in the face of present conditions at home and abroad. And it violates every principle of popular rule on which free governments are based. It is the "tyranny of the minorities" we suffer from.

The central defect of the modern Congress is that it permits a minority determined on inaction to frustrate the will of the majority which desires to act. All the majority wants to do is to work the will of the people it represents. Minority obstructionism has merely reinforced that Congressional lag which gets us into trouble. We can reflect soberly today on the results of the bitterest Senate filibuster of the nineteenth century, which in 1890-91 defeated a bill, already passed by the House, to give the federal government supervision over Congressional elections. How much rancor and discord in our century would have been avoided had the majority in the Senate been able to pass this bill, aimed at eliminating Negro disqualification and intimidation in the South.

Those who delight in the fear of "majority tyranny" should seek election to a major governmental post under conditions of genuine political competition. They would soon learn how varied are the interests that must be conciliated if success is to be achieved at the polls. There is nothing monolithic and therefore no basis for "tyranny" in the majorities put together by Congressmen from two-party states and districts today. Potential tyranny is a characteristic of minorities like the John Birch Society or the Communists, not the mark of the representatives of a major party seeking the support of a national electorate.

It is the dynamics of democratic politics, not the erection of legal barriers to action, that make for moderation in our public life and provide the real protection from majority tyranny. In fact, while both major parties have extremists in their ranks, those extremists have never represented orthodoxy in the parties to which they belonged. Their very power emerged from their exploitation of devices aimed at protecting the minority. Huey Long and his one-man filibusters or Joe McCarthy arrogating to himself the investigatory power of the Senate and temporarily usurping executive prerogatives never seriously threatened to assume leadership of either party. There is an old saying in England that the House of Commons has more sense than anyone in it. The same thing can be said of any legislative body where a consensus is permitted to develop and take action. It is, therefore, a grave error not to establish procedures which permit the good sense of a majority to prevail.

Congressional preoccupation with legal checks on the majority is superimposed on functional checks implicit in the separation of powers, including the Presidential veto. Moreover, our strongly held respect for minorities gives them additional protection. It is the strength of that tradition which provides the moral support for the effort to integrate the Negro into American life. It is indeed ironic that this effort on behalf of our most disadvantaged minority is frustrated by devices ostensibly aimed at preventing "majority tyranny."

The obstructionist policies encouraged by those same devices are in the long run self-defeating. In 1925 Vice President Dawes advised the Senate that "under the inexorable laws of human nature and human reaction, the Senate rules, unless changed, could only lessen the effectiveness, prestige, and dignity of that body."[1] There can be no doubt that the Dawes warning was prophetic, if unheeded. A legislature which denies itself the power to act, particularly when the obstacles to action are so obvious and so publicly demeaning as the filibuster, merits only disrespect and the loss of popular esteem it has achieved.

Max Lerner's harsh description is a typical reaction:

> Congress has become a problem child of the American governmental family. It is noisy, volatile, vulnerable to pressure groups and lobbies, often parochial in its outlook, jealous of its prerogatives, insecure about its position, implacable in its vendettas, bewildered by its mounting tasks. It has lost its reputation for great debate, has become intractable to party leadership and discipline and incapable of disciplining itself, and in recent generations it has developed fewer examples of the great leadership it once possessed.[2]

Vesting the veto power in a minority goes far to destroy that spirit of desirable compromise which is one of the hallmarks of a democratic legislative assembly. A minority bent on inaction finds it unnecessary to compromise with a majority which is powerless to act. The Congress of the United States is, within very broad limits, favorably disposed to accommodate a wide spectrum of opinion. There is no compulsion to agree on moderate and reasonable action, however, when the rules offer hope that nothing at all need be agreed to. Defiance by the minority breeds in the end vindictiveness in the majority. Neither sentiment is congenial to useful action.

The risk of tyranny by the majority over the minority is today small indeed. Tocqueville's fears of democracy have proved groundless. It is a minority, not a majority, which imposes sterile uniformity. Today the Negro minority is tyrannized by a white minority. National democracy has had no fair chance to do justice.

Another obstacle to clear thinking about Congressional reorganization is the ancient and slightly dishonorable doctrine of "states' rights." We tend to forget that our venerated Constitution was a wise reaction to states' rights pressed to the verge of chaos under the Articles of Confederation. It was states' rights which nearly disrupted the union at the Hartford Convention in 1814; which took South

Carolina down the primrose path of nullification in Jackson's first term; which, raised in defense of human slavery, played a major part in bringing on the Civil War; which has been the shield of the selfish men who have fought against social reform ever since; and which, today, is used as a major argument against that strengthening of the power of the legislative branch to act when its majority is ready for the action so necessary to national security and well-being.

As Henry Steele Commager has noted,

> For well over a century now, this pernicious doctrine [states' rights] has been invoked for two major purposes . . . to weaken government and to endanger freedom. A states' rights philosophy which is never inspired by generosity, never excited by a passion for freedom or for justice, never exalted by magnanimity but takes refuge in narrowness, selfishness and vindictiveness, exhausts its claim to tolerance.[3]

There is no greater nonsense circulated today than the theory that the states are the defenders of freedom and the national government its enemy. The fact is just the opposite. The growth of the power of the national government has secured an increase in individual freedom, social, economic and political. The effect of national power has been benign, not malign. It is a shame that the Congress has not sensed this basic political truth until long after it occurred to both the Supreme Court and the President. The use of states' rights as a rallying cry for those who desire to perpetuate an inept Congress unable to deal with pressing national problems is a cry to perpetuate plutocracy and greed and to protect those who are today violating civil rights and civil liberties with impunity. To rely upon the states for a solution of problems essentially national in their scope such as education, unemployment and social security is to insure that these problems will not be solved. Those who advocate states' rights are, therefore, in the vanguard of the opponents of Congressional reform. As long as they can keep the Congress negative their status quo philosophy is safe. It is state debt and state government employment which have risen almost astronomically in the postwar years, not the federal government's. Yet this enormous increase has not been sufficient to make appreciable inroads toward solution of the domestic problems which beset us. Letting the states do it is tantamount to letting the problems remain unsolved.

Closely related to the states' rights argument is the nightmare of "federal control" over individual liberties which haunts the dreams of our conservative friends. This is a sheer hallucination. I cannot think of one current program in which the "heavy hand of the federal government reaching out into our private lives" has actually been restrictive of our personal freedoms or detrimental to our economy—if, that is, one accepts the need for a justly organized society in a civilized world. The problem of protecting liberty against the demands of society is difficult and delicate, as John Stuart Mill made clear long ago. "Government, like dress," said Tom Paine, "is the badge of lost innocence." Sometimes the choice between liberty and order is difficult. In the great struggle for civil rights for all Americans, for example, it has been argued that equal access to public accommodations is an infringement on the liberty of the individual who owns or manages the facility. I would argue that the individual right of every American to the use of that facility is an *ex-*

pansion of basic liberty, not a *denial* of liberties. But the question is not easy.

The concern over minority rights and regional interests is understandable enough in view of our history. For the descendants of Southern planters, steerage immigrants, British convicts, African slaves and New England Puritans to live and work in peace and harmony, and pursue happiness together, is no easy thing. No other nation has had to attempt it. On the whole we have been successful, but we still have some miles to go on the road to the good society.

The motto carved on the New Senate Office Building is "The Senate is the Living Symbol of the Union of the States." That pretty well sums up the Congressional attitude. But time and history and world responsibility have made us a nation, and it is time that in our thinking and in our behavior we recognized contemporary fact. We must move toward national federalism, accepting the federal structure, but emphasizing the national.

There are many who persist in the mistaken view that the problems of Congress, like the poor, will always be with us. But the Congress has not always been as incapable of action as it is now, and majority rule has not always been so successfully thwarted. Like the tradition of Jim Crow in the South, which is not nearly so old as it is iniquitous, there is a tendency to accept as age-old and hallowed traditions the habits of a few decades. Most of the unfortunate traditions of Congress are not very old and not very hallowed. In a culture confronted with constant change it is surprising that so many still believe change in Congress is not possible.

Procedural reform in the Congress has a history at least as old as the practices which led to it. In the past hundred years, important procedural reforms have often been successfully accomplished as the need became clear.

How was it done before? There have been two classic instances of procedural reform in the House of Representatives. The rules and practices of the House grew like weeds from the First Congress until March of 1860, when a largely technical revision of the rules in the interest of clarity was adopted. Twenty years later the job was done again when the House approved a recodification recommended by a committee whose members included, among others, Samuel J. Randall of Pennsylvania, Alexander H. Stephens of Georgia, and James A. Garfield of Ohio, who shortly afterward was elected President. The committee's report consolidated in 44 rules what had formerly been 167, thus securing "accuracy in business, economy of time, order, uniformity and impartiality."[4] But the 1880 rules revision left untouched such dubious practices as riders on appropriations bills and the disappearing quorum—a technique of a minority under which members who were present refused to vote and thus invalidated the vote of the House for want of a quorum (in effect a filibuster).

All this history was preliminary to the first major reform of House procedures, "Reed's Rules" of 1890. Thomas Brackett Reed of Maine was a man of strong character and determined purpose. A large, stout, bald man with a walrus mustache typical of his day, and an acid tongue which withered opponents with invective and sarcasm, he believed that the duty of a legislature was to legislate. He became an expert on rules procedures and precedents.

In 1889, after twelve years in the House, he was elected Speaker. In those days the House, at the beginning of a new session, operated under general parliamentary procedure and, in due course and in leisurely fashion, eventually adopted rules which were generally, but not always, identical with those of the last preceding Congress. Shortly after the House met in 1889 the election case of Smith *vs.* Jackson was called up for consideration. Mr. Crisp of Georgia, a Democrat, raised the question of consideration. A roll call was ordered which resulted in 161 votes to take up the case, 2 opposed, with 163 not voting. The Democrats, who desired to stall, raised the question of no quorum.

Ever since the 1830s the practice had prevailed of all members of the minority party refusing to vote when they believed that not enough majority party members were present to make a quorum. Frequently, when the parties were fairly evenly divided, this tactic would be successful because some members from the majority party would fail to show up. Then a minority member would raise the question of "no quorum" and the presiding officer would rule the vote was invalid because a majority of the House had not voted. This despite the fact that enough members were present on the floor (though silent) to create a quorum had they responded when their names were called. Following this technique, a bill to admit California as a state in 1850 failed of passage on thirty-one roll calls in a single day. For this filibustering technique the House had no answer until Reed appeared on the scene.

When the suggestion of no quorum was made in the Smith *vs.* Jackson election case, Reed directed the clerk of the House to record the members on the floor who were present but not voting. He called off the names of forty-one of them, then announced that a quorum was present and that the resolution had been passed.

Bedlam broke out. The Democratic minority denounced the Speaker as a "scoundrel" and a "czar." "What becomes of the rights of the minority?" one member demanded. "The right of the minority," Reed replied mockingly, "is to draw its salaries and its function is to make a quorum."[5]

The near riot continued for three days. One key Democrat, with the parliamentary manual in his hand, addressed the Speaker:

> "I deny your right, Mr. Speaker, to count me present. . . ."
>
> "The Chair is making a statement of fact that the gentleman from Kentucky is present," Reed retorted. "Does he deny it?"[6]

The doors of the House were customarily locked when a roll call was ordered. As Reed persisted on subsequent roll calls in directing members present and not voting to be recorded as present for the purposes of making a quorum, a rush for the doors would follow to get out before they were locked in and counted during the roll call. Congressman Constantine Buckley Kilgore of Texas carried, for the rest of his life, the nickname "Kicking Buck Kilgore" for having kicked down a locked door to the House to make his escape.

In the end the uproar subsided, Democrats acquiesced, the filibuster power departed for all time from the House, and Reed reigned supreme as Speaker. The following year, 1890, the Reed Rules were adopted after full debate. They did more than destroy the practice of filibuster. They placed the Speaker in control of the House with almost dictatorial powers.

Reed acquired almost unlimited control over floor action. He would confer with William McKinley of Ohio, later to be President, Uncle Joe Cannon of Illinois, subsequently Speaker of the House, and one or two others on the Rules Committee, and then Reed would call in the minority leadership and say, "Gentlemen, we have decided to perpetrate the following outrage."[7]

Congressman Joseph Cannon became Speaker of the House in 1903. For seven years he ruled in the best Reed tradition. He was a genial man of strong conservative bent. He loved to play poker and drink whiskey. Senior Congressmen who shared the Speaker's political views and enjoyed similar habits formed a small oligarchy which under Cannon's direction ran the House. They had no program they were interested in enacting. They wanted to pass only such legislation as was absolutely essential, approve the appropriations bills and go home.

A number of insurgent Republicans and Democrats had been elected to the House during the Theodore Roosevelt years, however, and strong resentment against Cannon's dictatorial tactics built up. Cannon was using his power to defy members of his own party, the President included.

On March 16, 1910, a coalition led by liberal Republican George Norris of Nebraska, later to become Senator and the father of the TVA, initiated rule changes to cut the Speaker down to size. Cannon was removed from the Rules Committee, of which he had formerly been chairman.[8] Henceforth the Rules Committee was to consist of ten members, six from the majority party and four from the minority party, elected by the House itself, and it was to elect its own chairman. Cannon's power to appoint the standing committees of the House and their chairmen was turned over to the Ways and Means Committee.

It took a long debate and a continuous session lasting twenty-nine hours to accomplish these quite drastic reforms by a vote of 191–156 on March 19, 1910. The effect was to destroy a large part of the system of strong party government, party discipline and majority rule which the Republicans had erected under the leadership of Speakers Reed and Cannon. Insurgent Republicans, who had smarted under the Old Guard discipline, played a large part in the new reforms. As one of them, Congressman Nelson of Wisconsin, explained, "Members long chairmen of important committees . . . with records of faithful and efficient party service . . . have been ruthlessly removed, deposed, and humiliated before their constituents and the country because, forsooth, they would not cringe or crawl before the arbitrary power of the Speaker and his House machine. . . . We are fighting with our Democratic brethren for the common right of equal representation in this House, and for the right of way of progressive legislation in Congress."

Cannon continued as Speaker with substantially curtailed powers until the Democrats captured control of the House in November of 1910. When the Sixty-second Congress convened the following year, Champ Clark was elected Speaker. The Democratic majority then adopted its own rules, which retained all the curbs on the Speaker's power adopted the previous year. The day has come when it is obvious that these new rules are themselves insufficient. The trouble with these rules is that they continue the breach between the President and the House by making the Rules Committee and the chairmen of legislative committees immune to the pleas of the party leaders responsible for enactment of the President's program.

These two "revolutions" in the

House were paralleled by an equally drastic revolution in the Senate in 1913.

After the election of 1912 the Senate of the Sixty-third Congress contained fifty-one Democrats, forty-four Republicans and one Progressive. As usual the ranks in both parties were split into liberals, or administration men, and conservatives. The Democratic National Convention which nominated Woodrow Wilson for President at Baltimore in 1912 had adopted a liberal platform on which he ran under the slogan of "the New Freedom." Forty Democrats, ten Republicans and the one Progressive—the elder La Follette of Wisconsin—were in sympathy with the platform, whose principal planks dealt with child labor, women's suffrage, the tariff, monetary reform, antitrust legislation, strengthened Civil Service and pure food and health legislation.

Then, as now, conservatism in the Democratic party centered in the South, and, through seniority, controlled the party chairmanships, where much power resided. With a liberal majority of only fifty-one to forty-nine it was obviously going to be impossible to push the New Freedom program through the Senate unless Wilson's men could be put in charge and be prepared to cooperate with the progressive Republicans.

Thirty Democrats met at the home on Massachusetts Avenue of the youthful Senator from Tennessee, Luke "Young Thunderbolt" Lea, on a Sunday late in February, shortly before the members of the newly elected Congress were to take their oaths of office on March 4, 1913. Lea had first been elected to the Senate in 1910.

It was obviously going to be a tight squeeze to organize the Senate for Wilson. The first objective, they decided, must be to elect a strong Majority Leader to preside over the caucus and manage the strategy of the legislative program. Senator Thomas Staples Martin of Virginia, a conservative, had been Caucus and hence Minority Leader for some time. While he was a man of pleasing personality and unfailing courtesy and was personally popular with his colleagues, it was felt necessary to replace him with a man who would support the President. The group decided on John Worth Kern of Indiana, who was not present at the meeting, being preoccupied with the trial of a lawsuit.

To say that Senator Martin was unhappy is to understate the case. But the Wilson men had the votes, and the Senator from Indiana was duly elected Caucus (Majority) Leader.

Kern was also serving his first term in the Senate. But he was a national figure, having been the Democratic candidate for Vice President in 1908. He was the oldest of the men committed to enact the New Freedom program into law. His mustache and Vandyke beard embellished his obvious dignity. He was a man of infinite tact and patience. Well liked by his colleagues, he had a reputation for sound common sense. He needed all these qualities, for never before, or for that matter since, had a Senator been called to the majority leadership after only two years of service.

His task was formidable. Three of the fifty-one Democrats were disaffected. Eight more were in the doubtful category. He would have to rally the remaining forty, hold as many of the doubters as possible, woo the ten liberal Republicans and the one Progressive to squeeze through with the necessary majorities on the floor. The rules of the Senate, then as now, were archaic and made for delay and inaction.

But with the staunch support of his colleagues he got the job done. The

Steering Committee which he appointed was safely progressive but included two conservatives. Five of the nine members had served two years or less in the Senate. In assigning committee seats it set seniority aside without compunction when necessary to assure a majority for the President's program. Special committees controlled by liberals were created to deal with the Federal Reserve Bill and the constitutional amendment for women's suffrage. The reorganization of the Senate had been accomplished in a way paralleling the overturn of Cannonism in the House by the practical abolition of the seniority rule in making up committees.

"The Senate," said Kern, "will be Democratic not only in name but in practical results."[9]

The next step was the adoption of new rules which gave a majority of a committee authority to call meetings and dispose of pending business, a power hitherto vested in the chairman. They placed in the majority power to name subcommittees, to select conferees to meet with Representatives of the House and generally democratized Senate procedures. The result was to eliminate the power of a committee chairman to postpone action indefinitely on any bill which did not appeal to him. Committee chairmen became little more than presiding officers.

Yet these revolutionary changes were accomplished with a minimum of friction. Within a week the Democratic majority presented a solid front. Party discipline was maintained through the caucus.

The result is history. The Underwood Tariff, the Federal Reserve Act, the Federal Trade Commission Act, the Clayton Antitrust Act, the Seaman's Act, the Child Labor Law were among the major pieces of legislation adopted in a session lasting 567 days. The Congress met continuously from April 7, 1913, to October 24, 1914.* During that session and indeed for several years thereafter democracy with a small "d" and cooperation with the President of the United States combined to produce a legislative record in both houses worthy of a great nation.

There was another important Senatorial reform during Wilson's day. In 1917 a controversy arose over the President's request for legislation authorizing him to arm American merchant ships. They were being sunk with considerable regularity by German submarines imposing a blockade on Great Britain to starve her into submission. Popular opinion was outraged at the German action and strongly in support of the President.

There was at that time no way of terminating debate in the Senate in order to bring a bill to a vote. Twelve "peace" Senators were determined to hold off the vote on the President's bill by talking continuously until adjournment. And this they did, to the fury of the President, despite the fact that seventy-five Senators signed a declaration that they were prepared to vote for the bill if given an opportunity.

President Wilson denounced in words now famous "the little band of willful men" who had frustrated the national will. He described the Senate of the United States as "the only legislative body in the world which is unable to act when its majority is ready for action." Then he proceeded to arm the merchant ships anyway by executive action under his constitutional powers as Commander in Chief after Congress had adjourned.

* There was no adjournment at the end of 1913.

But this was not good enough for Senator Thomas J. Walsh of Montana, who was later to become, shortly before his death, Franklin Roosevelt's first Attorney General. Walsh was determined not to permit the blot on the Senate's reputation to remain uncleansed. At the beginning of the Sixty-fifth Congress in April of 1917 he brought out of committee the first cloture rule in the Senate since the "motion for the previous question" had been abandoned in 1807. The seventy-five Senators who had been denied an opportunity to vote, most of whom continued to serve in the succeeding Congress, were in a mood for action. Walsh pressed to passage the most celebrated of all Senate rules, Rule XXII. It provided that two-thirds of the whole Senate could, by a vote taken without debate, on a petition filed by sixteen Senators, impose cloture and require a vote on any pending matter after each Senator had spoken for no more than an hour.

The Kern and Walsh reforms were the only occasions during more than one hundred and fifty years, from the founding of the Republic to the end of World War II, that the United States Senate bestirred itself sufficiently to make action possible when action was needed, and to render a Presidential program immune from sabotage by a small minority.

Vice President Charles G. Dawes made an earnest and logical, but wholly unsuccessful, effort to persuade the Senate to modernize its rules in 1925. The bipartisan Establishment of that day, which had moved back into power with the election of ex-Senator Warren G. Harding to the Presidency in 1920, laughed him into silence.

A generation later, after a depression, a Second World War and the emergence of the United States as the leader of the free world, there was another round of Congressional reform. A public demand arose for the modernization of Congressional rules, procedures, precedents and customs. It found two staunch supporters in Senator Robert M. La Follette, Jr., Wisconsin Progressive Republican, and Representative A. S. Mike Monroney, Oklahoma Democrat. With the blessing of the majority and minority leadership they steered through both houses in 1945 a concurrent resolution creating a joint Congressional committee of twelve (six from each House, evenly divided as to party) authorized to "make a full and complete study of the organization and operations of the Congress and to recommend improvements to enable it better to meet its obligations under the Constitution." Unfortunately, the charge to the committee excluded consideration of the rules, practices, procedures and floor action of either House. This exception eliminated the area where reform was most needed, but did leave the committee considerable scope in other directions. Members of the committee who signed the report and still serve in Congress are Senator Richard Russell of Georgia, Senator Everett Dirksen of Illinois, then a Representative, Senator Monroney, then a Representative, and Representative Claude Pepper of Florida, then a Senator.

As the committee stated in its practically unanimous report,*

> Our Committee was created in response to a widespread Congressional and public belief that a grave constitutional crisis exists in which the fate of representative government itself is at stake. The course of events has created a breach between

* Representative Thomas J. Lane of Massachusetts dissented from the otherwise unanimous recommendation that Congressional salaries should be raised.

government and the people. Behind our inherited Constitutional pattern, a new political order has arisen which constitutes a basic change in the Federal design.

Strong words, and true.

After an extended and comprehensive series of hearings the committee recommended a number of drastic reforms, many but not all of which were enacted into law in the Legislative Reorganization Act of 1946. The committee structure of both Houses was simplified. Unnecessary committees were abolished, overlapping jurisdiction was eliminated. The staffs of committees and individual Congressmen were strengthened. The Office of Legislative Counsel, which renders invaluable service in the drafting of bills, was enlarged. The power of committee chairmen to pickle bills was to some small extent curtailed. Lobbies were required to register and thus become visible.

But some of the most important recommendations of the committee were either defeated on the floor or not pressed to a record vote because of the bipartisan opposition of the Establishment of that day.

Thus the committee had referred to the "need for the formal expression within the Congress of the main policies of the majority and minority parties." Its recommendations called for some mechanism which could bring about more party accountability for pledges made in the national platforms of the major political parties.

The committee wanted each House to create at the beginning of each Congress a majority and minority policy committee made up of seven members, membership thereon to expire at the end of each Congress, since the policy committees were to be representative of the members of that particular Congress only. The two policy committees of the party holding the White House were to meet regularly with the President and his principal advisers to improve relationships between the executive and legislative branches. The group would be called the Joint Executive-Legislative Council and would be created and financed by statute. "By giving Congressional leaders a part in the formulation of policy, instead of calling upon them to enact programs prepared without their participation, better cooperation can be obtained."

But that was as far as it got. The Establishment was not interested in responsible cooperation with the executive to enact the platform of the winning political party. The last thing it wanted was a move toward national party responsibility.

Another series of recommendations of the La Follette-Monroney Committee dealt with the more efficient use of Congressional time. "Prolonged sessions resulting from improper organization of the [Congressional] work load," said the committee report, " . . . are keeping members away from the people they represent for more than 10 to 11 months out of every year."

The committee recommended that Congress "provide for a regular recess period at the close of each fiscal year to insure the return of members to their constituents at definite intervals each year . . . their return is not required for 'fence building' or 'vacations' but is in fact the essence of representative democracy."

Congress acted on this recommendation. The Reorganization Act of 1946 requires that Congress shall go home on July 31 of each year, having passed all appropriations bills and other necessary legislation. Yet in the years I have served in the Senate we have never yet obeyed the law we passed to discipline ourselves. And, as every law student knows, you can't mandamus a legislature. Both the courts and the President are powerless to make us keep faith with ourselves.

A third recommendation of the La Follette-Monroney Committee dealt with fiscal control. It was proposed that the Congress, within sixty days of convening, should act on a joint resolution, recommended by joint action of the two Appropriations Committees, the Ways and Means Committee of the House and the Finance Committee of the Senate, fixing a maximum sum for appropriations for the next fiscal year. If this sum should be exceeded, all appropriations would be cut back pro-rata to bring them within the agreed total unless the Congress should by resolution authorize an increase in the national debt in the amount of the excess of appropriations over estimated revenues. This reform was enacted but never became meaningful. A number of other sound fiscal reforms were recommended by the committee. All were stricken from the bill when it came to the floor for action.

The matters discussed by the committee, but with respect to which no recommendations were made, are also of considerable interest. They included: (1) seniority of committee chairmen; (2) the powers of the House Rules Committee; (3) establishing a regular procedure for the questioning on the floor of the heads of executive departments; (4) limitation of debate in the Senate.

Most of the study committee's recommendations survived the scutiny of the Senate Special Legislative Committee, chaired by Senator La Follette, which reported the bill to the floor. The language of this Legislative Committee Report is also prophetic:

> Devised to handle the simpler task of an earlier day, our legislative machinery and procedures are by common consent no longer competent to cope satisfactorily with the grave and complex problems of the post-war world. They must be modernized if we are to avoid an imminent breakdown of the legislative branch of the national government. . . . Democracy itself is in grave danger of disintegrating from internal dissensions under the terrific pressures of the post-war world.

So it is again today.

NOTES

1. Franklin L. Burdette, *Filibustering in the Senate* (Princeton: Princeton University Press, 1940), pp. 224–25.
2. Max Lerner, *America as a Civilization* (New York: Simon & Schuster, 1957), p. 416.
3. Henry Steele Commager, "To Form a Much Less Perfect Union," *New York Times Magazine*, July 14, 1963, pp. 40, 42.
4. George B. Galloway, *History of the House of Representatives* (New York: Thomas Y. Crowell Co., 1961), p. 51.
5. This account is drawn from Galloway, *op. cit.*, pp. 52–53, and Neil MacNeil, *The Forge of Democracy* (New York: McKay, 1963), pp. 51 ff.
6. This colloquy is reported in Samuel W. McCall, *The Life of Thomas Brackett Reed* (Boston: Houghton Mifflin, 1914), pp. 167–68.
7. Quoted by MacNeil, *op. cit.*, from George Rothwell Brown, *The Leadership of Congress* (Indianapolis: Bobbs-Merrill, 1922), p. 88.
8. This account is taken largely from Galloway, *op. cit.*, pp. 54 ff.
9. Claude G. Bowers, *The Life of John Worth Kern* (Indianapolis: The Hollenbeck Press, 1918), p. 293.

SELECTED BIBLIOGRAPHY

Binkley, Wilfred E. *President and Congress.* 3rd rev. ed. New York: Vintage Books, 1962. Analyzes the constitutional basis of the relation between Congress and the President. Also examines the historical development of this relationship from the first administration of George Washington to the second Eisenhower administration.

Bolling, Richard W. *House Out of Order.* New York: Dutton, 1965. Argues that although Congress is not a rubber stamp, both structural and procedural reforms are necessary if the national legislature is to be an effective, democratic institution. Concludes that as the executive becomes more assertive, it is imperative for Congress to act effectively.

Bone, Hugh A. "Introduction to the Senate Policy Committees," *American Political Science Review,* 50 (June 1956), 339–359. Describes the development of the policy committees of the parties in the Senate after the passage of the Legislative Reorganization Act of 1946. Also examines some of the differences between the operations of the Democratic and Republican committees.

Burns, James MacGregor. *Congress on Trial.* New York: Harper, 1949. Questions the role of Congress as an effective instrument of democracy. Argues that the present age of crises requires the radical transformation of Congress and other governmental institutions. Especially criticizes the fragmented and irresponsible party system in Congress.

Cummings, Milton C. *Congressmen and the Electorate.* New York: Free Press, 1966. A study of congressional elections between 1920 and 1964. Analyzes the relationship between the congressional and presidential vote. Particularly concerned with the long-run trends in electoral politics in Congress and their implications for the party system.

Dahl, Robert A. *Congress and Foreign Policy.* New York: Harcourt Brace Jovanovich, 1950. Argues that Congress is remarkably ill-suited to exercise intelligent control over the nation's foreign policy in an age of crisis. Suggests a number of criteria for evaluating the role of Congress in making foreign policy.

Fenno, Richard F. *The Power of the Purse.* Boston: Little, Brown, 1966. Describes the appropriations process in Congress. Examines the relations between the appropriations committees and their respective houses and the executive agencies with which they interact. Argues that the appropriations process is the key to legislative control of the executive.

Fiellin, Alan. "Functions of Informal Groups in Legislative Institutions," *Journal of Politics,* 24 (February 1962), 72–91. Describes the role that state delegations play as informal groups in the House of Representatives.

Froman, Lewis A., Jr. *Congressmen and Their Constituencies.* Chicago: Rand McNally, 1963. Examines the relations between congressional voting behavior and the demographic composition of representatives' districts.

———, and Randall B. Ripley. "Conditions for Party Leadership: The Case of the House Democrats," *American Political Science Review,* 59 (March 1965), 52–63. Explores the conditions under which party leadership is strong or weak in the House of Representatives.

Goodwin, George. "The Seniority System in Congress," *American Political Science Review,* 53 (June 1959), 412–436. Describes and analyzes the historical development and the operation of the seniority system. Examines the pros and cons of the seniority system in terms of its alternatives.

Gross, Bertram M. *The Legislative Struggle.* New York: McGraw-Hill, 1953. Emphasizes the need to understand Congress in terms of the participants' interactions in the legislative process: party leaders, executive agency heads, the President, and so forth. Focuses on their strategies and tactics in particular combative situations.

Huitt, Ralph K. "The Congressional Committee: A Case Study," *American Political Science Review,* 48 (June 1954), 340–365. Views the congressional committee in terms of small group dynamics. Sees committee members as active, interested participants rather than advocates of the general interest.

———. "Democratic Party Leadership in the Senate," *American Political Science*

Review, 55 (June 1961), 333–344. Examines the pattern of Democratic party leadership under Lyndon B. Johnson's tenure as floor leader. Critical of reformers' model of responsible party leadership for its failure to consider the congressional context.

———. "Outsider in the Senate: An Alternative Role," *American Political Science Review,* 55 (September 1961), 566–575. Argues that the outsider, or maverick, performs an acceptable, alternative role. Concludes that legislative effectiveness should be measured by more than legislative output, for Congress is more than a bill-and-resolution factory.

Jones, Charles O. "Joseph G. Cannon and Howard W. Smith: An Essay on the Limits of Leadership in the House of Representatives," *Journal of Politics,* 30 (August 1968), 617–646. Examines the conditions under which leaders of the House may exceed the limits of their authority and consequently lose supporting majorities.

———. "Representation in Congress: The Case of the House Agriculture Committee," *American Political Science Review,* 55 (June 1961), 358–367. Examines committee members' representative functions in relation to their policy constituencies. Argues that the organization of the committee's subcommittees along commodity lines encourages such interest representation.

Kofmehl, Kenneth T. *Professional Staffs of Congress.* West Lafayette, Ind.: Purdue University Press, 1962. Analyzes and describes the professional staffs in Congress following the Legislative Reorganization Act of 1946.

Matthews, Donald R. *U.S. Senators and Their World.* Chapel Hill: University of North Carolina Press, 1960. Examines and describes the members of the Senate. Contains a good description of its norms. Argues that legislative effectiveness is determined by conformity with these norms.

Miller, William E., and Donald E. Stokes. "Constituency Influences in Congress," *American Political Science Review,* 57 (March 1963), 45–56. Compares the theory of representation with an empirically derived model of representation. Indicates a strong relation between a representative's roll call votes and his perception of his constituency's attitudes on issues.

Peabody, Robert L. "Party Leadership Change in the United States House of Representatives," *American Political Science Review,* 61 (September 1967), 675–693. Explores the bases of leadership change and stability in the House.

Robinson, James A. *Congress and Foreign Policy-Making.* Homewood, Ill.: Dorsey Press, 1967. Argues that the role of Congress is primarily to amend, legitimate, or both, but not to initiate, foreign policy decisions.

———. *The House Rules Committee.* Indianapolis, Ind.: Bobbs-Merrill, 1963. Analyzes the power of the Rules Committee. Examines its historical development. Explores the conditions under which it may be an independent power center, an instrument of party leadership, or a servant of a bipartisan House majority.

Truman, David B. *The Congressional Party.* New York: Wiley, 1959. Examines the party basis of congressional behavior. Suggests that a legislator's party identification is the best predictor of his behavior. Concludes that the leadership's power is highly personal rather than institutionalized. Finds that the party leadership occupies an important mediate role.

four

The Presidency

Presidential Elections

Every fourth year millions of Americans troop to the polls to elect a President. In the villages of Vermont, the industrial slums and suburbs of New York, the farms and trading centers of Illinois, and the megalopolis of southern California, from dawn in the East until night in the West, they participate in the transfer of power from one man to another. In thousands of places—schools, libraries, churches, store fronts—Americans decide who, for the next four years, will make war or peace, spend billions on defense, welfare, and foreign aid, direct the operations of a vast bureaucracy, and do battle with Congress over myriad programs and policies. Just when and where on election night this transfer of power occurs, which vote is decisive, no one knows and few probably care. The transfer of power in a presidential election is, as Theodore White has observed, an invisible and, generally, a peaceful act. Presidential elections in the United States usually have not been attended by barricades in the streets and the use of military force. Until recently presidential election campaigns have appeared more like a carnival than a serious political contest.

On election night citizens return to their homes to witness an event that has already occurred and whose outcome is beyond their control. Watching the election returns is a national pastime that gives Americans a sense of participation in the election of a President. The drama of election night, however, is an anticlimax to the months and years of planning and campaigning that make up a presidential election. John F. Kennedy and Richard M. Nixon's race to the White House began years before as each man carefully picked his way through the maze of American electoral politics. Both men traveled thousands of miles to speak to local party activists, to garner state convention votes, and to galvanize the masses of voters. Kennedy and Nixon pursued delegates anxiously in an attempt to hold their coalitions together during the national conventions. They spent millions on radio, television, newspaper, and other forms of political advertising, to attract the voters' attention. Although pursuing varying strategies and traveling different routes to the President's office at 1600 Pennsylvania Avenue, their choices were dictated by the same set of facts: the American political system.

There are two features of American politics, which, more than any others, shape presidential elections—the federal system and the electoral college. The federal system deliberately fragments power and thereby localizes presidential election contests. The electoral college determines the President's effective constituency, which is less than a national one. These two features shape both the contest for and the conduct of the presidential office. As a result of the federal structure and the electoral college, the President is somewhat less than a spokesman for the national interest. He becomes one voice, albeit more powerful than the others, among a chorus proclaiming the nation's interests.

The federal system, along with the separation of executive, legislative, and judicial power, disperses power throughout the government. In response to this highly decentralized system, American political parties themselves have become fragmented and localized. Possessing few resources with which they can reward or punish local party leaders and activists, national party spokesmen have adopted a posture of "benign neglect" toward local party organizations, which, however, control the nomination of candidates for public office and representatives to district, state, and national party conventions. While national party leaders, including the President, cannot control local organizations, the latter have often dictated presidential nominations. Furthermore, the conduct of elections in the United States is primarily a local affair; although elections are closely regulated by state laws, they are conducted by local officials. The national government imposes relatively few limitations, with the exception of recent civil rights legislation, on the conduct of elections.

Presidential hopefuls are afforded numerous pathways and multiple strategies to the White House by the fragmentation of the party and electoral systems. The presidential primary in Wisconsin, for example, is open to any registered voter without regard to party registration. In Pennsylvania, however, it is only open to registered members of a party. In sixteen states delegates to national party conventions are selected in a bewildering variety of primaries. Some are instructed to vote for the winner of the presidential primary on at least one ballot at the national convention. Others are advised, rather than required, to vote for the winner of the primary. In the remaining states, delegates to the national conventions are chosen by an equally bewildering variety of local, district, and state party meetings, primaries, and conventions. In reality, there are fifty different systems for selecting convention delegates.

The nominating process establishes a political marathon that exhausts candidates in the race to the White House; forces presidential hopefuls to spend vast sums of money to woo voters and capture convention delegates; and requires a potential President who claims to possess a national mandate to concentrate on local and, often, parochial concerns. This fragmented process also encourages internecine warfare among rival factions in state parties, for whose support presidential nominees must appeal. Furthermore, the system proliferates the number of candidates. Favorite sons and other "false" candidates are encouraged to run in order to maximize their delegation's influence at the national conventions. Although the mixed primary-convention system poses numerous problems for candidates, it virtually assures that there is no single road to the presidency; only the most adept and shrewd political strategist can make his way through the maze. Political incompetence is, therefore, usually eliminated from the contest. In order to be successful, a candidate must satisfy the demands of a broad range of groups in the party and among the electorate, which means that successful presidential candidates are most likely to represent a mediate, or moderate, political position. The complicated nature of presidential nominations reduces the possibility of both a politically incompetent candidate and a politically extreme President.

Whereas the federal system fragments party organization and localizes presidential campaigns, the electoral college narrows the President's constituency. After the national convention the presidential candidate of a party may, as Richard Nixon attempted in 1960, choose to visit all fifty states before the November election, although the electoral college system does not encourage a nationwide campaign strategy. A presidential hopeful must concentrate his campaign efforts on the large, urban, and politically marginal industrial states if he is to capture a majority of the electoral votes. Under the winner-take-all general ticket arrangement, presidential candidates are also encouraged to focus their attention on the large, politically competitive urban centers of industrial states. A candidate can, of course, pursue a strategy of capturing a larger number of the electoral votes of small states, as Nixon did in 1968, but such a strategy is fairly risky. It is probably more difficult to put together a larger and more diverse electoral constituency. Since 1932 both Democratic and Republican candidates have more often pursued the former rather than the latter strategy.

Since the 1930s radio and television have reshaped both pre- and postelection campaign strategies. Not only has the use of these media increased the cost of campaigning, but it has also shifted control from many disparate party organizations to small groups of men who surround each presidential hopeful. Today, as Aldous Huxley notes, "Orpheus has entered into an alliance with Pavlov" to package political issues and candidates. A relative unknown who has access to financial resources can be projected to the public by advertising. The importance of advertising and professional public relations men increases after the party's national convention when the two candidates attempt to capture the attention of a broader electorate. The adman's importance also increases in a close campaign, as in 1960 or 1968, for example, when a small number of undecided, but maleable, voters made the difference between defeat and victory. The advent of radio and television has created a new climate for presidential election campaigns, a climate that is conditioned by professional imagemakers.

Many of these features of presidential election campaigns also affect the conduct of postelection politics. The electoral college system, for example, continues to shape the President's relations with Congress. The President's electoral constituency may be primarily an urban, industrial one, while congressional constituencies range from the most rural (such as South Carolina) to the most urban (such as New York). These differences were greater before the Supreme Court ordered congressional redistricting in 1963. In the House of Representatives the rural areas of the nation were overrepresented due to the general shift in population toward the urban centers since the end of World War II. Differences between the electoral constituencies of the President and Congress often created serious tensions between the two branches in the postwar era. Although these tensions still exist, they probably have been mitigated by congressional redistricting.

Since 1945 numerous proposals have been introduced in Congress to reform or abandon the electoral college system. Critics of the electoral college usually have charged that the system is undemocratic, magnifies the winning candidate's popular mandate, and sometimes results in the election of minority presidents (that is, presidents who capture a majority of the electoral vote but fail to carry a popular majority). Reformers, however, usually do not consider the political consequences of their proposed change. One proposal (the Lodge-Gossett plan) "would abolish the general ticket system, by which a candidate with the popular plurality in a state is credited with all of the state's electoral votes." Under this plan, as Ruth C. Silva has noted, "the electoral votes of each state would be apportioned among the candidates in exact ratio to the popular vote." Professor Silva, who has applied the Lodge-Gossett formula to all presidential elections between 1880 and 1948, concludes that the plan would have been to the advantage of the Democrats. Another proposed reform (the Mundt plan) might favor the Republicans, enabling them to win "the presidency without carrying certain huge urban areas if districts were gerrymandered to favor Republicans." In any event, each of these proposed reforms would affect the balance of power within and between the two national parties. Both the Mundt and the Lodge-Gossett formulas would also change the President's constituency. Their consequences would extend beyond presidential elections to affect the whole structure of American national politics.

The electoral college is an integral part of the system of selecting a President that is acceptable to the American people. The purpose of the electoral system is not merely to select a leader; it is designed to choose a leader whose legitimacy will be accepted by millions of citizens. Presidential elections are a means to the peaceful transfer of power from one man to another. The final act in this transfer of power is the inaugural ceremony. A presidential inauguration, as Theodore White comments, "is a ceremony of state, of the visible majesty of power." If power passes invisibly from one man to the next in the dark hours of election night, the inaugural ceremony, with its color and pageantry, is the visible, symbolic ascension to power. The ceremony is deliberately conducted in public, for millions of Americans to witness on television, under the aegis of the Chief Justice of the Supreme Court, the high priest of American politics. During a few moments an ordinary man is invested with extraordinary power to make war and to keep the peace.

No sooner than this visible, symbolic act is completed, the new President must face a variety of perplexing decisions. How will he deal with the Congress? In what ways will he try to shape or modify the budget, which was prepared by his predecessor? Which campaign promises will he present to Congress as policy recommendations? How will he deal with friend and foe abroad? All these are important decisions, but they are contingent upon his choice of the three hundred or more key advisers, Cabinet secretaries, agency heads, and high-ranking diplomats that he must appoint if his programs and policies are ever to be realized. Some appointments may have already been filled between the election and the inauguration; other key positions will have to be filled immediately; still others may be deferred for days or even months. In filling these positions, the President will not only determine the character and direction of his administration, but will attempt to satisfy the wings, or factions, of his party; major interest groups; and requests from his personal friends, campaign staff, and family. Each of these key positions constitutes a scarce, nonrecurring resource that a President must exploit in order to assure his effectiveness as a national leader.

Presidential Power

A new President, as John F. Kennedy remarked after one year in office, is initially impressed with the enormous power of his office. After a while, however, he becomes aware of the numerous limitations on presidential power, or so Kennedy concluded. A new President soon discovers that he is not the only major actor in the American political system. Once again he is confronted with a basic fact of American politics: the fragmentation of power. The President's programs and policies may be frustrated by Congress through the appropriations process; his appointments to important executive positions may be delayed by the Senate; his nomination of Supreme Court justices and other judicial personnel may be rejected by a truculent Senate. Although the President may be the most visible and powerful political actor in the United States, he must deal with other actors whose power bases he does not, and cannot, control.

In addition to the Congress the President must deal with the bureaucracy of the vast executive branch. As John Kennedy, Lyndon Johnson, and Richard Nixon all learned, a President's orders are not self-executing. His directives may not be communicated to the appropriate bureaucrat; or if they are communicated, they may be misunderstood. Occasionally, a presidential appointee or a high-level civil servant may resist a President's directives. Some executive agents, the director of the Federal Bureau of Investigation or the head of the Corps of Army Engineers, for example, may be powerful in their own right; and because of their special relationships with Congress, they may be especially well insulated from presidential rewards and punishments. A new President will soon find, as Kennedy did, that he must use his resources carefully to plead, cajole, and threaten subordinates to assure their compliance with his directives. In other words, as Richard Neustadt observes, presidential power is the power to persuade others to comply with the President's orders, policies, and directives.

But the President is not alone in this struggle with the executive branch. The contest is not one between equal political actors. The *institutionalized* presidency includes a vast array of formal and informal advisers and agencies, such as the Bureau of the Budget, the National Security Council, and the Council of Economic Advisers, which surround the President in the Executive Office and are the arms with which he reaches out in his attempts to control the executive branch. Through the Bureau of the Budget, for example, the President attempts to gain control over the programs of agencies by cutting or increasing their budget recommendations. He may also influence governmental programs by recommending, through the organization and management division of the Bureau of the Budget that agencies reorganize their structure. These individuals and agencies in the executive office also keep the President informed about the operation of the government, and provide political information that is an important presidential resource. A well-informed President can avoid both surprise and scandal, two features of public life that jeopardize his power, reputation, and place in history.

The institutionalized presidency offers the man in the White House the tools that he requires to perform his job. Whether and how a particular President employs these tools depends upon his style, personality, and view of the office. Although there are many differences in style and personality among the thirty-seven men who have occupied the office, two major types of Presidents can be identified. They have been described by Erwin C. Hargrove as "Presidents of Action" (such as the two Roosevelts and Wilson) and "Presidents of Restraint" (such as Taft, Hoover, and Eisenhower). The Presidents of Action had a personal need to exercise power, to identify themselves intensely with the institution, and, generally, to expand the President's power and office. The two Roosevelts used presidential power aggressively in the pursuit of national policy. By contrast, the Presidents of Restraint were insensitive to the personal need for power, regarded themselves as presiding magistrates or dispassionate rulers, and found the exercise of power for personal advantage distasteful. Taft, Hoover, and Eisenhower were restrained in their exercise of power, ever mindful of the coordinate role of the Congress and the Supreme Court.

A President's style and personality also determine his use of other existing institutions such as the Cabinet. The President's Cabinet, which includes the heads of major executive departments and agencies, is not comparable to the British Cabinet system of government. The members of the President's Cabinet share no collective responsibility; that is, they are not directly responsible to the majority party in Congress. The Cabinet is an informal institution that is neither constitutionally nor statutorily prescribed or defined; how the President employs it is largely a matter of style. Eisenhower established the post of Cabinet secretary, formalized Cabinet meetings, and attempted to use the Cabinet to exchange information and coordinate the administration's program. Kennedy informalized it and frequently invited nonmembers in to keep him better informed. Franklin Roosevelt often encouraged controversy among his officers in order to maximize his freedom of choice and action. There are, however, limitations to its utility that are beyond the President's control. The Cabinet meeting is not really a place in which the free exchange of information occurs. Its members sometimes do not trust each other, often jealously guard information from each other, and are loathe to talk freely to other Cabinet officers who do not understand their problems. Thus, its utility to the President is limited, and it is not an especially useful mechanism for gathering information, coordinating programs, and promoting presidential control over policy.

In addition to the problems posed by the regular line agencies, the President must also reach out to control the so-called independent regulatory agencies (such as the Federal Communications Commission, the Federal Aviation Agency, and the Securities and Exchange Commission), whose directors or boards of governors are appointed by Congress for fixed terms. Not being entirely responsible to the President, they are quasi-independent judicial, legislative, and executive agencies. Although the President nominates their directors, he does not have the power to remove them from office. At times the agencies may pursue policies directly opposed to the President's. During the Kennedy administration, for example, the Department of Justice opposed the merger of the Pennsylvania and the New York Central railroads (as a violation of the antitrust acts), while the Interstate Commerce Commission gave its approval to the plan. When such conflicts occur, the President may intervene personally to resolve interagency disputes, or, occasionally, interagency battles are resolved by the courts, if a judicially cognizable conflict exists. The independent regulatory agency structure restricts a President's power or influence over public policy, sometimes frustrates his programs and political ambitions, and frequently promotes inaction in the American political system.

As John F. Kennedy learned during his brief tenure, a President may capture the nation's imagination with sparkling rhetoric and at the same time fail to realize "national goals" and ambitions because he is unable to win support in Congress or is frustrated by the many features of American politics that limit his power to make policy. The limited presidency, an eighteenth-century creation, was designed to protect and promote a liberal society. It was not fashioned for a complex, industrial order in which a cacophony of voices competes for the President's ear.

A major problem confronting the American people and their President is the integration of a large, complex, and diverse polity. In an age of more or less permanent crises, as Wilfred Binkley has observed, "the American people are rather reduced to the necessity of hoping for the good luck of getting a competent leader along with a major crisis." Some observers and would-be reformers have called for more explicit means of integration, such as the establishment of presidential and Cabinet responsibility to the Congress. Others, including Binkley, have urged strong presidential leadership as a means of dealing with and avoiding national crises. And a few, having concluded that we have the best of all possible types of presidencies, are willing to rely upon luck to produce "Presidents with capacity for leadership," which "ought not to be unwelcome even in 'normal' times."

In the following selections several historians and political scientists examine the nature of presidential elections, the President's power and style, the institutionalized presidency, and presidential policy making.

33

A Bad Idea Whose Time Has Come

IRVING KRISTOL AND PAUL WEAVER

In the excerpt that follows, Irving Kristol and Paul Weaver discuss the current proposal for direct, popular election of the President, finding it to be a simple-minded, vulgarized, and trivialized distortion of the democratic ideal of popular sovereignty. They argue that direct popular election of the President will destroy incentives supporting the two-party system; diminish the legitimacy of presidential succession; and prove to be deleterious to federalism, political moderation, and presidential leadership. The authors ask for, but do not expect, a more careful examination of this "reform," anticipating that the consequences of it might be a constitutional revolution of the first magnitude.

Kristol, Henry R. Luce Professor of Urban Values at New York University, is editor of The Public Interest, *a journal of contemporary urban political, social, and economic problems. He has served as a member of the Rand Corporation Study Group on Urban Problems, the Vice-President's Task Force on Income Maintenance, President-elect Nixon's Task Force on Voluntary Urban Action, and the Conference on the Future of New York City, among other committees. He is the author of numerous articles in* The New York Times Magazine, Harper's, Atlantic Monthly, Foreign Affairs, The Public Interest, New York Review of Books, *and the* Yale Review. *Paul H. Weaver, Assistant Professor of Government at Harvard University, is also the author of articles in* The New York Times Magazine, The Public Interest, *and the* New Leader.

It now seems very likely that, before too many years have passed, this nation will be electing its President in a new way. The House of Representatives has recently approved, by the overwhelming margin of 339 to 70 votes, a constitutional amendment that would abolish the Electoral College and replace it with a system of direct election by the people as a whole. Endorsed by President Nixon and former President Johnson, by the American Bar Association, by most of the mass media, and supported (according to the polls) by roughly four-fifths of the American people, the amendment seems to have an excellent chance of getting Senate approval—if not immediately, then eventually—and a better than even chance of ratification by the necessary three-quarters of the State Legislatures. Direct election of the President looks very much like one of those ideas whose time has come.

It is also one of those ideas which, if realized, is bound to have far-reaching implications for the nature of the American democracy. One cannot casually tinker with the political origins of the nation's most important governmental institution without also affecting its powers, its ideological complexion, and the quality of its leadership. Under these circumstances, one would expect the American people to be engaged in a lively discussion of the pros and cons—the potential costs and benefits—of the direct-election amendment. But such discussion is close to nonexistent. Despite the fact that constitutional reform is the chanciest kind of political surgery, this nation, on this occasion, seems willing to operate upon its Constitution without much fear or trembling. In a way, this dogmatic self-confidence is itself the most interesting, the most revealing, and the most frightening aspect of the entire episode.

To be sure, one reason for this lack of anxiety is the fact that many Americans are under the impression that the people as a whole already elect the President and that the purpose of the amendment is merely to sanction traditional—if nonconstitutional—practice. This impression is understandable, since under present arrangements things usually work out as if the people did elect their President. Yet the process by which this is worked out is itself of no little significance, even though popular opinion pays it so little heed.

For the fact is that, interposed between the people and the Presidency, there does exist—has always existed—a peculiar institution called the Electoral College, which is made up of representatives from each of the states, one elector for each Senator and Congressman. It is for state electors, not the Presidential candidates themselves, that the people vote on Election Day.[1] About six weeks after the election, the electors convene at their respective State Capitols and cast their votes for President. Whoever receives a majority of the electors' votes is President. If there is no majority, the task of selecting the President devolves upon the House of Representatives with each state delegation casting one vote and with an absolute majority (26 today) required for election.

Now, this Electoral-College system has never had a particularly firm hold on the loyalty and respect of the American people. Since 1824, when Senator Thomas Hart Benton led the first concerted movement for its abolition, more than 500 constitutional amendments have been introduced in

Congress to alter or eliminate it. Today it is widely denounced as a standing invitation to trouble and crisis; it is ridiculed as a creaky anachronism, a dusty relic of the "powdered wig and snuff-box era." Critics point out that even the Founding Fathers, who thought it up in the first place and wrote it into the Constitution, were ambivalent about it. The Constitutional Convention had a very difficult time making up its mind as to how the President would be chosen, and the device of the Electoral-College system was a compromise which few delegates found fully satisfying.

There are two major objections that have been raised against the Electoral College. The first is practical in its basis and technical in its focus. It accepts the fact that since ratification, the Electoral College has evolved from an assembly of independent electors, free to vote as they pleased, into a more or less automatic mechanism for registering the popular vote for the presidential candidates of the two major parties. It holds simply that the Electoral College is an imperfect and unreliable way of tallying the popular vote.

To begin with, it can happen that the candidate with the largest popular vote will fail to be elected President by the Electoral College. This has actually happened at least twice in our history—once in 1876, when Rutherford B. Hayes was elected although his opponent, Samuel J. Tilden, had a considerably larger popular vote, and again in 1888 when Benjamin Harrison was elected, although his opponent, Grover Cleveland, outpolled him by about 100,000 votes.[2]

In addition, it can happen that electors will not vote the way they are supposed to vote. Virtually all the men who run for the office of elector today are pledged to vote for the candidate of one party or another. In some states, such as Oklahoma, electors are even required by state law to vote for the candidate to whom they are pledged. But all such pledges and state laws have no standing in the Constitution. If an elector votes for some candidate other than the one to whom he is pledged, there is no constitutional way to invalidate that vote, and Congress must count it as cast.

Such a situation actually developed in 1968, when Dr. Lloyd Bailey of North Carolina broke his pledge to vote for Richard Nixon and cast his electoral vote for George Wallace instead. This kind of perfidy is extremely rare. Out of more than 15,000 electoral votes cast from 1824 to 1964, no more than 12 (by one interpretation of the record, only four) have gone to a candidate other than the one to whom the elector was pledged. No "faithless elector" has ever affected the outcome of a Presidential election.

A further practical objection is directed at the procedure to be followed in the case that no one receives an absolute majority in the Electoral College. If this happens, the House of Representatives then chooses a President from among the three leading candidates. The last time this happened—in 1824—there ensued an unseemly spectacle of influence-peddling and back-door-dealing which resulted in the election of John Quincy Adams, who had run a weak second to Andrew Jackson in the popular vote. Adams took office under a cloud of suspicion, and his Administration never fully recovered from the harm done to its claim to legitimacy. Having a President with a questionable claim to office was bad enough in the early 19th century; today it would be an unmitigated disaster.

There can be no doubt that these shortcomings in our current constitutional mode of electing the President are matters for authentic worry. They certainly constitute grounds for reforming the present system; but it is not so clear that they are sufficient reason for abolishing it altogether. One must take care to distinguish the defects of the present system from those which are inherent in *any* electoral system. In a very close election, after all, any method for deciding the winner is open to criticism and doubt. Indeed, it is at least arguable that, with respect to close elections, the most important virtue of a system for deciding the winner is the clarity and decisiveness with which the verdict is rendered. And, in this respect, the Electoral College is not without its value. Not only does it tend to magnify the margin of victory. It also sharply limits the number of popular votes which are likely to be challenged by the losing candidate.

A system of direct election, by contrast, invites every single vote cast in the entire nation to be challenged, a process that could take months or even years, and which would be likely to divide the nation far more deeply than would having a President who ran a close second in the popular vote.

As for the faithless elector, it is impossible to see any objection to a constitutional amendment which would nullify his potential for mischief. But there is a world of difference between enacting such a relatively minor reform of the current system and instituting direct popular election of the President. They are not at all the same thing—though, in current discussion, an awful lot of intelligent people seem to have got it into their heads that they must be the same thing.

The Electoral-College system has always been subjected to a second, more radical kind of criticism—a criticism which calls into question the justification for having any kind of Electoral College, reformed or unreformed. If the Presidency is a popular national office, the reasoning goes, the only just and logical way to elect the President is by direct popular vote. To the extent that the Electoral College introduces certain inequalities into the electoral process, it systematically distorts the popular will which is expressed on Election Day. So, instead of improving the Electoral College, the argument continues, we ought simply to abolish it altogether. This, it should be noted, is not a new opinion; its first famous exponent was none other than James Madison, who argued it before the Constitutional Convention. But in recent years its popularity has grown enormously, and today it clearly is the conventional and unthinking view of an overwhelming majority. This is something of a pity; that view really ought to be more controversial than it is.

Now, it is quite true that the current system establishes substantial inequalities among the Presidential votes of individual American citizens. First of all, there is the inequality flowing from the fact that the Constitution allocates to each state the same number of electoral votes as there are Senators and Congressmen. This gives (as the Founding Fathers intended it should) the smaller states—who have two Senators, just like the big states—a bit more "Presidential electoral power" than their population alone entitles them to. A second source of inequality is the practice, which has long prevailed in every state, of awarding the state's entire electoral vote to the winner of the popular vote in that state. This "winner-take-all" principle confers a decided advantage on the big, populous states with a large number of electoral votes.

Theoretically, it would be possible for a President to get barely more than half the popular vote in each of our 11 most populous states (which have 58 per cent of the nation's population), an additional bare majority in one small state, no votes at all in the other 38 states—and find himself declared the victor by the Electoral College while having received only something like 30 per cent of the total popular vote! Such a possibility, needless to say, is exceedingly remote in practice.

Weighing these two inequalities, one discovers that the winner-take-all principle more than compensates the larger states for the disproportionate numbers of electors allocated to the small states. This calculation, moreover, takes no account of the fact that our largest states tend to be the most evenly divided between the two parties, while our smaller states tend to give a large majority to one party or the other most of the time. The effect of this even division in the large states is to give any small, organized "swing" group—ethnic or racial minorities, the trade-union votes, etc.—an extraordinary influence over the outcome of Presidential elections.

The winner-take-all principle introduces another kind of inequality. Citizens whose opinions place them at the extremes of the ideological spectrum are almost automatically denied any hope of making their electoral weight felt in the Electoral College, even when their numbers in the nation as a whole are fairly substantial. In 1912, the Socialist candidate Eugene V. Debs received 900,000 votes, or 6 per cent of the total popular vote; in 1948, Henry Wallace won 1.2 million votes, which amounted to 2.4 per cent of the total vote. Neither received a single electoral vote. Sectional minorities, by contrast, find it much easier to register their numbers in the Electoral College. The same year Henry Wallace failed to win a single electoral vote, for example, Strom Thurmond, running for President on the States' Rights ticket, received 39 electoral votes although his popular vote was only a few thousand larger than Wallace's.

Direct election would wipe out all such disproportions and inequalities of electoral influence. Everyone would have one vote, and each vote would count equally in determining the winner of the Presidential campaign. Small states would lose their constitutional edge; big states would have no more influence than their numbers warrant, and neither would organized "swing" groups; ideological minorities would have as much electoral vigor as sectional ones. There would also be other apparent advantages. The current practice, nearly universal among Presidential hopefuls, of concentrating their personal campaign efforts in the big states would come to an end; candidates would be forced to make genuinely national campaigns. Everything then, would be fairer. Why should anyone object?

Well, there are quite a few good reasons. To see what they are, let us assume that America were to adopt the direct-election system. And now let us imagine how this change could affect the Presidency and in what way it might reshape our national politics.

Consider first the Presidential campaign itself. Under the current electoral system, candidates concentrate their time, money and personal effort in the big states. But with direct election, all this will change. A vote in California or New York will be no more valuable than a vote in Alaska or Nevada. One result will be that the cost of a Presidential campaign—it is already extremely high, around $20- or $30-million—will rise to astronomical proportions. Big money—whether the President's own or someone else's—will become even more influential in Presidential elections than it now is.

Certainly another result will be to accelerate the trend toward campaigning through television, with all that implies about the substitution of the artfulness of Madison Avenue for the more traditional arts of political persuasion. Personal appearances by candidates will undoubtedly be reduced; so, too, will candidates' knowledge of or care for special local conditions and problems. One can almost imagine that we will witness a revival of the old front-porch Presidential campaign, except that instead of staying at home, candidates will ensconce themselves in a television studio in New York from which they will rarely emerge. Everyone will have more equal "access" to the candidate and the campaign—which is to say that everyone will have equally little access to a campaign of minimal political substance. Things will be "fairer," but will they really be better?

* * *

. . . It is virtually certain that the structure of political influence in these conventions will undergo a quiet but significant shift. Under the current electoral system, party leaders from the big states possess a disproportionate share of influence. Partly this is because their states have large numbers of votes in the convention. But another reason for their influence is that no candidate can hope to win the general election without complete cooperation from party organizations in the fiercely competitive big states, which is where the outcome of the election is decided.

One may deplore the methods or opinions of political bosses in the big states and cities. Yet those who are quickest to deplore may yet be soonest moved to nostalgia. After all, every single one of our most revered recent Presidents and Presidential candidates has owed his nomination to the sponsorship of one or another boss: F.D.R. was the candidate of boss Ed Flynn; Adlai Stevenson was catapulted into the national picture by Jake Arvey, and John Kennedy would never have been nominated without Richard Daley and John Bailey.

Under a system of direct election, the big-state party leaders would still have the influence in the nominating convention that the numbers of their delegates warranted. But the cooperation of the big-state party organizations would be vastly less important than it is now. For, with direct election, a small margin of victory in a big state would have no particular significance. Accordingly, it is the party organizations in the *one-party* states that would become particularly important to a successful campaign effort. Instead of needing the cooperation of the party leaders in New York or Chicago, the Democratic candidates will especially need the help of leaders in Louisiana, in Alabama, in Mississippi, while the Republican candidates will be especially beholden to party influentials in Utah, Nebraska and other rock-ribbed Republican states where a strong get-out-the-vote effort will pay off handsomely. If this be progress, a great many progressives are going to find themselves mightily bewildered.

And here we touch on one of the most important likely consequences of direct election. The Presidency in the 20th century has been the source of almost every important piece of reform legislation enacted by our national Government. It is hard to imagine that an activist, liberal Presidency would have emerged—let alone persisted over the decades—had it not been for the preponderance of the big states under our current electoral system, and the special influence of minority groups in these big states. Public opinion polls have persistently revealed that the special brand of activism which has typified the Presidential wing of the Democratic (and, to a lesser extent, the Republican) party has never enjoyed the sustained support of a clear numerical majority of our citizens. It seems altogether probable that, under a system of direct election, the President could assume more of the character of an umpire among contending interests, less of the character of a leader who mobilizes the national will for public purposes. This is, after all, usually the case with our popularly elected mayors and governors.

One could understand, then, if liberals were opposing the direct election of the President, while conservatives were agitating for it. But, paradoxically, the situation is just the reverse. And this should give us a clue, that a high order of ideological passion is abroad in the land, and that the movement to abolish the Electoral College has a thrust that goes far beyond its ostensible purpose of modernizing an old institution.

At least as important in the long run—and important to every one of us, whether liberal or conservative—is the likely influence of direct popular election on our two-party system. We all tend to take it for granted that the two-party system is somehow sewn into the very fabric of our character as a politically "moderate" people, committed to the politics of "consensus." This is almost surely a delusion. The most important factor making for a two-party system has been the winner-take-all feature of our electoral system.

To be elected to Congress, to a state legislature, or to the Presidency, a candidate must win a plurality (or, in the case of the Presidency, a majority) on the first ballot—with the first ballot being the only ballot. A candidate who is serious about winning, therefore, has a very strong incentive to establish as broad an appeal as he can, both to his own diverse constituency and to potential defectors from the "other side." Inevitably—and this is something political scientists are nearly unanimous about—any single-member, single-ballot district system of election tends to encourage a two-party vote. After its fashion, the Electoral College has done much to insure that, despite the political fragmentation caused by division of powers and federalism, despite our racial and ethnic and regional heterogeneity, this nation as a whole has had but two major, permanent parties—disorganized and even inchoate, perhaps, but nevertheless two parties and not a mass of parties that intransigently reflect every fine color in the political spectrum.

As Prof. Alexander Bickel of the Yale Law School has eloquently argued, direct election of the President and the establishment of a runoff system (to replace the current procedure of sending an inconclusive election to the House of Representatives) will destroy many of the incentives supporting a two-party system, in which, precisely because the gulf between the parties is not too vast, the transfer of power can be accomplished without social convulsion or civil strife. The runoff provision, for example, gives every extremist leader the hope which the Electoral College's winner-take-all system denied him: that of being able, by bargaining prior to the runoff, to exert some leverage in the final choice of the President. Presidential elections are quite close, more often than not; and there would have been many occasions in the past century when, under direct election, a runoff would have been probable and bargaining with minority candidates inevitable. In contrast, under the present system, no election has been thrown into the House during all that time.

And the direct-election system will have its own direct effects on the parties. It could happen that protest candidates who are animated by the demands of conscience, and who fail to win their party's nomination, might in the name of conscience nevertheless present themselves to the electorate in the November election.

The current system makes such a strategy extremely difficult technically and, usually, suicidal politically. The direct-election method would remove the technical necessity of meeting the different requirements of each state for getting on the ballot, and it would also render the option of running in the general election, despite failing of nomination, far more appealing.

Who, for example, can doubt that, under a direct-election system, Eugene McCarthy would have run as an independent in the last general election? If he had, Humphrey's vote would certainly have been diminished sharply, and, quite possibly, Nixon's too, if to a lesser extent. George Wallace's vote, by contrast, would have been little affected. It is entirely likely that a runoff would have been necessary, and, though Wallace would not have been in the runoff, he would unquestionably have been in a position to influence—perhaps decisively—its outcome. Yet it is the supporters of Senator McCarthy who now most strongly press for direct election because of the role Wallace might have played had there been no initial majority in the Electoral College in 1968, with the election being then thrown into the House!

Among the many scholars who have studied the various methods for electing the President, the preponderant opinion is that direct election would, in the long run, fragment our party system and diminish the legitimacy of the Presidential succession. The curious thing is how people react to such predictions—or, more precisely, how they fail to react. During this past spring's hearings of the House Judiciary Committee, for example, all the arguments for and against the various modes of election were set forth, and the Congressmen appeared to understand them perfectly well.

Yet time and again, the committee members showed a profound reluctance to appreciate the importance and seriousness of the criticisms of direct Presidential election. They kept coming back to a single, abstract political dogma: one man, one vote, and each vote to be weighed in the same balance. The anticipated consequences of direct popular election seemed unable to affect their judgment; it was as if it had been divinely ordained that only one factor, only one criterion was properly involved in deciding how we, as citizens of a democracy, should elect our President.

This obsession—it can hardly be called anything else—testifies to the extent to which, in recent decades, the democratic idea has been vulgarized and trivialized. From being a complex idea, implying a complex mode of government, appropriate to a large and complex society, the idea of democracy has been debased into a simple-minded, arithmetical majoritarianism —government by adding machine. Just how far popular opinion has moved in this direction can be seen in the mythical history which our modern critics of American politics have spun about the Electoral College itself.

At the heart of this mythical history lies the belief, repeated again and again by men who ought to know better, that the Electoral College was intended to be an explicitly elitist and antidemocratic institution, an assembly of wise establishmentarians who, with cool deliberation, would make a choice too important and too difficult to be left to the common man. Just how mythical this image is can be judged from two simple facts. First, under the Constitution, the Electoral College never assembles to deliberate as a body—the electors go to their respective State Capitols, and no farther. Secondly, the Constitution leaves it to the states to decide *how* the electors are to be chosen—they can be appointed by the Governor, elected by the state legislature, or elected by the people as a whole, either as a slate, or individually, or by proportional representation, or in any other way.

Indeed, the one thing that practically all the delegates to the Constitutional Convention were clear on was that they were establishing a "popular government," or a system of representative democracy. It is true that they believed mankind to be weak and easily corrupted. But their solution to this problem was *not* peremptorily to exclude any part of the population from participation in political life. In fact, the Founding Fathers' distinctive contribution to the theory of constitutional democracy was the idea that the best way to correct for the weaknesses of human judgment was to open up the political process to every group, large and small, and that the more groups there are with access to governmental institutions, and the more various the modes of access, the wiser and more just a popular goverment would be.

But the Founders were further intent on assuring that this system of popular government would also be a system of *liberal* government—one in which the individual would enjoy massive protection against unjust infringement by government of his rights and liberties. The "popular" character of the new government ensured that no minority could easily use public power to such an end. But what of tyrannical actions taken by a temporary majority? The Convention's answer to this possibility was to divide sovereign power among various institutions so that not one but several majorities, each differently constituted, would have to concur before a law could be enacted. *That* is why the House, the Senate, and the Presidency are all elected in different ways. And *that* is the general idea —not any dark, antidemocratic intention—behind the original constitutional procedures for electing the Presidents, and it is still the effective import of those procedures, as adapted through almost two centuries' evolution, today.[3]

The persistence of a mythical history of the Electoral College shows how much we tend to reduce complex issues of government and politics into a mere catechism of simple questions and of stock, moralizing answers.

Such an approach to political life is disheartening enough in even the best of circumstances. But applied to our most important governmental institution, in a most difficult time, it is little short of scandalous. As The New Republic—which, on this issue, has been superbly intelligent (and, since its constituency is liberal to the core, courageous too)—recently remarked in an editorial:

". . . Throughout our history we have perceived other values in government than its reflection of simple majorities of the moment, which are in any event not easy to find or may be whipped up on demand. We have lived in this democracy as a rather complex sum of these values, not just as uncompromising majoritarianism. We have, since Madison, understood that people tend to act politically not so much as individuals as in groups; that they have opinions, preferences and interests which vary in intensity, thus calling for varying degrees of respect and forbearance on the part of others, even if these others constitute a majority; that majorities sometimes act rashly and even mindlessly, and may need to be given pause; that, in short, influence and even power should be distributed more widely than they would be in rigid adherence to the majoritarian principle, so that government may rest on widespread consent rather than teetering on the knife-edge of a transient 51 per cent.... Practical men interested in perfecting the American democracy are well-advised to disenthrall themselves from the romance of pure majoritarianism."

These are sensible words. But it is clear the *Zeitgeist* seems determined that they should fall on deaf ears.

NOTES

1. There is no such thing as an official "total popular vote" for the various Presidential candidates; there are only state-by-state totals for different slates of electors. Thus, when the Library of Congress supplied the House Judiciary Committee this year with the total popular vote in recent Presidential elections, the source of these statistics was not any official agency of government, but—The New York Times.
2. By one interpretation, the 1960 election was a third such occasion. In that year, Alabama elected 5 electors pledged to John F. Kennedy and 6 electors who were unpledged and who eventually voted for Senator Harry F. Byrd. If one allocates five-elevenths of the total Democratic vote in Alabama to Kennedy, instead of giving him all of the Democratic vote (as the media did), then the winner of the total popular vote in 1950 was Richard Nixon, by about 60,000 votes.
3. The fact that the present Electoral-College system is as much a product of American history as it is of the Constitution is frequently overlooked. As has been noted, neither the popular election of electors nor the winner-take-all principle is in the Constitution. The Electoral College, whatever its deficiencies, is no mere archaism.

34

Fourth Annual Message, December 3, 1860

JAMES BUCHANAN

The following selection is from President James Buchanan's Fourth Annual Message to Congress, delivered on December 3, 1860, in which he explained some of the problems posed by violations of the fugitive-slave law and presented his views on the limited scope of presidential power to deal with the crisis. Denying that the President had the power to resolve the conflict, Buchanan asked Congress to solve the problem.

* * *

Upon their [the American people's] good sense and patriotic forbearance I confess I still greatly rely. Without their aid it is beyond the power of any President, no matter what may be his own political proclivities, to restore peace and harmony among the States. Wisely limited and restrained as is his power under our Constitution and laws, he alone can accomplish but little for good or for evil on such a momentous question.

And this brings me to observe that the election of any one of our fellow-citizens to the office of President does not of itself afford just cause for dissolving the Union. This is more especially true if his election has been effected by a mere plurality, and not a majority of the people, and has resulted from transient and temporary causes, which may probably never again occur. In order to justify a re-

Reprinted from *A Compilation of the Messages and Papers of the Presidents*, edited by James D. Richardson (Washington, D.C.: Bureau of National Literature, 1897), Vol. 7, pp. 3157–3184.

sort to revolutionary resistance, the Federal Government must be guilty of "a deliberate, palpable, and dangerous exercise" of powers not granted by the Constitution. The late Presidential election, however, has been held in strict conformity with its express provisions. How, then, can the result justify a revolution to destroy this very Constitution? Reason, justice, a regard for the Constitution, all require that we shall wait for some overt and dangerous act on the part of the President elect before resorting to such a remedy. It is said, however, that the antecedents of the President elect have been sufficient to justify the fears of the South that he will attempt to invade their constitutional rights. But are such apprehensions of contingent danger in the future sufficient to justify the immediate destruction of the noblest system of government ever devised by mortals? From the very nature of his office and its high responsibilities he must necessarily be conservative. The stern duty of administering the vast and complicated concerns of this Government affords in itself a guaranty that he will not attempt any violation of a clear constitutional right.

After all, he is no more than the chief executive officer of the Government. His province is not to make but to execute the laws. . . .

* * *

The most palpable violations of constitutional duty which have yet been committed consist in the acts of different State legislatures to defeat the execution of the fugitive-slave law. It ought to be remembered, however, that for these acts neither Congress nor any President can justly be held responsible. Having been passed in violation of the Federal Constitution, they are therefore null and void. All the courts, both State and national, before whom the question has arisen have from the beginning declared the fugitive-slave law to be constitutional. . . . the fugitive-slave law has been the law of the land from the days of Washington until the present moment. Here, then, a clear case is presented in which it will be the duty of the next President, as it has been my own, to act with vigor in executing this supreme law against the conflicting enactments of State legislatures. Should he fail in the performance of this high duty, he will then have manifested a disregard of the Constitution and laws, to the great injury of the people of nearly one-half of the States of the Union. . . .

* * *

What, in the meantime, is the responsibility and true position of the Executive? He is bound by solemn oath, before God and the country, "to take care that the laws be faithfully executed," and from this obligation he can not be absolved by any human power. But what if the performance of this duty, in whole or in part, has been rendered impracticable by events over which he could have exercised no control? Such at the present moment is the case throughout the State of South Carolina so far as the laws of the United States to secure the administration of justice by means of the Federal judiciary are concerned. All the Federal officers within its limits through whose agency alone these laws can be carried into execution have already resigned. We no longer have a district judge, a district attorney, or a marshal in South Carolina. In fact, the whole machinery of the Federal Government necessary for the distribution of remedial justice among the people has been demolished, and it would be difficult, if not impossible, to replace it.

The only acts of Congress on the

statute book bearing upon this subject are those of February 28, 1795, and March 3, 1807. These authorize the President, after he shall have ascertained that the marshal, with his *posse comitatus,* is unable to execute civil or criminal process in any particular case, to call forth the militia and employ the Army and Navy to aid him in performing this service, having first by proclamation commanded the insurgents "to disperse and retire peaceably to their respective abodes within a limited time." This duty can not by possibility be performed in a State where no judicial authority exists to issue process, and where there is no marshal to execute it, and where, even if there were such an officer, the entire population would constitute one solid combination to resist him.

The bare enumeration of these provisions proves how inadequate they are without further legislation to overcome a united opposition in a single State, not to speak of other States who may place themselves in a similar attitude. Congress alone has power to decide whether the present laws can or can not be amended so as to carry out more effectually the objects. . . .

* * *

Apart from the execution of the laws, so far as this may be practicable, the Executive has no authority to decide what shall be the relations between the Federal Government and South Carolina. He has been invested with no such discretion. He possesses no power to change the relations heretofore existing between them, much less to acknowledge the independence of that State. This would be to invest a mere executive officer with the power of recognizing the dissolution of the confederacy among our thirty-three sovereign States. It bears no resemblance to the recognition of a foreign *de facto* government, involving no such responsibility. Any attempt to do this would, on his part, be a naked act of usurpation. . . .

* * *

35

Special Session Message, July 4, 1861

ABRAHAM LINCOLN

This excerpt is from President Lincoln's Special Session Message of July 4, 1861. In his message Lincoln informed the members of Congress how he had strained executive authority in his efforts to suppress the rebellion. Lincoln prefaced his enumeration of the steps he had taken without congressional authorization by posing the question of whether a republic must be either too strong for the liberties of its own people or too weak to maintain its own existence. He reported that this issue left him with no choice "but to call out the war powers of the government" to preserve the Union against force employed for its destruction.

* * *

Recurring to the action of the Government, it may be stated that at first a call was made for 75,000 militia, and rapidly following this a proclamation was issued for closing the ports of the insurrectionary districts by proceedings in the nature of blockade. So far all was believed to be strictly legal. At this point the insurrectionists announced their purpose to enter upon the practice of privateering.

Other calls were made for volunteers to serve three years unless sooner discharged, and also for large additions to the Regular Army and Navy. These measures, whether strictly legal or not, were ventured

Reprinted from *A Compilation of the Messages and Papers of the Presidents*, edited by James D. Richardson (Washington, D.C.: Bureau of National Literature, 1897), Vols. 7 and 8, pp. 3221–3232.

upon under what appeared to be a popular demand and a public necessity, trusting then, as now, that Congress would readily ratify them. It is believed that nothing has been done beyond the constitutional competency of Congress.

Soon after the first call for militia it was considered a duty to authorize the Commanding General in proper cases, according to his discretion, to suspend the privilege of the writ of *habeas corpus*, or, in other words, to arrest and detain without resort to the ordinary processes and forms of law such individuals as he might deem dangerous to the public safety. This authority has purposely been exercised but very sparingly. Nevertheless, the legality and propriety of what has been done under it are questioned, and the attention of the country has been called to the proposition that one who is sworn to "take care that the laws be faithfully executed" should not himself violate them. Of course some consideration was given to the questions of power and propriety before this matter was acted upon. The whole of the laws which were required to be faithfully executed were being resisted and failing of execution in nearly one-third of the States. Must they be allowed to finally fail of execution, even had it been perfectly clear that by the use of the means necessary to their execution some single law, made in such extreme tenderness of the citizen's liberty that practically it relieves more of the guilty than of the innocent, should to a very limited extent be violated? To state the question more directly, Are all the laws *but one* to go unexecuted, and the Government itself go to pieces lest that one be violated? Even in such a case, would not the official oath be broken if the Government should be overthrown when it was believed that disregarding the single law would tend to preserve it? But it was not believed that this question was presented. It was not believed that any law was violated. The provision of the Constitution that "the privilege of the writ of *habeas corpus* shall not be suspended unless when, in cases of rebellion or invasion, the public safety may require it" is equivalent to a provision—is a provision—that such privilege may be suspended when, in cases of rebellion or invasion, the public safety *does* require it. It was decided that we have a case of rebellion and that the public safety does require the qualified suspension of the privilege of the writ which was authorized to be made. Now it is insisted that Congress, and not the Executive, is vested with this power; but the Constitution itself is silent as to which or who is to exercise the power; and as the provision was plainly made for a dangerous emergency, it can not be believed the framers of the instrument intended that in every case the danger should run its course until Congress could be called together, the very assembling of which might be prevented, as was intended in this case, by the rebellion.

No more extended argument is now offered, as an opinion at some length will probably be presented by the Attorney-General. Whether there shall be any legislation upon the subject, and, if any, what, is submitted entirely to the better judgment of Congress.

The forbearance of this Government had been so extraordinary and so long continued as to lead some foreign nations to shape their action as if they supposed the early destruction of our National Union was probable. While this on discovery gave the Executive some concern, he is now happy to say that the sovereignty and rights of the United States are now everywhere practically respected by foreign powers, and a general sympathy with the country is manifested throughout the world.

The reports of the Secretaries of the Treasury, War, and the Navy will give the information in detail deemed necessary and convenient for your deliberation and action, while the Executive and all the Departments will stand ready to supply omissions or to communicate new facts considered important for you to know.

It is now recommended that you give the legal means for making this contest a short and a decisive one; that you place at the control of the Government for the work at least 400,000 men and $400,000,000. That number of men is about one-tenth of those of proper ages within the regions where apparently *all* are willing to engage, and the sum is less than a twenty-third part of the money value owned by the men who seem ready to devote the whole. A debt of $600,000,000 *now* is a less sum per head than was the debt of our Revolution when we came out of that struggle, and the money value in the country now bears even a greater proportion to what it was *then* than does the population. Surely each man has as strong a motive *now* to *preserve* our liberties as each had *then* to *establish* them.

* * *

It was with the deepest regret that the Executive found the duty of employing the war power in defense of the Government forced upon him. He could but perform this duty or surrender the existence of the Government. No compromise by public servants could in this case be a cure; not that compromises are not often proper, but that no popular government can long survive a marked precedent that those who carry an election can only save the government from immediate destruction by giving up the main point upon which the people gave the election. The people themselves, and not their servants, can safely reverse their own deliberate decisions.

As a private citizen the Executive could not have consented that these institutions shall perish; much less could he in betrayal of so vast and so sacred a trust as these free people had confided to him. He felt that he had no moral right to shrink, nor even to count the chances of his own life, in what might follow. In full view of his great responsibility he has so far done what he has deemed his duty. You will now, according to your own judgment, perform yours. He sincerely hopes that your views and your action may so accord with his as to assure all faithful citizens who have been disturbed in their rights of a certain and speedy restoration to them under the Constitution and the laws.

And having thus chosen our course, without guile and with pure purpose, let us renew our trust in God and go forward without fear and with manly hearts.

36

Letter to A. G. Hodges

ABRAHAM LINCOLN

In this letter to A. G. Hodges dated April 4, 1864, Abraham Lincoln contends "that measures otherwise unconstitutional might become lawful by becoming indispensable to the preservation of the Constitution through the preservation of the nation."

Executive Mansion, April 4, 1864.

My dear Sir: You ask me to put in writing the substance of what I verbally said the other day in your presence, to Governor Bramlette and Senator Dixon. It was about as follows:

"I am naturally antislavery. If slavery is not wrong, nothing is wrong. I cannot remember when I did not so think and feel, and yet I have never understood that the presidency conferred upon me an unrestricted right to act officially upon this judgment and feeling. It was in the oath I took that I would, to the best of my ability, preserve, protect, and defend the Constitution of the United States. I could not take the office without taking the oath. Nor was it my view that I might take an oath to get power, and break the oath in using the power. I understand, too, that in ordinary civil administration this oath even forbade me to practically indulge my primary abstract judgment on the moral question of slavery. I had publicly declared this many times, and in many ways. And I aver that, to this day, I have done no official act in mere deference to my abstract judg-

Reprinted from *The Complete Works of Abraham Lincoln*, edited by John Nicolay and John Hay (New York: Francis G. Tandy, 1894), Vol. 10, pp. 65–68.

ment and feeling on slavery. I did understand, however, that my oath to preserve the Constitution to the best of my ability imposed upon me the duty of preserving, by every indispensable means, that government—that nation, of which that Constitution was the organic law. Was it possible to lose the nation and yet preserve the Constitution? By general law, life and limb must be protected, yet often a limb must be amputated to save a life; but a life is never wisely given to save a limb. I felt that measures otherwise unconstitutional might become lawful by becoming indispensable to the preservation of the Constitution through the preservation of the nation. Right or wrong, I assume this ground, and now avow it. I could not feel that, to the best of my ability, I had even tried to preserve the Constitution, if, to save slavery or any minor matter, I should permit the wreck of government, country, and Constitution all together. When, early in the war, General Frémont attempted military emancipation, I forbade it, because I did not then think it an indispensable necessity. When, a little later, General Cameron, then Secretary of War, suggested the arming of the blacks, I objected because I did not yet think it an indispensable necessity. When, still later, General Hunter attempted military emancipation, I again forbade it, because I did not yet think the indispensable necessity had come. When in March and May and July, 1862, I made earnest and successive appeals to the border States to favor compensated emancipation, I believed the indispensable necessity for military emancipation and arming the blacks would come unless averted by that measure. They declined the proposition, and I was, in my best judgment, driven to the alternative of either surrendering the Union, and with it the Constitution, or of laying strong hand upon the colored element. I chose the latter. In choosing it, I hoped for greater gain than loss; but of this, I was not entirely confident. More than a year of trial now shows no loss by it in our foreign relations, none in our home popular sentiment, none in our white military force—no loss by it anyhow or anywhere. On the contrary it shows a gain of quite a hundred and thirty thousand soldiers, seamen, and laborers. These are palpable facts, about which, as facts, there can be no caviling. We have the men; and we could not have had them without the measure.

"And now let any Union man who complains of the measure test himself by writing down in one line that he is for subduing the rebellion by force of arms; and in the next, that he is for taking these hundred and thirty thousand men from the Union side, and placing them where they would be but for the measure he condemns. If he cannot face his case so stated, it is only because he cannot face the truth."

I add a word which was not in the verbal conversation. In telling this tale I attempt no compliment to my own sagacity. I claim not to have controlled events, but confess plainly that events have controlled me. Now, at the end of three years' struggle, the nation's condition is not what either party, or any man, devised or expected. God alone can claim it. Whither it is tending seems plain. If God now wills the removal of a great wrong, and wills also that we of the North, as well as you of the South, shall pay fairly for our complicity in that wrong, impartial history will find therein new cause to attest and revere the justice and goodness of God.

Yours truly,

A. LINCOLN.

37

Presidential Power: The Stewardship Theory

THEODORE ROOSEVELT

In the following excerpt from his Autobiography, *Theodore Roosevelt explains his stewardship theory of the presidency. Extending Lincoln's argument, Roosevelt asserted that it was not only the President's "right but his duty to do anything that the needs of the Nation demanded unless such action was forbidden by the Constitution or by the laws."*

* * *

The most important factor in getting the right spirit in my Administration, next to the insistence upon courage, honesty, and a genuine democracy of desire to serve the plain people, was my insistence upon the theory that the executive power was limited only by specific restrictions and prohibitions appearing in the Constitution or imposed by the Congress under its Constitutional powers. My view was that every executive officer, and above all every executive officer in high position, was a steward of the people bound actively and affirmatively to do all he could for the people, and not to content himself with the negative merit of keeping his talents undamaged in a napkin. I declined to adopt the view that what was imperatively necessary for the Nation could not be done by the President unless he could find some specific authorization to do it. My belief was that it was not only his right but his duty to do anything that the needs of the Nation demanded unless such action was forbidden by the Constitution or by the laws. Under this interpretation of executive power I did and caused to be done many things not previously done by the President and the heads of the departments. I did not usurp power, but I did greatly broaden the use of executive power. In other words, I acted for the public welfare, I acted for the common well-being of all our people, whenever and in whatever manner was necessary, unless prevented by direct constitutional or legislative prohibition.

* * *

. . . The course I followed, of regarding the executive as subject only to the people, and, under the Constitution, bound to serve the people affirmatively in cases where the Constitution does not explicitly forbid him to render the service, was substantially the course followed by both Andrew Jackson and Abraham Lincoln. Other honorable and well-meaning Presidents, such as James Buchanan, took the opposite and, as it seems to me, narrowly legalistic view that the President is the servant of Congress rather than of the people, and can do nothing, no matter how necessary it be to act, unless the Constitution explicitly commands the action. Most able lawyers who are past middle age take this view, and so do large numbers of well-meaning, respectable citizens. My successor in office took this, the Buchanan, view of the President's powers and duties.

For example, under my Administration we found that one of the favorite methods adopted by the men desirous of stealing the public domain was to carry the decision of the Secretary of the Interior into court. By vigorously opposing such action, and only by so doing, we were able to carry out the policy of properly protecting the public domain. My successor not only took the opposite view, but recommended to Congress the passage of a bill which would have given the courts direct appellate power over the Secretary of the Interior in these land matters. . . . Fortunately, Congress declined to pass the bill. Its passage would have been a veritable calamity.

I acted on the theory that the President could at any time in his discretion withdraw from entry any of the public lands of the United States and reserve the same for forestry, for water-power sites, for irrigation, and other public purposes. Without such action it would have been impossible to stop the activity of the land thieves. No one ventured to test its legality by lawsuit. My successor, however, himself questioned it, and referred the matter to Congress. Again Congress showed its wisdom by passing a law which gave the President the power which he had long exercised, and of which my successor had shorn himself.

Perhaps the sharp difference between what may be called the Lincoln-Jackson and the Buchanan-Taft schools, in their views of the power and duties of the President, may be best illustrated by comparing the attitude of my successor toward his Secretary of the Interior, Mr. Ballinger, when the latter was accused of gross misconduct in office, with my attitude towards my chiefs of department and other subordinate officers. More than once while I was President my officials were attacked by Congress, generally because these officials did their duty well and fearlessly. In every such case I stood by the official and refused to recognize the right of Congress to interfere with me excepting by impeachment or in other Constitutional manner. On the other hand, wherever I found the officer unfit for his position, I promptly removed him, even although the most influential men in Congress fought for his retention. The Jackson-Lincoln view is that a President who is fit to do good work should be able to form his own judgment as to his own subordinates, and, above all, of the subordinates standing highest and in closest and most intimate touch with him. My secretaries and their subordinates were responsible to me, and I accepted the responsibility for all their deeds. As long as they were satisfactory to me I stood by them against every critic or assailant, within or without Congress; and as for getting Congress to make up my mind for me about them, the thought would have been inconceivable to me. My successor took the opposite, or Buchanan, view when he permitted and requested Congress to pass judgment on the charges made against Mr. Ballinger as an executive officer. These charges were made to the President; the President had the facts before him and could get at them at any time, and he alone had power to act if the charges were true. However, he permitted and requested Congress to investigate Mr. Ballinger. The party minority of the committee that investigated him, and one member of the majority, declared that the charges were well founded and that Mr. Ballinger should be removed. The other members of the majority declared the charges ill founded. The President abode by the view of the majority. Of course believers in the Jackson-Lincoln theory of the Presidency would not be content with this town meeting majority and minority method of determining by another branch of the Government what it seems the especial duty of the President himself to determine for himself in dealing with his own subordinate in his own department.

* * *

38

Limitations of the President's Powers

WILLIAM HOWARD TAFT

In this brief selection from his book Our Chief Magistrate and His Powers, *William Howard Taft directly answers Roosevelt's stewardship theory of the presidency. Taft argues that the President's powers are constrained by the Constitution and acts of Congress. The President, according to this viewpoint, may not appropriate broad powers, that is, powers not specifically defined by the Constitution.*

* * *

The true view of the Executive functions is, as I conceive it, that the President can exercise no power which cannot be fairly and reasonably traced to some specific grant of power or justly implied and included within such express grant as proper and necessary to its exercise. Such specific grant must be either in the Federal Constitution or in an act of Congress passed in pursuance thereof. There is no undefined residuum of power which he can exercise because it seems to him to be in the public interest, and there is nothing in the Neagle case and its definition of a law of the United States, or in other precedents, warranting such an inference. The grants of Executive power are necessarily in general terms in order not to embarrass the Executive within the field of action plainly marked for him, but his jurisdiction must be justified and vindicated by affirmative constitutional or statutory provision, or it

Reprinted in abridged form from *Our Chief Magistrate and His Powers* by William Howard Taft (New York: Columbia University Press, 1916), pp. 139–145, by permission of the publisher.

does not exist. There have not been wanting, however, eminent men in high public office holding a different view and who have insisted upon the necessity for an undefined residuum of Executive power in the public interest. They have not been confined to the present generation. We may learn this from the complaint of a Virginia statesman, Abel P. Upshur, a strict constructionist of the old school, who succeeded Daniel Webster as Secretary of State under President Tyler. He was aroused by Story's commentaries on the Constitution to write a monograph answering and criticizing them, and in the course of this he comments as follows on the Executive power under the Constitution:

> The most defective part of the Constitution beyond all question, is that which related to the Executive Department. It is impossible to read that instrument, without being struck with the loose and unguarded terms in which the powers and duties of the President are pointed out. So far as the legislature is concerned, the limitations of the Constitution, are, perhaps, as precise and strict as they could safely have been made; but in regard to the Executive, the Convention appears to have studiously selected such loose and general expressions, as would enable the President, by implication and construction either to neglect his duties or to enlarge his powers. *We have heard it gravely asserted in Congress that whatever power is neither legislative nor judiciary, is of course executive, and, as such, belongs to the President under the Constitution.* How far a majority of that body would have sustained a doctrine so monstrous, and so utterly at war with the whole genius of our government, it is impossible to say, but this, at least, we know, that it met with no rebuke from those who supported the particular act of Executive power, in defense of which it was urged. Be this as it may, it is a reproach to the Constitution that the Executive trust is so ill-defined, as to leave any plausible pretense even to the insane zeal of party devotion, for attributing to the President of the United States the powers of a despot; powers which are wholly unknown in any limited monarchy in the world.

The view that he takes as a result of the loose language defining the Executive powers seems exaggerated. But one must agree with him in his condemnation of the view of the Executive power which he says was advanced in Congress. In recent years there has been put forward a similar view by executive officials and to some extent acted on. Men who are not such strict constructionists of the Constitution as Mr. Upshur may well feel real concern if such views are to receive the general acquiescence. . . .

* * *

. . . Mr. Roosevelt, by way of illustrating his meaning as to the differing usefulness of Presidents, divides the Presidents into two classes, and designates them as "Lincoln Presidents" and "Buchanan Presidents." In order more fully to illustrate his division of Presidents on their merits, he places himself in the Lincoln class of Presidents, and me in the Buchanan class. The identification of Mr. Roosevelt with Mr. Lincoln might otherwise have escaped notice, because there are many differences between the two, presumably superficial, which would give the impartial student of history a different impression. It suggests a story which a friend of mine told of his little daughter Mary. As he came walking home after a business day, she ran out from the house to greet him, all aglow with the importance of what she wished to tell him. She said, "Papa, I am the best scholar in the class." The father's heart throbbed with pleasure as he inquired, "Why, Mary, you surprise me. When did the teacher tell you? This afternoon?" "Oh, no," Mary's reply was, "the teacher didn't tell me—I just noticed it myself."

My judgment is that the view of . . . Mr. Roosevelt, ascribing an undefined residuum of power to the President is an unsafe doctrine and that it might lead under emergencies to results of an arbitrary character, doing irremediable injustice to private right. The mainspring of such a view is that the Executive is charged with responsibility for the welfare of all the people in a general way, that he is to play the part of a Universal Providence and set all things right, and that anything that in his judgment will help the people he ought to do, unless he is expressly forbidden not to do it. The wide field of action that this would give to the Executive one can hardly limit. . . .

* * *

I have now concluded a review of the Executive power, and hope that I have shown that it is limited, so far as it is possible to limit such a power consistent with that discretion and promptness of action that are essential to preserve the interests of the public in times of emergency, or legislative neglect or inaction.

There is little danger to the public weal from the tyranny or reckless character of a President who is not sustained by the people. The absence of popular support will certainly in the course of two years withdraw from him the sympathetic action of at least one House of Congress, and by the control that that House has over appropriations, the Executive arm can be paralyzed, unless he resorts to a coup d'état, which means impeachment, conviction and deposition. The only danger in the action of the Executive under the present limitations and lack of limitation of his powers is when his popularity is such that he can be sure of the support of the electorate and therefore of Congress, and when the majority in the legislative halls respond with alacrity and sycophancy to his will. This condition cannot probably be long continued. We have had Presidents who felt the public pulse with accuracy, who played their parts upon the political stage with histrionic genius and commanded the people almost as if they were an army and the President their Commander-in-Chief. Yet in all these cases, the good sense of the people has ultimately prevailed and no danger has been done to our political structure and the reign of law has continued. In such times when the Executive power seems to be all prevailing, there have always been men in this free and intelligent people of ours, who apparently courting political humiliation and disaster have registered protest against this undue Executive domination and this use of the Executive power and popular support to perpetuate itself.

The cry of Executive domination is often entirely unjustified, as when the President's commanding influence only grows out of a proper cohesion of a party and its recognition of the necessity for political leadership; but the fact that Executive domination is regarded as a useful ground for attack upon a successful administration, even when there is no ground for it, is itself proof of the dependence we may properly place upon the sanity and clear perceptions of the people in avoiding its baneful effects when there is real danger. Even if a vicious precedent is set by the Executive, and injustice done, it does not have the same bad effect that an improper precedent of a court may have, for one President does not consider himself bound by the policies or constitutional views of his predecessors.

The Constitution does give the President wide discretion and great power, and it ought to do so. It calls from him activity and energy to see that within his proper sphere he does what his great responsibilities and opportunities require. He is no figurehead, and it is entirely proper that an energetic and active clear-sighted people, who, when they have work to do, wish it done well, should be willing to rely upon their judgment in selecting their Chief Agent, and having selected him, should entrust to him all the power needed to carry out their governmental purpose, great as it may be.

39

Presidents of Action and Presidents of Restraint

ERWIN C. HARGROVE

In the following selection, Erwin C. Hargrove compares three "Presidents of Action" (the two Roosevelts and Wilson) with three "Presidents of Restraint" (Taft, Hoover, and Eisenhower) in terms of their drives, skills, and values. He develops several generalizations about each type of "political personality" and style of leadership for the presidential office. Hargrove's model of political personality, which includes four variables (psychological needs, mental traits, values, and "ego integration"), is used as a framework of analysis of biographical materials and the political subculture to which the particular President belonged. His analysis also provides a basis to evaluate a President's impact on the office and the times in which he lived.

Hargrove, Professor of Political Science at Brown University, has been a reporter for the Baltimore Sun *and a Washington correspondent. He has contributed articles to scholarly journals, including the* Canadian Journal of Economics and Political Science.

[I]

This . . . is a study of the men who have shaped the modern Presidency. The focus is on their personalities and skills as they have helped or hindered

Presidential leadership. Presidents of Action are compared to Presidents of Restraint in terms of the personal drives, skills, and values they have brought to the office, and conclusions are drawn about the consequences of each type of "political personality" and style of leadership for the office.

The three Presidents of Action who have most shaped the Presidential office are the two Roosevelts and Wilson. Each, in his own way, greatly amplified Presidential power. Each was a political artist whose deepest needs and talents were served by a political career. Presidents Truman, Kennedy, and Johnson are considered briefly as Presidents in this tradition.

The Presidents of Restraint—Taft, Hoover, and Eisenhower—went to the White House from careers as nonpolitical technicians. They did not put a high value on personal or Presidential power, and in the course of their careers they did not develop political skills. Their values were hostile to strong Presidential leadership, to the manipulation of others, to popular emotion, and to politics in general.

American political culture contains two important and conflicting views of the Presidency. The Whig theory, seen in the Presidents of Restraint, is almost an anti-theory, for it preaches that the incumbent should deliberately exercise restraint on his power and influence. It was shaped out of a fear of a strong, popular Presidency. This tradition does not value political skill in the President but rather stresses rectitude and dignity.

The irony is that such a view of the Presidency impedes an effective discharge of Presidential tasks. A sense of power and the willingness to search for it and use it with political skill are essential today.

The other tradition calls for strong Presidential leadership, for the Presidency to be the agency of popular reform. However, within this tradition the Presidents of Action who reflect it must continually do battle with those in Congress and the public who hold to the opposing model of Presidential leadership. The Presidents of Action often cause counterreactions that may eventually throw up Presidents of Restraint.

This lack of congruence between the political culture and the central political office exists in none of the other English-speaking democracies. It is in part a function of the dual nature of the Presidential office which is that of both a national symbol and a partisan leader. It also reflects differing views of the importance of government action. Progressives favor Presidential leadership and conservatives are skeptical of it.

Almost all students of the modern Presidency agree that the President today must be strong and skillful in his leadership of public opinion, of Congress, and of the bureaucracy beneath him. Skill has two components: a sensitivity to power relationships and the ability to act to maximize personal, that is, Presidential, power in each of these areas. The President has relatively little formal power to win compliance for his policies from publics, Congress, or administrators. He must find informal ways to persuade them to support him and this requires political skill.

A set of explicit norms for the conduct of each of these Presidential roles runs throughout this [essay]. The Presidents are compared and judged in terms of the capacity their political personalities and, therefore, their skills give them to play these roles.

It is assumed that the President must lead and educate public opinion. It is his chief source of power in Washington in his dealings with other holders of power. He needs technical skill, for example, speaking ability, a sense of timing, and empathy for public moods. But, more than this, he needs the ability and will to fit his policy leadership to an over-all strategy of leadership of public opinion. He must put events and policies in context and must gradually prepare the public for new departures. He must not continually lay his reputation on the line without success, but he must try to lead if he wants to be effective. If the President did not articulate the needs of the nation our democracy would be poorer.

All Presidents are now expected to be legislative leaders. Congress requires such leadership in order to be effective in its operation because it is not organized to lead. However, the internal organization and processes of Congress and the perspectives of its members, which are so different from those of the White House, present real obstacles to Presidential legislative leadership. He can use his messages, his budget, bills drafted in the executive branch, the veto power, and open appeal to the people as levers against Congress. He can also use patronage, the pork barrel, personal persuasion, accommodation and compromise, and the extraction of agreement out of collective bargaining. He must never cease to press for action and yet he cannot seem to dominate for fear of injuring Congressional pride. It is a job for a man who delights in the political process.

The President has difficulty in controlling the federal executive because of its size, variety, and complexity and the fact that much of it is independent of him in law and in fact because of long-established ties with Congress. He cannot simply issue commands and expect compliance within his own branch. He cannot count on receiving the information he needs from official channels. Officials beneath him are always tempted to go into business for themselves and to tell him only what they want him to know. In addition, they are not likely to see what he needs to know. The President must ensure that the essential decisions of state remain in his hands and he must also ensure that he receives the information necessary for such decisions, as well as seeing that the decisions are implemented once they are made. Thus, he needs as many sources of information as possible, including unofficial channels. And he must so organize his administration that the major decisions come to him and he can make his presence felt throughout bureaucracy as a galvanizing force. There is no one form of organization that will do all these things, but the test of Presidential skill in administration is his sensitivity and response to these inherent problems.

It is contended here that the first requisite for doing these tasks well is a sense of personal—and thus, Presidential—power. This sense of power is a function of "political personality," which is an amalgam of the drives, values, and traits of the leader. It is our premise that the skills of leadership are rooted in political personality.

The model of political personality used in this study contains four variables: needs, mental traits, values, and the ego, or unifying agent, which joins the first three factors into a recognizable personality. In practice these variables so interlace that they cannot be separated and this is the value of the concept of "ego integration." We avoid the error of reducing our explanations of behavior to any one factor. The personality acts as a unity.[1]

We do not see "needs." They are constructs inferred from observation of behavior. A leader who continually seeks attention in private and public life is said to have a need for attention that his dramatizing behavior serves. Needs and mental qualities, of course, fuse together but our use of the latter term is a common sense one. Does a man's mind seem to have been logical and rigorous or illogical, impressionistic and empathetic? Did he feel at home in flux or seek ordered relationships? It is obvious that mental traits may reflect needs or may have been instrumental in the development of some needs over others. This is a chicken-egg question. Certainly, mental traits serve needs and from the combination abilities develop. It is postulated that leaders seek to gratify their needs in the playing of political roles. They find some roles more congenial than others and shape roles to fit their predispositions of need, mentality, and ability.

The category of political values, or ideology, has two components: beliefs about policy and beliefs about proper behavior of the leader. Ideology is often congruent with needs and abilities. It cannot be reduced to a projection of personality needs. In the process of personal development, needs and mental traits shape abilities and all of these blend with a congenial set of values, which in turn help shape needs and mental traits. The edges of each factor are softened so that all can live together in varying degrees of comfort. The ego is the component of personality that organizes and directs these forces and mediates between them and the world. We shall assume in this study that political acts are most often a compound of several levels of political personality. It is interesting that these levels seem to reinforce each other as factors in motivation.

The choices that go into political artistry are rooted in stable predispositions, and in this sense they are intuitive as much as they are calculated. The situation helps shape the strategy and tactics of leadership but the skill in strategy or tactics is likely to be summoned forth from the reservoir of the unconscious. Most people who are quite good at something do not know why it is so. They work hard to refine their talent but the talent originally existed. Neustadt contends that the choices that go into the pursuit of Presidential "power" are a function of "perception," that is, whether or not the President is sensitive to power relationships, both potential and actual.[2] Perception is a function of personality. Some people are more sensitive to power relationships than others because of the differences in their unconscious adaptive mechanisms, implicit values, mental qualities, goals, and so forth.

In this study a biographical approach is used to describe political personality. We can see it develop in early life until a relatively consistent set of adult patterns exists. The method of analysis is to look for recurring patterns of skill and strategies of leadership and to relate them to political personality. Of course, situational and institutional factors must also be taken into account. But, Presidential personality, as an independent variable, has been neglected by political scientists, although not by historians and biographers.

This . . . is not a study of political biography for its own sake, but rather, it is an attempt to learn more about the qualities of personality required for the staggering tasks of the Presidency. The temperament and skills of one man are more important today than ever before. If we begin our analyses with consideration of the characters of private men, we finish with conclusions about their impact on public office.

In a sense, the Presidential office is shapeless, and each President fills it out to suit himself. Personality is certainly the chief factor. But, in another sense, the office has continuity in that succeeding Presidents make permanent contributions to the institution itself in the form of precedents of behavior or new powers. This has been particularly true of the Presidents of Action. Theodore Roosevelt created the modern Presidency as an agency of popular government. Woodrow Wilson institutionalized the President as chief legislator. Franklin D. Roosevelt provided the model of the President as an administrator of a giant bureaucracy. The Presidents of Restraint were generally reluctant to create these kinds of precedents. By holding to the Whig theory they fought against the tendency to make the office an agency of popular reform. This is a losing fight. It raises the possibility that the Presidency may not be a congenial place for American conservatives.

There are three levels of analysis and comparison in this [essay]. We compare political personalities and assess the consequences of different kinds of personalities for style and skill. In this regard we also compare political subcultures, since each set of leaders embodies a different subculture. We compare these types of political personality in the playing of Presidential roles, and again assess the consequences, and, finally, we assess the impact of each type on the Presidency itself.

* * *

[II]

The two Roosevelts and Wilson shaped the modern Presidency and we shall look at the institutional contributions of each in detail. Our theme here is the qualities they had in common that made them political "masters." Their political skill was the primary factor in their policy achievements and their impact on the Presidency. They developed a tradition of skill and a set of ground rules for Presidential effectiveness that have greatly influenced succeeding Presidents of Action. In fact, they influenced each other. Wilson took his ideas of strong Presidential leadership, in part, from the example of Theodore Roosevelt in office. Franklin Roosevelt admired and copied both "Uncle Ted" and Wilson, whom he served. What characteristics of political personality did they have in common?

1. They were driven by the need for personal power and this was the initial reason for their choice of a political career. In each man the quality of the need to influence and direct others was different but this kind of drive is essential to great political skill.

2. Their needs seem to have stimulated them to develop their abilities to influence others. In their youth and early careers they gradually shaped themselves into effective leaders in response, not to their policy ideals, but to their inner imperatives, that is, the needs for power and attention.

The developing relationships between needs, natural abilities, and skills of leadership are charted in each chapter. An example of this interaction would be Theodore Roosevelt's dramatizing ability. A need for attention seemed to be at the root of this skill, and out of that need acting and self-dramatizing talents were developed. Perhaps the talents stimulated the need. This is not important. What is important is that this private skill was eventually used for political goals. Roosevelt served his own need for attention while he served his goals for achievement. We can see in each of these men that beneath the threshold of public action there was a second level of private need, that is, to influence others, that was always pushing, reinforcing, and guiding their public actions. The private need increased their public effectiveness. These private needs cannot be explained by their public roles. They antedated these roles and reinforced them.

3. Mental traits, another component of political personality, also contributed to political skill. In each case, qualities of mind and of temperament fitted together, for example, Franklin Roosevelt was empathetic and intuitive in his human relations and flexible and an empiricist in his mode of thinking. . . . this congruence was important for the performance of Presidential roles. Needs and drives and intellectual qualities gave these men a sensitivity to power relationships.

4. Values gave them a sense of purpose in the Presidency that increased their effectiveness as leaders. Technical skill alone would not have been enough to account for their policy achievements. They came to office in periods of American history when there was need for national innovation and a redefinition of national goals. All were equal to the task. The fact that they were all "cultural outsiders" to American business civilization may help to explain their role as reformers. The two Roosevelts were aristocrats with roots in a preindustrial way of life. Wilson, a Southerner by birth and upbringing, and an academic by profession, was also an outsider in his era. Each man, therefore, found one variety or another of progressivism congenial because of its criticism of the values and practices of a business civilization. However, they had "conservative" roots as well. They were not radicals but rather reformers who were well equipped to be brokers between the past and future. They were also "marginal men" who lived and worked in several American worlds without being fully committed to any particular world. This gave them a perspective for the role of broker leaders.

5. Each man was favored by the times in which he became President. This was less true of Theodore Roosevelt than the other two, and his achievements were correspondingly less. But, in all three instances, skills of leadership were most effective when supported by favorable situations.

6. Their strengths were also their weaknesses. The same intense drives that sent them into political life and accounted for their skill and success were also their undoing at times. Theodore Roosevelt kept restraint on his ruder impulses while in the White House because he loved and gloried in the job. Out of office, at a relatively young age, he was unhappy and frustrated because his talents had no outlet. His subsequent bid to return to power smashed his own party and ruined his political career. Woodrow Wilson built many of his successes on his moral rigidity and refusal to compromise. But, in the fight for Senate approval of the League of Nations, his rigidity defeated him. Franklin Roosevelt's self-confidence was a source of national strength in time of crisis, but in the fight to pack the Supreme Court it betrayed him. There was a tragic flaw in the character of each of these men that was bound up with their talent. However, their darker qualities were not harmful to democratic institutions. When these drives got out of control they were self-defeating. The man and his policies suffered but American institutions

were not harmed. The most important restraints on the drive for power, in each case, were not institutional but personal. They could not have succeeded as democratic leaders without self-control and conscience and belief in democracy as a way of life.

7. The unique contribution of each man to the institution of the Presidency was a consequence of his political personality. They shaped Presidential roles in ways that were congenial to them.

* * *

[III]

Taft, Hoover, and Eisenhower had much in common. They were eminently non-political Presidents.

1. None had a drive for personal power like that seen in the Presidents of Action. Nor did they have self-dramatizing impulses. They shared a desire for order, harmony, and self-restraint.

2. Their needs stimulated them to develop abilities but they were not political abilities. Taft became a good judge, Hoover a fine engineer, and Eisenhower an able military leader. In each case, they emphasized technical skills in their pre-Presidential work and did not spend years developing the skills of moving others by speaking, bargaining, and manipulating as did the Presidents of Action. Hoover and Eisenhower did develop considerable ability to make large organizations work smoothly but this was solely administrative ability in Hoover's case and diplomatic skill in Eisenhower's case. Their philosophies of personal behavior made the manipulation of others by political skill distasteful to them.

3. Each exhibited mental qualities of order, logic, and regularity. They were good with tangible matters but poor at perceiving intangibles. They were strong in structured situations, when they could exercise some control over alternatives, but weak in unstructured situations. They did not enjoy the fast moving political process. They had little tactical skill and lacked the ability to conceive and carry out complex strategies of leadership. Because of their mental traits and character structures they could not ride many horses at once.

4. Their values complemented this style of leadership. Their conservatism often made them skeptical of the need for government action. Their Whig theory of the Presidency undermined their effectiveness in behalf of the ends they did seek. They put great emphasis on personal rectitude and the wrongness of trying to influence others by any means other than reasonable argument. Because they were technical men they overestimated the power of reason in the political process and underestimated the facts of power and conflicts of interest and values. They did not value political craftsmanship.

They were political "outsiders" unlike the Presidents of Action, but they were cultural "insiders" in the sense that they were not marginal men. Each had a stable social identity rooted in the Middle Western boyhood they experienced. They grew up in simple homogeneous environments and were trained in maxims of "Americanism," which they never really lost. This was especially true of Hoover, who lived abroad for some years, and of Eisenhower, who lived within a military world. Cut off from American life in many ways, each held to the simple maxims of his youth. This was the political culture they reflected in their values and character traits. Their view of the Presidency had its roots here.

5. Taft and Hoover did not serve in times favorable to their goals or styles of leadership. Eisenhower was luckier in this regard. Taft ran up against the progressive movement and Hoover against a depression. In both cases, their conservative values and style of leadership were not what was felt to be needed in the White House. This must be taken into account when we judge their skills of leadership. Situations did not favor the exercise of the skills they did possess. Eisenhower benefitted by and helped to create the era of political good feeling in the 1950's. He saw it as one of his greatest accomplishments that he had helped to unify the nation after the harsh political warfare of the last Truman years. This was the kind of skill he valued. In this sense he was a successful President by his own lights.

6. None of these men made important contributions to the powers or operation of the Presidency. Given their Whig theory, we would not expect them to have done so. In different ways, and for varying reasons, each was reluctant to play all Presidential roles to the hilt. Just as they resisted the tide of the progressive movement in its many forms, so did they resist the trend toward greater Presidential power, which was carried along by the Presidents of Action.

* * *

[IV]

We have compared six Presidents in terms of a model of political personality and a model of Presidential roles. We have postulated norms of skill for each role and asked how personality contributed to skill. By itself a static model will not tell us about dynamic relationships. But by joining the two models we can draw out propositions about personality and skill. The number of cases reinforces the propositions if the relationships are repeated in more than one case.

These models are put forward as frameworks for the analysis of past, and perhaps present, Presidents. They may not help to predict how men will behave in office in the future. Any predictive value of our propositions is very general. They suggest the kinds of skills to expect in certain kinds of men. Perhaps political scientists can use biographical and historical case studies on a wide comparative scale to say more about the interaction of personalities, institutions, and culture. Our concern here is to say a few things about the Presidency.

Personality, Skill, and Roles

Our six subjects have been grouped into two "types," which are only labels for a number of characteristics shared by those in each grouping. Obviously all past and future Presidents will not fall within each of these types. These are relatively pure types in the Presidency. They seem to reflect strong tendencies in American political culture. But we can compare these, and other, Presidents in terms of needs, mental traits, values, and skills, and assess the consequences of different kinds of personality for office.

1. LEADERSHIP OF PUBLIC OPINION. The Presidents of Action were skillful in this role. The two Roosevelts developed dramatizing skills in initial response to the need for attention. These skills were first developed in private life and then used in politics. They had great intuitive sensitivity as to how to get and keep the attention of others in the playing of political roles. Certainly the way in which

they led public opinion reflected this sensitivity. This need was the root of their great empathy for the thoughts and moods of others, which was a staple in their political style. Wilson did not seem to have the need for self-advertisement and his political style reflected this fact. His technical skill at leading public opinion was rooted in his drive for power over the minds of men and he developed oratorical skill in response to this imperative. But his was not a dramatizing style.

Skill in leading public opinion in all three men was also a function of their larger sense of political leadership. Their conception of the Presidency and their sense of purpose in their programs were also important factors. Needs for attention and power were likewise a part of this larger set of motivations.

The Presidents of Restraint did not have the technical skills that we value in leading public opinion because none had the needs that stimulate such skills. If anything, their personalities would not permit self-dramatization. None of their pre-Presidential training encouraged them to develop such skills. Their values also were a handicap. They deprecated drama, emotion in politics, and tricks and manipulations.

Eisenhower is a possible exception to this. He was personable and popular and liked to show himself to crowds. This reflected his general liking for people and his desire to be liked. But he seems to have underestimated his ability to move people in large numbers and to have felt uncomfortable as a popular hero. His needs did not drive him to dramatize himself.

However, more important for him as well as for Taft and Hoover is the fact that none of them had very well-developed strategic ideas about how to lead public opinion. Their conception of the Presidency, their distrust of many techniques of leadership, and their resistance to popular reform suggests that this kind of President finds it most congenial to be a symbolic leader above the political strife. The hard tasks of political leadership would seem to be more congenial to those leaders who are initially propelled to win public acceptance of themselves as persons. In them this search becomes part of the fight to win acceptance for policy. In both cases, the larger conception of leadership complements needs.

2. LEGISLATIVE LEADERSHIP. The Presidents of Action possessed technical skill in leading Congress. This skill was initially rooted in their needs for personal power. Over the years, and especially in their early careers, they developed abilities that served this need. This emotional imperative can be seen as a consistent undercurrent in their legislative leadership. It was an extra incentive.

The need for power had a different quality in each case. The two Roosevelts were perhaps not so driven as Wilson and therefore they could enjoy the process of leading for its own sake without having to feel that they must win every fight. They were capable of greater flexibility than Wilson. In this sense they were more fitted for the demands of Presidential legislative leadership. Wilson's inner demands were too rigid at times. He could lead Congress effectively only in certain kinds of situations. This suggests that the need for personal power, although necessary to skill, can be so intense that it becomes self-defeating. It may be that the kind of personality seen in modern dictators such as Hitler cannot rise to the top in stable democracies. Their demands for power are too intense.

The strategic skill of the Presidents of Action was rooted in the drive for personal power, but also in their conceptions of Presidential leadership, their sense of purpose, and their experience in developing strategies by which to lead others. Needs supplied the technical skill but not the larger sense of strategy and purpose. Their values reinforced their skills. They saw themselves as midwives of history. The fact that other men accepted this as true helps to explain their success but the certainty itself was a factor in their sense of efficacy and thus in their skill.

The Presidents of Restraint were not driven by the need for personal power and therefore lacked the skills that follow from such a need. Not driven by the need for personal power and coming from technical professions, they emphasized reason, appeals to unity, and morality as the means of persuasion and they down graded manipulative leadership.

Of course their lack of a larger sense of legislative strategy was due to their conception of the Presidency, their deference to Congress, and their desire to be Presidents above the political struggle. They also put less emphasis on dominating Congress because they wanted less government action than the Presidents of Action. Taft and Eisenhower lacked a sure sense of legislative purpose, which weakened their ability to lead. Hoover's sense of purpose was so rigid as to be disabling. It is interesting that the self-defeating qualities in the leadership styles of both Hoover and Wilson seem to have been rooted in similar traits of political personality, their compulsive stubbornness, mental rigidity, and moralism.

3. ADMINISTRATIVE LEADERSHIP. The drive for personal power of the Presidents of Action informed their sense of Presidential power. As in legislative leadership, the two Roosevelts loved process for its own sake more than Wilson, who was more a prisoner of his need to dominate than they. This was a handicap to him in controlling bureaucracy.

Each of them saw administration as a political dimension, and saw that their control was by no means automatic. Thus, while their need for power gave them a sensitivity to Presidential power, their conception of the Presidency as the center of decision was the dominant and guiding factor in their style of administration.

It is not clear that there was any relationship between their policy ideals and programs and their style of administration.

The lack of need for power in the Presidents of Restraint seems to have dulled their sense of Presidential power. Hoover might seem an exception to this since he was so determined to dominate his administration. But he did not so much want power over persons as authority over organization and mastery of problems. He saw associates and subordinates as means to these ends.

As we have seen in the performance of every Presidential role, for both types, the sensitivity to and need for personal power was only one part of a larger conception of administrative leadership. Conceptions of the Presidency, a dislike of conflict, a technical background, and qualities of intellect all caused these Presidents to fail to see the political dimension of administration.

As with the Presidents of Action, there does not seem to have been any relationship between their policies and programs and their administrative style.

Real consequences follow from the administrative styles of each type of President. The two Roosevelts kept superb control over bureaucracy by treating it as a political area in which the problems of Presidential power were essentially the same as those in other areas. This strategy not only made for control but it also pushed information up to the chief executive and gave him channels by which to implement policy. Taft and Eisenhower did not keep sufficient control over bureaucracy and thus tended to deny themselves needed information and have difficulty implementing policies once they were made. Wilson and Hoover were similar in their type of administration, which was "close to the vest," and both suffered from their unwillingness to delegate authority. This common style was perhaps rooted in their common rigidity of mind and ideology. Wilson was perhaps a less effective administrator than Hoover because of his drive for power. It was almost too intense to be useful.

4. AN IDEAL TYPE OF PRESIDENT. The two Roosevelts came closest to having the kinds of political personalities that can best perform Presidential roles by the criteria that have been advanced. They needed attention and power and these needs shaped their skills of leadership. However, these needs were not so intense as to be self-defeating. They had flexible, empirical minds, which permitted them to be adaptable and resourceful in finding solutions to problems. They seldom strayed too far in their thinking from what the traffic would bear but they were always pushing to go a little beyond that point. Their conceptions of the Presidential office, as a place for political leadership, informed and guided all their efforts. They were "political men" whose image of the Presidency was of themselves in the White House. These men are rare but they are essential to effective Presidential leadership.

We can expect certain consequences for the conduct of the office from such men. They will try to lead the nation in new directions, to educate the public. They will try to dominate Congress, with varying degrees of success, depending upon general political conditions. They will increase bureaucratic vitality and innovation by their catalytic style of administration. In sum, they will serve the principal purpose that a President of Action can serve, of being a catalyst to the national life.

Truman, Kennedy, and Johnson

Our analytic models may help to understand the three most recent Presidents of Action. They have not been treated in full for several reasons. Truman was originally President by accident and would never have normally been in the office. Kennedy was not permitted a full opportunity to develop. Johnson is too recent to be judged. However, a brief look at them in terms of our categories may suggest the utility of this approach. Any propositions suggested are only hypotheses.

Harry S. Truman never wanted to be President and often yearned to return to the Senate. He had none of the psychological needs that we have tied to skill. However, he was a reader of history, an admirer of Wilson and Roosevelt, and he venerated the Presidential office. He had the conception of the Presidency of the two Roosevelts and Wilson without their skills of leadership.

Certain personal qualities reinforced this respect for Presidential power. He loved to make decisions and he was aggressive. Therefore, he organized his administration for the making of decisions and he defended Presidential prerogatives and powers against everyone. He was most successful as an administrator. Although he valued system and organization much as Eisenhower did he was more accessible and fonder of reaching out for information and decisions. Thus he was more on top of his job than was Eisenhower.

However, he did not have Roosevelt's sense of personal power stakes in the administrative process. He had no sense of strategy but made decisions as they came to him without considering their relationship to other decisions. Thus, he often let the initiatives of other men time his decisions and his political strategy suffered because of it.[3]

His manner of leading public opinion was much like his decision-making. He had no sense of grand strategy but took each case as it came. He seldom prepared the public in advance for policy departures. Of course, he had to face more crises than F. D. R., who excelled at such preparation, but Truman's episodic approach to leadership was also responsible.[4]

Cornwell finds that Truman failed to use his press conferences for educating public opinion. He made brief responses to the questions and did not voluntarily add additional information. He approached the conferences as an ordeal. Evidently, the subtle prod of a need for attention was not present in him. The same was true of his use of television. He treated it as an adjunct to radio. Of course, he had had little experience with the projecting of ideas and personality on a national stage and it was too late to learn. It is interesting that the public podium on which he was most at home was the campaign trail.

His leadership of Congress was very uneven. In general, he felt it was his duty to advocate policies in a forthright manner. If Congress did not respond, at least he had done his duty. He had no gift for elaborate legislative strategy. His forthrightness served him well when Congress could be persuaded to act, for example, in the adoption of the Marshall Plan. At times, his combativeness was to his political advantage. He drew much political benefit from his attacks on the Republican 80th Congress. But, at other times, he wrangled and fought with Congress in a petty and unnecessary manner, such as his bypassing of Congress in the decision to go into Korea and the subsequent wrangling about it, or his disregard for Congressional prerogatives in the decision to send troops to Europe. He was simply doing his duty as he saw it, but with a conspicuous lack of skill.

His view of the Presidency fitted his times. The man who liked decisions had many crucial ones to make: to drop the first atomic bomb, to rescue Berlin, to continue nuclear research, to contain Communism in Europe and Asia. He made these decisions squarely and bravely. But, on balance, he cannot be seen as politically skillful. He had half the equipment for Presidential skill, that is, the necessary conception of the office. But he was not a completely "political man" in terms of his needs and drives and his political style revealed this.

John F. Kennedy had drives for action, challenge, and excellence in achievement. He had all the ambitions of the Kennedys. But he does not seem to have had a strong need to influence or win power over others for its own sake. He was primarily interested in meeting and solving problems.

He was a rationalist, who distrusted emotion in politics and liked to apply the yardstick of reason and factual analysis against every proposal. Similarly, he tried to use reason in his persuasion of men.

His values were a blend of the skeptic and the romantic. He was skeptical of popular courage and wisdom and did not expect too much of the political process. Yet, his romantic aspect caused him to love excellence and to preach visions.

His conception of the Presidency was that of past Presidents of Action, but he does not seem to have felt that the fulfillment of the office was himself in the White House. Rather, he saw it simply as a hard but exciting job. He wanted to be in the thick of thc action and that was in the White House.

As a leader of public opinion he was not a dramatist. Although he was extremely adept at public relations techniques he seems to have had a deeply rooted disinclination to dramatize himself. He was intellectual in his approach to public opinion and was happier in the cut and thrust of the press conference than he was barnstorming.

He was afraid to carry too many issues to the public because he felt the public mood was against new departures. In this he may have been accurate. However, it is hard to imagine him as a crusader. His gift was to break the ice on many new issues, for example, civil rights and economic questions, in his cool, analytic way. He was a good catalytic leader rather than a crusader or prophet.

He never enjoyed Congress when he served in it. It was too provincial and gave too little free scope to the individual member who wanted to rise. He was a natural executive. During his administration Congress was largely unfriendly to his New Frontier legislative proposals. Much of this was not his fault. The supporting votes were too often not there. However, many observers have speculated this his heart was not in the leadership of Congress. He was more interested in foreign affairs, an area in which he had more control. He did not find Congressional personalties congenial. He was too much a rationalist to appeal to congressmen in terms of their own perspectives. He had little skill at elaborate legislative strategies. He used the standard techniques but some felt he did so too mechanically and without artistic flair. These hypotheses deserve examination in light of the suggested relationship between the ability to lead Congress and the need for personal power.

His chief strength was administration. His driving energy, rational intelligence, and conception of the Presidency served him well. He cut back the institutionalization of the White House and personally dipped into administration at many levels. He read much and sought information from many sources. Gradually, through trial and error, he developed a system of relying on key subordinates to enhance his power over key decisions. This entire system of control and implementation was shown at its very best in the efficient response of the government to the Cuban missile crisis. Kennedy ran the entire operation himself.

Kennedy as President was intelligent and energetic. His conception of the Presidency and his drive for decisions were great virtues. But perhaps his lack of the needs for attention and power were handicaps to him. This is only a hypothesis to be examined.

Lyndon Johnson seems to have wanted power and influence over others for as long as anyone can remember. He is a thoroughgoing "political man," who has worked throughout his entire career at mastering the skills by which to manipulate others. As a Congressional secretary, a Congressman, a Senator, and finally Senate majority leader, he worked at the mastery of process rather than at substantive issues.

His mind is highly flexible, operational, empirical, and sensitive to the strengths and weaknesses of others and how they can be used for his own purposes.

His values are those of consensus. As a Texan, he was a broker between the South and other regions in Congress. As President he stresses the importance of national consensus over and above American pluralism. This is an attitude that is congenial to his skills as a broker.

As Senate majority leader he dominated that chamber by a combination of hard work, bargaining ability, persuasive power, willingness to use coercive sanctions, and, perhaps most important, the ability to fit the self-interest of many senators into a common pattern on particular pieces of legislation. Of course, this involved considerable watering down of legislation and the charge was made that Johnson, the broker who liked to manipulate, sought agreement at the expense of substance.

This charge is relevant for his Presidency because he has made it clear that he hopes to be a great President, but the skeptical have asked if his methods are not too geared to the production of minimal agreement to permit great creativity or innovations? This question has yet to be answered.

He has taken an active role as leader of public opinion. He does have the ability to dramatize himself and issues, and it seems to be based on a need for attention similar to Theodore Roosevelt's. He has shown an intense hunger for popularity. In the 1964 election campaign he was badly hurt by the reports of newsmen that the crowds did not love him, and his grandstand campaigning seemed designed in part to prove that this was not the case. Often he would taunt newsmen with the facts of his success with huge crowds.

He seems to have the ability to pursue a strategy of leadership on important issues. In March, 1965, Alabama state police committed violence against civil rights demonstrators in Selma, Alabama, and the scene was recorded on television. Johnson seized that opportunity to go before Congress at night, in a televised address, and ask for a voting rights bill. He put the issue in the context of American history and ideals, identified himself with the civil rights movement, and demanded that Congress act in response to outraged public opinion. His position was a strong one because of the nature of the issue and the recent dramatic events, and he took the opportunity to use his strength to the fullest. What was important for our understanding here was his ability to use the maximum leverage on Congress and to arouse public opinion in terms of American principles. He could not have picked a better case by which to advance the cause of civil rights.

Johnson had considerable success in getting his measures through Congress after Kennedy's death, in part because the measures were those of the dead leader. He was equally successful in the 1965 legislative session because of the large increase of Northern Democrats in the 1964 election. However, in both cases, his own skill at legislative manipulation was a factor. He exploited his close and long-standing ties with Congressional leaders, and he used all the standard manipulations and coercions known. But he also gave Congress a sense of participation in the policy-making process. He knows how to flatter Congressional pride and reward Congressional loyalties. And, beyond this, he has a skill at devising compromises that unite diverse men and groups in terms of the self-interest of each. This strategy has brought the same charge that was made against Johnson's Senate majority leadership, that is, he waters down policy to get agreement.

It is too soon to evaluate Johnson as an administrator. A new President requires considerable time to find his way in his own branch. Johnson is a fiercely energetic worker who makes great demands in time, energy, and loyalty upon his staff and associates. He certainly has a sense of personal power in the Presidency. At times it is argued that his egotism is so immense that it stifles the creativity of those beneath him. It will be interesting to see if the supremely legislative man can change over to an effective administrator.

Johnson seems to have the temperament and skills to be one of the great Presidents. He has the drive for personal power that is required. Much more than either Truman or Kennedy he is a craftsman in the art of influencing men. However, this is precisely his public image and he suffers from the fact. Many people deprecate him as a mere "politician" who is lacking in the dignity necessary to a President. This is the paradox we have been discussing all along. His obvious political skill is too obvious. He does not hide it with non-political qualities as the two Roosevelts and Wilson did.

Our models have certainly not explained these three Presidents but they have perhaps provided a framework for comparative study. It is an open question whether enough can ever be known about Presidential candidates to predict their general level of skill as President. It might be interesting to try to do so.

Personality and Situation

There is a pitfall to the kind of analysis of Presidential actions that has been employed in this study. It can easily overemphasize personality as a determinant of Presidential acts and ignore situational considerations, the advice of others to Presidents, and so forth. This is more of a problem when one is trying to give all the causes of specific past actions. That has not been the central purpose of this study. Rather, we have been concerned with the existence or nonexistence of skill. Situational factors influence actions but they are executed with varying degrees of skill and over time, by many cases, one can say whether a leader is skillful or not.

However, skill will not guarantee success in terms of winning approval for one's policy. The record would indicate that the great periods of Presidential leadership have been due as much to favorable situational climates as well as to the skill of Presidents. Wilson, F. D. R., and Truman were in office at times of great popular demand for government action. They rode the tide and took the credit. Theodore Roosevelt and John Kennedy came too soon for these groundswells and their successes, despite their skills, were more modest.

It is doubtful if either Taft or Hoover could have salvaged their situations even if they had been extremely skillful. Taft was fighting against the dominant political movement of his day. Hoover was saddled with the first years of a depression at a time when there was very little knowledge about how to respond. Eisenhower was helped by the climate of his times. The public seemed to want stability and consolidation and he gave it to them. A more vigorous kind of leadership might have failed.

Therefore, it is important to remember that leaders must never be given all the credit for their successes or failures. In fact, the same set of skills may be judged more favorably at one time than another in history. One suspects that Eisenhower could have made the decisions that Truman made and thus left office with a stronger professional reputation, had he been President right after the war. However, in general it is hard to imagine the men studied here being basically different kinds of Presidents than they were, regardless of the situation.

* * *

NOTES

1. This model is drawn from Henry Murray's theory of needs, Henry A. Murray, *Explorations in Personality* (New York: Oxford University Press, 1938), and from the concept of the ego as an integrating mechanism in M. Brewster Smith, Jerome S. Bruner, and Robert W. White, *Opinions and Personality* (New York: John Wiley and Sons, 1956).
2. Richard E. Neustadt, *Presidential Power* (New York: John Wiley and Sons, Inc., 1960).
3. Neustadt, *Presidential Power*, pp. 163, 164.
4. Cornwell, *Presidential Leadership*, p. 269.

40

Two Presidential Styles: Franklin D. Roosevelt and Dwight D. Eisenhower

RICHARD E. NEUSTADT

In the following excerpt, Richard E. Neustadt compares the presidential styles of Franklin D. Roosevelt and Dwight D. Eisenhower. Roosevelt, Neustadt argues, understood and manipulated presidential power in a way that no other modern President has used the office and its powers. By viewing the "job of being President as being F.D.R.," Roosevelt was able to exercise power effectively in the pursuit of his New Deal program. In contrast to Roosevelt's personal need to exercise power, Eisenhower, according to Neustadt, remained insensitive to the President's need for power, viewing himself as a presiding magistrate, a dispassionate ruler who finds the exercise of power for personal advantage distasteful.

These two conceptions of the President's role, style, and power resulted in very different modus operandi *in the presidential office. Whereas Roosevelt continually sought conflicting advice and information, Eisenhower preferred the brief (less than a single page, if possible) memorandum as a means of keeping himself informed. Roosevelt frequently assigned the same task to several individuals in order to maximize his freedom of choice. Eisenhower established a military chief-of-staff system to facilitate decision making. The following comparison of Roosevelt's and Eisenhower's differing conceptions of the presidential role and use of power also demonstrates the important relation between a President's personality and his use of the office.*

Neustadt is Professor of Government at the John F. Kennedy School of Government, Harvard University, and Director of the Institute of Politics. He was Special Assistant to President Truman from 1950 to 1953 and was a Section Chief of the Bureau of the Budget from 1946 to 1950. Neustadt is also the author of articles in such scholarly journals as the American Political Science Review *and* The Public Interest.

* * *

Roosevelt's methods were the product of his insights, his incentives, and his confidence. No President in this century has had a sharper sense of personal power, a sense of what it is and where it comes from; none has had more hunger for it, few have had more use for it, and only one or two could match his faith in his own competence to use it. Perception and desire and self-confidence, combined, produced their own reward. No modern President has been more nearly master in the White House.

Roosevelt had a love affair with power in that place. It was an early romance and it lasted all his life. Behind his sensitivity there lay a long and relevant experience: seven years of bureaucratic free-wheeling as *the* Assistant Secretary of the Navy, four years as the Governor of New York State, a quarter-century in party politics, and with it all, an "Uncle Ted." Experience informed a temperament precisely suited to absorb what it could teach about the nature and the uses of real power in high office. For Roosevelt, this was fun. Experience also informed a fixed *intention* to possess the power of the highest office. Roosevelt always wanted the Presidency and mastery was what he wanted from it.

He wanted power for its own sake; he also wanted what it could achieve. The challenge and the fun of power lay not just in having, but in doing. His private satisfactions were enriched by public purposes and these grew more compelling as more power came his way. Political experience and private life created in him not an ideology but a decided feeling for what government should be and where its policies should lead. In terms of fixed commitments to particular solutions he was neither a "New Dealer" nor an "internationalist." But he shared with men in both of these camps a feeling of direction. And happily for him, his own sense of direction coincided, in the main, with the course of contemporary history. His purposes ran with and not against the grain of what was going to happen in his time. His sense of power thus was reinforced by his sense of direction. Unlike a Herbert Hoover he was not caught in the trap of fighting history. But neither was he caught asleep and left behind.

Roosevelt had another ground for wanting to be President: it seemed to him so fitting. The White House was for him almost a family seat and like the other Roosevelt he regarded the whole country almost as a family property. Once he became the President of the United States that sense of fitness gave him an extraordinary confidence. Roosevelt, almost alone among our Presidents, had no conception of the office to live up to; he was it. His image of the office was himself-in-office. The memoirs left by his associates agree on this if nothing else: he saw the job of being President as being F.D.R. He wanted mas-

Reprinted in abridged form from *Presidential Power: The Politics of Leadership* by Richard E. Neustadt (New York: Wiley, 1960), pp. 152–171, by permission of the publisher.

tery, projected that desire on the office and fulfilled it there with every sign of feeling he had come into his own. Self-confidence so based was bound to reinforce his sense of purpose and to guarantee reliance on his sense of power. His methods of self-help in seeking power were precisely what one would expect from such a combination of interior resources. Where Roosevelt let his channels and advisers become orderly he acted out of character.

With Eisenhower, seemingly, the case is quite the opposite. Apparently he had a sense of power and a source of confidence as unlike Roosevelt's as were the two men's methods. For Eisenhower the promotion of disorder was distinctly out of character. When he could not work through a set procedure, or when channels failed him, or when his associates quarreled openly, he grew either disheartened or enraged. As Robert Donovan attests, reactions of both sorts were characteristic of this President from his first days in office.[1] All indications are that they remained in character throughout the following years. If Eisenhower's "system" did not help him see his power stakes, the reason, basically, is that this help was not the sort he wanted. His sensitivities did not prompt him to want it and his confidence was highest when he could assure himself that *personal* advantage had no place among his aims. So, at least, it seems.

* * *

Through Eisenhower's first six years his power sense was blunt in almost the degree that F.D.R.'s was sharp. As late as 1958 he had not quite got over "shocked surprise" that orders did not carry themselves out. Apparently he could not quite absorb the notion that effective power had to be extracted out of other men's self-interest; neither did he quite absorb the notion that nobody else's interest could be wholly like his own. And he seems to have been unaware of all his natural advantages in turning different interests toward his own. By 1959 he certainly had learned to use the veto as a vantage point, but other points less obviously "constitutional" appear to have eluded him. . . .

This relative insensitivity can be explained, at least in part, by Eisenhower's background. He lacked Roosevelt's experience. Instead he had behind him the irrelevancy of an army record compiled for the most part outside Washington. As a member of his entourage once told me:

> In the Army—at least in the old Army, Eisenhower's Army—everybody knew everybody, and knew what kind of job the other fellow had, and how he was supposed to do it. . . . Responsibility was a two way flow, with the lower echelons acting in terms of what the boss wanted as laid down in his master plan—and with the boss out in the field making inspections. Here [in civil government] there's no master plan, no two way flow, and no inspections. Besides, nobody fathoms the boss's job and he's never done theirs. And they haven't been together since West Point. They don't expect to stay together, either. The Army was full of politics, sure, but it was personality politics; everybody knew the game and knew who he was playing with and for what—and it was all inside the *family*. Here, there's no family.

Coming to the White House from that background, Eisenhower also lacked Roosevelt's enjoyment. As least until his seventh year the politics of power in the Presidency never was his sport; not recreation for him; certainly not fun. Like most politically inexperienced Americans, he seems to have thought party politics a "dirty" business (which may explain why his campaigning sometimes was so disingenuous). And the politics of self-aggrandizement as Roosevelt practiced it affronted Eisenhower's sense of personal propriety. Besides, the General seems to have had mental reservations about politicians as a class, mistrusting not alone their business but their characters. To quote the private comment of another of his aides:

> It really surprises me how mad he gets and the things that upset him. . . . He won't say anything personal against a member of Congress in public, but in private he can get much madder than any "pro" would. . . . And it isn't just the Democrats; deep down I think he feels the same way about Republicans.

Robert Donovan supplies us Eisenhower's answer when it was suggested to him a few weeks before his heart attack that Congress might be called back for a special session in the fall of 1955:

> He slowly twisted his head around to [Arthur] Burns and told him painfully that the cost of a special session might be the sanity and possibly the life of one Dwight D. Eisenhower.[2]

Such comments . . . strengthen the suggestion . . . that this man neither liked the game he was engaged in nor had gained much understanding of its rules.

Yet Eisenhower was not dragged protesting to the White House and he was not kept there against his will. In 1952 he actively sought nomination; in 1956 he actively sought re-election. By the time of his first campaign his candidacy had been debated publicly and privately for some five years.[3] By the time of his second campaign he had been President for almost a full term. By then he was no longer "inexperienced." His fingertips, however, remained blunt. . . .

What kept experience from sharpening his sense of power and his taste for it? The answer, seemingly, turns on a single point: Eisenhower wanted to be President, but what he wanted from it was a far cry from what F.D.R. had wanted. Roosevelt was a politician seeking personal power; Eisenhower was a hero seeking national unity. He came to crown a reputation not to make one. He wanted to be arbiter, not master. His love was not for power but for duty—and for status. Naturally, the thing he did not seek he did not often find.

The most inhibiting effect of Eisenhower's past career lay not in its irrelevance for presidential politics but its influence upon his image of himself as President. He genuinely thought himself the hero others thought him. In Marquis Childs's chilling words, "his view of himself was the official view of the Eisenhower personality, the view seen through channels."[4] And he genuinely thought the Presidency was, or ought to be, the source of unifying, moderating influence above the struggle, on the model of George Washington—the Washington, that is to say, of legend, not of life. As Eisenhower told the press in 1955:

> . . . in the general derogatory sense you can say that, of course, I do not like politics.
>
> Now on the other hand, any man who finds himself in a position of authority where he has a very great influence in the efforts of people to work toward a peaceful—a peaceful world—toward international relationships that will eliminate or minimize the chances of war, all that sort of thing, of course, it is a fascinating business. . . .
>
> There are in this office thousands of unique opportunities to meet especially interesting people, . . . leaders in culture, in health, in governmental action, and from all over the world.
>
> There are many things about the office and the work, the work with your associates, that are, well, let's say, at least intriguing, even if at times they are very fatiguing. But they are—it is a wonderful experience.

> But the word "politics" as you use it, I think the answer to that one, would be, no, I have no great liking for that.[5]

What drew him to the Presidency and held him there, it seems, was a conception of the good man above politics, emulating the Father of his Country.

With this image before him his self-confidence was high when he took office; higher still, perhaps, when he acceded to a second term. With this to guide him he could not dispute the arguments of all his friends that his "place in the world was unique," that he had "a God-given ability for reconciling differences among . . . nations," and for "healing divisions among the American people"—and, inferentially, that he fulfilled the Presidency just by being there.[6] But the reverse side of the coin was a diminished confidence when he dealt with the hard, divisive issues forced upon a President by dates and by events. His heightened confidence in 1956, after three years of office, suggests no change of image but a trick of history. When he decided on a second term the signs abounded that to be there was enough: "peace" in Korea, prosperity at home, the "spirit of Geneva," the censure of McCarthy, all these signs and others made beneficence appear its own reward. But precisely at the moment of his re-election, history caught up with him in giant jumps: Hungary, and Suez, and George Humphrey. Others followed after.

So long as he could play the statesman and the moderator, Eisenhower's sense of fitness for his job seems to have been no less than F.D.R.'s. His confidence, like Roosevelt's, was rooted in a sense of being naturally equipped to match his image of the office. But quite unlike the Roosevelt image, Eisenhower's, seemingly, did not delineate the politician and initiator in that lonely place where no one else's interests are one's own and no one else's expertise is expert. Thus the source of his self-confidence was frequently *an enemy of his power sense* and not, as with Roosevelt, a constant ally. Only in Eisenhower's seventh year, with his last congressional campaign behind him and his re-election barred by Constitutional Amendment, did his image of himself enhance his sensitivity to power in one sphere, the sphere of congressional relations. By then he could assure himself—reportedly he did—that "politics" played no part in his reach for personal influence.

Had Eisenhower been more purposeful as President his own sense of direction might have come to the rescue of his power sense. Occasionally this seems to have occurred, but not often. His purposes were not well suited to the task. His public statements, taken altogether, show he very much desired peace-with-honor both at home and abroad. He was more or less committed to the aims of foreign policy he had inherited, and more or less committed to maintain the welfare heritage from the New Deal. He was committed, also, to his party as the safest source of leadership for the United States; he hoped to see Republicans in office after he was gone. Taken on their face, such goals as these might have sufficed a man with a keen sense of power. Eisenhower's purposes seem tangible enough to have kept such a man in motion without being so precise as to impel him down blind alleys or to turn him against history. Their very imprecision, though, made them unsuitable to sharpen a dull power sense. If anything, they dulled it more. Eisenhower often seemed to mistake generalities for concrete undertakings; when he did pursue a concrete aim he often seemed to lose sight of his broad objectives.

Throughout Eisenhower's years of office there can be no doubt that peace, in the sense of a fundamental easing of the threat of war, was the broad objective he had most in mind, the one that stirred and interested him most, the one for which he felt himself particularly fitted. The thought that he, uniquely, could contribute to the cause of peace may have decided him upon a second term. As Robert Donovan reports in tracing that decision, "Constantly Eisenhower heard this appeal repeated, sometimes expressed in terms of duty to which he seemed peculiarly responsive. 'It was this advice,' an intimate said later, 'that he took to bed with him when he was making up his mind.' "[7] Yet both before and after 1956, this personal commitment seemed to guide him only on the mountaintop of general goals; down in the valley of specific applications he often appeared lost. In 1955 he personally was at great pains to create and to gain credit for the "spirit of Geneva." But in the weeks between the summit conference and his heart attack he gave no sign of knowing what he meant to do with either the creation or the credit. In 1957, during the London disarmament talks, Eisenhower backed Dulles over Stassen on approaches to the Russians without disallowing Stassen's premises. At the same time Eisenhower moved toward a Treasury view on defense budgeting which did not square at all with Dulles's premises. That year—among others—foreign policy disputes in his Administration found the President committed and uncertain on both sides. . . . Results were somewhat similar. Even in the sphere of peace which mattered to him most, Eisenhower's purposes were frequently too general to provide a guide line for him on specific undertakings.

It is no wonder that in other spheres of policy and politics which meant far less to Eisenhower than did peace, there should have been still greater gaps between his advocacy of a general goal and his sense of direction on particulars. When broad objectives were inapplicable or in conflict—as broad objectives usually are—he was inclined to throw the issue to the experts and to follow where the men he thought most expert chose to lead. He had enormous respect for successful businessmen, the more so as their manner matched the layman's expectations; if he did not equally admire politicians, he accorded them a layman's deference in what he took to be *their* line of work. When Eisenhower dealt with the particulars of home affairs and party politics, these were the experts he inclined to follow. They took him rather far, sometimes, from his avowed objectives.

It would be a distortion of the Eisenhower record to suggest that he invariably acted in this fashion. Intermittently, specifics came to interest him, even the political specifics. Sometimes his energies and personal enthusiasm fastened upon very concrete aims. Particularly in the months before his heart attack and, again, after the Democratic landslide in 1958, one senses that his own assertiveness about specific aims was definitely on the rise. His aides report that when and as this happened he was frequently quite capable of being his own guide, of taking his direction on particulars from his own sense of where and how to go. But it appears that these excursions to the realm of the specific often disengaged his mind from general aims. The classic instance seems to be his concentration on the budget in the seventh year of his Administration.

In part, perhaps, because his time was running out; in part, perhaps, because the Democratic victories of 1958 roused his combative instincts, Eisenhower turned his mind to budget-balancing with the enthusiasm once reserved for peace alone. By 1959 he was as purposeful about his budget aim as Humphrey had been two years earlier. What Humphrey then had advocated, Eisenhower made his own: an effort to keep *future* budgets balanced by resisting new commitments and reducing those on hand; in long-run terms an effort to keep spending down so that the rising revenues from economic growth could be applied to debt and tax reduction without adding to inflationary pressures. . . . the President pursued this negative objective with a fervor—and a skill in utilizing vantage points—which made him seem a "changed man" from the hesitant performer of 1957. By the same token, though, the positive objectives that had caused his hesitations in the first year of his second term seem almost to have vanished from his mind.

Eisenhower did not change the labels on his broader aims. In 1959 he still avowed the goals of 1956: peace, prosperity, and Modern Republicanism. But the meaning of those goals was altered rather markedly when each became identified with holding down the budget. Whether he was conscious of that alteration is an open question. And whether the new meanings were compatible with Soviet containment, with American advance, and with Republican advantage is decidedly in doubt. The answer will be given in the 1960's. Meanwhile, an affirmation of compatibility is only credible on the assumption that the Eisenhower program at the outset of his second term was based on faulty premises in almost every sphere—and that the reports of the Rockefeller Brothers Fund are fantasy. To assume otherwise is to conclude that Eisenhower's campaign for a balanced budget, with its pressure wholly on the spending side, involved a risk not only to his other goals of policy but also to the power prospects *after* 1960 of the Republican he hoped would follow him into the White House. For if Eisenhower's budgeting promoted expectations which the future could not meet, his political legacy was likely to be popular frustration in the time of the next President. Reportedly, the moral was not lost on either Rockefeller or Nixon. But there are no reports that Eisenhower saw the risk he ran, if not for himself then for them, in anything like these terms. On the contrary, by 1959 he seems to have been satisfied that Humphrey's aim was not merely good policy but quite sufficient as a base for White House power politics.

Conceivably, the "new" Eisenhower of 1959 bespeaks a change of outlook more profound than the foregoing analysis suggests. Conceivably, this President in his last years came to perceive his office and his power very differently than he had done before. It is conceivable but unlikely. A sympathetic member of his Administration told me:

> This is the Eisenhower of North Africa and Normandy, motivated by the same belief: that the only battle that counts is the last battle. After 1958 he knew the war was nearly over and the time was now or never for the final fight.

But in political warfare, the outcome for a President depends as much or more on the *first* battles. These are the battles that decide his public image and create a pattern for his Washington reputation. A President who makes himself a "new" man in his *seventh* year must be presumed a stranger, still, to politics and power.

With Eisenhower as with F.D.R., performance on the job reflected qualities inside the man which shaped his whole approach to personal power. In Roosevelt's case a striking sensitivity to power was heightened by vast confidence in using it, and by his sense of what to use it for. In Eisenhower's case a relative *in*sensitivity was reinforced by a self-confidence that wavered least when "politics" was farthest off, and by a set of purposes that either raised his eyes too high or cast them down too low to see the middle ground where strategy and tactics meet. It is no wonder that an F.D.R. on most occasions seemed acutely conscious of his power risks, whereas an Eisenhower frequently seemed unaware of them. Nor is it any wonder that the one man's methods helped him see his stakes of power, while the other man worked in a manner likely to obscure them. Roosevelt always knew what power was and always wanted it.

* * *

NOTES

1. See Robert J. Donovan, *Eisenhower: The Inside Story*, New York: Harper, 1956, chaps. 2, 4, 6, 10, 23, 25.
2. *Ibid.*, p. 357.
3. For a summary of Eisenhower's political involvement as a potential candidate from 1947 on see Marquis Childs, *Eisenhower: Captive Hero*, New York: Harcourt Brace, 1958, chaps. 6–7.
4. *Ibid.*, p. 177
5. Transcript of presidential press conference, May 31, 1955, as reported in the *New York Times*, June 1, 1955.
6. The quotations are from Robert Donovan's account of Eisenhower's conference with twelve close associates in January 1956, on the question of a second term. See Donovan, *Eisenhower*, pp. 394–395.
7. *Ibid.*, p. 402.

41

The Institutionalized Presidency

EDWARD S. CORWIN

In this selection, Edward S. Corwin expresses his concern over the aggrandizement of personalized presidential power in the era prior to the Eisenhower administration. His fear of "presidential dictatorship" was prompted by the great expansion of executive power during times of war and economic depression. The growth of governmental and, therefore, presidential power, according to Corwin, has resulted from "the demand that government assume an active *role in matters of general concern, and especially in matters affecting the material welfare of the great masses of the people." Inasmuch as expansion of the government's role is inevitable, he concludes, the answer is to bring the President's power "under some kind of institutional control."*

Corwin, among other scholars, finds the answer to the arbitrary exercise of presidential power to be an institutionalized presidency. The development of the Bureau of the Budget, Eisenhower's implementation of the chief-of-staff system, and the rapprochement between the White House and Capitol Hill in the 1950s were all encouraging signs to Corwin. Although he was well aware of the personalized nature of presidential power, he was hopeful that the institutionalized presidency would become structured enough to restrain incumbents in office. He failed to realize, however, that the institutionalized presidency was largely the product of Dwight D. Eisenhower's personality.

Edward Corwin was one of the most prolific students of American politics. In addition to The President: Office and Powers *(from which the following excerpt is taken),* Corwin wrote *more than eighteen books on American politics, among which are* National Supremacy *(1913),* The Doctrine of Judicial Review *(1914),* The President's Control of Foreign Relations *(1917),* The Twilight of the Supreme Court *(1934),* Court Over Constitution *(1938),* Constitutional Revolution *(1946),* Liberty Against Government *(1948),* A Constitution of Powers in a Secular State *(1951), and* The Constitution and What It Means Today *(1958). Corwin was Professor of Government at Princeton University.*

The President as "Dictator" Versus the President as Leader—A New Type of Cabinet

The growth of presidential participation in legislation,[1] and indeed the vast expansion in recent decades of the President's role in all the departments of national power, invites our attention afresh to a question repeatedly raised regarding the presidency in the past, but never with more insistency than in recent years, or for more cogent reasons. This is the question whether the presidency is a potential matrix of dictatorship; and, if it is, whether there is a remedy.

"Dictatorship," I hardly need point out, is a word with a highly ambiguous connotation, so much so in fact that I propose to dismiss it at the outset in favor of a less colorful word, "domination." "A nation," it has been well said, "does not have to have a genuine dictator in order to suffer some of the evils of too great executive domination." Imagine an historically minded member of Congress seeking nowadays to emulate Henry Dunning's exploit in 1781 of bringing George III's domination of Parliament to an end and with it, ultimately, British resistance to American independence. It would be the part of such a member to move a resolution declaring that "the power of the President has increased, is increasing, and ought to be diminished," and he would have little difficulty in making out an arresting case.

First off, he would point out that impeachment, the weapon that the Constitution provides against presidential "high crimes and misdemeanors," is, as Jefferson early discovered, a "scarecrow," and that to galvanize this scarecrow into life would be to run the risk of reducing the presidency to a nullity, as almost happened in 1868. Then, noting the decision in *Mississippi v. Johnson*[2] shortly after the Civil War, he would assert, and quite correctly, that the President has no judicially enforcible responsibility either for nonperformance of his duties or for exceeding his powers. Congress's power of the purse, to be sure, still offers, he would concede, an obstacle to presidential usurpation that only an outright *coup d'état* could entirely overcome. Nevertheless, as Dr. Wilmerding points out in his volume on *The Spending Power,*[3] not only have Presidents been able repeatedly to break over statutory controls on expenditure, but such controls are usually much abated by Congress itself in times of emergency, exactly when expenditures are heaviest and presidential dominance is at its zenith. Indeed, generalizing from what happened during the Great Depression, the honorable member might urge that congressional largess in such situations, by the hold that it gives the executive branch on millions of votes, enables the President to tighten his hold on Congress, and so creates a vicious circle whereby Congress pays for its own slow enslavement. And, continues our orator, when war activates the President's powers as Commander-in-Chief, the situation is still more disastrous from the point of view of opposing the power of the purse to presidential dominance. The sums that Congress is at such times under every compulsion to vote are colossal. The needs that they are designed to meet are forcefully represented, and are believed by the public, to be most urgent, while itemization is put out of the question by the demands of military secrecy; and unexpected turns in the military situation can aggravate all these difficulties. Moreover, the criticism that overworked congressional committees of varying competence can offer to the demands of the executive branch under such conditions will be haphazard in the extreme. An item of $50,000 may get more consideration, and certainly far better informed consideration, than a presidential demand for billions.

Turning then to the course that constitutional interpretation has taken more and more pronouncedly in consequence of our participation in two world wars and under the stimulation of economic crisis, our fictioned Dunning will sketch a system of constitutional law that attributes to Congress a legislative power of indefinite scope and the further power to delegate this indefinite power to the President *ad libitum*, and attributes to the President in his own right an indefinite power to proclaim "emergencies" and thereby appropriate an indefinite "aggregate of powers" in meeting them. At the same time he will show that the President, not without judicial encouragement, has been able to cut loose from the two most important controls that the Constitution originally imposed on his direction of foreign policy. With our four greatest wars directly ascribable to presidential policies, the exercise by Congress of its power "to declare war" has become, he will assert, an empty formality; while by means of the executive-agreement device the President has emancipated himself from his constitutional partner in pledging the national faith.

And at this point our hypothetical member will perhaps devote a word or two to the advantages that a President today enjoys in appealing to the multitude. Propaganda, he will point out, once the casual art of a gifted few, has been within recent times converted into a skilled technique supplemented by the most ingenious gadgets of mechanical science. Today the President of the United States can at any time request that the nation's broadcasting channels be cleared so that he may "chat" with the people, and the request will be granted pronto, for are not all the available frequencies allocated to companies on federal licenses that terminate every six months? Besides, every member of his administration is a propagandist and has access to the radio at will, although a first-class radio voice may not be the heaven-sent gift of all.

The picture is unquestionably overdrawn in some of its details. Thus, if it is true that impeachment is no longer to be reckoned with as an effective weapon in the arsenal of liberty, this is partly due to the fact that Presidents have in the past kept pretty clear of courses that might make people think seriously of so extreme a discipline. Again, although there is no court entitled to order a President to perform his duties or to enjoin him from exceeding his powers, the subordinates through whom he must ordinarily act do not share his immunity in this respect; and his orders are at all times subject to judicial inquiry into their validity when anybody bases on them any claim or justification whatsoever.[4] Also, his subordinates are, ordinarily, liable at any time to be summoned before a congressional investigating committee and put to the question regarding their official conduct.[5]

Nor is it by any means the fact that Congress's control of the purse strings is ineffective as a restraint on the executive branch. On the contrary, it is potentially a highly effective restraint, which with improved machinery within the power of Congress to provide could be made actual. Again, our orator did not find it to his purpose to mention that in the "concurrent resolution" a device today exists by which sweeping delegations of power to the President can be recalled by the houses without the necessity of obtaining presidential consent; and other lesser exaggerations or omissions might be indicated were it worth while.

Moreover, that is a seriously contracted point of view from which presidential domination appears as solely a *menace* to democratic institutions. Why, in the face of our democratic institutions, has presidential domination attained its present proportions? Must not this development be considered as a fulfillment in a measure of those institutions, and as an answer to some demand from public opinion, on which by hypothesis they are grounded? Without doubt, such is the fact, and especially as regards presidential leadership in legislation. Nor is it difficult to identify this demand: it is the demand that government assume an *active* role in matters of general concern, and especially in matters affecting the material welfare of the great masses of the people.

We are, then, not free to blame presidential leadership as such for those intrusions on "liberty," as it has sometimes been understood, that present expanded theories of governmental function entail. This at least must be conceded. We are free, on the other hand, to ask whether presidential leadership, as we know it, is as good an instrument of the demand that brought it into existence as conceivably it might be. Presidential leadership sets itself the task of guiding legislation; and the critics are numerous who say that it does the job badly. To make the indictment more specific, it is asserted that presidential leadership is discontinuous, not to say spasmodic; that it is too dependent on the personality of the President rather than on the authority of the office; that it is often insufficiently informed, especially as regards the all-important matter of administrative feasibility; and, finally, that the contact between the President and Congress is most faulty, being, in fact, at the mercy of either's whim. These contentions also have too much obvious validity to make it worth while to attempt to refute them or even to qualify them nicely.

In short, we are confronted, not with a *single* problem, but with *two* problems: first, that of bringing presidential power in *all* its reaches under some kind of institutional control; secondly, that of relieving presidential leadership in the legislative field of its excessive dependence on the accident of personality and the unevenness of performance that this involves. Is it possible that these two problems admit of a common solution? At least, so far as they do it is evident what form the solution must take: the *pro-*

vision, namely, of some kind of improved relationship between President and Congress.

* * *

"The Institutionalized Presidency"

There are . . . those who today contend that the problem of the "Personalized Presidency" has already been solved, or at least put well on the road to solution, by the "Institutionalized Presidency." . . .

The "Institutionalized Presidency" pivots, so to speak, on two hinges. The first is the Executive Office of the President, the product chiefly of legislation; the second is the White House Office, which has taken on unprecedented importance under President Eisenhower.

Dealing with the former, a recent writer remarks:

> We have routinized the President's responsibility to take the policy lead. And at the same time, we have institutionalized, in marked degree, the exercise of that responsibility. President and presidency are synonymous no longer; the office now comprises an officialdom twelve-hundred strong. For almost every phase of policy development there is now institutional machinery engaged in preparations on the President's behalf; for the financial and administrative workplan of the government, the Budget Bureau; for the Administration's legislative program, the White House counsel and the Budget's clearance organization; for programming in economic and social spheres, the Council of Economic Advisers (and to some degree the Cabinet, Eisenhower-style); in foreign and military fields, the National Security Council; in spheres of domestic preparedness, the Office of Defense Mobilization; these pieces of machinery among others, each built around a program-making task, all lumped together, formally, under the rubric "The Executive Office of the President," an institutional conception and a statutory entity less than two decades old.
>
> These are significant developments, this routinizing, institutionalizing, of the initiative. They give the presidency nowadays a different look than it has worn before, an aspect permanently "positive." But the reality behind that look was not just conjured up by statutes or by staffing. These, rather are *responses* to the impacts of external circumstance upon our form of government; not causes but effects.[6]

The legislative history of the Executive Office may be said to have begun with the Reorganization Act of 1939.[7] . . . For present purposes I shall devote major attention to the White House Office and to President Eisenhower's contribution to its emergence as an outstanding feature of the governmental machine.[8]

Presidents have, of course, "always had some kind of help in the discharge of their duties," but it was not until 1857 that Congress appropriated money for a presidential clerk. Earlier "some Presidents hired relatives or friends to do clerical work, paying them out of personal salary." Others, like Jackson, set up "kitchen cabinets," advisers who "kept backstage," but aided the President in various capacities.[9] Grant presided over "the great barbecue," comprising six White House assistants whose salaries totaled $13,900. McKinley lavished $44,340 on a staff of 27; Coolidge was given 46 employees, costing the public exchequer $93,520; F.D.R. ran the show before the Second World War with 37 employees, then stepped the number up to 55, including a number "on loan" from other agencies. Under Truman a budget of $957,836 initially sufficed for 282 employees; in 1952 these figures were 383 employees and $1,883,615.[10]

But it is in the Eisenhower regime that tendencies toward bureaucratization, exhibited during the incumbencies of Truman and F.D.R., have become controlling, thanks in part to

Mr. Eisenhower's military experience with the Chief of Staff work concept, in part to his settled preference for consensus and security as against debate and adventuring, and in part to intervals of bad health. In consequence of all these factors combined, the institutionalizing process has been carried beyond the Truman model in four respects: (1) in the employment of Sherman Adams as Chief of Staff; (2) in use of the Cabinet for collective consultation; (3) in more effective use of the Vice-President; and (4) in regular, planned consultation with congressional leaders on legislative policies.

Sherman Adams is, in fact if not in name, the "Chief of Staff" called for by the First Hoover Commission. Today he is accorded the title and enjoys a power in the White House second only to that of the President himself. Indeed, in light of what is now known about the matter it would seem that Mr. Adams was for all practical purposes President during the early stages of Mr. Eisenhower's illness.

Furthermore, to a far greater degree than any of his predecessors President Eisenhower has endeavored to employ the Cabinet as an instrument of collective policy-making. The revitalized Cabinet possesses a secretariat and confronts an agenda at its regular meetings. At the same time, each member is expected to assume full responsibility for the conduct of the affairs of his department. Cabinet meetings, if reports can be credited, are now more meaningful than they ever were under F.D.R., and they are often attended by the President's top advisers discharging responsibilities outside the departments. Not for Eisenhower the example of Lincoln's presentation of the Emancipation Proclamation to his Cabinet: "I have got you together to hear what I have written down. I do not wish your advice about the main matter, for that I have determined for myself."

Eisenhower has also made the conspicuous use of the Vice-President, not only inviting him to Cabinet meetings, but assigning him to preside over meetings of the Cabinet and the National Security Council when the President does not attend, and giving him a succession of extracongressional duties.

As befits the conciliatory tone of his regime, Eisenhower also holds regularly scheduled weekly conferences with congressional leaders, continuing the practice, even when the political complexion of the legislature has shifted against him, by including leaders of the opposition. Likewise, committee chairmen with a vested interest in subjects the President wishes discussed are also frequently invited to these meetings.[11] To be sure, the idea of such a conference is not a new one. The outstanding departure is Mr. Eisenhower's willingness to listen to as well as to instruct the congressmen. Moreover, results have been measured far less in legislative coups for presidential policy than in the comparative absence of strident discord between White House and Capitol Hill.[12]

Another marked characteristic of the Eisenhower administration is the frequent detachment of the President from the conduct of his subordinates. On several occasions he appears to have accomplished what President Truman and many commentators have said was impossible, "passing the buck" to the Secretary of Agriculture, the Secretary of State, the Secretary of the Army, the Attorney General. Each of these gentlemen, according to the President, is an independent officeholder with his own views of appropriate policy, with which the President has no warrant to interfere.

The same detachment, the same attitude of reigning rather than ruling, when coupled with efficient staff work, had already been carried so far by the time of the President's critical illness in midterm that the "administration" went on notwithstanding the disaster with scarcely a tremor. The persons most seriously inconvenienced were those whose commissions had to be signed by the President in person. It is true that at one time the suggestion was advanced within the administration itself that the Attorney General should explore the possibility of delegating further presidential power, totally ignoring the Vice-President. The idea was quickly dropped, however, on receipt of the first encouraging medical bulletin; and, Donovan writes, there was a further reason:

> This was that no papers of any great consequence awaited the President's signature. A key to the whole problem was the fact that his illness struck at the lowest period of government activity. Congress had adjourned. The President had acted on all bills requiring his attention. The Big Four Foreign Ministers' meeting was still nearly a month away. Many high officials had just got off on vacation. Preparation of the major messages to be submitted by the President to Congress in January was in the earliest stages. Even if he had been in the best of health, it was a time when the President's participation in the routine business of government would have been at a minimum.[13]

Meanwhile the American public, bemused by bulletins purveying medical detail, concentrated on the President's illness and left Sherman Adams a free hand. When the President had recovered sufficiently to work an hour at a time, nearly six weeks after the onset of his illness, the official biographer of his first term commented:

> Adams, as usual, was the channel through which work flowed to and from Eisenhower, and in this period the influence of the Assistant to the President upon the operations of the government was very considerable. Working in a plain office . . . Adams was on the phone to Washington from morning until night, giving instructions, arranging conferences, summoning officials to see the President and making innumerable administrative decisions. He would lay out areas of policy in which the President alone must make decisions and then see to it that decisions were reached on matters beyond these boundaries. In Denver, as in Washington, his authority was enhanced by his unique prerogative in speaking for the President—"It is the President's wish that . . ." or "The President hopes you will . . ." and so forth.[14]

Possibly a slight understatement! Eisenhower himself laughingly suggested that "there might even have been a few hints that the Cabinet did better without him" and expressed surprise that anyone should be surprised that "the Cabinet worked harmoniously and successfully in following the administration's familiar and practicable middle course between the extremes of too little and too much."[15]

Just how durable is President Eisenhower's impact on the presidency apt to be? Certainly the time is long past when the conception of the President as a sort of "boss of the works" had convincing connection with reality.[16]

Rather, I suggest, there is a long-term trend at work in the world that consolidates power in the executive departments of all governments, first in the person of one individual, then in an "administration." The era of Roosevelt, Churchill, Stalin, Hitler, Mussolini—each a cornerstone of the national "cult of personality"—has been followed by collegial rule, collective responsibility, and *ad hoc* policies flowing out of completed staff work. Saying this, however, is something different from planning the presidential office with a view to sterilizing it from the contaminating influence of its incumbent, or creating machinery so unwieldly that a new presidential personality can take hold only after a series of exhausting bureaucratic contests within the walls of the White House.

That Congress in setting up the principal constituent elements of the Executive Office of the President may have been motivated in part by the idea of aggrandizing its own power at the expense of the presidency, rather than by that of assisting him in his task of leading the nation and managing the government, may be conceded.[17] For all that, the office remains highly personal. F.D.R. showed that one could speak powerfully and in personal accents through ghost writers. Harry Truman, who felt and expressed his inadequacies in the job, nevertheless insisted on its high personal quotient:

> . . . after all, every final important decision has to be made right here on the President's desk, and only the President can make it. Nobody else can do it for him, and his decisions affect millions not only in his own country but throughout the world. No one man can really fill the Presidency. The Presidency has too many and too great responsibilities. All a man can do is to try to meet them. He must be able to judge men, delegate responsibility and back up those he trusts.[18]

And not even the spectacle of an actor coaching the President on his TV lines and mannerisms has dissuaded the people from looking upon the Chief Executive as the author of peace, prosperity, and good crops, or, in the alternative, of war, depression, and famine.

The compromising character of Mr. Eisenhower, built into his administration, *a fortiori* supports the view that the presidency is still very much a matter of who is President. In the pertinent words of a recent writer:

> Each President has organized the Presidency to conform to his own peculiar whims and talents. Mr. Hoover made of it a hair shirt. Mr. Roosevelt, at least in his earlier years, endowed it with a sort of chaotic exuberance. In Mr. Truman's time it had something of the quality of a state of siege, defensive and suspicious.
>
> Mr. Eisenhower's concept is that of an efficient and all-comprehending machine which embraces features both of the military staff and the corporate board of directors. He has brought this concept to a high state of operational perfection and relies upon it with confidence. So much so, indeed, that the job—"splendid misery" or not—never seems to get him down.[19]

At the same time, it was not an *"institution"* that received last November six million more votes for President than his competitor. The President, *this* President at least, is still very much a person.[20]

* * *

The great accession to presidential power in recent decades has . . . taken place in the *internal* equally with the *external* field of government, and has been signalized by the breakdown of the two great structural principles of the American Constitutional System, the doctrine of dual federalism and the doctrine of the Separation of Powers; while along with this breakdown has gone an even more fundamental change in popular outlook regarding the purpose and scope of governmental power. I mean, of course, the replacement of the *laissez-faire* theory of government with the idea that government should make itself an *active, reforming* force in the field of economic enterprise, which means necessarily that the *national government* should be active in this way, inasmuch as the field in question has long since come to transcend state lines.

The result for the presidency has been twofold. On the one hand, Presidents have made themselves spokesmen of the altered outlook, have converted their parties to it—a conversion not infrequently accompanied by backsliding—and, with the popular support thus obtained, have asserted a powerful legislative initiative. On the other hand, Congress, in responding to the President's leadership in its own peculiar field, has found it convenient to aggrandize his executive role enormously, by delegating to him the power to supplement its measures by a type of sublegislation called "administrative regulations." Not all this delegated power, it is true, has gone to the President, but a vast proportion of it has; and it constitutes a realm of presidential power of which the Framers had little prevision, although it began to appear in the field of foreign relations even as early as Washington's second administration.

The first exponent of the new presidency was Theodore Roosevelt, but his achievement was to some extent negated by faults of method. Woodrow Wilson was enabled by the advantage of having critically observed his predecessor, by his knowledge of political methods abroad, by a taste for institution-building, which was later to divert him into an abortive effort at world organization, and finally by the opportunity afforded by our entrance into the First World War, to illustrate on an unprecedented scale both the new roles of the President—that of legislative leader and that of recipient of delegated legislative power. The First World War was prosecuted for the most part under laws drafted under the appraising eye of the President and conferring on him far greater powers than those Lincoln had exercised as Commander-in-Chief.

But it is the second Roosevelt who beyond all twentieth-century Presidents put the stamp both of *personality* and *crisis* on the presidency. In the solution of the problems of an economic crisis—"a crisis greater than war"—he claimed for the national government in general and for the President in particular powers hitherto exercised only on the justification of war. Then when the greatest crisis in the history of our international relations arose he imparted to the President's diplomatic powers new extension, now without consulting Congress, now with Congress's approval; and when at last we entered the Second World War he endowed the precedents of both the Civil War and the First World War with unprecedented scope.

The presidency of this present year of grace, so far as it is explicable in terms of American constitutional law and theory, is the product of the following factors: (1) social acceptance of the idea that government should be active and reformist, rather than simply protective of the established order of things; (2) the breakdown of the principle of dual federalism in the field of Congress's legislative powers; (3) the breakdown of the principle of the Separation of Powers as defining the relation of President and Congress in lawmaking; (4) the breakdown of the corollary principle that the legislature may not delegate its powers; and (5) the impact on the President's power as Commander-in-Chief and the organ of foreign relationship of two world wars and the vastly enlarged role of the United States in the international field.

Does the presidency, then, in the light of these facts, constitute a standing menace to popular government and to those conceptions of personal liberty to which popular government is, in part, traceable? So far as concerns popular government in the sense of majority rule, the exact contrary is the case: all the developments named are the direct consequence of democracy's emergence from the constitutional chrysalis. That, on the other hand, these developments leave private and personal rights in the same strong position as they once enjoyed would be quite impossible to maintain. Nor is it feasible in this connection to distinguish too acutely between the property and other rights. Not only in the past, but today as well, the property right is the right best capable of holding its own against political power. This is the principal lesson to be drawn from the history of Liberalism.

As matters have stood till the other day, presidential power has been at times dangerously *personalized,* and this in two senses: first, that the leadership that it affords was dependent altogether on the accident of personality, against which our haphazard method of selecting Presidents offers no guarantee; and, secondly, that there is no governmental body that could be relied on to give the President independent advice and that he was nevertheless bound to consult. As a remedy calculated to meet both phases of the problem I have suggested a new type of Cabinet. At least, if a solution is to be sought in *institutional* terms, it must consist in *stabilizing* in some way or other the relationship between President and Congress.

Recent developments, however, may have relegated my proposal, even if it ever had any real prospect of acceptance, to the limbo of happy untried ideas—happy, perhaps, because untried. In the "Institutionalized Presidency" the President becomes merged with—albeit not submerged in—a cluster of institutions designed to base government in the national area on conference and consensus. The "Institutionalized Presidency" is the contribution of Congress and of recent Presidents, but particularly of President Eisenhower, whose temperament, training, and needs it obviously meets. But is it a permanent structure? In our "world in transition" no confident prediction can be safely vouchsafed. The incalculables are too many and too formidable.

NOTES

1. The most careful attempt to evaluate presidential leadership in terms of legislative product is that of Professor Lawrence H. Chamberlain in *The President, Congress and Legislation* (Columbia University Press, 1946). Tracing the history of the conception, gestation, and birth of ninety major acts of Congress, the earliest of which became law in 1882, the latest in 1940, Professor Chamberlain finds that "presidential influence" was "preponderant" in the enactment of nineteen of these measures, that "congressional influence" was "preponderant" in the enactment of thirty-five, that "joint presidential-congressional influence" brought about the enactment of twenty-nine and that "pressure group influence" was "preponderant" in the case of seven measures. The tests by which presidential preponderance is determined are liberal (*ibid.,* pp. 26–27), but in reaching so far back the investigation unmistakably favors congressional claims. Of the nineteen measures in the enactment of which presidential influence is reckoned to have been preponderant, ten became law betwen 1932 and 1938, while only two of the thirty-five credited to Congress were enacted during these years. Nor is this more than partially compensated for by the fact that twelve of the twenty-nine measures credited to the President and Congress jointly belong to the same period. *Ibid.,* pp. 450–52.

In his own evaluation of his results Professor Chamberlain points out the important difference between regarding the President as the *creator of legislation* and as *catalyst* bringing to fruition earlier ineffective efforts in and out of Congress. As is apparent, the latter is the vastly more important role. Except in wartime or extreme crisis, like that of 1933, few measures of the scope and importance of those treated by Professor Chamberlain have undergone a long term of incubation in congressional committee files before their final enactment.

Professor Chamberlain's volume supplies a needed corrective to swollen ideas of accomplishment of Presidents as legislators, but has not avoided altogether the opposed error. One can readily agree that the President frequently appears to be "the initiating agent of a particular law when as a matter of fact he is little more than the conveyance—sometimes the reluctant one—upon which it moves to fruition," that "presidential leadership has been and probably will continue to be uneven"—a matter that is considered in the text—and that "the atomized nature of the congressional approach to our legislative needs has supplied something without which the executive leadership would be less effective," "an inexhaustible flood of observations, suggestions, and proposals." *Ibid.*, pp. 463–64. Three things, however, Professor Chamberlain seems to me to overlook. One is that in our crisis-driven world time is often of the essence. The second is that the President occupies a superior position from which to descry the approach of crisis, especially crisis in the international field. The third is the concentrated political weight that the presidential office alone can bring to bear in support of an urgently needed measure. For all these reasons presidential leadership is a factor of ever increasing indispensability to the adequate functioning of the legislative process, and so of its survival.

With Mr. Chamberlain's volume it is interesting to compare on the subject of executive leadership in legislation Emile Giraud's *La Crise de la démocratie et le renforcement du pouvoir exécutif* (Paris, 1938). While the argument is mainly directed against the deficiencies of the French constitution—now defunct—it is rich in observations of interest to American readers, as that the executive must direct the legislature, being the organ with "unity of thought," "capacity to acquire a view of the whole" (p. 110), and possessing, by virtue of its participation in administrative and diplomatic activities, adequate information (p. 115). M. Giraud systematically attacks the *laissez-faire* conception of democracy as "the organization of resistance to power" (p. 72, n. 2). To the contrary, he asserts, it is "a power of action and realization" (p. 99). "A feeble executive," he continues, "means a feeble state, one which fulfills badly its function of protecting the individual against political, economic, and social forces which, without the state, tend to swallow him up, to exploit and oppress him" (pp. 101–2). All of which is true within limits, but furnishes no reason for compressing the Constitution into the opening clause of Article II.

2. *Mississippi v. Johnson*, 4 Wall. 475 (1867).
3. Lucius Wilmerding, *The Spending Power; A History of the Efforts of Congress to Control Expenditures* (Yale University Press, 1943).
4. Ever since the time of the great leading case of *Marbury v. Madison*, 1 Cr. 137 (1803), heads of departments have occasionally been subjected to proceedings, brought usually in the first instance in a District of Columbia court, in which a writ of mandamus or a writ of injunction was sought, and such writs have now and then been awarded against them. See, for example, *Kendall v. Stokes*, 12 Pet. 524; *Decatur v. Paulding*, 14 Pet. 497; *Garfield v. United States*, 211 U.S. 249; *Smith et al. v. Hitchcock*, 226 U.S. 53; *Morgan v. United States*, 304 U.S. 1. Two cases 130 years apart in which presidential orders were held by the Court to be without legal warrant are *Little v. Barreme*, 2 Cr. 170 (1804), and *Panama Refining Co. v. Ryan*, 293 U.S. 388 (1934). See also *Ex parte Orozco*, 201 F. 106 (1912).
5. See generally Marshall E. Dimock, *Congressional Investigations* (Johns Hopkins Press, 1926); M. Nelson McGeary, *The Development of Congressional Investigative Power* (Columbia University, 1940); and George B. Galloway, "The Investigative Function of Congress," 21 *American Political Science Review*, 46–70.

"A careful survey of the history of committee activity from 1789 to the expiration of the Sixty-eighth Congress in 1925 discloses that there have been, all told, about 285 investigations by the select and standing committees of the House and Senate. Only three Congresses have been barren of legislative inquests, while no administration has been immune. The high-water mark was reached during Grant's eight turbulent years, when incompetence and corruption ran riot through public life; between 1869 and 1877 Congress undertook thirty-seven different inquiries aimed at remedying bad conditions in the administration.

"Much American history can be gleaned from the reports of these nearly three hundred investigating committees. For the houses of Congress have employed the inquisitorial function over a wide range of governmental activity. Beginning with the inquiry into the defeat of General St. Clair by the Indians in 1792, and continuing down to the current investigation of the Tariff Commission, this device has been put to many uses. The record shows that the War Department has come most frequently under the inquiring eye. Congressional committees have scrutinized the conduct of all the wars in which the United States has engaged except the Spanish-American war, when President McKinley forestalled legislative inquiry by appointing the Dodge commission. They were responsible for the impeachment of President Johnson and Secretary of War Belknap. They have examined the conduct of the Treasury Department fifty-four times and of the Interior Department forty-one times, with attention centered most frequently on the Indian Bureau and the Pension and Patent Offices. The Government Printing Office has also been submitted to frequent inspection; likewise the Navy and Postoffice Departments. The President has been the subject of investigation twenty-three times, commencing with John Adams and ending with Woodrow Wilson. In fact, no department or activity of the government has escaped inquiry unless it be the Departments of Commerce and Labor since their separation in 1913." Galloway, *ibid.*, 47–48.

. . . I know of no instance in which a head of department has testified before a congressional committee in response to a subpoena or been held for contempt for refusal to testify. All appearances by these high officials seem to have been voluntary.

6. Richard E. Neustadt, "The Presidency at Mid-Century," *Law and Contemporary Problems*, XXI (Autumn, 1956), pp. 609–45. See also "The President and His Political Executives," Stephen K. Bailey, *The Annals of The American Academy of Political and Social Science* (September, 1956), pp. 24–36. The locale of the Executive Office of the President is the old building at the corner of Pennsylvania Avenue and 17th St. that once housed the State, Army, and Navy Departments.
7. 53 Stat. 561.
8. In this connection I have been greatly aided by Mr. Paul Tillett of the Department of Politics of Princeton University.
9. See Bailey *et al.*, *Government in America* (Henry Holt and Company, 1957), p. 338.
10. See Edward H. Hobbs, *Behind the President* (Washington, Public Affairs Press, 1954), pp. 91–92.
11. *Ibid.*, p. 215.
12. "President to Face Old Attitudes in New House," *Congressional Quarterly Weekly Report* (November 23, 1956), p. 1379.
13. Robert J. Donovan, *Eisenhower, The Inside Story* (New York Herald Tribune, Inc., 1956), p. 370.
14. *Ibid.*, p. 378.
15. *Ibid.*, pp. 385–86.
16. Even F.D.R. said that the two years between the Brownlow report and the enactment of the Reorganization Act of 1939 had deepened his "conviction that it is necessary for the President to have the machinery to enable him to carry out his constitutional responsibilities." Franklin D. Roosevelt, Message accompanying Reorganization Plan No. 1 of 1939. 76th Cong., 1st sess. (House Doc. 262).
17. Lester G. Seligman, "Presidential Leadership: The Inner Circle and Institutionalization," *Journal of Politics*, X, No. 3 (August, 1956), pp. 418–21.
18. William Hillman, *Mr. President* (New York, 1952), p. 10.
19. Cabell Phillips, *The New York Times Magazine*, February 3, 1957. See also R. H. Pear, "The American Presidency Under Eisenhower," 28 *The Political Quarterly* (British), (January-March, 1957), pp. 5–12.
20. Henry Jones Ford, who exhumed the presidency from the accumulated detritus of its failures, prophesied that it would eventually "assume an honorary and ceremonial character." *Rise and Growth*, p. 369.

Professor Rossiter, whose work on *The American Presidency* became a classic on publication, teaches, in effect, that the presidency is pervaded with a principle of meliorism that guarantees that it will always be just right. His motto is "Leave Your Presidency Alone," Clinton Rossiter, *The American Presidency,* 1st ed. (New York: Harcourt, Brace, 1956), p. 162.

Professor Stratton of Wellesley College feels that the presidency is gradually being ground into insignificance by Congress. "It is not impossible," he says, "if present trends continue, that the President will be reduced to laying cornerstones and giving commencement speeches while the leaders of Congress fight for spoils in some sort of hybrid parliamentary regime in which all the real governing gets done by the permanent civil service. Altogether this prospect is frightening enough to be called a nightmare." *The New York Times Magazine,* Jan. 20, 1957, p. 38.

At the other extreme M. Amaury de Riencourt contends in *The Coming Caesars* (New York: Coward-McCann, 1957) that the American people are already headed toward the fate that overtook the Roman Republic.

42

Thoughts on the Presidency

HENRY FAIRLIE

In the following selection, Henry Fairlie argues that the institutionalized presidency is more a myth than a reality. The exercise of executive power in the United States depends on the needs and personality of the President. In contrast to England's permanent civil service, which remains relatively stable as governments change, the American President's White House staff and Cabinet members shift with each new administration. The American presidency, according to Fairlie, has all of the elements of Caesaropapism; it reflects the will and needs of the incumbent.

Fairlie's essay attempts to refute Corwin's argument that the development of the Bureau of the Budget and other executive White House agencies serves to restrain the use of presidential power. If Fairlie is correct, then what internal restraints exist in the executive branch to limit the President? Many observers point to the existence of multiple power centers in the executive—the numerous departments and quasi-independent regulatory agencies—that limit the President's influence. Others argue that the American political system does not produce presidents who want to exercise unlimited, dictatorial power. Finally, it may be said that the President's power is far more limited than most critics believe. The President may be the most important political actor in Washington, but he is not the only *political actor.*

Fairlie, a British journalist and keen observer of the contemporary American political scene, is also the author of The Life of Politics. *His numerous articles on politics have appeared in both British and American newspapers and magazines.*

I have never understood why radicals in England object to the banal clichés which the Queen normally utters to her subjects. The English, after all, fought a civil war, executed one king and sent another king packing, precisely to be sure that monarchs in the future would not say anything which had any meaning. They then made doubly sure of this by giving the crown to a Hanoverian who could speak barely a word of English. When the Queen's consort to-day, a man of continental upbringing and notions, accentuated by an education at Gordonstoun, does say something in public which appears to carry some meaning, both Parliament and the press call for the executioner: only a 20th-century half-heartedness prevents the Duke of Edinburgh's head from rolling. It could, indeed, be said that the reason why the English fought their passionate, but still rather scholarly, civil war, and laboriously carried through what deserves to be known as the Inglorious Revolution, was primarily to make certain that those on the throne, and those near the throne, would not communicate intelligently with their subjects, but only with pedigree cattle, horses, and gun dogs.

So unused is an Englishman to the idea that a Head of State can do and say things of political importance that he is at something of a disadvantage (or is it an advantage?) when he contemplates a Presidency, whether the Presidency of the Fifth Republic or the Presidency of the United States. He does not really understand an elected and powerful Head of State. President Lebrun, in his frock coat, comes much more easily in his range of vision than President de Gaulle; and an English friend of mine likes to observe that *Mrs.* Calvin Coolidge seems to him very much what an ideal Head of State should be. Whenever there has been a national crisis (real or supposed) during my stay in America, I have found myself worried by the interventions and appearances of the President. Who, I always want to know, is speaking? The Head of State? The Commander-in-Chief? The head of a temporary administration? The temporary head of a political party? It is never quite clear; at least, I am never clear. All right: "Hail to the Chief." But what chief, I ask, and chief of what?

The Improbable United States

I first observed the . . . President of the United States on my first Saturday in this country. It was in March, 1965, just after the disturbances at Selma, Alabama, and he was giving a televised press conference in the Rose Garden of the White House. The impression which it made will never leave me, especially the extraordinary discordance between the decorousness of the surroundings and the almost Barnum and Bailey vigour with which the whole ceremony—for a ceremony it was, and was intended to be—was conducted. I remember turning to an English colleague, who had been in America for some time, and asking him why the American journalists stood when the President entered, a salute which no English journalist would give to any politician. "Because, you fool, he is the Head of State," my colleague whispered back. "But he is not to-day," I answered. "He is a party leader announcing a new party policy." Two days later, to my utter amazement, this same party

Reprinted from *The Public Interest* (Fall 1967), pp. 28–48, by permission of the publisher.

leader was allowed to address a joint meeting of both Houses of Congress, again conferring on a party policy something of the dignity which only a Head of State can offer.

It will seem to some that I am labouring an obvious and not very important point. I can only answer that the combination of Head of State and party leader is to me the most improbable feature of what I regard as a most improbable political office. Indeed I would, after two years, still find it hard to explain why the United States exists at all. I can find no manifest reason why it should have been the destiny of this subcontinent to become, and remain, one nation, under God or not. Nor can I find any satisfactory explanation of how this same nation survived the colossal strain of the mass immigration which took place in the last quarter of the 19th century, and the first twenty years of this. (When I read Richard Hofstadter's *The Paranoid Style in American Politics,* my first and main reaction was, not that there have been so many "kooks" on the American political scene, but that there have been so few, and especially that there were so few during and immediately after the period of mass immigration.) The real miracle of the United States—and the source of its perpetual fascination over the minds of other peoples, "more powerful than the eloquence of Mirabeau or the sword of Napoleon," as Archibald Alison said in 1833—is its mere existence; and, the more I ponder this improbable existence, the more I am convinced that *one* key to it lies in the most improbable of its political offices: the Presidency.

In fact, when I have gone back, with the slight experience of the United States which I have so far accumulated, to a rereading of *The Federalist,* I find in it this same awareness of the improbability of the whole business in which the constitution-makers were engaged. *The Federalist,* indeed, draws much of its power from the fact that it is a series of prudent essays on the improbable; and when I describe the Presidency as an improbable office in an improbable country, it is, of course, the fact and the nature of federalism (itself an improbable form of government, quite alien to English concepts, even though the English did assist in creating federal governments in Canada and Australia) which is attracting and holding my attention.

It was David Hume who foretold that the fruitful combination of the two ideas of representation and federation would enable—would *alone* enable—popular government to adapt itself to a vast continent. An outside observer, on his first encounter with it, must be allowed a little bemusement at the fact that the combination has worked, that the attempt was ever made, and that the achievement is so far there to see.

A Mythical Institution

First, however, there is demolition work to be done. A myth has been created since the Second World War—and is again being fostered—that the Presidency has become and is becoming "institutionalized." It is a myth worth destroying, for it is already distorting political observation. The truth is the opposite. There is no high political office which is less institutionalized.

I take an institution to be a body—an establishment, if one likes; I happen to dislike—which has a corporate existence of its own, independent of its supreme (but temporary) office-holder (or office-holders). A permanent civil service, as strongly entrenched, as formally and informally assured of its position, its influence, and its powers as is the English civil service, is quite clearly an institution. So, now, is the English monarchy; for, although the personality of the monarch may play some part in determining what she says and does (and, especially, how), it is obvious now that the heart of the monarchy lies, not in the person of the monarch, but in the office of her Private Secretary, which has built up, by precedent piled minutely on precedent, a body of rules and conventions which are self-perpetuating. To make the point amply clear, one can say that the English cabinet is an institution, that it has been "institutionalized" in the office of the Secretary to the Cabinet—but that the office of prime minister is not a political institution. Nor is the office of President of the United States.

The myth that the Presidency is being "institutionalized" is based, as far as I understand it, on the following claims:

1. That the President's personal staff, the formidable array of special assistants and counsellors in the White House, represents a qualitative, and not merely a quantitative, change in the character and activity of the Presidency;
2. That various traditional activities of the President—for example, his relations with Congress—have been "institutionalized" in a particular office in the White House: for example, Lawrence O'Brien's while he was there, and even now that, formally, he is not there;
3. That the Presidency, through various instruments, such as the rapidly developing Bureau of the Budget, has "institutionalized" its relationship with the various government departments and agencies;
4. That a body of White House lore is being built up, perpetuating itself in successive Presidencies, and exemplified by the close contact which was established between November, 1960 and January, 1961, between the staff of the out-going President in the White House and the (constitutionally nonexistent) staff of the in-coming one.

That is it; and, for the life of me, I cannot see that it adds up to saying much more than that the President does many things which the President did not do before, and needs a larger staff to help him. One specific claim I intend to keep separate, because it helps to make a separate and important point: namely, that the activities of the Bureau of the Budget, the Council of Economic Advisors, and the Office of Scientific Advisor to the President together constitute a form of "institutionalizing."

The White House Staff

I have to admit that there is, at first, the charm of novelty about the special assistants and counsellors who have become such a much-publicized element of government in the past seven years. The roll call of these Presidential assistants since 1961 is, indeed, stirring: Theodore C. Sorensen, Arthur M. Schlesinger, Jr., Lawrence F. O'Brien, McGeorge Bundy, Carl Kaysen, Richard Goodwin, Jack J. Valenti, Bill D. Moyers, Walt W. Rostow, John P. Roche. . . . the list is extensible, the names well known. But one must beware of being seduced by the publicity which has attended them, and which some of them have done much to create. ("While few of us had a 'passion for anonymity,' most of us had a preference in that direction," says Sorensen in *Kennedy,* words which one would like to believe contain a dash of deliberate irony.) On the whole, glamour and publicity are unreliable evidence of influence and power.

Yet it is as such that they are taken, for example, by Theodore H. White:

> The White House [under Kennedy] was a community. The politics of America were discussed not only at the White House and in its offices but were chewed over for hours in the evenings and over weekends by men who were transfixed by their participation in the thrill of power. . . . It was as if, under Kennedy, a fourth branch had been added to the traditional trio of executive, legislative and judicial branches. The new fourth branch was the policy-making branch of government.

It is a startlingly naive remark. Yet the leap which White makes—the leap from a description of the atmosphere which Kennedy's White House staff brought with them to the claim that a new political institution had been created, a new branch of government—is much the same as that made by other observers who argue that the increased number of special assistants and counsellors to the President, and the proliferation and variety of their roles, represent an "institutionalizing" of the Presidency.

It is with no disrespect that I suggest that the nearest parallel, in previous systems of government, to the nature of these men and their role, is to be found in the eunuchs who wielded such power and influence in many of the ancient empires. Eunuch rule, in the Chinese or the Turkish, in the Roman or the Mogul, empires was the most straight-forward device which emperors found for keeping power in their own court, away from a bureaucracy or an aristocracy (or even an army) which might challenge them. The eunuchs accumulated power and influence and wealth, and one T'ang eunuch gathered so large a hoard of gold and silver, jewels and silks, that thirty carts were needed for thirty days to move them—without his even writing a biography of his emperor.

The usefulness of this parallel is that it emphasizes the personal nature of the relationship between the President and his special assistants and counsellors. The ancient emperors wanted men whom they could trust—and who could be trusted more than those of poor origins, whom they had mutilated for their convenience and peace of mind, and then raised to the highest positions? The system and the methods are not precisely the same to-day, but the degree of personal dependence remains. "Kennedy wanted his staff to be small, in order to keep it more personal than institutional," Sorensen says, and then, in a vital and emphatic passage, he hammers the point home:

> . . . From the outset he abandoned the notion of a collective, institutionalized Presidency. He ignored Eisenhower's farewell recommendation to create a First Secretary of Government to oversee all foreign affairs agencies. He abandoned the practice of the Cabinet's and the National Council's making group decisions like corporate boards of directors. He abolished the White House practice of White House staff meetings and weekly Cabinet meetings. He abolished the pyramid structure of the White House staff, the Assistant President-Sherman Adams-type job, the Staff Secretary, the Cabinet Secretariat, the NSC Planning Board and the Operations Coordinating Board, all of which imposed, in his view, needless paperwork and machinery between the President and his responsible officers. . . . He relied instead on informal meetings and direct contacts—on a personal White House staff, the Budget Bureau and *ad hoc* task forces, to probe and define issues for his decision. . . .

Both Sorensen and Schlesinger emphasise that the special assistants in the White House, in those days, were for the most part *generalists,* whereas the most obvious attribute of "institutionalizing" is *specialization,* the codification of areas and boundaries of responsibility, the strict observance of precedent and record (as in the minutes of English cabinet meetings), and an almost hierarchical accountability.

None of these features of an institution, of "institutionalizing," was present in President Kennedy's White House staff; and, although something of the air, of the atmosphere, of the wide-ranging generalist has disappeared, none of them is present in President Johnson's White House staff, either.

It is absurd to talk of the "institutionalizing" of the Presidency through the White House staff, when that staff is liable to be changed from top to bottom with each change of President, and certain to be changed from top to bottom with a change of President which also involves a change of party; when men make the office, as Lawrence O'Brien emphatically did, as McGeorge Bundy did in a way very different from that of his successor, and as John Roche has done in a way very different from that of his predecessor; when the President can reach out and recruit almost at whim, as President Johnson did when he plucked back McGeorge Bundy during the Middle East crisis; and when the men themselves may resign almost at whim, as in the gradual withdrawal, between 1964 and 1966, of most of the "Kennedy men."

It will, I hope, eventually be seen why I regard the noninstitutional character of the Presidency as of such importance. For the moment, it is enough to say that the Presidency, *as organised in the White House,* seems to me a form of unencumbered, arbitrary, personal rule. "Institutionalization," precisely because it is based on precedent and hierarchy and codification, is the very opposite of arbitrariness; and it is with the arbitrary nature of the Presidency that I am at this point concerned.

An Instrument of Political Will

The other supposed evidence of the "institutionalizing" of the Presidency can be disposed of quickly. It was President Eisenhower who first established a special office in the White House to handle its relations with Congress. It was Lawrence O'Brien, under President Kennedy and then under President Johnson, who transformed that office into a formidable operation. But I must insist that the existence of this office, and others similar to it, is no evidence of "institutionalizing" *unless* it can be shown that it has changed the nature of the President's relationship with Congress, or the sanctions which either President or Congress can employ, or the nature of the Presidential *act* itself. The evidence is already in. It has done none of those things.

First, under President Eisenhower, the office became more a channel for Congress (i.e., Senator Lyndon Johnson) to run the White House rather than *vice versa;* while, under President Kennedy and President Johnson, it became the channel for O'Brien to work prodigious miracles in the art of directing by subtle indirection. In other words, it is the character of the President, and the character which he gives his Presidency, which has determined the role of the office—which is the very opposite of "institutionalization."

Secondly, the noninstitutional character of the office could not be clearer than it is to-day, when it can hardly be said to exist outside the person of the Postmaster-General, who is, of course, Lawrence F. O'Brien. In fact, there is some evidence that, faced with a difficult 90th Congress, President Johnson has increasingly fallen back on more traditional channels of communication with Congress, and has even bothered to remember that his Vice-President is also President of the Senate.

Thirdly, if the offices in the White House are made partly by the men who hold them, and partly by the character of the President and his Presidency, they are also made partly by situations and events. The handling of the 90th Congress in 1967 was an entirely different political task from the handling of the 89th in 1965, or the 88th in 1963. All these considerations, which apply to the legislative office in the White House, apply equally to all its other offices. With a new President, with the end of the war in Vietnam, with the definition of different national "goals," the organisation of the White House would immediately look very different from its organisation under President Eisenhower, President Kennedy, or President Johnson, when the "institutionalizing" of the Presidency is supposed to have occurred. We are not, in fact, gazing on an institution at all, but on an arbitrary flexible instrument of political will.

D.O.D. and B.O.B.

The rapid development of the power of certain departments and agencies—the Bureau of the Budget and the Department of Defense are the most obvious—is clearly an important example of "institutionization." But the "institutionalizing" of what? It is this question which must be considered carefully, for it is not enough to show that these agencies have become more effective instruments of the political will of the President. If the claim that the Presidency is being "institutionalized" is to be sustained, it has to be shown that their own "institutionalization" has significantly altered the conditions in which the Presidential will operates: that it has significantly altered the character of the Presidential act.

Robert McNamara's assertion of the power of the Department of Defense over the established Service departments is, of course, an indirect assertion of the Presidential power within his administration. But I am not in the least clear how significant this assertion is: how much of it is merely a reflection of the character of McNamara himself, of his "special relationship with the President," and of the wholly unmanageable nature of the war in Vietnam. I am not prepared to say, from my own observation, that the present character of the relationship of the President with his Service departments and his Service chiefs would survive the removal of any of these factors; that there has yet been an institutional change amounting (which is the argument I am contesting) to a constitutional change. (It is worth noticing, here, the role of the Department of Justice under Robert Kennedy: because of his personal relations with the President, even the most acute observers talked about it as an arm of the Presidency. But it was R. F. Kennedy who was the arm; not the Department.)

Similarly, the very significant development of the Bureau of the Budget—under two creative directors, and now, which is equally important, under a tough and skilled consolidating one—has obviously made the potential effectiveness of the Presidency much greater. Although President Truman relied on it, and therefore strengthened it a great deal, its nearly "institutional" development began, as so much else did, with President Eisenhower, in his attempt to create a Presidency which dispensed with the necessity for a President. (In much the same way, as is too seldom pointed out, the genius of his "military" leadership in the Second World War was to try and remove the necessity for generals. One always gets the impression from his memoirs that he could not understand why it was necessary to have a Bradley or a Patton or a Montgomery actually at the front.) From one Presidential memorandum—a significantly institutional method of proceeding—the Bureau of the Budget has moved, with the same pertinence and determination as the clerical bureaucracy under the medieval English kings, into feudal domains which previously seemed impregnable, and do not yet seem ripe to fall.

The extension of the activities and power of the Bureau of the Budget is the most obviously unexplored political development in the history of the United States in the past quarter of a century. Perhaps it is because it seems a dull subject: it is as "dull" as ditchwater, teeming with microbe, insect, and reptile life. Tadpoles, in the Bureau of the Budget, are frogs the next day—and all by virtue of the scribbled memoranda which are the hallmark of all institutional power, in any system, in any age. Climbing the steps of the Executive Office Building to visit the Bureau of the Budget is very like what it must have been to call on the scarcely known men who constituted the pertinacious bureaucracy of Henry II. At any moment, when they talk of Commerce or Agriculture or Health, Education and Welfare as if these were part of a rebellious (ecclesiastical or lay) baronage, one expects to hear the cry, "Who will rid me of this turbulent priest?"; and one would not be in the least surprised if five knights rode immediately down Pennsylvania Avenue to butcher the department heads in the sanctuary of their departments.

The instruments of pain which the Bureau of the Budget has devised in its battle with the feudal departments of government are many and terrible. The whole mysterious eschatology (for so they represent it, as a doctrine concerning last, or final, matters) of cost-effectiveness has become an almost sublime machine of torture, which the Inquisition would not have disdained. Moreover, the Bureau is reaching, not only to the obvious feudal domains, the hitherto largely independent departments or agencies, but beyond them to the Congressional committees with whom the departments have elaborately feudal relationships of mutual right and obligation. There is no doubt, in fact, that the power of the Bureau of the Budget has changed so much in recent years that a proper Whig (if any were left) in a proper Whig assembly (if any still existed) would introduce a motion simply announcing that its power has increased, is increasing, and ought to be diminished. But I am still not certain that the change has been a radical institutional or constitutional one. The present Director, certainly, has fought enough battles during the past year, and lost enough, to make one remember that a baronage, even in a republic, has deep reserves of that irresistible form of energy: total inaction.

The Doorkeepers

Lastly, there is no evidence that any White House lore, any body of precedent or rules or conventions, is being built up, to be passed on from one Presidency to the next. The passage from Sorensen's *Kennedy,* which has been quoted above, makes it amply clear that President Kennedy ripped apart the elaborate White House staff system which President Eisenhower had constructed, and established another which suited his own needs, methods, and appetites. The peculiar circumstances of President Johnson's succession, and especially the retention, for a number of months and, in some cases, for years, of many of President Kennedy's own staff, concealed an equally personal reorganization. It was not merely that Valenti and Moyers, for example, were hardly the same kind of men as Sorensen and O'Donnell; it was that what was asked and expected of them were different. No description of the roles of Valenti and Moyers—the scope and manner and impact of their activities—would bear any institutional relationship to the roles of Sorensen and O'Donnell.

Similarly, to-day, now that Valenti and Moyers have gone, who would be bold enough to try and define, in sensible institutional terms, the role of Marvin Watson? That he is a powerful and influential doorkeeper (as was O'Donnell, as was Moyers) does not say enough. In every system of government, there have been people intelligent enough to realize that keeping the monarch's door is a source of power. It was not for nothing that, in the Middle Ages, the period in all history which has been most fertile in the creation of political institutions, the most powerful official was frequently called by the title of chamberlain (*chamber:* room; *-ling:* one concerned with); and it is no surprise, therefore, to find that, in as personal a system of government as the Presidency, the office of chamberlain still exists.

But the doorkeeper, as eunuch after eunuch in the ancient empires, and busy cleric after busy cleric in the Middle Ages, quickly discovered, can make the most flexible use of his opportunities. His post, in other words, is not an institutional one at all; it depends far too much on personal influence and opportunity; and the White House is pre-eminently a staff of competing doorkeepers.

> Goosey, goosey, gander,
> Whither shall I wander?
> Upstairs and downstairs,
> And in my lady's chamber.

The nursery rhyme, it is believed, had a precise political application when it was composed. It still has, to-day, a general political application; not least in the Executive Mansion of the President of the United States of America.

Disguising Constitutional Change

Still, it is said, one cannot brush aside, in this way, the cumulative "institutionalization" which is represented, not only by the Bureau of the Budget, but by the Council of Economic Advisors and the Office of the Scientific Advisor to the President. There is no intention, here, of brushing aside anything that happens within the Executive Office Building, behind its 900 Doric columns, at the head of its four heroic cantilevered staircases. Henry Adams called the building itself "an architectural infant asylum." That the offices within it are not political infant asylums hardly needs stating.

I have dealt with the Bureau of the Budget, and acknowledged possible evidence of "institutionalization" there. (One of the obvious signs is the attractiveness of the Bureau to *career* civil servants in Washington. It can, more or less, pick and choose; and its staff has the positive bearing of an elite corps, much as Strategic Air Command once used to have in the armed services.) But, for all its obvious importance, it is hard to describe the Council of Economic Advisors as an "institution." If, as I have said, I am to recognize an institution, I wish to be shown a body whose *functions* and *attitudes* and *methods of procedure* exist, and remain very much the same, independently of the actual persons who staff them, or the actual politicians to whom they are responsible. I have followed, as closely as possible, somc of the internal debates which have taken place about economic policy during the time I have been in the United States, and which have resulted in Presidential economic decisions of varying timeliness and effectiveness. But the bodies which, in these debates, have acted as "institutions," with permanent habits of address have been—lo and behold!—the Treasury and the Federal Reserve; and, of course, to meet members of the Federal Reserve System, not merely in its headquarters in Washington, but scattered across the states, is to realise exactly what a formidable institution it is.

As for the Scientific Advisor to the President, and his office, their importance has declined as rapidly as it rose, during the period when science seemed to be the breastplate of the New Frontier. It may, of course, regain its importance, in new conditions, under another President, and its office, certainly, will survive, if only because the scientific community in the country expects it, and wants it. It has clients, in short, just as much as Commerce or Agriculture has always had them; and as even the Council of Economic Advisors may be said to have them now, among those who do not find the Treasury or the Federal Reserve congenial channels for expressing their interests or their opinions. These client relationships help to emphasise that the new arms of the Presidency are important, not because they represent its "institutionalization," but because they are a response to the expansion of its functions, and especially of the functions *it is expected to perform*, either by client bodies (e.g., the scientific community) or by the public at large. An expansion of functions *may* be a result of "institutionalization," and they *may* result in "institutionalization": this is the two-way story of all great bureaucracies. But a significant expansion of functions is the expression, primarily, not of institutional, but of constitutional change. Function, in a political process, is best defined in terms of expectation: of what people (either in the general public or as specific bodies) expect this or that part of the political process to do. In short, the powers of the constitution are redistributed because the expectation of performance by different bodies under the constitution has been redistributed. "Institutionalization" is a euphemism for disguising profound constitutional change.

A last example may be given. It could be said—it is said—that the President's supervision of foreign policy is being increasingly "institutionalized": in the National Security Council, for example, and almost physically in the Operations Room. But one should notice one feature of this development. The State Department itself increasingly leans on those in the White House who are concerned with foreign policy. The State Department itself has a heightened expectation of, not only what the White House will do, but what the White House should do. This raised expectation might seem, at first, to be only an internal, institutional, redistribution of functions. But it is much more. It is the result of a general—public—expectation of the role and powers of the President in a situation (only 25 years old) in which the definition of the national interest abroad and the creation and execution of a national policy abroad have become (as they were not before) such an unavoidable function of the political process, and one of such magnitude, that it is the Presidency which is expected to bear and perform it.

The change (like all the changes discussed), if it is institutional at all, is only secondarily so. It is primarily a constitutional change; for, a constitution may define functions, but it is itself made by expectations.

Presidential Energy

Some of the importance of Richard E. Neustadt's *Presidential Power* was that it was a restatement of the entirely personal, entirely accidental, entirely improvising nature of the supreme political office in the United States, this nature being unavoidable because it is confronted, not only by Congress, but by a score of other repositories of power and influence usually (as has been said) "in combat postures." He never boldly takes it on, but he is restless with the idea of an "institutionalized" Presidency. Machiavelli wrote a prescription for the "new men" of the "new prince." Neustadt, in terms suitable to our more commonplace age, but with similar anticipation, wrote a prescription for the "new men" of the "new president."

Properly and significantly, Neustadt directed his attention (in the three central chapter headings) to: Persuasion; Reputation; Prestige. None of them is an institutional quality. None of them can be "institutionalized." In fact, Neustadt was writing about exactly what Hamilton and Madison and Jay wrote about in *The Federalist.* The two most remarkable features of *The Federalist,* in its discussion of the Presidency, are, first, that they discussed it so little and, secondly, that the only really extended discussion of its nature (Nos. 70–77) is a discussion of Presidential *energy.*

"The necessity of an energetic executive . . ."; "energy as the most necessary qualification . . ."—it was on this that Hamilton (they were Hamilton's papers) fixed his mind. And so (not surprisingly, for he was writing at the end of President Eisenhower's artful, but not fully satisfying, exercise in relaxed government) did Neustadt; and so, of course, did President Kennedy.

It is impossible to ignore his Uncompleted Presidency. I have not the slightest doubt that much of its importance derives from the fact that it was uncompleted: that now, and for ever more, it can be maintained that, given two full terms, this exceptionally gifted politician could have moved, convincingly and successfully, to the full realization of his policies and his hopes. I have to demur, if only on the grounds I have already suggested: that inaction is the only inexhaustible form of political energy. But the Uncompleted Presidency has enabled a constitutional legend to be created. The legend is that the personal energy of the President can overcome the energy of the other political bodies in the country whose primary interest is either in inaction or in different action. An Uncompleted Presidency is necessary to such a myth because it means that no final account can be rendered, that no final adding up of the credit and debit columns can be made. It means that the benefit of the doubt can be given to exaggerated and even exotic claims.

Would President Kennedy's second term have been the record of achievement which Sorensen and Schlesinger and Neustadt (in the afterword to *Presidential Power*) ask us to believe? I doubt it, and I am grateful for their spirits that the disillusionment never came: disillusionment, not with the man, but with the capacity of the office. How would Lincoln have handled Reconstruction? It is the question which I never cease to ask myself as I pass the Lincoln Memorial, and watch the tourists taking their snapshots with their Polaroids. He might well have handled it superbly, but one must be given leave to doubt it. In a list of the ten greatest men the world has ever known, Lincoln would be my only confident entry as a politician (except, possibly, Elizabeth I who, in difficult and alarming circumstances, created a nation and the idea of nation which were to flower for another three and a half centuries). Yet, even our awareness of the vast achievement of Lincoln depends partly to-day on the fact that it was an Uncompleted Presidency, that the final account could never be rendered.

* * *

Popular Will and Representative Assemblies

. . . it is time that we rid our minds altogether of the idea that, in our age, the popular will or the popular voice find their true or convincing or authoritative expression in representative assemblies. It is certainly not true of France, which has returned, with an equanimity born of indolence, to its (revolutionary *and* Napoleonic) belief that government is "the incontrovertible agent of the . . . organic people." It is certainly not true of England, where representation has ceased to be a serious consideration in the political system, and the nature of the constitution is, with only marginal restraints, plebiscitary in its nature, a direct transference of power taking place from the people to the government. It is a *little* more true of the United States, because the two Houses of Congress can still exercise considerable restraints; but the fact remains that the popular will, in any energizing form, is again transferred directly from the people to the executive.

* * *

It is not strange that the idea of the executive as the energetic and energizing influence in a political system should crop up in both *The Federalist* and Amery's *Thoughts on the Constitution.* The idea of an initiating and directing executive is essential to the notion of the national state; and where it has always, in England, reflected what Dicey called the "omnipotence and undisputed supremacy throughout the whole country of the central government," it must increasingly come to reflect the same in the United States, whatever the distribution of powers in its constitution. It is essential, also, to the notion of democracy; for the one inescapable fact about a democracy is that its appetite for government is insatiable. "On, on and on—up, up, and up"—to use Ramsey MacDonald's favourite flourish of rhetoric—it goes: free enterprise creates the popular motor car; free citizens buy it; and, in a trice, both free enterprise and free citizens are demanding federally supported highways to be built through their states. The conservative critics of democracy in the 19th century were right in their forebodings: merely by allowing rein to insatiable popular appetites, strong government would become inevitable.

At the height of the city riots in 1967, Bill D. Moyers called, publicly, for Robert McNamara to be made *tsar* in charge of clearing the city slums and ghettoes. Popular appetite had been expressed—there is no doubt that much of the looting was the simplest expression of the simplest appetites—and immediately came democracy's only response to popular appetite: the request for a *tsar*.

After Hiroshima and Nagasaki, Earl Long buttonholed one of the most violent supporters of state rights in Louisiana. "What are you going to do now," he asked, "now that the Feds have the atom bomb?" It was an extreme example, but a dry recognition, of the "omnipotence and undisputed supremacy throughout the whole country" of a national and democratic government, even under the "written" constitution of the United States. A strong executive, *The Federalist* continually argued, is threatened by "the maxims of republican jealousy." Who is jealous, now, of the power of the federal executive, when popular appetites want what only it can supply, because it "has the ships, it has the men, it has the money, too"?

"As One People . . ."

I do not wish it to be thought that, in my ignorance of American politics, I am not aware of the pluralist nature of American society, and the remnants of pluralism in its constitution. I am merely asserting that the executive energy which a national and democratic state needs for its survival is now to be found only in the federal executive and the federal judiciary. I know that it is possible to point to individual states, individual governors, individual mayors who still give fitful demonstrations that executive energy does not yet reside solely in Washington, D. C. But this is not enough. The more energetic, for example, that the schemes of Mayor Lindsay of New York City and Governor Rockefeller of New York State become—the more ambitious in their objectives, and the more extensive in their scope—the larger and more urgent become their pleas for federal help and federal money. In short, the multiplication of interests now able to mobilise in such a way that they have direct access to the central government, in order to press their demands on society, is not going to result in a corresponding diversity and complexity of political institutions and activity, but only in the strengthening of one institution and one kind of activity: not in a variety of "plebiscites," but in one plebiscite.

Where, then, does the source of energy of the Presidency reside? Quite obviously, it resides, first, in the actual and symbolic importance of the fact that he is the "Head of State." "America has no more solemn rite than the inauguration of a President," says Arthur Schlesinger, Jr. in his introduction to a collection of the inaugural addresses of the Presidents of the United States:

Every four years since 1789 the austere ceremony has suspended the passions of politics to permit an interlude of national reunion . . . the nation listens for a moment as one people. . . .

To whom?

* * *

. . . the character of the Presidency is such that the majority of the people can be persuaded to look to it for a kind of leadership which no politician, in my opinion, should be allowed, let alone invited, to give. "If people want a sense of purpose," Harold Macmillan once said to me, "they should get it from their archbishops": a remark of recognizably English accent, finely delimiting the area of politics. This delimitation is essential to a free society, and it is the most obvious mark of a society that cares more for other things than freedom that its political leaders try to give the nation, the people, "a sense of purpose," and so justify any interference with their private pursuits, inclinations, and morals.

Caesaropapism?

The Presidency seems to me to be a seed bed for, and already to have in it some of the seeds of, the most refined of all absolutist systems: Caesaropapism. Some American political scientists have tried to persuade me that it is really a constitutional monarchy, stuck more or less where the English monarchy was stuck in 1688. But no one (except Macaulay, writing his absurd eulogies a century and a half later) ever looked for "a sense of purpose" to William III, a tedious *statdholder* from the Netherlands. It was the true achievement of the Whigs to make the English monarchy dull and boring (and rather vulgar as well) and, in the process, to eliminate all concern with national and moral purpose from English politics—which does not mean from English society—for ever.

The Presidency, as we are coming to know it, is very different. When, some time ago, I expressed the view that President Kennedy reminded me of Justinian, it was drawn to my attention that another English journalist, Patrick O'Donovan of the London *Observer*, had, while he was in Washington, compared President Johnson with Justinian. I do not think this coincidence can be altogether dismissed. Historical analogies can, of course, be pushed too far. But Americans are either unable or afraid to make them at all; and, as a result, they sacrifice some of the perceptions these can offer. O'Donovan made his comparison in 1965, when President Johnson seemed to be an Emperor on the Potomac; and both he and I were commenting on the energy, equal to Justinian's, which two successive Presidents appeared to be bringing to the overdue business of the consolidation of an empire. The more I consider the work of the Presidency in the past seven years, the more it seems to me to be embarked on a consolidation (or codification) of imperial (or federal) law and administration, with the purpose of creating, as Justinian set out to do, a commonwealth of citizens under one law, all of them persuaded of the ultimate justice, in doctrine and in practice, of the regime to which they consent.

If this interpretation is correct, then the position of the President as Head of State is going to become of increasing importance. Of all the multiple facets of Caesaropapism—instructive even to-day, because it attempted to work out the relations between people, emperor, pope, and God, in one constitution—the one which matters here is that it managed to achieve a surprisingly convincing combination between the *ascending* and *descending* theories of government: between the belief that power is conferred from below by the people, and the belief that it is conferred from above, by a superior force, i.e. God. The throne in the Byzantine Empire was elective: the people were the electors, and they could take the crown away. Indeed "the legal right to revolution" was recognized, and was voiced, for example, by the Patriarch, Nicholas Mysticus, in the 10th century. But—and it was by this trick that the Byzantine Emperors sustained themselves for so long—the people were also the Christian Commonwealth, and when they gave their assent to the Emperor at his coronation, they in fact acknowledged him as the representative of the Christian Commonwealth, and therefore as the Viceroy of God. His power having been given to him from below, the Emperor then exercised it as being confirmed from above. It was a brilliant device.

The Organic People

More and more, it seems to me, the Presidency in the United States, having originally received power from below, according to an *ascending* theory of government, will act, and is already acting, according to a *descending* theory, as if power is confirmed to it from above, by the law, the nation, the allegedly manifest (one is tempted to say, revealed) goals of the organic people. This is a recent development, and my description will be resisted by those who still emphasise the atomised nature of American society: a society of expectant capitalists and their institutions, able to buck the power of the state. I can only reply that I think their picture is already out of date (as both extreme right and new left instinctively recognise). The enmeshing of big business and the universities with the federal government hardly fits their picture. It fits the portents I am trying to describe here.

In England, the myth is still sustained that the executive is continually subject, from day to day, to a reaffirmation of assent from below, through the votes of the House of Commons. In practice, this is no longer true. But the myth is still useful. Although Harold Wilson from time to time tries it, no Prime Minister can announce a policy in the House of Commons (which is the only place he can announce it) as if he were a national leader, the Head of State; for there, opposite him, is the Opposition, representing half of the nation, and ready with a motion of censure and rejection. We know, anyhow, that the real Head of State is not there, but at the race-course, and the majority of the "organic people" are there, in spirit, with her.

In contrast, of course, President de Gaulle, having had power conferred on him from below (he uses the mandate like a coronation), has proceeded to act as if it had been confirmed to him from above: as if he were "the incontrovertible agent . . . of the organic people," the representative of *la France douce*—or rather, these days, *la France aigre*. Similarly, the President of the United States increasingly acts, in day-to-day matters, under the same claim, that he represents a superior national will —a claim which, in a moment of national crisis, President Lincoln felt bound to assert. (In terms of political theory, Lincoln claimed to represent a national will, the *real* will, even, of the organic people, at a moment when it could reasonably have been claimed that both national will and organic people had been shown not to exist. But he won, and so we know him to be great.)

I must emphasize again that I am fully aware of the countless bodies of interest which exist in this country, able to resist and obstruct the claims of the Presidency to exercise the national or popular will. But the fact remains that these bodies, even when they are organized in the two Houses of Congress, cannot and do not claim to represent the organic people. In fact their strength lies in the quite opposite claim: that they represent the people divided into separate and local interests, its organic unity destroyed. Again, therefore, the constitution of the United States might seem to combine two opposite theories of government: organic and inorganic representation of the people. But, in the modern age, no national state, and no democratic state of any size has been able to face the problems of government without, in practice, falling back more and more on the theory that a direct transference of power takes place from the people to the executive, that there is a direct transformation of popular energy into executive energy. In the United States, the difference in the political theory is evident in the difference between the methods of the New Deal and those of the Great Society. Roosevelt, for all his improvisation and his creative political genius, really manipulated the traditional political system. But the instinct of the administration of President Johnson has been to wrench both the theory and practice of the federal constitution almost to the point of annihilating it.

Of course, the effort has had more failures than successes. Of course, President Johnson has encountered the inexhaustible reserves of inaction and obstruction which separate and local interests possess in a country as large as the United States. But the effort, in future Presidencies, will continue. The theory of the American constitution needs urgently to be restated in terms of the democratic, and not liberal, assumptions which now prevail in the Western world. But political theory, in the United States, is not taken very seriously.

The Need for Political Theory

There are several obvious results of the working of the American Presidency in these conditions. In the first place, people come to expect too much of it: no sooner is a need demonstrated, an appetite expressed, than there is a demand for a presidential *tsar*. Secondly, and of course related to the first, the federal government itself tries to do too much: thus, there is a profound constitutional, as well as any political or personal, reason why the present administration is burdening itself with so many tasks. Thirdly, the available talent in the country, if attracted to public service, drifts more and more to the federal government, thus weakening all other sources of executive energy. Both the exaggerated elevation which the "new men" felt in the presidency of Kennedy, and the exaggerated disappointment so many of them feel in that of his successor, are explicable in terms of the "new presidency" itself, what is demanded of it and what it expects to do, and of the constitutional assumptions which increasingly support it.

Constitutions do matter. We spend far too much time these days examining political institutions—hence making the faulty analysis of an "institutionalized" Presidency—instead of the constitution which determines the relationship between them. Moreover, in examining constitutions, political theory is ultimately the only true assistance. If I have concentrated, in this article, on the combination of roles in the Presidency, it is because I believe that that combination lends itself, as in France, to the kind of distortion of a liberal constitution which the appetites of a democracy in a national state always demand: to the elevation of the descending over the ascending theory of government.

I am new to the Presidency. I have deliberately emphasized, perhaps over-emphasized, the one aspect of it which has most forcibly struck me: the elements in it which could lead to a form of Caesaropapism (which is a very different matter from the simple Caesarism which has always been feared to lie latent in the American Presidency, not least by the English Whigs in the early 19th century). In my edition of the *Encyclopaedia Britannica*, the article on Justinian is still the one composed by Lord Bryce. "Justinian's age," he says, "was quite unequal in intellect to so vast an undertaking as the fusing on scientific principles into one organic whole of the entire law of the empire." They are words of warning, worth addressing to the "new men" of our own age. (Was there not a hint of such a warning in Aaron Wildavsky's "The Political Economy of Efficiency" in *The Public Interest,* Summer 1967?) For, with all my selection and over-emphasis, I would add in conclusion that there is no aspect of the Presidency which does not seem to me to invite, as urgently, the assistance of political theory. The difference, in organization and role, between the national parties, on which the President relies, and the state and local parties is an obvious area in which political theory can offer illumination. So is the whole of the nominating (and, indeed, electing) process, which no longer performs, in theory or practice, what was originally expected of it.

When the two principles of representation and federation, which Hume said would alone enable a popular government to adapt itself to a vast continent, are to-day so changed and weakened, one can indeed question whether the federal constitution, as originally conceived, will survive. I am convinced only that its condition is critical, and that it requires, not only empirical observation, but the kind of political theory which makes even the prudent *Federalist* timeless.

43

The President and Congress: An Historic Perspective

WILFRED E. BINKLEY

In the following excerpt, Wilfred E. Binkley summarizes the historic balance between Congress and the President from 1789 to 1961. He views the President as the spokesman for the commercial, financial, and greater planter interests of the East Coast and Congress as the voice of agrarian interests until 1828, when Jackson's candidacy forced the presidential and congressional branches of government to exchange roles. Since that time, Binkley contends, strong Presidents have been the tribunes of the people, of the small agrarians and urban working classes, while Congress has represented the vested interests. There are, of course, numerous exceptions to this generalization; many of Franklin Roosevelt's emergency anti-Depression measures, for example, were as important to the vested interests as to the "little people." These exceptions to the contrary, Binkley has accurately described the changing presidential and congressional constituencies.

Although he accepts the efficacy of parliamentary government as a means of integrating the executive and legislative branches in England, he doubts its utility in the United States. The pattern of integration he suggests for the United States is one of strong presidents who are capable of exercising leadership and directing Congress' legislative programs. Binkley remains positively disposed toward "strong Presidents" who "promote the public welfare amid the mosaic of conflicting interests represented in Congress." In an age of more or less permanent crisis, he concludes, the American nation must increasingly rely on strong presidential leadership.

Binkley was Professor of Economics and Political Science from 1921 to 1927 and Professor of Political Science and History from 1927 to 1941 at Ohio Northern University, and a visiting lecturer at Oxford University in 1949–1950. He was also the author of The Powers of the President *(1937),* A Grammar of American Politics *(1949),* The Man in the White House *(1958), and* American Political Parties *(1962).*

The American presidency is an office rooted deep in colonial experience. Its prototype is the colonial governor who, as the representative of the Crown and agent of the dominant economic interests of Britain, was constantly confronted with the counterforces of emerging American democracy represented in the elective assembly in each of the colonies. Here was a conflict that ended only with the flight of the royal governors when the patriots seized power at the opening of the Revolutionary War and set up their own state governments. They made their state legislatures "omnipotent," while they reduced the state governors to mere agents of the legislatures except in New York and Massachusetts where the governors were popularly elected. The shadowy government of the Continental Congress and the Articles of Confederation proved satisfactory enough to the democratic forces of the post-Revolutionary period, since it left them quite securely intrenched in power in the omnipotent state legislatures. However, as the years of the 1780's slipped by, this governmental set-up grew increasingly obnoxious to the very strong commercial, financial, and greater planter interests of the coastal communities.

The framing and ratification of the Constitution were largely the work of coastal interests and it represented remarkably well the consummation of their desires. The debates of the Philadelphia Convention reveal a powerful and concerted drive against "democracy" which the delegates identified with the state legislatures, unrestrained by any central government. The specific evidence that they achieved the satisfaction of their desires is found in such provisions of the Constitution as the federal power to regulate commerce and thereby end the chaos of state regulations, the treaty-making power by which commercial agreements might be made with foreign nations, the prohibition of the states' power to emit bills of credit or make anything but gold or silver a tender in the payment of debts, or enact laws impairing the obligation of contracts.

Furthermore, the Constitution authorized the enactment of federal statutes and the establishment of enforcement agencies acting directly on the individual. Thus for the first time in American history a powerful set of distinctly American executive agencies was created, potentially, if not actually, popular in its nature. It apparently made necessary a Chief Executive. The proponents of the Constitution, the Federalists, thus became champions of the idea of a vigorous national executive and the anti-Federalists were closely identified and more or less satisfied with the powerful unchecked legislatures of the states and the feeble Congress of the Confederation.

When the time came to establish the government under the Constitution it was extremely fortunate for the Fed-

From *President and Congress*, Third Edition, by Wilfred E. Binkley. Copyright 1937, 1947, © 1962 by Wilfred E. Binkley. Reprinted by permission of Alfred A. Knopf, Inc.

eralists that they had within their group the leader to whom all turned as the one man for the presidency. George Washington was a national hero endeared to the masses as the father of his country. He was fitted by character, aptitude, and appropriate experience for the office of Chief Executive. He had served a magnificent apprenticeship in administration on a large scale by his exceptionally shrewd management of his vast plantation and by his performance of duties as Commander in Chief of the Continental army. His dealing with the Continental Congress had afforded him an invaluable experience with politicians and given him a foretaste of the difficulties inseparable from the office of President. Ever mindful of the proper subordination of the military to the civil authority, he had yet learned the bitter lesson of governmental impotence as manifested by the Congress during and after the Revolutionary War. Moreover, the character of the executive office devised by the constitutional framers would certainly have been less imposing if it had not been created in the full understanding that its first incumbent would be General Washington himself. Thus the personality of this remarkable man contributed to the strengthening of the Executive.[1]

After ample opportunity to survey the evidence in the case, the late Albert J. Beveridge came to the conclusion that the lifelong determination of John Marshall to obtain a strong national government derived from the profound impression made on him by the incompetence of the civil administration under the Continental Congress during the Revolution.[2] He had served as a soldier under Washington, as had also young Alexander Hamilton, who came in contact with the same executive futility under the Congress. These three key men of the Federalist party, Washington, Marshall, and Hamilton, no doubt saw eye to eye when their thoughts turned to legislatures. They were also affiliated with the economic and social groups that had charge of the government during the first decade under the Constitution.

Circumstances of various sorts, then —the previous experience of these outstanding Federalists in the Continental army, the interests of several powerful economic and social groups, the unrestrained conduct of some of the state legislatures dominated by the debtor element—these and other factors combined to induce the Federalists to assign to the Executive the function of leadership in the new government. The Federalist scheme of government was apparent from the very beginning. Congress, of course, created the departments and prescribed their functions and President Washington nominated the heads. The Treasury Department was the most important. Hamilton was placed at its head and in accordance with instructions from Congress made his famous Reports and followed them up with appropriate measures supported through his active influence on congressmen. The product was the remarkable financial program ever since associated with Hamilton's name. This was the Federalists' idea of executive leadership and their correspondence of the period revealed that they believed it to be the ultimate solution of the problem of the proper relationship to be maintained between the political branches of the government.[3] The executive heads of the departments under the President's titular leadership constituted a ministry which was to function freely and frankly in the full light of publicity. Congress was to have in this ministry a legislative reference bureau plus an active political leadership unencumbered by congressional committees.

In this matter, however, the agrarians had been taken off their guard. So far from suspecting peril to their interests in the Federalist pattern of government, they had even played into the hands of their opponents by consenting to the referring of matters to the executive heads instead of organizing the House internally for handling such matters by establishing a system of standing committees.[4] The landed gentry of Virginia had found themselves able to get along at home in the House of Delegates, working through the Committee of the Whole and as the largest delegation in the federal House of Representatives they had succeeded in imposing this procedure on Congress.[5] There was, however, a vital difference between the situations in Virginia and in the federal government. In the former the agrarians encountered no significant commercial interests in opposition. In Congress they faced the vigilant, intelligent, and powerfully motivated commercial interests and, moreover, the administration was in the latter's hands. The agrarians were as yet inadequately organized and led, their future chief, Thomas Jefferson, being in a sense a captive of the Federalists as Washington's Secretary of State, even victimized, so he thought later, by Hamilton's political trade of the location of the capital on the Potomac in return for Jefferson's delivery of the votes of some Southern congressmen for the assumption of state debts.

Exasperated by the manner in which they had unwittingly contributed to the success of Hamilton's program, the agrarians soon awakened to the disadvantage under which they were placed by the Federalist method of executive leadership. Under the astute but secret generalship of Jefferson their strategy began to take shape. Not the least significant feature of it was, as might have been expected, a drive against the Executive, not as a person—Washington's prestige made that too perilous—but as a branch of the government, particularly as represented in the Treasury Department. From that vantage point Hamilton had exercised almost a mastery of the government, easily putting through Congress the measures that the agrarians believed rendered them tributary to the financial interests. On that stronghold of Federalism, the agrarians large and small concentrated the attack that did not slacken until Hamilton had been driven back to private life. Jefferson sought to discredit the Federalists by denominating them "monocrats" while he led the "Republicans." This latter term meant to imply the advocates of a type of government in which the main organ was the legislature. The agrarians thus claimed to be the champions of legislative authority. As they conceived it, Congress, composed of representatives of the numerous communities of the country, was decentralizing in its tendency while the Executive had already proved to be a tremendous factor in nationalizing the government in the interest of the commercial and financial classes.

It is almost certain that the Federalists were blind to the spirit of the times and overplayed their hand. They defeated their purposes by the vigor with which they exercised the power of the executive office as well as by the inordinate claims they publicly made for that branch of the government. The landed gentry of the South and the agrarians generally were exasperated by Hamilton's claims for the Executive as set forth in his letters signed "Pacificus." Perhaps, plausible as the reasoning seemed, it was imprudent for him to point out that while the powers of Congress are specifically enumerated, the President is not thus limited but is under oath to "execute the office of President," thus implying a vast uncharted field of executive prerogative.[6] It has long been customary to regard the display of force, fifteen thousand militiamen, against the "whisky rebels" as a prudent demonstration of the authority of the national government but the Federalists paid a heavy price for it in the loss of prestige—it seemed to confirm the direst predictions of the agrarians as to the designs of the military monocrats against the people. It was Jefferson's testimony concerning the Whiskey Rebellion that: "The information of our militia returned from the westward is uniform, that though the people there let them pass quietly they were the objects of their laughter not their fear."[7] It almost certainly marks the turning point of Federalist power. Henceforth the party was on the defensive. The final piece of folly was the Alien and Sedition Acts, the latter of which conferred dictatorial power on the President with respect to deporting resident aliens. Unquestionably the personality of John Adams was not adequate in the presidential office, as the successor of Washington, to maintain the great prestige of the presidency. He failed to retain the support of his Cabinet and left the office with the Executive decidedly on the decline.

In 1801 Thomas Jefferson was elected to the presidency by the agrarians of both large and small holdings. He entered office determined to put the ship of state "on the Republican tack." No single element in the Republican party had been more influential than the Virginia gentry. Their delegation in Congress had been most persistent in checking the executive "usurpations" of Secretary of the Treasury Hamilton. They would not have permitted Jefferson to pursue a policy of bold leadership even if he had desired. He chose instead a role admirably suited to his temperament and managed Congress through secret influence somewhat after the manner of a political boss, although without any implication of corruption. Congress, however, was getting out of hand by the end of his administration, and under his successor, Madison, leadership in the government passed quite definitely to Congress. The House was thoroughly organized for action independent of the Executive and took the initiative in determining public policies. The trans-Allegheny West came into control and under the Speakership of Henry Clay the coastal gentry saw the reins of Congress pass permanently from their hands. So completely did the Republicans now succeed in the application of their doctrine of congressional "sovereignty" that for a quarter of a century the President was by election or nomination the choice of Congress. While not actually an agency of Congress, the presidency had nevertheless come to have a distinctly subordinate place in the government.

The subordination of the presidency was destined, however, to pass. The agrarians had reduced it and now they restored it and gave it a preeminent place in the federal government. The pioneer farmers of the West had enjoyed universal white manhood suffrage for years and in the hope of checking migration the older states had been compelled reluctantly to grant it. This created a situation suitable for the election to the presidency of a popular hero, a champion of the masses consisting of the urban working classes and the little agrarians everywhere, in short, the "underdogs." The landed gentry did not welcome such an innovation, but they were helpless when Andrew Jackson was a candidate in 1828. His election marked the beginning of the idea that the President is a "tribune of the people," privileged to exercise a vigorous veto in the people's behalf. The party of the agrarians had made a direct about-face on the doctrine of congressional sovereignty.

The now-defunct Federalist party finally got a successor in the Whigs, particularly the Northern wing of that party. Here reappeared as a political party an economic group combination that had once championed the Executive and profited so much by Hamilton's initiative and leadership in that branch of the government. This was the combination that had suffered so much from legislative excesses during the "critical period" of the Confederacy. One might expect them now to manifest once again their historic distrust of the legislature. But something had happened to induce an about-face in this group also. The threat of populism, once so imminent in legislatures, had now passed to the presidency. The commercial and industrial interests felt impelled to transfer their allegiance from the federal executive to the federal legislature. The eloquence of Clay and Webster, both figuratively and literally agents of these interests, was directed against the Executive as a governmental agency dangerous to the liberties of the "people." Something far deeper than the exigencies of politics and economics in that day is necessary to account for this historic reversal in the attitude of business toward the presidency. Ever since the days of Andrew Jackson the business interests of the United States have always been uncomfortable when a popular, aggressive leader has reached or even threatened to reach the office of President. Every "tribune of the people" from Jackson to Franklin D. Roosevelt has looked like a potential if not an actual "rabble rouser" to the capitalistic interests. Such an Executive, fearless both in initiative and in the use of the veto power, puts the control of the government quite definitely beyond their power.

The Whigs and, of course, the business interests generally, sought in vain to subordinate the Executive once more to the control of Congress and were finally reduced to the necessity of depending on capturing the presidency through a resort to rabble rousing on their own part. Accordingly in 1840 they offered as their candidate a military hero, General William Henry Harrison, and after the most boisterous campaign in our history elected him. In his inaugural address he promised to be the kind of a President the Whigs prescribed, duly subservient to Congress, but he did not live long enough to show how that would be done. The four-year term was completed by the Vice President, John Tyler, a strong-willed, Virginia, states-rights Democrat affiliated with the Whigs but who used the veto with deadly effect on the Whig program.

Throughout the first generation of the industrial revolution in the United States the political party of commerce, finance, and the industrial interests was pretty completely frustrated in its efforts to secure the legislation it desired from the federal government. It was able frequently to control Congress but the new type of Executive, ready with a veto message when he felt impelled to use it, either checked or prevented measures for internal improvements, a new Bank of the United States, and high protective tariffs. The second Whig President, General Zachary Taylor, was ready to use the veto himself on the Compromise Bill of 1850, designed by Clay and supported by Webster, and was only prevented from doing so by his untimely death. Almost all the experience the Whigs ever had with the presidency inclined them to look on that office with extreme distrust.

By the forties the Southern slavocracy managed to wrest control of the Democratic party from the masses that had shouted for Jackson. The preservation of the institution of slavery became their paramount political passion. Numerically a minority, they could not hope to control Congress, which, in any case, would have been insufficient for their purpose. They must obtain and maintain control of the presidency since the Jacksonian type of Executive had come to stay. Their master stratagem for this purpose was the fastening of the two-thirds rule for presidential nominations on the Democratic National Nomination Convention. The result was that even when they could not nominate a slaveholder they could, at any rate, prevent the nomination of a candidate inhospitable to slavery. In time the typical Democratic candidate became the "doughface," a Northern man with Southern principles. No matter what party controlled Congress, the veto power in the hands of a Pierce or a Buchanan made the slavocracy secure against legislation disadvantageous to their interests. Moreover, the most capable statesmen of the South, even if denied the presidency, found positions of commanding influence in the Cabinets of the "doughface" Presidents. Outnumbered in both House and Senate, the slave power had come to depend for the protection of their institution on the control of the presidency and thereby maintain the rule of a minority. The failure to retain this control in 1860 threw them into the panic that precipitated the secession movement.

The platform on which Lincoln was elected appealed strongly to the masses of free laborers and little farmers, because of its proposal to keep the territories free from the odium of slavery and to open them to settlers through homestead legislation of the type which Buchanan, under the influence of the slave power, had recently vetoed.[8] Industrial interests were attracted to the party by the promise of protective tariffs and railroad promoters by the promise of a Pacific railroad. The campaign was waged along the lines of the one by which Harrison had been elected twenty years before. Lincoln was presented as preeminently a man of the people. He readily accepted the idea and as President conducted himself as a tribune of the people. This doctrine was the beginning of his difficulty with the directorate of the Republican party. It was a democratic dogma repulsive to the former Whigs, from whose ranks many of the leaders of the Republican party had come. A list of the Republicans in Congress who at one time or another used against Lincoln's conduct as President the dogma of congressional superiority to the Executive included such names as those of Senators B. F. Wade, Charles Sumner, Zachary Chandler, James W. Grimes, and William Pitt Fessenden, and such members of the House of Representatives as Thaddeus Stevens and Henry Winter Davis. Not one of these former Whigs had divested himself of the fundamental Whig doctrine that the President is more or less responsible to Congress, which alone was assumed to be representative of the people. Most of them were lawyers whose clients were often the business interests. Taken by and large, they represented ideas that had always been basic policies of the Northern Whigs. These politicians welcomed no popular leader of the type Lincoln was assuming to be in the presidential office. The real Lincoln could never be a satisfactory type of President to the great industrial and financial leaders that came in time to constitute such an influential element in the Republican party. Only a mythical Lincoln could make that group happy at any time before or since his death. While never actually a rabble rouser, he could not play the role of a tribune of the people without seeming to be a potential one. The danger may have seemed implicit in the well-known passage in his first annual message to Congress: "Labor is prior to and independent of capital. Capital is only the fruit of labor, and could never have existed if labor had not first existed. Labor is the superior of capital, and deserves much the higher consideration."[9]

The haunting specter of populism has induced the business interests since the Civil War to seek constantly to put "safe and sane" men in the White House. Grant was quite satisfactory. He was almost infatuated with men of wealth and usually let Congress have its way, happily, however, checking the inflationists with a veto of the greenback "heresy." Cleveland was the independent type, dangerous at first because of his unorthodox views on protective tariffs manifested in his shocking tariff message of December, 1887, but he redeemed himself in his second term with his anti-inflation policy and his vigorous employment of federal authority in labor disturbances[10] and he consequently occupies today a secure place in their hall of fame. McKinley was "safe"; he worked with Congress. He saved the country from what the business interests regarded as the most dangerous arouser of the masses in our history. In 1896 William Jennings Bryan threw the business interests of the United States into a panic almost incomprehensible today.[11] Some were planning to leave the country if Bryan were elected. It was felt that such a candidate had to be defeated for the presidency to save society from dissolution.

Theodore Roosevelt had a similar capacity for arousing popular enthusiasm with his "big stick," his "square deal," his program of social reform, and his remarkably successful leadership in legislation. He was the least typical of the Republican Presidents. By 1912 he looked to the Old Guard like another Bryan and, despite the strong demand of the rank-and-file Republicans, they, nevertheless, defeated his nomination in the convention. The business interests were then willing to see the Republican party reduced temporarily to the rank of a third party in the hope of permanently eliminating such a "dangerous" man from party leadership. Woodrow Wilson's capacity to get the public ear, focus attention on the disorders and abuses of business, and compel prompt enactment of such measures as the Underwood Tariff, the Clayton Act, the Federal Trade Act, and the Federal Reserve Banking Act in the face of the powerful opposition of the business interests made him worthy to be placed in the great succession of Democratic Presidents following Jefferson and Jackson and to be considered just as obnoxious to the "interests" as his predecessors. Franklin Delano Roosevelt, hailed first as a savior of all, took his place with the other outstanding Democratic Presidents. Elevated to the presidency by a combination of farmers, laborers, and the disappointed middle class, he was bound sooner or later to arouse the resentment of powerful business interests. The determined but futile insistence on the "death sentence" for utility holding companies would make a marked man of any President. The whispering campaign against "that man" that followed was perhaps as inevitable as in the case of Woodrow Wilson or even Jackson and Jefferson, except that in those early days they shouted instead of whispered.

The cult of isolationism in America virtually ended with the 1930's and this profoundly affected the presidency. Not only did the burden of the office increase enormously during the presidencies of Truman and Eisenhower but its very nature underwent a profound change. War, both hot and cold, shifted the center of gravity of the presidential office from domestic issues into the very midst of world problems with the eyes of the human race centered on the President. To him fell decisions as to whether to contribute aid to save the post-war European economy from collapse and chaos, whether to repel communist aggression in Korea, to act promptly to save Greece and Turkey from inclusion within the Russian sphere, to land American forces in the Near East or suddenly to decide whether the moment of all-out attack had arrived that called for letting loose the American nuclear arsenal against the assumed attack. Meanwhile he may be perplexed by domestic issues that persist in having planet-wide implications, whether it be slums, labor strife, or desegregation riots.

The gigantic change within the lifetime of millions of Americans living today can be measured by the fact that President Cleveland managed the presidential office with a single secretary, when he had any at all, while in 1960 the Executive Office of the President contained half a dozen agencies with a total personnel of 2,814 while the White House Office, his immediate staff, the counterpart of Cleveland's single secretary, had a personnel of over 400. And with it all the President is overburdened.

A President who considers himself a tribune of the people, when possessed with flair for publicity and a fearless personality will inevitably start powerful interests demanding that Congress resume its "proper" function of legislation and cease being a "rubber stamp." The "dictator" has been violently condemned in the case of every President of the type under consideration. The words of Henry Clay, uttered a century ago, sound like an extract from a campaign philippic against Franklin Roosevelt: "We are in the midst of a Revolution, hitherto bloodless, but rapidly tending toward a total change of the pure republican character of the government, and to the concentration of all power in the hands of one man. The powers of Congress are paralyzed, except when exerted in conformity with his will. . . ."[12] Every President who has exercised any degree of leadership has inevitably provoked an outburst of "constitutionalism." Democrats in the first decade of the twentieth century condemned Theodore Roosevelt as intemperately as Republicans attacked his cousin in the 1940's.

The experience under the Constitution certainly reveals that the problem of integrating the executive and legislative branches has not yet been solved. There are those who confidently propose resort to the magic formula of a parliamentary system in which the executive can dissolve the legislature and "appeal to the country" in a general election. There was an epidemic of such proposals when Roosevelt and Truman in turn were deadlocked with Congress by the alliance of Southern Democratic with Republican congressmen which prevented extension of the presidential program of social legislation.

The theory of the English parliamentary system is fascinating to amateurs who know neither its historical evolution nor its prosaic practical operation. Of course it was by no means a product of planning but is instead a natural outgrowth of the experience of Britain's peculiar society groping through the centuries for adjustments, expedients, and makeshifts that would solve immediate governmental problems. Out of such innumerable trials do constitutions emerge and evolve. Whenever transplanted elsewhere the original parliamentary system may behave as an exotic plant. It could not do otherwise in America. This does not signify that it would be impossible here but that its performance would be unpredictable.

The American constitutional system is just as much the product of our own society and environment as the parliamentary is of another. Certainly our federal government today is no artificial creature. It, too, is rather the result of innumerable fortuitous day-to-day adjustments over three and a half centuries of governmental experience in the American environment. Such is the complexity of American society, with its conflicts of interests and of sections, that a resort to prompt settlement of its major issues by the simple majorities implicit in a parliamentary system might prove positively explosive. Conflicts inherent in our society are not to be resolved by a simple shift in the mechanics of government. These very conflicts, indeed, determined the nature of our constitution, and this constitution cannot be held responsible for such clashes.

A practicable national policy, translated into a federal statute, represents rather the net results of the concurrences and balances of the dominant interests of the sections, states, and congressional districts. Congress functions at its best when its statutes are most successful in striking an approximate equilibrium of these interests. It was a shrewd observation of the late Frederick Jackson Turner that our federal statutes resemble the international adjustments of general European treaties. So continental in its character is the United States that Turner further concluded, "The more the nation is organized on the principle of direct majority rule and consolidation the more sectional resistance is likely to manifest itself."

It may then be that the very opportunity our system gives for such a phenomenon as the "unholy alliance" of Southern Democrats with Northern Republicans provides the safety valve for what would otherwise be irreconcilable minorities in a parliamentary system. Doubtless the bloc represents ideologies already becoming obsolete. Local pressures may yet produce the "concurrent majorities" which, in contrast with simple national majorities, provide the only sound basis of national legislation in the United States.

In any case, whatever its merits, a parliamentary system is out of the question in the United States in the foreseeable future. There are, however, feasible reforms called for clearly within the framework of our traditional constitutional system. Rural population is over-represented in both Houses of Congress. In the

Senate, on the other hand, the cities make themselves felt through the balances of urban voting strength that the Senators in many states disregard only at their peril. In the House the effect of poll taxes is to give to a handful of voters in certain agrarian states gross over-representation. Moreover, the rural population in many states is given an advantage in congressional representation through the failure of state legislatures during the last generation to redistrict the state in accordance with the enormous growth of city populations.

The function of the President in our system is to discover and somehow or other to promote the public welfare amid the mosaic of conflicting interests represented in Congress. No one has expressed it better than President Coolidge in his statement, "It is because in their hours of timidity the Congress becomes subservient to the importunities of organized minorities that the President comes more and more to stand as the champion of the rights of the whole country."[13] We need Presidents expert in the kind of leadership that make this championship effective. Let us see what our experience has been.

Since the Civil War the training school for successful Presidents has been the gubernatorial office in the states, where they seem to serve an incomparable executive apprenticeship. The list of governors elevated to the presidency since 1865 is indeed impressive: Hayes, Cleveland, McKinley, Theodore Roosevelt, Wilson, Coolidge, and Franklin Roosevelt. While they varied in quality, not one failed, and several belong among the great Presidents. Elected to fill intervals between these abler Chief Executives were Grant, Garfield, Benjamin Harrison, Taft, Harding, and Hoover.[14] So striking is the contrast of the latter list to the former that it might be mistaken for a deliberate attempt to catalogue the less happy choices of the American electorate for the presidency. It is, however, merely a list of the Chief Executives who lacked experience as governors of their states. With rare exceptions, in the half century following the Civil War the American people alternated the two types of President.

Commencing with Harding, the alternation ceased. Three Presidents, each conforming closely to the Republican type and "safe" from the point of view of business, not at all disposed to rouse the populace, came in succession to the presidency. There has perhaps never been a decade in our history when business was more contented with the conduct of government than during the "prosperous" twenties. Government in its operation conformed to the Whig-Republican model. Congress legislated with no pronounced leadership on the part of any of the three Presidents. Harding, Coolidge, and Hoover were "constitutional" Presidents so far as any disposition to lead Congress was concerned. The decade of the twenties was one of relative economic calm, sometimes spoken of as the era of "Coolidge prosperity." Business got the protective tariffs it wanted and the Presidents vetoed "dangerous heresies" such as "uneconomic" farm relief or "heretical" ventures in government ownership. The era was singularly barren of regulative legislation. Not a single one of the great statutes of the kind that stand forth as landmarks in the legislation of the twentieth century was enacted in this decade of the 1920's.

There are those today who are disposed to put the cart before the horse and assume that this type of government brought economic calm, instead of economic calm determining the character of the government. They are forgetful of the fact that it was under this very regime that the great depression began and the kind of government then existing did not demonstrate its capacity to deal with the economic catastrophe it encountered. It may be, after all, but a fair-weather type of government. Surely it will not suffice as "crisis government." It is perhaps a truism that crises call for leaders in the presidential office capable of commanding confidence, and since the old myth that every great crisis brings forth a great leader was long ago exploded, the American people are rather reduced to the necessity of hoping for the good luck of getting a competent leader along with a major crisis. And Presidents with capacity for leadership ought not to be unwelcome even in "normal" times.

NOTES

1. See letter of P. Butler, May 5, 1788, in Max Farrand, *The Records of the Federal Convention*, 3 vols. (New Haven, 1911), III, p. 301.
2. *The Life of John Marshall*, I, pp. 146, 147.
3. See *supra*, p. 40.
4. *Supra*, p. 42.
5. *Supra*, p. 41.
6. *Supra*, p. 52.
7. Jefferson to Madison, Thomas Jefferson, *Writings* (1903), IX, pp. 293–97.
8. James D. Richardson, *Messages and Papers of the Presidents, 1789–1897*, 10 vols. (Washington, D.C., 1897), V, pp. 608–14.
9. Richardson, *op. cit.*, VI, p. 57.
10. In addition to keeping mails moving by use of federal troops at the Chicago R.R. strike of 1894, an army officer boasted of the purpose to "break the strike." C. A. Beard, "Emerging Issues in America," *Current History*, Nov., 1934, p. 203.
11. The reader may judge for himself the hysteria of the commercial East by an editorial from the New York *Tribune* written just after Bryan's defeat for the presidency in 1896: "He was only a puppet in the blood imbued hands of Altgeld, the anarchist, and Debs, the revolutionist, and other desperadoes of that type. . . . He goes down with the cause and must abide with it in the history of infamy. He had less provocation than Benedict Arnold, less intellectual force than Aaron Burr, less manliness than Jefferson Davis. He was the rival of them all in deliberate wickedness and treason to the republic." Quoted, H. F. Pringle, *Theodore Roosevelt*, p. 162.
12. *Supra*, p. 96.
13. Calvin Coolidge, "The President Lives Under a Multitude of Eyes," *The American Magazine* 108, Aug., 1929, p. 146.
14. Since only "elected" Presidents are considered, Arthur and Truman are omitted.

44

The President as International Leader

RICHARD P. LONGAKER

In the following selection, Richard P. Longaker contends that the emergence of the United States as a world power in the twentieth century has reshaped the office and powers of the President. Although Woodrow Wilson regarded the President's international role as an exigency of war, more than half a century of international crises has permanently transformed the President's position as both a world and domestic leader. In addition to expanding the President's power, these crises—such as the steel seizure case, the Bricker Amendment, intervention in Korea, the dispatch of troops to Europe, and the Gulf of Tonkin Resolution—have provoked serious constitutional and political struggles in the American political system. In each crisis the President's responses were shaped by the forces of domestic politics, for example, his relation to the Congress and the Supreme Court. In this article, Longaker demonstrates the close relationship between the movement of international events and the transformation of the presidency. Although the historic examples he employs occurred during the 1940s and 1950s, this selection highlights many contemporary problems in foreign policy making.

Richard Longaker is Professor of Political Science at the University of California at Los Angeles. He is the author of The Presidency and Individual Liberties *(1961),* Recent Trends in American Government *(1960), and several articles in such scholarly journals as the* Political Science Quarterly, Law and Contemporary Society, *and the* Mississippi Valley Historical Review.

Before taking office in 1913, Woodrow Wilson remarked to a friend: "It would be the irony of fate if my administration had to deal chiefly with foreign affairs."[1] Today, a President comes to office assured that he will spend most of his time and make his most difficult decisions in the field of global politics. Wilson's hopes were shattered by the First World War; Roosevelt's similar hopes by the Second; and within the last ten years, international leadership—a function that was thought to be temporary—has become a firm institutional addition to the American Presidency. Any President taking office today knows that one of his major responsibilities will be to *attempt* to exert leadership abroad, if not actually to lead. The emergence of this presidential function in recent years has added to the already distended powers of the chief executive, has changed in important respects the nature of the office, and has complicated the already complex problems of the Presidency. That this is true is demonstrated by the fact that the major constitutional struggles since the Second World War—the Bricker amendment, the Steel seizure, the Great Debate over presidential dispatch of troops to Europe, the McCarthy episode, and the intervention in the Korean War—were provoked by presidential responses to the demands of the new role. The purpose here is to identify the conditions under which the President can most successfully function as an international leader, to sketch briefly the historical development, to analyze the constitutional and institutional setting of his leadership, and to discuss some of the effects his new responsibility has on his traditional functions as a domestic leader.

The phrases used to describe the President's new role are various and frequently misleading. Some speak of the President as world leader, or as exercising world leadership. The existence of the Soviet Union, of course, precludes the use of this term, if taken literally. Others depict him as "leader of a coalition of free nations" or of a "coalition of the free,"[2] a title which is closer to the truth but overlooks the conflicting pressures of coalition leadership, the persuasion of neutrals, and the fact that the President tries to lead those, like Tito and Franco, who are not, ideologically speaking, free. The only term reasonably free from ambiguity is international leader, and even this phrase requires severe qualification, for the President's offer of leadership is often rejected. But still, the phrase implies at least an attempt by the President to work in concert with other nations in order to defend the national interest. It implies, moreover, that he becomes, on occasion, a vital influence in the policy making of other governments. The President can no longer stay at home; instead, he must journey beyond the boundaries of the United States in an effort to tip the balance of world power in favor of the United States. To assert that the President can no longer be passive director of American foreign relations is only to raise the question of how and when his leadership should be exercised. It is also to ask whether or not the President can, as the leader of a democratic nation in a constantly shifting international setting, exert leadership in a sustained fashion.

One President has stated that the

Reprinted from a symposium "The Presidential Office," in *Law and Contemporary Problems*, 21 (Autumn 1956), 735–752, published by the Duke University School of Law, Durham, N.C., by permission of the publisher and the author.

essence of presidential leadership is to "persuade [people] to do what they ought to do without persuasion."[3] In the international field, the essence of leadership is to persuade other leaders that the self-interest of all dictates a common course of action. Persuasion is facilitated if the group is held together by common beliefs and common dangers and if the President can articulate, forcibly and clearly, mutual hopes and fears. Presidential leadership abroad, in other words, depends on the world situation, his own ability, and the political and economic circumstances in the United States. As contemporary restlessness in Europe indicates, both in Western Europe's renewed interest in a European union and the Anglo-French attack on Egypt, the President is inevitably involved in foreign affairs and must attempt to lead, but he is not inevitably an international leader. Like presidential leadership in Congress, presidential international leadership is potential and conditional. Too frequently it is suggested that the need inevitably produces the result.

The Foundations of Effective International Leadership

What then produces the potential and what factors must be present to transform the potential into effective leadership? Obviously, the major factor in the President's potential for leadership is the enormous strength of the United States, the productive skill of her people, her size, resources, and population. But other conditions are almost as essential.

Among the most important is the existence of a common threat and fear of the consequences of acting alone or—and this is much less cohesive—the existence of a common, positive policy that is based not on an external threat, but on common ideals and purposes. Fear of Soviet domination has led to the provisional acceptance of American leadership in the past and, as fear has dwindled, American leadership has dwindled with it. Another condition, closely related to the first, is that basic agreement on goals and strategy must be possible. Under present conditions, the common goal, to prevent the extension of Soviet influence, is provided, but there must also be the possibility of agreement on methods. Once again, when the possibility does not exist—as in the recent Anglo-French and American differences over policy in the Middle East, or British-American differences over Formosan policy—the conditions for effective leadership are undermined. The same may be said for the political situation within the United States. If the President is to lead abroad, there must be common agreement among the important sectors of American society on the goals of his leadership and the methods to be used; in turn, his capacity for leadership is increased if there is a clear and tangible foreign threat to the nation's security. American leadership after 1945 was possible only because of the Vandenberg point of view; conversely, if there is any justification for Franklin D. Roosevelt's wavering before 1940, it is his awareness of the deep division within the United States over the question of American involvement abroad. Leadership, to be effective, requires the possibility of reaching fundamental agreement among those to be led.

Ideally, international leadership also assumes the balanced use, under unified presidential direction, of industrial resources and skills, sound administrative techniques, military power, and an idea. In our recent history, the Marshall Plan and NATO illustrate the balanced application of the four essentials. Industrial resources and skill produce international reliance, if not dependence, upon the nation possessing them and upon the President who directs their export. Although there are exceptions, it is generally true that the curve of presidential leadership is tied to the curve of American economic and military assistance. It is possible, in other words, to purchase the right to lead, although the purchase is seldom directly over the counter. But economic persuasion must be supplemented by proper administrative techniques at home and abroad to allow for sound planning and unobtrusive execution of the President's leadership. Conflicting policy statements, such as the contrary views of President Eisenhower and his Secretary of State concerning the moral posture of "neutrals," can upset in a day prestige constructed over a period of months.

The willingness to use military force—or at least the determination not to renounce outright the use of force—is an essential condition of leadership. It is arguable that the excessively peaceful atmosphere at the "summit meetings" in Geneva and American guarantees that force would not be used during the recent Suez crisis were instrumental in cutting into the substance of presidential leadership. On the other hand, unwarranted truculence and overemphasis on military means can be as damaging as a faint military heart. The Berlin airlift and the use of the Seventh Fleet in the Formosa Straits are the best recent examples of the judicious use of military and industrial potential while avoiding, at the same time, the excesses of a shooting war. In order to maintain leadership, the President must follow the dictum of Theodore Roosevelt concerning soft speaking and the big stick, which, despite constant repetition, cannot be improved upon. Unobtrusively, but none the less clearly, the President must base his leadership on a firm military foundation. This raises the question of the adequacy of nuclear strategy as a support for presidential leadership. Does overdependence on the nuclear counterblow reduce the flexibility of the President's international leadership? The President's leadership, if it is to be sustained and effective, must be based on a tactical air arm and mobile naval force, as well as powerful ground forces. If the President bases his leadership solidly on the ultimate weapon, he is likely to be frozen in a position of inaction as lesser wars swirl about him and lose initiative to allies who expect small fires to be quenched by carefully controlled methods, not a deluge. The police action and the use of "volunteers," not nuclear war, have become the standard for military involvement in recent years and if the President is to maintain initiative, there cannot be sole reliance on nuclear strategy. As the American intervention in Korea, among other crises, proves, the path of leadership follows a swath cut by infantrymen as well as the threat of ultimate nuclear war. The President has the unenviable task of finding a balance between the two.

Military might, industrial strength, and administrative techniques must be tied to an idea, both to activate those who are implementing policy and to assist in the persuasion of those who are willing to follow presidential leadership. Wilson's Fourteen Points, the Four Freedoms, the defensive Atlantic alliance, Point Four, and Atoms for Peace are all ideas which aroused attention and hope, have helped to persuade, and have symbolized presidential initiative and firm intentions. The idea must be transcendent and mix national interest and humanitarianism in an attractive blend. It must possess the elasticity which admits Titoists, Falangists, and Syngman Rhee and yet avoid the imputation of opportunism. The proposal to admit Eastern European nations into the Marshall Plan—so quickly rejected by the Soviet Union—allowed this program to meet this difficult test.

Successful presidential leadership, besides requiring harmony of military, administrative, industrial, and ideological effort, requires the adroit use of propaganda weapons to articulate the presidential effort. His leadership can fail if the goals are not made known or if they are not understood, enlivened, and protected against counterattack. The long struggle to reactivate the propaganda services, which were temporarily abandoned in 1945, reached a turning point in the first month of the Eisenhower administration with the establishment of the United States Information Service and the appointment of a special assistant to the President on propaganda matters.[4] Unfortunately for presidential efficiency in this field, the chief executive of a democratic state can never be the single voice heard overseas. Much of the propaganda effort cannot be positive presentation of principles and presidential programs, but must be directed toward counteracting the exploitable weaknesses—as in the field of civil rights or outbursts of McCarthyism—in the United States. Even though a democratic society compounds the difficulties, this does not obviate the necessity for the effective use of propaganda techniques as an active support for international leadership.

Finally, in the domestic sphere, sound international leadership by the President presupposes a substantial degree of institutional harmony between the President and both parties in Congress as well as presidential willingness to sacrifice short-term political advantage in the interests of consistent leadership abroad. Many instances can be cited of a breakdown in congressional-executive relations which have temporarily disabled the President's leadership overseas—the League fight in the Senate in 1919, the isolationist power in Congress in 1940–41, the Taft-Wherry resistance to the dispatch of American troops in support of NATO, the right wing Republican attack on American foreign policy in the Far East, and, more recently, the strong congressional protests against foreign aid appropriations. Congressional criticism of the President, when not blatantly partisan, is helpful, and fortunately there are many examples of cooperation, particularly under the guidance of Senators Vandenberg and George. In Congress, the President must satisfy the demands of what one commentator calls "extra-partisanship," the ambidextrous posture of using his party but not as a partisan, working "outside party lines while maintaining a base of support in [his] party."[5] Effective leadership abroad must first meet the test of effective leadership within the United States, in the parties, in Congress, and among the public at large.

What has been said about the necessary conditions for effective international leadership by the President is, of course, the counsel of perfection. Because the conditions are affected by the global balance or imbalance, by the necessities of popular government, including the separation of powers, and by the intangible quality of many of the problems to be solved, it is patently impossible for a President to meet all of the requirements fully. But since he is constitutionally responsible for defending the national interest, he is, nevertheless, obliged to make the attempt.

The Historical Development of the President's Role as International Leader

Every President since Washington has been committed to the defense of America's national interest, although from Washington's time until recent years, Presidents performed their duty by withdrawing from permanent international involvement and active intervention as international leaders. The policies in Latin America during the first one hundred and thirty years of United States history provided a severely limited dress rehearsal for later international leadership by the President. From the Monroe Doctrine through the Venezuela crisis and the Roosevelt corollary to the seizing of Panama, there was no lack of recognition of American interest to the south, even though the methods fell far short of the modern tests of constructive leadership. The subsequent Good Neighbor policy and the cooperative efforts culminating in the Rio Pact in 1947, mark the emergence of American leadership based on factors other than force and dollar diplomacy. In the Spanish-American War, the United States came of age as an international military power if only, among the many tangled motives, to continue a pattern of American hegemony in the Western Hemisphere. If there is similarity between the Presidents' experience in Latin America and the broad international commitments of today, it lies in the fact that American policy in most instances—the Monroe Doctrine, the Roosevelt corollary, Caribbean intervention, and even the more recent Guatemala intervention—was a reaction against outside pressure and not a product of positive presidential initiative. The Presidents' involvement in the Western Hemisphere differed from today's international leadership not only in the restricted geographical commitment, but in the methods and spirit underlying that leadership. The policies, except for the Spanish-American War, were basically unilateral executive actions with limited congressional participation, the part played by the *Government* was largely diplomatic and military, not economic, and the settlements were imposed unilaterally by the United States from a position of uncompromising strength.

Not until after the Second World War did the President assume the full obligation of international leadership in situations where the force or the threat of force is inadequate in itself, where Congress is a continually active partner, and where there is a complete industrial commitment and association with permanent alliances. The first President, in other words, to accept international leadership as a full-time job was President Truman, although his predecessors haltingly prepared the way. The only President to have positive enthusiasm for the role was Theodore Roosevelt; all others were drawn into leadership initially because of the failure of leadership elsewhere and in reaction to external pressure. Only Theodore Roosevelt attempted international leadership, in the first instance, because of his own sense of enterprise.

Most Presidents, seemingly, have been reluctant to try to lead abroad because they have realized from the beginning—as Wilson did too late—the limitations which the constitutional system and America's fundamental noninterventionism would impose on their leadership. And many have shared with their compatriots an aversion to "foreign" entanglements. Wilson moved hesitatingly, and only after agonizing reflection, to shatter the stalemate of the First World War and to secure the balance of power in the moral world he envisioned.[6] FDR was less hesitant but reaped Wilson's whirlwind and struggled against this before participating in the destruction of governments whose hostility to the United States had long been known. And Harry Truman moved to check anti-Communist forces in Greece and Turkey and Europe only in the face of British withdrawal and near chaos in Europe. American leadership, since Theodore Roosevelt, has been, in short, the leadership of counterattack. The first Roosevelt understood the demands of leadership as well as any President but although he had the script—except for Algeciras and Portsmouth—he did not have the world stage. There was no need for the President to direct the forces of stability when the world was already stable.

The history of presidential leadership from Wilson to Truman can be described—to borrow a phrase from an authority on diplomacy—as a shift in emphasis from the search for justice to the search for security.[7] Woodrow Wilson, the first President to become actively engaged on the entire world stage, did not fully appreciate either. The principal characteristic of Wilson's leadership abroad was its excessively sanguine and moral quality. He recognized as early as 1900 that the "plunge into international politics" in the war with Spain had "greatly increased [the President's] power and opportunity for constructive statesmanship. . . ."[8] Until 1917, however, he was extremely reluctant to intervene outside the Western Hemisphere, although his later attitude was foreshadowed by his moral crusade in Mexico. He assumed a commanding role in the First World War only at the last moment, but with the Fourteen Points, the negotiations in Paris, and during the League fight, he accepted the presidential obligation of international leadership with a vengeance. His failure or the failure of his less optimistic compatriots brought about a reaction against presidential involvement abroad which only Pearl Harbor and the fear of Soviet absorption of Europe after 1945 could dispel.

It is significant that American efforts in leadership in the interwar period are associated with the names of Secretaries of State: Hughes with the Washington Conference, Stimson with Manchuria, Hull with the London Economic Conference and the more successful Reciprocal Trade Program. Presidents did not seem to sense the obligation, and if they did, public opinion and not the President, set the tone. One need only cite FDR's attitude toward the London Economic Conference, his failure to offset the Nye investigations by a public statement warning of the fatal weakness of its conclusions,[9] or his support of the Neutrality Act in the campaign of 1940[10] to realize both public and presidential abdication of international responsibility. Only the timid foray of the "quarantine" speech, the quiet preparation for war by the joint Anglo-American staff after January 1941, and the *Curtiss-Wright* decision stand out as reminders that the President possessed the potential to lead.

The Lend-Lease Act, combining as it did the essentials of industrial power, administrative techniques, cautious military support, and an idea, marks the breakthrough. The President's international leadership under Roosevelt was characterized by its personal quality, as Churchill's leadership was. There is little doubt that FDR was the dominant leader—if only by Churchill's conscious submission to the fact of American industrial and military superiority. Because of Roosevelt's administrative methods and his shortsighted evaluation of postwar conditions, presidential leadership was not institutionalized; however, the combination of Truman's administrative methods, the National Security Act of 1947, the Marshall Plan, and NATO, finally brought about the institutionalization of the President's new role. The British retreat from international leadership and the realities of a bipolar world made clear that the President's responsibility was neither temporary nor could it afford to be merely personal. The easy adaptability of Roosevelt's leadership was gradually exchanged for the sometimes excessively institutionalized and security-conscious presidential leadership of today. Recent and past experience suggests that contemporary international leadership cannot depend alone on military security or moral leadership. Neither will it succeed if it is merely personal or rigidly institutional. It requires the difficult mixture of sound institutional support, of personal leadership, and the balanced application of justice and security.

The Constitutional Basis

The constitutional basis for the President's role as leader is no more than an extension and broadening of his traditional responsibilities as chief of foreign relations. There is no better description of this function than in *Durand v. Hollins*:[11]

> As the Executive head of the nation, the President is made the only legitimate organ of the General Government, to open and carry on correspondence or negotiations with foreign nations, in matters concerning the interests of the country or of its citizens. It is to him, also, that citizens abroad must look for protection of person and property, and for the faithful execution of the laws existing and intended for their protection. For this purpose, the whole executive power of the country is placed in his hands, under the Constitution, and the laws passed in pursuance thereof. . . . The great object and duty of Government is the protection of the lives, liberty, and property of the people composing it, whether abroad or at home; and any Government failing in the accomplishment of the object, or the performance of the duty, is not worth preserving.

In the first instance, the President's power to assume the responsibilities of international leader arises from his constitutional status as the executive head of the nation. As Hamilton pointed out in the Pacificus-Helvidius exchange with Madison, the President is not merely the instrument of Congress in foreign relations, but the possessor of independent executive power of which the specifically mentioned subsidiary powers to appoint ambassadors and to make treaties are minor manifestations.[12] The notion was reaffirmed in the Hoover Commission Task Force Report on Foreign Affairs:[13]

> The Constitution has left a great area of unassigned powers in which someone must act for the United States from time to time, and in the absence of any other assignment, the President, in his capacity as executive, is the only one able to act.

Possession of independent executive power means that the President cannot be satisfied in following a course set by the legislature in foreign affairs, but must search actively for the path leading to national advancement and preservation. In turn, he is not limited to action approved by Congress, but can employ any means not prohibited by the Constitution or the laws "to safeguard the nation."[14] The constitutional reasoning that vests *positive* executive power in the President and thus bestows on him the responsibility for all positive action not prohibited by the Constitution or statutes, including leadership abroad, rests on a practical foundation that was clearly described by John Jay in *Federalist 64*—namely, that the President, as distinguished from Congress, can bring to bear on foreign affairs secrecy, dispatch, and unity. The unity of the executive—the single voice and hand of leadership—the necessity for secrecy, a center of information and coordination of policy, and dispatch in implementing policy and protecting the nation in times of crisis have all received the sanction of custom. This has been demonstrated in recognition policy, in the right of the President to withhold documents from Congress, in statutes (generous delegations of power by Congress in foreign affairs), and in judicial decisions (from *Martin v. Mott*[15] to *United States v. Curtiss-Wright Export Corp.*[16]) over the years.

The broad interpretation of the opening words of Article II vesting the executive power in the President, buttressed by the practical arguments for presidential direction of foreign affairs, does not provide the only constitutional permission for presidential involvement in leadership abroad. He is also supported by the specific grants of power to see to the faithful execution of the laws and his function as commander-in-chief. The presidential obligation faithfully to execute the laws is a formidable grant of power in an era of extensive treaty-making; whether action is taken under Article V of the North Atlantic treaty, the United Nations treaty and the UN Participation Act, or lesser agreements, the President is as likely to move into a position of international leadership in executing the treaties as he was while negotiating them. President Truman based American entry into one of the nation's most frustrating but perhaps most fruitful wars, the "police" action in Korea, on his obligation to accomplish the faithful execution of the laws—in this case, the UN Charter. Because of American military and economic power, the President, in this instance, and potentially under the NATO system, has become the executive representative of the signatory nations in enforcing international law.

Moreover, it is a settled principle of constitutional law that the President's power as commander-in-chief is a broad discretionary grant permitting the President to deploy the armed forces in peacetime as well as war, for his own chosen diplomatic or strategic purposes. The Eisenhower administration has imposed limitations on itself in this regard by declaring that any movement of troops that might involve the United States in war should follow a congressional resolution bestowing discretion on the President. This procedure was followed in the Formosa crisis, for Quemoy and Matsu in the Pescadores, but it is more a product of domestic political tactics than constitutional law. And President Eisenhower and his Secretary of State have specifically reserved the plenary power of the President on occasions when Congress cannot be consulted and have denied that Congress must be consulted to determine the disposition of forces when there is no proximity to actual conflict.[17] President Truman relied, in part, on his power as commander-in-chief—independent of prior congressional approval—to send United States troops into Korea. The role of the commander-in-chief in *peacetime* was exhaustively considered during the Great Debate in Congress in 1951 over presidential assignment of troops to Europe without express congressional approval and was finally settled to presidential advantage. At that time, the President and his advisers contended that his power to dispatch troops was plenary, and the extent to which the commander-in-chief clause contributes to the President's function as leader, in peacetime, is clear in the following statement, one of many similar declarations to appear during the Great Debate:[18]

> In time of peace the President is just as much Commander in Chief as he is in time of war. His power over the Armed Forces remains the same. But in time of peace the exercise of that power is directed, not at subduing an enemy, but at broader considerations of national policy in general. In particular, the peacetime functions of the Commander in Chief are related to our defense needs and to the responsibilities of the President in the field of foreign affairs.

Finally, some Presidents have contended that the constitutional foundations for leadership abroad are supplemented, indirectly, by the President's oath of office. As Robert Sherwood states in *Roosevelt and Hopkins:* "Having taken the oath of office as President three times, he knew it by heart, and was well aware that he was sworn not only to 'uphold' but to '*defend*' the Constitution of the United States. It was a matter of his own judgment—and the judgment of his advisers whom he was empowered to appoint—as to where that defense should begin."[19] The oath to defend the Constitution is, in effect, the oath to defend the sovereign integrity of the United States. It can be—if only indirectly—an additional support for presidential initiative in bringing other nations together in defense of mutual global interests.

Besides the constitutional basis for presidential leadership in foreign affairs, the President gains authority from statutory grants of power. His authority is also reinforced by treaties, by executive agreements, by establishing or giving the President power to establish agencies to assist him in his foreign responsibilities, and by appropriations. And it was settled in the *Curtiss-Wright* case that statutory gifts of discretion in foreign affairs are not to be judged by the ordinary interpretation of delegated powers. Affirming "the very delicate, plenary and exclusive power of the President as the sole organ of the federal government in the field of international relations," Justice Sutherland went on to declare that it was unwise for Congress to stipulate narrow and definite standards in delegating power to the President:[20]

> It is quite apparent that if, in the maintenance of our international relations, embarrassment—perhaps serious embarrassment—is to be avoided and success for our aims achieved, congressional legislation which is to be made effective, through negotiation and inquiry within the international field must often accord to the President a degree of discretion and freedom from statutory restriction which would not be admissible were domestic affairs alone involved.

The Institutional Background

Today, the most impressive characteristic of presidential leadership in the international field is the high degree of institutionalization. In contrast with the situation before the

First World War, when our international commitments were hardly greater than the Pan American Union and the International Postal Union, and when Wilson depended on Colonel House and the Department of State, the President today is indirect or direct participant in at least five treaty organizations (ANZUS, SEATO, NATO, the Rio Pact, UN) and numerous specialized international organizations and eight domestic agencies devoted solely to assisting him in his international duties and numberless others that assist him indirectly. The complicated structure that stands behind the President's international leadership has increased in size, if not in efficiency, with the growth of presidential responsibility abroad, and nearly all agencies have come to participate actively in support of the President's leadership. That the Department of State and the military departments have become only partial contributors to the making and execution of foreign policy is as much of a truism as the statement that all aspects of domestic affairs in the United States have a direct or indirect effect on America's global position. In recent years, for example, the Departments of Agriculture, State, and Treasury have been, on occasion, intimately involved with questions influencing the President's position overseas; Agriculture in the proper use of farm surpluses and technical aid; the Treasury —as the active life of Secretary Humphrey indicates—in the task of finding a balance between domestic economic health and commitments abroad; and Justice in the production of legal opinions—such as the "destroyers for bases" contribution of Attorney General Jackson.

Hand in hand with the deeper involvement of the traditional departments in providing assistance to the President in his new role, efforts have been made to adjust institutions in the more immediate presidential family to the urgent demands for advice and the coordination of policy making and execution. Though some of these agencies, such as the Council of Economic Advisers and the Bureau of the Budget, were established by Congress to deal predominantly with domestic problems, they have necessarily felt the weight of the President's international obligation. Others were designed specifically to help the President shoulder this weight. The Atomic Energy Commission, the Central Intelligence Agency, the Joint Chiefs of Staff, the Office of Defense Mobilization, and the National Security Council with its helpmeet, the Operations Coordinating Board, have appeared and developed since 1947, the year when the President learned that leadership abroad was to be more than a temporary responsibility. Other offices, commissions, and *ad hoc* individual assignments, such as Harold Stassen's job as Secretary of Peace, or Disarmament, Clarence Randall's Commission on Foreign Trade and his more recent appointment as Special Adviser to the President on Foreign Economic Affairs, and the Office of the Special Assistant to the President in National Security Affairs appear and dissolve depending on the degree of presidential need and favor. No more compelling evidence is required of the existence of the President's new responsibility or the personal and institutional burden it places on him than the increase in the number of individuals reporting to him in this field.

How these agencies are used or if they are used at all depends, in the first instance, on international conditions and the administrative preference of the President and his immediate staff. There is no *best* way to arrange institutional support for presidential international leadership without considering the person in office or the problem at hand. There are principles of coordination of the international effort, the establishment of clear lines of responsibility and action, and the requirement that adequate information gets to the President; but each President has tended in the past, and doubtless will tend in the future, to shape the institutions to fit his workaday world.

Woodrow Wilson delegated much authority in foreign affairs to Secretary of State Bryan until the situation in Mexico and the threat of American involvement in Europe produced a change. Cordell Hull, among others, has given adequate testimony of FDR's frequent by-passing of the State Department in his exercise of leadership,[21] substituting Harry Hopkins, personal contact with foreign executives, and the Naval communications system for the traditional State Department channels. The National Security Council, under Truman, according to one set of authorities, tended to become "a sifter of staff memoranda,"[22] and the most momentous decision of the Truman administration, the intervention in Korea, was made without consultation with the Council meeting as such, although weekly meetings were made routine after that decision.[23] President Eisenhower, with his reliance on an almost air-tight staff system, has elevated and formalized the advisory role of the Council. Although he overruled the Council on the question of American intervention in Indo-China, consultation preceded the decision, and it is permissible to guess that he relies heavily on Council staff work and on the discussion and final opinions of the participants. He maintains, as Truman did not, a Special Assistant on National Security Affairs who directs the work of the Council, and has established the Operations Coordinating Board to try to insure the execution of decisions made by the Council. There is no assurance, however, that Eisenhower's changes or his reliance on the Council will set the pattern for his successor.

These aids to the President, in other words, have no life of their own, but live in prosperity or poverty depending on the working habits of the President or the situation at hand. Much the same can be said for the utilization of international agencies, although here international conditions and the nature of the issue are as important as personal preference in conditioning presidential choice. The United States, perhaps more than any other nation, has depended on the United Nations for its institutional leadership abroad. The original Baruch Plan, the United Action for Peace Plan, intervention in Korea, the recent resolutions condemning the Anglo-French involvement in Egypt, and the Atoms for Peace program were all initiated by American Presidents in the international agency. Presidential dependence on the United Nations has been based on the voting support in the General Assembly—as the United Action for Peace Plan illustrates—of the generally sympathetic South American and Western European blocs. With the addition of sixteen new states by the Eleventh General Assembly, a reliable majority may not henceforth be available, and, thus, presidential use of the United Nations may become less frequent, demonstrating again that the institutional expression of presidential leadership abroad is relative to the international circumstances. Two examples will perhaps emphasize the point. Notwithstanding President Truman's reliance on the United Nations, it is clear that United States forces would have been committed to Korea even without United Nations support. Only the fortuitous absence of the Soviet Union from the Security Council permitted the President to add the prestige of the United Nations to the prestige of the United States in this crisis. Secondly, the importance of NATO has declined as a vehicle of presidential leadership as disagreements within the Western alliance have increased in frequency and intensity. There can be, in sum, no set institutional pattern for the application of international leadership in Washington or overseas. This factor puts additional strain on presidential decisiveness and imagination.

The Impact of International Leadership on the Presidency

What have been the consequences of the President's attempts to fill his new role, and what problems are created for the presidential office? The changes in the Presidency within the last ten years, largely because of the new responsibility, have been as great as the change in the preceding fifty years. It can be said that in most respects Franklin Roosevelt's first term and the years of the Hoover administration bear a greater resemblance to the Presidency of Grover Cleveland than to that of Harry Truman. Just as America's involvement in world affairs has affected the entire governmental system, the President's new responsibility has had a strong impact on the traditional functions of the President and intensified old problems. It is not as if one more function had been added to total one more than the previous number of duties; rather, all of the traditional duties have been immersed in and distorted by the overriding function of international leadership. To illustrate how complete the invasion of his other responsibilities has been, it is only necessary to mark the relatively new presidential obligations of maintaining national prosperity and promoting civil liberties. The interrelationship between the President's international responsibility and his national obligations is apparent. The one complicates and intensifies the other. If the President avoids acting in the interest of civil liberties by not enforcing the law or does not stand as a defender of civil rights and legislative leader of reform in that field or if he does not take an active role in promoting economic health at home, his leadership abroad suffers through the loss of national prestige and power. In fact, it can be asserted that the President's role as international leader has been instrumental in the firm establishment of these other two twentieth-century additions to the President's duties.[24] A sick economy or a vacillating policy in civil rights can be as damaging to the President's efforts to lead abroad as the lack of adequate military power. In sum, none of his duties are free from international consequences.

This is apparent as one observes the impact of international leadership on the traditional presidential functions. The addition of a fluctuating international constituency to the President's national constituency has strengthened Congress, has heaped new administrative problems on an already overburdened office and has stultified the theory of less strenuous years that the President is to follow and represent public opinion rather than lead or oppose, even in the field of foreign affairs, where popular self-interest is not always enlightened and apathy, misinformation, and prejudice frequently hold sway.[25] A new and complicating ingredient has been added to presidential decision-making, an ingredient which has had a considerable, and a still unmeasurable impact, on the tactics of leadership at home and the institutions through which the leadership must be exercised. The executive, in the period since 1945, has been confronted with a decisive gain in the power of Congress, a gain which is, paradoxically, largely the result of increased presidential power and responsibility. Even in delegated legislative power, particularly in foreign affairs and beginning significantly with the Lend-Lease Act, Congress is making more and more use of joint or concurrent resolutions to provide for the withdrawal, at short notice, of power granted to the President.[26] The major reason for the increase in congressional power is the monetary necessities of leadership and consequent executive dependence on congressional appropriations. The power of the Senate over treaties is now shared with the entire Congress, since the implementation of treaties depends on appropriations. This reinvigoration of congressional power in the cold war manifests itself in numberless investigations by congressional committees, concessions made by the President to Congress on appointments, and—a development of better promise—the active participation of congressional leaders of both parties in executive foreign policy councils. The reinvigorated power of Congress calls for subdued use of the old weapons of legislative leadership and a new emphasis on collaboration and conciliation in achieving crucial foreign policy goals. In his role as legislative leader, the President must be more cautious than formerly and depend on his position as the best informed observer on foreign affairs in the United States to carry the day in Congress. His most effective weapon today is an appeal to Congress on the basis of national security and survival. He may appeal indirectly to Congress through the electorate or to the consciences of individual Congressmen. But this appeal must be used sparingly. Ultimately, he can by-pass the Congress, as President Roosevelt did in 1942;[27] but when there is no hot war, this road can lead directly to a legislative dead end. Unless the President wishes to take this chance, he can no longer be cavalier in his legislative leadership. And, if changed tactics are one of the results of the President's international role, it should be added that the President is forced, at times, to give less emphasis than he otherwise would to domestic legislation. In some cases, the *quid pro quo* of international leadership does mean the partial dissolution of leadership in the domestic field and the delegation of this traditional responsibility to others, either in or out of the presidential household.[28]

Recent Presidents have recognized the increased power of Congress by supporting greater collaboration between congressional committees and the executive agencies and closer contact between the President and congressional leaders at a higher level. What once was desirable is now essential. His relationship to his party and interest groups has also been affected by his new international role. Directly, and through Congress and his party, the President feels the pressure of group demands and particularism which frequently run counter to the interests of sound international leadership. Important contributors to his party, loyal followers, and important groups in pivotal states lay claim to presidential allegiance. Members of Congress, party leaders, and pressure groups—whether they are bicycle manufacturers interested in special tariff consideration, farmers demanding quotas or destructive dumping, Zionists, Irish-Americans, Slavic-Americans, or others sharing common loyalties with groups or nations abroad—complicate and can obstruct, by the very nature of their particularistic point of view, the President's efforts toward sound international leadership. He must make the choice, and if it is against the group interest, more often than not it will be a politically unpleasant one. In years past, the President faced the relatively less difficult task of balancing the interests of this national constituency against sectional or economic particularism; today, he must include his international constituency in the equation. The Democratic Party's policy toward Israel and the Republican commitment to "liberation" indicate that partisan considerations can never be suppressed, but as long as the cold war lasts, the President cannot return to the free wheeling party leadership of an earlier day without harming vital American interests and seriously jeopardizing his own success as international leader.

The administrative consequences of the President's assumption of the role of international leader are as striking as the effects on his traditional roles as party and legislative leader. The growth of the bureaucracy in recent years is largely a product of the President's need for help in fulfilling his new international responsibility. Help indeed has been given, but the very increase in size has tended to put the President in the center of a milling throng of unknown faces and has raised seemingly insuperable problems of coordination and implementation. Conflicting policies and statements are unavoidable even at the highest level, as the recent controversy over the state of American defenses indicates. When deeply felt professional and departmental loyalties are at stake, as they have been within the Department of State or in the controversies between State, Defense, and Agriculture, coordination and willing implementation are doubly difficult. Institutionalization of the President's role as international leader is a partial answer as the development of the staff system and more extensive use of the National Security Council and such agencies as the Operations Coordinating Board under President Eisenhower demonstrate. But institutionalization can never be the complete answer, partly because no amount of institutionalization can suppress the centrifugal forces within such a large institutional group, and partly because institutionalization itself can breed currents of inefficiency.

Some critics contend that inflexibility and lack of imagination have been the fruits of excessive institutionalization under President Eisenhower's leadership. Whether this specific charge is valid or not, it seems quite certain that overdependence on the channels of the National Security Council, a staff system, along with limited access to a busy President, can create obstructions to creative thinking as well as remove them. There can be no substitute for the haphazard, sometimes accidental, gifts of information that can come to a President from unexpected places. Presidents Roosevelt and Truman depended on side-door informants whose ideas, had the doors not been opened, might have been smothered in institutional channels. President Eisenhower's informal dinners at the White House have also served this purpose, and all Presidents have benefited from the weekly press conference which should share honors with congressional visitors as a method for breaking down institutional barriers. Similarly, as the

President's leadership can be distorted in institutional channels, his active leadership abroad can wane if it becomes impersonal. The President cannot speak continually through the Department of State or indirectly through his press secretary. By clever use of the press conference, appearances before international agencies, and occasional trips to the summit, the President can avoid being mired down in an administration designed to liberate him.

A final administrative problem that has been intensified by the President's responsibilities abroad is presidential control of specialists within his own administration—whether they are of the economic, scientific, or military variety. Lacking special knowledge in one or more of these fields, the President must be on guard constantly against the necessarily one-sided view of experts. From a military or scientific viewpoint, for example, the continued testing of the hydrogen bomb may seem sound, and yet, if the decision is made on technical grounds alone, the President's prestige abroad may suffer. President Eisenhower has avoided the dilemma of overdependence on expert advice in a technical world because of his own unique military and diplomatic experience. President Truman depended on many hours of study and an awareness that even a technical decision was his alone. As he describes his first day in office:[29]

> . . . on that first full day as President I did more reading that I ever thought I could. I even selected some papers to take home so that I might study them before retiring and upon waking. This was the first step in a routine of nightly work that I found to be one of the most trying but also one of the necessary duties of a President.

Difficult as it may be to resist the apparent certainties of technical advice, expert opinion can never substitute for the reflective over-all view of the President. With his new responsibility, in an increasingly complex world, the President is forced to redouble his efforts to escape from the narrow, technical point of view. Living as he does in an administrative labyrinth lined with the opinions of experts and specialists, this requires administrative skill, some audacity, and perhaps super-human wisdom.

Finally, the President's international role has placed in a new perspective the relationship of the President to public opinion. Before the President had assumed the obligation to try to lead other nations, he could afford to follow public opinion and define the relationship with the public as one of translating electoral sentiment into governmental action. When international leadership was added, however, other factors came into play: the necessity for being aware of sentiment outside the United States and being the active guide of opinion, and, on occasion, to be willing to act against immediate popular wishes. The President's obligation to his national constituency is no longer one of reflecting sentiment, but forming it. He must articulate for the public in understandable terms the reason for presidential involvement abroad. He must be able to establish in the public mind the consequences of a failure to lead and make dramatically clear what Lippmann calls "the intangible realities" of international power.[30]

Under any circumstances, guiding public opinion is more difficult than transforming public wishes into legislation. The difficulty is compounded in foreign affairs because the issues, except in the pure air of an emergency, are not clear or easily clarified. They are obscured by distance and their own complexity, while the alternatives presented to the public are not between the pleasant and unpleasant but between the least unpleasant and the most unpleasant. The President must have a rich fund of popular support if his leadership is to be sustained, but at the same time he must be prepared to act without popular support if reflection and sound advice dictate action in the national interest. Popularity is no measure of sound public policy in this field. The crux of the President's relationship with the public in this new situation is, in fact, the long-term preparation of public opinion for the unpopular action by a careful mixture of exhortation and appeals to self-preservation. The President can no longer permit the quality of his leadership to be molded by powerful interest groups; he can no longer be the passive receptacle of active public opinion, partly because in foreign affairs there is oftentimes no public opinion. He must create public opinion and yet refuse to yield to public voices which, if followed, would cast doubt on his capacity to lead abroad. The President must take full account of the palatable or unpalatable truth of America's international position and make that position forcefully clear in the public mind. As Thucydides remarked of Pericles, "Certainly when he saw that they were going too far in a mood of over-confidence, he would bring back to them a sense of their dangers; and when they were discouraged for no good reason he would restore their confidence." And he must be willing to accept the short-run political sacrifices that international leadership demands.

Since President Eisenhower's illness in 1955, it is impossible to discuss the Presidency without recognizing that the President's efforts to direct unpredictable international forces in the face of resourceful maneuvers by the Soviet Union, the contradictory interests of American allies and neutrals, and a complex constitutional system contribute more than any other activity to the tense weariness associated with the modern Presidency. If the Presidency is today, as Harry Truman described it, "like riding a tiger," it is because the President must deal with gargantuan imponderables which frequently cannot be reflected upon or completely understood but only inspected hurriedly before a decision is made. Perhaps history will conclude that the job is beyond the capacity of the man and the office, even though costly adjustments have been made to meet the President's new role. When one recalls the optimum conditions for effective international leadership—harmonious congressional-executive relations, effective administrative planning and coordination, the presence of a cohesive force abroad, among others—it is quite apparent that the President will never reach the exalted position of sustained international leadership, even if this were desirable, short of a severe world crisis or actual war. The present cold war environment requires that the President attempt to lead in the interest of American security, even though the attempt alone complicates his other presidential functions. He can only hope, when the anti-Soviet forces need leadership, that for an undetermined period of time his leadership will take hold.

NOTES

1. Wilson to E. G. Conklin, in 4 Ray S. Baker, *Woodrow Wilson: Life and Letters* 55 (1931).
2. See, for example, 2 Harry S. Truman, *Memoirs* 232 (1956); Robert J. Donovan, *Eisen-*

hower: The Inside Story 353 (1956); Nitze, "The Modern President as a World Figure," 307 *Annals* 114, 115 (1956); and Clinton L. Rossiter, *The American Presidency* 28 (1956).

3. Rossiter, *op. cit. supra* note 2, at 122.
4. Sargeant, "Information and Cultural Representation Overseas," in *The Representation of the United States Abroad* 71 (1956).
5. Bradford Westerfield, *Foreign Policy and Party Politics* 16 (1955).
6. See 1 Charles Seymour, *The Intimate Papers of Colonel House* 296–98 (1926); and 2 *id.* at 228.
7. Buchrig, "Idealism and Statecraft," 5 *Confluence* 252 (1956).
8. Woodrow Wilson, *Congressional Government* 22 (Meridian Books, 1956).
9. James MacGregor Burns, *Roosevelt: The Lion and the Fox* 254 (1956).
10. Robert E. Sherwood, *Roosevelt and Hopkins* 189 (1948).
11. 8 Fed. Cas. No. 4186, at 112 (C. C. S. D. N. Y. 1860). See Edward S. Corwin, *The President* c. 5 (1948).
12. 4 *The Works of Alexander Hamilton* 438–40 (Lodge ed. 1885).
13. Commission on Organization of the Executive Branch, Task Force Report on Foreign Affairs 47 (1949).
14. This theory is associated with Theodore Roosevelt but has been adopted by most strong Presidents. 2 Truman, *op. cit. supra* note 2, at 473, 478 (1956).
15. 25 U.S. (12 Wheat.) 19 (1827).
16. 299 U.S. 304 (1936).
17. Statement by Secretary of State Dulles at the Nine Power Conference on Western Defense, Sept. 29, 1954, 31 *Dep't State Bull.* 523 (1924); Message to Congress on the Formosan Situation, Jan. 24, 1955, "Security of the United States of America," H. Doc. No. 76, 84th Cong., 1st Sess. (1955), 32 *Dep't State Bull.* 211 (1955); and presidential press conference, Dec. 2, 1954, N.Y. Times, Dec. 3, 1954, p. 18, cols. 2–7.
18. Committee on Foreign Relations and Committee on the Armed Services, "Powers of the President to Send the Armed Forces Outside the United States," 82nd Cong., 1st Sess. 5 (1951).
19. Sherwood, *op. cit. supra* note 10, at 274.
20. 299 U.S. at 320.
21. 2 *The Memoirs of Cordell Hull* 1109–11 (1948); Burns, *op. cit. supra* note 9, at 383.
22. William Y. Elliott, *United States Foreign Policy: Its Organization and Control* 71 (1952).
23. Truman, *op. cit. supra* note 2, at 59–60, 333, 334 (1956).
24. *President's Committee on Civil Rights, To Secure These Rights,* 146–48 (1948).
25. Walter Lippmann, *Essays in the Public Philosophy* cc. 1–2 (1955).
26. Ginnane, "The Control of Federal Administration by Congressional Resolutions and Committees," 66 Harv. L. Rev. 569 (1953).
27. Message to Congress, Sept. 7, 1942, "Domestic Economy of the United States," H. Doc. 834, 77th Cong., 2d Sess. (1942), 88 *Cong. Rec.* 7052 (1942).
28. Referring to a dispute between two department heads, Sherman Adams is said to have remarked: "Either make up your mind or else tell me and I will do it. We cannot bother the President with this. He is trying to keep the world from war." Donovan, *op. cit. supra* note 2, at 71.
29. 1 Truman, *op. cit. supra* note 2, at 26–27 (1956).
30. Lippmann, *op. cit. supra* note 25, at 55.

SELECTED BIBLIOGRAPHY

Barber, James D. "Classifying and Predicting Presidential Styles," *Journal of Social Issues,* 24 (July 1968), 51–80. Develops a typological framework for classifying presidents according to their political styles. Analyzes biographical data on Coolidge and Hoover to determine how men exercise presidential power.

Blackman, Paul H. "Presidential Disability and the Bayh Amendment," *Western Political Quarterly,* 20 (June 1967), 440–455. Analyzes how the Twenty-fifth Amendment could, and is likely to, affect the presidency. Concludes that Section 4 of the amendment will both threaten the integrity of the presidential office and seriously alter presidential-congressional relations.

Corwin, Edward S. *The President: Office and Powers.* 4th ed. New York: New York University Press, 1957. The most original, stimulating, and monumental monograph on the presidency. The four editions of this book should be compared in order to understand Corwin's changing views of the presidency.

Evans, Rowland, and Robert Novak. *Lyndon B. Johnson: The Exercise of Power.* New York: New American Library, 1966. Shows how Johnson achieved, maintained, and dispensed power from 1931, when he was a freshman member of the House, until mid-1966, when events in Vietnam refused to respond to his mastery and exercise of presidential power. Concludes that Johnson's flexibility, temperament, and bargaining techniques developed during his congressional career made him a successful President in handling domestic problems but were disastrous in foreign affairs.

Falk, Stanley L. "The National Security Council Under Truman, Eisenhower, and Kennedy," *Political Science Quarterly,* 74 (September 1964), 403–434. Shows how each of three presidents organized the National Security Council (NSC) and used it to satisfy his own needs, style, and perception of his office. Carefully examines the changes in the structure and organization of the NSC. Provides a useful analysis of the NSC as a part of the institutionalized presidency.

Fenno, Richard F., Jr. *The President's Cabinet.* Cambridge, Mass.: Harvard University Press, 1959. Uses three levels of analysis—Cabinet as a discrete institution, President-Cabinet relationship, and Cabinet in the total government process—to study the membership, strengths, and weaknesses of the Cabinet during the period from Wilson to Eisenhower. Shows how proposals for altering the Cabinet's relation to the President and the Congress are likely to alter the President's relation to the Congress.

Hamilton, Alexander. "The Federalist No. 70 (March 17, 1787)," in John Jay, Alexander Hamilton, and James Madison, *The Federalist.* New York: Modern Library, n.d. The best and most perceptive of Hamilton's eleven essays on the presidency. The clearest statement of the advantages of a single executive—unity, energy, decision, dispatch, and responsibility—as opposed to the alleged factionalism, dissension, feebleness, dilatoriness, buck-passing, and irresponsibility of a collegial executive.

Harris, Joseph P. *The Advice and Consent of the Senate.* Berkeley and Los Angeles: University of California Press, 1953. Examines the operation and the effects of the confirmation of presidential appointments by the Senate. Takes a dim view of senatorial confirmation. Argues that it has hindered, rather than helped, the President win support for his legislative program, has caused party disunity, has not resulted in the high qualifications of nominees, has transferred the nominating function from the President to individual senators, and has weakened presidential responsibility.

Kallenbach, Joseph E. *The American Chief Executive: The Presidency and the Governorship.* New York: Harper & Row, 1966. Probably the best, most monumental, and most encyclopedic of the recent books on the American presidency. Contains references to the most significant literature on the subject until 1966.

May, Ernest R. "The Development of Political-Military Consultation in the United States," *Political Science Quarterly,* 70 (June 1955), 161–180. Presents the rationale for the National Security Council. Describes the haphazard communication between the diplomatic and military agencies in an earlier era. Traces the evolution of political-military consultation during World War I until the creation of the NSC after World War II. Points out the continuing problems in the council's efforts to coordinate military strategy and foreign policy.

Morgenthau, Hans J. "Conduct of American Foreign Policy," *Parliamentary Affairs,* 3 (1949), 147–161. Discusses how the conditions required to gain popular support for foreign policy limit the pursuit of a policy that astute policy makers would deem in the national interest. Argues that the evils inherent in the democratic conduct of foreign policy—hysteria, routine, and inertia—are aggravated by the constitutional separation of powers peculiar in America and the attendant political practices, which have a distorting and paralyzing influence.

Neustadt, Richard E. *Presidential Power: The Politics of Leadership.* New York: Wiley, 1960. A study of the status, prestige, and influence that actually enable a man to exercise presidential power. A Machiavellian handbook for Neustadt's "Prince" telling him how to get power, how to use it, and how to keep it—how to influence others to do what the President wants them to do. Also discusses the President's various constituencies, the relationships among them, and the importance of the President's personal image in each of them.

———. "Presidency and Legislation: The Growth of Central Clearance," *American Political Science Review,* 48 (September 1954), 641–671. Traces the development of the Bureau of the Budget as the President's clearing house for legislative proposals and enrolled bills presented for presidential signature or veto from 1921 to 1954. Also describes how Harding, Coolidge, Hoover, Roosevelt, Truman, and Eisenhower used this machinery for legislative clearance and, in the process, reveals a great deal about the different styles of these six presidents.

———. "Presidency and Legislation: Planning the President's Program," *American Political Science Review,* 49 (December 1955), 980–1021. Uses Eisenhower's 1954 legislative program as a case study in, and point of departure for, discussing the institutionalization of presidential program making. Observes that presidential legislative programming has become widely accepted as an elaboration of the President's constitutional right to recommend legislation.

Riker, William H., and William Bast. "Presidential Action on Congressional Nominations," in Aron Wildavsky (ed.), *The Presidency.* Boston: Little, Brown, 1969, 250–267. Examines the President's role as leader of his party, tabulates and discusses the thirty-nine instances from 1913 to 1960 when the President has publicly endorsed candidates in congressional primaries of his own party, and gives attention to the reasons for presidential reluctance to intervene in congressional primaries.

Rossiter, Clinton. *The American Presidency,* 2nd ed. New York: New American Library, 1960. A good, brief, and readable synthesis of the subject that is useful to both political scientist and interested citizen. Contains a selective but excellent bibliography.

Rourke, Francis E. "Administrative Secrecy: A Congressional Dilemma," *American Political Science Review,* 54 (September 1960), 684–694. Deals with executive privilege as a problem of reconciling the publicity of democracy with the privacy of liberty. Shows that Congress itself is largely responsible for the withholding of information by the executive, although representatives of both parties frequently call for disclosure. Argues that Congress is willing to go further than the executive branch in protecting the secrecy of executive records.

Saloma, John S., III. *Congress and the New Politics.* Boston: Little, Brown, 1969. Posits four models of legislative-executive relations as an analytical framework for studying the American dual system of representation and decision making.

Schwartz, Bernard. "Executive Privilege and Congressional Investigatory Power," *California Law Review,* 47 (1959), 3–50. Deals with the alleged right of the executive to withhold information from the public, the courts, and the Congress. Rejects the unfettered discretion of the executive to surround all its activities with secrecy. Argues that the assertion of executive privilege is inconsistent with the rule of law, has no basis in history or in case or statute law, and cannot be justified on the vague claim of executive prerogative.

Silva, Ruth C. "The Lodge-Gossett Resolution: A Critical Analysis," *American Political Science Review,* 44 (1950), 86–99. Speculates about the possible and anticipated consequences of the adoption of the Lodge-Gossett proposal on the basis of a statistical treatment of data resulting from application of the formula to election data from all presidential elections between 1880 and 1948.

———. *Presidential Succession.* Ann Arbor: University of Michigan Press, 1951. Has become the classic on the subject. Discusses many of the constitutional and political problems of succession. Proposes solutions to the problems of presidential disability and succession, some of which have become incorporated in the Twenty-fifth Amendment to the Constitution.

Sindler, Allan P. "Presidential Election Methods and Urban-Ethnic Interests," *Law and Contemporary Problems,* 27 (Spring 1962), 213–233.

U. S. Senate, Committee on the Judiciary, Subcommittee on Constitutional Amendments. *Electing the President: Hearings.* 91st Cong., 1st sess., 1969, 1–1053. Discusses various proposals for changing or abolishing the electoral college with its general ticket system, by which the candidate who polls a popular plurality in a state wins all the electoral votes of that state. Analyzes the outcome of the application of various proposals to the popular vote for President from 1948 through 1968.

five

The Judiciary

The Federal Courts

For many Americans the dual system of state and federal courts seems an incomprehensible tangle, yet it is an arrangement rooted in the historical tradition of the country. It would have been possible, of course, for the framers of the Constitution to have foregone the creation of a federal judicial branch and to have relied upon the state courts to interpret and enforce both the laws of Congress and the laws of the states. But the concern of those assembled at Philadelphia was to secure the power of the new national government, and they knew well the lesson of Bishop Hoadly's sermon that "whoever hath an absolute authority to interpret any written or spoken laws, it is he who is truly the lawgiver."

The delegates at the Constitutional Convention of 1787 feared that the states, jealous of their prerogatives, would decide questions of law in a way that would diminish the authority of the new national government. Furthermore, they sought to ensure justice through national courts for citizens in interstate conflicts because of the fear, for example, that a citizen of Maryland who pressed a claim against a Virginian in the courts of the Old Dominion would meet with bias in favor of the Virginian. Lastly, the framers were interested in the problem of uniformity. They realized that if each state had the final authority to interpret federal laws, the laws might come to have as many meanings as there were states. These reasons impelled the framers to provide for a national judiciary.

The authority of the national judiciary rests in constitutional language. The federal courts are empowered by Article III, Section 2, to hear two categories of cases: one determined by the parties to the litigation, the other determined by its subject matter. The case is within the jurisdiction of the federal courts if the United States is a party; if one of the states brings a lawsuit; if the litigation involves citizens of one state and another or a foreign country; if the dispute involves an ambassador or a minister of another country; and, finally, if it is a controversy between two citizens of the same state involving land grants claimed under titles of two or more states (a little-known provision that has been obscured by the passage of time). The federal courts may also hear cases that arise under the Constitution, laws, or treaties of the United States or that involve admiralty or maritime laws. All other matters rest in the state courts.

The issues over which the federal courts have jurisdiction can also be heard in state courts, however. Under the Supremacy Clause (Article VI, Section 2), the Constitution, laws, and treaties of the United States "shall be the supreme Law of the Land; and the Judges in every State shall be bound thereby." The important difference is, of course, that when these issues are heard by state courts they can be appealed to the federal courts for a final decision, whereas in other matters state judicial decisions are final.

The framers left broad discretion to the Congress in structuring the federal judicial system. In Article III, Section I, they provided that "The judicial Power of the United States, shall be vested in one supreme Court, and in such inferior Courts as the Congress may from time to time ordain and establish." Judges are nominated by the President and confirmed by the Senate. To insulate the judges from political pressures, judges "shall hold their Offices during good Behaviour" (that is, until death or retirement, unless impeached by Congress), and their compensation cannot be diminished during their term of office.

Under the broad mandate of the Constitution, Congress has established a three-tier system of federal courts. At the base are the district courts, which are trial courts that have jurisdiction over a defined geographical region—such as an entire state (for example, the United States District Court for Connecticut) or a portion of a state (for example, the United States District Court for the Eastern District of Wisconsin). Where caseloads are high, several district judges may be members of the same court, and cases are distributed among them.

The district courts are grouped into ten "circuits," and each circuit is provided with a court of appeals. All the districts in Illinois, Indiana, and Wisconsin, for instance, comprise the Seventh Circuit. These appellate courts ordinarily sit as three-man bodies to hear appeals from district court decisions. Again, where the caseload is heavy, there may be a larger number of judges so that appeals can be divided among a number of three-judge panels.

Finally, of course, there is the Supreme Court, the court of last resort in the national judicial system. Because of the enormous volume of appeals, the Supreme Court must exercise its discretion to refuse to hear a large number of cases. In such instances, the decision in the court below is final. Presently, the Congress has provided for nine seats on the Supreme Court, but the size of its membership is not fixed in the Constitution. The legislature has the power to alter the number of justices; this sometimes gives rise to the practice of "court packing," in which Congress and the President enlarge the number of justices in order to win the decision they favor.

In addition to this basic court structure, Congress has provided for certain specialized courts. Most important is the three-judge district court (actually consisting in most cases of two district judges and a court of appeals judge), which is convened when a party seeks to enjoin the enforcement of a state or national law on the ground that it is unconstitutional. Other special courts include the United States Court of Claims, the United States Court of Customs and Patent Appeals, the United States Tax Court, the United States Court of Military Appeals, and whatever courts Congress may provide to try cases in the territories of the United States. The jurisdictions of these courts as well as certain specialized responsibilities of the district and circuit courts are complicated subjects, which are beyond the scope of this book but are essential to the lawyer and the scholar of public law.

Judicial Review

If the federal courts were empowered only to interpret statutes and treaties, the judiciary would not loom so large in American politics. The judges would, of course, still be engaged in policy making, for, as Jack W. Peltason points out, a judicial decision that interprets a statute in one way rather than another advantages one party, interest, or value at the expense of the other. In many cases the law permits several interpretations; and the discretion in distributing advantages and disadvantages lies with the men on the bench. Thus, it rests with a court to decide, for example, whether an employee who works on a dock transferring goods from train cars to the cranes that load the goods aboard a ship can be compensated for on-the-job injuries under the Longshoremen's and Harbor Workers' Compensation Act of 1927; this act provides compensation "if the disability or death results from an injury occurring upon the navigable waters of the United States (including any dry dock)." In the case of *Nacirema Operating Co. v. Johnson,* 24 L.Ed. 2d 371 (1969) the Supreme Court held that such a dock worker's injury did not occur upon the navigable waters of the United States. But any decision the court had made would have been the law.

The Congress and the President can, of course, pass a new law or negotiate a new treaty to provide a more precise or a different meaning if a court interprets the existing language in a way that conflicts with the intention of the elected branches. But the power of judicial review, the power to interpret the meaning of the Constitution, is not subject to any similar check by the popular branches, and it is this great power that has thrust the judiciary—especially the Supreme Court—into the center of the American political arena.

Although the judges had hinted from time to time that they possessed the power to strike down laws contrary to the Constitution, judicial review was not clearly established until the landmark case of *Marbury v. Madison,* 2 L.Ed. 60 (1803). Speaking for a unanimous Court, Chief Justice John Marshall struck down a provision of the Judiciary Act of 1789, which had been passed by Congress and signed by the President. He declared:

> [T]he particular phraseology of the Constitution of the United States confirms and strengthens the principle, supposed to be essential to all written constitutions, that a law repugnant to the Constitution is void; and that courts, as well as other departments, are bound by that instrument.

Marshall's argument did not rest on a specific provision of the Constitution empowering the Supreme Court to invalidate laws that violate the Constitution. Instead, he based his stand on the inferences he drew from such provisions as those declaring that the "judicial Power shall extend to all Cases . . . arising under this Constitution" and providing that judicial officers shall be bound by oath to support the Constitution. Marshall did not point out that the existence of a conflict between the Constitution and a law depends primarily upon the judges' interpretation of the language of each document; thus, it lies within judicial discretion to create or avoid such conflicts by the manner in which the language of the statutes and the Constitution is interpreted.

In a long line of subsequent cases, the Supreme Court has established its authority to overrule executive as well as legislative acts that the justices deem contrary to the Constitution. It has also asserted and exercised the power to strike down provisions of state constitutions, acts of state legislatures, actions of state executives, and decisions of state courts that are deemed incompatible with the language of the Constitution or, for that matter, federal laws or treaties. Thus, the Supreme Court has become the arbiter of power in American government, deciding which powers rest with the states and which with the nation; determining the prerogatives of the executive and those of the legislature; and drawing the line between the areas in which government can act and those in which it cannot because such power is denied by the Bill of Rights and other guarantees of individual freedom. It is not surprising that Thomas Jefferson was moved to exclaim about the decision in *Marbury v. Madison* that "The Constitution, on this hypothesis, is a mere thing of wax in the hands of the judiciary which they may twist and shape into any form they please."

Edward S. Corwin, one of the greatest American constitutional scholars, once wrote of judicial review that "The people who say the Framers intended it are talking nonsense and the people who say they did not intend it are talking nonsense"—which nicely captures the incertitude surrounding the historical roots of judicial review. There was (and is) no judicial review in England; therefore, this power that American judges hold does not derive from the Anglo-Saxon legal tradition. On the other hand, the English Privy Council and the Board of Trade reviewed laws passed by colonial assemblies to ascertain that they neither exceeded the powers granted by charter nor conflicted with English law. This kind of "judicial review" might have established expectations in the colonies that did not exist in the mother country. At the time of ratification of the Constitution, there had been two or three (the precise figure is a subject of dispute among historians) instances in which state courts had struck down laws of state legislatures. But the adverse reaction to these decisions was so great and swift that they can scarcely be held to have established judicial review as an accepted function of the courts.

In 1912 Charles Beard published a summary of members of the Constitutional Convention who he alleged were advocates of judicial review; although his list did not constitute a majority of the convention, it did include a majority of the leaders. Other historians, including Corwin and Louis Boudin, have argued that Beard's list is too inclusive and that it counts as advocates men whose positions were not known (and perhaps not fixed) until after the convention. In any case, if the convention majority intended to establish judicial review, it certainly chose a circumspect manner of saying so, for there is no explicit warrant of the power in the Constitution. Even Chief Justice Marshall was compelled to work mightily to establish the necessary inferences and implications from the existing language.

It has also been pointed out that proposals for a Council of Revision which would be empowered to revise or veto legislation in conflict with the Constitution were defeated in the convention. On the other hand, it has been argued that Hamilton's "The Federalist No. 78," published during the debate on ratification in New York, explicitly states the power of judges to overrule legislative action contrary to the Constitution. But it must be remembered that Hamilton, though a giant in the fight for ratification, was not a figure of consequence at the convention, and that his own proposal for a constitution, which was rejected by the convention, did not include a provision establishing judicial review.

Though the intention of the framers and the historical roots of judicial review thus remain in doubt, the political power of the judiciary in America is a reality. Since *Marbury v. Madison* the power of judicial review has been exercised time and again. Today, it is commonly accepted by Americans as part of our Constitution, even if it is not explicitly granted in the Constitution.

This great power has plunged the Court into the center of every political crisis in American history, grave or small. It is simple enough to accept Peltason's argument that every judicial decision advances some interests or values and retards others, thus engaging judges in policy making "not as a matter of choice but of function." But judges are policy makers by choice as well as by function. Charles Evans Hughes, who had previously served as Associate Justice and was later to be named Chief Justice, said during his 1916 presidential campaign that "We are under the Constitution, but the Constitution is is what the judges say it is." And Harlan Fiske Stone, later to be Chief Justice, dissented from the decision of his brethren striking down a part of the New Deal by recognizing the awesome power of judges and warning that "the only check on our own exercise of power is our own sense of self-restraint."

In one aspect of judicial review the political implications are not so apparent. When the justices decide whether a power properly belongs to the legislature or the executive or to the national government or the states, they place power in the hands of quite different constituencies. The President's constituency tends to lie disproportionately in the great metropolitan states of the nation with their large blocs of electoral votes. Influence in Congress tends to rest in the more rural and socially homogeneous districts, where congressmen are continually returned to office, because men of long seniority are invested with power in committees. Similarly, the policies that might be adopted by the states will often be quite different from those adopted in Congress. If the Supreme Court had decided that the interstate commerce power did not permit Congress to prohibit racial discrimination in restaurants, motels, and so forth, these so-called public accommodations would have remained solely within the jurisdiction of the states, and their desegregation in many southern states would still lie in the future.

The Politics of the Judicial Process

Politics pervade not only the policies made by the courts, but also the appointment of judges, their deliberations, the process of litigation that brings cases to them, and the compliance with whatever decisions they announce. Henry Abraham demonstrates the political considerations involved in appointing a Supreme Court justice. Presidents and senators are concerned with the "real politics" of the nominees—with the kinds of decisions they are likely to make on the bench. In this century, three presidential nominees have been rejected outright by the Senate, and in each case ideology was a significant factor. John J. Parker, Clement Haynsworth, and Harrold Carswell were all strongly opposed by organized labor and by black groups who felt that their views were hostile to unions and to civil rights. In each instance, the appointing President also knew the views of the nominees. Nixon has said, in fact, that he intended to appoint "strict constructionists," men who would "be very conservative in overthrowing a law passed by the elected representatives at the state or Federal level."

Justices, of course, do not always conform to the expectations of presidents or senators. After his rejection for the Supreme Court, Parker made a strong record in defense of civil liberties and rendered several judicial blows against racial segregation on the Fourth Circuit Court of Appeals where he had sat and continued to sit. Thomas Jefferson was terribly disappointed that Joseph Story, whom he had appointed, soon joined in the nationalist outlook of Jefferson's archrival Chief Justice John Marshall. Theodore Roosevelt was angered when Oliver Wendell Holmes, whom he had elevated to the high court, rendered a decision weakening the antitrust laws during Roosevelt's "trust-busting" campaign.

The politics of appointment are equally matched by the politics of litigation. Cases that reach the Supreme Court are often sponsored by special interest groups seeking to sustain victories they have won in other forums or to reverse defeats suffered elsewhere. When the NAACP was unsuccessful in obtaining civil rights legislation in Congress and in the state legislatures, it turned to the courts and scored notable victories. Groups that do not sponsor test cases can file amicus curiae (friend of the court) briefs explaining their position on cases pending before the judges. The American Civil Liberties Union is one of the busiest filers of such briefs in both the federal and state courts. The role of interest groups in litigation is treated by Clement E. Vose.

It is sometimes alleged that interest groups seek to publish views favorable to their interpretation of the Constitution or the statutes in law journals and law reviews, which are widely read by lawyers and judges and are often cited in briefs and in judicial opinions. Congressman Wright Patman took the floor of the House of Representatives in 1957 to denounce "the Court's consideration of unknown, unrecognized and nonauthoritative textbooks, Law Review articles, and other writings of propaganda artists and lobbyists." Such sources, he argued, had helped shape antitrust decisions in a way that weakened the federal government's prosecution of monopolies.

Even the selection of a court in which to initiate a lawsuit involves political considerations, for astute lawyers know that judges of different courts have quite different attitudes about the law. When the National Labor Relations Board (NLRB) handed down its decision giving victory on almost all points to the United Automobile Workers in the prolonged and bitter strike between the union and the Kohler Plumbingware Company, both sides scrambled to file their appeal papers, but in different courts. The company hastened to the chambers of the Seventh Circuit Court of Appeals, known for its willingness to overturn NLRB decisions, while the union lawyers, desirous of a more complete victory, sped to the chambers of the Court of Appeals for the District of Columbia, which had concurrent jurisdiction and a much friendlier attitude toward the labor board. The union lawyers proved more fleet-footed and ultimately won their case in the forum they had selected. The Supreme Court subsequently refused to grant a writ of certiorari to review the decision of the court of appeals in *Kohler Co. v. N.L.R.B.*, 15 L.Ed. 2d 79 (1965).

Other influences enter into the process of litigation in ways that are indirect and difficult to measure, but that contribute nonetheless to the environment in which decision making occurs. These include newspaper comment and other public responses; the opinion of the bar and the bench, for judges seek and need the approval of their peer group; and the law schools, whose recognition and praise of justices reflect their concurrence with the dominant legal philosophy among the faculty. For some years it was apparent that Justice William O. Douglas and, to a lesser extent, Justice Hugo Black were favorites of the

Yale Law Faculty and were hailed at the Yale Law School because of their views on the "absolute" nature of rights guaranteed in the Bill of Rights. Justice Felix Frankfurter, who insisted on judicial restraint and was inclined to balance declarations of rights against the policies established by elected officials, was widely acclaimed at the Harvard Law School. (It may have been an influential factor in these faculty allegiances that Justice Douglas had been a member of the Yale Law Faculty and that Justice Frankfurter had taught at Harvard.) In addition, the great forces of social and economic change, often accompanied by dramatic changes in national politics, influence the decisions of judges. Justice Benjamin Cardozo captured this in his remark that "The great tides and currents which engulf the rest of men, do not turn aside in their course, and pass the judges idly by."

The process of decision within the courts is also intensely political. Walter F. Murphy demonstrates the range of tactics open to justices who wish to influence the course of a decision. The casting of a vote may often be accompanied by bargaining about the doctrine upon which the decision will be based. The modification of a concurring or dissenting opinion or its complete withdrawal may be made through the same process of arriving at an acceptable rationale for decision.

The Chief Justice, as David Danelski clearly shows, plays a central role in the internal politics of the Supreme Court. He is entitled to assign the opinion among the justices who vote for the same disposition of the case as he. This power has sometimes been used to assign an opinion to a justice who will ground the decision in a doctrine preferred by the Chief Justice rather than in an alternative and equally proper legal principle. The influence that accrues to a Chief Justice who assumes task and social leadership on the Court is well illustrated by Danelski's discussion of Charles Evans Hughes.

In addition, justices of common views tend to band together as blocs in the conduct of the Court's business. C. Herman Pritchett of the University of Chicago has shown the formation of such blocs in the Supreme Court from the New Deal through the Chief Justiceship of Fred M. Vinson (1946–1953). Table 1 portrays the line-up on the Court during the troubled years of the New Deal. In casting dissenting votes, Justices Stone, Cardozo, and Brandeis clearly formed a bloc, dissenting frequently and often together. As the history of that period makes plain, they were the "liberal" minority on the Supreme Court. Time and again they voted to sustain the social and economic regulations and programs enacted by the New Deal and the states to combat the Great Depression.

Justices Willis Van Devanter, George Sutherland, Pierce Butler, and James McReynolds were, on the other hand, the core of the "conservative" bloc. They dissented far less frequently, for they were often able to win the crucial fifth vote, usually from Justice Owen J. Roberts, that sanctified their view as constitutional doctrine. It was this majority, holding fast to constitutional doctrines which sharply restricted the regulatory powers of the government, that precipitated the famous struggle between Franklin D. Roosevelt and the Supreme Court. In 1937 this struggle culminated in the "court-packing" fight, in which Roosevelt threatened to pack the Court in order to get it to reverse itself on the constitutionality of the major New Deal programs.

In addition to showing the two strong voting blocs on the Court, the table

Table 1
Participation of and Agreements Among Supreme Court Justices in Dissenting Opinions, 1931–35 Terms*

	Stone	*Car-dozo*	*Bran-deis*	*Hughes*	*Rob-erts*	*Van De-vanter*	*Suther-land*	*But-ler*	*Mc-Reyn-olds*
No. dissents	67	55	57	15	15	17	23	36	33
Stone	(4)	51	53	12	6			1	
Cardozo	51	(3)	40	12	2	1		1	
Brandeis	53	40	(1)	10	8		1	3	
Hughes	12	12	10	(2)	1	1			
Roberts	6	2	8	1	(1)		5	7	3
Van Devanter		1		1		(1)	13	13	11
Sutherland			1		5	13	(1)	19	13
Butler	1	1	3		7	13	19	(5)	17
McReynolds					3	11	13	17	(13)

* Justice Holmes, who served part of the 1931 term, is excluded from the table.

Source: C. Herman Pritchett, *Civil Liberties and the Vinson Court* (Chicago: The University of Chicago Press, 1954), p. 178.

reveals how infrequently a liberal and conservative justice were joined together in dissent. The "roll call" of the justices shows a higher unity score among liberals and conservatives than is common even in such obviously political forums as the Congress. The center roles of Chief Justice Hughes and Justice Roberts are also apparent. When Hughes dissented, it was usually in conjunction with liberal members, whereas Roberts split his dissents about evenly between the two blocs. The infrequency with which Hughes and Roberts dissented reflects that their votes usually made the majority. The two blocs remained cohesive, and the decision of the Court thus rested on the votes of the two "swing" justices. Although bloc voting on the Court is not always as cohesive or sustained as it was in the New Deal period, subsequent studies continue to show a high degree of bloc action in the judicial process.

Compliance with the decisions and rules announced by the courts is also a complex and highly political process. The Supreme Court possesses neither the power of the purse nor of the sword. As a result, it is entirely dependent on other agencies in the government to execute its judgments. In the most flagrant cases of resistance, others may refuse to carry out a court's order. This occurred in 1861, for example, when President Lincoln refused to comply with a writ of habeas corpus issued by Chief Justice Roger Taney. The incident, explained more fully by Robert H. Jackson, was a test of the President's power to suspend the so-called Great Writ, which empowers judges to order public officials to present prisoners in court to determine whether they are being properly held. Lincoln asserted the authority of the executive to suspend the writ in time of emergency, but Taney ruled that such suspensions must be concurred in by the Congress. Lincoln's refusal to honor the writ overrode Taney's determination. More often, however, compliance is delayed and evaded by legal means. Since the Supreme Court usually states a legal principle and then remands the particular case to the appropriate lower court for further proceedings, the subordinate courts have innumerable opportunities to thwart Supreme Court mandates.

Judicial decisions, like constitutions and statutes, leave room for interpretation, and lower courts can read higher court opinions in ways contrary to their spirit and intention. Many southern district courts applied the Supreme Court's mandate for desegregation of schools "with all deliberate speed" in a manner that effectively defeated the purpose. Lower courts can also delay compliance by extending proceedings upon remand. The case of a young Negro named Virgil Hawkins is instructive. In 1949 he applied for admission to the University of Florida Law School and was rejected; on appeal to the Supreme Court his case was remanded to the Florida courts, which delayed and extended the proceedings until 1958, when Hawkins was finally able to obtain an order admitting him to the law school.

General principles announced by the Supreme Court often remain unenforced in many areas of the country because no one cares enough, or is bold enough, to insist on his rights. For example, in many communities, prayers are still a regular feature of the public school regime because no parent or child has raised the issue or chosen to take it to court.

It has been suggested that compliance with judicial policies is speedier and more complete when they do not affect large numbers of people directly and when they can be effectuated by a reasonably small number of officials. The reapportionment cases, for instance, did not require large-scale changes in the everyday living conditions of Americans, and they could be enforced simply by directing orders to the chief election officials in the states (usually the secretary of state). The Supreme Court's decisions rendering new procedural safeguards to criminal defendants are similar: most Americans are not affected in their daily lives, and those judges and lawyers in a position to assure the newly granted rights are within the reach of court orders and are likely to respect judicial decisions, even if they disagree with them. The desegregation decisions and the cases banning prayers in the public schools, on the other hand, require obedience by many local school officials and a change in social practices for millions of Americans. Delay, resistance, and nonenforcement have characterized the response to both decisions, and the Court's policies are still not fully in effect.

Judicial Review and Democracy

Recognizing that the courts are policy makers and deeply involved in politics, what can be the justification for investing them with the enormous power of judicial review? Oliver Wendell Holmes drew the distinction between judicial review of state action and of the policies of the national executive and legislature. The former was necessary, he argued, to preserve the power of the national government and to maintain the balance in the federal system. But the nation would have flourished as well, in his view, without review of the judicial branch. It is this power of the judges to oversee the Congress and the President that raises the most difficult questions for the American form of democratic government.

Henry Steele Commager puts the conflict between judicial review and democracy sharply: "the one non-elective and non-removable element in the government rejects the conclusions as to constitutionality arrived at by the two elective and removable branches." Justice Felix Frankfurter referred to the Supreme Court as "inherently oligarchic" and "the non-democratic organ of our Government." Certainly the power of judges, who are neither elected nor subject to popular recall in elections, to review and veto the actions of popularly elected officials in the national government and the states is difficult to square with majority rule and the principle of popular sovereignty.

The foremost justification offered by advocates of judicial review has been that the Supreme Court protects minority rights. It is the balance wheel in the majority rule system that assures that the guarantees of individual rights written into the Constitution will not be infringed upon by popular government. Robert A. Dahl suggests the discomfort caused by this argument when he says that

> to affirm that the Court supports minority preferences against majorities is to deny that popular sovereignty and political equality, at least in the traditional sense, exist in the United States; and to affirm that the Court *ought* to act in this way is to deny that popular sovereignty and political equality *ought* to prevail. . . . In a country that glories in its democratic tradition, this is not a happy state of affairs for the Court's defenders. . . .[1]

Furthermore, since the language of the Constitution is vague and broad (for example, it grants to the government the power to "regulate interstate and foreign commerce," and to persons the guarantee of "due process of law"), such things as the protection of "minority rights" can become whatever the Court wishes to interpret them to be. Favored minorities find themselves with judicially declared constitutional rights; other minorities are not so fortunate. But the minority rights justification need not become entangled in such theoretical considerations, for both Dahl and Commager have shown that the history of judicial activism does not confirm it. When Commager reviewed the seventy-five instances of "judicial nullification" of congressional action that had occurred prior to the publication of his *Majority Rule and Minority Rights* in 1943, he concluded that the record

> . . . discloses not a single case, in a century and a half, where the Supreme Court has protected freedom of speech, press, assembly, petition or religion against Congressional attack. It reveals no instance, with [one] possible exception . . . , where the Court has intervened on behalf of the underprivileged—the Negro, the alien, women, children, workers, tenant-farmers. It reveals, on the contrary, that the Court has effectively intervened, again and again, to defeat Congressional attempts to free the slave, to guarantee civil rights to Negroes, to protect workingmen, to outlaw child labor, to assist hard-pressed farmers, and to democratize the tax system.[2]

It can be argued, of course, that in recent years the Supreme Court has been a champion of minority rights. The Court has protected "minority rights" in ordering racial desegregation; in insisting upon the one-man, one-vote rule for legislative districting; in banning prayers in the public schools; in expanding

1 Robert A. Dahl, "Decision-Making in a Democracy: The Supreme Court as a National Policy-Maker," *Journal of Public Law*, 6 (1958), 283.

2 Henry Steele Commager, *Majority Rule and Minority Rights* (New York: Oxford University Press, 1943), p. 55.

the freedom of speech to prevent the harassment of unpopular political sects; and in extending the rights of criminal defendants. But the sixteen years of the Warren Court do not make the minority rights justification true for all time; and, indeed, the record shows that the time of the Warren Court is the exceptional period in the history of judicial policy making. Moreover, that period may already be drawing to a close with the determination of President Nixon to appoint "conservatives" and "strict constructionists" to the Supreme Court.

However, even if the activism on behalf of minority rights were to continue, the troublesome problem of squaring democracy with a minority veto power would remain, as would the question of which minorities would be entitled to such protection. Why should doctors not be saved from Medicare and businessmen from antitrust laws as criminal defendants are from self-incrimination and city dwellers from malapportionment?

One answer to the conflict between judicial review and majority rule has been based on Justice Stone's comments in a footnote in *United States v. Carolene Products Co.*, 82 L.Ed. 1234 (1938), the so-called Footnote Four Doctrine. Stone raised, but did not settle, the issue of whether there should be a narrower presumption of the constitutionality of legislation that seems to violate specific constitutional prohibitions (such as the Bill of Rights), to restrict the political processes through which majority rule is exercised, or to be directed at particular religions, ethnic groups, races, or "discrete and insular minorities." At least the second of these categories seems consistent with the concept of popular rule: the Court would protect voting rights, freedom of speech and petition, and other guarantees necessary to permit minorities to strive to gain majority status and to change policies that they find repugnant.

The vigorous application of explicit constitutional rights (such as "Congress shall make no law . . . abridging the freedom of speech . . .") would seem to be consistent with a view that the Constitution is the supreme law of the land and overrides ordinary legislation that conflicts with it. But it would not answer Commager's insistence that "legislative bodies, state and national, have been throughout our history profoundly conservative and constitution-minded," and that judicial review in such cases merely substitutes the judges' reading of the Constitution for the interpretation given it by elected officials.

The same problem of discretion in interpretation arises with regard to the rights of religious, ethnic, racial, and insular minorities. In 1896 the Supreme Court decided that the Fourteenth Amendment guarantee that "No State shall . . . deny to any person within its jurisdiction the equal protection of the laws" permitted segregated railway cars (and subsequently segregated schools, public accommodations, and so forth) as long as the separate facilities were equal. Although the language of the amendment was not altered during the intervening fifty-eight years, the Supreme Court decided in 1954 that segregated schools were "inherently unequal," and it subsequently applied this ruling to parks, courthouses, swimming beaches, and so on. There is no guarantee that the general clauses of the Constitution, which in recent years have been the basis for so many extensions of minority rights, will always be interpreted to protect the rights of political, religious, ethnic, racial, or insular minorities. Indeed, the Supreme Court's 1896 interpretation of those clauses is a lesson in point.

A somewhat different defense of judicial review emphasizes the numerous checks that the popular branches can impose upon the judiciary. Among them, refusing to comply with judicial decisions—as several strong presidents have done—is the most extreme. Court packing is another. There is no clearer case of court packing than that which took place in 1870, when the Supreme Court, by a vote of four to three, held unconstitutional the Legal Tender Act insofar as it provided that greenbacks should be legal tender for payment of debts incurred before the act's passage. In 1866, Congress had passed legislation providing that no new appointments be made to the then nine-member Court until, through death and resignation, it had been reduced to seven members. In 1870, the Radical Republicans in Congress passed a law increasing the membership of the Court to nine. President Grant promptly appointed two new justices—there is strong evidence that he knew the new justices' views on the legal tender issue before he nominated them—and in 1871 the Court reversed its previous decision on that issue.

The passage of a constitutional amendment is another device for overriding the Court. The judiciary has been overridden in this manner five times in American history and on major issues of national policy in four of these instances (the three Civil War amendments and the income tax amendment). But the amendment process is cumbersome and time consuming. Furthermore, a small minority in either house of Congress and an even smaller minority of states can block an amendment; thus the amendment process is a relatively ineffective majority tool against a Supreme Court that represents a well-rooted minority.

The Congress can also modify the appellate jurisdiction of the Supreme Court by passing legislation to take certain policy matters from the Court's purview. According to Article III, Section 2, of the Constitution "the supreme Court shall have appellate Jurisdiction. . . . with such Exceptions, and under such Regulations as the Congress shall make." In 1869 the Congress deprived the Court of appellate jurisdiction in certain habeas corpus cases in order to defeat judicial review of one of the Reconstruction acts. This was fully achieved when the Court held that it was not empowered to decide such a case even though the justices had already heard argument and voted upon it, but had not yet announced their decision.

Such weapons as constitutional amendments, court packing, open defiance, and jurisdictional limitations do not in fact provide effective checks by the popular branches upon the Court. Seldom are the issues great enough to warrant such drastic actions, and seldom do the other branches wish to inflict such severe wounds on the status of the third branch in order to attain a particular policy victory. In the final analysis the only check upon the Court that is both effective and feasible is the appointment of new justices to fill the seats of those who die or retire. Ordinarily such vacancies occur on the average of one every twenty-three months, so that a President can expect to name two justices each term. Since the Court is usually divided on grave issues, the President's appointments are often sufficient to tip the balance.

Two persuasive arguments have been advanced by advocates of judicial review who rely upon this ultimate power of the elected branches, through the regular appointment process, to bring the Court into line. Alexander Bickel has argued strongly that "government should serve not only what we conceive from time to time to be our immediate material needs but also certain enduring values." However, in the legislature "when the pressure for immediate results is strong enough and emotions ride high enough, men will ordinarily prefer to act on expediency rather than take the long view." Judges, on the other hand, have the leisure, the training, and the insulation to sort out the enduring values of society and to invoke judicial review to protect society from the momentary passions of the legislature. In the longer term, of course, the people can always override these judicial determinations by taking advantage of the natural turnover on the Court. It is in this short-term protection of long-term values that the merit of judicial review lies.

Robert Dahl also relies on the final power of the popular branches to staff the Court. On matters of great policy importance, the popular branches ultimately have their way, despite the checks sometimes imposed by judicial review. When the Court strikes down legislation within four years of its enactment, and thus presumably at a time when the lawmaking majority that passed it is still intact, the popular branches are usually soon vindicated by the Court's reversal of its decision. In a few cases—most notably those involving compensation for injured longshoremen, income tax, and child labor—the Court's veto was not finally reversed for more than a decade.

Because the popular branches are ordinarily sustained on major policy, and often reasonably quickly, Dahl does not find that the Court is as great a barrier to majority rule as is alleged by the enemies of judicial review. He also feels that it serves a vital purpose in a democratic society by conferring legitimacy upon the majority policy. In a nation of constitution worshipers, the declaration that legislation is constitutional gains it widespread acceptance. Since the Court's policies usually coincide with those of the lawmaking majority, its role in America is one of declaring the constitutionality, and thus the legitimacy, of the policies of majorities; and, in particular, it gains acceptance for the policies enacted by new majority regimes. Where there are policy differences within the lawmaking majority, the Court can sometimes take the lead in making policy, for although there is not enough support for such a policy to obtain legislative sanction, neither is there sufficient opposition to overrule policy innovation by the Court.

These elaborate rationales for judicial review are not, however, beyond challenge. Both assume that judges are particularly competent to make policy, either by protecting long-term values or by innovating within the broad confines of the majority coalition. Commager bitingly rejects the view that judges can be trusted more than legislators or executives to act independently, objectively, or dispassionately. The courts, he notes, are deeply political, and the justices have strong policy biases. Why should their biases be accorded more weight (indeed, as much weight) as those of men who are elected by the people?

Robert H. Jackson condemns the special competence of the justices from another perspective. Judicial review involves matters of social and economic policy, not mere mechanical applications of the Constitution. Yet the judicial process is narrow in its perspective, for it welcomes only lawyers as pleaders when the views of economists, sociologists, and other specialists may have as much or even greater relevance to the issues. Furthermore, lawsuits that establish general policy are fought over narrow sets of facts involving particular litigants. This does little to encourage policy making consistent with the larger reality of American life. Even the fact-gathering method of the courts—a trial with adversary presentations and rigid rules of evidence—is scarcely as useful for policy making as the methods of inquiry employed by the executive and legislative branches. Thus, rather than being competent to make policy, even in the short run, the courts may be less competent than the popular branches, whose conclusions they set aside in favor of their own.

There is another aspect of judicial review that needs attention. Even if Bickel and Dahl are correct that the Supreme Court cannot long withstand the preferences of a determined majority, it may also be true that even in the short run judicial review threatens democracy. When major national crises occur, there are upheavals in party politics in which the majority party is replaced by its rival. Examples of such realigning elections include the victory of the Jeffersonian Republicans over the issue of popular democracy, the emergence of Jacksonian democracy over the issues of expansion and national economic policy, the rise of the Republicans in the sectional crisis, and the reemergence of the Democrats in the Great Depression. The new majority party is then expected to act swiftly to meet the crisis that has shattered the old majority's standing. Yet at precisely this crucial time, the Supreme Court continues, by the rule of life tenure, to be dominated by men of the old coalition. Because of the nation's reverence for the Constitution and the legitimacy that the Court's role as constitutional interpreter confers upon judicial policy, the new majority finds itself hindered in facing the crisis by the agents of a majority now dissolved. Robert H. Jackson puts it eloquently:

> The judiciary is thus the check of a preceding generation on the present one; a check of conservative legal philosophy upon a dynamic people and nearly always the check of a rejected regime on the one in being.[3]

At each turn in American history, the great presidents who led the new majority coalitions were forced to battle the Court: Jefferson by suspending the Court's term for a year and threatening noncompliance with its orders; Jackson by outright defiance; Lincoln, too, by disobedience; and Franklin D. Roosevelt by the threat of court packing.

Even in the long run, the Court's role as a legitimacy-conferring institution may be more chimerical than real. Kenneth Dolbeare reports that the public has little knowledge about judicial decisions. Respondents to a public opinion survey were presented a list of eight public policy areas and asked to indicate whether the Court had rendered decisions in each of them. In four the Court had acted and in the remaining four it had not. Only 15 percent of those interviewed made correct statements about whether there had been judicial action in any four of the eight areas.

Dolbeare also shows that attitudes toward the Supreme Court are greatly influenced by the respondents' party identifications and by the party of the incumbent President. Democrats, on the whole, evaluated the Court favorably, and Republicans viewed it unfavorably, although Republican hostility was substantially moderated when the President was a Republican.

[3] Robert H. Jackson, *The Struggle for Judicial Supremacy* (New York: Vintage Books, 1941), p. 315.

Dahl's defense of the Supreme Court as a legitimacy-conferring institution is certainly weakened by these findings. How can the Supreme Court confer legitimacy either on specific policies or on whole regimes when the public lacks so much knowledge about the Court's decisions? Furthermore, if a citizen's party identification and the party of the President are significant in shaping attitudes toward the Court, it may be that the judiciary is legitimated by the other branches rather than conferring legitimacy on them, as Dahl argues.

The effectiveness of the judiciary in conferring legitimacy is made even more doubtful by the finding that it ranks last among the three branches in public confidence. In response to the question "Would you be likely to think the right thing had been done in Washington if the action had been taken by the Supreme Court (President, Congress)?" respondents expressed the greatest confidence in Congress, then in the President, and last in the Court. A study by Walter F. Murphy and Joseph Tanenhaus[4] heightens still further the skepticism about the Supreme Court's legitimacy-conferring function. The authors conclude that for the Supreme Court to confer legitimacy upon regimes, the public must know something of its work, recognize the Court as the interpreter of the Constitution, and favorably view the Court's particular decisions or its overall performance. Less than 13 percent of the public meets all three prerequisites.

The Supreme Court emerges from these conflicting appraisals without a well-articulated role. Although it has sometimes defended minorities, minorities have found the Court an inconstant ally at best. Unable, finally, to resist a purposeful and determined majority, it nonetheless has often frustrated majority rule and intervened against the new leadership mandated by emerging majorities in times of national crisis.

The Supreme Court's role in the long, stable eras of party rule also is not well defined. Its efficacy as a legitimacy-conferring institution is in doubt, and its competence as a policy innovator within the majority coalition is seriously challenged. It can scarcely pretend to be as responsive to the people as to the elected branches, yet it shares the powers of the elected branches in a polity widely considered democratic. It should perhaps be regarded as an anomalous institution in a democratic society, and one whose decisions must be subjected to the same searching review as the policies of the other branches. Public review of judicial policy is more awkward than is review of the more obviously political branches, but in a democracy the people need be no more tremulous in imposing their will on justices than they are on presidents or legislators.

[4] Walter F. Murphy and Joseph Tanenhaus, "Public Opinion and the United States Supreme Court," *Law and Society Review*, 2 (May 1968), 357-384.

45

The Study of Judicial Decision-Making

JACK W. PELTASON

In the brief selection that follows, Jack W. Peltason demonstrates that in making policy the courts are deeply involved in "politics." Because their decisions advantage some interests in society and defeat others, judges are engaged in policy making "not as a matter of choice but of function." When a judge decides to give a statute or a constitutional provision one interpretation rather than another, he gives victory to one interest in society rather than to its adversary. But judges are not merely creatures of their positions; they are —as the introduction suggests—aware of their policy-making role, and many of them welcome it. Their role as policy makers is often assumed as a matter of choice as well as of function.

Nonetheless, many Americans cling to the "orthodox ideology" that judges apply law rather than make it. This insistent belief that judges are not engaged in politics is the greatest weapon of the courts in the policy-making struggle, for their decisions often are not subject to the same criticism that other decision makers must accept.

Peltason is Professor of Political Science and Chancellor of the Champaign-Urbana campus of the University of Illinois. He is the author of Fifty-Eight Lonely Men: Southern Federal Judges and School Desegregation *(1961), coauthor of* Understanding the Constitution *(1967) and* Government by the People *(1966), and editor of* Essays on the American Constitution *(1964).*

The purpose of this essay is to describe federal judges as participants in the political process....

As Tocqueville observed, "Scarcely any political question arises in the United States that is not resolved sooner or later, into a judicial question." Is it not then appropriate to describe the activity of judges in the same terms that are used to discuss legislators and administrators? In so doing we provide a common frame of description which might lead the observer to ask certain questions that might be missed in a narrower focus. Furthermore, by describing the political role of the judges, analysis of the political process will be more complete.

Studies that are primarily concerned with legal doctrines—tracing their historical development and discussing their desirability—or studies that deal with individual judges—examining the influences that molded their thoughts, discovering what they "really meant," applauding or criticizing their decisions—are very important. But these studies do not, except incidentally, provide a framework in which judicial activity can be related to the behavior of other branches of government. They still leave the judges outside the political process.

* * *

Politics as Conflict of Interests

Politics can be viewed in many ways. To some it is a struggle between the good and the bad, between the defenders of the national interest and the spokesmen of selfish pressure groups. To others politics is the conflict between "the people" on the one hand and "the government" on the other. Still other students of politics assume that public officials should be studied in terms of their motives, purposes, biases, and personalities, with only incidental reference to activity outside the formal institutions of government.

In this essay that portion of human activity denominated "politics" is conceptualized as a conflict among interests (or values, rights, demands). An interest consists of all kinds of activity of all kinds of people, some of whom may be public officials, in conflict with an opposed array of activities. For example, all the activity—talking, writing, voting, litigating, or whatever—to secure state ownership of the oil under the marginal seas makes up the state-control interest, which is in conflict with the anti-state-control interest.

An interest is group activity. The activity of a single human being may be of great significance, especially if that individual is a President, Supreme Court justice, trade-union official, or the like. But only as the action of that one human being is related to and supported by the activity of others does it become relevant for our study of the political process.

An interest gets its significance in terms of its opposite, and politics is the process of group or interest conflict. For each interest there is analytically established a contrary interest, although there may be little or no activity to be observed. In such an event there is a *general* interest, activity so widely supported that there is little or no sign of a contrary interest within the community.

Interest is used here in a descriptive and not a normative sense. An interest is a category used by the observer to relate and group various

From *Federal Courts in the Political Process*, by Jack W. Peltason, pp. 1–5.

kinds of activities of various kinds of people. *Special interest* refers to the action of a part of those who make up the community. Interest does not here mean selfish. It is not used in contrast to ideals. Hence the term *national interest,* as used within this framework of description, would not refer to that which the author thinks to be good for the country, but to denote or describe activities of those who represent the nation or those who make up the nation.

An interest is to be distinguished from a physical collection of human individuals whose aggregate activities make up the interest. More important, an interest should not be confused with a formal organization or association. For example, the Taft-Hartley-repeal interest is composed, in part, of some action of most trade-union leaders and a little action of some of their followers. It also includes the activity of many who do not belong to trade unions. On the other hand, some trade unionists' activity is part of the anti-Taft-Hartley-repeal interest. Although officials of formal associations are often active participants in interest conflicts, for some interests there is no formally organized support.

In this essay *government* denotes the activity of men known as governmental officials. These officials are described not above or outside the group conflict, but as participants in it. Their activity is interest activity. Governmental officials are to be described as representing particular interests when they act in such a way as to support that interest. The official becomes a member of the group and his action becomes a part of the interest. Public officials represent many interests and are parts of many groups which may or may not be identical with or include the group which selected the officials.

Legislative votes, court decisions, presidential vetoes are to be described as interest activity. However there is no implication that these officials have "sold out to the selfish interests" or that their conduct is other than it should be. All that is noted is that when these officials make decisions, pass statutes, issue orders, write speeches, and so on, their action promotes some interests and demotes others. When the United States Attorney General, for example, argued before the United States Supreme Court that public-school segregation should be declared unconstitutional, his argument was part of the desegregation interest; so, of course, was the Supreme Court decision that public-school segregation is unconstitutional and so was the opinion written to justify that decision (and so were the actions of thousands of others).

Judges in the Political Process

A judge is in the political process and his activity is interest activity not as a matter of choice but of function. Judicial participation does not grow out of the judge's personality or philosophy but out of his position. A judge who defers to the legislature is engaging in interest activity just as much as the judge who avowedly writes his own preferences into his opinions. A Supreme Court composed of Holmeses and Frankfurters would be just as much a part of the policy-making process as one composed of Sutherlands and Murphys.

However, even in this enlightened day of social science one feels compelled to explain and justify an essay that attempts to describe judges and law as human institutions. Despite the washing of mechanical jurisprudence in the acid of critical observation, the notion persists that judges should not be studied in the same terms as other politicians.

James Madison long ago pointed out in *Federalist* No. 10 that the most important acts of legislation are "but so many judicial determinations . . . concerning the rights of large bodies of citizens," but students of politics, willing to describe legislators in terms of group conflict still resist applying these categories to judges. They argue that legislators are concerned with political controversies which are resolved by group struggle, but judges are concerned with legal controversies which are resolved by applying the "law." Legislators choose among competing values; judges apply the law.

Of course, most political scientists and legal scholars do not believe that "the law" is an external objective phenomenon that controls judges. The traditional explanations of judicial behavior are no longer in good standing among sophisticates. Yet judges will not admit to judicial legislation and the official explanation of public men and practicing lawyers is that the law is independent of the judge and controls his behavior. This explanation is ideological, not theoretical, and although it affects conduct, it does not describe the behavior of public men, practicing lawyers, or deciding judges.

Many skeptics of the orthodox ideology, after admitting that judges sometimes do make value choices and that the law does not necessarily control judges, nevertheless explain that in most cases a properly trained judge can determine the proper rule and arrive at the correct decision by looking at statutes or at past judicial decisions. The policy-making activity of judges is thought to be an exception to the general course of judicial business and not to justify treatment of the judiciary as an integral part of the political system. Some scholars would hold that courts are political agencies when deciding constitutional questions, but should be described dif ferently when deciding nonconstitutional matters.

It is of course true that judges make their decisions in terms of the law. The prevailing ideology requires that choices be so stated. And in many areas there is no conflict within the community about the interest to be supported. The law to be applied is clear. The judge's task is to apply rules about which there is little dispute. Judges who make decisions contrary to the widely accepted meaning of the law will discover that these decisions do not long survive. Where there is widespread agreement as to the rules which should be applied, the judge's task is relatively simple, his behavior predictable. However, whenever there is serious contention, he must choose, and he will find that he cannot turn to deductive logical machines for answers. The law becomes the judge's conclusion, not his starting point.

Compare, for example, the status of the separate-but-equal formula in 1910 with its status in the 1930s. In 1910 the formula was securely established, there was little agitation for change, the segregation interest was dominant, the law clear, the decisions predictable. By the 1930s the group struggle had unsettled the law. In 1910 there was substantial agreement on the interest to be supported, the rule or major premise was settled, and the conclusion was inevitable. By the 1930s there was conflict over the major premise, the particular interest the judge would support became less predictable. But whether the judge speaks for an interest supported by the entire community or for an interest supported by a small portion, it is necessary to describe his activities as participation in the group struggle.

More important, in order to justify an attempt to describe judges as participants in interest conflict, a discussion of whether judges discover or make law is somewhat beside the point. Whether judges make the choices or the law through the judges makes the choices, the choices are interest activity. It may be comforting to the group adversely affected to believe that the decision came not from men making value choices, but from scientific technicians. But this comfort-providing function of the official explanation of judicial behavior does not bear on or negate the importance of describing judicial choice-making in the same descriptive system used to describe other agencies of government.

To recognize that judges represent values and make choices is not to recognize that they are free to choose as they want. But then neither are legislators free. Both judges and legislators are required by the community to behave in certain ways. Both are required to explain their conduct and justify it in terms of some long-range considerations other than personal preference. A legislator explains his votes as being "required by the national interest" or "against the selfish special interests"—seldom as purely personal preferences. A judge is required to explain his decisions in terms of precedents, "intent of the framers," "intent of the legislators," "plain words of the statute." Failure to conform to the role imposed by the community can result in various kinds of sanctions.

Again, to recognize that judges participate in the political process as legislators do is not to assert that judges necessarily represent the same interests as legislators or that the consequences of judicial representation are the same as the consequences of legislative representation. Relations among judges and other decision-makers, public expectations about judicial behavior, functions allotted to judges, these and many other factors make the pattern of interest activity of judges different from that of legislators. Both judge and legislator are engaged in the group struggle, but the manner of participation varies.

* * *

46

Qualifications and Motivations: The United States

HENRY J. ABRAHAM

In the following selection, Henry J. Abraham reviews the factors that are considered by the President in nominating Supreme Court justices and by the Senate in acting upon these nominations. His exposition is dotted with historical examples that confirm that the naming of judicial officers is essentially a political process.

The concern of the President and the Senate with the "real politics" of judicial appointees has important implications for a democracy. Because federal judges "hold their Offices during good Behaviour" (in effect, for life or until retirement), they often have policy views that no longer command majority support among the public. The appointment of new judges whose real politics are acceptable to the popularly elected branches helps to bring the courts into line with majority opinion. When judicial vacancies do not occur at a time of rapid changes in public opinion, the stage is set for conflict between the popular branches, which reflect the current majority view, and the courts, which are dominated by the appointees of bygone majorities.

Abraham, Professor of Political Science at the University of Pennsylvania, has written on judicial process in America and Europe. He is author of Freedom and the Court *(1967),* Courts and Judges *(1959), and* The Judiciary *(1965), and a coauthor of* Elements of Democratic Government *(1964).*

Basic Prerequisites?

. . . there is but one standardized prerequisite for qualification as a *federal* judge today—the LL.B. degree of the aspirant. The possession of that degree is neither a constitutional nor a statutory requirement for appointment, but custom would automatically veto anyone without it for judicial service at the federal level. Moreover, the legal profession, which ... has a very real voice in today's appointive process, would remonstrate so determinedly that the political powers of the government involved would assuredly acquiesce....

Theoretically, any graduate of an accredited bona fide school of law with his eye on a federal judgeship may thus look forward to an appointment to the coveted niche—provided that he is politically "available" *and* acceptable to the executive, legislative, and private forces that, in the order enumerated, constitute the powers-that-be which underlie the paths of selection, nomination, and appointment in the judicial process. In the final analysis, of course, it is the President and his immediate advisers concerned—here the Attorney General and his Deputy—who take the crucial step of submitting the nominee to the Senate. Thus, all of America's chief executives, except William Henry Harrison, Zachary Taylor, and Andrew Johnson, have had an opportunity to designate at least one nominee for membership in the highest court of the land.... Table 1 illustrates thc number of justices each

Table 1
Number of Presidential Appointments of United States Supreme Court Justices Who Actually Served on the Court (arranged chronologically)

President	*Number of Successful Appointments*
Washington	10
J. Adams	3
Jefferson	3
Madison	2
Monroe	1
J. Q. Adams	1
Jackson	6
Van Buren	2
W. H. Harrison	0
Tyler	1
Polk	2
Taylor	0
Fillmore	1
Pierce	1
Buchanan	1
Lincoln	5
Johnson	0
Grant	4
Hayes	2
Garfield	1
Arthur	2
Cleveland	4
B. Harrison	4
McKinley	1
T. Roosevelt	3
Taft	6

Table 1 *(Continued)*

President	*Number of Successful Appointments*
Wilson	3
Harding	4
Coolidge	1
Hoover	3
F. D. Roosevelt	9
Truman	4
Eisenhower	5
Kennedy	2
Johnson	2
	99

President appointed and who *actually served*, including those not ultimately confirmed by the Senate....

Judicial Experience and Its Absence

In view of the minimal, formal basic requirement, it is hardly astonishing that many a newly appointed United States jurist lacks practical judicial experience.[1] ... Among the ninety-six individual justices who had served on the Supreme Court between 1789 and the end of 1967, only twenty had had ten or more years of previous judicial experience on any lower level, federal or state, at the time of their appointment, and forty had no judicial experience whatsoever. Yet, as Table 2

Table 2
Prior Judicial Experience of U.S. Supreme Court Justices and Their Subsequent Service

		Number of Years of Prior Judicial Experience			*Years of Service on Supreme Court*
Justice	*Year Appointed*	*Federal*	*State*	*Total*	
Jay*	1789	0	2	2	6
J. Rutledge*	1789 and 1795*	0	6	6	½
Cushing	1789	0	29	29	21
Wilson	1789	0	0	0	9
Blair	1789	0	11	11	7
Iredell	1790	0	½	½	9
T. Johnson	1791	0	1½	1½	2
Paterson	1793	0	0	0	13
S. Chase	1796	0	8	8	15
Ellsworth*	1796	0	5	5	4
Washington	1798	0	0	0	31
Moore	1799	0	1	1	5
Marshall*	1801	0	0	0	34

* Indicates Chief Justice and date of his appointment and/or promotion.

Table 2 *(Continued)*

Justice	*Year Appointed*	*Number of Years of Prior Judicial Experience* Federal	State	Total	*Years of Service on Supreme Court*
W. Johnson	1804	0	6	6	30
Livingston	1806	0	0	0	17
Todd	1807	0	6	6	19
Story	1811	0	0	0	34
Duval	1811	0	6	6	24
Thompson	1823	0	16	16	20
Trimble	1826	9	2	11	2
McLean	1829	0	6	6	32
Baldwin	1830	0	0	0	14
Wayne	1835	0	5	5	32
Taney*	1836	0	0	0	28
Barbour	1836	6	2	8	5
Catron	1837	0	10	10	28
McKinley	1837	0	0	0	15
Daniel	1841	4	0	0	19
Nelson	1845	0	22	22	27
Woodbury	1845	0	6	6	6
Grier	1846	0	13	13	24
Curtis	1851	0	0	0	6
Campbell	1853	0	0	0	8
Clifford	1858	0	0	0	23
Swayne	1862	0	0	0	19
Miller	1862	0	0	0	28
Davis	1862	0	14	14	15
Field	1863	0	6	6	34½
S. P. Chase*	1864	0	0	0	9
Strong	1870	0	11	11	10
Bradley	1870	0	0	0	22
Hunt	1872	0	8	8	10
Waite*	1874	0	0	0	14
Harlan, Sr.	1877	0	1	1	34
Woods	1880	12	0	12	7
Matthews	1881	0	4	4	8
Gray	1881	0	18	18	21
Blatchford	1882	15	0	15	11
L. Q. C. Lamar	1888	0	0	0	5
Fuller*	1888	0	0	0	22
Brewer	1889	6	22	28	21
Brown	1890	16	0	16	16
Shiras	1892	0	0	0	11
H. E. Jackson	1893	7	0	7	2
White*	1894 and 1910*	0	1½	1½	27
Peckham	1895	0	9	9	14
McKenna	1898	5	0	5	27
Holmes	1902	0	20	20	30

* Indicates Chief Justice and date of his appointment and/or promotion.

Table 2 *(Continued)*

Justice	*Year Appointed*	*Number of Years of Prior Judicial Experience*			*Years of Service on Supreme Court*
		Federal	*State*	*Total*	
Day	1903	4	3	7	19
Moody	1906	0	0	0	4
Lurton	1909	16	10	26	5
Hughes*†	1910 and 1930*	0	0	0	17
Van Devanter	1910	7	1	8	27
J. R. Lamar	1910	0	2	2	6
Pitney	1912	0	11	11	10
McReynolds	1914	0	0	0	27
Brandeis	1916	0	0	0	23
Clarke	1916	4	0	4	6
Taft*	1921	8	5	13	9
Sutherland	1922	0	0	0	16
Butler	1922	0	0	0	17
Sanford	1923	14	0	14	7
Stone*†	1923 and 1941*	0	0	0	23
Roberts	1930	0	0	0	15
Cardozo	1932	0	18	18	6
Black	1937	0	1½	1½	
Reed	1937	0	0	0	19
Frankfurter	1939	0	0	0	23
Douglas	1939	0	0	0	
Murphy	1940	0	7	7	9
Byrnes	1941	0	0	0	1
R. H. Jackson	1941	0	0	0	13
W. Rutledge	1943	4	0	4	6
Burton	1945	0	0	0	13
Vinson*	1946	5	0	5	7
Clark	1949	0	0	0	18
Minton	1949	8	0	8	7
Warren*	1953	0	0	0	
Harlan	1955	1	0	1	
Brennan	1956	0	7	7	
Whittaker	1957	3	0	3	5
Stewart	1958	4	0	4	
White	1962	0	0	0	
Goldberg	1962	0	0	0	3
Fortas	1965	0	0	0	
Marshall	1967	3½	0	3½	

* Indicates Chief Justice and date of his appointment and/or promotion.
† Indicates no judicial experience when appointed as *Associate* Justice.

demonstrates the totally inexperienced group contains many of the greatest and most illustrious names in America's judicial history. Among them are six of the fourteen Chief Justices (eight if one does not "count" Hughes's and Stone's years as Associate Justices)—Marshall, Taney, S. P. Chase, Waite, Fuller, and Warren—and Associate Justices such as Story, Miller, Bradley, Brandeis, and Frankfurter, to name a few.

In a learned essay, calling for selection of Supreme Court justices "wholly on the basis of functional fitness," Mr. Justice Frankfurter argued keenly that no judicial experience nor political affiliation nor geographic considerations ought to play a significant role in the appointment of these highest jurists, whose job he viewed as necessarily requiring the qualities of *philosopher*—"but not too philosophical," commented his student Paul A. Freund—*historian, and prophet*.[2] Thus he asserted:

> One is entitled to say without qualification that the *correlation between prior judicial experience and fitness for the Supreme Court is zero*. The significance of the greatest among the Justices who had such experience, Holmes and Cardozo, derived not from that judicial experience but from the fact that they were Holmes and Cardozo. They were thinkers, and more particularly, legal philosophers.[3]

Attitudes Toward Experience

Yet the experience factor for Supreme Court justices, although more or less dormant during some Administrations, such as those of President Franklin D. Roosevelt, is sometimes revitalized by others, as it was by that of President Eisenhower. Roosevelt paid little, if any heed to it, whereas Eisenhower, after his initial appointment of Mr. Chief Justice Warren, insisted that his nominees have at least *some* judicial experience, no matter how slight. Of the nine men who sat on the Court as a result of President Roosevelt's appointments (or promotion to Chief Justice in the case of Stone), neither Mr. Chief Justice Stone nor Associate Justices Reed, Frankfurter, Douglas, Byrnes, and Jackson had any judicial experience whatsoever, while Mr. Justice Rutledge served on the Court of Appeals for the District of Columbia for four years, and Justice Black served one and a half years and Justice Murphy seven years on state tribunals. President Truman followed his predecessor's habit of ignoring judicial background: of his four appointees, Associate Justices Burton and Clark had none at all, Mr. Chief Justice Vinson had five years, and Associate Justice Minton had eight years of prior service on the lower federal bench. President Eisenhower's four appointees subsequent to that of the Chief Justice, Associate Justices Harlan, Brennan, Whittaker, and Stewart, all had seen some prior service although the total number of years for the four comprised but fifteen. Neither Associate Justices White and Goldberg, appointed by President Kennedy, nor Fortas appointed by President Lyndon B. Johnson, had any judicial experience.

Congress, too, is hardly of one mind on the matter of the necessity or even the desirability of judicial experience as a prerequisite for appointment to the highest court in the land. Bills are continually introduced that would require future nominees to the Supreme Court to have upwards of five years of experience on lower court benches. In the 89th Congress, for example, thirteen bills of this type were sponsored by members on both sides of the aisle in both houses of Congress. But all of these measures failed of enactment. Moreover, many legislators agree with what is clearly a majority of the closest observers of the Supreme Court as well as with the thesis of Mr. Justice Frankfurter just described, that judicial experience, because of the peculiar nature of that Court's work, is not essential. The Supreme Court is not a trial court in the sense of the federal district courts below, nor is it called upon to deal with a particular judicial constituency as are these courts of first instance and, to a considerably lesser extent, the federal courts of appeals that lie immediately above the district courts in the judicial heirarchy. Further, there is very little transition or connection between the experience in the lower and the highest federal constitutional court—the procedural and jurisdictional frameworks are quite different. The type of private litigation at common law, so prevalent below, is practically extinct at the bar of today's Supreme Court; the latter is almost exclusively occupied with questions of public law, led by cases at constitutional law or with constitutional overtones, review of administrative actions, and other related questions. Experience on the courts below may well be theoretically desirable—although there are some observers who would not even grant that much—but it should not become a *requirement* for qualification for the Supreme Court....

A Case Study

A brief survey of the judicial experience factor in connection with the members of the 1967–68 Supreme Court may aid in demonstrating that even if that specific qualification is largely, or even wholly, absent in many instances, experience in other relevant areas of public service is often abundantly present. Of the members of that 1967–68 Court, which began its term on October 2, 1967, only five had past judicial experience, and in all but one of these cases it was rather negligible.... Only Mr. Justice Brennan, a protégé of long-time New Jersey Chief Justice Arthur T. Vanderbilt, with a record of seven years on State of New Jersey benches, could lay claim to relatively extensive judicial background....

Yet *all* of the members of the 1967–68 Court had a record of considerable experience in public life, frequently of an administrative nature, in addition to or in place of whatever judicial experience they might have had. Thus, upon his designation as Chief Justice at the age of sixty-two by President Eisenhower in 1953, Earl Warren had practised law and then devoted thirty-four years of his full life to public office, eleven of these as Republican Governor of California—always with strong bipartisan support. Mr. Justice Hugo L. Black had practised law for seventeen years and had been a Democratic Senator from Alabama for ten when he was appointed to the Court. Mr. Justice William O. Douglas had practised law, taught it for almost a decade, and had been both a member and chairman of the U.S. Securities and Exchange Commission for three years when President Roosevelt appointed him in 1939 at a youthful forty-one (only four justices were appointed at a younger age). Before he entered the federal judicial service in 1954, Mr. Justice John Marshall Harlan . . . had practised private law and had served the State of New York in a host of capacities over a period of thirty years. Mr. Justice William J. Brennan, Jr., had practised law for fifteen years, was a decorated army officer during World War II, and had served the State of New Jersey when Governor Driscoll appointed him to the state bench in 1949. Mr. Justice Potter Stewart had practised law for more than a decade and had served on the City Council of Cincinnati for five years, when he first entered the federal judiciary in 1954. Byron R. White—that rare phenomenon of both Rhodes Scholar and professional athlete (known as "Whizzer White")—had practised law for fourteen years and was U.S. Deputy Attorney General when his wartime friend President Kennedy sent him to the highest bench in 1962 at the age of forty-five. Abe Fortas, sent to the Court as the first Johnson appointment, in 1965, to succeed Arthur J. Goldberg, brought with him years of experience in the Department of Interior and Agriculture and on the faculty of the Yale Law School, and had had an eighteen-year-long senior partnership in one of the foremost law firms of the nation, Arnold, Fortas, and Porter. And President Johnson's second appointment, Thurgood Marshall—the first Negro to reach the highest Court—had practised law for three decades, much of it constitutional law at the bar of the Court he was destined to join; had been a nationally known leader in the civil rights movement; had served on the Second Circuit Court of Appeals from 1962 to 1965; and was the U.S. Solicitor-General when the President thus honored him in 1967.

If—for the sake of argument—one were to grant the wisdom of judicial experience as a pertinent requirement for Supreme Court nominees, a background rich in nonjudicial experience, such as that just described, does not compensate in and of itself for the lack of actual experience on a lower bench. However it does indicate that the men ... who come to the Supreme Court of the United States ... have had lengthy *legal* experience. Moreover, *all* of the 96 individuals who have sat on the highest bench, except Mr. Justice George Shiras (1892–1903), had engaged in at least *some* public service at various levels of government, often elective, or had actively participated in political activity.... Table 3 indicates the occupations of the individuals (using the full figure 99 here) as of the time of their appointment to the Supreme Court.

* * *

Motivations Underlying Appointments

Regardless of learned commentaries and "inside information" revelations, it is obvious that the only person who knows with certainty why he appointed an individual to the Supreme

Table 3
Occupations* of Supreme Court Designees at Time of Appointment†

Federal Officeholder in Executive Branch	21
Judge of State Court	21
Judge of Inferior Federal Court	19
Private Practice of Law	17
U.S. Senator	8
U.S. Representative	4
State Governor	3
Professor of Law	3
Associate Justice of U.S. Supreme Court§	2
Justice of the Permanent Court of International Justice	1

* Many of the appointees had held a variety of federal or state offices, or even both, prior to their selection.

† In general, the appointments from state office are clustered at the beginning of the Court's existence, those from federal office are more recent.

§ Justices White and Stone, who were *promoted* to the Chief Justiceship in 1910 and 1930, respectively.

Court of the United States—and, for that matter, to the lower federal courts, although his involvement is likely to be far less direct there—is the President of the United States who signed the commission. All the student of constitutional law or the historian can do with honesty and conviction is to hazard a reasonable inference based upon the facts at his disposal....

... there is normally more than simply one motive behind any human decision. Idealism, altruism, and selfishness are all constituent aspects of the human personality, and a particular action may result from the interplay of a myriad of motivations arising from each or all of these factors. In other words, the reasons for the appointment to the Supreme Court by a particular Chief Executive of a particular individual are usually multiple rather than single, although one motive may, of course, be predominant. Generally speaking, five factors have been taken into account, singly or severally, by the thirty-five presidents when making selections for the ninety-nine vacancies that existed during the history of the Court down to the end of 1967. They are the same factors that may be expected to govern lower appointments as well, but they stand out more, and are more "interesting" when applied to the level of the highest bench, where appointments naturally come infrequently. Other factors exist, of course; no claim to exclusiveness is made at all, but the five that follow—not necessarily in order of importance—represent unquestionabily those of greatest moment: (1) objective merit; (2) political availability of the designee; (3) his ideological appropriateness; (4) personal factors; and (5) geographical, religious, and other sociopolitical considerations. Something should be said about each of these, and some examples given.

(1) OBJECTIVE MERIT. This factor simply poses the question of whether the candidate possesses the ability and the background essential to an understanding of the complicated questions that come before the Court.... To determine whether or not the individual under consideration does possess these qualifications, the President could look to the nominee's basic intellectual capacity, his reputation for legal scholarship, his competence in a particular area of law, his experience as a judge, lawyer, or public official, his reputation in and out of his vocational sphere, his temperament. Age may well also be relevant here. If the potential nominee is too young, he may be deemed to lack maturity of judgment and wisdom; if he is too old, he may retire or die before he has acquired the experience —one may call it the style—necessary to bring to the fore his full talent as a member of that tribunal. Judge Learned Hand, universally recognized as one of the jewels in America's judicial crown, was usually regarded as "too old" when he was deemed "politically available," which he was never deemed to be when there was no issue of age.

* * *

Probably the most illustrative example of the objective merit factor and its recognition by the bar, the public, and the political elements alike was that of Mr. Justice Cardozo, whose selection was all but forced upon President Hoover by the country, and who was confirmed unanimously by the Senate the instant the nomination reached the floor. This despite the fact—conceivably detrimental or even fatal in the case of other nominees, depending upon circumstances—that the nominee came from New York, already "represented" on the bench at that time by Mr. Chief Justice Hughes and Mr. Justice Stone, and that he was Jewish, a religion already "represented" by Mr. Justice Brandeis. Hoover raised these points during a command-visit by Republican Senator Borah of Idaho, chairman of the Committee on Foreign Relations, who had been very vocal in urging the Cardozo appointment—along with many others, including Mr. Justice Stone. (The latter, who was to play a major role in persuading the President to designate the man whom he had introduced to him initially, even offered to resign his own seat on the Court if that was what it would take to see his fellow New Yorker nominated.) Hoover handed Senator Borah a list, indicating the names of several prominent individuals he was considering for the vacancy on the Court left by Mr. Justice Holmes's resignation. The last name on the list was that of the Chief Judge of the New York State Court of Appeals, Benjamin N. Cardozo. "Your list is all right," commented Senator Borah, "but you handed it to me upside down!"[4] When the President then strongly urged that his visitor consider the geographical situation involved, and mentioned "possible religious and sectarian repercussions," Senator Borah told him in no uncertain terms that "Cardozo belonged as much to Idaho as to New York" and that geography should no more bar him than the presence of two Virginians on the high bench—John Blair and Bushrod Washington—should have prevented President John Adams from naming John Marshall Chief Justice.[5] Furthermore, Borah told Hoover, "... anyone who raises the question of race [*sic*] is unfit to advise you concerning so important a matter."[6] When the President bowed to what was all but unanimous professional as well as popular clamor for the Cardozo appointment, he became the recipient of much praise, typical of which was Senator Clarence Dill of Washington's remark that "... when President Hoover appointed Judge Cardozo ... he performed the finest act of his career as President."[7]

(2) AND (3) POLITICAL AVAILABILITY AND IDEOLOGICAL APPROPRIATENESS. These two criteria often go hand in hand. They include considerations such as whether the choice of an individual will render the President popular, or more popular, among certain groups in the body politic; whether the President is indebted to the potential nominee for political services rendered; whether the nominee has been a loyal member of the President's political party; whether, as was so true of President Kennedy's selection of White in 1962,[8] he favors the President's policies and programs—his *Weltanschauung*—regardless of his party membership; and whether he is acceptable, or at least not "personally obnoxious," to the kindred home state politicos, notably those in the Senate. It is a rather firmly adhered to unwritten law of the judicial nominating process at the level of the Supreme Court, that as a rule, the President will not normally select a man from the political opposition. To assuage charges of "packing the courts" ..., this rule is relaxed purposely now and then at the level of the federal district courts and even at that of the courts of appeals, but only within "political reason." Nevertheless, it has also happened twelve or thirteen times on the Supreme Court including two promotions to Chief Justice....

* * *

The emphasis placed above on the twelve or thirteen deviations from membership in the political party of the appointing President is not intended to convey the impression that there is a national trend in that direction. Far from it! There will presumably always be some crossing of party lines, particularly at the district court level, in order to maintain overall harmony, to placate the opposition, and to establish a measure of bipartisanship, but the practice may be safely predicted to remain exceptional. After all, as many a President has been told by his political advisers, Republican or Democratic as the case may be, ". . . why should we give these plums to the other guys? . . . surely there are just as many good and deserving lawyers on *our side of the fence.*" More often than not this is probably true, and no doubt political patronage will continue to govern as an appointment-maxim in the judicial process. Thus, Wilson appointed 73 Democrats and 1 Republican to the federal courts; Harding, Coolidge, and Hoover selected 198 Republicans and 20 Democrats; F. D. Roosevelt 194 Democrats and 13 Republicans; Truman 128 Democrats and 13 Republicans; Eisenhower 178 Republicans and 11 Democrats; Kennedy 105 Democrats, 10 Republicans, and 1 member of the New York State Liberal party; and by October 1967 President Johnson had sent 130 Democrats and 10 Republicans to the federal bench. It is simply axiomatic that judicial appointments will go predominantly to members of the party in power. However, when it comes to nominees to the Supreme Court, of the greatest importance to the designating President is what Theodore Roosevelt referred to as the nominee's "real politics"—of which more below.

(4) PERSONAL FACTORS. Although it is perhaps something of an oversimplification, the basic point here is the close personal regard the President may have for an individual—a factor that may well override all other considerations. Although this concept is understandably impossible to measure, there is no doubt that it has played, and will continue to play, a very real role in individual cases. . . . it figured prominently in President Taft's appointment of Mr. Justice Lurton and, somewhat less so, in those of Mr. Justice Burton by President Truman and Mr. Justice Brandeis by President Wilson. Some other obvious examples of the personal friendship factor's undoubted significance are the Truman nominations of Mr. Chief Justice Vinson and Associate Justices Clark and Minton—it was probably *the* crucial factor in the latter appointment, although Minton was, of course, a good Democrat and had seen eight years of service, however colorless, on the federal appellate bench—and the L. B. Johnson appointment of his long-time friend and adviser, Abe Fortas (who also conveniently happened to be Jewish), to the seat vacated by Mr. Justice Goldberg's transfer to the post of United States Ambassador to the United Nations.

(5) GEOGRAPHICAL, RELIGIOUS, AND OTHER SOCIO-POLITICAL CONSIDERATIONS. We have already observed in the case of several nominees that a President is less likely to look favorably upon a candidate who comes from an area in which reside one or more justices already on the Court. But, again, if he is determined to appoint a certain individual—for example, President Wilson's choice of Mr. Justice Brandeis—geography will not be permitted to stand in the way. And in the case of

Mr. Justice Cardozo, the country would not *permit* President Hoover to allow it to do so. It might well be argued that the consideration of geography is relevant merely to the political propriety of the appointment and, thus, should be relegated to the second and third categories discussed above. However, the notion that all sections of the country should be "represented" on the Court—to date the justices have come from thirty of the fifty states—has the advantage of being equitable as well as having a political appeal. . . . Furthermore, in the earlier days of the Republic when the justices used to ride circuit, it was obviously desirable to appoint for a given circuit a jurist who would be familiar with its area. The last appointees to the Supreme Court literally to ride circuit were Associate Justices John Catron, John McKinley, and Peter V. Daniel, who came to the Court in 1837, 1837, and 1841, respectively, all Van Buren appointees. Geographical considerations, in other words, must not be regarded as the equivalent of political considerations, and should hence be viewed as related to equitable factors generally.

The same considerations apply, both more and less, to the religious factor. It is at once closely related to the political factor and represents one of the equitable considerations that have entered the governmental sphere. It is undoubtedly here to stay, for better or for worse—and surely for worse in this instance. Hence there exists the notion of both a "Roman Catholic" seat and a "Jewish seat" on the Supreme Court. Not a healthy development, the religious-group representation concept has become one of *the* facts of American political life, and it was probably a foregone conclusion that it would one day reach the Court as well. Although less of a problem or consideration there than in the make-up of election slates where, in some instances, such as the City of New York, it has become a maxim of politics, religious affiliation is a definite factor regarding Supreme Court nominees. With the exception of the seven years between Mr. Justice Murphy's death in 1949 and Mr. Justice Brennan's nomination in 1956—when, perhaps oddly in view of the charges

Table 4
The 30 States from Which the 99 Supreme Court Appointments Were Made

New York	13	Illinois	3
Ohio	10	North Carolina	2
Massachusetts	8	Iowa	2
Tennessee	7	Michigan	2
Pennsylvania	6	New Hampshire	1
Kentucky	5	Maine	1
Maryland	5	Mississippi	1
New Jersey	4	Kansas	1
Virginia	3	Wyoming	1
South Carolina	3	Utah	1
Connecticut	3	Minnesota	1
Georgia	3	Texas	1
Alabama	3	Indiana	1
California	3	Missouri	1
Louisiana	3	Colorado	1

Table 5
Acknowledged Religion of the 96 Individual Justices of the Supreme Court (at time of appointment)

Unspecified Protestant	25
Episcopalian	24
Presbyterian	16
Unitarian	6
Roman Catholic	6
Baptist	5
Jewish	5
Congregationalist	3
Methodist	3
Disciples of Christ	2
Quaker	1

of "politics" so frequently voiced against him, President Truman evidently deliberately ignored the practice—members of *both* the Roman Catholic and the Jewish faith have been on the Court ever since Mr. Justice Brandeis's ascent in 1916. (Roman Catholic: Mr. Chief Justice Taney, Mr. Chief Justice White, Associate Justices McKenna, Butler, Murphy, and Brennan; Jewish: Associate Justices Brandeis, Cardozo, Frankfurter, Goldberg, and Fortas.) The first Roman Catholic to be appointed was Mr. Chief Justice Taney[9] in 1835, by President Andrew Jackson, and since Mr. Justice McKenna's appointment by President McKinley in 1898, a member of that faith has always been on the Court, save for the seven-year interval of the Truman Administration. Whatever the merit or demerit of the religious factor, it will very likely remain as one of the elements of the sociopolitical aspects of judicial appointments that the nominating authorities, rightly or wrongly, have decided to take into account. And a new factor, that of *race,* entered upon the scene when in June 1967, on the retirement of Mr. Justice Clark, President Johnson designated as his replacement the first Negro ever to be nominated to the Supreme Court—the then U.S. Solicitor-General, Thurgood Marshall. The President, leaving no doubt that the nominee's race was a major, if not *the* major, factor in his selection, told the country: "It is the right thing to do and it is the right time. He is the right man in the right place."

"Packing the Court" and the Nominees' "Real Politics"

Regardless of the significance and the role each or all of the five factors may play in the President's selection of justices of the Supreme Court and the lower courts, especially at the highest level, the most important consideration is the nominee's "real politics"—his future voting behavior on the bench. If an appointing President had the power of clairvoyance coupled with that of a check upon the judicial decision-making process, that consideration would present no problem; but in their absence it is entirely normal for him to endeavor to "pack" the bench to a greater or lesser extent.

The practice of "packing," or of filling vacancies with individuals presumably safely of the President's own views and persuasion, has been associated in the popular mind most prominently with President Franklin D. Roosevelt, who presided over the transition of the "Old" to the "New" Court from 1937 on. Deaths and resignations permitted him to fill nine vacancies—a total exceeded only by President Washington. Moreover, his attempt to have his way all at once by virtue of his "Court Packing Bill" of 1937—which was reported adversely by the Senate Judiciary Committee and was defeated on the floor by a vote of 70:20 to recommit to the Committee—designed to permit him to appoint an additional justice for each incumbent above seventy years of age up to a total Court membership of fifteen, has closely linked him with the packing concept. Yet it is an historical fact that Presidents Jefferson, Jackson, and Lincoln, facing similar problems of what they viewed as Court opposition, followed solutions that were basically analogous. And the first President, George Washington himself, who is somehow placed on a pedestal far removed from what the public usually views as "politics," insisted that his nominees to the Supreme Court—and he nominated ten, even eleven if John Rutledge is counted twice—meet the following five criteria: (1) advocacy of federalism; (2) a record of active support of the Revolution, preferably as a "fighting participant"; (3) "fitness"; (4) past judicial service; (5) proper geographical apportionment. Every President is necessarily guilty of some packing—it is merely a matter of degree. In short, similarities of view of nominator and nominee are understandably and customarily a controlling factor; membership in the same political party is one as well, and an important one, as are some of the other factors discussed earlier—but far less so than that of the nominee's "real politics." . . .

The Nominee's "Real Politics"

One of those who endeavored to probe hard for that crucial factor on sundry occasions was President Theodore Roosevelt—and not always successfully. In discussing a potential nominee with his good friend, Republican Senator Henry Cabot Lodge of Massachusetts, the "All-American Boy President" put the matter well:

> . . . the *nominal* politics of the man [Horace H. Lurton, a Democrat] has nothing to do with his actions on the bench. His *real* politics are all important. . . . He is right on the Negro question; he is right on the power of the federal government; he is right on the Insular business; he is right about corporations; and he is right about labor. On every question that would come before the bench, he has so far shown himself to be in much closer touch with the policies in which you and I believe.

Table 6
Avowed Political Affiliation of the 99 Appointed Supreme Court Justices (at time of selection)

Federalists	13
Whig	1
Democrats	48
Republicans	36
Independent	1

Although concurring in substance, Lodge replied, however, that he could not "see why Republicans cannot be found who hold those opinions as well as Democrats,"[10] and he strongly supported the candidacy of another possibility for the position, the Republican Attorney General, William H. Moody of Massachusetts, whom Roosevelt then nominated. (Lurton, as we have seen, was subsequently sent to the Court, anyway—as the first appointment of another Republican, President Taft.)

Nevertheless, in the words of that eminent student of the Supreme Court, Charles Warren:

> . . . nothing is more striking in the history of the Court than the manner in which the hopes of those was expected a judge to follow the political views of the President appointing him have been disappointed.[11]

Few felt the immediate truth of that statement more keenly than did Teddy Roosevelt with his nomination of the great Oliver Wendell Holmes, Jr., whose early "anti-Administration" opinions in anti-trust cases, notably in the *Northern Securities* case,[12] were entirely unexpected.[13] President Madison was similarly chagrined with his appointment of Mr. Justice Story in the face of Jefferson's warning that the nominee was a Tory, and as predicted by Madison's political mentor, Story not only became an immediate supporter of John Marshall, their political and judicial nemesis, but he even "out-Marshalled" the Chief Justice in his nationalism. . . .

Surely, there is a very considerable element of unpredictability in the judicial appointing process. To the oft-heard "Does a man become any different when he puts on a gown?",

Mr. Justice Frankfurter's pungent reply was always: "If he is any good, he does!" As for the Chief Executive, he is of necessity a politician and the leader of his party as well as the leader of the nation. To play the first two roles successfully, he must pay at least some attention to "politics"—real and nominal—in his choice of judges. But he will probably be a failure in the judge-naming role if he employs only that criterion in making his selections.

On the Role of the United States Senate

Enough has been said throughout these pages about the general role of the Senate in the judicial appointive process to obviate an extended discussion. But a few additional comments would seem to be called for, especially regarding lengthy delays in confirmation and rejection of presidential nominees to the highest bench.[14] There is no question, of course, that the Senate possesses a veto over a nomination to the Court—and to the lower federal courts. Certainly in theory, it may exercise this veto for whatever reason it chooses—and it has done so on occasion. "Senatorial courtesy" . . . looms large here, particularly at the level of the federal district courts, where the patronage factor is more overt and more prominent than higher up. Conversely, the Senate will almost inevitably treat as a *cas d'honneur* the presidential designation of one of their own members to the Supreme Court—witness the cases of the then Senators Byrnes of South Carolina and Burton of Ohio. Byrnes was confirmed unanimously without even being scrutinized by the Committee on the Judiciary, that stern and powerful stumbling block of quite a few nominations. And the Burton appointment was confirmed unanimously on the same day it reached the Senate. A notable exception to this unwritten rule was the controversial appointment of Mr. Justice Black by President Franklin D. Roosevelt, which was referred to the Judiciary Committee for full hearings. The initial reason for that unusual action was Senator Black's strong support of the President's Court Packing bill, which was anathema to a majority of the Senate. But the controversy over the nomination was compounded by the subsequent revelation during the committee's hearings that Black had once been a member of the Ku Klux Klan in Alabama. Nevertheless, the committee ultimately voted 13:4 in his favor, Black explained his then-defunct membership in a candid broadcast to the nation, and the Senate confirmed the appointment by a vote of 66:15.

Two aspects of the Senate's role will be considered here: *unusual delays* and *rejections* encountered by appointees to the Supreme Court. Fifteen nominations were characterized by what were clearly "unusual delays." Nineteen failed to win approval—*not* counting the ultimately confirmed though once rejected Justices Paterson, Taney, Matthews, and Butler—of whom nine were rejected outright by an adverse vote on the motion to confirm, whereas in the instances of ten others the Senate either refused to act or "postponed" action, thus resulting in rejection in all but name.

Unusual Delays in Confirmation

For our purposes an "unusual delay" is one which is markedly longer than that which normally took place during the period in which the appointment was made. . . . An examination of the fifteen nominations at issue indicates not only that the periods of delay have tended to lengthen, but more significantly, that there has been a definite pattern of causes for these unusual delays. . . .

First, *involvement with a political question or problem,* on which there is a strong feeling on the part of the public, some senators, or organized pressure groups. For example, . . . Mr. Justice Benjamin Curtis's confirmation was delayed for three months in 1851 by senators who believed that he opposed the abolitionist cause and supported the Fugitive Slave Law. It was poetic justice that Curtis turned out to be one of only two members of the Court to oppose the *Dred Scott* decision;[15] in fact he felt so strongly about it and the entire slavery controversy that he resigned from the bench in 1861.

[Among] others whose appointments were delayed because of the political factor were Justices Joseph P. Bradley, by "hard money" Easterners for what was—correctly—believed to be his "soft money" philosophy; . . . Joseph McKenna by anti-trust and anti-railroad interests (and some anti-Catholics) who feared his close friendship with railroad magnate Leland Stanford; . . . Louis D. Brandeis, by a host of elements in the legal and business community (and some anti-Semites) because of his long, outspoken activities as a champion of the social and economic underdog, for over four months in 1916—still the longest battle in the history of the Court; . . . and, in 1967, Thurgood Marshall, by implacable racists: he was the first Negro to be nominated—the great-grandson of a Congo slave.

Second, *opposition to the appointing President,* manifesting itself in opposition to the nominee. Probably the best cases in point here are the appointments of Mr. Chief Justice Roger B. Taney and Associate Justice Philip P. Barbour, whose confirmation in each instance was delayed for two and a half months in 1835. The opposition against the two men was not so much directed against them as nominees as it was against the nominator, President Andrew Jackson. However, the powerful anti-Jackson faction in the Senate—led by the three great names of the time, Clay, Webster, and Calhoun—failed to prevail against Jackson's strong leadership and drive, which was backed by his immense popularity with the electorate.

Third, *personal senatorial vendettas.* Thus, Mr. Justice Robert H. Jackson's confirmation was delayed over a month in 1941, chiefly because of the vehement opposition of Democratic Senator Millard Tydings of Maryland, who had a long-standing personal feud with the nominee, based on the latter's failure as Attorney General to prosecute two Washington columnists for what Tydings alleged was a libelous radio broadcast. Mr. Chief Justice Earl Warren was delayed for almost two months in 1954, chiefly because of a fight against his confirmation by Republican Senator William Langer of North Dakota, a senior member of the Senate's Judiciary Committee. Langer and some Southern Democrats went so far as to impugn the nominee's loyalty because of his alleged "left wing" or "liberal" views. It was then and is now widely assumed that the main motivation for the Langer attack was his long-standing wish to secure the appointment for someone, almost anyone, from North Dakota. . . .

Rejections

Including under this heading so-called postponements, which in fact were never acted upon and/or were withdrawn, an examination of the reasons for these direct or indirect Senate vetoes points to five major factors. Again, more than one factor was often present, but the five to be discussed comprise the principal ones for the rejection on record:

First, *opposition to the nominating President,* manifesting itself in opposition to his nominee. Five Chief Executives were affected in this way. President John Quincy Adams's nomination of John J. Crittenden in 1828 was "postponed" by the Senate by a strictly partisan vote of 17:23 two months after the nomination. The Democrats in the Senate thus foiled a last-minute Whig appointment by the outgoing President and preserved the vacancy so that it could be filled by the incoming President-elect, Democrat Andrew Jackson. . . .

Assuredly, in many of these cases, the opposition to the nominee also had other important political connotations in that major policy issues were involved, and these issues were naturally connected with the opposition to the President concerned. Hence it was not, of course, simply blind opposition to, or dislike of, the President which resulted in the rejections.

Second, *involvement with a political question or problem,* on which there is a strong feeling on the part of the public, some senators, or organized pressure groups. Thus, John Rutledge's nomination as Chief Justice in 1795 was rejected by a vote of 10:14. Already serving on a recess appointment, and having been *confirmed* six years earlier as Associate Justice—a position he resigned, however, without ever sitting—Rutledge was rejected primarily because of a speech he had made in opposition to the Jay Treaty. Despite the fact that both he and his nominator, President George Washington, were Federalists, the Federalist senators refused to confirm a man who had actively opposed the treaty which they supported so wholeheartedly. . . .

. . . The last nominee to be rejected, U.S. Circuit Court of Appeals Judge John J. Parker, designated by President Herbert Hoover in 1930, was the victim of the narrow adverse vote of 39:41. Parker—the 107th Supreme Court nominee as of then—was opposed by organized labor because, as a judge, he had handed down an opinion affirming the upholding of "yellow dog" contracts by a lower court;[16] by Negro groups because he had allegedly made anti-Negro remarks in his campaign for Governor of North Carolina ten years earlier; by Progressive Republicans who deemed his economic views too conservative. Ironically, it was to be Judge Parker who wrote some of the earliest "pro-Negro" opinions in the segregation-desegregation realm, including *Rice v. Elmore,*[17] which sustained United States District Court Judge J. Waties Waring's 1947 outlawing of South Carolina's primary machinations designed to bar Negroes from the polls.[18]

Third, *"senatorial courtesy."* This custom accounted for several rejections. It appears to have been the *sole* factor involved in the unsuccessful nominations of William B. Hornblower and Wheeler H. Peckham of New York by President Grover Cleveland in 1893–94, by adverse votes of 24:30 and 32:41, respectively. In both instances, the rejection was directly attributable to the outspoken opposition of Senator Hill of New York, who was instrumental initially in Hornblower's defeat on grounds of senatorial courtesy, and who successfully applied the same magic concept when Cleveland substituted another New Yorker, Peckham, four months later. The doctrine was also invoked, although on a secondary basis, in the already described cases of Walworth and Woodward.

Fourth, *the limited ability of the nominee,* considered entirely objectively, has played a definite part in some rejections. In the face of swelling protests by the legal profession and the public, President Grant withdrew his 1873 nomination of George H. Williams five weeks after he made it. Williams's talents as a lawyer were mediocre; he had lost several important cases; and the bar simply adjudged him unqualified for this high office. Woolcott's rejection was also due, in part, to the lack of support of his fellow Republicans, who considered him to be a man of limited ability.

Fifth, *political unreliability of the nominee.* The best illustration of this factor in rejections of nominees to the highest bench is another among the several unsuccessful Grant nominations that of Caleb Cushing. Nominated in 1874, after the furor of the Williams designation had subsided somewhat, Cushing's age—seventy-four at the time—was used against him repeatedly in the confirmation debate. But the outstanding reason for the opposition to him was his political instability. A veritable political chameleon, Cushing had been, in turn, a Whig, a Tyler Whig, a Democrat, a Johnson Constitutional Conservative, and a Republican. (Shades of the Vicar of Bray!) No one really knew what his political and ideological positions were, and, with opposition from almost all political factions mounting daily, Grant withdrew his name.

Some Concluding Thoughts

Only two individuals both nominated *and* confirmed as Justice of the Supreme Court of the United States have declined to accept that august office. William Smith in 1837 and Roscoe Conkling in 1882; both men wished to stay in the active political arena. To them, as well as to others who declined to serve during the first half-century of the Court's existence, e.g. John Rutledge (as Associate Justice), John Jay, Levi Lincoln, John Quincy Adams, offices such as Chief Justice of South Carolina (Rutledge), Governor of New York (Jay), or active political federal office (Adams), seemed infinitely more inviting and important than that of Supreme Court Justice. For the Court did not really come into its own until the long Chief Justiceship of John Marshall raised it to the level of power and esteem it enjoys today.

The appointment procedure was evidently more casual in the early days of the country, for today, if a nomination is made, the President knows that the man will accept if confirmed. This indicates that the office is held in higher esteem, as well as the fact that communications are vastly improved. Of course, we have no way of knowing how many men decline presidential offers of appointment to the Supreme Court or their reasons for doing so, but speculation would indicate that there are not many who would turn down the post if offered to them.

* * *

In general, opposition to the confirmation of a Supreme Court Justice seems to reflect the existence of deep-seated concern in the nation. In the early years of the Court's history, relatively little concern was shown about the potentially "unfortunate effects" of justices of uncertain, or certain, convictions. It became more frequent and noticeable as the influence of the Court became more apparent. At the present time, when there are so many issues in which large numbers of people are deeply concerned, almost every appointee is made to run the gauntlet; he may even feel slighted if his appointment is unopposed, since this could be interpreted as a sign that he is not regarded as a man who carries very much weight. The nomination and confirmation procedure has become one more battleground on which large issues are fought out before the public eye.

NOTES

1. By way of contrast, in addition to other requirements, nominees to the intermediate appellate judiciary in Pakistan, for example, must have a minimum of ten years of judicial experience; and they need fifteen years for appointment to the Pakistan Supreme Court (including five years at the intermediate appellate level).
2. To which, in a conversation with the author in May 1954, Mr. Justice Brennan added "inordinate patience."
3. Felix Frankfurter, "The Supreme Court in the Mirror of Justices," 105 *University of Pennsylvania Law Review* 781 (1957). (Italics supplied.)
4. Claudius O. Johnson, *Borah of Idaho* (New York: Longman's, Green and Co., 1936), p. 452.
5. *The New York Times*, January 30, 1932.
6. Johnson, loc. cit. p. 453.
7. *The New York Times*, March 2, 1932.
8. As *Washington Star* reporter James E. Clayton reported the decision: "Thinking back on the process months later, the Attorney General [Robert F. Kennedy] tilted back in his chair and said: 'You wanted someone who generally agreed with you on what role government should play in American life, what role the individual in society should have. You didn't think about how he would vote in a reapportionment case or a criminal case. You wanted someone who, in the long run, you could believe would be doing what you thought was best. You wanted someone who agreed generally with your views of the country.' Both he and the President believed that White and Arthur J. Goldberg met that test. They could not be as sure of the others on the list [Paul A. Freund of Harvard University and Judge William H. Hastie of the U.S. Court of Appeals for the Third Circuit]." Quoted in Clayton's *The Making of Justice: The Supreme Court in Action* (New York: E. P. Dutton & Co., 1964), p. 52.
9. Taney married a Protestant, Anne Key of Frederick, Maryland. They had seven children, all of whom eventually joined Protestant churches.
10. Henry Cabot Lodge, *Selections from the Correspondence of Theodore Roosevelt and Henry Cabot Lodge, 1884–1918* (New York: Charles Scribner's Sons, 1925), Vol II, p. 228, and pp. 230–31.
11. *The Supreme Court of the United States,* rev. ed. (Boston: Little, Brown and Co., 1926), Vol. II, p. 22.
12. *Northern Securities v. United States,* 193 U. S. 197 (1904).
13. "T. R." was furious about Holmes's "anti-anti-trust" vote in that case and reportedly stormed: "I could carve out of a banana a Judge with more backbone than that!"—hardly a very appropriate remark in the light of Mr. Justice Holmes's lifelong reputation. (As quoted by Clayton, op. cit. p. 47.)
14. These points are discussed in considerable detail in Henry J. Abraham and Edward M. Goldberg, "A Note on the Appointment of Justices of the Supreme Court of the United States," 46 *American Bar Association Journal* 147 (February 1960) and, more generally, in Robert B. McKay, "Selection of United States Supreme Court Justices," 9 *Kansas Law Review* 109 (No. 2, 1960).

15. *Dred Scott v. Sandford,* 19 Howard 393 (1857).
16. *United Mine Workers v. Red Jacket Consolidated Coal and Coke Co.,* 18F.839 (1927), based on a U.S. Supreme Court precedent of 1917 (*Hitchman Coal and Coke Co. v. Mitchell,* 245 U.S. 229).
17. 165 F.2d 387 (1947).
18. *Rice v. Elmore,* 72 F. Supp. 516 (1947).

47

Excerpts from Account of Nixon's Comments in Informal Meeting with Reporters

THE NEW YORK TIMES

The following report on President Richard Nixon's discussion with the press on the appointment of Chief Justice Warren E. Burger illustrates many of the points made by Henry Abraham in the preceding selection. Nixon speaks directly about his desire to name a "strict constructionist" who agrees with the President on important constitutional and legal issues.

Nixon also discusses the practice of maintaining ethnic group and religious representation on the Court. At the time he appointed Mr. Burger to replace Chief Justice Earl Warren, Justice Abraham Fortas, a Jew, had also left the Court. With the appointment of Chief Justice Burger and, subsequently, of Justice Harry A. Blackmun, Nixon broke the tradition of having a Jewish member of the Court; a tradition that had been uninterrupted since the appointment of Justice Louis Brandeis in 1916.

The President explains his intention to name men with prior judicial experience to the Supreme Court. This qualification is at odds with the view (recounted in Abraham's discussion) of the late Felix Frankfurter and other students of the judiciary that prior judicial experience is not particularly relevant to the Court's primary role as a constitutional policy maker. Nonetheless, President Nixon has been firm on this point: all four of his Supreme Court nominees—Warren E. Burger, Clement Haynsworth, Harrold Carswell, and Harry A. Blackmun—have been judges of the United States Court of Appeals. However, in asserting that the nomination of Warren Burger was "one of the first times" that a judge of the Court of Appeals has been named Chief Justice, the President overlooked that among the fourteen previous chief justices, Chief Justice William Howard Taft and Chief Justice Fred M. Vinson had served as circuit court judges.

The President's description of the nomination procedure provides insight into the selection of judges. The distinction made by Nixon between senatorial clearance of Supreme Court justices and of lower court judges reflects the President's wide discretion in filling vacancies on the high court. Although Nixon did not mention it, clearance through the American Bar Association is standard practice for federal judges; however, this may come after the announcement of the nomination rather than before.

The President began by saying he would try to spell out the processes that he went through in making the decision [on the Chief Justice]. He said that at the time of the exchange of letters with the Chief Justice, before the inauguration, he knew that he would have this decision to make.

He also knew at that time that he did not have to make it in a hurry. In fact, he thought it was very wise not to make it too soon, because he thought that it would not be a proper mark of respect for the Court and for the Chief Justice to have a nomination go down, say, in February or March, and then have the possibility of Senate hearings and the like at a time that the Court was sitting.

So, from the beginning, while he did not pick any certain deadline date, he felt that the decision should be made before the term of Court ended so that the new Chief Justice could be indoctrinated, in effect, about the rules of the Court and so forth, by the outgoing Chief Justice.

Choice of Chief Justice

But this turned out to be the right time, he said, and that is why it came in the middle of May, although it could have come May 1. He said that he always thought between May 1 and June 1, but that is how this came about.

The President said that he had spelled out in the campaign his thinking with regard to the kind of man that should be Chief Justice. He wanted to differentiate two things here: There is a different standard for a Chief Justice than there is for a Justice, not in terms of intellectual qualifications, not in terms of knowledge of law, not in terms of the character, and that sort of thing, but in terms of what he described as a leadership quality. The Chief Justice is the leader of the Court, the chief administrative officer of the Court, he said.

In talking to Chief Justice Warren, for example, he found that there is an enormous amount of administrative responsibility which rests with the Chief Justice. So the Chief Justice must be a man who can be an equal to all the other justices in terms of education, and above all else, however, have that special quality, in addition, of commanding the respect and being able to lead the Court, he said.

The Chief Justice cannot, as is known, always get unanimity, he said. He added he wished to get one thing very clear, the Warren Court is not the first one that had five-to-four decisions. When the President was studying law in 1930, there were five-to-four decisions, when four dissented and five voted the other way, he said.

Leadership Quality

But this leadership quality is what he was looking for, beyond the bare essentials, which he or anybody would look for in appointing a Justice to the Supreme Court, he continued.

There are several things that he thought should be clarified at the beginning. There were no political clearances in this case, and there will be none for any Justices of the Supreme Court that he appoints, he said.

By a political clearance, he said, he meant that neither Minnesota nor Virginia Senators were informed, noting that Judge Burger comes from Minnesota and now lives in Virginia. They knew nothing about it and no further appointments will be cleared.

With regard to Circuit Court and District Court Judges, he said the custom was to clear appointments. The custom has varied with the Supreme Court but he felt very strongly that Supreme Court Justices should be appointed by the President without going through the political processes.

Above Politics

The Supreme Court must be above politics he said. This does not mean that the Supreme Court Justices are not Republicans, as was Mr. Burger when he was named, or Democrats, as was Justice Black when he was appointed, he said. But he thought it is very important that once they are appointed, and once they sit on the Court, that they sit there without owing that appointment to any political clearance process.

So there was no clearance with any Senators, no clearance with the national committee, and there will be none as far as any other Justices he names, he said.

He said that another factor that should be discussed is this: He noticed Arthur Goldberg's statement with regard to whether or not there was to be—as some members described it—a Jewish seat on the Court. He subscribes to Arthur Goldberg's conclusion. There is [not] a Jewish seat or a Catholic seat or a Negro seat on the Court, he said. He said he made this appointment and will make other ones based on the consideration of their competence.

He will see to it, of course, that he considers judges or people who might be qualified, representing all segments of the country, but in the final analysis the Court will not be used for the purpose of racial, religious or geographical balance, at least not while he is President, he said.

The Fortas Matter

He said that because of the Fortas matter, he determined that the appointee should not be a personal friend. He said he also determined that, if possible, he should avoid appointing somebody who would be a political friend or, using the Washington vernacular, "crony."

He said that he felt it was vitally important that it be a man who, if possible, could be approved by the Senate without violent controversy, and if possible, with a strong—well, not unanimous—but a strong vote of approval.

Mr. Nixon said it seemed to him that the Court, at this time, needs to have, particularly at the Chief Justice level, a man who has wide support in the nation and wide support in the Senate.

This does not mean that you could find any man who would satisfy this great spectrum of views in the Senate on economic and social philosophy or even legal philosophy, he said, adding he felt that in the appointment of Judge Burger he had been able to find a man who will command respect in these areas that he believed are so important.

Philosophy on Judges

During the campaign he set forth, as some may remember, he said, his own philosophy with regard to what he thought the role of a judge should be, a judge particularly of the Supreme Court, and for that matter, of other courts where they interpret constitutional matters, where they rule on constitutional cases, as distinguished from civil cases involving parties that don't have constitutional issue. He said he thought he used the term that he was a strict constructionist.

He said that he believed that the Constitution should be strictly interpreted as did Mr. Justice [Felix] Frankfurter. [Mr. Nixon said he used Mr. Frankfurter only as an example, because most of the judges in our courts over the years have held this philosophy.] Mr. Justice Frankfurter felt it was his responsibility to interpret the Constitution, he said, and it was the right of the Congress to write the laws and have great leeway to write those laws, and he should be very conservative in overthrowing a law passed by the elected representatives at the state or Federal level.

Appointments Discussed

He said he wanted to give a blow-by-blow as to when the Burger appointment was decided.

First, the only man that he discussed the appointments to the Supreme Court with in any detail was the Attorney General, he said, and this was quite deliberate.

He told all the members of the Senate and the House, Democrat and Republican, and many personal friends who were lawyers around the country, and non-lawyers who wrote him, that he wanted them to submit their recommendations and their arguments to the Attorney General for his evaluation, he said.

The Attorney General, however, had the responsibility not to recommend a man but to submit the case for each man to the President, and then he made the decision. He did this, he said, because he did not want to become personally involved in the contest, the very lively contest among several very well-qualified people for this position.

Every President works differently, he said, but he likes to be detached and stand back from it and decided as coolly and objectively as possible.

He then discussed what happened with regard to several of those that you [newsmen] speculated about very properly.

For example, Mr. Rhyne, he noted. A man who was perhaps his closest friend among all of those who were considered was Charles S. Rhyne, he said. Mr. Rhyne, he noted, went to law school with Mr. Nixon and was head of Citizens for Nixon in '60 and '68 and has argued cases before the Supreme Court; a very distinguished lawyer.

But Mr. Rhyne was a personal friend, and the President said that he felt that the appointment of a personal friend to the Supreme Court, particularly at this time in our history, would not be in the best interests of the Court.

Then, he continued, something should be reported with regard to four other men who were under consideration and what they did and how, on their own initiative, they affected Mr. Nixon's decision.

Incidentally, he added. In these times it is quite a tribute to each of these men in its own way. He characterized the four as four men who, at this time in their lives, each one of them would probably rather be Chief Justice than President of the United States. So that shows you how much they would have wanted to be Chief Justice, he said, and yet each one of them asked him not to consider them, either directly or indirectly."

Some Declined

He said that he did not talk personally to some of them and would not indicate which, except for one that he did talk to personally. Each one of them let him know they did not feel they should be considered because they felt it would not be best for the Court for any one of them to be on the Supreme Court.

He mentioned the high regard he had for Herbert Brownell. He was the man, next to Attorney General Mitchell, who was his closest adviser in selecting the Cabinet. And who would have made a superb Chief Justice, he said.

But, Mr. Nixon said, former Attorney General Brownell said, quite directly in that candid way of his, that he thought if he were nominated that there would be a controversy in the Senate—not because of any personal criticism of him, but because of the roles he played while Attorney General.

The President said he told Mr. Brownell on that scope that he was sure that the Senate would approve the nomination, but he felt it would not be in the interest of the Court to have a sharp partisan or personal controversy and, therefore, asked not to be considered.

Dewey Cited Age

Tom [Thomas E.] Dewey wrote himself out because of age, Mr. Nixon said. Mr. Dewey said that he felt the man who should be Chief Justice should be able to serve at least 10 years in that position, Mr. Nixon said, and there may have been other considerations. Mr. Nixon said he did not discuss this with him directly.

Of Mr. Justice Potter Stewart, Mr. Nixon said he asked to come to see the President two or three weeks ago. It was really quite a moving experience to see this young man [he is 45] who knew that he had tremendous support for this position, Mr. Nixon said, to come in and he said that he felt it would be in the best interest of the Court not to appoint a sitting judge on the Court to Chief Justice.

Justice Stewart, Mr. Nixon said, went over the history of the Court and said on only two occasions has it happened. But he said that, generally speaking, because of the special role that the Chief Justice has to play as the leader of the Court, it would be very difficult to take a man from the Court and put him above the others, the President said.

Justice Stewart said it would be better to bring a man from the outside rather than one from the Court and with that he took himself out and asked the President not to consider him, Mr. Nixon said.

Mitchell Had Support

Attorney General John N. Mitchell had very great support from the beginning. When they first discussed it, Mr. Mitchell said he did not want himself considered, Mr. Nixon added.

Incidentally, Mr. Mitchell is superbly qualified and is Mr. Nixon's closest adviser, as you know, on all legal matters and on many other matters as well, the President said. He said he does not know of any man in the Administration whose views on the law are closer to Mr. Nixon's than Attorney General Mitchell's.

But Mr. Mitchell said quite bluntly that it would not be good for the Court to have a political friend, as distinguished from a personal friend in the case of Charley Rhyne, appointed as Chief Justice at this time, the President said.

With regard to Mr. Justice Burger, Mr. Nixon said he felt for a long time that Circuit or District Court judges who have proved themselves on the line of battle, on the firing line, to be capable, able judges who have a track record, should be elevated.

It has been done in some cases, but more often than not Circuit Court judges do not go to the Supreme Court, and very, very seldom does a judge of the Circuit Court go to the Chief Justice, Mr. Nixon said, adding this is one of the first times.

Moved Toward Burger

Mr. Nixon said that in looking over all the Circuit Court Judges [not] in terms of age, 61 or 62, but in terms of his legal qualifications, in [terms] of his background, integrity, he determined over the weekend at Camp David [he said gave a lot of thought to it] that he should move toward Mr. Chief Justice—well, who will be Mr. Chief Justice—toward Judge Burger.

This will be hard to believe, Mr. Nixon [said], but at no time over these past few months up until three minutes before they went down to meet the press did he talk to Judge Burger, who did not know that he was being considered.

The first conversation that the President had with him was when he came upstairs at the White House last night.

As far as the decision made, the President said that on Monday morning [May 19] he called the Attorney General. He also called him from Camp David to discuss it, and said that quietly he wanted the Attorney General to begin the investigation processes that were necessary—referring to the F.B.I. investigation that was up in a Senate hearing.

Investigation Made

The Attorney General made that investigation, Mr. Nixon related, and then on Wednesday at approximately 12:30 the Attorney General had then met, was meeting at that time at the President's request with Judge Burger, and he called here and said that Judge Burger would be prepared to accept the appointment.

It was then that the President said he made the decision that the appointment would be announced at the press conference that evening. Mr. Nixon said he did not discuss this appointment with any members of the White House staff and with no Cabinet officers except with the Attorney General.

The final point, the President said he wished was with regard to the relationship he now has with Judge Burger. Mr. Nixon said it will show why he did not want to see him beforehand. While, the President said, his study of his opinions and knowledge of his views would indicate that they shared many views, he thought it is vitally important that the Chief Justice and all judges of the Supreme Court know that they are absolutely independent of the executive and legislative.

48

Litigation as a Form of Pressure Group Activity

CLEMENT E. VOSE

The following article by Clement E. Vose describes the activities of three interest groups—the American Liberty League, the National Consumers' League, and the National Association for the Advancement of Colored People—in seeking their policy objectives in the courts. By sponsoring test cases, supporting individual litigation, filing amicus curiae briefs, and engaging in other tactics to gain a favorable judicial decision, political interest groups strive in the courts to sustain gains made in other forums or to reverse defeats previously suffered. Just as judicial appointments are essentially political, so, frequently, are the sponsorship and conduct of litigation. Because lawsuits require special skills and substantial funds, not all interest groups or individuals have equal access to the judicial process, which again reflects the scope and bias of the pressure system (discussed in Part II).

Vose is John E. Andrus Professor of Government at Wesleyan University. Caucasians Only: The Supreme Court, the NAACP, and the Restrictive Covenant Cases, *his pioneering work on the role of interest groups in the judicial process, was published in 1959. He has written many articles on the judicial process and is currently the director of a Twentieth Century Fund project on constitutional change in the United States.*

The conventional judicial process is distinguished from legislative and administrative processes by features

Reprinted from *The Annals* of the American Academy of Political and Social Science, 319 (September 1958), 20–31, by permission of the author and the publisher.

which forbid, conceal, or control the participation of organized pressure groups. Justice Robert H. Jackson warned that "perhaps the most significant and least comprehended limitation upon the judicial power is that this power extends only to cases and controversies."[1] This limitation has meant that the Supreme Court of the United States refuses to provide advisory opinions and avoids what judges are fond of calling "political questions." It cannot be overstressed that the Supreme Court's only power is to decide lawsuits between adversaries with real interests at stake. Under the case system that marks American jurisprudence, a court is a "substantially passive instrument, to be moved only by the initiative of litigants."[2] This contrasts with the power of the President and the Congress to deal with any subject as desired.

Despite this limiting prerequisite, the Supreme Court does possess considerable control over the particular cases to be decided. The Judiciary Act of 1925 gave the Court almost complete discretionary control of its appellate business through grant or denial of the writ of certiorari. This statute settled the modern principle that the Supreme Court's function was

> not to see justice done in every case, but to decide the more important policy issues presented within the frame of a "case" or "controversy," concerning the federal balance, the relations of the branches of the federal government, or the fundamental rights of the individual in relation to government.[3]

Elaborating upon the function of deciding important policy issues, Chief Justice Fred M. Vinson, in 1949, told the bar that the Supreme Court is interested only in "those cases which present questions whose resolution will have immediate importance beyond the particular facts and parties involved."[4] Vinson added that "what the Court is interested in is the actual practical effect of the disputed decision—its consequences for other litigants and in other situations." This meant that lawyers whose petitions for certiorari were granted by the Supreme Court were representing not only their clients, "but tremendously important principles, upon which are based the plans, hopes and aspirations of a great many people throughout the country."

It is the thesis of this article that organizations—identifiable by letterhead—often link broad interests in society to individual parties of interest in Supreme Court cases. Since the American judicial system is built upon specific cases with specific facts, it is assumed that study of the role of specific organizations is relevant to understanding.[5]

Reasons Organizations Go to Court

Organizations support legal action because individuals lack the necessary time, money, and skill. With no delays a case takes an average of four years to pass through two lower courts to the Supreme Court of the United States. A series of cases on related questions affecting the permanent interest of a group may extend over two decades or more. The constant attention that litigation demands, especially when new arguments are being advanced, makes the employment of regular counsel economical. This may be supplemented by a legal staff of some size and by volunteer lawyers of distinction. Parties also pay court costs and meet the expense of printing the record and briefs. Organizations are better able to provide the continuity demanded in litigation than individuals. Some individuals do maintain responsibility for their own cases even at the Supreme Court level, but this is difficult under modern conditions.

The form of group participation in court cases is set by such factors as the type of proceeding, standing of the parties, legal or constitutional issues in dispute, the characteristics of the organization, and its interest in the outcome. Perhaps the most direct and open participation has been by organizations which have been obliged to protect their own rights and privileges. Robert A. Horn has shown that a modern constitutional law of association has developed out of Supreme Court cases concerning churches, trade unions, political parties, and other organizations.[6] The cases have sometimes placed organizations as parties, but more often the organization supports a member or an officer in litigation. One example must suffice.

The constitutional concept of religious freedom has been broadened in recent years by the Supreme Court decisions in cases involving members of the sect known as Jehovah's Witnesses. Most of the cases began when a Jehovah's Witness violated a local ordinance or state statute. Since 1938, the Witnesses, incorporated as the Watch Tower Bible and Tract Society and represented by its counsel, Hayden Cooper Covington, have won forty-four of fifty-five cases in the United States Supreme Court. As a result Jehovah's Witnesses now enjoy

the rights to solicit from house to house, to preach in the streets without a license, to canvass apartment buildings regardless of the tenants' or owners' wishes, to be recognized as ministers of an accredited religion and thus be exempt from the draft, to decline to serve on juries, and to refuse to salute or pledge allegiance to the flag.[7]

The NAACP

Since 1909 the National Association for the Advancement of Colored People has improved the legal status of Negroes immeasurably by the victories it has won in more than fifty Supreme Court cases.[8] During its early years, the NAACP relied upon prominent volunteer lawyers like Moorfield Storey, Louis Marshall, and Clarence Darrow to represent Negroes in the courts. Limited success coupled with its failure to win gains from Congress led the NAACP in the 1930's to make court litigation fundamental to its program. A separate organization, the NAACP Legal Defense and Educational Fund, was incorporated for this purpose. The goal of the NAACP was to make Negroes "an integral part of the nation, with the same rights and guarantees that are accorded to other citizens, and on the same terms."[9] This ambition meant that beginning in 1938 Thurgood Marshall as special counsel for the NAACP Legal Defense and Educational Fund held what was "probably the most demanding legal post in the country."[10]

In aiming to establish racial equality before the law on a broad basis, the Legal Defense Fund has not functioned as a legal aid society. Limited resources have prevented the Fund from participating in all cases involving the rights of Negroes. As early as 1935 Charles Houston, an imaginative Negro lawyer who preceded Marshall as special counsel, set the tone of NAACP efforts when he declared that the legal campaign against inequality should be carefully planned "to secure decisions, rulings and public opinion on the broad principle instead of being devoted to merely miscellaneous cases."[11]

By presenting test cases to the Supreme Court, the NAACP has won successive gains protecting the right of Negroes in voting, housing, transportation, education, and service on juries.[12] Each effort has followed the development of new theories of legal interpretation and required the preparation of specific actions in the courts to challenge existing precedent. The NAACP Legal Defense Fund has accomplished these two tasks through the co-operation of associated and allied groups. First, as many as fifty Negro lawyers practicing in all parts of the country have been counsel in significant civil rights cases in the lower courts. Many of these men received their legal education at the Howard University Law School in Washington, D.C., and have shared membership in the National Bar Association since its founding in 1925. These common associations have contributed to the consensus among Negro lawyers on timing their quest for equality through litigation. Second, the NAACP has long benefited from its official advisory group, the National Legal Committee composed of leading Negro and white lawyers. Today Lloyd Garrison is Chairman of the National Legal Committee of forty-five attorneys located in twenty-three cities. This is the nucleus of the many volunteers in many fields who have contributed ideas, often at national conferences, to the planning of litigation. Third, other organizations with no direct connection with the Legal Defense Fund have sponsored a few cases. State and local chapters of the NAACP have often aided Negroes who were parties in cases, especially in the lower courts. The St. Louis Association of Real Estate Brokers was the chief sponsor of the important restrictive covenant case of *Shelley* v. *Kraemer*.[13] A Negro national college fraternity, Alpha Phi Alpha, sponsored quite completely the successful attack on discrimination in interstate railway dining cars.[14]

Individual Test Cases

Winning new constitutional protections for Negroes has depended on the development of individual test cases with a Negro as party in each. There is no chronicle of the human interest stories contained in the roles of Negroes in historic Supreme Court cases. But what is known reveals many difficulties to be inherent in improving the legal status of a group of fifteen million persons through individual court cases. In a suit by a single plaintiff, the case may become moot as the passage of time makes the remedy sought inapplicable. This danger, though avoided by the co-operation of state officials, was created in the Missouri Law School case of 1938 when the plaintiff, Lloyd Gaines, disappeared just as the case was completed.[15] Also the concerted efforts of authorities to deny Negroes participation in the Texas white Democratic primary kept Dr. L. A. Nixon from voting even though he was the plaintiff in two Supreme Court victories.[16] Furthermore there is always the temptation for compromise by the original plaintiff which would accomplish his narrow purpose but stop the litigation before the broad constitutional issue was before the appellate court.

These dangers were largely overcome in the School Segregation Cases[17] when federal court actions were instituted by individual plaintiffs both on their own behalf and on behalf of persons similarly situated.

Since 1955, in the expanding litigation over race relations, the class action has become a procedural device of growing importance. Rule 23 (a) of the Federal Rules of Civil Procedure provides under certain circumstances that

> if persons constituting a class are so numerous as to make it impracticable to bring them all before the court, such of them, one or more, as will fairly insure the adequate representation of all may, on behalf of all, sue or be sued.[18]

One authority has said that "school segregation is a group phenomenon which is peculiarly suited to resolution in a class action."[19] As Negroes enter a new generation of litigation, their cases are apt increasingly to take the form of the class action.

The American Liberty League

The experience of the American Liberty League, organized in 1934 by conservative businessmen to oppose the New Deal, provides another variation on the theme of organizations in litigation.[20] When the League proved unable to prevent enactment of economic regulation by Congress, a National Lawyers' Committee was formed to question the constitutionality of the legislation. In August 1935, the National Lawyers' Committee of fifty-eight members announced plans to prepare a series of reports to the public on whether particular federal laws were "consonant with the American constitutional system and American traditions."[21] These reports "would be of a strictly professional nature and would in no case go into the question of social and economic advisability or the need for constitutional change to meet new conditions." This intention led the Committee during the next two years to conclude that a dozen New Deal statutes were unconstitutional.

The most celebrated Liberty League "brief" prepared by the National Lawyers' Committee questioned the constitutionality of the National Labor Relations Act. That analysis was prepared by a subcommittee of eight attorneys under the chairmanship of Earl F. Reed. It was then submitted to the other members and made public by Raoul E. Desverine, Chairman of the entire group, on Constitution Day, 1935.[22] The reports of the Committee were given wide publicity through press releases, the distribution of pamphlets, and radio talks by leading conservative lawyers like James M. Beck. Critics of these reports feared that they had two purposes: "to influence the federal courts when such legislation shall be presented for consideration" and "to arouse public sentiment so that confidence in the courts will be impaired should the legislation be held constitutional."[23]

Members of the National Lawyers' Committee of the American Liberty League, but not the organization itself, participated in litigation. The Committee's first public announcement had stated that "it will also contribute its services in test cases involving fundamental constitutional questions." Although the intention was to offer free legal services to citizens without funds to defend their constitutional rights, members of the National Lawyers' Committee actually represented major corporations which challenged the constitutionality of New Deal legislation in the Supreme Court. Earl F. Reed simply adapted the Liberty League report to apply to the specific facts of the case when he represented the Jones and Laughlin Steel Corporation against the National Labor Relations Board.[24] Another member of the National Lawyer's Committee, John W. Davis, represented the Associated Press in a companion case.[25]

Aiding the Government Defense

Judicial review in the United States constitutes an invitation for groups whose lobbying fails to defeat legislation to continue opposition by litigation. The NAACP has taken advantage of this in questioning state segregation laws, and, especially before 1937, business groups of various sizes—the American Liberty League, trade associations, and corporations—contested the constitutionality of state and federal regulatory legislation. This exploitation of judicial review has been balanced by the practice of victorious groups in legislation continuing to support administrative agencies in charge of enforcement. When statutes are challenged, organizations often support the Justice Department in Washington or a state Attorney General in defending them. This is to say that when losers in legislation have brought test cases in the courts, the legislative winners have aided the official legal defense.

The National Consumers' League

The efforts of the National Consumers' League to defend the validity of protective labor legislation affords an example of this private organizational aid to the public defense of legislation.[26] Organized by society women in 1899 to improve the lot of women and children in industry, the National Consumers' League sought first to boycott goods produced under substandard conditions and then to persuade state legislatures to control factory practices through legislation. When employers in the hotel and laundry business organized to defeat legislation in the courts, the National Consumers' League, in 1908, organized a Committee on Legislation and Legal Defense of Labor Laws to "assist in the defense of the laws by supplying additional legal counsel and other assistance."[27]

The leaders of the National Consumers' League, especially Mrs. Florence Kelley and Miss Josephine Goldmark, learned to prod state Attorneys General in order to gain adequate defense for statutes under fire in the courts. They also made two positive contributions. First, arrangements were made to provide distinguished outside counsel—most importantly, Louis D. Brandeis; but also Felix Frankfurter, Newton D. Baker, and Dean Acheson—to supervise the preparation of briefs and to make oral arguments for a state. Second, the sociological material which was the mark of the Brandeis brief was prepared by Miss Josephine Goldmark and the staff of the National Consumers' League. The first four briefs that were successful were then collected with additional material and published by Miss Goldmark as *Fatigue and Efficiency*.[28] Attorneys General in states whose labor laws were under attack could then invite Consumers' League attorneys to manage the defense or else use the sociological materials prepared by the League in the preparation of their own brief. As a result, the League contributed to the successful defense of state statutes in more than fifteen important cases.

Like most organizations with a long-range interest in litigation, the National Consumers' League believed that publicity was vital. Criticizing the Illinois Supreme Court for invalidating an eight-hour law for women, Florence Kelley wrote in 1905 that when time

> shall have convinced the medical profession, the philanthropists, and educators, as experience has already convinced the factory employees themselves, that it is a matter of life and death to young people who form so large a proportion of their

> numbers, to have a working day of reasonable length guaranteed by law, it will be found possible to rescue the fourteenth amendment to the Constitution of the United States from the perverted interpretation upon which this decision rests.[29]

Mrs. Kelley's view was adopted in Illinois in 1910, but the full Consumers' League program of child labor, maximum hour, and minimum wage regulation was not accommodated by the United States Supreme Court for three more decades. In that period the League stressed education on the subject and for this purpose distributed extra copies of its briefs to law schools, colleges, and public libraries.

No catalogue exists of government relations with private interests concerned with the conduct of litigation. The National Consumers' League experience suggests similar practices on other subjects at all government levels. At the municipal level, an attorney for a local milk producers association acted "of counsel" on the city's brief defending a favorable ordinance.[30] At the state level, the segregation interest has been closely associated with various Attorneys General in the South.[31] And a prominent attorney with national standing, John W. Davis, rendered free services to South Carolina in the School Segregation Cases.[32] At the federal level, the Justice Department has often been urged by organizations to initiate action to enforce federal statutes.[33]

Organizations as "Friends of the Court"

The appearance of organizations as *amici curiae* has been the most noticed form of group representation in Supreme Court cases.[34] This does not concern the technical office of *amicus curiae* for which an attorney is appointed to assist the court in deciding complex and technical problems. Today, the Supreme Court does sometimes, as in formulating its decree in the School Segregation Cases, issue a special invitation to the Solicitor General or to state Attorneys General to act as *amici curiae*. Of interest here is the rule under which individuals, organizations, and government attorneys have been permitted to file briefs and/or make oral argument in the Supreme Court. During the last decade *amici curiae* have submitted an average of sixty-six briefs and seven oral arguments in an average total of forty cases a term.[35]

The frequent entrance of organizations into Supreme Court cases by means of the *amicus curiae* device has often given litigation the distinct flavor of group combat. This may be illustrated by the group representation in quite different cases. In 1943, when a member of the Jehovah's Witnesses challenged the constitutionality of a compulsory flag salute in the schools, his defense by counsel for the Watchtower Bible and Tract Society was supported by separate *amici curiae*, the American Civil Liberties Union and the Committee on the Bill of Rights of the American Bar Association.[36] The appellant state board of education was supported by an *amicus curiae* brief filed by the American Legion. In 1951, in a case testing state resale price maintenance, the United States was an *amicus* against a Louisiana statute while the Commonwealth of Pennsylvania, the Louisiana State Pharmaceutical Association, American Booksellers, Inc., and the National Association of Retail Druggists entered *amici curiae* briefs in support of the statute.[37]

Many *amici curiae* briefs are workmanlike and provide the Court with helpful legal argument and material.

Yet writers who favor their use by organizations and recognize that "the *amici curiae* has had a long and respected role in our own legal system and before that, in the Roman law" believe that many briefs in recent years display a "timewasting character."[38] Another authority has said that after 1947 there were multiplying signs "that the brief *amicus curiae* had become essentially an instrumentality designed to exert extrajudicial pressure on judicial decisions."[39] Concern over this by the members of the Supreme Court was shown in 1946 when Justice Robert H. Jackson, in a dissenting opinion, criticized an *amicus curiae* brief by the American Newspaper Publishers Association:[40]

> . . . Of course, it does not cite a single authority not available to counsel for the publisher involved, and does not tell us a single new fact except this one: "This membership embraces more than 700 newspaper publishers whose publications represent in excess of eighty per cent of the total daily and Sunday circulation of newspapers published in this country. The Association is vitally interested in the issue presented in this case, namely, the right of newspapers to publish news stories and editorials pending in the courts."

Justice Jackson told his colleagues, "this might be a good occasion to demonstrate the fortitude of the judiciary."

Regulation of Organizations in the Courts

Judges, lawyers, legislators, and citizens have reacted to appearances that organizational activity in court cases touches the integrity of the judicial process. A number of limitations have resulted. But in protecting the legal system against these dangers, regulations may be too harsh on organizations and interfere unduly with the freedom of association their functioning represents. Especially is this true when the barriers against group participation in litigation are erected by legislative bodies, but it is not entirely absent when the rules are established by bar associations or by courts themselves. Some practices by organizations require control, but most of the practices of organizations in conducting litigation are perfectly compatible with an independent judiciary. Life tenure and other traditions of Anglo-American jurisprudence will attend to that. This should be borne in mind in evaluating controls placed on the practices discussed below.

Picketing of Federal Courthouses

During the trial of the leaders of the Communist party under the Smith Act in the Federal District Court for the Eastern District of New York located at Foley Square in New York City, picketing and parading outside the court was a daily occurrence. When the Senate Judiciary Committee was considering bills to limit this practice, it received many statements like the following: "Assuming under our form of representative government pressure groups must be tolerated in our legislative and executive branches, I feel there is no good reason why our courts should be subjected to such pressures."[41] In accord with this view, Congress, in 1950, enacted legislation prohibiting any person from parading, picketing, or demonstrating in or near a federal courthouse with the intent of "interfering with, obstructing, or impeding" the administration of justice or of "influencing any judge, juror, witness, or court officer" in the discharge of his duty.[42]

Mass Petitions to the Supreme Court

In 1953, the National Committee to Secure Justice in the Rosenberg Case addressed a petition claimed to have the support of 50,000 persons to the Supreme Court. Among many condemnations of this was one urging that "the Court must consult its own collective conscience on such matters without reference to the number of persons who are willing to sign a petition."[43] No rule prevents groups from such indecorous action but Justice Hugo Black has expressed the intense disapproval of the Supreme Court. In 1951, when granting a stay of execution to Willie McGhee, a Negro under the death penalty in Mississippi, Justice Black lamented the "growing practice of sending telegrams to judges in order to have cases decided by pressure."[44] Declaring that he would not read them, he said that "the courts of the United States are not the kind of instruments of justice that can be influenced by such pressures." Justice Black gave an implied warning to the bar by noting that "counsel in this case have assured me they were not responsible for these telegrams."

Organization Abuse of the Amicus Curiae Function

Supreme Court rules long provided that "a brief of an *amicus curiae* may be filed when accompanied by written consent of all parties to a case."[45] Until 1949 permission was freely granted. In that year, the filing of briefs by forty organizations in the case of the "Hollywood Ten" who had declined to testify before the House Un-American Activities Committee was widely regarded as an excessive use of the *amici curiae* procedure.[46] The Supreme Court thereupon called attention to the "rule of consent" by elaborating the procedures and permitting persons denied consent by a party to seek leave from the Court itself to act as *amicus curiae.* The Solicitor General, as the legal representative of the United States in the Supreme Court, took the 1949 rule change to mean that he should exercise the "rule of consent" against persons or groups wishing to be *amici curiae* in all cases. Since the United States government is a party in approximately 50 per cent of all cases before the Supreme Court the universal refusal of consent cut the number of organizations filing *amici curiae* briefs rather drastically. This rigid policy was adhered to by a succession of Solicitors General until August 1952. Complaints by Justices Black and Frankfurter then led the Solicitor General to modify the practice and exercise administrative discretion in passing upon requests of organizations to file briefs *amici curiae.*[47] This practice satisfied a majority of the Supreme Court for its 1949 rule change was incorporated into the full revision of the Court's rules which went into effect on July 1, 1954. However, Justice Black was still dissatisfied and, on adoption of the 1954 rules, declared:

> . . . I have never favored the almost insuperable obstacle our rules put in the way of briefs sought to be filed by persons other than the actual litigants. Most of the cases before this Court involve matters that affect far more than the immediate record parties. I think the public interest and judicial administration would be better served by relaxing rather than tightening the rule against *amicus curiae* briefs.[48]

The standard governing grant or denial of consent to file *amicus curiae* briefs has been elaborated upon in a statement of policy issued by the Office of the Solicitor General.[49] While espousing a liberal attitude, the Solicitor General frowns on applicants with "a general, abstract or academic interest" in a case and on "a brief which is 'a vehicle for propaganda efforts.'" Nor is a brief that merely repeats the arguments of the parties well regarded. On the other hand, consent is given "where the applicant has a concrete, substantial interest in the decision of the case, and the proposed brief would assist the Court by presenting relevant arguments or materials which would not otherwise be submitted." Furthermore, in recent years when the Solicitor General has refused consent, the Supreme Court in some cases has granted permission to an organization to file a brief *amicus curiae.*

Efforts to regulate the indiscriminate filing of *amici curiae* briefs prevent organizations on about ten occasions each term from participating in cases. For example, an American Legion post was refused consent to file an *amicus curiae* brief in the Steel Seizure Case while the Congress of Industrial Organizations was permitted to do so.[50] The most active organizations in filing *amici curiae* briefs in recent years have been the American Civil Liberties Union, the American Federation of Labor-Congress of Industrial Organizations, the American Jewish Congress, and the National Lawyers Guild. Yet under the "rule of consent" by parties to the case each of these organizations has sometimes been denied leave to file briefs.

Offer of Legal Aid by the Liberty League

The offer of the National Lawyers' Committee of the American Liberty League to donate its services in test cases led a critic to make a formal complaint to the American Bar Association. The League was charged with unethical conduct for having "organized a vast free lawyers service for firms and individuals 'bucking' New Deal laws on constitutional grounds."[51] The ABA Committee on Professional Ethics and Grievances ruled, in a formal opinion, that the activities of the Liberty League were perfectly proper, even laudable.[52] The Committee found that neither the substance of the offer, to provide legal defense for "indigent citizens without compensation," nor the "proffer of service," even when broadcast over the radio, was offensive to the ethical code of the American bar.

Barratry and the NAACP

Since 1954, eleven Southern states have acted separately through legislation or litigation to restrict the efforts of the National Association for the Advancement of Colored People to proceed with court cases aimed at ending segregation.[53] The NAACP frankly admits the deliberate and conscious use of litigation to secure economic, social, and political gains for Negroes. In some states, registration laws—similar to federal and state lobby registration provisions—require the filing of information by organizations which might participate in desegregation litigation. The common law crime of barratry, usually defined as the fomenting, soliciting, or inciting of unjustified litigation, has been outlawed by new statutes in other states. Legislative investigating committees have sought to expose NAACP practices in litigation as unethical and illegal. State Attorneys General have brought actions against the NAACP in state courts while the NAACP has brought suits in federal courts to secure declaratory judgments and injunctions against the enforcement of state statutes which would restrict their activities.

In June, the Supreme Court overruled as an unconstitutional violation of freedom of association a contempt fine of $100,000 imposed by Alabama on the NAACP for refusing to disclose its membership lists.[54] Two similar Virginia cases have been docketed with petitions for certiorari awaiting action when the Supreme Court convenes for its October 1958 term. In one, the NAACP has asked for review of a Supreme Court of Appeals of Virginia decision enabling a legislative committee to use subpoenas to secure the names of NAACP members and affiliates.[55] In the other case, Virginia has asked the Supreme Court to review the decision of a three-judge federal district court in which the majority concluded that acts punishing barratry and requiring registration could not constitutionally be applied to the normal activities of the NAACP.[56]

Conclusion

There is a logical relationship of organizational interest in litigation and the importance of courts in forming public policy. Although courts act only in cases between parties with concrete interests at stake, organizations concerned with the impact of the outcome may become quite active participants. Organizations may do this by sponsoring a "test case" brought in the name of a private party, they may aid the government attorney in a case, or they may file a brief as an *amicus curiae.* Considering the importance of the issues resolved by American courts, the entrance of organizations into cases in these ways seems in order. Indeed the essential right of organizations to pursue litigation would appear to follow from the generous attitude of American society toward the freedom of individuals to form associations for the purpose of achieving common goals. Of course, traditional judicial procedures should be followed and the attorneys for organizations, as well as for individuals, must address their arguments to reason. If these standards of conduct are followed there is no incompatibility between the activity of organizations in litigation and the integrity or independence of the judiciary.

NOTES

1. *The Supreme Court in the American System of Government* (Cambridge: Harvard University Press, 1955), p. 11.
2. *Ibid.*, p. 12.
3. James Willard Hurst, *The Growth of American Law* (Boston: Little, Brown & Co., 1950), p. 119.
4. Vinson, "Work of the Federal Courts," 69 S. Ct. v (1949).
5. For treatments of pressure groups in litigation, see Arthur F. Bentley, *The Process of Government* (Chicago: Universtiy of Chicago Press, 1908), pp. 382–99; David Truman, *The Governmental Process* (New York: Alfred A. Knopf, 1950), pp. 497–98; Donald C. Blaisdell, *American Democracy Under Pressure* (New York: Ronald, 1957), pp. 261–68; Jack W. Peltason, *Federal Courts in the Political Process* (Garden City, N.Y.: Doubleday & Company, 1955); Mark DeWolfe Howe, "Political Theory and the Nature of Liberty," *Harvard Law Review*, Vol. 67 (November 1953), pp. 91–95; Joseph B. Robinson, "Organizations Promoting Civil Rights and Liberties," *The Annals*, Vol.

275 (May 1951), pp. 18–26; Comment, "Private Attorneys-General: Group Action in the Fight for Civil Liberties," *Yale Law Journal,* Vol. 58 (March 1949), pp. 574–98. In criticism, see Walter Berns, *Freedom, Virtue and the First Amendment* (Baton Rouge: Louisiana State University Press, 1957), pp. 130–33, 160–62.

6. *Groups and the Constitution* (Stanford, Calif.: Stanford University Press, 1956). See also: Elias Lieberman, *Unions Before the Bar* (New York: Harper & Brothers, 1950).
7. Richard Harris, "I'd Like to Talk With You for a Minute," *New Yorker,* Vol. 32 (June 16, 1956), pp. 72, 88.
8. See Herbert Hill and Jack Greenberg, *Citizen's Guide to De-Segregation* (Boston: Beacon Press, 1955); Clement E. Vose, "NAACP Strategy in the Covenant Cases," *Western Reserve Law Review,* Vol. 6 (Spring 1955), pp. 101–45.
9. Roy Wilkins, "The Negro Wants Full Equality," in *What the Negro Wants,* Rayford W. Logan (Ed.) (Chapel Hill: University of North Carolina Press, 1944), pp. 113, 118.
10. Saunders Redding, *The Lonesome Road: The Story of the Negro's Past in America* (Garden City, N.J.: Doubleday & Company, 1958), p. 321.
11. Hill and Greenberg, *op. cit.* (note 8 *supra*), pp. 56–57.
12. For a survey, see Robert E. Cushman, *Civil Liberties in the United States* (Ithaca: Cornell University Press, 1956), pp. 211–24.
13. 334 U.S. 1 (1948).
14. Henderson v. United States, 339 U.S. 816 (1950).
15. Missouri ex. rel. Gaines v. Canada, 305 U.S. 337 (1937). See Walter White, *A Man Called White* (New York: Viking Press, 1948), p. 162.
16. Nixon v. Herndon, 273 U.S. 536 (1927); Nixon v. Condon, 286 U.S. 73 (1932). See *Louis Marshall, Champion of Liberty,* Charles Reznikoff (Ed.) (Philadelphia: Jewish Publication Society, 1957), pp. 426–47, *passim.*
17. 347 U.S. 483 (1954).
18. See "Class Actions: A Study of Group-Interest Litigation," *Race Relations Law Reporter,* Vol. 1 (October 1956), pp. 991–1010.
19. Robert B. McKay, " 'With all Deliberate Speed,' A Study of School Desegregation," *New York University Law Review,* Vol. 31 (June 1956), pp. 992, 1086.
20. See Benjamin R. Twiss, *Lawyers and the Constitution: How Laissez Faire Came to the Supreme Court* (Princeton, N.J.: Princeton University Press, 1942), pp. 241–49; Frederick Rudolph, "American Liberty League, 1934–1940," *American Historical Review,* Vol. 56 (October 1950), pp. 19–33.
21. For the announcement and list of members of the Committee, see *New York Times,* Aug. 22, 1935, pp. 1, 6.
22. *New York Times,* Sept. 19, 1935, pp. 1, 10.
23. Editorial in *United States Law Review* (October 1935), quoted in Thomas Reed Powell, "Fifty-eight Lawyers Report," *New Republic,* Vol. 85 (December 11, 1935), p. 120.
24. N.L.R.B. v. Jones & Laughlin Steel Corp., 301 U.S. 1, 12 (1937).
25. Associated Press v. N.L.R.B., 301 U.S. 103 (1937).
26. Clement E. Vose, "The National Consumers' League and the Brandeis Brief," *Midwest Journal of Political Science,* Vol. 1 (November 1957), pp. 267–90; Josephine Goldmark, *Impatient Crusader; Florence Kelley's Life Story* (Urbana: University of Illinois Press, 1953), pp. 143–79.
27. National Consumers' League, *Sixth Annual Report* (1908). The first N.C.L. victory was in Muller v. Oregon, 208 U.S. 412 (1908).
28. (New York: Russell Sage Foundation, 1912).
29. *Some Ethical Gains Through Legislation* (New York: The Macmillan Co., 1905), p. 141. Mrs. Kelley was criticizing the decision in Ritchie v. People, 155 Ill. 98, 40 N.E. 454 (1895), *reversed by* Ritchie v. Wayman, 244 Ill. 509, 91 N.E. 695 (1910).
30. Dean Milk Co. v. Madison, 340 U.S. 349 (1951).
31. See Samuel Krislov, ". . . Southern Attorneys General and Their Stand on Desegregation," unpublished paper read before the American Political Science Association, New York City, Sept. 7, 1957.
32. The South Carolina Case, Briggs v. Elliott, was joined with Brown v. Board of Education, and others, 347 U.S. 483 (1954). See *New York Times,* April 14, 1953, p. 11; "May It Please the Court," *Time,* Vol. 62 (December 21, 1953), p. 18.
33. Philip B. Perlman, Solicitor General, 1947–1952, in a letter to the author, Feb. 6, 1953.

See Perlman's testimony, *Hearings before Subcommittee of the House Committee on Appropriations,* Jan. 12, 1950, 81st Cong., 2nd Sess. (1950), pp. 101, 105.

34. Fowler V. Harper and Edwin D. Etherington, "Lobbyists Before the Court," *University of Pennsylvania Law Review,* Vol. 101 (June 1953), pp. 1172–1177; Peter H. Sonnenfeld, "Participation of *Amici Curiae* . . . in Decisions of the Supreme Court, 1949–1957," Government Research Bureau, Working Papers, No. 2 (East Lansing, Michigan, January 1958); Johanna Bernstein, "Volunteer *Amici Curiae* in Civil Rights Cases," New York University *Student Law Review,* Vol. 1 (Spring 1952), pp. 95–102.
35. Sonnenfeld, *op. cit.* (note 34 *supra*), p. 4.
36. West Virginia State Board of Education v. Barnette, 319 U.S. 624 (1943).
37. Schwegmann Brothers v. Calvert Distillers Corp., 341 U.S. 384 (1951).
38. Harper and Etherington, *op. cit.* (note 34 *supra*), p. 1172.
39. Frederick Bernays Wiener, "The Supreme Court's New Rules," *Harvard Law Review,* Vol. 68 (November 1954), pp. 20, 80.
40. Craig v. Harney, 331 U.S. 367, 397 (1946).
41. Communication of Judge F. Ryan Duffy (Federal Court of Appeals, 6th Circuit), Joint Hearings before the Subcommittee of the Committee on the Judiciary on S. 1681 and H.R. 3766, *To Prohibit the Picketing of Courts,* 81st Cong., 1st Sess. (June 15, 1949), p. 5.
42. 18 U.S.C. Sec. 1507 (1952), added in 1950 by 64 Stat. 1018; 63 Stat. 1616 (1949), 40 U.S.C. Secs. 13f–p (1952).
43. Harper and Etherington, *op. cit.* (note 34 *supra*), p. 1173, n. 4.
44. *New York Times,* March 16, 1951, p. 1.
45. In the old Supreme Court Rules, effective Feb. 27, 1939, section 27 (9), 306 U.S. 708–09 (1939). This section was amended on Nov. 14, 1949, 338 U.S. 959–60 (1949). All existing provisions were rescinded when new Supreme Court Rules became effective on July 1, 1954, 346 U.S. 951 (1954). Rules 42 and 44 govern *amicus curiae* procedure, 346 U.S. 951, 933, 996.
46. Lawson v. United States, 339 U.S. 934 (1949); Marshall v. United States, 339 U.S. 933 (1949). See Harper and Etherington, *op. cit.* (note 34 *supra*), p. 1173.
47. Sonnenfeld, *op. cit.* (note 34 *supra*), pp. 2, 3, 8, 10. For criticism by the justices, see Lee v. United States, 343 U.S. 924 (1952); United States v. Lovknit, 342 U.S. 915 (1952).
48. Justice Black's objection is appended to the Order Adopting Revised Rules of the Supreme Court, 346 U.S. 947 (1954).
49. Statement of the Office of the Solicitor General, issued May 1957, quoted in Sonnenfeld, *op. cit.* (note 34 *supra*), Appendix C, pp. 25–26.
50. Youngstown Sheet and Tube Co. v. Sawyer, 343 U.S. 579 (1952).
51. *New York Times,* Nov. 18, 1935, p. 15.
52. Opinion 148 in *American Bar Association Canons of Professional and Judicial Ethics —Opinions of Committee on Professional Ethics and Grievances* (Chicago: American Bar Association, 1957), pp. 308–12.
53. For a three-year summary of developments, see *Race Relations Law Reporter,* Vol. 2 (August 1957), pp. 892–94. Examples of the charges being made against the NAACP are seen in the Report of the Joint Committee on Offenses Against the Administration of Justice of the General Assembly of Virginia, filed on Nov. 13, 1957, *Race Relations Law Reporter,* Vol. 3 (February 1958), pp. 98–111. For defenses, see Robert L. Carter, "The Role of the NAACP in the School Segregation Cases," unpublished paper read before the American Political Science Association, New York City, Sept. 6, 1957; American Jewish Congress, *Assault upon Freedom of Association: A Study of the Southern Attack on the National Association for the Advancement of Colored People* (New York, 1957).
54. NAACP v. Alabama, No. 91, U.S. Sup. Ct., June 30, 1958 (26 U.S. Law Week 4489).
55. NAACP v. Committee on Offenses Against the Administration of Justice, 101 S.E. 2d 631 (Va. Sup. Ct. App., 1958).
56. NAACP v. Patty (Harrison), 159 F. Supp. 503 (E. D. Va., 1958).

49

Marshalling the Court

WALTER F. MURPHY

In the following essay, Walter F. Murphy discusses the tactics of individual justices and analyzes bloc formation on the Court, the influence of the Chief Justice, and the role of "professional reputation" in court decision making.

According to Murphy, justices engage in political maneuvering within the confines of the Court to gain policy outcomes that they prefer. Whether by using superior intellectual ability or legal craftsmanship, seeking to gain the personal esteem of other justices, bargaining about the casting of a vote or the writing of an opinion, or appealing to loyalty to the Court as an institution, a justice strives for a decision that accords with his view of "right" policy. Since justices in the American system are usually skillful and determined politicians, it is not surprising that such tactics are not only available but are well and readily used.

Murphy, Professor of Politics at Princeton, is one of the leading contemporary scholars on the Supreme Court. He is the author of Congress and the Court *(1962) and* Wiretapping on Trial *(1965) and is coeditor of* Courts, Judges, and Politics *(1961).*

Since he shares decision-making authority with eight other judges, the first problem that a policy-oriented Justice would confront is that of obtaining at least four, and hopefully eight, additional votes for the results

Abridged from *Elements of Judicial Strategy* by Walter F. Murphy.

he wants and the kinds of opinions he thinks should be written in cases important to his objectives. Moreover, because he faces other problems as well, he must try to influence* his colleagues with as little expenditure of time and energy as possible.

His initial step would be to examine the situation on the Court. In general three sets of conditions may obtain. There may be complete coincidence of interest with the other Justices, or at least with the number of associates he feels is necessary to attain his aim. Second, the interests of the other Justices, or a majority of them, may be indifferent to his objective. Third, the interests of his colleagues may be in opposition to his own. Since there are varying degrees of coincidence, indifference, and opposition, each represents a range rather than a pin-pointed position. The coincidence may be such that the Justice need only bring the facts or implications of a specific situation to the attention of his colleagues, or it may be so imperfect that the term coincidence can be used only in the sense of an analogy. Under the latter circumstances, the Justice may have to do a great deal of persuading to convince his colleagues that their objectives are not incongruous and that it is important to their interests that they support his suggestions.

Indifference may be, as one might assume, the situation in which attempts to exercise influence would be most necessary and would pay the biggest dividends; but influence could also have a major effect where interests were in opposition. Where the opposition was intense a Justice might still be able to lessen its impact on his policy aims by decreasing its intensity. Where the opposition was mild, a Justice might conceivably convince his associates that they were mistaken, or he might offer a concession in another area which they valued more highly in exchange for a concession here.

Influence, of course, does not simply come into existence.[1] It is the result of interaction among human beings, of their individual interests, values, and concepts of what moral rules, if any, ought to be controlling, and of their different perceptions of the situations in which they are operating. A policy-oriented Justice must therefore want to know what factors predispose one actor to respond positively to the suggestions, wishes, requests, or commands of another. Where actors are behaving rationally in terms of their particular goals, the question, "What shall I gain if I do *x* because actor A suggests, wishes, requests, or commands it?" is crucial. Personal esteem can also be important in gauging reactions, and it is often tied to self-interest. We tend to like those whose actions have benefited us in the past, to interpret as beneficial the actions of those whom we like, and, in turn, to help those whom we like. In addition, we frequently find ourselves liking another person for no apparent reason at all. In the process of reacting favorably to the suggestions of those we like, we may be unconsciously reckoning on intangible as well as tangible gains, such as an increase in affection. The desire to be loved seems as important as it is widespread in our society. Furthermore, once our affections have become attached to another person,

* In [one] sense influence . . . can be distinguished from leadership only if one restricts leadership to the exercise of influence within a specific group. As used in this chapter, the two terms are interchangeable. I prefer to use influence because, to most persons not trained in social psychology, leadership usually connotes a formal position in a hierarchy.

whether or not because of rational considerations, what Pepitone has called "facilitative distortion" may set in.[2] That is, we tend to attribute to persons to whom we are emotionally drawn the virtues and talents we would like them to have.

Thus, in disposing an actor to respond positively to the attempts at influence by another actor, personal esteem may merge with professional esteem—respect for judgment, knowledge, or skills—in that we might see those whom we like as having somewhat more of these qualities than they perhaps possess. Self-interest, as has already been indicated, may also be involved in professional evaluations. It is easier to esteem the abilities of those whose previous actions have been beneficial to one's own interests than to esteem the abilities of those whose actions have been harmful or indifferent. This is not to deny that such respect may be based on purely professional standards, largely apart from interest or affection, and still influence our decisions. In addition, such respect, no matter how generated, can lead to influence insofar as it operates as an economizing device. An actor might conclude that "A is an expert in this field, and I am not. The cost of becoming an expert is so high that I find it more efficient to follow A than to become an expert myself."

The concept of "oughtness" also plays a role in disposing an actor to respond to the suggestions of another. One might react positively or negatively to a suggestion because one feels that because of broad moral precepts or because of one's particular role in society, one should or should not perform such an act. In a more specific fashion, when he is a member of an institutional hierarchy, an actor might feel that he ought to carry out the wishes of those further up the hierarchy than he, at least in those matters relating to the superiors' areas of authority. Fear, too, can be a significant factor in determining influence. The question, "What reprisals shall I be risking if I do not do *x* at actor A's suggestion?" is central to any rational process of decision-making. And, in politics, sanctions can take forms ranging all the way from a decrease in affection to physical violence.

Since the Justices are largely equal in authority, an appeal by one Justice to his position on the Court is not likely to be an effective means of increasing influence with his associates, except perhaps in those few fields in which tradition has given the Chief Justice certain prerogatives. The Justices, however, are not equal in intellectual ability, in perspicacity, learning, legal craftsmanship, persuasive talents, energy, determination, ambition, or social skills; nor do they hold each other in equal personal and professional esteem. Thus a Justice has considerable opportunity to try to exercise influence over his colleagues. He could attempt: to appeal to their interests—to convince them that their interests would gain from furthering his interests or that their interests would suffer injury if they oppose his; to increase or create and then appeal to their personal and professional esteem for him; and to appeal to their concepts of duty and moral obligation.

The peculiar formal rules and informal norms of the Court would allow a Justice to operate under one or more of several simple strategies to exploit each of these possible appeals. First, he might try by force of his intellect and will to convince his colleagues not only that what he wanted was in the best interests of themselves, the Court, the country, humanity, or whatever other goals they might wish to foster, but also that it was morally incumbent upon them to act in the fashion he was proposing.

Second, a Justice might plan so to endear himself to the other Justices that they would be reluctant to vote against him in matters he considered to be vital. Conversely, he might try to capitalize on fear rather than affection and try to bludgeon his colleagues into agreement by threatening them with use of the sanctions available to him. Fourth, he might conclude that the only viable way to come near achieving his goal would be to negotiate: to compromise with those who were less intensively opposed to his policies. Last, he might decide that the best way of securing approval of his policies would be to secure new men for the Court, men whose interests would coincide closely with his own.

Taken alone, none of these simple strategies seems very promising. Occasionally a giant like Marshall can dominate the Court, but the great Chief Justice was blessed with several co-operative colleagues as well as with a magnificent sense of statecraft. As Justice Johnson explained to Jefferson:[3]

> While I was on our state-bench I was accustomed to delivering seriatim opinions . . . and was not a little surprised to find our Chief Justice in the Supreme Court delivering all the opinions in cases in which he sat, even in some instances when contrary to his own judgment and vote. But I remonstrated in vain; the answer was he is willing to take the trouble and it is a mark of respect to him. I soon found out however the real cause. Cushing was incompetent. Chase could not be got to think or write—Patterson [*sic*] was a slow man and willingly declined the trouble, and the other two judges [Marshall and Bushrod Washington] you know are commonly estimated as one judge. . . .

On the other hand, it is difficult to imagine any judge, even a Marshall, dominating men like Johnson, Taney, Field, Miller, Bradley, Brewer, Harlan, Holmes, Hughes, Brandeis, Sutherland, Van Devanter, Cardozo, or Stone. It is equally difficult to imagine any Justice getting passive acquiescence, for any length of time, on important and controversial issues from a Court composed of Justices as brilliant, individualistic, and strong-willed as Black, Douglas, Frankfurter, and Jackson.

Similarly, Supreme Court Justices are as unlikely to be swayed by personal esteem alone as solely by the threat of sanctions being applied against them. Bargaining, too, hardly seems to be the golden key to success, unless accompanied by high personal or professional esteem, some measure of coincidence or indifference of interests, and perhaps, by some fear of the application of sanctions.

Last, staffing the Court with men whose interests coincided with the policy-oriented Justice's would undoubtedly be very effective. It would depend, however, on (1) the Justice's being gifted with better vision than most Presidents have had in foreseeing how future judges would behave once securely on the bench, (2) enough vacancies occurring to permit a favorable majority to be formed, (3) the President and the general political environment allowing the Justice to play the chief role in the appointing process. The necessity of all three conditions happening simultaneously is a severe limitation on the practicality of sole reliance on this strategy.

It is obvious that in most circumstances a Justice would be far more prudent to pursue a mixed strategy employing some elements of each of these simple approaches. . . .

Tactics

Once he has decided on a strategic plan to secure a majority within the Court—and integrated that plan into his larger scheme to meet the other obstacles in his path—a Justice would have to consider the tactics open to him to carry out his efforts to persuade on the merits of his policy choice, to capitalize on personal regard, to bargain, to threaten, and if possible to have a voice in the selection of new personnel.

Persuasion on the Merits

To date all the Justices have been lawyers, and whatever the status of their technical knowledge when appointed, their work, their friends, their critics, their pride, and their clerks have forced most of them to become competent and usually highly competent lawyers. Traditional overemphasis on the logical element in judicial decision-making has been ridiculed by Legal Realists. Yet, while it is true that the work of courts revolves around basically subjective value judgments, judgments conditioned by all sorts of subconscious drives shaped in part by childhood experiences, no evidence has yet been adduced to show that judges decide cases through some automatic operation of emotional prejudices. To a significant extent judges can and do weigh such factors as legal principles and precedents and well thought-out ideas of proper public policy.

Furthermore, judges can be persuaded to change their minds about specific cases as well as about broad public policies, and intellectual persuasion can play an important role in such shifts. As Robert Jackson once commented from the bench: "I myself have changed my opinion after reading the opinions of the other members of this Court. And I am as stubborn as most. But I sometimes wind up not voting the way I voted in conference because the reasons of the majority didn't satisfy me."[4] An examination of the notes of conference discussions which Justice Murphy filed with his papers and the memoranda in this and in other collections of judicial papers show that time and again positions first taken at conference are changed as other Justices bring up new arguments. Perhaps most convincing in demonstrating the impact of intellectual factors are the numerous instances on record in which the Justice assigned the opinion of the Court has reported back to the conference that additional study had convinced him that he and the rest of the majority had been in error. A few examples will have to suffice:

When, in May, 1922, Taft circulated his opinion in *Hill* v. *Wallace*, he attached a statement summarizing the history of the Court's handling of the dispute.[5]

> . . . we voted first that there was equitable jurisdiction by a vote of 7 to 1, Justice Brandeis voting "No" and Justice Holmes being doubtful. On the question of whether [the congressional statute regulating trading in grain futures] could be sustained as a taxing act, the vote stood 7 to 1, Justice McKenna casting the negative vote, and Justice Brandeis not voting. Later we took a vote as to whether the act could be sustained as a regulation of interstate commerce. At first, by a vote of 5–4, it was held that it could not be so sustained. Later there was a change, and by a vote of 5 to 3, Justice Brandeis not voting, its validity as a regulation of interstate commerce was sustained.

Taft then pointed out that he had changed his mind and asked the Court to go along with him. "On a close examination of the case, the law and the record, I have reached the conclusion that the law is invalid as a taxing law and that it can not be sustained as a valid regulation of interstate commerce." When the opinion came down three days later, the statute was declared unconstitutional as a taxing act, under the authority of the Child Labor Tax Case. The vote was 8–1, with Brandeis agreeing in a separate opinion that the statute was unconstitutional but doubting that the plaintiffs had standing to sue.

* * *

As in all phases of human activity, eloquence and charm would be valuable additions to professional competence. One might suspect that Hughes's opening remarks to the conference when the troublesome issue of a compulsory flag salute was first discussed increased the predisposition of the other Justices to accept his reasoning. "I come up to this case," Justice Murphy recorded the Chief Justice as saying, "like a skittish horse to a brass band."[6]

It does not follow, to be sure, that all or even four Justices would be open to persuasion on the policy which the Justice wanted adopted. . . . Thus a Justice would also have to consider exploiting the vulnerability of any of his colleagues to non- or extrarational arguments. He would probably feel it unethical to appeal to the strong personal dislike of one Justice for another, though there may have been occasions when such an appeal would have been effective.

Less distasteful would be an appeal to loyalty to the Court as an institution, though it would normally be possible for a Justice to utilize this argument fully only when he was in the majority and was trying to pick up additional votes or was trying to get a majority to agree to an institutional opinion in preference to a seriatim expression of views. Similarly, in situations where the Justice feels that the general political environment requires unanimity, he might play on the isolation of a would-be dissenter.

Hirabayashi v. *United States* provides one example of a combination of such tactics. After reading a draft of Stone's opinion for the Court sustaining the conviction of a Nisei for violating the curfew imposed by the military on all West Coast Japanese Americans—an opinion which ducked the more serious question of the constitutionality of the evacuation and internment aspects of the program—Justice Murphy began writing a dissent. Hearing of this, Frankfurter sent him a plea to close ranks with his colleagues:[7]

> Please, Frank, with your eagerness for the austere functions of the Court and your desire to do all that is humanly possible to maintain and enhance the *corporate* reputation of the Court, why don't you take the initiative with the Chief Justice in getting him to take out everything that either offends you or that you would want to express more ironically.

Even after an exchange of several other notes, Murphy remained adamant, and he circulated a blistering opinion branding the whole Nisei program as "utterly inconsistent with our ideals and traditions" and "at variance with the principles for which we are fighting."[8] Frankfurter read Murphy's protest in horror, and he immediately wrote another impassioned plea:[9]

> Of course I shan't try to dissuade you from filing a dissent in that case—not because I do not think it highly unwise but because I think you are immovable. But I would like to say two things to you about the dissent: (1) it has internal contradictions which you ought not to allow to stand, and (2) do you really think it is conducive to the things you care about, including the great reputation of this Court, to suggest that everybody is out

of step except Johnny, and more particularly that the Chief Justice and seven other Justices of this Court are behaving like the enemy and thereby playing into the hands of the enemy?

Murphy was apparently moved at least to second thoughts about the possible implications of what he was doing. Within a few days he had switched his vote and had modified his dissent into a concurrence, though one which still expressed concern over the "melancholy resemblance" between United States treatment of the Nisei and Nazi treatment of the Jews.

* * *

A Justice might appeal to other emotions, for example, patriotism in cases involving issues of national security. In *Ex parte Quirin*, the Justices were unanimous in their conclusion that the government could try captured Nazi saboteurs in military tribunals rather than in regularly constituted civil courts, but they could not agree on an opinion explaining why such trials were constitutional. After the Chief Justice had circulated three different drafts of an opinion without securing full assent, one of the other members of the Court sent a long memorandum to all of his colleagues. He began by pointing out that most of the discussion was now approaching mere quibbling about words, since the Justices were agreed that the only real point of difference, the extent to which Congress could bind the President as Commander-in-Chief, should not be decided. As the clearest way of explaining his own views, the Justice offered a dialogue between himself and the saboteurs, a dialogue in which he rejected their claims out of hand, describing them as "damned scoundrels" who were attempting to create a conflict between the President and Congress which would continue long "after your bodies will be rotting in lime." At the conclusion of the dialogue, the Justice again spoke directly to his brethren:[10]

Some of the very best lawyers I know are now in the Solomon Island battle, some are seeing service in Australia, some are subchasers in the Atlantic, and some are on the various air fronts. It requires no poet's imagination to think of their reflections if the unanimous result reached by us in these cases should be expressed in opinions which would black out agreement in result and reveal internecine conflict about the manner of staffing that result. I know some of these men very, very intimately. I think I know what they would deem to be the governing canons of constitutional adjudication in a case like this. And I almost hear their voices were they to read more than a single opinion in this case. They would say something like this but in language hardly becoming a judge's tongue: "What in hell do you fellows think you are doing? Haven't we got enough of a job trying to lick the Japs and Nazis without having you fellows on the Court dissipate thoughts and feelings and energies of the folks at home by stirring up a nice row as to who has what power . . . ? Haven't you got any more sense than to get people by the ear on one of their favorite American pastimes—abstract constitutional discussions? . . . Just relax and don't be too engrossed in your own interests in verbalistic conflicts because the inroads on energy and national unity that such conflict inevitably produces, is a pastime we had better postpone until peacetime."

Stone, too, was hard at work trying to woo the doubtful Justices by means of what he described as "patient negotiations."[11] Eventually the opinion which came down was unanimous.

Increasing Personal Regard

Some people are blessed with a warmth and a sincerity that immediately attract other human beings. It is improbable that even a sophisticated version of a Dale Carnegie course, whether or not self-taught, could build up anything approaching the personal magnetism that such people have by nature. Observance of the simple rules of human courtesy and thoughtfulness, however, can do much to keep interpersonal relations on a plane where a meaningful exchange of ideas is possible.

When a new Justice comes to the Court, an older colleague might try to charm his junior brother. A gracious letter of welcome may make the new Justice more disposed to trust another's judgment or at least more disposed to compromise without rancor. . . .

. . . when Frankfurter's nomination was confirmed by the Senate, Hughes, despite the fact that his work on the Court had been sharply criticized by Frankfurter, immediately wrote a welcoming note:[12]

> Let me extend to you a warm welcome to collaboration in our work—for which you are so exceptionally qualified. We need you and I trust you will be able to take your seat at the opening of our next session on January 30th. If there is anything that I can do to aid in making your arrangements here, command me.
>
> With kindest regards, and looking forward with the greatest of pleasure to the renewal, in this relation, of the association with you that I had when you were with the Department of Justice many years ago. . . .

Once on the Court, the freshman Justice, even if he has been a state or lower federal court judge, moves into a strange and shadowy world. An occasional helping hand—a word of advice about procedure and protocol, a warning about personal idiosyncrasies of colleagues, or the trustworthiness of counsel—can be helpful and appreciated. Particularly if a new Justice comes to Washington in mid-term, aid in securing clerical assistance and law clerks can be a means of establishing good will—with the new Justice as well as with his staff.

The new Justice may also feel it necessary to establish warm social relations with his brethren. When he first came to the Court, Justice Stone asked several of his associates for pictures of themselves. . . .

Notations on slip opinions provide another avenue of social access. A large ego seems to be a prerequisite of political success, and large egos bruise easily—though the exigencies of American politics probably sift out most of those people with slow recuperative powers. In any event, a judicial opinion represents considerable labor, and it would be a rare man who did not enjoy appreciation of his intellectual offspring. Remarks on slip opinions are frequently glowing in their praise. Holmes could be as charmingly eloquent in his editorial comments as in his other writing. He told Taft in 1921, "I cling to my preceptor's hand and follow him through the dark passages to the light."[13] Stone received his full share of such encomia. On the back of the draft of the opinion in *United States* v. *Darby*, Douglas write: "I heartily agree. This has the master's real touch!" Frankfurter added: "This is a grand plum pudding. There are so many luscious plums in it that it's invidious to select. But I especially rejoice over (1) the way you buried *Hammer* v. *Dagenhart* and (2) your definitive exposure of the empty hobgoblin of the 10th Amendt. It's a superb job." On the back of Stone's dissent in *Cloverleaf Butter Co.* v. *Patterson,* Frank Murphy said: "This seems to me the finest kind of writing and it is sound too." . . . Certainly such comments make for an easier exchange of views than remarks like McReynolds' about an opinion of which he did not approve: "This statement makes me sick."[14]

Similarly, suggestions for changes in opinion should be made with tender regard for the feelings of the writer. Stone, for example, wrote Douglas about the latter's opinion[15] in a 1942 term case:[16]

I have gone over your opinion in this case with some care, and I congratulate you on your lucid and penetrating analysis and the great thoroughness with which you have done a difficult job. If Justice Brandeis could read it he would be proud of his successor.

Stone then quietly added to these gallantries a single-spaced typewritten page of suggestions for revision.

When a Justice has won a fight over a decision, he may be well advised to offer the olive branch to the loser, knowing that today's opponent will often be tomorrow's ally. After their failure to agree in the first Flag Salute case, Frankfurter wrote Stone a gentle note: "Though we read the scales differently in weighing these 'imponderables,' I cannot but feel confident that our scales are the same. In any event our ways do not part and we care no differently for the only things that give dignity to man—the things of the spirit."[17]

A somewhat different way for a Justice to build up a reservoir of good will for later use would be to accede frequently to the majority, and to let the majority know that although acquiescence goes against his better judgment, he is stifling his doubts for the sake of harmony. As Pierce Butler once wrote on the back of one of Stone's slip opinions:[18]

I voted to reverse. While this sustains your conclusion to affirm, I still think reversal would be better. But I shall in silence acquiesce. Dissents seldom aid in the right development of statement of the law. They often do harm. For myself I say: "Lead us not into temptation."

* * *

If such concessions as these are made on issues which a Justice does not think important—or on which he would have been in a small minority anyway—he has lost very little and may have put himself in an excellent position to win reluctant votes from colleagues on other issues. Certiorari voting supplies an opportunity for such tactics.[19] The Court's rules require a vote of four Justices to bring up a case, but where one or two members feel strongly about granting certiorari in a case, another Justice—providing the final decision in the litigation is not likely to affect detrimentally his cause—can capitalize on the situation by graciously saying something to the effect that he is willing to defer to the judgment of the minority.

Members of the Court should be sufficiently sophisticated to take praise and apparent deference from colleagues no more seriously than do most senators.... Yet, as has already been pointed out, friendship and the social amenities, especially when coupled with genuine intellectual respect, can play an important auxiliary role in the judicial process insofar as they help determine with whom a Justice is more apt to interact and with whom he will probably continue to negotiate even after an impasse has seemingly been reached.

When Stone first came to the Court, he was, as Taft thought, fundamentally a conservative. Within a very few years, however, Stone had joined Holmes and Brandeis in what the Chief Justice considered "radical" constitutional opinions. In part this change reflected Stone's capacity for intellectual growth, but the warm and stimulating companionship of Holmes and to a lesser extent Brandeis may also have been a decisive factor. As Thomas Reed Powell, a long-time confidant of Stone, commented, it was "respect and liking for Holmes and

Brandeis that turned him from his earlier attitudes."[20] On the other hand, Stone probably had slight intellectual respect for Taft. This fact, coupled with McReynolds' bigoted attitude toward Brandeis as well as his continual carping at Stone's opinions,[21] did little to keep the new Justice in the conservative camp.

Stone's change of viewpoint may be an unusual case. Probably more typical is that of the Justice who finds it easier to compromise with a colleague who has shown him respect and consideration than with an associate who has been coldly formal or even impolite. . . .

Use of Sanctions

The two major sanctions which a Justice can use against his colleagues are his vote and his willingness to write opinions which will attack a doctrine the minority or majority wishes to see adopted. The effectiveness of the first sanction usually depends on the closeness of the vote, though there may be special situations, as with Brandeis in the Child Labor Tax Case, where a particular Justice's vote will greatly increase the impact of the arguments of one side or the other, or where, as in the school segregation cases, the general political environment in which the Court functions makes unanimity or near unanimity extraordinarily desirable.

The effectiveness of the second sanction depends largely on the literary and forensic skill of the particular judge. A threat of a separate opinion from one Justice may be a matter hardly worth considering where the vote is not close, while a similar threat from a Johnson, a Field, a Bradley, a Harlan, a Brandeis, or a Black may menace both one's intellectual pride and policy objectives.

A Justice may employ sanctions which are even stronger—and more dangerous—than these. In 1893, Justice Field took what might be termed extreme measures against Justice Gray. After reading Field's dissent in *Fong Yue Ting* v. *United States*, Gray changed a sentence in his opinion for the majority. Feeling this modification took some of the sting out of his dissent, Field wrote Chief Justice Fuller that if Gray did not restore the sentence as originally written, he —Field—would add a footnote to his opinion explaining that Gray had corrected his error under fire. Gray consulted with the Chief Justice and backed down, leaving the sentence as originally written.[22] . . .

* * *

Similarly, but in one swift blow, Justice Jackson lashed out at Justice Black in 1946. Roosevelt had promised Jackson—or led Jackson to think that he had promised—to promote him to the chief justiceship when Stone stepped down, but Stone outlived Roosevelt by eleven months. When Stone died, Jackson was at Nürnberg finishing his work as chief American prosecutor of the Nazi war criminals, and he heard rumors that Black and his friends were feverishly lobbying against his promotion. Infuriated, Jackson cabled a long letter to the chairmen of the House and Senate judiciary committees, charging that Black had made "public threats to the President" to resign if Jackson were appointed Chief Justice. Jackson then offered a detailed explanation of the feud between himself and Black, accusing Black of "bullying" tactics and of dealings of questionable propriety in sitting in a case argued by a former law partner.[23]

Like massive retaliation, the threat of airing disputes in public is effective to the extent that it is never actually applied. Its use may embarrass one's adversary, but even a threat to use it may enrage him to the point of total alienation as far as future consultation or compromise is concerned. More important—since, if the Justice employing such a sanction were acting rationally, he would not make the threat unless relations with the target Justice had already reached a hopeless point—public use or threats of sanctions may damage the Court's prestige and so weaken its institutional power and thereby the Justice's ability to use that power for his own ends. . . .

Ridicule can be a lethal weapon in undermining the professional esteem in which an opposing Justice is held, although it is also a most dangerous device in that it will undoubtedly provoke the man against whom it is directed, and its clumsy use can engender sympathy for the target Justice even among those who disagree with him on the merits of a case. Occasionally, however, a Justice may accept these risks, as did the author of the following memorandum.[24]

Mr. Justice ——, concurring.

I greatly sympathize with the essential purpose of my Brother . . .'s dissent. His roundabout and turgid legal phraseology is a *cri de cœur*. "Would I were back in the Senate," he means to say, "so that I could put on the statute books what really ought to be there. But here I am, cast by Fate into a den of judges devoid of the habits of legislators, simple fellows who have a crippling feeling that they must enforce the laws as Congress wrote them and not as they ought to have been written. . . ."

Bargaining

Bargaining is most likely to occur when men agree on some matters, disagree on others, and still feel that further agreement would be profitable.[25] Where the disputants are of approximately equal authority, they must, if persuasion has failed and force is not a feasible alternative, either turn to bargaining or reconcile themselves to loss of the advantages which they would accrue from compromising over the remaining points of difference. Disputants in posts of political authority who fail to achieve some sort of *modus vivendi* will frequently find that the problem at hand will be solved by other actors —with perhaps no profit and some loss to the original disputants or to their policy goals.

For Justices, bargaining is a simple fact of life. Despite conflicting views on literary style, relevant precedents, procedural rules, and substantive policy, cases have to be settled and opinions written; and no opinion may carry the institutional label of the Court unless five Justices agree to sign it. In the process of judicial decision-making, much bargaining may be tacit,[26] but the pattern is still one of negotiation and accommodation to secure consensus. Thus how to bargain wisely—not necessarily sharply—is a prime consideration for a Justice who is anxious to see his policy adopted by the Court. A Justice must learn not only how to put pressure on his colleagues but how to gauge what amounts of pressure are sufficient to be "effective" and what amounts will overshoot the mark and alienate another judge. In many situations a Justice has to be willing to settle for less than he wants if he is to get anything at all. As Brandeis once remarked, the "great difficulty of all group action, of course, is when and what concession to make."[27]

To bargain effectively, one must have something to trade and also a sanction to apply if the offer is rejected or if there is a renege on a promise. The personal honor of the Justices minimizes the possibility of a renege in the usual sense of the term, but under existing Supreme Court practice a Justice is free to change his vote—and perhaps the disposition of a case—up to the minute the decision is announced in the courtroom. Beyond this, he may even change his position and vote for a rehearing and a reversal if such a petition is filed after a case has been decided. Equally important, he may shift his doctrinal position the next time the basic issue is before the Court.

The most significant items a Justice has to offer in trade are his vote and his concurrence in an opinion. Conversely, as the last section pointed out, threats to change a vote or to write a separate opinion, dissenting or concurring, are the sanctions most generally available to a Justice. When the Court is sharply divided any Justice can wield great influence. In 1889 Justice Gray deftly pressured Miller:[28]

> After a careful reading of your opinion in *Shotwell* v. *Moore,* I am very sorry to be compelled to say that the first part of it (especially in the passage which I have marked in the margin) is so contrary to my convictions, that I fear, unless it can be a good deal tempered, I shall have to deliver a separate opinion on the lines of the enclosed memorandum.
>
> I am particularly troubled about this, because, if my scruples are not removed, and Justices Field, Bradley and Lamar adhere to their dissent, your opinion will represent only four judges, half of those who took part in the case.

Faced with the defection of one of his narrow majority, Miller had little choice but to adopt Gray's views.

It is also clear that where the Court is closely divided an uncommitted Justice has great bargaining advantages, advantages which a deeply committed Justice might assume by appearing unsure. . . .

* * *

All intra-Court bargaining takes place with the understanding that if the opinion writer ignores the suggestions which his colleagues scribble on slip opinions, he risks the disintegration of his majority. The threat to pull out normally need not be expressed, though some Justices have preferred to be very explicit about their intentions. Stone, for example, once wrote Frankfurter:[29]

> If you wish to write, placing the case on the ground which I think tenable and desirable, I shall cheerfully join you. If not, I will add a few observations for myself.

Only slightly less direct was the note, attached to a draft of a concurring opinion, which Stone sent Roberts:

> I doubt if we are very far apart in the Cantwell case, but in order that you might get exactly my views, I have written them out and enclosed them herewith.
>
> If you feel that you could agree with me, I think you would find no difficulty in making some changes in your opinion which would make it unnecessary for me to say anything.

While it is probably true that accommodation within the Court more often prevents a majority from splintering into concurring factions, compromise can also serve to mute dissent. In either case the threat of a separate opinion may create a bargaining situation in which both minority and majority may gain something. Fearing that publication of a dissent or concurrence might cause the author of the prevailing opinion to make his pronouncements more rigid or perhaps draw attention to and emphasize an "erroneous" ruling, a minority Justice might reason that it would be more prudent to suppress his disagreement if he can win concessions from the majority.

Justice Johnson had the opportunity to explain one such occasion, *Sturges v. Crowninshield,* and to live to see a new majority erode the disputed policy. As he later wrote: "The Court was, in that case, greatly divided in their views of the doctrine, and the judgment partakes as much of a compromise as of a legal adjudication. The minority thought it better to yield something than risk the whole."[30] . . .

Publication of a dissent and *circulation within the Court* of a separate opinion serve two different functions. The latter is essentially an effort to resolve conflict within the Court by persuading, in one fashion or another, other Justices. The former is basically an attempt to shift the arena of combat. Having lost in the Court, a dissenting opinion is, as Cardozo said, an appeal to history, particularly to future judges.[31] But a dissent can be more. Whether the author intends it or not, a dissent can become an appeal to contemporaries—to members of Congress, to the President and executive officials, to lower court judges, to the bar or other interest groups, or to the public at large—to change the decision of the majority. As Frankfurter explained to Murphy in discussing a dissent in *Harris* v. *United States:*[32]

> This is a protest opinion—a protest at the Bar of the future—but also an effort to make the brethren realize what is at stake. Moreover, a powerful dissent in a case like that is bound to have an effect on the lower courts as well as on the officers of the law, just as a failure to speak out vigorously against what the Court is doing will only lead to further abuse. And so in order to impress our own brethren, the lower courts, and enforcement officers, it seems to me vital to make the dissent an impressive document.

Although dissent is a cherished part of the common law tradition, a Justice who persistently refuses to accommodate his views to those of his colleagues may come to be regarded as an obstructionist. A Justice whose dissents become levers for legislative or administrative action reversing judicial policies may come to be regarded as disloyal to the bench. . . . Justice Johnson explained to Jefferson that he had found that one had to be wary of writing separate opinions "or become such a cypher in our consultations as to effect no good at all."[33]

At this time we lack sufficient empirical knowledge about the norms of intra-Court behavior to know how far a Justice would have to go in writing separate opinions before alienating his associates. It is possible that a reputation for writing dissents which result in favorable legislative and/or executive action might actually increase the Justice's bargaining power. A Justice who tried to build up such a reputation would have to be aware that, damage to personal relations within the Court aside, frequent appeals, especially if they were successful, to other branches of government or to public opinion to change what the Court was doing could severely injure the prestige of the Court and thus the Justice's chances of utilizing judicial power to achieve his own goals.

A Justice has to be concerned also about the attention outside the Court which his dissents will gain. As in all aspects of life, overexposure can lead to boredom. Stone explained this to Karl Llewellyn: "You know, if I should write in every case where I do not agree with some of the views expressed in the opinions, you and all my other friends would stop reading them."[34]

Another factor which might prod a minority Justice into accepting compromise is psychological. Most people experience anxiety when they find themselves in sharp disagreement with a group with whom they are intimately associated. Supreme Court Justices tend to be highly independent and individualistic men, but they may not be completely immune to this distaste for isolation. . . .

The strength of this tug toward agreement will vary according to the Justice's reliance on the Court as a reference group, and this reliance in turn will largely be a function of the personal and professional esteem in which he holds his colleagues. Where another reference group, either outside the Court or in the minority on the Court, is equally or more important to the Justice than the Court majority and where his views are applauded by that other group, he is very likely be more persistent in asserting his views. Stone's reference group* of law school professors such as John Bassett Moore, Edward Borchard, Thomas Reed Powell, Herman Oliphant, Karl Llewellyn, and Felix Frankfurter made it easier for him to maintain his position in the old Court, as did his friendship with Holmes and Brandeis and later Cardozo.

By recognizing the existence of this tug toward agreement and the factors which affect it, a Justice might be better able to control it in himself and able to use it to his advantage. Where a Justice is one of a minority group on the Court, his friends in academic life—and many Justices have had close ties with major universities, either through their previous careers or their law clerks—might build themselves into a reference group for the minority by writing encouraging letters and publishing laudatory articles about the minority's work. When the Justice is in the majority he might further isolate the minority by having his friends write critical articles, or he might try to cut the minority off from access to their academic connections.[35] More simply, where he thought the Court was the other Justices' reference group, he might stress loyalty to the Court as an institution and the implications of isolation from the majority, as Frankfurter did with Murphy in *Hirabayashi.*

On the other hand, there are factors which push the majority Justices, especially the opinion writer, to accept accommodation. An eloquent, tightly-reasoned dissent can be an upsetting force. Stone's separate opinions during the thirties pointed up more sharply the folly of the conservative Justices than did any of the attacks on the Court by elected politicians. The majority may thus find it profitable to mute criticism from within the Court by giving in on some issues. The Justice who has been assigned the task of writing the opinion of the Court may see himself as a broker adjusting the interests of his associates as well as of himself. His problems, of course, are dynamic rather than static. By making a change in an opinion to pick up one vote he may lose another. Moreover, by compromising and incorporating several different lines of reasoning in his opinion he may expose himself to even more damaging dissent. . . .

Most important, a Justice would want to avoid having to water down his policy to the point where it ceased to be an operational doctrine—though it is possible that emasculation may be the only alternative to an outright rejection of his policy by the major-

* The term "reference persons" might be equally appropriate here.

ity. As Stone wrote a colleague about the draft opinion in *Hirabayashi:* "I am anxious as far as I reasonably can to meet the views of my associates, but it seems to me that if I accepted your suggestions very little of the structure of my opinion would be left, and that I should lose most of my adherents. It seems to me, therefore, that it would be wiser for me to stand by the substance of my opinion and for you to express your views in your concurrence as you have already done."[36]

The opinion writer can apply some sort of marginal analysis to the alternatives he confronts. His minimum need—his essential need—is for four additional votes if he is to speak with the institutional authority of the Court. Thus, given the high value of these first four votes, he should rationally be willing to pay a relatively high price in accommodation to secure them. Once majority acquiescence has been obtained, the marginal value of any additional vote declines perceptibly, as would the price which an opinion writer should be willing to pay. However, the marginal value of another vote is never zero, though the asking price may exceed its real value and may have to be rejected. In the judicial process a 5–4 decision emphasizes the strength of the losing side and may encourage resistance and evasion. The greater the majority, the greater the appearance of certainty and the more likely a decision will be accepted and followed in similar cases. One hesitates to imagine how much more difficult implementation of the school segregation decisions would be had there been a four or three or even a two judge minority willing to claim in public that "separate but equal" was a valid constitutional doctrine.

A further bargaining complication may arise when a Justice who at first noted his dissent is persuaded that the majority is right, and, like many converts, is willing to take a firmer stand than some of the original believers with whom the opinion writer has had to negotiate. Here the opinion writer faces a most delicate choice between publication of a more forceful assertion of the doctrine which he is advocating and potential alienation of one or more relatively lukewarm members of his coalition who may view strengthening the majority opinion as a breach of faith or at least cause for a separate statement of views.

There is also the question of with whom to bargain. If a Justice were in the minority and trying to lessen the damage the majority opinion would do to the chances of achieving his objective, the obvious person whom he would have to influence would be the Justice assigned the task of writing the opinion of the Court. It would not, however, always be necessary to approach the opinion writer directly. The minority Justice might exploit his social relations with a Justice who was also on close terms with the opinion writer and have that third Justice act as an intermediary. Then, too, if the opinion writer were handling a particularly controversial case or were the kind of person who put a very high value on unanimity, it might be most prudent for the minority Justice to wait to be approached rather than make the first overtures himself. The same sort of considerations would apply to a majority Justice who wished the Court to issue a stronger statement than he thought the opinion writer would draft.

If a Justice were in the minority and trying to pick up an extra vote to give the appearance of more solidity to his protest or to turn his minority into a majority, or if the author of the opinion of the Court were attempting to increase his majority, the obvious colleague to approach—again directly or through an intermediary—would be one who had expressed some uncertainty during or after conference or whose voting record indicated ambiguous commitments to the side with which he had actually voted. Having attended the conference and having talked probably with several colleagues in private, a Justice would normally have a good idea of who might be wavering. . . .

The writer of the majority opinion who wished to squelch a dissent might also have the option of contacting the dissenter directly or working through an intermediary or, if he strongly suspected that the dissent was being circulated merely for bargaining purposes, of sitting back and waiting to be approached. Probably the most ticklish situation, from the point of view of interpersonal relations, in which a Justice might find himself is when he is with the majority but not writing the majority opinion, and he fears that the opinion writer is about to win over a dissenter by conceding more than the value of the additional vote. Under such circumstances, a Justice would have to proceed most cautiously in order to avoid the twin perils of appearing to be a busybody interfering at every stage of the negotiations and at the other extreme of sulking behind the threat of writing a separate concurrence. Either course might annoy the opinion writer to the extent that he would give up the chance of having that Justice's vote and make even greater concessions to win the former dissenter.

* * *

Co-option

It would be much easier for a Justice to vote and join in opinions with a judge whose policy goals were identical or very similar to his own* than with a colleague with contrary aims. It is possible, under the sort of favorable political circumstances discussed earlier . . . for a policy-oriented Justice to exert influence in the executive process and to have a voice in choosing a new colleague, a colleague who, hopefully, will agree with him on decisions and opinions important to his policy goals. Gratitude, especially if it were coupled with deep intellectual respect, might play a role in increasing the helping Justice's influence with the new appointee, but its role would probably be minor. As Presidents have often painfully learned, gratitude is usually a weak emotion in judges who have what amounts to life tenure. Although gratitude might make social relations easier, certainly it would not be comparable in effect to a basic agreement on policy.

Many members of the Court have become embroiled in appointment politicking. Miller,[37] Fuller,[38] and Brown[39] tried it with varying degrees of success, but the most systematic efforts along these lines were made by William Howard Taft.[40] Probably no judge ever came to the bench with a clearer conception of the "proper" role of the individual Justice within the Court or the "proper" role of the Court in the American political system than Taft. "Teamwork" was the Chief Justice's overriding value in

* This relationship might not constitute influence in any formal sense of the term, but by definition the policy-oriented Justice would prefer efficient achievement of his policy objective over merely increasing his personal influence, since the first would be the end and the second only a means.

intra-Court relations, and he saw the protection of property rights through the Fifth and Fourteenth Amendments as the Court's principal task.

Since Harding had promised Sutherland the first place on the Court, Taft had little to do with the former Senator's appointment—except perhaps in a negative way in that both Taft and Sutherland had been candidates for the chief justiceship. The center chair had been Taft's avowed lifelong ambition, and Sutherland, so Harding said, was "crazy" for the office.[41] Taft gave a broad hint about his alert interest in the appointing process when, after his own selection, he wrote a gracious letter to George Sutherland expressing the hope that Sutherland would soon join him on the bench. "Our views," the new Chief Justice noted, "are very much alike and it is important that they prevail."[42]

When Justice Day retired, Taft, knowing that Harding was not committed to any candidate, began to work feverishly to find a suitable nominee. After failing to interest John W. Davis, the Chief Justice and Van Devanter decided that "Pierce Butler is our man." Taft then opened an intensive campaign to bring off the nomination. He called on the President and wrote him several letters lavishly praising Butler and criticizing other candidates. The Chief Justice also carried on a lengthy correspondence with Butler, giving him news on events in Washington and plying him with advice on how to advance his cause. Taft's suggestions included not only the best way for Butler to deploy his political assets but also how to exploit his religious assets as well. The Chief Justice believed that Harding wanted to appoint a Catholic (Justice McKenna was expected to retire soon); Taft also knew that Archbishop Hayes of New York was pushing Judge Martin Manton of the United States Circuit Court of Appeals for the Second Circuit. To counter this activity, Taft urged Butler to line up the Catholic hierarchy in the Middle West. Butler protested that he abhorred the thought of involving clergymen in politics, but he did supply the names of one cardinal, two archbishops, and three bishops, plus the bishops in the archdiocese of St. Paul, with whom Harding could consult.

After Harding nominated Butler, the Chief Justice switched his attention to the Senate and once again gave Butler detailed advice on which senators were important and how they might be approached. Taft talked with his own friends on Capitol Hill and arranged a quick judiciary committee meeting to approve the nomination.

* * *

When McKenna retired—also with Taft's assistance, this time in the form of a positive suggestion to the Justice that he was too infirm to perform his duties in a satisfactory manner[43]—the Chief Justice once more took part in choosing a colleague. He visited Coolidge and claimed to have "rather forced" the President to appoint Stone.[44] Fourteen years later, when Stone heard of Taft's statement, he said he doubted that Taft had been influential with Coolidge or that Coolidge had needed anyone to recommend his Attorney General to him.[45] Taft, however, persisted in asserting responsibility for Stone's selection, even after he became convinced that he had made a serious error in the choice.[46]

Stone, in turn, played a major part in Cardozo's nomination. Taking advantage of his close relationship with Hoover, Stone introduced Cardozo to the President. As Stone recalled the incident, "I seized the opportunity to make the President acquainted with the kind of a judge he ought to appoint and prefaced the call by expatiating on that topic at some length."[47] On several later occasions Stone reminded Hoover of Cardozo's fitness[48] and strongly recommended him when Holmes retired. Hoover, however, wavered, fearing to offend the Senate by having three New York men (Stone and Hughes were also from New York) and two Jews (Brandeis was still on the bench) on the Court.

Stone then took a bold course of action:[49]

> I was apprehensive lest a selection should be made which would emphasize the Court's conservative tendencies, and feeling that they were already over-emphasized, I feared that great harm might result and that some sort of an explosion would occur not unlike that which actually took place after the decisions in the *A.A.A.* case and the *Tipaldo Women's Wage* case. In a conversation with President Hoover intended to emphasize both the importance of the appointment and Judge Cardozo's fitness I intimated to him that if he feared criticism because of the addition of a New York man to the Court when there were two other New Yorkers already there, I would be willing to retire from the Court. Later, in conversation with Senator Wagner, who was then about to discuss the matter with President Hoover, I made the same suggestion.

It is impossible to determine whether Stone was merely trying to put additional pressure on Hoover or was really tired of the frustrations of judicial work.[50] Other men and forces were also at work in the appointment and Stone never claimed full—or even much—credit, though when the nomination was announced Frankfurter wired him: "The country is your debtor for your decisive help in achieving a great national good."[51]

* * *

Some judicial efforts have been successful, others may not have been. . . . Some Justices, like Taft or Stone or perhaps Butler, have been in an excellent position to influence appointments; other Justices have not. But, since most members of the Court come to the bench only after extensive political experience,[52] the average Justice must be aware of the informal as well as the formal channels through which influence can be exerted. Most important, it is quite clear that if a Justice wishes to enter the appointing process—and is able to do so—he can make ideology a prime factor in determining who will receive his support.

Although many Justices are in a position where they can affect appointments, it does not necessarily follow that any particular Justice will always, often, or even ever have a voice in the selection of other members of the Court. Nor does it mean that those Justices who can exert influence will choose to do so. There are dangers in participating in the political processes, and a judge may reasonably conclude in many situations that, all questions of ethics aside, the risk of high costs in possible requests for a *quid pro quo* from executive officials is not worth the benefit that may be derived.[53] This sort of assessment is especially likely to occur when the Justice has good reason to believe that the administration will select the "right" kind of man without assistance from the bench.

* It should be noted that Justice Frankfurter later changed his mind. In a letter to me of Sept. 27, 1961, he stated that he had come to believe that the "decisive help" had been supplied by Senators Borah and Watson.

NOTES

1. The literature on influence is vast. Among the works which I have found most helpful are: Fritz Heider, *The Psychology of Interpersonal Relations* (New York: John Wiley & Sons, Inc., 1958); Sidney Verba, *Small Groups and Political Behavior:*

A Study of Leadership (Princeton: Princeton University Press, 1961); Robert F. Bales, *Interaction Process Analysis* (Cambridge, Mass.: Addison-Wesley Press, 1950); George C. Homans, *The Human Group* (New York: Harcourt, Brace & World, 1950); Bernard Bass, *Leadership, Psychology, and Organizational Behavior* (New York: Harper & Bros., 1960); Paul Hare, E. F. Borgatta, and R. Bales (eds.), *Small Groups: Studies in Social Interaction* (New York: A. A. Knopf, 1955); and David Danelski, "The Influence of the Chief Justice in the Decisional Process of the Supreme Court" (paper delivered to the 1960 meeting of the American Political Science Association), a shorter version of this paper appears in Walter F. Murphy and C. Herman Pritchett, *Courts, Judges, and Politics* (New York: Random House, 1961), pp. 497–508.

2. Albert Pepitone, "Motivational Effects in Social Perception," 3 *Hum. Rels.* 57, 71–75 (1950).
3. Quoted in Donald Morgan, *Justice William Johnson* (Columbia: University of South Carolina Press, 1954), pp. 181–82.
4. It is interesting to observe that not only in their memoranda to one another but also in conference, the Justices argue in terms of such categories as "intent of the framers," the meaning of legislative history or previous Court decisions as well as in terms of the policy implications of possible decisions. This evidence indicates, of course, that the real process of judicial policy-making is a very subtle business, that judges often think largely in traditional legal categories, though their behavior may actually be more accurately described under different concepts.
5. Memorandum of Taft to the other Justices, May 12, 1922, Taft Papers. The memorandum was addressed to all members of the Court except John Clarke. Since the U.S. Reports do not note that Clarke did not participate, the omission was probably due to an oversight by the Chief Justice's secretary.
6. Box 4, West Virginia v. Barnette file, Frank Murphy Papers, Michigan Historical Collections, Ann Arbor, Mich. The Murphy Papers used in this [essay] are arranged in boxes by terms of the Court, with each case having a separate file or set of files. The Taft Papers are arranged chronologically, with no topical order whatever. The Stone Papers are arranged in several different ways. Some correspondence is contained in files organized according to person; other correspondence and slip opinions are filed according to term; and some files are arranged by subject matter.
7. Frankfurter to Murphy, June 5, 1943, Box 4, Hirabayashi file, Murphy Papers.
8. Draft opinion, *ibid.*
9. June 10, 1943, *ibid.*
10. Box 4, Ex parte Quirin file, Murphy Papers. Although this memorandum was initialed and the style is unmistakable, I think the Justice who wrote it would prefer to remain anonymous.
11. Stone to Roger Nelson, Nov. 30, 1942, Stone Papers. Alpheus T. Mason, *Harlan Fiske Stone: Pillar of the Law* (New York: Viking Press, 1956), chap. xxxix, presents a detailed account of the way the case was handled.
12. Hughes to Frankfurter, Jan. 18, 1939, Charles Evans Hughes Papers, Library of Congress.
13. Yazoo & Miss. V. Rr. v. Clarksdale (1921); quoted in David Danelski, "The Chief Justice and the Supreme Court" (Ph.D. diss., University of Chicago, 1961), p. 179.
14. Quoted in Merlo Pusey, *Charles Evans Hughes* (New York: Macmillan Co., 1951) II, 671.
15. Institutional Investors v. Chi., Milwaukee, St. Paul & Pac. Rr. (1943).
16. Feb. 20, 1943, Stone Papers.
17. The note is dated only "Friday." From its place in the Stone Papers, I judge the year to be 1940.
18. The Malcomb Baxter (1928), Stone Papers. The final decision was unanimous.
19. Professor Glendon Schubert has been exploring the relevance of game theory to certiorari decisions. See his *Quantitative Analysis of Judicial Behavior* (New York: Free Press of Glencoe, 1959) and "Policy without Law: An Extension of the Certiorari Game," 14 *Stan. L. Rev.* 284 (1962).
20. Quoted in Mason, *op. cit.*, p. 254.
21. Few of Stone's early opinions escaped criticism from McReynolds, criticism of a kind which can best be described as "picky." In McReynolds' defense, however, it should be said that he believed—though he was not always able to translate his belief into

practice—that a judicial opinion should say no more than was absolutely necessary to decide a specific case. "When a judge fully appreciates that every unnecessary word in an opinion hurts it, he may be relied upon to write with good effect. But when vanity, or an itch to throw off new and striking phrases and shine in the books, troubles him, his outgivings are apt to be noxious." McReynolds to Judge Hollzer, Aug. 31, 1933, James C. McReynolds Papers, Alderman Library, University of Virginia. McReynolds felt (quite correctly) that Stone often put more into his opinions than the cases demanded. . . .

22. The story is told in Willard L. King, *Melville Weston Fuller* (New York: Macmillan Co., 1950), pp. 185–86.
23. For an account sympathetic to Jackson, read Eugene Gerhart, *America's Advocate: Robert H. Jackson* (Indianapolis: Bobbs Merrill, Inc., 1958), chap. xv; for an account sympathetic to Black, see John P. Frank, *Mr. Justice Black: The Man and His Opinions* (New York: A. A. Knopf, 1948), chap. vii.
24. This memorandum is filed in the Stone Papers. I would suspect that, as with the Quirin memorandum cited in note 10, the Justice would prefer to remain anonymous. Moreover, unlike the Quirin memorandum, this one is not initialed, so it may not have been written by the purported author.
25. See generally, Robert A. Dahl and Charles Lindblom, *Politics, Economics, and Welfare* (New York: Harper & Bros., 1953), chap. xii.
26. The concept of tacit bargaining is ably developed in Thomas Schelling, *The Strategy of Conflict* (Cambridge, Mass.: Harvard University Press, 1960), chap. i.
27. Quoted in Alexander Bickel, *Unpublished Opinions of Mr. Justice Brandeis* (Cambridge, Mass.: Belknap Press of Harvard University Press, 1957), p. 18.
28. Quoted in Charles Fairman, *Mr. Justice Miller and the Supreme Court 1862–1890* (Cambridge, Mass.: Harvard University Press, 1939), p. 320.
29. Jan. 20, 1941, Stone Papers.
30. Ogden v. Saunders (1827).
31. B. N. Cardozo, "Law and Literature," 14 *Yale Rev.* 699, 715–16 (1925). Charles Evans Hughes made much the same comment in his book *The Supreme Court of the United States* (New York: Columbia University Press, 1928), p. 68.
32. Feb. 15, 1947, Box 8, Harris file, Murphy Papers.
33. Quoted in Morgan, *Justice William Johnson*, p. 182.
34. Feb. 4, 1935, Stone Papers.
35. Taft thought that Brandeis was supported by a "claque" of liberal professors who wrote for law reviews. Taft to W. L. Phelps, May 30, 1927, Taft Papers. More recently, other Justices have sometimes been alleged to have used their law-school connections to reward friends and punish enemies, or at least to carry on a fight from the conference room or the pages of the U.S. Reports to the pages of law reviews.
36. Stone to Douglas, June 9, 1943, Stone Papers.
37. Fairman, *op. cit.*, pp. 349–68, 370–71, 381, 429.
38. King, *op. cit.*, pp. 180–81.
39. *Ibid.*
40. For studies of Taft's activities in the appointing process and the criteria which he applied, see my "In His Own Image," *1961 Supreme Court Review* 159; and "Chief Justice Taft and the Lower Court Bureaucracy," 24 *J. of Pols.* 453 (1962). David Danelski, *A Supreme Court Justice Is Appointed* (New York: Random House, 1964), has an intricately detailed examination of the appointment of Pierce Butler.
41. Taft's old friend and former White House Press Secretary, Gus Karger, wrote Taft that Harding had told him this. Karger to Taft, May 25, 1921, Taft Papers.
42. Taft to Sutherland, July 2, 1921, George Sutherland Papers, Library of Congress.
43. Taft left a remarkable memorandum describing the background to and the actual discussion with McKenna about his resignation; see my "In His Own Image," *loc. cit.*
44. Taft to Robert A. Taft, July 2, 1925, Taft Papers.
45. See Mason, *Harlan Fiske Stone*, p. 184.
46. Taft to Horace Taft, June 8, 1928, Taft Papers.
47. Stone to G. Helman, May 29, 1939, Stone Papers.
48. Stone to B. Shein, Feb. 3, 1942, *ibid.* As other possibilities Stone also mentioned Newton D. Baker and Learned Hand. Stone to R. Hale, Feb. 15, 1932, *ibid.*

49. Stone to G. Helman, Nov. 30, 1939, *ibid.*
50. In 1939 Stone, disclaiming any altruism in offering to resign, said that he would not have been sorry to leave the Court because "I felt mine was a voice crying in the wilderness so far as the tendencies of the Court were concerned, and I had numerous opportunities to do worthwhile things." Stone to G. Helman, *ibid.* In 1929, less than three years before the Cardozo nomination, Stone faced no less opposition on the Court—indeed Hughes and Roberts were not as conservative as Taft and Sanford had been—but he turned down several opportunities to leave the bench for lucrative private practice as well as offers to become Secretary of State and head of the National Law Reform Committee. These persistent refusals do not appear to indicate an anxiousness to throw off the cares of the Court. On the other hand, Stone had ambitions to become Chief Justice and his name had been frequently mentioned as Taft's successor. Hughes's appointment to the center chair may well have dampened Stone's enthusiasm for judicial work.
51. Feb. 15, 1932, *ibid.*
52. John Schmidhauser, "The Justices of the Supreme Court: A Collective Portrait," 3 *Midw. J. of Pol. Sci.* 1 (1959).
53. Taft, for instance, was asked several favors by politicians whose aid he had sought. See my "In His Own Image," *loc. cit.*

50

The Influence of the Chief Justice in the Decisional Process

DAVID J. DANELSKI

In the following selection, David J. Danelski reports on the Chief Justice's limited formal powers, such as the initial presentation of each case for consideration and the assignment of the opinion. Danelski's more important contribution, however, is his description of the influence that the Chief Justice possesses if he is able to combine his formal powers with informal task and social leadership. The effectiveness of the Supreme Court as a policy-making body depends in substantial measure on the Chief Justice's ability to perform these leadership roles or upon their exercise by some other member of the Court. When the Chief Justice fails, the Court may be greatly hindered in meeting its caseload and badly divided in its decisions, as during the term of Chief Justice Harlan F. Stone.

Because this essay describes the influence of the Chief Justice in decision making within the Supreme Court, it should be regarded as a companion piece to Walter F. Murphy's discussion of tactics on the Court.

Danelski, Professor of Government at Cornell University, has written numerous papers and articles on the Supreme Court. He has published A Supreme Court Justice Is Appointed *(1964) and* Judicial Behavior *(forthcoming), and he is coeditor of* Comparative Judicial Behavior *(1969).*

The Chief Justice of the United States has a unique opportunity for leadership in the Supreme Court. He pre-

From *Courts, Judges and Politics,* edited by Walter F. Murphy and C. Herman Pritchett, pp. 497–508.

sides in open court and over the secret conferences where he usually presents each case to his associates, giving his opinion first and voting last. He assigns the Court's opinion in virtually all cases when he votes with the majority; and when the Court is divided, he is in a favorable position to seek unity. But his office does not guarantee leadership. His actual influence depends upon his esteem, ability, and personality and how he performs his various roles.

In Conference

The conference is the matrix of leadership in the Court.[1] The Court member who is able to present his views with force and clarity and defend them successfully is highly esteemed by his associates. When perplexing questions arise, they turn to him for guidance. He usually makes more suggestions than his colleagues, gives more opinions, and orients the discussion more frequently, emerging as the Court's task leader. In terms of personality, he is apt to be somewhat reserved; and, in concentrating on the decision of the Court, his response to the emotional needs of his associates is apt to be secondary.

Court members frequently disagree in conference and argue their positions with enthusiasm, seeking to persuade their opponents and the undecided brethren. And always, when the discussion ends, the vote declares the victor. All of this gives rise to antagonism and tension, which, if allowed to get out of hand, would make intelligent, orderly decision of cases virtually impossible. However, the negative aspects of conference interaction are more or less counterbalanced by activity which relieves tension, shows solidarity, and makes for agreement. One Court member usually performs more such activity than the others. He invites opinions and suggestions. He attends to the emotional needs of his associates by affirming their value as individuals and as Court members, especially when their views are rejected by the majority. Ordinarily he is the best-liked member of the Court and emerges as its social leader. While the task leader concentrates on the Court's decision, the social leader concentrates on keeping the Court socially cohesive. In terms of personality, he is apt to be warm, receptive, and responsive. Being liked by his associates is ordinarily quite important to him; he is also apt to dislike conflict.

As presiding officer of the conference, the Chief Justice is in a favorable position to assert task and social leadership. His presentation of cases is an important task function. His control of the conference's process makes it easy for him to invite suggestions and opinions, seek compromises, and cut off debate which appears to be getting out of hand, all important social functions.

It is thus possible for the Chief Justice to emerge as both task and social leader of the conference. This, however, requires the possession of a rare combination of qualities plus adroit use of them. Normally, one would expect the functions of task and social leadership to be performed by at least two Court members, one of whom might or might not be the Chief Justice. As far as the Chief Justice is concerned, the following leadership situations are possible:

	Task Leadership	*Social Leadership*
I	+	+
II	−	+
III	+	−
IV	−	−

In situation I, the Chief Justice is a "great man" leader, performing both leadership functions. The consequences of such leadership, stated as hypotheses, are: (1) conflict tends to be minimal; (2) social cohesion tends to increase; (3) satisfaction with the conference tends to increase; (4) production, in terms of number of decisions for the time spent, tends to increase. The consequences in situations II and III are the same as in I, particularly if the Chief Justice works in coalition with the associate justice performing complementary leadership functions. However, in situation IV, unless the task and social functions are adequately performed by associate justices, consequences opposite to those in situations I, II, and III tend to occur....

Situation II prevailed in the Taft Court (1921–1930): Chief Justice Taft was social leader, and his good friend and appointee, Justice Van Devanter, was task leader. Evidence of Van Devanter's esteem and task leadership is abundant. Taft, for example, frequently asserted that Van Devanter was the ablest member of the Court. If the Court were to vote, he said, that would be its judgment too. The Chief Justice admitted that he did not know how he could get along without Van Devanter in conference, for Van Devanter kept the Court consistent with itself, and "his power of statement and his immense memory make him an antagonist in conference who generally wins against all opposition." At times, Van Devanter's ability actually embarrassed the Chief Justice, and he wondered if it might not be better to have Van Devanter run the conference himself. "Still," said Taft, "I must worry along until the end of my ten years, content to aid in the deliberation when there is a difference of opinion." In other words, Taft was content to perform the social functions of leadership. And he did this well. His humor soothed over the rough spots in conference. "We are very happy with the present Chief," said Holmes in 1922. "He is good-humored, laughs readily, not quite rapid enough, but keeps things moving pleasantly."

Situation I prevailed in the Hughes Court (1930–1941): task and social leadership were combined in Chief Justice Hughes. He was the most esteemed member of his Court. This was due primarily to his performance in conference. Blessed with a photographic memory, he would summarize comprehensively and accurately the facts and issues in each case he presented. When he finished, he would look up and say with a smile: "Now I will state where I come out." Then he would outline his views as to how the case should be decided. Sometimes that is all the discussion a case received, and the justices proceeded to vote for the disposition suggested by the Chief. Where there was discussion, the other Court members gave their views in order of seniority without interruption, stating why they concurred or dissented from the views of the Chief Justice. After they had their say, Hughes would review the discussion, pointing out his agreement and disagreement with the views expressed. Then he would call for a vote.

As to the social side of Hughes' leadership, there is the testimony of Justice Roberts: never in the eleven years Roberts sat with Hughes in conference did he see him lose his temper. Never did he hear him pass a personal remark or even raise his voice. Never did he witness him interrupting or engaging in controversy with an associate. Despite Hughes' popular image of austerity, several of his associates have said that he had a keen sense of humor which aided in keeping differences in conference from becoming discord. Moreover, when discussion showed signs of deteriorating into wrangling, Hughes would cut it off. On the whole, he was well-liked. Justice Roberts said: "Men whose views were as sharply opposed as those of Van Devanter and Brandeis, or those of Sutherland and Cardozo, were at one in their admiration and affectionate regard for their presiding officer." Roberts could have well added Justices Holmes, Black, Reed, Frankfurter, Douglas, McReynolds, and perhaps others.

Situation IV prevailed during most of Stone's Chief Justiceship (1941–1946). When Stone was promoted to the center chair, Augustus Hand indicated in a letter to Hughes that Stone did not seem a sure bet as task leader because of "a certain inability to express himself orally and maintain a position in a discussion." Hand proved to be correct. Stone departed from the conference role cut out by Hughes. When he presented cases, he lacked the apparent certitude of his predecessor; and, at times, his statement indicated that he was still groping for a solution. In that posture, cases were passed on to his associates for discussion. Court members spoke out of turn, and Stone did little to control their debate. Instead, according to Justice Reed, he would join in the debate with alacrity, "delighted to take on all comers around the conference table." "Jackson," he would say, "that's damned nonsense." "Douglas, *you* know better than that."

In other words, Stone was still acting like an associate justice. Since he did not assume the Chief Justice's conference role as performed by Hughes, task leadership began to slip from his grasp. Eventually, Justice Black emerged as the leading contender for task leadership. Stone esteemed Black, but distrusted his unorthodox approach; thus no coalition occurred as in the Taft Court. Justices Douglas, Murphy, Rutledge, and, to a lesser degree, Reed acknowledged Black's leadership which he was able to reinforce by generally speaking before them in conference. Justices Roberts, Frankfurter, and Jackson, however, either looked to Stone for leadership or competed for it themselves.

The constant vying for task leadership in the Stone conference led to serious conflict, ruffled tempers, severe tension, and antagonism. A social leader was badly needed. Stone was well-liked by his associates and could have performed this function well, but he did not. He did not use his control over the conference process to cut off debates leading to irreconcilable conflict. He did not remain neutral when controversies arose so that he could later mediate them. As his biographer, Alpheus T. Mason, wrote: "He was totally unprepared to cope with the petty bickering and personal conflict in which his Court became engulfed." At times, when conference discussion became extremely heated, Justice Murphy suggested that further consideration of certain cases be postponed. Undoubtedly others also performed social functions of leadership, but in this regard, Stone was a failure.

A consideration of the personalities of the task and social leaders on the Court from 1921 to 1946 is revealing. Of his friend, task leader Van Devanter, William D. Mitchell said: "Many thought him unusually austere, but he was not so with his friends. He was dignified and reserved." Of task leader Black, his former law clerk, John P. Frank, wrote: "Black has firm personal dignity and reserve.... [He] is a very, very tough man. When he is convinced, he is cool hard steel. . . . His temper is usually in close control, but he fights, and his words may occasionally have a terrible edge. He can be a rough man in an argument." On the other hand, social leader Taft was a warm, genial, responsive person who disliked conflict of any kind. Stone had a similar personality. He, too, according to Justice Jackson, "dreaded conflict." Hughes' personality contained elements conducive to both task and social leadership. He was "an intense man," said Justice Roberts; when he was engrossed in the work of the Court, "he had not time for lightness and pleasantry." Nonetheless, added Roberts, Hughes' relations with "his brethren were genial and cordial. He was considerate, sympathetic, and responsive."

The consequences of the various Court leadership configurations from 1921 to 1946 may be summarized as follows:

	Taft (II)	*Hughes (I)*	*Stone (IV)*
Conflict	Present but friendly.	Present but bridled by CJ.	Considerable; unbridled and at times unfriendly.
Cohesion	Good; teamwork and compromise.	Fair; surface personal cordiality; less teamwork than in Taft Court.	Poor; least cohesion in 25-year period; personal feuds in the Court.
Satisfaction	Considerable.	Mixed; Stone dissatisfied prior to 1938; Frankfurter, Roberts, and others highly satisfied.	Least in 25-year period; unrelieved tension and antagonism.
Production	Fair; usually one four- to five-hour conference a week with some items carried over.	Good; usually one conference a week.	Poor; frequently more than one conference a week; sometimes three and even four.

Except in production, the Taft Court fared better than the Courts under his two successors. The consequences of leadership in the Stone Court were predictable from the hypotheses, but Hughes' "great man" leadership should have produced consequences more closely approximating those in the Taft Court. The difference in conflict, cohesion, and satisfaction in the two Courts can be perhaps attributed to the fact that Taft was a better social leader than Hughes.

Opinion Assignment

The Chief Justice's power to assign opinions is significant because his designation of the Court's spokesman may be instrumental in:

(1) Determining the value of a decision as a precedent, for the grounds of a decision frequently depend upon the justice assigned the opinion.
(2) Making a decision as acceptable as possible to the public.
(3) Holding the Chief Justice's majority together when the conference vote is close.
(4) Persuading dissenting associates to join in the Court's opinion.

The Chief Justice has maximal control over an opinion when he assigns it to himself; undoubtedly Chief Justices have retained many important cases for that reason. The Chief Justice's retention of "big cases" is generally accepted by his associates. In fact, they expect him to speak for the Court in those cases so that he may lend the prestige of his office to the Court's pronouncement.

When the Chief Justice does not speak for the Court, his influence lies primarily in his assignment of important cases to associates who generally agree with him. From 1925 to 1930, Taft designated his fellow conservatives, Sutherland and Butler, to speak for the Court in about half of the important constitutional cases[2] assigned to associate justices. From 1932 to 1937, Hughes, who agreed more with Roberts, Van Devanter, and Sutherland than the rest of his associates during this period, assigned 44 per cent of the important constitutional cases to Roberts and Sutherland. From 1943 to 1945, Stone assigned 55.5 per cent of those cases to Douglas and Frankfurter. During that period, only Reed agreed more with Stone than Frankfurter, but Douglas agreed with Stone less than any other justice except Black. Stone had high regard for Douglas' ability, and this may have been the Chief Justice's overriding consideration in making these assignments.

It is possible that the Chief Justice might seek to influence dissenting justices to join in the Court's opinion by adhering to one or both of the following rules:

Rule 1: Assign the case to the justice whose views are the closest to the dissenters on the ground that his opinion would take a middle approach upon which both majority and minority could agree.

Rule 2: Where there are blocs on the Court and a bloc splits, assign the opinion to a majority member of the dissenters' bloc on the grounds that (a) he would take a middle approach upon which both majority and minority could agree and (b) the minority justices would be more likely to agree with him because of general mutuality of agreement.

There is some evidence that early in Taft's Chief Justiceship he followed Rule 1 occasionally and assigned himself cases in an effort to win over dissenters. An analysis of his assignments from 1925 to 1930, however, indicates that he apparently did not adhere to either of the rules with any consistency. The same is true for Stone's assignments from 1943 to 1945. In other words, Taft and Stone did not generally use their assignment power to influence their associates to unanimity. However, an analysis of Hughes' assignments from 1932 to 1937 indicates that he probably did. He appears to have followed Rule 1 when either the liberal or conservative blocs dissented intact. When the liberal bloc dissented, Roberts, who was then a center judge, was assigned 46 per cent of the opinions. The remaining 54 per cent were divided among the conservatives, apparently according to their degree of conservatism: Sutherland, 25 per cent; Butler, 18 per cent; McReynolds, 11 per cent. When the conservative bloc dissented,

Hughes divided 63 per cent of those cases between himself and Roberts.

Hughes probably also followed Rule 2. When the left bloc split, Brandeis was assigned 22 per cent of the cases he could have received compared with his 10 per cent average for unanimous cases. When the right bloc split, Sutherland was assigned 16 per cent of the decisions he could have received compared with his 11 per cent average for unanimous cases. He received five of the six cases assigned the conservatives when their bloc split.

Of course, there are other considerations underlying opinion assignment by the Chief Justice, such as equality of distribution, ability, and expertise. It should be noted that opinion assignment may also be a function of social leadership.

Uniting the Court

One of the Chief Justice's most important roles is that of Court unifier. Seldom has a Chief Justice had a more definite conception of that role than Taft. His aim was unanimity, but he was willing to admit that at times dissents were justifiable and perhaps even a duty. Dissents were proper, he thought, in cases where a Court member strongly believed the majority erred in a matter involving important principle or where a dissent might serve some useful purpose, such as convincing Congress to pass certain legislation. But, in other cases, he believed a justice should be a good member of the team, silently acquiesce in the views of the majority, and not try to make a record for himself by dissenting.

Since Taft's conception of the function of the dissent was shared by most of his associates, his efforts toward unity were well received. Justices joining the Taft Court were indoctrinated in the "no dissent unless absolutely necessary" tradition, most of them learning it well. Justice Butler gave it classic expression on the back of one colleague's opinions in 1928:

> I voted to reverse. While this sustains your conclusion to affirm, I still think reversal would be better. But I shall in silence acquiesce. Dissents seldom aid in the right development or statement of the law. They often do harm. For myself I say: "lead us not into temptation."

Hughes easily assumed the role of Court unifier which Taft cut out for him, for his views as to unanimity and dissent were essentially the same as Taft's. Believing that some cases were not worthy of dissent, he would join in the majority's disposition of them, though he initially voted the other way. For example, in a 1939 case involving statutory construction, he wrote to an associate: "I choke a little at swallowing your analysis, still I do not think it would serve any useful purpose to expose my views."

Like Taft, Hughes mediated differences of opinion between contending factions, and in order to get a unanimous decision, he would try to find common ground upon which all could stand. He was willing to modify his own opinions to hold or increase his majority; and if this meant he had to put in some disconnected thoughts or sentences, in they went. In cases assigned to others, he would readily suggest the addition or subtraction of a paragraph in order to save a dissent or a concurring opinion.

When Stone was an associate justice, he prized the right to dissent and occasionally rankled under the "no dissent unless absolutely necessary" tradition of the Taft and Hughes Courts. As Chief Justice, he did not believe it appropriate for him to dissuade Court members from dissenting in individual cases by persuasion or otherwise. A Chief Justice, he thought, might admonish his associates generally to exercise restraint in the matter of dissents and seek to find common ground for decision, but beyond that he should not go. And Stone usually went no further. His activity or lack of it in this regard gave rise to new expectations on the part of his associates as to their role and the role of the Chief Justice regarding unanimity and dissent. In the early 1940's, a new tradition of freedom of individual expression displaced the tradition of the Taft and Hughes Courts. This explains in part the unprecedented number of dissents and separate opinions during Stone's Chief Justiceship.

Nonetheless, Stone recognized that unanimity was desirable in certain cases. He patiently negotiated a unanimous decision in the Nazi Saboteurs case.[3] It should be pointed out, however, that this case was decided early in his Chief Justiceship before the new tradition was firmly established. By 1946, when he sought unanimity in the case of General Yamashita,[4] the new tradition of freedom was so well established that Stone not only failed to unite his Court, but the dissenters, Murphy and Rutledge, apparently resented his attempt to do so.

The unprecedented number of dissents and concurrences during Stone's Chief Justiceship can be only partly attributed to the displacing of the old tradition of loyalty to the Court's opinion. A major source of difficulty appears to have been the free-and-easy expression of views in conference. Whether the justices were sure of their grounds or not, they spoke up and many times took positions from which they could not easily retreat; given the heated debate which sometimes occurred in the Stone conference, the commitment was not simply intellectual. What began in conference frequently ended with elaborate justification as concurring or dissenting opinions in the United States Reports. This, plus Stone's passiveness in seeking to attain unanimity, is probably the best explanation for what Pritchett characterized as "the multiplication of division" in the Stone Court.

Conclusion

Interpersonal influence in the Supreme Court is an important aspect of the judicial process which has been given little attention. Of course, the "why" of the Court's decisions cannot be explained solely or even predominantly in those terms. Yet interpersonal influence is a variable worthy of consideration. Take, for example, the Court's about-face in the flag salute cases. With task leader Hughes presiding in 1940, not a single justice indicated in conference that he would dissent in the Gobitis[5] case. Subsequently, Stone registered a solo dissent, but such militant civil libertarians as Black, Douglas, and Murphy remained with Hughes. Only three years later, the Court reversed itself in the Barnette[6] case with Black, Douglas, and Murphy voting with Stone. One might seriously ask whether the presence of Hughes in the first case and not in the second had something to do with the switch. Much more work has to be done in this area, but it appears that in future analyses of the Court's work, task and social leadership will be useful concepts.

The importance of the Chief Justice's power to assign opinions is obvious. Equally if not more important is his role in unifying the Court. Taft's success in this regard greatly contributed to the Court's prestige, for unanimity reinforces the myth that the law is certain. In speaking of the Court in 1927, Hughes said that "no institution of our government stands higher in public confidence." As Court unifier, he sought to maintain that confidence after his appointment in 1930. That the Court's prestige is correlated with unanimity was demonstrated in Stone's Chief Justiceship: as dissent rose, the Court's prestige declined.

Thus the activity of the Chief Justice can be very significant in the judicial process. If he is the Court's task leader, he has great influence in the allocation of political values which are inevitably involved in many of the Court's decisions. More than any of his associates, his activity is apt to affect the Court's prestige; this is important, for ultimately the basis of the Court's power is its prestige.

NOTES

1. This study is based largely on private papers of members of the Supreme Court from 1921 to 1946. The theory of conference leadership is derived primarily from the work of Robert F. Bales. See his "Task Roles and Social Roles in Problem-Solving Groups" in Maccoby *et al.*, *Readings in Social Psychology* (New York, 1958), pp. 437–447.
2. "Important constitutional cases" were determined by examination of four recent leading works on the Constitution. If a case was discussed in any two of the works, it was considered an "important constitutional case."
3. *Ex parte Quirin* (1942).
4. *In re Yamashita* (1946).
5. *Minersville School District* v. *Gobitis* (1940).
6. *West Virginia* v. *Barnette* (1943). . . .

51

Government by Lawsuit

ROBERT H. JACKSON

In the following excerpts, Robert H. Jackson elegantly argues that the Supreme Court's role in national policy making is contrary to democratic principles, brings about disastrous policy decisions, and is marred by severe procedural shortcomings. Constitutional adjudication, he points out, tends to fix much more rigid limits on popular government than does statutory interpretation. Statutes can be rewritten if the Court mistakes the legislature's intention, but the Constitution can be changed only with great difficulty. Jackson does not say what checks should be imposed on the Court, however, or whether the Court should be deprived of the power of judicial review. He makes a compelling case against "government by lawsuit," but his prescription that the Court should only exercise the power of judicial review in "clear" cases seems a lame corrective.

Perhaps Jackson's most important contribution to the discussion of judicial review in a democracy is that he forcefully brings to the public's attention all the shortcomings of judicial policy making. Such knowledge can open the way for appropriate correctives (perhaps even the court-packing plan in 1937) at appropriate times. Ultimately, the Supreme Court cannot prevail against a sustained and determined public effort to curb its powers or reverse its policies.

Jackson served as Assistant Attorney General, Solicitor General, and Attorney General of the United States under Franklin D. Roosevelt. In the first position he was a prominent participant in the "court-packing" fight of 1937. His first book, The Struggle for Judicial Supremacy, *sharply attacks judicial policy making in the United States and points out its impact during the crisis of the 1930s.*

Jackson subsequently wrote The Case Against the Nazi War Criminals *(1946),* The Nürnberg Case, *(1947), and* The American Supreme Court *(1954). Appointed Associate Justice of the Supreme Court by President Roosevelt in 1945, he served on the Court until his death in 1954. Jackson was the chief American representative at the Nürnberg war trials.*

[I]

The long struggle between the Supreme Court and the Roosevelt administration is over. I have not recited the legal battles of that conflict for their own sakes. Each of the great cases of this period would merit a volume of its own. But from the aggregate experience there seem to me to emerge large questions that relate to the extent to which we are governed by judgments in lawsuit, the fitness of the judicial process for such a function, the restraint shown by the Court toward problems within its scope, and the very urgent necessity for improving the procedures of constitutional litigation.

We have seen a harassed government take a series of legislative actions to relieve economic depression and prevent social demoralization. For the questions I now raise it makes no difference whether one regards these measures separately or collectively as wise or unwise, and it makes no difference whether one regards any one or more of the decisions as correct.

A judgment in a lawsuit ended the N.R.A. experiment, and another ended the Agricultural Adjustment Act. One lawsuit killed railway pensions, another ended minimum wages, and another struck down municipal bankruptcy relief. Another lawsuit restored the right to minimum wages, railway pensions or municipal bankruptcy. Whether we might organize the soft coal industry, regulate labor relations, pay old-age benefits, regulate utility holding companies or have a system of unemployment insurance has depended in each instance on the outcome of a litigation. *This is government by lawsuit.*

These constitutional lawsuits are the stuff of power politics in America. Such proceedings may for a generation or more deprive an elected Congress of power, or may restore a lost power, or confirm a questioned one. Such proceedings may enlarge or restrict the authority of an elected President. They settle what power belongs to the Court itself and what it concedes to its "coordinate" departments. Decreases in litigation write the final word as to distribution of powers as between the Federal Government and the state governments and mark out and apply the limitations and denials of power constitutionally applicable to each. To recognize or to deny the power of governmental agencies in a changing world is to sit as a continuous allocator of power in our governmental system. The Court may be, and usually is, above party politics and personal politics, but the politics of power is a most important and delicate function, and adjudication of litigation is its technique.

Those who understand the characteristics and limitations of the con-

Abridged from *The Struggle for Judicial Supremacy* by Robert H. Jackson. Copyright 1941 and renewed 1969 by William E. Jackson and Mary Jackson Craighill. Reprinted by permission of Alfred A. Knopf, Inc.

ventional lawsuit technique recognize it as a very dubious instrument for the control of governmental policies. Not only are the effects and consequences of any given decision obscure to the masses of the people, but few lawyers follow the Court closely enough to sense its underlying trends and pressures. This alone makes it a somewhat irresponsible force in public affairs.

Judicial justice is well adapted to ensure that established legislative rules are fairly and equitably applied to individual cases. But it is inherently ill suited, and never can be suited, to devising or enacting rules of general social policy. Litigation procedures are clumsy and narrow, at best; technical and tricky, at their worst.

* * *

Let us examine the practical weakness in operation of the litigation technique when it is used to review far-flung economic and social conditions which vex modern government.

Government Policy Cannot Be Tested by Legal Doctrine Alone

Custom decrees that the Supreme Court shall be composed only of lawyers, though the Constitution does not say so. Those lawyers on the bench will hear only from lawyers at the bar. If the views of the scientist, the laborer, the business man, the social worker, the economist, the legislator, or the government executive reach the Court, it is only through the lawyer, in spite of the fact that the effect of the decision may be far greater in other fields than in jurisprudence. Thus government by lawsuit leads to a final decision guided by the learning and limited by the understanding of a single profession—the law.

It is no condemnation of that profession to doubt its capacity to furnish single-handed the rounded and comprehensive wisdom to govern all society. No more, indeed not nearly so much, would I entrust only doctors, or economists, or engineers, or educators, or theologians, to make a final review of our democratically adopted legislation. But we must not blink the fact that legal philosophy is but one branch of learning with peculiarities of its own and that judicial review of the reasonableness of legislation means the testing of the whole social process by the single standard—of men of the law.

The legal profession, like many another, tends to become over-professionalized. We forget that law is the rule for simple and untaught people to live by. We complicate and over-refine it as a weapon in legal combat until we take it off the ground where people live and into the thin atmosphere of sheer fiction. If you doubt this statement, listen to the Supreme Court session of May 29, 1939. Speaking of intangible rights, Mr. Justice Stone, in one case, declared:[1] "These are not in any sense *fictions*. They are indisputable realities,"* and added, "While *fictions* are sometimes invented in order to realize the judicial conception of justice, we cannot define the constitutional guaranty in terms of a *fiction* so unrelated to reality. . . ."*

On the same day, in a second case, Mr. Chief Justice Hughes said:[2] "I think that the decision in this case pushes the *fiction*. . . to an unwarranted extreme . . ." *

In presenting his views in a third case, Mr. Justice Reed said:[3] "It is not the substitution of a new *fiction* as

* Italics supplied.

to the mass of [choices] in action for the established *fiction* of a tax situs at the place of incorporation."*

Of course *fictions* played a more prominent part than usual in the pronouncements of that day, but lawyers and judges do think in terms of fictions quite as readily as in terms of realities.

These fictions tend to mischief whenever they are accepted as having a validity of their own apart from any purpose they serve. Of course the flexibility of the process and its capacity to do justice has often been achieved only by setting up a fiction as a bridge with the past in order to reach new ground. Thus, there may be preserved a measure of continuity while the law advances. John Doe and Richard Roe, those fictional gentlemen of the law, are men of straw where once they were flesh and blood, but they enable lawyers to use old forms and procedures to gain new ends. Fictions are often the hostages that the forces of movement give to the forces of position. But frequently lawyers' fictions serve no such useful purpose; too often they are employed as a screen to cover up a retreat. To regard a giant corporation, with its stockholders, directors and employees, as a single person is a useful and convenient fiction to enable the corporation to sue and be sued as simply as any individual; but to maintain that a worker dealing with his corporation is dealing with simply another individual like himself is to pervert a fiction as only a legal mind could do with solemnity.

When this process is carried too far in common law, legislative representatives of enfranchised men can correct the profession. Legislation rooted out the fictional doctrines about assumed risk and the acts of a fellow servant as factors in employers' liability and substituted the simple realism of workmen's compensation. The capricious capers of that "reasonably prudent man" who is the fictional standard of conduct in negligence trials is now creating a demand for automobile accident compensation. The doctrine of *caveat emptor*—let the buyer beware—became so unreal in modern marketing that it was set aside by legislation like the Securities Act.

But when such fictions as "freedom of contract" are introduced into the law of the Constitution to test the validity of legislation, the remedy is not so easy—it requires a constitutional amendment or a courageous and realistic Court to correct that.

In addition to resorting to fiction to explain facts where modern learning would resort to facts to clarify fictions, legal doctrine has another characteristic which sets it quite apart from all science and from most philosophy. Legal learning is largely built around the principle known as *stare decisis*. It means that on the same point of law yesterday's decision shall govern today's decision. Like a coral reef, the common law thus becomes a structure of fossils. Preparation for admission to the bar is largely a study of old authorities. At the bar, cases are won by finding in the maze of legal literature a controlling case or by distinguishing or discrediting the case found by an adversary. Precedents largely govern the conclusions and surround the reasoning of lawyers and judges. In the field of common law they are a force for stability and predictability, but in constitutional law they are the most powerful influence in forming and supporting reactionary opinions. The

* Italics supplied.

judge who can take refuge in a precedent does not need to justify his decision to the reason. He may "reluctantly feel himself bound" by a doctrine, supported by a respected historical name, that he would not be able to justify to contemporary opinion or under modern conditions.

Under this doctrine decisions made today become the guide and precedent by which future similar cases will be governed. So, when the Court announces a rule that strikes down a law, it not only binds the executive and judicial departments; it does far more than this. It binds *itself* and its *successors* and all inferior courts and future judges to decide similar cases by like logic. It not only limits the judgment of other judges, but, so long as the rule stands, it destroys the discretion even of the men who made it.

It was this paralyzing influence of the precedent that made the series of decisions outlawing New Deal experiments so serious. These decisions became precedents for limitations upon the power of all future Congresses. Their cumulative effect aroused apprehensions as to the ability of representative democracy to meet the future problems that beset its people in a day of change.

It was this process of whittling down by precedent that led Chief Justice Hughes, on behalf of himself and Justices Brandeis, Stone, and Cardozo, to protest in *Railroad Retirement Board* v. *Alton R. R. Co.*[4] He said: ". . . the majority finally raise a barrier against all legislative action of this nature by declaring that the subject matter itself lies beyond the reach of the congressional authority to regulate interstate commerce. . . . That is a conclusion of such serious and far-reaching importance that it overshadows all other questions raised by the Act. . . . I think that the conclusion thus reached is a departure from sound principles and places an unwarranted limitation upon the commerce clause of the Constitution."

This was a paraphrase by the Chief Justice of Portia's:

> " 'Twill be recorded for a precedent;
> And many an error, by the same
> example,
> Will rush into the state: it can not be."

Of course, such judicial misconstruction theoretically can be cured by constitutional amendment. But the period of gestation of a constitutional amendment, or of any law reform, is reckoned in decades usually; in years, at least. And, after all, as the Court itself asserted in overruling the minimum-wage cases, it may not be the Constitution that was at fault.

It is also true that the Court can limit its deference to precedent if it is composed of Justices who are so inclined. Mr. Justice Stone has said that the doctrine "has only a limited application in the field of constitutional law."[5]

Mr. Chief Justice Taney has said:[6] "I . . . am quite willing that it be regarded hereafter as the law of this court, that its opinion upon the construction of the Constitution is always open to discussion when it is supposed to have been founded in error, and that its judicial authority should hereafter depend altogether on the force of the reasoning by which it is supported."

Mr. Justice Brandeis on another occasion said:[7] "But in cases involving the Federal Constitution, where correction through legislative action is practically impossible, this Court has often overruled its earlier decisions. The Court bows to the lessons of experience and the force of better reasoning, recognizing that the process of trial and error, so fruitful in the physical sciences, is appropriate also in the judicial function."

But these were daring judges. Such are not always in a majority. And if, in the language of Justice Brandeis, the Court is to bow "to the lessons of experience and the force of better reasoning," may we ask whose experience? And whose reasoning? Can the lawyer qualify to speak for all society?

The Conventional "Case" or "Controversy" Procedure Is Inadequate to Collect, Summarize, and Interpret the Experience and Reason of Our Society

Justices generally are learned in the theories of the law—but they cannot know the conditions in every industry or the experiences in every social layer of our national life. No form of lawsuit has yet been devised suitable to inform them adequately, with judicial standards of proof, of the factors in our mass problems. To follow the effects of a minimum-wage policy, for example, through our business and social structure or to establish the effects of the Socal Security Act on the general welfare by legal testimony and exhibits would produce a mass that would be incomprehensible and exhausting.

The vice of the litigation process in broad constitutional questions is that since we cannot expand the lawsuit process to include an era, a people, and a continent, we simply cut down the problem to the scope of a lawsuit. The cases we have recited demonstrate how the broad and impersonal policy that moved Congress became subjected to the procedures of a very narrow, individual, and legalistic controversy.

The deficiencies of this lawsuit method appear clearly when we look to the make-up of the information that it provides for the judges.

Important constitutional decisions are sometimes rendered on a legal record consisting chiefly of two documents drawn by opposing lawyers. It may be an indictment and a demurrer, or it may be a bill of complaint and a motion to dismiss. These amount to little more than the conflicting and unsupported assertions of two attorneys. This really gives the Court little information apart from the situation of the party and the consequences to him of the act challenged. It personalizes the controversy. In some cases the Supreme Court has refused to decide constitutionality on such a basis and has returned the parties to the lower courts with an admonition to develop their facts.[8]

When it is attempted to prove broad assertions by legal evidence, the record usually becomes large and forbidding. Either it must contain a vast amount of testimony difficult to summarize and evaluate, or it must state agreed facts which each side thinks important. In the test of the Public Utility Holding Company Act this latter method condensed the factual background into two thousand printed pages. Records in bitterly contested cases run into lengths that defeat their very purpose. Justice Brandeis complained that the record and briefs in one rate case weighed sixty-seven pounds avoirdupois.[9]

Counsel appreciates the narrowness of the process when he begins to select the little part of the appropriate background that he can present in a "brief." At best, our presentation of economic and social backgrounds is elementary and amateurish—and generally apologetically relegated to an appendix. Most Justices have little time for supplemental reading. A few regard economic information as an "ostentatious parade of irrelevant statistics."[10]

Then comes the dramatic and decisive day of argument in the Supreme Court. No experience can be more challenging to the advocate. Counsel will have from one to four hours for argument, depending on the grace of the Court for anything more an hour. His own preparations will be superficial as compared with those of the men who have specialized in the theory or the administration of the questioned Act. But only a fraction, even of his own background knowledge, can be imparted to the Court. To select the materials and arguments that will carry conviction, to omit nothing necessary to the persuasion of any judge, to answer off-hand the doubts and questions from the bench in so grave a cause is a responsibility no lawyer ought to be required or allowed to assume. Constitutionality should not depend on an advocate's judgment, or want of it, in argument. The Justices' avenues of information should not be so restricted or so formalized.

Such a process is utterly inadequate to educate an uninformed judge or to overcome old convictions or predilections, or to win a conversion to a new viewpoint. Success in such an enterprise is apt to be accidental or the result of pre-determination. The judge goes to conference with too little except his predilections to guide his vote. Argument is likely to leave each judge just where it found him. The wonder is, not that our courts have lately been obliged frequently to confess error, but that the instances are so few. The limitations on the litigation procedure emphasize the unheeded wisdom given to the Supreme Court by James C. Carter, leader of the bar of his day, in arguing the constitutionality of the income tax:[11] "Nothing could be more unwise and dangerous—nothing more foreign to the spirit of the Constitution—than an attempt to baffle and defeat a popular determination by a judgment in a lawsuit."

Delay, Doubt, and Confusion

We have considered limitations inherent in legal procedures which make the lawsuit an unfit channel for exercise of political power, and which suggest that those who possess no other implements should scrupulously avoid judgments for which it is not adequate. But even if the precaution is faithfully observed, there remains a wide field in which our constitutional system requires interpretative adjudications.

Constitutional litigation is so important to the preservation of the equilibrium between departments of government, between state and nation, and between effective authority and individual liberty that no effort should be spared to make it modern, systematic, expeditious, and simple. That has not been done and the New Deal experience shows the points of weakness.

The district courts of the United States are not institutional in their proceedings so much as they are personal. Each such court is an individual, in fact, with a life tenure and independence of every other district court. The district judges, about one hundred seventy-five in number, include at all times a wide range of abilities, experiences, party affiliations and loyalties, local connections, and economic views and prejudices. A litigant may often exercise a good deal of choice as to the judge or judges who will first hear his challenge to an act of Congress. The lower court thus settled upon admits or excludes evidence, expedites or delays proceedings, finds the facts, makes the first decision on the law, and controls provisional and temporary remedies. But these lower court decisions have no finality as to the law. The lawyers who fight for them and the judges who write them know that they are inconclusive.

A statute involving a major policy is likely to be the subject of a number of attacks at about the same time in different courts. Then begins confusion. No district judge is required to, and few do, yield obedience or even respect to the decision of another. One local judge may sustain the legislation; another may hold the act partly good and partly bad; and another may hold it all unconstitutional. For a considerable period in 1939, the Agricultural Marketing Act, governing the sale of milk to handlers, was unconstitutional in New York State and constitutional in Massachusetts because the federal district judges came to opposite conclusions about the same question. Opinion and counter-opinion bewilder the citizen who wants to obey the law but who does not know what to do when one judicial star differeth from another.

Then come appeals; proceedings are printed; and, in due time, the cases are argued in the United States Circuit Court of Appeals. There are ten of these intermediate courts, and conflicting opinions are likely to issue; but they settle nothing. The Judiciary Act of 1937 authorizes in some cases that this intermediate court be passed by, and the Supreme Court has long had discretion to order it skipped, but even in cases where both government and an industry agree in urging that the time be saved, the Court often majestically refuses to be hurried.

After these court of appeals decisions, briefs are rewritten and reprinted, and the case reaches the Supreme Court. Once there it is promptly heard and soon decided. The delay is in the interminable lower court proceedings. This delay, doubt, and confusion has a social and economic cost.

New Deal legislation was often held in a long period of suspense and uncertainty. The *Gold Clause Cases* were decided one year and eight months after the Joint Resolution struck down the Gold Clauses. Meanwhile, all forward commitments of the business world were subject to a possible infirmity, so substantial that it was finally resolved by a majority of only one vote.

After almost two years of vigorous administration, the N.R.A. was held at all times to have been invalid. A myriad of transactions had been closed and thousands of persons had altered their positions in reliance on it.

Two and a half years after its adoption, the A.A.A. was struck down by a sharply divided Court with havoc to existing commitments.

While most of this delay is in the lower courts, the Supreme Court has itself delayed decision. It has a philosophy that while it has a duty to decide constitutional questions, it must escape the duty if possible.

An eminently qualified and not unfriendly authority writes:[12] "But the Court has improved upon the common law tradition and evolved rules of judicial administration especially designed to postpone constitutional adjudications and therefore constitutional conflicts until they are judicially unavoidable. The Court will avoid decision on grounds of constitutionality if a case may go off on some other ground, as, for instance, statutory construction.

"The Court has thus evolved elaborate and often technical doctrines for postponing if not avoiding constitutional adjudication. In one famous controversy, involving a conflict between Congress and the president, the Supreme Court was able until recently to avoid decision of a question that arose in the First Congress. Such a system inevitably introduces accidental factors in decision making. So much depends on how a question is raised and when it is raised."

Nevertheless, Mr. Frankfurter thought this prolonged uncertainty less harmful than "the mischief of premature judicial intervention." By the latter he thinks the "Court's prestige within its proper sphere would be inevitably impaired."

Must we choose between *"premature judicial intervention"* on one hand and *"technical doctrines for postponing if not avoiding constitutional adjudication"* on the other? If that were our choice I would think Mr. Frankfurter had chosen wisely. But need we be gored by either horn of such a dilemma? Can we not establish a procedure for determination of substantial constitutional questions at the suit of real parties in interest which will avoid prematurity or advisory opinions on the one hand and also avoid technical doctrines for postponing inevitable decisions? Should we not at least try to lay inevitable constitutional controversies to early rest?

An important reason for doing so is that Supreme Court law is retroactive in its operation, and that is one of the perils and inconveniences of constitutional litigation. Normally, judicial decision is law-making after the event. The function of judges is to decide controversies, and their decisions must necessarily be made to relate back to govern the transaction which provoked the controversy. This led Bentham to assert that judges make the common law "just as a man makes laws for his dog. When your dog does anything you want to break him of, you wait till he does it, and then beat him for it."[13] But the judicial conscience is eased by a theory which denies personal guilt. "But even in such cases the subsequent judges do not pretend to make a new law, but to vindicate the old one from misrepresentation. For if it be found that the former decision is manifestly absurd or unjust, it is declared, not that such a sentence was *bad law,* but that it was *not law.* . . ."[14] This sort of theoretical fol-de-rol about a "transcendental body of law" was called by Justice Holmes a "fallacy and illusion."[15]

On some occasions, the Supreme Court has refused to allow state court decisions to become effective retroactively[16] and it has held that the Federal Constitution permits a state to provide against retroactive effect of state court decisions if it so desires. Justice Cardozo, for a unanimous court, wrote:[17] "A state in defining the limits of adherence to precedent may make a choice for itself between the principle of forward operation and that of relation backward. It may say that decisions of its highest court, though later overruled, are law none the less for intermediate transactions."

It is hard to see why a similar choice should not be open to the Federal Government. The task of doing practical justice does not depend on solving a riddle as to whether an overruling decision serves to correct wrong law or simply to correct a wrong judge. As Solicitor General I urged that "this Court has, and should have, as an incident of its power to overrule prior decisions, the power in particular cases to prevent an overruling decision from being an instrument of injustice or hardship."[18] But, there must be definite limitations in applying such a rule, and the particular case was not appropriate for its application.

Later, the Court considered the effects of retroactivity created by holding enactments unconstitutional, in a vein that indicates that the Court will strive to mitigate hardships caused thereby.

Mr. Chief Justice Hughes wrote:[19] "The Courts below have proceeded on the theory that the Act of Congress, having been found to be unconstitutional, was not a law; that it was inoperative, conferring no rights and imposing no duties, and hence affording no basis for the challenged decree. . . . It is quite clear, however, that such broad statements as to the effect of a determination of unconstitutionality must be taken with qualifications. The actual existence of a statute, prior to such a determination, is an operative fact and may have consequences which cannot justly be ignored. The past cannot always be erased by a new judicial declaration. The effect of the subsequent ruling as to invalidity may have to be considered in various aspects,—with respect to particular relations, individual and corporate, and particular conduct, private and official. Questions of rights claimed to have become vested, of status, of prior determinations deemed to have finality and acted upon accordingly, of public policy in the light of the nature both of the statute and of its previous application, demand examination. These questions are among the most difficult of those which have engaged the attention of courts, state and federal, and it is manifest from numerous decisions that an all-inclusive statement of a principle of absolute retroactive invalidity cannot be justified."

* * *

[II]

The political nature of judicial review generally is either unrecognized or ignored. But it is that which gives significance to constitutional litigation and which makes it transcend mere legal proceedings.

The Supreme Court, to which this essential function is committed, is an institution of distinctive characteristics which were intended to give it independence and detachment, but which also tend to make it anti-democratic. To review the functions of the Court in conjunction with its peculiar qualities will explain its repeated drift into struggles with strong Executives and will reveal the dangers that beset its future.

The ultimate function of the Supreme Court is nothing less than the arbitration between fundamental and ever-present rival forces or trends in our organized society. The technical tactics of constitutional lawsuits are part of a greater strategy of statecraft in our system. Supreme Court decrees pick out roughly the drifts of national policy. Every really important movement has been preceded by "leading cases" and has left others in its wake, even as will the New Deal. Conflicts which have divided the Justices always mirror a conflict which pervades society. In fact, it may be said that the Supreme Court conference chamber is the forum where each fundamental cause has had its most determined and understanding championship. The student of our times will nowhere find the deeper conflicts of American political philosophy and economic policy more authentically and intelligently portrayed than in the opinions and dissents of members of the Supreme Court. Justices such as Holmes and Brandeis have not only furnished the highest expression but they have been the very source and the intellectual leaders of recent liberalism in the United States. And nowhere can one find the philosophy of conservatism and opposition to the Administration's policy more intelligently or earnestly expressed than in the opinions of Justices Sutherland and Butler. The Constitution, in making the balance between different parts of our government a legal rather than a political question, casts the Court as the most philosophical of our political departments. It keeps the most fundamental equilibriums of our society, such as that between centralization and localism, between liberty and authority, and between stability and progress. These issues underlie nearly every movement in an organized society.

The Court has as its highest responsibility the duty to hold every such movement, in its legislative and executive phases, within all express bounds of the Constitution. Whether or not the Justices avow such an end, whether or not they are even aware of it, their acts and pronouncements often do tip the balance between these irrepressible forces, even in matters of constitutionally permissible policy. It is safer that they be conscious of the ultimate implications and the weight of their decisions and the tensions and pressures in a democratic society which they influence.

These important functions devolve upon a Supreme Court which was intended to be, and by its inherent nature always will prove to be, over the years, a relatively conservative institution. This was assured by the provisions that its Justices should receive office through appointment and should hold it for life.

Another assurance, not provided by the Constitution, but supplied by custom, is that such Justices are drawn only from the legal profession. The entire philosophy, interest, and training of the legal profession tend toward conservatism. As I have already remarked, it is much concerned with precedents, authorities, existing customs, usages, vested rights, and established relationships. Its method of thinking, accepted by no other profession, cultivates a supreme respect for the past, and its order. Justice Cardozo has well said that the "power of precedent, when analyzed, is the power of the beaten track."[20] No lawyer sufficiently devoted to the law to know our existing rules, the history of them, and the justification for them, will depart from them lightly. The contribution of legal philosophy to the balance of social forces will always be on the conservative side.

This trend to conservatism in the profession of the law is intensified in the case of judges by the weight of the official tradition of social and intellectual isolation. Mr. Taft compared Court life to life in a monastery.[21]

The operation of our two-party system has also tended to separate the judiciary from the elective branches and to place them in opposition. The party system often serves to bridge the constitutional division between the executive and legislative branches. Adherence to a common party organization and tradition and program tends to weld the executive departments and the majority of Senators and Congressmen into a cohesive group, and thus to supply cooperation between otherwise detached units.

This extra-constitutional inducement to cooperation has at all critical times operated in reverse between the judiciary and the elective branches of government. The Federalist Party Executives, Washington and Adams, had no differences with the judiciary. They appointed all of the judges. But at every turn in national policy where the cleavage between the old order and the new was sharp, the new President has faced a judiciary almost wholly held over from the preceding regime. Whatever influence party background may have on judicial trends, whether great or little, it has been an estranging influence between the Court and the great Presidents, Jefferson, Jackson, Lincoln, and Franklin D. Roosevelt.

The Court, moreover, is almost never a really contemporary institution. The operation of life tenure in the judicial department, as against elections at short intervals of the Congress, usually keeps the average viewpoint of the two institutions a generation apart. The judiciary is thus the check of a preceding generation on the present one; a check of conservative legal philosophy upon a dynamic people, and nearly always the check of a rejected regime on the one in being. And the search for Justices of enduring liberalism has usually ended in disappointment.

This conservative institution is under every pressure and temptation to throw its weight against novel programs and untried policies which win popular elections. Its plain duty to enforce explicit constitutional provisions even in opposition to the majority is easily rationalized into enforcing its own views of good policy. To the extent that it does so, it defeats government by representative democracy.

Our representative federation was not devised to arrest change, but to provide peaceful and orderly methods for the continuous changes which were recognized to be inevitable. The device of periodic election was chosen to register and remedy discontents and grievances in time to prevent them from growing into underground or violent revolutionary movements. An election that can turn out one regime and install another is a revolution—a peaceful and lawful revolution. By such method we give flexibility and a measure of popular responsibility to our federated system and maintain a continuity of the government, even though the governors be turned out from time to time. The measure of success of a democratic system is found in the degree to which its elections really reflect rising discontent before it becomes unmanageable, by which government responds to it with timely redress, and by which losing groups are self-disciplined to accept election results.

It must be remembered that our democratic system can succeed in composing oppositions only if the effort is made while the separation is not extreme. When the separation becomes wide or deep, as that over slavery finally became, the contest gets beyond the capacity of elective processes to compose.

* * *

. . . The very ability of democracies to settle issues peaceably may depend on responding to them before they have developed the bitterness which comes of long-endured injustices.

Our American elections have been fought between parties which, roughly, have represented the forces advocating change and those preferring stability.

* * *

But election as a device to defend against violence by registering and responding to this "scattered discontent and diffuse enthusiasm" fails, if the popularly elected regime is to be prevented judicially from putting its policies into force. It should, of course, be so restrained where its program violates clear and explicit terms of the Constitution, such as the specific prohibitions in the Bill of Rights. But to use vague clauses to import doctrines of restraint, such as "freedom of contract," is to set up the judiciary as a check on elections, a nullification of the process of government by consent of the governed. It leaves the grievances of the frustrated majority to grow, and more extreme remedies to commend themselves to those who would have been satisfied with more moderate, if more timely, ones.

I have little fear of legislative or political clashes between the forces of liberalism and those of conservatism in the present state of our American society. Each is subject to moderating influences from a constituency which has not often in substantial numbers approved real radicalism or extreme reactionism. The Senator in our National Congress has faced his constituents not over six years before, and on average much more recently, and the conservative Representative is not over two years from his ballot box. They are all parts of a political party that never more than four years previously has faced a Presidential election and at least within that period must do so again. Hence, the conservatism of legislators is moderated by elimination and by expediency, just as liberalism among them is restrained by the average opinion of electors. Whatever other defects the elective process under a two-party system may present, it does temper extremes of legislative opinion. By it, if at all, issues may be compromised out and a balance struck between the forces of stability and those of progress.

But, after this political and legislative process has taken place, to add another and more extreme and inflexible hurdle in the form of judicial review of social policy loads the dice in favor of the *status quo* and makes the constructive task of liberal leadership impossible. It is always the dynamic party of change which is frustrated by the Court's attitude, for the conservative party, resting on the policy of letting well enough alone, presents for review little legislation that is untried or novel. Liberal leadership exhausts its power to persuade the discontented and the have-nots to accept ballot-box disappointments or compromises if their victories are to be nullified and if elections are effective in shaping policy only when conservatives win. This was the problem that confronted the New Deal leadership in 1937—either the election was only a mirage to winning progressive forces or the Court must yield.

The Supreme Court can maintain itself and succeed in its tasks only if the counsels of self-restraint urged most earnestly by members of the Court itself are humbly and faithfully heeded. After the forces of conservatism and liberalism, of radicalism and reaction, of emotion and of self-interest are all caught up in the legislative process and averaged and come to rest in some compromise measure such as the Missouri Compromise, the N.R.A., the A.A.A., a minimum-wage law, or some other legislative policy, a decision striking it down closes an area of compromise in which conflicts have actually, if only temporarily, been composed. Each such decision takes away from our democratic federalism another of its defenses against domestic disorder and violence. The vice of judicial supremacy, as exerted for ninety years in the field of policy, has been its progressive closing of the avenues to peaceful and democratic conciliation of our social and economic conflicts.

In stressing this I do not join those who seek to deflate the whole judicial process. It is precisely because I value the role that the judiciary performs in the peaceful ordering of our society that I deprecate the ill-starred adventures of the judiciary that have recurringly jeopardized its essential usefulness.

Nor am I unmindful of the hard-won heritage of an independent judiciary which for over two hundred years has maintained the "rule of law" in England, the living principle that not even the king is above the law. But again, the rule of law is in unsafe hands when courts cease to function as courts and become organs for control of policy. . . .

With us, what is wanted is not innovation, but a return to the spirit with which our early judges viewed the function of judicial review of legislation—the conviction that it is an awesome thing to strike down an act of the legislature approved by the Chief Executive, and that power so uncontrolled is not to be used save where the occasion is clear beyond fair debate.

If the judiciary attempts to enforce a judicial conservatism after legislative and political conservatism has decided to yield and compromise, it will jeopardize its power to serve the Republic in high and undisputed functions which only it can perform. By impairing its own prestige through risking it in the field of policy, it may impair its ability to defend our liberties.

I yield to the lawyer's impulse to prove my point by citing a precedent. The lowest point in the history of the federal judiciary was May 1861. Roger B. Taney, the aged Chief Justice of the United States, was sitting in Masonic Hall in Baltimore to hear the return to a writ of habeas corpus, "that traditional bulwark of individual liberty," which he had issued. An aide-de-camp in full military uniform and appropriately wearing a sword,[22] appeared and declined obedience to the ancient writ of freedom, upon the ground that it had been "suspended." Let the Chief Justice state the case:[23] "The case, then, is simply this: a military officer, residing in Pennsylvania, issues an order to arrest a citizen of Maryland, upon vague and indefinite charges, without any proof, so far as appears; under this order, his house is entered in the night, he is seized as a prisoner, and conveyed to Fort McHenry, and there kept in close confinement; and when a habeas corpus is served on the commanding officer, requiring him to produce the prisoner before a justice of the supreme court, in order that he may examine into the legality of the imprisonment, the answer of the officer, is that he is authorized by the president to suspend the writ of habeas corpus at his discretion, and in the exercise of that discretion, suspends it in this case, and on that ground refuses obedience to the writ.

"As the case comes before me, therefore, I understand that the president not only claims the right to suspend the writ of habeas corpus himself, at his discretion, but to delegate that discretionary power to a military officer, and to leave it to him to determine whether he will or will not obey judicial process that may be served upon him."

And he further recites: "But the documents before me show, that the military authority in this case has gone far beyond the mere suspension of the privilege of the writ of habeas corpus. It has, by force of arms, thrust aside the judicial authorities and officers to whom the constitution has confided the power and duty of interpreting and administering the laws, and substituted a military government in its place, to be administered and executed by military officers.

"Yet, under these circumstances, a military officer, stationed in Pennsylvania, without giving any information to the district attorney, and without any application to the judicial authorities, assumes to himself the judicial power in the district of Maryland; undertakes to decide what constitutes the crime of treason or rebellion; what evidence (if indeed he required any) is sufficient to support the accusation and justify the commitment; and commits the party, without a hearing, even before himself, to close custody, in a strongly garrisoned fort, to be there held, it would seem, during the pleasure of those who committed him."

Shorn of power, but not of courage, Taney, "a great Chief Justice,"[24] in full expectation that he, too, would be imprisoned, thundered forth the fundamental and eternal principles of civilian freedom from military usurpation. But with a confession of helplessness and despair, he closed an opinion which must rank as one of the most admirable and pathetic documents in American judicial annals:[25] "In such a case, my duty was too plain to be mistaken. I have exercised all the power which the constitution and laws confer upon me, but that power has been resisted by a force too strong for me to overcome."

And so he sent his opinion to President Lincoln in the hope that "that high officer" would "determine what measures he will take to cause the civil process of the United States to be respected and enforced."

The answer, if any, was drowned out by the measured tread of marching feet. Judicial power was all but extinct. Nothing but the indispensable necessity for its function could bid it rise again.

Did the lonely and frustrated Chief Justice recall the tragic part that he, more than any other, had played in starting that march? Only four years before he had read the opinion in the *Dred Scott* case,[26] in which his Court had held the Missouri Compromise to be unconstitutional. The Missouri Compromise itself had ceased to be important. But there was still hope that American forbearance and statesmanship would prove equal to finding some compromise between the angry forces that were being aroused by the slave issue. That hope vanished when the Supreme Court held that the Constitution would allow no compromise about the existence of slavery in the territories. Taney had attempted to forestall the anticipated verdict of coming elections—the verdict that came with the election of 1860. Now the weary and weather-beaten old Chief Justice was overmastered by the violence of forces that he had himself turned away from compromise in legislative halls and had hurried toward war.

One such precedent is enough!

NOTES

1. *Curry* v. *McCanless*, 307 U.S. 357, 366, 374.
2. *Graves* v. *Elliott*, 307 U.S. 383, 387.
3. *Newark Fire Ins. Co.* v. *State Board*, 307 U.S. 313, 321.

4. 295 U.S. 330, 375.
5. *St. Joseph Stock Yards Co.* v. *United States,* 298 U.S. 38, 94.
6. *The Passenger Cases,* 7 How. 283, 470.
7. *Burnet* v. *Coronado Oil & Gas Co.,* 285 U.S. 393, 406.
8. See *Borden's Co.* v. *Baldwin,* 293 U.S. 194.
9. *Baltimore and Ohio R. Co.* v. *United States,* 298 U.S. 349, 381.
10. Mr. Justice McReynolds in *Steward Machine Co.* v. *Davis,* 301 U.S. 548, 599.
11. See *Pollock* v. *Farmers' Loan & Trust Co.,* 157 U.S. 429, 531.
12. Frankfurter, Felix: *Law and Politics.* New York: Harcourt, Brace and Company; 1939, p. 25.
13. See Kocourek, Albert: "Retrospective Decisions and Stare Decisis and a Proposal," 17 *A. B. A. Journal,* 180.
14. See Blackstone: *Commentaries.* Philadelphia: Rees, Welsh & Company; 1897. Vol. I, pp. 69–70.
15. See dissenting opinions, *B. & W. Taxi. Co.* v. *B. & Y. Taxi. Co.,* 276 U.S. 518, 533.
16. *Gelpcke* v. *Dubuque,* 1 Wall. 175.
17. *Great Northern Ry.* v. *Sunburst Co.,* 287 U.S. 358, 364.
18. See Reply to Petition for Rehearing in *Helvering* v. *Gerhardt.* Rehearing denied 305 U.S. 669.
19. *Chicot County* v. *Baxter Bank, No. 122,* October Term, 1939. Decided January 2, 1940.
20. Cardozo, Benjamin N.: *The Growth of the Law.* New Haven: Yale University Press; 1939, p. 62.
21. Pringle, Henry F.: *The Life and Times of William Howard Taft.* New York, Toronto: Farrar and Rinehart; 1939. Vol. II, p. 961.
22. Swisher, Carl B.: *Roger B. Taney.* New York: The Macmillan Company; 1936, p. 551.
23. *Ex parte Merryman,* 17 Fed. Cas. 144, 147. Case No. 9,487.
24. See Tribute to Taney by Chief Justice Hughes, *A.B.A. Journal,* Vol. XVII, pp. 785–790.
25. *Ex parte Merryman,* 17 Fed. Cas. 144, 153; Case No. 9,487.
26. *Dred Scott* v. *Sandford,* 19 How. 393.

52

Decision-Making in a Democracy: The Supreme Court as a National Policy-Maker

ROBERT A. DAHL

In the following, widely republished article on the Supreme Court, Robert A. Dahl shows that the Supreme Court is a significant national policy maker. He rejects the argument that the Supreme Court's policy-making power is justified by the need to protect minority rights. He believes that majority rule, an essential democratic principle, is not consistent with a veto power for the minority; in fact, the Supreme Court's history does not show that it has been vigilant in protecting personal and political freedoms. Because of the President's appointive power, the Supreme Court is seldom at odds for long with the "lawmaking majority" on major policy questions. Furthermore, as part of the nation's majority political coalition, the Supreme Court adds legitimacy to the policies of government by validating them as constitutional. In a nation of constitution worshipers, this validation vastly increases acceptance of majority rule.

Dahl overlooks the strong possibility that at those historical moments, when the Court and the lawmaking majority are in conflict, the delay entailed in awaiting vacancies on the Court is least tolerable to the public and most dangerous to the stability of the nation. Furthermore, as Kenneth Dolbeare suggests in the next article, the public visibility of the Court may be so slight that its legitimacy-conferring capability is doubtful indeed.

Dahl, Sterling Professor of Political Science at Yale University, is one of the most eminent American political scientists. He has published Congress and Foreign Policy *(1950),* Who Governs? *(1961),* A Preface to Democratic Theory *(1956),* Modern Political Analysis *(1963), and* Pluralist Democracy in the United States *(1967). He is coauthor of* Economics, Politics and Welfare *(1953) and editor of* Oppositions in Western Democracies *(1966).*

To consider the Supreme Court of the United States strictly as a legal institution is to underestimate its significance in the American political system. For it is also a political institution, an institution, that is to say, for arriving at decisions on controversial questions of national policy. As a political institution, the Court is highly unusual, not least because Americans are not quite willing to accept the fact that it *is* a political institution and not quite capable of denying it; so that frequently we take both positions at once. This is confusing to foreigners, amusing to logicians, and rewarding to ordinary Americans who thus manage to retain the best of both worlds.

I

A policy decision might be defined as an effective choice among alternatives about which there is, at least initially, some uncertainty. This uncertainty may arise because of inadequate information as to (a) the alternatives that are thought to be "open"; (b) the consequences that will probably ensue from choosing a given alternative; (c) the level of probability that these consequences will actually ensue; and (d) the relative value of the different alternatives, that is, an ordering of the alternatives from most preferable to least preferable, given the expected consequences and the expected probability of the consequences actually occurring. An *effective* choice is a selection of the most preferable alternative accompanied by measures to insure that the alternative selected will be acted upon.

No one, I imagine, will quarrel with the proposition that the Supreme Court, or indeed any court, must make and does make policy decisions in this sense. But such a proposition is not really useful to the question before us. What is critical is the extent to which a court can and does make policy decisions by going outside established "legal" criteria found in precedent, statute and constitution. Now in this respect the Supreme Court occupies a most peculiar position, for it is an essential characteristic of the institution that from time to time its members decide cases where legal criteria are not in any realistic sense adequate to the task. A distinguished associate justice of the present Court has recently described the business of the Supreme Court in these words:

> It is essentially accurate to say that the Court's preoccupation today is with the application of rather fundamental aspirations and what Judge Learned Hand calls "moods," embodied in provisions like the due process clauses, which were designed not to be precise and positive directions for rules of action. The judicial process in applying them involves a judgment. . . . that is, on the views of the direct representatives of the people in meeting the needs of society, on the views of Presidents and Governors, and by their construction of the will of legislatures the Court breathes life, feeble or strong, into the inert pages of the Constitution and the statute books.[1]

Very often, then, the cases before the Court involve alternatives about which there is severe disagreement in the society, as in the case of segregation or economic regulation; that is, the setting of the case is "political." Moreover, they are usually cases where competent students of constitutional law, including the learned justices of the Supreme Court themselves, disagree; where the words of the Constitution are general, vague,

Reprinted from *Journal of Public Law*, 6 (1958), 279–295, by permission of the author and publisher.

ambiguous, or not clearly applicable; where precedent may be found on both sides; and where experts differ in predicting the consequences of the various alternatives or the degree of probability that the possible consequences will actually ensue. Typically, in other words, although there may be considerable agreement as to the alternatives thought to be open [(a)], there is very serious disagreement as to questions of fact bearing on consequences and probabilities [(b) and (c)], and as to questions of value, or the way in which different alternatives are to be ordered according to criteria establishing relative preferability [(d)].

If the Court were assumed to be a "political" institution, no particular problems would arise, for it would be taken for granted that the members of the Court would resolve questions of fact and value by introducing assumptions derived from their own predispositions or those of influential clienteles and constituents. But, since much of the legitimacy of the Court's decisions rests upon the fiction that it is not a political institution but exclusively a legal one, to accept the Court as a political institution would solve one set of problems at the price of creating another. Nonetheless, if it is true that the nature of the cases arriving before the Court is sometimes of the kind I have described, then the Court cannot act strictly as a legal institution. It must, that is to say, choose among controversial alternatives of public policy by appealing to at least some criteria of acceptability on questions of fact and value that cannot be found in or deduced from precedent, statute, and Constitution. It is in this sense that the Court is a national policy-maker, and it is this role that gives rise to the problem of the Court's existence in a political system ordinarily held to be democratic.

Now I take it that except for differences in emphasis and presentation, what I have said so far is today widely accepted by almost all American political scientists and by most lawyers. To anyone who believes that the Court, is not, in at least some of its activities, a policy-making institution, the discussion that follows may seem irrelevant. But to anyone who holds that at least one role of the Court is as a policy-making institution in cases where strictly legal criteria are inadequate, then a serious and much debated question arises, to wit: Who gets what and why? Or in less elegant language: What groups are benefited or handicapped by the Court and how does the allocation by the Court of these rewards and penalties fit into our presumably democratic political system?

II

In determining and appraising the role of the Court, two different and conflicting criteria are sometimes employed. These are the majority criterion and the criterion of Right or Justice.

Every policy dispute can be tested, at least in principle, by the majority criterion, because (again: in principle) the dispute can be analyzed according to the numbers of people for and against the various alternatives at issue, and therefore according to the proportions of the citizens or eligible members who are for and against the alternatives. Logically speaking, except for a trivial case, every conflict within a given society must be a dispute between a majority of those eligible to participate and a minority or minorities; or else it must be a dispute between or among minorities only.[2] Within certain limits, both possibilities are independent of the number of policy alternatives at issue, and since the argument is not significantly affected by the number of alternatives, it is convenient to assume that each policy dispute represents only two alternatives.[3]

If everyone prefers one of two alternatives, then no significant problem arises. But a case will hardly come before the Supreme Court unless at least one person prefers an alternative that is opposed by another person. Strictly speaking, then, no matter how the Court acts in determining the legality or constitutionality of one alternative or the other, the outcome of the Court's decision must either (1) accord with the preferences of a minority of citizens and run counter to the preferences of a majority; (2) accord with the preferences of a majority and run counter to the preferences of a minority; or (3) accord with the preferences of one minority and run counter to the preferences of another minority, the rest being indifferent.

In a democratic system with a more or less representative legislature, it is unnecessary to maintain a special court to secure the second class of outcomes. A case might be made out that the Court protects the rights of national majorities against local interests in federal questions, but so far as I am aware, the role of the Court as a policy-maker is not usually defended in this fashion; in what follows, therefore, I propose to pass over the ticklish question of federalism and deal only with "national" majorities and minorities. The third kind of outcome, although relevant according to other criteria, is hardly relevant to the majority criterion, and may also be passed over for the moment.

One influential view of the Court, however, is that it stands in some special way as a protection of minorities against tyranny by majorities. In the course of its 167 years, in seventy-eight cases, the Court has struck down eighty-six different provisions of federal law as unconstitutional,[4] and by interpretation it has modified a good many more. It might be argued, then, that in all or in a very large number of these cases the Court was, in fact, defending the rights of some minority against a "tyrannical" majority. There are, however, some exceedingly serious difficulties with this interpretation of the Court's activities.

III

One problem, which is essentially ideological in character, is the difficulty of reconciling such an interpretation with the existence of a democratic polity, for it is not at all difficult to show by appeals to authorities as various and imposing as Aristotle, Locke, Rousseau, Jefferson, and Lincoln that the term democracy means, among other things, that the power to rule resides in popular majorities and their representatives. Moreover, from entirely reasonable and traditional definitions of popular sovereignty and political equality, the principle of majority rule can be shown to follow by logical necessity.[5] Thus to affirm that the Court supports minority preferences against majorities is to deny that popular sovereignty and political equality, at least in the traditional sense, exist in the United States; and to affirm that the Court *ought* to act in this way is to deny that popular sovereignty and political equality *ought* to prevail in this country. In a country that glories in its democratic tradition, this is not a happy state of affairs for the Court's defenders; and it is no wonder that a great deal of effort has gone into the enterprise of proving that, even if the Court consistently defends minorities against majorities, nonetheless it is a thoroughly "democratic" institution. But no amount of tampering with democratic theory can conceal the fact that a system in which the policy preferences of minorities prevail over majorities is at odds with the traditional criteria for distinguishing a democracy from other political systems.[6]

Fortunately, however, we do not need to traverse this well-worn ground; for the view of the Court as a protector of the liberties of minorities against the tyranny of majorities is beset with other difficulties that are not so much ideological as matters of fact and logic. If one wishes to be at all rigorous about the question, it is probably impossible to demonstrate that any particular Court decisions have or have not been at odds with the preferences of a "national majority." It is clear that unless one makes *some* assumptions as to the kind of evidence one will require for the existence of a set of minority and majority preferences in the general population, the view under consideration is incapable of being proved at all. In any strict sense, no adequate evidence exists, for scientific opinion polls are of relatively recent origin, and national elections are little more than an indication of the first preferences of a number of citizens—in the United States the number ranges between about forty and sixty per cent of the adult population—for certain candidates for public office. I do not mean to say that there is no relation between preferences among candidates and preferences among alternative public policies, but the connection is a highly tenuous one, and on the basis of an election it is almost never possible to adduce whether a majority does or does not support one of two or more policy alternatives about which members of the political elite are divided. For the greater part of the Court's history, then, there is simply no way of establishing with any high degree of confidence whether a given alternative was or was not supported by a majority or a minority of adults or even of voters.

In the absence of relatively direct information, we are thrown back on indirect tests. The eighty-six provisions of federal law that have been declared unconstitutional were, of course, initially passed by majorities of those voting in the Senate and in the House. They also had the president's formal approval. We could, therefore, speak of a majority of those voting in the House and Senate, together with the president, as a "lawmaking majority." It is not easy to determine whether any such constellation of forces within the political elites actually coincides with the preferences of a majority of American adults or even with the preferences of a majority of that half of the adult population which, on the average, votes in congressional elections. Such evidence as we have from opinion polls suggests that Congress is not markedly out of line with public opinion, or at any rate with such public opinion as there is after one discards the answers of people who fall into the category, often large, labelled "no response" or "don't know." If we may, on these somewhat uncertain grounds, take a "lawmaking majority" as equivalent to a "national majority," then it is possible to test the hypothesis that the Supreme Court is shield and buckler for minorities against national majorities.

Under any reasonable assumptions about the nature of the political process, it would appear to be somewhat naive to assume that the Supreme Court either would or could play the role of Galahad. Over the whole history of the Court, on the average one new justice has been appointed every twenty-two months. Thus a president can expect to appoint about two new justices during one term of office; and if this were not enough to tip the balance on a normally divided Court, he is almost certain to succeed in two terms. Thus, Hoover had three appointments; Roosevelt, nine; Truman, four; and Eisenhower, so far, has had four. Presidents are not famous for appointing justices hostile to their own views on public policy nor could they expect to secure confirmation of a man whose stance on key questions was flagrantly at odds with that of the dominant majority in the Senate. Justices are typically men who, prior to appointment, have engaged in public life and have committed themselves publicly on the great questions of the day. As Mr. Justice Frankfurter has recently reminded us, a surprisingly large proportion of the justices, particularly of the great justices who have left their stamp upon the decisions of the Court, have had little or no prior judicial experience.[7] Nor have the justices—certainly not the great justices—been timid men with a passion for anonymity. Indeed, it is not too much to say that if justices were appointed primarily for their "judicial" qualities without regard to their basic attitudes on fundamental questions of public policy, the Court could not play the influential role in the American political system that it does in reality play.

The fact is, then, that the policy views dominant on the Court are never for long out of line with the policy views dominant among the lawmaking majorities of the United States. Consequently it would be most unrealistic to suppose that the Court would, for more than a few years at most, stand against any major alternatives sought by a lawmaking majority. The judicial agonies of the New Deal will, of course, quickly come to mind; but Mr. Roosevelt's difficulties with the Court were truly exceptional. Generalizing over the whole history of the Court, the chances are

Table 1
The Interval Between Appointments to the Supreme Court

Interval in Years	*Per Cent of Total Appointments*	*Cumulative Per Cent*
Less than 1	21	21
1	34	55
2	18	73
3	9	82
4	8	90
5	7	97
6	2	99
—	—	—
12	1	100
Total	100	100

Note: The table excludes the six appointments made in 1789. Except for the four most recent appointments, it is based on data in the *Encyclopedia of American History*, 461–62 (Morris ed., 1953). It may be slightly inaccurate because the source shows only the year of appointment, not the month. The twelve-year interval was from 1811 to 1823.

about one out of five that a president will make one appointment to the Court in less than a year, better than one out of two that he will make one within two years, and three out of four that he will make one within three years. Mr. Roosevelt had unusually bad luck: he had to wait four years for his first appointment; the odds against this long an interval are four to one. With average luck, the battle with the Court would never have occurred; even as it was, although the "court-packing" proposal did formally fail, by the end of his second term Mr. Roosevelt had appointed five new justices and by 1941 Mr. Justice Roberts was the only remaining holdover from the Hoover era.

It is to be expected, then, that the Court is least likely to be successful in blocking a determined and persistent lawmaking majority on a major policy and most likely to succeed against a "weak" majority; e.g., a dead one, a transient one, a fragile one, or one weakly united upon a policy of subordinate importance.

IV

An examination of the cases in which the Court has held federal legislation unconstitutional confirms, on the whole, our expectations. Over the whole history of the Court, about half the decisions have been rendered more than four years after the legislation was passed.

Of the twenty-four laws held unconstitutional within two years, eleven were measures enacted in the early years of the New Deal. Indeed, New Deal measures comprise nearly a

Table 2
Percentage of Cases Held Unconstitutional Arranged by Time Intervals Between Legislation and Decision

Number of Years	*New Deal Legislation %*	*Other %*	*All Legislation %*
2 or Less	92	19	30
3–4	8	19	18
5–8	0	28	24
9–12	0	13	11
13–16	0	8	6
17–20	0	1	1
21 or More	0	12	10
Total	100	100	100

Table 3
Cases Holding Legislation Unconstitutional Within Four Years After Enactment

	New Deal		*Other*		*Total*	
Interval in Years	*No.*	*%*	*No.*	*%*	*No.*	*%*
2 or Less	11	29	13	34	24	63
3 to 4	1	3	13	34	14	37
Total	12	32	26	68	38	100

third of all the legislation that has ever been declared unconstitutional within four years after enactment.

It is illuminating to examine the cases where the Court has acted on legislation within four years after enactment—where the presumption is, that is to say, that the lawmaking majority is not necessarily a dead one. Of the twelve New Deal cases, two were, from a policy point of view, trivial; and two, although perhaps not trivial, were of minor importance to the New Deal program.[8] A fifth[9] involved the NRA, which was to expire within three weeks of the decision. Insofar as the unconstitutional provisions allowed "codes of fair competition" to be established by industrial groups, it is fair to say that President Roosevelt and his advisers were relieved by the Court's decision of a policy they had come to find increasingly embarrassing. In view of the tenacity with which Mr. Roosevelt held to his major program, there can hardly be any doubt that had he wanted to pursue the major policy objective involved in the NRA codes, as he did, for example, with the labor provisions, he would not have been stopped by the Court's special theory of the Constitution. As to the seven other cases,[10] it is entirely correct to say, I think, that whatever some of the eminent justices might have thought during their fleeting moments of glory, they did not succeed in interposing a barrier to the achievement of the objectives of the legislation; and in a few years most of the constitutional interpretation on which the decisions rested had been unceremoniously swept under the rug.

The remainder of the thirty-eight cases where the Court has declared legislation unconstitutional within four years of enactment tend to fall into two rather distinct groups: those involving legislation that could reasonably be regarded as important *from the point of view of the lawmaking majority* and those involving minor legislation. Although the one category merges into the other, so that some legislation must be classified rather arbitrarily, probably there will be little disagreement with classifying the specific legislative provisions involved in eleven cases as essentially minor from the point of view of the lawmaking majority (however important they may have been as constitutional interpretations).[11] The specific legislative provisions involved in the remaining fifteen cases are by no means of uniform importance, but with one or two possible exceptions it seems reasonable to classify them as major policy issues from the point of view of the lawmaking majority.[12] We would expect that cases involving major legislative policy would be propelled to the Court much more rapidly than cases involving minor policy, and, as the table below shows, this is in fact what happens.

Thus a lawmaking majority with

Table 4

Number of Cases Involving Legislative Policy Other than Those Arising Under New Deal Legislation Holding Legislation Unconstitutional Within Four Years After Enactment

Interval in Years	*Major Policy*	*Minor Policy*	*Total*
2 or Less	11	2	13
3 to 4	4	9	13
Total	15	11	26

major policy objectives in mind usually has an opportunity to seek for ways of overcoming the Court's veto. It is an interesting and highly significant fact that Congress and the president do generally succeed in overcoming a hostile Court on major policy issues. It is particularly instructive to examine the cases involving major policy. In two cases involving punitive legislation enacted by Radical Republican Congresses against supporters of the Confederacy during the Civil War, the Court faced a rapidly crumbling majority whose death knell as an effective national force was sounded with the election of 1876.[11] Three cases are difficult to classify and I have labelled them "unclear." Of these, two were decisions made in 1921 involving a 1919 amendment to the Lever Act to control prices.[15] The legislation was important, and the provision in question was clearly struck down, but the Lever Act terminated three days after the decision and Congress did not return to the subject of price control until World War II, when it experienced no constitutional difficulties arising from these cases (which were primarily concerned with the lack of an ascertainable standard of guilt). The third case in this category successfully eliminated stock dividends from the scope of the Sixteenth Amendment, although a year later Congress enacted legislation taxing the actual income from such stock.[16]

The remaining ten cases were ultimately followed by a reversal of the actual policy results of the Court's action, although not necessarily of the specific constitutional interpretation. In four cases,[17] the policy consequences of the Court's decision were overcome in less than a year. The other six required a long struggle. Workmen's compensation for longshoremen and harbor workers was invalidated by the Court in 1920;[18] in 1922 Congress passed a new law which was, in its turn, knocked down by the Court in 1924;[19] in 1927 Congress passed a third law, which was finally upheld in 1932.[20] The notorious income tax cases[21] of 1895 were first somewhat narrowed by the Court itself;[22] the Sixteenth Amendment was recommended by President Taft in 1909 and was ratified in 1913, some eighteen years after the Court's decisions. The two child labor cases represent the most effective battle ever waged by the Court against legislative policy-makers. The original legislation outlawing child labor, based on the commerce clause, was passed in 1916 as a part of Wilson's New Freedom. Like Roosevelt later, Wilson was somewhat unlucky in his Supreme Court appointments; he made only

Table 5
Type of Congressional Action Following Supreme Court Decisions Holding Legislation Unconstitutional Within Four Years After Enactment (Other than New Deal Legislation)

Congressional Action	*Major Policy*	*Minor Policy*	*Total*
Reverses Court's Policy	10[a]	2[d]	12
Changes Own Policy	2[b]	0	2
None	0	8[e]	8
Unclear	3[c]	1[f]	4
Total	15	11	26

Note: For the cases in each category, see footnote 13.

three appointments during his eight years, and one of these was wasted, from a policy point of view, on McReynolds. Had McReynolds voted "right," the subsequent struggle over the problem of child labor need not have occurred, for the decision in 1918 was by a Court divided five to four, McReynolds voting with the majority.[23] Congress moved at once to circumvent the decision by means of the tax power, but in 1922 the Court blocked that approach.[24] In 1924 Congress returned to the engagement with a constitutional amendment that was rapidly endorsed by a number of state legislatures before it began to meet so much resistance in the states remaining that the enterprise miscarried. In 1938, under a second reformist president, new legislation was passed, twenty-two years after the first; this a chastened Court accepted in 1941,[25] and thereby brought to an end a battle that had lasted a full quarter-century.

The entire record of the duel between the Court and the lawmaking majority, in cases where the Court has held legislation unconstitutional within four years after enactment, is summarized in Table 6.

Thus the application of the majority criterion seems to show the following: First, if the Court did in fact uphold minorities against national majorities, as both its supporters and critics often seem to believe, it would be an extremely anomalous institution from a democratic point of view. Second, the elaborate "democratic" rationalizations of the Court's defenders and the hostility of its "democratic" critics are largely irrelevant, for lawmaking majorities generally have had their way. Third, although the Court seems never to have succeeded in holding out indefinitely, in a very small number of important cases it has delayed the application of policy up to as much as twenty-five years.

V

How can we appraise decisions of the third kind just mentioned? Earlier I referred to the criterion of Right or Justice as a norm sometimes invoked to describe the role of the Court. In accordance with this norm, it might be argued that the most important policy function of the Court is to protect rights that are in some sense basic or fundamental. Thus (the argument might run) in a country where basic rights are, on the whole, respected, one should not expect more than a small number of cases where the Court has had to plant itself

Table 6
Type of Congressional Action After Supreme Court Decisions Holding Legislation Unconstitutional Within Four Years After Enactment (Including New Deal Legislation)

Congressional Action	*Major Policy*	*Minor Policy*	*Total*
Reverses Court's Policy	17	2	19
None	0	12	12
Other	6*	1	7
Total	23	15	38

* In addition to the actions in Table 5 under "Changes Own Policy" and "Unclear," this figure includes the NRA legislation affected by the *Schechter Poultry* case.

firmly against a lawmaking majority. But majorities may, on rare occasions, become "tyrannical"; and when they do, the Court intervenes; and although the constitutional issue may, strictly speaking, be technically open, the Constitution assumes an underlying fundamental body of rights and liberties which the Court guarantees by its decisions.

Here again, however, even without examining the actual cases, it would appear, on political grounds, somewhat unrealistic to suppose that a Court whose members are recruited in the fashion of Supreme Court justices would long hold to norms of Right or Justice substantially at odds with the rest of the political elite. Moreover, in an earlier day it was perhaps easier to believe that certain rights are so natural and self-evident that their fundamental validity is as much a matter of definite knowledge, at least to all reasonable creatures, as the color of a ripe apple. To say that this view is unlikely to find many articulate defenders today is, of course, not to disprove it; it is rather to suggest that we do not need to elaborate the case against it in this essay.

In any event the best rebuttal to the view of the Court suggested above will be found in the record of the Court's decisions. Surely the six cases referred to a moment ago, where the policy consequences of the Court's decisions were overcome only after long battles, will not appeal to many contemporary minds as evidence for the proposition under examination. A natural right to employ child labor in mills and mines? To be free of income taxes by the federal government? To employ longshoremen and harbor workers without the protection of workmen's compensation? The Court itself did not rely upon such arguments in these cases, and it would be no credit to their opinions to reconstruct them along such lines.

So far, however, our evidence has been drawn from cases in which the Court has held legislation unconstitutional within four years after enactment. What of the other forty cases? Do we have evidence in these that the Court has protected fundamental or natural rights and liberties against the dead hand of some past tyranny by the lawmakers? The evidence is not impressive. In the entire history of the Court there is not one case arising under the First Amendment in which the Court has held federal legislation unconstitutional. If we turn from these fundamental liberties of religion, speech, press and assembly, we do find a handful of cases—something less than ten—arising under Amendments Four to Seven in which the Court has declared acts unconstitutional that might properly be regarded as involving rather basic liberties.[26] An inspection of these cases leaves the impression that, in all of them, the lawmakers and the Court were not very far apart; moreover, it is doubtful that the fundamental conditions of liberty in this country have been altered by more than a hair's breadth as a result of these decisions. However, let us give the Court its due; it is little enough.

Over against these decisions we must put the fifteen or so cases in which the Court used the protections of the Fifth, Thirteenth, Fourteenth and Fifteenth Amendments to preserve the rights and liberties of a relatively privileged group at the expense of the rights and liberties of a submerged group: chiefly slaveholders at the expense of slaves,[27] white people at the expense of colored people,[28] and property holders at the expense of wage earners and other groups.[29]

These cases, unlike the relatively innocuous ones of the preceding set, all involved liberties of genuinely fundamental importance, where an opposite policy would have meant thoroughly basic shifts in the distribution of rights, liberties, and opportunities in the United States—where, moreover, the policies sustained by the Court's action have since been repudiated in every civilized nation of the Western world, including our own. Yet, if our earlier argument is correct, it is futile —precisely because the basic distribution of privilege *was* at issue—to suppose that the Court could have possibly acted much differently in these areas of policy from the way in which it did in fact act.

VI

Thus the role of the Court as a policy-making institution is not simple; and it is an error to suppose that its functions can be either described or appraised by means of simple concepts drawn from democratic or moral theory. It is possible, nonetheless, to derive a few general conclusions about the Court's role as a policy-making institution.

National politics in the United States, as in other stable democracies, is dominated by relatively cohesive alliances that endure for long periods of time. One recalls the Jeffersonian alliance, the Jacksonian, the extraordinarily long-lived Republican dominance of the post-Civil War years, and the New Deal alliance shaped by Franklin Roosevelt. Each is marked by a break with past policies, a period of intense struggle, followed by consolidation, and finally decay and disintegration of the alliance.

Except for short-lived transitional periods when the old alliance is disintegrating and the new one is struggling to take control of political institutions, the Supreme Court is inevitably a part of the dominant national alliance. As an element in the political leadership of the dominant alliance, the Court of course supports the major policies of the alliance. By itself, the Court is almost powerless to affect the course of national policy. In the absence of substantial agreement within the alliance, an attempt by the Court to make national policy is likely to lead to disaster, as the *Dred Scott* decision and the early New Deal cases demonstrate. Conceivably, the cases of the last three decades involving the freedom of Negroes, culminating in the now famous decision on school integration, are exceptions to this generalization; I shall have more to say about them in a moment.

The Supreme Court is not, however, simply an *agent* of the alliance. It is an essential part of the political leadership and possesses some bases of power of its own, the most important of which is the unique legitimacy attributed to its interpretations of the Constitution. This legitimacy the Court jeopardizes if it flagrantly opposes the major policies of the dominant alliance; such a course of action, as we have seen, is one in which the Court will not normally be tempted to engage.

It follows that within the somewhat narrow limits set by the basic policy goals of the dominant alliance, the Court *can* make national policy. Its discretion, then, is not unlike that of a powerful committee chairman in Congress who cannot, generally speaking, nullify the basic policies substantially agreed on by the rest of the dominant leadership, but who can, within these limits, often determine important questions of timing, effectiveness, and subordinate policy. Thus the Court is least effective against a current lawmaking majority—and evidently least inclined to act. It is most effective when it sets the bounds of policy for officials, agencies, state governments or even regions, a task that has come to occupy a very large part of the Court's business.[30]

Few of the Court's policy decisions can be interpreted sensibly in terms of a "majority" versus a "minority." In this respect the Court is no different from the rest of the political leadership. Generally speaking, policy at the national level is the outcome of conflict, bargaining, and agreement among minorities; the process is neither minority rule nor majority rule but what might better be called *minorities* rule, where one aggregation of minorities achieves policies opposed by another aggregation.

The main objective of presidential leadership is to build a stable and dominant aggregation of minorities with a high probability of winning the presidency and one or both houses of Congress. The main task of the Court is to confer legitimacy on the fundamental policies of the successful coalition. There are times when the coalition is unstable with respect to certain key policies; at very great risk to its legitimacy powers, the Court can intervene in such cases and may even succeed in establishing policy. Probably in such cases it can succeed only if its action conforms to and reinforces a widespread set of explicit or implicit norms held by the political leadership; norms which are not strong enough or are not distributed in such a way as to insure the existence of an effective lawmaking majority but are, nonetheless, sufficiently powerful to prevent any successful attack on the legitimacy powers of the Court. This is probably the explanation for the relatively successful work of the Court in enlarging the freedom of Negroes to vote during the past three decades and in its famous school integration decisions.[31]

Yet the Court is more than this. Considered as a political system, democracy is a set of basic procedures for arriving at decisions. The operation of these procedures presupposes the existence of certain rights, obligations, liberties and restraints; in short, certain patterns of behavior. The existence of these patterns of behavior in turn presupposes widespread agreement (particularly among the politically active and influential segments of the population) on the validity and propriety of the behavior. Although its record is by no means lacking in serious blemishes, at its best the Court operates to confer legitimacy, not simply on the particular and parochial policies of the dominant political alliance, but upon the basic patterns of behavior required for the operation of a democracy.

NOTES

1. Frankfurter, *The Supreme Court in the Mirror of Justices*, 105 U. of Pa. L. Rev. 781, 793 (1957).
2. Provided that the total membership of the society is an even number, it is technically possible for a dispute to occur that divides the membership into two equal parts, neither of which can be said to be either a majority or minority of the total membership. But even in the instances where the number is even (which should occur on the average only half the time), the probability of an exactly even split, in any group of more than a few thousand people, is so small that it may be ignored.
3. Suppose the number of citizens, or members eligible to participate in collective

decisions, is *n*. Let each member indicate his "most preferred alternative." Then it is obvious that the maximum number of most preferred alternatives is *n*. It is equally obvious that if the number of most preferred alternatives is more than or equal to $n/2$, then no majority is possible. But for all practical purposes those formal limitations can be ignored, for we are dealing with a large society where the number of alternatives at issue before the Supreme Court is invariably quite small. If the number of alternatives is greater than two, it is theoretically possible for preferences to be distributed so that no outcome is consistent with the majority criterion, even where all members can rank all the alternatives and where there is perfect information as to their preferences; but this difficulty does not bear on the subsequent discussion, and it is disregarded. For an examination of this problem, consult Arrow, *Social Choice and Individual Values* (1951).

4. Actually, the matter is somewhat ambiguous. There appear to have been seventy-eight cases in which the Court has held provisions of federal law unconstitutional. Sixty-four different acts in the technical sense have been construed, and eighty-six different provisions in law have been in some respects invalidated. I rely here on the figures and the table given in Library of Congress, Legislative Reference Service, *Provisions of Federal Law Held Unconstitutional by the Supreme Court of the United States* 95, 141–47 (1936), to which I have added *United States v. Lovett*, 328 U.S. 303 (1946), and *United States ex rel. Toth v. Quarles*, 350 U.S. 11 (1955). There are some minor discrepancies in totals (not attributable to the differences in publication dates) between this volume and *Acts of Congress Held Unconstitutional in Whole or in Part by the Supreme Court of the United States*, in Library of Congress, Legislative Reference Service, *The Constitution of the United States of America, Analysis and Interpretation* (Corwin ed., 1953). The difference is a result of classification. The latter document lists seventy-three acts held unconstitutional (to which *Toth v. Quarles*, supra, should be added) but different sections of the same act are sometimes counted separately.
5. Dahl, *A Preface to Democratic Theory*, c. 2 (1956).
6. Compare Commager, *Majority Rule and Minority Rights* (1943).
7. Frankfurter, *op. cit.* supra note 1, at 782–84.
8. *Booth v. United States*, 291 U.S. 339 (1934), involved a reduction in the pay of retired judges. *Lynch v. United States*, 292 U.S. 571 (1934), repealed laws granting to veterans rights to yearly renewable term insurance; there were only twenty-nine policies outstanding in 1932. *Hopkins Federal Savings & Loan Ass'n v. Cleary*, 296 U.S. 315 (1935), granting permission to state building and loan associations to convert to federal ones on a vote of fifty-one per cent or more of votes cast at a legal meeting. *Ashton v. Cameron County Water Improvement District*, 298 U.S. 513 (1936), permitting municipalities to petition federal courts for bankruptcy proceedings.
9. *Schechter Poultry Corp. v. United States*, 295 U.S. 495 (1935).
10. *United States v. Butler*, 297 U.S. 1 (1936); *Perry v. United States*, 294 U.S. 330 (1935); *Panama Refining Co. v. Ryan*, 293 U.S. 388 (1935); *Railroad Retirement Board v. Alton R. Co.*, 295 U.S. 330 (1935); *Louisville Joint Stock Land Bank v. Radford*, 295 U.S. 555 (1935); *Rickert Rice Mills v. Fontenot*, 297 U.S. 110 (1936); *Carter v. Carter Coal Co.*, 298 U.S. 238 (1936).
11. *United States v. Dewitt*, 9 Wall. (U.S.) 41 (1870); *Gordon v. United States*, 2 Wall. (U.S.) 561 (1865); *Monongahela Navigation Co. v. United States*, 148 U.S. 312 (1893); *Wong Wing v. United States*, 163 U.S. 228 (1896); *Fairbank v. United States*, 181 U.S. 283 (1901); *Rassmussen v. United States*, 197 U.S. 516 (1905); *Muskrat v. United States*, 219 U.S. 346 (1911); *Choate v. Trapp*, 224 U.S. 665 (1912); *Evans v. Gore*, 253 U.S. 245 (1920); *Untermyer v. Anderson*, 276 U.S. 440 (1928); *United States v. Lovett*, 328 U.S. 303 (1946). Note that although the specific legislative provisions held unconstitutional may have been minor, the basic legislation may have been of major policy importance.
12. *Ex parte Garland*, 4 Wall. (U.S.) 333 (1867); *United States v. Klein*, 13 Wall. (U.S.) 128 (1872); *Pollock v. Farmers' Loan & Trust Co.*, 157 U.S. 429 (1895), rehearing granted 158 U.S. 601 (1895); *Employers' Liability Cases*, 207 U.S. 463 (1908); *Keller v. United States*, 213 U.S. 138 (1909); *Hammer v. Dagenhart*, 247 U.S. 251 (1918); *Eisner v. Macomber*, 252 U.S. 189 (1920); *Knickerbocker Ice Co. v. Stewart*, 253 U.S. 149 (1920);*United States v. Cohen Grocery Co.*, 255 U.S. 81 (1921); *Weeds, Inc. v. United States*, 255 U.S. 109 (1921); *Bailey v. Drexel Furniture Co.*, 259 U.S. 20 (1922); *Hill v.*

Wallace, 259 U.S. 44 (1922); *Washington v. Dawson & Co.* 264 U.S. 219 (1924); *Trusler v. Crooks,* 269 U.S. 475 (1926).

13a. *Pollock v. Farmers' Loan & Trust Co.,* 157 U.S. 429 (1895); *Employers' Liability Cases,* 207 U.S. 463 (1908); *Keller v. United States,* 213 U.S. 138 (1909); *Hammer v. Dagenhart,* 247 U.S. 251 (1918); *Bailey v. Drexel Furniture Co.,* 259 U.S. 20 (1922); *Trusler v. Crooks,* 269 U.S. 475 (1926); *Hill v. Wallace,* 259 U.S. 44 (1922); *Knickerbocker Ice Co. v. Stewart,* 253 U.S. 149 (1920); *Washington v. Dawson & Co.,* 264 U.S. 219 (1924).

b. *Ex parte Garland,* 4 Wall. (U.S.) 333 (1867); *United States v. Klein,* 13 Wall. (U.S.) 128 (1872).

c. *United States v. Cohen Grocery Co.,* 255 U.S. 81 (1921); *Weeds, Inc. v. United States,* 255 U.S. 109 (1921); *Eisner v. Macomber,* 252 U.S. 189 (1920).

d. *Gordon v. United States,* 2 Wall. (U.S.) 561 (1865); *Evans v. Gore,* 253 U.S. 245 (1920).

e. *United States v. Dewitt,* 9 Wall. (U.S.) 41 (1870); *Monongahela Navigation Co. v. United States,* 148 U.S. 312 (1893); *Wong Wing v. United States,* 163 U.S. 228 (1896); *Fairbank v. United States,* 181 U.S. 283 (1901); *Rassmussen v. United States,* 197 U.S. 516 (1905); *Muskrat v. United States,* 219 U.S. 346 (1911); *Choate v. Trapp,* 224 U.S. 665 (1912); *United States v. Lovett,* 328 U.S. 303 (1946).

f. *Untermyer v. Anderson,* 276 U.S. 440 (1928).

14. *Ex parte Garland,* 4 Wall. (U.S.) 333 (1867); *United States v. Klein,* 13 Wall. (U.S.) 128 (1872).

15. *United States v. Cohen Grocery Co.,* 255 U.S. 81 (1921), *Weeds, Inc. v. United States,* 255 U.S. 109 (1921).

16. *Eisner v. Macomber,* 252 U.S. 189 (1920).

17. *Employers' Liability Cases,* 207 U.S. 463 (1908); *Keller v. United States,* 213 U.S. 138 (1909); *Trusler v. Crooks,* 269 U.S. 475 (1926); *Hill v. Wallace,* 259 U.S. 44 (1922).

18. *Knickerbocker Ice Co. v. Stewart,* 253 U.S. 149 (1920).

19. *Washington v. Dawson & Co.,* 264 U.S. 219 (1924).

20. *Crowell v. Benson,* 285 U.S. 22 (1932).

21. *Pollock v. Farmers' Loan & Trust Co.,* 157 U.S. 429 (1895).

22. *Nicol v. Ames,* 173 U.S. 509 (1899); *Knowlton v. Moore,* 178 U.S. 41 (1900); *Patton v. Brady,* 184 U.S. 608 (1902); *Flint v. Stone Tracy Co.,* 220 U.S. 107 (1911).

23. *Hammer v. Dagenhart,* 247 U.S. 251 (1918).

24. *Bailey v. Drexel Furniture Co.,* 259 U.S. 20 (1922).

25. *United States v. Darby,* 312 U.S. 100 (1941).

26. The candidates for this category would appear to be *Boyd v. United States,* 116 U.S. 616 (1886); *Rassmussen v. United States,* 197 U.S. 516 (1905); *Wong Wing v. United States,* 163 U.S. 228 (1896); *United States v. Moreland,* 258 U.S. 433 (1922); *Kirby v. United States,* 174 U.S. 47 (1899); *United States v. Cohen Grocery Co.,* 255 U.S. 81 (1921); *Weeds, Inc. v. United States,* 255 U.S. 109 (1921); *Justices of the Supreme Court v. United States ex rel. Murray,* 9 Wall. (U.S.) 274 (1870); *United States ex rel. Toth v. Quarles,* 350 U.S. 11 (1955).

27. *Dred Scott v. Sandford,* 19 How. (U.S.) 393 (1857).

28. *United States v. Reese,* 92 U.S. 214 (1876); *United States v. Harris,* 106 U.S. 629 (1883); *United States v. Stanley* (Civil Rights Cases), 109 U.S. 3 (1883); *Baldwin v. Franks,* 120 U.S. 678 (1887); *James v. Bowman,* 190 U.S. 127 (1903); *Hodges v. United States,* 203 U.S. 1 (1906); *Butts v. Merchants & Miners Transportation Co.,* 230 U.S. 126 (1913).

29. *Monongahela Navigation Co. v. United States,* 148 U.S. 312 (1893); *Adair v. United States,* 208 U.S. 161 (1908); *Adkins v. Children's Hospital,* 261 U.S. 525 (1923); *Nichols v. Coolidge,* 274 U.S. 531 (1927); *Untermyer v. Anderson,* 276 U.S. 440 (1928); *Heiner v. Donnan,* 285 U.S. 312 (1932); *Louisville Joint Stock Land Bank v. Radford,* 295 U.S. 555 (1935).

30. "Constitutional law and cases with constitutional undertones are of course still very important, with almost one-fourth of the cases in which written opinions were filed [in the two most recent terms] involving such questions. Review of administrative action . . . constitutes the largest category of the Court's work, comprising one-third of the total cases decided on the merits. The remaining . . . categories of litigation . . . all involve largely public law questions." Frankfurter, *op. cit.* supra note 1, at 793.

31. *Rice v. Elmore,* 165 F.2d 387 (C.A. 4th, 1947), cert. denied 333 U.S. 875 (1948); *United States v. Classic,* 313 U.S. 299 (1941); *Smith v. Allwright,* 321 U.S. 649 (1944); *Grovey v. Townsend,* 295 U.S. 45 (1935); *Brown v. Board of Education,* 347 U.S. 483 (1954); *Bolling v. Sharpe,* 347 U.S. 497 (1954).

53

The Public Views the Supreme Court

KENNETH M. DOLBEARE

The following essay by Kenneth M. Dolbeare strongly suggests that the Supreme Court, like most other political institutions in America, is judged through a partisan screen: Democrats tend to have favorable attitudes toward the Court, while Republicans hold less sympathetic views. The party affiliation of the incumbent President also shapes attitudes toward the Court. When General Eisenhower held the presidency, Republicans took a more favorable view of the Court than they did during the terms of Democratic presidents.

Dolbeare also shows that Americans have little knowledge about decisions of the Supreme Court. Even those who view the Court favorably are seldom able to mention specific decisions on which their approval is based.

The role of party identification and the presidency in shaping attitudes toward the Court and the scant information possessed by most Americans about the Court's work raise substantial doubts about Robert A. Dahl's thesis (in the preceding selection) that the Supreme Court confers legitimacy upon the policies of the lawmaking majority in the popular branches of the government. Except in a few highly controversial areas, such as racial segregation and religious exercises in public schools, the Court's decisions are virtually unknown to the American public.

Furthermore, since partisan identification and the party of the President are so important in shaping public attitudes toward the Court, it is plausible to hypothesize that the legitimacy of the Supreme Court's decisions and the acceptance of its orders derive from other political institutions. If this is the case, then the asserted legitimacy-conferring func-

tion of the Court appears to be negligible.

Dolbeare is Professor of Political Science at the University of Washington. He is the author of Trial Courts in Urban Politics *(1967), coauthor of* Little Groups of Neighbors *(1968), and the author of articles on the judicial process.*

Scholars and laymen alike have long been captivated by the attempt to define the part played by the United States Supreme Court in the American political process. Some have treated it as an organ of government operating in a context of other institutions and forces,[1] while others have tried to grapple with such elusive intangibles as its democratic or symbolic qualities.[2] One dimension common to both of these approaches involves the nature of public response to the Court's actions; in both approaches, assumptions are made about public attentiveness, evaluation, and probable reaction to the Court and its decisions.

Because there has been little evidence concerning how much the public knows or cares about the Supreme Court, lively arguments based on assumptions about the nature of public response have developed and endured. Legal scholars and judges differ over whether the Justices should exercise self-restraint and avoid exposing themselves to possible public disfavor, or whether they should be "activists" and do what they deem necessary in hopes that the public will ultimately acquiesce.[3] Insofar as this argument involves expectations about public response, it seems to hinge upon the question of possible public antipathy to judicial willingness to decide controversial issues. Others insist upon "neutral principles"[4] as the basis for decisions, by which is meant formulating a rule of general applicability rather than "result-oriented" decision-making geared to the circumstances of particular cases. In part, this argument is based on the question of whether public acquiescence is related to an image of the Court as an institution whose decisions embody some higher justification than reasonableness or propriety. Another frequently debated issue is whether the apparently anti-democratic character of judicial review can be legitimated as serving the cause of popular sovereignty; frequently this takes the form of arguing that the Court is really representing the will of the people in its actions.[5] Whether it is or not, of course, is a matter which has never been subjected to direct proof.

Political scientists are more inclined to be interested in the Court's political role and its impact in the political system. Some have attempted to set up a characterization of the Court as one among several governmental institutions, all of which interact with each other in a context of public opinion.[6] At least one has been courageous enough to talk in terms of the Court's "constituency,"[7] a concept so suggestive of representation and responsibility that most have assiduously avoided it in respect to the Court. More current is a view of the Court that sees it as a body of decision-makers who act within a framework of "demands" and "supports" arising out of the remainder of the political system.[8] All these approaches implicitly assume that sufficient public awareness and knowledge about the Court exist so that the public will react to unpopular Court decisions. In addition, some now fear that respect for the institution and/or its symbolic role may be undermined by an excessively clear revelation of the fact that the Justices sometimes make law, and that compliance with its decisions may therefore be endangered.[9]

This paper reports some highlights of an attempt to find evidence bearing on these important issues.[10] It seeks to answer such questions as, How much does the general public know about the Supreme Court? What factors affect attitudes toward the Court? Does acceptance of the "myths" of nonpolitical, mechanical jurisprudence affect evaluation of the Court or the prospect of compliance with its decisions? Who are the Court's opponents, and what are their prospects for effective resistance?

For evidence that will permit even speculative answers to these questions, we must turn to various forms of public-opinion research. Our data here include reanalyzed national sample surveys conducted by the American Institute of Public Opinion (Gallup) organization reaching back to 1937,[11] combined with national survey results of 1964.[12] The best data, however, were produced through a much more detailed and multi-dimensional inquiry conducted with a cross section of the adult population of Wisconsin by the University of Wisconsin Survey Research Laboratory.[13]

The review of the data follows a four-stage format. First, we examine the perception of the Court as an institution distinct from the other branches of national government. Next, cognition is explored—the extent and nature of the public's knowledge about the Court and its actions. Then the evaluations which have emerged from the public as a whole and from special segments of it are investigated across a substantial period of time. The bases and correlations of these evaluations are explored and related to the problems of compliance and resistance. Finally, there is an attempt to suggest some implications for students of American legal and political processes.

I

We begin by attempting to sort out the public's view of the Court from its perceptions of the Congress and the Presidency: How distinctively is the Court seen? Does the public conceive it to be more or less important, powerful, or trustworthy than the others? While these are partly evaluative dimensions, we are concerned here only with the evidence these responses offer of a capacity to conceive of the Court as a particular entity, distinguishable from but comparable to the other branches.

In terms of the public's view of its importance in deciding how Ameri-

Table 1
Branch of Government Which "Does the Most Important Things"*

Congress	52%
Supreme Court	6
President	27
Depends	3
Don't Know	12
	100%
	N=627

* Q. "Which branch of government would you say does the most important things in deciding how Americans are going to live . . . the Congress, the Supreme Court, or the President?" Wisconsin Survey, 1966.

Table 2
Confidence in Actions Taken by Institutions of the National Government*

	By Congress?	*By President?*	*By Supreme Court?*
Yes	50%	35%	28%
Depends	20	17	13
No	16	33	39
Don't Know	14	15	20
	100%	100%	100%
	N=627	N=627	N=627

* Wisconsin Survey, 1966.

cans are going to live, the Supreme Court trails far behind the other institutions. At the same time, 71 percent of this sample answered affirmatively to the abstract question of whether the Supreme Court could make important changes in the way people live. Perhaps it is more significant, however, that 16 percent denied that the Court had this potential.

In order to reach beyond the symbolization of government toward a sense of relative trust in institutions, a series of questions was asked about respondents' confidence in the actions of the three major institutions. This question was repeated (with the institutions rotated) in the form, "Would you be likely to think the right thing had been done in Washington if the action had been taken by the Supreme Court (President, Congress)?" Once again, the Court appears distinguishable and, more surprisingly, to trail the others in the public's confidence. One cannot help sympathizing with the respondent's problem here, in that no suggestion was offered as to *what* had been done. A "depends" answer would seem to be the only logical solution to the dilemma presented by the question. This was deliberate, however, in order to reach generalized institutionally-related attitudes and not specific issue dimensions; the sharp differences in responses suggest that respondents held distinctive attitudes toward the institutions as such, though there is no certainty that it is only relative trust which is measured here. Nevertheless, the Court appears to be the only institution whose actions respondents, without further information, were prepared to question. Put another way, only the question about the Court elicited more No answers than Yes answers.

Some further insight into the bases of these differences in response is available from a comparison of the political party identification of each set of respondents. We find that the nature of responses to the institution is related to the respondents' own partisan identification. There is a definite shift on the part of Republicans from confidence in the Congress to doubts about the President, probably attributable to the salience of partisanship with respect to the latter. Members of the party out of power in the White House have traditionally associated themselves with the Congress. All respondents were inclined to distrust the Court, with Republicans displaying the widest disparity—a disparity closely related to the proportions of distrust of the President. In summary, at least in the eyes of this Wisconsin sample, the Court is per-

Table 3
Confidence in Action Taken by Institutions, by Political Party*

	By Congress?			*By President?*			*By Supreme Court?*		
	Dem.	*Ind.*	*Rep.*	*Dem.*	*Ind.*	*Rep.*	*Dem.*	*Ind.*	*Rep.*
Yes	59%	57%	61%	58%	35%	24%	39%	41%	30%
Depends	20	22	24	17	23	22	14	16	17
No	21	21	15	25	42	54	47	43	53
	100%	100%	100%	100%	100%	100%	100%	100%	100%

* Wisconsin Survey, 1966. "Don't Knows" eliminated. Democrats: N=188 to 198; Independents: N=109 to 122; Republicans: N=149 to 158.

ceived separately from the other institutions: it is relatively unimportant (though capable of effecting significant changes in people's lives) and relatively untrustworthy.

So far we have noted that the public's capacity to distinguish the Court from other institutions of government does not mean that it sees the Court in more favorable terms than it does the others. Before carrying this further, we shall examine the extent of public knowledge about the Court and its work.

II

Opinion studies contain few enough questions about the Supreme Court in any form, but there are almost none concerning the extent of knowledge about the Court and its work. And yet this is a highly significant datum: what credence should be placed on approval or disapproval in the absence of information as to the knowledge of the Court's actions possessed by the respondents? Are there gains to be realized in terms of support for the Court (or at least greater acquiescence in its decisions) from expansion of public awareness and knowledge about the Court?[14]

National studies reveal that most people *do* know the name of the highest court in the land (86 percent, AIPO, 1949), although not many knew the number of judges on the Court (40 percent, AIPO, 1945). The only other inquiry directed at knowledge as such occurred in 1945 on Justice Roberts' retirement, when a national sample was asked how many judges of each political party were then on the bench. Normally a rather exotic question, this was more meaningful at the time because there had been considerable media discussion of the fact that Republican Supreme Court Justices were becoming extinct, and calls for appointment of a Republican were being made. Chief Justice Stone's credentials as a Republican might have been suspect by this time, inasmuch as he had been elevated to the center chair by President Franklin Roosevelt, but even accepting the prospect of some confusion over his party loyalties, the 5 percent accuracy in naming the number of Republican judges is not impressive under the circumstances.

A much more satisfying line of inquiry was pursued with respect to the Wisconsin sample. Respondents were asked to say simply whether the Supreme Court had made decisions (not how the decisions had gone) in recent years in each of eight subject areas, and some surprising limitations of knowledge became apparent. Table 4 displays this generally low level of knowledge. The prayer decisions have apparently been one of the most salient actions of the Court, being unknown only to the same seemingly irreducible number of persons who have managed to remain unaware of the segregation decisions. Less anticipated were the remarkably low levels of knowledge about the highly publicized reapportionment and defendants' rights cases. Wisconsin had both redistricted and experienced its full share of denunciations of the Court for placing limits on law-enforcement officials, but the public did not link these to the Court in any clear fashion. Perhaps defendants' rights issues are the private preserve of policemen and editorial writers. In any event, other activities of the national government, such as federal aid to education and Medicare, are attributed to the Court (wrongly) much more often than are apportionment and defendants' rights. That there is a residuum of assumption that the Court has acted—or a willingness of respondents to say Yes to interviewers—is indicated by the relatively high affirmative responses to the questions involving the urban renewal program and the John Birch Society. That the defendants' rights decisions receive no greater affirmative response than these two seems to relegate them to a specially insignificant status in the public mind.

On the basis of these responses, it was possible to set up an index of knowledge about Supreme Court decisions which would serve to distinguish those with higher levels of knowledge and permit comparison of such people with other knowledge-level groupings in various ways. In terms of number correct out of eight questions (and, it might be well to note again, respondents needed only to know that the Court had made decisions, not how the cases were decided), the percentages in each category were as follows:

8 correct	2%
7 correct	3%
6 correct	2%
5 correct	8%
4 correct	13%
3 correct	23%
2 correct	26%
1 correct	12%
0 correct	12%

Table 4
Knowledge of Court's Decisions,* Eight Areas

Subject	*Yes: Made Decision*	*No: No Decisions*	*Don't Know*
Rights of defendants accused of crimes	26%	7%	66%
Federal aid to education	45	10	45
Redistricting for state legislatures	35	9	56
Medical care for the aged	52	24	24
Prayers in public schools	71	7	22
Segregation in public schools	72	7	21
Urban renewal program	26	15	59
John Birch Society	23	19	58

* Q. "Do you happen to recall whether the Supreme Court made a decision in recent years on . . . ?" Wisconsin Survey, 1966. N=627 in all cases.

The paucity of numbers in the upper levels led to a generous characterization of "high knowledge" as including all with five or more correct answers. "Medium" includes those with three and four correct answers, and all others are "low." As might be expected, high-knowledge people are quite disproportionately the better educated, wealthier people. About half of them are Republicans, about 5 percent independents, and the rest Democrats. Since there were more Democrats than Republicans (plus a substantial number of independents) in the sample, this is a distinct over-representation of Republicans. These high-knowledge people are the ones with a high sense of political efficacy, for they are also the ones who say that they would act in some way to change a Court decision of which they disapprove. The relevance of these demographic and attitudinal characteristics will become clearer as we look at differential evaluations of the Court's performance.

III

The evidence to this point suggests separate perception of the Court but a low level of knowledge about what it has done in specific subject areas. The results from questions calling for evaluative responses should be read in the light of these findings. Opinion not rooted in knowledge could be changeable if more information were provided, or high-knowledge persons might be sufficiently influential as to render the opinion of others relatively inconsequential. The findings presented in this section suggest that the Court suffers under any combination of circumstances, including both of the above. Let us first look at the general pattern of public approval and disapproval over the last twenty years, then at the specific content of reactions in recent years, and finally at the part played by knowledge, party identification, and other factors in the creation of attitudes.

Evaluative dimensions appear in most AIPO questions concerning the Supreme Court, as we noted in section I above. In order to concentrate on evaluation with as few extraneous elements as possible, therefore, this analysis is based on questions which ask essentially only whether the respondent approves or disapproves of the Court and whether his opinion has risen or fallen in recent years. With these limitations, it is still possible to set up a time continuum of twenty years with four national surveys. Because of the difference in the wording of questions (and because, while all ask whether attitudes have changed, only two precede this by asking whether general evaluation is favorable or unfavorable on balance), Table 5 presents them separately but as closely grouped for comparison as possible.

Confining our analysis for the moment to the totals involved, we find a consistent pattern of downward change in respect or regard for the Court. But it is not clear from these data whether this indicates a net shift toward generally lower evaluations of the Court over time. It may simply be an enduring phenomenon of attitudes toward the Court that they always appear to be heading down for some segment of the population but general evaluation remains constant and favorable overall.

The two most recent surveys offer the best opportunity to explore reasons for approval or disapproval of the Court. In Wisconsin in 1966, re-

Table 5
Evaluations of the Supreme Court, 1946–1964

1946: Attitude Change and Direction[a]

	Higher Regard	*Lower Regard*	*Total Changing*	*Total Don't Know; No Answer*
Democrats	6%	18%	24%	76%
Republicans	3	43	46	54
All Respondents	3	28	31	69

1949: Opinion of Court, Attitude Change and Direction[b]

	Opinion of Court				*Attitude Change, Direction*		
	Very High	*Favorable*	*Disapproval*	*No Opinion*	*Respect Increased*	*Respect Decreased*	*Same or No Opinion*
Democrats	17%	47%	8%	27%	27%	12%	61%
Republicans	16	41	24	19	18	33	49
All Respondents	17	43	14	26	22	22	56

1957: Respect for Court v. Congress, Attitude Change and Direction[c]

	Greater Respect for:				*Respect for Court:*	
	Congress	*Court*	*Same*	*Don't Know*	*Increased*	*Decreased*
Democrats	34%	28%	22%	16%	3%	18%
Republicans	26	32	26	16	3	15
All Respondents	29	30	23	17	3	16

1964: Attitude Directions[d]

	Affirmative	*Negative*	*Mixed*	*No Interest*
Democrats	12%	22%	5%	62%
Republicans	10	37	6	47
All Respondents	12	26	5	57

[a] 1946, AIPO: Q. "Has your attitude toward the Supreme Court changed in recent years? Do you have a higher regard or a lower regard for the Supreme Court now?" N=1553.

[b] 1949, AIPO: Q. "What is your opinion of the U.S. Supreme Court? Would you say that your respect for the U.S. Supreme Court has increased or decreased in recent years?" Two surveys with the same questions were conducted three days apart; combined N=2919.

[c] 1957, AIPO: Q. "Which do you have greater respect for, Congress or the Supreme Court? Has your attitude toward the Supreme Court changed in recent years?" N=1016.

[d] 1964, Michigan SRC: Q. "We are all pretty busy these days and can't be expected to keep up on everything. Have you had time to pay any attention to what the Supreme Court of the United States has been doing in the past few years? (If yes) Is there anything in particular that it has done that you have liked or disliked? (What is that?) (Anything else?)"

spondents were first asked to rate the Court's performance and then to specify what it had done that was good and what it had done that was bad. Ratings of the Court's job were as follows:

Very good	8%
Good	42
Fair	25
Poor	6
Don't know	19
	100%
	N=627

When those respondents who rated the Court were asked to name a good thing the Court had done, the only subject that came to mind (and then only to 19 percent of those who rated the Court) was civil rights and integration. No other subject was mentioned by more than 1 percent of respondents. The capacity to name a *bad* thing was even lower, with only 9 percent able to name anything at all (two-thirds of these specified the prayer decisions). For the Wisconsin sample, ratings of the Court rested on scant linkage with specific aspects of its decisions.

The same was true of the Survey Research Center's national sample in 1964, from which a remarkably similar pattern of response emerges. Respondents' reactions to an evaluative question (see note to Table 5 above) were classified into affirmative and negative categories. Only 9 percent responded affirmatively, and almost all were on the subject of civil rights and integration. A full 23 percent responded negatively, with the prayer decisions the basis for the majority and a scattering of other cases being mentioned.

If ratings of the Court's performance, and presumably approval-disapproval reactions as well, are thus devoid of informed content or even interest, to what factors may they be attributed? The answer inherent in the four-survey table above is political partisanship, but before we examine this, let us conclude our consideration of the part played by knowledge.

Our knowledge index comes entirely from the responses of the Wisconsin sample, but there is no apparent reason to doubt its generality, since the Wisconsin results have conformed to national results in all respects where comparison was possible. Table 6 indicates that high knowledge correlates with relatively greater disapproval of the Court. Table 7 shows that this is only partly due to the fact that the better educated and more knowledgeable persons were Republicans, and Republicans tended to be less favorable toward the Court.

These findings require that the role of political partisanship in determining attitudes toward the Court be con-

Table 6
Knowledge and Rating of the Court*

Rating	*Very Good and Good*	*Fair*	*Poor*		
Knowledge:					
High	54%	28%	18%	100%	N=92
Medium	65	29	7	101	N=196
Low	64	33	4	101	N=221

* Wisconsin Survey, 1966.

Table 7
Party Affiliation, Knowledge, and Rating of the Court

	Republicans		*Democrats*	
Rating of Court	*High Knowledge**	*Low Knowledge*	*High Knowledge*	*Low Knowledge*
Very good and good	51%	58%	70%	72%
Fair	28	34	23	24
Poor	21	8	7	4
	100%	100%	100%	100%
	N=67	N=93	N=73	N=141

* "High" knowledge here includes four or more correct, "low" all others. Wisconsin Survey, 1966.

sidered in detail. This has been done in depth elsewhere,[15] but sufficient data are available here to sketch the outlines of a close association between respondents' party affiliation and attitudes toward the Supreme Court.

A glance at Table 7 shows Democrats approving the Court more strongly than Republicans. Reference back to Table 5 shows that this has been the case at least since 1946. Negative changes in attitudes occur disproportionately among Republicans also, with the exception of 1957. In the Wisconsin Survey, where measures of intensity of party identification were available, rating of the Court was lowest among the strong Republicans and highest among the strongest Democrats. A simple comparison based on these data shows differentials of this order [see table below].

	Republicans	*Democrats*
Very good and good	55%	72%
Fair	32	24
Poor	13	5
	100%	101%

Why are respondents' party affiliations related to attitudes toward the Court? Party membership does not seem to be merely a cover for other factors, such as conservatism/liberalism, for several reasons. An index of conservatism/liberalism, constructed out of the Wisconsin data, showed some differences between conservatives and liberals with respect to the Court but distinctly less than between Republicans and Democrats. Conservatives and liberals differed from each other sharply according to party affiliation.

The 1957 survey, in which there was only minimal difference between Republicans and Democrats as to the proportion experiencing negative attitude changes (and that due to Southerners), presents a special problem here but also provides a clue: with Republicans presumably of the same general mind as in 1946, 1949, and 1964 in terms of conservatism/liberalism, what accounts for the complete absence of the otherwise consistent differential between the parties? Surely the Court's decisions in the 1956 Term were enough to awaken conservative antipathies, but there was no evidence of this in June of 1957 when this survey was taken. (Inclusion of the preponderantly Democratic South changes the national percentages by only 2 or 3 points in any case, so that Southern resentment of the desegregation decisions cannot be the primary cause of this difference.)

One speculative hypothesis may be offered. Attitudes toward the Court seem to be strongly party-related, but perhaps not just in the sense of Democrats favoring the Court and Republicans disapproving it. Attitudes and attitude change toward the Court seem to be related also to the party affiliation of the President, with respondents being more inclined to view the Court favorably when their party controls the White House. Support for the hypothesis that there is an association in the public mind between the President and the Supreme Court may be found from the fact that in the Wisconsin sample, those who were inclined to think the right thing had been done if the action were taken by the President (about one-third of the sample) were dramatically the most likely of any group to think the same of the Supreme Court. The 1957 results discussed above may be understandable in the light of this hypothesis, and two other results during the Eisenhower incumbency provide further support. Republicans and Democrats are virtually indistinguishable in these two surveys, in sharp contrast to the otherwise "normal" Republican level of disapproval. If the South were included in Table 8, Republicans would appear as decidedly more favorable to the Court than Democrats. These are the only times that Republicans have not been distinctly more negative, and/or changing in the negative direction, in the twenty years examined. The generally conservative nature of the Court's decision-making in the early 1950's might be credited with moderating Republican opposition, but this would require assumptions about attentiveness and knowledge wholly at odds with the findings of the previous section. Nor are Republicans likely to be such overwhelming supporters of *Brown v. Board of Education* that all else would be overridden.

Table 8
Party-Based Opinion during Republican Presidency, 1952-1960, South Excluded

1954: Approval of Segregation Decision[a]			
	Approve	*Disapprove*	*No Opinion*
Democrats	66%	31%	3%
Republicans	64	30	6

1956: Belief That the Court is Taking on More Authority Than the Constitution Intended[b]			
	Court Is	*Court* Is Not	*No Opinion*
Democrats	18%	58%	24%
Republicans	20	57	23

[a] 1954, AIPO: Q. "The U.S. Supreme Court has ruled that racial segregation in the public schools is illegal. This means that all children, no matter what their race, must be allowed to go to the same schools. Do you approve or disapprove of the decision?" N=807.
[b] 1956, AIPO: Q. "Do you think the Supreme Court is taking on more authority than the Constitution intended it to have?" N=1018.

The evidence for Presidential associations is by no means conclusive, nor is it intended to suggest that other factors are not also at work. There is evidence of some effect of conservatism/liberalism attitudes, and clear indication of an independent effect of the degree of knowledge possessed. But party affiliation seems clearly the dominant variable in determining evaluation of the Court, with the possible Presidential association as part of that party-based attitudinal complex.

IV

So far, we have found evaluative opinion to be generally favorable, though based on very low levels of knowledge. Those with relatively high levels of knowledge were inclined to be least favorable towards the Court. Changes in attitudes seem to be dependent more on party identifications as focussed through the vehicle of the President than on any other factors. We are still left with some important questions: Who are the Court's opponents in the general public? What are the prospects for resistance to the Court's rulings? Do the so-called "myths" of Court neutrality, nonpartisanship, and mechanical law-giving contribute to a more favorable view of the Court and a readier propensity to comply with its decisions?

In order to locate those persons most opposed to the Court as an institution, we isolated those who rated the Court's performance as "fair" or "poor" and *also* said they would *not* "be likely to think the right thing had been done by the government in Washington, if the action had been taken by the Supreme Court." Somewhat surprisingly, these "anti-Court" people were almost a perfect cross section of the sample. There was a lower proportion of conservatives in this group than in the sample as a whole. It is probable that Wisconsin is thinner in right-wing sentiment than some other states, but this still seems to suggest that conservative opposition to the Court is less widespread in the general public than the outcries of proponents would suggest. At the same time, some liberals may be less than satisfied with the pace of Court movement in their direction and should be numbered among those unhappy with the Court. Throughout the Wisconsin data, and by several different measures, liberals continued to make up substantial proportions of those people who expressed less favorable attitudes toward the Court.

What are the prospects for resistance to the Court's rulings? The very small number of persons with strong anti-Court attitudes (12 percent of the sample, using the definition of the preceding paragraph) might be swelled by people aggrieved at a particular decision, with resultant defiance of the Court. The experience after the anti-segregation decision of 1954 is too recent to overlook this possibility, but the evidence of low levels of knowledge suggests that few issues indeed would have this potential. Respondents were asked, "If the U.S. Supreme Court made a decision which affected you personally, and you felt this was a wrong decision, do you think you would do anything to try to change the Court's decision?" A full 36 percent said that they would. Again, these people represent an almost perfect cross section of the sample in all respects except that they came disproportionately from the higher knowledge levels.

Probably affirmative answers to this question represent respondents' sense of political efficacy rather than particular evaluative attitudes toward the

Court. This is confirmed by the means which these people volunteered that they would take to try to change the Court's decision. Fully half would act through their representatives in Congress, about a quarter would act within the established legal processes, and only a scattered few would have recourse to agitation with the general public to develop opposition to the Court. This is quiescence indeed. Those who rate the Court's performance as poor are the most likely to act to change a decision, but they are neither numerous nor particularly rebelliously inclined. Those who indicated that they would do nothing to change a decision gave answers that paint a classic picture of the dimensions of the feeling of powerlessness which are possible in modern society.

Is there any connection between this quiescence and adherence to the "myths" of mechanical jurisprudence? The Wisconsin sample was asked, "Some people say that the judges of the U.S. Supreme Court decide cases strictly on the basis of what the Constitution says, while others say that they decide on the basis of what they think is right for the country. Which comes closest to the way you feel?" The sample divided 48 percent to 38 percent in favor of strictly Constitution-based decision-making, with only low-knowledge Democrats feeling that the judges' view of the good of the country was the dominant factor. An index of acceptance-rejection of these "myths" was constructed from responses to this question and the respondents' agree-disagree reactions to the statement, "Since U.S. Supreme Court judges don't have many of the political attitudes and pressures which elected officials have, the Supreme Court judges can do things more fairly." Those who agreed "very much" or "on the whole" were taken as having internalized the myths relatively strongly and, if they also answered the previous question in favor of strict, Constitution-based decisions, were categorized as "strong myth holders." Those who agreed only a little or disagreed to any extent, and who felt the judges decide on the basis of what they think is right for the country, were categorized as "myth rejecters." Table 9 compares the two groups in terms of their evaluation of the Court's recent performance. The acceptance of these myths seems to correlate with higher ratings of the Court, but again, we cannot be certain whether the former causes the latter or whether one is inclined to endorse the myths because of satisfaction with the Court. There is little or no difference between the two groups in terms of levels of knowledge, liberalism/conservatism, or propensity to act to change a decision. Strong acceptance of the myths does seem in

Table 9
Relation of Myth-Holding to Rating of the Court

	How Good a Job Has Court Been Doing?			
Group	*Very Good or Good*	*Fair*	*Poor*	
Strong Myth Holders	75%	25%	1%	101% N=148
Myth Rejecters	43	37	20	100% N= 98

fact to bear an independent relationship to evaluation of the Court. But we may well doubt that the procedures followed by the Court or the character of its decision-making are relevant to the extent of myth-holding in the general public, except in the most extreme situation; knowledge levels are too low and the structuring effects of party affiliation and Presidential polarization too great to permit us to envision anything but the respondent's educational experience behind his acceptance or rejection of the myths.

Can we identify sectors of the general public which give particular support to the Court? The evidence so far suggests that the public is inattentive and uninformed about the Court, but that there exists a generalized sense of confidence in the institution, particularly among the lowest knowledge levels. We cannot find support for the Court in knowledge alone, and images of a ring of knowledgeable defenders protecting the Court from attacks by the uninformed and the right-wing ideologue are apparently false. We have instead a dialogue between a small number of attentive people, in which numbers are on the side of the Court's opponents, a group not limited to conservatives alone. The Court's opponents are unsuccessful in generating significant support because the general public is simply unaware of, but generally favorable toward, the Supreme Court. The major sources of support for the Court, then, are found in the lower knowledge levels of the mass public.

This support is expressed only in a generalized way, however, and then through a perhaps unanticipated channel. The link between an inattentive general public and the Supreme Court seems to be the political parties. Early-acquired party loyalties become relevant to attitudes toward the Court because of the salience of the party identification of the President. Changes in attitude toward the Court and levels of opinion toward it are chiefly affected by party and by presidential associations. Occasionally an issue with dramatic impact cuts through the general pattern and succeeds in restructuring attitudes, but this is extremely rare and only the segregation cases in recent history have had real effects on evaluations of the Court.

V

If we were social scientists unfamiliar with the arguments over the Court's relationship with the people, we would probably have anticipated these results. The voting studies and other recent research[16] have documented the structuring effects of party identification, and here, where visibility is so low and issue and candidate orientations foreclosed, party might be expected to be even more influential. The only findings even relatively inconsistent with other opinion studies are those about the effects of high knowledge and the degree of disinterest and ignorance about the Court. But in some respects even the effect of knowledge fits into familiar patterns, because Republicans generally have higher levels of information than Democrats, and we have noted the disapproval tendencies of Republicans. The paucity of knowledge is probably related to the lack of personal impact of the Court's activities. The pro-Court specifiers of civil rights and integration may be responding partly to the massive publicity of twelve years since the Brown decision. The anti-Court specifiers of the prayer decision may be responding to a specially personalized issue area, a subject which has greater capacity to touch people's lives and create discussion and/or action at the local level. Certainly areas such as apportionment and defendants' rights are not ones in which average citizens are as likely to become engaged.

The lack of personalization of Court impact may also be accountable for its relative success in gaining compliance in recent years with such sweeping policy changes as apportionment and defendants' rights. Where the responsibility to act in accordance with the Court's requirements rests on public officials (for example, legislators and law-enforcement officials) with relatively little public action required, compliance is high and the public is relatively unengaged. Where change in behavioral patterns by large numbers of people is involved, such as in the segregation and prayer instances, the general public is more intimately impacted, and compliance is more difficult to secure. Thus it would seem possible to hypothesize that the Court's successful policy initiatives of recent years were owing to the institutional and official acquiescence it has received, rather than to any real public approval of its actions. When the public *has* become engaged, it is quite likely to be in opposition, and decisions in such areas have led to negative trends in attitudes toward the Court. The downturn in reactions to the Court is such a consistent feature of American public opinion, however, and the public is so uninvolved in Court matters except for generalized approval of the institution, that it would be wrong to argue that the Court was in disfavor or that such disfavor would have an effect on its capacity to act. The general public is just too far removed from the Court and its work to be relevant to it in any major way, either as a controlling factor or as a measure of the propriety of its decisions. The Court can take far-reaching action, such as in the matters of apportionment or defendants' rights, without ever making a dent in the public consciousness.

This is not to deny, of course, that the Supreme Court is an important institution of the American political process. It *does* suggest that the Court acts free of the people's specific reactions, and that its institutional context, its personnel, and its procedures are relatively more important. The people view the Court just about as they do other political objects, and not in any special terms. Their attitudes toward it are shaped by the same broad agents that shape their party allegiances and voting behavior, and they judge the Court—when they do—just as they do their other leading politicians. Distinctive in so many ways, the Court is in the long run rendered essentially comparable to the other institutions by the unconscious act of the people.

NOTES

1. See Samuel Krislov, *The Supreme Court in the Political Process* (New York: Macmillan, 1965) or, for a more dramatic, participant's account, Robert H. Jackson, *The Struggle for Judicial Supremacy* (New York: A. A. Knopf, 1941).
2. See Max Lerner, "The Constitution and the Court as Symbols," *Yale Law Journal*, XLVI (1937), pp. 1290–1319 or, for a summary, Alpheus T. Mason, "Myth and Reality in Supreme Court Decisions," *Virginia Law Review*, XLVIII (December 1962), pp. 1385–1406, or any of the works cited in note 5 below.
3. See Wallace Mendelson, *Justices Black and Frankfurter* (Chicago: University of

Chicago Press, 1961), or "Justice Black and First Amendment Absolutes: A Public Interview," *New York University Law Review*, XXXVII (1962), pp. 569–73.

4. See Herbert Wechsler, *Principles, Politics and Fundamental Law* (Cambridge, Mass.: Harvard University Press, 1961); Arthur S. Miller and Ronald Howell, "The Myth of Neutrality in Constitutional Adjudication," *University of Chicago Law Review*, XXVII (1960), p. 661; or Alexander M. Bickel, *The Least Dangerous Branch* (New York: Bobbs-Merrill, 1962).
5. See Charles L. Black, *The People and the Court* (New York: Macmillan, 1960); E. V. Rostow, "The Democratic Character of Judicial Review," *Harvard Law Review*, LXVI (1952), p. 193; Robert H. Jackson, *The Supreme Court in the American System of Government* (New York: Harper & Row, 1955); Robert G. McCloskey, *The American Supreme Court* (Chicago: University of Chicago Press, 1960); or Learned Hand, *The Bill of Rights* (Cambridge, Mass.: Harvard University Press, 1958).
6. See Jack Peltason, *Federal Courts in the Political Process* (New York: Random House, 1955); Alan Westin, *The Anatomy of a Constitutional Law Case* (New York: Macmillan, 1961); or, for more explicit treatments, Walter Murphy, *Congress and the Court* (Chicago: University of Chicago Press, 1962), and *Elements of Judicial Strategy* (Chicago: University of Chicago Press, 1964).
7. Martin Shapiro, *Law and Politics in the Supreme Court* (New York: Free Press of Glencoe, 1964), pp. 8–9.
8. See Glendon W. Schubert, *Judicial Policy-Making* (Chicago: Scott, Foresman, 1965), or Herbert Jacob, *Justice in America* (Boston: Little, Brown, 1965).
9. See Arthur S. Miller, "Some Pervasive Myths About the U.S. Supreme Court," *St. Louis University Law Journal*, X (Winter 1965), pp. 153–189, or, for a summary of the opposing arguments, Arthur S. Miller, "On the Need for 'Impact Analysis' of Supreme Court Decisions," *Georgetown Law Journal*, LIII (Winter 1965), pp. 365–401.
10. For another effort to develop evidence, see John Kessel, "Public Perceptions of the Supreme Court," *Midwest Journal of Political Science*, X (1966), pp. 167–91, a study conducted in a single city. Other political scientists who have sought to integrate public opinion data into their analyses of the actions of the Court and its judges include Murphy, *Congress and the Court*, p. 264, and *Elements of Judicial Strategy*, pp. 19–20, and Krislov, *op. cit.*, pp. 151–55.
11. These data were made available through the courtesy and cooperation of the Roper Center in Williamstown, Mass.
12. These data were made available through the courtesy and cooperation of the Inter-University Consortium, Ann Arbor, Mich.
13. This study, a clustered area probability sample of 627 adults, was conducted under the direction of Harry Sharp. His assistance as well as that of the staff of the Laboratory are gratefully acknowledged.
14. Concern is sometimes expressed about the quality of reporting about the Court, based in part on the concern that people may get erroneous impressions about the Court as a result of errors in reporting. See Chester Newland, "Press Coverage of the United States Supreme Court," *Western Political Quarterly*, XVII (1964), p. 15.
15. Kenneth M. Dolbeare and Phillip E. Hammond, "The Political Party Basis of Attitudes Toward the United States Supreme Court" (forthcoming, *Public Opinion Quarterly*).
16. See Angus Campbell, Gerald Gurin, Warren Miller, and Donald E. Stokes, *The American Voter* (New York: John Wiley & Sons, 1960), and Fred Greenstein, *Children and Politics* (New Haven: Yale University Press, 1963).

SELECTED BIBLIOGRAPHY

Beard, Charles A. "The Supreme Court—Usurper or Grantee," *Political Science Quarterly*, 27 (March 1912), 1–34. An argument by the prominent historian that the Founding Fathers did indeed intend the Supreme Court to exercise the power of judicial review.

Becker, Theodore, ed. *The Impact of Supreme Court Decisions*. New York: Oxford University Press, 1969. An unusually good collection of writings on the problems of compliance with judicial decisions. Deals with the courts as they make policy decisions, but points out the meaninglessness of those decisions unless they are complied with. Asks to what extent in a democracy the courts can expect their policy mandates to be obeyed, without the powers of sword or purse.

Bickel, Alexander M. *The Least Dangerous Branch.* New York: Bobbs-Merrill, 1962. Makes an eloquent defense of judicial review, arguing that judge-made policy cannot succeed against deeply felt and sustained contrary popular opinion. Also argues that the Court enunciates the long-term values of the society at times when the legislative branch may be moved by short-term political pressures.

Black, Charles L., Jr. *The People and the Court.* Englewood Cliffs, N.J.: Prentice-Hall, 1960. Argues cogently for judicial activism in the area of civil liberties and opposes judicial review in matters of economic policy. May be the best defense for the contemporary Supreme Court against the accusation that it is as much a usurper of popular power as was the conservative Court of the 1930s.

Boudin, Louis B. "Government by Judiciary," *Political Science Quarterly,* 26 (June 1911), 238–70. A strong historical argument that the Constitutional Convention did not intend the Supreme Court to have the power of judicial review.

Commager, Henry Steele. *Majority Rule and Minority Rights.* New York: Oxford University Press, 1943. Criticizes judicial review as an obstruction to popular sovereignty. Rejects the assertion that the Supreme Court has been a protector of minority rights by analyzing the cases in which the Court has struck down congressional enactments. Argues that the Congress is sufficiently "Constitution minded" to preserve civil liberties.

Danelski, David J. *A Supreme Court Justice Is Appointed.* New York: Random House, 1964. A thorough study of the appointment of Justice Pierce Butler. A good history, illustrating the intensely political nature of judicial appointments.

Jacob, Herbert. *Justice in America.* Boston: Little, Brown, 1965. A good survey of the judicial process. Concerned with the relationship of the courts to other institutions in the society. Shows the role of lawyers, litigants, lower and appellate courts, and such processes as negotiation and trial in the American judicial system.

Krislov, Samuel. *The Supreme Court in the Political Process.* New York: Macmillan, 1965. A useful, brief survey of the Supreme Court as a political institution. Discusses both the internal politics of the Court and the politics of recruitment, litigation, and compliance. Includes short chapters on recent judicial decisions in the area of governmental power and civil liberties.

Lewis, Anthony. *Gideon's Trumpet.* New York: Vintage Books, 1966. An insightful case study of the litigation, from beginning to conclusion, that established the right of indigent defendants in criminal cases to be represented by counsel.

Lockhart, William B., Yale Kamisar, and Jesse H. Choper. *The American Constitution.* Rochester, Minn.: West Publishing Co., 1967, and *Supplement,* 1970. An outstanding collection of cases on constitutional law and civil liberties. Includes excerpted essays and law review articles. Contains notes and questions that render this a brilliant study of the problems of constitutional doctrine.

Mason, Alpheus Thomas, and William M. Beaney. *The Supreme Court in a Free Society.* New York: Norton, 1968. An excellent survey of the political and legal history of the Supreme Court. Relates constitutional doctrine to politics in the Supreme Court and in the other branches of the government.

McCloskey, Robert G. *The American Supreme Court.* Chicago: University of Chicago Press, 1964. Divides constitutional history into four periods and argues that the Supreme Court's decisions in each period reflected predominant values in the society. A defense of judicial review on the premise that the Court has been responsive to prevailing opinion in the nation.

Miller, Charles A. *The Supreme Court and the Uses of History.* Cambridge, Mass.: Belknap Press of the Harvard University Press, 1969. A superb analysis of the Supreme Court's use and misuse of history in deciding cases.

Murphy, Walter F. *Congress and the Court.* Chicago: University of Chicago Press, 1962. An important study of the relationship between congressional and judicial power showing that a determined legislature can defeat, at least temporarily, an activist Court. Focuses primarily on the struggle between the branches in 1957 and 1958, but presents a complete narrative on the history of legislative-judicial conflict. Brings together survey data, analyses of judicial doctrine, reports on legislation, and description of the maneuvering within the Court and the Congress. A highly readable and rewarding study of the power relationship between the Congress and the Supreme Court.

Pritchett, C. Herman. *The Roosevelt Court: A Study in Judicial Politics and Values.* New York: Macmillan, 1948. A pioneering study of the Supreme Court during the New Deal era. Applies a form of roll call (bloc voting) analysis to the conduct of Supreme Court justices.

Rodell, Fred. *Nine Men.* New York: Vintage Books, 1955. A straightforward political history of the Supreme Court that is sharply critical of the tendency of justices to obstruct popular democracy.

Schmidhauser, John R. *The Supreme Court: Its Politics, Personalities, and Procedures.* New York: Holt, Rinehart and Winston, 1960. A broad study of the Supreme Court as a political institution with a notable discussion of the recruitment pattern of justices throughout the Court's history.

Schubert, Glendon. *Judicial Policy-Making.* Glenview, Ill.: Scott, Foresman and Co., 1965. Uses the behavioral approach to the judiciary; describes the relationship between the courts and other institutions in the political system as well as between lower courts and the Supreme Court. Treats judges who make policy as political actors, rather than as law givers. Includes insightful discussions of judicial activism and restraint and of the dominant value systems of the Supreme Court in various eras of American history.

Vose, Clement E. *Caucasians Only: The Supreme Court, the NAACP, and the Restrictive Covenant Cases.* Berkeley: University of California Press, 1959. A seminal work in the study of the judicial process. Shows in detail the role that an interest group played in laying the foundations for, and pursuing successful litigation to achieve, its policy goals. A fascinating account of the story of the NAACP's strategy of winning equal rights for Negroes through the judiciary.

A Note on the Type

The text of this book was set on the Linotype in Aster, a typeface designed by Francesco Simoncini for Ludwig and Mayer, the German type foundry. Starting out with the basic old-face letterforms that can be traced back to Francesco Griffo in 1495, Simoncini emphasized the diagonal stress by the simple device of extending diagonals to the full height of the letterforms and squaring off. By modifying the weights of the individual letters to combat this stress, he has produced a type of rare balance and vigor.

This book was composed by Cherry Hill Composition, Pennsauken, New Jersey. Printed and bound by The Kingsport Press, Kingsport, Tenn.

Design by Karin Batten